C ... ON

T

IN ... XT

By

Eleanor M. Fox

Walter J. Derenberg Professor of Trade Regulation,
New York University School of Law

AMERICAN CASEBOOK SERIES®

WEST®

A Thomson Reuters business

Mat #40778231

Thomson Reuters created this publication to provide you with accurate and authoritative information concerning the subject matter covered. However, this publication was not necessarily prepared by persons licensed to practice law in a particular jurisdiction. Thomson Reuters does not render legal or other professional advice, and this publication is not a substitute for the advice of an attorney. If you require legal or other expert advice, you should seek the services of a competent attorney or other professional.

610 Opperman Drive
St. Paul, MN 55123
1–800–313–9378

Printed in the United States of America

ISBN: 978–0–314–19992–8

in memory of
Lawrence A. Sullivan
(1923-2007)

PREFACE AND ACKNOWLEDGMENTS TO THE THIRD EDITION

Larry Sullivan and I wrote the first edition of this casebook in the late 1980s. It was published in 1989.

The year 1980 had marked a turning point in U.S. antitrust law. The heritage of the 1960s with its mission for equal opportunity was still very much with us, and Lewis D. Brandeis' notion of a clearer path for "the little man" as well as William O. Douglas' notion of autonomy and freedom through diversity still infused American antitrust. But these notions were quickly being overtaken. Globalization was shrinking the world; lower trade barriers meant fierce competition from abroad and new opportunities beyond borders. Efficiency became the mantra. The new paradigm for U.S. antitrust was consumer welfare—focusing on how business could gain market power and harm consumers. The new paradigm rationalized U.S. antitrust law and tended to ensure that antitrust law would help and not hurt efficiency—of firms and markets.

Thus it was in the context of change that we wrote the first volume. We included much of the history and evolution of the antitrust law along with the most current cases so that the students could not only grasp the currents of the political economy but predict the direction of the law.

When it came time for the second edition Larry Sullivan was already nearing the last years of his life and we were fortunate to be able to collaborate with Rudolf Peritz, who added much to the book. The second edition was published in 2004. The antitrust law was still evolving from the path of pluralism and distrust of bigness to the path of efficiency and trust in the market. Up to the last month of preparing our manuscript for the second edition, there had been only a few new Supreme Court antitrust decisions and these often favored the plaintiff; for example, *Aspen Skiing*, a unanimous judgment for the complainant against an exclusionary refusal to cooperate in issuing a multi-mountain ticket to all of the Aspen slopes, and *Eastman Kodak*, declining to uphold the district court's grant of summary judgment for Kodak against independent servicers of Kodak equipment who had been cut off from Kodak-brand repair parts. The *Kodak* case, however, was decided 5–4, and the dissent by Justice Scalia was the handwriting on the wall of the approaching millennium. Just days before the printing of the second edition, the Supreme Court decided its head-turning *Trinko* case; and our publisher allowed us to include it—in an appendix.

What else occurred in this more-than-decade between the first and second editions? In the same year as publication of our first edition, the Berlin wall fell. Most of the world became democratized. Scores of nations that had distrusted markets began to nurture markets, more or less; and almost all of these nations adopted competition (antitrust) laws. By the time of the second edition, antitrust was well on its way to becoming internationalized.

Larry Sullivan passed away on October 7, 2007. His mark is deeply impressed on this book, on antitrust law in general (his treatise has been cited by the Supreme Court and other federal courts hundreds of times), and, more importantly, on the many of us who loved him and appreciated his humanism, his intellect, his Irish raconteurism, and simply his qualities as a human being. I dedicate this volume to him.

Meanwhile, in the eight years since the publication of the second edition, the Supreme Court decided 11 antitrust cases, 10 in favor of the defendant, overruling precedents and resetting the perspectival compass. All of them followed the footprint of *Trinko*.

On the world front, antitrust law has become significantly internationalized. The United States has lost some of the sheen of hegemony. U.S. antitrust and European Union competition law remain the models for the world, with EU outpacing the U.S. Scores of developing counties are injecting their needs into their competition laws, including distributional concerns and other public interests. The huge, rapidly emerging developing economies of China, India and Brazil may in some ways be setting a pace of their own.

On the new economy/technology front, the world continues its pace of rapid change. Apple has sold its twenty–fifth billion iPad. Google makes 34,000 searches per second. Microsoft, the "monopolist" of the last two decades, is seeking to enlist the antitrust authorities in the U.S. and the EU to stop Google from allegedly manipulating the market in web search and expanding its power into adjacent markets that might be the pathways to control the future of information and communication technologies in the world.

It is in this context that I write this third edition. How have I changed the book? I have reduced, but retained, historical coverage. All chapters are modernized; they include all of the latest Supreme Court cases and many instructive lower court cases. I have added a number of problems including an inspired one created by the International Competition Network—a virtual organization of the competition authorities of the world. I have retained, although reduced, excerpts from all of the old flagship cases including *Alcoa* and *Standard Oil*, and mined the philosophic premises of the Justices, highlighting the threads that have woven their way into the modern Court opinions. I have incorporated many non-U.S. references, showing contrasts and convergences and helping explain not only what U.S. antitrust law is but what it might be and what some of the rest of the world thinks it should be. I have incorporated contemporary economic thinking in an accessible and non-technical way, retaining the perspective that antitrust is *law* heavily influenced by generalized principles of economics, and not the other way around.

My goal is and has been, and Larry's was, to educate the student in the fullness of American antitrust; to show its place in domestic policy and in the world; to train the student in the analytics of contemporary antitrust law and practice, and to prepare the student to think about antitrust in the larger context, however that context might change.

I owe enormous thanks to Dan Crane for his very helpful comments on the second edition of the book; to my excellent student research assistant, Robert R. Miller; to Denise Junqueira (NYU LL.M. 2010) for her excellent work on the book when she was my student; and as always to my superb assistant Linda Smalls for helping me prepare the manuscript.

One mechanical note: In the case excerpts, brackets are used for summaries or insertions by the editor; ellipses (. . .) indicate omitted words and asterisks (***) indicate omitted paragraphs. Citations and footnotes are omitted without indication.

ELEANOR M. FOX
New York, New York

May 2012

Preface and Acknowledgments to the Second Edition

Much has changed in the last decade, raising the profile of antitrust. We would highlight four key developments.

First, the pace of globalization has quickened, making many more markets global. Second, Internet and telecommunications technologies have exponentially increased the speed of communication across the globe, creating new opportunities both for competition and its restraint. Third, antitrust law itself has "gone global," with approximately 100 countries adopting and maintaining antitrust laws. Fourth, Chicago school economics, which dominated much of 1980s U.S. antitrust, has been tempered by "post-Chicago" economics, which relaxes many of the faith-in-markets assumptions of Chicago school and gives greater credence to market realities.

We have revised the casebook with these changes very much in mind. We stated in the preface to the first edition: "In this book of history, economics, politics, and law, we have steered an eclectic course." In this edition, we have retained the mix of history, economics, politics, and law. To this, we have added some geo-politics, we have given the book a comparative and international dimension, and we have posed frequent queries meant to focus attention on global or at least cross-border welfare and to trigger your thoughts about the relationship between national sovereignty and the economic welfare of the citizen of the world.

Antitrust was one of the first interdisciplinary law school subjects, integrating law, economics and political science. The interdisciplinary pulls of antitrust are even more compelling in the globalized world. The antitrust student and the antitrust lawyer are no mere technicians—although they must be that, too. They easily become internationalists.

We are deeply indebted to Poonam Gupta for her excellent research assistance, to Linda Smalls for her extraordinary expert and patient assistance in preparing the manuscript, and to the Filomen D'Agostino and Max E. Greenberg Research Fund, the Milton & Miriam Handler Foundation, the New York University Law School Foundation, and New York Law School, for generous research support.

In our edits of the cases, we omit citations without ellipses. Otherwise, we show omissions of words by three dots and omissions of paragraphs by asterisks.

Eleanor M. Fox
Lawrence A. Sullivan
Rudolph J.R. Peritz

PREFACE AND ACKNOWLEDGMENTS TO THE FIRST EDITION

Antitrust law once reflected broad, value-based policy, informed by the enacting Congresses' distrust of bigness and power and their concern for economic opportunity on the merits. But in the mid to late 1970s, the Supreme Court put a cap on the growing body of antitrust constraints, and in the early 1980s, a new Administration turned the old antitrust on its head. In 1981 the Justice Department, taking a leaf from Chicago School economics, proclaimed that the sole role for antitrust is to stop inefficient transactions; and it asserted that few transactions are inefficient because the market is a robust check on inefficient behavior. Government enforcement since 1981 has focused almost entirely on blatant cartelization. As this book goes to press, minimal antitrust is still the rule of thumb amid speculation about what changes further time may bring.

There are compelling reasons to study antitrust. First, antitrust is a unique blend of intellectual theory, social policy, political economy, microeconomics and law. Thus, to study antitrust law is to engage in an interdisciplinary enterprise that informs the study of law, legal institutions, and social policy. Second, the study of antitrust prepares the student for the practice of antitrust law, which is a field of great intellectual and practical interest and excitement; it may involve one in government service, counselling, practice before an administrative agency, analytical discussions and negotiations with the Justice Department, and federal court litigation. Moreover, the practice of antitrust law provides the constant challenge of learning facts about the functioning of whole industries. Third, as we approach the centennial of the Sherman Antitrust Law, antitrust is at a cusp where different social forces meet; future developments will be interesting to observe, and perhaps even to shape.

In this book of history, economics, politics, and law, we have steered an eclectic course. Our goal is to provide the student with sufficient background to understand the intellectual history, the evolution, and the state of the law of antitrust; to excite the student to question the path the law has taken and to consider the paths it might take. We also hope to give the student a simple introduction to economic thinking and to illuminate the process of choosing the assumptions that shape economic analysis, so that the emerging antitrust lawyer or scholar can ask the right questions and, as well, appreciate the policy choices that underlie competing styles of antitrust economics.

We are deeply indebted to Jed Davis, Randall M. Fox, Katharine Lauer, Vickie Saker and Anita Stork for their indispensable research assistance, to Rita Tidwell and Simpson Thacher & Bartlett for aid and assistance in preparing the manuscript, and to the Filomen D'Agostino and Max E. Greenberg Research Fund, New York University and to the Committee on Research, University of California, Berkeley, for their generous research support.

ELEANOR M. FOX
LAWRENCE A. SULLIVAN

New York City, New York
Berkeley, California
June 1989

SUMMARY OF CONTENTS

Table of Contents

TABLE OF CASES

The principal cases are in bold type. Cases cited or discussed in the text are in roman type. References are to pages. Cases cited in principal cases and within other quoted materials are not included.

CASES AND MATERIALS ON

U.S. ANTITRUST IN GLOBAL CONTEXT

Third Edition

This casebook focuses on American antitrust, which has its unique history and evolution. But we should not and do not ignore antitrust in the rest of the world. Nor do we ignore global competition—which crosses all boundaries in this world of fast changing technologies, easy trade, and relative freedom of firms to move headquarters or build supply chains wherever conditions are most propitious. Accordingly, comparative and international references are woven into the book throughout.

In twenty-first century antitrust we meet questions such as whether the world's greatest stock exchanges can merge and whether Google can give preference to its own applications. We ask how deeply hospitals can collaborate to provide health care services, and whether global victims of globally price-fixed vitamins can get recompense. But we also deal with the same basic industries that have erected some of the biggest barriers to competition over time—some of which have also contributed important innovations—such as oil, steel, transportation and communications.

While times have changed, barriers have fallen, and technological advances can cure some monopolistic restraints faster than antitrust, most of the questions of antitrust remain the same, even while modes of analysis have changed.

For this introductory chapter, we present five early, still classic cases—railroad self-regulation by price fixing, a steel pipe cartel in "only" a section of the country, a great railroad consolidation, the famous Standard Oil trust, and U.S. Steel's notorious acquisition of 180 competitors. All five cases tested the reach of the fledgling U.S. antitrust laws. All five cases tested the limits of appropriate government intervention in the economy and the balance between personal freedoms and law. In all five cases the Court was struggling with basic questions that we still struggle with today. What is economic power and what is its significance? What is the significance of market structure? defendants' intent? competitive effects? Are bad acts necessary for a violation of the law? Indeed, what does it mean to be "bad"? The questions persist, even in a now part-virtual economy; and the early inquiries and answers lay the foundation for modern antitrust.

At the end of this first segment, we include a note on economics. We proceed to study cartels, monopoly, mergers, competitor collaborations other than cartels, and vertical restraints. We end with a wrap-up on globalization and what it means for antitrust.

First, a few words about the passage of the Sherman Antitrust Act.

B. THE INDUSTRIAL REVOLUTION, THE TRUSTS, AND THE PASSAGE OF THE SHERMAN ACT

1. THE BIRTH OF THE TRUSTS AND THE ENACTMENT OF THE SHERMAN ACT

In the second half of the nineteenth century, industrialization changed the face of business. During the period 1865–1900 the nation rapidly rose to the status of the world's industrial leader. American entrepreneurs took advantage of abundant resources, developed new production technologies, and expanded commercial markets, increasing the nation's economic output.[1] Natural resources drove settlement westward across the continent. Federal homesteading programs opened the frontier to agriculture, mining, petroleum, lumber, and water development.[2]

Mass production became commonplace. Innovations in communication and transportation provided the infrastructure necessary to enable business to respond to growing urban markets. Railroad mileage doubled between 1865 and 1873. By the early 1890s, businesses could ship goods more quickly, cheaply and dependably throughout the year. The modernization of the telegraph and the invention of the telephone in 1876 made available more rapid, accurate information about the market and further increased the volume of possible business transactions.[3]

The railroads—the nation's first "big business," according to Alfred Chandler—were first to confront the problem of ruinous competition. Railroads required a high initial investment for construction of fixed assets and their maintenance. To offset the high capital and operating costs, railroad companies vied for a large volume of business at low rates. Often, railroads set differential rates, lowering prices for large volume shippers and long hauls.[4] Responding to low-priced competition, railroads formed pools or cartels. These were loosely structured combinations of competitors and became regionally dominant systems.[5]

But the pools were unstable; there was widespread cheating. Prominent corporations turned to a new, tighter form of combination—the trust. The trust was created when a number of corporations, erstwhile pool members, "turned their stock over to a board of trustees receiving in

---

1. See H. Scheiber, H. Vatter, and H. Faulkner, AMERICAN ECONOMIC HISTORY, 159–161, 193–194 (1976) (hereafter Scheiber, AMERICAN ECONOMIC HISTORY).

2. L.E. Davis, et al., AMERICAN ECONOMIC GROWTH: AN ECONOMIST'S HISTORY OF THE U.S., 106–09 (1972) (hereafter Davis, AMERICAN ECONOMIC GROWTH); see generally P.W. Gates, HISTORY OF PUBLIC LAND LAW DEVELOPMENT (1968).

3. *Id.* at 195–97.

4. G. Miller, RAILROADS AND THE GRANGER LAWS, 16–23 (1971) (hereafter Miller, GRANGER LAWS); A.D. Chandler, THE VISIBLE HAND: THE MANAGERIAL REVOLUTION IN AMERICAN BUSINESS, ch. 5, 140–42, 148–51, 156–64 (1977) (hereafter Chandler, VISIBLE HAND).

5. See Chandler, VISIBLE HAND.

return trust certificates of equivalent value."[6] Each participating corporation retained its individual state charter, but all participants were subject to the control of the newly formed, unincorporated entity that held their stock. Some corporations combined vertically, integrating the entire production and distribution process from obtaining raw materials to providing structured marketing systems. As markets gradually expanded, despite recurring periods of overcapacity and depression, vertical integration permitted businesses to squeeze out unintegrated rivals by reducing costs and prices. Vertical combinations (usually combined with acquisitions of competitors) were more successful than purely horizontal (competitor) pools in reducing costs, increasing productivity, and eliminating competition.[7]

Standard Oil, the best known of the great trusts, was formed in 1882. It successfully captured the petroleum industry and maintained its control for many years. Other refining and distilling companies adopted this new form of organization.[8] After consolidating horizontally, trusts would often attempt to gain control over the input resources and the marketing system needed for their particular industry.[9] Again, Standard Oil was the model that many imitated.

Trusts were formed not only in oil but also in steel, electric power and other public utility industries. The rise of the trusts in the 1880s fed widespread fears about the economic implications of the combination movement. Economic change during this period had wrought a new social order. Tradition had been up-ended. The individual worker and independent artisan were displaced by a specialized, wage-earning industrial labor force.

To many, the trust had become a symbol of a new order. To its supporters, it signified wealth, cooperation, and progressive development. To its detractors, the trust was a monolithic, impersonal, centrally administered organization that represented greed, inhumanity, and economic stratification. Despite the fact that only eight industrial consolidations during the 1880s actually took the form of trust,[10] the term "trust" came to denote more than a specific legal device for corporate combination. It became the catch-phrase in a public debate over the course of economic growth and the distribution of wealth.

The belief that free competition was essential to a thriving, efficient economy was widely held in the nineteenth century. Business people argued that competition was the "great regulator"; it led to economic natural selection, the survival of the most efficient. Because competition was thought to be governed by natural laws, any attempts to impose

6. *Id.*, 319.

7. *Id.* at 285–289.

8. *Id.* at 320.

9. *Id.* at 315.

10. Chandler, VISIBLE HAND at 320.

"artificial" restraints would, it was feared, hinder progress.[11] But there was a contradiction: large businesses were consolidating to avoid the assertedly immutable law of competition.

At first business people and economists resolved the contradiction in favor of the trusts. Primarily, they argued that trusts were inevitable growths, dictated by the same forces that governed the evolution of the biological world. The evolutionary argument affirmed the positive nature of the trust. The appearance of the trust signaled that social evolution had reached a new stage. In this schema, the trust was a way of eliminating excessive competition and restoring balance and efficiency to the economic order.[12]

But many farmers, laborers, and small business owners rejected these justifications. Newspapers published exposés of the unscrupulous methods used by trust leaders to quash their competitors and to force smaller businesses to cooperate with them. Henry Demarest Lloyd argued that the trusts had achieved their size and power through secret, illegal means. He fueled the growing antitrust movement with tales of the corrupt methods used by the leaders of the most infamous trust—the Standard Oil Company.[13]

Also, opponents of the trust directly challenged the natural-growth conception.[14] Populist leader William Jennings Bryan maintained that trusts were unnatural growths.[15] Opponents of trusts also rejected the classical theorists' claim that when a business serves its own interest it inevitably serves the public.[16] It was observed that the threat of potential competition did not constrain trusts; merely, the trusts responded to the threat by acquiring the potential competitors and continuing to restrict entry.[17]

Public opinion turned against the trusts. Small business owners viewed the expansion of big business with apprehension, fearing that the trusts would either absorb them or drive them out of business. Small retailers, jobbers, and traveling salespeople found their businesses severely

---

11. S. Fine, LAISSEZ-FAIRE AND THE GENERAL WELFARE STATE 100–03 (1956) (hereafter Fine, LAISSEZ-FAIRE). For an interesting review of economic views during this period, and for a useful bibliography, see J. May, ANTITRUST PRACTICE AND PROCEDURE IN THE FORMATIVE ERA: THE CONSTITUTIONAL AND CONCEPTUAL REACH OF STATE ANTITRUST LAW, 1880–1918, 135 U.Pa.L.Rev. 56171 (1987) (hereafter May, ANTITRUST PRACTICE AND PROCEDURE).

12. See generally Fine, LAISSEZ-FAIRE at 110–11, 221–25, 338; and W. Letwin, LAW AND ECONOMIC POLICY IN AMERICA, 75–77 (1965) (hereafter Letwin, LAW AND ECONOMIC POLICY).

13. H.D. Lloyd, The Story of a Great Monopoly, in LORDS OF INDUSTRY, 1–46 (1910) (hereafter Lloyd, LORDS OF INDUSTRY).

14. See James B. Dill, remarks made to Lincoln Steffens:

> Trusts are natural, inevitable growths out of our social and economic conditions.... You cannot stop them by force, with laws. They will sweep down like glaciers upon your police, courts, and states, and wash them into flowing rivers.

Quoted in Lincoln Steffens, THE AUTOBIOGRAPHY OF LINCOLN STEFFENS, 196 (1931).

15. CHICAGO CONFERENCE ON TRUSTS, 510 (1900).

16. H.D. Lloyd, Wealth Against Commonwealth, in THE POPULIST MIND, 496, 501–02 (N. Pollack ed. 1967).

17. Alfred Eichner, EMERGENCE OF OLIGOPOLY 124 (1978).

challenged by the new chain stores and mail-order firms.[18] Many shippers, angered by the discriminatory railroad rates, agitated for local and national government regulation.[19] Farmers were plagued by the high costs of consumer products and the low prices of their crops. They complained that their situation was "aggravated by ... trusts ... that sold farmers bags and bought their linseed oil and cottonseed,"[20] and by "middlemen and commodity speculators who handled their crops."[21] The Grange and the Farmers Alliance rallied around proposals to control big business. The emergence of national labor unions by the 1880s and the more frequent occurrence of strikes attested to the economic problems of the new industrial workers.[22]

The trusts' ability to obtain favorable political treatment rekindled the traditional American hostility towards monopoly and special privilege. As William Letwin commented, "Hatred of monopoly is one of the oldest American political habits...."[23] (Is it still?)

Many solutions were proposed, including attacking the trusts under state corporate law or restraint-of-trade law. But no state solution seemed adequate.

2. PASSAGE OF THE SHERMAN ACT

By the time of the election of 1888, which brought Benjamin Harrison to the presidency, it was commonly acknowledged that "the public had found the trusts to be a growing and intolerable evil."[24] The candidates of all three political parties supported a national antitrust law. Even big business advocates reconciled themselves to a law against the trusts, perhaps convinced that Congress would not vote for the tariff they wanted unless domestic competition was protected.

In 1889, Senator John Sherman introduced the Sherman Antitrust Act, which was redrafted largely through the efforts of Senators Edmunds and Hoar. During Congressional debate, Senator Sherman reiterated that the purpose of the bill was to contain the concentration of economic power. He said:

> The popular mind is agitated with problems that may disturb social order, and among them all none is more threatening than the inequality of condition, of wealth, and opportunity that has grown within a single generation out of the concentration of capital into vast combi-

---

18. Chandler, VISIBLE HAND at 233.

19. L. Benson, MERCHANTS, FARMERS AND RAILROADS, 13 (1955); see also GRANGER LAWS at 16–23.

20. Letwin, LAW AND ECONOMIC POLICY at 59.

21. Scheiber, AMERICAN ECONOMIC HISTORY at 214.

22. D. Brody, STEELWORKERS IN AMERICA: THE NONUNION ERA, 159–60 (1960); A. Paul, CONSERVATIVE CRISIS AND THE RULE OF LAW: ATTITUDES OF BAR AND BENCH, 1887–1895, 128–30 (1960).

23. Letwin, LAW AND ECONOMIC POLICY at 59.

24. See W.H. Taft, THE ANTI-TRUST ACT AND THE SUPREME COURT, 2 (1914); H. Thorelli, THE FEDERAL ANTITRUST POLICY, 129 (1955) (hereafter Thorelli, FEDERAL ANTITRUST POLICY).

nations to control production and trade and to break down competition. These combinations already defy or control powerful transportation corporations and reach State authorities. They reach out their Briarean arms to every part of our country.... Congress alone can deal with them, and if we are unwilling or unable there will soon be a trust for every product and a master to fix the price for every necessity of life.[25]

The legislative history of the act is replete with such rhetoric. As Robert H. Bork has written:

In looking to the legislative history, one discerns repeated concern for the welfare of consumers and also for the welfare of small business and for various other values—a potpourri of other values. So far as I'm aware, Congress, in enacting these statutes, never faced the problem of what to do when values come into conflict in specific cases. Legislators appear to have assumed, as it is most comfortable to assume, that all good things are always compatible.[26]

Little in the legislative history illuminates what Congress meant by "restraint of trade" in Section 1 of the Sherman Act or what "monopolization" meant in Section 2. Virtually every reference says, in effect, that Congress left the task of interpretation to the courts, through case-by-case application.

Despite the deep ambiguity about what the statute meant or was expected to accomplish, on July 2, 1890 Congress passed the Sherman Antitrust Act. Sections 1 and 2 were and are still the most important sections of the U.S. antitrust laws. They read as follows today, having been revised to upgrade the offense from a misdemeanor to a crime, and to increase the allowable fines and jail terms.[27]

"An act to protect trade and commerce against unlawful restraints and monopolies.

"SEC. 1. Every contract, combination in the form of trust or otherwise, or conspiracy, in restraint of trade or commerce among the several States, or with foreign nations, is hereby declared to be illegal. Every person who shall make any such contract or engage in any such combination or conspiracy hereby declared to be illegal shall be deemed guilty of a felony, and, on conviction thereof, shall be punished by a fine not exceeding 100 million dollars if a corporation, or, if any other person, one million dollars, or by imprisonment not exceeding 10 years, or by both said punishments, in the discretion of the court.

---

25. 21 Cong.Rec. 2,460 (1890).

26. Robert Bork, The Role of the Courts in Applying Economics, 54 Antitrust L.J. 21, 24 (1985).

27. Relevant portions of the Sherman Act, as amended, appear in Appendix B. The prohibitory language remains the same as in the 1890 law. The offense is now a felony, and the levels of fines and prison terms have increased.

"SEC. 2. Every person who shall monopolize, or attempt to monopolize, or combine or conspire with any other person or persons, to monopolize any part of the trade or commerce among the several States, or with foreign nations, shall be deemed guilty of a felony, and, on conviction thereof, shall be punished by fine not exceeding 100 million dollars if a corporation, or, if any other person, one million dollars, or by imprisonment not exceeding 10 years, or by both said punishments, in the discretion of the court."

As seen, the act reflected a complex range of ideals, goals and practical necessities. It was greeted with hostility by economists.[28] That it was passed at all is a tribute to the widely held antitrust sentiment.

The courts took on the mantle of interpretation. The cases presented in the pages immediately following show the Justices of the Supreme Court in the throes of trying to solve the riddle of antitrust: What motivates and should motivate the law? You will see, before long, the currently articulated anchor of the law: efficiency and consumer welfare (both of which need definition, a subject on which we will spend time). In the earlier days, the Justices debated within a wider range. As you read the cases that follow, we ask you to do two things: 1) Pay attention to the values and perceptions debated, and not just history. Perceptions regarding how much to trust the market and how much to trust antitrust intervention to correct market failures underlie definitions of consumer welfare and efficiency and how to reach those goals even today. 2) Always consider what is best for consumers, and be ready to identify any application of law that seems to harm consumers.

C. THE FIRST FEW DECADES

1. WHAT THE LAW PROHIBITS: DEVELOPING THE RULE AGAINST CARTELS

During its first decade, the Sherman Act was not invoked to challenge any of the notorious trusts, such as oil, tobacco or farm machinery. These cases were to be prosecuted early in the twentieth century. The Supreme Court first considered the meaning of "restraint of trade" in a railroad price-fixing case.

As you read the early cases, consider what was at stake. Note the defendants' arguments, which were offered more than once on the blank slate of the Sherman Act: competition is not all good; especially when it may become ruinous, it is reasonable for the industry to regulate it.

The case that follows contains the germ of a per se rule—i.e. a rule of blanket illegality. The universe for its application would remain to be refined. The warring philosophies of political economy—how much trust

28. "The historians of American antitrust policy have emphasized the lack of enthusiasm, and often downright hostility, with which economists greeted the Sherman Act." G. Stigler, THE ECONOMIST AS PREACHER, AND OTHER ESSAYS, 41–42 (1982).

in the market and how much intervention by the state—emerged from day one in the application of the Sherman Act.

UNITED STATES v. TRANS–MISSOURI FREIGHT ASSOCIATION

166 U.S. 290 (1897).

JUSTICE PECKHAM: [The railroad companies, which were competitors, agreed to set rates for freight traffic. The rates were to be "reasonable". Rate changes were to be voted upon at monthly meetings. All parties were to be bound unless they gave written notice within 10 days from the time a change was agreed. Price cutting not in good faith to meet competition was subject to fines. The United States sued to have the agreement set aside as void and the association dissolved.]

. . . The next question to be discussed is as to what is the true construction of the statute, assuming that it applies to common carriers by railroad. What is the meaning of the language as used in the statute, that "every contract, combination in the form of trust or otherwise, or conspiracy, in restraint of trade or commerce among the several states or with foreign nations is hereby declared to be illegal?" Is it confined to a contract or combination which is only in unreasonable restraint of trade or commerce, or does it include what the language of the act plainly and in terms covers—all contracts of that nature?

[*The Railroads argue: Sherman § 1 cannot mean what it says*]

We are asked to regard the title of this act as indicative of its purpose to include only those contracts which were unlawful at common law, but which require the sanction of a Federal statute in order to be dealt with in a Federal court. [The Court proceeds to reject that interpretation. It rejected the view that the statute could not mean what it says; the view that the statute prohibits only contracts in *unreasonable* restraint of trade. The Court declared that it must respect "the plain and ordinary meaning" of the statute, which prohibits *all* contracts in restraint of trade. This broad prohibition, however, does not necessarily encompass sale of a business with a limited covenant not to compete. Such covenant "in effect is collateral to such sale, and where the main purpose of the whole contract is accomplished by such a sale, [the contract] might not be included, within the letter or spirit of the statute in question."]

* * *

[*The Railroads argue: Too much competition is not good; it will lead to financial ruin; courts must determine whether restraints are reasonable*].

To the question why competition should necessarily be conducted to such an extent as to result in this relentless and continued war, to eventuate only in the financial ruin of one or all of the companies indulging in it, the answer is made that if competing railroad companies be left subject to the sway of free and unrestricted competition the results above foreshadowed necessarily happen from the nature of the case; that competition being the rule, each company will seek business to the extent of its power, and will underbid its rival in order to get the business, and such underbidding will act and react upon each company until the prices are so reduced as to make it impossible to prosper or live under them; that it is too much to ask of human nature for one company to insist upon charges sufficiently high to afford a reasonable compensation, and while doing so to see its patrons leave for rival roads who are obtaining its business by offering less rates for doing it than can be afforded and a fair profit obtained therefrom. Sooner than experience ruin from mere inanition, efforts will be made in the direction of meeting the underbidding of its rival until both shall end in ruin. The only refuge, it is said, from this wretched end lies in the power of competing roads agreeing among themselves to keep up prices for transportation to such sums as shall be reasonable in themselves, so that companies may be allowed to save themselves from themselves, and to agree not to attack each other, but to keep up reasonable and living rates for the services performed....

* * *

[*The court responds*]

There is another side to this question, however, and it may not be amiss to refer to one or two facts which tend to somewhat modify and alter the light in which the subject should be regarded. If only that kind of contract which is in unreasonable restraint of trade be within the meaning of the statute, and declared therein to be illegal, it is at once apparent that the subject of what is a reasonable rate is attended with great uncertainty. What is a proper standard by which to judge the fact of reasonable rates? Must the rate be so high as to enable the return for the whole business done to amount to a sum sufficient to afford the shareholder a fair and reasonable profit upon his investment? If so, what is a fair and reasonable profit? That depends sometimes upon the risk incurred, and the rate itself differs in different localities. Which is the one to which reference is to be made as the standard? Or is the reasonableness of the profit to be limited to a fair return upon the capital that would have been sufficient to build and equip the road, if honestly expended? ... It is quite apparent, therefore, that it is exceedingly difficult to formulate even the terms of the rule itself which should govern in the matter of determining what would be reasonable rates for transportation. While even after the standard should be determined there is such an infinite variety of facts entering into the question of what is a reasonable rate, no matter what standard is adopted, that any individual shipper would in most cases be apt to abandon the effort to show the unreasonable character of a charge, sooner than hazard the great expense in time and money necessary to prove the fact, and at the same time incur the ill-will of the road itself in all his future dealings with it. To say, therefore, that the act excludes agreements which are not in unreasonable restraint of trade, and which tend simply to keep up reasonable rates for transportation, is substantially to leave the question of reasonableness to the companies themselves.

* * *

Upon the subject now under consideration it is well said by Judge Oliver P. Shiras, United States district court judge, northern district of Iowa, in his very able dissenting opinion in this case in the United States circuit court of appeals, as follows:

> "... It may be entirely true that as we proceed in the development of the policy of public control over railway traffic, methods will be devised and put in operation by legislative enactment whereby railway companies and the public may be protected against the evils arising from unrestricted competition and from rate wars which unsettle the business of the community, but I fail to perceive the force of the argument that because railway companies *through their own action cause evils to themselves* and the public by sudden changes or reductions in tariff rates they must be permitted to deprive the community of the benefit of competition in securing reasonable rates for the transportation of the products of the country. Competition, free and unrestricted, is the general rule which governs all the ordinary business pursuits and transactions of life. Evils, as well as benefits, result therefrom. In the fierce heat of competition the stronger competitor may crush out the weaker; fluctuations in prices may be caused that result in wreck and disaster; yet, balancing the benefits as against the evils, the law of competition remains as a controlling element in the business world. That free and unrestricted competition in the matter of railroad charges may be productive of evils does not militate against the fact that such is the law now governing the subject. No law can be enacted nor system be devised for the control of human affairs that in its enforcement does not produce some evil results, no matter how beneficial its general purpose may be. There are benefits and there are evils which result from the operation of the law of free competition between railway companies. The time may come when the companies will be relieved from the operation of this law, but they cannot, by combination and agreements among themselves, bring about this change...."

The arguments which have been addressed to us against the inclusion of all contracts in restraint of trade, as provided for by the language of the act, have been based upon the alleged presumption that Congress, notwithstanding the language of the act, could not have intended to embrace all contracts, but only such contracts as were in unreasonable restraint of trade. Under these circumstances we are, therefore, asked to hold that the act of Congress excepts contracts which are not in unreasonable restraint of trade, and which only keep rates up to a reasonable price, notwithstanding the language of the act makes no such exception....

This we cannot and ought not to do....

It may be that the policy evidenced by the passage of the act itself will, if carried out, result in disaster to the roads and in a failure to secure the advantages sought from such legislation. Whether that will be the result or not we do not know and cannot predict. These considerations are, however, not for us. If the act ought to be read as contended for by defendants, Congress is the body to amend it and not this court, by a process of judicial legislation wholly unjustifiable. . . .

. . . In the view we have taken of the question, the intent alleged by the government is not necessary to be proved. The question is one of law in regard to the meaning and effect of the agreement itself, namely: Does the agreement restrain trade or commerce in any way so as to be a violation of the act? We have no doubt that it does. The agreement on its face recites that it is entered into "for the purpose of mutual protection by establishing and maintaining reasonable rates, rules, and regulations on all freight traffic, both through and local." To that end the association is formed and a body created which is to adopt rates, which, when agreed to, are to be the governing rates for all the companies, and a violation of which subjects the defaulting company to the payment of a penalty, and although the parties have a right to withdraw from the agreement on giving thirty days' notice of a desire so to do, yet while in force and assuming it to be lived up to, there can be no doubt that its direct, immediate, and necessary effect is to put a restraint upon trade or commerce as described in the act.

For these reasons the suit of the Government can be maintained without proof of the allegation that the agreement was entered into for the purpose of restraining trade or commerce or for maintaining rates above what was reasonable. The necessary effect of the agreement is to restrain trade or commerce, no matter what the intent was on the part of those who signed it. . . .

JUSTICE WHITE, dissenting: . . . The plain intention of the law was to protect the liberty of contract and the freedom of trade. Will this intention not be frustrated by a construction which, if it does not destroy, at least gravely impairs, both the liberty of the individual to contract and the freedom of trade? If the rule of reason no longer determines the right of the individual to contract or secures the validity of contracts upon which trade depends and results, what becomes of the liberty of the citizen or the freedom of trade? Secured no longer by the law of reason, all these rights become subject, when questioned, to the mere caprice of judicial authority. Thus, a law in favor of freedom of contract, it seems to me, is so interpreted as to gravely impair that freedom. Progress and not reaction was the purpose of the act of Congress. The construction now given the act disregards the whole current of judicial authority and tests the right to contract by the conceptions of that right entertained at the time of the year books instead of by the light of reason and the necessity of modern society. To do this violates, as I see it, the plainest conception of public policy, for, as said by Sir G. Jessel, Master of the Rolls, in *Printing & N. Registering Co. v. Sampson,* L.R. 19 Eq. 465, "if there is one thing which more than another public policy requires it is that men of full age and competent understanding shall have the utmost liberty of contracting, and their contracts when entered into freely and voluntarily shall be held sacred and shall be enforced by courts of justice."

The remedy intended to be accomplished by the act of Congress was to shield against the danger of contract or combination by the few against the interest of the many, and to the detriment of freedom. The construction now given, I think, strikes down the interest of the many to the advantage and benefit of the few. It has been held in a case involving a combination among workingmen that such combinations are embraced in the act of Congress in question, and this view was not doubted by this court. *In re Debs*, 158 U. S. 564, 565.* The interpretation of the statute, therefore, which holds that reasonable agreements are within its purview, makes it embrace every peaceable organization or combination of the laborer to benefit his condition either by obtaining an increase of wages or diminution of the hours of labor.... It follows that the construction which reads the rule of reason out of the statute embraces within its inhibition every contract or combination by which workingmen seek to peaceably better their condition. It is, therefore, as I see it, absolutely true to say that the construction now adopted ... makes the statute tend to an end never contemplated, and against the accomplishment of which its provisions were enacted ..... * * *

[Quoting from a letter from a Kansas City businessman printed in the second annual report of the Interstate Commerce Commission:] "The frequent and violent changes in railway rates which have taken place during the past few years ... are ruinous to all business men, as well as the railways, and are the cause of great discontent among shippers everywhere, and especially to the farmers. What is needed is a fixed, permanent rate, which shall be reasonable, and which can be counted upon by any one engaging in business."

"... [C]ompetition for business between railroad companies is often pushed to ruinous extremes, and the most serious difficulty in the way of securing obedience to the law may be traced to this fact. When competition degenerates to rate wars, they are as unsettling to the business of the country as they are mischievous to the carriers, and the spirit of existing law is against them." * * *

QUESTIONS AND COMMENTS

1. The Interstate Commerce Act was enacted in 1887, but the Interstate Commerce Commission (ICC) did not then have the power to fix and enforce rates.

* Editors' note: In *Debs* (1895), the Court upheld a contempt citation against Eugene Debs for exhorting the rank and file railroad workers to continue their strike against Pullman after the district court had enjoined it. The initial targets of the Sherman Act were the workers; workers' combinations were held to restrain trade and violate the Sherman Act—even while Justice White and others thought it much more doubtful that large business combinations offended the law. See R. Peritz, COMPETITION POLICY IN AMERICA: HISTORY, RHETORIC, LAW (rev. ed. 2001), 32B36. Congress later adopted a labor exemption, in Clayton Act § 6.

2. What was the crux of the disagreement between Justice Peckham and Justice (Edward D.) White? What basic philosophies of economic regulation and personal and business freedom were at stake?

3. What was the purpose and probable effect of the price fixing? Was there a good policy argument, or not, that competitors should have the right to overcome forces of ruinous competition by agreement among themselves? Who would be helped or hurt by the agreement?

4. At issue was the then critical question of construction of Section 1 of the Sherman Act. Should it be construed to embody the common law, which had largely developed in England and was somewhat ambiguous but may have allowed certain price fixing? If not, should the statute be construed in accordance with its letter (*all* restraints are illegal), or should it be construed according to "reason"? Should the type of restraint matter? Notice that Justice Peckham distinguishes the railroads' price fixing (a direct restraint) from restraints collateral to a wholly appropriate main purpose.

5. We have omitted the portion of the opinion rejecting defendants' argument that railroads, being subject to special regulation (the Interstate Commerce Act), were not subject to the antitrust laws. In this portion of its opinion, the Court said:

> [Business combinations may even reduce prices] by reducing the expense inseparable from the running of many different companies for the same purpose. Trade or commerce under those circumstances may nevertheless be badly and unfortunately restrained by driving out of business the small dealers and worthy men whose lives have been spent therein, and who might be unable to readjust themselves to their altered surroundings. Mere reduction in the price of the commodity dealt in might be dearly paid for by the ruin of such a class, and the absorption of control over one commodity by an all-powerful combination of capital.... A change from stage coaches and canal boats to railroads threw at once a large number of men out of employment.... These are the misfortunes which seem to be the necessary accompaniment of all great industrial changes.... It is a misfortune, but yet in such cases it seems to be the inevitable accompaniment of change and improvement.
>
> It is wholly different, however, when such changes are effected by combinations of capital....

The concern that great combinations might drive out of business "small dealers and worthy men" had resonance in U.S. antitrust for most of a century, and you will see the theme reappearing in many cases. The words touched and reflected the populist chord of antitrust. The inverse relationship between protectionism and efficiency was not to be seriously confronted in U.S. antitrust law until the third quarter of the twentieth century. Competition and efficiency are deeply in tension with protectionism.

But what is protectionism? Was Justice Pekham protectionist, or was a different value embedded in his words? Recall the context of the passage: If small dealers and worthy men are hurt by a cartel, as opposed to their being hurt by the forces of economic progress, that is yet another reason not to tolerate the cartel. Was Justice Peckham reflecting the value of entrepreneurialism; the perspective that society will be better off if we trust the entrepreneurial spirit, more than giant combinations of capital, to provide goods and services at reasonable prices and to open new pathways of invention? A focus on entrepreneurship and open markets was to produce the "free trader doctrine"—which emerged and survived from 1911 (see *Dr. Miles*, p. 615 infra) to 1977 (see *GTE Sylvania*, p. 641 infra). The free trader doctrine has only muted resonance in U.S. antitrust today, the common wisdom being that concern for the freedom of competitors who have no market power is indistinguishable from protectionism.[56] Is it?

Shortly after the decision in *Trans–Missouri,* a case involving a secret iron pipe cartel came before the Court of Appeals for the Sixth Circuit. Judge (later President, and later still, Chief Justice) William Howard Taft wrote the Court's opinion. Taft took the occasion to address these questions.

Judge Taft's decision is a famous one, and it is still cited with admiration. The modern concept of naked restraints versus ancillary restraints, the first being illegal on their face, is traced to Judge Taft's opinion. Further, in analyzing the predictable effect of the bid rigging conspiracy before the court, Judge Taft's opinion is classic.

UNITED STATES v. ADDYSTON PIPE & STEEL CO.

85 F. 271 (6th Cir.1898), *modified* and *aff'd,* 175 U.S. 211 (1899).

JUDGE TAFT: . . . The argument for defendants is that their contract of association was not, and could not be, a monopoly, because their aggregate tonnage capacity did not exceed 30 per cent. of the total tonnage capacity of the country; that the restraints upon the members of the association, if restraints they could be called, did not embrace all the states, and were not unlimited in space; that such partial restraints were justified and upheld at common law if reasonable, and only proportioned to the necessary protection of the parties; that in this case the partial restraints were reasonable, because without them each member would be subjected to ruinous competition by the other, and did not exceed in degree of stringency or scope what was necessary to protect the parties in securing prices for their product that were fair and reasonable to themselves and the public; that competition was not stifled by the association because the prices fixed by it had to be fixed with reference to the very active competition of pipe companies which were not members of the association, and which had more than double the defendants' capacity; that in this way the association only modified and restrained the evils of ruinous competition, while the public had all the benefit from competition which public policy demanded.

56. The German Ordoliberal notion of the importance of preserving the individual's freedom of trade (see D. Gerber, LAW AND COMPETITION IN TWENTIETH CENTURY EUROPE: PROTECTING PROMETHEUS (1998)), is sympathetic with the (once popular) American free trader doctrine

From early times it was the policy of Englishmen to encourage trade in England, and to discourage those voluntary restraints which tradesmen were often induced to impose on themselves by contract. Courts recognized this public policy by refusing to enforce stipulations of this character. The objections to such restraints were mainly two. One was that by such contracts a man disabled himself from earning a livelihood with the risk of becoming a public charge, and deprived the community of the benefit of his labor. The other was that such restraints tended to give to the covenantee, the beneficiary of such restraints, a monopoly of the trade, from which he had thus excluded one competitor, and by the same means might exclude others. * * *

The inhibition against restraints of trade at common law seems at first to have had no exception.... After a time it became apparent to the people and the courts that it was in the interest of trade that certain covenants in restraint of trade should be enforced. It was of importance, as an incentive to industry and honest dealing in trade, that, after a man had built up a business with an extensive good will, he should be able to sell his business and good will to the best advantage, and he could not do so unless he could bind himself by an enforceable contract not to engage in the same business in such a way as to prevent injury to that which he was about to sell. It was equally for the good of the public and trade, when partners dissolved, and one took the business, or they divided the business, that each partner might bind himself not to do anything in trade thereafter which would derogate from his grant of the interest conveyed to his former partner. Again, when two men became partners in a business, although their union might reduce competition, this effect was only an incident to the main purpose of a union of their capital, enterprise, and energy to carry on a successful business, and one useful to the community. Restrictions in the articles of partnership upon the business activity of the members, with a view of securing their entire effort in the common enterprise, were, of course, only ancillary to the main end of the union, and were to be encouraged.... * * *

It would be stating it too strongly to say that these ... covenants in restraint of trade include all of those upheld as valid at the common law; but it would certainly seem to follow from the tests laid down for determining the validity of such an agreement that no conventional restraint of trade can be enforced unless the covenant embodying it is merely ancillary to the main purpose of a lawful contract, and necessary to protect the covenantee in the enjoyment of the legitimate fruits of the contract, or to protect him from the dangers of an unjust use of those fruits by the other party....

This very statement of the rule implies that the contract must be one in which there is a main purpose, to which the covenant in restraint of trade is merely ancillary.... But where the sole object of both parties in making the contract as expressed therein is merely to restrain competition, and enhance or maintain prices, it would seem that there was nothing to justify or excuse the restraint, that it would necessarily have a tendency to monopoly, and therefore would be void. In such a case there is no measure of what is necessary to the protection of either party, except the vague and varying opinion of judges as to how much, on principles of political economy, men ought to be allowed to restrain competition. There is in such contracts no main lawful purpose, to subserve which partial restraint is permitted, and by which its reasonableness is measured, but the sole object is to restrain trade in order to avoid the competition which it has always been the policy of the common law to foster.

Much has been said in regard to the relaxing of the original strictness of the common law in declaring contracts in restraint of trade void as conditions of civilization and public policy have changed, and the argument drawn therefrom is that the law now recognizes that competition may be so ruinous as to injure the public, and, therefore, that contracts made with a view to check such ruinous competition and regulate prices, though in restraint of trade, and having no other purpose, will be upheld. We think this conclusion is unwarranted by the authorities when all of them are considered. * * *

It is true that there are some cases in which the courts, mistaking, as we conceive, the proper limits of the relaxation of the rules for determining the unreasonableness of restraints of trade, have set sail on a sea of doubt, and have assumed the power to say, in respect to contracts which have no other purpose and no other consideration on either side than the mutual restraint of the parties, how much restraint of competition is in the public interest, and how much is not.

The manifest danger in the administration of justice according to so shifting, vague, and indeterminate a standard would seem to be a strong reason against adopting it. [Emphasis added.]

* * *

Upon this review of the law and the authorities, we can have no doubt that the association of the defendants, however reasonable the prices they fixed, however great the competition they had to encounter, and however great the necessity for curbing themselves by joint agreement from committing financial suicide by ill-advised competition, was void at common law, because in restraint of trade, and tending to a monopoly. But the facts of the case do not require us to go so far as this, for they show that the attempted justification of this association on the grounds stated is without foundation.

The defendants, being manufacturers and vendors of cast-iron pipe, entered into a combination to raise the prices for pipe for all the states west and south of New York, Pennsylvania, and Virginia, constituting considerably more than three-quarters of the territory of the United States, and significantly called by the associates "pay territory." Their joint annual output was 220,000 tons. The total capacity of all the other cast-iron pipe manufacturers in the pay territory was 170,500 tons. Of this, 45,000 tons was the capacity of mills in Texas, Colorado, and Oregon, so far removed from that part of the pay territory where the demand was considerable that necessary freight rates excluded them from the possibility of competing, and 12,000 tons was the possible annual capacity of a mill at St. Louis, which was practically under the same management as that of one of the defendants' mills. Of the remainder of the mills in pay territory and outside of the combination, one was at Columbus, Ohio, two in northern Ohio, and one in Michigan. Their aggregate possible annual capacity was about one-half the usual annual output of the defendants' mills. They were, it will be observed, at the extreme northern end of the pay territory, while the defendants' mills at Cincinnati, Louisville, Chattanooga, and South Pittsburg, and Anniston, and Bessemer, were grouped much nearer to the center of the pay territory. The freight upon cast-iron pipe amounts to a considerable percentage of the price at which manufacturers can deliver it at any great distance from the place of manufacture. Within the margin of the freight per ton which Eastern manufacturers would have to pay to deliver pipe in pay territory, the defendants, by controlling two-thirds of the output in pay territory, were practically able to fix prices. The competition of the Ohio and Michigan mills, of course, somewhat affected their power in this respect in the northern part of the pay territory; but, the further south the place of delivery was to be, the more complete the monopoly over the trade which the defendants were able to exercise, within the limit already described. Much evidence is adduced upon affidavit to prove that defendants had no power arbitrarily to fix prices, and that they were always obliged to meet competition. To the extent that they could not impose prices on the public in excess of the cost price of pipe with freight from the Atlantic seaboard added, this is true; but, within that limit, they could fix prices as they chose. The most cogent evidence that they had this power is the fact, everywhere apparent in the record, that they exercised it. The details of the way in which it was maintained are somewhat obscured by the manner in which the proof was adduced in the court below, upon affidavits solely, and without the clarifying effect of cross-examination, but quite enough appears to leave no doubt of the ultimate fact. The defendants were, by their combination, therefore able to deprive the public in a large territory of the advantages otherwise accruing to them from the proximity of defendants' pipe factories, and, by keeping prices just low enough to prevent competition by Eastern manufacturers, to compel the public to pay an increase over what the price would have been, if fixed by competition between defendants, nearly equal to the advantage in freight rates enjoyed by defendants over Eastern competitors. The defendants acquired this power by voluntarily agreeing to sell only at prices fixed by their committee, and by allowing the highest bidder at the secret "auction pool" to become the lowest bidder of them at the public letting. Now, the restraint thus imposed on themselves was only partial. It did not cover the United States. There was not a complete monopoly. It was tempered by the fear of competition, and it affected only a part of the price. . . .

It has been earnestly pressed upon us that the prices at which the cast-iron pipe was sold in pay territory were reasonable. A great many affidavits of purchasers of pipe in pay territory, all drawn by the same hand or from the same model, are produced, in which the affiants say that, in their opinion, the prices at which pipe has been sold by defendants have been reasonable. We do not think the issue an important one, because, as already stated, we do not think that at common law there is any question of reasonableness open to the courts with reference to such a contract. Its tendency was certainly to give defendants the power to charge unreasonable prices, had they chosen to do so. But, if it were important, we should unhesitatingly find that the prices charged in the instances which were in evidence were unreasonable. The letters from the manager of the Chattanooga foundry written to the other defendants, and discussing the prices fixed by the association, do not leave the slightest doubt upon this point, and outweigh the perfunctory affidavits produced by the defendants. The cost of producing pipe at Chattanooga, together with a reasonable profit, did not exceed $15 a ton. It could have been delivered at Atlanta at $17 to $18 a ton, and yet the lowest price which that foundry was permitted by the rules of the association to bid was $24.25. The same thing was true all through pay territory to a greater or less degree, and especially at "reserved cities." . . . * * *

QUESTIONS AND COMMENTS

1. Judge Taft distinguished between "the covenant in restraint of trade [that] is merely ancillary," and an agreement "merely to restrain competition" (often called, today, a "naked restraint"). What is a naked restraint? Was the pipe producers' bidding compact a naked restraint? Was the railroads' "self regulation" (of prices) (*Trans–Missouri*) a naked restraint? Is a lawyer's agreement not to compete against his or her partners a naked restraint? Describe the difference in treatment between a naked and an ancillary (or collateral) restraint.

2. What was the market (the area within which defendants allegedly exercised power to raise price)? In this market, what was the relationship between supply and demand? Why does the Court use, as a basis for comparison, capacity of non-member producers and output of member producers? If member producers raised their prices above cost,[57] what would (did) happen? Would geographically distant sellers come quickly and easily into the market? What was the lid on the bid riggers' ability to charge supracompetitive prices? Did it adequately protect the consumer?

3. If defendants had been able to show that potential competition protected the consumer, would they have prevailed?

4. After the Taft opinion in *Addyston Pipe,* the Supreme Court decided its second railroad price-fixing case. The members of the Joint Traffic Association (railroads east of the Mississippi River) had a rate-fixing agreement similar to that in *Trans–Missouri,* except that a member could deviate from

57. "Cost" includes a return on investment sufficient to draw capital to the market.

the association's rate schedule if its board of directors adopted a resolution to do so and served notice on the association. While defendants claimed that this right to deviate was material, the railroads' principal argument did not depend upon factual distinctions. Their principal argument was that the Supreme Court could not have meant what it said in *Trans–Missouri*. The principle of *Trans–Missouri,* they argued, unreasonably interfered with liberty and property and with most normal business transactions.

Justice Peckham again wrote for the Supreme Court. The Court reaffirmed *Trans–Missouri*, with Justice White and others again dissenting. The Court, however, softened its dictum that *all* restraints are illegal, stating that the formation of corporations, partnership agreements, joint sales agencies, and sales or leases with ancillary covenants not to compete had never been regarded as contracts in restraint of trade. The Court once again rejected the defense of ruinous competition. *United States v. Joint–Traffic Association*, 171 U.S. 505 (1898).

Did the Court in *Trans–Missouri* and *Joint–Traffic* treat the railroads' argument of ruinous competition too cavalierly? Was the Court's position wise even if the railroads' prediction was credible? Suppose there is too much capital in an industry; over-capitalization is temporary; there is a short-term downturn in demand. Can competitor price-fixing be defended as a way of holding capacity in the market until demand rises again? Some European and Asian antitrust systems authorize "crisis cartels" in exceptional cases. Should the United States authorize crisis cartels? Who should decide when and how competition should be moderated?

In 1906 the Interstate Commerce Commission was given the power to set railroad rates. In 1948, Congress passed the Reed–Bulwinkle Act, allowing railroads to fix rates collectively through rate bureaus and giving them antitrust immunity for doing so. The Staggers Rail Act of 1980 eliminated most antitrust immunity.

5. In *Addyston Pipe,* defendants appealed to the Supreme Court from the judgment against them. They argued that Congress had no power under the Commerce Clause of the Constitution to prohibit their agreement; they claimed that the exercise of such power would impair their constitutional guarantee of liberty of contract. They also argued that their arrangement had no direct effect on interstate commerce. The Supreme Court rejected all of these contentions. In another opinion by Justice Peckham, the Court quoted approvingly from Judge Taft's lower court opinion. It affirmed the judgment for plaintiff, modifying it only to exclude wholly intrastate activities. *Addyston Pipe & Steel Co. v. United States*, 175 U.S. 211 (1899).

Thus, at the turn of the century, all agreements among competitors that had the "direct and immediate" [purpose and] effect of restraining trade (essentially cartels, in modern language) were banned by Section 1 of the Sherman Act, whereas agreements reasonably collateral to legitimate business transactions were not. The Taft opinion in *Addyston Pipe* convincingly argues that this development is generally consistent with the American common law tradition, to which Congress was apparently pointing. And as we saw, a divided Court had rejected the view that all agreements—even price-fixing agreements—must be tested by a standard of reasonableness.

2. TRUST BUSTING, BIG COMBINATIONS, AND THEODORE ROOSEVELT

In the election of 1900, both parties took stands against the trusts. The Republicans were elected and upon the assassination of President McKinley a few months after his inauguration, the vice-president, Theodore Roosevelt, took office. Roosevelt offered a simple and vivid dichotomy. While condemning the unscrupulous tactics of "bad" trusts, he balanced his attack with praise for "good" trusts. Good trusts made possible great material development, and they increased the nation's international prestige. The nation, he thought, should accept large size as an unavoidable characteristic of the then new economy.

Roosevelt was a friend of business (at least of "good" business). Although called the "great trust buster," he prosecuted relatively few antitrust cases. His first was *Northern Securities*—a consolidation of great railroads by the purchase of stock. According to Letwin:

> It was the first antitrust case in which those cast as villains were celebrities.... James J. Hill, the swashbuckling railroad man who had built the Great Northern ... and J. Pierpont Morgan, the Goliath of bankers. Each was accompanied by a host of minor moguls.... The drama was staged ... as a conflict between Reason and Extravagance, between the respectable requirements of the common good and the wilfulness of colorful, but dangerous, buccaneers.[20]

The case was a landmark for holding or confirming that neither liberty of contract or property, nor the spector of ruinous competition, exonerated the defendants from antitrust liability. It is included here to illuminate the intellectual and ideological debate about the proper scope and limits of antitrust in view of constitutional freedoms. Some of these arguments resonate today, even though it is clear that antitrust law can prohibit anticompetitive acquisitions—by stock purchase or otherwise.

NORTHERN SECURITIES CO. v. UNITED STATES

193 U.S. 197 (1904).

JUSTICE HARLAN: [By 1901, J.P. Morgan and James J. Hill had acquired majority interests in three regionally dominant railroad companies: The Northern Pacific, the Great Northern, and the Chicago, Burlington, and Quincy. E.H. Harriman, owner of the Union Pacific, initiated a bitter, costly fight to obtain complete control of the Northern Pacific, his primary competitor. The threat of cut-throat competition and substantial losses in investments to all three industrialists led to a settlement, brokered by "reigning" banker J.P. Morgan, in the form of a holding company, the Northern Securities Company. Chartered in New Jersey, the corporation held the stock of the Northern Pacific, Great Northern, and Burlington lines. Suit was brought to dissolve the combination on grounds that it violated the Sherman Act.]

20. Letwin, LAW AND ECONOMIC POLICY at 182. See 182–95, 200–37.

... Necessarily by this combination or arrangement the holding company in the fullest sense dominates the situation in the interest of those who were stockholders of the constituent companies; as much so, for every practical purpose, as if it had been itself a railroad corporation which had built, owned, and operated both lines for the exclusive benefit of its stockholders. Necessarily, also, the constituent companies ceased, under such a combination, to be in active competition for trade and commerce along their respective lines, and have become, practically, one powerful consolidated corporation, by the name of a holding corporation the principal, if not the sole, object for the formation of which was to carry out the purpose of the original combination under which competition between the constituent companies would cease.... No scheme or device could more certainly come within the words of the act—"combination in the form of a trust or otherwise ... in restraint of commerce among the several States or with foreign nations,"—or could more effectively and certainly suppress free competition between the constituent companies. This combination is, within the meaning of the act, a "trust;" but if not, it is a *combination in restraint of interstate and international commerce;* and that is enough to bring it under the condemnation of the act. The mere existence of such a combination and the power acquired by the holding company as its trustee, constitute a menace to, and a restraint upon, that freedom of commerce which Congress intended to recognize and protect, and which the public is entitled to have protected. If such combination be not destroyed, all the advantages that would naturally come to the public under the operation of the general laws of competition, as between the Great Northern and Northern Pacific Railway companies, will be lost, and the entire commerce of the immense territory in the northern part of the United States between the Great Lakes and the Pacific at Puget Sound will be at the mercy of a single holding corporation, organized in a State distant from the people of that territory. * * *

[F]rom the former opinions of this court ... certain propositions are plainly deducible and embrace the present case. Those propositions are: ...

That *every* combination or conspiracy which would extinguish competition between otherwise competing railroads engaged in *interstate trade or commerce,* and which would *in that way* restrain *such* trade or commerce, is made illegal by the act; ...

That the natural effect of competition is to increase commerce, and an agreement whose direct effect is to prevent this play of competition restrains instead of promotes trade and commerce;

That to vitiate a combination, such as the act of Congress condemns, it need not be shown that the combination, in fact, results or will result in a total suppression of trade or in a complete monopoly, but it is only essential to show that by its necessary operation it tends to restrain interstate or international trade or commerce or tends to create a monopoly in such trade or commerce and to deprive the public of the advantages that flow from free competition; that the constitutional guaranty of liberty of contract does not prevent Congress from prescribing the rule of free competition for those engaged in *interstate and international* commerce; . . .

Many suggestions were made in argument based upon the thought that the Anti–Trust Act would in the end prove to be mischievous in its consequences. Disaster to business and wide-spread financial ruin, it has been intimated, will follow the execution of its provisions. Such predictions were made in all the cases heretofore arising under that act. But they have not been verified. It is the history of monopolies in this country and in England that predictions of ruin are habitually made by them when it is attempted, by legislation, to restrain their operations and to protect the public against their exactions. In this, as in former cases, they seek shelter behind the reserved rights of the States and even behind the constitutional guarantee of liberty of contract. But this court has heretofore adjudged that the act of Congress did not touch the rights of the States, and that liberty of contract did not involve a right to deprive the public of the advantages of free competition in trade and commerce. Liberty of contract does not imply liberty in a corporation or individuals to defy the national will, when legally expressed. Nor does the enforcement of a legal enactment of Congress infringe, in any proper sense, the general inherent right of every one to acquire and hold property. That right, like all other rights, must be exercised in subordination to the law.

* * *

Justice Brewer concurred, objecting to the sweeping language of the plurality opinion and stating that the act is limited by the power of each individual to manage his own property. "Freedom of action in these respects is among the inalienable rights of every citizen." If this case were about a single individual's investment rather than a combination, he said, the antitrust law could not infringe that right.

JUSTICE WHITE, joined by CHIEF JUSTICE FULLER and JUSTICES PECKHAM and HOLMES, dissenting:

. . . [T]he principle that the ownership of property is embraced within the power of Congress to regulate commerce, whenever that body deems that a particular character of ownership, if allowed to continue, may restrain commerce between the states or create a monopoly thereof, is, in my opinion, in conflict with the most elementary conceptions of rights of property. For it would follow if Congress deemed that the acquisition by one or more individuals engaged in interstate commerce of more than a certain amount of property would be prejudicial to interstate commerce, the amount of property held or the amount which could be employed in interstate commerce could be regulated. . . . * * *

If the principle were adopted, and the power which would arise from so doing were exercised, the result would be not only to destroy the state and Federal governments, but, by the implication of authority, from which the destruction would be brought about, there would be erected upon the ruins of both a government endowed with the arbitrary power to disregard the great guaranty of life, liberty, and property and every other safeguard upon which organized civil society depends.... * * *

JUSTICE HOLMES, joined by the CHIEF JUSTICE and JUSTICES WHITE and PECKHAM, dissenting:

I am unable to agree with the judgment of the majority of the court, and although I think it useless and undesirable, as a rule, to express dissent, I feel bound to do so in this case and to give my reasons for it.

Great cases, like hard cases, make bad law. For great cases are called great, not by reason of their real importance in shaping the law of the future, but because of some accident of immediate overwhelming interest which appeals to the feelings and distorts the judgment. These immediate interests exercise a kind of hydraulic pressure which makes what previously was clear seem doubtful, and before which even well settled principles of law will bend. What we have to do in this case is to find the meaning of some not very difficult words ... * * *

... This act is construed by the Government to affect the purchasers of shares in two railroad companies because of the effect it may have, or, if you like, is certain to have, upon the competition of these roads. If such a remote result of the exercise of an ordinary incident of property and personal freedom is enough to make that exercise unlawful, there is hardly any transaction concerning commerce between the States that may not be made a crime by the finding of a jury or a court.... * * *

[After pointing out that "The act says nothing about competition" and arguing that the transaction did not involve a contract or conspiracy in restraint of trade:]

If the statute applies to this case it must be because the parties, or some of them, have formed, or because the Northern Securities Company is, a combination in restraint of trade among the States, or, what comes to the same thing in my opinion, because the defendants, or some or one of them, are monopolizing or attempting to monopolize some part of the commerce between the States. But the mere reading of those words shows that they are used in a limited and accurate sense. According to popular speech, every concern monopolizes whatever business it does, and if that business is trade between two States it monopolizes a part of the trade among the States. Of course the statute does not forbid that. It does not mean that all business must cease....

... [T]he act of Congress will not be construed to mean the universal disintegration of society into single men, each at war with all the rest, or even the prevention of all further combinations for a common end.

There is a natural feeling that somehow or other the statute meant to strike at combinations great enough to cause just anxiety on the part of those who love their country more than money, while it viewed such little ones as I have supposed with just indifference. This notion, it may be said, somehow breathes from the pores of the act, although it seems to be contradicted in every way by the words in detail. And it has occurred to me that it might be that when a combination reached a certain size it might have attributed to it more of the character of a monopoly merely by virtue of its size than would be attributed to a smaller one. I am quite clear that it is only in connection with monopolies that size could play any part. But my answer has been indicated already. In the first place size in the case of railroads is an inevitable incident and if it were an objection under the act, the Great Northern and the Northern Pacific already were too great and encountered the law. In the next place in the case of railroads it is evident that the size of the combination is reached for other ends than those which would make them monopolies. * * *

In view of my interpretation of the statute I do not go further into the question of the power of Congress. That has been dealt with by my brother White and I concur in the main with his views. I am happy to know that only a minority of my brethren adopt an interpretation of the law which in my opinion would make eternal the *bellum omnium contra omnes* and disintegrate society so far as it could into individual atoms. If that were its intent I should regard calling such a law a regulation of commerce as a mere pretense. It would be an attempt to reconstruct society. I am not concerned with the wisdom of such an attempt, but I believe that Congress was not entrusted by the Constitution with the power to make it and I am deeply persuaded that it has not tried.

QUESTIONS AND COMMENTS

1. Consider the fundamental rights arguments advanced by the railroads and by five of the Justices (Brewer included). Did the Justices have a point (at least at the dawn of the twentieth century)? Did application of the antitrust laws to invalidate stock transfers possibly infringe constitutional rights of contract or property? If basic freedoms were not infringed, were they nonetheless implicated? Consider the relationship between competition and robust rights of contract and property. Do legal protections of contract and property rights enhance competition and efficiency? Consider the relationship between freedoms of contract and property and economic regulation. Might we (some of us) be willing to tolerate harms to competition and efficiency in order to preserve "rights"? Which did the Justices have in mind—the synergy or the trade-off?

Note that the synergy hypothesis—a society enhances competition by protecting rights of contract and property—is invoked today. See Justice Breyer's opinion in *NYNEX v. Discon, Inc.*, 525 U.S. 128 (1998), infra at 653, quoting from *Standard Oil*: "the freedom of the individual right to contract when not unduly or improperly exercised [is] the most efficient means for the prevention of monopoly." *Id.* at 137. Microsoft, in its arguments before the D.C. Circuit Court of Appeals, invoked the importance to competition of intellectual property protection. See *United States v. Microsoft Corp.*, 253 F.3d 34, 49–50, 62–64 (D.C.Cir.), cert. denied, 534 U.S. 952 (2001). Many scholars and policymakers advising post-Communist nations stressed, as a first step towards a democratic, market-based economy: clear and well protected rights of property and contract. When a society absolutely denies contract and property rights, there are no markets. When a society is founded on freedoms of property and contract, among others, is the correlation more attenuated?

2. Was the turn-of-the-century combination of the great railroads likely to cause the price of freight shipments to rise? Why? Would such a price rise be likely to encourage new entry by another railroad? Would it cause a shift by shippers to other forms of transportation? Did the Court know? Did it care?

3. Did this merger place enormous wealth in the control of a few? Did the merger's contribution to the concentration of wealth condemn it? Does an increase in the wealth controlled by a few correlate with a lessening of competition?

4. Which is correct: Harlan's view that all combinations of competitors (or of large competitors) deprive the public of the advantages of free competition, or Holmes' view that the antitrust law is not about competition, and that in order to maintain a proper regard for liberty no combination should be illegal, regardless of its effect on competition, unless some act is done with the sinister intent to keep rivals out of the business or to ruin those already in it?

Is Justice Holmes correct that the natural result of the Court's holding is to atomize society? How about: The natural result of the Court's decision is to tend to preserve existing pluralism? Should antitrust preserve pluralism (business diversity)?

5. Holmes had been appointed to the Court by Theodore Roosevelt, who had made a large political investment in the *Northern Securities* case. Seldom reticent, Roosevelt commented publicly on Holmes' dissent. He thought that Holmes showed "all the spirit of a banana."[21] That judgment is probably as unfair to Holmes as it is characteristic of Roosevelt. What Holmes sought to do in *Northern Securities* was consistent with his own libertarian philosophy. He thought the antitrust laws were "humbug."[22]

3. THE RULE OF REASON IS BORN: JUDGING "BY THE LIGHT OF REASON"

The Taft Presidency; The Rule of Reason

William Howard Taft, a former federal judge and future U.S. Chief Justice, was Roosevelt's hand-picked successor as President. Although Taft had supported Roosevelt's trust policy, he had reservations about both its wisdom and legality. Taft's legalistic world view led him to discard Roosevelt's moralistic distinctions among trusts. Taft outlined a functional distinction between combinations established specifically to eliminate competition, and those that happened to restrict trade en route to efficient production.[23]

---

21. C.D. Bowen, YANKEE FROM OLYMPUS, 370 (1944).

22. HOLMES-POLLOCK LETTERS, 163 (M. Howe ed., 1941).

23. See W.H. Harbaugh, POWER AND RESPONSIBILITY: THE LIFE AND TIMES OF THEODORE ROOSEVELT (1961) (hereafter Harbaugh, POWER AND RESPONSIBILITY) 403–07; Letwin, LAW AND ECONOMIC POLICY at 252.

Still, the courts lacked a legal formula that would make interpretation of the Sherman Act consistent and effective. The early restraint of trade cases showed that the Supreme Court was divided between two views of the Sherman Act. By one view the act was a dramatically new law that prohibited combinations that produced power. Alternatively, the act was regarded as a federal codification of English common law, tolerant of combinations unless they deprived outsiders of the freedom to practice their trades. From 1888 to 1910, when Melville W. Fuller was Chief Justice, a majority of the Court had the first conception. Associate Justice Edward D. White was among the dissenters. Oliver Wendell Holmes was appointed to the Court in 1902, and joined the dissenters. Fuller died in 1910, and President Taft elevated White to Chief Justice. As you will see, a new majority emerged. The case in which the new majority emerged involved the oil industry. To place the case in economic context, a little historical background may be helpful.

Oil was discovered in the northwestern corner of Pennsylvania in 1859. John D. Rockefeller, a young merchant in Cleveland, was at first skeptical about investing in the oil business, which was marked by the anarchy of drillers and diggers, by fires and disasters, and by the abrupt rise and fall of prices by several hundred percent.

But by 1862, prospects seemed more favorable. Rockefeller met and teamed up with a technologist, Andrews, who devised methods for obtaining a high yield of kerosene oil from crude oil. Rockefeller and Andrews established a refinery. They, and a new partner, Flagler, soon had the largest oil refinery in Cleveland.

Matthew Josephson, in The Robber Barons (1962), continues the story as follows. Consider, as you read the excerpt, which of Rockefeller's strategies were good, hard competition (they might hurt less efficient competitors but would benefit people and firms who wanted oil)? Which strategies were likely to hurt the market and hurt users of oil? These are the main inquiries in monopolization cases today.

THE ROBBER BARONS, excerpt

Rockefeller and Flagler approached the railroad which carried so many carloads of their oil toward the seaboard, and whose tariff figured heavily in the ultimate cost. They demanded from it concessions in freight rates that would enable them to meet the advantages of other refining centers such as Pittsburgh, Philadelphia and New York. Their company was now large enough to force the hand of the railroad, in this case, a branch of Vanderbilt's New York Central system; and they were granted their demands: a secret reduction or "rebate" on all their shipments of oil. "Such was the railroad's method," Rockefeller himself afterward admitted. He relates:

A public rate was made and collected by the railroad companies, but so far as my knowledge extends, was seldom retained in full; a portion of it was repaid to the shipper as a rebate. By this method the real rate of freight which any shipper paid was not known by his competitors, nor by other railroads, the amount being a matter of bargain with the carrying companies.

Once having gained an advantage Rockefeller pressed forward relentlessly. The volume of his business increased rapidly. Thanks to the collaboration of the railroad, he had placed his rivals in other cities and in Cleveland itself under a handicap, whose weight he endeavored to increase.

The railroads, as we see, possessed the strategic power, almost of life and death, to encourage one industrial group or cause another to languish. Their policy was based on the relative costs of handling small or large volume shipments. Thus as the Rockefeller company became the largest shipper of oil, its production rising in 1870 to 3,000 barrels a day, and offered to guarantee regular daily shipments of as much as sixty carloads, the railroads were impelled to accept further proposals for rebates. It was to their interest to do so in view of savings of several hundred thousand dollars a month in handling. On crude oil brought from the Oil Regions, Rockefeller paid perhaps 15 cents a barrel less than the open rate of 40 cents; on refined oil moving from Cleveland toward New York, he paid approximately 90 cents against the open rate of $1.30. These momentous agreements were maintained in utter secrecy, perhaps because of the persisting memory of their illegality, according to the common law ever since Queen Elizabeth's time, as a form of "conspiracy" in trade.

In January, 1870, Rockefeller, Flagler & Andrews were incorporated as a joint-stock company, a form increasingly popular, under the name of the Standard Oil Company of Ohio. At this time their worth was estimated at one million dollars; they employed over a thousand workers and were the largest refiners in the world. Despite deeply disturbed conditions in their trade during 1870, profits came to them in a mounting flood, while in the same year, it is noteworthy, four of their twenty-nine competitors in Cleveland gave up the ghost. The pious young man of thirty who feared only God, and thought of nothing but his business, gave not a sign of his greatly augmented wealth, which made him one of the leading personages of his city. His income was actually a fabulous one for the time. The Standard Oil Company from the beginning earned something like 100 per cent on its capital; and Rockefeller and his brother owned a full half-interest in it in 1870. But with an evangelistic fervor John Rockefeller was bent only upon further conquests, upon greater extensions of the power over industry which had come into the hands of the group he headed.

In the life of every conquering soul there is a "turning point," a moment when a deep understanding of the self coincides with an equally deep sense of one's immediate mission in the tangible world. For Rockefeller, brooding, secretive, uneasily scenting his fortune, this moment came but a few years after his entrance into the oil trade, and at the age of thirty. He had looked upon the disorganized conditions of the Pennsylvania oil fields, the only source then known, and found them not good: the guerilla fighting of drillers, of refining firms, of rival railroad lines, the mercurial changes in supply and market value—very alarming in 1870—offended his orderly and methodical spirit. But one could see that petroleum was to be the light of the world. From the source, from the chaotic oil fields where thousands of drillers toiled, the grimy stream of the precious commodity, petroleum, flowed along many diverse channels to narrow into the hands of several hundred refineries, then to issue once more in a continuous stream to consumers throughout the world. Owner with Flagler and Harkness of the largest refining company in the country, Rockefeller had a strongly entrenched position at the narrows of this stream. Now what if the Standard Oil Company should by further steps of organization possess itself wholly of the narrows? In this period of anarchic individual competition, the idea of such a movement of rationalization must have come to Rockefeller forcibly, as it had recently come to others.[1] * * *

This grand idea of industrial rationalization owed its swift, ruthless, methodical execution no doubt to the firmness of character we sense in Rockefeller, who had the temper of a great, unconscionable military captain, combining audacity with thoroughness and shrewd judgment. His plan seemed to take account of no one's feelings in the matter. Indeed there was something revolutionary in it; it seemed to fly in the face of human liberties and deep-rooted custom and common law. The notorious "South Improvement Company," with its strange charter, ingeniously instrumenting the scheme of combination, was to be unraveled amid profound secrecy. By conspiring with the railroads (which also hungered for economic order), it would be terribly armed with the power of the freight rebate which garrotted all opposition systematically. . . .

I had our plan clearly in mind. It was right. I knew it as a matter of conscience. It was right between me and my God. If I had to do it tomorrow I would do it again in the same way—do it a hundred times.

The broad purpose was to control and direct the flow of crude petroleum into the hands of a narrowed group of refiners. The refiners would be supported by the combined railroad trunk lines which shipped the oil; while the producers' phase of the stream would be left unorganized—*but with power over their outlet to market* henceforth to be concentrated into the few hands of the refiners.

---

1. The English economist J.A. Hobson has written in this connection: "Each kind of commodity, as it passes through the many processes from the earth to the consumer, may be looked upon as a stream whose channel is broader at some points and narrow at others. Different streams of commodities narrow at different places. Some are narrowest and in fewest hands at the transport stage, others in one of the processes of manufacture, others in the hands of export merchants. . . ." In the case of petroleum the logical "narrows" was at the point of refinery; and inevitably, Rockefeller and Flagler set in motion their great plan to control the stream. "Just as a number of German barons planted their castles along the banks of the Rhine, in order to tax the commerce between East and West which was obliged to make use of this highway, so it is with these economic 'narrows.' Wherever they are found, monopolies plant themselves in the shape of 'rings,' 'corners,' 'pools,' 'syndicates,' or trusts.' " ("The Evolution of Modern Capitalism," p. 142.) (Footnote from original.)

Saying nothing to others, bending over their maps of the industry, Rockefeller and Flagler first drew up a short list of the principal refining companies who were to be asked to combine with them. Then having banded together a sufficient number, they would persuade the railroads to give them special freight rates—on the ground of "evening" the traffic—guaranteeing equitable distribution of freight business; and this in turn would be a club to force other elements needed into union with them. They could control output, drive out competitors, and force all foreign countries throughout the world to buy their product from them at their own terms. They could finally dictate market prices on crude oil, stabilize the margin of profit at their own process, and do away at last with the dangerously speculative character of their business.

Their plans moved forward rapidly all through 1871. For a small sum of money the "conspirators" obtained the Pennsylvania charter of a defunct corporation, which had been authorized to engage in almost any kind of business under the sun. Those who were approached by the promoters, those whom they determined to use in their grand scheme, were compelled in a manner typical of all Rockefeller's projects to sign a written pledge of secrecy:

I, ______, do solemnly promise upon my honor and faith as a gentleman that I will keep secret all transactions which I may have with the corporation known as the South Improvement Company; that should I fail to complete any bargains with the said company, all the preliminary conversations shall be kept strictly private; and finally that I will not disclose the price for which I dispose of any products or any other facts which may in any way bring to light the internal workings or organization of the company. All this I do freely promise.

At the same time, in confidential pourparlers with the officials of the Erie, the Pennsylvania and the New York Central Railroads, the men of the Standard Oil represented themselves as possessing secret control of the bulk of the refining interest. Thus they obtained conditions more advantageous than anything which had gone before; and this weapon in turn of course ensured the triumph of their pool.

The refiners to be combined under the aegis of the South Improvement Company were to have a rebate of from 40 to 50 per cent on the crude oil they ordered shipped to them and from 25 to 50 per cent on the refined oil they shipped out. The refiners in the Oil Regions were to pay *twice as much* by the new code (though nearer to New York) as the Standard Oil Company at Cleveland. But besides the rebate the members of the pool were to be given also a "drawback" consisting of part of the increased tariff rate which "outsiders" were forced to pay. Half of the freight payments of a rival refiner would in many cases be paid over to the Rockefeller group. Their competitors were simply to be decimated; and to make certain of this the railroads agreed—all being set down in writing, in minutest detail—"to make manifests or way-bills of all petroleum or its product transported over any portion of its lines . . . which manifests shall state the name of the consignee, the place of shipment and the place of destination," this information to be furnished faithfully to the officers of the South Improvement Company.

The railroad systems, supposedly public-spirited and impartial, were to open all their knowledge of rival private business to the pool, thus helping to concentrate all the oil trade into the few hands chosen. In return for so much assistance, they were to have their freight "evened," and were enabled at last to enter into a momentous peace pact with each other by which the oil traffic (over which they had quarreled bitterly) was to be fairly allotted among themselves.

By January, 1872, after the first decade of the oil business, John Rockefeller, with the aid of the railroad captains, was busily carrying out a most "elaborate national plan" of his own for the control of his industry—such planned control as the spokesman of the business system asserted ever afterward was impossible. The first pooling of 1872, beautiful as was its economic architecture and laudable its motive, had defects which were soon plainly noticeable. All the political institutions, the whole spirit of American law still favored the amiable, wasteful individualism of business, which in Rockefeller's mind had already become obsolete and must be supplanted by a centralized, one might say almost *collectivist*—certainly cooperative rather than competitive—form of operation. Moreover, these "revolutionists" took little account of the social dislocations their juggernaut would bring. Like the railroad baron, Vanderbilt, working better than they knew, their eyes fixed solely upon the immediate task rather than upon some millennium of the future, they desired simply, as they often said, to be "the biggest refiners in the world. . . ."

To the principal oil firms in Cleveland Rockefeller went one by one, explaining the plan of the South Improvement Company patiently, pointing out how important it was to oppose the crew refiners and save the Cleveland oil trade. . . .

Then if the men demurred, according to much of the testimony at the Senate Investigation of 1876, he would point out suavely that it was useless to resist; opposition would certainly be crushed. The offers of purchase usually made were for from a third to a half the actual cost of the property.

Now a sort of terror swept silently over the oil trade. In a vague panic, competitors saw the Standard Oil officers come to them and say (as Rockefeller's own brother and rival, Frank, testified in 1876): "if you don't sell your property to us it will be valueless, because we have got the advantage with the railroads."

The railroad rates indeed were suddenly doubled to the outsiders, and those refiners who resisted the pool came and expostulated; then they became frightened and disposed of their property. One of the largest competitors in Cleveland, the firm of Alexander, Scofield & Co., held out for a time, protesting before the railroad officials at the monstrous unfairness of the deal. But these officials when consulted said mysteriously: "*Better sell—better get clear*—better sell out—no help for it." Another powerful refiner, Robert Hanna, uncle of the famous Mark Alonzo, found that the railroads would give him no relief, and also was glad to sell out at 40 or 50 cents on the dollar for his property value. To one of these refiners, Isaac L. Hewitt, who had been his employer in boyhood, Rockefeller himself spoke with intense emotion. He urged Hewitt to take stock. Hewitt related: "He told me that it would be sufficient to take care of my family for all time ... and asking for reasons, he made this expression, I remember: '*I have ways of making money that you know nothing of.*' "....

During forty years the Standard Oil men marched from trial to trial like habitual felons, before the public was convinced that it was not dealing with the archcriminals of the age, but with destiny. The opposition was always on behalf of a laissez-faire individualism. Miss Tarbell, in her crusading days, before she turned official apologist for famous capitalists, was but championing (and in the name of her expropriated father) the wastefulness, the competitive anarchy of the independent Pennsylvania oil-producers. Rockefeller, on the other hand, was literally the instrument of economic determinism; he was the more or less conscious guiding genius of a process of concentration which held in view the national (and even international) rather than the local organization of oil exploiting. Under his example American capitalism advanced swiftly toward a new phase, transforming, as the most profound social prophet of the century was saying at this very time, "the pigmy property of the many into the titan property of the few, transforming the individual and scattered means of production into socially concentrated forms." This is the true character of the historic process which passes before our eyes in the American scene of the '70's and '80's.

It was an age which seemed "gilded" or "tarnished" or "dreadful" or "tragic" by turns; yet an immensely fruitful age, under whose surface movements of strife and confusion, of repulsion and attraction, one capitalist expropriated others, the strong steadily went on destroying the individual independence of the weak, and in systematic fashion "the large capitals got the better of the smaller ones." Thus all the scattered individual means of production were being brought together, as Marx wrote, into the "new centralization," hastening the development of society, breeding the new technical means for "those tremendous industrial undertakings which can only arise as the outcome of the centralization of capital." And the birth-throes of a new social order but added to the turbulence of the age, with its sounds of ringing arms, its shouts of the conquerors, groans of the fallen. Under Rockefeller, a giant industrial machine was raising itself over the land.

Thenceforth, though persecuted and pilloried, himself the most hated man of the age, he would retain his lead, hang on like death to his great unifying idea, advancing anew after each momentary retreat, evading all attempts at regulation, until the Standard Oil, with its refineries, pipe lines, tank wagons, ships and foreign terminals, had become an industrial empire as far-spreading as the British Empire, until Babylon and Nineveh and Peiping were illuminated by Standard kerosene. Rockefeller's organizing genius would create the "mother of Trusts," soon to spawn a score of other great "Trusts" in whiskey, cattle, beef, sugar, coal, iron and copper. The Standard Oil "Trust," as a corporate device, as a capitalist construction, had the beauty of one of the new steel suspension bridges. A bridge between the past and the future.*

Standard Oil, for all of its sins and virtues, was Exhibit A to the Sherman Act. The legislators may not have known exactly what their antitrust proscription meant, but they seem to have known that Standard Oil violated it. The real question was how to formulate the rule of law. This challenge was not easy. Indeed, perhaps predictably, it resulted in two quite different formulations, one in the majority opinion written by Chief Justice White. The other was by Justice Harlan in concurrence and dissent. Consider the political philosophy tension between the two formulations—a difference in perception, approach and underlying values that was to resurface through time and that can help to explain divergent opinions to the present day.

The opinion itself is long, dense, and sometimes confusing. We have selected excerpts to give you a bird's-eye view of the Court's effort to draw a line between what is permitted and what is prohibited. You should not spend too much time parsing the Court's words. Rather, think about the values the Court was trying to exonerate (a view of individual and business freedom) and the evil it was trying to define. Was the Court concerned that the law might condemn too much good or benign business conduct? If so, at what cost?

STANDARD OIL CO. OF NEW JERSEY v. UNITED STATES

221 U.S. 1 (1911).

CHIEF JUSTICE WHITE: The Standard Oil Company of New Jersey and 33 other corporations, John D. Rockefeller, William Rockefeller and five other individual defendants prosecute this appeal to reverse a decree of the court below....

The bill ... was filed on November 15, 1906.... The detailed averments concerning the alleged conspiracy were arranged with reference to three periods, the first from 1870 to 1882, the second from 1882 to 1899, and the third from 1899 to the time of the filing of the bill. * * *

... [O]n the one hand, with relentless pertinacity and minuteness of analysis, it is insisted that the facts establish that the assailed combina-

* Matthew Josephson, THE ROBBER BARONS: THE GREAT AMERICAN CAPITALISTS 1861–1901 (1934, 1962), pp. 112–119, 161–163, reprinted by permission of Harcourt Brace Jovanovich, Inc.; media/digital rights by permission of Harold Ober Associates, Inc.

tion took its birth in a purpose to unlawfully acquire wealth by oppressing the public and destroying the just rights of others, and that its entire career exemplifies an inexorable carrying out of such wrongful intents, since, it is asserted, the pathway of the combination from the beginning to the time of the filing of the bill is marked with constant proofs of wrong inflicted upon the public and is strewn with the wrecks resulting from crushing out, without regard to law, the individual rights of others. Indeed, so conclusive, it is urged, is the proof on these subjects that it is asserted that the existence of the principal corporate defendant—the Standard Oil Company of New Jersey—with the vast accumulation of property which it owns or controls, because of its infinite potency for harm and the dangerous example which its continued existence affords, is an open and enduring menace to all freedom of trade and is a byword and reproach to modern economic methods. On the other hand, in a powerful analysis of the facts, it is insisted that they demonstrate that the origin and development of the vast business which the defendants control was but the result of lawful competitive methods, guided by economic genius of the highest order, sustained by courage, by a keen insight into commercial situations, resulting in the acquisition of great wealth, but at the same time serving to stimulate and increase production, to widely extend the distribution of the products of petroleum at a cost largely below that which would have otherwise prevailed, thus proving to be at one and the same time a benefaction to the general public as well as of enormous advantage to individuals. It is not denied that in the enormous volume of proof contained in the record in the period of almost a lifetime to which that proof is addressed, there may be found acts of wrongdoing, but the insistence is that they were rather the exception than the rule, and in most cases were either the result of too great individual zeal in the keen rivalries of business or of the methods and habits of dealing which, even if wrong, were commonly practised at the time. And to discover and state the truth concerning these contentions both arguments call for the analysis and weighing, as we have said at the outset, of a jungle of conflicting testimony covering a period of forty years, a duty difficult to rightly perform and, even if satisfactorily accomplished, almost impossible to state with any reasonable regard to brevity. * * *

The debates show that doubt as to whether there was a common law of the United States which governed the subject in the absence of legislation was among the influences leading to the passage of the act. They conclusively show, however, that the main cause which led to the legislation was the thought that it was required by the economic condition of the times, that is, the vast accumulation of wealth in the hands of corporations and individuals, the enormous development of corporate organization, the facility for combination which such organizations afforded, the fact that the facility was being used, and that combinations known as trusts were being multiplied, and the wide-spread impression that their power had been and would be exerted to oppress individuals and injure the public generally.... * * *

Generalizing these considerations, the situation is this: 1. That by the common law monopolies were unlawful because of their restriction upon individual freedom of contract and their injury to the public. 2. That as to necessaries of life the freedom of the individual to deal was restricted where the nature and character of the dealing was such as to engender the presumption of intent to bring about at least one of the injuries which it was deemed would result from monopoly, that is an undue enhancement of price. 3. That to protect the freedom of contract of the individual not only in his own interest, but principally in the interest of the common weal, a contract of an individual by which he put an unreasonable restraint upon himself as to carrying on his trade or business was void....

... It is remarkable that nowhere at common law can there be found a prohibition against the creation of monopoly by an individual. This would seem to manifest, either consciously or intuitively, a profound conception as to the inevitable operation of economic forces and the equipoise or balance in favor of the protection of the rights of individuals which resulted. That is to say, as it was deemed that monopoly in the concrete could only arise from an act of sovereign power, and, such sovereign power being restrained, prohibitions as to individuals were directed, not against the creation of monopoly, but were only applied to such acts in relation to particular subjects as to which it was deemed, if not restrained, some of the consequences of monopoly might result. After all, this was but an instinctive recognition of the truisms that the course of trade could not be made free by obstructing it, and that an individual's right to trade could not be protected by destroying such right. * * *

Without going into detail and but very briefly surveying the whole field, it may be with accuracy said that the dread of enhancement of prices and of other wrongs which it was thought would flow from the undue limitation on competitive conditions caused by contracts or other acts of individuals or corporations, led, as a matter of public policy, to the prohibition or treating as illegal all contracts or acts which were unreasonably restrictive of competitive conditions, either from the nature or character of the contract or act or where the surrounding circumstances were such as to justify the conclusion that they had not been entered into or performed with the legitimate purpose of reasonably forwarding personal interest and developing trade, but on the contrary were of such a character as to give rise to the inference or presumption that they had been entered into or done with the intent to do wrong to the general public and to limit the right of individuals, thus restraining the free flow of commerce and tending to bring about the evils, such as enhancement of prices, which were considered to be against public policy.... * * *

... The statute under this view [in the first section] evidenced the intent not to restrain the right to make and enforce contracts, whether resulting from combination or otherwise, which did not unduly restrain interstate or foreign commerce, but to protect that commerce from being restrained by methods, whether old or new, which would constitute an interference that is an undue restraint.

... [I]t inevitably follows that the provision necessarily called for the exercise of judgment which required that some standard should be resorted to for the purpose of determining whether the prohibitions contained in the statute had or had not in any given case been violated. Thus not specifying but indubitably contemplating and requiring a standard, it follows that it was intended that the standard of reason which had been applied at the common law and in this country in dealing with subjects of the character embraced by the statute, was intended to be the measure used for the purpose of determining whether in a given case a particular act had or had not brought about the wrong against which the statute provided. * * *

Undoubtedly, the words "to monopolize" and "monopolize" as used in the [second] section reach every act bringing about the prohibited results.... [B]y [the statute] the omission of any direct prohibition against monopoly in the concrete indicates a consciousness that the freedom of the individual right to contract when not unduly or improperly exercised was the most efficient means for the prevention of monopoly, since the operation of the centrifugal and centripetal forces resulting from the right to freely contract was the means by which monopoly would be inevitably prevented if no extraneous or sovereign power imposed it and no right to make unlawful contracts having a monopolistic tendency were permitted. In other words that freedom to contract was the essence of freedom from undue restraint on the right to contract.... * * *

We see no cause to doubt the correctness of these conclusions [defendants violated Sections 1 and 2], ... for the following reasons:

a. Because the unification of power and control over petroleum and its products which was the inevitable result of the combining in the New Jersey corporation by the increase of its stock and the transfer to it of the stocks of so many other corporations, aggregating so vast a capital, gives rise, in and of itself, in the absence of countervailing circumstances, to say the least, to the *prima facie* presumption of intent and purpose to maintain the dominancy over the oil industry, not as a result of normal methods of industrial development, but by new means of combination which were resorted to in order that greater power might be added than would otherwise have arisen had normal methods been followed, the whole with the purpose of excluding others from the trade and thus centralizing in the combination a perpetual control of the movements of petroleum and its products in the channels of interstate commerce.

b. Because the *prima facie* presumption of intent to restrain trade, to monopolize and to bring about monopolization resulting from the act of expanding the stock of the New Jersey corporation and vesting it with such vast control of the oil industry, is made conclusive by considering, *1,* the conduct of the persons or corporations who were mainly instrumental in bringing about the extension of power in the New Jersey corporation before the consummation of that result and prior to the formation of the trust agreements of 1879 and 1882; *2,* by considering the proof as to what was done under those agreements and the acts which immediately preceded the vesting of power in the New Jersey corporation as well as by weighing the modes in which the power vested in that corporation has been exerted and the results which have arisen from it.

... [W]e think no disinterested mind can survey the period in question without being irresistibly driven to the conclusion that the very genius for commercial development and organization which it would seem was manifested from the beginning soon begot an intent and purpose to exclude others which was frequently manifested by acts and dealings wholly inconsistent with the theory that they were made with the single conception of advancing the development of business power by usual methods, but which on the contrary necessarily involved the intent to drive others from the field and to exclude them from their right to trade and thus accomplish the mastery which was the end in view.... The exercise of the power which resulted from that organization fortifies the foregoing conclusions, since the development which came, the acquisition here and there which ensued of every efficient means by which competition could have been asserted, the slow but resistless methods which followed by which means of transportation were absorbed and brought under control, the system of marketing which was adopted by which the country was divided into districts and the trade in each district in oil was turned over to a designated corporation within the combination and all others were excluded, all lead the mind up to a conviction of a purpose and intent which we think is so certain as practically to cause the subject not to be within the domain of reasonable contention. * * *

JUSTICE HARLAN, concurring in part and dissenting in part: In order that my objections to certain parts of the court's opinion may distinctly appear, I must state the circumstances under which Congress passed the Anti-trust Act, and trace the course of judicial decisions as to its meaning and scope. This is the more necessary because the court by its decision, when interpreted by the language of its opinion, has not only upset the long-settled interpretation of the act, but has usurped the constitutional functions of the legislative branch of the Government. With all due respect for the opinions of others, I feel bound to say that what the court has said may well cause some alarm for the integrity of our institutions. Let us see how the matter stands.

All who recall the condition of the country in 1890 will remember that there was everywhere, among the people generally, a deep feeling of unrest. The Nation had been rid of human slavery—fortunately, as all now feel—but the conviction was universal that the country was in real danger from another kind of slavery sought to be fastened on the American people, namely, the slavery that would result from aggregations of capital in the hands of a few individuals and corporations controlling, for their own profit and advantage exclusively, the entire business of the country, including the production and sale of the necessaries of life. Such a danger was thought to be then imminent, and all felt that it must be met firmly and by such statutory regulations as would adequately protect the people against oppression and wrong. Congress therefore took up the matter and gave the whole subject the fullest consideration. All agreed that the National Government could not, by legislation, regulate the domestic trade carried on wholly within the several States; for, power to regulate such trade remained with, because never surrendered by, the States. But, under authority expressly granted to it by the Constitution, Congress could regulate commerce among the several States and with foreign states. Its authority to regulate such commerce was and is paramount, due force being given to other provisions of the fundamental law devised by the fathers for the safety of the Government and for the protection and security of the essential rights inhering in life, liberty and property.

Guided by these considerations, and to the end that the people ... might not be dominated by vast combinations and monopolies, having power to advance their own selfish ends, regardless of the general interests and welfare, Congress passed the Anti-trust Act of 1890....

[M]y brethren, in their wisdom, have ... now said to those who ... object to all legislative prohibitions of contracts, combinations and trusts in restraint of interstate commerce, "You may *now* restrain such commerce, provided you are reasonable about it; only take care that the restraint in not undue." The disposition of the case under consideration, according to the views of the defendants, will, it is claimed, quiet and give rest to "the business of the country." On the contrary, I have a strong conviction that it will throw the business of the country into confusion and invite widely-extended and harassing litigation, the injurious effects of which will be felt for many years to come. When Congress prohibited *every* contract, combination or monopoly, in restraint of commerce, it prescribed a simple, definite rule that all could understand, and which could be easily applied by everyone wishing to obey the law, and not to conduct their business in violation of law. But now, it is to be feared, we are to have, in cases without number, the constantly recurring inquiry—difficult to solve by proof—whether the particular contract, combination, or trust involved in each case is or is not an "unreasonable" or "undue" restraint of trade....[*]

[*] [Editors' note:] Two weeks later the Court decided *United States v. American Tobacco Co.*, 221 U.S. 106 (1911). Reiterating the rule of reason and stressing again the importance of freedom of contract, the Court, by Chief Justice White, held that the five major tobacco companies and American Tobacco Company, the firm into which they had merged, violated Sections 1 and 2 of the Sherman Act. The five majors merged after a period of fierce competition. They increased capital and spent "enormous" amounts of money to buy some 40 competitors. They exacted covenants not to compete from the sellers, and they closed down many of the purchased businesses. When competitors refused to sell to the tobacco combination, defendants started price wars, bankrupted the recalcitrants, and bought their remaining assets. The opinions by Chief Justice White in both *Standard Oil* and *American Tobacco* emphasize the importance of evaluating the defendants' conduct and intent, thus differing significantly from Justice Harlan's almost exclusive focus on the evil of large aggregations of power.

QUESTIONS AND COMMENTS

1. The *Standard Oil* case elicited strong responses. In announcing the "rule of reason," Chief Justice White broke the interpretational logjam that had characterized restraint of trade jurisprudence. But White's reasonableness standard differed from Taft's conception of the meaning of the Sherman Act. Although President Taft clearly wanted judicial enforcement of the Sherman Act to be the cornerstone of his antitrust policy, he thought legality should turn on whether the defendants' restraint was an end in itself (naked) or was imposed in the service of other legitimate business goals (ancillary). Taft believed that the new "rule of reason" gave the courts open-ended and arbitrary "power to say what was a reasonable restraint or a reasonable monopoly."[1] Would Taft's factors be relevant considerations under White's rule of reason? How does Harlan's approach differ from Chief Justice White's? What value does each put on price levels? distributional concerns, including wealth and power?

According to the majority, what was the legal basis for Standard Oil's violation of the law? Did Standard Oil violate the law because it gained monopoly? because it had a "bad" intent? because it engaged in "bad acts"?

What is bad intent? What are bad acts? Does the end result, monopoly, make acts bad? Is an act bad if it hurts competitors? Can it be bad if it does not hurt consumers? Look back at the *Robber Barons* excerpt. Which of the described acts are bad acts—according to White? Harlan? Taft?

2. Rockefeller brought oil to the American people at a lower price than anyone had done before. May we assume that Standard Oil could price below its competitors because it had achieved economies of scale and they had not? that it was able to obtain a low rate from the railroads because it cost the railroads less to carry a unit of oil shipped by Standard Oil (given the assured large and continuous supply) than a unit of oil shipped by its small competitors? Suppose that Standard Oil had been able to get lower prices from railroads because the railroads, needing Standard Oil's business, had to curry good will and were prepared to take a lower return on its traffic than on the traffic of smaller oil companies. Was the success of Standard Oil a triumph of power and leverage or a triumph of efficiencies? See Ron Chernow, TITAN: THE LIFE OF JOHN D. ROCKEFELLER, SR. (Random House 1998).

How does the rule of reason apply to the efficient but unscrupulous competitor?

3. Note the Court's reference to sovereign power. If we preserve business freedom, ban only those contracts that unreasonably restrain trade, and keep government out, the market will work to protect the public. Is this statement correct? Is it empirically verifiable? Does it reflect a philosophy of political economy?

Scholars debate the economic wisdom of the *Standard Oil* decision. In an influential article that became a cornerstone for "Chicago" antitrust theory, John McGee contends that the Standard Oil Company never priced below its

1. Letwin, LAW AND ECONOMIC POLICY at 252, 267.

cost. He concludes that Standard Oil's ability to engage in low pricing must have derived from its efficiencies.[2]

4. Pursuant to the court's decree, the Standard Oil combination was dissolved. The assets of the parent company were distributed to its stockholders. The Rockefellers, the dominant holders of stock in the parent company, retained control of the oil business. They became the controlling shareholders in each of the subsidiaries after dissolution. Each subsidiary (the "seven sisters") remained dominant in its region.[3] The *Standard Oil* decree did not greatly affect Standard Oil's powerful position within the oil industry, until, years later, the discovery of new oil fields brought new entry, and, over time, common control of subsidiary companies eroded through stock trading.[4] In 1960, however, the oil producing nations, led by Saudi Arabia, formed OPEC (Organization of Petroleum Exporting Countries), a cartel to exploit the production of oil for the benefit of its members. At the turn of the twentieth century, in the shadow of OPEC and also in the wake of development of new sources of energy, the U.S. oil industry re-consolidated. Among the mergers—all cleared by the Federal Trade Commission—were successors to the seven sisters, including Exxon (formerly ESSO [S.O.]) and Mobil.

5. Like John D. Rockefeller, Bill Gates was a young man not yet 30 years old when he demonstrated an uncanny perception of the needs and directions of industry—for him, computers and high technology. Like John D. Rockefeller, he assembled a small team, focused on ideas that would revolutionize business, and pursued them doggedly and ruthlessly, crushing and suppressing challengers. But with good or bad intent? good or bad effects? by anticompetitive or deeply competitive means? Was Microsoft a predatory monopolist that deserved to broken up, or a gift of the gods that deserved to be nurtured? We treat the *Microsoft* case in Chapter 3. The old questions recur.

6. The idea of a central role for bad intent pervades *Standard Oil*. What does the Court mean by intent to restrain trade? Bear in mind that the Court was setting limits to the reach of the Sherman Act in favor of freedom of business to "reasonably forward ... personal interest and develop trade." You will meet the word "intent" throughout the study of antitrust. In contemporary times, the antitrust officials and jurists often express the significance of intent as follows: Intent to kill the competitor tells you nothing at all. You need to ask: How? Killing the competitor by meritorious acts, such as low prices made possible by efficiencies, is not a "bad" act. Nonetheless, intent—when it is revealed—can be very important; it can give good clues about probable effects of certain conduct on competition and consumers and can help predict those effects. Are the words of Chief Justice White in *Standard Oil* consistent or inconsistent with contemporary usage?

---

2. J. McGee, Predatory Price Cutting: The Standard Oil (N.J.) Case, 1 J. of Law & Econ. 137 (1958).

3. See J. Blair, ECONOMIC CONCENTRATION: STRUCTURE, BEHAVIOR AND PUBLIC POLICY 563 (1972).

4. Harbaugh, POWER AND RESPONSIBILITY at 405.

THE INTENT BAROMETER

	good	bad
1. Intent to crush the competitors by lower prices?	☐	☐
a. by lower prices that, it is well known, the smaller competitors cannot meet?	☐	☐
2. Intent to help the smaller competitors by charging a price high enough to keep them in the market?	☐	☐
3. Intent to save the industry from a disastrous financial crisis?	☐	☐
4. Intent to sell more of your goods at the expense of your competitors?	☐	☐
5. Intent to get a monopoly?	☐	☐

Discuss the antitrust significance of your answers. As to each "intent," add a story about the context. E.g., A monopolist, faced with competition, charges a price below that which its new competitor can afford.

4. LEGISLATIVE REFORMS IN THE WAKE OF STANDARD OIL

a. The 1912 Campaign and Antitrust Policy

Standard Oil's rule of reason produced uncertainty. The decision displeased enforcers and victims because its stress on intent would make antitrust lawsuits more difficult to win. It displeased firms, even large firms, because it gave them no guidance as to what they could or could not legally do. During the 1912 presidential campaign, moderates in both parties called for more explicit definition of illegal business conduct. The election of Woodrow Wilson seemed to express a national sentiment in favor of legislative amplification of antitrust.[5]

With the help of Louis Brandeis, his chief economic advisor during the campaign, Wilson developed his antitrust policies. Wilson's program was called the "New Freedom." He wanted the federal government to ensure economic opportunity by enacting "a body of laws which will look after the men who are on the make rather than the men who are already made."[6] The government was to liberate business from the "shackles of monopoly and special privilege" and to enable the exercise of individual energy.[7] Wilson wanted to eliminate the influence of special interest

5. *Id.*

6. Woodrow Wilson, THE NEW FREEDOM 17 (1917).

7. Arthur Stanley Link, WOODROW WILSON AND THE PROGRESSIVE ERA 21 (1963).

groups, including labor, farm organizations, and large corporations. He initially opposed federal regulatory commissions because of the risk that special interests would control them. He said: "If the government is to tell big business how to run their business, then don't you see that big businessmen have to get [even] closer to the government than they are now? Don't you see that they must capture the government, in order not to be restrained by it?"[8] Thus a strong, active government was dangerous; but massive corporate bureaucracies were dangerous, too.[9]

Wilson's goal was an open, competitive marketplace in which new players—men on the make—had the opportunity to thrive and innovate. His object was not to shackle business but to ensure that it played by the rules of fair competition.[10]

In 1914, Congress enacted two new antitrust statutes—the Clayton Act and the Federal Trade Commission Act, which would complement, not replace, the Sherman Act. Although the new statutes reflected different approaches to antitrust enforcement, they shared the purpose of limiting the Court's discretion under the rule of reason.

b. Wilson's Legislative Record

i. The Clayton Act

The Clayton Act prohibited, and prohibits, price discrimination, tying, exclusive dealing and mergers that may substantially lessen competition.

The statute also exempted (and exempts) labor unions, which were then a primary target of antitrust enforcement. However, the exemption was interpreted narrowly and it was not until the 1930s when new labor laws and a differently constituted Supreme Court created a regime more sympathetic to labor. (The Clayton Act was to be amended again in 1936 to toughen the anti-price discrimination provision, in 1950 to strengthen the merger provision, and in 1976 to add a requirement for pre-merger notification to the Justice Department and the Federal Trade Commission.)

Relevant provisions of the Clayton Act are printed in Appendix B. Most important to this study of antitrust is Clayton § 3, prohibiting exclusive dealing and tying whose effect may be substantially to lessen competition, and Clayton § 7, prohibiting mergers whose effect may be to lessen competition. See Chapters 4 and 6 infra. Also of particular importance in practice is the amended provision on price discrimination.

ii. The Federal Trade Commission Act

In 1914 Congress also passed the FTC Act. The Act created an agency to investigate and enjoin "unfair methods of competition." The FTC was

---

8. *Id.* at 176.

9. Louis Hacker, THE COURSE OF AMERICAN ECONOMIC GROWTH AND DEVELOPMENT 269 (1970).

10. J.P. Miller, Woodrow Wilson's Contribution to Antitrust Policy, in THE PHILOSOPHY AND POLICIES OF WOODROW WILSON, 132, 134 (E. Latham ed. 1958).

empowered to develop expertise and to promulgate guidelines for particular industries and for the competitive process more broadly. The FTC was designed as a more cutting-edge authority than the Antitrust Division of the Department of Justice. It had no fining power and no criminal enforcement power, and, unlike judgments of the courts at the close of Justice Department cases, which were prima facie evidence of antitrust violations, FTC orders could not be relied on by private parties seeking compensation for antitrust harms.

The passage of the Clayton and FTC Acts ended Wilson's legislative reforms. The administration became decidedly congenial to business. An era of government-business cooperation had arrived.[11] By 1920 the Supreme Court reflected this mood of the times.

The *U.S. Steel Case*, which follows, involves the first stage of a huge consolidation of the steel industry. If, at the time of the case, there remained any remnant of the idea that "big was bad" (an idea inherent in early railroad merger cases), *U.S. Steel* dispelled the notion. The case has landmark status regarding the big-may-not-be-bad proposition. Think, as you read the case: Might the numerous, cumulative acquisitions of competitors by U.S. Steel have harmed competition, in spite of the Court's conclusion? If so, how? Or was this just a case of 180 efficient acquisitions?

UNITED STATES v. UNITED STATES STEEL CORP.

251 U.S. 417 (1920).

JUSTICE MCKENNA: The case [filed in 1911 under President Taft], was heard in the District Court by four judges. They agreed that the bill should be dismissed; they disagreed as to the reasons for it. One opinion (written by Judge Buffington and concurred in by Judge McPherson) expressed the view that the Steel Corporation was not formed with the intention or purpose to monopolize or restrain trade, and did not have the motive or effect "to prejudice the public interest by unduly restricting competition or unduly obstructing the course of trade." The corporation, in the view of the opinion, was an evolution, a natural consummation of the tendencies of the industry on account of changing conditions, practically a compulsion from "the metallurgical method of making steel and the physical method of handling it," this method, and the conditions consequent upon it, tending to combinations of capital and energies rather than diffusion in independent action....

The other opinion (by Judge Woolley and concurred in by Judge Hunt) was in some particulars, in antithesis to Judge Buffington's. The view was expressed that neither the Steel Corporation nor the preceding combinations, which were in a sense its antetypes, had the justification of industrial conditions, nor were they or it impelled by the necessity for integration, or compelled to unite in comprehensive enterprise because

11. Arthur Stanley Link, WOODROW WILSON AND THE PROGRESSIVE ERA 72–76 (1963).

such had become a condition of success under the new order of things. On the contrary, that the organizers of the corporation and the preceding companies had illegal purpose from the very beginning, and the corporation became "a combination of combinations, by which, directly or indirectly, approximately 180 independent concerns were brought under one business control," which, measured by the amount of production, extended to 80% or 90% of the entire output of the country, and that its purpose was to secure great profits which were thought possible in the light of the history of its constituent combinations, and to accomplish permanently what those combinations had demonstrated could be accomplished temporarily, and thereby monopolize and restrain trade.[1]

The organizers, however (we are still representing the opinion), underestimated the opposing conditions and at the very beginning the Corporation instead of relying upon its own power sought and obtained the assistance and the cooperation of its competitors (the independent companies). In other words the view was expressed that the testimony did "not show that the corporation in and of itself ever possessed or exerted sufficient power when acting alone to control prices of the products of the industry." Its power was efficient only when in cooperation with its competitors, and hence it concerted with them in the expedients of pools, associations, trade meetings, and finally in a system of dinners inaugurated in 1907 by the president of the company, E.H. Gary, and called "the Gary Dinners." The dinners were congregations of producers and "were nothing but trade meetings," successors of the other means of associated action and control through such action. They were instituted first in "stress of panic," but, their potency being demonstrated, they were afterwards called to control prices "in periods of industrial calm." "They were pools without penalties" and more efficient in stabilizing prices. But it was the further declaration that "when joint action was either refused or withdrawn the Corporation's prices were controlled by competition."

The Corporation, it was said, did not at any time abuse the power or ascendency it possessed. It resorted to none of the brutalities or tyrannies that the cases illustrate of other combinations. It did not secure freight rebates; it did not increase its profits by reducing the wages of its employees—whatever it did was not at the expense of labor; it did not increase its profits by lowering the quality of its products, nor create an artificial scarcity of them; it did not oppress or coerce its competitors—its

1. As bearing upon the power obtained and what the Corporation did we give other citations from Judge Woolley's opinion as follows:

"... As a last analysis of this testimony, it is sufficient to say it shows that, large as was the corporation, and substantial as was its proportion of the business of the industry, the corporation was not able in the first ten years of its history to maintain its position in the increase of trade. During that period, its proportion of the domestic business decreased from 50.1 per cent. to 40.9 per cent. and its increase of business during that period was but 40.6 per cent. of its original volume. Its increase of business, measured by percentage, was exceeded by eight of its competitors, whose increase of business, likewise measured by percentage, ranged from 63 to 3779. This disparity in the increase of production indicates that the power of the corporation is not commensurate with its size, and that the size and the consequent power of the corporation are not sufficient to retard prosperous growth of efficient competitors...."

competition, though vigorous, was fair; it did not undersell its competitors in some localities by reducing its prices there below those maintained elsewhere, or require its customers to enter into contracts limiting their purchases or restricting them in resale prices; it did not obtain customers by secret rebates or departures from its published prices; there was no evidence that it attempted to crush its competitors or drive them out of the market, nor did it take customers from its competitors by unfair means, and in its competition it seemed to make no difference between large and small competitors. Indeed it is said in many ways and illustrated that "instead of relying upon its own power to fix and maintain prices, the corporation, at its very beginning sought and obtained the assistance of others." It combined its power with that of its competitors. It did not have power in and of itself, and the control it exerted was only in and by association with its competitors. Its offense, therefore, such as it was, was not different from theirs and was distinguished from theirs "only in the leadership it assumed in promulgating and perfecting the policy." This leadership it gave up, and it had ceased to offend against the law before this suit was brought. It was hence concluded that it should be distinguished from its organizers and that their intent and unsuccessful attempt should not be attributed to it, that it "in and of itself is not now and has never been a monopoly or a combination in restraint of trade," and a decree of dissolution should not be entered against it....

It is the contention of the Corporation ... (to quote the words of Judge Buffington, he quoting those of a witness,) ... "that instead, as was then the practice, of having one mill to make 10 or 20 or 50 products, the greatest economy would result from having one mill make one product, and make that product continuously." In other words, that there was a necessity for integration, and rescue from the old conditions—from their improvidence and waste of effort; and that, in redress of the conditions, the Corporation was formed, its purpose and effect being "salvage not monopoly," to quote the words of counsel. It was, is the insistence, the conception of ability, "a vision of a great business which should embrace all lines of steel and all processes of manufacture from the ore to the finished product and which by reason of the economies thus to be effected and the diversity of products it would be able to offer, could successfully compete in all the markets of the world."

... We have seen that the judges of the District Court unanimously concurred in the view that the Corporation did not achieve monopoly, and such is our deduction, and it is against monopoly that the statute is directed, not against an expectation of it, but against its realization, and it is certain that it was not realized.... What then can now be urged against the Corporation? ... It is greater in size and productive power than any of its competitors, equal or nearly equal to them all, but its power over prices was not and is not commensurate with its power to produce.

... The company's officers and, as well, its competitors and customers, testified that its competition was genuine, direct and vigorous, and was reflected in prices and production. No practical witness was produced by the Government in opposition. Its contention is based on the size and asserted dominance of the Corporation—alleged power for evil, not the exertion of the power in evil. Or as counsel put it, "a combination may be illegal because of its purpose; it may be illegal because it acquires a dominating power, not as a result of normal growth and development, but as a result of a combination of competitors." Such composition and its resulting power constitute, in the view of the Government, the offence against the law, and yet it is admitted "no competitor came forward and said he had to accept the Steel Corporation's prices." But this absence of complaint counsel urge against the Corporation. Competitors, it is said, followed the Corporation's prices because they made money by the imitation. Indeed the imitation is urged as an evidence of the Corporation's power. "Universal imitation," counsel assert, is "an evidence of power." In this concord of action, the contention is, there is the sinister dominance of the Corporation—"its extensive control of the industry is such that the others [independent companies] follow." * * *

. . . The Government does not hesitate to present contradictions, though only one can be true, such being we were told in our school books the "principle of contradiction." In one competitors (the independents) are represented as oppressed by the superior power of the Corporation; in the other they are represented as ascending to opulence by imitating that power's prices which they could not do if at disadvantage from the other conditions of competition; and yet confederated action is not asserted. If it were this suit would take on another cast. The competitors would cease to be the victims of the Corporation and would become its accomplices. And there is no other alternative. The suggestion that lurks in the Government's contention that the acceptance of the Corporation's prices is the submission of impotence to irresistible power is, in view of the testimony of the competitors, untenable. They, as we have seen, deny restraint in any measure or illegal influence of any kind. The Government, therefore, is reduced to the assertion that the size of the Corporation, the power it may have, not the exertion of the power, is an abhorrence to the law, or as the Government says, "the combination embodied in the Corporation unduly restrains competition by its *necessary effect,* [the italics are the emphasis of the Government] and therefore is unlawful regardless of purpose." "A wrongful purpose," the Government adds, is "matter of aggravation." The illegality is statical, purpose or movement of any kind only its emphasis. To assent to that, to what extremes should we be led? Competition consists of business activities and ability—they make its life; but there may be fatalities in it. Are the activities to be encouraged when militant, and suppressed or regulated when triumphant because of the dominance attained? To such paternalism the Government's contention, which regards power rather than its use the determining consideration, seems to conduct. Certainly conducts we may say, for it is the inevitable logic of the Government's contention that competition must not only be free, but that it must not be pressed to the ascendency of a competitor, for in ascendency there is the menace of monopoly. * * *

The Corporation was formed in 1901, no act of aggression upon its competitors is charged against it, it confederated with them at times in offence against the law, but abandoned that before this suit was brought, and since 1911 no act in violation of law can be established against it except its existence be such an act. This is urged, as we have seen, and that the interest of the public is involved, and that such interest is paramount to corporation or competitors. Granted—though it is difficult to see how there can be restraint of trade when there is no restraint of competitors in the trade nor complaints by customer—show can it be worked out of the situation and through what proposition of law? . . . [S]hall we declare the law to be that size is an offence even though it minds its own business because what it does is imitated? The Corporation is undoubtedly of impressive size and it takes an effort of resolution not to be affected by it or to exaggerate its influence. But we must adhere to the law and the law does not make mere size an offence or the existence of unexerted power an offence. It, we repeat, requires overt acts and trusts to its prohibition of them and its power to repress or punish them. It does not compel competition nor require all that is possible. . . . * * *

We think, therefore, that the decree of the District Court should be affirmed.

QUESTIONS AND COMMENTS

1. U.S. Steel acquired 180 competitors, bringing under its control at least 50% and as much as 90% of the domestic steel business; this in the wake of the Gary (price-fixing) dinners. What would it have taken, according to the Court, to make such acquisitions illegal? Would anything condemn them? Did U.S. Steel try to achieve monopoly, but fail? Might it have succeeded in organizing an oligopoly?

2. What was so good about the fact that U.S. Steel never undersold its competitors or departed from published prices? never tried to crush competitors or drive them from the market? Was this an efficient merger, an anticompetitive merger, or both?

3. Might the Court have embraced the view that mere size is no offence and still have declared the merger illegal?

4. Apply the analysis of White, of Taft, of Harlan. Was Chief Justice White's opinion in *Standard Oil* part of the problem?

5. The declaration that "the law does not make mere size an offence" continues to be cited with approval. But mergers, especially of competitors, can produce market structures and incentives that cause prices to rise. There may be no trace of intent to harm competition. Is this concern with "mere size"?

Remember the *U.S. Steel* opinion. We will ask you to consider an alternative analysis when we deal with cartels and cartel-like (oligopoly) behavior.

In later years the Court would focus more seriously on the *effects* of mergers in concentrated markets and would condemn those mergers that induce competitor cooperation, whether or not they threaten to produce monopoly.

5. ADDENDUM ON HISTORY

Prosperity, and little antitrust enforcement, followed World War I. Then, in 1929, the stock market crashed. The Great Depression followed. Franklin D. Roosevelt was elected President in 1933 and ushered in a vast scheme of government-supported cartelization as the means (now seen as misguided) to get business back on its feet. See Daniel Crane, Antitrust Enforcement during National Crises: An Unhappy History, in GLOBAL COMPETITION POLICY, release 1 December 2008.

The years of and just following World War II were marked by fears of fascism and communism. Antitrust (the economic democracy of markets) was embraced as a protection against the country's slipping into authoritarian rule. The political context provided motivation for the strengthening of the merger law in 1950, as we note in the merger chapter, below.

After the Great Depression, antitrust regained its place. In the face of fascist and communist threats in the 1940s and 1950s, antitrust became a policy instrument of choice to contain power.

The late 1970s brought a different turn of events. With lower trade barriers and rapid globalization, the country began to see efficiency and competitiveness as its priority. Murmurings of globalization and discontent of business with overregulation led to a new, more market-trusting paradigm.

Through all the twists and turmoils of the years, lessons of *Trans–Missouri*, *Addyston Pipe*, *Standard Oil*, *Northern Pacific*, and *U.S. Steel*[12] remain strong.

Through all of the iterations of American antitrust, economics has played a significant role. We turn to a brief overview of antitrust and economics, in broad outline.

D. THE ECONOMICS OF COMPETITION

Certain basic economic principles undergird competition law as an instrument for efficiency. Moreover, economics can be applied to help a society achieve its goals, whatever they are, more directly and at lower cost.

A system of free enterprise (markets) with competition law may help to obtain a more efficient allocation of resources, keep prices down for

---

12. Except: Contrary to *U.S. Steel*, bad acts are not necessary to condemn a merger as anticompetitive. Moreover, in tension with *Standard Oil*, the emphasis on intent has given way to an emphasis on effects, while in cartel cases all that is necessary is that defendants agreed to the cartel (e.g., price-fixing).

buyers, and foster incentives to innovate. These are the goals, in modern times, of U.S. antitrust. Competition law may have other goals as well. In the European Union, goals include market integration, openness, control of dominance, fairness, and competitiveness (the growth of efficient, dynamic and responsive firms for the sake of European economic strength in world markets). Pursuit of many of these goals tends to produce allocative efficiency or prevent consumer price-rises; thus the goals share common ground. But sometimes goals other than efficiency (in its various forms) may be in tension with efficiency goals, and a society may choose them nonetheless. In either event, it is important to understand the basic principles of the economics of competition law in the service of efficiency.

Firms with sustained market power may have an incentive to act inefficiently, both in the sense of letting costs rise and in the sense of using their power to exploit buyers. Firms with monopoly power may have the incentive to preserve their monopolies by eliminating competitors or blocking them from markets. Firms that have grown to monopoly or dominant size under conditions of free enterprise may have achieved their positions by competition on the merits. To preserve incentives to excel as well as to preserve a firm's organic efficiencies, we may wish to control a dominant firm's anticompetitive behavior and to work on other fronts to reduce barriers, rather than to attack the structure itself. This is the direction of U.S. law for unilateral conduct cases (monopolization). This section deals largely with the less ambiguous economic problem of cartels.

Here, then, is a brief introduction to market economics.

Classically, in a system of perfect competition, there would be a number of sellers, a number of buyers, and perfect market information available to all. The sellers, competing among themselves for business, would be induced to make and provide what their customers want. To do so they would aspire to be inventive and progressive and to minimize costs. The pressures of competition would keep prices near costs. The producers would make and provide as many units of a product as the buyers wanted and were willing to buy at cost or more. Consumers would be sovereign.

The same responsiveness would be observed even in a market of few sellers if there were no significant barriers to entry into the market and if entry were very quick and easy. In that case, potential competitors would (in theory, for barriers are seldom so inconsequential) provide the same pressures as do actual competitors. Also, in theory, sophisticated and powerful buyers could provide the same pressures on sellers to behave competitively, especially if the buyers were in a position to enter the market themselves or to finance entry by others if they were not satisfied with the performance of the existing sellers. Further, in high technology markets marked by rapid changes in technology (new economy markets), the threat of break-through innovations by potential competitors may provide the pressure to induce responsiveness of even a dominant firm.

If all markets in the world were characterized by effective competition—with efficient and fully responsive sellers—competition itself would allocate resources to the production and distribution of all goods and services in the proportions buyers demanded. The fullest possible production would then be squeezed out of the world's scarce resources. Demand would remain a function of the existing distribution of wealth, however, for what people choose to buy is a function of their wealth.

Real markets deviate substantially from the ideal. Nonetheless, competition tends to produce an efficient allocation of resources, push costs downwards, and help intermediate the process whereby buyers and ultimately consumers get what they want and at a price more or less near cost (including a reasonable return on investment). Competition is one of the most important mechanisms on which society relies to produce efficiency and serve consumers.

Competition also tends to keep markets free and open, and thereby to provide opportunities for entrepreneurs and small and medium-sized firms. Also, competition is a product of freedom of enterprise. It fosters diversity and pluralism, and it provides rewards based on merit. Therefore, competition both reflects and tends to support democratic institutions. Finally, forces of competition know no artificial divisions, such as national borders. If American car makers need steel, and lowest priced steel (always, at the desired quality) can be obtained in Germany or Japan, the market will drive the German and Japanese steel over the national border lines (unless U.S. steelmakers lobby for and get protection, as they are wont to do, raising the price of U.S. cars).

While competition and freedom to compete on the merits serve all of the above objectives, private firms can sometimes restrain competition and thereby undermine the objectives of competition policy. The most obvious way in which firms can restrain competition and harm consumers is by forming a cartel, which is a combination of competitors to eliminate the competition among them. The classic form of cartel is a price-fixing or market division agreement by all significant firms in the market. In theory, competitors could agree to charge a certain high price and not to compete on price. If buyers have no good substitutes and barriers to entry are high, the conspirators would have the power to raise prices considerably above the competitive price (i.e., considerably higher than the cost of efficient firms to make and sell the product, including a reasonable return on investment)—as long as they all stick to their agreement. The cartel members would naturally be able to sell less of their goods at this higher price. They would have to prevent outsiders from producing or selling more units of the product, for extra production would drive the price back down. The cartel members would hold back output, and they would exploit the buyers that stay in the market (these customers keep buying because they have no good alternative) even though they must pay a higher price. Essentially the same thing would happen if the parties agree to divide geographic markets ("You take east of the Mississippi; I take west of the Mississippi"). If outsiders face insurmountable barriers and the insiders keep to their pact, each would become the monopolist in its market and would have the power and incentive to raise prices; buyers would demand less of the goods at the supracompetitive price, and the firms would reduce their output.

This phenomenon may be depicted graphically as:

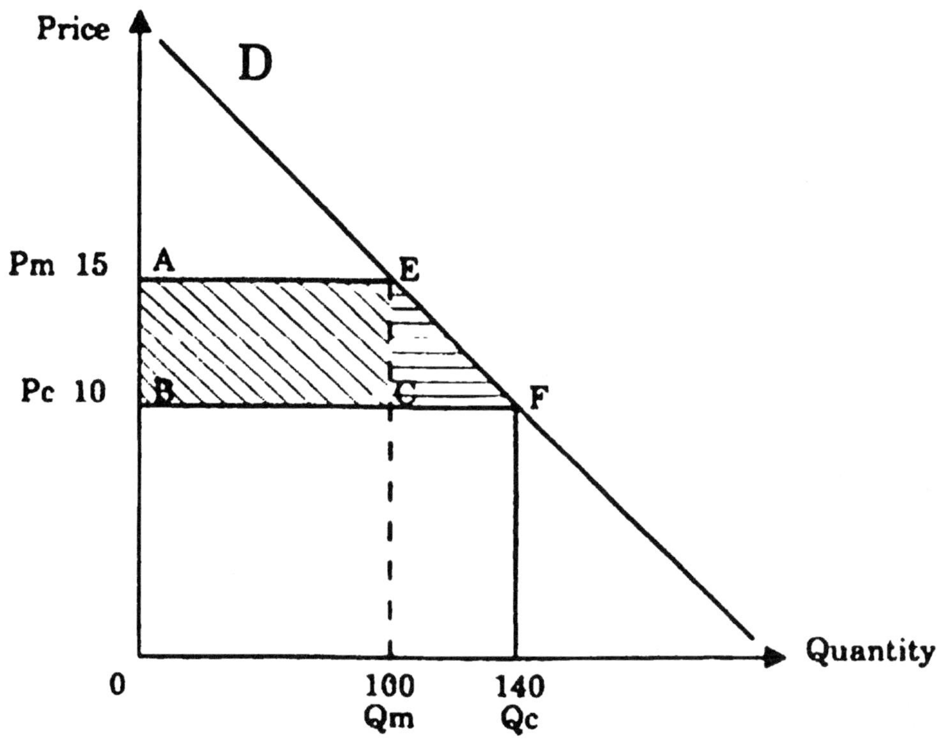

The demand curve (D) slopes downward. The base line represents the quantity demanded at a given price. The vertical line at the left represents the price. Less is demanded as price rises. Therefore higher price yields lower quantity. If the firms' cost is 10 (the competitive price), and upon forming a cartel their profit-maximizing price is 15 (the monopoly price), given the depicted demand function, the cartel members would reduce production from 140 units to 100 units. They would make more money by producing less because of their ability to exploit the remaining customers. Society loses. Triangle CEF is called the dead weight or welfare loss. People wanted to buy the amount depicted by the triangle, and they were willing to buy it at cost or more, but this amount was never produced. Rectangle ABCE represents the product sold at the extra-high price, and it represents a wealth transfer. Under conditions of competition buyers would have kept the money represented by rectangle ABCE. The cartel empowered the sellers to extract this surplus from the buyers.

You will frequently encounter the term "consumer surplus". Under conditions of competition, all of the space in the triangle above line BCF is consumer surplus. Under cartel conditions, where price rises from 10 to 15, everything above line AE is consumer surplus. Consumer surplus represents the money that consumers were willing to spend but did not have to spend in order to purchase the product. When economists say that conduct or a transaction does not harm or lessen consumer welfare, they usually mean that the conduct or transaction does not cause a decrease in consumer surplus.

As noted, cartelists can use mechanisms other than price fixing to achieve the same ends. They can allocate territories so that each becomes a monopolist in its own territory. They can allocate customers, creating monopoly power over each customer. Or they can parcel out production quotas—one of the devices used by the cartel of the oil producing and exporting countries (OPEC). Setting quotas as a means of limiting output is the other side of the price-fixing coin. By setting a high price, the quantity demanded will fall. By setting quotas, the collaborators create scarcity and the price will rise. Several devices can be used in tandem. Cartelists often fix prices and then set quotas, to avoid squabbling about who gets to enjoy the high price. Moreover, if no member can sell more than a fixed quota, it will not be able to cheat on its co-conspirators (i.e., secretly violate its cartel obligations) by selling more goods at a lower price.

We have spoken above of the static effect of cartels; that is, a cartel will normally cause the price of a known good, produced in known ways, to be higher and output to be lower than under conditions of independent decision-making. Cartels also have a negative dynamic effect. If firms have agreed not to compete and do not anticipate rivalry, they tend to let costs rise and their incentives to find new and better ways of pleasing their customers are muted. This effect is called x-inefficiency.

The objectives of the cartel can sometimes be achieved through means short of conspiracy. If a market is highly concentrated (i.e., there are few firms; thus, an oligopoly) and incumbents are insulated by barriers to entry—especially if the sellers are relatively similar to one another in cost structure and the product is homogeneous—the price and output moves of the incumbents may be relatively transparent to one another. The price that will maximize the profits of each is likely to be approximately the same, or at least in many circumstances it is. Under these conditions, no firm would charge a price higher than the common price because it would be out-competed and it would lose its sales. None would venture to charge a lower price because competition would break out and all producers would be worse off: they would sell approximately the same quantity of goods but at a lower price. The firms may find it both possible and profitable to behave like a cartel—higher price, lower output, lower dynamism—even without an agreement. They may count on one another not to steal their customers or start a price war because if any firm does so they will end up sharing the same pie at a lower price and they all will be worse off. This parallelism and detente is called interdependence.

In an oligopolistic market, firms may coordinate their actions by price leadership. Also, they may coordinate by staying within their own traditional territories. A territorial strategy has often been employed by firms in Europe, where national markets were historically isolated by trade barriers. French firms feared that if they began to sell in Germany, German firms, in retaliation, would sell at low prices in the French market, and vice versa. Patterns of mutual deference or spheres of influence developed, reinforcing oligopoly behavior. The more concentrated the market, the less need there was for an explicit agreement, because the result could be achieved without one. This presents a dilemma for antitrust, as we will see, for there may be no agreement to challenge.

Since merging is one way to reduce the number of players in the market, and fewness of players makes anticompetitive coordination easier, mergers that result in high concentration may produce cartel effects; i.e. the firms left in the market may adopt cooperative rather than competitive modes of behavior. Moreover, mergers between two leading head-to-head players may harm competition and consumers by eliminating their own important rivalry. Mergers, however, are integrative and may produce synergies and other efficiencies, while cartels are virtually always inefficient and are by definition formed to suppress competition. Therefore the law treats cartels much more harshly and summarily than it treats mergers.

Likewise, achieving a monopoly may produce higher prices and lower output. Indeed, in economic textbooks, it does so paradigmatically. But a monopoly may be achieved by competition itself and dominant firm conduct that hurts competitors may bring consumers lower prices and better products. For these reasons and others we will study, monopoly cases often contain many nuances. Consequently, the law treats cartels much more harshly and summarily than most cases of alleged monopoly conduct.

There are many books on antitrust economics. One helpful collection is HANDBOOK OF ANTITRUST ECONOMICS (Paolo Buccirossi, ed., MIT 2008), which is comprised of chapters by some of the most prominent scholars in the field. See *http://mitpress.mit.edu/catalog/item/default.asp?ttype=2&tid=11509*. Also helpful is Michael D. Whinston, LECTURES ON ANTITRUST ECONOMICS (MIT 2006), covering the economics of price fixing, horizontal mergers, and exclusionary vertical contracts. See *http://mitpress.mit.edu/catalog/item/default.asp?tid=10866&ttype=2*.

What Is Efficiency?

The several faces of efficiency

What does efficiency mean?

There are two separate questions:

1. What are the kinds of efficiency?

2. How can a competition law system facilitate efficient conduct and an efficiently functioning market?

The kinds of efficiency

THE EFFICIENCY PARADOX

Eleanor Fox

in B. Pitofsky, ed., HOW THE CHICAGO SCHOOL OVERSHOT THE MARK 77 (2008) (excerpt, edited)

Mapping efficiency

Efficiency is often categorized as allocative, productive or dynamic. Allocative efficiency refers to the allocation of resources to their most valued uses in view of the choices buyers make given their ability and willingness to pay at least cost for goods and services.

Productive efficiency refers to a firm's production and distribution at the lowest feasible cost. Given the cost of inputs and the quality desired of outputs, a firm is productively efficient when it produces and distributes a good or service at the lowest cost possible.

Innovative or dynamic efficiency refers to the efficiency benefits achieved through research, development and innovation, including the diffusion of technology to produce new products and processes. It includes firms' production of knowledge (of what to make and how to make it), and cross-fertilization among firms to enhance the body of knowledge, all leading to improvements in the state of art.

Dynamic efficiency gains can easily swamp static efficiency gains; that is, they can swamp the gains that result from pushing price closer to costs.

Efficiency is sometimes assessed in terms of total welfare. For example, will a particular merger or course of conduct cause the sum of consumer plus producer surplus to shrink? Sometimes it is assessed in terms of consumer welfare. For example, will the merger or conduct cause *consumer* surplus to shrink? Even jurisdictions that define antitrust as a consumer welfare prescription (rather than a total welfare prescription) seldom focus only on whether consumer surplus will shrink. They also—at least sometimes—value consumer choice, both in terms of the variety of goods and services and the autonomy of consumers to choose. Moreover, they value producer incentives to invest and to innovate, which will normally inure to consumer benefit.

In large economies such as the United States, conduct and transactions seldom lessen consumer welfare without also lessening total welfare, so the distinction between consumer and total welfare is often moot. The distinction is most likely to be material in merger analysis, and even then it is usually insignificant because the parties to a price-raising merger usually cannot prove that their merger is likely to produce net efficiencies that could not otherwise be achieved.

Efficiency also applies to the form and formulation of rules and standards in view of administrative capabilities—the ease or difficulty of applying the law. As applied to conduct that is almost always harmful and almost never beneficial, a rule of per se illegality or quick look (and quick condemnation) is efficient. It saves enforcement resources, gives business greater certainty, and more effectively deters inefficient conduct. If the category is well-drawn, the bright-line rule will not be inefficient in the sense of condemning pro-competitive and efficient conduct; but if it is overbroad—a problem produced by the growing per se category in the 1960s, per se illegality will handicap efficiency.

How to achieve efficiency

How to achieve efficiency is a complex question. In a market economy, many factors and arrangements drive towards efficiency, in all of its senses. Eliminating unnecessary regulation produces substantial efficiency gains. A robust corporate take-over market spurs firms to achieve more productive and dynamic efficiency. Intellectual property protection can spur innovation—although too much protection can create perverse counter-incentives, frustrating innovative moves by outsiders. Competition policy, such as policy to dismantle anti-dumping duties on low-priced imports, can significantly unleash efficient firm behavior.

It is easy to see how competition *policy* can increase efficiency; but what can antitrust *law* do?

Antitrust *law* does not necessarily *produce* efficiency because it is proscriptive, not prescriptive. But antitrust law can prevent harms to efficiency. Antitrust law can preserve an environment in which firms have the incentive to behave rivalrously and in which upstarts have a clear and open path to wage their challenges. Open markets help to preserve the incentives that produce productive, dynamic and market efficiency. But antitrust law needs a limiting principle, lest the law interfere with transactions that benefit consumers and the market. Since about 1980, U.S. courts shifted from a tradition of protecting the competition process (rivalry) and the openness of markets to a different and more specific inquiry: Will the *outcome* of a particular merger or conduct be inefficient by inducing producers to reduce the total amount of the relevant good (i.e., will it lower market output)? Under this framework, if the answer is affirmative, the merger or conduct is likely to be characterized as anticompetitive, at least unless firm efficiencies outweigh consumer loss or the conduct otherwise serves consumers and the market. If not, the merger or conduct is likely to be characterized as procompetitive or neutral.

Chicago and Other "Schools"

You will frequently hear about Chicago School and antitrust. What is Chicago School?

First, there is no monolithic Chicago School. Chicago School encompasses a group of thinkers whose perspectives span a spectrum. On the notional right end of the spectrum are individuals who may have voted against the antitrust laws if they had had the chance—matching the sympathies of most economists at the time when Congress enacted the Sherman Act. Just in from the right, individuals may at least have voted against the monopolization and merger laws.

Many Chicago scholars bring to their analysis strong default presumptions that cartels are inherently unstable, markets work very well, business actors are rational profit-maximizers, business acts are virtually always efficient, and government enforcement is virtually always inefficient except in hard core cartel cases. Judge Posner, for one, a foremost contributor to Chicago School thinking and to antitrust thinking, is not at this end of the spectrum. He does not apply a strong presumption that markets virtually always work well. But despite some diversity, Chicago School is normally associated with strong pro-market presumptions.

A second aspect of Chicago School is how it defines the appropriate scope for antitrust. That scope is informed by non-interventionist first premises and is best captured by a negative: If the conduct or transaction does not lessen output or if it has significant pro-efficiency, pro-innovation qualities, it is not inefficient and should not be proscribed. This paradigm broadens the scope of freedom from antitrust.

Chicago School has contributed important insights to U.S. antitrust, not least by focusing us on key questions: Why did the firm engage in the questioned behavior? Was it a response to the market? Would it help the firm deliver something new and better to the market? What is the probable effect of the antitrust *enforcement*? Will the enforcement help consumers or hurt them? Will it incentivize firms to innovate, or will it chill innovation? Chicago School opened up rigid formulations of law that previously had no room for these questions. The questions are now firmly embedded in U.S. antitrust law and analysis.

A good recent sampling of Chicago School scholarship is contained in a special issue of the Journal of Competition Law & Economics celebrating the twenty-fifth anniversary of the famous article by Judge Frank Easterbrook, The Limits of Antitrust, 63 Texas L. Rev. 1 (1984–1985). The special issue, The Limits of Antitrust Revisited, is 6 J. Competition Law & Economics (March 2010).

There is also a perspective called "post-Chicago." Post–Chicagoans relax the free-market assumptions and pay much more attention to context and facts than to theory of what efficient firms and efficient markets would do. What firms and people really do is also a question asked by behavioral economics, which demonstrates that people are not always rational profit-maximizers.

There was once a perspective called the Harvard School, which drew inferences of anticompetitive incentives from concentrated market structure. The Harvard School initiated the Structure–Conduct–Performance paradigm: market structure influences conduct which influences performance. The understanding was, at the time, that these influences were strong and often determinative. The old Harvard School does not exist today, but the law—which it deeply influenced—still gives credence to a concern that high market concentration with high barriers to entry tend to insulate the market from the forces of competition and to set the stage for non-competitive performance and anticompetitive conduct.

Analysis taking issue with Chicago School is collected in the essays of a number of experts in Pitofsky, ed., HOW THE CHICAGO SCHOOL OVERSHOT THE MARK: THE EFFECT OF CONSERVATIVE ECONOMIC ANALYSIS ON U.S. ANTITRUST (2008). Also, you may want to become familiar with several perspectives on antitrust that incorporate post-Chicago insights and yet offer a specific lens. See, for example, Neil W. Averitt and Robert H. Lande, Using the "Consumer Choice" Approach to Antitrust Law, 74 Antitrust L.J. 175 (2007) (arguing that the currently popular price and efficiency paradigms do not work well enough; they are confusing and nontransparent and are unable to handle issues of non-price competition; and that they should be replaced by a consumer choice framework, which includes cost and other measures); Maurice E. Stucke, Behavioral Economists at the Gate: Antitrust in the Twenty–First Century, 38 Loyola U. Chicago L.J. 513 (2007) (exploring paradoxes and anomalies raised by application of Chicago School rational choice theories and noting corporate behavior in connection with mergers that rationality models do not explain).

E. WHO ENFORCES THE LAW?

The enforcement system for U.S. antitrust law is complex. The Justice Department enforces the Sherman and Clayton Acts by bringing cases to federal court. It may sue criminally—which it does only for egregious conduct such as price-fixing conspiracies—or civilly; for example to stop a merger or monopolistic practice. The Federal Trade Commission may bring proceedings for Clayton Act violations, including anticompetitive mergers, and for violations of the Federal Trade Commission Act, which prohibits unfair methods of competition. DOJ and FTC jurisdiction may overlap substantially and apportionment of cases, especially mergers, is worked out between the agencies. Also, private parties may sue when they are in the line of antitrust injury; they must be harmed or likely to be harmed by that which makes the challenged act illegal. Successful private plaintiffs are entitled to treble damages—three times their injury. They may also get an injunction in a proper case. Finally, state attorneys general may sue under the federal antitrust laws for harm to their residents, as long as interstate commerce is affected, and they may also sue under their own state's antitrust law.

Sectoral regulators, such as the Federal Communications Commission, may also be charged with considering the competitive effects of transactions.

A longer description of enforcement appears in Appendix A, The Framework for U.S. Antitrust Law, part III. Read this now. Throughout the casebook you will read cases that bear on the enforcement system; for example, the Justice Department's criminal enforcement program is treated in Chapter 2, and the limits of private actions to contest mergers of competitors are covered in Chapter 4.

CHAPTER 2

CARTELS AND CLOSELY RELATED AGREEMENTS

■ ■ ■

A. INTRODUCTION

We saw in Chapter 1 that, almost from the start, the Sherman Act condemned hard-core price-fixing and bid rigging cartels—the kind of arrangement encountered in *Trans-Missouri* and *Addyston Pipe and Steel*. This chapter is devoted to the law of cartels and closely related agreements.

Under U.S. law and policy, cartels are the worst kind of antitrust violation. In other nations they are at least one of the worst restraints. The anti-cartel principle has been the unwavering antitrust prohibition throughout U.S. history, even while ascendant political philosophies and economic conditions have shifted and the shifts have brought different notions of what constitutes illegal monopolization and mergers.

Why has the anti-cartel principle been so strong and unwavering? Consider the threads of conflicting philosophy as well as the premises of economics that we have reviewed. Combinations of competitors to control the market raise the power concerns of Justice Harlan, the freedom of trade and property concerns of Justice White, the consumer (price) concerns of Judge Taft, the entrepreneurial concerns of Justice Peckham, and the bullying concerns of Justice McKenna. Think about antitrust economics. Assume a market of vigorous competition with prices at competitive levels. The competitors decide that they want a softer life and they jointly raise the price of their product to a monopoly price. They "rob" consumers. This is the wealth transfer rectangle, page 51 supra—a distributional effect that Justice Harlan worried about. Also, they impair efficiency. See the welfare triangle—resources that would naturally have flowed into the market do not go into the market; this is an allocative loss that worries economists and is compatible with the [libertarian] freedom concerns of Justices White and Holmes.

Cartels are often targeted at the most vulnerable people in society and in that sense they are instruments to rob the poor. Even in the twenty-first century, cartelists tend to target less developed countries because less developed countries are less likely to catch them and bring them to account.

In the great quinine cartel of the 1960s, conspiring chemical companies in Europe "caused" malaria deaths of soldiers in Vietnam by reducing the supply of the only known cure for malaria. And of more recent memory, pharmaceutical companies in Europe and Asia, and their subsidiaries in the United States, undermined health by combining to raise the price of vitamins.

Cartels were used politically in the past to co-opt free nations and compromise their defense production, as did German-run cartels in the 1940s, which were prosecuted by Franklin D. Roosevelt's antitrust chief Thurman Arnold. The German-led cartels facilitated Hitler's war effort. And in the European Community of the 1960s and '70s, market division cartels were the biggest private-power threat to the central goal of integrating the nations of Europe.

Thus, there is enormous support for law against cartels, in the United States and the world. In the United States, hard core cartels (meaning: agreements designed to control the market, not ambiguous conduct that could be serving the market) are normally prosecuted criminally rather than civilly by the Department of Justice,[1] and offenders are subjected to large fines and may go to jail.

In this chapter we explain the forms of cartels, the U.S. law applicable to cartels, the world approach to cartels, and important legal issues, including proof, justifications, exemptions, and cooperation among agencies across the world.

Forms and tasks of cartels. Cartels are agreements among competitors to control the market. They can take several forms. In the United States, the most common form is price-fixing; the competitors decide on their joint profit maximizing price (as best they can) and they enforce their agreement. In the European Union, at least soon after the national laws erecting trade barriers were abolished, the most common form was market division ("You take your home market and I'll take my home market.") Alternatively, competitors might allocate quotas: "You mine no more than x tons of potash, I'll mine no more than y tons, Z will mine up to z tons." As another alternative, competitors might allocate customers. Whatever the form, the participants, if successful, will lower the total output of their product and raise its price.

In each case, however, certain conditions are necessary to make the cartel work. First, the cartel must include all significant producers. If it is a buyers' cartel, everything works in reverse; the cartel must include all significant buyers. Second, barriers must keep non-cartel members out of the market or assure that they don't expand, for otherwise outsiders will

---

1. See Framework Essay, Appendix A, as to the powers of the Justice Department and the Federal Trade Commission. Only the Justice Department may sue criminally. The Justice Department may choose, in any particular case, whether to prosecute criminally or sue civilly. By tradition, it reserves its criminal authority for hard core cartels.

simply enter and increase total production, which will push price back down, spoiling the cartel. Sometimes there are natural barriers or government barriers; sometimes the cartel members can carry out a boycott to keep outsiders from entering or expanding. Third, the cartel members must have good means to administer the cartel: determine the "right" price or quotas (often done through an intensive information exchange); publish the price or other scheme to one another; police all members to detect cheating on the cartel (e.g., secretly charging below the cartel price); and punish cheaters. These tasks are difficult to accomplish. They are greatly facilitated by the existence of no more than a few competitors. Too many players may make the coordination impossible and cheaters undetectable. Moreover, simplicity facilitates the tasks of cartelists. If the products are homogeneous it will be much easier for them to find a joint profit-maximizing price than if the products are differentiated.

We note these conditions here for several reasons. First, if you are a prosecutor, you must be something of a sleuth. Cartels are not easy to prove. You may need to find pieces of a puzzle that fit together. If, for example, you observe an intricate information exchange among competitors, this may be a clue that the firms are not competing at all.

Second, there are roughly two routes to antitrust violations: one through competitor coordination (oligopoly, cartels, and conduct or transactions creating or entrenching oligopolistic behavior), and the other by monopoly or other single-firm power. For the first route, the conditions conducive to cartels are exactly the conditions conducive to other offenses based on oligopoly. Thus, for mergers that may induce oligopolistic behavior (less rivalry, more interdependence or cooperation, and as a result inferior results for consumers), we ask whether the conditions are present that would be likely to lead to cartel-like or other non-rivalrous behavior, usually raising prices. The U.S. antitrust agencies—the Antitrust Division of the Department of Justice and the FTC—have issued merger guidelines advising how the agencies analyze mergers to determine if they are anticompetitive. Take a look now at the 2010 Horizontal Merger Guidelines, Appendix C, § 7. Coordinated Effects. You will see the relationship between cartel conduct, on the one hand, and mergers that are anticompetitive because they induce oligopoly behavior.

The U.S. law. You have read *Trans–Missouri* and *Addyston Pipe*. These cases are a good introduction to the U.S. rule on cartels: Cartels, which are by definition naked restraints, are illegal on their face. "Ruinous competition" is no defense. Judge Taft, in *Addyston Pipe*, not only articulated the rule against cartels, but he showed why it should be so; that is, why and how cartels raise prices.

Standard Oil's rule of reason, inviting inquiry into defendants' purpose and intent, the power of the parties, and the agreement's actual effect, may have temporarily weakened *Trans–Missouri* and *Addyston Pipe*, giving some support to defendants' launching a defense of "reasonableness." But not for long, as we shall see.

Cartels and the world. Globalization has increased the interdependence of the nations of the world. Cartels are increasingly global. If one nation alone (say, the United States) had a law against cartels but could not enforce its law against foreign firms, cartelists would always ply their work offshore. Absent an international regime the whole world would be cartelized. In the 1940s through 1960s, a principal question was the extraterritorial reach of the U.S. antitrust law. Today, when approximately 120 countries have antitrust laws, the principal global antitrust questions are how to coordinate enforcement, how to deal with the proliferation of exemptions including for export cartels, and whether there should be any international rules or framework, particularly against cartels.

Major legal questions. Hard core cartel law is different from most other aspects of antitrust law. It is different because other areas typically involve difficult analytical questions as to whether certain conduct or transactions are anticompetitive on the one hand, or procompetitive and good for consumers, on the other. Cartels are, by definition, anticompetitive. For hard core cartels our questions are:

(1) Did the suspected firms actually form a cartel? That is, did they agree? This is a question of proof. The problem is fact-specific. There is a growing body of law dismissing cases before trial for insufficient evidence of agreement, and even insufficient allegations of one.

(2) If there is a cartel, can it be justified? Can it be justified by proof of crisis, depression, government involvement? Is the particular cartel exempt, for example under sector regulatory law or for reasons of industrial policy or sovereign immunity?

(3) Who can sue to enforce the U.S. law against cartels? For sure, the U.S. government, attorneys general in harmed states, and private parties who are direct buyers (who are entitled to treble their damages).[2] Can a foreign person, injured abroad by a price-rise in the U.S. market, take advantage of U.S. antitrust law? If the goal is world cartel deterrence (is it?) is there an optimal allocation of cases to jurisdictions?

(4) Competitors often make agreements with one another; but is their agreement a cartel? Is their enterprise so obviously destructive of competition that it should be condemned without serious analysis? This is a characterization question. On its face, the agreement may fall into a grey area. If it is not clearly a cartel, defendants are entitled to a rule of reason analysis sometimes quickly applied to determine whether on balance the agreement is good or bad for consumers and the market. But if it is a cartel, the agreement is simply condemned.

We treat the major characterization cases in this chapter. There are many other cases of competitor collaboration which we treat in Chapter 5, after the study of monopolization and mergers.

---

2. See Framework Essay, Appendix A, for the rights of private parties including their standing to sue.

In the following cases, we see the crystallization of the per se rule against cartels, and the cautious treatment of conduct that may not deserve condemnation.

B. REHABILITATING *TRANS-MISSOURI*: NAKED RESTRAINTS VERSUS REASONABLE AGREEMENTS

Standard Oil (1911) announced "the rule of reason." Did this apply to cartels? Did it put a major dent in the rule of *Trans-Missouri*? In the next major case, the Court punted. The Court applied the rule of reason and tried to articulate its content. But were the facts entirely different from those in *Trans-Missouri*?

BOARD OF TRADE OF THE CITY OF CHICAGO v. UNITED STATES

246 U.S. 231 (1918).

JUSTICE BRANDEIS: [Chicago was the leading grain market in the world. Most grain trading was done on its Board of Trade. The Board, something like a stock exchange, was open from 9:30 A.M. to 1:15 P.M. At the close of the regular session, sales of grain to arrive were made at sessions called "The Call." These purchases were made largely from country dealers and farmers. Four or five big Chicago warehouses had been exploiting the farmers by buying up grain "to arrive" after the close of the Call at very low prices. The Board adopted the Call Rule, requiring that any purchases made after the close of the Call and before the next session of the exchange had to be made at the price established at the close of the Call. The United States (Justice Department) sought to enjoin the Call Rule as price fixing illegal per se. The Court denied application of the per se rule.]

... The Government proved the existence of the rule and described its application and the change in business practice involved. It made no attempt to show that the rule was designed to or that it had the effect of limiting the amount of grain shipped to Chicago; or of retarding or accelerating shipment; or of raising or depressing prices; or of discriminating against any part of the public; or that it resulted in hardship to anyone. The case was rested upon the bald proposition, that a rule or agreement by which men occupying positions of strength in any branch of trade, fixed prices at which they would buy or sell during an important part of the business day, is an illegal restraint of trade under the Anti-Trust Law. But the legality of an agreement or regulation cannot be determined by so simple a test, as whether it restrains competition. Every agreement concerning trade, every regulation of trade, restrains. To bind, to restrain, is of their very essence. The true test of legality is whether the restraint imposed is such as merely regulates and perhaps thereby promotes competition or whether it is such as may suppress or even destroy competition. To determine that question the court must ordinarily consider the facts peculiar to the business to which the restraint is applied; its condition before and after the restraint was imposed; the nature of the restraint and its effect, actual or probable. The history of the restraint, the evil believed to exist, the reason for adopting the particular remedy, the purpose or end sought to be attained, are all relevant facts. This is not because a good intention will save an otherwise objectionable regulation or the reverse; but because knowledge of intent may help the court to interpret facts and to predict consequences. The District Court erred, therefore, in striking from the answer allegations concerning the history and purpose of the Call rule and in later excluding evidence on that subject. But the evidence admitted makes it clear that the rule was a reasonable regulation of business consistent with the provisions of the Anti–Trust Law. * * *

QUESTIONS AND COMMENTS

1. How is the Call Rule different from the competitors' agreement in *Trans–Missouri* and in *Addyston Pipe*? In each case, were the competitors facilitating the market or overriding it? Who set the price?

2. Did the Court succeed in giving content to the rule of reason? to the significance of intent? Take note of the statement on intent. It remains a helpful guide.

3. In the next case, invoking the *Standard Oil* rule of reason, defendants once again raised the defense that the prices they fixed were reasonable.

UNITED STATES v. TRENTON POTTERIES CO.

273 U.S. 392 (1927).

JUSTICE STONE: [Twenty individuals and 23 corporations, controlling 82% of the market, fixed the prices of sanitary pottery (toilet bowls). After conviction, defendants argued that the trial court should have submitted to the jury the question whether the agreement was reasonable.]

... Whether this type of restraint is reasonable or not must be judged in part at least in the light of its effect on competition, for whatever difference of opinion there may be among economists as to the social and economic desirability of an unrestrained competitive system, it cannot be doubted that the Sherman Law and the judicial decisions interpreting it are based upon the assumption that the public interest is best protected from the evils of monopoly and price control by the maintenance of competition.

The aim and result of every price-fixing agreement, if effective, is the elimination of one form of competition. The power to fix prices, whether reasonably exercised or not, involves power to control the market and to fix arbitrary and unreasonable prices. The reasonable price fixed today may through economic and business changes become the unreasonable price of tomorrow. Once established, it may be maintained unchanged because of the absence of competition secured by the agreement for a price reasonable when fixed. Agreements which create such potential power may well be held to be in themselves unreasonable or unlawful restraints, without the necessity of minute inquiry whether a particular price is reasonable or unreasonable as fixed and without placing on the government in enforcing the Sherman Law the burden of ascertaining from day to day whether it has become unreasonable through the mere variation of economic conditions. Moreover, in the absence of express legislation requiring it, we should hesitate to adopt a construction making the difference between legal and illegal conduct in the field of business relations depend upon so uncertain a test as whether prices are reasonable—a determination which can be satisfactorily made only after a complete survey of our economic organization and a choice between rival philosophies.... * * *

Meanwhile, after a period of prosperity, the Great Economic Depression hit the country.

Crisis

APPALACHIAN COALS, INC. v. UNITED STATES

288 U.S. 344 (1933).

CHIEF JUSTICE HUGHES: [Defendants were 137 producers of bituminous coal in Appalachia, which had been particularly hard hit by the depression. Capacity for coal far exceeded demand, due partly to the industrial condition and partly to shift of demand to other energy sources such as oil, natural gas, and water power. The unfavorable conditions were aggravated by distress coal—by-products of producing particular sizes of coal. There were no storage facilities, and the by-product shapes were shipped unsold. Conditions were aggravated also by "pyramiding"—the producer would authorize several dealers to sell the same coal, putting the coal into competition with itself. To alleviate the problems, the producers organized Appalachian Coals. They planned for it to function as the exclusive sales agent for them and others, together to represent 70–80% of the tonnage in the territory. Most Appalachian coal was sold outside of the territory, however, in the highly competitive region to the east and north, under an adverse freight rate. The Appalachian producers solicited approval of their plan from the Department of Justice, but the DOJ disapproved.]

First. There is no question as to the test to be applied in determining the legality of the defendants' conduct. The purpose of the Sherman Anti–Trust Act is to prevent undue restraints of interstate commerce, to maintain its appropriate freedom in the public interest, to afford protection from the subversive or coercive influences of monopolistic endeavor. As a charter of freedom, the Act has a generality and adaptability comparable to that found to be desirable in constitutional provisions. It does not go into detailed definitions which might either work injury to legitimate enterprise or through particularization defeat its purpose by providing loopholes for escape. The restrictions the Act imposes are not mechanical or artificial. Its general phrases, interpreted to attain its fundamental objects, set up the essential standard of reasonableness. They call for vigilance in the detection and frustration of all efforts unduly to restrain the free course of interstate commerce, but they do not seek to establish a mere delusive liberty either by making impossible the normal and fair expansion of that commerce or the adoption of reasonable measures to protect it from injurious and destructive practices and to promote competition upon a sound basis.

* * *

Fifth. We think that the evidence requires the following conclusions:

(1) With respect to defendant's purposes, we find no warrant for determining that they were other than those they declared. Good intentions will not save a plan otherwise objectionable, but knowledge of actual intent is an aid in the interpretation of facts and prediction of consequences. Chicago Board of Trade v. United States [246 U.S. 231]. The evidence leaves no doubt of the existence of the evils at which defendants' plan was aimed. The industry was in distress. It suffered from over-expansion and from a serious relative decline through the growing use of substitute fuels. It was afflicted by injurious practices within itself, practices which demanded correction. If evil conditions could not be entirely cured, they at least might be alleviated. The unfortunate state of the industry would not justify any attempt unduly to restrain competition or to monopolize, but the existing situation prompted defendants to make, and the statute did not preclude them from making, an honest effort to remove abuses, to make competition fairer, and thus to promote the essential interests of commerce. The interests of producers and consumers are interlinked. When industry is grievously hurt, when producing concerns fail, when unemployment mounts and communities dependent upon profitable production are prostrated, the wells of commerce go dry. So far as actual purposes are concerned, the conclusion of the court below was amply supported that defendants were engaged in a fair and open endeavor to aid the industry in a measurable recovery from its plight. The inquiry then, must be whether despite this objective the inherent nature of their plan was such as to create an undue restraint upon interstate commerce.

(2) The question thus presented chiefly concerns the effect upon prices. The evidence as to the conditions of the production and distribution of bituminous coal, the available facilities for its transportation, the extent of developed mining capacity, and the vast potential undeveloped capacity, makes it impossible to conclude that defendants through the operation of their plan will be able to fix the price of coal in the consuming

markets. The ultimate finding of the District Court is that the defendants "will not have monopoly control of any market, nor the power to fix monopoly prices;" and in its opinion the court stated that "the selling agency will not be able, we think, to fix the market price of coal." Defendants' coal will continue to be subject to active competition. In addition to the coal actually produced and seeking markets in competition with defendants' coal, enormous additional quantities will be within reach and can readily be turned into the channels of trade if an advance of price invites that course.... * * *

... We think that the Government has failed to show adequate grounds for an injunction in this case. We recognize, however, that the case has been tried in advance of the operation of defendants' plan, and that it has been necessary to test that plan with reference to purposes and anticipated consequences without the advantage of the demonstrations of experience. If in actual operation it should prove to be an undue restraint upon interstate commerce, if it should appear that the plan is used to the impairment of fair competitive opportunities, the decision upon the present record should not preclude the Government from seeking the remedy which would be suited to such a state of facts.... * * *

QUESTIONS AND COMMENTS

1. Was the agreement in *Appalachian Coals* a naked restraint? an ancillary restraint? a reasonable naked restraint? simply a joint venture in a highly competitive market? Is it distinguishable from the agreements in *Trans–Missouri* and *Addyston Pipe*? What would Judge Taft (*Addyston Pipe*) say? What would Chief Justice White (*Standard Oil*) say? On balance, is the rule of *Appalachian Coals* a good, flexible rule of a sort that makes the Sherman Act liveable? Or was it a "sneaky" treatment of a cartel as not a cartel because, on some reckoning, the Court thought this was a reasonable plan that could help the poor coal producers and the economy?

2. *Appalachian Coals* was a child of the Great Economic Depression of the 1930s. It reached the Supreme Court during the depression. *Socony–Vacuum* (below) was a depression case that reached the Supreme Court after the depression. Consider whether, after *Socony–Vacuum* (which has not been undermined by subsequent law), there is room any more for an *Appalachian Coals* analysis.

3. As you would expect, there is pressure to soften competition rules in times of crisis even in modern times. In Ireland in 2002, the Irish beef processors faced debilitating oversupply and, with the encouragement of their government, devised a plan under which "goers" would shut down their plants and "stayers" would pay them to do so. The processors argued that this was an agreement to save the industry and improve the functioning of the market. The European Court held that this was an agreement to restrict competition by object. Competition Authority of Ireland v. Beef Industry Development Society Ltd. (BIDS), Case C–209/07, [2008] ECR I–8637, ECJ. In

theory, under the competition law of the European Union, an agreement to restrict competition by object can possibly be justified; there is no per se rule; but justification of a cartel, even a crisis cartel, cannot be expected.

UNITED STATES v. SOCONY-VACUUM OIL CO.

310 U.S. 150 (1940).

JUSTICE DOUGLAS: Respondents were convicted by a jury under an indictment charging violations of 1 of the Sherman Anti-trust Act. The Circuit Court of Appeals reversed and remanded for a new trial [to determine whether the oil companies' agreement was reasonable].

[The depression caused a crisis in the oil market. The crisis was intensified by "hot oil"—surreptitiously produced in violation of state law, shipped in violation of federal law and dumped on the market. The wholesale price of oil had fallen below the cost of manufacture. Congress passed the National Industrial Recovery Act, which authorized self help by the petroleum industry, working with government officials. The Secretary of the Interior, who was administrator of a code of fair competition for the petroleum industry, established a Petroleum Administrative Board, which was charged with the task to advise and make recommendations to him. Charles Arnott, a vice-president of Socony Vacuum, was appointed chairman of the planning and coordination committee. Arnott, in close touch with the Secretary of the Interior, appointed a Tank Car Committee.]

The first meeting of the Tank Car Committee was held February 5, 1935, and the second on February 11, 1935. At these meetings the alleged conspiracy was formed, the substance of which, so far as it pertained to the Mid-Continent phase, was as follows:

It was estimated that there would be between 600 and 700 tank cars of distress gasoline produced in the Mid-Continent oil field every month by about 17 independent refiners. These refiners, not having regular outlets for the gasoline, would be unable to dispose of it except at distress prices. Accordingly, it was proposed and decided that certain major companies (including the corporate respondents) would purchase gasoline from these refiners. The Committee would assemble each month information as to the quantity and location of this distress gasoline. Each of the major companies was to select one (or more) of the independent refiners having distress gasoline as its "dancing partner,"[20] and would assume responsi-

20. Respondent R.W. McDowell, a vice president of Mid-Continent, testified as follows respecting the origin and meaning of this term:

> "The phrase 'dancing partners' came up right there after Mr. Ashton had gone around the room. There were these 7 or 8 small refiners whom no one had mentioned. He said this situation reminded him of the dances that he used to go to when he was a young fellow. He said, 'Here we are at a great economic ball.' He said, 'We have these major companies who have to buy gasoline and are buying gasoline, and they are the strong dancers.' And he said, 'They have asked certain people to dance with them. They are the better known independent refiners.' He said, 'Here are 7 or 8 that no one seems to know.' He said, 'They remind me of the wallflowers that always used to be present at those old country dances.' He said, 'I think it is going to be one of the jobs of this Committee to introduce some of these wallflowers to some of

bility for purchasing its distress supply.... Purchases were to be made at the "fair going market prices." * * *

... [T]he final details of the Mid-Continent buying program were worked out, including an assignment of the "dancing partners" among the major companies.... Before the month was out all companies alleged to have participated in the program (except one or two) made purchases; 757 tank cars were bought from all but three of the independent refiners who were named in the indictment as sellers.

V. APPLICATION OF THE SHERMAN ACT, CHARGE TO THE JURY

The court charged the jury that it was a violation of the Sherman Act for a group of individuals or corporations to act together to raise the prices to be charged for the commodity which they manufactured where they controlled a substantial part of the interstate trade and commerce in that commodity.... It also charged that there was no evidence of governmental approval which would exempt the buying programs from the prohibitions of the Sherman Act; and that knowledge or acquiescence of officers of the government or the good intentions of the members of the combination would not give immunity from prosecution under that Act.

The Circuit Court of Appeals held this charge to be reversible error, since it was based upon the theory that such a combination was illegal *per se*. In its view respondents' activities were not unlawful unless they constituted an unreasonable restraint of trade. Hence, since that issue had not been submitted to the jury and since evidence bearing on it had been excluded, that court reversed and remanded for a new trial so that the character of those activities and their effect on competition could be determined. In answer to the government's petition respondents here contend that the judgment of the Circuit Court of Appeals was correct, since there was evidence that they had affected prices only in the sense that the removal of the competitive evil of distress gasoline by the buying programs had permitted prices to rise to a normal competitive level; that their activities promoted rather than impaired fair competitive opportunities; and therefore that their activities had not unduly or unreasonably restrained trade.... * * *

... [F]or over forty years this Court has consistently and without deviation adhered to the principle that price-fixing agreements are unlawful per se under the Sherman Act and that no showing of so-called competitive abuses or evils which those agreements were designed to eliminate or alleviate may be interposed as a defense.... * * *

The elimination of so-called competitive evils is no legal justification for such buying programs. The elimination of such conditions was sought primarily for its effect on the price structures. Fairer competitive prices, it is claimed, resulted when distress gasoline was removed from the market. But such defense is typical of the protestations usually made in price-

the strong dancers, so that everybody can dance.' And from that simile, or whatever you want to call it, the term 'dancing partner' arose."

fixing cases. Ruinous competition, financial disaster, evils of price cutting and the like appear throughout our history as ostensible justifications for price-fixing. If the so-called competitive abuses were to be appraised here, the reasonableness of prices would necessarily become an issue in every price-fixing case. In that event the Sherman Act would soon be emasculated; its philosophy would be supplanted by one which is wholly alien to a system of free competition; it would not be the charter of freedom which its framers intended.

The reasonableness of prices has no constancy due to the dynamic quality of business facts underlying price structures. Those who fixed reasonable prices today would perpetuate unreasonable prices tomorrow, since those prices would not be subject to continuous administrative supervision and readjustment in light of changed conditions. Those who controlled the prices would control or effectively dominate the market. And those who were in that strategic position would have it in their power to destroy or drastically impair the competitive system. But the thrust of the rule is deeper and reaches more than monopoly power. Any combination which tampers with price structures is engaged in an unlawful activity. Even though the members of the price-fixing group were in no position to control the market, to the extent that they raised, lowered, or stabilized prices they would be directly interfering with the free play of market forces. The Act places all such schemes beyond the pale and protects that vital part of our economy against any degree of interference. Congress has not left with us the determination of whether or not particular price-fixing schemes are wise or unwise, healthy or destructive. It has not permitted the age-old cry of ruinous competition and competitive evils to be a defense to price-fixing conspiracies. It has no more allowed genuine or fancied competitive abuses as a legal justification for such schemes than it has the good intentions of the members of the combination. If such a shift is to be made, it must be done by the Congress. Certainly Congress has not left us with any such choice....

Nor is it important that the prices paid by the combination were not fixed in the sense that they were uniform and inflexible.... In this case, the result was to place a floor under the market—a floor which served the function of increasing the stability and firmness of market prices. That was repeatedly characterized in this case as stabilization. But in terms of market operations stabilization is but one form of manipulation. And market manipulation in its various manifestations is implicitly an artificial stimulus applied to (or at times a brake on) market prices, a force which distorts those prices, a factor which prevents the determination of those prices by free competition alone.... * * *

Under the Sherman Act a combination formed for the purpose and with the effect of raising, depressing, fixing, pegging, or stabilizing the price of a commodity in interstate or foreign commerce is illegal per se.... Proof that a combination was formed for the purpose of fixing prices and that it caused them to be fixed or contributed to that result is proof of the completion of a price-fixing conspiracy under § 1 of the Act.[59] The indictment in this case charged that this combination had that purpose and effect. And there was abundant evidence to support it. Hence the existence of power on the part of members of the combination to fix prices was but a conclusion from the finding that the buying programs caused or contributed to the rise and stability of prices.

As to knowledge or acquiescence of officers of the Federal government little need be said. The fact that Congress through utilization of the precise methods here employed could seek to reach the same objectives sought by respondents does not mean that respondents or any other group may do so without specific congressional authority. Admittedly no approval of the buying programs was obtained under the National Industrial Recovery Act prior to its termination on June 16, 1935, (§ 2(c)) which would give immunity to respondents from prosecution under the Sherman Act. Though employees of the government may have known of those programs and winked at them or tacitly approved them, no immunity would have thereby been obtained. For Congress had specified the precise manner and method of securing immunity. None other would suffice. Otherwise national policy on such grave and important issues as this would be determined not by Congress nor by those to whom Congress had delegated authority but by virtual volunteers. The method adopted by Congress for alleviating the penalties of the Sherman Act through approval by designated public representatives would be supplanted by a foreign system. But even had approval been obtained for the buying programs, that approval would not have survived the expiration in June 1935 of the Act which was the source of that approval. As we have seen the buying program continued unabated during the balance of 1935 and far into 1936....

Accordingly we conclude that the Circuit Court of Appeals erred in reversing the judgments on this ground....

QUESTIONS AND COMMENTS

1. Since *Socony–Vacuum*, it has been clear that agreements to fix prices are illegal per se and are not exonerated by an economic crisis.

---

59. Under this indictment proof that prices in the Mid–Western area were raised as a result of the activities of the combination was essential, since sales of gasoline by respondents at the increased prices in that area were necessary in order to establish jurisdiction in the Western District of Wisconsin. Hence we have necessarily treated the case as one where exertion of the power to fix prices (i.e., the actual fixing of prices) was an ingredient of the offense. But that does not mean that both a purpose and a power to fix prices are necessary for the establishment of a conspiracy under § 1 of the Sherman Act.... [It is] well-settled that conspiracies under the Sherman Act are not dependent on any overt act other than the act of conspiring.... [A] conspiracy to fix prices violates § 1 of the Act though no overt act is shown, though it is not established that the conspirators had the means available for accomplishment of their objective, and though the conspiracy embraced but a part of the interstate or foreign commerce in the commodity.... Whatever economic justification particular price-fixing agreements may be thought to have, the law does not permit any inquiry into their reasonableness. They are all banned because of their actual or potential threat to the central nervous system of the economy ...

2. Consider the defenses: This was a severe crisis; prices were not actually fixed; the price paid for the distress gas was the market price; and government officials supported the plan. Did the Court do the right thing? Was it too inflexible, and indeed unfair? Did the industry do what was widely perceived as socially beneficial at the time?

3. The Court distinguishes *Appalachian Coals*, stating that that plan did not contemplate or involve the fixing of market prices. Is this a fair distinction? Despite the apparent clarity of a per se rule for naked restraints and a rule of reason for other restraints during the years following *Socony–Vacuum,* cases such as *Appalachian Coals* and even *Chicago Board of Trade* left areas of doubt about which rule applied.

4. In contrasting *Appalachian Coals* with *Socony–Vacuum*, one should be mindful of history. Each case is a product of convictions dominant at the time it was decided. During the early New Deal period the national administration was committed to the idea that industry-wide cooperation among businesses and unions was essential to promote economic recovery. By 1940, when *Socony–Vacuum* was decided, the country was recovering from the economic trauma of the 1930s. The enemy was not the Depression, but Nazi Germany. Attorney General Thurman Arnold was aggressively attacking national and international cartels, many of which had created shortages of materials critical to the war effort. The titanium cartel was a notorious example. See *United States v. National Lead Co.*, 63 F.Supp. 513 (S.D.N.Y. 1945), *aff'd*, 332 U.S. 319 (1947). Is it a surprise that *Socony–Vacuum* makes no concessions to claims by competitors that competition will harm the public interest?

5. See Daniel Crane, The Story of *United States v. Socony–Vacuum*: Hot Oil and Antitrust in the Two New Deals, Chapter 3 in ANTITRUST STORIES, E. Fox and D. Crane eds. (Foundation 2007).

Market Division

Before the European Community was formed in 1957, producers in each European nation were protected from outsiders by high barriers to trade. When the trade barriers fell, the producers formed agreements to keep their markets to themselves. Market division cartels were formed, and successfully challenged, in sugar, quinine, and dyestuffs, among others. See excerpts from the European cartel cases in Eleanor Fox, THE COMPETITION LAW OF THE EUROPEAN UNION IN COMPARATIVE PERSPECTIVE, CASES AND MATERIALS (West 2009), Chap. 2.

Geographic market division cartels are less common in the United States, but they do occur. Indeed, the principal case involves bar review courses. BRG of Georgia pioneered a popular bar review course in Georgia. Bar/Bri (the nationally known bar review program of Harcourt Brace Janovich) entered the Georgia market on a limited basis and found BRG to be a fierce competitor selling at a much lower price. Soon thereafter, Harcourt Brace Janovich made a deal with BRG. It gave BRG an exclusive license to market HBJ's materials in Georgia, and each agreed to stay out of one another's territory. The price of BRG's course rose from $150 to more than $400. The

Supreme Court held that plaintiff was entitled to summary judgment. *Palmer v. BRG of Georgia, Inc.*, 498 U.S. 46 (1990), relying on *United States v. Topco Associates, Inc.*, 405 U.S. 596 (1972).

The Naked Boycott

In *Socony*, the competitors attempted to control the market through buying up excess supply, which was called "tamper[ing] with price structures" and came to be lumped with price fixing. But the evil the Court identified was more general than price fixing. The evil was "*[a]ny combination which ... directly interfere[s] with the free play of market forces.*" Competitors can directly interfere with market forces in other equally harmful ways; for example, market division. By dividing markets geographically, competitors can become monopolists in "their own" markets, and the effect on price can be virtually the same as price fixing. Assigning production quotas is another equivalent device; it is a more direct obstruction than price fixing because the device itself creates the scarcity that causes prices to rise.

Yet another device can directly obstruct the market: boycotting outsiders, especially mavericks. When used against innovators, this device can be more serious even than price fixing, because price fixing has a static implication—we are talking about the price of known products made in known ways. The big break-throughs for markets and consumers come when a firm offers new products, or old products in new ways. Gains from opening the market to innovation tend to overwhelm gains from deterring price fixing. See Michael Porter & Scott Stern, The New Challenge to America's Prosperity: Findings From the Innovation Index (Council on Competitiveness 1999).

A year after *Socony*, the Supreme Court examined a boycott.

Fashion Originators' Guild of America ("FOGA") v. FTC, 312 U.S. 457 (1941). The designers, manufacturers and distributors of fashion textiles and fashion womens' clothes were alarmed by the "style pirates," who copied the fashion designs and sold them cheaply. Taking matters into their own hands, they organized and policed an intricate system whereby none of the Guild's members or cooperators (including 12,000 retailers) could buy from or sell to any of the "pirates" at any part of the chain of design, manufacture or distribution, nor could they buy from or sell to any of their own numbers who violated the rules of the boycott. The 176 manufacturers who were members of the Guild occupied a commanding position in the trade. Violators were heavily fined, in addition to being ostracized from the supply chain. The FTC enjoined the system as an unfair method of competition. FOGA appealed on grounds that the FTC had not proved a price rise, output limitation, or quality deterioration. The Supreme Court affirmed. Justice Black wrote for the Court:

> ... [T]he findings of the Commission bring petitioners' combination in its entirety well within the inhibition of the policies declared by the Sherman Act itself.... Among the many respects in which the Guild's plan runs contrary to the policy of the Sherman Act are these: it narrows the outlets to which garment and textile manufacturers can sell and the sources from which retailers can buy; subjects all retailers and manufacturers who decline to comply with the Guild's program to an organized

> boycott; takes away the freedom of action of members by requiring each to reveal to the Guild the intimate details of their individual affairs; and has both as its necessary tendency and as its purpose and effect the direct suppression of competition from the sale of unregistered textiles and copied designs. In addition to all this, the combination is in reality an extra-governmental agency, which prescribes rules for the regulation and restraint of interstate commerce, and provides extra-judicial tribunals for determination and punishment of violations, and thus "trenches upon the power of the national legislature and violates the statute." [Citing *Addyston Pipe*.]
>
> Petitioners, however, argue that the combination cannot be contrary to the policy of the Sherman and Clayton Acts, since the Federal Trade Commission did not find that the combination fixed or regulated prices, parcelled out or limited production, or brought about a deterioration in quality. But action falling into these three categories does not exhaust the types of conduct banned by the Sherman and Clayton Acts. . . .

Would you have predicted an anticompetitive effect? What effect?

FOGA was invoked in *Klor's v. Broadway–Hale Stores*, 359 U.S. 207 (1959), where Klor's, a small retail store on Mission Street in San Francisco, alleged that its neighbor Broadway–Hale, a chain department store, had organized an agreement among their common suppliers (e.g., GE, RCA, Zenith) to jointly refuse to supply Klor's with radios, TV sets, refrigerators and other household goods or to supply Klor's only at higher prices. When Klor's sued Broadway–Hale for a violation of the Sherman Act, Broadway–Hale moved for summary judgment on grounds that there were hundreds of other competing retailers within a few blocks and competition could not have been hurt. The district court agreed and dismissed the case. The Supreme Court reversed. Group boycotts, it said, are per se illegal. Among other things, they "cripple the freedom of traders and thereby restrain their ability to sell in accordance with their own judgment."

Did the FOGA boycott harm consumers? Did the Court care whether the Broadway–Hale (suppliers') boycott harmed consumers? At the time of *Klor's*, the antitrust laws protected traders (including competitors) from coercive action against them. Often there is synergy between the interests of boycotted sellers and the interests of consumers. Is there synergy in *FOGA*? in *Klors*?

Why would big GE, RCA, Zenith and others agree among themselves (as well as with Broadway–Hale) to discriminate against little George Klor? If we take the allegations in the complaint at face value, the complaint alleged a hard core competitors' agreement to boycott a customer.

If Klor's had alleged only separate agreements between Broadway–Hale and each of the big suppliers to refuse to supply George Klor, would the complaint have stated a claim for a per se illegal group boycott? Is a vertical (buyer-supplier) agreement different from a horizontal (competitors') agreement? Consider incentives, power and effects. We treat the vertical issue in Chapter 6.

Other Devices

Some cartel cases have involved intellectual property, and some have involved standard-setting conspiracies. Patents grant the patentee exclusive rights for a term of years (20 years in the United States) to make, use and sell the patented product or process. Sometimes patents block one another, and sometimes they are complements, meriting cross-licensing. See Chapter 5C.4. At various times in our history, competing patent holders have cartelized under the cover of a patent pool. Virtually all of the competitors in a market would pool their patents as a strategy to avoid competition. A number of these cartels were international. See, e.g., *Zenith Radio Corp. v. Hazeltine Research, Inc.*, 395 U.S. 100 (1969); *Standard Oil Co. (Indiana) (Oil Cracking) v. United States*, 283 U.S. 163 (1931). Patent pooling cases can be complicated by (as noted above) the need to access complementary technologies. These more complicated cases are treated in Chapter 5.

Standard-setting by competitors, likewise, while often important to facilitate competition, has frequently been abused as a means to keep out competitors. The insiders set standards to block new entrants. For example, in *Allied Tube & Conduit Corp. v. Indian Head, Inc.*, 486 U.S. 492 (1988) (p. 166 infra), the incumbents rigged the process so that a cheaper substitute would fail to meet safety standards.

In short, long before the end of the first 50 years of antitrust, cartels were recognized as a heinous antitrust offense. Absent an exemption (such as for cooperatives of agricultural producers and labor unions), cartels are illegal per se.

C. CHARACTERIZATION CASES (IS THIS A CARTEL?)

Socony–Vacuum is the law of the land. At least this is true of clear cartels. *Socony is* a case of a clear cartel. However sympathetic their plight, the competitors were trying to manipulate the market. But what did the Court mean in *Socony* when it said: "[*Any* agreement] with the purpose . . .[2] of raising, depressing, fixing, pegging, or stablizing the price of a commodity in interstate or foreign commerce is illegal per se"? Is this language overbroad? Throughout the 1940s, '50s, and '60s, until the mid 1970s, courts tended to give this language broad scope and indeed to read the words as if they said: "with the purpose *or* with the effect." Beginning in 1978, a series of Supreme Court cases put limits on the *Socony* dictum, refined the scope of the per se rule against price-fixing, and clarified the scope of defenses to agreements that have anticompetitive aspects.

Ethics, professionalism, and "reasonable" self-regulation

In a surprising number of contemporary cases, the restraint is imposed by professionals in the name of self-regulation. Why? Perhaps because steel makers understood that *Socony* applied to them, while

2. We eliminate "and with the effect" because footnote 59 makes clear that proof of anticompetitive effect is not necessary. It was required in the *Socony* case for venue purposes.

professionals did not. For many years, the traditional professions (doctors, lawyers, accountants) asserted with some success that their activities were not business in the commercial sense and that Congress could not have intended the antitrust laws to apply to them. The contention that the professions were immune from the antitrust laws had some currency at least until 1975, when the Court decided *Goldfarb v. Virginia State Bar,* 421 U.S. 773 (1975). In *Goldfarb,* lawyers' price fixing resulted from the bar's promulgation of minimum fee schedules and accompanying "ethics" rules. The Supreme Court held that professionals (like others) could not fix prices. In *Goldfarb*, the Virginia lawyers protested that they acted solely in the public interest in devising and enforcing their minimum fee schedule. However, their ethics rules left little to the imagination. The Supreme Court notes in footnote 4:

> In 1962 the State Bar published a minimum-fee-schedule report that listed a series of fees and stated that they "represent the considered judgment of the Committee [on Economics of Law Practice] as to [a] fair minimum fee in each instance." ... [S]hortly thereafter the County Bar adopted its own minimum-fee schedule that purported to be "a conscientious effort to show lawyers in their true perspective of dignity, training and integrity." The suggested fees for title examination were virtually identical to those in the State Bar report. In accord with Opinion 98 of the State Bar Committee on Legal Ethics the schedule stated that, although there is an ethical duty to charge a lower fee in a deserving case, if a lawyer
>
>> " 'purely for his own advancement, intentionally and regularly bills less than the customary charges of the bar for similar services ... [in order to] increase his business with resulting personal gain, it becomes a form of solicitation contrary to Canon 27 and also a violation of Canon 7, which forbids the efforts of one lawyer to encroach upon the employment of another.' "
>>
>> [The State Bar subsequently scaled up suggested fees. The County Bar published the new schedule, stating] that lawyers should feel free to charge more than the recommended fees; and to avoid condemnation of higher fees charged by some lawyers, it cautioned County Bar members that "to ... publicly criticize lawyers who charge more than the suggested fees herein might in itself be evidence of solicitation...."

After *Goldfarb*, the appropriate treatment of a variety of other restraints by professionals, however, remained open to question. In the following case the restraint was not identified as a cartel (although it was close to being one). The Court assumed that a justification may have been permissible. The question was: If so, what kind of defense or justification was admissible?

NATIONAL SOCIETY OF PROFESSIONAL ENGINEERS v. UNITED STATES

435 U.S. 679 (1978).

JUSTICE STEVENS: This is a civil antitrust case brought by the United States to nullify an association's canon of ethics prohibiting competitive bidding by its members. The question is whether the canon may be justified under the Sherman Act because it was adopted by members of a learned profession for the purpose of minimizing the risk that competition would produce inferior engineering work endangering the public safety. The District Court rejected this justification without making any findings on the likelihood that competition would produce the dire consequences foreseen by the association. The Court of Appeals affirmed. We granted certiorari to decide whether the District Court should have considered the factual basis for the proffered justification before rejecting it. Because we are satisfied that the asserted defense rests on a fundamental misunderstanding of the Rule of Reason frequently applied in antitrust litigation, we affirm.

I

Engineering is an important and learned profession. . . .

The National Society of Professional Engineers (Society) was organized in 1935 to deal with ... the promotion of the professional, social, and economic interests of its members. . . .

The charges of a consulting engineer may be computed in different ways. . . . Suggested fee schedules for particular types of services in certain areas have been promulgated from time to time by various local societies. This case does not, however, involve any claim that the National Society has tried to fix specific fees, or even a specific method of calculating fees. It involves a charge that the members of the Society have unlawfully agreed to refuse to negotiate or even to discuss the question of fees until after a prospective client has selected the engineer for a particular project. Evidence of this agreement is found in § 11(c) of the Society's Code of Ethics, adopted in July 1964.[3]

---

3. That section, which remained in effect at the time of trial, provided:

"Section 11—The Engineer will not compete unfairly with another engineer by attempting to obtain employment or advancement or professional engagements by competitive bidding. . . .

"c. He shall not solicit or submit engineering proposals on the basis of competitive bidding. Competitive bidding for professional engineering services is defined as the formal or informal submission, or receipt, of verbal or written estimates of cost or proposals in terms of dollars, man days of work required, percentage of construction cost, or any other measure of compensation whereby the prospective client may compare engineering services on a price basis prior to the time that one engineer, or one engineering organization, has been selected for negotiations. The disclosure of recommended fee schedules prepared by various engineering societies is not considered to constitute competitive bidding. An Engineer requested to submit a fee proposal or bid prior to the selection of an engineer or firm subject to the negotiation of a satisfactory contract, shall attempt to have the procedure changed to conform to ethical practices, but if not successful he shall withdraw from consideration for the proposed work. These principles shall be applied by the Engineer in obtaining the services of other professions."

The District Court found that the Society's Board of Ethical Review has uniformly interpreted the "ethical rules against competitive bidding for engineering services as prohibiting the submission of any form of price information to a prospective customer which would enable that customer to make a price comparison on engineering services." If the client requires that such information be provided, then § 11(c) imposes an obligation upon the engineering firm to withdraw from consideration for that job....[4]

In 1972 the Government filed its complaint against the Society alleging that members had agreed to abide by canons of ethics prohibiting the submission of competitive bids for engineering services and that, in consequence, price competition among the members had been suppressed and customers had been deprived of the benefits of free and open competition. The complaint prayed for an injunction terminating the unlawful agreement.

In its answer the Society admitted the essential facts alleged by the Government and pleaded a series of affirmative defenses, only one of which remains in issue. In that defense, the Society averred that the standard set out in the Code of Ethics was reasonable because competition among professional engineers was contrary to the public interest. It was averred that it would be cheaper and easier for an engineer "to design and specify inefficient and unnecessarily expensive structures and methods of construction." Accordingly, competitive pressure to offer engineering services at the lowest possible price would adversely affect the quality of engineering. Moreover, the practice of awarding engineering contracts to the lowest bidder, regardless of quality, would be dangerous to the public health, safety, and welfare. For these reasons, the Society claimed that its Code of Ethics was not an "unreasonable restraint of interstate trade or commerce."

... The District Court did not, however, make any finding on the question whether, or to what extent, competition had led to inferior engineering work which, in turn, had adversely affected the public health, safety, or welfare. That inquiry was considered unnecessary because the court was convinced that the ethical prohibition against competitive bidding was "on its face a tampering with the price structure of engineering fees in violation of § 1 of the Sherman Act."

... [T]he Court of Appeals affirmed its conclusion that the agreement was unlawful on its face and therefore "illegal without regard to claimed or possible benefits."

II

In *Goldfarb v. Virginia State Bar,* 421 U.S. 773, the Court held that a bar association's rule prescribing minimum fees for legal services violated

4. Having been selected, the engineer may then, in accordance with the Society's canons of ethics, negotiate a satisfactory fee arrangement with the client. If the negotiations are unsuccessful, then the client may withdraw his selection and approach a new engineer.

§ 1 of the Sherman Act. In that opinion the Court noted that certain practices by members of a learned profession might survive scrutiny under the Rule of Reason even though they would be viewed as a violation of the Sherman Act in another context. The Court said:

> "The fact that a restraint operates upon a profession as distinguished from a business is, of course, relevant in determining whether that particular restraint violates the Sherman Act. It would be unrealistic to view the practice of professions as interchangeable with other business activities, and automatically to apply to the professions antitrust concepts which originated in other areas. The public service aspect, and other features of the professions may require that a particular practice, which could properly be viewed as a violation of the Sherman Act in another context, be treated differently. We intimate no view on any other situation than the one with which we are confronted today." 421 U.S., at 788–789, n. 17.

Relying heavily on this footnote, and on some of the major cases applying a Rule of Reason ... petitioner argues that its attempt to preserve the profession's traditional method of setting fees for engineering services is a reasonable method of forestalling the public harm which might be produced by unrestrained competitive bidding. To evaluate this argument it is necessary to identify the contours of the Rule of Reason and to discuss its application to the kind of justification asserted by petitioner.

A. The Rule of Reason.

One problem presented by the language of § 1 of the Sherman Act is that it cannot mean what it says. The statute says that "every" contract that restrains trade is unlawful. But, as Mr. Justice Brandeis perceptively noted [in *Chicago Board of Trade*], restraint is the very essence of every contract; read literally, § 1 would outlaw the entire body of private contract law. Yet it is that body of law that establishes the enforceability of commercial agreements and enables competitive markets—indeed, a competitive economy—to function effectively.

... The legislative history [of the Sherman Act] makes it perfectly clear that courts [are] to give shape to the statute's broad mandate by drawing on common-law tradition. The Rule of Reason, with its origins in common-law precedents long antedating the Sherman Act, has served that purpose.... [T]he Rule ... focuses directly on the challenged restraint's impact on competitive conditions.

This principle is apparent in even the earliest of cases applying the Rule of Reason, *Mitchel v. Reynolds,* [1 P.Wms. 181 (1711)]. *Mitchel* involved the enforceability of a promise by the seller of a bakery that he would not compete with the purchaser of his business. The covenant was for a limited time and applied only to the area in which the bakery had operated. It was therefore upheld as reasonable, even though it deprived the public of the benefit of potential competition. The long-run benefit of enhancing the marketability of the business itself—and thereby providing incentives to develop such an enterprise—outweighed the temporary and limited loss of competition.

The Rule of Reason suggested by *Mitchel v. Reynolds* has been regarded as a standard for testing the enforceability of covenants in restraint of trade which are ancillary to a legitimate transaction, such as an employment contract or the sale of a going business. Judge (later Mr. Chief Justice) Taft so interpreted the Rule in his classic rejection of the argument that competitors may lawfully agree to sell their goods at the same price as long as the agreed-upon price is reasonable. *United States v. Addyston Pipe & Steel Co.,* 85 F. 271, 282–283 (CA6 1898), aff'd, 175 U.S. 211. That case, and subsequent decisions by this Court, unequivocally foreclose an interpretation of the Rule as permitting an inquiry into the reasonableness of the prices set by private agreement.

The early cases also foreclose the argument that because of the special characteristics of a particular industry, monopolistic arrangements will better promote trade and commerce than competition. . . . * * *

There are, thus, two complementary categories of antitrust analysis. In the first category are agreements whose nature and necessary effect are so plainly anticompetitive that no elaborate study of the industry is needed to establish their illegality—they are "illegal *per se.*" In the second category are agreements whose competitive effect can only be evaluated by analyzing the facts peculiar to the business, the history of the restraint, and the reasons why it was imposed. In either event, the purpose of the analysis is to form a judgment about the competitive significance of the restraint; it is not to decide whether a policy favoring competition is in the public interest, or in the interest of the members of an industry. Subject to exceptions defined by statute, that policy decision has been made by the Congress.

B. The Ban on Competitive Bidding.

Price is the "central nervous system of the economy," *United States v. Socony-Vacuum Oil Co.,* 310 U.S. 150, 226 n. 59, and an agreement that "interfere[s] with the setting of price by free market forces" is illegal on its face. In this case we are presented with an agreement among competitors to refuse to discuss prices with potential customers until after negotiations have resulted in the initial selection of an engineer. While this is not price fixing as such, no elaborate industry analysis is required to demonstrate the anticompetitive character of such an agreement. It operates as an absolute ban on competitive bidding, applying with equal force to both complicated and simple projects and to both inexperienced and sophisticated customers. . . .

The Society's affirmative defense confirms rather than refutes the anticompetitive purpose and effect of its agreement. The Society argues that the restraint is justified because bidding on engineering services is inherently imprecise, would lead to deceptively low bids, and would thereby tempt individual engineers to do inferior work with consequent risk to public safety and health. The logic of this argument rests on the assumption that the agreement will tend to maintain the price level; if it had no such effect, it would not serve its intended purpose. . . .

It may be, as petitioner argues, that competition tends to force prices down and that an inexpensive item may be inferior to one that is more costly. There is some risk, therefore, that competition will cause some suppliers to market a defective product. Similarly, competitive bidding for engineering projects may be inherently imprecise and incapable of taking into account all the variables which will be involved in the actual performance of the project. Based on these considerations, a purchaser might conclude that his interest in quality—which may embrace the safety of the end product—outweighs the advantages of achieving cost savings by pitting one competitor against another. . . .

The Sherman Act does not require competitive bidding; it prohibits unreasonable restraints on competition. Petitioner's ban on competitive bidding prevents all customers from making price comparisons in the initial selection of an engineer, and imposes the Society's views of the costs and benefits of competition on the entire marketplace. It is this restraint that must be justified under the Rule of Reason, and petitioner's attempt to do so on the basis of the potential threat that competition poses to the public safety and the ethics of its profession is nothing less than a frontal assault on the basic policy of the Sherman Act. * * *

. . . [T]he cautionary footnote in *Goldfarb,* 421 U.S., at 788–789, n. 17, quoted *supra,* cannot be read as fashioning a broad exemption under the Rule of Reason for learned professions. We adhere to the view expressed in *Goldfarb* that, by their nature, professional services may differ significantly from other business services, and, accordingly, the nature of the competition in such services may vary. Ethical norms may serve to regulate and promote this competition, and thus fall within the Rule of Reason. But the Society's argument in this case is a far cry from such a position. We are faced with a contention that a total ban on competitive bidding is necessary because otherwise engineers will be tempted to submit deceptively low bids. Certainly, the problem of professional deception is a proper subject of an ethical canon. But, once again, the equation of competition with deception, like the similar equation with safety hazards, is simply too broad; we may assume that competition is not entirely conducive to ethical behavior, but that is not a reason, cognizable under the Sherman Act, for doing away with competition.

In sum, the Rule of Reason does not support a defense based on the assumption that competition itself is unreasonable. Such a view of the Rule would create the "sea of doubt" on which Judge Taft refused to embark in *Addyston* and which this Court has firmly avoided ever since. * * *

JUSTICE BLACKMUN, with whom JUSTICE REHNQUIST joined, concurring in part and concurring in the judgment: * * *

My skepticism about ... shaping the Rule of Reason to such a narrow last as does the majority, arises from the fact that there may be ethical rules which have a more than *de minimis* anticompetitive effect and yet are important in a profession's proper ordering. A medical association's prescription of standards of minimum competence for licensing or certification may lessen the number of entrants. A bar association's regulation of the permissible forms of price advertising for nonroutine legal services or limitation of in-person solicitation, see *Bates v. State Bar of Arizona,* 433 U.S. 350 (1977),[*] may also have the effect of reducing price competition. In acknowledging that "professional services may differ significantly from other business services" and that the "nature of the competition in such services may vary," but then holding that ethical norms can pass muster under the Rule of Reason only if they promote competition, I am not at all certain that the Court leaves enough elbowroom for realistic application of the Sherman Act to professional services. * * *

QUESTIONS AND COMMENTS

1. The challenged agreement assured that no engineer would engage in competitive bidding before being selected by a client for negotiations. Did the Court treat this as per se illegal? as subject to the rule of reason? something in between? Why does the Court even allow for the possibility of a justification of defendants' rule? Why is the rule of reason relevant at all?

2. The Engineers asserted that intense price competition would lead to vigorous efforts by engineers to cut their costs and thus would consistently produce inferior engineering work. If the ethical rule was a good faith response to this problem, what result? What should be the result? What would Justices Blackmun and Rehnquist decide? If price competition does tend to produce inferior engineering work and thus impair safety, how should society deal with this problem? How has society dealt with similar contentions about the effect of competition in the airline industry?

3. Does *Professional Engineers* hold that competitors may not interfere with price competition in order to achieve some non-economic social good, such as safer bridges or better public health and safety? Does it hold that, even in full blown rule-of-reason analysis, such social benefits may not be weighed on the scale against competitive harms? Is this consistent or inconsistent with *Chicago Board of Trade?*

4. Analyze the restraint in terms of purpose and intent, power, and effect on competition, assuming that at least most of the engineers devised, approved of, and implemented their Code of Ethics as public-spirited citizens.

5. The Engineers' Code of Ethics was a loose-knit agreement. Shortly thereafter a tighter-knit agreement came before the Court—one that involved some integration of functions but that could affect price or influence other outcomes of the competitive process.

---

* *Editors' note*: The Arizona court's approval of the bar rule against advertising routine legal services was held to be a violation of the Constitutional right to free commercial speech.

Making a market

It may not be obvious to you how CBS, in the case presented below, came to assert that the music licensors' practice of offering blanket licenses for background music to the television broadcasters was credibly illegal per se. You may observe that this mode of business operation is entirely different from the agreements designed to squelch a form of competition. The explanation is: Especially from the mid–1960s to the mid–1970s, the per se rule had been ever expanding. It had expanded far beyond cartels. If the lawyers could devise an argument that seemed to give an arrangement some resemblance to price fixing (e.g., the creators of the musical compositions stopped price-competing with one another), there was a chance that this then-elastic per se rule would apply. *BMI* became a vehicle for rationalizing the per se rule.

BROADCAST MUSIC, INC. v. COLUMBIA BROADCASTING SYSTEM, INC.

441 U.S. 1 (1979).

JUSTICE WHITE: This case involves an action under the antitrust and copyright laws brought by respondent Columbia Broadcasting System, Inc. (CBS), against petitioners, American Society of Composers, Authors and Publishers (ASCAP) and Broadcast Music, Inc. (BMI), and their members and affiliates. The basic question presented is whether the issuance by ASCAP and BMI to CBS of blanket licenses to copyrighted musical compositions at fees negotiated by them is price fixing *per se* unlawful under the antitrust laws.

I

CBS operates one of three national commercial television networks, supplying programs to approximately 200 affiliated stations and telecasting approximately 7,500 network programs per year. Many, but not all, of these programs make use of copyrighted music recorded on the soundtrack. CBS also owns television and radio stations in various cities. It is " 'the giant of the world in the use of music rights,' " the " 'No. 1 outlet in the history of entertainment.' "

Since 1897, the copyright laws have vested in the owner of a copyrighted musical composition the exclusive right to perform the work publicly for profit, but the legal right is not self-enforcing. In 1914, Victor Herbert and a handful of other composers organized ASCAP because those who performed copyrighted music for profit were so numerous and widespread, and most performances so fleeting, that as a practical matter it was impossible for the many individual copyright owners to negotiate with and license the users and to detect unauthorized uses. "ASCAP was organized as a 'clearing-house' for copyright owners and users to solve these problems" associated with the licensing of music. As ASCAP operates today, its 22,000 members grant it nonexclusive rights to license nondramatic performances of their works, and ASCAP issues licenses and distributes royalties to copyright owners in accordance with a schedule reflecting the nature and amount of the use of their music and other factors.

BMI, a nonprofit corporation owned by members of the broadcasting industry, was organized in 1939, is affiliated with or represents some 10,000 publishing companies and 20,000 authors and composers, and operates in much the same manner as ASCAP. Almost every domestic copyrighted composition is in the repertory either of ASCAP, with a total of three million compositions, or of BMI, with one million.

Both organizations operate primarily through blanket licenses, which give the licensees the right to perform any and all of the compositions owned by the members or affiliates as often as the licensees desire for a stated term. Fees for blanket licenses are ordinarily a percentage of total revenues or a flat dollar amount, and do not directly depend on the amount or type of music used. Radio and television broadcasters are the largest users of music, and almost all of them hold blanket licenses from both ASCAP and BMI. Until this litigation, CBS held blanket licenses from both organizations for its television network on a continuous basis since the late 1940's and had never attempted to secure any other form of license from either ASCAP or any of its members.

The complaint filed by CBS charged various violations of the Sherman Act and the copyright laws.... [After trial] the court dismissed the complaint. * * * [T]he Court of Appeals [reversed, holding] that the blanket license issued to television networks was a form of price fixing illegal per se under the Sherman Act. * * * Because we disagree with the Court of Appeals' conclusions with respect to the per se illegality of the blanket license, we reverse its judgment and remand the cause for further appropriate proceedings.

II

In construing and applying the Sherman Act's ban against contracts, conspiracies, and combinations in restraint of trade, the Court has held that certain agreements or practices are so "plainly anticompetitive," and so often "lack ... any redeeming virtue," that they are conclusively presumed illegal ... This per se rule is a valid and useful tool of antitrust policy and enforcement. ... But easy labels do not always supply ready answers.

A

... As generally used in the antitrust field, "price fixing" is a shorthand way of describing certain categories of business behavior to which the per se rule has been held applicable. The Court of Appeals' literal approach does not alone establish that this particular practice is one of those types or that it is "plainly anticompetitive" and very likely without "redeeming virtue." ... When two partners set the price of their goods or services they are literally "price fixing," but they are not per se in violation of the Sherman Act.... Thus, it is necessary to characterize the challenged conduct as falling within or without that category of behavior to which we apply the label "per se price fixing." That will often, but not always, be a simple matter. * * *

B

* * * ... [I]n 1941, the United States charged that the blanket license, which was then the only license offered by ASCAP and BMI, was an illegal restraint of trade and that arbitrary prices were being charged as the result of an illegal copyright pool. The Government sought to enjoin ASCAP's exclusive licensing powers and to require a different form of licensing by that organization. The case was settled by a consent decree that imposed tight restrictions on ASCAP's operations....

Under the [decree as amended in 1950], members may grant ASCAP only nonexclusive rights to license their works for public performance. Members, therefore, retain the rights individually to license public performances, along with the rights to license the use of their compositions for other purposes.... ASCAP is required to grant to any user making written application a nonexclusive license to perform all ASCAP compositions, either for a period of time or on a per-program basis. ASCAP may not insist on the blanket license, and the fee for the per-program license, which is to be based on the revenues for the program on which ASCAP music is played, must offer the applicant a genuine economic choice between the per-program license and the more common blanket license. * * *

Finally, we note that Congress, itself in the new Copyright Act, has chosen to employ the blanket license and similar practices.... * * *

III

* * *

A

As a preliminary matter, we are mindful that the Court of Appeals' holding would appear to be quite difficult to contain. If, as the court held, there is a per se antitrust violation whenever ASCAP issues a blanket license to a television network for a single fee, why would it not also be automatically illegal for ASCAP to negotiate and issue blanket licenses to individual radio or television stations or to other users who perform copyrighted music for profit? Likewise, if the present network licenses issued through ASCAP on behalf of its members are per se violations, why would it not be equally illegal for the members to authorize ASCAP to issue licenses establishing various categories of uses that a network might have for copyrighted music and setting a standard fee for each described use?

Although the Court of Appeals apparently thought the blanket license could be saved in some or even many applications, it seems to us that the per se rule does not accommodate itself to such flexibility and that the observations of the Court of Appeals with respect to remedy tend to impeach the per se basis for the holding of liability.

CBS would prefer that ASCAP be authorized, indeed directed, to make all its compositions available at standard per-use rates within negotiated categories of use. But if this in itself or in conjunction with blanket licensing constitutes illegal price fixing by copyright owners, CBS urges that an injunction issue forbidding ASCAP to issue any blanket license or to negotiate any fee except on behalf of an individual member for the use of his own copyrighted work or works. Thus, we are called upon to determine that blanket licensing is unlawful across the board. We are quite sure, however, that the per se rule does not require any such holding.

B

... [N]othing in the Copyright Act of 1976 indicates in the slightest that Congress intended to weaken the rights of copyright owners to control the public performance of musical compositions. Quite the contrary is true. Although the copyright laws confer no rights on copyright owners to fix prices among themselves or otherwise to violate the antitrust laws, we would not expect that any market arrangements reasonably necessary to effectuate the rights that are granted would be deemed a per se violation of the Sherman Act....

C

More generally, in characterizing this conduct under the per se rule, our inquiry must focus on whether the effect and, here because it tends to show effect, ... the purpose of the practice are to threaten the proper operation of our predominantly free-market economy—that is, whether the practice facially appears to be one that would always or almost always tend to restrict competition and decrease output, and in what portion of the market, or instead one designed to "increase economic efficiency and render markets more, rather than less, competitive." ...

The blanket license, as we see it, is not a "naked restrain[t] of trade with no purpose except stifling of competition," but rather accompanies the integration of sales, monitoring, and enforcement against unauthorized copyright use. See L. Sullivan, Handbook of the Law of Antitrust § 59, p. 154 (1977). As we have already indicated, ASCAP and the blanket license developed together out of the practical situation in the marketplace: thousands of users, thousands of copyright owners, and millions of compositions. Most users want unplanned, rapid, and indemnified access to any and all of the repertory of compositions, and the owners want a reliable method of collecting for the use of their copyrights. Individual sales transactions in this industry are quite expensive, as would be individual monitoring and enforcement, especially in light of the resources of single composers. Indeed, as both the Court of Appeals and CBS recognize, the costs are prohibitive for licenses with individual radio stations, nightclubs, and restaurants, and it was in that milieu that the blanket license arose.

A middleman with a blanket license was an obvious necessity if the thousands of individual negotiations, a virtual impossibility, were to be avoided. Also, individual fees for the use of individual compositions would presuppose an intricate schedule of fees and uses, as well as a difficult and expensive reporting problem for the user and policing task for the copyright owner. Historically, the market for public-performance rights organized itself largely around the single-fee blanket license, which gave unlimited access to the repertory and reliable protection against infringement. When ASCAP's major and user-created competitor, BMI, came on the scene, it also turned to the blanket license. * * *

D

This substantial lowering of costs ... differentiates the blanket license from individual use licenses. The blanket license is composed of the individual compositions plus the aggregating service. Here, the whole is truly greater than the sum of its parts; it is, to some extent, a different product. The blanket license has certain unique characteristics: It allows the licensee immediate use of covered compositions, without the delay of prior individual negotiations, and great flexibility in the choice of musical material. Many consumers clearly prefer the characteristics and cost advantages of this marketable package, and even small performing-rights societies that have occasionally arisen to compete with ASCAP and BMI have offered blanket licenses....

E

Finally, we have some doubt—enough to counsel against application of the per se rule—about the extent to which this practice threatens the "central nervous system of the economy," that is, competitive pricing as the free market's means of allocating resources. Not all arrangements among actual or potential competitors that have an impact on price are per se violations of the Sherman Act or even unreasonable restraints. Mergers among competitors eliminate competition, including price competition, but they are not per se illegal, and many of them withstand attack under any existing antitrust standard. Joint ventures and other cooperative arrangements are also not usually unlawful, at least not as price-fixing schemes, where the agreement on price is necessary to market the product at all.

Here, the blanket-license fee is not set by competition among individual copyright owners, and it is a fee for the use of any of the compositions covered by the license. But the blanket license cannot be wholly equated with a simple horizontal arrangement among competitors. ASCAP does set the price for its blanket license, but that license is quite different from anything any individual owner could issue. The individual composers and authors have neither agreed not to sell individually in any other market nor use the blanket license to mask price fixing in such other markets.

Moreover, the substantial restraints placed on ASCAP and its members by the consent decree must not be ignored. The District Court found that there was no legal, practical, or conspiratorial impediment to CBS's obtaining individual licenses; CBS, in short, had a real choice. * * * [Reversed and remanded for rule of reason analysis.]

QUESTIONS AND COMMENTS

1. What was CBS's strongest argument that the arrangements constituted price fixing? By reason of the arrangement, individual musical compositions and composers did not compete against one another on price. Was this a problem for the ultimate buyer? To the extent that they suppressed some competition, did the combinations have redeeming virtues?

2. Note carefully the Court's test for when conduct is illegal per se. The *BMI* formulation became the new and predominant test for per se illegality—at least in rhetoric if not always in application. Note how hard core cartels fit easily and precisely within the terms of the test. Is the *Socony* formulation (see page 68 supra) a superior or inferior formulation? Why?

3. What are the main factors that place the BMI (ASCAP) arrangements outside of the per se rule?

4. The case was remanded and tried under a rule of reason. Under a rule of reason analysis, the court must define the market and then consider, given the forces of competition and the prospect of efficiencies, whether the arrangement helps or hurts competition to the ultimate benefit of consumers. See Chapter 5 for analysis under the rule of reason.

5. After the Supreme Court decided *BMI,* some claimed that the per se rule was so narrowly cabined that it was virtually dead. This proposition was tested by beleaguered beer wholesalers in Fresno, California. They had been competing fiercely by extending more and more credit to the local beer retailers. Finally, they agreed to stop granting credit to the retailers, thus requiring the retailers to pay for the beer on delivery. They contended that their agreement did not lessen competition but increased it.

CATALANO, INC. v. TARGET SALES, INC.

446 U.S. 643 (1980).

PER CURIAM: Petitioners, ... beer retailers ..., brought suit against respondent wholesalers alleging that they had conspired to eliminate short-term trade credit formerly granted on beer purchases in violation of § 1 of the Sherman Act. The District Court entered an interlocutory order, which ... denied petitioners' "motion to declare this a case of *per se* illegality," and then certified to the United States Court of Appeals for the Ninth Circuit the question whether the alleged agreement among competitors fixing credit terms, if proved, was unlawful on its face. The Court of Appeals granted permission to appeal, and, with one judge dissenting, agreed with the District Court that a horizontal agreement among competitors to fix credit terms does not necessarily contravene the antitrust laws. We ... reverse....

[Petitioners allege and we assume:] ... [B]eginning in early 1967, respondent wholesalers secretly agreed, in order to eliminate competition among themselves, that as of December 1967 they would sell to retailers only if payment were made in advance or upon delivery. Prior to the agreement, the wholesalers had extended credit without interest up to the 30– and 42–day limits permitted by state law. According to the petition, prior to the agreement wholesalers had competed with each other with respect to trade credit, and the credit terms for individual retailers had varied substantially. After entering into the agreement, respondents uniformly refused to extend any credit at all.

The Court of Appeals decided that the credit-fixing agreement ... might actually enhance competition (1) "by removing a barrier perceived by some sellers to market entry," and (2) "by the increased visibility of price...."

In dissent, Judge Blumenfeld expressed the opinion that an agreement to eliminate credit was a form of price fixing....

Our cases fully support Judge Blumenfeld's analysis and foreclose both of the possible justifications on which the majority relied....

It is virtually self-evident that extending interest-free credit for a period of time is equivalent to giving a discount equal to the value of the use of the purchase price for that period of time. Thus, credit terms must be characterized as an inseparable part of the price. An agreement to terminate the practice of giving credit is thus tantamount to an agreement to eliminate discounts, and thus falls squarely within the traditional *per se* rule against price fixing. While it may be that the elimination of a practice of giving variable discounts will ultimately lead in a competitive market to corresponding decreases in the invoice price, that is surely not necessarily to be anticipated. It is more realistic to view an agreement to eliminate credit sales as extinguishing one form of competition among the sellers. In any event, when a particular concerted activity entails an obvious risk of anticompetitive impact with no apparent potentially redeeming value, the fact that a practice may turn out to be harmless in a particular set of circumstances will not prevent its being declared unlawful *per se*.

The majority of the panel of the Court of Appeals suggested, however, that a horizontal agreement to eliminate credit sales may remove a barrier to other sellers who may wish to enter the market. But in any case in which competitors are able to increase the price level or to curtail production by agreement, it could be argued that the agreement has the effect of making the market more attractive to potential new entrants. If that potential justifies horizontal agreements among competitors imposing one kind of voluntary restraint or another on their competitive freedom, it would seem to follow that the more successful an agreement is in raising the price level, the safer it is from antitrust attack. Nothing could be more inconsistent with our cases.

Nor can the informing function of the agreement, the increased price visibility, justify its restraint on the individual wholesaler's freedom to select his own prices and terms of sale. For, again, it is obvious that any industrywide agreement on prices will result in a more accurate understanding of the terms offered by all parties to the agreement. As the *Sugar Institute* case demonstrates, however, there is a plain distinction between the lawful right to publish prices and terms of sale, on the one hand, and an agreement among competitors limiting action with respect to the published prices, on the other. * * *

Accordingly, the judgment of the Court of Appeals is reversed, and the case is remanded for further proceedings consistent with this opinion.

QUESTIONS AND COMMENTS

1. Defendants invoked arguments from economic theory that sellers cannot effectively fix the price of a product by fixing the price of only one component. If they fix the price of the component, they will focus their competition on the price of the product. Suppose plywood is sold and delivered pursuant to an invoice that specifies the price for the wood and the price for delivery. If the sellers tried to price fix by fixing the delivery charge alone, the attempt (it is claimed) would be abortive; if the fixed delivery component exceeded the cost of delivery, competition would force down the price for the wood. Is this the way markets work? If so, would plywood sellers bother to fix the price of delivery? If beer sellers could not reduce competitive pressure on price by agreeing to deny credit, why would they bother to do so?

2. Compare *In re Plywood Antitrust Litigation*, 655 F.2d 627 (5th Cir.1981), *cert. dismissed*, 462 U.S. 1125 (1983): The plywood manufacturers cartelized through the following device: The price was set by the price leader in the West Coast market. When sellers sprang up in the Southeast, the Southeast sellers charged near-by customers the traditional base price plus "phantom freight," i.e., the freight costs that would have to be incurred by the West Coast sellers. If barriers to enter Southeast production were low, as defendants contended, would the market prove that there was no phantom freight? that higher quality must have accounted for the higher Southeast price? that an agreement to charge phantom freight could not have existed because it would not have made economic sense?

* * *

Meanwhile, for more than 30 years the Court had not decided a case involving maximum price-fixing by competitors. In *Kiefer–Stewart Co. v. Joseph E. Seagram & Sons,* 340 U.S. 211 (1951), the Court, relying on the dictum in *Socony* (all price fixing is illegal, whether raising, lowering, or stabilizing prices) had held that maximum price fixing by competitors is illegal per se despite the fact that it may put a lid on prices. The greatest fear was that a minimum price would masquerade as a maximum price. In the years following, however, scholars argued that maximum price fixing can be economically beneficial and that courts should carefully analyze the facts before condemning it. See Frank Easterbrook, *Maximum Price Fixing*, 48 U. CHI. L. REV. 886 (1981).

Against this background, the *Maricopa County* case came to the Supreme Court. The State of Arizona had sued two medical foundations and moved for partial summary judgment declaring maximum-fee agreements illegal per se. The district court denied the motion, and the Court of Appeals for the Ninth Circuit affirmed.

ARIZONA v. MARICOPA COUNTY MEDICAL SOCIETY

457 U.S. 332 (1982).

JUSTICE STEVENS: The question presented is whether § 1 of the Sherman Act has been violated by an agreement among competing physicians setting, by majority vote, the maximum fees that they may claim in full payment for health services provided to policyholders of specified insurance plans. The United States Court of Appeals for the Ninth Circuit held that the question could not be answered without evaluating the actual purpose and effect of the agreement at a full trial. Because the undisputed facts disclose a violation of the statute, we granted certiorari, and now reverse. * * *

II

The Maricopa Foundation for Medical Care is a non-profit Arizona corporation composed of licensed doctors of medicine, osteopathy, and podiatry engaged in private practice. Approximately 1,750 doctors, representing about 70% of the practitioners in Maricopa County, are members.

The Maricopa Foundation was organized in 1969 for the purpose of promoting fee-for-service medicine and to provide the community with a competitive alternative to existing health insurance plans. The foundation performs three primary activities. It establishes the schedule of maximum fees that participating doctors agree to accept as payment in full for services performed for patients insured under plans approved by the foundation. It reviews the medical necessity and appropriateness of treatment provided by its members to such insured persons. It is authorized to draw checks on insurance company accounts to pay doctors for services performed for covered patients. . . .

The Pima Foundation for Medical Care, which includes about 400 member doctors, performs similar functions. For the purposes of this litigation, the parties seem to regard the activities of the two foundations as essentially the same. . . .

* * *

The fee schedules limit the amount that the member doctors may recover for services performed for patients insured under plans approved by the foundations. To obtain this approval the insurers—including self-insured employers as well as insurance companies[11]—agree to pay the

11. . . . The record contains no firm data on the portion of the health care market that is covered by [insurance plans approved by the Maricopa or Pima foundations.] The State relies upon a 1974 analysis indicating that the insurance plans endorsed by the Maricopa foundation

doctors' charges up to the scheduled amounts, and in exchange the doctors agree to accept those amounts as payment in full for their services. The doctors are free to charge higher fees to uninsured patients and they also may charge any patient less than the scheduled maxima. A patient who is insured by a foundation-endorsed plan is guaranteed complete coverage for the full amount of his medical bills only if he is treated by a foundation member. He is free to go to a nonmember physician and is still covered for charges that do not exceed the maximum fee schedule, but he must pay any excess....

The impact ... is a matter of dispute. The State of Arizona contends that the periodic upward revisions of the maximum fee schedules have the effect of stabilizing and enhancing the level of actual charges by physicians, and that the increasing level of their fees in turn increases insurance premiums. The foundations, on the other hand, argue that the schedules impose a meaningful limit on physicians' charges, and that the advance agreement by the doctors to accept the maxima enables the insurance carriers to limit and to calculate more efficiently the risks they underwrite and therefore serves as an effective cost containment mechanism that has saved patients and insurers millions of dollars.... [We] must assume that the respondents' [Maricopa's] view of the genuine issues of fact is correct.

This assumption presents, but does not answer, the question whether the Sherman Act prohibits the competing doctors from adopting, revising, and agreeing to use a maximum fee schedule in implementation of the insurance plans.

III

The respondents recognize that our decisions establish that price fixing agreements are unlawful on their face. But they argue that the *per se* rule does not govern this case because the agreements at issue are horizontal and fix maximum prices, are among members of a profession, are in an industry with which the judiciary has little antitrust experience, and are alleged to have procompetitive justifications....

A * * *

The application of the *per se* rule to maximum price fixing agreements in *Kiefer–Stewart Co. v. Seagram & Sons*, 340 U.S. 211 (1951), followed ineluctably from *Socony–Vacuum*:

> "For such agreements, no less than those to fix minimum prices, cripple the freedom of traders and thereby restrain their ability to sell in accordance with their own judgment. We reaffirm what we said in *United States v. Socony–Vacuum Oil Co.*, 310 U.S. 150, 223: 'Under the Sherman Act a combination formed for the purpose and with the effect of raising, depressing, fixing, pegging, or stabilizing the price of

had about 63% of the prepaid health care market, but the respondents contest the accuracy of this analysis.

a commodity in interstate or foreign commerce is illegal *per se*.' " *Id.*, at 213.

* * * We have not wavered in our enforcement of the *per se* rule against price fixing....

B

Our decisions foreclose the argument that the agreements at issue escape *per se* condemnation because they are horizontal and fix maximum prices....

Nor does the fact that doctors—rather than nonprofessionals—are the parties to the price fixing agreements support the respondents' position.... The price fixing agreements in this case ... are not premised on public service or ethical norms. The respondents do not argue ... that the quality of the professional service that their members provide is enhanced by the price restraint.... [T]he claim that the price restraint will make it easier for customers to pay does not distinguish the medical profession from any other provider of goods or services.

We are equally unpersuaded by the argument that we should not apply the *per se* rule in this case because the judiciary has little antitrust experience in the health care industry.... [T]he result of this reasoning was the adoption by the Court of Appeals of a legal standard based on the reasonableness of the fixed prices, an inquiry we have so often condemned....

The respondents' principal argument is that the *per se* rule is inapplicable because their agreements are alleged to have procompetitive justifications.... The anticompetitive potential inherent in all price fixing agreements justifies their facial invalidation even if procompetitive justifications are offered for some. Those claims of enhanced competition are so unlikely to prove significant in any particular case that we adhere to the rule of law that is justified in its general application. Even when the respondents are given every benefit of the doubt, the limited record in this case is not inconsistent with the presumption that the respondents' agreements will not significantly enhance competition.

The respondents contend that their fee schedules are pro-competitive because they make it possible to provide consumers of health care with a uniquely desirable form of insurance coverage that could not otherwise exist. The features of the foundation-endorsed insurance plans that they stress are a choice of doctors, complete insurance coverage, and lower premiums. The first two characteristics, however, are hardly unique to these plans. Since only about 70% of the doctors in the relevant market are members of either foundation, the guarantee of complete coverage only applies when an insured chooses a physician in that 70%. If he elects to go to a non-foundation doctor, he may be required to pay a portion of the doctor's fee. It is fair to presume, however, that at least 70% of the doctors in other markets charge no more than the "usual, customary, and reasonable" fee that typical insurers are willing to reimburse in full....

. . . Even if a fee schedule is . . . desirable, it is not necessary that the doctors do the price fixing. The record indicates that the Arizona Comprehensive Medical/Dental Program for Foster Children is administered by the Maricopa foundation pursuant to a contract under which the maximum fee schedule is prescribed by a state agency rather than by the doctors. . . . [I]nsurers are capable not only of fixing maximum reimbursable prices but also of obtaining binding agreements with providers guaranteeing the insured full reimbursement of a participating provider's fee. . . .

The most that can be said for having doctors fix the maximum prices is that doctors may be able to do it more efficiently than insurers. The validity of that assumption is far from obvious[28] but in any event there is no reason to believe that any savings that might accrue from this arrangement would be sufficiently great to affect the competitiveness of these kinds of insurance plans. . . .

C

Our adherence to the *per se* rule is grounded not only on economic prediction, judicial convenience, and business certainty, but also on a recognition of the respective roles of the Judiciary and the Congress in regulating the economy. Given its generality, our enforcement of the Sherman Act has required the Court to provide much of its substantive content. By articulating the rules of law with some clarity and by adhering to rules that are justified in their general application, however, we enhance the legislative prerogative to amend the law. . . .

IV

Having declined the respondents' invitation to cut back on the *per se* rule against price fixing, we are left with the respondents' argument that their fee schedules involve price fixing in only a literal sense. For this argument, the respondents rely upon *Broadcast Music, Inc. v. Columbia Broadcasting System, Inc.*, 441 U.S. 1 (1979). * * *

This case is fundamentally different. Each of the foundations is composed of individual practitioners who compete with one another for patients. Neither the foundations nor the doctors sell insurance, and they derive no profits from the sale of health insurance policies. The members of the foundations sell medical services. Their combination in the form of the foundation does not permit them to sell any different product. Their combination has merely permitted them to sell their services to certain customers at fixed prices and arguably to affect the prevailing market price of medical care.

---

28. In order to create an insurance plan under which the doctor would agree to accept as full payment a fee prescribed in a fixed schedule, someone must canvass the doctors to determine what maximum prices would be high enough to attract sufficient numbers of individual doctors to sign up but low enough to make the insurance plan competitive. In this case that canvassing function is performed by the foundation; the foundation then deals with the insurer. It would seem that an insurer could simply bypass the foundation by performing the canvassing function and dealing with the doctors itself. . . .

The foundations are not analogous to partnerships or other joint arrangements in which persons who would otherwise be competitors pool their capital and share the risks of loss as well as the opportunities for profit. In such joint ventures, the partnership is regarded as a single firm competing with other sellers in the market. The agreement under attack is an agreement among hundreds of competing doctors concerning the price at which each will offer his own services to a substantial number of consumers. It is true that some are surgeons, some anesthesiologists, and some psychiatrists, but the doctors do not sell a package of three kinds of services. If a clinic offered complete medical coverage for a flat fee, the cooperating doctors would have the type of partnership arrangement in which a price fixing agreement among the doctors would be perfectly proper. But the fee agreements disclosed by the record in this case are among independent competing entrepreneurs. They fit squarely into the horizontal price fixing mold.

* * *

JUSTICE POWELL, with whom CHIEF JUSTICE BURGER and JUSTICE REHNQUIST join, dissenting: The medical care plan condemned by the Court today is a comparatively new method of providing insured medical services at predetermined maximum costs. It involves no coercion. Medical insurance companies, physicians, and patients alike are free to participate or not as they choose. On its face, the plan seems to be in the public interest.

... [R]ather than identifying clearly the controlling principles and remanding for decision on a completed record, this Court makes its own *per se* judgment of invalidity. The respondents' contention that the "consumers" of medical services are benefitted substantially by the plan is given short shrift. The Court concedes that "the parties conducted [only] a limited amount of pretrial discovery", leaving undeveloped facts critical to an informed decision of this case. I do not think today's decision on an incomplete record is consistent with proper judicial resolution of an issue of this complexity, novelty, and importance to the public. I therefore dissent. * * *

II

* * * Several ... aspects of the record are of key significance.... First, the foundation arrangement forecloses *no* competition. Unlike the classic cartel agreement, the foundation plan does not instruct potential competitors: "Deal with consumers on the following terms and no others." Rather, physicians who participate in the foundation plan are free both to associate with other medical insurance plans—at any fee level, high or low—and directly to serve uninsured patients—at any fee level, high or low. Similarly, insurers that participate in the foundation plan also remain at liberty to do business outside the plan with any physician—foundation member or not—at any fee level. Nor are physicians locked into a plan for more than one year's membership. Thus freedom to compete, as well as freedom to withdraw, is preserved.

Second, on this record ... insurers represent consumer interests.... [O]nce a consumer ... has chosen a medical insurance plan ... he is largely indifferent to the amount that his physician charges.... The insurer, however, is *not* indifferent. To keep insurance premiums at a competitive level and to remain profitable, insurers—including those who have contracts with the foundations—step into the consumer's shoes with his incentive to contain medical costs....

III

It is settled law that once an arrangement has been labeled as "price fixing" it is to be condemned *per se*. But it is equally well settled that this characterization is not to be applied as a talisman to every arrangement that involves a literal fixing of prices. Many lawful contracts, mergers, and partnerships fix prices. But our cases require a more discerning approach Before characterizing an arrangement as a *per se* price fixing agreement meriting condemnation, a court should determine whether it is a "naked restrain[t] of trade with no purpose except stifling of competition." ...

As part of this inquiry, a court must determine whether the procompetitive economies that the arrangement purportedly makes possible are substantial and realizable in the absence of such an agreement. * * *

QUESTIONS AND COMMENTS

1. Was the Maricopa Foundation a cartel? Apply the test for per se illegality as formulated in *BMI*. Does such a foundation suppress the competition among the doctors? Might it, to the contrary, be viewed as a method of competition—against HMOs and other prepaid medical care? If so, is competition through insured health care one of the competitive forces that doctors are likely to take into account in setting their fees? Is it obvious that the Maricopa formula degrades health care and harms consumers/patients? Might it help them?

2. What would happen to the levels of insurance premiums (and thus to the salability of the insurance plans) if the doctors set the maximum prices higher than the market price? What would happen if an insurance plan that guarantees full reimbursement of doctors' fees and forbids doctors' balance billing set the maximum lower than market?

3. Is the basic problem here the concept of the foundation or merely who sets the maximum fee? Is that a big antitrust problem or a small detail?

4. Note that Justice Stevens wrote the opinion for the Court, and that Justice Stevens seems to prefer a more flexible *per se* rule than does Justice Powell (see *BMI*). Justice Stevens respects the formulation in *Socony*; he is wary of competitors' agreement on prices; he is wary of competitors' tampering with this central nerve of the competition process. Do Powell and Stevens have a disagreement about the relationship between competition and efficiencies? About the importance of the competition process and the threat of private power? Which approach is wiser? The next opinion, too, is authored by Justice Stevens.

NATIONAL COLLEGIATE ATHLETIC ASSOCIATION v. UNIVERSITY OF OKLAHOMA

468 U.S. 85 (1984).

JUSTICE STEVENS: [The NCAA regulates amateur collegiate sports. It includes most colleges with major athletic programs. For each season, it adopts a plan for the televising of college football games by television networks, with a view to reducing the adverse effects of live television on football game attendance.

The plan requires the television networks that agree to carry the games to schedule at least 82 different member institutions during each 2–year period, with no member eligible to appear more than six times, and none more than four times nationally.

The Universities of Oklahoma and Georgia are major football playing schools. They challenge the limitations on their appearances.

The district court held that the NCAA plan was a cartel; a pact among competing schools to limit television exposure of games and raise price. It held the restrictions illegal.]

II

. . . By participating in an association which prevents member institutions from competing against each other on the basis of price or kind of television rights that can be offered to broadcasters, the NCAA member institutions have created a horizontal restraint—an agreement among competitors on the way in which they will compete with one another. . . . Because it places a ceiling on the number of games member institutions may televise, the horizontal agreement places an artificial limit on the quantity of televised football that is available to broadcasters and consumers. By restraining the quantity of television rights available for sale, the challenged practices create a limitation on output. . . . Moreover, . . . the minimum aggregate price . . . preclude[s] any price negotiation. . . .

Horizontal price fixing and output limitation are ordinarily . . . "illegal *per se*" . . . without inquiry into the particular market context. . . . Nevertheless, we have decided that it would be inappropriate to apply a *per se* rule . . . [because] this case involves an industry in which horizontal restraints on competition are essential if the product is to be available at all.

. . . [T]he NCAA seeks to market a particular brand of football—college football. The identification of this "product" with an academic tradition differentiates college football from and makes it more popular than professional sports to which it might otherwise be comparable, such as, for example, minor league baseball. In order to preserve the character and quality of the "product," athletes must not be paid, must be required to attend class, and the like. And the integrity of the "product" cannot be preserved except by mutual agreement. . . .

Broadcast Music squarely holds that a joint selling arrangement may be so efficient that it will increase sellers' aggregate output and thus be procompetitive. Similarly, ... a restraint in a limited aspect of a market may actually enhance marketwide competition.... Thus, despite the fact that this case involves restraints on the ability of member institutions to compete in terms of price and output, a fair evaluation of their competitive character requires consideration of the NCAA's justifications for the restraints. * * *

III

Because it restrains price and output, the NCAA's television plan has a significant potential for anticompetitive effects. The findings of the District Court indicate that this potential has been realized. The District Court found that if member institutions were free to sell television rights, many more games would be shown on television, and that the NCAA's output restriction has the effect of raising the price the networks pay for televisions rights. Moreover, courts found that by fixing a price for television rights to all games, the NCAA creates a price structure that is unresponsive to viewer demand and unrelated to the prices that would prevail in a competitive market. And, of course, since as a practical matter institutions need NCAA approval, members have no real choice but to adhere to the NCAA's television controls.

The anticompetitive consequences of this arrangement are apparent. Individual competitors lose their freedom to compete. Price is higher and output lower than they would otherwise be, and both are unresponsive to consumer preference. This latter point is perhaps the most significant, since "Congress designed the Sherman Act as a 'consumer welfare prescription.'" *Reiter v. Sonotone Corp.*, 442 U.S. 330, 343. A restraint that has the effect of reducing the importance of consumer preference in setting price and output is not consistent with this fundamental goal of antitrust law. Restrictions on price and output are the paradigmatic examples of restraints of trade that the Sherman Act was intended to prohibit. See *Standard Oil Co. v. United States*, 221 U.S. 1, 52–60 (1911). At the same time, the television plan eliminates competitors from the market, since only those broadcasters able to bid on television rights covering the entire NCAA can compete. Thus, as the District Court found, many telecasts that would occur in a competitive market are foreclosed by the NCAA's plan.

Petitioner argues, however, that its television plan can have no significant anticompetitive effect since the record indicates that it has no market power—no ability to alter the interaction of supply and demand in the market. We must reject this argument for two reasons, one legal, one factual.

As a matter of law, the absence of proof of market power does not justify a naked restriction on price or output. To the contrary, when there is an agreement not to compete in terms of price or output, "no elaborate industry analysis is required to demonstrate the anticompetitive character of such an agreement." *Professional Engineers*, 435 U.S., at 692. Petitioner does not quarrel with the District Court's finding that price and output are not responsive to demand. Thus the plan is inconsistent with Sherman Act's command that price and supply be responsive to consumer preference. We have never required proof of market power in such a case. This naked restraint on price and output requires some competitive justification even in the absence of a detailed market analysis

As a factual matter, it is evident that petitioner does possess market power. The District Court employed the correct test for determining whether college football broadcasts constitute a separate market—whether there are other products that are reasonably substitutable for televised NCAA football games. Petitioner's argument that it cannot obtain supracompetitive prices from broadcasters since advertisers, and hence broadcasters, can switch from college football to other types of programming simply ignores the findings of the District Court.... Indeed, the District Court's subsidiary finding that advertisers will pay a premium price per viewer to reach audiences watching college football because of their demographic characteristics is vivid evidence of the uniqueness of this product....

We turn now to the NCAA's proffered justifications.

IV

[The Court rejects defendants' analogy to BMI; NCAA is not an integrated joint venture; the schools are individual agents. Nor were there procompetitive efficiencies; NCAA football could be marketed just as effectively without the plan.] * * *

V

Throughout the history of its regulation of intercollegiate football telecasts, the NCAA has indicated its concern ... that fan interest in a televised game may adversely affect ticket sales for games that will not appear on television.

... Under the current plan, games are shown on television during all hours that college football games are played. The plan simply does not protect live attendance....

There is, however, a more fundamental reason for rejecting this defense. The NCAA's argument that its television plan is necessary to protect live attendance is not based on a desire to maintain the integrity of college football as a distinct and attractive product, but rather on a fear that the product will not prove sufficiently attractive to draw live attendance when faced with competition from televised games. At bottom the NCAA's position is that ticket sales for most college games are unable to compete in a free market. The television plan protects ticket sales by limiting output—just as any monopolist increases revenues by reducing output....

VI

* * * ... It is reasonable to assume that most of the regulatory controls of the NCAA are justifiable means of fostering competition among amateur athletic teams and therefore procompetitive because they enhance public interest in intercollegiate athletics. The specific restraints on football telecasts that are challenged in this case do not, however, fit into the same mold as do rules defining the conditions of the contest, the eligibility of participants, or the manner in which members of a joint enterprise shall share the responsibilities and the benefits of the total venture.

The NCAA does not claim that its television plan has equalized or is intended to equalize competition within any one league. The plan is nationwide in scope and there is no single league or tournament in which all college football teams compete. There is no evidence of any intent to equalize the strength of teams in [different divisions].... * * * Affirmed.

Justice White, a former all-star football player, dissented. He believed the Court erred in treating intercollegiate athletics as an enterprise pursued solely or even primarily for profit. He thought that the NCAA needed to impose restraints in order to prevent competitive excesses harmful to the students and the institutions; that each of the NCAA regulations was a legitimate attempt to keep university athletes from becoming professionalized, overshadowing the educational mission; that the output measured by the Court was not the proper one, and that NCAA had no monopoly power when competing as it does against many other types of entertainment.

QUESTIONS AND COMMENTS

1. Notice who sued: predictably, the "best" competitors—more of whose games would have been demanded if the NCAA had not restricted their freedom to compete. If the district court's findings were correct, the NCAA cartel would have raised the TV license fee for the games above the competitive level precisely because output—especially of the most attractive games—was limited. Did plaintiffs prove competitive harm?

2. How would you characterize the rule of *NCAA*? Does the case apply an almost per se rule? a strong presumption? Does the Court's methodology differ from its approach in *Maricopa*? (i.e., the *NCAA* Court listened to arguments on efficiency, necessity, and even reasonableness before deciding that the conduct was illegal.)

3. Note the Court's formulation of why application of a strict per se rule would have been inappropriate: The "case involves an industry in which horizontal restraints on competition are essential if the product is to be available at all." As you would expect, future defendants would try to make the most of this gateway. It has not proved to be a wide gateway.

4. Two years after *NCAA* the Supreme Court decided a case in which a federation of dentists jointly refused to supply their patients' x rays to the patients' insurers. The insurers wanted to use the x rays to double check whether procedures for which reimbursement was requested, such as fillings, were necessary. The dentists claimed that the x rays were a poor source for this information and would mislead. The case was tried before an FTC administrative law judge, not as a per se violation but as a presumptive violation. Relatively little evidence was introduced on each point. The FTC upheld the finding that the joint refusal was illegal. The Supreme Court affirmed. It noted that the conduct resembled per se illegal group boycotts, but it had two distinguishing features: the dentists' conduct was not an attempt to harm a competitor, and the defendant was a professional association. Nonetheless, the Court said, applying "the Rule of Reason to these facts is not a matter of any great difficulty." The agreement "limit[ed] consumer choice by impeding the 'ordinary give and take of the market place' " and the dentists showed no efficiencies or procompetitive effect. We will study the decision in Chapter 5, page 447 infra, under rule of reason analysis. *FTC v. Indiana Federation of Dentists*, 476 U.S. 447 (1986).

Problem

Can colleges fix financial aid packages?

Prospective college students may be admitted to more than one college. This is "the overlap" group. The top colleges are competing for these students. Their admissions' officers compare notes; they make an overlap list. They agree not to compete for these students on the basis of financial aid (which may be seen as a discount from tuition). Rather, they will compete on the basis of the merits of the college. This way, the colleges will avoid price wars for the students they all want the most and there will be more financial aid to go around.

Is this plan illegal on its face?

Are there any crucial facts you want to know before you (possibly) declare the plan illegal?

Is any one of the following cases decisive: *Professional Engineers*, *Catalano*, *NCAA*?

Student 1: The plan is illegal on its face and should be enjoined.
Student 2: The plan is not illegal on its face and a trial court should consider . . . [what facts and circumstances?]
Students 3, 4 and 5: You are the judges.

[Remember your analysis and conclusions. You will meet this case later in the materials.]

We present two more important contemporary Supreme Court cases on competitor price restraints. The first decision solidifies the anti-cartel rule, despite equities that might have weakened it. The second questions the wisdom of rigid rules, outside of the area of hard core cartels. *Superior Court Trial Lawyers*, below, centers on boycotting conduct more than it does on price fixing; but as you will see, the two are integral. The boycott was against the buyer of the lawyer's services and was solely a method to obtain a price rise.

FTC v. SUPERIOR COURT TRIAL LAWYERS ASSOCIATION

493 U.S. 411 (1990).

JUSTICE STEVENS: [The group of lawyers in Washington, D.C., who regularly accepted court appointments to represent criminal defendants ("CJA regulars") engaged in a boycott; they agreed with one another not to accept any new cases until their fees ($30 per hour for court time, $20 per hour for out-of-court time) were raised. The authority to raise the fees resided in the D.C. Council. The boycott created a crisis in the D.C. justice system. The D.C. Council raised the fees, and the lawyers again accepted their usual appointments.

The FTC sued and found a violation of the Federal Trade Commission Act. The appellate court remanded on grounds that the lawyers had engaged in an expressive boycott and the FTC should have examined whether the lawyers had market power and should have dismissed the case if the lawyers did not have market power, so as not to intrude unnecessarily on First Amendment freedoms. Reversing the appellate court, the Supreme Court held that the boycott, which was also a price-fixing cartel, was illegal per se.]

... Respondents' boycott may well have served a cause that was worthwhile and unpopular. We may assume that the pre-boycott rates were unreasonably low, and that the increase has produced better legal representation for indigent defendants. Moreover, given that neither indigent criminal defendants nor the lawyers who represent them command any special appeal with the electorate, we may also assume that without the boycott there would have been no increase in District CJA fees at least until the Congress amended the federal statute. These assumptions do not control the case, for it is not our task to pass upon the social utility or political wisdom of price-fixing agreements.... [R]espondents' boycott "constituted a classic restraint of trade within the meaning of Section 1 of the Sherman Act." As such, it also violated the prohibition against unfair methods of competition in § 5 of the FTC Act. Prior to the boycott CJA lawyers were in competition with one another, each deciding independently whether and how often to offer to provide services to the District at CJA rates. The agreement among the CJA lawyers was designed to obtain higher prices for their services and was implemented by a concerted refusal to serve an important customer in the market for legal services and, indeed, the only customer in the market for the particular services that CJA regulars offered. "This constriction of supply is the essence of 'price-fixing,' whether it be accomplished by agreeing upon a price, which will decrease the quantity demanded, or by agreeing upon an output, which will increase the price offered." The horizontal arrangement among these competitors was unquestionably a "naked restraint" on price and output. See National Collegiate Athletic Assn. v. Board of Regents of Univ. of Okla., 468 U.S. 85, 110 (1984).

It is of course true that the city purchases respondents' services because it has a constitutional duty to provide representation to indigent defendants. It is likewise true that the quality of representation may improve when rates are increased. Yet neither of these facts is an acceptable justification for an otherwise unlawful restraint of trade....

The social justifications proffered for respondents' restraint of trade thus do not make it any less unlawful ... Respondents' argument, like that made by the petitioners in Professional Engineers, ultimately asks us to find that their boycott is permissible because the price it seeks to set is reasonable. But it was settled shortly after the Sherman Act was passed that it "is no excuse that the prices fixed are themselves reasonable." See, e.g., United States v. Trenton Potteries Co., 273 U.S. 392, 397–398 (1927).... * * *

Equally important is the second error implicit in respondents' claim to immunity from the per se rules. In its opinion, the Court of Appeals assumed that the antitrust laws permit, but do not require, the condemnation of price fixing and boycotts without proof of market power. The opinion further assumed that the per se rule prohibiting such activity "is only a rule of 'administrative convenience and efficiency,' not a statutory command." This statement contains two errors. The per se rules are, of course, the product of judicial interpretations of the Sherman Act, but the rules nevertheless have the same force and effect as any other statutory commands. Moreover, while the per se rule against price fixing and boycotts is indeed justified in part by "administrative convenience," the Court of Appeals erred in describing the prohibition as justified only by such concerns. The per se rules also reflect a long-standing judgment that the prohibited practices by their nature have "a substantial potential for impact on competition." Jefferson Parish Hospital District, 466 U.S. [2, 16 (1984)]. * * *

... Every such horizontal arrangement among competitors poses some threat to the free market. A small participant in the market is, obviously, less likely to cause persistent damage than a large participant. Other participants in the market may act quickly and effectively to take the small participant's place. For reasons including market inertia and information failures, however, a small conspirator may be able to impede competition over some period of time. Given an appropriate set of circumstances and some luck, the period can be long enough to inflict real injury upon particular consumers or competitors. * * *

Of course, some boycotts and some price-fixing agreements are more pernicious than others; some are only partly successful, and some may only succeed when they are buttressed by other causative factors, such as political influence. But an assumption that, absent proof of market power, the boycott disclosed by this record was totally harmless—when overwhelming testimony demonstrated that it almost produced a crisis in the administration of criminal justice in the District and when it achieved its economic goal—is flatly inconsistent with the clear course of our antitrust jurisprudence. Conspirators need not achieve the dimensions of a monopoly, or even a degree of market power any greater than that already disclosed by this record, to warrant condemnation under the antitrust laws.

QUESTIONS AND COMMENTS

1. In addition to contending that they had no power to harm competition and that their action did not harm competition, defendants sought to justify their conduct on grounds of freedom of expression and the right to petition government (the *Noerr* defense, see p. 163 infra), but they failed. The portion of the case regarding the trial lawyers' justifications is at p. 173 infra. They were not protected by the labor exemption, Clayton Act § 6, because they were independent contractors, not employees. Clayton § 6 protects, among other things, collective bargaining negotiations.

2. The FTC and Department of Justice have broad discretion in deciding what cases to bring. Why would the FTC choose to bring this case?

3. What was the purpose of the lawyers' strike and boycott? What was the effect? Does it matter whether some CJA lawyers wanted solely to help indigent defendants; that some of these lawyers did not care at all about their own fees but knew that $20/$30 an hour was not enough money to draw a sufficient number of qualified lawyers into the market? Did these strikers have "good" intent and strikers who only wanted more money have "bad" intent? If this is not the relevant "intent," what is?

A few years later the FTC challenged dental association by-laws that limited the dentists' advertising. The Supreme Court had already intimated that an agreement among professionals to suppress truthful price advertising was a serious restraint on competition. Such a restraint denies information to consumers; it reduces incentives to compete; it eliminates a force that could reduce the cost of services, and it eliminates opportunities for new entrants to enter the market, thus perpetuating the market position of established incumbents. *Bates v. State Bar of Arizona*, 433 U.S. 350, 374–78 (1977) (prohibiting a *state* restraint; namely, the Arizona court's authorization of the bar association's "ethical" rules). Suppression of price advertising might thus be compared with the suppression of price bidding in *National Society of Professional Engineers*.

Although *California Dental Association* is not a classic cartel case, it and *The Three Tenors* case that follows will provide a fitting end point to our per se analysis and a segue to the cases on rule of reason that we will study in Chapter 5.

CALIFORNIA DENTAL ASSOCIATION v. FTC

526 U.S. 756 (1999).

[The California Dental Association (CDA) was a professional association with 19,000 members, comprising about 75% of the dentists in California. The CDA had rules of ethics which, among other things, prohibited false and misleading advertising. Members agreed to abide by the rules, and the association expelled members who violated them. The challenged rules:

1. effectively prohibited advertising across-the-board discounts, such as for senior citizens and new patients,*
2. prohibited promotional statements about price levels, such as "inexpensive fees" and "reasonable prices,"
3. prohibited claims about quality or superiority of a dentist's services,
4. discouraged solicitation, such as reporting results of free screening of school children on forms bearing the dentist's name and address, and
5. imposed disclosure requirements for the advertising of discounts, including the term of the discount, the amount of the nondiscounted fee, and all restrictions qualifying the discount.

The Commission, by Chairman Robert Pitofsky, first separated the restraints on price advertising (see 1, 2, and 5 above) from the other restraints and stated that the price restraints fall within the category of per se illegality. It held the non-price restraints to be illegal after a "quick look" under the rule of reason. As to the non-price restraints, the Commission said:

> As our quick look under the rule of reason reveals, the advertising restrictions are likely to have anticompetitive effects, CDA has the necessary market power to harm competition by adopting the restraints, and there are no countervailing efficiencies or other business justifications that would justify the imposition of this kind of ban on broad categories of truthful and nondeceptive advertising. In short, CDA's advertising restrictions are unreasonable, make out a violation of Section 1 of the Sherman Act, and therefore violate Section 5 of the FTC Act....

The Court of Appeals affirmed the result under a quick-look analysis.]

JUSTICE SOUTER: ... The case before us ... fails to present a situation in which the likelihood of anticompetitive effects is [intuitively] obvious. Even on Justice Breyer's [dissenting] view that bars on truthful and

* This was an effective prohibition because so much additional information was required that simple advertising was not possible.

verifiable price and quality advertising are *prima facie* anticompetitive ... and place the burden of procompetitive justification on those who agree to adopt them, the very issue at the threshold of this case is whether professional price and quality advertising is sufficiently verifiable in theory and in fact to fall within such a general rule. Ultimately our disagreement with Justice Breyer turns on our different responses to this issue. Whereas he accepts, as the Ninth Circuit seems to have done, that the restrictions here were like restrictions on advertisement of price and quality generally ..., it seems to us that the CDA's advertising restrictions might plausibly be thought to have a net procompetitive effect, or possibly no effect at all on competition. The restrictions on both discount and nondiscount advertising are, at least on their face, designed to avoid false or deceptive advertising in a market characterized by striking disparities between the information available to the professional and the patient.... In a market for professional services, in which advertising is relatively rare and the comparability of service packages not easily established, the difficulty for customers or potential competitors to get and verify information about the price and availability of services magnifies the dangers to competition associated with misleading advertising. What is more, the quality of professional services tends to resist either calibration or monitoring by individual patients or clients, partly because of the specialized knowledge required to evaluate the services, and partly because of the difficulty in determining whether, and the degree to which, an outcome is attributable to the quality of services (like a poor job of tooth-filling) or to something else (like a very tough walnut).... * * *

[The appellate court's observations of the anticompetitive effect of the restrictions on price advertising] brush over the professional context and describe no anticompetitive effects. Assuming that the record in fact supports the conclusion that the CDA disclosure rules essentially bar advertisement of across-the-board discounts, it does not obviously follow that such a ban would have a net anticompetitive effect here. Whether advertisements that announced discounts for, say, first-time customers, would be less effective at conveying information relevant to competition if they listed the original and discounted prices for checkups, Xrays, and fillings, than they would be if they simply specified a percentage discount across the board, seems to us a question susceptible to empirical but not *a priori* analysis. In a suspicious world, the discipline of specific example may well be a necessary condition of plausibility for professional claims that for all practical purposes defy comparison shopping. It is also possible in principle that, even if across-the-board discount advertisements were more effective in drawing customers in the short run, the recurrence of some measure of intentional or accidental misstatement due to the breadth of their claims might leak out over time to make potential patients skeptical of any such across-the-board advertising, so undercutting the method's effectiveness.... It might be, too, that across the-board discount advertisements would continue to attract business indefinitely, but might work precisely because they were misleading customers, and thus just because their effect would be anticompetitive, not procompetitive. Put another way, the CDA's rule appears to reflect the prediction that any costs to competition associated with the elimination of across-the-board advertising will be outweighed by gains to consumer information (and hence competition) created by discount advertising that is exact, accurate, and more easily verifiable (at least by regulators). As a matter of economics this view may or may not be correct, but it is not implausible, and neither a court nor the Commission may initially dismiss it as presumptively wrong. * * *

The Court of Appeals was comparably tolerant in accepting the sufficiency of abbreviated rule-of-reason analysis as to the nonprice advertising restrictions. The court began with the argument that "[t]hese restrictions are in effect a form of output limitation, as they restrict the supply of information about individual dentists' services." *Ibid.* (citing P. Areeda & H. Hovenkamp, Antitrust Law ¶ 1505, pp. 693–694 (1997 Supp.)). Although this sentence does indeed appear as cited, it is puzzling, given that the relevant output for antitrust purposes here is presumably not information or advertising, but dental services themselves. The question is not whether the universe of possible advertisements has been limited (as assuredly it has), but whether the limitation on advertisements obviously tends to limit the total delivery of dental services. The court came closest to addressing this latter question when it went on to assert that limiting advertisements regarding quality and safety "prevents dentists from fully describing the package of services they offer," 128 F.3d, at 728, adding that "[t]he restrictions may also affect output more directly, as quality and comfort advertising may induce some customers to obtain nonemergency care when they might not otherwise do so," *ibid.* This suggestion about output is also puzzling. If quality advertising actually induces some patients to obtain more care than they would in its absence, then restricting such advertising would reduce the demand for dental services, not the supply; and it is of course the producers' supply of a good in relation to demand that is normally relevant in determining whether a producer-imposed output limitation has the anticompetitive effect of artificially raising prices....

Although the Court of Appeals acknowledged the CDA's view that "claims about quality are inherently unverifiable and therefore misleading," 128 F.3d, at 728, it responded that this concern "does not justify banning all quality claims without regard to whether they are, in fact, false or misleading," *ibid.* As a result, the court said, "the restriction is a sufficiently naked restraint on output to justify quick look analysis." *Ibid.* The court assumed, in these words, that some dental quality claims may escape justifiable censure, because they are both verifiable and true. But its implicit assumption fails to explain why it gave no weight to the countervailing, and at least equally plausible, suggestion that restricting difficult-to-verify claims about quality or patient comfort would have a procompetitive effect by preventing misleading or false claims that distort the market. It is, indeed, entirely possible to understand the CDA's restrictions on unverifiable quality and comfort advertising as nothing more than a procompetitive ban on puffery.... * * *

Saying here that the Court of Appeal's conclusion at least required a more extended examination of the possible factual underpinnings than it received is not, of course, necessarily to call for the fullest market analysis. Although we have said that a challenge to a "naked restraint on price and output" need not be supported by "a detailed market analysis" in order to "requir[e] some competitive justification," *National Collegiate Athletic Assn.*, 468 U.S., at 110, it does not follow that every case attacking a less obviously anticompetitive restraint (like this one) is a candidate for plenary market examination. The truth is that our categories of analysis of anticompetitive effect are less fixed than terms like "per se," "quick look," and "rule of reason" tend to make them appear. We have recognized, for example, that "there is often no bright line separating *per se* from Rule of Reason analysis," since "considerable inquiry into market conditions" may be required before the application of any so-called "per se" condemnation is justified. *Id.*, at 104, n. 26. "[W]hether the ultimate finding is the product of a presumption or actual market analysis, the essential inquiry remains the same—whether or not the challenged restraint enhances competition." *Id.*, at 104. Indeed, the scholar who enriched antitrust law with the metaphor of "the twinkling of an eye" for the most condensed rule-of-reason analysis himself cautioned against the risk of misleading even in speaking of a 'spectrum' of adequate reasonableness analysis for passing upon antitrust claims: "There is always something of a sliding scale in appraising reasonableness, but the sliding scale formula deceptively suggests greater precision than we can hope for.... Nevertheless, the quality of proof required should vary with the circumstances." P. Areeda, Antitrust Law ¶ 1507, p. 402 (1986).... As the circumstances here demonstrate, there is generally no categorical line to be drawn between restraints that give rise to an intuitively obvious inference of anticompetitive effect and those that call for more detailed treatment. What is required, rather, is an enquiry meet for the case, looking to the circumstances, details, and logic of a restraint. The object is to see whether the experience of the market has been so clear, or necessarily will be, that a confident conclusion about the principal tendency of a restriction will follow from a quick (or at least quicker) look, in place of a more sedulous one. And of course what we see may vary over time, if the rule-of reason analyses in case after case reach identical conclusions. For now, at least, a less quick look was required for the initial assessment of the tendency of these professional advertising restrictions. Because the Court of Appeals did not scrutinize the assumption of relative anticompetitive tendencies, we vacate the judgment and remand the case for a fuller consideration of the issue.

* * *

JUSTICE BREYER, joined by JUSTICES STEVENS, KENNEDY and GINSBURG, concurring and dissenting: * * *

Do each of the three [price] restrictions mentioned have "the potential for genuine adverse effects on competition"? *Indiana Federation,* 476 U.S., at 460. I should have thought that the anticompetitive tendencies of the three restrictions were obvious. An agreement not to advertise that a fee is reasonable, that service is inexpensive, or that a customer will receive a discount makes it more difficult for a dentist to inform customers that he charges a lower price. If the customer does not know about a lower price, he will find it more difficult to buy lower price service. That fact, in turn, makes it less likely that a dentist will obtain more customers by offering lower prices. And that likelihood means that dentists will prove less likely to offer lower prices. But why should I have to spell out the obvious? To restrain truthful advertising about lower prices is likely to restrict competition in respect to price—"the central nervous system of the economy." *United States v. Socony–Vacuum Oil Co.,* 310 U.S. 150, 226, n. 59 (1940).... I need not decide whether the Commission was right in applying a *per se* rule. I need only assume a rule of reason applies, and note the serious anticompetitive tendencies of the price advertising restraints.

The restrictions on the advertising of service quality also have serious anticompetitive tendencies. This is not a case of "mere puffing," as the FTC recognized. The days of my youth, when the billboards near Emeryville, California, home of AAA baseball's Oakland Oaks, displayed the name of "Painless" Parker, Dentist, are long gone—along with the Oakland Oaks. But some parents may still want to know that a particular dentist makes a point of "gentle care." Others may want to know about 1–year dental work guarantees. To restrict that kind of service quality advertisement is to restrict competition over the quality of service itself, for, unless consumers know, they may not purchase, and dentists may not compete to supply that which will make little difference to the demand for their services. That, at any rate, is the theory of the Sherman Act. And it is rather late in the day for anyone to deny the significant anticompetitive tendencies of an agreement that restricts competition in any legitimate respect, ... let alone one that inhibits customers from learning about the quality of a dentist's service.

Nor did the Commission rely solely on the unobjectionable proposition that a restriction on the ability of dentists to advertise on quality is likely to limit their incentive to compete on quality. Rather, the Commission pointed to record evidence affirmatively establishing that quality-based competition is important to dental consumers in California. Unsurprisingly, these consumers choose dental services based at least in part on "information about the type and quality of service." Similarly, as the Commission noted, the ALJ [Administrative Law judge at FTC] credited testimony to the effect that "advertising the comfort of services will 'absolutely' bring in more patients," and, conversely, that restraining the ability to advertise based on quality would decrease the number of patients that a dentist could attract. Finally, the Commission looked to the testimony of dentists who themselves had suffered adverse effects on their business when forced by petitioner to discontinue advertising quality of care.

The FTC found that the price advertising restrictions amounted to a "naked attempt to eliminate price competition." It found that the service quality advertising restrictions "deprive consumers of information they value and of healthy competition for their patronage." It added that the "anticompetitive nature of these restrictions" was "plain." The Court of Appeals agreed. I do not believe it possible to deny the anticompetitive tendencies I have mentioned.

We must also ask whether, despite their anticompetitive tendencies, these restrictions might be justified by other procompetitive tendencies or redeeming virtues. This is a closer question—at least in theory.... * * *

With one exception, my own review of the record reveals no significant evidentiary support for the proposition that the Association's members must agree to ban truthful price and quality advertising in order to stop untruthful claims. The one exception is the obvious fact that one can stop untruthful advertising if one prohibits all advertising ... * * *

QUESTIONS AND COMMENTS

1. Who is more convincing, Justice Souter or Justice Breyer? Identify the essential differences between them, in perspective, assumptions, starting points. Understanding these differences can be helpful throughout the study of antitrust.

2. Does *California Dental* affect analysis of facts such as those in *National Society of Professional Engineers*? Would the engineers' health and safety claims now get sympathetic scrutiny under a *California Dental* framework?

3. Does *California Dental* affect analysis of facts such as those in *Maricopa*? Would the doctors' argument that the foundation's scheme increases competition and provides more availability of insured health services now be entitled to greater credence?

4. Other jurisdictions, too, are respectful of professional restraints. In *J.C.J. Wouters v. Algemene Raad van de Nederlandse Orde van Advocaten,* Case C–309/99, [2002] ECR I–1577, the European Court of Justice held that decisions of the Amsterdam and Rotterdam bar associations forbidding lawyers from practicing in full partnership with accountants was so clearly reasonable regulation for the "necessary and proper practice of the legal profession" as to be beyond antitrust scrutiny. In *Arduino*, Case C–35/99, [2002] ECR I–1529, and *Cipolla and Macrino*, Case C–94/04 and 202/04, [2006] ECR I–11421, the Italian bar set mandatory fee schedules for lawyers practicing in Italy. The European Court ruled that mandatory minimum fees set by a professional body could be upheld as long as the state retains the decision-making power and establishes sufficient control mechanisms. Has the law gone too far, or appropriately far, in insulating professional restraints from antitrust? Are lawyer minimum fee schedules naked restraints in the guise of public interest—or are they in the public interest? In the United

States, if lawyers' restraints get state court approval they are likely to be insulated from the antitrust laws under the state action doctrine. See F.1 below. But suppose there is no state-approval mechanism. Is an agreement among lawyers not to form partnerships with economists or accountants a naked restraint? Is it a division of markets? How would it fare under U.S. law?

POLYGRAM HOLDING, INC. v. FTC
(The Three Tenors)

416 F.3d 29 (D.C. Cir. 2005).

CHIEF JUDGE DOUGLAS GINSBURG: [The three tenors—José Carreras, Placido Domingo, and Luciano Pavarotti—presented world acclaimed concerts at the 1990 soccer World Cup, the 1994 World Cup, and the 1998 World Cup. PolyGram, one of the world's largest music companies, distributed the audio and video recordings of the 1990 concert. Warner Communications, another of the world's largest music companies, distributed the recordings of the 1994 concert. In 1997, PolyGram and Warner formed a joint venture to distribute the recordings of the 1998 concert. Concerned that the 1998 concert was neither as original nor as appealing as the 1990 and 1994 concerts, PolyGram and Warner agreed to a moratorium on price discounting and advertising of the 1990 and 1994 recordings before and just after the release of the 1998 recordings. PolyGram and Warner, as joint venturers, characterized the moratorium as an ancillary restraint necessary to prevent either of them from free riding on the release of the 1998 recordings.] * * *

The Supreme Court's approach to evaluating a § 1 claim has gone through a transition over the last twenty-five years, from a dichotomous categorical approach to a more nuanced and case-specific inquiry. In 1978, just before the transition began, the Court summarized its doctrine as follows:

> There are ... two complementary categories of antitrust analysis. In the first category are agreements whose nature and necessary effect are so plainly anticompetitive that no elaborate study of the industry is needed to establish their illegality—they are "illegal per se." In the second category are agreements whose competitive effect can only be evaluated by analyzing the facts particular to the business, the history of the restraint, and the reasons why it was imposed. [quoting from *National Society of Professional Engineers*]

Courts and commentators have recognized the trade-offs inherent in each category. *Per se* analysis, which requires courts to generalize about the utility of a challenged practice, reduces the cost of decision-making but correspondingly raises the total cost of error by making it more likely some practices will be held unlawful in circumstances where they are harmless or even procompetitive. *See, e.g., Arizona v. Maricopa County Med. Soc.*, 457 U.S. 332, 344 (1982) ("For the sake of business certainty and litigation efficiency, we have tolerated the invalidation of some agreements that a fullblown inquiry might have proved to be reasonable"); Phillip E. Areeda & Herbert Hovenkamp, *Antitrust Law*, ¶ 1509c (2d ed. 2003) (observing that *per se* analysis "dispenses with costly proof requirements, such as proof of market power," but consequently "produces a certain number of false positives"). The converse—increased litigation cost but reduced cost of error—obtains under the rule of reason, which requires an exhaustive inquiry into all the myriad factors "bearing on whether the conduct is on balance anticompetitive or procompetitive." Donald F. Turner, *The Durability, Relevance, and Future of American Antitrust Policy*, 75 CAL. L. REV. 797, 800 (1987); *see* Frank H. Easterbrook, *The Limits of Antitrust*, 63 Tex. L. Rev. 1, 12–13 (1984) ("When everything is relevant, nothing is dispositive.... Litigation costs are the product of vague rules combined with high stakes, and nowhere is that combination more deadly than in antitrust litigation under the Rule of Reason").

Since *Professional Engineers* the Supreme Court has steadily moved away from the dichotomous approach—under which every restraint of trade is either unlawful *per se,* and hence not susceptible to a procompetitive justification, or subject to full-blown rule-of-reason analysis—toward one in which the extent of the inquiry is tailored to the suspect conduct in each particular case. For instance, the Court did not hold unlawful *per se* an agreement limiting the number of football games each participating college could sell to television, which agreement was challenged in *NCAA v. Board of Regents*, 468 U.S. 85, 100 (1984) (recognizing but declining to apply doctrine that "[h]orizontal price-fixing and output limitation are ordinarily condemned as a matter of law under an 'illegal *per se*' approach"); or the refusal of an organization of dentists to provide x-rays to dental insurers, which was at issue in *IFD*, 476 U.S. at 458 ("Although this Court has in the past stated that group boycotts are unlawful *per se*, we decline to resolve this case by forcing the Federation's policy into the 'boycott' pigeonhole and invoking the *per se* rule").

At the same time, however, in *NCAA* and *IFD* the Court did not insist upon the elaborate market analysis ordinarily required under the rule of reason to prove the defendant had market power and the restraint it imposed had an anticompetitive effect. *See NCAA*, 468 U.S. at 109–10 (rule of reason analysis unnecessary in light of district court's finding price and output not responsive to demand); *IFD*, 476 U.S. at 459 ("While this is not price fixing as such, no elaborate industry analysis is required to demonstrate the anticompetitive character of such an agreement"). The Court instead adopted an intermediate inquiry, since dubbed the "quick look," to evaluate horizontal restraints of trade. *See, e.g.*, Areeda & Hovenkamp, *Antitrust Law*, ¶ 1911a.

It would be somewhat misleading, however, to say the "quick look" is just a new category of analysis intermediate in complexity between "*per se*" condemnation and full-blown "rule of reason" treatment, for that would suggest the Court has moved from a dichotomy to a trichotomy, when in fact it has backed away from any reliance upon fixed categories and toward a continuum....

In this case, as we have said, the Commission analyzed PolyGram's conduct under the legal framework it had devised in *Mass. Board* (1988), which it maintains is consistent with the Supreme Court's teaching of more than a decade later in *California Dental* (1999). FTC Op. at 28–29. The *Mass. Board* analysis proceeds in several distinct steps: First, the Commission must determine whether it is obvious from the nature of the challenged conduct that it will likely harm consumers. If so, then the restraint is deemed "inherently suspect" and, unless the defendant comes forward with some plausible (and legally cognizable) competitive justification for the restraint, summarily condemned. "Such justifications," the Commission explained, "may consist of plausible reasons why practices that are competitively suspect as a general matter may not be expected to have adverse consequences in the context of the particular market in question, or they may consist of reasons why the practices are likely to have beneficial effects for consumers." *Id.* at 29.

If the defendant does offer such an explanation, then the Commission "must address the justification" in one of two ways. First, the Commission may explain why it can confidently conclude, without adducing evidence, that the restraint very likely harmed consumers. *Id.* at 33–34. Alternatively, the Commission may provide the tribunal with sufficient evidence to show that anticompetitive effects are in fact likely. *Id.* at 33. If the Commission succeeds in either way, then the evidentiary burden shifts to the defendant to show the restraint in fact does not harm consumers or has "procompetitive virtues" that outweigh its burden upon consumers. *Id.* at 34 n. 45.

PolyGram argues the Commission's framework conflicts with Supreme Court precedent by condemning a restraint that is not *per se* illegal without the Commission having to prove the restraint actually harms competition. According to PolyGram, "proof of actual anticompetitive effect (or market power as its surrogate) is required in *any* Rule of Reason case."

For reasons we have already explained, we reject PolyGram's attempt to locate the appropriate analysis, and the concomitant burden of proof, by reference to the vestigial line separating *per se* analysis from the rule of reason.... At bottom, the Sherman Act requires the court to ascertain whether the challenged restraint hinders competition; the Commission's framework, at least as the Commission applied it in this case, does just that.

We therefore accept the Commission's analytical framework. If, based upon economic learning and the experience of the market, it is obvious that a restraint of trade likely impairs competition, then the restraint is presumed unlawful and, in order to avoid liability, the defendant must either identify some reason the restraint is unlikely to harm consumers or identify some competitive benefit that plausibly offsets the apparent or anticipated harm. That much follows from the caselaw; for instance, in *NCAA* the Court held that a "naked restraint on price and output requires some competitive justification even in the absence of a detailed market analysis." 468 U.S. at 110. Similarly, in *IFD*, the Supreme Court ruled a horizontal agreement to withhold services could not be sustained because the dentists failed to advance any "credible argument" that "some countervailing procompetitive virtue ... [redeemed] an agreement limiting consumer choice by impeding the 'ordinary give and take of the market place.'" 476 U.S. at 459; *see also California Dental*, 526 U.S. at 771 (remanding for closer look at challenged advertising restrictions after concluding they "might plausibly be thought to have a net procompetitive effect, or possibly no effect at all on competition").

Although the Commission uses the term "inherently suspect" to describe those restraints that judicial experience and economic learning have shown to be likely to harm consumers, *see* FTC Op. at 29, we note that, under the Commission's own framework, the rebuttable presumption of illegality arises not necessarily from anything "inherent" in a business practice but from the close family resemblance between the suspect practice and another practice that already stands convicted in the court of consumer welfare. The Commission appears to acknowledge, as it must, that as economic learning and market experience evolve, so too will the class of restraints subject to summary adjudication....

That said, we have no difficulty with the Commission's conclusion that PolyGram's agreement with Warner in all likelihood had a deleterious effect upon consumers—unless, that is, PolyGram comes forward with some plausible explanation to the contrary. An agreement between joint venturers to restrain price cutting and advertising with respect to products not part of the joint venture looks suspiciously like a naked price fixing agreement between competitors, which would ordinarily be condemned as *per se* unlawful. The Supreme Court has recognized time and again that agreements restraining autonomy in pricing and advertising impede the "ordinary give and take of the market place." *IFD*, 476 U.S. at 459; *see also NCAA*, 468 U.S. at 107 ("[r]estrictions on price and output are the paradigmatic examples of restraints of trade that the Sherman Act was intended to prohibit"); *Bates v. State Bar of Ariz.*, 433 U.S. 350, 364 (1977) (advertising "serves to inform the public of the availability, nature, and prices of products and services, and thus performs an indispensable role in the allocation of resources in a free enterprise system").

PolyGram's fate in this case therefore rests upon the plausibility of the sole competitive justification it proffered for the moratorium agreement, namely, that the restrictions on discounting and advertising enhanced the long-term profitability of all three concert albums and promoted the "Three Tenors" brand. According to PolyGram, each company was concerned the other would "free ride" on the promotional activities of the joint venture by promoting its own earlier concert album; as a result fewer Three Tenors albums would be sold overall and the joint venture would be less likely to create future products, such as a "greatest hits" album or a boxed set. Thus, PolyGram likens the moratorium agreement here to the restraint at issue in *Polk Brothers, Inc. v. Forest City Enterprises*, 776 F.2d 185 (7th Cir. 1985), where two potential retail competitors collaborated to build a store offering some of each company's products but agreed not to sell competing products at the new store. Because the restraint arguably promoted productivity and output by controlling each participant's ability to free-ride on the other's promotional efforts, the court, rather than condemning the restraint summarily, went on to evaluate it under the rule of reason. *Id.* at 190.

At first glance PolyGram's contention has some force; the moratorium appears likely to have mitigated the "spillover" effects that could be expected to follow an aggressive launch of the 1998 album. Absent the moratorium, that is, a consumer, after learning of the new album through the joint venture's advertising, might decide that he would be just as happy with an older concert album, especially if the older album were then available at a discount. The "free-riding" to be eliminated by the moratorium agreement, however, was nothing more than the competition of products that were not part of the joint undertaking. Why not an agreement by which PolyGram and Warner would eliminate advertising and price competition on all their records for a time while they focused exclusively upon promoting the new Three Tenors album? The "procompetitive" justification PolyGram offers is "nothing less than a frontal assault on the basic policy of the Sherman Act." *Nat'l Soc'y of Prof'l Engineers*, 435 U.S. at 695.

To take the Commission's example, if General Motors were vigorously to advertise the release of a new model SUV, other SUV manufacturers would no doubt reap some of the benefit of GM's efforts. FTC Op. at 43. But that would not mean General Motors and its competitors could lawfully agree to restrict prices and advertising on existing SUV models in return for General Motors giving its rivals a share of its profit on the new model. Nor would an agreement to restrain prices and advertising on existing SUVs be lawful if General Motors were to release the new model SUV as a joint venture with one of its competitors. *Id.* at 45. A restraint cannot be justified solely on the ground that it increases the profitability of the enterprise that introduces the new product, regardless whether that enterprise is a joint venture or a solo undertaking. And it simply does not matter whether the new SUV would have been profitable absent the restraint; if the only way a new product can profitably be introduced is to restrain the legitimate competition of older products, then one must seriously wonder whether consumers are genuinely benefitted by the new product. As the Supreme Court said in *Catalano, Inc. v. Target Sales, Inc.*, 446 U.S. 643, 649 (1980),

> in any case in which competitors are able to increase the price level or to curtail production by agreement, it could be argued that the agreement has the effect of making the market more attractive to potential new entrants. If that potential justifies horizontal agreements among competitors imposing one kind of voluntary restraint or

> another on their competitive freedom, it would seem to follow that the more successful an agreement is in raising the price level, the safer it is from antitrust attack. Nothing could be more inconsistent with our cases.

See also Law v. NCAA, 134 F.3d 1010, 1023 (10th Cir. 1998) ("While increasing output, creating operating efficiencies, making a new product available, enhancing service or quality, and widening consumer choice have been accepted by courts as justifications for otherwise anticompetitive agreements, mere profitability or cost savings have not qualified as a defense under the antitrust laws").

In sum, because PolyGram has failed to identify any competitive justification for its agreement with Warner to refrain from advertising or discounting their competitive Three Tenors products, we hold it violated § 5 of the FTC Act.... * * *

Per Se and Rule of Reason

Per se: The agreement is condemned without investigation into purpose or effect. Intention to (e.g.) fix prices is enough.

Rule of reason: This much-used phrase is a misnomer. It is not a rule. It simply denotes the wide category for analysis that is operative in all cases where the per se rule is not applicable. The question is how to analyze the problem to determine whether the agreement is anticompetitive and should be proscribed.

Obviously anticompetitive: When an agreement, on its face, has strong anticompetitive properties and no (or no important) obviously procompetitive properties, as in *National Society of Professional Engineers*, the burden shifts to the defendant to demonstrate procompetitive/efficiency aspects. Absent such a showing, the agreement is condemned. This is called a "quick look" analysis. The Supreme Court seems to prefer more nuance, but language of "quick look" is still helpful.

Not-so-obviously anticompetitive; but maybe: For cases in this category a full analysis may be necessary. A full analysis usually entails: definition of the relevant market, calculation of market shares, assessment of market power, and attention to all anticompetitive and procompetitive aspects. If anticompetitive aspects are serious but procompetitive aspects are also weighty, you will want to ask whether an obvious less restrictive alternative is available. As the Supreme Court said in *California Dental Association,* what is needed "is an enquiry meet for the case."

QUESTIONS AND COMMENTS

1. Why does the appellate court reject the FTC's language: "inherently suspect"? Is "quick look" retained or abandoned as a category for analysis? What are the benefits of moving to a continuum from more bounded categories? According to the D.C. Circuit, does a *per se* category still exist?

2. Did the court adequately distinguish *California Dental*? Is its opinion more sympathetic with Justice Souter's majority opinion in *California Dental* or with Justice Breyer's dissent?

3. Suppose this case had been brought in federal court by Discount Music Co. and Discount Music Co. moved for summary judgment on grounds that the moratorium agreement was illegal per se. If you were the judge, would you grant the motion for judgment on the no-discount claim? Does *Palmer v. BRG of Georgia*, 498 U.S. 46 (1990) (supra at 72, help? How would you treat the motion for summary judgment regarding the agreement not to advertise?

4. Did the court dispense with the need for proof of market power? Can market power be presumed from the necessary effect—e.g., 3T1 and 3T2 would have sold more albums and at lower prices but for the moratorium clause?

5. Which of the cases in this chapter are true hard core cartel cases and which are not? How would you now formulate the per se rule? How would you describe the type of conduct that, while not illegal per se, is so essentially anticompetitive that it deserves to be condemned unless justified by procompetitive/efficiency aspects?

6. The Supreme Court reversed the 96–year old *per se* rule against vertical minimum resale price fixing in *Leegin v. PSKS*, infra page 630, stating: "Resort to *per se* rules is confined to restraints, like those mentioned [competitor price-fixing or market division], 'that would always or almost always tend to restrict competition and decrease output.' "

7. Recurring issues have involved reverse payment settlements between branded and generic pharmaceutical manufacturers. Typically, a maker of a generic pharmaceutical files a new drug application under the Hatch–Waxman Act, a statute designed to facilitate entry by generics. (Generic medicines sell at a fraction of the price of the corresponding branded drug.) Hatch–Waxman gives the first generic manufacturer who files a new drug application a 180–day exclusivity over other generic versions of the brand. Under the statute, the filing is a constructive infringement and the brand manufacturer virtually automatically sues the generic for infringement. The brand manufacturer and the generic manufacturer settle the action by an agreement in which the generic manufacturer affirms the validity of the patent and agrees not to put the generic medicine on the market for a period typically within the term of the patent, and the brand manufacturer agrees to make a large payment (typically hundreds of millions of dollars) to the generic company. The Federal Trade Commission is committed to ending this practice, which it regards as gaming the Hatch–Waxman Act by a pay-off to delay entry. It calculates that the settlements cost American consumers $3.5 billion a year. See FTC Press Release, June 23, 2009, *http://www.ftc.gov/opa/2009/06/capspeech.shtm.* The FTC asserts that these settlements are illegal per se. The FTC has not fared well in the courts, which generally see the matter as a complex one involving the interplay of patent laws and antitrust, and implicating the limits of courts in considering the validity and worth of patents. See, e.g., *Arkansas Carpenters Health and Welfare Fund v. Bayer AG* ("Cipro"), 604 F.3d 98 (2d Cir. 2010), *cert. denied*, ___ U.S. ___, 131 S.Ct. 1606 (2011), treated in Chapter 5

infra. The FTC has been lobbying Congress to declare pay-for-delay settlements illegal. Should Congress adopt such a law?

* * *

A recent Supreme Court case in which plaintiffs asserted an illegal-per-se agreement between competitors involved two major oil and gas companies, Texaco and Shell. Texaco and Shell formed a marketing joint venture, which was approved by the Justice Department. Texaco and Shell retained the trade marks of their brands and apparently jointly instructed the joint venture to sell Texaco-brand gas and Shell-brand gas at the same price. See Dagher v. Saudi Refining Inc., 369 F.3d 1108 (9th Cir. 2004) (reversed by the Supreme Court, infra). They maintained that each of their brands was a distinct product with "its own unique chemical composition . . . trademark, and marketing strategy."

Here is the relevant excerpt from the opinion of the Supreme Court, which ignored the fact that the joint venture's uniform price for the two brands was the result of the competitors' agreement.

TEXACO INC. v. DAGHER

547 U.S. 1 (2006)

JUSTICE THOMAS: From 1998 until 2002, petitioners Texaco Inc. and Shell Oil Co. collaborated in a joint venture, Equilon Enterprises, to refine and sell gasoline in the western United States under the original Texaco and Shell Oil brand names. Respondents, a class of Texaco and Shell Oil service station owners, allege that petitioners engaged in unlawful price fixing when Equilon set a single price for both Texaco and Shell Oil brand gasoline. We granted certiorari to determine whether it is *per se* illegal under § 1 of the Sherman Act, 15 U. S. C. § 1, for a lawful, economically integrated joint venture to set the prices at which the joint venture sells its products. We conclude that it is not, and accordingly we reverse the contrary judgment of the Court of Appeals.

I

Historically, Texaco and Shell Oil have competed with one another in the national and international oil and gasoline markets. Their business activities include refining crude oil into gasoline, as well as marketing gasoline to downstream purchasers, such as the service stations represented in respondents' class action.

In 1998, Texaco and Shell Oil formed a joint venture, Equilon, to consolidate their operations in the western United States, thereby ending competition between the two companies in the domestic refining and marketing of gasoline. Under the joint venture agreement, Texaco and Shell Oil agreed to pool their resources and share the risks of and profits from Equilon's activities. Equilon's board of directors would comprise representatives of Texaco and Shell Oil, and Equilon gasoline would be sold to downstream purchasers under the original Texaco and Shell Oil brand names. The formation of Equilon was approved by consent decree, subject to certain divestments and other modifications, by the Federal Trade Commission, see *In re Shell Oil Co.*, 125 F. T. C. 769 (1998), as well as by the state attorneys general of California, Hawaii, Oregon, and Washington. Notably, the decrees imposed no restrictions on the pricing of Equilon gasoline.

After the joint venture began to operate, respondents brought suit in district court, alleging that, by unifying gasoline prices under the two brands, petitioners had violated the *per se* rule against price fixing that this Court has long recognized under § 1 of the Sherman Act. See, *e.g.*, *Catalano, Inc.* v. *Target Sales, Inc.*, 446 U. S. 643, 647 (1980) *(per curiam)*. The District Court awarded summary judgment to Texaco and Shell Oil. It determined that the rule of reason, rather than a *per se* rule or the quick look doctrine, governs respondents' claim, and that, by eschewing rule of reason analysis, respondents had failed to raise a triable issue of fact. The Ninth Circuit reversed, characterizing petitioners' position as a request for an "exception to the *per se* prohibition on price fixing," and rejecting that request. We consolidated Texaco's and Shell Oil's separate petitions and granted certiorari to determine the extent to which the *per se* rule against price fixing applies to an important and increasingly popular form of business organization, the joint venture.

II

Section 1 of the Sherman Act prohibits "[e]very contract, combination in the form of trust or otherwise, or conspiracy, in restraint of trade or commerce among the several States." This Court has not taken a literal approach to this language, however. See, *e.g.*, *State Oil Co.* v. *Khan*, 522 U. S. 3, 10 (1997) ("[T]his Court has long recognized that Congress intended to outlaw only *unreasonable* restraints" (emphasis added)). Instead, this Court presumptively applies rule of reason analysis, under which antitrust plaintiffs must demonstrate that a particular contract or combination is in fact unreasonable and anticompetitive before it will be found unlawful. See, *e.g.*, *id.*, at 10–19 (concluding that vertical price-fixing arrangements are subject to the rule of reason, not *per se* liability). *Per se* liability is reserved for only those agreements that are "so plainly anticompetitive that no elaborate study of the industry is needed to establish their illegality." *National Soc. of Professional Engineers* v. *United States*, 435 U. S. 679, 692 (1978). Accordingly, "we have expressed reluctance to adopt *per se* rules . . . 'where the economic impact of certain practices is not immediately obvious.' " *State Oil*, *supra*, at 10 (quoting *FTC* v. *Indiana Federation of Dentists*, 476 U.S. 447, 458–459 (1986)).

Price-fixing agreements between two or more competitors, otherwise known as horizontal price-fixing agreements, fall into the category of arrangements that are *per se* unlawful. See, *e.g.*, *Catalano*, *supra*, at 647. These cases do not present such an agreement, however, because Texaco and Shell Oil did not compete with one another in the relevant market—namely, the sale of gasoline to service stations in the western United

States—but instead participated in that market jointly through their investments in Equilon. In other words, the pricing policy challenged here amounts to little more than price setting by a single entity—albeit within the context of a joint venture—and not a pricing agreement between competing entities with respect to their competing products. Throughout Equilon's existence, Texaco and Shell Oil shared in the profits of Equilon's activities in their role as investors, not competitors. When "persons who would otherwise be competitors pool their capital and share the risks of loss as well as the opportunities for profit ... such joint ventures [are] regarded as a single firm competing with other sellers in the market." *Arizona* v. *Maricopa County Medical Soc.*, 457 U.S. 332, 356 (1982). As such, though Equilon's pricing policy may be price fixing in a literal sense, it is not price fixing in the antitrust sense. See *Broadcast Music, Inc.* v. *Columbia Broadcasting System, Inc.*, 441 U.S. 1, 9 (1979) ("When two partners set the price of their goods or services they are literally 'price fixing,' but they are not *per se* in violation of the Sherman Act").

This conclusion is confirmed by respondents' apparent concession that there would be no *per se* liability had Equilon simply chosen to sell its gasoline under a single brand. We see no reason to treat Equilon differently just because it chose to sell gasoline under two distinct brands at a single price. As a single entity, a joint venture, like any other firm, must have the discretion to determine the prices of the products that it sells, including the discretion to sell a product under two different brands at a single, unified price. If Equilon's price unification policy is anticompetitive, then respondents should have challenged it pursuant to the rule of reason. But it would be inconsistent with this Court's antitrust precedents to condemn the internal pricing decisions of a legitimate joint venture as *per se* unlawful.

The court below reached the opposite conclusion by invoking the ancillary restraints doctrine. That doctrine governs the validity of restrictions imposed by a legitimate business collaboration, such as a business association or joint venture, on nonventure activities. Under the doctrine, courts must determine whether the nonventure restriction is a naked restraint on trade, and thus invalid, or one that is ancillary to the legitimate and competitive purposes of the business association, and thus valid. We agree with petitioners that the ancillary restraints doctrine has no application here, where the business practice being challenged involves the core activity of the joint venture itself—namely, the pricing of the very goods produced and sold by Equilon. And even if we were to invoke the doctrine in these cases, Equilon's pricing policy is clearly ancillary to the sale of its own products. Judge Fernandez, dissenting from the ruling of the court below, put it well:

> "In this case, nothing more radical is afoot than the fact that an entity, which now owns all of the production, transportation, research, storage, sales and distribution facilities for engaging in the gasoline business, also prices its own products. It decided to price them the same, as any other entity could. What could be more

integral to the running of a business than setting a price for its goods and services?" 369 F. 3d, at 1127.

See also *Broadcast Music, supra*, at 23 ("Joint ventures and other cooperative arrangements are ... not usually unlawful, at least not as price-fixing schemes, where the agreement on price is necessary to market the product at all"). * * *

Because the pricing decisions of a legitimate joint venture do not fall within the narrow category of activity that is *per se* unlawful under § 1 of the Sherman Act, respondents' antitrust claim cannot prevail. Accordingly, the judgment of the Court of Appeals is reversed.

QUESTIONS AND COMMENTS

1. If the Court had acknowledged that Texaco and Shell agreed to require the joint venture to sell both brands at the same price, would this have made a difference? Why did Texaco and Shell not leave the pricing of the gas to the joint venture? Why might Texaco and Shell have had an incentive to remove price disparity between their brands, while the joint venture might not have shared this incentive?

2. Make an argument under *Texaco v. Dagher*, combined with *California Dental Association*, that *Maricopa* has been effectively overruled. Does the argument convince you?

Problem

Is this lawyers' agreement illegal per se?

The Association of the Bar of the City of New York (City Bar), a private organization, decides to offer a pre paid insurance plan for routine legal services for low and middle income clients: house closings and property transfers, wills and probate, tax consultations and minor litigations. Its purpose is to serve the public interest in affordable legal services.

To make its insurance product attractive, the City Bar wants to set a guaranteed reimbursable legal fee for each service insured, and wants to require all lawyers who agree to participate in the plan as service providers to accept the insurance reimbursement as full payment for the service. It knows that setting the guaranteed reimbursable amount (whether in terms of dollars per hour or a percentage of the value of a transaction) will not be easy. It proposes to delegate the function to each City Bar committee that has expertise in the particular area—e.g., the Trusts and Estates Committee for T&E services—asking that committee to ascertain what is a fair charge for the service, particularly through questionnaires sent to the committee members and then to the bar more broadly. All committees are comprised of practicing lawyers; most are public spirited lawyers. It is contemplated that the City Bar Executive Committee (elected from the Association's membership) will normally accept the recommendation of the relevant committee, adjusting the reimbursable fees upwards only as and if necessary to attract a sufficient number of qualified lawyers, and downwards wherever possible while still providing acceptable service.

The City Bar asks your firm for a written opinion as to the permissibility of the plan under the antitrust laws. You are asked by your senior partner to address the more limited questions: Is this plan illegal per se? If not strictly illegal per se, is a court likely to find it illegal after a quick look? (If your answers are No, your senior partner is prepared to convince a court that the agreement is reasonable.)

Student 1 argues: This agreement is illegal per se or illegal after a quick look.
Student 2 argues the contrary.
Students 3, 4 and 5 are the judges. They may question the litigators before rendering their decision.

D. IS THE DEFENDANT ONE "PERSON"? OR MULTIPLE PARTIES WHO CAN CONSPIRE?

Are the parties capable of conspiring with one another? As the Supreme Court held in *Copperweld Corp. v. Independence Tube Corp.*, 467 U.S. 752 (1984), a corporation and its wholly owned subsidiary are not capable of conspiring with one another. They are a single enterprise and their act is a unilateral act. The breadth of the single-enterprise doctrine was tested in *American Needle, Inc. v. National Football League*, wherein the 32 separately-owned professional football teams formed a new entity, National Football League Properties (NFLP), to market the teams' names, logos, trademarks and related intellectual property. NFLP had granted non-exclusive licenses to use the logos for items such as caps and T-shirts to American Needle and others. Subsequently it withdrew the non-exclusive licenses and gave an exclusive license to Reebok. American Needle sued, alleging among other things a conspiracy of the teams. Defendants moved to dismiss on grounds that NFLP was a single entity and the teams could not conspire.

AMERICAN NEEDLE, INC. v. NATIONAL FOOTBALL LEAGUE

560 U.S. ___, 130 S.Ct. 2201 (2010)

JUSTICE STEVENS:

"Every contract, combination in the form of a trust or otherwise, or, conspiracy, in restraint of trade" is made illegal by § 1 of the Sherman Act. The question whether an arrangement is a contract, combination, or conspiracy is different from and antecedent to the question whether it unreasonably restrains trade. This case raises that antecedent question about the business of the 32 teams in the National Football League (NFL) and a corporate entity that they formed to manage their intellectual property. We conclude that the NFL's licensing activities constitute concerted action that is not categorically beyond the coverage of § 1. The legality of that concerted action must be judged under the Rule of Reason.

I

Originally organized in 1920, the NFL is an unincorporated association that now includes 32 separately owned professional football teams. Each team has its own name, colors, and logo, and owns related intellectual property. Like each of the other teams in the league, the New Orleans Saints and the Indianapolis Colts, for example, have their own distinctive names, colors, and marks that are well known to millions of sports fans.

Prior to 1963, the teams made their own arrangements for licensing their intellectual property and marketing trademarked items such as caps and jerseys. In 1963, the teams formed National Football League Properties (NFLP) to develop, license, and market their intellectual property. Most, but not all, of the substantial revenues generated by NFLP have either been given to charity or shared equally among the teams. However, the teams are able to and have at times sought to withdraw from this arrangement.

Between 1963 and 2000, NFLP granted nonexclusive licenses to a number of vendors, permitting them to manufacture and sell apparel bearing team insignias. Petitioner, American Needle, Inc., was one of those licensees. In December 2000, the teams voted to authorize NFLP to grant exclusive licenses, and NFLP granted Reebok International Ltd. an exclusive 10–year license to manufacture and sell trademarked headwear for all 32 teams. It thereafter declined to renew American Needle's nonexclusive license.

American Needle filed this action in the Northern District of Illinois, alleging that the agreements between the NFL, its teams, NFLP, and Reebok violated §§ 1 and 2 of the Sherman Act. In their answer to the complaint, the defendants averred that the teams, NFL, and NFLP were incapable of conspiring within the meaning of § 1 "because they are a single economic enterprise, at least with respect to the conduct challenged." After limited discovery, the District Court granted summary judgment on the question "whether, with regard to the facet of their operations respecting exploitation of intellectual property rights, the NFL and its 32 teams are, in the jargon of antitrust law, acting as a single entity." The court concluded "that in that facet of their operations they have so integrated their operations that they should be deemed a single entity rather than joint ventures cooperating for a common purpose." *Ibid.*

The Court of Appeals for the Seventh Circuit affirmed. The panel observed that "in some contexts, a league seems more aptly described as a single entity immune from antitrust scrutiny, while in others a league appears to be a joint venture between independently owned teams that is subject to review under § 1." Relying on Circuit precedent, the court limited its inquiry to the particular conduct at issue, licensing of teams' intellectual property. The panel agreed with petitioner that "when making a single-entity determination, courts must examine whether the conduct in question deprives the marketplace of the independent sources of economic control that competition assumes." The court, however, discounted the significance of potential competition among the teams regarding the use of their intellectual property because the teams "can function only as one source of economic power when collectively producing NFL football." The court noted that football itself can only be carried out jointly. ("Asserting that a single football team could produce a football game ... is a Zen riddle: Who wins when a football team plays itself"). Moreover, "NFL teams share a vital economic interest in collectively promoting NFL football ... [to] compet[e] with other forms of entertainment." "It thus follows," the court found, "that only one source of economic power controls the promotion of NFL football," and "it makes little sense to assert that each individual team has the authority, if not the responsibility, to promote the jointly produced NFL football." Recognizing that NFL teams have "license[d] their intellectual property collectively" since 1963, the court held that § 1 did not apply.

We granted certiorari.

II

As the case comes to us, we have only a narrow issue to decide: whether the NFL respondents are capable of engaging in a "contract, combination ..., or conspiracy" as defined by § 1 of the Sherman Act, 15 U.S.C. § 1, or, as we have sometimes phrased it, whether the alleged activity by the NFL respondents "must be viewed as that of a single enterprise for purposes of § 1." *Copperweld Corp. v. Independence Tube Corp.*, 467 U.S. 752, 771 (1984). Taken literally, the applicability of § 1 to "every contract, combination ... or conspiracy" could be understood to cover every conceivable agreement, whether it be a group of competing firms fixing prices or a single firm's chief executive telling her subordinate how to price their company's product. But even though, "read literally," § 1 would address "the entire body of private contract," that is not what the statute means.... * * *

Congress used [the] distinction between concerted and independent action to deter anticompetitive conduct and compensate its victims, without chilling vigorous competition through ordinary business operations. The distinction also avoids judicial scrutiny of routine, internal business decisions.

Thus, in § 1 Congress "treated concerted behavior more strictly than unilateral behavior." [467 U.S.] at 768. This is so because unlike independent action, "[c]oncerted activity inherently is fraught with anticompetitive risk" insofar as it "deprives the marketplace of independent centers of decision making that competition assumes and demands." *Id.*, at 768–

769. And because concerted action is discrete and distinct, a limit on such activity leaves untouched a vast amount of business conduct. As a result, there is less risk of deterring a firm's necessary conduct; courts need only examine discrete agreements; and such conduct maybe remedied simply through prohibition. . . .

III

We have long held that concerted action under § 1 does not turn simply on whether the parties involved are legally distinct entities. Instead, we have eschewed such formalistic distinctions in favor of a functional consideration of how the parties involved in the alleged anticompetitive conduct actually operate. * * *

We finally reexamined the intraenterprise conspiracy doctrine in *Copperweld Corp. v. Independence Tube Corp.*, 467 U.S. 752 (1984), and concluded that it was inconsistent with the " 'basic distinction between concerted and independent action.' " *Id.*, at 767. Considering it "perfectly plain that an internal agreement to implement a single, unitary firm's policies does not raise the antitrust dangers that § 1 was designed to police," *id.*, at 769, we held that a parent corporation and its wholly owned subsidiary "are incapable of conspiring with each other for purposes of § 1 of the Sherman Act," *id.*, at 777. We explained that although a parent corporation and its wholly owned subsidiary are "separate" for the purposes of incorporation or formal title, they are controlled by a single center of decisionmaking and they control a single aggregation of economic power. Joint conduct by two such entities does not "depriv[e] the marketplace of independent centers of decisionmaking," *id.*, at 769, and as a result, an agreement between them does not constitute a "contract, combination . . . or conspiracy" for the purposes of § 1.

IV

* * *

Because the inquiry is one of competitive reality, it is not determinative that two parties to an alleged § 1 violation are legally distinct entities. Nor, however, is it determinative that two legally distinct entities have organized themselves under a single umbrella or into a structured joint venture. The question is whether the agreement joins together "independent centers of decisionmaking." *Id.*, at 769. If it does, the entities are capable of conspiring under § 1, and the court must decide whether the restraint of trade is an unreasonable and therefore illegal one.

V

The NFL teams do not possess either the unitary decisionmaking quality or the single aggregation of economic power characteristic of independent action. Each of the teams is a substantial, independently owned, and independently managed business. "[T]heir general corporate actions are guided or determined" by "separate corporate consciousnesses," and "[t]heir objectives are" not "common." *Copperweld*, 467 U.S., at 771.... The teams compete with one another, not only on the playing field, but to attract fans, for gate receipts and for contracts with managerial and playing personnel.

Directly relevant to this case, the teams compete in the market for intellectual property. To a firm making hats, the Saints and the Colts are two potentially competing suppliers of valuable trademarks. When each NFL team licenses its intellectual property, it is not pursuing the "common interests of the whole" league but is instead pursuing interests of each "corporation itself," *Copperweld*, 467 U.S., at 770; teams are acting as "separate economic actors pursuing separate economic interests," and each team therefore is a potential "independent cente[r] of decisionmaking," *id.*, at 769. Decisions by NFL teams to license their separately owned trademarks collectively and to only one vendor are decisions that "depriv[e] the marketplace of independent centers of decisionmaking," *ibid.*, and therefore of actual or potential competition. See NCAA, 468 U.S., at 109, n. 39 (observing a possible § 1 violation if two separately owned companies sold their separate products through a "single selling agent"); cf. Areeda & Hovenkamp ¶ 1478a, at 318 ("Obviously, the most significant competitive threats arise when joint venture participants are actual or potential competitors").

In defense, respondents argue that by forming NFLP, they have formed a single entity, akin to a merger, and market their NFL brands through a single outlet. But it is not dispositive that the teams have organized and own a legally separate entity that centralizes the management of their intellectual property. An ongoing § 1 violation cannot evade § 1 scrutiny simply by giving the ongoing violation a name and label....

The NFL respondents may be similar in some sense to a single enterprise that owns several pieces of intellectual property and licenses them jointly, but they are not similar in the relevant functional sense. Although NFL teams have common interests such as promoting the NFL brand, they are still separate, profit-maximizing entities, and their interests in licensing team trademarks are not necessarily aligned.... Common interests in the NFL brand "*partially* unit[e] the economic interests of the parent firms," Brodley, Joint Ventures and Antitrust Policy, 95 Harv. L. Rev. 1521, 1526 (1982) (emphasis added), but the teams still have distinct, potentially competing interests.

It may be, as respondents argue, that NFLP "has served as the 'single driver'" of the teams' promotional vehicle, "'pursu[ing] the common interests of the whole.'" Brief for NFL Respondents 28 (quoting *Copperweld* ...). But illegal restraints often are in the common interests of the parties to the restraint, at the expense of those who are not parties. It is true, as respondents describe, that they have for some time marketed their trademarks jointly. But a history of concerted activity does not immunize conduct from § 1 scrutiny....

Respondents argue that nonetheless, as the Court of Appeals held, they constitute a single entity because without their cooperation, there would be no NFL football. It is true that "the clubs that make up a professional sports league are not completely independent economic competitors, as they depend upon a degree of cooperation for economic survival." *Brown*, 518 U.S., at 248. But the Court of Appeals' reasoning is unpersuasive. * * *

The question whether NFLP decisions can constitute concerted activity covered by § 1 is closer than whether decisions made directly by the 32 teams are covered by § 1. This is so both because NFLP is a separate corporation with its own management and because the record indicates that most of the revenues generated by NFLP are shared by the teams on an equal basis. Nevertheless we think it clear that for the same reasons the 32 teams' conduct is covered by § 1, NFLP's actions also are subject to § 1, at least with regards to its marketing of property owned by the separate teams. NFLP's licensing decisions are made by the 32 potential competitors, and each of them actually owns its share of the jointly managed assets. Apart from their agreement to cooperate in exploiting those assets, including their decisions as the NFLP, there would be nothing to prevent each of the teams from making its own market decisions relating to purchases of apparel and headwear, to the sale of such items, and to the granting of licenses to use its trademarks.

We generally treat agreements within a single firm as independent action on the presumption that the components of the firm will act to maximize the firm's profits. But in rare cases, that presumption does not hold. Agreements made within a firm can constitute concerted action covered by § 1 when the parties to the agreement act on interests separate from those of the firm itself, and the intrafirm agreements may simply be a formalistic shell for ongoing concerted action. See, *e.g.*, *Topco Associates, Inc.*, 405 U.S., at 609; *Sealy*, 388 U.S., at 352–354. * * *

If the fact that potential competitors shared in profits or losses from a venture meant that the venture was immune from § 1, then any cartel "could evade the antitrust law simply by creating a 'joint venture' to serve as the exclusive seller of their competing products." *Major League Baseball Properties, Inc. v. Salvino, Inc.*, 542 F.3d 290, 335 (CA2 2008) (Sotomayor, J., concurring in judgment). "So long as no agreement," other than one made by the cartelists sitting on the board of the joint venture, "explicitly listed the prices to be charged, the companies could act as monopolies through the 'joint venture.' " *Ibid.* (Indeed, a joint venture with a single management structure is generally a better way to operate a cartel because it decreases the risks of a party to an illegal agreement defecting from that agreement). However, competitors "cannot simply get around" antitrust liability by acting "through a third-party intermediary or 'joint venture'." *Id.*, at 336.

VI

Football teams that need to cooperate are not trapped by antitrust law. "[T]he special characteristics of this industry may provide a justification" for many kinds of agreements. *Brown*, 518 U.S., at 252 (STEVENS, J., dissenting). The fact that NFL teams share an interest in making the entire league successful and profitable, and that they must cooperate in the production and scheduling of games, provides a perfectly sensible justification for making a host of collective decisions. But the conduct at issue in this case is still concerted activity under the Sherman Act that is subject to § 1 analysis.

When "restraints on competition are essential if the product is to be available at all," *per se* rules of illegality are inapplicable, and instead the restraint must be judged according to the flexible Rule of Reason. NCAA, 468 U.S., at 101; see *id.*, at 117 ("Our decision not to apply a *per se* rule to this case rests in large part on our recognition that a certain degree of cooperation is necessary if the type of competition that petitioner and its member institutions seek to market is to be preserved"); see also *Dagher*, 547 U.S., at 6. In such instances, the agreement is likely to survive the Rule of Reason. See *Broadcast Music, Inc. v. Columbia Broadcasting System, Inc.*, 441 U.S. 1, 23 (1979) ("Joint ventures and other cooperative arrangements are also not usually unlawful ... where the agreement ... is necessary to market the product at all"). And depending upon the concerted activity in question, the Rule of Reason may not require a detailed analysis; it "can sometimes be applied in the twinkling of an eye." *NCAA*, 468 U.S., at 109, n. 39.

Other features of the NFL may also save agreements amongst the teams. We have recognized, for example, "that the interest in maintaining a competitive balance" among "athletic teams is legitimate and important," NCAA, 468 U.S., at 117. While that same interest applies to the teams in the NFL, it does not justify treating them as a single entity for § 1 purposes when it comes to the marketing of the teams' individually owned intellectual property. It is, however, unquestionably an interest that may well justify a variety of collective decisions made by the teams.... * * *

Accordingly, the judgment of the Court of Appeals is reversed, and the case is remanded for further proceedings consistent with this opinion.

QUESTIONS AND COMMENTS

1. How is *American Needle* (multiple entities) to be distinguished from *Texaco v. Dagher* (one entity)?

2. Does the Court's test work? Doesn't a joint venture, such as Equilon in *Dagher*, always combine independent centers of decision-making?

3. What was at stake? Wouldn't the exclusive licensing agreement be judged under a rule of reason even if the NFLP were considered one entity?

4. There remained a question of major importance: the fate of the agreement on remand. You will want to analyze this question after you have

studied horizontal and vertical restraints. To anticipate your later analysis: You will want to determine whether, by the agreement, the teams gained market power and if so was it possibly offset by efficiencies. You will want to know: To what extent are the teams' products competitive and to what extent are they complements? Does each prospective licensee want, in effect, a blanket license so it can produce and sell football caps and shirts efficiently? How did (1) the formation of NFLP, and (2) the shift to a single licensee, affect the price of the caps and shirts to consumers? You need not dwell on how to analyze these issues now. We study rule of reason analysis in Chapter 5.

E. PLEADING AND PROVING AGREEMENT

1. PROVING A CARTEL

Thus far we have examined the rule against cartels. We have embarked on sometimes difficult analysis to determine when competitors' collaborations are or are not cartels; and we have examined some attempted defenses.

We now reach an intensely practical subject. What constitutes sufficient allegations and proof of concertation (agreement or understanding, e.g. to fix prices or divide markets)? We start with high price conspiracies, a category that includes most price-fixing cases, and work up to the more difficult and complicated challenge of proving a low price conspiracy.

A cartel is hard to prove in the absence of direct evidence. Direct evidence, when it is available, usually comes from the cartel members themselves; possibly a disgruntled employee or other whistle blower. For many years, direct evidence was very hard to obtain. Then, beginning in 1978, the United States Justice Department inaugurated a program of leniency. The first cartel member to report on the cartel in sufficient detail for prosecution gets freedom from fines and jail. The U.S. leniency program has been extremely successful in uncovering cartels, and indeed in destabilizing cartels, as members compete to be the first one in the door. Leniency programs have spread throughout the world.

Nonetheless, there remain many cartels that are suspected on the basis of circumstantial evidence alone. This section is about proof by circumstantial evidence. As we have just implied, "contract, combination or conspiracy," for purposes of Section 1 of the Sherman Act (or otherwise), may be proved by direct or circumstantial evidence. In some cases, conspirators leave a trail of evidence behind them. In the infamous world lysine cartel case, a whistle-blowing employee of ADM who became an informant for the government surreptitiously taped the cartel meetings through a mysteriously re-appearing (but unnoticed) lamp in hotel meeting rooms around the world. See remarks of Scott D. Hammond, Deputy Assistant Attorney General for Criminal Enforcement, U.S. Department of Justice, Caught in the Act: Inside an International Cartel, Paris, Oct. 18, 2005, *at http://www.justice.gov/atr/public/speeches/212266.htm*. Watch the tape, which may be found at *http://www.youtube.com/watch?v=wDH0Rv8 R0SQfeature=related*. See John Connor, *Global Price Fixing: Our Customers are the Enemy* (2002), for a riveting account of recent global cartels and their detection. Other times, information that might have proved a cartel seems to evaporate. In a trans-world industrial diamond cartel case, the key witness from France failed to appear at trial, documents located abroad could not be obtained, and the case for the prosecution was lost. See *United States v. General Electric Co.*, 869 F.Supp. 1285 (S.D. Ohio 1994); Connor, supra, at 68, 134.

Problems regarding proof fall into three categories. First, what level of agreement or understanding is necessary to constitute the foundation for a violation of Section 1 of the Sherman Act? Must it be a real "meeting of the minds," with each party giving commitment to and getting commitment from the other parties (e.g., to fix prices); or is it enough that the structure of the market conduces to interdependent oligopolistic behavior (i.e., acting in a parallel manner, knowing that it is also in interests of the few competitors to follow suit)? You will see that mere interdependence is not enough; but keep your mind open as you read the cases. It is clear, also, that an express agreement is not necessary; the parties may give their assent to one another in more subtle ways. Second, what evidence is sufficient to infer agreement, express or tacit? This question is the subject of much contemporary case law, which addresses two questions: 1) What is the legal standard regarding sufficiency of evidence of agreement to go to the jury; and 2) On particular sets of facts, is defendant entitled to summary dismissal? Does the plaintiff get to the jury? A third question is of a different order: How to get the necessary evidence, particularly in a globalized world where knowledgeable people and critical documents are likely to be in another country? This problem, often arising in the context of criminal conspiracies, involves government leniency programs (inviting whistle blowing) and coordination with sister antitrust agencies all over the world. In this section we deal with case law largely responsive to problem two, but problem one is intertwined.

For many years, the most important case on point was *Interstate Circuit*. Consider, as you read this case: It was not clear at the time whether the vertical resale price fixing (movie companies dictating the ticket price in the movie theatres) was permissible. The legality of vertical price fixing is not part of the problem we present; it was not challenged in this case, so do not spend time thinking about the vertical aspects. The question presented here is: Did the movie distributors have a horizontal agreement among themselves to fix and raise the box office price at which the movie theaters must sell their tickets? If they did, it was facilitated by the affiliated exhibitor groups, Interstate Circuit and Texas Consolidated and their officers, whom you may treat as one person for resolving the issue of the case: Did the movie distributors collude? Was there sufficient evidence for the district court to find a distributor conspiracy?

INTERSTATE CIRCUIT, INC. v. UNITED STATES

306 U.S. 208 (1939).

JUSTICE STONE: ... The case is now before us on findings of the District Court specifically stating that appellants did in fact agree with each other to enter into and carry out the contracts, which the court found to result in unreasonable and therefore unlawful restraints of interstate commerce.

Appellants comprise the two groups of defendants in the District Court.... The distributor appellants are engaged in the business of distributing in interstate commerce motion picture films, copyrights on which they own or control, for exhibition in theatres throughout the United States. They distribute about 75 per cent of all first-class feature films exhibited in the United States....

The exhibitor group of appellants consists of Interstate Circuit, Inc., and Texas Consolidated Theatres, Inc., and Hoblitzelle and O'Donnell, who are respectively president and general manager of both and in active charge of their business operations. The two corporations are affiliated with each other and with Paramount Pictures Distributing Co., Inc., one of the distributor appellants.

Interstate operates forty-three first-run and second-run motion picture theatres, located in six Texas cities.[1] It has a complete monopoly of first-run theatres in these cities, except for one in Houston operated by one distributor's Texas agent....

Texas Consolidated operates sixty-six theatres, some first- and some subsequent-run houses, in various cities and towns in the Rio Grande Valley and elsewhere in Texas and in New Mexico. In some of these cities there are no competing theatres, and in six leading cities there are no competing first-run theatres. It has no theatres in the six Texas cities in which Interstate operates. That Interstate and Texas Consolidated dominate the motion picture business in the cities where their theatres are located is indicated by the fact that at the time of the contracts in question Interstate and Consolidated each contributed more than 74 per cent, of all the license fees paid by the motion picture theatres in their respective territories to the distributor appellants.

On July 11, 1934, following a previous communication on the subject to the eight branch managers of the distributor appellants, O'Donnell, the manager of Interstate and Consolidated, sent to each of them a letter on the letterhead of Interstate, each letter naming all of them as addressees, in which he asked compliance with two demands as a condition of Interstate's continued exhibition of the distributors' films in its 'A' or first-run theatres at a night admission of 40 cents or more. One demand

1. A first-run theatre is one in which a picture is first exhibited in any given locality. A subsequent-run theatre is one in which there is a subsequent exhibition of the same picture in the same locality.

was that the distributors "agree that in selling their product to subsequent runs, that this 'A' product will never be exhibited at any time or in any theatre at a smaller admission price than 25 for adults in the evening." The other was that "on 'A' pictures which are exhibited at a night admission of 40 or more—they shall never be exhibited in conjunction with another feature picture under the so-called policy of double features."....

.... The trial court found that the proposed restrictions constituted an important departure from prior practice.

The local representatives of the distributors, having no authority to enter into the proposed agreements, communicated the proposal to their home offices. Conferences followed between Hoblitzelle and O'Donnell, acting for Interstate and Consolidated, and the representatives of the various distributors. In these conferences each distributor was represented by its local branch manager and by one or more superior officials from outside the state of Texas. In the course of them each distributor agreed with Interstate for the 1934–35 season to impose both the demanded restrictions upon their subsequent-run licensees in the six Texas cities served by Interstate, except Austin and Galveston. While only two of the distributors incorporated the agreement to impose the restrictions in their license contracts with Interstate, the evidence establishes, and it is not denied, that all joined in the agreement .....

The trial court drew the inference of agreement from the nature of the proposals made on behalf of Interstate and Consolidated; from the manner in which they were made; from the substantial unanimity of action taken upon them by the distributors; and from the fact that appellants did not call as witnesses any of the superior officials who negotiated the contracts with Interstate or any official who, in the normal course of business, would have had knowledge of the existence or non-existence of such an agreement among the distributors....

The O'Donnell letter named on its face as addressees the eight local representatives of the distributors, and so from the beginning each of the distributors knew that the proposals were under consideration by the others. Each was aware that all were in active competition and that without substantially unanimous action with respect to the restrictions for any given territory there was risk of a substantial loss of the business and good will of the subsequent-run and independent exhibitors, but that with it there was the prospect of increased profits. There was, therefore, strong motive for concerted action, full advantage of which was taken by Interstate and Consolidated in presenting their demands to all in a single document.

There was risk, too, that without agreement diversity of action would follow. Compliance with the proposals involved a radical departure from the previous business practices of the industry and a drastic increase in admission prices of most of the subsequent-run theatres....

... It taxes credulity to believe that the several distributors would, in the circumstances, have accepted and put into operation with substantial unanimity such far-reaching changes in their business methods without some understanding that all were to join, and we reject as beyond the range of probability that it was the result of mere chance....

[The inference of agreement] was supported and strengthened when the distributors, with like unanimity, failed to tender the testimony, at their command, of any officer or agent of a distributor who knew, or was in a position to know, whether in fact an agreement had been reached among them for concerted action. When the proof supported, as we think it did, the inference of such concert, the burden rested on appellants of going forward with the evidence to explain away or contradict it. They undertook to carry that burden by calling upon local managers of the distributors to testify that they had acted independently of the other distributors, and that they did not have conferences with or reach agreements with the other distributors or their representatives. The failure under the circumstances to call as witnesses those officers who did have authority to act for the distributors and who were in a position to know whether they had acted in pursuance of agreement is itself persuasive that their testimony, if given, would have been unfavorable to appellants. The production of weak evidence when strong is available can lead only to the conclusion that the strong would have been adverse. Silence then becomes evidence of the most convincing character.

While the District Court's finding of an agreement of the distributors among themselves is supported by the evidence, we think that in the circumstances of this case such agreement for the imposition of the restrictions upon subsequent-run exhibitors was not a prerequisite to an unlawful conspiracy. It was enough that, knowing that concerted action was contemplated and invited, the distributors gave their adherence to the scheme and participated in it. Each distributor was advised that the others were asked to participate; each knew that coöperation was essential to successful operation of the plan. They knew that the plan, if carried out, would result in a restraint of commerce, which ... was unreasonable within the meaning of the Sherman Act, and knowing it, all participated in the plan. The evidence is persuasive that each distributor early became aware that the others had joined. With that knowledge they renewed the arrangement and carried it into effect for the two successive years.

It is elementary that an unlawful conspiracy may be and often is formed without simultaneous action or agreement on the part of the conspirators. Acceptance by competitors, without previous agreement, of an invitation to participate in a plan, the necessary consequence of which, if carried out, is restraint of interstate commerce, is sufficient to establish an unlawful conspiracy under the Sherman Act .....

QUESTIONS AND COMMENTS

1. *Interstate Circuit* is called the "rimless wheel" case. It is also called a hub-and-spoke case. O'Donnell is the hub. Each of the big eight distributors—Columbia, Fox, Loews, Paramount, RKO, United Artists, Universal and Warner—stands on a point along the imaginary rim, and each is joined to the hub by its own spoke. The question is whether the fact-finder can link the big eight; can you join the dots on the rim? As you see, the fact-finder did "discover" the rim, and the Supreme Court agreed that the evidence supported the finding.

2. From what evidence does the Court infer that the distributors agreed among themselves to common prices at the box office? Did the Court infer that the distributors must have expressly agreed to fix these prices?

The Court in *Interstate Circuit* assumed—and stressed—that the parallel conduct of the movie distributors would have been profitable only if all of the distributors took the same course of action. Could any one of the distributors profitably have said "yes" to Interstate if all others had said "no"? But didn't each have the incentive to say "yes," knowing that it was in everyone's interest to say "yes"? Isn't this the essence of oligopolistic interdependence? Can interdependence occur without agreement?

3. Read again the last two paragraphs in the excerpt of the case. What does Justice Stone mean by the dictum that agreement is "not a prerequisite to an unlawful conspiracy"? Does he mean only that an express agreement is not essential and that an implied agreement would be enough? He continues: "It was enough that, knowing that concerted action was contemplated and invited, the distributors gave their adherence to the scheme and participated in it." Is interdependent but non-conspiratorial adoption of a new market strategy treated the same way as an actual agreement to implement the strategy? Suppose in a tight oligopoly one firm acted as price leader, others followed, and supracompetitive pricing was maintained. Does such conduct fall within Justice Stone's condemnation? How should the court frame injunctive relief against the violation?

4. Factors other than collusion—such as competition itself and non-collusive oligopolistic behavior—can often explain uniformity of price or conduct; they might explain even conscious uniformity. Accordingly, courts require a plaintiff relying on conscious parallelism to introduce some "plus" factor to raise a jury question of collusion. A plus factor can be any fact that makes the inference of collusion stronger than the inference of independent choice. For example: (1) The day before they all raised their prices, the competitors held a secret meeting to discuss prices. (This provided an opportunity for collusion under circumstances that cast suspicion). (2) The defendants' identical bids were sealed, and there was no apparent non-collusive way they could have known the bids of one another. (This was conformity under circumstances making it unlikely to be mere coincidence). (3) If any one competitor had pursued the course of conduct alone, it would have been unprofitable or economically not feasible, but if all or most followed the same course, all would gain.

In *C–O–Two Fire Equip. Co. v. United States,* 197 F.2d 489, 497 (9th Cir.), cert. denied, 344 U.S. 892 (1952), the court said:

> .... [The] question is not whether identical prices throughout the industry in and of itself establishes a conspiracy.... Here ... we have in addition to price uniformity, the other so-called plus factors.... They include a background of illegal licensing agreements containing minimum price maintenance provisions, an artificial standardization of product, a raising of prices at a time when a surplus existed in the industry, and a policing of dealers to effectuate the maintenance of minimum price provisions in accordance with price lists published and distributed by the corporate defendants, including appellant C–O–Two. Other factors which convinced the trial court, beyond a reasonable doubt, that the conspiracy did in fact exist, as charged, were the use of a delivered price system which resulted in price identity to the customer for the products sold, regardless of where they were manufactured, and the submitting of identical bids to public agencies. We think that the facts are not only consistent with the guilt of appellants, but also inconsistent with any other reasonable hypothesis.

5. When plaintiff's evidence raises an inference of collusion, defendant may introduce evidence that tends to rebut that inference. Does the defendant rebut the inference that may arise from factor (3) in paragraph 4 above by showing that the market structure and product characteristics were so conducive to oligopolistic interdependence that defendants did not *have* to agree in order to embark upon a price-raising course of behavior; that each would be aware (and would be aware that all others would be aware) that a rise in price would be in their common interest? Indeed, does factor (3) raise an inference of collusion?

6. One way that competitors have sought to organize price uniformity is by adopting a standard set of freight rates, particularly in industries such as cement and steel, where freight charges reflect a large portion of the delivered price. In a single basing point system, industry members agree to charge one set of freight rates. For example, steel manufacturers in the Northeast and Midwest signed on to the so-called "Pittsburgh Plus" plan, agreeing to charge freight from Pittsburgh, regardless of the actual shipping point, to the buyer's place of business. *U.S. Steel*, 8 FTC 1 (1924). Recall the discussion of the tasks of cartelists in Chapter 1. The conspirators must have a methodology, as simple as possible, to decide on the "right" price and to detect cheating from it. Basing point pricing is one such methodology.

But inference of agreement in view of uniformity is not always a simple proposition.

THEATRE ENTERPRISES, INC. v. PARAMOUNT FILM DISTRIBUTING CORP.

346 U.S. 537 (1954).

JUSTICE CLARK: Petitioner brought this suit for treble damages and an injunction under §§ 4 and 16 of the Clayton Act, alleging that respondent motion picture producers and distributors had violated the antitrust laws by conspiring to restrict "first-run" pictures to downtown Baltimore theatres, thus confining its suburban theatre to subsequent runs and unreasonable "clearances."[5] [The trial judge entered judgment on a verdict for respondents—the movie distributors, denying petitioner's motion for a directed verdict. The court of appeals affirmed.]....

... Petitioner now urges, as it did in the Court of Appeals, that the trial judge should have directed a verdict in its favor and submitted to the jury only the question of the amount of damages....

... [P]etitioner owns and operates the Crest Theatre, located in a neighborhood shopping district some six miles from the downtown shopping center in Baltimore, Maryland. The Crest, possessing the most modern improvements and appointments, opened on February 26, 1949. Before and after the opening, petitioner, through its president, repeatedly sought to obtain first-run features for the theatre. Petitioner approached each respondent separately, initially requesting exclusive first-runs, later asking for first-runs on a "day and date" basis.[7] But respondents uniformly rebuffed petitioner's efforts and adhered to an established policy of restricting first-runs in Baltimore to the eight downtown theatres. Admittedly there is no direct evidence of illegal agreement between the respondents and no conspiracy is charged as to the independent exhibitors in Baltimore, who account for 63% of first-run exhibitions. The various respondents advanced much the same reasons for denying petitioner's offers. Among other reasons, they asserted that day-and-date first-runs are normally granted only to noncompeting theatres. Since the Crest is in "substantial competition" with the downtown theatres, a day-and-date arrangement would be economically unfeasible. And even if respondents wished to grant petitioner such a license, no downtown exhibitor would waive his clearance rights over the Crest and agree to a simultaneous showing. As a result, if petitioner were to receive first-runs, the license would have to be an exclusive one. However, an exclusive license would be economically unsound because the Crest is a suburban theatre, located in a small shopping center, and served by limited public transportation facilities; and, with a drawing area of less than one-tenth that of a downtown theatre, it cannot compare with those easily accessible theatres in the power to draw patrons. Hence the downtown theatres offer far greater opportunities for the widespread advertisement and exploitation of newly released features, which is thought necessary to maximize the overall return from subsequent runs as well as first-runs. The respondents, in the light of these conditions, attacked the guaranteed offers of petitioner, one of which occurred during the trial, as not being made in good faith. Respondents Loew's and Warner refused petitioner an exclusive license

5. "A clearance is the period of time, usually stipulated in license contracts, which must elapse between runs of the same feature within a particular area or in specified theatres." *United States v. Paramount Pictures, Inc.*, 334 U.S. 131, 144, n. 6 (1948).

7. A first run "day and date" means that two theatres exhibit a first-run at the same time. Had petitioner's request for a day-and-date first-run been granted, the Crest and a downtown theatre would have exhibited the same features simultaneously.

because they owned the three downtown theatres receiving their first-run product.

The crucial question is whether respondents' conduct toward petitioner stemmed from independent decision or from an agreement, tacit or express. To be sure, business behavior is admissible circumstantial evidence from which the fact finder may infer agreement. But this Court has never held that proof of parallel business behavior conclusively establishes agreement or, phrased differently, that such behavior itself constitutes a Sherman Act offense. Circumstantial evidence of consciously parallel behavior may have made heavy inroads into the traditional judicial attitude toward conspiracy; but "conscious parallelism" has not yet read conspiracy out of the Sherman Act entirely. Realizing this, petitioner attempts to bolster its argument for a directed verdict by urging that the conscious unanimity of action by respondents should be "measured against the background and findings in the *Paramount* case." In other words, since the same respondents had conspired in the *Paramount* case to impose a uniform system of runs and clearances without adequate explanation to sustain them as reasonable restraints of trade, use of the same device in the present case should be legally equated to conspiracy. But the *Paramount* decrees, even if admissible, were only prima facie evidence of a conspiracy covering the area and existing during the period there involved. Alone or in conjunction with the other proof of the petitioner, they would form no basis for a directed verdict. Here each of the respondents had denied the existence of any collaboration and in addition had introduced evidence of the local conditions surrounding the Crest operation which, they contended, precluded it from being a successful first-run house. They also attacked the good faith of the guaranteed offers of the petitioner for first-run pictures and attributed uniform action to individual business judgment motivated by the desire for maximum revenue. This evidence, together with other testimony of an explanatory nature, raised fact issues requiring the trial judge to submit the issue of conspiracy to the jury....

QUESTIONS AND COMMENTS

1. If, at the close of the evidence, defendants in *Theatre Enterprises* had moved to dismiss for insufficiency of the evidence, should the trial judge have granted the motion?

2. From the 1950s to 1970s, following the holding and spirit of *Interstate Circuit*, judges liberally sent to the jury cases in which plaintiffs showed suspicious circumstances of commonality. Indeed, when judges gave summary judgment to defendants, courts of appeal were often quick to reverse. Even the Supreme Court declared that questions of combination or conspiracy are questions for the jury, and that summary judgment should not be lightly given. See *First National Bank of Arizona v. Cities Service Company*, 391 U.S. 253 (1968). As time went on, pressures began to push doctrine in the other direction. The increasing complexity of cases imposed new burdens on the federal judicial system. Massive discovery and econometrics attending rule of

reason analysis made antitrust cases more complex and more expensive. The prospect of treble damage judgments, combined with other pro-plaintiff rules and procedures, sometimes led to large settlements even of nuisance lawsuits. By the mid 1970s, courts were beginning to read more narrowly the Supreme Court's language that discouraged the use of summary judgment in antitrust cases. Then, in the mid 1980s, the *Japanese Electronics* case (*Matsushita*) came before the Supreme Court.

The Japanese television manufacturers had been "invading" the U.S. market, and, with prices below or nearly below what the U.S. manufacturers could bear, the Japanese firms were seriously injuring the American industry. The American manufacturers sued, alleging a low-price conspiracy. On the basis of a voluminous factual record, Judge Becker of the Eastern District of Pennsylvania granted summary judgment for defendants, finding that plaintiffs failed to raise a genuine issue of material fact to support their claim that there was a conspiracy that could have harmed them. The Court of Appeals for the Third Circuit reversed. The Supreme Court granted certiorari.

At first blush, you will regard this as much more than a proof-of-conspiracy case, and it is. The Court engages in a complex analysis of why the alleged conspiracy (low pricing by 21 firms over 20 years) would not have made economic sense. The Court's conclusion—the alleged conspiracy would not have made sense—becomes a major factor in the Court's ultimate decision that the conspiracy did not happen (more accurately, it was not proved). The case has become a major authority on predatory pricing—a subject we meet again in Chapter 4, as well as on the sufficiency of evidence to get to the jury in the case of an agreement based on circumstantial evidence.

We have not yet reached the subject of predatory pricing—pricing below cost, usually by a monopolist, with a view towards eliminating the competition and raising price. The *Matsushita* case involves claims that a number of firms (the Japanese firms) conspired to price below cost to eliminate the American firms. A large part of the case analyzes why this goal would be particularly difficult for conspirators to achieve. If the Japanese firms could not expect to achieve this goal by conspiracy, why would they have conspired?

MATSUSHITA ELECTRIC INDUSTRIAL CO. v. ZENITH RADIO CORP.

475 U.S. 574 (1986).

JUSTICE POWELL: This case requires that we again consider the standard district courts must apply when deciding whether to grant summary judgment in an antitrust conspiracy case.

I

... Petitioners, defendants below, are 21 corporations that manufacture or sell "consumer electronic products" (CEPs)—for the most part, television sets. Petitioners include both Japanese manufacturers of CEPs and American firms, controlled by Japanese parents, that sell the Japanese-manufactured products. Respondents, plaintiffs below, are Zenith

Radio Corporation (Zenith) and National Union Electric Corporation (NUE). Zenith is an American firm that manufactures and sells television sets. NUE is the corporate successor to Emerson Radio Company, an American firm that manufactured and sold television sets until 1970, when it withdrew from the market after sustaining substantial losses. Zenith and NUE began this lawsuit in 1974, claiming that petitioners had illegally conspired to drive American firms from the American CEP market. According to respondents, the gist of this conspiracy was a " 'scheme to raise, fix and maintain artificially *high* prices for television receivers sold by [petitioners] in Japan and, at the same time, to fix and maintain *low* prices for television receivers exported to and sold in the United States.' " These "low prices" were allegedly at levels that produced substantial losses for petitioners. The conspiracy allegedly began as early as 1953, and ... was in full operation by sometime in the late 1960's .....

The District Court [decided] petitioners' motions for summary judgment. In an opinion spanning 217 pages, the court found that the admissible evidence did not raise a genuine issue of material fact as to the existence of the alleged conspiracy....

On the merits ... the [Third Circuit] found that the ... summary judgment decision was improper. The court acknowledged that "there are legal limitations upon the inferences which may be drawn from circumstantial evidence," but it found that "the legal problem ... is different" when "there is direct evidence of concert of action." ..... [T]he Court of Appeals concluded that a reasonable factfinder could find a conspiracy to depress prices in the American market in order to drive out American competitors, which conspiracy was funded by excess profits obtained in the Japanese market .....

We reverse....

II

We begin by emphasizing what respondents' claim is *not*. Respondents cannot recover antitrust damages based solely on an alleged cartelization of the Japanese market, because American antitrust laws do not regulate the competitive conditions of other nations' economies. Nor can respondents recover damages for any conspiracy by petitioners to charge higher than competitive prices in the American market. Such conduct would indeed violate the Sherman Act, but it could not injure respondents: as petitioners' competitors, respondents stand to gain from any conspiracy to raise the market price in CEPs. Finally, for the same reason, respondents cannot recover for a conspiracy to impose nonprice restraints that have the effect of either raising market price or limiting output. Such restrictions, though harmful to competition, actually *benefit* competitors by making supracompetitive pricing more attractive. Thus, neither petitioners' alleged supracompetitive pricing in Japan, nor the five company rule*

* By their agreement, each Japanese producer was permitted to sell only to five American distributors. [eds.]

that limited distribution in this country, nor the check prices** insofar as they established minimum prices in this country, can by themselves give respondents a cognizable claim against petitioners for antitrust damages. The Court of Appeals therefore erred to the extent that it found evidence of these alleged conspiracies to be "direct evidence" of a conspiracy that injured respondents.

Respondents nevertheless argue that these supposed conspiracies, if not themselves grounds for recovery of antitrust damages, are circumstantial evidence of another conspiracy that *is* cognizable: a conspiracy to monopolize the American market by means of pricing below the market level. The thrust of respondents' argument is that petitioners used their monopoly profits from the Japanese market to fund a concerted campaign to price predatorily and thereby drive respondents and other American manufacturers of CEPs out of business. Once successful, according to respondents, petitioners would cartelize the American CEP market, restricting output and raising prices above the level that fair competition would produce. The resulting monopoly profits, respondents contend, would more than compensate petitioners for the losses they incurred through years of pricing below market level.

The Court of Appeals found that respondents' allegation of a horizontal conspiracy to engage in predatory pricing, if proved,[9] would be a *per se* violation of § 1 of the Sherman Act. Petitioners did not appeal from that conclusion. The issue in this case thus becomes whether respondents adduced sufficient evidence in support of their theory to survive summary judgment....

III

To survive petitioners' motion for summary judgment, respondents must establish that there is a genuine issue of material fact as to whether petitioners entered into an illegal conspiracy that caused respondents to suffer a cognizable injury. This showing has two components. First, respondents must show more than a conspiracy in violation of the antitrust laws; they must show an injury to them resulting from the illegal conduct. Respondents charge petitioners with a whole host of conspiracies in restraint of trade. Except for the alleged conspiracy to monopolize the American market through predatory pricing, these alleged conspiracies could not have caused respondents to suffer an "antitrust injury," because they actually tended to benefit respondents. Therefore, unless, in context, evidence of these "other" conspiracies raises a genuine issue concerning

---

** By formal agreements arranged in cooperation with Japan's Ministry of International Trade and Industry (MITI), petitioners fixed minimum prices for CEPs exported to the American market. The parties refer to these prices as the "check prices," and to the agreements that require them as the "check price agreements." [eds.]

9. We do not consider whether recovery should ever be available on a theory such as respondents' when the pricing in question is above some measure of incremental cost. As a practical matter, it may be that only direct evidence of below-cost pricing is sufficient to overcome the strong inference that rational businesses would not enter into conspiracies such as this one.

the existence of a predatory pricing conspiracy, that evidence cannot defeat petitioners' summary judgment motion.

Second, the issue of fact must be "genuine." . . .

It follows from these settled principles that if the factual context renders respondents' claim implausible—if the claim is one that simply makes no economic sense—respondents must come forward with more persuasive evidence to support their claim than would otherwise be necessary. . . .

. . . [The] antitrust law limits the range of permissible inferences from ambiguous evidence in a § 1 case. Thus, in *Monsanto Co. v. Spray–Rite Service Corp.,* 465 U.S. 752 (1984), we held that conduct as consistent with permissible competition as with illegal conspiracy does not, standing alone, support an inference of antitrust conspiracy. To survive a motion for summary judgment or for a directed verdict, a plaintiff seeking damages for a violation of § 1 must present evidence "that tends to exclude the possibility" that the alleged conspirators acted independently. Respondents in this case, in other words, must show that the inference of conspiracy is reasonable in light of the competing inferences of independent action or collusive action that could not have harmed respondents. * * *

IV

A predatory pricing conspiracy is by nature speculative. Any agreement to price below the competitive level requires the conspirators to forgo profits that free competition would offer them. The forgone profits may be considered an investment in the future. For the investment to be rational, the conspirators must have a reasonable expectation of recovering, in the form of later monopoly profits, more than the losses suffered. . . . The success of any predatory scheme depends on *maintaining* monopoly power for long enough both to recoup the predator's losses and to harvest some additional gain. . . . For this reason, there is a consensus among commentators that predatory pricing schemes are rarely tried, and even more rarely successful. . . .

These observations apply even to predatory pricing by a *single firm* seeking monopoly power. In this case, respondents allege that a large number of firms have conspired over a period of many years to charge below-market prices in order to stifle competition. Such a conspiracy is incalculably more difficult to execute than an analogous plan undertaken by a single predator. The conspirators must allocate the losses to be sustained during the conspiracy's operation, and must also allocate any gains to be realized from its success. Precisely because success is speculative and depends on a willingness to endure losses for an indefinite period, each conspirator has a strong incentive to cheat, letting its partners suffer the losses necessary to destroy the competition while sharing in any gains if the conspiracy succeeds. The necessary allocation is therefore difficult to accomplish. Yet if conspirators cheat to any substantial extent, the conspiracy must fail, because its success depends on depressing the market price for *all* buyers of CEPs. If there are too few goods at the artificially low price to satisfy demand, the would-be victims of the conspiracy can continue to sell at the "real" market price, and the conspirators suffer losses to little purpose.

Finally, if predatory pricing conspiracies are generally unlikely to occur, they are especially so where, as here, the prospects of attaining monopoly power seem slight. In order to recoup their losses, petitioners must obtain enough market power to set higher than competitive prices, and then must sustain those prices long enough to earn in excess profits what they earlier gave up in below-cost prices. Two decades after their conspiracy is alleged to have commenced, petitioners appear to be far from achieving this goal: the two largest shares of the retail market in television sets are held by RCA and respondent Zenith, not by any of the petitioners. Moreover, those shares, which together approximate 40% of sales, did not decline appreciably during the 1970's. Petitioners' collective share rose rapidly during this period, from one-fifth or less of the relevant markets to close to 50%. Neither the District Court nor the Court of Appeals found, however, that petitioners' share presently allows them to charge monopoly prices; to the contrary, respondents contend that the conspiracy is ongoing—that petitioners are still artificially *depressing* the market price in order to drive Zenith out of the market. The data in the record strongly suggest that that goal is yet far distant.

The alleged conspiracy's failure to achieve its ends in the two decades of its asserted operation is strong evidence that the conspiracy does not in fact exist. Since the losses in such a conspiracy accrue before the gains, they must be "repaid" with interest. And because the alleged losses have accrued over the course of two decades, the conspirators could well require a correspondingly long time to recoup. Maintaining supracompetitive prices in turn depends on the continued cooperation of the conspirators, on the inability of other would-be competitors to enter the market, and (not incidentally) on the conspirators' ability to escape antitrust liability for their *minimum* price-fixing cartel. Each of these factors weighs more heavily as the time needed to recoup losses grows. If the losses have been substantial—as would likely be necessary in order to drive out the competition—petitioners would most likely have to sustain their cartel for years simply to break even.

Nor does the possibility that petitioners have obtained supracompetitive profits in the Japanese market change this calculation. Whether or not petitioners have the *means* to sustain substantial losses in this country over a long period of time, they have no *motive* to sustain such losses absent some strong likelihood that the alleged conspiracy in this country will eventually pay off. The courts below found no evidence of any such success, and—as indicated above—the facts actually are to the contrary: RCA and Zenith, not any of the petitioners, continue to hold the largest share of the American retail market in color television sets. More important, there is nothing to suggest any relationship between petitioners' profits in Japan and the amount petitioners could expect to gain from a conspiracy to monopolize the American market. In the absence of any such evidence, the possible existence of supracompetitive profits in Japan simply cannot overcome the economic obstacles to the ultimate success of this alleged predatory conspiracy.

In *Monsanto,* we emphasized that courts should not permit factfinders to infer conspiracies when such inferences are implausible, because the effect of such practices is often to deter procompetitive conduct.... [C]utting prices in order to increase business often is the very essence of competition. Thus, mistaken inferences in cases such as this one are especially costly, because they chill the very conduct the antitrust laws are designed to protect.

In most cases, this concern must be balanced against the desire that illegal conspiracies be identified and punished. That balance is, however, unusually one-sided in cases such as this one. As we earlier explained, predatory pricing schemes require conspirators to suffer losses in order eventually to realize their illegal gains; moreover, the gains depend on a host of uncertainties, making such schemes more likely to fail than to succeed. These economic realities tend to make predatory pricing conspiracies self-deterring: unlike most other conduct that violates the antitrust laws, failed predatory pricing schemes are costly to the conspirators. Finally, unlike predatory pricing by a single firm, *successful* predatory pricing conspiracies involving a large number of firms can be identified and punished once they succeed, since some form of minimum price-fixing agreement would be necessary in order to reap the benefits of predation. Thus, there is little reason to be concerned that by granting summary judgment in cases where the evidence of conspiracy is speculative or ambiguous, courts will encourage such conspiracies.

V

* * * The "direct evidence" on which the court relied was evidence of *other* combinations, not of a predatory pricing conspiracy. Evidence that petitioners conspired to raise prices in Japan provides little, if any, support for respondents' claims: a conspiracy to increase profits in one market does not tend to show a conspiracy to sustain losses in another. Evidence that petitioners agreed to fix *minimum* prices (through the "check price" agreements) for the American market actually works in petitioners' favor, because it suggests that petitioners were seeking to place a floor under prices rather than to lower them. The same is true of evidence that petitioners agreed to limit the number of distributors of their products in the American market—the so-called five company rule. That practice may have facilitated a horizontal territorial allocation, but its natural effect would be to raise market prices rather than reduce them....

... [I]n light of the absence of any rational motive to conspire, neither petitioners' pricing practices, nor their conduct in the Japanese market, nor their agreements respecting prices and distribution in the American market, suffice to create a "genuine issue for trial."

On remand, the Court of Appeals is free to consider whether there is other evidence that is sufficiently unambiguous to permit a trier of fact to find that petitioners conspired to price predatorily for two decades despite the absence of any apparent motive to do so. The evidence must "ten[d] to exclude the possibility" that petitioners underpriced respondents to compete for business rather than to implement an economically senseless conspiracy. *Monsanto,* 465 U.S., at 764. In the absence of such evidence, there is no "genuine issue for trial"....

Justices White, Brennan, Blackmun and Stevens dissented. They believed that the plaintiffs had introduced sufficient evidence to go to the jury. They cited, among other things, direct evidence that the defendants colluded, e.g. in Japan and on the five-company rule, the economist's (de Podwin) report finding long-term below cost sales in the United States, and the following statement of the appellate court:

> "[A] factfinder might reasonably infer that the allocation of customers in the United States, combined with price-fixing in Japan, was intended to permit concentration of the effects of dumping upon American competitors while eliminating competition among the Japanese manufacturers in either market."

QUESTIONS AND COMMENTS

1. Under *Matsushita*, what is the standard that plaintiffs must meet to get to the jury on the question whether defendants had an agreement? Does this differ from the standard in *Interstate Circuit*?

2. Do you agree that plaintiffs failed to meet the standard? Was there evidence from which a jury could infer that the Japanese producers agreed to a price that was lower than the price that competition would have produced? If so, what was that evidence?

3. Did the Court legitimately use the neoclassical competition model to predict behavior of Japanese producers? Is it "implausible" to suppose that Japanese producers would *not* behave like American short-term profit maximizers?

But does the Court's decision depend on the assumption that the Japanese behaved like the Americans? Even if the assumption is wrong, is the hypothesis that the low prices resulted from competition at least equally as strong as the hypothesis that they resulted from conspiracy?

4. Suppose that the cost of the American producers (including a sufficient return to survive) was $100 per TV set; the cost to the Japanese firms was $90; competition among the Japanese producers would have driven price to $90; the Japanese producers in fact conspired to hold price at $98. Was this combination illegal *in a way that inflicted antitrust harm on the plaintiffs*?

5. Read again the dissenting Justices' quote from the court of appeals. If the fact-finder found just such a conspiracy to injure the American competitors, but there remained so many Japanese competitors competing against one another that the overall intensity of competition in the marketplace was not reduced, did the Americans prove a conspiracy illegal under the U.S. antitrust laws, or did they prove merely unfair competition? Do you suspect that the majority and dissenting Justices had different views?

The law of the European Union took a turn similar to that of the law of the United States. In early cartel cases, notably the *Sugar* case, *Suiker Unie v. Commission* (Sugar Cartel), Cases 40–48, 50, 54–56, 111, 113–114/73, [1975] ECR 1663, the Court of Justice articulated a definition of "concert" (paras. 172–174) that was similar to the loose and broad definition in *Interstate Circuit*. In 1993, the Court of Justice decided the *Wood pulp* case.

As you read the case, consider how U.S. courts would decide.

Å. ÅHLSTRÖM OSAKEYHTIÖ & ORS v. COMMISSION (Wood pulp; proof of agreement)

Cases C–89, 104, 114, 116–117, 125–129/85, [1993] ECR I–1307 (European Court of Justice 1993).

[U.S., Canadian, Finnish, Swedish and Norwegian firms shipped wood pulp into the European Community at virtually uniform prices with virtually uniform and sometimes simultaneous changes in price. The producers all made quarterly price announcements. Prices were nearly always quoted in dollars. The European Commission found a price-fixing arrangement. Most of its decision was annulled by the European Court of Justice, which found the producers' story more convincing.]

(a) System of price announcements * * *

76 The experts [appointed by the Court] observe first that the system of announcements at issue must be viewed in the context of the long-term relationships which existed between producers and their customers and which were a result both of the method of manufacturing the pulp and of the cyclical nature of the market. In view of the fact that each type of paper was the result of a particular mixture of pulps having their own characteristics and that the mixture was difficult to change, a relationship based on close co-operation was established between the pulp producers and the paper manufacturers. Such relations were all the closer since they also had the advantage of protecting both sides against the uncertainties inherent in the cyclical nature of the market: they guaranteed security of supply to buyers and at the same time security of demand to producers.

77 The experts point out that it is in the context of those long-term relationships that, after the Second World War, purchasers demanded the introduction of that system of announcements. Since pulp accounts for between 50–75 per cent of the cost of paper, those purchasers wished to ascertain as soon as possible the prices which they might be charged in order to estimate their costs and to fix the prices of their own products. However, as those purchasers did not wish to be bound by a high fixed price in the event of the market weakening, the announced price was regarded as a ceiling price below which the transaction price could always be renegotiated.

78 The explanation given for the use of a quarterly cycle is that it is the result of a compromise between the paper manufacturers' desire for a degree of foreseeability as regards the price of pulp and the producers' desire not to miss any opportunities to make a profit in the event of a strengthening of the market.

79 The US dollar was, according to the experts, introduced on the market by the North American producers during the 1960s. That development was generally welcomed by purchasers who regarded it as a means of ensuring that they did not pay a higher price than their competitors. * * *

(c) Parallelism of announced prices * * *

101 It is apparent from the [Court's] expert's report, together with the ensuing discussion, that the experts regard the normal operation of the market as a more plausible explanation for the uniformity of prices than concertation. The main thrust of their analysis may be summarised as follows.

102 The experts describe the market as a group of oligopolies-oligopsonies consisting of certain producers and of certain buyers and each corresponding to a given kind of pulp. That market structure results largely from the method of manufacturing paper pulp: since paper is the result of a characteristic mixture of pulps, each paper manufacturer can deal only with a limited number of pulp producers and, conversely, each pulp producer can supply only a limited number of customers. Within the groupings so constituted, co-operation was further consolidated by the finding that it offered both buyers and sellers of pulp security against the uncertainties of the market.

103 That organisation of the market, in conjunction with its very high degree of transparency, leads in the short term to a situation where prices are slow to react. The producers know that, if they were to increase their prices, their competitors would no doubt refrain from following suit and thus lure their customers away. Similarly, they would be reluctant to reduce their prices in the knowledge that, if they did so, the other producers would follow suit, assuming that they had spare production capacity. Such a fall in prices would be all the less desirable in that it would be detrimental to the sector as a whole:

since overall demand for pulp is inelastic, the loss of revenue resulting from the reduction in prices could not be offset by the profits made as a result of the increased sales and there would be a decline in the producers' overall profits.

104 In the long term, the possibility for buyers to turn, at the price of some investment, to other types of pulp and the existence of substitute products, such as Brazilian pulp or pulp from recycled paper, has the effect of mitigating oligopolistic trends on the market. That explains why, over a period of several years, fluctuations in prices have been relatively contained.

105 Finally, the transparency of the market could be responsible for certain overall price increases recorded in the short term: when demand exceeds supply, producers who are aware—as was the case on the pulp market—that the level of their competitors' stocks is low and that their production capacity utilisation rate is high would not be afraid to increase their prices. There would then be a serious likelihood of their being followed by their competitors. * * *

Conclusions

126 Following that analysis, it must be stated that, in this case, concertation is not the only plausible explanation for the parallel conduct. To begin with, the system of price announcements may be regarded as constituting a rational response to the fact that the pulp market constituted a long-term market and to the need felt by both buyers and sellers to limit commercial risks. Further, the similarity in the dates of price announcements may be regarded as a direct result of the high degree of market transparency, which does not have to be described as artificial. Finally, the parallelism of prices and the price trends may be satisfactorily explained by the oligopolistic tendencies of the market and by the specific circumstances prevailing in certain periods. Accordingly, the parallel conduct established by the Commission does not constitute evidence of concertation.

QUESTIONS AND COMMENTS

1. In para. 71 the Court Justice declared that parallel conduct cannot furnish proof of concertation "unless concertation constitutes the only plausible explanation for such conduct.... [The Treaty] does not deprive economic actors of the right to adapt themselves intelligently to the existing and anticipated conduct of their competitiors." Compare this standard with the standard of *Matsushita*. Do you think the European Court meant what it said regarding "the only plausible explanation"? If agreement was the most probable explanation of the parallel price moves, although not the only plausible one, should the Court have drawn an inference of a concerted practice? It is clear, however, that, in the judgment of the Court of Justice, the Commission's proof did not meet the standard of *Matsushita*. The judges did not believe that the conspiracy story was more plausible than the non-conspiracy story.

2. *Wood Pulp* is a high price case; *Matsushita* is a low price case. Might this difference affect the legal standard? Is a high-price case or a low-price case easier to prove, in a situation of conscious parallelism? Should it matter whether, in the high price case, the industry is an oligopoly prone to interdependence? Which way does the fact of oligopoly structure cut?

3. Lower court cases in the United States are not uniform. The Court of Appeals for the Eighth Circuit affirmed dismissal before trial in the case of an alleged potash conspiracy, despite parallel pricing plus price verification telephone calls among high level executives, discussions among competitors about a Canadian potash export association, "excess capacity; a sudden end to a price war; the industry giant's publicly avowed ambition to lead the industry to higher prices; large price rises . . . and a pattern of competitors threatening and rebuking each other's pricing conduct," all against a background of antidumping actions and their settlement. *Blomkest Fertilizer, Inc. v. Potash Corp. of Saskatchewan, Inc.,* 203 F.3d 1028 (8th Cir.2000), cert. denied, 531 U.S. 815 (2000).

The United States Court of Appeals for the Seventh Circuit reversed a dismissal under the following circumstances: Buyers of high fructose corn syrup (HFCS) sued the five principal manufacturers of HFCS for a price-fixing conspiracy resulting in substantial overcharges. They presented no direct evidence that the defendants conspired. They showed, however, that the structure of the market was favorable to secret price fixing, and economic evidence demonstrated that defendants were not competing. There were few sellers and the product was highly standardized, making collusion easy (but there were some large buyers such as Coca–Cola and Pepsi). There were no close substitutes for HFCS and demand was inelastic, making attainable profits from collusion high. Defendants had significant excess capacity, making price competition risky. The defendants bought some HFCS from one another even though they could have produced it at a lower cost. At the outset of the alleged conspiracy, defendant ADM announced that it was raising its price for the lower of the two grades of HFCS to 90% of the price of the higher grade and the other defendants quickly followed, even though the cost of the lower grade was only 65% of the cost of the higher grade. The court, by Judge Posner, said:

> To summarize the discussion to this point, there is evidence both that the HFCS market has a structure that is auspicious for price fixing and that during the period of the alleged conspiracy the defendants avoided or at least limited price competition. But as the defendants point out (when they are not arguing, inconsistently, that the industry was in fact fiercely competitive), all of this evidence is consistent with the hypothesis that they had a merely tacit agreement, which at least for purposes of this appeal the plaintiffs concede is not actionable under section 1 of the Sherman Act. The question then becomes whether there is enough evidence for a reasonable jury to find that there was an explicit agreement, not merely a tacit one. To repeat, there is evidence that the defendants were not competing; we might go so far as to say they had tacitly agreed not to compete, or at least to compete as little as possible; but the plaintiffs must prove that there was an actual, manifest agreement not to compete. Another and equivalent way to put this is that they

must present evidence that would enable a reasonable jury to reject the hypothesis that the defendants foreswore price competition without actually agreeing to do so. See, e.g., *Matsushita Electric Industrial Co. v. Zenith Radio Corp.*, 475 U.S. 574, 588 (1986).

More evidence is required the less plausible the charge of collusive conduct. In *Matsushita*, for example, the charge was that the defendants had conspired to lower prices below cost in order to drive out competitors, and then to raise prices to monopoly levels. This was implausible for a variety of reasons, such as that it would mean that losses would be incurred in the near term in exchange for the speculative possibility of more than making them up in the uncertain and perhaps remote future—when, moreover, the competitors might come right back into the market as soon as (or shortly after) prices rose above cost, thus thwarting the conspirators' effort at recouping their losses with a commensurate profit. But the charge in this case involves no implausibility. The charge is of a garden-variety price-fixing conspiracy orchestrated by a firm, ADM, conceded to have fixed prices on related products (lysine and citric acid) during a period overlapping the period of the alleged conspiracy to fix the prices of HFCS.

High Fructose Corn Syrup Antitrust Litigation, 295 F.3d 651 (7th Cir. 2002).

Is Judge Posner faithful to the test laid down by the Supreme Court in *Matsushita*? If not, what is his test, and which test is superior?

Judge Posner wrote the opinion, also, in *JTC Petroleum Company*. *JTC Petroleum* adds the dimension of standing of the plaintiff and whether it suffered antitrust injury (also a factor in *Matsushita*). As in *Matsushita*, plaintiff was suing its competitors; this time not only for price fixing but also for enlisting the producers of a necessary input (asphalt for road repair) to boycott the plaintiff. Could plaintiff defeat a motion for summary judgment? As you read the case, consider whether the evidence gave rise to an inference that defendants probably conspired in ways that caused plaintiff antitrust injury.

JTC PETROLEUM CO. v. PIASA MOTOR FUELS, INC.

190 F.3d 775 (7th Cir. 1999).

CHIEF JUDGE POSNER:

The plaintiff seeks damages for violations of sections 1 and 2 of the Sherman Act arising out of the road-repair business in southern Illinois. There are two groups of defendants: the road contractors themselves, called "applicators", and producers of the emulsified asphalt that the applicators apply to the surface of the roads. After the plaintiff, itself an applicator, settled with all three of the producers and three of the six applicator defendants, the district court granted summary judgment for the remaining applicator defendants, who are the appellees in this court.

* * *

The plaintiff presented evidence both that the applicator defendants had agreed not to compete with one another in bidding on local government contracts and that the producers had agreed not to compete among each other either, both agreements being (if proved) per se violations of section 1 of the Sherman Act..... These are local markets, with a limited number of competitors, selling a rather standardized service to local governments constrained to give their business to the lowest bidder, a constraint that makes it easy for colluding bidders to determine whether one of their number is cheating on the agreement to divide markets. The conditions are thus ripe for effective collusion, making it unsurprising that there is evidence that the applicator defendants in fact colluded with one another to allocate the applicator business in their region. (In discussing the evidence, we emphasize that we are construing it in the light most favorable to the plaintiff, as we are required to do in reviewing the grant of summary judgment to the defendants.)

As for the producers of the asphalt used by these applicators, the record contains evidence that the product is both heavy relative to value and prone to deteriorate when transported long distances, and that as a result the practical radius within which a plant can supply applicators is only about 70 miles. This has limited to three the number of producers that can supply applicators in the region served by the plaintiff and by the applicator defendants. The plants are specialized to the production of emulsified asphalt, meaning that they can't readily be switched to producing other products. This gives the producers an incentive to produce emulsified asphalt up to the capacity of their plants (because there is no profitable use of the plants other than producing this product), and, since it is a fungible product, about the only way of increasing output is by cutting price. But since the demand for emulsified asphalt is inelastic—that is, lower prices do not yield commensurate increases in volume—the effect of price competition would be to diminish profits. So the producers, like the applicators, have much to gain by eliminating competition among themselves. And since the product is standard and the number of competing producers few, an agreement not to compete should not be too difficult to enforce; that is, at the producer level as at the applicator level, cheating should be readily observable and hence quickly checked by a retaliatory price cut. Therefore a cartel agreement would not be quickly eroded by cheating, and so again the conditions for collusion are ripe and again the record contains evidence of such collusion.

But the only defendants remaining in the case are applicators, which is to say the plaintiff's competitors. The producers have settled out. Suppose that all that the plaintiff were complaining about, therefore, was a conspiracy of the applicators to raise prices or (what amounts to the same thing) to allocate customers or markets. The complaint would fail at the threshold. A conspiracy of a firm's competitors to do these things could only help the firm, by providing an umbrella under which it could sell a large quantity at a supracompetitive price generating supracompetitive profits just by setting price in between the conspirators' price and the lower, competitive price that would prevail in the absence of the conspiracy. You *want* your competitors to charge high prices.

The fact that it was in JTC's interest that the other applicators agree not to compete with each other would be irrelevant if the Department of Justice were suing the applicators, but it is not; this is a private suit by a competitor that, since it cannot show harm to itself from its competitors' eliminating competition among themselves, cannot obtain relief under the antitrust laws. To put it bluntly, you cannot obtain damages without proving injury. (This is a general principle of both common law tort law and statutory tort law, rather than anything special to antitrust.) As a purchaser of emulsified asphalt, JTC could of course be hurt by a producers' cartel, but, to repeat, no producer remains as a defendant.

So what JTC has tried to show is that the applicators enlisted the producers in their conspiracy, assigning them the role of policing the applicators' cartel by refusing to sell to applicators who defied the cartel—such as JTC, which has bid for jobs that the cartel had assigned to other applicators. JTC, a maverick, was a threat to the cartel—but only if it could find a source of supply of emulsified asphalt. The claim is that the applicators got the producers to deny JTC this essential input into its business, and as a result injured it. The producer was the cat's paw; the applicators were the cat.

Matsushita Electric Industrial Co. v. Zenith Radio Corp., however, teaches that an antitrust claim which makes no economic sense can on that ground be dismissed on summary judgment. And it might seem to make no sense from the producers' standpoint to shore up a cartel of their customers. Cartels, as we have pointed out, raise price above the competitive level and by doing so reduce the demand for their product. The less asphalt the members of the applicators' cartel sell (perhaps because the higher, cartel price induces municipalities to defer road maintenance), the less they will buy, and so the producers will be hurt. But if the producers have nowhere else to turn to sell their product, as may be the case here because of the specialized character of their plants and the limited radius within which they can ship their product from the plant, the applicator defendants may be able to coerce them into helping to police their cartel by threatening to buy less product from them or pay less for it.....

Alternatively, and more plausibly (at least on this record), the cartelists may have been paying the producers to perform the policing function, rather than coercing them, by threats, to do so. If by refusing to sell to mavericks the producers increase the profits of the applicators' cartel, they create a fund out of which the cartel can compensate them, in the form of a higher price for the purchase of the product, for their services to the cartel. The record contains evidence that one of the producers obtained from applicators in the cartel area prices that were 4 to 18 (or maybe even 28) percent higher than the prices it obtained from presumably noncolluding applicators in the adjacent region, though there is no suggestion that the producer's costs were any higher in that region. The evidence is contested by the defendants, but the resolution of the contest is for trial. There is also evidence (again contested, and again this is irrelevant to whether summary judgment was properly granted) that the reasons the producers gave for refusing to sell to JTC were pretextual.... for example, that JTC was not a good credit risk, even though when JTC offered to pay cash the producers still refused to sell to it. This suggests that the real reason for the refusal was one that the producers didn't want to acknowledge—namely that they were being compensated by the cartel for refusing to sell to a customer whom otherwise they would have been happy to sell to. The combination of the price difference with the evidence of pretext supports an inference that the producers were being compensated by the applicators for shoring up the cartel by boycotting an applicator that was competing with the cartel. If so—if the producers were working for the cartel—they were part of the applicators' conspiracy, and for the injury that they inflicted on JTC as agents of the applicators' cartel by denying JTC a source of supply the members of the cartel, three of which are the remaining defendants, would be culpable under elementary principles of both conspiracy law and agency law.

There may be an innocent explanation for why producers would charge lower prices elsewhere or why they refused to sell to JTC. But the only issue for us, in reviewing the grant of summary judgment for these defendants, is whether a rational jury, having before it the evidence developed to date, could conclude (construing the evidence as favorably to the plaintiff as the record permits) that the reason for the producers' refusal to deal with JTC was that they were in cahoots with the cartel to discourage competition in the applicator market. Given the evidence of cartelization at both the applicator and producer level, the suspicious producer price behavior (suggestive of the producers' having been "paid off" by the cartel to boycott JTC and other upstarts), and the pretextual character of the reasons the producers gave for the refusal to deal, a rational jury could conclude that JTC was indeed the victim of a producers' boycott organized by the applicator defendants.

All the evidence that we have discussed is circumstantial, but of course an inference of conspiracy—of, in this case, an informal agreement among the applicators and the producers to deny supply to firms that tried to break into the applicators' cosily divided market—can be drawn from circumstantial evidence as well as from admissions or other direct testimony of the conspirators' communications with each other. * * *

Reversed.

QUESTIONS AND COMMENTS

1. Explain why this market was particularly susceptible to collusion and how this circumstance was relevant to plaintiff's case.

2. Why did the settlement with the producers make this a hard case for plaintiff?

3. How did the plaintiff and Judge Posner maneuver around the problem that plaintiff was complaining about a cartel of its competitors?

4. Judge Posner held that the facts raised an inference of an agreement that caused antitrust harm to plaintiff sufficient to defeat defendants' summary judgment motion. What was the argument to the contrary?—an argument that had obviously appealed to the district court. Who had the better side of the argument?

---

2. PLEADING FACTS SUFFICIENT FOR PLAUSIBLE INFERENCE OF AGREEMENT

A class of telephone users brought a treble damage action against four Baby Bells—the Incumbent Local Exchange Carriers, or ILECs. The ILECs were authorized monopolists of telecommunications services in their local and regional markets for many years. This all changed when new technologies made possible efficient competition in local service. In 1996, Congress passed the Telecommunications Act to facilitate entry into the local markets by CLECs—competitive local exchange carriers. The ILECs were the best equipped and positioned entrants into the markets of one another. ILECs' territories adjoined and sometimes wound around each other; one even had an "island" of its service area surrounded by the territory of another. Qwest's CEO, Notebaert, said: "This [entering another's market] might be a good way to turn a quick dollar but that doesn't make it right."

The plaintiffs alleged: Each ILEC engaged in parallel exclusionary conduct in its service area to inhibit the growth of CLECs in its territory; the ILEC's flagrantly resisted the 1996 Act's command to share the local loop without favoring itself; and each assiduously refrained from entering the service area of the other despite the financially attractive opportunity to do so. They alleged also that the ILECs communicated among themselves through numerous industry associations and that they *agreed* to refrain from competing with one another in the territories of the other as indicated by the above facts. Plaintiffs alleged on information and belief that the ILECs conspired to divide customers and territories and to prevent competitive entry.

The federal rules of pleading authorize "notice" pleading, rather than requiring pleading all of the facts on which a claim is based. More than half a century ago, the Supreme Court held, in *Conley v. Gibson*, 355 U.S. 41 (1957), that a complaint may not be dismissed for failure to state a claim unless "no set of facts . . . would entitle him to relief."

The ILECs moved to dismiss the *Twombly* complaint. The district court granted the motion. The appellate court reversed. The Supreme Court held that the complaint should be dismissed. The complaint was based only on parallel conduct, the Court said; plaintiffs did not plead "plausible grounds to infer an agreement." [at n. 4]

BELL ATLANTIC CORP. v. TWOMBLY

550 U.S. 544 (2007).

JUSTICE SOUTER: * * * In applying these general standards to a § 1 claim, we hold that stating such a claim requires a complaint with enough factual matter (taken as true) to suggest that an agreement was made. Asking for plausible grounds to infer an agreement does not impose a probability requirement at the pleading stage; it simply calls for enough facts to raise a reasonable expectation that discovery will reveal evidence of illegal agreement. * * *

We think that nothing contained in the complaint invests either the action or inaction alleged with a plausible suggestion of conspiracy. As to the ILECs' supposed agreement to disobey the 1996 Act and thwart the CLECs' attempts to compete, we agree with the District Court that nothing in the complaint intimates that the resistance to the upstarts was anything more than the natural, unilateral reaction of each ILEC intent on keeping its regional dominance. The 1996 Act did more than just subject the ILECs to competition; it obliged them to subsidize their competitors with their own equipment at wholesale rates. The economic incentive to resist was powerful, but resisting competition is routine market conduct, and even if the ILECs flouted the 1996 Act in all the ways the plaintiffs allege, ... there is no reason to infer that the companies had agreed among themselves to do what was only natural anyway; so natural, in fact, that if alleging parallel decisions to resist competition were enough to imply an antitrust conspiracy, pleading a § 1 violation against almost any group of competing businesses would be a sure thing.

The complaint makes its closest pass at a predicate for conspiracy with the claim that collusion was necessary because success by even one CLEC in an ILEC's territory "would have revealed the degree to which competitive entry by CLECs would have been successful in the other territories." But, its logic aside, this general premise still fails to answer the point that there was just no need for joint encouragement to resist the 1996 Act; as the District Court said, "each ILEC has reason to want to avoid dealing with CLECs" and "each ILEC would attempt to keep CLECs out, regardless of the actions of the other ILECs." ...

Plaintiffs' second conspiracy theory rests on the competitive reticence among the ILECs themselves in the wake of the 1996 Act, which was supposedly passed in the " 'hop[e] that the large incumbent local monopoly companies ... might attack their neighbors' service areas, as they are the best situated to do so.' " ... Based on this state of affairs, and perceiving the ILECs to be blessed with "especially attractive business opportunities" in surrounding markets dominated by other ILECs, the plaintiffs assert that the ILECs' parallel conduct was "strongly suggestive of conspiracy."

But it was not suggestive of conspiracy, not if history teaches anything. In a traditionally unregulated industry with low barriers to entry, sparse competition among large firms dominating separate geographical segments of the market could very well signify illegal agreement, but here we have an obvious alternative explanation. In the decade preceding the 1996 Act and well before that, monopoly was the norm in telecommunications, not the exception. The ILECs were born in that world, doubtless liked the world the way it was, and surely knew the adage about him who lives by the sword. Hence, a natural explanation for the noncompetition alleged is that the former Government-sanctioned monopolists were sitting tight, expecting their neighbors to do the same thing.

In fact, the complaint itself gives reasons to believe that the ILECs would see their best interests in keeping to their old turf. Although the complaint says generally that the ILECs passed up "especially attractive business opportunit[ies]" by declining to compete as CLECs against other ILECs, it does not allege that competition as CLECs was potentially any more lucrative than other opportunities being pursued by the ILECs during the same period, and the complaint is replete with indications that any CLEC faced nearly insurmountable barriers to profitability owing to the ILECs' flagrant resistance to the network sharing requirements of the 1996 Act. Not only that, but even without a monopolistic tradition and the peculiar difficulty of mandating shared networks, "[f]irms do not expand without limit and none of them enters every market that an outside observer might regard as profitable, or even a small portion of such markets." Areeda & Hovenkamp ¶ 307d, at 155 (Supp. 2006).... The upshot is that Congress may have expected some ILECs to become CLECs in the legacy territories of other ILECs, but the disappointment does not make conspiracy plausible. * * *

... Because plaintiffs have not nudged their claims across the line from conceivable to plausible, their complaint must be dismissed.

QUESTIONS AND COMMENTS

1. The Supreme Court overruled the 50–year old precedent, *Conley v. Gibson*, 355 U.S. 41 (1957). Under *Conley*, a complaint was dismissible for factual insufficiency only if it appeared beyond doubt that plaintiff could prove "no set of facts" that would entitle it to relief.

2. The Court referred at length to the ease with which plaintiffs can get discovery, burdening defendants with huge costs, and the ease with which plaintiffs—especially in a case like *Twombly* where the class represented 90% of all telephone users in the country—can pressure huge nuisance settlements. More than once the Court referenced abuse of discovery.

3. What does the Court mean by its new test of "plausibility"? Was an agreement among the ILECs to make life tough for new entrants plausible?

Was an agreement between the ILECs to stay out of one another's territory plausible? Does the Court require more than the common understanding of plausibility? Does the Court require something akin to the *Matsushita* summary judgment standard, albeit with regard to *pleading* the basic facts rather than supporting them with evidence?

4. What is the significance of *Twombly*? Will it change antitrust litigation and outcomes?

In fact, the impact of *Twombly* has been huge. In the wake of *Twombly*, courts have dismissed numerous complaints, and plaintiffs have filed fewer cases. Defendants typically bring *Twombly* motions at the outset of a case.

5. In *Ashcroft v. Iqbal*, 556 U.S. 662 (2009), the Court held that the rule of *Twombly* applies to civil procedure generally. It clarified that: "The plausibility standard is not akin to a 'probability requirement,' but it asks for more than a sheer possibility that a defendant has acted unlawfully."

TEXT MESSAGING ANTITRUST LITIGATION

630 F.3d 622 (7th Cir. 2010).

JUDGE POSNER: * * **

The complaint in *Twombly* alleged that the regional telephone companies that were the successors to the Bell Operating Companies [the local telephone service providers] which AT&T had been forced to divest in settlement of the government's antitrust suit against it were engaged in "parallel behavior." Bluntly, they were not competing. But section 1 of the Sherman Act, under which the suit had been brought, does not require sellers to compete; it just forbids their agreeing or conspiring not to compete. So as the Court pointed out, a complaint that merely alleges parallel behavior alleges facts that are equally consistent with an inference that the defendants are conspiring and an inference that the conditions of their market have enabled them to avoid competing without having to agree not to compete. The core allegations of the complaint in *Twombly* were simply that "In the absence of any meaningful competition between the [defendants] in one another's markets, and in light of the parallel course of conduct that each engaged in to prevent competition from [other carriers] within their respective local telephone and/or high speed internet services markets and the other facts and market circumstances alleged above, Plaintiffs allege upon information and belief that [the defendants] have entered into a contract, combination or conspiracy to prevent competitive entry in their respective local telephone and/or high speed internet services markets and have agreed not to compete with one another and otherwise allocated customers and markets to one another." *Id.* at 551.

* * *

The second amended complaint [in this case, *Text Messaging*] alleges a mixture of parallel behaviors, details of industry structure, and industry practices, that facilitate collusion. There is nothing incongruous about such a mixture. If parties agree to fix prices, one expects that as a result they will not compete in price—that's the purpose of price fixing. Parallel behavior of a sort anomalous in a competitive market is thus a symptom of price fixing, though standing alone it is not proof of it; and an industry structure that facilitates collusion constitutes supporting evidence of collusion. An accusation that the thousands of children who set up makeshift lemonade stands all over the country on hot summer days were fixing prices would be laughed out of court because the retail sale of lemonade from lemonade stands constitutes so dispersed and heterogeneous and uncommercial a market as to make a nationwide conspiracy of the sellers utterly implausible. But the complaint in this case alleges that the four defendants sell 90 percent of U.S. text messaging services, and it would not be difficult for such a small group to agree on prices and to be able to detect "cheating" (underselling the agreed price by a member of the group) without having to create elaborate mechanisms, such as an exclusive sales agency, that could not escape discovery by the antitrust authorities.

Of note is the allegation in the complaint that the defendants belonged to a trade association and exchanged price information directly at association meetings. This allegation identifies a practice, not illegal in itself, that facilitates price fixing that would be difficult for the authorities to detect. The complaint further alleges that the defendants, along with two other large sellers of text messaging services, constituted and met with each other in an elite "leadership council" within the association—and the leadership council's stated mission was to urge its members to substitute "co-opetition" for competition.

The complaint also alleges that in the face of steeply falling costs, the defendants increased their prices. This is anomalous behavior because falling costs increase a seller's profit margin at the existing price, motivating him, in the absence of agreement, to reduce his price slightly in order to take business from his competitors, and certainly not to increase his price. And there is more: there is an allegation that all at once the defendants changed their pricing structures, which were heterogeneous and complex, to a uniform pricing structure, and then simultaneously jacked up their prices by a third. The change in the industry's pricing structure was so rapid, the complaint suggests, that it could not have been accomplished without agreement on the details of the new structure, the timing of its adoption, and the specific uniform price increase that would ensue on its adoption. A footnote in *Twombly* had described the type of evidence that enables parallel conduct to be interpreted as collusive: "Commentators have offered several examples of parallel conduct allegations that would state a [Sherman Act] § 1 claim under this standard ... [namely,] 'parallel behavior that would probably not result from chance, coincidence, independent responses to common stimuli, or mere interdependence unaided by an advance understanding among the parties' ... [;] 'conduct [that] indicates the sort of restricted freedom of action and sense of obligation that one generally associates with agreement.' The parties in this case agree that 'complex and historically unprecedented changes in pricing structure made at the very same time by multiple competitors, and made for no other discernible reason' would support a plausible inference of conspiracy." *Bell Atlantic Corp. v. Twombly*, *supra*, 550 U.S. at 557 n. 4 (citations omitted). That is the kind of "parallel plus" behavior alleged in this case.

What is missing, as the defendants point out, is the smoking gun in a price-fixing case: direct evidence, which would usually take the form of an admission by an employee of one of the conspirators, that officials of the defendants had met and agreed explicitly on the terms of a conspiracy to raise price. The second amended complaint does allege that the defendants "agreed to uniformly charge an unprecedented common per unit price of ten cents for text messaging services," but does not allege direct evidence of such an agreement; the allegation is an inference from circumstantial evidence. Direct evidence of conspiracy is not a sine qua non, however. Circumstantial evidence can establish an antitrust conspiracy.... We need not decide whether the circumstantial evidence that we have summarized is sufficient to *compel* an inference of conspiracy; the case is just at the complaint stage and the test for whether to dismiss a case at that stage turns on the complaint's "plausibility."

The Court said in *Iqbal* that the "plausibility standard is not akin to a 'probability requirement,' but it asks for more than a sheer possibility that a defendant has acted unlawfully." 129 S. Ct. at 1949. This is a little unclear because plausibility, probability, and possibility overlap. Probability runs the gamut from a zero likelihood to a certainty. What is impossible has a zero likelihood of occurring and what is plausible has a moderately high likelihood of occurring. The fact that the allegations undergirding a claim could be true is no longer enough to save a complaint from being dismissed; the complaint must establish a nonnegligible probability that the claim is valid; but the probability need not be as great as such terms as "preponderance of the evidence" connote.

The plaintiffs have conducted no discovery. Discovery may reveal the smoking gun or bring to light additional circumstantial evidence that further tilts the balance in favor of liability. All that we conclude at this early stage in the litigation is that the district judge was right to rule that the second amended complaint provides a sufficiently plausible case of price fixing to warrant allowing the plaintiffs to proceed to discovery.

QUESTIONS AND COMMENTS

1. What critical facts in *Messaging* distinguish it from the facts in *Twombly*? Why, under the facts in *Twombly*, was the conspiracy story not sufficiently plausible to entitle plaintiffs to discovery?

2. In *Messaging*, was the story of mere interdependence (no agreement) also plausible? What do the plaintiffs have to prove at trial to get to the jury on the question whether defendants had an agreement? Can they do so on the basis of the circumstantial evidence summarized?

3. The impact of *Twombly* cannot be understated. One example of its impact is *Minn–Chem Inc. v. Agrium Inc.*, 657 F.3d 650 (7th Cir. 2011) (*reh'g en banc granted*). There, the Court of Appeals held that *Twombly* (and a foreign trade antitrust act that you will meet below and that requires a direct U.S. effect) required dismissal of a case by U.S. potash buyers against members of a notorious Canadian potash cartel and their alleged Russian collaborators because the defendants did not sell the potash directly into the United States (to avoid U.S. antitrust laws?). Moreover, despite the fact that U.S. prices rose 600% during the cartel period, a general allegation that defendants conspired with respect to U.S. prices was deemed merely conclusory and thus insufficient.

F. STATE ACTION, POLITICAL ACTION

1. THE STATE ACTION DOCTRINE

We turn now from questions of fact to questions of law. Are certain private-firm agreements outside of the scope of the Sherman Act because of involvement of the state or the political nature of the conduct? Does state encouragement or command, or does solicitation of a state command, immunize the private party? A large portion of these cases arise in the context of private firms participating in a cartel. Therefore it is particularly appropriate to discuss the legal effect of state involvement here.

Another critical mass of state action cases has arisen in the context of resale price maintenance agreements, which are vertical agreements (treated in Chapter 6), and we continue the discussion at that point.

The subject is of major importance. It is often noted that state measures that lessen competition are much more enduring and harmful than private restraints; they cannot be overcome merely by creative competition. Moreover, they are often procured by vested interests; e.g. by "big steel," which doesn't like the competition of lower-priced imports. But on the other hand, the democratic state must have room to act in (a notion of) the public interest; and the people must have open channels to inform and convince the state actors.

We start with the landmark case, *Parker v. Brown*, followed by related cases of political action and the right to lobby, and possible limits on these rights in the presence of fraud and deceit.

PARKER v. BROWN

317 U.S. 341 (1943).

CHIEF JUSTICE STONE: [California adopted the Agricultural Prorate Act in 1933, setting forth a procedure for the adoption of a marketing program on petition of producers of any agricultural product and upon a showing that the program "will prevent agricultural waste and conserve agricultural wealth of the state without permitting unreasonable profits to producers." Raisin producers, facing a crisis of overproduction and declining prices, so petitioned, triggering the adoption of a raisin marketing program for the 1940 crop. The program was to be carried out by state officials "so as to restrict competition among the growers and maintain prices in the distribution of their commodities to packers." Under the program, all producers were required to deliver all raisins they wished to market to the Program Committee, which was to be made up of producers and one or two packers. The committee members were required to grade the raisins, to place all substandard raisins and at least 20% of the standard and substandard raisins in a surplus pool to be disposed of only for by-product purposes, and to place 50% of the crop in a stabilization pool. Each producer could sell the remaining 30% of its standard raisins through ordinary channels subject to obtaining a certificate and paying a fee. The committee would dispose of the pooled raisins in such a manner as to obtain stability; and they would pay the producers what the raisins earned, less administration costs. Violations by producers were punishable by fines and jail. As a result of the program, prices allegedly rose from $45 per ton to $55 per ton.

Almost all of the raisins consumed in the United States and nearly one-half of the world crop were produced in California Proration Zone No. 1. Approximately 95% of raisins grown in California were ultimately shipped in interstate or foreign commerce.

Brown was a producer and packer of raisins. He sued to enjoin State Director of Agriculture Parker, the Program Committee, and various other state officials from implementing the program, alleging it to be a violation of the commerce clause of the Constitution, to be preempted by the federal Agricultural Marketing Agreement, and to constitute a violation of the Sherman Act. Rejecting each of Mr. Brown's claims, the Court said of the Sherman Act:]

. . . In a dual system of government in which, under the Constitution, the states are sovereign, save only as Congress may constitutionally subtract from their authority, an expressed purpose to nullify a state's control over its officers and agents is not lightly to be attributed to Congress.

The Sherman Act makes no mention of the state as such, and gives no hint that it was intended to restrain state action or official action directed by the state. The Act is applicable to "persons" including corporations (§ 7), and it authorizes suits under it by persons and corporations (§ 15). . . .

There is no suggestion of a purpose to restrain state action in the Act's legislative history. The sponsor of the bill which was ultimately enacted as the Sherman Act declared that it prevented only "business combinations." . . .

True, a state does not give immunity to those who violate the Sherman Act by authorizing them to violate it, or by declaring that their action is lawful, and we have no question of the state or its municipality becoming a participant in a private agreement or combination by others for restraint of trade. Here the state command to the Commission and to the program committee of the California Prorate Act is not rendered unlawful by the Sherman Act since, in view of the latter's words and history, it must be taken to be a prohibition of individual and not state action. It is the state which has created the machinery for establishing the prorate program. Although the organization of a prorate zone is proposed by producers, and a prorate program, approved by the Commission, must also be approved by referendum of producers, it is the state, acting through the Commission, which adopts the program and which enforces it with penal sanctions, in the execution of a governmental policy. The prerequisite approval of the program upon referendum by a prescribed number of producers is not the imposition by them of their will upon the minority by force of agreement or combination which the Sherman Act prohibits. The state itself exercises its legislative authority in making the regulation and in prescribing the conditions of its application....

The state in adopting and enforcing the prorate program made no contract or agreement and entered into no conspiracy in restraint of trade or to establish monopoly but, as sovereign, imposed the restraint as an act of government which the Sherman Act did not undertake to prohibit....

* * *

QUESTIONS AND COMMENTS

1. Regarding the Commerce Clause, the Court said:

> ... When Congress has not exerted its power under the Commerce Clause, and state regulation of matters of local concern is so related to interstate commerce that it also operates as a regulation of that commerce, the reconciliation of the power thus granted with that reserved to the state is to be attained by the accommodation of the competing demands of the state and national interests involved.... * * *
>
> ... [T]he evidence ... leaves no doubt that the evils attending the production and marketing of raisins ... in that state present a problem local in character and urgently demanding state action for the economic protection of those engaged in one of its important industries.... 317 U.S. at 362, 363.

Was the prorate program an undue restraint on commerce, in modern terms? What is the proper balance between California's right to regulate a matter of local concern (a decent living for its farmers) and the interest of the American public in the free flow of trade? Who should pay for California's agricultural crisis?

2. How did the Court construe the Sherman Act? Is the holding merely that the state (acting in its sovereign capacity) is not "a person" within the meaning of: "No person shall ..."? Or is the holding broader?

Whatever the Court intended in *Parker v. Brown*, the case is read as providing a state action *defense* to claims of private anticompetitive action where the state has a clearly articulated policy that entails anticompetitive conduct and it supervises any private anticompetitive conduct. The defense would have been put into play if farmer Brown had sued his fellow producers who faithfully contributed their raisins to the raisin pool and got their (unjust) rewards. The defense is, in effect: "This is state action, not private action," or, if the action is compelled: "The state made me do it."

Later cases made it clear that no state action defense is available if the state encourages or even orders private parties to do an act such as price fixing, and purports to confer on the private parties immunity from federal law. Not only must the state have a clearly and affirmatively expressed state policy to replace competition with regulation but the state must supervise any private anticompetitive conduct taken to carry out that policy. The leading cases that establish the proposition that the state cannot confer immunity for private acts (*Schwegmann*, at page 618 infra; *Midcal* page 619 infra) are part of the vertical resale price-fixing story and are covered in the vertical restraints chapter, Chapter 6. See also the Framework Essay, Appendix A.

Later cases made it clear also that cities and municipalities do not have the stature of states. For local government to be entitled to immunity, the state must delegate to the city or municipality express authority to take action that foreseeably has anticompetitive effects. *Town of Hallie v. City of Eau Claire*, 471 U.S. 34 (1985). The Local Government Antitrust Act of 1984 provides that local governments and officials or employees acting in an official capacity are not liable for antitrust damages. Read the description of the state action cases in the Framework Essay.

3. If American raisin-eaters don't like subsidizing California raisin producers (by paying supra-competitive prices), do they have recourse? If you had the ear of your senator, what would you propose? Note that Congress has the power to preempt anticompetitive state action as long as it does not entrench unconstitutionally on state sovereign rights.

4. Suppose that 75% of California raisins are sold in international markets mostly to Mexicans and Canadians. What is the recourse for Mexican and Canadian raisin-lovers who don't like subsidizing California farmers?

5. The European Union imposes a stricter discipline on its member states (nations) than does the United States on U.S. states. If a (nation) state facilitates or even orders a private cartel, that state's antitrust authority and its national courts have the duty to "disapply" the state law. *Consorzio Industrie Fiammiferi and Autoritá Garanta della Concorrenza e del Mercato*, Case C–198/01, [2003] ECR I–8055. The state legislation would violate the state's duty of loyalty under the Treaty not to undermine effective enforcement of the EU competition laws. Moreover, a state-organized cartel with principal sales and thus principal effects in other member states would violate free movement principles of the Treaty. See E. Fox, What if *Parker v. Brown* were Italian?, Chapter 19 in 2003 Fordham Corporate Law Institute, International Antitrust Law & Policy (B. Hawk ed., 2004.)

6. The questions above suggest a dilemma in the globalized world. Cartels impose costs on others. (Negative externalities.) One solution is to forbid the conduct; i.e., to forbid state cartels that target or perhaps seriously affect commerce outside of that state. Another approach is for a community to examine the program more closely and to consider whether, despite its harms, the conduct or the freedom to engage in it has outbalancing benefits for the

community (jobs; sovereign rights of states). But what happens when virtually all of the costs are imposed on outsiders while all of the benefits are reaped by insiders? Would California have adopted the raisin cartel if it had to pay the costs? Can "state action" shield *all* state anticompetitive action no matter how large the externalities? Should a state (nation) be required to justify its restraint by identifying a legitimate, non-parochial state interest, and even then by applying a rule of proportionality (as in the EU internal market)? See Peter Oliver, Free Movement of Goods in the European Community, Chapters 6–8 (5th ed. 2010).

While the GATT/WTO goes part of the way to prohibit certain nation state import and export cartels, it does not tackle the problem of *Parker v. Brown* in a global economy.

2. POLITICAL ACTION

Cartel members and other antitrust defendants typically raise a companion claim to the state action defense. They claim that competitors' joint lobbying of legislators, trade associations' efforts to influence regulators, and other efforts to gain government protection from competition are protected political action. Where successful, such petitioning can lead to governmental restraints of trade more effective than private cartels. Defendants assert that their activity was political and, thus, that they were engaged in constitutionally protected political action rather than a prohibited restraint of trade. As we shall see, such claims have found a large measure of success.

In the 1950s, competition from truckers in the business of long-distance freight hauling threatened the major eastern railroads. The railroads banded together under the aegis of their trade association, the Eastern Railroad Presidents Conference, to encourage the passage of state laws that would limit the weight of trucks on the roads and that would tax heavy trucks. The conference enlisted a public relations firm to conduct a "dirty" campaign meant to foster public distrust of truckers. The railroads persuaded the Governor of Pennsylvania to veto a bill that would have allowed truckers in Pennsylvania to carry heavier loads.

The truckers sued the railroads for an antitrust conspiracy. The truckers won in the district court, and the railroads appealed.

EASTERN RAILROAD PRESIDENTS CONFERENCE v. NOERR MOTOR FREIGHT

365 U.S. 127 (1961).

JUSTICE BLACK: ... [T]he Sherman Act does not prohibit two or more persons from associating together in an attempt to persuade the legislature or the executive to take particular action with respect to a law that would produce a restraint or a monopoly. Although such associations could perhaps, through a process of expansive construction, be brought within the general proscription of "combination[s] ... in restraint of trade," they bear very little if any resemblance to the combinations normally held violative of the Sherman Act, combinations ordinarily characterized by an express or implied agreement or understanding that the participants will jointly give up their trade freedom, or help one another to take away the trade freedom of others through the use of such devices as price-fixing agreements, boycotts, market-division agreements, and other similar arrangements. This essential dissimilarity between an agreement jointly to seek legislation or law enforcement and the agreements traditionally condemned by § 1 of the Act, even if not itself conclusive on the question of the applicability of the Act, does constitute a warning against treating the defendants' conduct as though it amounted to a common-law trade restraint. And we do think that the question is conclusively settled, against the application of the Act, when this factor of essential dissimilarity is considered along with the other difficulties that would be presented by a holding that the Sherman Act forbids associations for the purpose of influencing the passage or enforcement of laws.

In the first place, such a holding would substantially impair the power of government to take actions through its legislature and executive that operate to restrain trade. In a representative democracy such as this, these branches of government act on behalf of the people and, to a very large extent, the whole concept of representation depends upon the ability of the people to make their wishes known to their representatives. To hold that the government retains the power to act in this representative capacity and yet hold, at the same time, that the people cannot freely inform the government of their wishes would impute to the Sherman Act a purpose to regulate, not business activity, but political activity, a purpose which would have no basis whatever in the legislative history of that Act. Secondly, and of at least equal significance, such a construction of the Sherman Act would raise important constitutional questions. The right of petition is one of the freedoms protected by the Bill of Rights, and we cannot, of course, lightly impute to Congress an intent to invade these freedoms. Indeed, such an imputation would be particularly unjustified in this case in view of all the countervailing considerations enumerated above. For these reasons, we think it clear that the Sherman Act does not apply to the activities of the railroads at least insofar as those activities comprised mere solicitation of governmental action with respect to the passage and enforcement of laws. We are thus called upon to consider whether the courts below were correct in holding that, notwithstanding this principle, the Act was violated here because of the presence in the railroads' publicity campaign of additional factors sufficient to take the case out of the area in which the principle is controlling.

The first such factor relied upon was the fact, established by the finding of the District Court, that the railroads' sole purpose in seeking to influence the passage and enforcement of laws was to destroy the truckers as competitors for the long-distance freight business. But we do not see how this fact, even if adequately supported in the record, could transform conduct otherwise lawful into a violation of the Sherman Act. All of the considerations that have led us to the conclusion that the Act does not apply to mere group solicitation of governmental action are equally applicable in spite of the addition of this factor. The right of the people to inform their representatives in government of their desires with respect to the passage or enforcement of laws cannot properly be made to depend upon their intent in doing so. It is neither unusual nor illegal for people to seek action on laws in the hope that they may bring about an advantage to themselves and a disadvantage to their competitors.... Indeed, it is quite probably people with just such a hope of personal advantage who provide much of the information upon which governments must act. A construction of the Sherman Act that would disqualify people from taking a public position on matters in which they are financially interested would thus deprive the government of a valuable source of information and, at the same time, deprive the people of their right to petition in the very instances in which that right may be of the most importance to them. We reject such a construction of the Act .....

QUESTIONS AND COMMENTS

1. In *United Mine Workers of America v. Pennington,* 381 U.S. 657 (1965), small coal producers sued large coal mine owners and union officials for having combined to persuade the Secretary of Labor to raise the minimum wage for coal miners, thus disproportionately raising the costs of the small coal producers, whose mining practices were more labor intensive. The Supreme Court extended *Noerr* to attempts to influence the executive branch. The now widely known *Noerr–Pennington* doctrine emerged.

2. Sometimes competitors *appear* to be petitioning government but they are actually acting to harm competition without regard to a favorable government response. Such was the case in *California Motor Transport Company v. Trucking Unlimited,* 404 U.S. 508 (1972). The defendant, California Motor Transport, automatically opposed every competitor's application for a license, knowing and intending that the mere opposition would impose costs on the competitors that would chill the application process. The court denied immunity to California Motor Transport. The case established the "sham" exception to the *Noerr–Pennington* doctrine.

3. In *California Motor Transport*, Justice Douglas distinguished the deception practiced in *Noerr* in the political arena from California Motor's baseless litigation: "... [U]nethical conduct in the setting of the adjudicatory process often results in sanctions.... There are many other forms of illegal and reprehensible practice which may corrupt the administrative or judicial processes and which may result in antitrust violations. Misrepresentations, condoned in the political arena, are not immunized when used in the adjudicatory process."

Does misrepresentation disqualify the use of the *Noerr* defense in non-judicial adjudicative proceedings as it does in judicial proceedings? The circuits are not uniform, but in general they disallow the *Noerr* defense in the case of a misrepresentation that "(1) was intentionally made, with knowledge of its falsity; and (2) was material, in the sense that it actually altered the outcome of the proceeding." *Mercatus Group, LLC v. Lake Forest Hosp.*, 641 F.3d 834, 843 (7th Cir. 2011). For contrasting interpretations of this standard, see also *Cheminor Drugs Ltd. v. Ethyl Corp.*, 168 F.3d 119 (3d Cir.1999); *In re Flonase Antitrust Litig.*, 795 F. Supp. 2d 300 (E.D. Pa. 2011); *Kottle v. Northwest Kidney Centers*, 146 F.3d 1056, 1063 (9th Cir. 1998).

Is *Noerr* applicable to standard-setting by a trade association whose model codes are routinely adopted by states? Can collaborators shield anti-competitive standard-setting by arguing that their conduct was equivalent to petitioning the states? *Allied Tube* addresses these questions.

ALLIED TUBE & CONDUIT CORP. v. INDIAN HEAD, INC.

486 U.S. 492 (1988).

JUSTICE BRENNAN: Petitioner contends that its efforts to affect the product standard-setting process of a private association are immune from antitrust liability under the *Noerr* doctrine primarily because the association's standards are widely adopted into law by state and local governments. The United States Court of Appeals for the Second Circuit held that *Noerr* immunity did not apply. We affirm.

The National Fire Protection Association (Association) is a private, voluntary organization with more than 31,500 individual and group members representing industry, labor, academia, insurers, organized medicine, firefighters, and government. The Association, among other things, publishes product standards and codes related to fire protection through a process known as "consensus standard making." One of the codes it publishes is the National Electrical Code, which establishes product and performance requirements for the design and installation of electrical wiring systems. Revised every three years, the National Electric Code (Code) is the most influential electrical code in the nation. A substantial number of state and local governments routinely adopt the Code into law with little or no change; private certification laboratories, such as Underwriters Laboratories, normally will not list and label an electrical product that does not meet Code standards; many underwriters will refuse to insure structures that are not built in conformity with the Code; and many electrical inspectors, contractors, and distributors will not use a product that falls outside the Code.

Among the electrical products covered by the Code is electrical conduit, the hollow tubing used as a raceway to carry electrical wires through the walls and floors of buildings. Throughout the relevant period, the Code permitted using electrical conduit made of steel, and almost all conduit sold was in fact steel conduit. Starting in 1980, respondent began to offer plastic conduit made of polyvinyl chloride. Respondent claims its plastic conduit offers significant competitive advantages over steel conduit, including pliability, lower installed cost, and lower susceptibility to short circuiting. In 1980, however, there was also a scientific basis for concern that, during fires in high-rise buildings, polyvinyl chloride conduit might burn and emit toxic fumes.

Respondent initiated a proposal to include polyvinyl chloride conduit as an approved type of electrical conduit in the 1981 edition of the Code. Following approval by one of the Association's professional panels, this proposal was scheduled for consideration at the 1980 annual meeting, where it could be adopted or rejected by a simple majority of the members present. Alarmed that, if approved, respondent's product might pose a competitive threat to steel conduit, petitioner, the nation's largest producer of steel conduit, met to plan strategy with, among others, members of the steel industry, other steel conduit manufacturers, and its independent sales agents. They collectively agreed to exclude respondent's product from the 1981 Code by packing the upcoming annual meeting with new Association members whose only function would be to vote against the polyvinyl chloride proposal.

Combined, the steel interests recruited 230 persons to join the Association and to attend the annual meeting to vote against the proposal. Petitioner alone recruited 155 persons—including employees, executives, sales agents, the agents' employees, employees from two divisions that did not sell electrical products, and the wife of a national sales director. Petitioner and the other steel interests also paid over $100,000 for the membership, registration, and attendance expenses of these voters. At the annual meeting, the steel group voters were instructed where to sit and how and when to vote by group leaders who used walkie-talkies and hand signals to facilitate communication. Few of the steel group voters had any of the technical documentation necessary to follow the meeting. None of them spoke at the meeting to give their reasons for opposing the proposal to approve polyvinyl chloride conduit. Nonetheless, with their solid vote in opposition, the proposal was rejected and returned to committee by a vote of 394 to 390. Respondent appealed the membership's vote to the Association's Board of Directors, but the Board denied the appeal on the ground that, although the Association's rules had been circumvented, they had not been violated.

In October 1981, respondent brought this suit in Federal District Court, alleging that petitioner and others had unreasonably restrained trade in the electrical conduit market in violation of § 1 of the Sherman Act . . . The jury . . . awarded respondent damages, to be trebled, of $3.8 million for lost profits resulting from the effect that excluding polyvinyl chloride conduit from the 1981 Code had of its own force in the marketplace. No damages were awarded for injuries stemming from the adoption of the 1981 Code by governmental entities.

The District Court then granted a judgment n.o.v. for petitioner, reasoning that *Noerr* immunity applied because the Association was "akin to a legislature" and because petitioner, "by the use of methods consistent with acceptable standards of political action, genuinely intended to influence the [Association] with respect to the National Electrical Code, and to thereby influence the various state and local legislative bodies which adopt the [Code]." The Court of Appeals reversed. . . .

Concerted efforts to restrain or monopolize trade by petitioning government officials are protected from antitrust liability under the doctrine established by *Noerr*. The scope of this protection depends, however, on the source, context, and nature of the anticompetitive restraint at issue . . . A publicity campaign directed at the general public, seeking legislation or executive action, enjoys antitrust immunity even when the campaign employs unethical and deceptive methods. But in less political arenas, unethical and deceptive practices can constitute abuses of administrative or judicial processes that may result in antitrust violations.

In this case, the restraint of trade on which liability was predicated was the Association's exclusion of respondent's product from the Code, and no damages were imposed for the incorporation of that Code by any government. The relevant context is thus the standard-setting process of a private association. Typically, private standard-setting associations, like the Association in this case, include members having horizontal and vertical business relations. There is no doubt that the members of such associations often have economic incentives to restrain competition and that the product standards set by such associations have a serious potential for anticompetitive harm. Agreement on a product standard is, after all, implicitly an agreement not to manufacture, distribute, or purchase certain types of products. Accordingly, private standard-setting associations have traditionally been objects of antitrust scrutiny. When, however, private associations promulgate safety standards based on the merits of objective expert judgments and through procedures that prevent the standard-setting process from being biased by members with economic interests in stifling product competition, those private standards can have significant procompetitive advantages. It is this potential for procompetitive benefits that has led most lower courts to apply rule of reason analysis to product standard-setting by private associations.

Given this context, petitioner does not enjoy the immunity accorded those who merely urge the government to restrain trade. We agree with the Court of Appeals that the Association cannot be treated as a "quasi-legislative" body simply because legislatures routinely adopt the Code the Association publishes. Whatever *de facto* authority the Association enjoys, no official authority has been conferred on it by any government, and the decisionmaking body of the Association is composed, at least in part, of persons with economic incentives to restrain trade. . . . [W]here, as here, the restraint is imposed by persons unaccountable to the public and without official authority, many of whom have personal financial interests in restraining competition, we have no difficulty concluding that the restraint has resulted from private action.

Noerr immunity might still apply, however, if, as petitioner argues, the exclusion of polyvinyl chloride conduit from the Code, and the effect that exclusion had of its own force in the marketplace, were incidental to a valid effort to influence governmental action. Petitioner notes that the lion's share of the anticompetitive effect in this case came from the predictable adoption of the Code into law by a large number of state and local governments. Indeed, petitioner argues that, because state and local governments rely so heavily on the Code and lack the resources or technical expertise to second-guess it, efforts to influence the Association's standard-setting process are the most effective means of influencing legislation regulating electrical conduit. This claim to *Noerr* immunity has some force. The effort to influence governmental action in this case certainly cannot be characterized as a sham given the actual adoption of the 1981 Code into a number of statutes and local ordinances. Nor can we quarrel with petitioner's contention that, given the widespread adoption of the Code into law, any effect the 1981 Code had in the marketplace of its own force was, in the main, incidental to petitioner's genuine effort to influence governmental action....

Nonetheless, the validity of petitioner's actions remains an issue. We cannot agree with petitioner's absolutist position that the *Noerr* doctrine immunizes every concerted effort that is genuinely intended to influence governmental action. If all such conduct were immunized then, for example, competitors would be free to enter into horizontal price agreements as long as they wished to propose that price as an appropriate level for governmental ratemaking or price supports. Horizontal conspiracies or boycotts designed to exact higher prices or other economic advantages from the government would be immunized on the ground that they are genuinely intended to influence the government to agree to the conspirators' terms. Firms could claim immunity for boycotts or horizontal output restrictions on the ground that they are intended to dramatize the plight of their industry and spur legislative action. Immunity might even be claimed for anticompetitive mergers on the theory that they give the merging corporations added political clout. Nor is it necessarily dispositive that packing the Association's meeting may have been the most effective means of securing government action, for one could imagine situations where the most effective means of influencing government officials is bribery, and we have never suggested that that kind of attempt to influence the government merits protection. We thus conclude that the *Noerr* immunity of anticompetitive activity intended to influence the government depends not only on its impact, but also on the context and nature of the activity.... * * *

... Although we do not here set forth the rules of antitrust liability governing the private standard-setting process, we hold that at least where, as here, an economically interested party exercises decision making authority in formulating a product standard for a private association that comprised market participants, that party enjoys no *Noerr* immunity from any antitrust liability flowing from the effect the standard has of its own force in the marketplace....

... What petitioner may not do (without exposing itself to possible antitrust liability for direct injuries) is bias the process by, as in this case, stacking the private standard-setting body with decisionmakers sharing their economic interest in restraining competition. . . .

Justice White, joined by Justice O'Connor, dissented. They would have applied *Noerr* immunity on grounds that petitioners' actions were a genuine attempt to influence governmental action; indeed it was a much more direct and focused attempt than in *Noerr* itself.

NOTE ON ***PROFESSIONAL REAL ESTATE INVESTORS v. COLUMBIA PICTURES,*** 508 U.S. 49 (1993)

Professional Real Estate Investors (PRE) operated resort hotels. PRE rented videodiscs to guests for use in videodisc players located in guests' rooms, and sought to develop a market for sale of videodisc players to other hotels. Columbia and other major motion picture studios held copyrights on motion pictures recorded on PRE's discs and licensed PRE and others to transmit these pictures to their hotel rooms. When Columbia and the other movie companies (collectively "Columbia") sued PRE for copyright infringement, PRE counterclaimed, alleging that the copyright action was a sham cloaking a conspiracy to monopolize and restrain trade in violation of the Sherman Act. The district court granted summary judgment to PRE on the copyright claim; that is, there was no infringement. The court of appeals affirmed the decision on the copyright and remanded the antitrust claim. On remand, the district court granted summary judgment to Columbia on PRE's antitrust claim. It found that Columbia had probable cause to bring the copyright claim and that the pursuit of litigation that is supported by probable cause and therefore is not baseless constitutes protected petitioning within the *Noerr* doctrine. Therefore Columbia's alleged intent to harm its competitors in providing movies to hotel rooms was irrelevant; even "bad" intent cannot turn a possibly meritorious litigation into a "sham." The appellate court affirmed. The Supreme Court, by Justice Thomas, affirmed.

The Court outlined a two part definition of "sham" litigation not entitled to *Noerr* immunity. The suit must be "objectively baseless in the sense that no reasonable litigant could realistically expect success on the merits"; and "the baseless suit conceals 'an attempt to interfere *directly* with the business relationships of a competitor,' [citing *Noerr*], through the 'use [of] the governmental *process*—as opposed to the *outcome* of the process ... as an anticompetitive weapon.' "

Justice Stevens, with whom Justice O'Connor joined, concurred, stating:

> While I agree with the Court's disposition of this case and with its holding "that an objectively reasonable effort to litigate cannot be sham regardless of subjective intent," I write separately to disassociate myself from some of the unnecessarily broad dicta in the Court's opinion. Specifically, I disagree with the Court's equation of "objectively baseless"

with the answer to the question whether any "reasonable litigant could realistically expect success on the merits." There might well be lawsuits that fit the latter definition but can be shown to be objectively unreasonable, and thus shams. It might not be objectively reasonable to bring a lawsuit just because some form of success on the merits—no matter how insignificant—could be expected. With that possibility in mind, the Court should avoid an unnecessarily broad holding that it might regret when confronted with a more complicated case.

Which is the better test?

Some years earlier, Otter Tail, a monopoly generator and reseller of electric energy, brought lawsuits against any town in its distribution area that proposed to build its own electricity distribution facilities, knowing that the town could not float bonds for the project if any suit was pending against it that could impair the value of the bonds. See *Otter Tail Power Co. v. United States*, 410 U.S. 366, 380 (1973). Otter Tail had investigated each such town and brought the "best" suit it could. The suits, as planned, deterred the towns' entry into distribution of electricity. Perhaps Otter Tail could realistically have expected a favorable outcome in some of the suits. Was all of the litigation a sham? Might Otter Tail be disentitled to *Noerr* immunity for its litigation strategy regardless of whether the lawsuits were without objective base? Or would such a rule fall into the subjectivity trap that the Court thinks is so important to avoid?

NOTE ON STATE OF MISSOURI v. NATIONAL ORGANIZATION FOR WOMEN

620 F.2d 1301 (8th Cir.1980), *cert. denied*,
449 U.S. 842 (1980)

In *Noerr*, *Pennington*, and *Indian Head*, defendants sought government action in order to hurt competitors. In *Missouri v. NOW*, defendants took concerted action that would hurt a state's economy to get government action. The National Organization For Women (NOW) invited would-be convention goers to boycott states that had not ratified the Equal Rights Amendment. NOW hoped that the resulting economic pressure on those states would convince their legislatures to ratify the ERA. Is such a political boycott covered by the antitrust laws? Should it be? The court held for NOW, asserting that resort to "a boycott in a non-competitive political arena for the purpose of influencing legislation is not proscribed by the Sherman Act." 620 F.2d 1301 at 1315. The court added in a footnote:

> The Sherman Act may apply in some situations to noncommercial and non-economic boycotts. However, we do not rest our decision in this case upon the basis that the boycott was noncommercial and non-economic. Our decision is based upon the right to use political activities to petition the government, as was the underlying factor in *Noerr*. Id. at n. 16.

Judge Gibson dissented. First, he noted, the court did not establish that NOW was exercising a protected constitutional right; the court found only that constitutionally protected interests were implicated. Second, Judge Gibson invoked the presumption against implied exclusions from the antitrust laws. Third:

> NOW may not have economic interests at stake in this controversy, but the boycott severely affects the competitive posture of Missouri convention interests and the overall economic welfare of Missouri residents. Thus, the technical characterization of the boycott as noncommercial and noneconomic is misleading and actually erroneous in important respects. The anticompetitive economic and commercial effects of the boycott on Missouri's legitimate business interests and welfare are identical, regardless of whether the motivation for the boycott is political or economic. The majority thus places the court's imprimatur upon a boycott with potentially severe economic and commercial consequences simply on the basis of the boycott's motivation. The precedential support for drawing this distinction is tenuous at best. Id. at 1322–23.

Who is right? Does *Indian Head* (see p. 166 supra) provide an answer? At what point, if any, does economic activity for political purposes become constitutionally protected, rather than being activity that merely implicates constitutional interests?

NOTE ON NAACP v. CLAIBORNE HARDWARE CO.

458 U.S. 886 (1982)

In March 1966, black citizens of Claiborne County, Mississippi, gave white elected officials a list of demands aimed at achieving racial equality. The white officials' response was unsatisfactory. At a meeting of the local NAACP, several hundred black citizens voted to boycott the white merchants in town.

In April 1969 when the boycott was still in effect, Charles Evers, Field Secretary for the NAACP, gave a speech in which he said: "If we catch any of you going in any ... racist stores, we're going to break your damn neck." Generally, however, the boycott was peaceful and orderly. Names of boycott violators were read aloud at church meetings and were published in a black newspaper. Violators were demeaned and ostracized. Four incidents of violence were reported, including shots fired at a house and a brick thrown through a windshield. The boycott caused substantial business to be diverted from the area's white merchants to its black merchants and to merchants outside of the area. The white merchants sued the NAACP for tortious conduct and a violation of Mississippi's antitrust law.

The lower courts found liability for violation of a Mississippi statute outlawing threats of bodily harm and coercion. They held that, since force and violence were involved, the First Amendment afforded no protection at all. Reversing, the Supreme Court said:

> We hold that the nonviolent elements of petitioners' activities are entitled to the protection of the First Amendment .....
>
> The First Amendment does not protect violence.... No federal rule of law restricts a State from imposing tort liability for business losses that are caused by violence and by threats of violence. When such conduct

occurs in the context of constitutionally protected activity, however, "precision of regulation" is demanded....

... Petitioners withheld their patronage from the white establishment of Claiborne County to challenge a political and economic system that had denied them the basic rights of dignity and equality that this country had fought a Civil War to secure. While the State legitimately may impose damages for the consequences of violent conduct, it may not award damages for the consequences of nonviolent protected activity. Only those losses proximately caused by unlawful conduct may be recovered.

The First Amendment similarly restricts the ability of the State to impose liability on an individual solely because of his association with another. *Id.* at 915–19 (1982).

Does *Claiborne* answer the questions the *NOW* court thought were still open? Is *Allied Tube/Indian Head* consistent with *Claiborne?* Is it possible to reconcile these cases by asking whether the boycotters had a constitutional right to engage in the joint action they undertook? Did NOW have a constitutional right to boycott states not ratifying the ERA? Did steel conduit makers have a constitutional right to pack the meeting of the standard setting association?

FTC v. SUPERIOR COURT TRIAL LAWYERS ASSOCIATION

493 U.S. 411 (1990) (alleged justifications).

JUSTICE STEVENS: [See facts above, at [p. 102.] The group of lawyers in Washington, D.C., who regularly accepted court appointments to represent criminal defendants ("CJA regulars") engaged in a boycott; they agreed with one another not to accept any new cases until their fees ($30 per hour for court time, $20 per hour for out-of-court time) were raised. The authority to raise the fees resided in the D.C. Council. The boycott created a crisis in the D.C. justice system. The D.C. Council raised the fees, and the lawyers again accepted their usual appointments. The FTC found a violation of Section 5 of the Federal Trade Commission Act, which prohibits unfair methods of competition (roughly commensurate with anticompetitive agreements or conduct under the Sherman Act). The appellate court reversed and remanded on grounds that the lawyers had engaged in an expressive boycott and the FTC should have examined whether the lawyers had market power and should have dismissed the case if the lawyers did not have market power so as not to intrude unnecessarily on First Amendment freedoms. The Supreme Court reversed, holding that the boycott, which was also a price-fixing cartel, was illegal per se. It then turned to the *Noerr* and free speech defenses.]

... Respondents' agreement is not outside the coverage of the Sherman Act simply because its objective was the enactment of favorable legislation.

Our decision in *Noerr* in no way detracts from this conclusion. In *Noerr*, we "considered whether the Sherman Act prohibited a publicity campaign waged by railroads" and "designed to foster the adoption of laws destructive of the trucking business, to create an atmosphere of distaste for truckers among the general public, and to impair the relationships existing between truckers and their customers." *Claiborne Hardware*, 458 U.S., at 913. Interpreting the Sherman Act in the light of the First Amendment's Petition Clause, the Court noted that "at least insofar as the railroads' campaign was directed toward obtaining governmental action, its legality was not at all affected by any anticompetitive purpose it may have had." 365 U.S., at 139–140.

It of course remains true that "no violation of the Act can be predicated upon mere attempts to influence the passage or enforcement of laws," id., at 135, even if the defendants' sole purpose is to impose a restraint upon the trade of their competitors, id., at 138–140. But in the *Noerr* case the alleged restraint of trade was the intended *consequence* of public action; in this case the boycott was the means by which respondents sought to obtain favorable legislation. The restraint of trade that was implemented while the boycott lasted would have had precisely the same anticompetitive consequences during that period even if no legislation had been enacted. In *Noerr*, the desired legislation would have created the restraint on the truckers' competition; in this case the emergency legislative response to the boycott put an end to the restraint.

Indeed, respondents' theory of *Noerr* was largely disposed of by our opinion in *Allied Tube & Conduit Corp. v. Indian Head Inc.*, 486 U.S. 492 (1988). We held that the *Noerr* doctrine does not extend to "every concerted effort that is genuinely intended to influence governmental action." 486 U.S., at 503. . . .

The lawyers' association argues that if its conduct would otherwise be prohibited by the Sherman Act and the Federal Trade Act, it is nonetheless protected by the First Amendment rights recognized in *NAACP v. Claiborne Hardware*, 458 U.S. 886 (1982). That case arose after black citizens boycotted white merchants in Claiborne County, Miss. The white merchants sued under state law to recover losses from the boycott. We found that the "right of the States to regulate economic activity could not justify a complete prohibition against a nonviolent, politically motivated boycott designed to force governmental and economic change and to effectuate rights guaranteed by the Constitution itself." Id., at 914. We accordingly held that "the nonviolent elements of petitioners' activities are entitled to the protection of the First Amendment." Id., at 915.

. . . It is, of course, clear that the association's efforts to publicize the boycott, to explain the merits of its cause, and to lobby District officials to enact favorable legislation—like similar activities in *Claiborne Hardware*—were activities that were fully protected by the First Amendment. But nothing in the FTC's order would curtail such activities, and nothing in the FTC's reasoning condemned any of those activities.

The activity that the FTC order prohibits is a concerted refusal by CJA lawyers to accept any further assignments until they receive an increase in their compensation; the undenied objective of their boycott was an economic advantage for those who agreed to participate. It is true that the *Claiborne Hardware* case also involved a boycott. That boycott, however, differs in a decisive respect. Those who joined the Claiborne Hardware boycott sought no special advantage for themselves....

The same cannot be said of attorney's fees. As we recently pointed out, our reasoning in *Claiborne Hardware* is not applicable to a boycott conducted by business competitors who "stand to profit financially from a lessening of competition in the boycotted market." *Allied Tube Corp. v. Indian Head, supra*, at 508....

Respondents' concerted action in refusing to accept further CJA assignments until their fees were increased was thus a plain violation of the antitrust laws. The exceptions derived from *Noerr* and *Claiborne Hardware* have no application to respondents' boycott. For these reasons we reject the arguments made by respondents in the cross-petition.

The Court of Appeals, however, crafted a new exception to the per se rules, and it is this exception which provoked the FTC's petition to this Court. The Court of Appeals derived its exception from *United States v. O'Brien*, 391 U.S. 367 (1968). In that case O'Brien had burned his Selective Service registration certificate on the steps of the South Boston Courthouse. He did so before a sizable crowd and with the purpose of advocating his antiwar beliefs. We affirmed his conviction. We held that the governmental interest in regulating the "nonspeech element" of his conduct adequately justified the incidental restriction on First Amendment freedoms.[13] Specifically, we concluded that the statute's incidental restriction on O'Brien's freedom of expression was no greater than necessary to further the Government's interest in requiring registrants to have valid certificates continually available.

However, the Court of Appeals held that, in light of *O'Brien*, the expressive component of respondents' boycott compelled courts to apply the antitrust laws "prudently and with sensitivity," with a "special solicitude for the First Amendment rights" of respondents. The Court of Appeals concluded that the governmental interest in prohibiting boycotts is not sufficient to justify a restriction on the communicative element of the boycott unless the FTC can prove, and not merely presume, that the boycotters have market power. Because the Court of Appeals imposed this special requirement upon the Government, it ruled that per se antitrust analysis was inapplicable to boycotts having an expressive component.

13. "This Court has held that when 'speech' and 'nonspeech' elements are combined in the same course of conduct, a sufficiently important governmental interest in regulating the nonspeech element can justify incidental limitations on First Amendment freedoms.... [We] think it clear that a government regulation is sufficiently justified if it is within the constitutional power of the Government; if it furthers an important or substantial governmental interest; if the governmental interest is unrelated to the suppression of free expression; and if the incidental restriction on alleged First Amendment freedoms is no greater than is essential to the furtherance of that interest." 391 U.S., at 376–377.

There are at least two critical flaws in the Court of Appeals' antitrust analysis: it exaggerates the significance of the expressive component in respondents' boycott and it denigrates the importance of the rule of law that respondents violated. Implicit in the conclusion of the Court of Appeals are unstated assumptions that most economic boycotts do not have an expressive component, and that the categorical prohibitions against price fixing and boycotts are merely rules of "administrative convenience" that do not serve any substantial governmental interest unless the price-fixing competitors actually possess market power.

It would not much matter to the outcome of this case if these flawed assumptions were sound. *O'Brien* would offer respondents no protection even if their boycott were uniquely expressive and even if the purpose of the per se rules were purely that of administrative efficiency. We have recognized that the Government's interest in adhering to a uniform rule may sometimes satisfy the *O'Brien* test even if making an exception to the rule in a particular case might cause no serious damage.... The administrative efficiency interests in antitrust regulation are unusually compelling....

In any event, however, we cannot accept the Court of Appeals' characterization of this boycott or the antitrust laws. Every concerted refusal to do business with a potential customer or supplier has an expressive component. At one level, the competitors must exchange their views about their objectives and the means of obtaining them. The most blatant, naked price-fixing agreement is a product of communication, but that is surely not a reason for viewing it with special solicitude. At another level, after the terms of the boycotters' demands have been agreed upon, they must be communicated to its target: "we will not do business until you do what we ask." That expressive component of the boycott conducted by these respondents is surely not unique. On the contrary, it is the hallmark of every effective boycott.

At a third level, the boycotters may communicate with third parties to enlist public support for their objectives; to the extent that the boycott is newsworthy, it will facilitate the expression of the boycotters' ideas. But this level of expression is not an element of the boycott. Publicity may be generated by any other activity that is sufficiently newsworthy. Some activities, including the boycott here, may be newsworthy precisely for the reasons that they are prohibited: the harms they produce are matters of public concern. Certainly that is no reason for removing the prohibition.

In sum, there is thus nothing unique about the "expressive component" of respondents' boycott. A rule that requires courts to apply the antitrust laws "prudently and with sensitivity" whenever an economic boycott has an "expressive component" would create a gaping hole in the fabric of those laws. Respondents' boycott thus has no special characteristics meriting an exemption from the per se rules of antitrust law.

Justices Blackmun, Brennan and Marshall dissented in part. They would have required rule of reason analysis in deference to the expressive nature of the boycott. They believed that success of the boycott could have been attributable to "persuasiveness of the message rather than any coercive economic force." Justice Blackmun stressed that the boycotters could not have coerced the District. They had no market power. The District could have broken the boycott at will by requiring members of the bar—including the members of the SCTLA—to represent indigent defendants pro bono.

QUESTIONS AND COMMENTS

1. Was the Court too dismissive of the argument that this was a uniquely expressive boycott (to improve the disastrous quality of legal representation of indigent defendants) and that the governmental interest in regulating the non-expressive aspects (the interest in keeping CJA lawyers at work in the short term) was not sufficient to condemn the expressive aspects? Would recognition of a Constitutional defense have created a gaping hole in the fabric of antitrust?

2. Do *Superior Court Trial Lawyers* and *Allied Tube/Indian Head* raise doubt about the soundness of *Missouri v. NOW*? Are grass roots consumer boycotts permissible, and can a principled distinction be made between them and political boycotts by traders who stand to profit from a lessening of competition?

3. The *Noerr* doctrine is founded upon the right to petition *U.S.* governments. What if firms petition foreign governments to restrain U.S. trade? The Justice Department and Federal Trade Commission announced, in their 1995 International Guidelines, that they will apply the doctrine to the petitioning of foreign governments. *Id.*, 3.34, Appendix F.

4. In the 1970s Bechtel Corporation, along with other U.S. construction firms, sought to preserve their important business relationships with the Arab League countries by agreeing with the Arab League countries to boycott (e.g., not to choose as subcontractors) all friends of Israel. Was this boycott illegal? If otherwise illegal, was it protected by *Noerr* immunity? by *Claiborne* political action immunity? See *United States v. Bechtel Corp.*, 1979–1 Trade Cas. (CCH) ¶ 62,429 (N.D.Cal.1979).

G. THE INTERNATIONAL DIMENSION

1. EXTRATERRITORIAL REACH AND ENFORCEMENT

The Sherman Act expressly applies to restraints of trade or commerce "among the several States or with foreign nations."

For many years it was highly controversial as to whether national law could reach foreign persons conspiring in foreign nations to fix prices on goods bound for (for example) the United States. In *United States v.*

Aluminum Co. of America (Alcoa), 148 F.2d 416 (2d Cir.1945), the United States pioneered the "effects doctrine," which holds that U.S. antitrust laws apply to foreign actors who conspire abroad when the actors intend to and do affect U.S. commerce. The rule has been softened by a doctrine of comity, which holds that a nation with lesser interests at stake should normally defer to a nation with greater interests at stake in the event of conflict. See *Timberlane Lumber Co. v. Bank of America*, 549 F.2d 597 (9th Cir. 1976).

In the 1940s, nations widely disagreed on the value of competition as opposed to business cooperation, making the *Alcoa* rule a sensitive one. Why should, for example, British firms be caught in the web of U.S. antitrust when the acts they did on British soil were perfectly legal under British law?

But by the late twentieth century, things had changed. Not only was the competition ethic spreading but foreign cartels, including cartels emanating from the United States, were threatening Europe. In 1988 in the European *Wood Pulp* cartel case, *Å. Åhlström Osakeyhtiö & Ors v. Commission*, Cases C–89, 104, 114, 116–117, 125–129/85 [1988] ECR 5193, the European Court of Justice held that the Treaty of Rome applied to offshore agreements (the alleged cartelists being North American and Scandinavian) as long as the concertation was "implemented" in the European Union.

In *Hartford Fire Ins. Co. v. California,* 509 U.S. 764 (1993), the U.S. Supreme Court reaffirmed the effects test for the United States: "[I]t is well established by now that the Sherman Act applies to foreign conduct that was meant to produce and did in fact produce some substantial effect in the United States." *Id.* at 796.

Thus, the United States and the European Union are in relative agreement (with some nuanced differences) that they can reach world or offshore cartels that harm their citizens. Since *Wood pulp,* the cries of impermissible extraterritoriality for cartels with domestic effect have been muted. The policy conversations have turned to enforcement; typically, issues of enforcement of national law against international cartels.

For private parties injured by a cartel and seeking recompense, the United States is the most attractive forum in the world, with class actions, treble damages, broad discovery, and lawyers' contingent fees. Can *everyone* injured directly by a cartel that harms the U.S. sue under U.S. law? This question was raised by cartel members sued by non-U.S. plaintiffs who bought goods at foreign locations at prices directly inflated by price fixing conspiracies in world markets that importantly included the United States.

Defendants sought to dismiss these lawsuits on grounds that their (acknowledged) conspiracy was beyond the reach of the U.S. antitrust law. They relied on the Foreign Trade Antitrust Improvement Act of 1982 (FTAIA).

The FTAIA cut back (or clarified) the reach of the Sherman Act in matters involving foreign commerce, principally to protect U.S. sellers from Sherman Act challenges for their activity abroad. The statute, first, carves out import commerce—which remains subject to preexisting rules. Acts entailing sufficiently direct, substantial and foreseeable harms to U.S. commerce are within the reach of the U.S. law. As to all other commerce with foreign nations, the FTAIA provides, in relevant part, that the Sherman Act shall not apply unless:

> "(1) such conduct has a direct, substantial and reasonably foreseeable effect—
>
> (A) on [domestic or (B) export] commerce . . . [and]
>
> (2) such effect gives rise to a claim under [the Sherman Act], other than this section."

There was a notorious worldwide vitamin cartel, leading to convictions and jail terms as a result of prosecutions in the United States and elsewhere. Vitamin distributors from Ecuador, Panama, the Ukraine, and Australia who bought price-fixed vitamins outside of the United States sued for treble damages under the Sherman Act. Defendants, principally from Europe and Japan and including U.S. subsidiaries of Japanese firms, moved to dismiss. They claimed that plaintiffs failed to satisfy FTAIA paragraph (2) [see above], on grounds that the U.S. effects of the vitamins cartel did not give rise to the particular plaintiffs' claims.

The plaintiffs disputed the interpretation of paragraph (2). They argued that paragraph (2) simply means that *any* U.S. effect (e.g., an effect on jobs) is not enough to convey Sherman Act jurisdiction. Rather, the effect must be one proscribed by a section of the Sherman Act other than the FTAIA. Plaintiffs further argued that the FTAIA reads on the reach of the Sherman Act, not who sues to enforce it—which could be a question of standing or comity. The Act says nothing about who can sue to enforce the Sherman Act against conspiracies that harm the U.S.

In setting about to analyze the case, the Supreme Court first assumed that "the adverse foreign effect [in the case before it] was independent of any adverse domestic effect." (Nonetheless it left this factual question open; it turned out not to be the case that the two effects were independent.) The Court then interpreted the FTAIA, with respect to activity other than imports, as excluding from the reach of the Sherman Act all foreign commerce except that which the FTAIA expressly allows to be caught by the Sherman Act. It then characterized the FTAIA as a sweeping "exception" from the general rule that the Sherman Act does not reach U.S. foreign commerce. It asked whether plaintiffs' case came within the exception and held it did not for two reasons. The first reason focused on the language and history of the FTAIA; the Court found the language ambiguous and construed paragraph (2) in the spirit of a legislative attempt to cut back the law. The Court declared that "such effect" means: the effect on U.S. commerce must give rise to the particular plaintiff's claim. The second reason—what good policy requires—is presented below.

F. HOFFMANN-LA ROCHE v. EMPAGRAN S.A.

542 U.S. 155 (2004).

JUSTICE BREYER: * * * We turn now to the basic question presented, that of the exception's application. Because the underlying antitrust action is complex, potentially raising questions not directly at issue here, we reemphasize that we base our decision upon the following: The price-fixing conduct significantly and adversely affects both customers outside the United States and customers within the United States, but the adverse foreign effect is independent of any adverse domestic effect. In these circumstances, we find that the FTAIA exception does not apply (and thus the Sherman Act does not apply) for two main reasons.

First, this Court ordinarily construes ambiguous statutes to avoid unreasonable interference with the sovereign authority of other nations.... This rule of construction reflects principles of customary international law—law that (we must assume) Congress ordinarily seeks to follow....

This rule of statutory construction cautions courts to assume that legislators take account of the legitimate sovereign interests of other nations when they write American laws. It thereby helps the potentially conflicting laws of different nations work together in harmony—a harmony particularly needed in today's highly interdependent commercial world.

No one denies that America's antitrust laws, when applied to foreign conduct, can interfere with a foreign nation's ability independently to regulate its own commercial affairs. But our courts have long held that application of our antitrust laws to foreign anticompetitive conduct is nonetheless reasonable, and hence consistent with principles of prescriptive comity, insofar as they reflect a legislative effort to redress *domestic* antitrust injury that foreign anticompetitive conduct has caused. See *United States* v. *Aluminum Co. of America*, 148 F. 2d 416, 443–444 (CA2 1945) (L. Hand, J.)....

But why is it reasonable to apply those laws to foreign conduct *insofar as that conduct causes independent foreign harm and that foreign harm alone gives rise to the plaintiff's claim?* Like the former case, application of those laws creates a serious risk of interference with a foreign nation's ability independently to regulate its own commercial affairs. But, unlike the former case, the justification for that interference seems insubstantial. See Restatement [(Third) of Foreign Relations Law of the United States (1986)] 403(2) (determining reasonableness on basis of such factors as connections with regulating nation, harm to that nation's interests, extent to which other nations regulate, and the potential for conflict). Why should American law supplant, for example, Canada's or Great Britain's or Japan's own determination about how best to protect Canadian or

British or Japanese customers from anticompetitive conduct engaged in significant part by Canadian or British or Japanese or other foreign companies?

We recognize that principles of comity provide Congress greater leeway when it seeks to control through legislation the actions of *American* companies, see Restatement § 402; and some of the anticompetitive price-fixing conduct alleged here took place in *America*. But the higher foreign prices of which the foreign plaintiffs here complain are not the consequence of any domestic anticompetitive conduct *that Congress sought to forbid*, for Congress did not seek to forbid any such conduct insofar as it is here relevant, *i.e.*, insofar as it is intertwined with foreign conduct that causes independent foreign harm. Rather Congress sought to *release* domestic (and foreign) anticompetitive conduct from Sherman Act constraints when that conduct causes foreign harm. Congress, of course, did make an exception where that conduct also causes domestic harm. See House Report 13 (concerns about American firms' participation in international cartels addressed through "domestic injury" exception). But any independent domestic harm the foreign conduct causes here has, by definition, little or nothing to do with the matter.

We thus repeat the basic question: Why is it reasonable to apply this law to conduct that is significantly foreign *insofar as that conduct causes independent foreign harm and that foreign harm alone gives rise to the plaintiff's claim?* We can find no good answer to the question.

The Areeda and Hovenkamp treatise notes that under the Court of Appeals' interpretation of the statute

> "a Malaysian customer could ... maintain an action under United States law in a United States court against its own Malaysian supplier, another cartel member, simply by noting that unnamed third parties injured [in the United States] by the American [cartel member's] conduct would also have a cause of action. Effectively, the United States courts would provide worldwide subject matter jurisdiction to any foreign suitor wishing to sue its own local supplier, but unhappy with its own sovereign's provisions for private antitrust enforcement, provided that a different plaintiff had a cause of action against a different firm for injuries that were within U.S. [other-than-import] commerce. It does not seem excessively rigid to infer that Congress would not have intended that result." P. Areeda & H. Hovenkamp, Antitrust Law ¶ 273, pp. 51–52 (Supp. 2003).

We agree with the comment. We can find no convincing justification for the extension of the Sherman Act's scope that it describes.

Respondents reply that many nations have adopted antitrust laws similar to our own, to the point where the practical likelihood of interference with the relevant interests of other nations is minimal. Leaving price fixing to the side, however, this Court has found to the contrary. See, *e.g.*, *Hartford Fire*, 509 U. S. at 797–799 (noting that the alleged conduct in the London reinsurance market, while illegal under United States antitrust laws, was assumed to be perfectly consistent with British law and policy); see also, *e.g.*, 2 W. Fugate, Foreign Commerce and the Antitrust Laws § 16.6 (5th ed. 1996) (noting differences between European Union and United States law on vertical restraints).

Regardless, even where nations agree about primary conduct, say price fixing, they disagree dramatically about appropriate remedies. The application, for example, of American private treble-damages remedies to anticompetitive conduct taking place abroad has generated considerable controversy.... And several foreign nations have filed briefs here arguing that to apply our remedies would unjustifiably permit their citizens to bypass their own less generous remedial schemes, thereby upsetting a balance of competing considerations that their own domestic antitrust laws embody. *E.g.*, Brief for Federal Republic of Germany et al. as *Amici Curiae* 2 (setting forth German interest "in seeing that German companies are not subject to the extraterritorial reach of the United States' antitrust laws by private foreign plaintiffs—whose injuries were sustained in transactions entirely outside United States commerce—seeking treble damages in private lawsuits against German companies"); Brief for Government of Canada as *Amicus Curiae* 14 ("treble damages remedy would supersede" Canada's "national policy decision"); Brief for Government of Japan as *Amicus Curiae* 10 (finding "particularly troublesome" the potential "interfere[nce] with Japanese governmental regulation of the Japanese market").

These briefs add that a decision permitting independently injured foreign plaintiffs to pursue private treble-damages remedies would undermine foreign nations' own antitrust enforcement policies by diminishing foreign firms' incentive to cooperate with antitrust authorities in return for prosecutorial amnesty....

Respondents alternatively argue that comity does not demand an interpretation of the FTAIA that would exclude independent foreign injury cases *across the board*. Rather, courts can take (and sometimes have taken) account of comity considerations case by case, abstaining where comity considerations so dictate....

In our view, however, this approach is too complex to prove workable. The Sherman Act covers many different kinds of anticompetitive agreements. Courts would have to examine how foreign law, compared with American law, treats not only price fixing but also, say, information-sharing agreements, patent-licensing price conditions, territorial product resale limitations, and various forms of joint venture, in respect to both primary conduct and remedy. The legally and economically technical nature of that enterprise means lengthier proceedings, appeals, and more proceedings—to the point where procedural costs and delays could themselves threaten interference with a foreign nation's ability to maintain the integrity of its own antitrust enforcement system. Even in this relatively simple price-fixing case, for example, competing briefs tell us (1) that potential treble-damage liability would help enforce widespread anti-price-fixing norms (through added deterrence) and (2) the opposite, namely that such liability would hinder antitrust enforcement (by reducing incentives to enter amnesty programs).... How could a court seriously interested in resolving so empirical a matter—a matter potentially related to impact on foreign interests—do so simply and expeditiously?

We conclude that principles of prescriptive comity counsel against the Court of Appeals' interpretation of the FTAIA. Where foreign anticompetitive conduct plays a significant role and where foreign injury is independent of domestic effects, Congress might have hoped that America's antitrust laws, so fundamental a component of our own economic system, would commend themselves to other nations as well. But, if America's antitrust policies could not win their own way in the international marketplace for such ideas, Congress, we must assume, would not have tried to impose them, in an act of legal imperialism, through legislative fiat. * * *

QUESTIONS AND COMMENTS

1. The Court remanded the case for a determination 1) whether plaintiffs had preserved their claim that the vitamin conspiracy's domestic effects were linked to the foreign price rise in that, without higher prices in the United States, defendants could not have maintained higher prices abroad; and 2) whether proof of these facts would satisfy the FTAIA's test. On remand, the Court of Appeals for the District of Columbia held that the plaintiffs had preserved this claim, but that, in light of the Supreme Court's construction of paragraph (2), they failed to satisfy the FTAIA's requirements. The FTAIA requirement that the domestic effects "give rise to" the plaintiffs' claim means, said the appellate court, that the domestic effects must "proximately" cause the foreign price rise. It is not enough that, "but for" the U.S. effects, the prices would not have risen in the foreign markets (e.g., but for the U.S. effects, arbitrage based upon competitively low U.S. prices would have defeated the price rise). The D.C. Circuit Court held as a matter of law that the U.S. domestic effect did not *proximately* cause the foreign harm, and it dismissed the case. 417 F.3d 1267 (D.C. Cir. 2005), cert. denied, 546 U.S. 1092 (2006). A number of foreign restraint cases have been dismissed under the FTAIA on grounds that a foreign plaintiff's harm was not proximately caused by the harm in the U.S. market, or that the U.S. harm from a foreign cartel was not sufficiently direct.

2. After deciding that FTAIA paragraph (2) was ambiguous, the Supreme Court decided *Empagran* on policy grounds. Did it make the right policy choice? How strong is the argument that closing the U.S. courthouse door to victims of the world conspiracy who purchased their price-fixed vitamins abroad is necessary to avoid unreasonable interference with the sovereignty of the harmed nations? Would Ecuador (which had no antitrust law at the time) have objected if U.S. courts provided compensation (or threefold compensation) to the Ecuadorian victims? Which was a stronger case for a finding of no jurisdiction on the basis of sovereign rights of other nations: *Hartford Fire*, in which the UK insisted that application of the Sherman Act

would conflict with its own regulation authorizing collaborative conduct in the UK by members of its Lloyds of London insurance market (the Court found that the Sherman Act reached the off-shore collaboration and rejected the claim that comity required dismissal), or *Empagran*?

3. The *Empagran* Court noted the arguments of Germany, Canada and the United States that permitting foreign buyers who bought their price-fixed products abroad to recover treble damages would diminish cartel members' incentives to blow the whistle on their cartel in return for leniency and thus undercut detection and deterrence. A U.S. statute (ACPERA, see App. B) now forgives treble damage claims (but not single damage liability) of cooperating leniency applicants. In view of this statute, does the deterrence question tip decisively the other way; i.e., is it now obvious that more rather than less treble damage exposure will deter cartels?

4. How and where should a court draw the line between buyers who make purchases abroad and are entitled to sue under the U.S. antitrust laws and those not entitled? Consider, for example, the buyers from Christie's and Sotheby's who were harmed by the New York–London auction houses' price-fixing conspiracy. Some buyers bought art in both New York and London auctions and sometimes had art works shipped to New York for viewing before they decided to place a bid at the London auction site. Did the high New York prices proximately cause the London price-rise? Is it possible to separate the New York transactions from a unitary trans-Atlantic conspiracy?

5. In view of the growing number of transnational cartels, the world consumer interest to deter them, the fact that the U.S. enforcement system is still the strongest in the world, and the fact that some of U.S. trading partners jealously guard their right to apply their own enforcement systems, what is the wisest and best rule? Should Congress rewrite the FTAIA? Suppose that Congress wishes to do so. It asks you to draft a replacement statute. Do so.

6. A number of foreign commerce cases do not invoke the FTAIA because they concern products directly imported into the United States. In these cases defendants not uncommonly raise defenses of Act of State, foreign sovereign compulsion, and comity. One of the most closely watched of these cases is *Vitamin C Antitrust Litigation*, 810 F. Supp. 2d 522 (E.D.N.Y. 2011). Chinese vitamin C producers fixed prices into the United States. The Chinese government filed an amicus brief in their defense, alleging that it had approved and encouraged the companies to export their vitamin C at a fixed minimum price as a self-discipline mechanism under supervision of the ministry to ease China's transition to a market system. The court denied defendants' motion for summary judgment. It concluded that the price fixing had not been compelled and therefore a true conflict did not exist. Defendants could have complied with U.S. and Chinese law at the same time.

7. Meanwhile, antitrust agencies of the world engage in intense cooperation in coordinating the detection and prosecution of international cartels, subject to requirements of confidentiality owed to the targets. For a fact-intensive and colorful state-of-play of criminal antitrust enforcement and cooperation, see Scott D. Hammond, Deputy Assistant Attorney General for

Criminal Enforcement, Antitrust Division, U.S. Department of Justice, Feb. 25, 2010, available at *http://www.justice.gov/atr/public/speeches/255515.htm*.

8. For additional treatment of extraterritorial jurisdiction and its limits, see the Framework Essay, Appendix A.

2. THE OECD HARD CORE CARTEL RECOMMENDATION

Through the mid to late 1900s, many nations condoned cartels as an acceptable way of economic life. That time has largely passed. There is increasing recognition in the world that cartels are a source of illegitimate market power; that they raise prices for business buyers and consumers; that they deaden initiative and stand in the way of progress. Even in developing countries—some of which may see cartels as a way of exploiting their own scarce resources and standing up to the industrialized world—it is widely accepted that domestic cartels undercut their ability to adjust to global markets, and it is well known that international cartels target the vulnerable, i.e., less developed countries.

In the 1990s, with the fall of Soviet communism and command-and-control economies, the widespread acceptance of markets, and the significant lowering of barriers to trade, nations gained a new awareness of their economic interdependence. They adopted many bilateral cooperation agreements, which became a framework for cooperative efforts to (among other things) challenge cartels that spanned continents. Antitrust authorities began to discuss convergence of national competition laws in order to avoid systems friction and to realize the possibility of a more nearly seamless world. The principal substantive rule on which nations have agreed, albeit informally and with much room for derogations, is a recommendation against hard core cartels.

The recommendation was adopted in 1998 in the context of the Organization for Economic Cooperation and Development, an organization of developed countries that increasingly reaches out to developing countries.

RECOMMENDATION OF THE COUNCIL CONCERNING EFFECTIVE ACTION AGAINST HARD CORE CARTELS

OECD, Paris, 27–28 April 1998.

THE COUNCIL,

Having regard to Article 5 b) of the Convention on the Organisation for Economic Co-operation and Development of 14th December 1960;

Having regard to previous Council Recommendations' recognition that "effective application of competition policy plays a vital role in promoting world trade by ensuring dynamic national markets and encouraging the lowering or reducing of entry barriers to imports"; and that "anticompetitive practices may constitute an obstacle to the achievement of economic growth, trade expansion, and other economic goals of Member countries";

Having regard to the Council Recommendation that exemptions from competition laws should be no broader than necessary and to the agreement in the Communiqué of the May 1997 meeting of the Council at Ministerial level to "work towards eliminating gaps in coverage of competition law, unless evidence suggests that compelling public interests cannot be served in better ways";

Having regard to the Council's long-standing position that closer co-operation is necessary to deal effectively with anticompetitive practices in one country that affect other countries and harm international trade, and its recommendation that when permitted by their laws and interests, Member countries should co-ordinate investigations of mutual concern and should comply with each other's requests to share information from their files and to obtain and share information obtained from third parties;

Recognising that benefits have resulted from the ability of competition authorities of some Member countries to share confidential investigatory information with a foreign competition authority in cases of mutual interest, pursuant to multilateral and bilateral treaties and agreements, and considering that most competition authorities are currently not authorised to share investigatory information with foreign competition authorities;

Recognising also that co-operation through the sharing of confidential information presupposes satisfactory protection against improper disclosure or use of shared information and may require resolution of other issues, including potential difficulties relating to differences in the territorial scope of competition law and in the nature of sanctions for competition law violations;

Considering that hard core cartels are the most egregious violations of competition law and that they injure consumers in many countries by raising prices and restricting supply, thus making goods and services completely unavailable to some purchasers and unnecessarily expensive for others; and

Considering that effective action against hard core cartels is particularly important from an international perspective—because their distortion of world trade creates market power, waste, and inefficiency in countries whose markets would otherwise be competitive—and particularly dependent upon co-operation—because they generally operate in secret, and relevant evidence may be located in many different countries;

I. RECOMMENDS as follows to Governments of Member countries:

A. CONVERGENCE AND EFFECTIVENESS OF LAWS PROHIBITING HARD CORE CARTELS

1. Member countries should ensure that their competition laws effectively halt and deter hard core cartels. In particular, their laws should provide for:

a) effective sanctions, of a kind and at a level adequate to deter firms and individuals from participating in such cartels; and

b) enforcement procedures and institutions with powers adequate to detect and remedy hard core cartels, including powers to obtain documents and information and to impose penalties for non-compliance.

2. For purposes of this Recommendation:

a) a "hard core cartel" is an anticompetitive agreement, anticompetitive concerted practice, or anticompetitive arrangement by competitors to fix prices, make rigged bids (collusive tenders), establish output restrictions or quotas, or share or divide markets by allocating customers, suppliers, territories, or lines of commerce;

b) the hard core cartel category does not include agreements, concerted practices, or arrangements that (i) are reasonably related to the lawful realisation of cost-reducing or output-enhancing efficiencies, (ii) are excluded directly or indirectly from the coverage of a Member country's own laws, or (iii) are authorised in accordance with those laws. However, all exclusions and authorisations of what would otherwise be hard core cartels should be transparent and should be reviewed periodically to assess whether they are both necessary and no broader than necessary to achieve their overriding policy objectives. After the issuance of this Recommendation, Members should provide the Organisation annual notice of any new or extended exclusion or category of authorisation.

B. INTERNATIONAL CO-OPERATION AND COMITY IN ENFORCING LAWS PROHIBITING HARD CORE CARTELS

1. Member countries have a common interest in preventing hard core cartels and should cooperate with each other in enforcing their laws against such cartels. In this connection, they should seek ways in which co-operation might be improved by positive comity principles applicable to requests that another country remedy anticompetitive conduct that adversely affects both countries, and should conduct their own enforcement activities in accordance with principles of comity when they affect other countries' important interests.

2. Co-operation between or among Member countries in dealing with hard core cartels should take into account the following principles:

a) the common interest in preventing hard core cartels generally warrants co-operation to the extent that such co-operation would be consistent with a requested country's laws, regulations, and important interests;

b) to the extent consistent with their own laws, regulations, and important interests, and subject to effective safeguards to protect commercially sensitive and other confidential information, Member countries' mutual interest in preventing hard core cartels warrants co-operation that might include sharing documents and information in their possession with foreign competition authorities and gathering documents and information on behalf of foreign competition authorities on a voluntary basis and when necessary through use of compulsory process;

c) a Member country may decline to comply with a request for assistance, or limit or condition its co-operation on the ground that it considers compliance with the request to be not in accordance with its laws or regulations or to be inconsistent with its important interests or on any other grounds, including its competition authority's resource constraints or the absence of a mutual interest in the investigation or proceeding in question;

d) Member countries should agree to engage in consultations over issues relating to co-operation.

In order to establish a framework for their co-operation in dealing with hard core cartels, Member countries are encouraged to consider entering into bilateral or multilateral agreements or other instruments consistent with these principles.

3. Member countries are encouraged to review all obstacles to their effective co-operation in the enforcement of laws against hard core cartels and to consider actions, including national legislation and/or bilateral or multilateral agreements or other instruments, by which they could eliminate or reduce those obstacles in a manner consistent with their important interests.

4. The co-operation contemplated by this Recommendation is without prejudice to any other co-operation that may occur in accordance with prior Recommendations of the Council, pursuant to any applicable bilateral or multilateral agreements to which Member countries may be parties, or otherwise.

II. INSTRUCTS the Competition Law and Policy Committee:

1. to maintain a record of such exclusions and authorisations as are notified to the Organisation pursuant to Paragraph I. A 2(b);

2. to serve, at the request of the Member countries involved, as a forum for consultations on the application of the Recommendation; and

3. to review Member countries' experience in implementing this Recommendation and report to the Council within two years on any further action needed to improve co-operation in the enforcement of competition law prohibitions of hard core cartels.

III. INVITES non-Member countries to associate themselves with this Recommendation and to implement it.

QUESTIONS AND COMMENTS

1. What are the benefits and limits of the Hard Core Cartel Recommendation? Is it tough enough to be meaningful or do its derogations and qualifications diminish its strength (even apart from enforcement problems)?

2. Does the Recommendation apply to hard core export cartels?

3. The "Recommendation" is merely that; it is a recommendation to nations. Moreover, the OECD has no dispute settlement procedures and no enforcement powers. What are the implications of lack of enforcement mechanisms? Does this have benefits? costs?

4. The OECD is one of several fora in which the antitrust family of the world meets, shares experiences and cooperates. The other three prominent world fora are the International Competition Network, uniquely comprised of competition agencies, not states; the United Nations Conference on Trade and Development; and the World Trade Organization. The WTO seemed to hold the promise of a world competition law framework, but that promise has largely dissipated for the time being.

3. THE DOHA (WTO) DECLARATION

Since at least 1995, the European Union has recommended world competition rules in the context of the World Trade Organization, which has dispute settlement procedures and possible enforcement mechanisms. The EU proposed a building block approach, building from cooperation agreements to world rules on non-discrimination, national treatment, transparency and due process (typical in trade agreements), to, eventually, a full set of substantive rules with dispute settlement. The United States opposed the enterprise, wary about the need for any world rules, and concerned lest antitrust be subordinated to protectionist trade rules, and lest the U.S. be governed by unaccountable bureaucracies. Perhaps circumspect in view of U.S. opposition, the EU pared back its agenda and proposed a world anti-cartel rule, with rules on non-discrimination, national treatment, transparency, due process, and technical assistance and capacity building for nations in need of it. It proposed no dispute resolution except regarding the adoption and maintenance of the rules. At the GATT/WTO ministerial trade meeting in Doha, Qatar in November 2001, the ministers adopted an agenda for future negotiations.

The trade meeting in Doha came four years after the trade meeting in Seattle. The Seattle meeting had aborted without consensus, but, famously, it raised consciousness about the fact that the prior rounds had principally benefited the industrialized countries. The Doha round was planned to be "the development round."

Joseph Stiglitz has described the background of the round as follows:

> The global protests over globalization began at the WTO meetings in Seattle, Washington, because it was the most obvious symbol of the global inequities and the hypocrisy of the advanced industrial countries. While these countries had preached—and forced—the opening of the markets in the developing countries to their industrial products, they had continued to keep their markets closed to the products of the developing countries, such as textiles and agriculture. While they preached that developing countries should not subsidize their industries, they continued to provide billions in subsidies to their own farmers, making it impossible for the developing countries to compete. While they preached the virtues of competitive markets, the United States was quick to push for global cartels in steel and aluminum when its domestic industries seemed threatened by imports.... [S]o unfair has the trade agenda been that not only have the poorer countries not received a fair share of the benefits; the poorest region in the world, Sub-Saharan Africa, was actually made worse off as a result of the last round of trade negotiations.
>
> These inequities have increasingly been recognized, and that, combined with the resolve of some of the developing countries, resulted in the Doha "development" round of trade negotiations (November 2001), which put on its agenda the redressing of some of these past imbalances.[1]

The Doha agenda included the following:

DOHA MINISTERIAL DECLARATION

WTO, 14 November 2001.

1. The multilateral trading system embodied in the World Trade Organization has contributed significantly to economic growth, development and employment throughout the past fifty years. We are determined, particularly in the light of the global economic slowdown, to maintain the process of reform and liberalization of trade policies, thus ensuring that the system plays its full part in promoting recovery, growth and development. We therefore strongly reaffirm the principles and objectives set out in the Marrakesh Agreement Establishing the World Trade Organization, and pledge to reject the use of protectionism.

* * *

Interaction between trade and competition policy

23. Recognizing the case for a multilateral framework to enhance the contribution of competition policy to international trade and development, and the need for enhanced technical assistance and capacity-building in this area as referred to in paragraph 24, we agree that negotiations will take place after the Fifth Session of the Ministerial

1. See J. Stiglitz, Globalization and its Discontents, (2002), p. 244–45.

Conference on the basis of a decision to be taken, by explicit consensus, at that Session on modalities of negotiations.

24. Recognize the needs of developing and least-developed countries for enhanced support for technical assistance and capacity building in this area, including policy analysis and development so that they may better evaluate the implications of closer multilateral cooperation for their development policies and objectives, and human and institutional development. To this end, we shall work in cooperation with other relevant intergovernmental organisations, including UNCTAD, and through appropriate regional and bilateral channels, to provide strengthened and adequately resourced assistance to respond to these needs.

25. In the period until the Fifth Session, further work in the Working Group on the Interaction between Trade and Competition Policy will focus on the clarification of: core principles, including transparency, non-discrimination and procedural fairness, and provisions on hardcore cartels; modalities for voluntary cooperation; and support for progressive reinforcement of competition institutions in developing countries through capacity building. Full account shall be taken of the needs of developing and least-developed country participants and appropriate flexibility provided to address them.

QUESTIONS AND COMMENTS

1. The Fifth Session of the Ministerial Conference was held in Cancun in October 2003. The industrialized countries/regions, particularly the United States and the European Union, failed to offer commitments to reduce agricultural subsidies to a level satisfactory to the developing countries. The impass in Cancun led to a jettisoning of issues less central to the core work of the WTO. The competition program was a casualty. It was removed from the Doha Round agenda. Even after the passage of years, the parties failed to reach consensus on the trade issues central to the Doha agenda, and it appears at this writing that the Doha Round has failed.

2. Should there be a world rule against hard core cartels? Should all members of the WTO be required to adopt or maintain such a rule? What impact would such a requirement have on the United States? on developing countries?

3. If there should be an anti-cartel rule, what should it say? Should it be modeled after the OECD Hard Core Cartel Recommendation? Should it be simpler and tougher?

Meanwhile, international coordination proceeds at a considerable pace. The International Competition Network, for one, assists competition agencies to enhance their skills, and it seeks to foster convergence. The

ICN works through a number of working groups including the Cartel Working Group. The Cartel Working Group organizes annual cartel workshops at venues around the world. It has produced much useful work product, which is available on the ICN website, *http://www.internationalcompetitionnetwork.org*. This includes an Anti–Cartel Enforcement Manual, describing how to conduct raids and searches for documents and how to draft and implement leniency programs; providing templates for ICN members' anti-cartel enforcement regimes; and providing references for important practical issues such as how the various member agencies set fines, procedures for settlement, and modes for cooperation in investigations. Browse the ICN web pages on cartels.

Chapter 3

Monopoly and Dominance

■ ■ ■

A. INTRODUCTION

Section 2 of the Sherman Act provides that no person may "monopolize, attempt to monopolize, or conspire to monopolize." Article 102 of the European Treaty (Treaty on the Functioning of the European Union, or TFEU) prohibits "[a]ny abuse by one or more undertakings of a dominant position...." These two provisions are more or less the models, for the world, for law to control the behavior of dominant firms.

U.S. monopoly law has followed the swings of the socio-political pendulum. Concerns about concentrated economic power as a threat to political and economic democracy dominated the antitrust discourse in the 1960s. Contrapuntally, pursuit of efficiency and world competitiveness dominated the discourse in the 1980s. Despite the pendulum's swings,[1] there is a strong and stable core of anti-monopoly law in the United States and increasingly in the rest of the world. There is also a margin of instability, which we later identify.

At the core of the law are cases in which the defendant has real and enduring economic power, especially when bolstered or even conferred and protected by the state, and this monopoly firm engages in acts that enhance and maintain its monopoly and that do not qualify as competitive responses to markets and buyers. A paradigmatic example is the case of AT&T before the 1982 consensual break-up, when the feared and beloved Ma Bell, which invented great new technologies for the American people, also erected road-blocks against rivals' competing technologies that promised to change the face of the market. See *United States v. American Telephone and Telegraph Co.*, 524 F.Supp. 1336 (D.D.C.1981), treated in part below. Similarly, recall when the Standard Oil Trust procured the railroads' agreement to raise the rivals' costs of shipping their oil to refineries and to give the oil trust a cut of the higher prices in return for evening its traffic among the railroads. See page 30 supra.

---

1. This does not mean that the pendulum swings between two fixed points. It does not. We learn from history and adjust to modernization.

We might call AT&T's blatant market blockages and the Oil Trust's raising rivals' costs hard core monopolization (no purpose or effect except to harm competition). Europe has more paradigmatic examples than the United States in view of the pervasive state ownership and use of state-privileged power to block rivals, as in its several port and ferry cases. See, e.g., Port of Rødby, 94/119/EC, Commission decision of 21 Dec. 1993, O.J. L 055, 26 January 1994 at 0052 (port owner also operates a ferry and refuses to allow access to a would-be ferry competitor).

How far beyond hard core monopolization does the law extend? This is a hard question. U.S. monopoly law has at times enjoyed a wide domain to prohibit dominant firms from bullying and coercing powerless competitors. At other times, including the present, the monopoly law has contracted, in sympathy with monopoly firms' claims of efficiencies and need to compete in the world. Indeed, as the new millennium unfolds, U.S. antitrust has a favorite epithet: Antitrust law protects competition and consumers, not competitors; it is not a prescription against unfairness. Moreover, much of the contemporary caselaw assumes that freedom of conduct by even a dominant firm nearly always benefits consumers and that, if competitors complain, they must want protection from competition itself. Do you hear the voice of Justice Edward D. White dissenting in *Trans–Missouri* and later as Chief Justice authoring the Court's opinion in *Standard Oil*?

We begin with two classic cases that are household names in U.S. antitrust law—*Alcoa*, which confronts us with the question, What is monopolization?, and *du Pont–Cellophane*, which confronts us with the question, What is a market? Both cases, and particularly the questions they stimulate, are laboratories for the questions that underlie modern analysis. *Alcoa* arose in the long but now forsaken period of consensus that antitrust should protect competition and economic democracy through protection of the "competitive structure" of markets. While this older consensus has been replaced by more trustfulness in business to reach competitive results, a monopoly position not vulnerable to competitive challenge may still raise concerns, largely focusing on the conduct of the firm.

B. THE *ALCOA* CASE

In the late 1930s the United States brought suit against Aluminum Company of America (Alcoa) and its Canadian affiliate, Aluminum Limited. The suit charged that Alcoa monopolized the U.S. market for aluminum, and also that Aluminum Limited, with foreign co-conspirators, operated an international cartel that restrained imports and kept all but a small amount of foreign aluminum out of the United States.

The district court gave judgment for Alcoa. The Department of Justice appealed to the Supreme Court.[2] Due to recusals the Court lacked

2. Until an amendment in 1974, the Expediting Act provided for direct appeal from the district court to the Supreme Court in antitrust cases brought by the United States. The 1974

the quorum of six justices necessary to hear the case. It referred the appeal to the Court of Appeals for the Second Circuit. The ensuing appellate court opinion by Chief Judge Learned Hand did much to shape the law of monopolization, first as a beacon and later as a foil. We consider here the part of the opinion that deals with the charge of monopolization.[3]

As you read the case, think not only about the decision itself but also: Why do you think the Justice Department brought this suit? What did it want? Note that the case is an early flagship case struggling with the question: What is the monopoly law all about? What do *you* think should be the standard for violating the law against monopolization? As you consider this question, ask how your proposed standard affects incentives. Consider also the possible remedies for violation and how these remedies affect incentives. If a violation has no good remedy, you might want to reconsider the substantive standard.

UNITED STATES v. ALUMINUM CO. OF AMERICA

148 F.2d 416 (2d Cir.1945).

CHIEF JUDGE LEARNED HAND:

I.

"ALCOA'S" MONOPOLY OF "VIRGIN" INGOT

... Hall discovered a process by which [alumina could be isolated from bauxite and oxygen could be eliminated] and got a patent on April 2, 1889, which he assigned to "Alcoa." ... [U]ntil February 2, 1909, "Alcoa" had either a monopoly of the manufacture of "virgin" aluminum ingot, or the monopoly of a process which eliminated all competition.

The extraction of aluminum from alumina requires a very large amount of electrical energy, which is ordinarily, though not always, most cheaply obtained from water power. Beginning at least as early as 1895, "Alcoa" secured such power from several companies by contracts, containing in at least three instances, covenants binding the power companies not to sell or let power to anyone else for the manufacture of aluminum. "Alcoa"—either itself or by a subsidiary—also entered into four successive "cartels" with foreign manufacturers of aluminum by which, in exchange for certain limitations upon its import into foreign countries, it secured covenants from the foreign producers, either not to import into the United States at all, or to do so under restrictions, which in some cases involved the fixing of prices. These "cartels" and restrictive covenants and certain other practices were the subject of a suit filed by the United States against

amendment provides that appeal lies to a federal court of appeals unless a case is certified as one in which "immediate consideration of the appeal by the Supreme Court is of general public importance in the administration of justice," in which case appeal may proceed to the Supreme Court. Pub.L. 93–528, § 5, 88 Stat. 1708, 1709.

3. In the cartel part of the opinion, the court found an illegal international cartel. The cartel restrained imports into the United States. Alcoa's Canadian affiliate participated; but there was no proof of Alcoa's participation.

"Alcoa" on May 16, 1912, in which a decree was entered by consent on June 7, 1912, declaring several of these covenants unlawful and enjoining their performance; and also declaring invalid other restrictive covenants obtained before 1903 relating to the sale of alumina. * * *

[*Control of the market*]

There are various ways of computing "Alcoa's" control of the aluminum market—as distinct from its production—depending upon what one regards as competing in that market. The judge figured its share—during the years 1929–1938, inclusive—as only about thirty-three percent; to do so he included "secondary," [ingot made from aluminum scrap] and excluded that part of "Alcoa's" own production which it fabricated and did not therefore sell as ingot. If, on the other hand, "Alcoa's" total production, fabricated and sold, be included, and balanced against the sum of imported "virgin" and "secondary," its share of the market was in the neighborhood of sixty-four per cent for that period. The percentage we have already mentioned—over ninety—results only if we both include all "Alcoa's" production and exclude "secondary". That percentage is enough to constitute a monopoly; it is doubtful whether sixty or sixty-four percent would be enough; and certainly thirty-three per cent is not. Hence it is necessary to settle what [w]e shall treat as competing in the ingot market. That part of its production which "Alcoa" itself fabricates, does not of course ever reach the market as ingot.... However, even though we were to assume that a monopoly is unlawful under § 2 only in case it controls prices, the ingot fabricated by "Alcoa," necessarily had a direct effect upon the ingot market. All ingot—with trifling exceptions—is used to fabricate intermediate, or end, products; and therefore all intermediate, or end, products which "Alcoa" fabricates and sells, pro tanto reduce the demand for ingot itself.... We cannot therefore agree that the computation of the percentage of "Alcoa's" control over the ingot market should not include the whole of its ingot production. * * *

... The competition of "secondary" must ... be disregarded, as soon as we consider the position of "Alcoa" over a period of years; it was as much within "Alcoa's" control as was the production of the "virgin" from which it had been derived....

We conclude therefore that "Alcoa's" control over the ingot market must be reckoned at over ninety per cent; that being the proportion which its production bears to imported "virgin" ingot. If the fraction which it did not supply were the product of domestic manufacture there could be no doubt that this percentage gave it a monopoly—lawful or unlawful, as the case might be. The producer of so large a proportion of the supply has complete control within certain limits....

[*Significance of foreign sources of supply; effect on prices and power*]

The case at bar is however different, because, for aught that appears there may well have been a practically unlimited supply of imports as the price of ingot rose. Assuming that there was no agreement between "Alcoa" and foreign producers not to import, they sold what could bear the handicap of the tariff and the cost of transportation. For the period of eighteen years—1920–1937—they sold at times a little above "Alcoa's" prices, at times a little under; but there was substantially no gross difference between what they received and what they would have received, had they sold uniformly at "Alcoa's" prices. While the record is silent, we may therefore assume—the plaintiff having the burden—that, had "Alcoa" raised its prices, more ingot would have been imported. Thus there is a distinction between domestic and foreign competition; the first is limited in quantity, and can increase only by an increase in plant and personnel; the second is of producers who, we must assume, produce much more than they import, and whom a rise in price will presumably induce immediately to divert to the American market what they have been selling elsewhere. It is entirely consistent with the evidence that it was the threat of greater foreign imports which kept "Alcoa's" prices where they were, and prevented it from exploiting its advantage as sole domestic producer; indeed, it is hard to resist the conclusion that potential imports did put a "ceiling" upon these prices. Nevertheless, within the limits afforded by the tariff and the cost of transportation, "Alcoa" was free to raise its prices as it chose, since it was free from domestic competition, save as it drew other metals into the market as substitutes. Was this a monopoly within the meaning of § 2? The judge found that, over the whole half century of its existence, "Alcoa's" profits upon capital invested, after payment of income taxes, had been only about ten per cent, and, although the plaintiff puts this figure a little higher, the difference is negligible.... This assumed, it would be hard to say that "Alcoa" had made exorbitant profits on ingot, if it is proper to allocate the profit upon the whole business proportionately among all its products—ingot, and fabrications from ingot. A profit of ten per cent in such an industry, dependent, in part at any rate, upon continued tariff protection, and subject to the vicissitudes of new demands, to the obsolescence of plant and process—which can never be accurately gauged in advance—to the chance that substitutes may at any moment be discovered which will reduce the demand, and to the other hazards which attend all industry; a profit of ten per cent, so conditioned, could hardly be considered extortionate.

[*Why, apart from excessive pricing, the Act might condemn monopoly/ monopolization*]

... But ... it is no excuse for "monopolizing" a market that the monopoly has not been used to extract from the consumer more than a "fair" profit. The Act has wider purposes. Indeed, even though we disregarded all but economic considerations, it would by no means follow that such concentration of producing power is to be desired, when it has not been used extortionately. Many people believe that possession of unchallenged economic power deadens initiative, discourages thrift and depresses energy; that immunity from competition is a narcotic, and rivalry is a stimulant, to industrial progress; that the spur of constant stress is necessary to counteract an inevitable disposition to let well enough alone. Such people believe that competitors, versed in the craft as no consumer can be, will be quick to detect opportunities for saving and new shifts in production, and be eager to profit by them. In any event the mere fact that a producer, having command of the domestic market, has not been able to make more than a "fair" profit, is no evidence that a "fair" profit could not have been made at lower prices.... True, it might have been thought adequate to condemn only those monopolies which could not show that they had exercised the highest possible ingenuity, had adopted every possible economy, had anticipated every conceivable improvement, stimulated every possible demand. No doubt, that would be one way of dealing with the matter, although it would imply constant scrutiny and constant supervision, such as courts are unable to provide. Be that as it may, that was not the way that Congress chose; it did not condone "good trusts" and condemn "bad" ones; it forbad all. Moreover, in so doing it was not necessarily actuated by economic motives alone. It is possible, because of its indirect social or moral effect, to prefer a system of small producers, each dependent for his success upon his own skill and character, to one in which the great mass of those engaged must accept the direction of a few. These considerations, which we have suggested only as possible purposes of the Act, we think the decisions prove to have been in fact its purposes. * * *

We have been speaking only of the economic reasons which forbid monopoly; but, as we have already implied, there are others, based upon the belief that great industrial consolidations are inherently undesirable, regardless of their economic results. In the debates in Congress Senator Sherman himself in the passage quoted in the margin showed that among the purposes of Congress in 1890 was a desire to put an end to great aggregations of capital because of the helplessness of the individual before them.[1] ... That Congress is still of the same mind appears in the Surplus Property Act of 1944 and the Small Business Mobilization Act.... Throughout the history of these statutes it has been constantly assumed that one of their purposes was to perpetuate and preserve, for its own sake and in spite of possible cost, an organization of industry in small units which can effectively compete with each other. We hold that "Alcoa's" monopoly of ingot was of the kind covered by § 2.

It does not follow because "Alcoa" had such a monopoly, that it "monopolized" the ingot market: it may not have achieved monopoly; monopoly may have been thrust upon it. * * *

[*Defenses to monopolization*]

---

1. "If the concerted powers of this combination are intrusted to a single man, it is a kingly prerogative, inconsistent with our form of government, and should be subject to the strong resistance of the State and national authorities * * *." 21 Cong. Rec., 2457 (1890).

"The popular mind is agitated with problems that may disturb social order, and among them all none is more threatening than the inequality of condition, of wealth, and opportunity that has grown within a single generation out of the concentration of capital into vast combinations to control production and trade and to break down competition. These combinations ... reach out their Briarean arms to every part of our country. They are imported from abroad. Congress alone can deal with them, and if we are unwilling or unable there will soon be a trust for every production and a master to fix the price for every necessity of life. * * * " 21 Cong. Rec. 2460 (1890). See also 21 Cong. Rec. 2598 (1890).

[The Supreme Court has expressed compunctions against condemning size.] What engendered these compunctions is reasonably plain; persons may unwittingly find themselves in possession of a monopoly, automatically so to say: that is, without having intended either to put an end to existing competition, or to prevent competition from arising when none had existed; they may become monopolists by force of accident. Since the Act makes "monopolizing" a crime, as well as a civil wrong, it would be not only unfair, but presumably contrary to the intent of Congress, to include such instances. A market may, for example, be so limited that it is impossible to produce at all and meet the cost of production except by a plant large enough to supply the whole demand. Or there may be changes in taste or in cost which drive out all but one purveyor. A single producer may be the survivor out of a group of active competitors, merely by virtue of his superior skill, foresight and industry. In such cases a strong argument can be made that, although, the result may expose the public to the evils of monopoly, the Act does not mean to condemn the resultant of those very forces which it is its prime object to foster: finis opus coronat. The successful competitor, having been urged to compete, must not be turned upon when he wins ... [See] the gloss of Cardozo, J., in United States v. Swift & Co., 286 U.S. 106, p. 116, when he said, "Mere size ... is not an offense against the Sherman Act unless magnified to the point at which it amounts to a monopoly ... but size carries with it an opportunity for abuse that is not to be ignored when the opportunity is proved to have been utilized in the past." "Alcoa's" size was "magnified" to make it a "monopoly"; indeed, it has never been anything else; and its size not only offered it an "opportunity for abuse," but it "utilized" its size for "abuse," as can easily be shown.

It would completely misconstrue "Alcoa's" position in 1940 to hold that it was the passive beneficiary of a monopoly, following upon an involuntary elimination of competitors by automatically operative economic forces. Already in 1909, when its last lawful monopoly ended, it sought to strengthen its position by unlawful practices, and these concededly continued until 1912. In that year it had two plants in New York, at which it produced less than 42 million pounds of ingot; in 1934 it had five plants ..., and its production had risen to about 327 million pounds, an increase of almost eight-fold. Meanwhile not a pound of ingot had been produced by anyone else in the United States. This increase and this continued and undisturbed control did not fall undesigned into "Alcoa's" lap; obviously it could not have done so. It could only have resulted, as it did result, from a persistent determination to maintain the control, with which it found itself vested in 1912. There were at least one or two abortive attempts to enter the industry, but "Alcoa" effectively anticipated and forestalled all competition, and succeeded in holding the field alone. True, it stimulated demand and opened new uses for the metal, but not without making sure that it could supply what it had evoked. There is no dispute as to this; "Alcoa" avows it as evidence of the skill, energy and initiative with which it has always conducted its business; as a reason why, having won its way by fair means, it should be commended, and not dismembered. We need charge it with no moral derelictions after 1912; we may assume that all it claims for itself is true. The only question is whether it falls within the exception established in favor of those who do not seek, but cannot avoid, the control of a market. It seems to us that that question scarcely survives its statement. It was not inevitable that it should always anticipate increases in the demand for ingot and be prepared to supply them. Nothing compelled it to keep doubling and redoubling its capacity before others entered the field. It insists that it never excluded competitors; but we can think of no more effective exclusion than progressively to embrace each new opportunity as it opened, and to face every newcomer with new capacity already geared into a great organization, having the advantage of experience, trade connections and the elite of personnel. Only in case we interpret "exclusion" as limited to manoeuvres not honestly industrial, but actuated solely by a desire to prevent competition, can such a course, indefatigably pursued, be deemed not "exclusionary." So to limit it would in our judgment emasculate the Act; would permit just such consolidations as it was designed to prevent. * * *

We disregard any question of "intent." . . . In order to fall within § 2, the monopolist must have both the power to monopolize, and the intent to monopolize. To read [the language of Justice Holmes in the *Swift* case] as demanding any "specific" intent, makes nonsense of it, for no monopolist monopolizes unconscious of what he is doing. So here, "Alcoa" meant to keep, and did keep, that complete and exclusive hold upon the ingot market with which it started. That was to "monopolize" that market, however innocently it otherwise proceeded. So far as the judgment held that it was not within § 2, it must be reversed. * * *

II.

"ALCOA'S" UNLAWFUL PRACTICES

[The court affirmed the dismissal of all conduct claims, except for one.]

The plaintiff describes as the "Price Squeeze" a practice by which, it says, "Alcoa" intended to put out of business the manufacturers of aluminum "sheet" who were its competitors; for "Alcoa" was itself a large—in fact much the largest—maker of that product, and had been the first to introduce it many years before the period in question. . . . We shall not describe the manufacture of "sheet"—"sheet rolling"—beyond saying that "rolling ingot," not "notched bar ingot," must be used, and that it is forced between two rollers until it gets to the desired thickness: "gauge." It is made as "coiled sheet" or "flat sheet"; also the metal may be hardened by various alloys to bring up its tensile strength. The "squeeze" is asserted to have been exercised upon five "gauges" of "coiled sheet," four "gauges" of "flat sheet" and five "gauges" of alloyed metal—called "Duralumin." * * *

The plaintiff's theory is that "Alcoa" consistently sold ingot at so high a price that the "sheet rollers," who were forced to buy from it, could not pay the expenses of "rolling" the "sheet" and make a living profit out of the price at which "Alcoa" itself sold "sheet." To establish this the plaintiff asks us to take "Alcoa's" costs of "rolling" as a fair measure of its competitors' costs, and to assume that they had to meet "Alcoa's" price for all grades of "sheet," and could not buy ingot elsewhere. It seems to us altogether reasonable, in the absence of proof to the contrary, to suppose that "Alcoa's" "rolling" costs were not higher than those of other "sheet rollers". . . .

Compressing into reasonable compass what the tables show, the result is as follows. For all the five "gauges" of "coiled sheet" for eight years, 1925–1932, the average profit open to competing "rollers" was .84 cents a pound, as against 4.7 cents for the five succeeding years, 1933–1937. The corresponding figures for "flat sheet" were .59 cents and 4 cents; and for "Duralumin," 4.9 cents and 11.8 cents. Moreover, in 31 instances out of 112 there was no "spread" at all; that is, the cost of ingot plus the cost of "rolling" was greater than the price at which "Alcoa" was selling "sheet." Obviously, there was in the eight years little or no inducement to continue in the "sheet" business, and Baush, the only "roller" of "duralumin," gave up in 1931, although "Alcoa" insists, and the judge found, that this was because of its inefficiency. . . .

. . . That it was unlawful to set the price of "sheet" so low and hold the price of ingot so high, seems to us unquestionable, provided, as we have held, that on this record the price of ingot must be regarded as higher than a "fair price." True, this was only a consequence of "Alcoa's" control over the price of ingot, and perhaps it ought not to be considered as a separate wrong; moreover, we do not use it as part of the reasoning by which we conclude that the monopoly was unlawful. But it was at least an unlawful exercise of "Alcoa's" power after it had been put on notice by the "sheet rollers" complaints; and this is true, even though we assent to the judge's finding that it was not part of an attempt to monopolize the "sheet" market. * * *

QUESTIONS AND COMMENTS

What vision of the world (political economy) lies behind Judge Learned Hand's opinion? Is it the vision of the Congress that adopted the Sherman Act (in Hand's view)? Is there an alternative vision? Have the concerns of Hand, and of the Senators quoted, been overtaken by time? Are we not, or are not some of us, still concerned with the inequality of wealth and opportunity that has seemed to grow out of the concentration of capital? See *Alcoa*, note 1. See Charles M. Blow, Inconvenient Income Inequality, New York Times, Op-Ed, Dec. 16, 2011. Do we still believe that antitrust has relevance? that market control by dominant firms is part of the problem and that pushing back against it can be part of the solution? Or is/was this idea just empty, populist rhetoric, then and now?

Alcoa and the Power Issue

Did Alcoa have monopoly power (power to raise price significantly above cost and lower market output for a considerable period of time)? Did it command a supracompetitive price for its aluminum? What forces constrained its price?

Is very large market share (two-thirds or more) a good proxy for monopoly power? Is it a good first cut, if the market is well defined and barriers are high?[4] Or is it merely a device to shift the burden to the defendant? Can the defendant successfully defend by proving (if it can) that it made no more than a reasonable return on investment?

Judge Hand catalogued the evils of monopoly. Did Alcoa's conduct and performance reveal these evils?

Keep an open mind as to the legal standards for the offense of monopolization and for the more specific price-squeeze offense. The formalism of *Alcoa* and its inhospitality to monopoly structure has given way to more dynamic analysis that you will see in cases such as *Microsoft* below.

Alcoa and the Structure and Conduct Issues

Recall that the court holds the monopoly unlawful, and expressly does not include the price squeeze as a part of its reasoning. Was monopoly thrust upon Alcoa? What did it do wrong? What should it have done or not done, according to the court? Would this course of action have been better or worse for competition? for consumers?

The price squeeze: Why was Alcoa's high pricing of ingot to the sheet steel makers and low pricing of sheet steel to customers an unlawful exercise of its power? Note that the price squeeze was not part of an attempt to monopolize the sheet market.

Alcoa and the Remedy Issue

The remedy phase of antitrust cases is crucial. In civil cases (which constitute virtually all antitrust cases other than hard core cartels), the function of the remedy is not to punish; it is to restore the market to the condition it would have enjoyed had there been no violation, and to deter future violations.

In *Alcoa*, the remedy phase was deferred until after the end of World War II. During the war, the government itself had developed and operated large aluminum facilities. When the war was over the government sold these facilities to Reynolds and Kaiser. As a result, by 1948 Alcoa accounted for less than half of aluminum sales in the United States.

4. We treat market definition at C below. The market should include all products that are reasonably interchangeable and are good substitutes, tending to keep price near cost. Secondary aluminum was presumably not an adequate competitive constraint on the price of virgin aluminum.

In the relief proceedings, the government requested that Alcoa be broken up into two parts.

UNITED STATES v. ALUMINUM CO. OF AMERICA

91 F.Supp. 333 (S.D.N.Y.1950).

JUDGE KNOX: . . . While I am firmly convinced that the Government is entitled to some relief, I am as strongly persuaded that, for the present at least, the organization of Alcoa's physical properties should not be disturbed. . . .

[A] strong and resourceful domestic aluminum industry is a vital necessity, not alone from the standpoint of national security, but also for the peacetime welfare of the general public. . . . [T]he future development of the industry depends upon its being composed of financially sound and well-integrated organizations. One must constantly remember that aluminum products are in fierce rivalry with articles composed of other materials, and which are manufactured and sold by concerns that, in size, are fully equal to Alcoa. . . .

If the aluminum industry is to develop fully, and be able to satisfy the tremendous demands to which, in the natural course of events, it will be subjected, it must not be reduced to a state of relative impotence. On the contrary, the industry, if its present stature is to be maintained, must carry on a continuous process of encroachment upon the preserves of other industries whose products are manufactured by corporations that will not abjectly surrender the trade positions they now hold. The success of any such effort to encroach upon fields of endeavor that are now occupied by strongly entrenched competitors can be achieved only by companies that are rich in resources, and which are capable of undertaking extensive scientific and market experimentations. At the present juncture, the weakening of any aluminum producer would lessen the buoyancy of the industry as a whole. Rightly or wrongly, from an economic and social standpoint, big business in many industries is an actuality, and if such enterprises are to be subjected to effective competition, their trade rivals must be of somewhat comparable strength.

This situation imposes a minimum effective size on any aluminum producer if it be a real contributor to the growth of the industry, and be, as well, a lively competitor with the producers of other metals. Unless fully persuaded—as I am not—that a divestiture of Alcoa's properties should take place, I am most reluctant to attempt to tamper unnecessarily with economic and industrial forces from which the public has reaped substantial benefits, and from which, also, it can continue to be served, and without detriment, in my opinion, to the national welfare.

The vertical divestiture of an integrated concern so as to create, at a minimum, another fully integrated and effective competitor would be, in its nature, a highly speculative—and even hazardous—venture. A corporation, designed to operate effectively as a single entity, cannot readily be dismembered of parts of its various operations without a marked loss of efficiency. And, to be sure that the segmented portions, when combined in a new organization, will be able to cohere successfully, it may be necessary that they be provided with compensatory advantages.... These inherent difficulties are considerably magnified in the present context.

To the extent that Alcoa possesses duplicate and comparable facilities, the problem of divestiture would be less troublesome. But, in an extremely important stage of production, a major impediment to a successful divestiture is to be found. Alcoa has two alumina plants. The one located at Mobile, Alabama, is its only facility economically comparable to the alumina plants of Reynolds and Kaiser. In order to produce alumina at East St. Louis (Alcoa's other plant), at costs that approach the competitive level, the use of domestic bauxite would be required. The diminution of these already scarce reserves, under readily imaginable circumstances, might possibly take on the proportions of a calamity. Similar unequal concentrations by Alcoa of particular productive operations, at a single plant, likewise exist in certain fields of fabrication.

The insurance of successful competition by any dissociated portion of Alcoa would depend upon the ability of the new corporation to supply itself with efficient and experienced management. Since Alcoa, for so long, was the only domestic producer of aluminum, there is but a limited number of persons outside of its staff, and the officialdom of Reynolds and Kaiser, of which a large part was trained in the Alcoa organization, who are able efficiently to function as executives and managers in this industry. Thus, although the independence of the new firm would be the purpose for its creation, it could not, in the first instance, completely sever its ties with Alcoa.

When account is taken of the personnel and equipment presently employed in research, an equally grave problem must be faced. It would be a singular disservice to the public if the skill and technique of Alcoa's research department were impaired. Any divestiture which would extend to this activity, almost surely, would have a baneful effect upon the future of the industry. Nor would independence be fostered by tying two firms to the same research department. Yet, to recruit, outfit and finance a research organization which would not be under a serious disadvantage to that of Alcoa would, indeed, be close to an impossible task. * * *

Actually, any type of plan that would carry greater assurances for the success and independence of the new concern, and, at the same time, of necessity, be more crippling to Alcoa, is unnecessary in view of present competitive conditions, and the availability of other forms of relief. The Reynolds and Kaiser organizations are operating successfully and profitably, and there is little or no reason to think that either of them will be unable, under existing trade circumstances, to continue to thrive, and even to prosper. The Government disposal program has launched them with excellent properties, low investments, and safeguards for their future stability. The effective future competitive efforts of these two companies will be greatly enhanced if the shadow that now hangs over them in Alcoa's potential control of Aluminum Limited be removed. * * *

My present conclusion is that, in addition to the relief . . . [prohibiting patent grant-backs and permitting the disposition of the government's] St. Lawrence Plant, the shareholders of Alcoa be required to dispose of their stock interests either in Limited or in Alcoa. . . .

What is Judge Knox's perspective on political economy and the structure of business? Does it differ from Judge Hand's?

As would later be the case in *Microsoft* (p. 219 infra), identifying the appropriate remedy presented a dilemma. Monopoly may be evil because consumers lose the benefits of rivalry—including innovation and lower prices—that competition stimulates. But once monopoly exists, is a court order to dismember the monopolist likely to achieve social gains? Would it lead to lower prices? Would it encourage innovation? Would it foster more efficient management? Is there any way to know?

Judge Knox had a relatively easy task. The government had created competition by establishing and then selling aluminum facilities and the court could readily create yet more competition by ending Alcoa's control of its Canadian subsidiary. What if these options were not available? What would Judge Knox have done? What would you have done?

While the *Alcoa* case was being prosecuted, the government was also proceeding against cartels—in addition to the world aluminum cartel. It sued the major tobacco firms for combinations and conspiracies to restrain and monopolize trade. A year after the appellate court decided *Alcoa,* the Supreme Court reviewed a conviction in American Tobacco Co. v. United States, 328 U.S. 781 (1946). The Supreme Court affirmed the conviction and, in doing so, "welcome[d] the opportunity to endorse" the key passages in *Alcoa* describing the purposes of the Sherman Act and the elements of the offense of monopolization. 328 U.S. at 813–14.

Alcoa, endorsed by the Supreme Court in *American Tobacco* and supported by the work of influential industrial organization economists such as Edward S. Mason of Harvard and Joseph Bain of Berkeley, introduced a long period of "structural consensus." It was then common wisdom that industry structure (concentration and market share) significantly influenced a firm's conduct, which in turn influenced its performance; and that high concentration signaled a low level of competition and poor performance. This was called the structure-conduct-performance paradigm. The tightness of the relationship was later thrown into much doubt, but nonetheless, the structure of the market continues to be a touchstone of antitrust analysis.

Market definition delineates an area within which market forces can be examined. A market includes all products or services whose competition tends to keep prices down to cost. Antitrust outcomes frequently depend upon the market definition. In a broadly-defined market, a defendant firm may seem small; it might have an insignificant market share. In a narrowly defined market, the firm might seem monopoly-sized. Therefore it is important to delineate a realistic market definition. But what is realistic? It is becoming common cause today that market definition is an artificial construction; it is an indirect and circular way to try to decipher whether a putative violator has market power. Nonetheless, it is commonly required by courts as a first step in monopolization analysis and can provide an important point of focus.

The most important market definition case of the twentieth century was *DuPont/Cellophane*. Be critical as you read the case. Was the Court asking the right questions to determine whether duPont had market power? Would it have been more helpful to use more direct measures of duPont's market power? What might they be? (You will want to consult the dissenting opinion.)

C. MARKET DEFINITION AND MONOPOLY POWER

1. THE *DuPONT CELLOPHANE* CASE

UNITED STATES v. E.I. Du PONT De NEMOURS & CO.

351 U.S. 377 (1956).

JUSTICE REED: * * * The Government's direct appeal here ... "attacks only the ruling that du Pont has not monopolized trade in cellophane." ...

During the period that is relevant to this action, du Pont produced almost 75% of the cellophane sold in the United States, and cellophane constituted less than 20% of all "flexible packaging material" sales....

... The court below found that the "relevant market for determining the extent of du Pont's market control is the market for flexible packaging materials," and that competition from those other materials prevented du Pont from possessing monopoly powers in its sales of cellophane.

... Every manufacturer is the sole producer of the particular commodity it makes but its control in the [monopoly] sense of the relevant market depends upon the availability of alternative commodities for buyers: i.e., whether there is a cross-elasticity of demand between cellophane and the other wrappings. This interchangeability is largely gauged by the purchase of competing products for similar uses considering the price, characteristics and adaptability of the competing commodities. The court below found that the flexible wrappings afforded such alternatives. This Court must determine whether the trial court erred in its estimate of the competition afforded cellophane by other materials. * * *

III. THE SHERMAN ACT, § 2—MONOPOLIZATION ...

If cellophane is the "market" that du Pont is found to dominate, it may be assumed it does have monopoly power over that "market."

Monopoly power is the power to control prices or exclude competition. It seems apparent that du Pont's power to set the price of cellophane has been limited only by the competition afforded by other flexible packaging materials. Moreover, it may be practically impossible for anyone to commence manufacturing cellophane without full access to du Pont's technique. However, du Pont has no power to prevent competition from other wrapping materials. The trial court consequently had to determine whether competition from the other wrappings prevented du Pont from possessing monopoly power in violation of § 2. * * *

IV. THE RELEVANT MARKET

... [W]here there are market alternatives that buyers may readily use for their purposes, illegal monopoly does not exist merely because the product said to be monopolized differs from others. If it were not so, only physically identical products would be a part of the market. To accept the Government's argument [that substitutes must be substantially fungible to be included in the market], we would have to conclude that the manufacturers of plain as well as moistureproof cellophane were monopolists, and so with films such as Pliofilm, foil, glassine, polyethylene, and Saran, for each of these wrapping materials is distinguishable. These were all exhibits in the case. New wrappings appear, generally similar to cellophane: is each a monopoly? What is called for is an appraisal of the "cross-elasticity" of demand in the trade.

The varying circumstances of each case determine the result. In considering what is the relevant market for determining the control of price and competition, no more definite rule can be declared than that commodities reasonably interchangeable by consumers for the same purposes make up that "part of the trade or commerce," monopolization of which may be illegal. As respects flexible packaging materials, the market geographically is nationwide.

... Cellophane costs more than many competing products and less than a few. But whatever the price, there are various flexible wrapping materials that are bought by manufacturers for packaging their goods in their own plants or are sold to converters who shape and print them for use in the packaging of the commodities to be wrapped.

Cellophane differs from other flexible packaging materials. From some it differs more than from others. The basic materials from which the wrappings are made ... are aluminum, cellulose acetate, chlorides, wood pulp, rubber hydrochloride, and ethylene gas. It will adequately illustrate the similarity in characteristics of the various products by noting here Finding 62 as to glassine [detailing the qualities of glassine]. Its use is almost as extensive as cellophane and many of its characteristics equally or more satisfactory to users.

It may be admitted that cellophane combines the desirable elements of transparency, strength and cheapness more definitely than any of the others....

But, despite cellophane's advantages, it has to meet competition from other materials in every one of its uses.... Food products are the chief outlet, with cigarettes next. The Government makes no challenge to Finding 283 that cellophane furnishes less than 7% of wrappings for bakery products, 25% for candy, 32% for snacks, 35% for meats and poultry, 27% for crackers and biscuits, 47% for fresh produce, and 34% for frozen foods. Seventy-five to eighty percent of cigarettes are wrapped in cellophane. Finding 292. Thus, cellophane shares the packaging market with others. The over-all result is that cellophane accounts for 17.9% of flexible wrapping materials, measured by the wrapping surface....

Moreover a very considerable degree of functional interchangeability exists between these products.... It will be noted, that except as to permeability to gases, cellophane has no qualities that are not possessed by a number of other materials. Meat will do as an example of interchangeability. Although du Pont's sales to the meat industry have reached 19,000,000 pounds annually, nearly 35%, this volume is attributed "to the rise of self-service retailing of fresh meat." In fact, since the popularity of self-service meats, du Pont has lost "a considerable proportion" of this packaging business to Pliofilm. Pliofilm is more expensive than cellophane, but its superior physical characteristics apparently offset cellophane's price advantage. While retailers shift continually between the two, the trial court found that Pliofilm is increasing its share of the business....

An element for consideration as to cross-elasticity of demand between products is the responsiveness of the sales of one product to price changes of the other. If a slight decrease in the price of cellophane causes a considerable number of customers of other flexible wrappings to switch to cellophane, it would be an indication that a high cross-elasticity of demand exists between them; that the products compete in the same market. The court below held that the "[g]reat sensitivity of customers in the flexible packaging markets to price or quality changes" prevented du Pont from possessing monopoly control over price. The record sustains these findings.

We conclude that cellophane's interchangeability with the other materials mentioned suffices to make it a part of this flexible packaging material market.

The Government stresses the fact that the variation in price between cellophane and other materials demonstrates they are noncompetitive. As these products are all flexible wrapping materials, it seems reasonable to consider, as was done at the trial, their comparative cost to the consumer in terms of square area. Findings as to price competition are set out in the margin.[29] Cellophane costs two or three times as much, surface measure, as its chief competitors for the flexible wrapping market, glassine and greaseproof papers. Other forms of cellulose wrappings and those from

29. [Editor's note: We have omitted footnote 29 but summarize many of the findings in question 2 following the case.]

other chemical or mineral substances, with the exception of aluminum foil, are more expensive. The uses of these materials are largely to wrap small packages for retail distribution. The wrapping is a relatively small proportion of the entire cost of the article. Different producers need different qualities in wrappings and their need may vary from time to time as their products undergo change. But the necessity for flexible wrappings is the central and unchanging demand. We cannot say that these differences in cost gave du Pont monopoly power over prices in view of the findings of fact on that subject. * * *

The "market" which one must study to determine when a producer has monopoly power will vary with the part of commerce under consideration. The tests are constant. That market is composed of products that have reasonable interchangeability for the purposes for which they are produced—price, use and qualities considered. While the application of the tests remains uncertain, it seems to us that du Pont should not be found to monopolize cellophane when that product has the competition and interchangeability with other wrappings that this record shows. * * *

CHIEF JUSTICE WARREN, joined by JUSTICES BLACK and DOUGLAS, dissenting: This case, like many under the Sherman Act, turns upon the proper definition of the market. In defining the market in which du Pont's economic power is to be measured, the majority virtually emasculate § 2 of the Sherman Act. They admit that "cellophane combines the desirable elements of transparency, strength and cheapness more definitely than any of" a host of other packaging materials. Yet they hold that all of those materials are so indistinguishable from cellophane as to warrant their inclusion in the market.... * * *

During the period covered by the complaint (1923–1947) cellophane enjoyed phenomenal growth.... Yet throughout this period the price of cellophane was far greater than that of glassine, waxed paper or sulphite paper.... [I]n 1929 cellophane's price was seven times that of glassine; in 1934, four times, and in 1949 still more than twice glassine's price.... [C]ellophane had a similar price relation to waxed paper and ... sulphite paper sold at even less than glassine and waxed paper. We cannot believe that buyers, practical businessmen, would have bought cellophane in increasing amounts over a quarter of a century if close substitutes were available at from one-seventh to one-half cellophane's price. That they did so is testimony to cellophane's distinctiveness.

The inference yielded by the conduct of cellophane buyers is reinforced by the conduct of sellers other than du Pont.... Sylvania, the only other cellophane producer, absolutely and immediately followed every du Pont price change, even dating back its price list to the effective date of du Pont's change. Producers of glassine and waxed paper, on the other hand, displayed apparent indifference to du Pont's repeated and substantial price cuts.... [F]rom 1924 to 1932 du Pont dropped the price of plain cellophane 84%, while the price of glassine remained constant. And during the period 1933–1946 the prices for glassine and waxed paper actually increased in the face of a further 21% decline in the price of cellophane. If "shifts of business" due to "price sensitivity" had been substantial, glassine and waxed paper producers who wanted to stay in business would have been compelled by market forces to meet du Pont's price challenge just as Sylvania was. . . .

Du Pont's every action was directed toward maintaining dominance over cellophane. Its 1923 agreements with La Cellophane, the French concern which first produced commercial cellophane, gave du Pont exclusive North and Central American rights to cellophane's technology, manufacture and sale, and provided, without any limitation in time, that all existing and future information pertaining to the cellophane process be considered "secret and confidential," and be held in an exclusive common pool. In its subsequent agreements with foreign licensees, du Pont was careful to preserve its continental market inviolate. In 1929, while it was still the sole domestic producer of cellophane, du Pont won its long struggle to raise the tariff from 25% to 60%, ad valorem, on cellophane imports, substantially foreclosing foreign competition. When Sylvania became the second American cellophane producer the following year and du Pont filed suit claiming infringement of its moistureproof patents, they settled the suit by entering into a cross-licensing agreement. Under this agreement, du Pont obtained the right to exclude third persons from use of any patentable moistureproof invention made during the next 15 years by the sole other domestic cellophane producer, and, by a prohibitive royalty provision, it limited Sylvania's moistureproof production to approximately 20% of the industry's moistureproof sales. The record shows that du Pont and Sylvania were aware that, by settling the infringement suit, they avoided the possibility that the courts might hold the patent claims invalid and thereby open cellophane manufacture to additional competition. If close substitutes for cellophane had been commercially available, du Pont, an enlightened enterprise, would not have gone to such lengths to control cellophane.

As predicted by its 1923 market analysis, du Pont's dominance in cellophane proved enormously profitable from the outset. After only five years of production, when du Pont bought out the minority stock interests in its cellophane subsidiary, it had to pay more than fifteen times the original price of the stock. But such success was not limited to the period of innovation, limited sales and complete domestic monopoly. A confidential du Pont report shows that during the period 1937–1947, despite great expansion of sales, du Pont's "operative return" (before taxes) averaged 31%, while its average "net return" (after deduction of taxes, bonuses, and fundamental research expenditures) was 15.9%. Such profits provide a powerful incentive for the entry of competitors.[15] Yet from 1924 to 1951

15. See Stocking and Mueller, The Cellophane Case, XLV Amer. Economic Rev. 29, 60–63 (1955), where the authors compare the domestic economic history of rayon with that of cellophane. The first American rayon producer earned 64.2% on its investment in 1920, thereby attracting du Pont. After a loss in 1921, du Pont's average return for the next four years was roughly 32%. As more firms began rayon production, du Pont's and the industry's return on investment began to drop. When 6 new firms entered the industry in 1930, bringing the number only one new firm, Sylvania, was able to begin cellophane production. And Sylvania could not have entered if La Cellophane's secret process had not been stolen....

... The trial judge thought that, if du Pont raised its price, the market would "penalize" it with smaller profits as well as lower sales. Du Pont proved him wrong. When 1947 operating earnings dropped below 26% for the first time in 10 years, it increased cellophane's price 7% and boosted its earnings in 1948. Du Pont's division manager then reported that "If an operative return of 31% is considered inadequate then an upward revision in prices will be necessary to improve the return." It is this latitude with respect to price, this broad power of choice, that the antitrust laws forbid. Du Pont's independent pricing policy and the great profits consistently yielded by that policy leave no room for doubt that it had power to control the price of cellophane. * * *

If competition is at the core of the Sherman Act, we cannot agree that it was consistent with that Act for the enormously lucrative cellophane industry to have no more than two sellers from 1924 to 1951. The conduct of du Pont and Sylvania illustrates that a few sellers tend to act like one and that an industry which does not have a competitive structure will not have competitive behavior. The public should not be left to rely upon the dispensations of management in order to obtain the benefits which normally accompany competition. Such beneficence is of uncertain tenure. Only actual competition can assure long-run enjoyment of the goals of a free economy....

QUESTIONS AND COMMENTS

1. Market definition remains a central issue in modern antitrust litigation. Should so much turn on market definition? Is it relevant that du Pont did all that it could to protect its position in cellophane? If du Pont's conduct was reprehensible by some measure, should it be illegal?

2. Using *du Pont's* interchangeability and cross-elasticity approach, comment on whether or not you would infer from each of the following statements—the first 9 of which are derived from footnote 29—whether flexible wrappings other than cellophane tend to push the price of cellophane towards its cost and therefore should be included in the relevant market. If the statement is not in itself sufficient to enable you to draw an inference, what more do you need to know?

1. Buyers had and used substitutes for every one of cellophane's uses.

2. With one exception (permeability to gases), cellophane had no qualities not possessed by one or more of a number of other materials.

3. No other product had the same combination of qualities and characteristics as cellophane.

---

of producers to 20, average industry earnings for that year declined to 5% and du Pont suffered a net loss. "From the beginning of the depression in 1929 through the succeeding recovery and the 1938 recession du Pont averaged 29.6 per cent before taxes on its cellophane investment. On its rayon investment it averaged only 6.3 per cent." *Id.*, at 62–63.

4. As self-service meats became more popular, du Pont lost a considerable portion of its packaging business to pliofilm, a product more expensive than cellophane but with superior physical characteristics.

5. Cellophane was always priced higher than the other two largest selling flexible wrappings, wax paper and glassine, and if cellophane lowered its price somewhat it would have attracted more business from the buyers of these products.

6. When du Pont's costs declined between 1924 to 1935, it reduced its prices. When its costs increased after 1935, it made no further price reductions until 1938 and 1939.

7. During an eight-year period du Pont dropped the price of plain cellophane 84%; the price of glassine (which was far lower than the price of cellophane) remained constant.

8. Du Pont never priced below its costs.

9. As the trial judge observed on his visit to the Annual Packaging Show in Atlantic City, many flexible packaging materials were offered in competition with cellophane.

10. Sylvania, the only other producer of cellophane, followed every pricing move made by du Pont.

11. Du Pont made efforts to keep others from entering or expanding into the production and sale of cellophane.

12. From 1937 to 1947, du Pont's return before taxes was 31%; its return after taxes, bonuses, and basic research expense was 15.9%. Production of rayon is an industry with similar capital requirements and risks. Du Pont entered the rayon market in 1921. By the end of 1930, the rayon industry was competitively structured, with 20 producers. From 1929 through 1938, du Pont averaged 29.6% before taxes on its investment in cellophane and 6.3% on its investment in rayon.

Now consider: How useful has the exercise been? Was the result of the effort inclusion of many or most flexible wrappings? Did this help you to understand whether du Pont did or did not have monopoly power?

3. Judge Richard Posner has popularized the "*Cellophane* fallacy." If a firm has monopoly power, it is probably already pricing at a point reflecting the use of its monopoly power, and just below the level that will cause a critical mass of buyers to shift to substitutes. At that point, by definition, alternative products and their sellers will keep the monopolist's price at its current price and no higher. So one would expect an increase in a profit-maximizing monopolist's price to cause buyers to shift to an alternative product. Therefore cross-elasticity of demand for a product calculated on the basis of *current* price tells you only the outer limits of the power of a putative monopolist. R. Posner, Antitrust Law 150–51 (2d ed. 2001).

If cross-elasticity at current price is an inaccurate basis for measuring power, what is a better tool? You want to know the cross-elasticity of demand at defendant's cost (including a reasonable return on investment), but the data are difficult to obtain. Consider the *Cellophane* dissenters' benchmarks. Are they useful? Consider also the challenged acts, as described in the dissenting opinion. Can you draw any inferences from the conduct? Do du Pont's challenged acts help you to determine whether the company had market power? whether it thought it had market power? If a firm engages in acts or strategies that would not be profitable unless the firm had market power or the prospect of gaining it, is this relevant?

When product markets are defined en route to determining whether the putative monopolist had monopoly power, they should include all products that are good checks on exploitative pricing; i.e., all products that tend to keep prices down to cost.

4. Twenty-six years after *Cellophane*, the Justice Department published merger guidelines that set forth, among other things, a methodology for defining the market—which is a framework to help determine whether particular mergers create or enhance market power.[5] The current Guidelines are the 2010 Federal Agency Horizontal Merger Guidelines. See Chapter 4 and Appendix C. To define the market, one normally starts with the smallest credible market hypothesis. In the hypothetical case of a merger of du Pont and Sylvania in the 1950s, that hypothesis would have been cellophane. Then (hypothetically), the analyst imposes a SSNIP—a small but significant and nontransitory increase in price over current price (e.g. 5%). Then one observes (with the help of economists, etc.) whether, in the face of the price rise, a critical mass of buyers would shift to other alternatives (glassine, waxed paper) so as to make the price increase unprofitable. All such alternatives are included in the relevant market. Is the *Cellophane* test substantially a SSNIP test? Why is the *Cellophane* fallacy not a fallacy for market definition in merger analysis?Do you see why the SSNIP test is appropriate for merger analysis when the question is whether the merger will *increase* prices, but not necessarily helpful in monopoly cases to determine whether a putative monopolist *already has* monopoly power?

2. MODERN U.S. MARKET DEFINITION AND ASSESSMENT OF POWER

Despite its incompleteness, the *Cellophane* test gives important information. Reasonably interchangeable products (substitutability at current price) should be included in a first-cut market hypothesis, at least to determine the outer limits of a market. Cross-elasticity at current price similarly is helpful. It will reveal dynamics of market competition *given* the putative dominant firm's price. Still, we need to know whether defendant was pricing at a monopoly level. How can we get this information? There may be direct evidence that defendant derived supracompetitive profits from its distinctive product; there may be evidence of an elevated return on investment compared with a benchmark industry with similar characteristics including capital investment and risk (see the dissent in *Cellophane*); there may be evidence that defendant's prices rose after a competitive force was removed (see *Kodak*, below.)

5. Notably, the 2010 Horizontal Merger Guidelines take some stress off market definition and suggest other ways to determine if the merger creates market power and hurts consumers.

In a given case, two or more market delineations may be equally credible. If you, like Justice Scalia, deplore "the sledgehammer of § 2" (see his dissenting opinion in *Kodak*); or if you, like Justice Stevens, worry about the excesses of private power, would you have been moved towards an expansive or narrow market definition in the *Cellophane* case? Would your inclinations or assumptions be affected by the pace and character of technological change and thus the sustainability of any monopoly (cellophane was rapidly losing market share to newer wraps)? Consider two contemporary cases on market definition: *Kodak* and *Microsoft*.

EASTMAN KODAK CO. v. IMAGE TECHNICAL SERVICES, INC.

504 U.S. 451 (1992)
(market definition).

JUSTICE BLACKMUN: [Eastman Kodak Company entered the market for making and selling high-volume photocopying and micrographic equipment. It encouraged independent service companies (ISOs) to service and repair the Kodak machines. It sold repair parts to these firms, or made them available through manufacturers that it licensed to make certain parts. The ISOs provided good service at reasonable prices.

Some time later Kodak decided to undercut the ISOs and take most of the servicing businesses for itself. It advised its equipment customers that they now had two options; either they could repair their Kodak machines themselves, in which case Kodak or the licensed manufacturers would sell them the repair parts, or Kodak would service their machines. Kodak required the licensed manufacturers to stop supplying parts to the ISOs. Kodak's prices were higher than the ISOs' prices and its service was sometimes of inferior quality.

The ISOs sued Kodak for violations of Sections 1 and 2. They alleged that Kodak had monopolized the market for servicing and repair of the Kodak copying equipment. In support of their single-brand market definition, they introduced evidence that customers of the copying equipment, at the time of their purchase, could not feasibly obtain sufficient information about suppliers' performance in the aftermarket (service and repair) and their future repair needs; that once a customer bought a certain brand it was locked into the brand; it had no flexibility to switch just because a competitor offered lower-price upkeep; and that therefore the supplier of the brand (Kodak) had market power over service and repair in its own aftermarket.

Kodak argued that a brand cannot be a market. Kodak maintained that competition among copying machine competitors would necessarily cause it to behave responsively towards its customers for their servicing needs, and it stated that significant interbrand competition in the original-purchase market (which plaintiffs had not denied) is inconsistent with a firm's market power over its own brand in the aftermarket. Kodak moved for summary judgment. The district court granted the motion. The appellate court reversed.]

Kodak also contends that, as a matter of law, a single brand of a product or service can never be a relevant market under the Sherman Act. We disagree. The relevant market for antitrust purposes is determined by the choices available to Kodak equipment owners.... Because service and parts for Kodak equipment are not interchangeable with other manufacturers' service and parts, the relevant market from the Kodak-equipment owner's perspective is composed of only those companies that service Kodak machines. See *Du Pont*, 351 U.S., at 404 (The "market is composed of products that have reasonable interchangeability"). This Court's prior cases support the proposition that in some instances one brand of a product can constitute a separate market.... The proper market definition in this case can be determined only after a factual inquiry into the "commercial realities" faced by consumers. [Remanded for trial.]

* * *

JUSTICE SCALIA, joined by JUSTICES O'CONNOR and THOMAS, dissenting: The Court today finds in the typical manufacturer's inherent power over its own brand of equipment—over the sale of distinctive repair parts for that equipment, for example—the sort of "monopoly power" sufficient to bring the sledgehammer of § 2 into play.... In my opinion, this makes no economic sense. [B]ecause the sort of power condemned by the Court today is possessed by every manufacturer of durable goods with distinctive parts, the Court's opinion threatens to release a torrent of litigation and a flood of commercial intimidation that will do much more harm than good to enforcement of the antitrust laws and to genuine competition.... * * *

... Without even so much as asking whether the purposes of § 2 are implicated here, the Court points to Kodak's control of "100% of the parts market and 80% to 95% of the service market," markets with "no readily available substitutes," ... and finds that the proffer of such statistics is sufficient to fend off summary judgment. But this showing could easily be made, as I have explained, with respect to virtually any manufacturer of differentiated products requiring aftermarket support. By permitting antitrust plaintiffs to invoke § 2 simply upon the unexceptional demonstration that a manufacturer controls the supplies of its single-branded merchandise, the Court transforms § 2 from a specialized mechanism for responding to extraordinary agglomerations (or threatened agglomerations) of economic power to an all-purpose remedy against run-of-the-mill business torts....

QUESTIONS AND COMMENTS

1. Additional portions of both the majority and dissenting opinions in this case appear in the excerpt on tying, infra, at p. 671.

2. Who is correct, Blackmun or Scalia? What explains their differences? Values? Perspectives? Who has the better grasp of economics? Does Justice

Blackmun have a good point: The question, on a summary judgment motion, is whether plaintiffs have presented credible evidence that defendant has the power to exploit the buyers in the hypothesized market, and interbrand competition in an equipment market does not negate the possibility of power over buyers locked into a single brand. Does Justice Scalia have a good point about the torrent of litigation and intimidation (of defendants pressured to settle nuisance suits) likely to be unleashed by a routine recognition of single brand markets? Isn't nearly every buyer of expensive equipment locked into buying replacement parts from the manufacturer of its brand? Does this mean that every brand manufacturer is a monopolist? Is there a principled way to take account of both concerns?

3. Is *Kodak* consistent with *Cellophane*?

4. In the subsequent part of its opinion in *Kodak*, the Supreme Court held that the ISOs had assembled sufficient evidence to go to trial on both the monopolization claim and the tying claim. The Court's analysis of the law on tying is at p. 671 infra. At trial, the jury returned a unanimous verdict for the plaintiffs, with damages totalling $71.8 million after trebling. Appealing again, Kodak claimed among other things that its intellectual property ownership gave it the absolute right to refuse to supply spare parts to the ISOs. This part of the appellate court's opinion is at p. 298 infra.

5. Domino Pizza, Inc., a major fast-food pizza operator with franchisees operating 3500 Domino Pizza stores, required its franchisees to purchase from it or its designee all ingredients for their pizzas and all other supplies. The franchisees sued, claiming that they were overcharged and alleging that Domino Pizza had monopolized the $500 million aftermarket for supplies to Domino franchisees. Was there a relevant market for supplies to Domino Pizza franchisees? Can the franchisees prevail on their relevant market claim on the basis of *Kodak*? See *Queens City Pizza v. Domino's Pizza*, in Chapter 6 at p. 703.

UNITED STATES v. MICROSOFT CORP.

253 F.3d 34 (D.C.Cir.), cert. denied, 534 U.S. 952 (2001)
(market definition).

PER CURIAM: [The federal government, 20 states* and the District of Columbia sued Microsoft for violating Sections 1 and 2 of the Sherman Act by a series of exclusionary acts and threats designed to preserve its monopoly in Intel-compatible personal computer operating systems. Microsoft argued that this market definition was too narrow; that there were many sources of competitive pressures on Microsoft's Windows that should have been included.]

Monopoly Power

1. *Market Structure*

a. *Market definition*

"Because the ability of consumers to turn to other suppliers restrains a firm from raising prices above the competitive level," *Rothery Storage &*

* One state dropped out.

Van Co. v. Atlas Van Lines, Inc., 792 F.2d 210, 218 (D.C.Cir.1986), the relevant market must include all products "reasonably interchangeable by consumers for the same purposes." *du Pont*, 351 U.S. at 395. In this case, the District Court defined the market as "the licensing of all Intel-compatible PC operating systems worldwide," finding that there are "currently no products—and . . . there are not likely to be any in the near future—that a significant percentage of computer users worldwide could substitute for [these operating systems] without incurring substantial costs." *Conclusions of Law*, [87 F.Supp. 2d] at 36. Calling this market definition "far too narrow," . . . Microsoft argues that the District Court improperly excluded three types of products: non-Intel compatible operating systems (primarily Apple's Macintosh operating system, Mac OS), operating systems for non-PC devices (such as handheld computers and portal websites), and "middleware" products, which are not operating systems at all.

We begin with Mac OS. Microsoft's argument that Mac OS should have been included in the relevant market suffers from a flaw that infects many of the company's monopoly power claims: the company fails to challenge the District Court's factual findings, or to argue that these findings do not support the court's conclusions. The District Court found that consumers would not switch from Windows to Mac OS in response to a substantial price increase because of the costs of acquiring the new hardware needed to run Mac OS (an Apple computer and peripherals) and compatible software applications, as well as because of the effort involved in learning the new system and transferring files to its format. The court also found the Apple system less appealing to consumers because it costs considerably more and supports fewer applications. Microsoft responds only by saying: "the district court's market definition is so narrow that it excludes Apple's Mac OS, which has competed with Windows for years, simply because the Mac OS runs on a different microprocessor." . . . This general, conclusory statement falls far short of what is required to challenge findings as clearly erroneous. . . .

Microsoft's challenge to the District Court's exclusion of non-PC based competitors, such as information appliances (handheld devices, etc.) and portal websites that host serverbased software applications, suffers from the same defect: the company fails to challenge the District Court's key factual findings. In particular, the District Court found that because information appliances fall far short of performing all of the functions of a PC, most consumers will buy them only as a supplement to their PCs. The District Court also found that portal websites do not presently host enough applications to induce consumers to switch, nor are they likely to do so in the near future. . . .

This brings us to Microsoft's main challenge to the District Court's market definition: the exclusion of middleware. Because of the importance of middleware to this case, we pause to explain what it is and how it relates to the issue before us.

Operating systems perform many functions, including allocating computer memory and controlling peripherals such as printers and keyboards. Operating systems also function as platforms for software applications. They do this by "exposing"—*i.e.*, making available to software developers—routines or protocols that perform certain widely-used functions. These are known as Application Programming Interfaces, or "APIs." For example, Windows contains an API that enables users to draw a box on the screen. Software developers wishing to include that function in an application need not duplicate it in their own code. Instead, they can "call"—*i.e.*, use—the Windows API. Windows contains thousands of APIs, controlling everything from data storage to font display.

Every operating system has different APIs. Accordingly, a developer who writes an application for one operating system and wishes to sell the application to users of another must modify, or "port," the application to the second operating system. This process is both time consuming and expensive.

"Middleware" refers to software products that expose their own APIs. Because of this, a middleware product written for Windows could take over some or all of Windows's valuable platform functions—that is, developers might begin to rely upon APIs exposed by the middleware for basic routines rather than relying upon the API set included in Windows. If middleware were written for multiple operating systems, its impact could be even greater. The more developers could rely upon APIs exposed by such middleware, the less expensive porting to different operating systems would be. Ultimately, if developers could write applications relying exclusively on APIs exposed by middleware, their applications would run on any operating system on which the middleware was also present. Netscape Navigator and Java—both at issue in this case—are middleware products written for multiple operating systems.

Microsoft argues that, because middleware could usurp the operating system's platform function and might eventually take over other operating system functions (for instance, by controlling peripherals), the District Court erred in excluding Navigator and Java from the relevant market. The District Court found, however, that neither Navigator, Java, nor any other middleware product could now, or would soon, expose enough APIs to serve as a platform for popular applications, much less take over all operating system functions. Again, Microsoft fails to challenge these findings, instead simply asserting middleware's "potential" as a competitor. The test of reasonable interchangeability, however, required the District Court to consider only substitutes that constrain pricing in the reasonably foreseeable future, and only products that can enter the market in a relatively short time can perform this function. See *Rothery*, 792 F.2d at 218 ("Because the ability of consumers to turn to other suppliers restrains a firm from raising prices above the competitive level, the definition of the 'relevant market' rests on a determination of available substitutes."); see also *Findings of Fact* ¶ 29 ("[I]t would take several years for middleware . . . to evolve" into a product that can constrain operating system pricing.). Whatever middleware's ultimate potential, the District Court found that consumers could not now abandon their operating systems and switch to middleware in response to a sustained price for Windows above the competitive level. Nor is middleware likely to overtake the operating system as the primary platform for software development any time in the near future.

Alternatively, Microsoft argues that the District Court should not have excluded middleware from the relevant market because the primary focus of the plaintiffs' § 2 charge is on Microsoft's attempts to suppress middleware's threat to its operating system monopoly. According to Microsoft, it is "contradict[ory]" to define the relevant market to exclude the "very competitive threats that gave rise" to the action. The purported contradiction lies between plaintiffs' § 2 theory, under which Microsoft preserved its monopoly against middleware technologies that threatened to become viable substitutes for Windows, and its theory of the relevant market, under which middleware is not presently a viable substitute for Windows. Because middleware's threat is only nascent, however, no contradiction exists. Nothing in § 2 of the Sherman Act limits its prohibition to actions taken against threats that are already well-developed enough to serve as present substitutes. Because market definition is meant to identify products "reasonably interchangeable by consumers," *du Pont*, 351 U.S. at 395, and because middleware is not now interchangeable with Windows, the District Court had good reason for excluding middleware from the relevant market.

b. Market power

Having thus properly defined the relevant market, the District Court found that Windows accounts for a greater than 95% share. The court also found that even if Mac OS were included, Microsoft's share would exceed 80%. Microsoft challenges neither finding, nor does it argue that such a market share is not predominant.

Instead, Microsoft claims that even a predominant market share does not by itself indicate monopoly power. Although the "existence of [monopoly] power ordinarily may be inferred from the predominant share of the market," *Grinnell*, 384 U.S. at 571, we agree with Microsoft that because of the possibility of competition from new entrants, looking to current market share alone can be "misleading." ... In this case, however, the District Court was not misled. Considering the possibility of new rivals, the court focused not only on Microsoft's present market share, but also on the structural barrier that protects the company's future position. That barrier—the "applications barrier to entry"—stems from two characteristics of the software market: (1) most consumers prefer operating systems for which a large number of applications have already been written; and (2) most developers prefer to write for operating systems that already have a substantial consumer base. This "chicken-and-egg" situation ensures that applications will continue to be written for the already dominant

Windows, which in turn ensures that consumers will continue to prefer it over other operating systems.

Challenging the existence of the applications barrier to entry, Microsoft observes that software developers do write applications for other operating systems, pointing out that at its peak IBM's OS/2 supported approximately 2,500 applications. This misses the point. That some developers write applications for other operating systems is not at all inconsistent with the finding that the applications barrier to entry discourages many from writing for these less popular platforms. * * *

Microsoft next argues that the applications barrier to entry is not an entry barrier at all, but a reflection of Windows' popularity. It is certainly true that Windows may have gained its initial dominance in the operating system market competitively—through superior foresight or quality. But this case is not about Microsoft's initial acquisition of monopoly power. It is about Microsoft's efforts to maintain this position through means other than competition on the merits. Because the applications barrier to entry protects a dominant operating system irrespective of quality, it gives Microsoft power to stave off even superior new rivals. The barrier is thus a characteristic of the operating system market, not of Microsoft's popularity, or, as asserted by a Microsoft witness, the company's efficiency.

Finally, Microsoft argues that the District Court should not have considered the applications barrier to entry because it reflects not a cost borne disproportionately by new entrants, but one borne by all participants in the operating system market. According to Microsoft, it had to make major investments to convince software developers to write for its new operating system, and it continues to "evangelize" the Windows platform today. Whether costs borne by all market participants should be considered entry barriers is the subject of much debate. ... We need not resolve this issue, however, for even under the more narrow definition it is clear that there are barriers. When Microsoft entered the operating system market with MS–DOS and the first version of Windows, it did not confront a dominant rival operating system with as massive an installed base and as vast an existing array of applications as the Windows operating systems have since enjoyed. Moreover, when Microsoft introduced Windows 95 and 98, it was able to bypass the applications barrier to entry that protected the incumbent Windows by including APIs from the earlier version in the new operating systems. This made porting existing Windows applications to the new version of Windows much less costly than porting them to the operating systems of other entrants who could not freely include APIs from the incumbent Windows with their own.

2. *Direct Proof*

Having sustained the District Court's conclusion that circumstantial evidence proves that Microsoft possesses monopoly power, we turn to Microsoft's alternative argument that it does not behave like a monopolist. Claiming that software competition is uniquely "dynamic," the company suggests a new rule: that monopoly power in the software industry should be proven directly, that is, by examining a company's actual behavior to determine if it reveals the existence of monopoly power. According to Microsoft, not only does no such proof of its power exist, but record evidence demonstrates the absence of monopoly power. The company claims that it invests heavily in research and development ... (citing Direct Testimony of Paul Maritz ... testifying that Microsoft invests approximately 17% of its revenue in R&D), and charges a low price for Windows (a small percentage of the price of an Intel-compatible PC system and less than the price of its rivals ...).

Microsoft's argument fails because, even assuming that the software market is uniquely dynamic in the long term, the District Court correctly applied the structural approach to determine if the company faces competition in the short term. Structural market power analyses are meant to determine whether potential substitutes constrain a firm's ability to raise prices above the competitive level; only threats that are likely to materialize in the relatively near future perform this function to any significant degree. *Rothery*, 792 F.2d at 218 (only substitutes that can enter the market "promptly" should be considered). The District Court expressly considered and rejected Microsoft's claims that innovations such as handheld devices and portal websites would soon expand the relevant market beyond Intel-compatible PC operating systems. Because the company does not challenge these findings, we have no reason to believe that prompt substitutes are available. The structural approach, as applied by the District Court, is thus capable of fulfilling its purpose even in a changing market....

Even if we were to require direct proof, moreover, Microsoft's behavior may well be sufficient to show the existence of monopoly power. Certainly, none of the conduct Microsoft points to—its investment in R&D and the relatively low price of Windows—is inconsistent with the possession of such power. The R&D expenditures Microsoft points to are not simply for Windows, but for its entire company, which most likely does not possess a monopoly for all of its products. Moreover, because innovation can increase an already dominant market share and further delay the emergence of competition, even monopolists have reason to invest in R&D. Microsoft's pricing behavior is similarly equivocal. The company claims only that it never charged the short-term profit-maximizing price for Windows. Faced with conflicting expert testimony, the District Court found that it could not accurately determine what this price would be. In any event, the court found, a price lower than the short-term profit-maximizing price is not inconsistent with possession or improper use of monopoly power....

More telling, the District Court found that some aspects of Microsoft's behavior are difficult to explain unless Windows is a monopoly product. For instance, according to the District Court, the company set the price of Windows without considering rivals' prices, something a firm without a monopoly would have been unable to do. The District Court also found that Microsoft's pattern of exclusionary conduct could only be rational "if the firm knew that it possessed monopoly power." . . .

QUESTIONS AND COMMENTS

1. Traditionally, the market must include all significant competitive pressures that tend to push prices to cost. Is this the right perspective for new economy markets? If not, what is the right perspective? Can market power be proved directly? How?

2. How strong were Microsoft's arguments that the market must include *a*) Non–Intel compatible operating systems, principally Mac OS (Apple). *b*) Non–PC based competitors such as handheld devices. *c*) Middleware. Which of the three claims is strongest? Which is weakest? Does Microsoft have a good point that middleware had to be included since plaintiffs' theory of the case was based on Microsoft's conduct to eliminate the threat from middleware, which potentially could be written to run on all operating systems and if this occurred middleware would "commoditize" Microsoft?

3. Explain the relationship between market definition, market share, and market power. Does the Court use presumptions and burden-shifting? How? Is this justified?

4. What is the significance of an applications barrier to entry into the PC operating systems market?

5. Are you convinced that Microsoft had monopoly power? power to do what? How important are the following claims, if proven: *a*) Microsoft did not charge an exploitative price for its software. *b*) Microsoft had to keep innovating to satisfy computer users, or it would probably be overtaken by a rival's new technological paradigm. *c*) Microsoft had the power to hold at bay technological challengers who needed to rely in part on Microsoft's operating system or other support from Microsoft.

6. European Union law offers the following definition of dominance, first articulated in *Hoffmann–La Roche v. Commission*, Case 85/76, [1979] ECR 461, and quoted frequently thereafter.

> 38 The dominant position . . . referred to [in (now) Article 102] relates to a position of economic strength enjoyed by an undertaking which enables it to prevent effective competition being maintained on the relevant market by affording it the power to behave to an appreciable extent independently of its competitors, its customers and ultimately of the consumers.
>
> 39 Such a position does not preclude some competition, which it does where there is a monopoly or a quasi-monopoly, but enables the undertaking which profits by it, if not to determine, at least to have an appreciable influence on the conditions under which that competition will develop, and in any case to act largely in disregard of it so long as such conduct does not operate to its detriment. . . . * * *
>
> 40 A substantial market share as evidence of the existence of a dominant position is not a constant factor and its importance varies from market to market according to the structure of these markets, especially as far as production, supply and demand are concerned. . . .

41 . . . [A]lthough the importance of the market shares may vary from one market to another the view may legitimately be taken that very large shares are in themselves, and save in exceptional circumstances, evidence of the existence of a dominant position.

An undertaking which has a very large market share and holds it for some time, by means of the volume of production and the scale of the supply which it stands for—without those having much smaller market shares being able to meet rapidly the demand from those who would like to break away from the undertaking which has the largest market share—is by virtue of that share in a position of strength which makes it an unavoidable trading partner and which, already because of this secures for it, at the very least during relatively long periods, that freedom of action which is the special feature of a dominant position.

* * *

In the EU *AKZO* case, Case 62/86, [1991] ECR–I–3359, a market share of 50% was held to create a presumption of dominance.

U.S. caselaw tends to set the bar higher; e.g., a presumption at 70% where barriers are significant. ANTITRUST LAW DEVELOPMENTS 6th at 231 (2007).

Even though caselaw in numerous jurisdictions incorporates presumptions and accordingly a shift in the burden of coming forward with evidence, the U.S. antitrust agencies recognize that numerous factors are relevant to a prediction of significant sustainable market power. The agencies do the analysis and do not take a market-share short-cut. Thus, they ask: Does this firm have the power to raise price significantly above cost for a significant time?

A recommendation of the International Competition Network identifies the important factual inquiries. See International Competition Network, Recommended Practices for Dominance/Substantial Market Power Analysis (2008), at *http://www.internationalcompetitionnetwork.org/uploads/library/doc317.pdf*.

Watch the videos produced by ICN on market definition and market power. These may be found on the website of the International Competition Network, *http://www.internationalcompetitionnetwork.org*. Find ICN Curriculum Project and select Module 3, Market Definition, and Module 4, Market Power.

D. THE CONDUCT OFFENSE

1. THE PARADIGM

In *Alcoa* the court suggested that the Section 2 offense might be structural—attaining and preserving a monopoly position; for after all, monopoly normally leads to economic exploitation and inefficiency. Moreover, monopoly is akin to a dictatorship of the market. Therefore, the court suggested, *monopoly* was presumptively a wrong to society, although sometimes a firm could avoid condemnation by proving that it did not seek monopoly; that it was an accident or a fortuity.

This stark perspective—the monopoly structure offense—was challenged by observers and policymakers. It conflicted with a view of freedom of business enterprise, and it could undercut incentives to be the best. Moreover, many observers were skeptical that a firm could obtain more than transient power unless the *government* granted monopoly rights or erected barriers to entry, and they worried about judicial error in finding that a monopoly existed. If, however, a firm attained or maintained monopoly by reprehensible acts, these concerns would disappear; punishing bad acts would not punish meritorious behavior; incentives to succeed on the merits would be left untouched. Accordingly, even in the shadow of *Alcoa*, courts examined the conduct of the putative monopolist to determine whether that conduct was "wrongfully" anticompetitive. Some jurists (notably Judge Wyzanski) expressed the view that monopoly almost inevitably bred "wrongful" conduct, for such are the incentives; power tends to corrupt; the powerful tend to use the power they have. If this was so, it was a short step from monopoly power to abuse of that power.

"Bad conduct," however, proved hard to characterize. What is bad conduct and what is merely aggressive competition? What is anticompetitive, and what (even if unsavory) is at most a tort? If competitors are hurt by the acts of the dominant firm, are they hurt by competition or by predation? This debate did not fully crystallize until the 1980s, when the law sharpened its focus to protect consumers, and antitrust enforcers and later the Supreme Court cautioned sternly against using antitrust to "protect competitors" from efficient competition. Global competition put pressure on policymakers not to handicap success and not to blunt aggressive firms' competitiveness in international markets. As you read the cases exploring whether certain conduct is anticompetitive, bear in mind the possible tension between protecting consumers and preserving a clear and open path for competitors.

Monopolization and attempt to monopolize are two different offenses.[6] In the case of attempts to monopolize it is usually said that a firm must specifically intend to gain monopoly and its challenged acts must threaten to produce a dangerous probability of achieving monopoly. *Swift & Co. v. United States*, 196 U.S. 375, 396 (1905). Nonetheless, conduct that is anticompetitive for purposes of the attempt offense will also be anticompetitive for purposes of the monopolization offense, and to that rather large extent, the offenses merge. *Lorain Journal* is the first case we present. The offense alleged is attempt to monopolize. We present the case here generically, however, for deciphering whether the conduct is anticompetitive is equally relevant to the offense of monopolization. The important question is: What is anticompetitive conduct?

6. Section 2 of the Sherman Act also prohibits conspiracies to monopolize. Conspiracies to monopolize also run afoul of Section 1 of the Sherman Act.

While the analytical language in *Lorain Journal* is not entirely modern, pay attention to the conclusion: This conduct was anticompetitive and illegal under Section 2. It still is.

LORAIN JOURNAL CO. v. UNITED STATES

342 U.S. 143 (1951).

JUSTICE BURTON: . . . [W]e hold that the injunction [under Section 2 of the Sherman Act] was justified. * * *

The appellant corporation, here called the publisher, has published the Journal in the City of Lorain since before 1932. In that year it, with others, purchased the Times–Herald which was the only competing daily paper published in that city. Later, without success, it sought a license to establish and operate a radio broadcasting station in Lorain.

The court below describes the position of the Journal, since 1933, as "a commanding and an overpowering one." It has a daily circulation in Lorain of over 13,000 copies and it reaches ninety-nine percent of the families in the city. 92 F.Supp. at 796. . . . The Sunday News, appearing only on Sundays, is the only other newspaper published there. * * *

From 1933 to 1948 the publisher enjoyed a substantial monopoly in Lorain of the mass dissemination of news and advertising, both of a local and national character. However, in 1948 the Elyria–Lorain Broadcasting Company, a corporation independent of the publisher, was licensed by the Federal Communications Commission to establish and operate in Elyria, Ohio, eight miles south of Lorain, a radio station whose call letters, WEOL stand for Elyria, Oberlin and Lorain. Since then it has operated its principal studio in Elyria and a branch studio in Lorain. Lorain has about twice the population of Elyria and is by far the largest community in the station's immediate area. Oberlin is much smaller than Elyria and eight miles south of it. * * *

The court below found that appellants knew that a substantial number of Journal advertisers wished to use the facilities of the radio station as well. For some of them it found that advertising in the Journal was essential for the promotion of their sales in Lorain County. It found that at all times since WEOL commenced broadcasting, appellants had executed a plan conceived to eliminate the threat of competition from the station. Under this plan the publisher refused to accept local advertisements in the Journal from any Lorain County advertiser who advertised or who appellants believed to be about to advertise over WEOL. The court found expressly that the purpose and intent of this procedure was to destroy the broadcasting company.

. . . To carry out appellants' plan, the publisher monitored WEOL programs to determine the identity of the station's local Lorain advertisers. Those using the station's facilities had their contracts with the publisher terminated and were able to renew them only after ceasing to advertise through WEOL. The program was effective. Numerous Lorain

County merchants testified that, as a result of the publisher's policy, they either ceased or abandoned their plans to advertise over WEOL.

> "Having the plan and desire to injure the radio station, no more effective and more direct device to impede the operations and to restrain the commerce of WEOL could be found by the Journal than to cut off its bloodstream of existence—the advertising revenues which control its life or demise....
>
> "... [T]he very existence of WEOL is imperiled by this attack upon one of its principal sources of business and income."....

1. *The conduct complained of was an attempt to monopolize interstate commerce....* Because of the Journal's complete daily newspaper monopoly of local advertising in Lorain and its practically indispensable coverage of 99% of the Lorain families, this practice forced numerous advertisers to refrain from using WEOL for local advertising. That result not only reduced the number of customers available to WEOL in the field of local Lorain advertising and strengthened the Journal's monopoly in that field, but more significantly tended to destroy and eliminate WEOL altogether. Attainment of that sought-for elimination would automatically restore to the publisher of the Journal its substantial monopoly in Lorain of the mass dissemination of all news and advertising, interstate and national, as well as local. It would deprive not merely Lorain but Elyria and all surrounding communities of their only nearby radio station. * * *

... [T]he publisher's conduct was aimed at ... complete destruction and elimination of WEOL. The court found that the publisher, before 1948, enjoyed a substantial monopoly in Lorain of the mass dissemination not only of local news and advertising, but of news of out-of-state events transmitted to Lorain for immediate dissemination, and of advertising of out-of-state products for sale in Lorain. WEOL offered competition by radio in all these fields so that the publisher's attempt to destroy WEOL was in fact an attempt to end the invasion by radio of the Lorain newspaper's monopoly of interstate as well as local commerce. * * *

2. *The publisher's attempt to regain its monopoly of interstate commerce by forcing advertisers to boycott a competing radio station violated § 2....* Numerous Lorain advertisers wished to supplement their local newspaper advertising with local radio advertising but could not afford to discontinue their newspaper advertising in order to use the radio.

WEOL's greatest potential source of income was local Lorain advertising. Loss of that was a major threat to its existence. The court below found unequivocally that appellants' conduct amounted to an attempt by the publisher to destroy WEOL and, at the same time, to regain the publisher's pre–1948 substantial monopoly over the mass dissemination of all news and advertising.

To establish this violation of § 2 as charged, it was not necessary to show that success rewarded appellants' attempt to monopolize. The injunctive relief under § 4 sought to forestall that success. While appellants' attempt to monopolize did succeed insofar as it deprived WEOL of income, WEOL has not yet been eliminated. The injunction may save it. "[W]hen that intent [to monopolize] and the consequent dangerous probability exist, this statute [the Sherman Act], like many others and like the common law in some cases, directs itself against that dangerous probability as well as against the completed result." *Swift & Co. v. United States*, 196 U.S. 375, 396. * * *[8]

The publisher claims a right as a private business concern to select its customers and to refuse to accept advertisements from whomever it pleases. We do not dispute that general right. "But the word 'right' is one of the most deceptive of pitfalls.... The right claimed by the publisher is neither absolute nor exempt from regulation. Its exercise as a purposeful means of monopolizing interstate commerce is prohibited by the Sherman Act. The operator of the radio station, equally with the publisher of the newspaper, is entitled to the protection of that Act...."

Questions and Comments

1. There is a strong principle in U.S. law—unlike the law of certain European and other countries—that a firm, even a monopoly firm, has the right to choose its customers; it may deal or not, at its discretion. See *United States v. Colgate & Co.*, 250 U.S. 300 (1919). Is *Lorain Journal* a simple refusal-to-deal case? Did Lorain Journal simply want nothing to do with firms that advertised on WEOL, or did it want (and expect) its ultimatum to produce something else?

2. Would Lorain Journal have had the incentive to boycott customers who advertised on WEOL if WEOL had had an alternative source of ample advertising revenues and was sure to flourish?

3. What do you make of Lorain Journal's justification in footnote 8: it was protecting the businesses of Lorain (including its own business) from outside competition and was thereby protecting the Lorain community. Should this argument have helped or hurt the Journal? Does *National Society of Professional Engineers*, p. 77 supra, allow it?

4. *Lorain Journal* is a paradigmatic case of anticompetitive conduct. See R. Bork, The Antitrust Paradox: A Policy at War with Itself 344 (1978). The conduct had no purpose or expected effect but to handicap its competitor or put it out of business, thus preserving Lorain Journal's claim on the advertising budgets of the local businesses. The conduct did not respond to any needs and desires of its customers; quite to the contrary, the conduct was punishing.

---

8. Appellants have sought to justify their conduct on the ground that it was part of the publisher's program for the protection of the Lorain market from outside competition. The publisher claimed to have refused advertising from Elyria or other out-of-town advertisers for the reason that such advertisers might compete with Lorain concerns. The publisher then classified WEOL as the publisher's own competitor from Elyria and asked its Lorain advertisers to refuse to employ WEOL as an advertising medium in competition with the Journal. We find no principle of law which required Lorain advertisers thus to boycott an Elyria advertising medium merely because the publisher of a Lorain advertising medium had chosen to boycott some Elyria advertisers who might compete for business in the Lorain market. Nor do we find any principle of law which permitted this publisher to dictate to prospective advertisers that they might advertise either by newspaper or by radio but that they might not use both facilities.

The defendant had to pay a price—risking the good will of customers who shunned WEOL simply for the privilege of advertising in Lorain Journal, and losing some customers who preferred WEOL. But Lorain Journal undoubtedly calculated that the cost was worth it; most Lorain businesses could not afford not to advertize in the Journal, and the ultimatum could drain WEOL—its new and one serious competitor—of its life blood.

5. In the much later era of *Microsoft*, (former) Judge Robert Bork represented Netscape, pioneer of the browser for personal computers and especially for Microsoft's Windows. He argued that Microsoft's conduct that strategically excluded Netscape's Navigator browser from access to all efficient channels of distribution fit precisely within the *Lorain Journal* paradigm. See p. 692 infra. Did it?

2. EVOLUTION OF THE LAW

The monopoly law poses a conundrum. Monopoly is the perceived problem. Yet outlawing "monopoly" is also a problem.

Economically, monopoly is harmful because the monopolist can be expected to raise prices and lower output (and act sluggishly), thereby misallocating resources. But monopoly pricing—the paradigmatic consumer harm—is not illegal in the United States. Courts are ill equipped to be price regulators. The hope is that high pricing will invite competition, and the forces of competition will break the back of the monopoly. *Berkey Photo, Inc. v. Eastman Kodak Co.*, 603 F.2d 263, 294 (2d Cir.1979), *cert. denied*, 444 U.S. 1093 (1980).

Since simple, direct exploitation (monopoly pricing) is not illegal, courts called upon to apply Section 2 deal principally with conduct that excludes competitors and harms the market and consumers. This phenomenon has survived even the flowering of the Chicago School (protect consumers, not competitors).

European antitrust history differs on three counts. First, there is no European *Alcoa*. The founders of the European Community meant to *regulate* the conduct of the dominant firm, not to condemn dominance. Second, the founders were, in general, receptive to, not skeptical of, government regulation. For example, in the Treaty of Rome, now the Treaty on the Functioning of the European Union, they expressly made unfair pricing (excessively high or low pricing) an abuse-of-dominance offense. Third, the European system never begrudged law to protect opportunity, access, and openness for competitors. Rather, freedom of trade by business actors is treated as a component of the "free movement" law (freedom from state and private restraints) and as an important means of integrating the European economies into one common internal market. See E. Fox, What is Harm to Competition?—Exclusionary Practices and Anticompetitive Effect, 70 Antitrust L.J. 371 (2002).

The competition laws of many nations follow the EU in prohibiting excessive pricing, which is usually defined as pricing having no reasonable relationship to value, or pricing unreasonably high over costs.

We will reach the modern law on exclusionary conduct rather quickly. First we take a look at several landmarks that pave the way.

If these earlier cases are not entirely modern, it is because they spend little or no time on two additional inquiries which are essential today: 1) Was the challenged conduct efficient and helpful to consumers, and 2) Could the "foreclosed" competitors simply have competed harder and better and have maneuvered around the restraint? Add these two questions to your analytical toolbox as you read the pre–1980 cases.

UNITED STATES v. UNITED SHOE MACHINERY CORP.

110 F.Supp. 295 (D.Mass.1953) aff'd, 347 U.S. 521 (1954).

JUDGE WYZANSKI: [United Shoe Machinery (USM) manufactured more than 75% of all shoe-making machines. It had virtually a monopoly of the complex machines. Shoe manufacturers could normally not afford to buy the machines, and USM leased them, for 10–year terms. The lessee of a USM machine was required to use the machine to full capacity if it had work available. When a lessee desired to replace a machine, USM would give favorable terms if the machine was replaced with a USM machine. USM repaired the machines "free." The machines performed excellently and the repair service was prompt and efficient. USM's success with its complicated machines and its resulting good business relations with shoe factories enabled USM to sell or lease more simple machines to the shoe factories. USM took a lower rate of return where competition was greater. "Much of United's market power [was] traceable to the magnetic ties inherent in its system of leasing. . . ."]

* * *

In one sense, the leasing system and the miscellaneous activities just referred to (except United's purchases in the second-hand market) were natural and normal, for they were, in Judge Hand's words, "honestly industrial". They are the sort of activities which would be engaged in by other honorable firms. And, to a large extent, the leasing practices conform to long-standing traditions in the shoe machinery business. Yet, they are not practices which can be properly described as the inevitable consequences of ability, natural forces, or law. They represent something more than the use of accessible resources, the process of invention and innovation, and the employment of those techniques of employment, financing, production, and distribution, which a competitive society must foster. They are contracts, arrangements, and policies which, instead of encouraging competition based on pure merit, further the dominance of a particular firm. In this sense, they are unnatural barriers; they unnecessarily exclude actual and potential competition; they restrict a free market. While the law allows many enterprises to use such practices, the Sherman Act is now construed by superior courts to forbid the continuance of effective market control based in part upon such practices. Those courts hold that market control is inherently evil and constitutes a violation of § 2 unless economically inevitable, or specifically authorized and regulated by law.

* * *

Nor has United affirmatively proved that it has achieved spectacular results at amazing rates of speed, nor has it proved that comparable research results and comparable economies of production, distribution, and service could not be achieved as well by, say, three important shoe machinery firms, as by one. Compo with a much smaller organization indicates how much research can be done on a smaller scale.... [O]ne point is worth recalling. Compo's inventors first found practical ways to introduce the cement process which United had considered and rejected. This experience illustrates the familiar truth that one of the dangers of extraordinary experience is that those who have it may fall into grooves created by their own expertness. They refuse to believe that hurdles which they have learned from experience are insurmountable, can in fact be overcome by fresh, independent minds. * * * [USM violated § 2.]

Remedy ... In the anti-trust field the courts have been accorded, by common consent, an authority they have in no other branch of enacted law. Indeed, the only comparable examples of the power of judges is the economic role they formerly exercised under the Fourteenth Amendment, and the role they now exercise in the area of civil liberties. They would not have been given, or allowed to keep, such authority in the anti-trust field, and they would not so freely have altered from time to time the interpretation of its substantive provisions, if courts were in the habit of proceeding with the surgical ruthlessness that might commend itself to those seeking absolute assurance that there will be workable competition, and to those aiming at immediate realization of the social, political, and economic advantages of dispersal of power.

* * *

The court ordered only modest divestiture, along with injunctions requiring, among other things, that USM sell, rather than only lease, its complex machines to customers who wished to purchase them. But even after implementation of the remedy, the stronghold of USM persisted. The government moved for further divestiture, which it got by consent decree. 1969 Trade Cas. (CCH), ¶ 72,688 (D. Mass. 1969).

NOTE ON UNITED STATES v. GRINNELL CORP.
384 U.S. 563 (1966)

This case involved mergers and predatory pricing in central station protective services for fires and burglary. The case is most noteworthy for its formulation of the necessary conditions to violate Section 2:

> The offense of monopoly under § 2 of the Sherman Act has two elements: (1) the possession of monopoly power in the relevant market and (2) the

willful acquisition or maintenance of that power as distinguished from growth or development as a consequence of a superior product, business acumen, or historic accident.

Point (2) remained to be defined by subsequent caselaw. We will spend a good deal of time on what "willful acquisition or maintenance" means. Courts would later find it necessary to add to point (2), so as not to condemn procompetitive acts that are good for consumers: "by acts not on competitive merits."

Compare the *Grinnell* standard with the *Alcoa* test. Note that it is a step away from *Alcoa*'s strong skepticism toward "monopoly structure."

3. ESSENTIAL FACILITIES AND DUTIES TO DEAL

Until relatively recent times, U.S. antitrust law was not unsympathetic with the notion that a firm with monopoly power in one market which was competing in an adjacent market had duties to competitors in the adjacent market. The essential facilities doctrine embodied this notion. But as you read the cases, below, be aware that sympathies changed. The turning point is captured in *Verizon v. Trinko* (2004), p. 249 infra. As you read the following cases and excerpts, ask yourself the modern question: If the dominant firm is forced by law to deal with its competitors, or to deal with them on certain terms, what does this legal obligation do to the incentives of that firm to invest, invent, and compete as hard as it can?

United States v. Terminal Railroad Association of St. Louis, 224 U.S. 383 (1912). The Terminal Company—a joint venture—was organized in 1889 by six railroad companies. At first it controlled only one of three independent lines connecting railroads terminating on either side of the Mississippi River at St. Louis. At great expense it acquired the other two lines. Because of the topography of St. Louis and its environs, including the river, great hills, and already occupied valleys, no railroad could enter the City of St. Louis or provide means of connection to lines on the opposite side of the river except by using the terminal facilities controlled by the Terminal Company.

The railroads that organized the Terminal Company allowed others to join the joint venture provided there was unanimous consent to their admission. By the time the complaint alleging monopolization and combination was filed, 14 companies were joint owners. Nonproprietors were permitted to use the facilities for the same fee paid by the proprietors.

The Justice Department sued, alleging that the combination was illegal under Sections 1 and 2 of the Sherman Act. The Court agreed with the Justice Department:

> [T]he situation at St. Louis is most extraordinary, and we base our conclusion in this case, in a large measure, upon that fact. The "physical or topographical condition peculiar to the locality," which is advanced as a prime justification for a unified system of terminals, constitutes a most obvious reason why such a unified system is an obstacle, a hindrance and a restriction upon interstate commerce, unless it is the impartial agent of all who, owing to conditions, are under such compulsion, as here exists, to use its facilities....

For a remedy, recognizing the public utility of consolidated terminal facilities, the Court gave directions for a decree requiring the Terminal Railroad Association to give other railroad lines equal and nondiscriminatory access to the facilities. The terms, said the Court, must allow admission to joint ownership "upon a plane of equality" and must "place every [non-owner] company upon as nearly an equal plane as may be with respect to expenses and charges as that occupied by the proprietary companies."

In antitrust jurisprudence, *Terminal Railroad* transcended its heritage as a combination (Section 1) case. It became the paradigm for essential facility duties; i.e., if a single railroad controlled all access over the Missouri River at St. Louis and for miles around, it had the duty to grant reasonable access to competing railroads. If it denied such access, the only motivation could be to impose costs on competitors.

If there was one other paradigmatic case that stood for the essential facility doctrine, it was *MCI Communications v. AT&T Corp.*, 708 F.2d 1081 (7th Cir. 1983). AT&T held the monopoly connection of long distance telephone lines to local networks. AT&T refused to give MCI—a newer long distance service competitor—reasonable access to the local lines. The Court of Appeals held that AT&T's refusal was an act of monopolization. It identified four elements necessary to establish liability:

> "(1) control of the essential facility by a monopolist; (2) a competitor's inability practically or reasonably to duplicate the essential facility; (3) the denial of the use of the facility to a competitor; and (4) the feasibility of providing the facility."

Id. at 1132–33.

Otter Tail Power Co. v. United States, 410 U.S. 366 (1973). Otter Tail was an electric utility that generated and transmitted electric power and supplied electricity at retail to municipalities, their residents, and the commercial customers within their borders. In the late 1960s and early 1970s, many towns decided to build their own transmission systems—a move that the private power industry deemed socialistic. Elbow Lake and Hankinson, towns in Otter Tail's area, requested Otter Tail to supply it with electric power at wholesale. Otter Tail refused. The towns then approached the U.S. Bureau of Reclamation, which was willing to sell them power at wholesale, but the power would have to be wheeled over the lines of Otter Tail. Otter Tail refused to wheel the power at wholesale, although it could have done so with no interference with its business. The

Federal Power Commission had the power to order an interconnection of Otter Tail with the towns, and in the case of Elbow Lake it had done so. Hankinson was seeking an order of interconnection but the town council voted to withdraw it and to renew Otter Tail's contract to serve the town (410 U.S. at 371–72).

The Supreme Court upheld a finding of monopolization. Otter Tail had used its "strategic dominance in the transmission of power ... to foreclose potential entrants into the retail area from obtaining electric power from outside sources of supply ... [citing *Lorain Journal*]. [Its] refusals to sell at wholesale or to wheel were solely to prevent municipal power systems from eroding its monopolistic position."

Otter Tail has been frequently cited as an essential facility case (although the Supreme Court did not use those words): Otter Tail owned the only transmission lines that could carry the electricity to the municipalities and the municipalities had become potential competitors for the "right to monopolize" the local retail market. Otter Tail could transmit electric energy, or wheel the Bureau's energy on its lines, without interfering with its generation business. Therefore it had the duty to wheel to or deal with competitors or potential competitors in the vertically adjacent (retail) market.

Who was hurt by Otter Tail's refusals to deal; i.e. its decision to keep the retail business for itself? Does it matter whether output or price would change?

The essential facilities doctrine was an exception to the rule of no duty to deal. By 1980, lower courts had expanded the essential facilities doctrine, and many firms with sole control of a facility or function were faced with the obligation of non-discriminatory dealing. See Abbott Lipsky and Gregory Sidak, Essential Facilities, 51 Stan. L. Rev. 1187 (1999). The courts were looking for limits to the doctrine. One set of limits was imposed in *Official Airline Guides*.

OFFICIAL AIRLINE GUIDES, INC. v. FTC

630 F.2d 920 (2d Cir.1980).

JUDGE OAKES: [Before computerized airline reservation systems were devised, the Official Airline Guide was "the bible" of airline flight schedules and the standard reference for airline ticket offices, travel agents, businesses and business travelers. Reuben H. Donnelley Corp., itself not an air carrier, was the publisher. The Guide carried a listing of connecting flights, but Donnelley refused to list the flight services of commuter airlines in this section. Rather, it listed the commuter flights separately and at the end of the book, without giving information on their connections. As a result, users of the Guide were steered to the major carriers for connecting flights. Because the relevant information about commuter airlines was not accessible, the commuter carriers were placed at a competitive disadvantage. When asked to explain, Donnelley said that the commuter flights were less reliable and therefore travelers would be ill-served and dissatisfied if listings were integrated. The Commission found that the refusal was arbitrary, it harmed competition, and it constituted a violation.] * * *

We turn then to the crucial issue in the case, whether Donnelley as a monopolist had some duty under section 5 of the FTC Act not to discriminate unjustifiably between the competing classes of carriers so as to place one class at a significant competitive disadvantage. In other words, does the FTC Act authorize the Commission to find unlawful the type of challenged activity engaged in by petitioner? . . .

The Commission's brief . . . refers us to two lines of cases with which it claims its decision is consistent. The first line recognizes limitations that may be placed upon a monopolist's rights to affect competition. Thus, in *Lorain Journal Co. v. United States,* 342 U.S. 143 (1951), the Court held that a monopolist newspaper violated section 2 of the Sherman Act by refusing to sell advertising space to merchants who also purchased air advertising time from a local radio station. Though recognizing the general right of a private business to select its customers, the Court held that the exercise of this right for the purpose of monopolization violates the Sherman Act. . . . But *Lorain Journal,* unlike the present case, involved a monopolist seeking to preserve its *own* monopoly. The Commission similarly argues that its position is supported by *Otter Tail Power Co. v. United States,* 410 U.S. 366 (1973), where the Court held that a monopolist may not abuse its monopoly power in one market to gain an improper advantage or to destroy threatened competition in an adjacent market in which it also operates. . . . But as the Commission itself pointed out, the instant case "differs from ordinary monopolization cases where challenged acts or practices were engaged in to benefit the monopolist competitively, either in the market in which the monopoly power existed or in some adjacent market into which the monopolist had extended its operations." Donnelley, though possibly a monopolist in the airline schedule publishing industry, admittedly had no anticompetitive motive or intent with respect to the airline industry and is engaged in a different line of commerce from that of the air carriers.

The second line of cases relied upon in the Commission's brief recognizes the duty that the joint owners of a scarce resource have to make the resource available to all potential users on nondiscriminatory terms. * * *

Each of these cases, however, involved joint refusals to deal resulting in injury to the *defendants'* competitors, while the instant case involves only unilateral behavior by Donnelley which allegedly has affected competition among air carriers, a business in which Donnelley is not engaged. * * *

. . . We note that the FTC with some justification states that the arbitrary refusal of a monopolist to deal leaves the disadvantaged competitor, even though in another field, with no recourse to overcome the disadvantage, and the Commission wants us to take the "small step" in terms of "the fundamental goals of antitrust."

But we think enforcement of the FTC's order here would give the FTC too much power to substitute its own business judgment for that of the monopolist in any decision that arguably affects competition in another industry. Such a decision would permit the FTC to delve into, as the Commission itself put the extreme case, "social, political, or personal reasons" for a monopolist's refusal to deal. Professors Areeda and Turner give examples of a monopolist theater which refuses to admit men with long hair or a monopolist newspaper which refuses to publish advertising from cigarette manufacturers. The Commission says that neither of these examples would trigger antitrust scrutiny because there is no competition among persons who attend movies, and refusing to publish advertisements for all cigarette companies would not place any of them at a disadvantage *vis-a-vis* a competitor. Nevertheless, the Commission's own example of its opinion of a monopolist newspaper refusing to take advertisements from a particular cigarette company because of the style of prior advertisements or the political views of its president shows just how far the Commission's opinion could lead us. What we are doing, as the Commission itself recognized, is weighing benefits to competition in the other field against the detrimental effect of allowing the Commission to pass judgment on many business decisions of the monopolist that arguably discriminate among customers in some way. Thus, if the only supermarket in town decides to stock Birdseye vegetables but not Green Giant vegetables, the FTC would be able to require it to stock Green Giant vegetables if it were to find Green Giant competitively disadvantaged.

... We think that even a monopolist, as long as he has no purpose to restrain competition or to enhance or expand his monopoly, and does not act coercively, retains this right....

QUESTIONS AND COMMENTS

1. In what sense did Donnelley's refusal to deal with the commuter airlines on equal terms with the major carriers harm competition? Was it likely that air fares were higher? Was it unfair to the commuter airlines?

2. Was it good policy to let Donnelley decide how to satisfy its customers, since it had no interest in excluding a competitor in the air carrier market and therefore no conflict of interest? On the other hand, why shouldn't the owner of an essential facility have a duty not to discriminate? European law imposes this duty—although in the usual case the complainant is a competitor, the defendant is often a state enterprise, and often but not always the refusal harms consumers in the market of the competitor. See John Temple Lang, Defining Legitimate Competition: Companies' Duties to Supply Competitors, and Access to Essential Facilities, Ch. 12 in B. Hawk ed., International Antitrust Law & Policy, Fordham Corp. L. Inst. (1995).

3. Or might Donnelley have had an interest: currying good will with its big customers. How could this have been proved? Should it have been inferred? Would that have changed the outcome?

In the mid–1980s, *Aspen Skiing Co.* reached the Supreme Court. Aspen Skiing Co. had refused to cooperate with its smaller, single-mountain competitor, who wanted to give its customers easy access to Aspen Skiing's three slopes. The Court did not invoke the essential facilities doctrine, but, before *Trinko* (below), the decision was often interpreted as if it had done so.

ASPEN SKIING CO. v. ASPEN HIGHLANDS SKIING CORP.

472 U.S. 585 (1985).

JUSTICE STEVENS: In a private treble damages action, the jury found that petitioner Aspen Skiing Company (Ski Co.) had monopolized the market for downhill skiing services in Aspen, Colorado. The question presented is whether that finding is erroneous as a matter of law because it rests on an assumption that a firm with monopoly power has a duty to cooperate with its smaller rivals in a marketing arrangement in order to avoid violating § 2 of the Sherman Act.

I.

Aspen is a destination ski resort with a reputation for "super powder," "a wide range of runs," and an "active night life," including "some of the best restaurants in North America." Between 1945 and 1960, private investors independently developed three major facilities for downhill skiing: Aspen Mountain (Ajax), Aspen Highlands (Highlands), and Buttermilk. A fourth mountain, Snowmass, opened in 1967.

The development of any major additional facilities is hindered by practical considerations and regulatory obstacles. The identification of appropriate topographical conditions for a new site and substantial financing are both essential. Most of the terrain in the vicinity of Aspen that is suitable for downhill skiing cannot be used for that purpose without the approval of the United States Forest Service. That approval is contingent, in part, on environmental concerns. Moreover, the county government must also approve the project, and in recent years it has followed a policy of limiting growth.

Between 1958 and 1964, three independent companies operated Ajax, Highlands, and Buttermilk. In the early years, each company offered its own day or half-day tickets for use of its mountain. In 1962, however, the three competitors also introduced an interchangeable ticket. The 6–day, all-Aspen ticket provided convenience to the vast majority of skiers who visited the resort for weekly periods, but preferred to remain flexible about what mountain they might ski each day during the visit. * * *

In 1964, Buttermilk was purchased by Ski Co., but the interchangeable ticket program continued....

In the 1971–1972 season, the coupon booklets were discontinued and an "around the neck" all-Aspen ticket was developed. This refinement on the interchangeable ticket was advantageous to the skier, who no longer found it necessary to visit the ticket window every morning before gaining access to the slopes. Lift operators at Highlands monitored usage of the ticket in the 1971–1972 season by recording the ticket numbers of persons going onto the slopes of that mountain. Highlands officials periodically met with Ski Co. officials to review the figures recorded at Highlands, and to distribute revenues based on that count. * * *

... Ski Co. and Highlands [switched to random sample] surveys to allocate the revenues from the 4–area, 6–day ticket. Highlands' share of the revenues from the ticket was 17.5% in 1973–1974, 18.5% in 1974–1975, 16.8% in 1975–1976, and 13.2% in 1976–1977. During these four seasons, Ski Co. did not offer its own 3–area, multi-day ticket in competition with the all-Aspen ticket. By 1977, multi-area tickets accounted for nearly 35% of the total market. Holders of multi-area passes also accounted for additional daily ticket sales to persons skiing with them.

... [F]or the 1977–1978 season, Ski Co. offered to continue the all-Aspen ticket only if Highlands would accept a 13.2% fixed share of the ticket's revenues. * * *

In the 1970's the management of Ski Co. increasingly expressed their dislike for the all-Aspen ticket. They complained that a coupon method of monitoring usage was administratively cumbersome. They doubted the accuracy of the survey and decried the "appearance, deportment, [and] attitude" of the college students who were conducting it. In addition, Ski Co.'s President had expressed the view that the 4–area ticket was siphoning off revenues that could be recaptured by Ski Co. if the ticket was discontinued. In fact, Ski Co. had reinstated its 3–area, 6–day ticket during the 1977–1978 season, but that ticket had been outsold by the 4–area, 6–day ticket nearly two to one.

In March 1978, the Ski Co.... [made] Highlands "an offer that [it] could not accept" [12.5%; and it refused to consider counteroffers]. * * *

As far as Ski Co. was concerned, the all-Aspen ticket was dead. In its place Ski Co. offered the 3–area, 6–day ticket featuring only its mountains....

Ski Co. took additional actions that made it extremely difficult for Highlands to market its own multi-area package to replace the joint offering. Ski Co. discontinued the 3–day, 3–area pass for the 1978–1979 season, and also refused to sell Highlands any lift tickets, either at the tour operator's discount or at retail. Highlands finally developed an alternative product, the "Adventure Pack," which consisted of a 3–day pass at Highlands and three vouchers, each equal to the price of a daily lift ticket at a Ski Co. mountain. The vouchers were guaranteed by funds on deposit in an Aspen bank, and were redeemed by Aspen merchants at full value. Ski Co., however, refused to accept them. * * *

Without a convenient all-Aspen ticket, Highlands basically "becomes a day ski area in a destination resort." Highlands' share of the market for downhill skiing services in Aspen declined steadily after the 4–area ticket based on usage was abolished in 1977 . . ., to 11% in 1980–81.

II.

. . . Ski Co. does not challenge the jury's special verdict finding that it possessed monopoly power. Nor does Ski Co. criticize the trial court's instructions to the jury concerning the second element of the § 2 offense.

On this element, the jury was instructed that it had to consider whether "Aspen Skiing Corporation willfully acquired, maintained, or used that power by anti-competitive or exclusionary means or for anti-competitive or exclusionary purposes." The instructions elaborated:

> "In considering whether the means or purposes were anti-competitive or exclusionary, you must draw a distinction here between practices which tend to exclude or restrict competition on the one hand and the success of a business which reflects only a superior product, a well-run business, or luck, on the other. . . .
>
> "For example, a firm that has lawfully acquired a monopoly position is not barred from taking advantage of scale economies by constructing a large and efficient factory. These benefits are a consequence of size and not an exercise of monopoly power. Nor is a corporation which possesses monopoly power under a duty to cooperate with its business rivals. Also a company which possesses monopoly power and which refuses to enter into a joint operating agreement with a competitor or otherwise refuses to deal with a competitor in some manner does not violate Section 2 if valid business reasons exist for that refusal.
>
> ". . . We are concerned with conduct which unnecessarily excludes or handicaps competitors. This is conduct which does not benefit consumers by making a better product or service available—or in other ways—and instead has the effect of impairing competition. . . ."

The jury answered a specific interrogatory finding the second element of the offense as defined in these instructions.

. . . The District Court denied Ski Co.'s motion [for judgment] and entered a judgment awarding Highlands treble damages of $7,500,000, costs and attorney's fees.

The Court of Appeals affirmed in all respects. * * *

III. * * *

. . . Ski Co. . . . is surely correct in submitting that even a firm with monopoly power has no general duty to engage in a joint marketing program with a competitor. Ski Co. is quite wrong, however, in suggesting that the judgment in this case rests on any such proposition of law. For the trial court unambiguously instructed the jury that a firm possessing monopoly power has no duty to cooperate with its business rivals.

The absence of an unqualified duty to cooperate does not mean that every time a firm declines to participate in a particular cooperative venture, that decision may not have evidentiary significance, or that it may not give rise to liability in certain circumstances. The absence of a duty to transact business with another firm is, in some respects, merely the counterpart of the independent businessman's cherished right to select his customers and his associates. The high value that we have placed on the right to refuse to deal with other firms does not mean that the right is unqualified.

In *Lorain Journal v. United States,* 342 U.S. 143 (1951), we squarely held that this right was not unqualified. * * *

The qualification on the right of a monopolist to deal with whom he pleases is not so narrow that it encompasses no more than the circumstances of *Lorain Journal.* In the actual case that we must decide, the monopolist did not merely reject a novel offer to participate in a cooperative venture that had been proposed by a competitor. Rather, the monopolist elected to make an important change in a pattern of distribution that had originated in a competitive market and had persisted for several years. The all-Aspen, 6–day ticket with revenues allocated on the basis of usage was first developed when three independent companies operated three different ski mountains in the Aspen area. It continued to provide a desirable option for skiers when the market was enlarged to include four mountains, and when the character of the market was changed by Ski Co.'s acquisition of monopoly power. Moreover, since the record discloses that interchangeable tickets are used in other multi-mountain areas which apparently are competitive, it seems appropriate to infer that such tickets satisfy consumer demand in free competitive markets.

Ski Co.'s decision to terminate the all-Aspen ticket was thus a decision by a monopolist to make an important change in the character of the market.[31] Such a decision is not necessarily anticompetitive, and Ski Co. contends that neither its decision, nor the conduct in which it engaged to implement that decision, can fairly be characterized as exclusionary in this case....

... Since the jury was unambiguously instructed that Ski Co.'s refusal to deal with Highlands "does not violate § 2 if valid business reasons exist for that refusal," we must assume that the jury concluded that there were no valid business reasons for the refusal. The question then is whether that conclusion finds support in the record.

---

31. "In any business, patterns of distribution develop over time; these may reasonably be thought to be more efficient than alternative patterns of distribution that do not develop. The patterns that do develop and persist we may call the optimal patterns. By disturbing optimal distribution patterns one rival can impose costs upon another, that is, force the other to accept higher costs." Bork 156.

IV.

The question whether Ski Co.'s conduct may properly be characterized as exclusionary cannot be answered by simply considering its effect on Highlands. In addition, it is relevant to consider its impact on consumers and whether it has impaired competition in an unnecessarily restrictive way.[32] If a firm has been "attempting to exclude rivals on some basis other than efficiency,"[33] it is fair to characterize its behavior as predatory. It is, accordingly, appropriate to examine the effect of the challenged pattern of conduct on consumers, on Ski Co.'s smaller rival, and on Ski Co. itself.

Superior Quality of the All–Aspen Ticket * * *

... [T]he evidence supports a conclusion that consumers were adversely affected by the elimination of the 4–area ticket. In the first place, the actual record of competition between a 3–area ticket and the all-Aspen ticket in the years after 1967 indicated that skiers demonstrably preferred four mountains to three. Highlands' expert marketing witness testified that many of the skiers who come to Aspen want to ski the four mountains, and the abolition of the 4–area pass made it more difficult to satisfy that ambition. A consumer survey undertaken in the 1979–1980 season indicated that 53.7% of the respondents wanted to ski Highlands, but would not; 39.9% said that they would not be skiing at the mountain of their choice because their ticket would not permit it.

Expert testimony and anecdotal evidence supported these statistical measures of consumer preference. A major wholesale tour operator asserted that he would not even consider marketing a 3–area ticket if a 4–area ticket were available. During the 1977–1978 and 1978–1979 seasons, people with Ski Co.'s 3–area ticket came to Highlands "on a very regular basis" and attempted to board the lifts or join the ski school. Highlands officials were left to explain to angry skiers that they could only ski at Highlands or join its ski school by paying for a 1–day lift ticket. Even for the affluent, this was an irritating situation because it left the skier the option of either wasting one day of the 6–day, 3–area pass or obtaining a refund which could take all morning and entailed the forfeit of the 6–day discount. An active officer in the Atlanta Ski Club testified that the elimination of the 4–area pass "infuriated" him.

Highlands' Ability to Compete

The adverse impact of Ski Co.'s pattern of conduct on Highlands is not disputed in this Court. Expert testimony described the extent of its pecuniary injury....

---

32. "Thus, 'exclusionary' comprehends at the most behavior that not only (1) tends to impair the opportunities of rivals, but also (2) either does not further competition on the merits or does so in an unnecessarily restrictive way." 3 P. Areeda & D. Turner, Antitrust Law 78 (1978).

33. Bork 138.

Ski Co.'s Business Justification

Perhaps most significant, however, is the evidence relating to Ski Co. itself, for Ski Co. did not persuade the jury that its conduct was justified by any normal business purpose. Ski Co. was apparently willing to forgo daily ticket sales both to skiers who sought to exchange the coupons contained in Highlands' Adventure Pack, and to those who would have purchased Ski Co. daily lift tickets from Highlands if Highlands had been permitted to purchase them in bulk. The jury may well have concluded that Ski Co. elected to forgo these short run benefits because it was more interested in reducing competition in the Aspen market over the long run by harming its smaller competitor.

That conclusion is strongly supported by Ski Co.'s failure to offer any efficiency justification whatever for its pattern of conduct. In defending the decision to terminate the jointly offered ticket, Ski Co. claimed that usage could not be properly monitored [but its conduct showed this claim to be pretext]. . . .

In the end, Ski Co. was pressed to justify its pattern of conduct on a desire to disassociate itself from—what it considered—the inferior skiing services offered at Highlands. The all-Aspen ticket based on usage, however, allowed consumers to make their own choice on these matters of quality. Ski Co.'s purported concern for the relative quality of Highlands' product was supported in the record by little more than vague insinuations, and was sharply contested by numerous witnesses. Moreover, Ski Co. admitted that it was willing to associate with what it considered to be inferior products in other markets.

. . . [T]he record in this case comfortably supports an inference that the monopolist made a deliberate effort to discourage its customers from doing business with its smaller rival. The sale of its 3–area, 6–day ticket, particularly when it was discounted below the daily ticket price, deterred the ticket holders from skiing at Highlands. The refusal to accept the Adventure Pack coupons in exchange for daily tickets was apparently motivated entirely by a decision to avoid providing any benefit to Highlands even though accepting the coupons would have entailed no cost to Ski Co. itself, would have provided it with immediate benefits, and would have satisfied its potential customers. Thus the evidence supports an inference that Ski Co. was not motivated by efficiency concerns and that it was willing to sacrifice short run benefits and consumer good will in exchange for a perceived long-run impact on its smaller rival.

Because we are satisfied that the evidence in the record,[44] construed most favorably in support of Highlands' position, is adequate to support

44. Given our conclusion that the evidence amply supports the verdict under the instructions as given by the trial court, we find it unnecessary to consider the possible relevance of the "essential facilities" doctrine, or the somewhat hypothetical question whether nonexclusionary conduct could ever constitute an abuse of monopoly power if motivated by an anticompetitive purpose. If, as we have assumed, no monopolist monopolizes unconscious of what he is doing, that case is unlikely to arise.

the verdict under the instructions given by the trial court, the judgment of the Court of Appeals is *Affirmed*.

QUESTIONS AND COMMENTS

1. What did Aspen Skiing Co. do wrong? Did it control an essential facility (and therefore violate special essential facility duties)? Why did the Court not make use of the essential facility doctrine? Compare the essentiality of Highlands' customers' access to Aspen Skiing's slopes with that of Elbow Lake's and Hankinson's need to use Otter Tail's power lines (if they were to enter the market for local retail supply of electric power—and become *the* retail supplier in their towns).

2. If Aspen Skiing's slopes were not an essential facility, why wasn't Highlands obliged to "go it alone"? Isn't that what competitors normally must do? Are there costs of requiring a leading competitor to share facilities with a smaller competitor?

3. Are there facts—structure or conduct—that make this case different from a simple refusal to deal case, and that justify the result? What facts?

4. What is the rule of *Aspen Skiing?* Would the result have been the same if Aspen Skiing had never cooperated with Highlands?

5. Aspen Skiing had argued, unsuccessfully, that its mountains were more desirable physically and better maintained than Highlands', and that continued cooperation (after a change in ownership of Aspen Skiing and a new management strategy) would degrade Aspen Skiing. Is this an efficiency defense? A free rider defense? A non-efficiency legitimate business justification? Who would have the burden of proving this justification? Does it matter whether it is characterized as an efficiency justification? If the Court had accepted the justification in fact and in law, would Highlands still have had a chance to show that the consumer harm was weightier than the efficiency benefits? Or would Aspen Skiing have been entitled to judgment?

6. What must Aspen Skiing do as a result of the opinion? On what terms must it now deal with Highlands? Who decides?

7. When the case reached the Supreme Court, the relevant market had already been defined as skiing in Aspen. Thus, in the Supreme Court the market definition issue was no longer open. Was that a satisfactory state of affairs? If the market was destination ski resorts in the United States, what would have been the probable result?

Aspen Distinguished: More Limits to the Duty to Deal

OLYMPIA EQUIPMENT LEASING CO. v. WESTERN UNION TELEGRAPH CO.

797 F.2d 370 (7th Cir.1986).

JUDGE POSNER: [Western Union Telegraph Company created the Telex service. It leased Telex terminals, on which subscribers could send and receive messages to and from other Telex subscribers, and provided the transmission service. At a later date it decided to concentrate on the service, not the machines. To raise capital, it wanted to sell its supply of terminals. Accordingly, it decided to make a market for firms that would lease Telex equipment to others, for these were the firms that would buy the machines from Telex. It offered to put the names of such firms on a list that its sales force gave to new subscribers, and it provided seminars to its service, training, and referrals to these firms. Olympia took advantage of the offer and entered the market for leasing Telex machines.

Then Western Union changed course. Its own inventory of terminals was liquidating too slowly. It withdrew support services for its terminal-leasing competitors.

Olympia had depended almost entirely on Western Union's sales force for its business, and when that support was withdrawn, Olympia foundered. Olympia solicited Western Union's own terminal-leasing customers, prompting an enraged Western Union employee to say: "these turkeys ... ought to be flushed." Olympia's business failed, and Olympia sued Western Union for monopolizing the equipment leasing market by withdrawing its support.]

On these facts, could a rational trier of fact find that Olympia was a victim of monopolization?....

[I]f Western Union had monopoly power over telex service, it could use that power to curtail competition in the complementary equipment market.... [T]he record compiled in this case, which included evidence that even a steep increase in the price of telex service would not have caused many subscribers to switch to substitute services (thus implying a low elasticity of demand for telex service, and therefore monopoly power for the firm that controlled the service—Western Union), a rational jury could have found that Western Union had monopoly power in the market for telex service; so we must repress our skepticism.

But the bare fact that a firm has monopoly power in Market X does not imply that it will have an incentive to obtain monopoly power over Y, an input into X. In general a monopolist like any other firm wants to minimize its input costs; the lower those costs are, the greater the monopoly profits it will be able to make. Therefore the rational monopolist will usually want his input markets to be competitive, for competition usually will minimize the costs that he has to pay for his inputs. There are, however, special circumstances in which a rational monopolist may want to restrict competition in an input market; as it happens, one of those circumstances is where the monopolist's rates are regulated. Western Union's monopoly of telex service was a regulated monopoly, and a regulated monopolist may have an incentive to project its monopoly into related but unregulated markets. * * *

... Not the possession, but the abuse, of monopoly power violates section 2. And far from abusing any monopoly power it may have had, by excluding independent providers of terminal equipment from selling to its telex customers, Western Union encouraged the entry of independent providers.... The alleged violation came when, having created and nurtured new competition, Western Union stopped helping the new competitors because it found it could not liquidate its terminal inventory as rapidly as it had hoped to be able to do. * * *

Today it is clear that a firm with lawful monopoly power has no general duty to help its competitors, whether by holding a price umbrella over their heads or by otherwise pulling its competitive punches....

If a monopolist does extend a helping hand, though not required to do so, and later withdraws it as happened in this case, does he incur antitrust liability? We think not. Conceivably he may be liable in tort or contract law, under theories of equitable or promissory estoppel or implied contract (of which more shortly), or by analogy to the common law tort rule that though there is no duty to help a bystander in distress, once help is extended it may not be withdrawn, at least if the effect is to make the bystander's rescue by someone else less likely. But the controlling consideration in an antitrust case is antitrust policy rather than common law analogies. Since Western Union had no duty to encourage the entry of new firms into the equipment market, the law would be perverse if it made Western Union's encouraging gestures the fulcrum of an antitrust violation. Then no firm would dare to attempt a graceful exit from a market in which it was a major seller....

Some cases hold, however, that a firm which controls a facility essential to its competitors may be guilty of monopolization if it refuses to allow them access to the facility....

The present case would be an essential-facility case if Western Union had refused to supply telex service to a customer who got his terminal equipment from Olympia rather than from it, or if Olympia were a competing supplier of telex service who, like the specialized common carriers in the long-distance telephone market, depended on the owner of the local exchanges (here Western Union) to complete its service. Neither condition is satisfied. The essential feature of the refusal-to-deal cases—a monopoly supplier's discriminating against a customer because the customer has decided to compete with it—is missing here. * * *

Olympia analogizes access to all the major mountains at Aspen to Western Union's vendor list, and argues that just as Aspen Highlands could not survive without access to the mountains so Olympia could not survive without the list. The analogy lacks not only plausibility but also evidentiary support.... Although some customers of Western Union may not have known about alternative vendors, nothing prevented those vendors from acquainting the customers with their existence.... Brand-new firms are expected to make their own way in the market, by advertising or other means of promotion....

Aspen Highlands could not acquire three more mountains in the Aspen area in order to be able to compete more effectively with the Aspen Skiing Company but Olympia could and did hire salesmen to substitute for the Western Union sales force that had been helping it. If Western Union had tried to prevent Olympia from making the substitution it would have been guilty of exclusionary conduct. But Olympia had no right under antitrust law to take a free ride on its competitor's sales force. You cannot conscript your competitor's salesmen to sell your product even if the competitor has monopoly power and you are a struggling new entrant. Advertising a competitor's products free of charge is not a form of cooperation commonly found in competitive markets; it is the antithesis of competition....

Olympia cites *Aspen Highlands* for the proposition that if a firm with monopoly power cannot give a good business justification for not cooperating with a competitor, its refusal to cooperate violates antitrust law. Conjoined with other evidence, lack of business justification may indicate probable anticompetitive effect. But there is a clear business justification in this case: Western Union wanted to liquidate its supply of telex terminals faster, so it stopped promoting a competitor's supply. The main economic objection to monopoly is that the monopolist restricts output compared to what it would be under competition. The monopolist cannot be faulted for wanting to sell *more* output unless he is engaged in some predatory or exclusionary scheme the long-run effect of which may be to restrict output (perhaps in a different market, as in a case where the regulated monopolist takes over a related market in an effort to evade profit regulation and thus keep profits up, and output down, in the monopoly market). There is no such scheme here; Western Union's long-run design is to get out of the telex terminal market. The defendant in *Aspen Highlands* discontinued a service that its customers valued, thus forgoing normal competitive benefits in the hope (so the jury found at any rate) of reaping long-term anticompetitive gains; there is no prospect of such gains in the unusual case—which is the present case—of a monopolist who is voluntarily relinquishing his monopoly position. * * *

We add, what has become an antitrust commonplace, that if conduct is not objectively anticompetitive the fact that it was motivated by hostility to competitors ("these turkeys") is irrelevant. The importance of intent in such fields as tort and criminal law makes it natural to suppose that it should play an important role in antitrust law as well, for an antitrust violation is a statutory tort. But there is an insoluble ambiguity about anticompetitive intent that is not encountered in the ordinary tort case. If A strikes B deliberately, we are entitled to infer, first, that A's act was more dangerous than if the blow had been accidental (you are more likely to hurt someone if you are trying to hurt him than if you are trying, however ineptly, to avoid hurting him, as in the typical accident case), and, second, that the cost of avoidance to the injurer would have been less than if the blow had been accidental; indeed, the cost of forbearing to commit an act of deliberate aggression is negative, because the act requires effort. Similar inferences would be possible in antitrust cases if the purpose of antitrust law were to protect the prosperity or solvency (corresponding to the bodily integrity of potential tort victims) of competitors, but it is not. Competition, which is always deliberate, has never been a tort, intentional or otherwise.... If firm A through lower prices or a better or more dependable product succeeds in driving competitor B out of business, society is better off, unlike the case where A and B are individuals and A kills B for B's money. In both cases the "aggressor" seeks to transfer his victim's wealth to himself, but in the first case we applaud the result because society as a whole benefits from the competitive process. That Western Union wanted to "flush these turkeys" tells us nothing about the lawfulness of its conduct.

Most businessmen don't like their competitors, or for that matter competition. They want to make as much money as possible and getting a monopoly is one way of making a lot of money. That is fine, however, so long as they do not use methods calculated to make consumers worse off in the long run. Consumers would be worse off if a firm with monopoly power had a duty to extend positive assistance to new entrants, or having extended it voluntarily a duty to continue it indefinitely. The imposition of such a duty would make firms that possessed or might be thought to possess monopoly power, however laudably obtained, timid about relinquishing that power or, having done so, timid about competing with new entrants. The question therefore is not whether Western Union withdrew the vendor list in order to make money at the expense of Olympia, which of course it did, but whether such withdrawal was an objectively anticompetitive act. It was not, once the basic premise that monopolists are not required to help their competitors, but need only refrain from anticompetitive acts such as denial of access to essential facilities, is granted. * * *

Aspen was applied in *Eastman Kodak v. Image Technical Services, Inc.*, 504 U.S. 451 (1992) (see above at p. 214. Kodak had cut off independent servicers of Kodak copying equipment from access to repair parts, and the ISOs sued Kodak both for tying the repair parts to the Kodak service (see p. 671 below) and for monopolizing the service and repair of the Kodak copying equipment. Kodak sought dismissal of the complaint before trial, but the Supreme Court refused to grant dismissal. Regarding the standard for Section 2 illegality, the Court said:

> The second element of a § 2 claim is the use of monopoly power "to foreclose competition, to gain a competitive advantage, or to destroy a competitor." *United States v. Griffith*, 334 U.S. 100, 107 (1948). If Kodak adopted its parts and service policies as part of a scheme of willful acquisition or maintenance of monopoly power, it will have violated § 2....[32]
>
> ... [R]espondents have presented evidence that Kodak took exclusionary action to maintain its parts monopoly and used its control

32. It is true that as a general matter a firm can refuse to deal with its competitors. But such a right is not absolute; it exists only if there are legitimate competitive reasons for the refusal. See *Aspen Skiing Co.*

over parts to strengthen its monopoly share of the Kodak service market. Liability turns, then, on whether "valid business reasons" can explain Kodak's actions.... Factual questions exist ... about the validity and sufficiency of each claimed justification, making summary judgment inappropriate. *Id.*, 482–485.

In the pages below, you will come to grips with the modern rules and standards for Section 2 liability. Sometimes, as you will see, the analysis will be a function of the category of conduct that is challenged; for example, refusal to deal, predatory pricing, price squeeze, or exclusive dealing. Do not become attached to the fairly quick and easy shift of the burden from plaintiff to defendant that you have just seen in *Aspen* and *Kodak*, for later cases such as *Trinko* recalibrate the balance.

QUESTIONS AND COMMENTS

1. What was it about the market structure in *Aspen* and in *Olympia* that made a crucial difference between the two cases?

2. Explain why competition law is different from tort law and why intent (to kill the competitor) tells us little or nothing relevant to antitrust liability.

3. Apply the analysis in *Olympia* to *Kodak/ITS*.

4. In *Oscar Bronner,* the European Court of Justice rejected the claim of Bronner, owner of a small daily newspaper, that the distribution system of Mediaprint, the near-monopolist publisher and owner of the only nation-wide newspaper distribution system, was an essential facility to which he had a right of access. The Court said that Mediaprint's refusal to distribute Bronner's newspaper would not amount to an abuse of dominance in violation of (now) Article 101 of the Treaty unless it was likely to eliminate all competition in the daily newspaper market, access was indispensable to Bronner's business, and the refusal to deal could not be objectively justified. Bronner had not made this case. Among other things, there were no technical or legal obstacles preventing Bronner, alone or in combination with other small newspapers, from setting up an alternative distribution system. Oscar Bronner GmbH & Co. KG v. Mediaprint Zeitungs und Zeitschriftenverlag GmbH & Co., Case C–7/97, [1998] ECR I–7791.

Would the outcome be the same in the United States? Are consumers better off or worse off under the rule of *Bronner*? Can you justify the rule of *Bronner* even if consumers would get more choice and lower-priced papers if Bronner got access to the distribution system of Mediaprint? Would Bronner's access probably have produced lower distribution costs, wider availability of Bronner's paper, and head-on competition with Mediaprint?

Meanwhile, in the U.S., a big monopoly case in telecommunications was brewing. After the breakup of AT&T and for more than a decade thereafter, lawful regional monopolies occupied local land-line service markets. By 1996, given new technologies, these local markets were amenable to competition. The Telecommunications Act of 1996 liberalized telecommunications, opening local phone service markets to competition. It requires the carrier with the local phone service monopoly to provide competitors with fair, equal, non-discriminatory access to the local network (local "loop"—an infrastructure necessary to provide local service that cannot feasibly be duplicated).

Bell Atlantic, now Verizon, was the carrier with the local service monopoly in the New York area. AT&T, the long distance carrier surviving the 1982 break-up, entered the local market. Bell Atlantic failed to give AT&T and the other competing local exchange carriers (CLECs) access to the local loop equivalent to the access that Bell Atlantic enjoyed; it filled orders of CLEC customers after filling those for its own local service, and failed to fill a substantial number of orders in a timely manner.

The CLECs complained to the Federal Communications Commission. Bell Atlantic argued that, in the weeks following approval of its New York long distance application and in connection with steps it took to comply with regulatory demands, it encountered a problem with its computer support systems, affecting its service to the CLECs, and that within a few months the problem was fixed. The FCC rejected this story, and it found that Bell Atlantic had improperly failed to provide the CLECs with equal access. Bell Atlantic paid a fine of $3 million to the U.S. Treasury and $10 million to the CLECs injured by Bell Atlantic's misconduct.

Under interconnection agreements pursuant to the Telecoms Act, the CLECs' only recourse for disputes arising under the agreement was the dispute resolution process that resulted in the above fines. Thus, AT&T had given up its antitrust rights.

Lawyer Trinko, a customer of AT&T, claimed that his phone service was disrupted during this period by reason of Bell Atlantic's misconduct, that he lost clients and prospective clients as a result, and that he and other members of the class were entitled to treble damages.

Bell Atlantic moved to dismiss on grounds, among others, that the Telecoms Act preempted the antitrust laws, that in any event Trinko et al. had no standing to sue under the antitrust laws, and that the allegations did not make out a Sherman Act violation.

The district court dismissed the case. The Court of Appeals for the Second Circuit reversed, finding sufficient allegations of violation of essential facilities duties and monopoly leveraging. The Supreme Court granted certiorari—and ultimately handed down a decision that, to many observers, changed the face and rhetoric of Section 2 violations and, as well, rebalanced the relationship between sector regulation and antitrust.

VERIZON COMMUNICATIONS INC. v. LAW OFFICES OF CURTIS V. TRINKO

540 U.S. 398 (2004).

JUSTICE SCALIA:

The Telecommunications Act of 1996 imposes certain duties upon incumbent local telephone companies in order to facilitate market entry by competitors, and establishes a complex regime for monitoring and enforcement. In this case we consider whether a complaint alleging breach of the incumbent's duty under the 1996 Act to share its network with competitors states a claim under § 2 of the Sherman Act.

I.

Petitioner Verizon Communications Inc. is the incumbent local exchange carrier (LEC) serving New York State. Before the 1996 Act, Verizon, like other incumbent LECs, enjoyed an exclusive franchise within its local service area. The 1996 Act sought to "uproot" the incumbent LECs' monopoly and to introduce competition in its place. Central to the scheme of the Act is the incumbent LEC's obligation under 47 U.S.C. § 251(c) to share its network with competitors, see AT&T Corp. v. Iowa Utilities Bd., 525 U.S. 366, 371 (1999), including provision of access to individual elements of the network on an "unbundled" basis. § 251(c)(3). New entrants, so called competitive LECs, resell these unbundled network elements (UNEs), recombined with each other or with elements belonging to the LECs.

Verizon, like other incumbent LECs, has taken two significant steps within the Act's framework in the direction of increased competition. First, Verizon has signed interconnection agreements with rivals such as AT&T, as it is obliged to do under § 252, detailing the terms on which it will make its network elements available. (Because Verizon and AT&T could not agree upon terms, the open issues were subjected to compulsory arbitration under §§ 252(b) and (c).) In 1997, the state regulator, New York's Public Service Commission (PSC), approved Verizon's interconnection agreement with AT&T.

Second, Verizon has taken advantage of the opportunity provided by the 1996 Act for incumbent LECs to enter the long distance market (from which they had long been excluded). That required Verizon to satisfy, among other things, a 14–item checklist of statutory requirements, which includes compliance with the Act's network sharing duties. §§ 271(d)(3)(A) and (c)(2)(B). Checklist item two, for example, includes "nondiscriminatory access to network elements in accordance with the requirements" of § 251(c)(3). § 271(c)(2)(B)(ii). Whereas the state regulator approves an interconnection agreement, for long distance approval the incumbent LEC applies to the Federal Communications Commission (FCC). In December 1999, the FCC approved Verizon's § 271 application for New York.

Part of Verizon's UNE obligation under § 251(c)(3) is the provision of access to operations support systems (OSS), a set of systems used by incumbent LECs to provide services to customers and ensure quality. Verizon's interconnection agreement and long distance authorization each specified the mechanics by which its OSS obligation would be met. As relevant here, a competitive LEC sends orders for service through an electronic interface with Verizon's ordering system, and as Verizon completes certain steps in filling the order, it sends confirmation back through the same interface. Without OSS access a rival cannot fill its customers' orders.

In late 1999, competitive LECs complained to regulators that many orders were going unfilled, in violation of Verizon's obligation to provide access to OSS functions. The PSC and FCC opened parallel investigations, which led to a series of orders by the PSC and a consent decree with the FCC....

Respondent Law Offices of Curtis V. Trinko, LLP, a New York City law firm, was a local telephone service customer of AT&T. The day after Verizon entered its consent decree with the FCC, respondent filed a complaint in the District Court for the Southern District of New York, on behalf of itself and a class of similarly situated customers. The complaint, as later amended, alleged that Verizon had filled rivals' orders on a discriminatory basis as part of an anticompetitive scheme to discourage customers from becoming or remaining customers of competitive LECs, thus impeding the competitive LECs' ability to enter and compete in the market for local telephone service. According to the complaint, Verizon "has filled orders of [competitive LEC] customers after filling those for its own local phone service, has failed to fill in a timely manner, or not at all, a substantial number of orders for [competitive LEC] customers . . ., and has systematically failed to inform [competitive LECs] of the status of their customers' orders." The complaint set forth a single example of the alleged "failure to provide adequate access to [competitive LECs]," namely the OSS failure that resulted in the FCC consent decree and PSC orders. It asserted that the result of Verizon's improper "behavior with respect to providing access to its local loop" was to "deter potential customers [of rivals] from switching." The complaint sought damages and injunctive relief for violation of § 2 of the Sherman Act ....

The District Court dismissed the complaint in its entirety. As to the antitrust portion, it concluded that respondent's allegations of deficient assistance to rivals failed to satisfy the requirements of § 2. The Court of Appeals for the Second Circuit reinstated the complaint in part, including the antitrust claim. 305 F. 3d 89, 113 (2002). We granted certiorari, limited to the question whether the Court of Appeals erred in reversing the District Court's dismissal of respondent's antitrust claims.

II.

[*Does the 1996 Act preempt the Sherman Act? Implied immunity*]

To decide this case, we must first determine what effect (if any) the 1996 Act has upon the application of traditional antitrust principles. The Act imposes a large number of duties upon incumbent LECs—above and beyond those basic responsibilities it imposes upon all carriers, such as assuring number portability and providing access to rights of way, see 47 U.S.C. §§ 251(b)(2), (4). Under the sharing duties of § 251(c), incumbent LECs are required to offer three kinds of access. Already noted, and perhaps most intrusive, is the duty to offer access to UNEs on "just, reasonable, and nondiscriminatory" terms, § 251(c)(3), a phrase that the FCC has interpreted to mean a price reflecting long run incremental cost. A rival can interconnect its own facilities with those of the incumbent LEC, or it can simply purchase services at wholesale from the incumbent and resell them to consumers. See §§ 251(c)(2), (4). The Act also imposes upon incumbents the duty to allow physical "collocation" that is, to permit a competitor to locate and install its equipment on the incumbent's premises which makes feasible interconnection and access to UNEs. See § 251(c)(6).

That Congress created these duties, however, does not automatically lead to the conclusion that they can be enforced by means of an antitrust claim. Indeed, a detailed regulatory scheme such as that created by the 1996 Act ordinarily raises the question whether the regulated entities are not shielded from antitrust scrutiny altogether by the doctrine of implied immunity. See, e.g., United States v. National Assn. of Securities Dealers, Inc., 422 U.S. 694 (1975); Gordon v. New York Stock Exchange, Inc., 422 U.S. 659 (1975). In some respects the enforcement scheme set up by the 1996 Act is a good candidate for implication of antitrust immunity, to avoid the real possibility of judgments conflicting with the agency's regulatory scheme "that might be voiced by courts exercising jurisdiction under the antitrust laws." United States v. National Assn. of Securities Dealers, Inc., supra, at 734.

Congress, however, precluded that interpretation. Section 601(b)(1) of the 1996 Act is an antitrust specific saving clause providing that "nothing in this Act or the amendments made by this Act shall be construed to modify, impair, or supersede the applicability of any of the antitrust laws." 110 Stat. 143, 47 U.S.C. § 152, note. This bars a finding of implied immunity. As the FCC has put the point, the saving clause preserves those "claims that satisfy established antitrust standards."

But just as the 1996 Act preserves claims that satisfy existing antitrust standards, it does not create new claims that go beyond existing antitrust standards; that would be equally inconsistent with the saving clause's mandate that nothing in the Act "modify, impair, or supersede the applicability" of the antitrust laws. We turn, then, to whether the activity of which respondent complains violates preexisting antitrust standards.

III.

[*The Section 2 violation: "forced sharing" not required—no duty to deal with competitors*]

The complaint alleges that Verizon denied interconnection services to rivals in order to limit entry. If that allegation states an antitrust claim at all, it does so under § 2 of the Sherman Act, which declares that a firm shall not "monopolize" or "attempt to monopolize." It is settled law that this offense requires, in addition to the possession of monopoly power in the relevant market, "the willful acquisition or maintenance of that power as distinguished from growth or development as a consequence of a superior product, business acumen, or historic accident." United States v. Grinnell Corp., 384 U.S. 563, 570–571 (1966). The mere possession of monopoly power, and the concomitant charging of monopoly prices, is not only not unlawful; it is an important element of the free market system. The opportunity to charge monopoly prices at least for a short period is what attracts "business acumen" in the first place; it induces risk taking that produces innovation and economic growth. To safeguard the incentive to innovate, the possession of monopoly power will not be found unlawful unless it is accompanied by an element of anticompetitive conduct.

Firms may acquire monopoly power by establishing an infrastructure that renders them uniquely suited to serve their customers. Compelling such firms to share the source of their advantage is in some tension with the underlying purpose of antitrust law, since it may lessen the incentive for the monopolist, the rival, or both to invest in those economically beneficial facilities. Enforced sharing also requires antitrust courts to act as central planners, identifying the proper price, quantity, and other terms of dealing a role for which they are ill suited. Moreover, compelling negotiation between competitors may facilitate the supreme evil of antitrust: collusion. Thus, as a general matter, the Sherman Act "does not restrict the long recognized right of [a] trader or manufacturer engaged in an entirely private business, freely to exercise his own independent discretion as to parties with whom he will deal." United States v. Colgate & Co., 250 U.S. 300, 307 (1919).

[*Exception one: Aspen*]

However, "[t]he high value that we have placed on the right to refuse to deal with other firms does not mean that the right is unqualified." Aspen Skiing Co. v. Aspen High lands Skiing Corp., 472 U.S. 585, 601 (1985). Under certain circumstances, a refusal to cooperate with rivals can constitute anticompetitive conduct and violate § 2. We have been very cautious in recognizing such exceptions, because of the uncertain virtue of forced sharing and the difficulty of identifying and remedying anticompetitive conduct by a single firm. The question before us today is whether the allegations of respondent's complaint fit within existing exceptions or provide a basis, under traditional antitrust principles, for recognizing a new one.

The leading case for § 2 liability based on refusal to cooperate with a rival, and the case upon which respondent understandably places greatest reliance, is Aspen Skiing, supra. The Aspen ski area consisted of four mountain areas. The defendant, who owned three of those areas, and the plaintiff, who owned the fourth, had cooperated for years in the issuance of a joint, multiple day, all area ski ticket. After repeatedly demanding an increased share of the proceeds, the defendant canceled the joint ticket. The plaintiff, concerned that skiers would bypass its mountain without some joint offering, tried a variety of increasingly desperate measures to recreate the joint ticket, even to the point of in effect offering to buy the defendant's tickets at retail price. Id., at 593–594. The defendant refused even that. We upheld a jury verdict for the plaintiff, reasoning that "[t]he jury may well have concluded that [the defendant] elected to forgo these short run benefits because it was more interested in reducing competition ... over the long run by harming its smaller competitor." Id., at 608.

Aspen Skiing is at or near the outer boundary of § 2 liability. The Court there found significance in the defendant's decision to cease participation in a cooperative venture. See id., at 608, 610–611. The unilateral termination of a voluntary (and thus presumably profitable) course of dealing suggested a willingness to forsake short term profits to achieve an anticompetitive end. Ibid. Similarly, the defendant's unwillingness to renew the ticket even if compensated at retail price revealed a distinctly anticompetitive bent.

The refusal to deal alleged in the present case does not fit within the limited exception recognized in Aspen Skiing. The complaint does not allege that Verizon voluntarily engaged in a course of dealing with its rivals, or would ever have done so absent statutory compulsion. Here, therefore, the defendant's prior conduct sheds no light upon the motivation of its refusal to deal upon whether its regulatory lapses were prompted not by competitive zeal but by anticompetitive malice. The contrast between the cases is heightened by the difference in pricing behavior. In Aspen Skiing, the defendant turned down a proposal to sell at its own retail price, suggesting a calculation that its future monopoly retail price would be higher. Verizon's reluctance to interconnect at the cost based rate of compensation available under § 251(c)(3) tells us nothing about dreams of monopoly.

The specific nature of what the 1996 Act compels makes this case different from Aspen Skiing in a more fundamental way. In Aspen Skiing, what the defendant refused to provide to its competitor was a product that it already sold at retail to oversimplify slightly, lift tickets representing a bundle of services to skiers. Similarly, in Otter Tail Power Co. v. United States, 410 U.S. 366 (1973), another case relied upon by respondent, the defendant was already in the business of providing a service to certain customers (power transmission over its network), and refused to provide the same service to certain other customers. Id., at 370–371, 377–378. In the present case, by contrast, the services allegedly withheld are not otherwise marketed or available to the public. The sharing obligation imposed by the 1996 Act created "something brand new" "the wholesale market for leasing network elements." Verizon Communications Inc. v. FCC, 535 U.S., at 528. The unbundled elements offered pursuant to § 251(c)(3) exist only deep within the bowels of Verizon; they are brought out on compulsion of the 1996 Act and offered not to consumers but to rivals, and at considerable expense and effort. New systems must be designed and implemented simply to make that access possible indeed, it is the failure of one of those systems that prompted the present complaint.

[*Possibly, a second exception: essential facilities*]

We conclude that Verizon's alleged insufficient assistance in the provision of service to rivals is not a recognized antitrust claim under this Court's existing refusal to deal precedents. This conclusion would be unchanged even if we considered to be established law the "essential facilities" doctrine crafted by some lower courts, under which the Court of Appeals concluded respondent's allegations might state a claim. See generally Areeda, Essential Facilities: An Epithet in Need of Limiting Principles, 58 Antitrust L. J. 841 (1989). We have never recognized such a doctrine, see Aspen Skiing Co., 472 U.S., at 611, n. 44; AT&T Corp. v. Iowa Utilities Bd., 525 U.S., at 428 (opinion of Breyer, J.), and we find no need either to recognize it or to repudiate it here. It suffices for present purposes to note that the indispensable requirement for invoking the doctrine is the unavailability of access to the "essential facilities"; where access exists, the doctrine serves no purpose. Thus, it is said that "essential facility claims should ... be denied where a state or federal agency has effective power to compel sharing and to regulate its scope and terms." P. Areeda & H. Hovenkamp, Antitrust Law, p. 150, & 773e (2003 Supp.). Respondent believes that the existence of sharing duties under the 1996 Act supports its case. We think the opposite: The 1996 Act's extensive provision for access makes it unnecessary to impose a judicial doctrine of forced access. To the extent respondent's "essential facilities" argument is distinct from its general § 2 argument, we reject it.

IV.

[*No additional exception warranted where regulatory system is effective watchdog; problem of false positives; problem of continuing supervision*]

Finally, we do not believe that traditional antitrust principles justify adding the present case to the few existing exceptions from the proposition that there is no duty to aid competitors. Antitrust analysis must always be attuned to the particular structure and circumstances of the industry at issue. Part of that attention to economic context is an awareness of the significance of regulation. As we have noted, "careful account must be taken of the pervasive federal and state regulation characteristic of the industry." United States v. Citizens & Southern Nat. Bank, 422 U.S. 86, 91 (1975); see also IA P. Areeda & H. Hovenkamp, Antitrust Law, p. 12, & 240c3 (2d ed. 2000). "[A]ntitrust analysis must sensitively recognize and reflect the distinctive economic and legal setting of the regulated industry to which it applies." Concord v. Boston Edison Co., 915 F.2d 17, 22 (CA1 1990) (Breyer, C. J.).

One factor of particular importance is the existence of a regulatory structure designed to deter and remedy anticompetitive harm. Where such a structure exists, the additional benefit to competition provided by antitrust enforcement will tend to be small, and it will be less plausible that the antitrust laws contemplate such additional scrutiny. Where, by contrast, "[t]here is nothing built into the regulatory scheme which performs the antitrust function," Silver v. New York Stock Exchange, 373 U.S. 341, 358 (1963), the benefits of antitrust are worth its sometimes considerable disadvantages. . . .

The regulatory framework that exists in this case demonstrates how, in certain circumstances, "regulation significantly diminishes the likelihood of major antitrust harm." Concord v. Boston Edison Co., supra. Consider, for example, the statutory restrictions upon Verizon's entry into the potentially lucrative market for long distance service. To be allowed to enter the long distance market in the first place, an incumbent LEC must be on good behavior in its local market. Authorization by the FCC requires state by state satisfaction of § 271's competitive checklist, which as we have noted includes the nondiscriminatory provision of access to UNEs. . . .

The FCC's § 271 authorization order for Verizon to provide long distance service in New York discussed at great length Verizon's commitments to provide access to UNEs, including the provision of OSS. . . . Those commitments are enforceable by the FCC through continuing oversight; a failure to meet an authorization condition can result in an order that the deficiency be corrected, in the imposition of penalties, or in the suspension or revocation of long distance approval. . . .

The regulatory response to the OSS failure complained of in respondent's suit provides a vivid example of how the regulatory regime operates. When several competitive LECs complained about deficiencies in Verizon's servicing of orders, the FCC and PSC responded. The FCC soon concluded that Verizon was in breach of its sharing duties under § 251(c), imposed a substantial fine, and set up sophisticated measurements to gauge remediation, with weekly reporting requirements and specific penalties for failure. . . . In short, the regime was an effective steward of the antitrust function.

Against the slight benefits of antitrust intervention here, we must weigh a realistic assessment of its costs. Under the best of circumstances, applying the requirements of § 2 "can be difficult" because "the means of illicit exclusion, like the means of legitimate competition, are myriad." United States v. Microsoft Corp., 253 F.3d 34, 58 (CADC 2001) (en banc) (per curiam). Mistaken inferences and the resulting false condemnations "are especially costly, because they chill the very conduct the antitrust laws are designed to protect." Matsushita Elec. Industrial Co. v. Zenith Radio Corp., 475 U.S. 574, 594 (1986). The cost of false positives counsels against an undue expansion of § 2 liability. One false positive risk is that an incumbent LEC's failure to provide a service with sufficient alacrity might have nothing to do with exclusion. Allegations of violations of § 251(c)(3) duties are difficult for antitrust courts to evaluate, not only because they are highly technical, but also because they are likely to be extremely numerous, given the incessant, complex, and constantly changing interaction of competitive and incumbent LECs implementing the sharing and interconnection obligations. Amici States have filed a brief asserting that competitive LECs are threatened with "death by a thousand cuts," Brief for New York et al. as Amici Curiae 10 (internal quotation marks omitted) the identification of which would surely be a daunting task for a generalist antitrust court. Judicial oversight under the Sherman Act would seem destined to distort investment and lead to a new layer of interminable litigation, atop the variety of litigation routes already available to and actively pursued by competitive LECs.

Even if the problem of false positives did not exist, conduct consisting of anticompetitive violations of § 251 may be, as we have concluded with respect to above cost predatory pricing schemes, "beyond the practical ability of a judicial tribunal to control." Brooke Group Ltd. v. Brown & Williamson Tobacco Corp., 509 U.S. 209, 223 (1993). Effective remediation of violations of regulatory sharing requirements will ordinarily require continuing supervision of a highly detailed decree. We think that Professor Areeda got it exactly right: "No court should impose a duty to deal that it cannot explain or adequately and reasonably supervise. The problem should be deemed irremedia[ble] by antitrust law when compulsory access requires the court to assume the day to day controls characteristic of a regulatory agency." Areeda, 58 Antitrust L.J., at 853. In this case, respondent has requested an equitable decree to "[p]reliminarily and permanently enjoi[n] [Verizon] from providing access to the local loop market . . . to [rivals] on terms and conditions that are not as favorable" as those that Verizon enjoys. An antitrust court is unlikely to be an effective day to day enforcer of these detailed sharing obligations.[4]

The 1996 Act is in an important respect much more ambitious than the antitrust laws. It attempts "to eliminate the monopolies enjoyed by the inheritors of AT&T's local franchises." Verizon Communications Inc. v. FCC, 535 U.S., at 476. Section 2 of the Sherman Act, by contrast, seeks merely to prevent unlawful monopolization. It would be a serious mistake to conflate the two goals. The Sherman Act is indeed the "Magna Carta of free enterprise," United States v. Topco Associates, Inc., 405 U.S. 596, 610 (1972), but it does not give judges carte blanche to insist that a monopolist alter its way of doing business whenever some other approach might yield greater competition. We conclude that respondent's complaint fails to state a claim under the Sherman Act.

JUSTICE STEVENS, with whom JUSTICE SOUTER and JUSTICE THOMAS join, concurring in the judgment.

In complex cases it is usually wise to begin by deciding whether the plaintiff has standing to maintain the action. Respondent, the plaintiff in

---

4. The Court of Appeals also thought that respondent's complaint might state a claim under a "monopoly leveraging" theory. . . . We disagree. To the extent the Court of Appeals dispensed with a requirement that there be a "dangerous probability of success" in monopolizing a second market, it erred. . . .

this case, is a local telephone service customer of AT&T. Its complaint alleges that it has received unsatisfactory service because Verizon has engaged in conduct that adversely affects AT&T's ability to serve its customers, in violation of § 2 of the Sherman Act. Respondent seeks from Verizon treble damages, a remedy that § 4 of the Clayton Act makes available to "any person who has been injured in his business or property." The threshold question presented by the complaint is whether, assuming the truth of its allegations, respondent is a "person" within the meaning of § 4.

Respondent would unquestionably be such a "person" if we interpreted the text of the statute literally. But we have eschewed a literal reading of § 4, particularly in cases in which there is only an indirect relationship between the defendant's alleged misconduct and the plaintiff's asserted injury. Associated Gen. Contractors of Cal., Inc. v. Carpenters, 459 U.S. 519, 529–535 (1983). In such cases, "the importance of avoiding either the risk of duplicate recoveries on the one hand, or the danger of complex apportionment of damages on the other," weighs heavily against a literal reading of § 4. Id.

I would not go beyond the first step in this case. Although respondent contends that its injuries were, like the plaintiff's injuries in Blue Shield of Va. v. McCready, 457 U.S. 465, 479 (1982) [patient of psychologist gets damages from insurer for covering costs of psychiatrist but not of psychologist], "the very means by which ... [Verizon] sought to achieve its illegal ends," it remains the case that whatever antitrust injury respondent suffered because of Verizon's conduct was purely derivative of the injury that AT&T suffered. And for that reason, respondent's suit, unlike McCready, runs both the risk of duplicative recoveries and the danger of complex apportionment of damages. The task of determining the monetary value of the harm caused to respondent by AT&T's inferior service, the portion of that harm attributable to Verizon's misconduct, whether all or just some of such possible misconduct was prohibited by the Sherman Act, and what offset, if any, should be allowed to make room for a recovery that would make AT&T whole, is certain to be daunting. AT&T, as the direct victim of Verizon's alleged misconduct, is in a far better position than respondent to vindicate the public interest in enforcement of the anti trust laws. Denying a remedy to AT&T's customer is not likely to leave a significant antitrust violation undetected or unremedied, and will serve the strong interest "in keeping the scope of complex antitrust trials within judicially manageable limits." Associated Gen. Contractors, 459 U.S., at 543.

In my judgment, our reasoning in Associated General Contractors requires us to reverse the judgment of the Court of Appeals. I would not decide the merits of the § 2 claim unless and until such a claim is advanced by either AT&T or a similarly situated competitive local exchange carrier.

QUESTIONS AND COMMENTS

1. The Telecommunications Act of 1996 imposes on the incumbent local exchange carrier (Verizon) the very obligation that Trinko claims is also an antitrust obligation: to provide nondiscriminatory access to the elements of the infrastructure on an unbundled basis. What is the relationship between the regulatory statute and the antitrust laws? Should they normally be construed to work hand in hand, each bolstering the other (as they often do in Europe and routinely did pre-*Trinko* in the United States)? When does the regulatory statute preempt the antitrust laws? Why would the Court have favored preemption if the Telecommunications Act had not been explicit to the contrary?

2. What affect did the 1996 Act have on the Court's application of antitrust principles? Would the Court have dismissed the Section 2 charges on the merits (duty to provide nondiscriminatory access to an essential facility; duty not to leverage power over the local loop to procure advantages in the local service market) if there were no Telecommunications Act?

3. How would this Court have decided *Aspen Skiing*, supra p. 236? How would this Court have decided *Otter Tail*, supra p. 232 (wherein the Federal Power Commission had the power under the Federal Power Act to order Otter Tail to interconnect with the municipalities and sell power to them at wholesale and in fact had so ordered in the case of one town)? Did the Court, in footnote 4, overrule *Berkey v. Kodak*, supra p. 228, on the issue of leveraging?

4. The Court speaks in the language of "forced sharing" of one's property, which it identifies as the task of "central planners" (point III, para. 2), rather than in the language of duties that may derive from control of a facility essential to compete. What are the implications of this choice of words?

5. How does the Court think about the costs of antitrust intervention? Which are more costly: mistaken interventions (sometimes called type 1 errors) or mistaken failures to intervene (sometimes called type 2 errors)? How did the Court's concerns about mistaken interventions, combined with its concerns about the difficulties of judicial supervision of a decree, shape the Court's decision?

6. What is the role of economics in the Court's decision?

7. The Court states that even if "some other approach might yield greater competition," judges do not have "carte blanche to insist that a monopolist alter its way of doing business." Is the Court making a statement about the capacity of judges? about the robustness of markets? about the importance of business freedom and property rights? Does it regard positive duties (access and non discrimination) as social engineering?

8. Why is *Trinko* a duty-to-deal case? Bell Atlantic had not refused to deal with AT&T. Why isn't this a case of strategic use of leverage to raise rivals' costs? Would the argument or outcome be different if the matter had been framed as a raising-rivals'-costs case?

9. Justice Stevens, joined by Justices Souter and Thomas, would have dismissed Trinko's action on grounds of lack of standing to sue and would not have decided the merits of a case brought by a plaintiff without standing. Trinko, after all, was a lawyer who claimed he must have lost clients because his service provider, AT&T, was treated discriminatorily by Verizon. Trinko's harm was derivative of AT&T's. Moreover, litigating such a claim might have run the risk of duplicative recoveries, and deciphering what part of Trinko's harm was attributable to Verizon was "certain to be daunting." Was Stevens correct? By taking a quite different path, the majority set a new course for the law of monopolization.

10. After *Trinko*, what scope is there for a refusal-to-deal violation under U.S. law if the essential facility doctrine is not available? What is the controlling principle? Is it limited to the Court's statement (re-statement) of *Aspen*?

What is the scope for an essential facilities obligation? See Brett Frischmann and Spencer Weber Waller, Revitalizing Essential Facilities, 75 Antitrust L.J. 1 (2008).

11. After *Trinko*, the Supreme Court was confronted with a price-squeeze case. Pacific Bell, the incumbent provider of telephone service on the West Coast, which also competed in the market for broad band service for the Internet (DSL), charged its wholesale customers so much and its retail DSL customers so little that the wholesalers could not compete with Pacific Bell. Below, you will see the effects of *Trinko* in resolving the question, Was there a duty not to price-squeeze? *Pacific Bell Telephone v. linkLine Communications, Inc.* (*linkLine*), page 277 infra.

12. European Union law has taken a different path regarding duties to deal and also regarding the relationship between antitrust and regulation. EU law corresponds more closely with U.S. law at the time of *Otter Tail* (antitrust exists side-by-side regulation even when the regulator has the power to cure the problem) and *Aspen* (exclusionary acts are illegal unless justified). Thus, EU law corresponds more closely with U.S. law before *Trinko* and *linkLine*. See *Deutsche Telekom* (EU), infra at 285; *Microsoft* (EU), infra at 333.

We now put duties to deal to one side (until we return to the issue in intellectual property licensing cases) and turn to some difficult, recurrent issues regarding low pricing: When does the low pricing harm competition and when must it be regarded as benefitting competition—regardless of consequences to competitors?

4. STRATEGIC LOW PRICING—PREDATORY PRICING AND PRICE-DISCRIMINATION

Firms with market power may price low to eliminate or discipline their competitors. (Of course, they may price low, also, in order to compete.) Sometimes low pricing is also discriminatory pricing. For example, the seller may lower its price only selectively, in order to win particular business.

Is low and discriminatory pricing good or bad for competition? Low pricing is essentially good; price competition is at the heart of the competition system. But might it be bad because it may hurt and even eliminate competitors; and possibly the predator may raise prices and hurt consumers at the end of a predatory siege?

The *Standard Oil* case of 1911 is the most famous example of price discrimination and predation in violation of the Sherman Act. Standard Oil shipped huge quantities of oil on the railroads. It used its buying power to convince the railroads to charge low rates to it, to jack up the rates they charged to Standard Oil's competitors, and to rebate the overcharges to Standard Oil. Moreover, Standard Oil charged high prices to buyers of refined oil in monopoly areas, and, in competitive areas, it charged prices so low that its competitors were "forced" to sell their businesses to Standard Oil. See p. 33 supra. Were these strategies anticompetitive? Explain the ambiguities.

Price discrimination (predictably) persisted. In 1914 Congress passed the Clayton Act to target certain practices including price discrimination. Section 2 of the Clayton Act prohibited sellers from discriminating in price between different buyers of goods of like grade and quality "where the effect of such discrimination may be to substantially lessen competition or tend to create a monopoly in any line of commerce" unless the discrimination was cost justified. 38 Stat. 730. The measure was designed to protect small re-sellers from selective low pricing offered by dominant competitors to larger re-sellers. See H.R.Rep. No. 2287, 74th Cong., 2d Sess. 3–6 (1936).

In 1936 Congress amended Section 2 of the Clayton Act by the Robinson–Patman Act. The Robinson–Patman Act prohibits price discrimination (unless justified by cost savings or the need to meet competition) where the effect "may be substantially to lessen competition or tend to create a monopoly in any line of commerce, or to injure, destroy or prevent competition with any person who either grants or knowingly receives the benefits of such discrimination, or with customers of either of them. . . ."

Until the 1970s very little case law defined "substantial lessening of competition" for purposes of injury on the primary line; that is, injury to a competitor of the seller.[7] The most important case on point for a decade was *Utah Pie*. You will note that this was a case of the 1960s, when the Court was concerned with fairness to competitors—a value that may be seen as embedded in the Robinson–Patman Act by statutory literalists. Note that the Robinson–Patman Act does not require market power as an ingredient of the violation. Why, then, you ask, do we introduce *Utah Pie* at this point in the Casebook? The case is here because, as the decades wore on and efficiency/consumer welfare became the focus of the antitrust law, *Utah Pie* was held up as Exhibit A, along with two or three other cases you will meet such as *Von's Grocery* (merger of a 3% firm and a 4% firm, 384 U.S. 270 (1966)) and *Albrecht* (maximum resale price-fixing) (pages ___ infra) to the brief on why U.S. antitrust law had become perverse and why U.S. antitrust needed the "Chicago" revolution. *Utah*

7. For secondary line injury—i.e., injury to the disfavored firm in its downstream competition—see p. 717 infra.

Pie and the several cases that protected competitors became the flashpoint for the debate that enabled the emergence of a laissez faire jurisprudence of monopolization.

UTAH PIE CO. v. CONTINENTAL BAKING CO.

386 U.S. 685 (1967).

JUSTICE WHITE: [In 1957 Utah Pie pioneered frozen dessert pies in Salt Lake City. Within a year, just before the alleged predations, it accounted for two-thirds of the frozen dessert pie sales in Salt Lake City. Beginning in 1958, its position was challenged by Continental Baking Company, Carnation Company and Pet Milk Company. These firms, all of which sold frozen dessert pies in other areas, charged selective low prices in the area newly dominated by Utah Pie. This price competition reduced Utah Pie's share to almost 45%, although Utah Pie constantly increased its sales volume and continued to make a profit. Utah Pie sued for treble damages and injunctive relief for violations of Section 2(a) of the Clayton Act [the Robinson–Patman Act]. Utah Pie proved that each of the defendants contributed to a "deteriorating price structure," and that each sold frozen pies in the Salt Lake area at lower prices than those it charged in places closer to its plants. There was evidence that the discriminatory sales were unprofitable to Continental, that its price "was less than its direct cost plus an allocation for overhead. . . ."

The jury found for Utah Pie and the district court entered judgment on the verdict. The court of appeals reversed on the ground that the evidence did not support a finding of injury to competition. The Supreme Court reversed the appellate court. It stressed defendants' "predatory intent" to injure Utah Pie, which it gleaned from documents such as one by Pet Milk's management which "identified Utah Pie as an 'unfavorable factor,' one which 'd[u]g holes in our operation' and posed a constant 'check' on Pet's performance in the Salt Lake City market." The Court also noted that Continental made a price cut to a big buyer, Safeway, immediately after which Utah Pie made a deeper price cut.] * * *

. . . The jury could rationally have concluded that had Utah not lowered its price, Continental, which repeated its offer once, would have continued it, that Safeway would have continued to buy from Continental and that other buyers, large as well as small, would have followed suit. It could also have reasonably concluded that a competitor who is forced to reduce his price to a new all-time low in a market of declining prices will in time feel the financial pinch and will be a less effective competitive force.

. . . It is true that many of the primary line cases that have reached the courts have involved blatant predatory price discriminations employed with the hope of immediate destruction of a particular competitor. On the question of injury to competition such cases present courts with no difficulty, for such pricing is clearly within the heart of the proscription of the Act. Courts and commentators alike have noted that the existence of predatory intent might bear on the likelihood of injury to competition. In this case there was some evidence of predatory intent with respect to each of these respondents. There was also other evidence upon which the jury could rationally find the requisite injury to competition. The frozen pie market in Salt Lake City was highly competitive. At times Utah Pie was a leader in moving the general level of prices down, and at other times each of the respondents also bore responsibility for the downward pressure on the price structure. We believe that the Act reaches price discrimination that erodes competition as much as it does price discrimination that is intended to have immediate destructive impact. In this case, the evidence shows a drastically declining price structure which the jury could rationally attribute to continued or sporadic price discrimination. The jury was entitled to conclude that "the effect of such discrimination," by each of these respondents, "may be substantially to lessen competition ... or to injure, destroy, or prevent competition with any person who either grants or knowingly receives the benefit of such discrimination ...." The statutory test is one that necessarily looks forward on the basis of proven conduct in the past. Proper application of that standard here requires reversal of the judgment of the Court of Appeals.

QUESTIONS AND COMMENTS

1. What does the Court mean by a "drastically declining price structure"? Is it true that a firm forced by competition to reduce prices "will be a less effective competitive force"? Might the opposite be true? Whom or what does the rule of *Utah Pie* protect?

2. Identify any statements in the opinion with which you disagree or that you suspect are out of step with modern pro-consumer competition law. Explain.

The IBM Story

In the 1970s, IBM came to dominate the market for business computers, which were contained in large main frames that required various peripheral attachments, such as disks and memories. The market for peripheral equipment was lucrative. Small firms began to reverse engineer and copy (and improve) IBM's own peripherals. The small firms made good products, sold them to IBM main frame customers at prices substantially below IBM's prices, and made deep inroads into IBM's sales of peripheral attachments to the IBM main frame. Incensed, IBM officials organized a blue ribbon committee called SMASH, procured the secret financial records of IBM's competitors, and reduced IBM's prices to a point below that which the competitors could meet. But IBM never priced below its own costs. It did not have to do so because IBM was a very efficient producer. Several of the targeted competitors sued IBM for monopolizing the IBM-compatible peripherals market by predatory pricing strategies. The first of these cases to go to trial was brought by Telex. Telex won a $259.5 million judgment in the district court.

Some policy makers sympathized with Telex; others feared that a *Utah Pie*-type concern for competitors defeated by low prices would deeply undermine price competition. While the appeal in *Telex v. IBM* was pending, Professors Philip Areeda and Donald Turner published one of the most influential antitrust articles ever written, Predatory Pricing and Related Practices Under Section 2 of the Sherman Act, 88 Harv. L. Rev. 697 (1975). Areeda and Turner argued that predatory pricing was almost always a losing strategy and therefore would rarely be undertaken, and that low pricing was so important for competition and consumers that it must be safeguarded by a bright-line and prophylactic rule in favor of the low pricer. Accordingly, they proposed a test which (as later slightly modified) provided:

> (1) a short run profit-maximizing (or loss-minimizing) price is non-predatory even though below the short run average total cost of the firm;
>
> (2) either a price at or above short run average total cost or a price at or above reasonably anticipated short run marginal and average variable cost is non-predatory even if it is not profit-maximizing (or loss-minimizing) in the short run;
>
> (3) a price below the reasonably anticipated short run marginal cost is predatory, unless (because of a firm's high production level) the price is at or above short run average total cost;
>
> (4) where accounting records are not adequate to compute short run marginal cost, reasonably anticipated short run average variable cost may serve as a surrogate for short run marginal cost;
>
> (5) when average variable cost is substituted for marginal cost, the qualifying ("unless") clause in (3) is irrelevant and the norm becomes: *a price below reasonably anticipated short run average variable cost is predatory; a price at or above that level is non-predatory.*

Telex's victory against IBM was short-lived. The Court of Appeals for the Tenth Circuit reversed the judgment for Telex, 510 F.2d 894 (10th Cir.1975) (per curiam), in large part on the strength of the Areeda/Turner test. The new rule of law would weed out and disqualify predatory pricing claims by inefficient producers who could not withstand a barrage of low pricing that was above the alleged predator's marginal or average variable cost.

Telex v. IBM triggered an outpouring of scholarly literature on predatory pricing. Most scholars thought the *Utah Pie* rule was too soft on price competition. Some thought Areeda and Turner too forgiving of selective low pricing intended and likely to destroy the most feared smaller competitor. A few thought Areeda and Turner were too indulgent to plaintiffs and advocated a rule of per se legality for low pricing.

Several other predatory pricing suits against IBM were brought to court. The plaintiffs lost. In these cases, the courts articulated different formulations of the legal standard. For example, the court in *TransAmerica* (Transamerica Computer Co. v. IBM Corp., 698 F.2d 1377 (9th Cir.), cert. denied, 464 U.S. 955 (1983)), held:

> [T]o establish predatory pricing a plaintiff must prove that the anticipated benefits of defendant's price depended on its tendency to discipline or eliminate competition and thereby enhance the firm's long-term ability to reap the benefits of monopoly power. If the defendant's prices were below average total cost but above average variable cost, the plaintiff bears the

burden of showing defendant's pricing was predatory. If, however, the plaintiff proves that the defendant's prices were below average variable cost, the plaintiff has established a prima facie case of predatory pricing and the burden shifts to the defendant to prove that the prices were justified without regard to any anticipated destructive effect they might have on competitors. [quoting from *Inglis*, 668 F.2d 1014, 1035–36 (9th Cir. 1981).]* * *

... [T]he district court's *per se* test [for prices above average total costs] rests on the notion that price reductions to average total cost result from efficient production and harm only less efficient competitors. But companies may lower their prices for temporary strategic reasons as well. One critic of the Areeda–Turner test points out that a monopolist can employ price strategies that jeopardize consumers' long-run welfare without lowering prices below average total cost and concludes that "it is unrealistic and even analytically wrong to apply a simple short-run price-cost rule for determining whether exclusionary pricing by a monopolist is socially undesirable and therefore predatory." Scherer, *Predatory Pricing and the Sherman Act: A Comment,* 89 Harv.L.Rev. 869, 890 (1976). It may be difficult in many or most instances to assess the long-run consequences of challenged pricing policies. But where those difficulties can be overcome, the law should not prevent plaintiffs from proving antitrust violations. * * *

We therefore hold that if the challenged prices exceed average total cost, the plaintiff must prove by clear and convincing evidence—i.e., that it is highly probably true—that the defendant's pricing policy was predatory.

Judge Lucas, concurring, disagreed that pricing above cost could sometimes be predatory. He thought that pricing above total cost will rarely be anticompetitive; that the court's rule could inhibit procompetitive low pricing; and that the ruling "may well increase the number of meritless antitrust actions."

Judge Lucas' approach was mirrored in *Barry Wright Corp. v. ITT Grinnell Corp.*, 724 F.2d 227 (1st Cir.1983), wherein the court, by Judge (now Justice) Breyer, rejected the above-total-cost prong of the *Trans-America* rule as too soft on complaining competitors, and declared that a price that is above both incremental and total cost is per se lawful. Thus:

In sum, we believe that such above-cost price cuts are typically sustainable; that they are normally desirable (particularly in concentrated industries); that the "disciplinary cut" is difficult to distinguish in practice; that it, in any event, primarily injures only higher cost competitors; that its presence may well be "wrongly" asserted in a host of cases involving legitimate competition; and that to allow its assertion threatens to "chill" highly desirable procompetitive price cutting. For these reasons, we believe that a precedent allowing this type of attack on prices that exceed both incremental and average costs would more likely interfere with the procompetitive aims of the antitrust laws than further them. Hence, we conclude that the Sherman Act does not make unlawful prices that exceed both incremental and average costs. 724 F.2d at 235–36.

QUESTIONS AND COMMENTS

1. Justice Breyer's position has now been substantially adopted by the Supreme Court.

2. Compare Einer Elhauge, Why Above–Cost Price Cuts to Drive Out Entrants are not Predatory—and the Implications for Defining Costs and Market Power, 112 Yale L.J. 681 (2003), with Aaron S. Eldin, Stopping Above–Cost Predatory Pricing, 111 Yale L.J. 941 (2002).

3. After *Utah Pie*, the Supreme Court was not to deal with predatory pricing until the *Japanese Electronics* case (475 U.S. 574) in 1986, which you read at page 138 supra. The ultimate question there was not whether prices were predatory but whether there was evidence of a low-price conspiracy that anticompetitively harmed the American electronics producers. The economics and strategies of predatory pricing featured prominently in the Court's decision because the plaintiff's had alleged a predatory pricing conspiracy and because the Court seemed to assume that unless the low price was a predatory one there was no antitrust harm. In *Japanese Electronics* the Court declared that below-cost pricing by the several Japanese competitors was improbable; that it was unlikely to pay; and that below-cost pricing by oligopolists, as compared with one monopolist, was close to incredible. How could Japanese cartelists bent on squeezing out the Americans by below-cost pricing persuade one another to take losses as they pushed prices down, and persuade one another not to cheat as they later (if they could) elevated prices to monopoly levels? What difference did it make, to the proof-of-conspiracy question, if the Japanese electronics firms' low prices were not below their costs?

Costs

Costs are fixed or variable.

Fixed costs do not vary with changes in output.

Variable costs, by definition, vary with changes in output.

Total cost is the sum of fixed and variable costs.

Marginal cost (MC) is the cost of producing one more unit of output.

Average variable cost (AVC) is the sum of all variable costs divided by output. It is often used to approximate marginal cost.

Average avoidable cost (AAC) includes all costs that could have been avoided if a given quantity of output had not been produced. The category, by definition, does not include sunk costs, which are costs that cannot be recovered on exit or if the relevant amount of production is discontinued.

Long-run incremental cost includes all of the forward-looking costs of producing a given increment of output (e.g., the additional output that would be entailed by a predatory pricing strategy). This includes all fixed costs, and thus all sunk costs. For long-run average incremental costs (LRAIC), one divides the sum of all long-run incremental costs by the relevant increment in production. LRAIC is often used as the appropriate cost measure in predatory pricing cases when the relevant product has large fixed costs and a low marginal cost.

Average total cost is the sum of all costs divided by output.

Marginal and average variable costs are often almost identical. They begin to diverge when the cost of the last unit of output exceeds the average variable cost. At that point, the marginal cost of each additional unit will both exceed and raise the average. Firms will generally seek to produce up to the output at which the marginal cost does not exceed the price that can be obtained and the average cost does not rise sufficiently to cause diminishing returns. Both marginal and average variable cost can be very low as compared with full costs, especially when fixed costs are very high, as in air transport. Imagine an airplane just about to take off when, at the last minute, you buy your ticket (undoubtedly at a premium because getting on the flight was valuable to you); but the incremental cost to the airline of accommodating and serving you was close to 0.

Firms frequently price below full cost in order to get more business; but they cannot do so forever. They must eventually, or simultaneously by other higher-priced sales, cover their full costs in order to survive.

In 1993, the now flagship price predation case—*Brooke Group*—came before the Supreme Court. Much had happened since the 1960s and *Utah Pie*. The concern was no longer that low-price competition would eliminate competitors but that antitrust would eliminate low-price competition. Note that the question in the case was not whether prices, to be predatory, had to be below cost or even below average variable or marginal cost; they admittedly were, for 18 months. Note also that the case was brought under the Robinson–Patman Act rather than the Sherman Act because the defendant was not in a monopoly position and therefore Sherman Act Section 2 was not available. Nonetheless, this is the case that set the standard for Section 2 predation law.

At the Supreme Court, former Judge Robert Bork argued for defendant Brown & Williamson, and Professor Philip Areeda argued for plaintiff Liggett (which had been acquired by Brooke Group).

BROOKE GROUP LTD. v. BROWN & WILLIAMSON TOBACCO CORP.

509 U.S. 209 (1993).

JUSTICE KENNEDY: * * * Liggett contends that Brown & Williamson's discriminatory volume rebates to wholesalers threatened substantial competitive injury by furthering a predatory pricing scheme designed to purge competition from the economy segment of the cigarette market. This type of injury, which harms direct competitors of the discriminating seller, is known as primary-line injury.... We last addressed primary line injury over 25 years ago, in Utah Pie Co. v. Continental Baking Co., 386 U.S. 685 (1967).... We reversed the Court of Appeals and held that the evidence presented was adequate to permit a jury to find a likelihood of injury to competition.

Utah Pie has often been interpreted to permit liability for primary-line price discrimination on a mere showing that the defendant intended to harm competition or produced a declining price structure. The case had been criticized on the grounds that such low standards of competitive injury are at odds with the antitrust laws traditional concern for consumer welfare and price competition.... We do not regard the *Utah Pie* case itself as having the full significance attributed to it by its detractors. *Utah Pie* was an early judicial inquiry in this area and did not purport to set forth explicit, general standards for establishing a violation of the Robinson–Patman Act. As the law has been explored since *Utah Pie*, it has become evident that primary-line competitive injury under the Robinson–Patman Act is of the same general character as the injury inflicted by predatory pricing schemes actionable under § 2 of the Sherman Act.... There are, to be sure, differences between the two statutes. For example, we interpret § 2 of the Sherman Act to condemn predatory pricing when it poses "a dangerous probability of actual monopolization," *Spectrum Sports, Inc. v. McQuillan*, 506 U.S. 447, 455 (1993) whereas the Robinson–Patman Act requires only that there be "a reasonable possibility" of substantial injury to competition before its protections are triggered.... But whatever additional flexibility the Robinson–Patman Act standard may imply, the essence of the claim under either statute is the same: A business rival has priced its products in an unfair manner with an object to eliminate or retard competition and thereby gain and exercise control over prices in the relevant market.

Accordingly, whether the claim alleges predatory pricing under § 2 of the Sherman Act or primary-line price discrimination under the Robinson–Patman Act, two prerequisites to recovery remain the same. First, a plaintiff seeking to establish competitive injury resulting from a rival's low prices must prove that the prices complained of are below an appropriate measure of its rival's costs.... Although *Cargill* and *Matsushita* [the *Japanese Electronics* case] reserved as a formal matter the question " 'whether recovery should *ever* be available ... when the pricing in question is above some measure of incremental cost,' " *Cargill*, supra, at 117–118, n. 12 (quoting *Matsushita*, supra, [475 U.S.] at 585, n. 9), the reasoning in both opinions suggests that only below-cost prices should suffice, and we have rejected elsewhere the notion that above-cost prices that are below general market levels or the costs of a firm's competitors inflict injury to competition cognizable under the antitrust laws.... As a general rule, the exclusionary effect of prices above a relevant measure of cost either reflects the lower cost structure of the alleged predator, and so represents competition on the merits, or is beyond the practical ability of a judicial tribunal to control without courting intolerable risks of chilling legitimate price-cutting....

Even in an oligopolistic market, when a firm drops its prices to a competitive level to demonstrate to a maverick the unprofitability of straying from the group, it would be illogical to condemn the price cut: The antitrust laws then would be an obstacle to the chain of events most conducive to a breakdown of oligopoly pricing and the onset of competition. Even if the ultimate effect of the cut is to induce or reestablish supracompetitive pricing, discouraging a price cut and forcing firms to maintain supracompetitive prices, thus depriving consumers of the benefits of lower prices in the interim, does not constitute sound antitrust policy....

The second prerequisite to holding a competitor liable under the antitrust laws for charging low prices is a demonstration that the competitor had a reasonable prospect, or, under 2 of the Sherman Act, a dangerous probability, of recouping its investment in below-cost prices.... Recoupment is the ultimate object of an unlawful predatory pricing scheme; it is the means by which a predator profits from predation. Without it, predatory pricing produces lower aggregate prices in the market, and consumer welfare is enhanced. Although unsuccessful predatory pricing may encourage some inefficient substitution toward the product being sold at less than its cost, unsuccessful predation is in general a boon to consumers.

That below-cost pricing may impose painful losses on its target is of no moment to the antitrust laws if competition is not injured:....

Even an act of pure malice by one business competitor against another does not, without more, state a claim under the federal antitrust laws; those laws do not create a federal law of unfair competition....

For recoupment to occur, below-cost pricing must be capable, as a threshold matter, of producing the intended effects on the firm's rivals, whether driving them from the market, or, as was alleged to be the goal here, causing them to raise their prices to supracompetitive levels within a disciplined oligopoly. This requires an understanding of the extent and duration of the alleged predation, the relative financial strength of the predator and its intended victim, and their respective incentives and will.... The inquiry is whether, given the aggregate losses caused by the below-cost pricing, the intended target would likely succumb.

If circumstances indicate that below-cost pricing could likely produce its intended effect on the target, there is still the further question whether it would likely injure competition in the relevant market. The plaintiff must demonstrate that there is a likelihood that the predatory scheme alleged would cause a rise in prices above a competitive level that would be sufficient to compensate for the amounts expended on the predation, including the time value of the money invested in it. . . .

Evidence of below-cost pricing is not alone sufficient to permit an inference of probable recoupment and injury to competition. Determining whether recoupment of predatory losses is likely requires an estimate of the cost of the alleged predation and a close analysis of both the scheme alleged by the plaintiff and the structure and conditions of the relevant market. If market circumstances or deficiencies in proof would bar a reasonable jury from finding that the scheme alleged would likely result in sustained supracompetitive pricing, the plaintiff's case has failed. In certain situations—for example, where the market is highly diffuse and competitive, or where new entry is easy, or the defendant lacks adequate excess capacity to absorb the market shares of his rivals and cannot quickly create or purchase new capacity-summary disposition of the case is appropriate. . . .

These prerequisites to recovery are not easy to establish, but they are not artificial obstacles to recovery; rather, they are essential components of real market injury. As we have said in the Sherman Act context, "predatory pricing schemes are rarely tried, and even more rarely successful," *Matsushita, supra*, at 589, and the costs of an erroneous finding of liability are high. . . .

B.

Liggett does not allege that Brown & Williamson sought to drive it from the market but that Brown & Williamson sought to preserve supracompetitive profits on branded cigarettes by pressuring Liggett to raise its generic cigarette prices through a process of tacit collusion with other cigarette companies. Tacit collusion, sometimes called oligopolistic price coordination or conscious parallelism, describes the process, not in itself unlawful, by which firms in a concentrated market might in effect share monopoly power, setting their prices at a profit-maximizing, supracompetitive level by recognizing their shared economic interests and their interdependence with respect to price and output decisions. . . . *Matsushita* observed that such schemes are even more improbable when they require coordinated action among several firms. . . .

However unlikely predatory pricing by multiple firms may be when they conspire, it is even less likely when, as here, there is no express coordination. Firms that seek to recoup predatory losses through the conscious parallelism of oligopoly must rely on uncertain and ambiguous signals to achieve concerted action. The signals are subject to misinterpretation and are a blunt and imprecise means of ensuring smooth cooperation, especially in the context of changing or unprecedented market circumstances. This anticompetitive minuet is most difficult to compose and to perform, even for a disciplined oligopoly.

... In this case, for example, Brown & Williamson, with its 11–12% share of the cigarette market, would have had to generate around $9 in supracompetitive profits for each $1 invested in predation; the remaining $8 would belong to its competitors, who had taken no risk. Liggett suggests that these considerations led the Court of Appeals to rule out its theory of recovery as a matter of law. The final paragraph appears to state the holding: Brown & Williamson may not be held liable because oligopoly pricing does not "provide an economically rational basis" for recouping predatory losses.

To the extent that the Court of Appeals may have held that the interdependent pricing of an oligopoly may never provide a means for achieving recoupment and so may not form the basis of a primary-line injury claim, we disagree. A predatory pricing scheme designed to preserve or create a stable oligopoly, if successful, can injure consumers in the same way, and to the same extent, as one designed to bring about a monopoly. However unlikely that possibility may be as a general matter, when the realities of the market and the record facts indicate that it has occurred and was likely to have succeeded, theory will not stand in the way of liability. See *Eastman Kodak Co. v. Image Technical Services, Inc.*, 504 U.S. 451, 466–467 (1992). * * *

Having thus recognized the possibility of price predation aimed at assuring oligopolistic stability, the Court concluded that market realities precluded a finding of liability here. While a reasonable jury could conclude that Brown & Williamson's intent was anticompetitive and that the price of its generics was below its costs for 18 months, the evidence was inadequate to show a reasonable prospect of cost recoupment. No such finding was sustainable because no evidence suggests that Brown & Williamson was likely to obtain the power to raise the prices for generic cigarettes above a competitive level. The output and price information does not indicate that oligopolistic price coordination in fact produced supracompetitive prices in the generic segment. Nor does the evidence about the market and Brown & Williamson's conduct indicate that the alleged scheme was likely to have brought about tacit coordination and oligopoly pricing in that segment.

* * *

JUSTICE STEVENS, with whom JUSTICES WHITE and BLACKMUN joined, dissenting.

* * *

For a period of 18 months in 1984 and 1985, respondent Brown & Williamson Tobacco Corporation (B&W) waged a price war against petitioner, known then as Liggett & Myers (Liggett). Liggett filed suit claiming that B&W's pricing practices violated the Robinson–Patman Act. After a 115–day trial, the jury agreed, and awarded Liggett substantial damages. The Court of Appeals, however, found that Liggett could not succeed on its claim, because B&W, as an independent actor controlling only 12% of the national cigarette market, could not injure competition.

Today, the Court properly rejects that holding. Instead of remanding the case to the Court of Appeals to resolve the other issues raised by the parties, however, the Court goes on to review portions of the voluminous trial record, and comes to the conclusion that the evidence does not support the jury's finding that B&W's price discrimination "had a reasonable possibility of injuring competition." In my opinion the evidence is plainly sufficient to support that finding.

The fact that a price war may not have accomplished its purpose as quickly or as completely as originally intended does not immunize conduct that was illegal when it occurred. . . .

. . . . The rebate program was intended to harm Liggett and in fact caused it serious injury. The jury found that Liggett had suffered actual damages of $49.6 million, an amount close to, but slightly larger than, the $48.7 million trading profit B&W had indicated it would forgo in order to discipline Liggett. To inflict this injury, B&W sustained a substantial loss. During the full 18–month period, B&W's revenues ran consistently below its total variable costs, with an average deficiency of approximately $0.30 per carton and a total loss on B&W black and whites of almost $15 million. That B&W executives were willing to accept losses of this magnitude during the entire 18 months is powerful evidence of their belief that prices ultimately could be "managed up" to a level that would allow B&W to recoup its investment.

The Aftermath [of the Price War]

At the end of 1985, the list price of branded cigarettes was $33.15 per carton, and the list price of black and whites, $19.75 per carton. . . . Over the next four years, the list price on both branded and black and white cigarettes increased twice a year, by identical amounts. The June 1989 increases brought the price of branded cigarettes to $46.15 per carton, and the price of black and whites to $33.75—an amount even higher than the price for branded cigarettes when the war ended in December 1985. . . . Because the rate of increase was higher on black and whites than on brandeds, the price differential between the two types of cigarettes narrowed, from roughly 40% in 1985 to 27% in 1989.

The expert economist employed by Liggett testified that the post–1985 price increases were unwarranted by increases in manufacturing or other costs, taxes, or promotional expenditures. To be sure, some portion of the volume rebates granted distributors was passed on to consumers in the form of promotional activity, so that consumers did not feel the full brunt of the price increases. Nevertheless, the record amply supports the conclusion that the post–1985 price increases in list prices produced higher consumer prices, as well as higher profits for the manufacturers.

The legal question presented by this evidence is whether the facts as they existed during and at the close of the 18–month period, and all reasonable inferences to be drawn from those facts, justified the finding by the jury that B&W's discriminatory pricing campaign "had a reasonable possibility of injuring competition."

II.

The Sherman Act, enacted in 1890, the Clayton Act, enacted in 1914, and the Robinson–Patman Act, which amended the Clayton Act in 1936, ... prohibit the predatory practice of deliberately selling below cost to discipline a competitor, either to drive the competitor out of business or to raise prices to a level that will enable the predator to recover its losses and, in the long run, earn additional profits. Sales below cost and anticompetitive intent are elements of the violation of all three statutes. Neither of those elements, however, is at issue in this case.

The statutes do differ significantly with respect to one element of the violation, the competitive consequences of predatory conduct. Even here, however, the three statutes have one thing in common; not one of them requires proof that a predatory plan has actually succeeded in accomplishing its objective....

In this case, ... then, Liggett need not show any actual harm to competition, but only the reasonable possibility that such harm would flow from B&W's conduct. The evidence presented supports the conclusion that B&W's price war was intended to discipline Liggett for its unprecedented use of price competition in an industry that had enjoyed handsome supracompetitive profits for about half a century. The evidence also demonstrates that B&W executives were confident enough in the feasibility of their plan that they were willing to invest millions of company dollars in its outcome. And all of this, of course, must be viewed against a background of supracompetitive, parallel pricing, in which "prices for cigarettes increased in lock-step, twice a year ... irrespective of the rate of inflation, changes in the cost of production, or shifts in consumer demand," bringing with them dramatic increases in profit margins. * * *

QUESTIONS AND COMMENTS

1. Why would Brown & Williamson price below variable cost for 18 months if it could not expect the "investment in predation" to be worth it? Did it miscalculate? Or was it worth it? If the predation was worth it, where did the Court go wrong?

2. Why is the Court so confident that predation is rarely tried and even more rarely successful? Some respected scholars disagree. See Patrick Bolton, Joseph F. Brodley and Michael R. Riordan, Predatory Pricing: Strategic Theory and Legal Policy, 88 Geo. L.J. 2239 (2000); K. Elzinga and D. Mills, Predatory Pricing and Strategic Theory, reply to Bolton et al., 89 Geo. L.J. 2475 (2001); P. Bolton, et al., Predatory Pricing: Response to Critique and Further Elaboration, reply to K. Elzinga et al., 89 Geo. L.J. 2495 (2001). Why

might the *Brooke Group* rule survive (and it does survive) even if predation is not as rare as the Court supposed?

3. Should the rule be exported to the world? The European Court of Justice has considered the reasoning of *Brooke Group*, and has rejected the requirement that the plaintiff must prove a recoupment scenario. See France Télécom SA v. Comm'n, Case C–202/07 P, 2009 ECR I–02369 (European Court of Justice); TeliaSonera, Case C–52/09, 2011 ECR II–__ (European Court of Justice). See also E. Fox, Cases and Materials on the Competition Law of the European Union in Comparative Perspectives, 133–145 (West 2009).

5. PREDATORY BUYING

Predatory buying is the reverse of predatory selling. The buyer buys up inputs at a price that is "too high"—a price above market that its rivals in the downstream market cannot afford to pay. This buyer squeezes out its rivals, gaining monopsony (single buyer) power over its suppliers. Having monopsony power, it is able to squeeze its suppliers, who are now forced to sell to the monopsonist at a lower-than-competitive price.

Do the antitrust laws protect the squeezed out rivals? Do they protect the suppliers from exploitation by the "predatory" monopsonist? What if there is no harm to consumers? What if consumers will get a benefit from the now lower input prices?

In the early 2000s, Ross–Simmons and Weyerhaeuser operated sawmills in the Pacific Northwest. The predominant hardwood in the area was red alder. Ultimately, the logs were processed for hardwood lumber. Alder logs made up only a small part of hardwood lumber sales, and were not distinctive. The sale of hardwood lumber was a competitive market.

Weyerhaeuser was one of the largest manufacturers of hardwood lumber in the world. Its share of purchases of alder sawlogs in the Pacific Northwest was 65%, but its share of sales in North America for all hardwood lumber was less than 3%. Ross–Simmons claimed, and proved to a jury, that Weyerhaeuser overpaid for alder sawlogs and bought more alder sawlogs than it needed, intentionally squeezing Ross–Simmons, which could not pay so high a price, and causing the closure of its plant, thus monopolizing the Pacific Northwest alder sawlog market. The circuit court affirmed the judgment for plaintiff entered on the jury verdict. But Ross–Simmons had not shown that Weyerhaeuser had engaged in predatory bidding (buying at a price so high that its expenditures could not be recovered by its sales price) or that it was likely to recoup these losses, as would be required if the *Brooke Group* standard applied to predatory buying as well as to predatory selling.

WEYERHAEUSER COMPANY v. ROSS–SIMMONS HARDWOOD LUMBER CO.

549 U.S. 312 (2007).

JUSTICE THOMAS: * * *

IV. A. * * *

Tracking the economic similarity between monopoly and monopsony, predatory-pricing plaintiffs and predatory-bidding plaintiffs make strikingly similar allegations. A predatory-pricing plaintiff alleges that a predator cut prices to drive the plaintiff out of business and, thereby, to reap monopoly profits from the output market. In parallel fashion, a predatory-bidding plaintiff alleges that a predator raised prices for a key input to drive the plaintiff out of business and, thereby, to reap monopsony profits in the input market. Both claims involve the deliberate use of unilateral pricing measures for anticompetitive purposes. And both claims logically require firms to incur short-term losses on the chance that they might reap supracompetitive profits in the future.

B.

More importantly, predatory bidding mirrors predatory pricing in respects that we deemed significant to our analysis in *Brooke Group*. In *Brooke Group*, we noted that " 'predatory pricing schemes are rarely tried, and even more rarely successful.' " 509 U.S., at 226 (quoting Matsushita, 475 U.S., at 589). Predatory pricing requires a firm to suffer certain losses in the short term on the chance of reaping supracompetitive profits in the future. *Id.*, at 588–589. A rational business will rarely make this sacrifice. *Ibid.* The same reasoning applies to predatory bidding. A predatory-bidding scheme requires a buyer of inputs to suffer losses today on the chance that it will reap supracompetitive profits in the future. For this reason, "[s]ucccessful monopsony predation is probably as unlikely as successful monopoly predation." R. Blair & J. Harrison, Monopsony 66 (1993).

And like the predatory conduct alleged in *Brooke Group*, actions taken in a predatory-bidding scheme are often "the very essence of competition." Just as sellers use output prices to compete for purchasers, buyers use bid prices to compete for scarce inputs. There are myriad legitimate reasons—ranging from benign to affirmatively procompetitive—why a buyer might bid up input prices. A firm might bid up inputs as a result of miscalculation of its input needs or as a response to increased consumer demand for its outputs. A more efficient firm might bid up input prices to acquire more inputs as a part of a procompetitive strategy to gain market share in the output market. A firm that has adopted an input-intensive production process might bid up inputs to acquire the inputs necessary for its process. Or a firm might bid up input prices to acquire excess inputs as a hedge against the risk of future rises in input costs or future input shortages. There is nothing illicit about these bidding decisions. Indeed, this sort of high bidding is essential to competition and innovation on the buy side of the market.

Brooke Group also noted that a failed predatory-pricing scheme may benefit consumers. The potential benefit results from the difficulty an aspiring predator faces in recouping losses suffered from below-cost pricing. Without successful recoupment, "predatory pricing produces lower aggregate prices in the market, and consumer welfare is enhanced." *Ibid.* Failed predatory-bidding schemes can also, but will not necessarily, benefit consumers. In the first stage of a predatory-bidding scheme, the predator's high bidding will likely lead to its acquisition of more inputs. Usually, the acquisition of more inputs leads to the manufacture of more outputs. And increases in output generally result in lower prices to consumers. Thus, a failed predatory-bidding scheme can be a "boon to consumers" in the same way that we considered a predatory-pricing scheme to be.

In addition, predatory bidding presents less of a direct threat of consumer harm than predatory pricing. A predatory-pricing scheme ultimately achieves success by charging higher prices to consumers. By contrast, a predatory-bidding scheme could succeed with little or no effect on consumer prices because a predatory bidder does not necessarily rely on raising prices in the output market to recoup its losses. Even if output prices remain constant, a predatory bidder can use its power as the predominant buyer of inputs to force down input prices and capture monopsony profits.

C.

The general theoretical similarities of monopoly and monopsony combined with the theoretical and practical similarities of predatory pricing and predatory bidding convince us that our two-pronged *Brooke Group* test should apply to predatory-bidding claims.

* * *

QUESTIONS AND COMMENTS

1. Do you agree that predatory buying is the mirror image of predatory selling?

2. In *Brooke Group*, the Court expressed particular concern about enjoining low prices—the first leg of predatory selling—because this would entail an immediate and considerable consumer loss, and a later price rise is very speculative. How would the Court risk harming consumers by intervening against the first leg of predatory buying (bidding "too much")?

3. In *Weyerhaeuser*, since Weyerhaeuser accounted for only 3% of the output market, how could a predatory buying scheme make sense, and how could it ever hurt consumers? Suppose it worked only to transfer profits from the smaller alder sawlog firms (which were squeezed out) to Weyerhaeuser,

with no impact on consumers. If, as the jury found, Weyerhaeuser over-bought the logs precisely to squeeze out its competitors, should the squeezed-out firms have an antitrust remedy against Weyerhaeuser? Why does the Court reject this idea? Are the facts inherently not credible?

6. PRICE SQUEEZES

Recall that in *Alcoa* (1945), the appellate court based its holdings of violation on two separate offenses: 1) *Alcoa* had achieved monopoly actively; it was not thrust upon it; and 2) *Alcoa* had sold aluminum to the independent fabricators at a price so high, and had sold its own fabricated product on the market at a price so low, that the fabricators could not afford to stay in business. The first and principal holding has long since been overridden by modern law that bases liability on conduct, not structure. The second holding was generally accepted as the law, until . . .

In the wake of *Trinko*, supra at page 249, Pacific Bell, the incumbent telephone service provider on the West Coast, charged Internet service providers (ISPs) so much for the elements of DSL service (for broadband telephone Internet connection), and charged its own end users of DSL so little, that the ISPs could not provide the DSL service at a profit. LinkLine and other ISPs sued. Pacific Bell moved to dismiss. The district court denied the motion. The Ninth Circuit Court of Appeals affirmed.

Pacific Bell petitioned for certiorari. The U.S. Department of Justice urged the Supreme Court to grant certiorari, arguing that an antitrust price squeeze claim cannot stand when (as dictated by *Trinko*) the defendant has no antitrust duty to provide the wholesale input to the plaintiff at all. It said in its Amicus Brief:

> Section 2 of the Sherman Act does not provide a cause of action for "price-squeeze" claims of the type at issue here—namely, allegations that a vertically integrated company with an alleged monopoly at the wholesale level, but with no antitrust duty to provide that wholesale input to its retail competitors, engaged in a "price squeeze" by leaving insufficient margin between wholesale and retail prices to allow its retail competitors to compete. Accepting such a price-squeeze theory based solely on an inadequate margin between a defendant's wholesale and retail prices would recognize an antitrust claim involving no allegations of predatory pricing, no breach of an antitrust duty to deal, and no conduct that harms competition in a way the antitrust laws forbid. Such a theory of liability could not be reconciled with this Court's modern antitrust jurisprudence. The court of appeals' contrary holding is erroneous and is in conflict with the decisions of other courts of appeals. Despite the interlocutory posture of the case, review is warranted because the Ninth Circuit's endorsement of such a theory threatens to chill retail price-cutting by vertically integrated firms and encourage litigation designed to protect competitors at the expense of competition, thereby undermining the procompetitive pur-

poses of the antitrust laws and harming consumers. Accordingly, the petition should be granted.

An amicus brief in support of certiorari was filed also by a group of law and economics scholars, who argued that "*linkLine* is the most important antitrust case that the Court could take during the Fall 2007 Term." This brief was authored by Robert H. Bork and J. Gregory Sidak. Going further than the DOJ, the professors claimed that price squeeze as a theory of antitrust liability should be abolished; it makes sense only as a regulatory issue. The brief continues:

> [T]he Ninth Circuit's rule is of pressing concern precisely because it will deter efficiency-enhancing conduct and competitive pricing. Vertical integration and partial integration are ubiquitous, and firms need to be able to make decisions about such integration without the threat of liability. Vertically integrated firms likewise need to be free to cut retail prices (as long as the prices are not predatory) without concern for rivals.... * * *
>
> The alternative to consumer-welfare maximization is the view that antitrust law is simply one more tool of industrial policy, and thus its application may permissibly compromise consumer welfare to advance the welfare of competitors. Other nations evidently consider this normative proposition to be appropriate, if recent developments in the European Union are a valid indication. More than ever before, the United States and Europe appear to be at a fork in the road over whether the law of monopolization exists to protect consumers or to ensure that a specified number of firms will profitably populate a market. The Ninth Circuit's *linkLine* decision implicitly chooses the latter path, which leads to the Potemkin village of 'managed competition.'

The Federal Trade Commission parted ways with the Department of Justice and filed a statement (3–0) with the Supreme Court urging the Court to deny the petition for certiorari "because we disagree with DOJ's analysis, and because this case does not appear to be worthy of review at this time." The statement maintains that the Ninth Circuit "is unquestionably correct"; "claims of a predatory price squeeze in a partially regulated industry remain viable after *Trinko.*"

PACIFIC BELL TELEPHONE CO. v. LINKLINE COMMUNICATIONS, INC.

555 U.S. 438, 129 S.Ct. 1109 (2009).

CHIEF JUSTICE ROBERTS: The plaintiffs in this case, respondents here, allege that a competitor subjected them to a "price squeeze" in violation of § 2 of the Sherman Act. They assert that such a claim can arise when a vertically integrated firm sells inputs at wholesale and also sells finished goods or services at retail. If that firm has power in the wholesale market, it can simultaneously raise the wholesale price of inputs and cut the retail price of the finished good. This will have the effect of "squeezing" the profit margins of any competitors in the retail market. Those firms will have to pay more for the inputs they need; at the same time, they will have to cut their retail prices to match the other firm's prices. The question before us is whether such a price-squeeze claim may be brought under § 2 of the Sherman Act when the defendant is under no antitrust obligation to sell the inputs to the plaintiff in the first place. We hold that no such claim may be brought.

I.

This case involves the market for digital subscriber line (DSL) service, which is a method of connecting to the Internet at high speeds over telephone lines. AT&T owns much of the infrastructure and facilities needed to provide DSL service in California. In particular, AT&T controls most of what is known as the "last mile"—the lines that connect homes and businesses to the telephone network. Competing DSL providers must generally obtain access to AT&T's facilities in order to serve their customers.

Until recently, the Federal Communications Commission (FCC) required incumbent phone companies such as AT&T to sell transmission service to independent DSL providers, under the theory that this would spur competition. In 2005, the Commission largely abandoned this forced-sharing requirement in light of the emergence of a competitive market beyond DSL for high speed Internet service; DSL now faces robust competition from cable companies and wireless and satellite services. As a condition for a recent merger, however, AT&T remains bound by the mandatory interconnection requirements, and is obligated to provide wholesale "DSL transport" service to independent firms at a price no greater than the retail price of AT&T's DSL service.

The plaintiffs are four independent Internet service providers (ISPs) that compete with AT&T in the retail DSL market. Plaintiffs do not own all the facilities needed to supply their customers with this service. They instead lease DSL transport service from AT&T pursuant to the merger conditions described above. AT&T thus participates in the DSL market at both the wholesale and retail levels; it provides plaintiffs and other independent ISPs with wholesale DSL transport service, and it also sells DSL service directly to consumers at retail.

In July 2003, the plaintiffs brought suit in District Court, alleging that AT&T violated § 2 of the Sherman Act by monopolizing the DSL market in California. The complaint alleges that AT&T refused to deal with the plaintiffs, denied the plaintiffs access to essential facilities, and engaged in a "price squeeze." Specifically, plaintiffs contend that AT&T squeezed their profit margins by setting a high wholesale price for DSL transport and a low retail price for DSL Internet service. This maneuver allegedly "exclude[d] and unreasonably impede[d] competition," thus allowing AT&T to "preserve and maintain its monopoly control of DSL access to the Internet." *Ibid.*

... AT&T moved for judgment on the pleadings, arguing that the plaintiffs' claims in this case were foreclosed by *Trinko*. The District Court held that AT&T had no antitrust duty to deal with the plaintiffs, but it denied the motion to dismiss with respect to the price-squeeze claims. The court acknowledged that AT&T's argument "has a certain logic to it," but held that *Trinko* "simply does not involve price-squeeze claims." The District Court also noted that price-squeeze claims have been recognized by several Circuits and "are cognizable under existing antitrust standards." * * *

On interlocutory appeal, the Court of Appeals for the Ninth Circuit affirmed the District Court's denial of AT&T's motion for judgment on the pleadings on the price-squeeze claims.... * * *

We granted certiorari, to resolve a conflict over whether a plaintiff can bring price-squeeze claims under § 2 of the Sherman Act when the defendant has no antitrust duty to deal with the plaintiff. We reverse. * * *

III.

A.

Section 2 of the Sherman Act makes it unlawful to "monopolize, or attempt to monopolize, or combine or conspire with any other person or persons, to monopolize any part of the trade or commerce among the several States, or with foreign nations." Simply possessing monopoly power and charging monopoly prices does not violate § 2; rather, the statute targets "the willful acquisition or maintenance of that power as distinguished from growth or development as a consequence of a superior product, business acumen, or historic accident." *United States v. Grinnell Corp.*, 384 U.S. 563, 570–571 (1966).

As a general rule, businesses are free to choose the parties with whom they will deal, as well as the prices, terms, and conditions of that dealing. See *United States v. Colgate & Co.*, 250 U.S. 300, 307 (1919). But there are rare instances in which a dominant firm may incur antitrust liability for purely unilateral conduct. For example, we have ruled that firms may not charge "predatory" prices—below-cost prices that drive rivals out of the market and allow the monopolist to raise its prices later and recoup its losses. *Brooke Group*, 509 U.S., at 222–224....

There are also limited circumstances in which a firm's unilateral refusal to deal with its rivals can give rise to antitrust liability. See *Aspen Skiing Co. v. Aspen Highlands Skiing Corp.*, 472 U.S. 585, 608–611 (1985)....[3]

3. The Court of Appeals assumed that any duty to deal arose only from FCC regulations, and the question on which we granted certiorari made the same assumption. Even aside from the District Court's reasoning, it seems quite unlikely that AT&T would have an antitrust duty to deal with the plaintiffs. Such a duty requires a showing of monopoly power, but—as the FCC has recognized, the market for high-speed Internet service is now quite competitive; DSL providers face stiff competition from cable companies and wireless and satellite providers.

The challenge here focuses on retail prices—where there is no predatory pricing—and the terms of dealing—where there is no duty to deal. Plaintiffs' price-squeeze claims challenge a different type of unilateral conduct in which a firm "squeezes" the profit margins of its competitors. This requires the defendant to be operating in two markets, a wholesale ("upstream") market and a retail ("downstream") market. A firm with market power in the upstream market can squeeze its downstream competitors by raising the wholesale price of inputs while cutting its own retail prices. This will raise competitors' costs (because they will have to pay more for their inputs) and lower their revenues (because they will have to match the dominant firm's low retail price). Price-squeeze plaintiffs assert that defendants must leave them a "fair" or "adequate" margin between the wholesale price and the retail price. In this case, we consider whether a plaintiff can state a price-squeeze claim when the defendant has no obligation under the antitrust laws to deal with the plaintiff at wholesale.

B.

[*Claim challenging wholesale prices*]

1. A straightforward application of our recent decision in *Trinko* forecloses any challenge to AT&T's *wholesale* prices. In *Trinko*, Verizon was required by statute to lease its network elements to competing firms at wholesale rates. The plaintiff—a customer of one of Verizon's rivals—asserted that Verizon denied its competitors access to interconnection support services, making it difficult for those competitors to fill their customers' orders. The complaint alleged that this conduct in the upstream market violated § 2 of the Sherman Act by impeding the ability of independent carriers to compete in the downstream market for local telephone service.

We held that the plaintiff's claims were not actionable under § 2. Given that Verizon had no antitrust duty to deal with its rivals at all, we concluded that "Verizon's alleged insufficient assistance in the provision of service to rivals" did not violate the Sherman Act. *Trinko* thus makes clear that if a firm has no antitrust duty to deal with its competitors at wholesale, it certainly has no duty to deal under terms and conditions that the rivals find commercially advantageous.

In this case, as in *Trinko*, the defendant has no antitrust duty to deal with its rivals at wholesale; any such duty arises only from FCC regulations, not from the Sherman Act. There is no meaningful distinction between the "insufficient assistance" claims we rejected in *Trinko* and the plaintiffs' price-squeeze claims in the instant case. The *Trinko* plaintiffs challenged the quality of Verizon's interconnection service, while this case involves a challenge to AT&T's pricing structure. But for antitrust purposes, there is no reason to distinguish between price and nonprice components of a transaction.... The nub of the complaint in both *Trinko* and this case is identical—the plaintiffs alleged that the defendants (upstream monopolists) abused their power in the wholesale market to prevent rival firms from competing effectively in the retail market. *Trinko* holds that such claims are not cognizable under the Sherman Act in the absence of an antitrust duty to deal.

The District Court and the Court of Appeals did not regard *Trinko* as controlling because that case did not directly address price-squeeze claims. This is technically true, but the reasoning of *Trinko* applies with equal force to price-squeeze claims. AT&T could have squeezed its competitors' profits just as effectively by providing poor-quality interconnection service to the plaintiffs, as Verizon allegedly did in *Trinko*. But a firm with no duty to deal in the wholesale market has no obligation to deal under terms and conditions favorable to its competitors. If AT&T had simply stopped providing DSL transport service to the plaintiffs, it would not have run afoul of the Sherman Act. Under these circumstances, AT&T was not required to offer this service at the wholesale prices the plaintiffs would have preferred.

[*Claim challenging retail prices*]

2. The other component of a price-squeeze claim is the assertion that the defendant's *retail* prices are "too low." Here too plaintiffs' claims find no support in our existing antitrust doctrine.

"[C]utting prices in order to increase business often is the very essence of competition." *Matsushita Elec. Industrial Co. v. Zenith Radio Corp.*, 475 U.S. 574, 594 (1986). In cases seeking to impose antitrust liability for prices that are too low, mistaken inferences are "especially costly, because they chill the very conduct the antitrust laws are designed to protect." *Ibid*.... To avoid chilling aggressive price competition, we have carefully limited the circumstances under which plaintiffs can state a Sherman Act claim by alleging that prices are too low. Specifically, to prevail on a predatory pricing claim, a plaintiff must demonstrate that: (1) "the prices complained of are below an appropriate measure of its rival's [the alleged predator's] costs"; and (2) there is a "dangerous probability" that the defendant will be able to recoup its "investment" in below-cost prices. *Brooke Group* at 222–224. "Low prices benefit consumers regardless of how those prices are set, and so long as they are above predatory levels, they do not threaten competition." *Atlantic Richfield Co. v. USA Petroleum Co.*, 495 U.S. 328, 340 (1990).

In the complaint at issue in this interlocutory appeal, there is no allegation that AT&T's conduct met either of the *Brooke Group* requirements. Recognizing a price-squeeze claim where the defendant's retail price remains above cost would invite the precise harm we sought to avoid in *Brooke Group*: Firms might raise their retail prices or refrain from aggressive price competition to avoid potential antitrust liability. See 509 U.S., at 223 ("As a general rule, the exclusionary effect of prices above a relevant measure of cost either reflects the lower cost structure of the alleged predator, and so represents competition on the merits, or is beyond the practical ability of a judicial tribunal to control without courting intolerable risks of chilling legitimate price cutting").

3. Plaintiffs' price-squeeze claim, looking to the relation between retail and wholesale prices, is thus nothing more than an amalgamation of a meritless claim at the retail level and a meritless claim at the wholesale level. If there is no duty to deal at the wholesale level and no predatory pricing at the retail level, then a firm is certainly not required to price both of these services in a manner that preserves its rivals' profit margins.[4]

C.

1. Institutional concerns also counsel against recognition of such claims. We have repeatedly emphasized the importance of clear rules in antitrust law. Courts are ill suited "to act as central planners, identifying the proper price, quantity, and other terms of dealing." *Trinko*, 540 U.S., at 408. " 'No court should impose a duty to deal that it cannot explain or adequately and reasonably supervise. The problem should be deemed irremedia[ble] by antitrust law when compulsory access requires the court to assume the day-to-day controls characteristic of a regulatory agency.' " *Id.*, at 415 (quoting Areeda, Essential Facilities: An Epithet in Need of Limiting Principles, 58 Antitrust L.J. 841, 853 (1989)); see also *Town of Concord v. Boston Edison Co.*, 915 F. 2d 17, 25 (CA1 1990) (Breyer, C. J.) ("[A]ntitrust courts normally avoid direct price administration, relying on rules and remedies . . . that are easier to administer").

It is difficult enough for courts to identify and remedy an alleged anticompetitive practice at one level, such as predatory pricing in retail markets or a violation of the duty-to-deal doctrine at the wholesale level. See *Brooke Group* at 225 (predation claims "requir[e] an understanding of the extent and duration of the alleged predation, the relative financial strength of the predator and its intended victim, and their respective incentives and will"); *Trinko*, *supra*, at 408. Recognizing price squeeze claims would require courts simultaneously to police both the wholesale and retail prices to ensure that rival firms are not being squeezed. And courts would be aiming at a moving target, since it is the *interaction* between these two prices that may result in a squeeze.

Perhaps most troubling, firms that seek to avoid price-squeeze liability will have no safe harbor for their pricing practices. See *Town of Concord* at 22 (antitrust rules "must be clear enough for lawyers to explain them to clients"). At least in the predatory pricing context, firms know they will not incur liability as long as their retail prices are above

4. Like the Court of Appeals, 503 F. 3d, at 880, amici argue that price squeeze claims have been recognized by Circuit Courts for many years, beginning with Judge Hand's opinion in United States v. Aluminum Co. of America, 148 F. 2d 416 (CA2 1945) (Alcoa). In that case, the Government alleged that Alcoa was using its monopoly power in the upstream aluminum ingot market to squeeze the profits of downstream aluminum sheet fabricators. The court concluded: "That it was unlawful to set the price of 'sheet' so low and hold the price of ingot so high, seems to us unquestionable, provided, as we have held, that on this record the price of ingot must be regarded as higher than a 'fair price.' " Id., at 438. Given developments in economic theory and antitrust jurisprudence since Alcoa, we find our recent decisions in Trinko and Brooke Group more pertinent to the question before us.

cost. *Brooke Group* at 223. No such guidance is available for price-squeeze claims.

The most commonly articulated standard for price squeezes is that the defendant must leave its rivals a "fair" or "adequate" margin between the wholesale price and the retail price. See *Town of Concord* at 23–25; *Alcoa*, 148 F. 2d 416, 437–438 (CA2 1945). One of our colleagues has highlighted the flaws of this test in Socratic fashion:

> "[H]ow is a judge or jury to determine a 'fair price?' Is it the price charged by other suppliers of the primary product? None exist. Is it the price that competition 'would have set' were the primary level not monopolized? How can the court determine this price without examining costs and demands, indeed without acting like a rate-setting regulatory agency, the rate-setting proceedings of which often last for several years? Further, how is the court to decide the proper size of the price 'gap'? Must it be large enough for all independent competing firms to make a 'living profit,' no matter how inefficient they may be? . . . And how should the court respond when costs or demands change over time, as they inevitably will?" *Town of Concord*, *supra*, at 25.

Some amici respond to these concerns by proposing a "transfer price test" for identifying an unlawful price squeeze: A price squeeze should be presumed if the upstream monopolist could not have made a profit by selling at its retail rates if it purchased inputs at its own wholesale rates. Whether or not that test is administrable, it lacks any grounding in our antitrust jurisprudence. An upstream monopolist with no duty to deal is free to charge whatever wholesale price it would like; antitrust law does not forbid lawfully obtained monopolies from charging monopoly prices. *Trinko*, *supra*, at 407 ("The mere possession of monopoly power, and the concomitant charging of monopoly prices, is not only not unlawful; it is an important element of the free-market system"). Similarly, the Sherman Act does not forbid—indeed, it encourages—aggressive price competition at the retail level, as long as the prices being charged are not predatory. *Brooke Group*, 509 U.S., at 223–224. If both the wholesale price and the retail price are independently lawful, there is no basis for imposing antitrust liability simply because a vertically integrated firm's wholesale price happens to be greater than or equal to its retail price.

2. Amici assert that there are circumstances in which price squeezes may harm competition. For example, they assert that price squeezes may raise entry barriers that fortify the upstream monopolist's position; they also contend that price squeezes may impair nonprice competition and innovation in the downstream market by driving independent firms out of business.

The problem, however, is that amici have not identified any independent competitive harm caused by price squeezes above and beyond the harm that would result from a duty-to-deal violation at the wholesale level or predatory pricing at the retail level. See 3A P. Areeda & H. Hovenkamp, Antitrust Law ¶ 767c, p. 126 (2d ed. 2002) ("[I]t is difficult to see any *competitive* significance [of a price squeeze] apart from the consequences of vertical integration itself"). To the extent a monopolist violates one of these doctrines, the plaintiffs have a remedy under existing law. We do not need to endorse a new theory of liability to prevent such harm.

IV.

Lastly, as mentioned above, plaintiffs have asked us for leave to amend their complaint to bring a *Brooke Group* predatory pricing claim. We need not decide whether leave to amend should be granted. Our grant of certiorari was limited to the question whether price-squeeze claims are cognizable in the absence of an antitrust duty to deal....

... Even if the amended complaint is further amended to add a *Brooke Group* claim, it may not survive a motion to dismiss. For if AT&T can bankrupt the plaintiffs by refusing to deal altogether, the plaintiffs must demonstrate why the law prevents AT&T from putting them out of business by pricing them out of the market.... * * *

Trinko holds that a defendant with no antitrust duty to deal with its rivals has no duty to deal under the terms and conditions preferred by those rivals. 540 U.S., at 409–410. *Brooke Group* holds that low prices are only actionable under the Sherman Act when the prices are below cost and there is a dangerous probability that the predator will be able to recoup the profits it loses from the low prices. 509 U.S., at 222–224. In this case, plaintiffs have not stated a duty-to-deal claim under *Trinko* and have not stated a predatory pricing claim under *Brooke Group*. They have nonetheless tried to join a wholesale claim that cannot succeed with a retail claim that cannot succeed, and alchemize them into a new form of antitrust liability never before recognized by this Court. We decline the invitation to recognize such claims. Two wrong claims do not make one that is right.

The judgment of the Court of Appeals is reversed, and the case is remanded for further proceedings consistent with this opinion.

JUSTICE BREYER, joined by JUSTICES STEVENS, SOUTER, and GINSBURG, concurring in the judgment:

I would accept respondents' concession that the Ninth Circuit majority's "price squeeze" holding is wrong, I would vacate the Circuit's decision, and I would remand the case in order to allow the District Court to determine whether respondents may proceed with their "predatory pricing" claim....

* * *

QUESTIONS AND COMMENTS

1. Why would Bell Atlantic agree to provide the input to the customer/rival and then proceed to impose a price squeeze on the rival?

2. Remember that, under *Trinko*, the incumbent has no antitrust duty to deal if the regulator does (or perhaps could?) require dealing. In *linkLine*,

the FCC (during a discrete period that expired) required the monopolist/incumbent to deliver the service; AT&T thereafter agreed to an extension of this obligation in order to obtain clearance of a merger. The FCC could have prohibited but did not prohibit a price squeeze. Did the Court properly rely upon the non-existence of an antitrust duty to deal? Should it matter whether the regulator has addressed the problem, as it had in *Trinko*?

3. Applying the learning from *Trinko* and *linkLine*, give an example of a situation in which a dominant firm has an antitrust obligation to provide inputs to a customer who is also a rival. Does *AT&T* (1981) ("hard core monopolization"), see page 193 supra, qualify? If you cannot think of an example, does that mean that the Bork/Sidak position is the law? Is margin squeeze no longer a viable concept, apart from predatory pricing that meets the *Brooke Group* criteria—and maybe even predatory pricing will not qualify when there is no antitrust duty to deal?

4. Did the Court overrule *Alcoa* regarding price squeeze? See *linkLine* note 4.

* * *

In the European Union, the Court of Justice decided a case with very similar facts. The European Commission accused Deutsche Telekom of violating Article 82 of the Treaty of Rome establishing the European Community (now Article 102 of the Treaty on the Functioning of the European Union), which as we have seen prohibits abuse of dominance and is the closest counterpart to Section 2 of the Sherman Act. The European Commission found a violation, which was upheld by both the General Court and the Court of Justice.

DEUTSCHE TELEKOM AG v. COMMISSION

Case T–271/03, 2008 ECR II–00477 (General Court), appeal dismissed (i.e. judgment *aff'd*), Case C–280/08 P, 2010 ECR I ___, European Court of Justice.

[Deutsche Telekom (DT) was the dominant provider of telecommunications services in Germany and had sole access to the local loop. DT was regulated by the German regulatory authority, which imposed retail price ceilings. DT charged new entrants into the local telecom service market higher fees for wholesale access to the local loop than it charged its customers for fixed line subscriptions for broadband and narrow band access including DSL service for fast-speed Internet. This means DT charged its retail buyers of DSL service less than it charged its rivals for access to the local loop, which access was necessary to supply DSL service. DT had a duty under German regulatory legislation to provide competitors access to the local loop. Therefore, said the Court, it had an Article 82 (now 101) duty not to create a margin squeeze. DT had the power to eliminate the margin squeeze even within the existing confines of the German regulation or by applying to the German regulatory body for price adjustments.]

* * *

234 According to the Commission, the applicant's pricing practices restricted competition in the market for retail access services. It reaches that conclusion in the contested decision ... on the basis of the very existence of the margin squeeze. It maintains that it is not necessary to demonstrate an anti-competitive effect, although, in the alternative, it examines that effect in ... the contested decision.

235 Given that, until the entry of a first competitor on the market for retail access services, in 1998, the applicant had a monopoly on that retail market, the anti-competitive effect which the Commission is required to demonstrate relates to the possible barriers which the applicant's pricing practices could have created for the growth of competition in that market.

236 In that respect it must be borne in mind that the applicant owns the fixed telephone network in Germany and, moreover, that it is not disputed that, as the Commission notes ... there was no other infrastructure in Germany at the time of the adoption of the decision that would have enabled competitors of the applicant to make a viable entry onto the market in retail access services.

237 Having regard to the fact that the applicant's wholesale services are thus indispensible to enabling a competitor to enter into competition with the applicant on the downstream market in retail access services, a margin squeeze between the applicant's wholesale and retail charges will in principle hinder the growth of competition in the downstream markets. If the applicant's retail prices are lower than its wholesale charges, or if the spread between the applicant's wholesale and retail charges is insufficient to enable an equally efficient operator to cover its product-specific costs of supplying retail access services, a potential competitor who is just as efficient as the applicant would not be able to enter the retail access services market without suffering losses. * * *

239 ... [T]he small market shares acquired by the applicant's competitors in the retail access market since the market was liberalised by the entry into force of the TKG on 1 August 1996 are evidence of the restrictions which the applicant's pricing practices have imposed on the growth of competition in those markets.... * * *

261 [T]he applicant submits that RegTP [the German regulator] alone is responsible for the margin squeeze alleged by the Commission. The alleged margin squeeze is the direct consequence of regulatory decisions of RegTP and previously of the BMPT, and of the regulatory approach underpinning them. The Commission is wrong to find that the applicant has infringed Article 82 EC, because the applicant was simply complying with the binding decisions of RegTP, which gave rise to a legitimate expectation by the applicant. Through the medium of the contested decision, the Commission is subjecting the applicant's pricing practices to double regulation, thereby infringing the principle of proportionality and the legal certainty guaranteed by

the division of powers under Community law in relation to charges in the telecommunications sector. Furthermore, by adopting the contested decision, the Commission is trying to correct the German authorities' exercise of their own regulatory powers, whereas it should to that end have initiated proceedings for failure to fulfil obligations. By proceeding in this way, the Commission has misused its powers. * * *

263 In the first place, as regards the applicant's complaint that the Commission has subjected the applicant's pricing practices to double regulation and thereby infringed the principles of proportionality and of legal certainty, it must be held that the legal framework to which the applicant refers above does not affect the powers which the Commission derives directly from Article 7(1) of Council Regulation (EC) No 1/2003 to find infringements of Articles 81 EC and 82 EC.

264 It has already been held that, between 1 January 1998 and 31 December 2001, the applicant had sufficient scope to end the margin squeeze identified in the contested decision and, from 1 January 2002, sufficient scope to reduce that margin squeeze. [The applicant could have increased its retail prices; it could have applied for increases in the retail price cap; moreover, through its applications it influences the level of the prices set by the regulators; paras. 97–151; para. 104.] Its conduct therefore falls within the scope of Article 82 EC.

265 While it is not inconceivable that the German authorities also infringed Community law ... by opting for a gradual rebalancing of connection and call charges, such a failure to act, if it were to be established, would not remove the scope which the applicant had to reduce the margin squeeze. * * *

267 In the second place, as regards the complaint relating to the protection of legitimate expectations, it must be borne in mind that, in a number of decisions taken in the period covered by the contested decision, RegTP did in fact consider whether a margin squeeze resulted from the applicant's charges. However, in its decisions, after finding the negative spread between the applicant's wholesale and retail prices, RegTP took the view in each case that other operators should be able to offer their end-users competitive prices by resorting to cross-subsidisation of access services and call services.

268 The fact remains that RegTP's decisions do not include any reference to Article 82 EC. In addition, RegTP's statement that '[c]ompetitors are not so prejudiced with regard to their competitive opportunities in the local network by the slight difference between retail and wholesale prices as to make it economically impossible for them to enter the market successfully or even to remain in the market' does not imply that the applicant's pricing practices do not distort competition within the meaning of Article 82 EC. On the contrary, it follows implicitly but necessarily from RegTP's decisions that the applicant's pricing practices have an anti-competitive effect, since the applicant's

competitors have to resort to cross-subsidisation in order to be able to remain competitive on the market in access services. * * *

271 In the contested decision, the Commission refers only to the applicant's pricing practices and not to the decisions of the German authorities. Even if RegTP had infringed a Community rule and even if the Commission could have initiated proceedings against the Federal Republic of Germany for failure to fulfil obligations, such possibilities cannot affect the lawfulness of the contested decision. In that decision, the Commission merely found that the applicant had committed an infringement of Article 82 EC, a provision which concerns only economic operators, not the Member States. The Commission did not therefore misuse its powers by making that finding on the basis of Article 82 EC.

Welcoming the judgment, European Competition Commissioner Neelie Kroes said: "This [the margin squeeze] was clearly harmful to consumers, because competition between operators is the best means to bring overall prices down." MEMO/08/232 of 10/04/2008.

* * *

To what do you attribute the differences between *Deutsche Telecom* and *linkLine*? Different objectives? A different understanding of economics or its premises ? Differences in regulatory law? A different understanding of the relationship between the role of regulation and the role of antitrust? Was the professors' brief in *linkLine* right or wrong to accuse the European Union of protecting competitor welfare rather than consumer welfare?

7. LOYALTY REBATES, BUNDLED REBATES

May a dominant firm give rebates to customers based on their "loyalty" (not dealing with competitors)? May it offer loyalty rebates that progressively gain a greater hold on the loyal customer; e.g.: "When you reach X amount of purchases (X being calibrated to the customer's needs), you get a 10% rebate on all sales going back to day 1." Are loyalty rebates merely price competition, or are they exclusionary conduct foreclosing competitors from the chance to compete on the merits?

Le Page's Inc. v. 3M (Minnesota Mining & Manufacturing) Co., 324 F.3d 141 (3d Cir.2003) (en banc), *cert. denied,* 542 U.S. 953 (2004). 3M made and sold Scotch-brand tape for decades and it had significant market power in the transparent tape market, where it accounted for 90% of sales. Le Page's began to offer a private-label transparent tape at a much lower price and became quite successful at selling it to large retailers and chains such as K–Mart and CVS. 3M countered with bundled loyalty rebates on product groups including its famous Scotch tape, which nearly all retailers needed, and including a cheap private label tape, which it introduced as a fighting brand "to kill" Le Page's. The rebates were all-or-nothing rebates; the buyers got nothing back if they failed to meet their threshold for any one of six products. 3M never priced below its cost.

Le Page's big buyers dropped Le Page's in order to meet their targets with 3M. A divided court of appeals upheld a jury verdict for Le Page's, finding that the conduct was exclusionary and maintained 3M's monopoly in violation of Section 2 of the Sherman Act. Judge Sloviter said, for the court: "3M's incentive was ... to preserve the market position of Scotch-brand tape by discouraging widespread acceptance of the cheaper, but substantially similar, tape produced by Le Page's."

Summing up the case, Judge Sloviter said:

> Section 2, the provision of the antitrust laws designed to curb the excesses of monopolists and near-monopolists, is the equivalent in our economic sphere of the guarantees of free and unhampered elections in the political sphere. Just as democracy can thrive only in a free political system unhindered by outside forces, so also can market capitalism survive only if those with market power are kept in check. That is the goal of the antitrust laws.
>
> The jury heard the evidence and the contentions of the parties, accepting some and rejecting others. There was ample evidence that 3M used its market power over transparent tape, backed by its considerable catalog of products, to entrench its monopoly to the detriment of Le Page's, its only serious competitor, in violation of § 2 of the Sherman Act. We find no reversible error. Accordingly, we will affirm the judgment of the District Court.

Judge Greenberg, dissenting, argued that rebates are price competition and price competition is legal unless prices are predatory within the rule of *Brooke Group*; and Le Page's had not introduced evidence that 3M priced below its costs.

Other jurisdictions have been more reluctant to condemn rebates, even loyalty rebates, on grounds that they are price competition and generally good for consumers. See, e.g., *Cascade Health Solutions v. PeaceHealth*, 502 F.3d 895 (9th Cir. 2007), cautioning that courts should be hesitant to interfere with the benefits that flow to consumers from discounted pricing. In *PeaceHealth*, a hospital operator offered package discounts to insurers. A competitor complained. The court held that the competitor would have to prove that, after allocating the discount entirely to the competitive product, defendant's price for the competitive product would be below its average variable cost of production; thus, predatory pricing. Under this test, an inefficient competitor would not be protected; only those bundled rebates that are calculated to exclude an equally efficient competitor would be illegal. Here is the reasoning of the court.

CASCADE HEALTH SOLUTIONS v. PEACEHEALTH

515 F.3d 883 (9th Cir. 2008).

JUDGE GOULD: * * *

Bundling is the practice of offering, for a single price, two or more goods or services that could be sold separately. A bundled discount occurs when a firm sells a bundle of goods or services for a lower price than the seller charges for the goods or services purchased individually. *See* Daniel A. Crane, *Mixed Bundling, Profit Sacrifice, and Consumer Welfare,* 55 Emory L.J. 423, 425 (2006); David S. Evans & Michael Salinger, *Why Do Firms Bundle and Tie?,* 22 Yale J. on Reg. 37, 41 (2005); Thomas A. Lambert, *Evaluating Bundled Discounts,* 89 Minn. L.Rev. 1688, 1693 (2005). As discussed above, PeaceHealth offered bundled discounts to Regence and other insurers in this case. Specifically, PeaceHealth offered insurers discounts if the insurers made PeaceHealth their exclusive preferred provider for primary, secondary, and tertiary care.

Bundled discounts are pervasive, and examples abound. Season tickets, fast food value meals, all-in-one home theater systems—all are bundled discounts. Like individual consumers, institutional purchasers seek and obtain bundled discounts, too. . . .

* * *

Bundled discounts generally benefit buyers because the discounts allow the buyer to get more for less. . . . Bundling can also result in savings to the seller because it usually costs a firm less to sell multiple products to one customer at the same time than it does to sell the products individually. . . .

Not surprisingly, the Supreme Court has instructed that, because of the benefits that flow to consumers from discounted prices, price cutting is a practice the antitrust laws aim to promote. . . . Consistent with that principle, we should not be too quick to condemn price-reducing bundled discounts as anticompetitive, lest we end up with a rule that discourages legitimate price competition.

However, it is possible, at least in theory, for a firm to use a bundled discount to exclude an equally or more efficient competitor and thereby reduce consumer welfare in the long run. *See* Richard A. Posner, *Antitrust Law* 236 (2d ed.2001); Barry Nalebuff, *Exclusionary Bundling,* 50 Antitrust Bull. 321, 321 (2005). For example, a competitor who sells only a single product in the bundle (and who produces that single product at a lower cost than the defendant) might not be able to match profitably the price created by the multi-product bundled discount. *See Ortho Diagnostic Sys., Inc. v. Abbott Labs., Inc.,* 920 F.Supp. 455, 467 (S.D.N.Y.1996). This is true even if the post-discount prices for both the entire bundle and each product in the bundle are above the seller's cost. *See Ortho,* 920 F.Supp. at 467 (noting that "a firm that enjoys a monopoly on one or more of a group of complementary products, but which faces competition on others, can price all of its products above average variable cost and yet still drive an equally efficient competitor out of the market"). Judge Kaplan's opinion in *Ortho* provides an example of such a situation:

> Assume for the sake of simplicity that the case involved the sale of two hair products, shampoo and conditioner, the latter made only by A and the former by both A and B. Assume as well that both must be used to wash one's hair. Assume further that A's average variable cost for conditioner is \$2.50, that its average variable cost for shampoo is \$1.50, and that B's average variable cost for shampoo is \$1.25. B therefore is the more efficient producer of shampoo. Finally, assume that A prices conditioner and shampoo at \$5 and \$3, respectively, if bought separately but at \$3 and \$2.25 if bought as part of a package. Absent the package pricing, A's price for both products is \$8. B therefore must price its shampoo at or below \$3 in order to compete effectively with A, given that the customer will be paying A \$5 for conditioner irrespective of which shampoo supplier it chooses. With the package pricing, the customer can purchase both products from A for \$5.25, a price above the sum of A's average variable cost for both products. In order for B to compete, however, it must persuade the customer to buy B's shampoo while purchasing its conditioner from A for \$5. In order to do that, B cannot charge more than \$0.25 for shampoo, as the customer otherwise will find A's package cheaper than buying conditioner from A and shampoo from B. On these assumptions, A would force B out of the shampoo market, notwithstanding that B is the more efficient producer of shampoo, without pricing either of A's products below average variable cost. * * *

In this case, McKenzie asserts it could provide primary and secondary services at a lower cost than PeaceHealth. Thus, the principal anticompetitive danger of the bundled discounts offered by PeaceHealth is that the discounts could freeze McKenzie out of the market for primary and secondary services because McKenzie, like seller B in Judge Kaplan's example, does not provide the same array of services as PeaceHealth and therefore could possibly not be able to match the discount PeaceHealth offers insurers.

From our discussion above, it is evident that bundled discounts, while potentially procompetitive by offering bargains to consumers, can also pose the threat of anticompetitive impact by excluding less diversified but more efficient producers. These considerations put into focus this problem: How are we to discern where antitrust law draws the line between bundled discounts that are procompetitive and part of the normal rough-and-tumble of our competitive economy and bundled discounts, offered by firms holding or on the verge of gaining monopoly power in the relevant market, that harm competition and are thus proscribed by § 2 of the Sherman Act?

2

In this case, the district court based its jury instruction regarding the anticompetitive effect of bundled discounting on the Third Circuit's en banc decision in *LePages Inc. v. 3M,* 324 F.3d 141 (3d Cir.2003) (en banc). In that case, the plaintiff, LePage's, was the market leader in sales of "private label" (i.e., store brand) transparent tape. As LePage's market share fell and its profitability declined, it brought suit asserting that 3M, who manufactured Scotch tape, some private label tape, and many other products that LePage's did not produce (like healthcare products and retail automotive products), leveraged its monopoly over Scotch brand tape to monopolize the private label tape market. Specifically, LePage's alleged that 3M's multitiered bundled rebate structure was anticompetitive. The bundled rebate structure offered progressively higher rebates when customers increased purchases across 3M's different product lines—discounts LePage's could not offer because it did not sell the same diverse array of products as 3M. *See id.* A jury found that 3M's conduct violated § 2 of the Sherman Act and 3M appealed.

The primary issue before the Third Circuit was whether 3M unlawfully maintained its monopoly power through the bundled discount program. 3M argued that its bundled rebate structure was legal as a matter of law because it never priced below cost. 3M relied heavily on the United States Supreme Court's decision in *Brooke Group Ltd. v. Brown & Williamson Tobacco Corp.,* 509 U.S. 209 (1993). In *Brooke Group,* a primary-line price discrimination case brought under the Robinson–Patman Act, the Supreme Court held that, in a single product predatory pricing case, a plaintiff must prove (1) that its rival's low prices were below an appropriate measure of its rival's costs and (2) that its rival had a reasonable prospect, or, under § 2 of the Sherman Act, a dangerous probability, of recouping its investment in below-cost prices. *Id.* at 222, 224, 113 S.Ct. 2578. In *LePage's,* the Third Circuit, in a 7–3 en banc decision, refused to apply *Brooke Group*'s below-cost pricing requirement to bundled discounting.

The Third Circuit first distinguished *Brooke Group* by noting that the defendant in that case was an oligopolist while 3M was a monopolist. . . .

The court noted that "[t]he principal anticompetitive effect of bundled rebates as offered by 3M is that when offered by a monopolist they may foreclose portions of the market to a potential competitor who does not manufacture an equally diverse group of products and who therefore cannot make a comparable offer." The Third Circuit concluded that the jury could reasonably have found that 3M used its monopoly in transparent tape along with its extensive catalog of other products to exclude LePage's from the market and that 3M did not present any adequate business justification for its bundled discounting program. The court thus affirmed the jury verdict in LePage's favor, even though LePage's economist testified that LePage's was not as efficient a tape producer as 3M, *see id.* at 177 (Greenburg, J., dissenting).

In this case, the district court used *LePage's* to formulate its jury instruction. Specifically, the district court instructed the jury that

> plaintiff ... contends that defendant has bundled price discounts for its primary, secondary, and tertiary acute care products and that doing so is anticompetitive. Bundled pricing occurs when price discounts are offered for purchasing an entire line of services exclusively from one supplier. Bundled price discounts may be anti-competitive if they are offered by a monopolist and substantially foreclose portions of the market to a competitor who does not provide an equally diverse group of services and who therefore cannot make a comparable offer.

As 3M did in *LePage's*, PeaceHealth argues that the jury instruction incorrectly stated the law because it allowed the jury to find that a defendant with monopoly power (or, in the case of an attempted monopolization claim, a dangerous probability of achieving monopoly power) engaged in exclusionary conduct by simply offering a bundled discount that its competitor could not match. The instruction did not require the jury to consider whether the defendant priced below cost. *LePage's*, PeaceHealth asserts, was wrongly decided because it allows the jury to conclude, from the structure of the market alone, that a competitor has been anticompetitively excluded from the market....

As the bipartisan Antitrust Modernization Commission ("AMC") recently noted, the fundamental problem with the *LePage's* standard is that it does not consider whether the bundled discounts constitute competition on the merits, but simply concludes that all bundled discounts offered by a monopolist are anticompetitive with respect to its competitors who do not manufacture an equally diverse product line. Antitrust Modernization Comm'n, *Report and Recommendations* 97 (2007) [hereinafter AMC Report]. The *LePage's* standard, the AMC noted, asks the jury to consider whether the plaintiff has been excluded from the market, but does not require the jury to consider whether the plaintiff was at least as efficient of a producer as the defendant.... Thus, the *LePage's* standard could protect a less efficient competitor at the expense of consumer welfare. As Judge Greenberg explained in his *LePage's* dissent, the Third Circuit's standard "risks curtailing price competition and a method of pricing beneficial to customers because the bundled rebates effectively lowered [the seller's] costs." *LePage's,* 324 F.3d at 179 (Greenberg, J., dissenting).

The AMC also lamented that *LePage's* "offers no clear standards by which firms can assess whether their bundled rebates are likely to pass antitrust muster." AMC Report, *supra,* at 94. The Commission noted that efficiencies, and not schemes to acquire or maintain monopoly power, likely explain the use of bundled discounts because many firms without market power offer them. The AMC thus proposed a three-part test that it believed would protect procompetitive bundled discounts from antitrust scrutiny. The AMC proposed that:

> Courts should adopt a three-part test to determine whether bundled discounts or rebates violate Section 2 of the Sherman Act. To prove a violation of Section 2, a plaintiff should be required to show each one of the following elements (as well as other elements of a Section 2 claim): (1) after allocating all discounts and rebates attributable to the entire bundle of products to the competitive product, the defendant sold the competitive product below its incremental cost for the competitive product; (2) the defendant is likely to recoup these short-term losses; and (3) the bundled discount or rebate program has had or is likely to have an adverse effect on competition.

* * *

3

We must decide whether we should follow *LePage's* or whether we should part ways with the Third Circuit by adopting a cost-based standard to apply in bundled discounting cases.

* * *

One of the challenges of interpreting and enforcing the amorphous prohibitions of §§ 1 and 2 of the Sherman Act is ensuring that the antitrust laws do not punish economic behavior that benefits consumers and will not cause long-run injury to the competitive process. A bundled discount, however else it might be viewed, is a price discount on a collection of goods. The Supreme Court has undoubtedly shown a solicitude for price competition. In *Weyerhaeuser,* Justice Thomas, writing for the Court, reminded us that, in *Brooke Group,* the Court had cautioned that "the costs of erroneous findings of predatory-pricing liability were quite high because [t]he mechanism by which a firm engages in predatory pricing-lowering prices-is the same mechanism by which a firm stimulates competition, and therefore, mistaken findings of liability would chill the very conduct the antitrust laws are designed to protect." *Weyerhaeuser,* 127 S.Ct. at 1075 (internal quotations omitted, alteration in original).

Given the endemic nature of bundled discounts in many spheres of normal economic activity, we decline to endorse the Third Circuit's definition of when bundled discounts constitute the exclusionary conduct proscribed by § 2 of the Sherman Act. Instead, we think the course safer for consumers and our competitive economy to hold that bundled discounts may not be considered exclusionary conduct within the meaning of § 2 of the Sherman Act unless the discounts resemble the behavior that the Supreme Court in *Brooke Group* identified as predatory. Accordingly, we hold that the exclusionary conduct element of a claim arising under § 2 of the Sherman Act cannot be satisfied by reference to bundled discounts unless the discounts result in prices that are below an appropriate measure of the defendant's costs. * * *

One of the scholars cited by the court in *PeaceHealth* is Professor Daniel Rubinfeld, who wrote:

> This Essay has argued that because procompetitive conduct (such as "pure" above-cost low pricing or innovation) can weaken rivals, weakening rivals is not by any means sufficient to condemn a monopolist's conduct. And perhaps most strongly for monopolists that lack market discipline on their prices, it is very important not to have legal rules that deter price discounting. Any sensible price-discounting antitrust inquiry must proceed to a workable identification of the characteristics of pricing programs that are alleged to generate a rival-harming effect. In the bundling context as with "pure" predatory pricing—whether it is volume discounts or per-unit price lowering on a single product—it has been suggested that this crucial function be performed by a price-cost test for illegality. Using an appropriate measure of cost, the test would support illegality if the cost to the defendant of its rebate program (in term of discounts offered) would be greater than the benefit it achieved through increased sales.

Daniel Rubinfeld, 3M's Bundled Rebates: An Economic Perspective, 72 U. Chi. L. Rev. 243. 262–63 (2005) (footnotes omitted).

The International Competition Network accomplishes most of its work through working groups. Periodically, the working groups organize workshops for the education and networking of officials and staff of competition agencies around the world. One working group is the Unilateral Conduct Working Group, and one project of the Working Group was to examine standards for loyalty rebates around the world and consider whether common standards have emerged. The Working Group produced a Report on the Analysis of Loyalty Discounts and Rebates Under Unilateral Conduct Laws (2009), which may be found at *http://www.international competitionnetwork.org/uploads/library/doc357. pdf.*

Also, the Working Group developed a hypothetical, rich with facts and data sets, which was used for role-playing and analysis at an ICN workshop. The facts and data sets are printed in Appendix H of the Casebook, which is an important part of the problem that follows.

Problem

loyalty rebates

developed by the ICN Working Group on Unilateral Conduct

Cerveja, the largest brewer in ICNland, has a national market share of 73% of branded beer sales. Cerveja establishes a loyalty program, "So Hoppy Together," as described in Appendix H. Study the appendix.

Seventeen small local breweries complain to the competition authority that the program is eliminating them from the market. More than 70 small retailers complain that Cerveja has dropped them from the program.

ICNland has standards identical to Section 2 of the Sherman Act. Should the competition authority challenge the program?

Student 1: You represent the small local breweries. Try to convince the agency to sue.
Student 2: You represent competitor Hollandia. Try to convince the agency of your point of view.
Student 3: You represent Cerveja. Try to convince the agency that your program is procompetitive and pro-consumer and that the agency should welcome it.
Student 4: You represent the small retailers association. Tell the agency how your clients are affected and what this means for competition and consumers.
Students 5, 6 and 7: You are Commissioners. Question the lawyers who come before you. Then deliberate and decide whether to bring proceedings.

A little guidance for ICNLand

There is a serious question as to what is the correct legal standard for judging the Hoppy plan. (This is an unresolved question in the United States.) Cerveja will argue for a price predation rule. The complainants will argue for a standard more sympathetic to them. They should in any event be able to tell a story as to why beer consumers (now or in the middle term) will be worse off as a result of the Hoppy program. How will the Hoppy program give market power to Cerveja or maintain its existing market power? Will it push up the price of beer?

A note to the beer retailers: You may (think you) want to argue about your loss of autonomy, but this is not an antitrust concern in the United States.

A note to Hollandia: You think you are squeezed out of "space" for introducing new brands—and even for selling Hollandia Brew—but remember, you are big, well resourced, and more modern and lower cost than Cerveja. Can't you find a way to compete?

A note to Cerveja: Are you going to put up a strong argument that you do not have market power and cannot hope to get it by the Hoppy program? What are your arguments along these lines? And complainants, how do you plan to counter them?

What is the significance of the Cerveja document that envisions an end-game of live-and-let-live for Cerveja and Hollandia?

To the whole team: You will note that there are market definition issues as well as liability issues. You may want to start out with the hypothesis that beer in ICNLand is the market and begin discussion of the liability issue on that hypothesis. As you discuss the main question of whether the Hoppy program is anticompetitive—or procompetitive—you may want to bring in market issues, including whether states of ICNLand might be separate geographic markets. (Can Cerveja exploit beer drinkers in Agrilandia even if not in Urbania?)

And don't forget to mine the documents in the record for evidence of intent and probable effect of the Hoppy program. Consider: What is the significance of the intent evidence, and what should it be?

8. INTELLECTUAL PROPERTY: DUTY TO LICENSE?

Is there, and when is there, a duty to license a patent, copyright, or trade secret? When is there a right of access to IP-protected material? And when is there an IP defense to a duty to deal?

For a number of years, in the case of anticompetitive conduct other than simple, stand-alone refusal to sell or license intellectual property, antitrust was regarded as higher in the hierarchy than the protections of intellectual property, which grant exclusive rights to the intellectual property holder. For example, when U.S. Shoe Machinery Company was charged with monopolistic strategies to keep potential competitors from making complex shoe machinery, USM did not mount a defense that its machines were protected by copyrights and patents and that it alone had the right to decide how to use or dispose of its intellectual property. See *United States v. United Shoe Mach. Corp.*, 110 F.Supp. 295 (D. Mass. 1953) *aff'd*, 347 U.S. 521 (1954), supra p. 229.

Similarly, Eastman Kodak was charged with illegal tying and monopolization. Kodak, at the start of its business, invited independent service providers to service and repair its micrographic equipment. The independents (the ISOs) thereupon built up profitable businesses servicing the Kodak machines. Some time later, Kodak changed course, required its equipment buyers to get their service from Kodak, and cut off the independents from access to the Kodak repair parts. When sued, Kodak did not (for several years) allege that it held 220 patents covering 65 parts (of the thousands of machine parts) and that its diagnostic and service software were copyrighted, and it did not make the argument that *therefore* it had no duty to refrain from using its monopoly of the parts to monopolize the service. But times changed; intellectual property arguments gained greater traction. When the Supreme Court reversed dismissal of the ISOs complaint against Kodak and remanded the case for trial (see p. 214 supra), Kodak asserted the IP allegations and asked the trial court to charge the jury that illegal exclusionary conduct does not include "exercising lawful patents or copyrights." The trial court declined to give this instruction. It did instruct the jury that, if Kodak had engaged in monopolization by exercise of its alleged repair parts monopoly, "the fact that some of the replacement parts are patented or copyrighted does not provide Kodak with a defense against any of those antitrust claims." The jury returned a verdict for the ISOs. Kodak appealed. Plaintiffs asserted that Kodak's argument—"I was exercising my lawful IP rights"—was mere pretext. Here is the relevant part of the court's opinion. Recall that *Trinko* was decided in the interim. The case on remand concerned, among other things, Kodak's duty to deal with the ISOs in light of *Trinko.*

IMAGE TECHNICAL SERVICES, INC. v. EASTMAN KODAK CO.

125 F.3d 1195 (9th Cir.1997), cert. denied, 523 U.S. 1094 (1998).

JUDGE GILMORE: Kodak's challenge raises unresolved questions concerning the relationship between federal antitrust, copyright and patent laws. In particular we must determine the significance of a monopolist's unilateral refusal to sell or license a patented or copyrighted product in the context of a § 2 monopolization claim based upon monopoly leveraging. This is a question of first impression. * * *

Patent law seeks to protect inventions, while inducing their introduction into the market for public benefit. *SCM Corp.,* 645 F.2d at 1203. Patent laws "reward the inventor with the power to exclude others from making, using or selling [a patented] invention throughout the United States." *Id.*[7]

Federal copyright law "secures a fair return for an author's creative labor" in the short run, while ultimately seeking "to stimulate artistic creativity for the general public good." ... The Copyright Act grants to the copyright owner the exclusive right to distribute the protected work. 17 U.S.C. § 106. This right encompasses the right to "refrain from vending or licensing," as the owner may "content [itself] with simply exercising the right to exclude others from using [its] property." *Data General,* 36 F.3d at 1186. * * *

... Under the fact-based approaches of *Aspen Skiing* and *Kodak,* some measure must guarantee that the jury account for the procompetitive effects and statutory rights extended by the intellectual property laws. To assure such consideration, we adopt a modified version of the rebuttable presumption created by the First Circuit in *Data General,* and hold that "while exclusionary conduct can include a monopolist's unilateral refusal to license a [patent or] copyright," or to sell its patented or copyrighted work, a monopolist's "desire to exclude others from its [protected] work is a presumptively valid business justification for any immediate harm to consumers." *Data General,* 36 F.3d at 1187. * * *

Given this presumption, the district court's failure to give any weight to Kodak's intellectual property rights in the jury instructions constitutes an abuse of discretion. This error was, however, harmless. The ISOs maintain that Kodak argued protection of intellectual property as a business justification to the jury, which rejected this justification as

---

7. In 1988, Congress amended the patent laws to provide that "no patent owner otherwise entitled to relief for infringement ... of a patent shall be denied relief or deemed guilty of misuse or illegal extension of the patent right by reason of ... (4) [the patent owner's] refusal to license or use any rights to the patent." 35 U.S.C. § 271(d) (1988).

pretextual. An error in instructing the jury in a civil case does not require reversal if it is more probable than not harmless.

Kodak contends that the district court's jury instructions prevented it from arguing intellectual property to the jury. Although Kodak listed "Protect[ ] Kodak's R & D investment and intellectual property rights" among the seven business justifications it presented, the only argument Kodak made in closing was this:

> Protecting Investments. By itself, again, another legitimate business reason. You've already seen the size of the investments. And indeed, Plaintiffs themselves recognized that they wouldn't be in business unless Kodak made those investments.

Phrased in these broad terms, Kodak's argument repeats the "free-riding" justification rejected, as a matter of law, by the Supreme Court. *Kodak,* 504 U.S. at 485 [see page 671 infra]. The Supreme Court held that preventing the ISOs from "exploiting the investment Kodak has made in product development, manufacturing and equipment sales" does not suffice as a business justification. *Id.* ("This understanding of free-riding has no support in our case law.").

Given the interplay of the antitrust and intellectual property laws discussed above, Kodak's contention that its refusal to sell its parts to ISOs was based on its reluctance to sell its patented or copyrighted parts was a presumptively legitimate business justification. *See Data General,* 36 F.3d at 1187. Kodak may assert that its desire to profit from its intellectual property rights justifies its conduct, and the jury should presume that this justification is legitimately procompetitive. * * *

The *Data General* court noted that the presumption of legitimacy can be rebutted by evidence that the monopolist acquired the protection of the intellectual property laws in an unlawful manner. The presumption may also be rebutted by evidence of pretext. Neither the aims of intellectual property law, nor the antitrust laws justify allowing a monopolist to rely upon a pretextual business justification to mask anticompetitive conduct. See *Kodak*, 504 U.S. at 484 (Because "Kodak's willingness to allow self-service casts doubt on its quality claim ... a reasonable trier of fact could conclude that [this justification] is pretextual.") (citation omitted).

Kodak defends its intellectual property rights "justification" against claims of pretext. Kodak argues that its subjective motivation is irrelevant. Kodak also contends ... that a desire to best the competition does not prove pretext, nor does hostility to competitors. Kodak's argument and its accompanying authority stands for nothing more than the proposition that a desire to compete does not demonstrate pretext.

Evidence regarding the state of mind of Kodak employees may show pretext, when such evidence suggests that the proffered business justification played no part in the decision to act. Kodak's parts manager testified that patents "did not cross [his] mind" at the time Kodak began the parts policy. Further, no distinction was made by Kodak between "proprietary" parts covered by tooling or engineering clauses and patented or copyrighted products. In denying Kodak's motion for a new trial, the district court commented that Kodak was not actually motivated by protecting its intellectual property rights. Kodak argues that the district court should have allowed the jury to reach this conclusion.

Kodak photocopy and micrographics equipment requires thousands of parts, of which only 65 were patented. Unlike the other cases involving refusals to license patents, this case concerns a blanket refusal that included protected and unprotected products.... From this evidence, it is more probable than not that the jury would have found Kodak's presumptively valid business justification rebutted on the grounds of pretext. [Affirmed.]

* * *

The Federal Circuit, which is a specialized court entrusted with appeals regarding patents and trademarks, had a different point of view.

INDEPENDENT SERVICE ORGANIZATIONS ANTITRUST LITIGATION (CSU v. XEROX)

203 F.3d 1322 (Fed.Cir.2000), cert. denied, 531 U.S. 1143 (2001).

CHIEF JUDGE MAYER: [Xerox manufactures and sells high volume copiers and printers. For a number of years it encouraged independent service organizations (ISOs) to repair and service its machines. In 1984 it embarked on a policy of not selling parts to ISOs (to keep the servicing business for itself), thus threatening to ruin the business of CSU and other ISOs.

CSU sued for antitrust violations. Xerox counterclaimed for patent and copyright infringement, since CSU, needing the parts for its service and repair business, had cannabalized parts from used Xerox equipment and had obtained them by other means. The district court granted summary judgment to Xerox, dismissing CSU's antitrust claims.] * * *

A. * * *

CSU further relies on the Ninth Circuit's holding on remand in *Image Technical Services* that " 'while exclusionary conduct can include a monopolist's unilateral refusal to license a [patent] or to sell its patented ... work, a monopolist's desire to exclude others from its [protected] work is a presumptively valid business justification for any immediate harm to consumers.' " 125 F.3d at 1218. By that case, the Ninth Circuit adopted a rebuttable presumption that the exercise of the statutory right to exclude provides a valid business justification for consumer harm, but then excused as harmless the district court's error in failing to give any instruction on the effect of intellectual property rights on the application of the antitrust laws. It concluded that the jury must have rejected the presumptively valid business justification as pretextual. This logic requires an evaluation of the patentee's subjective motivation for refusing to sell or license its patented products for pretext. We decline to follow *Image Technical Services*.

We have held that "if a [patent infringement] suit is not objectively baseless, an antitrust defendant's subjective motivation is immaterial." *Nobelpharma*, 141 F.3d at 1072. We see no more reason to inquire into the subjective motivation of Xerox in refusing to sell or license its patented works than we found in evaluating the subjective motivation of a patentee in bringing suit to enforce that same right. In the absence of any indication of illegal tying, fraud in the Patent and Trademark Office, or sham litigation, the patent holder may enforce the statutory right to exclude others from making, using, or selling the claimed invention free from liability under the antitrust laws. We therefore will not inquire into his subjective motivation for exerting his statutory rights, even though his refusal to sell or license his patented invention may have an anticompetitive effect, so long as that anticompetitive effect is not illegally extended beyond the statutory patent grant. It is the infringement defendant and not the patentee that bears the burden to show that one of these exceptional situations exists and, in the absence of such proof, we will not inquire into the patentee's motivations for asserting his statutory right to exclude. Even in cases where the infringement defendant has met this burden, which CSU has not, he must then also prove the elements of the Sherman Act violation.

We answer the threshold question of whether Xerox's refusal to sell its patented parts exceeds the scope of the patent grant in the negative. Therefore, our inquiry is at an end. Xerox was under no obligation to sell or license its patented parts and did not violate the antitrust laws by refusing to do so.

B.

The Copyright Act expressly grants a copyright owner the exclusive right to distribute the protected work by "transfer of ownership, or by rental, lease, or lending." 17 U.S.C. § 106(3) (1996). "The owner of the copyright, if [it] pleases, may refrain from vending or licensing and content [itself] with simply exercising the right to exclude others from using [its] property." *Data General*, 36 F.3d at 1186.

The Supreme Court has made clear that the property right granted by copyright law cannot be used with impunity to extend power in the marketplace beyond what Congress intended. *See United States v. Loew's, Inc.*, 371 U.S. 38, 47–48 (1962) (block booking of copyrighted motion pictures is illegal tying in violation of Sherman Act). The Court has not, however, directly addressed the antitrust implications of a unilateral refusal to sell or license copyrighted expression. * * *

Perhaps the most extensive analysis of the effect of a unilateral refusal to license copyrighted expression was conducted by the First Circuit in *Data General Corp. v. Grumman Systems Support Corp.*, 36

F.3d 1147. There, the court noted that the limited copyright monopoly is based on Congress' empirical assumption that the right to "exclude others from using their works creates a system of incentives that promotes consumer welfare in the long term by encouraging investment in the creation of desirable artistic and functional works of expression.... We cannot require antitrust defendants to prove and reprove the merits of this legislative assumption in every case where a refusal to license a copyrighted work comes under attack." The court went on to establish as a legal standard that "while exclusionary conduct can include a monopolist's unilateral refusal to license a copyright, an author's desire to exclude others from use of its copyrighted work is a presumptively valid business justification for any immediate harm to consumers." The burden to overcome this presumption was firmly placed on the antitrust plaintiff. The court gave no weight to evidence showing knowledge that developing a proprietary position would help to maintain a monopoly in the service market in the face of contrary evidence of the defendant's desire to develop state-of-the-art diagnostic software to enhance its service and consumer benefit.

As discussed above, the Ninth Circuit adopted a modified version of this *Data General* standard. Both courts agreed that the presumption could be rebutted by evidence that "the monopolist acquired the protection of the intellectual property laws in an unlawful manner." *Image Technical Servs.*, 125 F.3d at 1219. The Ninth Circuit, however, extended the possible means of rebutting the presumption to include evidence that the defense and exploitation of the copyright grant was merely a pretextual business justification to mask anticompetitive conduct. The hazards of this approach are evident in both the path taken and the outcome reached. The jury in that case was instructed to examine each proffered business justification for pretext, and no weight was given to the intellectual property rights in the instructions. This permitted the jury to second guess the subjective motivation of the copyright holder in asserting its statutory rights to exclude under the copyright laws without properly weighing the presumption of legitimacy in asserting its rights under the copyright laws. While concluding that the failure to weigh the intellectual property rights was an abuse of discretion, the Ninth Circuit nevertheless held the error harmless because it thought the jury must have rejected the presumptive validity of asserting the copyrights as pretextual. This is in reality a significant departure from the First Circuit's central premise that rebutting the presumption would be an uphill battle and would only be appropriate in those rare cases in which imposing antitrust liability is unlikely to frustrate the objectives of the Copyright Act.

We believe the First Circuit's approach is more consistent with both the antitrust and the copyright laws and is the standard that would most likely be followed by the Tenth Circuit in considering the effect of Xerox's unilateral right to refuse to license or sell copyrighted manuals and diagnostic software on liability under the antitrust laws. We therefore reject CSU's invitation to examine Xerox's subjective motivation in asserting its right to exclude under the copyright laws for pretext, in the absence of any evidence that the copyrights were obtained by unlawful means or were used to gain monopoly power beyond the statutory copyright granted by Congress. In the absence of such definitive rebuttal evidence, Xerox's refusal to sell or license its copyrighted works was squarely within the rights granted by Congress to the copyright holder and did not constitute a violation of the antitrust laws. * * *

QUESTIONS AND COMMENTS

1. In each case, *ITS/Kodak* and *CSU/Xerox*, what is the case *for* an antitrust duty to license? Was the decision to decline to license the patents or copyrights anticompetitive or inefficient? Did refusal to license cause consumer harm?

2. Note that, even in the absence of IP protection, there is usually no duty to deal. Essential facilities (*Otter Tail*, and *AT&T* before the break-up, but see *Trinko*) is one exception. Refusal to deal in the context of affirmative anticompetitive strategies (*Aspen*) is another. Why is there usually no duty to deal, even when an obligation to deal might be efficient for the market and consumers (see, e.g., the facts of *Bronner*, p. 247 supra)?

3. Does intellectual property protection make the "no duty to deal" principle stronger or weaker? Remember that IP rights are granted by license of government. Is this relevant?

4. Does the rule of *Kodak* erode government-granted IP privileges? Is this good or bad, from the viewpoint of market competition, innovation, and performance? Is the court's holding with respect to "pretext" sound? Why should Kodak's intent to exclude competitors as opposed to its intent to protect or exercise IP rights matter? Is there a discernible adjudicable difference? Were there other grounds on which the *Kodak* court might have reached the same result?

5. Are you satisfied with the court's opinion in *CSU*? Are IP rights (and should they be) fairly sacrosanct? Are there any cases in which licensing would make markets and consumers so much better off as to warrant a duty to license?

In South Africa nearly five million of the country's 45 million people have HIV, the virus that causes AIDS. Thirty percent of all deaths are attributed to AIDS. The scourge is not only killing masses of people, it is undermining the social and economic structure of the economy. See Alex de Waal, "Why the HIV/AIDS Pandemic is a Structural Threat to Africa's Governance and Economic Development," 27 Fletcher Forum of World Affairs 6 (Summer/Fall 2003).

GlaxoSmithKline makes the most effective anti-retroviral drug. However, the supracompetitive price of the drug puts it out of reach for almost all South Africans who need it. The South African Competition Law declares that a company abuses its dominance if it "refus[es] to supply scarce goods to a competitor when supplying those goods is economically feasible," "unless the firm concerned can show technological, efficiency or other pro-competitive, gains which outweigh the anti-competitive effect of its act...." § 8(d).

Should the South African Competition Commission declare the high price an abusive price and order Glaxo to license its drug to generic manufacturers who wish to sell it into South Africa? See *Hazel Tau v. GlaxoSmithKline, http://www.tac.org.za/Documents/DrugCompaniesCC/TAU–GSK–Settlement–20031209.doc.*

6. The U.S. Federal Trade Commission has taken a view different from the U.S. Court of Appeals for the Federal Circuit. Intel, the dominant maker of the microprocessing chip that is the central nervous system of most personal computers, supplied the chip to various customers, such as Intergraph and Compaq. These firms incorporated the chip into their computers or work stations. Intel supplied them also with a flow of technical information that they needed to incorporate the chip. When three of the customers sued Intel for infringing their technology, Intel cut them off from the supply of knowhow, disadvantaging them in their competition. The FTC, under Chairman Pitofsky, brought proceedings against Intel, and prevailed upon it to enter into a consent order to cease and desist from its discriminatory cutoffs. *Intel Corp.*, FTC Dkt. No. 9288 (consent order to cease and desist, Aug. 3, 1999), summarized at Trade Reg. Rep. (CCH) [Transfer Binder 1997–2001] ¶ 25,575.

Intergraph then sued Intel in federal court for damages. The Court of Appeals for the Federal Circuit dismissed the case on the basis of reasoning similar to that in *CSU*. Even a monopolist has no affirmative duty to license its technology, the court said. *Intergraph Corp. v. Intel Corp.,* 195 F.3d 1346 (Fed.Cir.1999). Intergraph was one of a number of firms that could possibly invent around the Intel chip. If it continued to get the technological information from Intel it was more likely to be able to do so. Could Intergraph show harm to competition and consumers? How? Which rule makes consumers better off?

7. The law of the European Union also diverges from that of the Federal Circuit. In *Magill* (*Radio Telefis Eireann v. Commission*), cases C–241/91P and C–242/91P, [1995] ECR I–743, the European Court of Justice upheld a decision by the European Commission that TV broadcasters in Ireland had a duty to license their programming schedules (copyrighted under Irish law) to the producer of a weekly TV guide. Derogating from the usual rule of no duty to license intellectual property, the Court observed that there was consumer demand for a consolidated TV guide, and the broadcasters had "exclude[d] all competition on that market since they denied access to the basic information which is the raw material indispensable for the compilation of such a guide." para. 56. How would a U.S. court decide this case?

Rambus—Gaming the Standard–Setting Process

Rambus was a member of JEDEC (Joint Electron Device Engineering Council), a standard setting organization. JEDEC had a policy requiring its members to disclose in advance if they had intellectual property rights the use of which was necessary to comply with a proposed standard. In such a case, the member would accept a RAND obligation; i.e., licensing the technology on reasonable and non-discriminatory terms. According to the FTC, Rambus had such intellectual property rights but failed to disclose them. After the standard was adopted, Rambus sought supra-competitive royalties from the companies practicing the technology (a "patent ambush"). The FTC brought proceedings and found that Rambus had willfully and intentionally engaged in misrepresentations and omissions that misled JEDEC members about information "highly material" to the standard setting process, thereby either causing JEDEC to select the Rambus-based technology rather than a substitute or (if JEDEC would have selected the Rambus-based technology anyway) raising the cost of practicing the standard. The FTC enforces the Federal Trade Commission Act, which in Section 5(b) prohibits unfair methods of competition and unfair or deceptive acts or practices. While the FTC is not empowered to enforce the Sherman Act, it commonly imports the standards of the Sherman Act and thus alleges, as it did here, that the respondent's conduct was a violation of the Sherman Act and thus a violation of FTCA Section 5. The FTC found that Rambus' conduct was a violation of Sherman Section 2 and thus a violation of FTCA Section 5. It limited Rambus' royalties for three years (e.g. to 0.25% and 0.5% depending on the technology), and after that forbade the charging of royalties for the particular technology.

Rambus appealed. The Court of Appeals for the D.C. Circuit reversed. The court questioned the factual basis for finding that Rambus had breached an antitrust duty to provide information to its rivals. Separately, it found no antitrust violation. The Commission had not determined whether, if Rambus had disclosed the information, JEDEC would have incorporated the Rambus technology in the standard. Therefore, the court said, the FTC's case could stand only if each of the alternatives would constitute a violation of Section 2. If an informed JEDEC would have chosen non-proprietary technology instead of Rambus' technology, the court assumed arguendo that the deceit would have been exclusionary and the exclusion would have produced Rambus' market power, violating the law. But if JEDEC would still have chosen Rambus' technology, and if the problem was that Rambus failed to sign a RAND obligation, Rambus' conduct "merely" raised the price of a product. "Even if deception raises the price secured by a seller, but does so without harming competition, it is beyond the antitrust laws' reach." * * * "[A]n otherwise lawful monopolist's use of deception simply to obtain higher prices normally has no particular tendency to exclude rivals and thus to diminish competition." (citing NYNEX, see Casebook p. 653 infra). Rambus Inc. v. FTC, 522 F.3d 456 (D.C. Cir. 2008), cert. denied, 129 S.Ct. 1318 (2009).

Assume that Rambus had in fact engaged in a serious and material deception. Who is right, the Commission or the court? Why did Rambus' ambush not harm competition by raising the price?

Europe had its own *Rambus* case. Rambus settled the case, committing that it would offer worldwide licenses for the technology in question and would do so for five years at maximum rates, depending on the technology; e.g. 1.5%. Rambus, Case COMP/38.636, European Commission Decision of 9 Dec. 2009.

The European Union has shown a greater inclination than the United States to require a dominant firm to license intellectual property when licensing is indispensable to effective competition in an adjoining market and refusal to license prevents the emergence of new products. E.g., *IMS Health GmbH*, Case C–418/01, [2004] ECR I–5039 (European Court of Justice).

The story continues, for cases on complex strategies (below) often involve intellectual property, both in terms of whether the conduct amounts to an offense and in terms of an appropriate remedy.

9. COMPLEX STRATEGIES TO MAINTAIN MONOPOLY, INCLUDING PRODUCT CHANGE, EXCLUSIVE DEALING, TYING AND BUNDLING, ESPECIALLY IN HIGH TECH MARKETS

a. Introduction

Some of the most challenging cases involve a dominant firm whose product in one market is the industry standard and whose competitors in an adjacent market must make their product compatible with the industry standard. The dominant firm—often a highly inventive firm—has the power to create incompatibilities or otherwise strategically change its product design to marginalize competitors.

For a period in the 1970s extending into the early 1980s, cases against two major firms came within this category: AT&T and IBM.

In *United States v. American Telephone and Telegraph Company*, 524 F.Supp. 1336 (D.D.C.1981), denying AT&T's motion to dismiss at the close of the government's case, the court found evidence that AT&T (then the fully integrated Ma Bell) had engaged in numerous and continuous predatory and illegal practices, including strategies to block telephone manufacturing competitors from access to customers wishing to buy telephones, to prevent telephone wire and other hardware makers from access to their natural customers, and most importantly, to block emerging long distance competitors such as MCI from access to the local intercity loops necessary to complete long distance service. See *MCI Communications v. AT&T Corp.*, supra p. 232. See infra p. 423 for consideration of the legality of the vertical integration.

Famously, the case resulted in a consent decree whereby AT&T agreed to spin off the local telephone monopolies. AT&T remained a long distance carrier. The theory of the government's case was related to regulation: long distance service was becoming a competitive market that should be and would soon be freed of regulation. Local service appeared, at the time, to be a continuing natural monopoly, thus requiring continuing regulation. The combination of regulated with competitive markets created perverse incentives for overcharging (long distance), undercharging (local service was priced low under political pressures), and cross-subsidization. To meet competition in the emerging global long distance markets, U.S. carriers would need to be efficient, responsive and unhampered by regulation.

The *IBM* cases were themselves an "industry." They lasted for nearly two decades. IBM, the leading firm in "mainframes"—the newly invented computer processing unit, also made peripheral equipment such as disks and memories, compatible with its mainframes. Moreover, it made its CPUs (central processing units) available by long-term leases to minimize the market opportunities for possible competitors. It frequently changed the interfaces between its mainframes and peripheral devices, allegedly to throw off its peripheral competitors. And it "stole" financials of its fiercest competitors in order to price below those competitors where it hurt the most; but IBM was efficient and did not price below its own costs. See *TransAmerica Computer Co. v. IBM Corp.,* supra at 263.

IBM settled the most serious private cases against it, and won the others. The trial of the Justice Department case against it lasted 13 years. It appeared (to the outside world) that the government was winning and that there was a reasonably good chance that the court, by Judge Edelstein, would enter an order breaking up IBM. But two things changed: the market (IBM was losing its power) and the administration.

In 1981, the new (Reagan) administration withdrew the case against IBM. See L. Sullivan, Monopolization: Corporate Strategy, the IBM Cases, and the Transformation of the Law, 60 Texas L.Rev. 587, 599–604 (1982).

In the private cases against IBM, the courts struggled with the question of how to handle a dominant firm's product changes that threw the competitors off target. The firm labeled these changes innovation and the competitors labeled them predatory strategies to monopolize. The courts agreed that a firm, even a dominant firm, must have room to innovate. They also agreed that changes that degraded the firm's own product and thereby harmed competitors could be part of a predatory strategy. (At one point, IBM slowed down the speed of a function just short of the speed that would allow competitors' products to attach. See *In re IBM Peripheral EDP Devices Antitrust Litigation (TransAmerica)*, 481 F.Supp. 965, 1007–08 (N.D.Cal.1979), aff'd, 698 F.2d 1377 (9th Cir.), cert. denied, 464 U.S. 955 (1983)). But the courts disagreed on the appropriate standard for distinguishing product change innovation from product change predation; in particular, how much deference to give the dominant firm; should there be a prophylactic rule of non-intervention. Compare Judge Schnacke in *TransAmerica* with Judge Choy in *CalComp. California Computer Products, Inc. v. IBM Corp.,* 613 F.2d 727 (9th Cir.1979). The IBM story, and the split of the courts as to how to approach product change that may be inventive, exclusionary, or even both, was a precursor to the next big monopoly case, *Microsoft.*

b. Microsoft–U.S.

United States v. Microsoft Corporation: A Background Note

Through skill, focus, luck, and aggression, Microsoft came to dominate the market of operating systems for personal computers. Microsoft's products became nearly ubiquitous, and were much valued and needed by computer users. Microsoft also came to be seen as the market bully. Several high profile antitrust cases and many less notorious ones were brought against Microsoft, in the United States and in a number of other countries. As you contemplate the merits of the cases described below, ask yourself: What is the theory of the case? How is Microsoft (allegedly) using market power? Was the conduct likely to produce more market power or maintain its position of power, as opposed to neither increasing nor maintaining power? Who was likely to be hurt? Were computer users likely to be better or worse off? Was the conduct likely to affect price? innovation? Would a prohibition of the conduct affect price? innovation?

Here are some facts:

In the early 1990s, all manufacturers of personal computers (original equipment manufacturers, or "OEMs") needed a license from Microsoft in order to load computers with Microsoft's Windows. Microsoft agreed to give the OEMs licenses in bulk, charging them for its software on the basis of all computers the OEM sold, whether or not they were loaded with Microsoft's operating system. The pricing system made it uneconomical for the OEMs to use any other operating system, and thereby deepened Microsoft's hold on the market. Also, Microsoft required firms that made software applications for Windows to enter into broad covenants not to use any knowhow involved in those applications in connection with work for Microsoft's operating system competitors. This made it very difficult for the firms to make applications for Apple, IBM, or any emerging competitor. The Justice Department sued Microsoft. The European Commission, also, began proceedings. Both authorities settled with Microsoft, on similar terms—which were to be highly criticized as mere band-aids stuck on a rampaging dragon whose predations far exceeded the specific acts identified in the complaints. See *United States v. Microsoft Corp.*, 56 F.3d 1448 (D.C.Cir.1995).

Microsoft signed the U.S. consent decree in 1994. It agreed not to condition the licensing of its operating system on the licensing of any other product, "provided, however, that this provision ... shall not be construed to prohibit Microsoft from developing integrated products...." (Consent decree § IV(E)(I).)

Soon thereafter Netscape pioneered a powerful, attractive, and highly demanded browser, the Navigator. Microsoft thereupon introduced a browser of its own, Internet Explorer (IE), bundled IE with its operating system, and refused to let the OEMs include Netscape's Navigator on the Microsoft system. The Justice Department attacked this tie-in as a wilful violation of the consent decree. It sued Microsoft for contempt, and sought a preliminary injunction against the tie. The District Court for the District of Columbia (Judge Thomas Penfield Jackson) granted a preliminary injunction. The terms of the order provided that, if Microsoft chose to bundle its browser (Internet Explorer) with its operating system, it was required, also, to offer the two products separately, thus tending to assure access for outsiders. The Court of Appeals for the D.C. Circuit reversed the grant of the preliminary injunction.

The question in the consent decree litigation was one of construction of the consent decree—Was the bundle of operating system and browser two products or an integrated one? Was it *clearly* two products, so that Microsoft's conduct had to be an intentional flouting of the decree? In offering its opinion on the construction of the decree, the appellate court gave its opinion, also, on the *law* regarding product integration: If manufacturers do nothing more than bolt two products together, that is a tie, and here, because Microsoft presumably had market power, the tie would be illegal under the law as well as the decree. This tying conduct would be the same as "if Windows 95 were artificially rigged to crash if [Internet Explorer] were deleted." But, said the two-judge majority on the court, integration is "genuine if it is beneficial when compared to purchaser combination." Moreover, courts may not "embark on product design assessment." If there is a difference of engineering opinion about whether the integration is genuine (i.e. a superior design), and one view supports the genuineness of the integration, that is the end of the inquiry. *United States v. Microsoft Corp.*, 147 F.3d 935 (D.C.Cir.1998). Why? What is the case for judicial abstention from addressing the question whether a dominant firm's product combination is invention or predation? Judge Wald, the third member of the panel, dissented from the abstention approach. She would have balanced the positive and negative effects.

After this ruling, the Justice Department dropped the contempt charge. It and 20 states brought a plenary monopolization case against Microsoft. (One state later dropped out, and the District of Columbia joined the suit.) Microsoft moved for summary judgment and dismissal of the complaint. Judge Jackson denied the motion as to all claims but one. He dismissed the claim, brought by the states, challenging Microsoft's monopoly leveraging: use of leverage in the operating system market to gain a competitive advantage in the browser market, thus shifting significant share of browsers from Netscape to Microsoft. Note that this "mere leveraging" claim did not allege that the result of this conduct was to confer market power on Microsoft. Other claims—specifically, claims of attempt to monopolize the browser market and monopolization of the operating system market—included these further allegations. The leveraging claim was about the *use* of power to obtain an advantage, not the *increase* of power.

Dismissing the leveraging claim, Judge Jackson said:

> The D.C. Circuit has never spoken definitively on the leveraging theory, but has noted "substantial academic criticism cast upon the leveraging concept." ... Assuming that Microsoft has an operating

system monopoly and browsers are being sold competitively, Microsoft's incentive is to extract all available monopoly profits from the OS/browser *combination.* Accordingly, it already prices its operating system at the monopoly profit-maximizing price, considering what consumers are willing to pay for the entire package. Even if Microsoft were to obtain a monopoly in the market for browsers, the profit-maximizing price for the combination wouldn't change; Microsoft could not make additional monopoly profits even by monopolizing the browser market as well. . . .

The Court will grant Microsoft's motion for summary judgment on the States' leveraging claim. While the Supreme Court has not considered a leveraging claim *per se*, it has clearly stated that a firm violates § 2 only when it actually monopolizes or dangerously threatens to do so. . . .

United States v. Microsoft Corp., 1998–2 Trade Cas. ¶ 72,261 (D.D.C.1998). See *Trinko*, supra page 256, n. 4.[8]

The remaining claims against Microsoft went to trial. At the conclusion of the trial, Judge Jackson held that Microsoft had illegally maintained its operating system monopoly by various anticompetitive strategies designed to cripple the innovative efforts of Netscape, Sun Microsystems, Intel, and Apple; that it had illegally attempted to monopolize the browser market, and that it had illegally (per se) tied its browser to its operating system. It ordered that Microsoft be broken into two parts, one part for the operating system, the other for applications for the operating system. Microsoft appealed to the Court of Appeals for the D.C. Circuit.

UNITED STATES v. MICROSOFT CORPORATION

253 F.3d 34 (D.C.Cir.), cert. denied, 534 U.S. 952 (2001)
(monopolization).

(See the court's opinion on market definition and monopoly power at p. 216 supra).

PER CURIAM: * * *

---

8. Expressing its view of modern law, the court thus rejected a tradition that had been well articulated in the earlier monopolization case against Eastman Kodak, *Berkey Photo, Inc. v. Eastman Kodak Co.*, 603 F.2d 263 (2d Cir. 1979), cert. denied, 444 U.S. 1093 (1980). The Court of Appeals for the Second Circuit said in *Berkey/Kodak*:

> [We] must determine whether a firm violates § 2 by using its monopoly power in one market to gain a competitive advantage in another, albeit without an attempt to monopolize the second market. We hold, as did the lower court, that it does.
>
> This conclusion appears to be an inexorable interpretation of the antitrust laws. We tolerate the existence of monopoly power, we repeat, only insofar as necessary to preserve competitive incentives and to be fair to the firm that has attained its position innocently. There is no reason to allow the exercise of such power to the detriment of competition, in either the controlled market or any other. That the competition in the leveraged market may not be destroyed but merely distorted does not make it more palatable. Social and economic effects of an extension of monopoly power militate against such conduct. * * *
>
> . . . It is the use of economic power that creates the liability.

II. MONOPOLIZATION * * *

B. Anticompetitive Conduct

. . . [H]aving a monopoly does not by itself violate § 2. A firm violates § 2 only when it acquires or maintains, or attempts to acquire or maintain, a monopoly by engaging in exclusionary conduct "as distinguished from growth or development as a consequence of a superior product, business acumen, or historic accident." *Grinnell,* 384 U.S. at 571. . . .

In this case, after concluding that Microsoft had monopoly power, the District Court held that Microsoft had violated § 2 by engaging in a variety of exclusionary acts (not including predatory pricing), to maintain its monopoly by preventing the effective distribution and use of products that might threaten that monopoly. Specifically, the District Court held Microsoft liable for: (1) the way in which it integrated IE into Windows; (2) its various dealings with Original Equipment Manufacturers ("OEMs"), Internet Access Providers ("IAPs"), Internet Content Providers ("ICPs"), Independent Software Vendors ("ISVs"), and Apple Computer; (3) its efforts to contain and to subvert Java technologies; and (4) its course of conduct as a whole. Upon appeal, Microsoft argues that it did not engage in any exclusionary conduct.

Whether any particular act of a monopolist is exclusionary, rather than merely a form of vigorous competition, can be difficult to discern: the means of illicit exclusion, like the means of legitimate competition, are myriad. The challenge for an antitrust court lies in stating a general rule for distinguishing between exclusionary acts, which reduce social welfare, and competitive acts, which increase it.

From a century of case law on monopolization under § 2, however, several principles do emerge. First, to be condemned as exclusionary, a monopolist's act must have an "anticompetitive effect." That is, it must harm the competitive *process* and thereby harm consumers. In contrast, harm to one or more *competitors* will not suffice. "The [Sherman Act] directs itself not against conduct which is competitive, even severely so, but against conduct which unfairly tends to destroy competition itself." *Spectrum Sports, Inc. v. McQuillan,* 506 U.S. 447, 458 (1993)*; see also Brooke Group Ltd. v. Brown & Williamson Tobacco Corp.*, 509 U.S. 209, 225 (1993) ("Even an act of pure malice by one business competitor against another does not, without more, state a claim under the federal antitrust laws. . . .").

Second, the plaintiff, on whom the burden of proof of course rests, must demonstrate that the monopolist's conduct indeed has the requisite anticompetitive effect. In a case brought by a private plaintiff, the plaintiff must show that its injury is "of 'the type that the statute was intended to forestall,' " *Brunswick Corp. v. Pueblo Bowl–O–Mat, Inc.,* 429 U.S. 477, 487–88 (1977); no less in a case brought by the Government, it must demonstrate that the monopolist's conduct harmed competition, not just a competitor.

Third, if a plaintiff successfully establishes a *prima facie* case under § 2 by demonstrating anticompetitive effect, then the monopolist may proffer a "procompetitive justification" for its conduct. See *Eastman Kodak*, 504 U.S. at 483. If the monopolist asserts a procompetitive justification—a nonpretextual claim that its conduct is indeed a form of competition on the merits because it involves, for example, greater efficiency or enhanced consumer appeal—then the burden shifts back to the plaintiff to rebut that claim.

Fourth, if the monopolist's procompetitive justification stands unrebutted, then the plaintiff must demonstrate that the anticompetitive harm of the conduct outweighs the procompetitive benefit. In cases arising under § 1 of the Sherman Act, the courts routinely apply a similar balancing approach under the rubric of the "rule of reason." . . .

Finally, in considering whether the monopolist's conduct on balance harms competition and is therefore condemned as exclusionary for purposes of § 2, our focus is upon the effect of that conduct, not upon the intent behind it. Evidence of the intent behind the conduct of a monopolist is relevant only to the extent it helps us understand the likely effect of the monopolist's conduct. . . .

With these principles in mind, we now consider Microsoft's objections to the District Court's holding that Microsoft violated § 2 of the Sherman Act in a variety of ways.

1. Licenses Issued to Original Equipment Manufacturers

The District Court condemned a number of provisions in Microsoft's agreements licensing Windows to OEMs, because it found that Microsoft's imposition of those provisions (like many of Microsoft's other actions at issue in this case) serves to reduce usage share of Netscape's browser and, hence, protect Microsoft's operating system monopoly. The reason market share in the browser market affects market power in the operating system market is complex, and warrants some explanation.

Browser usage share is important because . . . a browser (or any middleware product, for that matter) must have a critical mass of users in order to attract software developers to write applications relying upon the APIs [applications programming interfaces] it exposes, and away from the APIs exposed by Windows. Applications written to a particular browser's APIs, however, would run on any computer with that browser, regardless of the underlying operating system. "The overwhelming majority of consumers will only use a PC operating system for which there already exists a large and varied set of . . . applications, and for which it seems relatively certain that new types of applications and new versions of existing applications will continue to be marketed. . . ." *Findings of Fact* ¶ 30. If a consumer could have access to the applications he desired—regardless of the operating system he uses—simply by installing a particular browser on his computer, then he would no longer feel compelled to select Windows in order to have access to those applications; he could select an operating system other than Windows based solely upon its quality and price. In other words, the market for operating systems would be competitive.

Therefore, Microsoft's efforts to gain market share in one market (browsers) served to meet the threat to Microsoft's monopoly in another market (operating systems) by keeping rival browsers from gaining the critical mass of users necessary to attract developer attention away from Windows as the platform for software development. Plaintiffs also argue that Microsoft's actions injured competition in the browser market—an argument we will examine below in relation to their specific claims that Microsoft attempted to monopolize the browser market and unlawfully tied its browser to its operating system so as to foreclose competition in the browser market. In evaluating the § 2 monopoly maintenance claim, however, our immediate concern is with the anticompetitive effect of Microsoft's conduct in preserving its monopoly in the operating system market.

In evaluating the restrictions in Microsoft's agreements licensing Windows to OEMs, we first consider whether plaintiffs have made out a *prima facie* case by demonstrating that the restrictions have an anticompetitive effect. In the next subsection, we conclude that plaintiffs have met this burden as to all the restrictions. We then consider Microsoft's proffered justifications for the restrictions and, for the most part, hold those justifications insufficient.

a. Anticompetitive effect of the license restrictions

The restrictions Microsoft places upon Original Equipment Manufacturers are of particular importance in determining browser usage share because having an OEM pre-install a browser on a computer is one of the two most cost-effective methods by far of distributing browsing software. (The other is bundling the browser with internet access software distributed by an IAP.) The District Court found that the restrictions Microsoft imposed in licensing Windows to OEMs prevented many OEMs from distributing browsers other than IE. In particular, the District Court condemned the license provisions prohibiting the OEMs from: (1) removing any desktop icons, folders, or "Start" menu entries; (2) altering the initial boot sequence; and (3) otherwise altering the appearance of the Windows desktop.

The District Court concluded that the first license restriction—the prohibition upon the removal of desktop icons, folders, and Start menu entries—thwarts the distribution of a rival browser by preventing OEMs from removing visible means of user access to IE. The OEMs cannot practically install a second browser in addition to IE, the court found, in part because "pre-installing more than one product in a given category . . . can significantly increase an OEM's support costs, for the redundancy can lead to confusion among novice users." That is, a certain number of novice computer users, seeing two browser icons, will wonder which to use when and will call the OEM's support line. Support calls are extremely expensive and, in the highly competitive original equipment market, firms have a strong incentive to minimize costs. * * *

As noted above, the OEM channel is one of the two primary channels for distribution of browsers. By preventing OEMs from removing visible means of user access to IE, the license restriction prevents many OEMs from pre-installing a rival browser and, therefore, protects Microsoft's monopoly from the competition that middleware might otherwise present. Therefore, we conclude that the license restriction at issue is anticompetitive. We defer for the moment the question whether that anticompetitive effect is outweighed by Microsoft's proffered justifications.

The second license provision at issue prohibits OEMs from modifying the initial boot sequence—the process that occurs the first time a consumer turns on the computer. Prior to the imposition of that restriction, "among the programs that many OEMs inserted into the boot sequence were Internet sign-up procedures that encouraged users to choose from a list of IAPs assembled by the OEM." Microsoft's prohibition on any alteration of the boot sequence thus prevents OEMs from using that process to promote the services of IAPs, many of which—at least at the time Microsoft imposed the restriction—used Navigator rather than IE in their internet access software. ... Microsoft does not deny that the prohibition on modifying the boot sequence has the effect of decreasing competition against IE by preventing OEMs from promoting rivals' browsers. Because this prohibition has a substantial effect in protecting Microsoft's market power, and does so through a means other than competition on the merits, it is anticompetitive. Again the question whether the provision is nonetheless justified awaits later treatment.

Finally, Microsoft imposes several additional provisions that, like the prohibition on removal of icons, prevent OEMs from making various alterations to the desktop: Microsoft prohibits OEMs from causing any user interface other than the Windows desktop to launch automatically, from adding icons or folders different in size or shape from those supplied by Microsoft, and from using the "Active Desktop" feature to promote third-party brands. These restrictions impose significant costs upon the OEMs; prior to Microsoft's prohibiting the practice, many OEMs would change the appearance of the desktop in ways they found beneficial. See, e.g., ... (March 1997 letter from Hewlett–Packard to Microsoft: "We are responsible for the cost of technical support of our customers, including the 33% of calls we get related to the lack of quality or confusion generated by your product.... We must have more ability to decide how our system is presented to our end users. If we had a choice of another supplier, based on your actions in this area, I assure you [that you] would not be our supplier of choice.").

The dissatisfaction of the OEM customers does not, of course, mean the restrictions are anticompetitive. The anticompetitive effect of the license restrictions is, as Microsoft itself recognizes, that OEMs are not able to promote rival browsers, which keeps developers focused upon the

APIs in Windows. . . . [B]ut for the restrictions in their licenses to use Windows, OEMs could promote multiple IAPs and browsers. By preventing the OEMs from doing so, this type of license restriction, like the first two restrictions, is anticompetitive: Microsoft reduced rival browsers' usage share not by improving its own product but, rather, by preventing OEMs from taking actions that could increase rivals' share of usage.

b. Microsoft's justifications for the license restrictions

Microsoft argues that the license restrictions are legally justified because, in imposing them, Microsoft is simply "exercising its rights as the holder of valid copyrights." Microsoft also argues that the licenses "do not unduly restrict the opportunities of Netscape to distribute Navigator in any event."

Microsoft's primary copyright argument borders upon the frivolous. The company claims an absolute and unfettered right to use its intellectual property as it wishes: "If intellectual property rights have been lawfully acquired," it says, then "their subsequent exercise cannot give rise to antitrust liability." That is no more correct than the proposition that use of one's personal property, such as a baseball bat, cannot give rise to tort liability. As the Federal Circuit succinctly stated: "Intellectual property rights do not confer a privilege to violate the antitrust laws." *In re Indep. Serv. Orgs. Antitrust Litig.*, 203 F.3d 1322, 1325 (Fed.Cir.2000). * * *

The only license restriction Microsoft seriously defends as necessary to prevent a "substantial alteration" of its copyrighted work is the prohibition on OEMs automatically launching a substitute user interface upon completion of the boot process. ("[A] few large OEMs developed programs that ran automatically at the conclusion of a new PC system's first boot sequence. These programs replaced the Windows desktop either with a user interface designed by the OEM or with Navigator's user interface."). We agree that a shell that automatically prevents the Windows desktop from ever being seen by the user is a drastic alteration of Microsoft's copyrighted work, and outweighs the marginal anticompetitive effect of prohibiting the OEMs from substituting a different interface automatically upon completion of the initial boot process. We therefore hold that this particular restriction is not an exclusionary practice that violates § 2 of the Sherman Act.

In a second variation upon its copyright defense, Microsoft argues that the license restrictions merely prevent OEMs from taking actions that would reduce substantially the value of Microsoft's copyrighted work: that is, Microsoft claims each license restriction in question is necessary to prevent OEMs from so altering Windows as to undermine "the principal value of Windows as a stable and consistent platform that supports a broad range of applications and that is familiar to users." Microsoft, however, never substantiates this claim, and, because an OEM's altering the appearance of the desktop or promoting programs in the boot sequence does not affect the code already in the product, the practice does not self-evidently affect either the "stability" or the "consistency" of the platform.... [W]e conclude Microsoft has not shown that the OEMs' liberality reduces the value of Windows except in the sense that their promotion of rival browsers undermines Microsoft's monopoly—and that is not a permissible justification for the license restrictions.

Apart from copyright, Microsoft raises one other defense of the OEM license agreements: It argues that, despite the restrictions in the OEM license, Netscape is not completely blocked from distributing its product. That claim is insufficient to shield Microsoft from liability for those restrictions because, although Microsoft did not bar its rivals from all means of distribution, it did bar them from the cost-efficient ones.

In sum, we hold that with the exception of the one restriction prohibiting automatically launched alternative interfaces, all the OEM license restrictions at issue represent uses of Microsoft's market power to protect its monopoly, unredeemed by any legitimate justification. The restrictions therefore violate § 2 of the Sherman Act.

2. Integration of IE and Windows

Although Microsoft's license restrictions have a significant effect in closing rival browsers out of one of the two primary channels of distribution, the District Court found that "Microsoft's executives believed ... its contractual restrictions placed on OEMs would not be sufficient in themselves to reverse the direction of Navigator's usage share. Consequently, in late 1995 or early 1996, Microsoft set out to bind [IE] more tightly to Windows 95 as a technical matter."

Technologically binding IE to Windows, the District Court found, both prevented OEMs from pre-installing other browsers and deterred consumers from using them. In particular, having the IE software code as an irremovable part of Windows meant that pre-installing a second browser would "increase an OEM's product testing costs," because an OEM must test and train its support staff to answer calls related to every software product preinstalled on the machine; moreover, pre-installing a browser in addition to IE would to many OEMs be "a questionable use of the scarce and valuable space on a PC's hard drive."

Although the District Court, in its Conclusions of Law, broadly condemned Microsoft's decision to bind "Internet Explorer to Windows with ... technological shackles," its findings of fact in support of that conclusion center upon three specific actions Microsoft took to weld IE to Windows: excluding IE from the "Add/Remove Programs" utility; designing Windows so as in certain circumstances to override the user's choice of a default browser other than IE; and commingling code related to browsing and other code in the same files, so that any attempt to delete the files containing IE would, at the same time, cripple the operating system. As with the license restrictions, we consider first whether the suspect actions had an anticompetitive effect, and then whether Microsoft has provided a procompetitive justification for them.

a. Anticompetitive effect of integration

As a general rule, courts are properly very skeptical about claims that competition has been harmed by a dominant firm's product design changes. In a competitive market, firms routinely innovate in the hope of appealing to consumers, sometimes in the process making their products incompatible with those of rivals; the imposition of liability when a monopolist does the same thing will inevitably deter a certain amount of innovation. This is all the more true in a market, such as this one, in which the product itself is rapidly changing. Judicial deference to product innovation, however, does not mean that a monopolist's product design decisions are per se lawful.

The District Court first condemned as anticompetitive Microsoft's decision to exclude IE from the "Add/Remove Programs" utility in Windows 98. Microsoft had included IE in the Add/Remove Programs utility in Windows 95, but when it modified Windows 95 to produce Windows 98, it took IE out of the Add/Remove Programs utility. This change reduces the usage share of rival browsers not by making Microsoft's own browser more attractive to consumers but, rather, by discouraging OEMs from distributing rival products. Because Microsoft's conduct, through something other than competition on the merits, has the effect of significantly reducing usage of rivals' products and hence protecting its own operating system monopoly, it is anticompetitive; we defer for the moment the question whether it is nonetheless justified.

Second, the District Court found that Microsoft designed Windows 98 "so that using Navigator on Windows 98 would have unpleasant consequences for users" by, in some circumstances, overriding the user's choice of a browser other than IE as his or her default browser. Plaintiffs argue that this override harms the competitive process by deterring consumers from using a browser other than IE even though they might prefer to do so, thereby reducing rival browsers' usage share and, hence, the ability of rival browsers to draw developer attention away from the APIs exposed by Windows. Microsoft does not deny, of course, that overriding the user's preference prevents some people from using other browsers. Because the override reduces rivals' usage share and protects Microsoft's monopoly, it too is anticompetitive.

Finally, the District Court condemned Microsoft's decision to bind IE to Windows 98 "by placing code specific to Web browsing in the same files as code that provided operating system functions." Putting code supplying browsing functionality into a file with code supplying operating system functionality "ensures that the deletion of any file containing browsing-specific routines would also delete vital operating system routines and thus cripple Windows. . . ." As noted above, preventing an OEM from removing IE deters it from installing a second browser because doing so increases the OEM's product testing and support costs; by contrast, had OEMs been able to remove IE, they might have chosen to pre-install Navigator alone. * * *

. . . [W]e conclude that such commingling has an anticompetitive effect; as noted above, the commingling deters OEMs from pre-installing rival browsers, thereby reducing the rivals' usage share and, hence, developers' interest in rivals' APIs as an alternative to the API set exposed by Microsoft's operating system.

b. Microsoft's justifications for integration

Microsoft proffers no justification for two of the three challenged actions that it took in integrating IE into Windows—excluding IE from the Add/Remove Programs utility and commingling browser and operating system code. Although Microsoft does make some general claims regarding the benefits of integrating the browser and the operating system, . . . it neither specifies nor substantiates those claims. Nor does it argue that either excluding IE from the Add/Remove Programs utility or commingling code achieves any integrative benefit. Plaintiffs plainly made out a *prima facie* case of harm to competition in the operating system market by demonstrating that Microsoft's actions increased its browser usage share and thus protected its operating system monopoly from a middleware threat and, for its part, Microsoft failed to meet its burden of showing that its conduct serves a purpose other than protecting its operating system monopoly. Accordingly, we hold that Microsoft's exclusion of IE from the Add/Remove Programs utility and its commingling of browser and operating system code constitute exclusionary conduct, in violation of § 2.

As for the other challenged act that Microsoft took in integrating IE into Windows—causing Windows to override the user's choice of a default browser in certain circumstances—Microsoft argues that it has "valid technical reasons." Specifically, Microsoft claims that it was necessary to design Windows to override the user's preferences when he or she invokes one of "a few" out "of the nearly 30 means of accessing the Internet." According to Microsoft:

> The Windows 98 Help system and Windows Update feature depend on ActiveX controls not supported by Navigator. . . . Lastly, Windows 98 does not invoke Navigator if a user accesses the Internet through "My Computer" or "Windows Explorer" because doing so would defeat one of the purposes of those features—enabling users to move seamlessly from local storage devices to the Web *in the same browsing window.*

. . . [P]laintiffs offer no rebuttal whatsoever. Accordingly, Microsoft may not be held liable for this aspect of its product design.

3. Agreements with Internet Access Providers

* * * The District Court condemned Microsoft's actions in (1) offering IE free of charge to IAPs and (2) offering IAPs a bounty for each customer the IAP signs up for service using the IE browser. In effect, the court concluded that Microsoft is acting to preserve its monopoly by offering IE to IAPs at an attractive price. Similarly, the District Court held Microsoft liable for (3) developing the IE Access Kit ("IEAK"), a software package

that allows an IAP to "create a distinctive identity for its service in as little as a few hours by customizing the [IE] title bar, icon, start and search pages," and (4) offering the IEAK to IAPs free of charge, on the ground that those acts, too, helped Microsoft preserve its monopoly. Finally, the District Court found that (5) Microsoft agreed to provide easy access to IAPs' services from the Windows desktop in return for the IAPs' agreement to promote IE exclusively and to keep shipments of internet access software using Navigator under a specific percentage, typically 25%. We address the first four items—Microsoft's inducements—and then its exclusive agreements with IAPs.

... [P]laintiffs argued that by pricing below cost on IE (indeed, even paying people to take it), Microsoft was able simultaneously to preserve its stream of monopoly profits on Windows, thereby more than recouping its investment in below-cost pricing on IE. The District Court did not assign liability for predatory pricing, however, and plaintiffs do not press this theory on appeal.

The rare case of price predation aside, the antitrust laws do not condemn even a monopolist for offering its product at an attractive price, and we therefore have no warrant to condemn Microsoft for offering either IE or the IEAK free of charge or even at a negative price. Likewise, as we said above, a monopolist does not violate the Sherman Act simply by developing an attractive product.... Therefore, Microsoft's development of the IEAK does not violate the Sherman Act.

We turn now to Microsoft's deals with IAPs concerning desktop placement. Microsoft concluded these exclusive agreements with all "the leading IAPs," including the major OLSs [Online Services]. The most significant of the OLS deals is with AOL [America Online], which, when the deal was reached, "accounted for a substantial portion of all existing Internet access subscriptions and ... attracted a very large percentage of new IAP subscribers." Under that agreement Microsoft puts the AOL icon in the OLS folder on the Windows desktop and AOL does not promote any non-Microsoft browser, nor provide software using any non-Microsoft browser except at the customer's request, and even then AOL will not supply more than 15% of its subscribers with a browser other than IE. * * *

In this case, plaintiffs allege that, by closing to rivals a substantial percentage of the available opportunities for browser distribution, Microsoft managed to preserve its monopoly in the market for operating systems. The IAPs constitute one of the two major channels by which browsers can be distributed. Microsoft has exclusive deals with "fourteen of the top fifteen access providers in North America[, which] account for a large majority of all Internet access subscriptions in this part of the world." By ensuring that the "majority" of all IAP subscribers are offered IE either as the default browser or as the only browser, Microsoft's deals with the IAPs clearly have a significant effect in preserving its monopoly; they help keep usage of Navigator below the critical level necessary for

Navigator or any other rival to pose a real threat to Microsoft's monopoly....

Plaintiffs having demonstrated a harm to competition, the burden falls upon Microsoft to defend its exclusive dealing contracts with IAPs by providing a procompetitive justification for them. Significantly, Microsoft's only explanation for its exclusive dealing is that it wants to keep developers focused upon its APIs—which is to say, it wants to preserve its power in the operating system market. That is not an unlawful end, but neither is it a procompetitive justification for the specific means here in question, namely exclusive dealing contracts with IAPs. Accordingly, we affirm the District Court's decision holding that Microsoft's exclusive contracts with IAPs are exclusionary devices, in violation of § 2 of the Sherman Act.

4. Dealings with Internet Content Providers, Independent Software Vendors, and Apple Computer

The District Court held that Microsoft engages in exclusionary conduct in its dealings with ICPs, which develop websites; ISVs, which develop software; and Apple, which is both an OEM and a software developer.... The District Court condemned Microsoft's deals with ICPs and ISVs, stating: "By granting ICPs and ISVs free licenses to bundle [IE] with their offerings, and by exchanging other valuable inducements for their agreement to distribute, promote[,] and rely on [IE] rather than Navigator, Microsoft directly induced developers to focus on its own APIs rather than ones exposed by Navigator."

With respect to the deals with ICPs, the District Court's findings do not support liability.... Because plaintiffs failed to demonstrate that Microsoft's deals with the ICPs have a substantial effect upon competition, they have not proved the violation of the Sherman Act.

As for Microsoft's ISV agreements[:] ... * * * The District Court did not specifically identify what share of the market for browser distribution the exclusive deals with the ISVs foreclose. Although the ISVs are a relatively small channel for browser distribution, they take on greater significance because, as discussed above, Microsoft had largely foreclosed the two primary channels to its rivals. In that light, one can tell from the record that by affecting the applications used by "millions" of consumers, Microsoft's exclusive deals with the ISVs had a substantial effect in further foreclosing rival browsers from the market.... Microsoft had an opportunity to, but did not, present the District Court with evidence demonstrating that the exclusivity provisions have some such procompetitive justification.

[W]e hold that those arrangements violate § 2 of the Sherman Act.

Finally, the District Court held that Microsoft's dealings with Apple violated the Sherman Act. Apple is vertically integrated: it makes both software (including an operating system, Mac OS), and hardware (the Macintosh line of computers). Microsoft primarily makes software, including, in addition to its operating system, a number of popular applications.

One, called "Office," is a suite of business productivity applications that Microsoft has ported to Mac OS. The District Court found that "ninety percent of Mac OS users running a suite of office productivity applications [use] Microsoft's Mac Office." Further, the District Court found that:

> In 1997, Apple's business was in steep decline, and many doubted that the company would survive much longer.... Many ISVs questioned the wisdom of continuing to spend time and money developing applications for the Mac OS. Had Microsoft announced in the midst of this atmosphere that it was ceasing to develop new versions of Mac Office, a great number of ISVs, customers, developers, and investors would have interpreted the announcement as Apple's death notice.

Microsoft recognized the importance to Apple of its continued support of Mac Office. ... ([Bill Gates said] "I think ... Apple should be using [IE] everywhere and if they don't do it, then we can use Office as a club.").

In June 1997 Microsoft Chairman Bill Gates determined that the company's negotiations with Apple " 'have not been going well at all.... Apple let us down on the browser by making Netscape the standard install.' Gates then reported that he had already called Apple's CEO ... to ask 'how we should announce the cancellation of Mac Office....' " The District Court further found that, within a month of Gates' call, Apple and Microsoft had reached an agreement pursuant to which [Microsoft agreed to continue supplying MAC Office and Apple agreed to bundle IE with MAC OS and not to install Navigator.] ...

This exclusive deal between Microsoft and Apple has a substantial effect upon the distribution of rival browsers. If a browser developer ports its product to a second operating system, such as the Mac OS, it can continue to display a common set of APIs. Thus, usage share, not the underlying operating system, is the primary determinant of the platform challenge a browser may pose. Pre-installation of a browser (which can be accomplished either by including the browser with the operating system or by the OEM installing the browser) is one of the two most important methods of browser distribution, and Apple had a not insignificant share of worldwide sales of operating systems. (Microsoft has 95% of the market not counting Apple and "well above" 80% with Apple included in the relevant market). Because Microsoft's exclusive contract with Apple has a substantial effect in restricting distribution of rival browsers, and because (as we have described several times above) reducing usage share of rival browsers serves to protect Microsoft's monopoly, its deal with Apple must be regarded as anticompetitive. ("By extracting from Apple terms that significantly diminished the usage of Navigator on the Mac OS, Microsoft helped to ensure that developers would not view Navigator as truly cross-platform middleware.").

Microsoft offers no procompetitive justification for the exclusive dealing arrangement.... Accordingly, we hold that the exclusive deal with Apple is exclusionary, in violation of § 2 of the Sherman Act.

5. Java

Java, a set of technologies developed by Sun Microsystems, is another type of middleware posing a potential threat to Windows' position as the ubiquitous platform for software development. The Java technologies include: (1) a programming language; (2) a set of programs written in that language, called the "Java class libraries," which expose APIs; (3) a compiler, which translates code written by a developer into "bytecode"; and (4) a Java Virtual Machine ("JVM"), which translates bytecode into instructions to the operating system. Programs calling upon the Java APIs will run on any machine with a "Java runtime environment," that is, Java class libraries and a JVM.

In May 1995 Netscape agreed with Sun to distribute a copy of the Java runtime environment with every copy of Navigator, and "Navigator quickly became the principal vehicle by which Sun placed copies of its Java runtime environment on the PC systems of Windows users." Microsoft, too, agreed to promote the Java technologies—or so it seemed. For at the same time, Microsoft took steps "to maximize the difficulty with which applications written in Java could be ported from Windows to other platforms, and vice versa." *Conclusions of Law,* at 43. Specifically, the District Court found that Microsoft took four steps to exclude Java from developing as a viable cross-platform threat: (a) designing a JVM incompatible with the one developed by Sun; (b) entering into contracts, the so-called "First Wave Agreements," requiring major ISVs to promote Microsoft's JVM exclusively; (c) deceiving Java developers about the Windows-specific nature of the tools it distributed to them; and (d) coercing Intel to stop aiding Sun in improving the Java technologies.

a. The incompatible JVM

The District Court held that Microsoft engaged in exclusionary conduct by developing and promoting its own JVM. Sun had already developed a JVM for the Windows operating system when Microsoft began work on its version. The JVM developed by Microsoft allows Java applications to run faster on Windows than does Sun's JVM, but a Java application designed to work with Microsoft's JVM does not work with Sun's JVM and vice versa. The District Court found that Microsoft "made a large investment of engineering resources to develop a high-performance Windows JVM," and, "by bundling its . . . JVM with every copy of [IE] . . . Microsoft endowed its Java runtime environment with the unique attribute of guaranteed, enduring ubiquity across the enormous Windows installed base." As explained above, however, a monopolist does not violate the antitrust laws simply by developing a product that is incompatible with those of its rivals. In order to violate the antitrust laws, the incompatible product must have an anticompetitive effect that outweighs any procompetitive justification for the design. Microsoft's JVM is not only incompatible with Sun's, it allows Java applications to run faster on Windows than does Sun's JVM. Microsoft's faster JVM lured Java developers into using Microsoft's developer tools, and Microsoft offered those tools deceptively, as we discuss below. The JVM, however, does allow applications to run more swiftly and does not itself have any anticompetitive effect. Therefore, we reverse the District Court's imposition of liability for Microsoft's development and promotion of its JVM.

b. The First Wave Agreements

The District Court also found that Microsoft entered into First Wave Agreements with dozens of ISVs to use Microsoft's JVM. ("In exchange for costly technical support and other blandishments, Microsoft induced dozens of important ISVs to make their Java applications reliant on Windows-specific technologies and to refrain from distributing to Windows users JVMs that complied with Sun's standards.").... * * *

... [T]he record indicates that Microsoft's deals with the major ISVs had a significant effect upon JVM promotion.... [T]he products of First Wave ISVs reached millions of consumers. The First Wave ISVs included such prominent developers as Rational Software, which, according to Microsoft itself, is "the leading supplier of utilities such as anti-virus software." Moreover, Microsoft's exclusive deals with the leading ISVs took place against a backdrop of foreclosure: the District Court found that "when Netscape announced in May 1995 [prior to Microsoft's execution of the First Wave Agreements] that it would include with every copy of Navigator a copy of a Windows JVM that complied with Sun's standards, it appeared that Sun's Java implementation would achieve the necessary ubiquity on Windows." As discussed above, however, Microsoft undertook a number of anticompetitive actions that seriously reduced the distribution of Navigator, and the District Court found that those actions thereby seriously impeded distribution of Sun's JVM. Because Microsoft's agreements foreclosed a substantial portion of the field for JVM distribution and because, in so doing, they protected Microsoft's monopoly from a middleware threat, they are anticompetitive.

... Because the cumulative effect of the deals is anticompetitive and because Microsoft has no procompetitive justification for them, we hold that the provisions in the First Wave Agreements requiring use of Microsoft's JVM as the default are exclusionary, in violation of the Sherman Act.

c. Deception of Java developers

Microsoft's "Java implementation" included, in addition to a JVM, a set of software development tools it created to assist ISVs in designing Java applications. The District Court found that, not only were these tools incompatible with Sun's cross-platform aspirations for Java—no violation, to be sure—but Microsoft deceived Java developers regarding the Windows-specific nature of the tools. Microsoft's tools included "certain 'keywords' and 'compiler directives' that could only be executed properly by Microsoft's version of the Java runtime environment for Windows." As a result, even Java "developers who were opting for portability over performance ... unwittingly [wrote] Java applications that [ran] only on

Windows." That is, developers who relied upon Microsoft's public commitment to cooperate with Sun and who used Microsoft's tools to develop what Microsoft led them to believe were cross-platform applications ended up producing applications that would run only on the Windows operating system.

When specifically accused by a *PC Week* reporter of fragmenting Java standards so as to prevent cross-platform uses, Microsoft denied the accusation and indicated it was only "adding rich platform support" to what remained a cross-platform implementation. An e-mail message internal to Microsoft, written shortly after the conversation with the reporter, shows otherwise. . . .

Finally, other Microsoft documents confirm that Microsoft intended to deceive Java developers, and predicted that the effect of its actions would be to generate Windows-dependent Java applications that their developers believed would be cross-platform; these documents also indicate that Microsoft's ultimate objective was to thwart Java's threat to Microsoft's monopoly in the market for operating systems. One Microsoft document, for example, states as a strategic goal: "Kill cross-platform Java by growing the polluted Java market."

Microsoft's conduct related to its Java developer tools served to protect its monopoly of the operating system in a manner not attributable either to the superiority of the operating system or to the acumen of its makers, and therefore was anticompetitive. Unsurprisingly, Microsoft offers no procompetitive explanation for its campaign to deceive developers. Accordingly, we conclude this conduct is exclusionary, in violation of § 2 of the Sherman Act.

d. The threat to Intel

The District Court held that Microsoft also acted unlawfully with respect to Java by using its "monopoly power to prevent firms such as Intel from aiding in the creation of cross-platform interfaces." In 1995 Intel was in the process of developing a high-performance, Windows-compatible JVM. Microsoft wanted Intel to abandon that effort because a fast, cross-platform JVM would threaten Microsoft's monopoly in the operating system market. . . .

Intel nonetheless continued to undertake initiatives related to Java. By 1996 "Intel had developed a JVM designed to run well . . . while complying with Sun's cross-platform standards." In April of that year, Microsoft again urged Intel not to help Sun by distributing Intel's fast, Suncompliant JVM. And Microsoft threatened Intel that if it did not stop aiding Sun on the multimedia front, then Microsoft would refuse to distribute Intel technologies bundled with Windows.

Intel finally capitulated in 1997, after Microsoft delivered the *coup de grace*. [Gates said: Back off from JAVA and I will stop supporting a technology competing with Intel.]

... [W]e affirm the conclusion that Microsoft's threats to Intel were exclusionary, in violation of § 2 of the Sherman Act. * * *

C. Causation

As a final parry, Microsoft urges this court to reverse on the monopoly maintenance claim, because plaintiffs never established a causal link between Microsoft's anticompetitive conduct, in particular its foreclosure of Netscape's and Java's distribution channels, and the maintenance of Microsoft's operating system monopoly. ("There is insufficient evidence to find that, absent Microsoft's actions, Navigator and Java already would have ignited genuine competition in the market for Intel-compatible PC operating systems.")....

Microsoft points to no case, and we can find none, standing for the proposition that, as to § 2 *liability* in an equitable enforcement action, plaintiffs must present direct proof that a defendant's continued monopoly power is precisely attributable to its anticompetitive conduct....

... To require that § 2 liability turn on a plaintiff's ability or inability to reconstruct the hypothetical marketplace absent a defendant's anticompetitive conduct would only encourage monopolists to take more and earlier anticompetitive action.

We may infer causation when exclusionary conduct is aimed at producers of nascent competitive technologies as well as when it is aimed at producers of established substitutes....

Given this rather edentulous test for causation, the question in this case is not whether Java or Navigator would actually have developed into viable platform substitutes, but (1) whether as a general matter the exclusion of nascent threats is the type of conduct that is reasonably capable of contributing significantly to a defendant's continued monopoly power and (2) whether Java and Navigator reasonably constituted nascent threats at the time Microsoft engaged in the anticompetitive conduct at issue. As to the first, suffice it to say that it would be inimical to the purpose of the Sherman Act to allow monopolists free reign to squash nascent, albeit unproven, competitors at will—particularly in industries marked by rapid technological advance and frequent paradigm shifts.... As to the second, the District Court made ample findings that both Navigator and Java showed potential as middleware platform threats.

Microsoft's concerns over causation have more purchase in connection with the appropriate remedy issue, *i.e.*, whether the court should impose a structural remedy or merely enjoin the offensive conduct at issue. [D]ivestiture is a remedy that is imposed only with great caution, in part because its long-term efficacy is rarely certain. Absent some measure of confidence that there has been an actual loss to competition that needs to be restored, wisdom counsels against adopting radical structural relief. ... But these queries go to questions of remedy, not liability. In short, causation affords Microsoft no defense to liability for its unlawful actions undertaken to maintain its monopoly in the operating system market.

III. ATTEMPTED MONOPOLIZATION [BROWSERS]

Microsoft further challenges the District Court's determination of liability for "attempting to monopolize ... any part of the trade or commerce among the several States." To establish a § 2 violation for attempted monopolization, "a plaintiff must prove (1) that the defendant has engaged in predatory or anticompetitive conduct with (2) a specific intent to monopolize and (3) a dangerous probability of achieving monopoly power." *Spectrum Sports, Inc. v. McQuillan*, 506 U.S. 447, 456 (1993). Because a deficiency on any one of the three will defeat plaintiffs' claim, we look no further than plaintiffs' failure to prove a dangerous probability of achieving monopoly power in the putative browser market. * * *

To establish a dangerous probability of success, plaintiffs must as a threshold matter show that the browser market can be monopolized, *i.e.*, that a hypothetical monopolist in that market could enjoy market power. This, in turn, requires plaintiffs (1) to define the relevant market and (2) to demonstrate that substantial barriers to entry protect that market. Because plaintiffs have not carried their burden on either prong, we reverse without remand.

A. Relevant Market * * *

Defining a market for an attempted monopolization claim involves the same steps as defining a market for a monopoly maintenance claim, namely a detailed description of the purpose of a browser—what functions may be included and what are not—and an examination of the substitutes that are part of the market and those that are not. The District Court never engaged in such an analysis nor entered detailed findings defining what a browser is or what products might constitute substitutes. * * *

B. Barriers to Entry

Because a firm cannot possess monopoly power in a market unless that market is also protected by significant barriers to entry, it follows that a firm cannot threaten to achieve monopoly power in a market unless that market is, or will be, similarly protected..... Plaintiffs have the burden of establishing barriers to entry into a properly defined relevant market.... Plaintiffs must not only show that barriers to entry protect the properly defined browser market, but that those barriers are "significant." ... [P]laintiffs ... failed to carry their burden on barriers to entry. * * *

... Accordingly, we reverse the District Court's determination of § 2 liability for attempted monopolization.

* * *

QUESTIONS AND COMMENTS

1. The Court of Appeals reversed and remanded the district court's holding that bundling the browser with the operating system was an illegal tie. See p. 680 infra.

For procedure and due process reasons, the Court of Appeals reversed and remanded the district court's order to break Microsoft into two parts, one for the operating system and one for the applications. It warned, however, that breakup is a drastic remedy and should not lightly be ordered. On remand, the district court entered an order that largely resembled the settlement agreement proposed by Microsoft and substantially agreed to by the federal government and nine of the plaintiff states. The order required non-discriminatory licensing of certain protocols necessary for interoperability. It prohibited Microsoft from retaliating against customers that used competitors' products. Also, among other things, Microsoft was required to allow end users and OEMs to enable and remove access to middleware products of competitors and to ensure that Windows did not automatically alter an OEM's configuration of icons, menu entries, and shortcuts. See final judgment, 2002–2 Trade Cas. (CCH) ¶s 73,854, 73,860 (D.D.C. 2002).

Is this an appropriate remedy? The best remedy? Would a breakup have been better (or worse) to induce the right incentives? See, for articles offering a range of viewpoints on the efficacy of the relief in the *Microsoft* case, Symposium: The End of the Microsoft Antitrust Case?, 75 Antitrust L.J. Issue 3 (2009).

2. Microsoft argued that it was under intense market pressures to invent and that if it should try to sit back on laurels it would find no laurels; some competitor would pioneer a technological breakthrough and Windows would be obsoleted. Microsoft argued also that its computer software was inexpensive; that Microsoft behaved like a competitor, not a monopolist, and that it was forced to do so by the intense pressures of potential competition that are endemic to high tech, fast-moving markets.

What is the significance of these arguments to the debate whether Section 2 is an appropriate instrument to regulate the conduct of firms in high tech, new economy markets?

Which is and should be more significant to competition policy: the fact that new technology could instantaneously obsolete the product of the incumbent, or the fact that network effects and the prime mover advantage tend to entrench the incumbent?

3. Compare Microsoft's claim that the decision effectively confiscates its intellectual property and that it deeply undercuts incentives to invent, with the governments' claim that Microsoft stifled innovation. Who has the better side of the argument? How do we balance incentives for the incumbent versus incentives for outsiders in trying to decide what is best for the market, in particular for a network market?

4. What is the one claim as to which the court upholds the copyright defense? By what principle is this copyright justification upheld and all others rejected? Is the court's general rejection of the copyright justification consistent with the Federal Circuit's opinion in *CSU/Xerox* (see 300 supra)? Since Microsoft may in theory refuse to license, must it be allowed to license on whatever conditions it chooses?

5. In each instance (taken separately) in which Microsoft's conduct had a substantial (or non trivial) negative impact on Netscape Navigator's share of

browsers, the court held that plaintiffs had demonstrated an anticompetitive effect in the operating system market. Do you agree?

6. Did the plaintiff governments (federal and state) prove that, as a result of the specific anticompetitive conduct, there was less output of computer software? Should it have been required to prove this effect? How strong was Microsoft's argument that its conduct had not harmed competition, even if it harmed a few competitors?

7. What do you expect will be the legacy of the D.C. Circuit's opinion in *Microsoft* for antitrust? for the competitiveness and innovativeness of firms? for antitrust compliance and deterrence? for the future of the complex monopoly case?

8. *United States v. Microsoft* was not, however, the end of the matter. Suits against Microsoft were brought by competitors, by consumers, by the European Commission, and by competition authorities in a number of other jurisdictions. We note three competitor actions below; then we describe the case by the European Commission.

Caldera, Inc. v. Microsoft Corp., 72 F.Supp.2d 1295 (D.Utah 1999), and 87 F.Supp.2d 1244 (D.Utah 1999). In 1976 Gary Kidall founded Digital Research, Inc. (DRI), which developed one of the first operating systems for personal computers. Even after Microsoft won the IBM contract to become the operating system on IBM PCs, DRI continued to develop its operating system and to offer significant competition. Microsoft thereupon embarked upon a strategy, which eventually worked, to oust DRI from the market. The strategy, as alleged, included: purposely creating incompatibilities; discontinuing disclosure of information necessary to beta test Windows (pre-release testing, which gives information on compatibility and technical issues); using per-processor licenses—requiring OEMs to pay as if they used MS DOS on all computers, whether they did so or not, thus inducing them to use MS DOS exclusively because they already had paid for it; flashing "error" messages on consumer screens when non-Microsoft software products were used and advising the user to remove the foreign product and contact Windows; adding a device making it impossible for Windows to install a DR DOS system; spreading "vaporware"—announcing non-existing products whenever DRI was launching a new product, and creating a campaign of "fear, uncertainty and doubt" (FUD) against DRI and its forthcoming versions of DR DOS; and tying MS DOS and Windows.

Microsoft moved for summary judgment on each claim. As to the claims regarding predisclosure and incompatibilities, Microsoft said it had no duty to aid competitors. As to the tying claim, Microsoft said it had created a new product; therefore it had not tied two products. As to error messages and FUD, Microsoft argued that the claim did not meet the requirements of the product disparagement (libel) tort. As to the per-processor licensing, Microsoft said: its agreements were not exclusive; the

OEMs were free to use operating systems of others; the contracts were reasonable.

Does each claim state a cause of action? Must each claim stand on its own, or can all be seen in context as an aggregate strategy of monopolization?

The district court denied Microsoft's motions. In January 2000, Microsoft settled with Caldera for $155 million. See S. Robinson, Microsoft and Caldera Settle Antitrust Suit, NY Times, Jan. 11, 2000, C2.

Sun Microsystems, Inc. v. Microsoft Corp., 333 F.3d 517 (4th Cir.2003). The two other competitors most clearly injured by Microsoft's exclusionary strategies were Netscape (browsers) and Sun Microsystems (JAVA language and computer workstations). Netscape, by its new parent AOL Time Warner, sued and then settled with Microsoft for $750 million and a variety of software development agreements. See S. Lohr and D. Kirkpatrick, Microsoft to Pay AOL $750 Million, NY Times, May 30, 2003, p. A1. Sun Microsystems' litigation is still pending at this writing.

Sun sought a mandatory preliminary injunction requiring Microsoft to incorporate Sun's JAVA software in every copy of its Windows PC operating system and its web browser so that Sun's JAVA could operate as middleware on top of every Microsoft operating system. Sun also sought a preliminary injunction against copyright infringement. The district court granted the mandatory preliminary injunction, as well as a preliminary injunction against copyright infringement resulting from Microsoft's uses of JAVA that exceeded the limited license granted by Sun to Microsoft in an agreement settling prior copyright infringement claims. The district court recognized that the "must carry" injunction was unprecedented, but stated that it was necessary to prevent "tipping" against JAVA and in favor of Microsoft's .NET in the emerging market for Internet-enabled distributed computing platforms. As related by the court of appeals, by Judge Niemeyer:

> Sun developed the Java platform as middleware that would permit software applications to be run on various operating systems. Proceeding under the motto "write once, run anywhere," Sun developed the Java platform to provide software developers with tools that would enable them to write applications software for any computer and operating system that includes Java middleware. Sun contends that Java's promise of cross-platform compatibility posed a competitive threat to Microsoft because of its potential to erode the requirement to tailor applications software to particular operating systems—an applications-software barrier to entry that was protecting Microsoft's monopoly in the PC operating systems market. It alleges that Microsoft responded to this threat with an "embrace and extend" strategy, described by the California district court in *Sun Microsystems, Inc. v. Microsoft Corp.,* 87 F.Supp.2d at 995, as follows:
>
> > First, Microsoft "embraced" the Java technology by licensing from Sun the right to use its Java Technology to develop and

> distribute compatible Products. Second, Microsoft "extended" the Java platform by developing strategic incompatibilities into its Java runtime and development tools products. According to Sun, these incompatibilities tied applications using Microsoft's Java development tools to Microsoft's virtual machine and the Windows platform. Third, Microsoft used its distribution channels to flood the market with its version of the Java Technology in [what Sun characterized as] an attempt to "hijack the Java Technology and transform it into a Microsoft proprietary programming and runtime environment."

The so-called "embrace" took place when Microsoft and Sun entered into a Technology License and Distribution Agreement ("License Agreement") on March 11, 1996, whereby Sun licensed Microsoft to make and distribute Java-based products. This License Agreement required Microsoft's implementations of the Java platform to meet compatibility standards set by Sun (now by the "Java Community Process," an organization of licensees and developers to whom Sun has turned over control of Java).

Using its access to Sun's proprietary code granted under the License Agreement, Microsoft allegedly developed a Java implementation—the primary component of which was the Microsoft Java Virtual Machine (MSJVM)—that was incompatible with the core Java platform. Microsoft also allegedly interfered with Sun's distribution channels for Java by damaging the market for Netscape's Navigator, a web browser that was at one time the principal vehicle for the distribution of Java. Additionally, Microsoft allegedly stunted further development of Java by preventing Intel Corporation from cooperating with Sun and Netscape in the development of a high-performance, Windows-compatible Java product.

Microsoft's alleged conduct prompted Sun to file suit against Microsoft in the Northern District of California, alleging trademark and copyright violations as well as unfair competition under California law. Following extensive litigation, Microsoft and Sun entered into a Settlement Agreement dated January 23, 2001 [granting Microsoft a limited right to continue distribution of MSJVM incorporated in certain products, and requiring Microsoft to pay $20 million to Sun.]

Shortly after Microsoft began the commercial distribution in February 2002 of Visual Studio .NET, a programming product containing Microsoft's own middleware—the .NET platform—to compete with the Java platform, Sun commenced this action....

The future harm alleged by Sun is "market tipping," which Sun's expert, Dr. Dennis Carlton, described as the expected end-state of a market that is subject to strong "feedback effects." According to Dr. Carlton, the feedback effects in the incipient competition between Java and .NET arise from the decisions of software developers to write applications for a particular platform:

> As more applications written to one platform arise, that increases the demand to have that platform. As the presence of that platform increases, then that creates a heightened incentive for developers toward deciding what platform to write to, to write to the platform that is increasing ... or [that] has the greater relative prevalence. And that is an effect that will feed back on itself because once there's a greater presence of a platform, it increases the incentives for more applications. The more applications there are, the more developers there are, it becomes more desirable to have the platform. And it will be a feedback like I described earlier, that will be mutually reinforcing.

The result of this cycle is what Sun and the district court refer to as "market tipping," which Dr. Carlton testified is "what other people would alternatively describe as a tendency for a dominant product or a dominant standard to emerge." Sun's theory for preliminary relief relied not only on the purported presence of these "feedback effects" in the emerging market for middleware but also on the theory that the feedback effects in this market would arise in the early stages of competition and entrench one dominant standard as the winner of the competition almost from the very beginning. Dr. Carlton testified:

> It's in the early stages that feedback effects can get set up. And once they're set up, they can lead to a market tipping. And once it tips, or once these feedback effects get set up, they may be hard to undo. And therefore, the market structure can be entrenched and the initial stages can be determinative of these final outcomes. That's why the initial stages can be quite important.

After canvassing the competing evidence offered by Sun and Microsoft, which included not only the testimony of Dr. Carlton but also the written and oral testimony of software developers, executives from Sun and Microsoft, and Microsoft's own economics expert, the district court observed:

> On this evidence I find there will be a substantial feedback effect in the market for general purpose, Internet-enabled distributed computing platforms as the competition between .NET and Java unfolds. I also find that, in accordance with the general economic principles cited by the D.C. Circuit in the Department of Justice case, .NET and Java will compete for the field rather than within the field. * * *
>
> Therefore, the genuine threat that market tipping presents cannot be dismissed on the ground that at the moment, before the competition has begun, a large number of software developers are still Java-oriented. Microsoft, Sun, and the developer community are all looking toward the future, and in order to determine whether a must-carry injunction is necessary and appropriate, a court must do so as well.

But even as the court accepted Sun's theory of relief, it limited the findings on which it based the relief:

> I do not suggest, however, it is inevitable that the market will tip in favor of .NET. Dennis Carlton, Sun's expert economist, has candidly acknowledged that he cannot determine whether tipping away from Java is more likely than not. It is possible that .NET and Java will both survive as competing platforms and that the new market will be a heterogeneous one.

The district court clarified the limitation of its finding in its legal analysis, stating that it did "*not find* that at this precise moment there is an *imminent threat* that the market for general purpose, Internet-enabled distributed computing platforms will tip in favor of .NET." [237 F.Supp.2d] at 651 (emphasis added). Rather, the court found that "unless Sun is given a fair opportunity to compete in a market untainted by the effects of Microsoft's past anti-trust violations, there is a *serious risk that in the near future* the market will tip in favor of .NET, that it is impossible to ascertain when such tipping might occur in time to prevent it from happening, and that if the market does tip in favor of .NET, Sun could not be adequately compensated in damages." *Id.* (emphasis added).

———

In view of these last observations, the court of appeals held that the harm claimed was not sufficiently imminent, and a mandatory injunction was not necessary to preserve the claim. Moreover, it held that the legal case was defective because the injunctive relief was not designed to protect competition in the relevant market (Intel-compatible PC operating systems) but was targeted toward an emerging collateral market. Most district and circuit courts, it said, reject the theory that monopoly leveraging into a collateral market is illegal. Accordingly, the court of appeals vacated the mandatory preliminary injunction.

Was the court correct to vacate the mandatory preliminary injunction? Is the threat of tipping always somewhat uncertain? Is it important, or not, for courts to nip in the bud threatened tipping of a network market through use of leverage?

c. Microsoft–Europe

The European Commission brought proceedings against Microsoft, a "super-dominant" firm with more than 90% of the personal computer (PC) operating systems market, for abusing its dominant position in violation of Article 82 of the Treaty of Rome. The Commission found two sets of Microsoft's practices illegal: 1) Bundling its media player with its operating system (Windows), which had become the standard in the market. RealNetworks had pioneered the media player and RealNetworks' player was popularly used with Windows. Thereafter Microsoft made its own media player and bundled it with Windows, foreclosing media player rivals from the most efficient channels to the market. 2) Refusal to deal, in the form of refusing to provide workgroup server software rivals with full interoperability information to connect with Windows and with Microsoft's workgroup server software. Workgroup servers are servers used by small enterprises to interconnect file, printing, document-sharing and management functions of all PCs within the enterprise. Novell and others had pioneered workgroup server software. Before Microsoft developed such software of its own, it gave full interoperability information to the workgroup server software providers. Then Microsoft made its own workgroup server software and withheld from its rivals the full information they needed for seamless interoperability, noting that it still provided a good deal of interoperability information and claiming that it had no legal duty to help its rivals. Belatedly, it also claimed that its interface protocols containing the withheld interoperability information contained intellectual property and that it had a right of absolute exclusivity of its intellectual property.

For remedies, the Commission ordered Microsoft to supply the full interoperability protocols, offer an unbundled version of Windows without the media player, and pay a fine of €497 million for the two violations. In response, Microsoft offered the unbundled version but at the same price that it offered the bundled version. Not surprisingly, almost no one chose the unbundled version. Microsoft provided interoperability protocols, but, according to the monitoring trustee, the information provided was not in a form developers would understand. The Commission imposed a €280 million fine for noncompliance with the interoperability mandate and an additional fine of €3 million per day until Microsoft should comply.

Microsoft appealed to the Court of First Instance (now the General Court). The Court affirmed. An appeal to the European Court of Justice regarding (only) the fine for noncompliance with the remedial order is pending.

MICROSOFT CORP. v. COMMISSION

Case T-201/04R, European General Court, 2004 ECR II-02977.

Refusal to deal, involving Microsoft's refusal to provide rivals with certain interoperability protocols; the protocols contained intellectual property

[The Court observed that only exceptionally does the holder of an intellectual property right have a duty to deal. It recited the requirements of the *IMS* and *Magill* precedents, which require that, to give rise to a duty to deal, four criteria must be satisfied: (1) access [here, to the complete interoperability information] must be indispensable to enable firms to carry on business, (2) the refusal must exclude any effective competition on a neighboring market, and (3) the refusal must prevent the appearance of a new product for which there is a potential consumer demand. (4) It would then fall to the dominant firm to prove an objective justification. After finding that the Commission had proved indispensability and that the refusal gave rise to a sufficient risk of the elimination of competition, the Court turned to whether the refusal limited production or technological development (for if it did it would prevent the appearance of new products).]

648 It was on that last hypothesis [prejudice to consumers may arise where there is a limitation not only of production or markets, but also of technical development] that the Commission based its finding in the contested decision. Thus, the Commission considered that Microsoft's refusal to supply the relevant information limited technical development to the prejudice of consumers within the meaning of Article 82(b) EC and it rejected Microsoft's assertion that it had not been demonstrated that its refusal caused prejudice to consumers.

649 The Court finds that the Commission's findings at the recitals referred to in the preceding paragraph are not manifestly incorrect.

650 Thus, in the first place, the Commission was correct to observe that '[owing] to the lack of interoperability that competing work group server operating system products can achieve with the Windows domain architecture, an increasing number of consumers are locked into a homogeneous Windows solution at the level of work group server operating systems'.

651 It must be borne in mind that . . . Microsoft's refusal prevented its competitors from developing work group server operating systems capable of attaining a sufficient degree of interoperability with the Windows domain architecture, with the consequence that consumers' purchasing decisions in respect of work group server operating systems were channelled towards Microsoft's products. The Court has also already observed that it was apparent from a number of documents in the file that the technologies of the Windows 2000 range, in particular Active Directory, were increasingly being taken up by organisations. As interoperability problems arise more acutely with work group server operating systems in that range of products than with those of the preceding generation, the increasing uptake of those systems merely reinforces the 'lock-in' effect referred to in the preceding paragraph.

652 The limitation thus placed on consumer choice is all the more damaging to consumers because . . . they consider that non-Microsoft work group server operating systems are better than Windows work group server operating systems with respect to a series of features to which they attach great importance, such as 'reliability/availability of the . . . system' and 'security included with the server operating system'.

653 In the second place, the Commission was correct to consider that the artificial advantage in terms of interoperability that Microsoft retained by its refusal discouraged its competitors from developing and marketing work group server operating systems with innovative features, to the prejudice, notably, of consumers. That refusal has the

consequence that those competitors are placed at a disadvantage by comparison with Microsoft so far as the merits of their products are concerned, particularly with regard to parameters such as security, reliability, ease of use or operating performance speed.

654 The Commission's finding that '[i]f Microsoft's competitors had access to the interoperability information that Microsoft refuses to supply, they could use the disclosures to make the advanced features of their own products available in the framework of the web of interoperability relationships that underpin the Windows domain architecture' is corroborated by the conduct which those competitors had adopted in the past, when they had access to certain information concerning Microsoft's products. The two examples which the Commission gives, 'PC NetLink' and 'NDS for NT', speak volumes in that regard. PC NetLink is software developed by Sun on the basis of AS/U, which had been developed by AT & T using source code which Microsoft had licensed to it in the 1990s. A document submitted by Microsoft during the administrative procedure shows that the innovative features and added value that PC NetLink brought to Windows work group networks was used as a selling point for that product. Likewise, in its marketing material, Novell highlighted the new features which NDS for NT—software which it had developed using reverse engineering—brought to the Windows domain architecture (in this instance Windows NT). * * *

664 Last, it must be borne in mind that it is settled case-law that Article 82 EC covers not only practices which may prejudice consumers directly but also those which indirectly prejudice them by impairing an effective competitive structure (Case 85/76 *Hoffmann–La Roche* v *Commission* [1979] ECR 461, paragraph 125, and *Irish Sugar* v *Commission*, paragraph 232). In this case, Microsoft impaired the effective competitive structure on the work group server operating systems market by acquiring a significant market share on that market.

665 The Court concludes from all of the foregoing considerations that the Commission's finding to the effect that Microsoft's refusal limits technical development to the prejudice of consumers within the meaning of Article 82(b) EC is not manifestly incorrect. The Court therefore finds that the circumstance relating to the appearance of a new product is present in this case.

Absence of objective justification

666 In the first place, Microsoft claims that the refusal to supply the information was objectively justified by the intellectual property rights which it holds over the 'technology' concerned. It has made significant investment in designing its communication protocols and the commercial success which its products have achieved represents the just reward. It is generally accepted, moreover, that an undertaking's refusal to communicate a specific technology to its competitors

may be justified by the fact that it does not wish them to use that technology to compete with it. * * *

690 The Court considers that, even on the assumption that it is correct, the fact that the communication protocols covered by the contested decision, or the specifications for those protocols, are covered by intellectual property rights cannot constitute objective justification within the meaning of *Magill* and *IMS Health*. Microsoft's argument is inconsistent with the *raison d'être* of the exception which that case-law thus recognises in favour of free competition, since if the mere fact of holding intellectual property rights could in itself constitute objective justification for the refusal to grant a licence, the exception established by the case-law could never apply. In other words, a refusal to license an intellectual property right could never be considered to constitute an infringement of Article 82 EC even though in *Magill* and *IMS Health*, the Court of Justice specifically stated the contrary.

691 It must be borne in mind that the Community judicature considers that the fact that the holder of an intellectual property right can exploit that right solely for his own benefit constitutes the very substance of his exclusive right. Accordingly, a simple refusal, even on the part of an undertaking in a dominant position, to grant a licence to a third party cannot in itself constitute an abuse of a dominant position within the meaning of Article 82 EC. It is only when it is accompanied by exceptional circumstances such as those hitherto envisaged in the case-law that such a refusal can be characterised as abusive and that, accordingly, it is permissible, in the public interest in maintaining effective competition on the market, to encroach upon the exclusive right of the holder of the intellectual property right by requiring him to grant licences to third parties seeking to enter or remain on that market. It must be borne in mind that it has been established above that such exceptional circumstances were present in this case. * * *

710 The Commission came to a negative conclusion [Microsoft failed to prove an objective justification] but not by balancing the negative impact which the imposition of a requirement to supply the information at issue might have on Microsoft's incentives to innovate against the positive impact of that obligation on innovation in the industry as a whole, but after refuting Microsoft's arguments relating to the fear that its products might be cloned, establishing that the disclosure of interoperability was widespread in the industry concerned and showing that IBM's commitment to the Commission in 1984 was not substantially different from what Microsoft was ordered to do in the contested decision and that its approach was consistent with Directive 91/250 [on the legal protection of computer programs, which considers disclosure of interoperability information beneficial to innovation].

* * *

Bundling the media player and the operating system

1036 The Commission's analysis of the foreclosure condition begins at recital 841 to the contested decision, where the Commission states that in the present case there are good reasons not to assume without further analysis that the bundling of Windows and Windows Media Player constitutes conduct which by its very nature is liable to foreclose competition. In substance, the conclusion which the Commission reached is based on the finding that the bundling of Windows Media Player with the Windows client PC operating system—the operating system pre-installed on the great majority of client PCs sold throughout the world—without the possibility of removing that media player from the operating system, allows Windows Media Player to benefit from the ubiquity of that operating system on client PCs, which cannot be counterbalanced by the other methods of distributing media players.

1037 The Court considers that that finding, which is the subject-matter of the first stage of the Commission's reasoning, is entirely well founded.

1038 Thus, in the first place, it is clear that owing to the bundling, Windows Media Player enjoyed an unparalleled presence on client PCs throughout the world, because it thereby automatically achieved a level of market penetration corresponding to that of the Windows client PC operating system and did so without having to compete on the merits with competing products. It must be borne in mind that it is common ground that Microsoft's market share on the client PC operating systems market is more than 90% and that the great majority of sales of Windows client PC operating systems (approximately 75%) are made through OEMs, who pre-install Windows on the client PCs which they assemble and distribute. Thus, the figures . . . show that in 2002 Microsoft had a market share of 93.8% by units shipped on the client PC operating systems market . . . and that Windows—and, as a result, Windows Media Player—was pre-installed on 196 million of the 207 million client PCs shipped in the world between October 2001 and March 2003.

1039 As will be explained in greater detail below, no third-party media player could achieve such a level of market penetration without having the advantage in terms of distribution that Windows Media Player enjoys as a result of Microsoft's use of its Windows client PC operating system.

1040 It should be added that Microsoft's combined offer of the Windows operating system and the NetShow 2.0 player from June 1998 did not guarantee NetShow 2.0 the same degree of presence on client PCs. . . . NetShow 2.0 was included on the Windows 98 installation CD but was not installed by any of the four default installations of that system. In other words, users had to make the effort to install NetShow 2.0 separately and could therefore decide not to install it.

Similarly, that combined offer did not prevent developers of third-party media players from competing with Microsoft on the intrinsic merits of their products or prevent OEMs from taking advantage of that competition.

1041 In the second place, it is clear that, as the Commission correctly states, '[u]sers who find [Windows Media Player] pre-installed on their client PCs are indeed in general less likely to use alternative media players as they already have an application which delivers media streaming and playback functionality'. The Court therefore considers that, in the absence of the bundling, consumers wishing to have a streaming media player would be induced to choose one from among those available on the market. * * *

1046 Thus, the release of the bundled version of Windows and Windows Media Player as the only version of the Windows operating system capable of being pre-installed by OEMs on new client PCs had the direct and immediate consequence of depriving OEMs of the possibility previously open to them of assembling the products which they deemed most attractive for consumers and, more particularly, of preventing them from choosing one of Windows Media Player's competitors as the only media player. On this last point, it must be borne in mind that at the time RealPlayer had a significant commercial advantage as market leader. As Microsoft itself acknowledges, it was only in 1999 that it succeeded in developing a streaming media player that performed well enough, given that its previous player, NetShow, 'was unpopular with customers because it did not work very well'. It must also be borne in mind that between August 1995 and July 1998 it was RealNetworks' products—first RealAudio Player, then RealPlayer—that were distributed with Windows. There is therefore good reason to conclude that if Microsoft had not adopted the impugned conduct competition between RealPlayer and Windows Media Player would have been decided on the basis of the intrinsic merits of the two products.

1047 Furthermore, even if developers of media players competing with Microsoft succeeded in reaching an agreement with OEMs for the pre-installation of their product, they would still be in a disadvantageous competitive position by comparison with Microsoft. First, as Windows Media Player cannot be removed by OEMs or by users from the package consisting of Windows and Windows Media Player, the third-party media player could never be the only media player on the client PC. In particular, the bundling prevents developers of third-party media players from competing with Microsoft for that purpose on the intrinsic merits of the products. Second, as the number of media players that OEMs are prepared to pre-install on client PCs is limited, developers of third-party media players compete with each other in order to have their products pre-installed, while, owing to the bundling, Microsoft evades that competition and the significant additional costs which it entails. On this last point, it is pertinent [that] ... the Commission mentions the distribution agreement for RealPlayer concluded in 2001 between RealNetworks and Compaq and also the fact that Microsoft acknowledged during the administrative procedure that RealNetworks paid OEMs to pre-install its products.

1048 It follows from those findings that the Commission was correct to conclude that 'the option of entering into agreements with OEMs [was] a less efficient and effective means of obtaining media player distribution in the face of Microsoft's tying'.

1049 In the fourth place, the Court finds that the Commission was also correct to find that methods of distributing media players other than pre-installation by OEMs could not offset Windows Media Player's ubiquity. * * *

Absence of objective justification

[Microsoft claimed that efficiency gains outweighed any anticompetitive effects; that consumers want one product, pre-installed; that the tying produces efficiencies and enhances technical performance; that adding components piecemeal can create conflicts and cause malfunction; and that removing components degrades the system. The court held that the Commission did not err in rejecting all of these arguments on the facts.]

* * *

QUESTIONS AND COMMENTS

1. How would U.S. courts have answered the interoperability question? the bundling question? For insight on the interoperability question, see *Trinko,* supra p. 249. For insight on the bundling question, see *Microsoft* (U.S.), supra p. 310, and *Illinois Tool Works*, infra, p. 684.

2. Thomas Barnett, then U.S. Assistant Attorney General for Antitrust, issued the following statement on September 17, 2007, immediately after the release of the European judgment:

"In light of the United States' own antitrust case and judgment against Microsoft, and the importance of the computer industry to consumers and to the global economy, the United States has a particular interest in today's CFI [Court of First Instance] decision. The decision is both lengthy and complex, as befits the importance and difficulty of the issues raised by the EC's case against Microsoft. It will therefore be some time before the full impact of today's decision on antitrust policy in Europe will be apparent. We are ... however, concerned that the standard applied to unilateral conduct by the CFI, rather than helping consumers, may have the unfortunate consequence of harming consumers by chilling innovation and discouraging competition.

"In the United States, the antitrust laws are enforced to protect consumers by protecting competition, not competitors. In the absence of demonstrable consumer harm, all companies, including dominant firms, are encouraged to compete vigorously. U.S. courts recognize the potential benefits to consumers when a company, including a dominant company, makes unilateral business decisions, for example to add features to its popular products or license its intellectual property to rivals, or to refuse to do so."

Explain how (according to Barnett) European law protects competitors and U.S. law protects consumers. Identify two or three paragraphs of the CFI (now General Court) judgment that Barnett would cite to make his point. What would be the response of the Director General of the Competition Directorate of the European Commission? Is one perspective sounder than the other?

3. In October 2007 Microsoft announced that it would not appeal from the CFI judgment and agreed to comply with the 2004 Commission decision. It agreed to make available to server software developers including open-source developers the protocols they need to interoperate as smoothly with Microsoft's operating system as Microsoft's own server software works with its operating system. It agreed further: Open source software developers will be able to access the protocols at no cost, and Microsoft will not assert patent rights against them. Commercial developers, such as IBM and Red Hat, must pay a license fee of 0.4% of revenues. However, those who do not need the protocols that involve patents will be able to obtain a license by paying a one-time nominal payment of 10,000 euros. Microsoft had already complied with the order regarding the bundling of the media player requiring that, if it chooses to bundle, it also must offer an unbundled version of its operating system.

4. What effect, do you predict, will these remedies have on competition? on innovation? on Microsoft?

5. Microsoft is a global company. If it harms the competition process and consumers in the United States, it may do so worldwide. Are proceedings against Microsoft a legitimate use of European antitrust powers? Does it matter whether the European law is or is not compatible with U.S. law? Does it matter whether European law does (or may be thought to) "protect competitors"? Does it matter whether the home country of a dominant firm may have (or may be seen to have) an incentive to protect its national champion?

6. In December 2008, after several years' study, the European Commission issued a Communication entitled "Guidance on the Commission's Enforcement Priorities in Applying Article 82 EC Treaty to Abusive Exclusionary Conduct by Dominant Undertakings." This Communication sets forth the analysis likely to be used by the European Commission in analyzing the range of exclusionary practices that may amount to an abuse of dominance under Treaty Article 82, now 102—the counterpart to Section 2 of the Sherman Act. These practices include exclusive dealing, exclusive purchasing, fidelity rebates, refusals to deal, and margin squeezes. The Guidance paper may be found at the link at *http://ec.europa.eu/competition/antitrust/art82/index.html*. The document confirms that the Commission's approach is economic and effects-based, and that exclusionary conduct harming *consumers* will be prioritized. Much of the analysis is virtually the same as U.S. analysis. In difficult areas, however, European analysis is more likely to lean on the side of protecting the competitive structure of the market than on the side of protecting the market from "erroneous" antitrust interventions.

d. The Intel Case, and the Revitalization of Section 5 of the Federal Trade Commission Act

Background: The Section 2 Report

Meanwhile, in 2008, at the end of the administration of President George W. Bush, the Justice Department Antitrust Division issued a report: "Competition and Monopoly: Single Firm Conduct Under Section 2 of the Sherman Act." The Report was intended to give guidance as to when conduct runs afoul of the law. The Report may be found at *http://www.usdoj.gov/atr/public/reports/236681.htm*.

The Report took a conservative view of the law, preferring to rely on business judgment than on antitrust intervention, and was centrally concerned that the prosecution of Section 2 actions would chill competitive conduct of dominant firms.

At the outset of the Obama Administration, the then new antitrust chief, Assistant Attorney General Christine Varney, withdrew the Report, saying:

> [E]ffective today, May 11, 2009, the Section 2 Report no longer represents the policy of the Department of Justice with regard to antitrust enforcement under Section 2 of the Sherman Act. The Report and its conclusions should not be used as guidance by courts, antitrust practitioners, and the business community....
>
> ... The Report ... reflects an excessive concern with the risks of over-deterrence and a resulting preference for an overly lenient approach to enforcement. The failing of this approach is that it effectively straightjackets antitrust enforcers and courts from redressing monopolistic abuses, thereby allowing all but the most bold and predatory conduct to go unpunished and undeterred.
>
> While the Department is not proposing any one specific test to govern all Section 2 matters at this time, I believe the balanced analyses reflected in the leading cases interpreting the reaches of the Sherman Act provide important guidance in this regard. In particular, leading Section 2 cases—from *Lorain Journal v. United States* to *Aspen Skiing Co. v. Aspen Highlands Skiing Corp.* to *United States v. Microsoft*—highlight a common concern regarding the harmful effects of a monopolist's exclusionary or predatory conduct on competition and, ultimately, consumers. Reinvigorated Section 2 enforcement will thus require the Division to go "back to the basics" and evaluate single-firm conduct against these tried and true standards that set forth clear limitations on how monopoly firms are permitted to behave....

Christine Varney, Vigorous Antitrust Enforcement in this Challenging Era, May 11, 2009, *http://www.justice.gov/atr/public/speeches/245711.htm*

Thus, the Section 2 Report was withdrawn. But the Supreme Court had already tightened the standards for proof of Section 2 violations.

There was, however, another tool lying in the antitrust enforcers' tool chest. This was Section 5 of the Federal Trade Commission Act. Section 5 of the FTC Act forbids "unfair methods of competition." For years, the FTC had used Section 5 authority to reprehend only conduct that would also violate the Sherman Act, Section 1 or 2. Now, thought the FTC officials, it was time to dust off the tool and use FTC Act Section 5 to catch conduct they regarded as anticompetitive but which was now possibly beyond reach of the Sherman Act.

The *Intel* case.

Intel is the largest manufacturer of the microchips inside computers. These chips are described as the brains of the computer. AMD was its closest rival. When AMD finally made an attractive new chip, Intel launched a series of strategies, allegedly including exclusive contracts, fidelity rebates, and deception and coercion of big customers not to use the new chip, in order to fence out AMD.

An FTC investigation of Intel had been pending for some time. Meanwhile, the European Commission brought proceedings against Intel and found that it had abused its dominance; it imposed a cease and desist order and a remarkably large fine (1.06 billion euros) on Intel. *http://europa.eu/rapid/pressReleasesAction.do?reference=IP/09/745*. Moreover, in November 2009, the New York State Attorney General sued Intel for violating the Sherman Act and New York State law, alleging "bribery and coercion to maintain a stranglehold on the market."

Finally, on December 16, 2009, the U.S. FTC brought an administrative complaint against Intel. It brought its case principally under Section 5 of the Federal Trade Commission, not limiting its claim (as it usually did) to a violation of Section 2 of the Sherman Act. The FTC Act prohibits unfair acts and practices and unfair methods of competition. Thus, it is broader than the Sherman Act. Unlike judgments enforcing the Sherman Act, orders of the FTC, even if affirmed by the federal courts, cannot be invoked by private parties as proof of a violation.

The FTC's statement on bringing the case, the statement of two Commissioners on the reasons for using Section 5 of the Federal Trade Commission Act, and the concurring and dissenting statement of Commissioner Rosch follow.

FTC CHALLENGES INTEL'S DOMINANCE OF WORLDWIDE MICROPROCESSOR MARKETS

FTC Charges Anticompetitive Tactics Have Stifled Innovation and Harmed Consumers

FTC Press Release, Dec. 16, 2009.

The Federal Trade Commission today sued Intel Corp., the world's leading computer chip maker, charging that the company has illegally used its dominant market position for a decade to stifle competition and strengthen its monopoly.

In its complaint, the FTC alleges that Intel has waged a systematic campaign to shut out rivals' competing microchips by cutting off their access to the marketplace. In the process, Intel deprived consumers of choice and innovation in the microchips that comprise the computers' central processing unit, or CPU. These chips are critical components that often are referred to as the "brains" of a computer.

According to the FTC complaint, Intel's anticompetitive tactics were designed to put the brakes on superior competitive products that threatened its monopoly in the CPU microchip market. Over the last decade, this strategy has succeeded in maintaining the Intel monopoly at the expense of consumers, who have been denied access to potentially superior, non-Intel CPU chips and lower prices, the complaint states.

> "Intel has engaged in a deliberate campaign to hamstring competitive threats to its monopoly," said Richard A. Feinstein, Director of the FTC's Bureau of Competition. "It's been running roughshod over the principles of fair play and the laws protecting competition on the merits. The Commission's action today seeks to remedy the damage that Intel has done to competition, innovation, and, ultimately, the American consumer."

The FTC's administrative complaint charges that Intel carried out its anticompetitive campaign using threats and rewards aimed at the world's largest computer manufacturers, including Dell, Hewlett–Packard, and IBM, to coerce them not to buy rival computer CPU chips. Intel also used this practice, known as exclusive or restrictive dealing, to prevent computer makers from marketing any machines with non-Intel computer chips.

In addition, allegedly, Intel secretly redesigned key software, known as a compiler, in a way that deliberately stunted the performance of competitors' CPU chips. Intel told its customers and the public that software performed better on Intel CPUs than on competitors' CPUs, but the company deceived them by failing to disclose that these differences were due largely or entirely to Intel's compiler design.

Having succeeded in slowing adoption of competing CPU chips over the past decade until it could catch up to competitors like Advanced Micro Devices, Intel allegedly once again finds itself falling behind the competition—this time in the critical market for graphics processing units, commonly known as GPUs, as well as some other related markets. These products have lessened the need for CPUs, and therefore pose a threat to Intel's monopoly power.

Intel has responded to this competitive challenge by embarking on a similar anticompetitive strategy, which aims to preserve its CPU monopoly by smothering potential competition from GPU chips such as those made by Nvidia, the FTC complaint charges. As part of this latest campaign, Intel misled and deceived potential competitors in order to protect its monopoly. The complaint alleges that there also is a dangerous probability that Intel's unfair methods of competition could allow it to extend its monopoly into the GPU chip markets.

According to the FTC's complaint, Intel's anticompetitive tactics violate Section 5 of the FTC Act, which is broader than the antitrust laws and prohibits unfair methods of competition, and deceptive acts and practices in commerce. Critically, unlike an antitrust violation, a violation of Section 5 cannot be used to establish liability for plaintiffs to seek triple damages in private litigation against the same defendant. The complaint also alleges that Intel engaged in illegal monopolization, attempted monopolization and monopoly maintenance, also in violation of Section 5 of the FTC Act.

To remedy the anticompetitive damage alleged in the complaint, the FTC is seeking an order which includes provisions that would prevent Intel from using threats, bundled prices, or other offers to encourage exclusive deals, hamper competition, or unfairly manipulate the prices of its CPU or GPU chips. The FTC also may seek an order prohibiting Intel from unreasonably excluding or inhibiting the sale of competitive CPUs or GPUs, and prohibiting Intel from making or distributing products that impair the performance—or apparent performance—of non-Intel CPUs or GPUs. * * *

Statement of Chairman Leibowitz and Commissioner Rosch

After a multi-year investigation, extensive discussions within the Commission—including an unprecedented four Commission meetings—and multiple meetings with Intel Corporation ("Intel") and other interested parties, the Commission has voted unanimously to challenge an alleged course of conduct undertaken by Intel. Broadly speaking, the complaint alleges that Intel fell behind in the race for technological superiority in a number of markets and resorted to a wide range of anticompetitive conduct, including deception and coercion, to stall competitors until it could catch up. If the allegations in the complaint are true, Intel's actions over a period of years and continuing up until today have diminished competition and harmed consumers.

The complaint challenges Intel's conduct as an unfair method of competition, both in violation of the Sherman Act and also as a "stand-alone" violation of Section 5 of the FTC Act, i.e. as an unfair method of competition independent of the Sherman Act. We focus this statement on the stand-alone Section 5 unfair method of competition claim because liability under that standard has the potential to protect consumers while at the same time limiting Intel's susceptibility to private treble damages cases.

Despite the long history of Section 5, until recently the Commission has not pursued free-standing unfair method of competition claims outside of the most well-accepted areas, partly because the antitrust laws themselves have in the past proved flexible and capable of reaching most anticompetitive conduct. However, concern over class actions, treble damages awards, and costly jury trials have caused many courts in recent decades to limit the reach of antitrust. The result has been that some conduct harmful to consumers may be given a "free pass" under antitrust jurisprudence, not because the conduct is benign but out of a fear that the harm might be outweighed by the collateral consequences created by private enforcement. For this reason, we have seen an increasing amount of potentially anticompetitive conduct that is not easily reached under the antitrust laws, and it is more important than ever that the Commission actively consider whether it may be appropriate to exercise its full Congressional authority under Section 5.

It has been understood for many years that Section 5 extends beyond the borders of the antitrust laws, and its broad reach is beyond dispute. Indeed, that broad authority is woven into the very framework of the Commission itself. When Congress passed the Federal Trade Commission Act in 1914, it specifically decided to create an agency that has broad jurisdiction to stop unfair methods of competition, and it balanced that broad authority by limiting the remedies available to the Commission.

Congress enacted Section 5 in light of court decisions whose reach had limited the effectiveness of the Sherman Act in contravention of Congressional intent. Thus, Section 5 was clearly a Congressional effort to bolster enforcement and provide protection for competition and consumers beyond the parameters of the Sherman Act. In fact, the Court's *Sperry & Hutchinson* holding regarding the broad sweep of Section 5 authority was based in part on the clear legislative history of the statute....

Of course, even though the Commission has broad authority under Section 5, the Commission is well aware of its duty to enforce Section 5 responsibly. We take seriously our mandate to find a violation of Section 5 only when it is proven that the conduct at issue has not only been unfair to rivals in the market but, more important, is likely to harm consumers, taking into account any efficiency justifications for the conduct in question. Section 5 is clearly broader than the antitrust laws, but it is not without boundaries, and the Commission will clearly describe and stay within those boundaries if this case comes before it to review. * * *

Concurring and Dissenting Statement of Commissioner J. Thomas Rosch

I.

I concur in the issuance of a Section 5 complaint challenging an alleged course of conduct by Intel Corporation ("Intel") to maintain monopoly power in the markets for central processing units ("CPUs") in computers and at least near-monopoly power in markets for computer graphics products. In accordance with Section 5, I have concluded that there is reason to believe that the alleged course of conduct occurred and that issuance of a pure Section 5 complaint challenging that alleged conduct would be in the public interest.... The Supreme Court has held that Section 5 is broader than the Sherman or Clayton Acts, which can be enforced by both private and public plaintiffs.... However, the reach of Section 5, like any other statute, is not unlimited. I think the Commission can and should define those limitations as they apply to this case.

In my view, there are four considerations that warrant the application of Section 5 here. First, this is not a case where harm to competition can easily be segregated from harm to competitors. The markets alleged in this case and Intel's alleged position in those markets are extraordinarily concentrated: the CPU markets are duopoly markets in which Intel and Advanced Micro Devices ("AMD") are the only meaningful participants; the graphics products markets are likewise highly concentrated markets in which Intel, AMD, and Nvidia Corporation ("Nvidia") are the only meaningful competitors. Significantly, Intel has monopoly power in the CPU markets and near-monopoly power in the computer graphics product markets and, judging from the allegations in the complaint, the entry barriers surrounding these markets are remarkably high. Under those unique circumstances, the oft-repeated admonition that the Sherman and Clayton Acts protect competition, not competitors, and the federal courts' attendant disinclination to protect competitors in cases brought under those statutes, do not fit well. If the firm with monopoly or near-monopoly power (here, allegedly Intel) engages in an exclusionary and unjustifiable course of conduct that hurts its only competitor in the CPU markets (here, allegedly AMD) or its only two competitors in the computer graphics product markets (here, allegedly AMD and Nvidia), given the uncommonly high entry barriers, that exclusionary conduct harms competition too, by inhibiting those rivals from constraining the exercise of monopoly power.

Second, although Intel's alleged conduct led to higher prices in the CPU markets, that alleged conduct can still be within the Commission's Section 5 powers even if Intel cannot be said to have caused price increases. To be sure, most conventional Section 2 cases alleging monopoly maintenance or attempted monopolization rise or fall on proof of higher prices—if for no other reason than that kind of injury is easiest to measure. But that is not the only kind of consumer injury with which a law enforcement agency like the Commission should be concerned. The Commission must also be concerned with whether a course of conduct by a firm with monopoly power reduces consumer choice by reducing alternatives. That is true whether the "consumer" suffering the reduction in choice is an original equipment manufacturer ("OEM") or an end user of computer equipment that buys equipment from the OEM. Thus, if and to the extent that an exclusionary course of conduct by a firm with monopoly power results in that less measurable form of consumer injury, Section 5 is the most appropriate vehicle for the analysis, and the Commission, with its expertise and experience, is the most appropriate plaintiff to make that determination.

Third, the complaint here alleges that Intel engaged in an exclusionary course of conduct. That is a claim with clearly identifiable elements that most logically resides in the Commission's Section 5 authority. Simply put, in my view it is improper to slice and dice each constituent part of the alleged course of conduct to determine whether it, standing alone, had the purpose or effect to hinder competition and injure consumers in violation of Section 2: the constituent parts did not stand alone, and both their effects on Intel's few alleged rivals and their consequent impact on consumer choice can only be assessed by examining the effects of Intel's alleged course of conduct as a whole. Although a number of courts have disparaged "course of conduct" claims made under Section 2 as mere "monopoly broth" claims or claims that "0 plus 0 plus 0 equal 1," that militates in favor of the Commission exercising its discretion and expertise to use Section 5 to reach such a course of conduct. Indeed, under those circumstances, a Section 5 "course of conduct" claim may be viewed much as the "invitation to collude" cases that the Commission has pursued as pure Section 5 cases in order to reach conduct that the Sherman Act may not otherwise reach. Lest there be any misunderstanding, Intel must be given the opportunity to show that any injury to competition or to consumers was offset by efficiencies that it reasonably could have achieved only by engaging in the conduct causing those consequences. But that defense does not justify altogether eschewing a course of conduct claim under Section 5.

Fourth, I believe that Intel's intent here is relevant in assessing its liability. The Second Circuit, for example, has held that a respondent's state of mind is not only relevant, but must be taken into account, to determine whether the respondent's conduct constitutes an "unfair method of competition" under Section 5. *E.I. DuPont de Nemours & Co. v. FTC*, 729 F.2d 128, 138–40 (2d Cir. 1984). Properly read, I think that *Aspen Skiing Co. v. Aspen Highlands Skiing Corp.*, 472 U.S. 585 (1985), holds that such an intent would be relevant in a Section 2 case. *Id.* at 610–11 (defendant's practices "support[ed] an inference that [the defendant] was not motivated by efficiency concerns and that it was willing to sacrifice short-run benefits and consumer goodwill in exchange for a perceived long-run impact on its smaller rival"). Yet some Section 2 cases have said that an analysis of the defendant's intent is irrelevant in a Section 2 case. Indeed, it can be argued that the Commission's antitrust expertise and experience makes it a more dispassionate and superior judge of that evidence than a lay jury in a Section 2 case.

II.

Although I concur in the issuance of a complaint based on pure Section 5 claims, I respectfully dissent insofar as the complaint also contains Section 2 "tag-along" claims. To be clear, my reasons for doing so are not based on the fact that I lack a "reason to believe" that a Section 2 violation has occurred; instead, I dissent from the addition of the Section 2 claims on public policy grounds.

First, I see no advantage to adding the Section 2 claims. To be sure, there is favorable Section 2 case law that supports each constituent part of the course of conduct that is pled....

Second, it cannot be said that including the Section 2 claims (as opposed to a clearly defined Section 5 course of conduct claim) means that the outcome of this litigation will provide more predictability to the business community by somehow providing better notice of the type of conduct that the antitrust laws preclude.... A well-defined Section 5 course of conduct claim can provide just as much guidance.

Third, and most importantly, the collateral consequences of including any Section 2 claims are very unfavorable for both Intel and the Commission. Intel currently faces the treble damage suits filed by the New York Attorney General under Section 2 in the United States District Court in Delaware in addition to a number of Section 2 treble damage class actions that have been filed there. The Commission should not enable those plaintiffs to free ride off of the Commission's work. Nor should it put itself in a position where an unfavorable outcome in those cases may be cited against it. Neither of those consequences can occur if the Commission proceeds solely under Section 5....

Beyond that, as my colleagues, Chairman Leibowitz and more recently Commissioner Kovacic have pointed out, the Supreme Court has steadily been "shrinking" the ambit of the Sherman Act both procedurally and substantively. *See, e.g., Bell Atl. Corp. v. Twombly*, 550 U.S. 544, 558–61 (2007); *Credit Suisse Sec. (USA) v. Billing*, 551 U.S. 264, 281–82 (2007). By all accounts, these changes are, partially at least, due to the Court's concern about the Sherman Act's application by juries and generalist federal district courts. Regardless of whether one shares that concern about private Sherman Act enforcement, it is undeniable that this jurisprudence "slops over" to public enforcement. That is so because insofar as the federal agencies prosecute their cases under the Sherman Act, they must proceed under the same statutes that private plaintiffs invoke. That consequence, however, can be minimized—if not avoided altogether—if the Commission proceeds under Section 5 alone.... * * *

Intel denied the charges, stating that it has always fairly and lawfully competed; that competition in the market was vigorous and dynamic; that chip prices had been declining rapidly and more so than for any other product tracked by the U.S., and that AMD's mismanagement had brought its troubles on itself. *http://www.ftc.gov/os/adjpro/d9341/091231respanswertocmplt.pdf*. Intel and its supporters also questioned the FTC's use of Section 5 of the FTCA unhinged to the Sherman Act, and saw it as overregulation and micro-management bound to retard innovation and harm consumers.

QUESTIONS AND COMMENTS

1. Consider the FTC's specific allegations. What would it have to prove to win its case? Must it prove more than that Intel made exclusive contracts with chip buyers? that Intel gave discounts for exclusive or fidelity contracts and those discounts hurt AMD, taking away some market share?

2. What is the significance of the constantly declining prices and increasing output of the chips?

3. How compelling was Intel's argument that Section 5 enforcement unlinked to the limits of the Sherman Act will harm competition and innovation?

The FTC settled the *Intel* case on the terms described in the following press release.

FTC SETTLES CHARGES OF ANTICOMPETITIVE CONDUCT AGAINST INTEL

Press Release, Aug. 4, 2010

Provisions are Designed to Foster Competition in the Computer Chip Business

The Federal Trade Commission approved a settlement with Intel Corp. that resolves charges the company illegally stifled competition in the market for computer chips. Intel has agreed to provisions that will open the door to renewed competition and prevent Intel from suppressing competition in the future.

The settlement goes beyond the terms applied to Intel in previous actions against the company and will help restore competition that was lost as a result of Intel's alleged past anticompetitive tactics. At the same time, the settlement will leave the company room to innovate and offer competitive pricing.

"This case demonstrates that the FTC is willing to challenge anticompetitive conduct by even the most powerful companies in the fastest-moving industries," said Chairman Job Leibowitz. "By accepting this settlement, we open the door to competition today and address Intel's anticompetitive conduct in a way that may not have been available in a final judgment years from now. Everyone, including Intel, gets a greater degree of certainty about the rules of the road going forward, which allows all the companies in this dynamic industry to move ahead and build better, more innovative products."

The FTC settlement applies to Central Processing Units, Graphics Processing Units and chipsets and prohibits Intel from using threats, bundled prices, or other offers to exclude or hamper competition or otherwise unreasonably inhibit the sale of competitive CPUs or GPUs. The settlement also prohibits Intel from deceiving computer manufacturers about the performance of non-Intel CPUs or GPUs.

The FTC settlement goes beyond those reached in previous antitrust cases against Intel in a number of ways. For example, the FTC settlement order protects competition and not any single competitor in the CPU, graphics, and chipset markets. It also addresses Intel's disclosures related to its compiler—a product that plays an important role in CPU performance. The settlement order also ensures that manufacturers of complementary products such as discrete GPUs will be assured access to Intel's CPU for the next six years.

The FTC sued Intel in December 2009 alleging that the company used anticompetitive tactics to cut off rivals' access to the marketplace and deprive consumers of choice and innovation in the microchips that comprise computers' central processing unit, or CPU. These chips are critical components that often are referred to as the "brains" of a computer. The action also challenged Intel's conduct in markets for graphics processing units and other chips.

The FTC alleged that Intel's anticompetitive practices violated Section 5 of the FTC Act, which is broader than the antitrust laws and prohibits unfair methods of competition and deceptive acts and practices in commerce. Unlike an antitrust violation, a violation of Section 5 cannot be used to establish liability for plaintiffs to seek triple damages in private litigation against the same defendant.

Under the settlement, Intel will be prohibited from:

- conditioning benefits to computer makers in exchange for their promise to buy chips from Intel exclusively or to refuse to buy chips from others; and
- retaliating against computer makers if they do business with non-Intel suppliers by withholding benefits from them.

In addition, the FTC settlement order will require Intel to:

- modify its intellectual property agreements with AMD, Nvidia, and Via so that those companies have more freedom to consider mergers or joint ventures with other companies, without the threat of being sued by Intel for patent infringement;
- offer to extend Via's x86 licensing agreement for five years beyond the current agreement, which expires in 2013;
- maintain a key interface, known as the PCI Express Bus, for at least six years in a way that will not limit the performance of graphics processing chips. These assurances will provide incentives to manufacturers of complementary, and potentially competitive, products to Intel's CPUs to continue to innovate; and
- disclose to software developers that Intel computer compilers discriminate between Intel chips and non-Intel chips, and that

they may not register all the features of non-Intel chips. Intel also will have to reimburse all software vendors who want to recompile their software using a non-Intel compiler.

The FTC adopted the consent order on Nov. 2, 2010, with a modification to allow Intel to manufacture and sell a chip that was in development and did not contain an interface otherwise required by the decree.

QUESTIONS AND COMMENTS

1. Comment on the FTC consent order in view of the theory of the case. Is it addressed to the problems of the complaint? Is it likely to solve the problems identified?

2. Should Section 5 of the FTC Act be construed to prohibit more conduct than the Sherman Act prohibits? You have read the Commissioners' arguments in the affirmative. What are the arguments in the negative? What do you think?

Problem

Abbott Labs made a popular cholesterol-reducing, capsule-form drug, TriCor. When the patent was about to expire and two firms were well positioned to enter the field with generic versions, Abbott Labs changed the capsule to a tablet and made minor improvements (including effectiveness of the tablet even when taken without food). It secured FDA approval of the tablet, listed its new formulation and new patent in the "Orange Book" of approved drug products, and removed the TriCor capsule formulation from the database that identifies FDA approved drugs. The effect of the removal was that pharmacies could not fill prescriptions for TriCor capsules with generic formulations. These moves pulled the rug out from under the would be generic entrants. The generic competitors and purchasers sue Abbott for preventing low-priced generic substitution by manipulating the regulatory law. Abbott Labs moves to dismiss.

Student 1: Argue for Abbott Labs.

Student 2: Argue for the generics, Gena and Teva.

Students 3, 4 and 5: You are the judges. Press the lawyers to tell you: By what standard or principle should this case be decided? Ask the generics' lawyer: What is the appropriate relief?

Problem

Search is the critical way in which computer users navigate the web. The object of a search engine, from the user's point of view, is to be directed as quickly as possible to the websites most likely to be relevant to the user's inquiry. Google pioneered search. It has collected trillions of pieces of data from the over one trillion websites, and it answers queries in megaseconds.

Google accounts for 79% of searches in the United States and 94% in the world, with Bing (Microsoft)/Yahoo a distant second. Google accounts for 80% of paid search advertising in the United States, and more in the world.

Recently, Google has expanded from being a pure search engine into provision of other services that involve the provision of information (e.g., Google News and YouTube) and services in specialized areas, such as maps and flight search.

Microsoft has complained of Google's practices to the U.S. Federal Trade Commission and to the Competition Directorate of the European Commission.

Allegations include:

1. Rigging search results. Google allegedly pushes natural (unpaid) results down to the bottom of the first results page or to a second page. Since 80% of users never click on the second page, website owners seeking more visibility are forced to spend more on Google advertising. When they do so, the Google algorithm moves up their positioning.

2. Rigging search results against Google competitors, such as maps and flight search. The competitors allege that Google slants its algorithms to position Google-owned or related services favorably and to position the competitors unfavorably.

3. Google puts links to its own products and services above the natural search results. Users are deceived into thinking that these are natural results of the search rather than self-interested results.

4. Google has a practice of scraping content from other websites and using it on its own pages; for example, taking content from TripAdvisor and using it on Google Fight Search. When TripAdvisor complained, Google responded that, if it stopped scraping, TripAdvisor would not appear as a result on any Google search because the process was integral (gathering information for Google search).

As a result of these practices, and in view of Google's using the same practices on the increasingly popular mobile search (for which Google accounts for about 98%), it is claimed, the price of search advertising will go up, consumers are and will be deceived, competitors will be set back by competition not on the merits, and innovation will be reduced.

[See Thomas O. Barnett, Testimony at Hearing before the Senate Judiciary Committee on Antitrust, Competition Policy and Consumer Rights, Sept. 21, 2011]

Google denies all facts material to a violation and insists that its algorithms select results neutrally to respond to users' queries.

Student 1: You are on the staff of the Federal Trade Commission. Argue to the Director of the Bureau of Competition that serious issues of possible antitrust violations have been raised and highlight the points on which you need more information in order to bring a case. Prepare a list of the information you need.

Student 2: You, too, are on the staff of the FTC. Argue to the Director of the Bureau of Competition that it should close its pending investigation against Google.

Student 3: You are the Director of the Bureau of Competition. Question your staff members. Then give your assessment.

10. SUMMING UP: WHAT STANDARDS FOR EXCLUSIONARY CONDUCT?

U.S. antitrust law does not have a single standard for analyzing exclusionary conduct. In 2004, the President of the United States convened a Commission to conduct a comprehensive review of the antitrust laws and to make recommendations for their modernization. The Antitrust Modernization Commission, Deborah Garza, chair, submitted its Report and Recommendations in 2007. Here is its summary and analysis of standards for Section 2:

Antitrust Modernization Commission Report and Recommendations

April 2007

(footnotes omitted)

* * *

Chapter I. C

Exclusionary Conduct

* * *

2. Tests for Particular Types of Conduct or a Single Test for All Conduct

15. **Additional clarity and improvement in Sherman Act Section 2 legal standards are desirable, particularly with respect to areas where there is currently a lack of clear and consistent standards, such as bundling and whether and in what circumstances (if any) a monopolist has a duty to deal with rivals.**

Many commentators are skeptical that any one legal standard should be used to evaluate the wide variety of different types of conduct that may be challenged under Section 2. Others, however, have urged the use of a single test. Two proposals—the "no economic sense" and "profit sacrifice" tests—have their genesis in the predatory pricing test, which implicitly defines "competition on the merits" as pricing that is above an appropriate measure of the defendant's costs. Those and other proposals are discussed below.

"No Economic Sense" Test. The DOJ has advocated the use of a "no economic sense" test, which asks "whether, on the basis of information available to a firm at the time of the challenged conduct, the challenged conduct would have made economic sense even if it did not reduce or eliminate competition." The test condemns conduct only when its anticompetitive objective is unambiguous because the conduct would not have been undertaken "but for" the prospect of obtaining or maintaining monopoly power. Although the DOJ has advanced this test in several cases, including *Microsoft*, *Dentsply*, and *Trinko*, no court has ever adopted it.

Proponents contend the test is consistent with existing case law and "can be administered effectively by courts and businesses alike" because the test essentially focuses on the economic rationality or profitability of the defendant's conduct from the defendant's perspective at the time the defendant decides whether to undertake a particular course of conduct. Although this test may not capture all anticompetitive single-firm conduct, proponents believe underinclusiveness is preferable to requirements for complex evidentiary judgments.

Others counter that the test can fail to capture substantially anticompetitive conduct by focusing exclusively on the profitability of the conduct for the defendant. Thus, the test fails to examine the challenged conduct's effects on consumer welfare, critics assert. The test exculpates conduct that offers some minimal efficiencies—that is, that makes *some* economic sense—even where the conduct may cause disproportionately great anticompetitive effects. In addition, in exclusive dealing cases the application of the "no economic sense" test is arguably unintelligible because exclusive dealing "makes economic sense" for the defendant "precisely through the mechanism of exclusion." "In most cases, there is no way to separate the economic benefit to the defendant from the exclusionary impact on rivals." This criticism suggests the test may be overinclusive as well as underinclusive.

"Profit Sacrifice" Test. The "profit sacrifice" test is closely related to the "no economic sense" test. One variant asks whether the defendant has sacrificed immediate profits as part of a strategy whose profitability depends on the recoupment of those profits through the exclusion of rivals. Although it has not specifically adopted this test, the Supreme Court has asked this question in refusal-to-deal cases, noting, for example, that the defendant in *Aspen* "was willing to sacrifice short-run benefits and goodwill in exchange for a perceived long-run impact on its smaller rival." Another variant asks "whether the allegedly anticompetitive conduct would be profitable for the defendant and would make good business sense even if it did not exclude rivals and thereby create or preserve

market power for the defendant."

As with the "no economic sense" test, proponents maintain the "profit sacrifice" test is easy to administer and provides clear guidance to businesses, thereby increasing the likelihood that businesses will engage in procompetitive conduct that other legal tests might misconstrue as anticompetitive. The test does not condemn all conduct that might reduce welfare overall, but proponents judge the test to be preferable to "market-wide balancing tests."

Opponents apply basically the same criticisms to the "profit sacrifice" test as to the "no economic sense" test. In particular, one commentator argues the test is "both too broad and too narrow." The test is too broad, this critic contends, because it could condemn a firm "invest[ing] heavily in designing a better mousetrap that, once marketed, will ruin rivals or significantly limit their sales." The test is too narrow, he asserts, "because some exclusionary practices don't involve sacrifice at all." He agrees the test is dispositive in predatory pricing cases, however, and also finds the test "quite helpful in cases involving unilateral refusals to deal."

Less Efficient Competitor Test. Judge Richard A. Posner has proposed that an unreasonably exclusionary practice is one that is "likely in the circumstances to exclude from the defendant's market an equally or more efficient competitor." Proponents see value in this test, but caution that it, too, may be too narrow "where the dominant firm is able to keep the output of rivals inefficiently low by engaging in practices that confer no significant social benefits." Others point out that exclusion of an inefficient rival may harm consumer welfare if the rival is excluded before it reaches minimum efficient scale, or if the less efficient rival has been keeping prices in the relevant market below the monopoly level. Critics also raise concern that the test may be very difficult administratively. Nonetheless, commentators and courts have found this test useful in evaluating bundled discounts or rebates.

Balancing Test. In its *Microsoft* decision, the D.C. Circuit employed a balancing test, which examines both competitive effects and efficiencies, to assess claims under Section 2. That test requires a plaintiff first to establish that the monopolist's conduct had an " 'anticompetitive effect.' That is, it must harm the competitive *process* and thereby harm consumers." Once the plaintiff establishes a prima facie case, to avoid liability the defendant must provide a procompetitive justification for its conduct, that is, "a nonpretextual claim that its conduct is indeed a form of competition on the merits because it involves, for example, greater efficiency or enhanced consumer appeal." If the defendant makes this showing, then the plaintiff either must rebut the claim of procompetitive benefits or show that the anticompetitive harm nevertheless "outweighs" those benefits. Proponents point out this is the basic rule of reason test that courts have applied for many years, and continue to apply, in Section 1 and Section 2 cases. They contend that use of this test is necessary to answer the basic question of whether the challenged conduct, on balance, harmed consumer welfare.

Opponents criticize this test as too complex and difficult to administer. They argue that, because businesses will be uncertain of how their course of conduct might be judged, they will be reluctant to undertake procompetitive conduct. Proponents respond that other tests, including the "no economic sense" and "profit sacrifice" tests, are equally complex and less accurate.

As this brief review of possible tests for evaluating conduct under Section 2 suggests, they each seek to identify conduct that harms consumer welfare. Some tests place greater value on the avoidance of chilling procompetitive conduct and undue enforcement costs than on ensuring that the test captures all or most instances of anticompetitive conduct. Others emphasize the importance of focusing on consumer welfare effects and contend that accuracy can be achieved without perverse influences on firms' incentives or undue enforcement costs.

Thus far, no consensus exists that any one test can suffice to assess all types of conduct that may be challenged under Section 2. The current test for predatory pricing, for example, works well in that context, but problems have been identified with the application of its progeny—the "no economic sense" and "profit sacrifice" tests—in some other contexts. The more extensive inquiry mandated by the *Microsoft* balancing test may be appropriate in some circumstances, but, as exemplified by the case of predatory pricing, is not necessarily warranted or desirable for all types of conduct challenged under Section 2. Some contend that the best approach is to develop different tests for different types of conduct.

As courts, antitrust agencies, and commentators continue to refine the antitrust standards for conduct challenged under Section 2, a focal point for their assessment should be whether a particular test is the one most likely to protect consumer welfare in the context of the type of conduct at issue. To answer this question will require, among other things, an evaluation of whether a particular test is likely to overdeter procompetitive, or underdeter anticompetitive, conduct. Particular attention should be given to long-run, as well as short-run, consumer interests. For example, any Section 2 test for refusals to deal with a rival should reflect proper consideration of consumers' long-run interests in maintaining firms' incentives to invest in valuable competitive assets—incentives that could be significantly diminished by forced sharing of assets with a rival in particular circumstances.

E. MONOPOLIZATION AND GLOBALIZATION

The global economy has produced two divergent forces. On the one hand, the opening up of the world to global competition increases the sources of competitive pressures and interactions, making it less likely for monopoly to emerge and be sustained. On the other hand, new technologies and network effects increase possibilities for cross border consequences of exclusionary practices. And with the adoption of the effects test (reach of national law to offshore acts based on market effects) around the world, we see challenges to the same or similar dominant firm practices by more than one jurisdiction. The U.S. and the EU proceedings against Microsoft are a famous example; challenges to Microsoft's various strategies were launched in other countries as well, including Japan, South Korea, and Taiwan.

There is much convergence but also a margin of divergence between the U.S. law of monopolization and the monopolization or abuse of dominance laws of many other nations. The United States is probably the jurisdiction most concerned that antitrust enforcement will protect inefficient firms from hard competition, and is more likely than some others to find an exclusionary practice to be predominantly procompetitive. EU law shows more systematic concern with dominant firm action that "abuses" competitors; for example, action that blocks competitors' pathways to contest markets and diminishes *their* incentives to invest and invent. Yet other jurisdictions, such as Indonesia, have demonstrated concern that large aggressive competitors will destroy the balance of markets and deprive entrepreneurs of their livelihoods, destabilizing fragile societies. See P.T. Indomarco Prismatama, 03/KPPUBLB1/2000 (Commission for the Supervision of Business Competition, Indonesia). Developing countries, worried about counteracting poverty and fostering inclusive growth in a context of blocked markets, may choose a different balance between allocative efficiency and distributional equity.

The International Competition Network has assembled material from around the world, which is available on the network's web site, *www.internationalcompetitionnetwork.org*. Select the Working Group on Unilateral Conduct.

CHAPTER 4

MERGERS

■ ■ ■

A. HISTORICAL PERSPECTIVE

1. INTRODUCTION—THE EARLY MERGER LAW

The history of U.S. merger law may be traced to the *Standard Oil* case of 1911. The Supreme Court upheld a district court finding that Standard Oil had violated Sections 1 and 2 of the Sherman Act by numerous acquisitions of competitors and suppliers, accompanied by various acts to monopolize oil refining by destroying its remaining competitors. Early law continued to evolve with the notorious case of *U.S. Steel* and its acquisitions of 180 competitors, in which the Supreme Court found that the combined firm did not abuse power; "it did not oppress or coerce its competitors." (See p. 44 supra).

In 1914, Congress passed the Clayton Act, which specifically prohibited certain acquisitions; namely, stock acquisitions whose effect may be to substantially lessen competition between the acquired and acquiring companies. The 1914 act proved to be toothless and porous. Moreover, in the years just following World War II, the country became increasingly fearful of large corporate consolidations that could play into the hands of another Hitler and tilt the country toward fascism if not communism. To plug a statutory loophole and to stem the "rising tide of economic concentration," the 1950 Congress passed the Celler–Kefauver Amendment to Section 7 of the Clayton Act, prohibiting mergers and acquisitions whose "effect ... may be substantially to lessen competition, or to tend to create a monopoly ... in any line of commerce in any section of the country."

This is the law that governs mergers today. The legislative history and motivations underlying the amended merger law were described at length by the Supreme Court in *Brown Shoe Co. v. United States,* 370 U.S. 294 (1962), the first Supreme Court case to apply the Celler–Kefauver Amendment. The *Brown Shoe* Court gave the following account before proceeding to condemn the rather insignificant merger of a leading shoe manufacturer and the eighth largest shoe retailer in the country:

> The dominant theme pervading congressional consideration of the 1950 amendments was a fear of what was considered to be a rising

tide of economic concentration in the American economy. Apprehension in this regard was bolstered by the publication in 1948 of the Federal Trade Commission's study on corporate mergers. Statistics from this and other current studies were cited as evidence of the danger to the American economy in unchecked corporate expansions through mergers. Other considerations cited in support of the bill were the desirability of retaining "local control" over industry and the protection of small businesses. Throughout the recorded discussion may be found examples of Congress' fear not only of accelerated concentration of economic power on economic grounds, but also of the threat to other values a trend toward concentration was thought to pose.

Most commentators regard the Supreme Court's summary of the legislative history as accurate,[1] albeit unattuned to the trade-offs between stemming concentration and protecting consumers. Former judge Robert Bork adds his perspective in his influential book, THE ANTITRUST PARADOX: A POLICY AT WAR WITH ITSELF (1978):

> Proponents of the bill discussed the alleged increase of overall concentration in the American economy, the increase in concentration in particular industries, the role of mergers in both types of concentration, the effects of big business on individuality and initiative, harm to civic responsibility, and so on, through a long catalog of the real and imagined economic and social consequences of mergers. Many commentators and courts rather uncritically assume that it is the duty of the courts in some way to reflect these woolly congressional concerns in deciding particular cases. In *Brown Shoe,* in fact, the Supreme Court went so far as to attribute to Congress a decision to prefer the interests of small, locally owned businesses to the interests of consumers. But to put the matter bluntly, there simply was no such congressional decision either in the legislative history or in the text of the statute.... The Warren Court was enforcing its own social preferences, not Congress's. Id. at 64–66.

2. EVOLUTION OF THE LAW

In the 1960s a remarkably large number of merger cases reached the Supreme Court. The Court's opinions during this period were responsive to then current enforcement attitudes and popular opinion and were faithful to the legislative spirit. They emphasized the dangers of high concentration and the goal of stopping incipient trends towards concentration. They expressed the purpose of the law in social and political terms, and incorporated economic assumptions and methodology sympathetic with the social policy objectives.

---

1. See, e.g., C. Kaysen and D. Turner, ANTITRUST POLICY, Ch. 3 (1959); R. Peritz, Competition Policy in AMERICA: HISTORY, RHETORIC, LAW (rev. ed. 2001) at 195–99; D. Bok, Section 7 of the Clayton Act and the Merging of Law and Economics, 74 Harv.L.Rev. 226 (1960); H. Blake, Conglomerate Mergers and the Antitrust Laws, 73 Colum.L.Rev. 555 (1973); J. Brodley, Potential Competition Mergers: A Structural Synthesis, 87 Yale L.J. 1 (1977).

Both social policy and the style of economic analysis have shifted radically since the 1960s. The cases before the mid–1970s must be read in part as history; but they also must be appreciated as part of the chain of precedent, especially since some of the early cases, including landmark *Brown Shoe*, continue to be cited for selective holdings and dictum.

We provide important excerpts from some of these early cases; first *Brown Shoe* (1962), which gave us a surprisingly long-lasting formulation of market definition as well as an epithet on the mission of antitrust—protect competition not competitors—which (taken out of the context of the opinion itself) applies robustly to this day; *Philadelphia National Bank* (1963), which gave us the much challenged but judicially recognized "Philadelphia National Bank presumption" impugning high concentration; *Consolidated Foods* (1965), which (now anachronistically) condemned a merger of leading firms in adjacent markets that created substantial opportunities for reciprocity; *Procter and Gamble* (1967), which (also anachronistically) planted fears of "deep pocket" mergers; and *Citizens Publishing Company* (1969), which announced the still existing (if extremely narrow) failing firm defense. We shall pass quickly through these cases, pausing a moment on *General Dynamics* (1974), which marks the turning of the tide from a hostile attitude towards big mergers to a cooler, technocratic analysis of whether the merger under review increases market power and is likely to harm market competition and consumers. We quickly proceed to modern analysis as reflected in the current merger guidelines, and then to the analytics of the cases.

Here is an excerpt from the much cited, and much reviled, *Brown Shoe* case, which laid the path of the merger law for two decades.

BROWN SHOE COMPANY v. UNITED STATES

370 U.S. 294 (1962).

CHIEF JUSTICE WARREN: [Brown was the fourth largest manufacturer of shoes in the United States, with a market share of 4%, and was a leading retailer. Kinney was the eighth largest shoe retailer in the United States and the leading family-style shoe store chain. It manufactured less than 0.5% of the nation's shoes, and retailed less than 2%. The top four U.S. shoe manufacturers produced 23% of the nation's shoes. There was a trend of shoe manufacturers' acquiring retail outlets. Brown was a major pace-setter of this trend.

Brown acquired Kinney after the United States sued under Section 7 of the Clayton Act and lost a motion for a preliminary injunction. The district court found no violation as a result of the combination of the firms' manufacturing facilities but found violations by reason of Brown's foreclosing rival manufacturers from selling their shoes to Kinney stores, and it found violations in shoe retailing markets in all cities of 10,000 or more population in which both Brown and Kinney stores were located. It ordered divestiture. The trial court found the merger illegal on grounds that it would foreclose Kinney's competitors from substantial outlets and it would eliminate important retailing competition where both companies were located.] * * *

The Product Market

The outer boundaries of a product market are determined by the reasonable interchangeability of use or the cross-elasticity of demand between the product itself and substitutes for it. However, within this broad market, well-defined submarkets may exist which, in themselves, constitute product markets for antitrust purposes. The boundaries of such a submarket may be determined by examining such practical indicia as industry or public recognition of the submarket as a separate economic entity, the product's peculiar characteristics and uses, unique production facilities, distinct customers, distinct prices, sensitivity to price changes, and specialized vendors. Because § 7 of the Clayton Act prohibits any merger which may substantially lessen competition "in *any* line of commerce" (emphasis supplied), it is necessary to examine the effects of a merger in each such economically significant submarket to determine if there is a reasonable probability that the merger will substantially lessen competition. If such a probability is found to exist, the merger is proscribed.

Applying these considerations to the present case, we conclude that the record supports the District Court's finding that the relevant lines of commerce are men's, women's, and children's shoes. These product lines are recognized by the public; each line is manufactured in separate plants; each has characteristics peculiar to itself rendering it generally noncompetitive with the others; and each is, of course, directed toward a distinct class of customers.

* * *

THE PROBABLE EFFECT OF THE MERGER . . .

The market share which companies may control by merging is one of the most important factors to be considered when determining the probable effects of the combination on effective competition in the relevant market. In an industry as fragmented as shoe retailing, the control of substantial shares of the trade in a city may have important effects on competition. If a merger achieving 5% control were now approved, we might be required to approve future merger efforts by Brown's competitors seeking similar market shares. The oligopoly Congress sought to avoid would then be furthered and it would be difficult to dissolve the combinations previously approved. Furthermore, in this fragmented industry, even if the combination controls but a small share of a particular market, the fact that this share is held by a large national chain can adversely affect competition. Testimony in the record from numerous independent retailers, based on their actual experience in the market, demonstrates that a strong, national chain of stores can insulate selected outlets from the vagaries of competition in particular locations and that the large chains can set and alter styles in footwear to an extent that renders the independents unable to maintain competitive inventories. A third significant aspect of this merger is that it creates a large national chain which is integrated with a manufacturing operation. The retail outlets of integrated companies, by eliminating wholesalers and by increasing the volume of purchases from the manufacturing division of the enterprise, can market their own brands at prices below those of competing independent retailers. Of course, some of the results of large integrated or chain operations are beneficial to consumers. Their expansion is not rendered unlawful by the mere fact that small independent stores may be adversely affected. *It is competition, not competitors, which the Act protects*. [Emphasis added by editor.] But we cannot fail to recognize Congress' desire to promote competition through the protection of viable, small, locally owned businesses. Congress appreciated that occasional higher costs and prices might result from the maintenance of fragmented industries and markets. It resolved these competing considerations in favor of decentralization. We must give effect to that decision.

. . . We cannot avoid the mandate of Congress that tendencies toward concentration in industry are to be curbed in their incipiency, particularly when those tendencies are being accelerated through giant steps striding across a hundred cities at a time. In the light of the trends in this industry we agree with the Government and the court below that this is an appropriate place at which to call a halt.

* * *

QUESTIONS AND COMMENTS

The market definition formulation, although often cited, is imprecise. Current practice would hypothesize a smallest credible market (e.g. retail sales of non-designer women's shoes in Chattanooga), and then measure whether a small but significant price rise would cause a significant shift of buyers to another product or territory. [It would not cause such a shift if, for example, other retailers would quickly move in.] See Part B infra.

The passage on competitive effects contains what may be the most quoted sentence in antitrust today: "It is competition, not competitors, which the Act protects." What did the Court mean by this sentence?

UNITED STATES v. PHILADELPHIA NATIONAL BANK

374 U.S. 321 (1963).

JUSTICE BRENNAN: [Philadelphia National Bank, the second largest commercial bank with headquarters in Philadelphia, sought to acquire Girard Trust Corn Exchange Bank, the third largest. The resulting bank would have been the largest commercial bank in the four-county area. It would have held 36% of commercial bank assets, 36% of deposits, and 34%

of loans. Post merger, the top two banks would have had 59% of commercial bank assets, 58% of deposits, and 58% of loans.]

* * *

We noted in *Brown Shoe Co., supra,* at 315, that "[t]he dominant theme pervading congressional consideration of the 1950 amendments [to § 7] was a fear of what was considered to be a rising tide of economic concentration in the American economy." This intense congressional concern with the trend toward concentration warrants dispensing, in certain cases, with elaborate proof of market structure, market behavior, or probable anticompetitive effects. Specifically, we think that a merger which produces a firm controlling an undue percentage share of the relevant market, and results in a significant increase in the concentration of firms in that market, is so inherently likely to lessen competition substantially that it must be enjoined in the absence of evidence clearly showing that the merger is not likely to have such anticompetitive effects.

Such a test lightens the burden of proving illegality only with respect to mergers whose size makes them inherently suspect in light of Congress' design in § 7 to prevent undue concentration. Furthermore, the test is fully consonant with economic theory. That "[c]ompetition is likely to be greatest when there are many sellers, none of which has any significant market share," is common ground among most economists, and was undoubtedly a premise of congressional reasoning about the antimerger statute.

The merger of appellees will result in a single bank's controlling at least 30% of the commercial banking business in the four-county Philadelphia metropolitan area. Without attempting to specify the smallest market share which would still be considered to threaten undue concentration, we are clear that 30% presents that threat. . . . * * *

. . . There is no reason to think that concentration is less inimical to the free play of competition in banking than in other service industries. On the contrary, it is in all probability more inimical. For example, banks compete to fill the credit needs of businessmen. Small businessmen especially are, as a practical matter, confined to their locality for the satisfaction of their credit needs. If the number of banks in the locality is reduced, the vigor of competition for filling the marginal small business borrower's needs is likely to diminish. At the same time, his concomitantly greater difficulty in obtaining credit is likely to put him at a disadvantage *vis-à-vis* larger businesses with which he competes. In this fashion, concentration in banking accelerates concentration generally. * * *

. . . [I]t is suggested that the increased lending limit of the resulting bank will enable it to compete with the large out-of-state banks, particularly the New York banks, for very large loans. We reject this application of the concept of "countervailing power." If anti-competitive effects in one market could be justified by pro-competitive consequences in another, the logical upshot would be that every firm in an industry could, without violating § 7, embark on a series of mergers that would make it in the end as large as the industry leader. For if all the commercial banks in the Philadelphia area merged into one, it would be smaller than the largest bank in New York City. . . .

This brings us to appellees' final contention, that Philadelphia needs a bank larger than it now has in order to bring business to the area and stimulate its economic development. We are clear, however, that a merger the effect of which "may be substantially to lessen competition" is not saved because, on some ultimate reckoning of social or economic debits and credits, it may be deemed beneficial. A value choice of such magnitude is beyond the ordinary limits of judicial competence, and in any event has been made for us already, by Congress when it enacted the amended § 7. Congress determined to preserve our traditionally competitive economy. It therefore proscribed anticompetitive mergers, the benign and the malignant alike, fully aware, we must assume, that some price might have to be paid.

* * *

Questions and Comments

We call your attention particularly to the *Philadelphia National Bank* presumption, a version of which you should look for in the current Horizontal Merger Guidelines, see below, § 5.3. You should also take note of the last two paragraphs of the case excerpt, rejecting, respectively, a countervailing power defense and a social policy defense. Both holdings are modern principles. But can the arguments of the merger partners be reframed as *efficiencies in the relevant market*? If so, they will get a more hospitable reception.

* * *

NOTE ON FTC v. CONSOLIDATED FOODS CORP.
380 U.S. 592 (1965)

Consolidated Foods, a major food processor with a network of wholesale and retail sales, acquired Gentry, the third largest maker of dehydrated onions and garlic. Consolidated was a large buyer from firms, such as meat packers, that made large purchases of dehydrated onions and garlic. Consolidated had used reciprocity programs in the past ("I will buy from you if you buy from me") and could be expected to continue to do so. The Court held the acquisition illegal, stating:

> We hold at the outset that the "reciprocity" made possible by such an acquisition is one of the congeries of anticompetitive practices at which the antitrust laws are aimed. The practice results in "an irrelevant and alien factor," intruding into the choice among competing products, creating at the least "a priority on the business at equal prices." *International Salt Co. v. United States,* 332 U.S. 392, 396–397; *Northern Pac. R. Co. v. United States,* 356 U.S. 1, 3, 6, 12. Reciprocal trading may ensue

not from bludgeoning or coercion but from more subtle arrangements. A threatened withdrawal of orders if products of an affiliate cease being bought, as well as a conditioning of future purchases on the receipt of orders for products of that affiliate, is an anticompetitive practice. * * *

. . . [T]he Commission was surely on safe ground in reaching the following conclusion:

> "If reciprocal buying creates for Gentry a protected market, which others cannot penetrate despite superiority of price, quality, or service, competition is lessened whether or not Gentry can expand its market share. . . . [Gentry's] loss of sales fails to refute the likelihood that Consolidated's reciprocity power, which it has shown a willingness to exploit to the full, will not immunize a substantial segment of the garlic market from normal quality, price, and service competition."

Consolidated Foods should help you understand the frame of reference in the 1960s. It does not fit the modern consumer welfare paradigm. Why not?

NOTE ON ***FTC v. PROCTER & GAMBLE CO.,*** 386 U.S. 568 (1967)

Procter & Gamble, one of the largest producers of soap products, acquired Clorox, the leading manufacturer of household liquid bleach. Clorox accounted for 48.8% of the market. Purex, the next largest firm, accounted for 15.7%. Four other firms, together, held 15%. The remaining 20% was divided among 200 small firms.

All liquid bleach is chemically identical. Clorox created a strong brand image by millions of dollars of advertising. Procter was the nation's largest advertiser and, in view of its tremendous volume, it received large discounts from the media. Procter was engaged in a program of diversifying into related lines. Household liquid bleach was an obvious candidate.

After the merger, producers other than Clorox were selling more bleach than ever before. Nonetheless, the Court held:

> . . . There is every reason to assume that the smaller firms would become more cautious in competing due to their fear of retaliation by Procter. It is probable that Procter would become the price leader and that oligopoly would become more rigid.
>
> The acquisition may also have the tendency of raising the barriers to new entry. The major competitive weapon in the successful marketing of bleach is advertising. Clorox was limited in this area by its relatively small budget and its inability to obtain substantial discounts. By contrast, Procter's budget was much larger; and, although it would not devote its entire budget to advertising Clorox, it could divert a large portion to meet the short-term threat of a new entrant. Procter would be able to use its volume discounts to advantage in advertising Clorox. Thus, a new entrant would be much more reluctant to face the giant Procter than it would have been to face the smaller Clorox.

Possible economies cannot be used as a defense to illegality. Congress was aware that some mergers which lessen competition may also result in economies but it struck the balance in favor of protecting competition. See *Brown Shoe Co. v. United States,* [370 U.S. 294 (1962)] at 358, 360.

The Commission also found that the acquisition of Clorox by Procter eliminated Procter as a potential competitor. The Court of Appeals declared that this finding was not supported by evidence because there was no evidence that Procter's management had ever intended to enter the industry independently and that Procter had never attempted to enter. The evidence, however, clearly shows that Procter was the most likely entrant. Procter had recently launched a new abrasive cleaner in an industry similar to the liquid bleach industry, and had wrested leadership from a brand that had enjoyed even a larger market share than had Clorox. Procter was engaged in a vigorous program of diversifying into product lines closely related to its basic products. Liquid bleach was a natural avenue of diversification. . . .

It is clear that the existence of Procter at the edge of the industry exerted considerable influence on the market. First, the market behavior of the liquid bleach industry was influenced by each firm's predictions of the market behavior of its competitors, actual and potential. Second, the barriers to entry by a firm of Procter's size and with its advantages were not significant. There is no indication that the barriers were so high that the price Procter would have to charge would be above the price that would maximize the profits of the existing firms. Third, the number of potential entrants was not so large that the elimination of one would be insignificant. Few firms would have the temerity to challenge a firm as solidly entrenched as Clorox. Fourth, Procter was found by the Commission to be the most likely entrant. These findings of the Commission were amply supported by the evidence.

The judgment of the Court of Appeals is reversed and remanded with instructions to affirm and enforce the Commission's order [of divestiture].

QUESTIONS AND COMMENTS

1. Note the Court's two concerns and, as well, its treatment of efficiencies. *Procter & Gamble* was much criticized for its refusal to consider the positive effects of efficiencies and for its assumption that deeper pockets would give market power to a dominant firm. It was criticized also, but less so, for its treatment of potential competition. Later, *Marine Bancorporation,* 418 U.S. 602 (1974), page 419 infra, tightened the standards for proving that loss of a merger partner's own potential competition harms competition.

2. The Chinese merger authority recently relied on *Procter & Gamble* to justify its prohibition of Coca–Cola's acquisition of Huiyuan, a major Chinese juice company. The Wall Street Journal, *China's Statement Blocking Coca–Cola Huiyuan*, March 18, 2009, available at *http://blogs.wsj.com/chinarealtime/2009/03/18/china% E2% 80% 99s-statement-blocking-coca-cola-huiyuan-deal/.*

CITIZEN PUBLISHING CO. v. UNITED STATES

394 U.S. 131 (1969).

JUSTICE DOUGLAS: [In 1940, the Citizen and the Star, the only two daily newspapers in Tucson, entered into a joint operating agreement providing for joint sale of advertising, joint distribution of the newspapers, and pooling of profits. As extended, the agreement was to run for 50 years. Prior to the joint operating agreement, the Citizen had annual losses of about $23,500. It owed $79,000 to its stockholders for advances of working capital, and its liabilities exceeded its assets by more than $53,000. Some years after the agreement was renewed, Citizen's shareholders acquired the stock of the Star.

The Court held that the agreement involved price fixing and profit pooling illegal per se under Section 1 of the Sherman Act.] * * *

The only real defense of appellants was the "failing company" defense—a judicially created doctrine.... That defense was before the Court in *International Shoe Co. v. FTC,* 280 U.S. 291, where § 7 of the Clayton Act was in issue. The evidence showed that the resources of one company were so depleted and the prospect of rehabilitation so remote that "it faced the grave probability of a business failure." 280 U.S., at 302. There was, moreover, "no other prospective purchaser." *Ibid.* It was in that setting that the Court held that the acquisition of that company by another did not substantially lessen competition within the meaning of § 7. 280 U.S., at 302–303.

In the present case the District Court found:

> "At the time Star Publishing and Citizen Publishing entered into the operating agreement, and at the time the agreement became effective, Citizen Publishing was not then on the verge of going out of business, nor was there a serious probability at that time that Citizen Publishing would terminate its business and liquidate its assets unless Star Publishing and Citizen Publishing entered into the operating agreement." 280 F.Supp., at 980.

The evidence sustains that finding. There is no indication that the owners of the Citizen were contemplating a liquidation. They never sought to sell the Citizen and there is no evidence that the joint operating agreement was the last straw at which the Citizen grasped. Indeed the Citizen continued to be a significant threat to the Star. How otherwise is one to explain the Star's willingness to enter into an agreement to share its profits with the Citizen? Would that be true if as now claimed the Citizen was on the brink of collapse?

The failing company doctrine plainly cannot be applied in a merger or in any other case unless it is established that the company that acquires the failing company or brings it under dominion is the only available purchaser. For if another person or group could be interested, a unit in the competitive system would be preserved and not lost to monopoly power. So even if we assume, *arguendo,* that in 1940 the then owners of the Citizen could not long keep the enterprise afloat, no effort was made to sell the Citizen; its properties and franchise were not put in the hands of a broker; and the record is silent on what the market, if any, for the Citizen might have been.

Moreover, we know from the broad experience of the business community since 1930, the year when the *International Shoe* case was decided, that companies reorganized through receivership, or through Chapter X or Chapter XI of the Bankruptcy Act often emerged as strong competitive companies. The prospects of reorganization of the Citizen in 1940 would have had to be dim or nonexistent to make the failing company doctrine applicable to this case.

The burden of proving that the conditions of the failing company doctrine have been satisfied is on those who seek refuge under it. That burden has not been satisfied in this case. * * *

Citizen Publishing is still the law. Although the Court seemed to ground the defense (if proved) on social values—saving the community and jobs—the merger guidelines, as you will see, take an economic tack and speak in terms of the remote likelihood that competition will be harmed if a company is failing.

3. THE TURNING OF THE TIDE

1974 was a watershed year. Supreme Court Justices Black, Harlan, Fortis, and Chief Justice Warren had recently retired. Justices Rehnquist and Stewart, along with Chief Justice Berger and Justices Powell and Blackmun, were to form a new majority—deferential to business interests, non-judgmental about bigness and industrial concentration, and demanding of plaintiffs in their proof that a merger would harm competition. Moreover, in the early to mid 1970s, barriers to trade were lowered, foreign competition was robust, U.S. firms that had seemed invincible in the 1960s were losing ground to their more efficient German and Japanese competitors, and the country was in economic recession.

In 1974, the Supreme Court decided *United States v. General Dynamics Corporation*, 415 U.S. 486 (1974). General Dynamics had acquired two major Illinois coal producers, creating a post-merger market share of 44.3%. The Justice Department sued, relying on its "statistical case." The district court found no harm to competition. The Supreme Court held that the statistics, if reliable as a proxy for future market shares, would have qualified for the *Philadelphia National Bank* presumption, but in this case the statistics did not suffice as a proxy. The market had changed. Coal was facing intense competition from other sources of energy. Moreover, the reserves of one of the acquired firms were depleted.

General Dynamics, the last horizontal merger case decided on the merits (as opposed to standing and antitrust injury) by the Supreme Court, provides a segue to the modern era. Many more changes were to come; the courts, the agencies, and the country moved farther away from the old structure-conduct-performance paradigm, in which market structure was deemed a powerful determinant of both conduct and performance. They began to demand harder proof from the plaintiff that any given merger would probably increase market power, raise prices and lower output (or lessen incentives to invent and invest). They began to give credence to the possibility that a given merger was efficient on grounds that it would save substantial costs, enable the firms to engage in lower-price competition, and in general serve consumers.

B. CONTEMPORARY LAW AND ENFORCEMENT

1. THE GUIDELINES: INTRODUCTION

The Department of Justice issued its first set of merger guidelines in 1968. It did so to give guidance to business and the bar as to how it intended to enforce the merger antitrust laws. The guidance was substantially revised in the 1980s to reflect the new focus on consumer welfare and a new appreciation of the importance of efficiencies.

In 2010, the federal agencies jointly issued revised guidelines covering mergers of competitors and potential competitors ("horizontal mergers"). These are printed in Appendix C. There are no current guidelines on vertical and conglomerate (all other) mergers. The 1984 guidelines covered non-horizontal mergers, and these are printed in Appendix D. In any event, horizontal mergers are clearly the principal category of concern. Mergers of buyers and suppliers (vertical) are more likely to be efficient and procompetitive, although it is possible for them to have serious foreclosing and barrier-raising effects or cartel facilitating effects. Conglomerate mergers are even less likely to be anticompetitive. They too could possibly lead to anticompetitive foreclosures, but, in the United States, this is considered a rare occurrence.

The European Union has issued merger guidelines for horizontal, vertical and conglomerate mergers. The EU horizontal merger guidelines are quite similar to the 1992 (just previous) U.S. merger guidelines.

In this section we first give a brief summary of the 2010 U.S. Horizontal Merger Guidelines. Following that, we review with you some examples for computing market concentration, since the Guidelines use the language of the "HHI" (Herfindahl–Hirschman Index) and you may find it helpful to become familiar with the numbers, how they are calculated, and what they signify. Thereafter, we turn to the case law, which is always fact intensive and provides a laboratory for applying the theories and concepts of anti-competitiveness (and pro-competitiveness) to the facts.

Here is a brief summary of what you will find in the Horizontal Merger Guidelines.

The Guidelines are intended principally as guidance for businesses and their lawyers in knowing how the agencies are likely to analyze horizontal mergers. They may also be useful to courts. In analyzing mergers, the agencies are seeking to identify a credible story that the merger will impose anticompetitive harm, principally on customers although it could also be on sellers, and then to assess the strength of the story. There are two anticompetitive scenarios. One is cartel-like ("*coordinated effects*") and the other is based on monopoly or single-firm power ("*unilateral effects*"). These are the two avenues for getting or increasing market power and thereby harming the market and consumers. Both depend upon the existence of barriers to entry or expansion so that outsiders cannot easily and quickly enter the market and fill the slack when prices rise.

How do the agencies reach the point at which they can predict a merger's probable effect? The traditional route is to define the market, measure the market concentration and its increase as a result of the merger, and, if the numbers are high enough, explore further whether the market environment is conducive to coordinated or unilateral price-raising behavior.

The Guidelines describe tools available to define the market. Hypothesize a market, assume a single monopolist who raises price 5% (or maybe 10%) (a "SSNIP", see page 817), and observe what will happen. Will a critical mass of buyers shift to another alternative so that our putative monopolist could not profitably hold the price increase? If so, include that next alternative in the market and proceed again with a SSNIP until the hypothetical price increase is (hypothetically) profitable, and you have your market (product and geographic). It may not be so simple. The Guidelines recognize that more than one set of market delineations may be equally plausible. The agencies may work with more than one market definition or even none at all in gauging the mergers effect, as we relate below.

Next, list the market participants and the shares of each, and measure concentration using the HHI. To do so, multiply each share by itself and add the squared shares, both before and after the merger. The resulting numbers are your Herfindahls (HHIs).

Then, as a rule of thumb:

1. If the increase in HHI from before to after the merger (the delta) is less than 100 or the post-merger HHI is below 1500, this is so small a change in the concentration or such a low level of concentration that there is unlikely to be a problem.
2. If the merger results in an HHI between 1500 and 2500 (a moderately concentrated market) and the delta will increase by more than 100 points, or if the merger results in an HHI above

2500 (a highly concentrated market) and the delta is between 100 and 200 points, the merger "potentially raises significant concerns and often warrants scrutiny."

3. "Mergers resulting in highly concentrated markets that involve an increase in the HHI of more than 200 points will be presumed to be likely to enhance market power." This presumption may be rebutted. Indeed, going outside the written words of the Guidelines, the presumption (which you will recognize as a form of the *Philadelphia National Bank* presumption, supra page 362) will probably not be used by the agency in its administrative function of analyzing the merger. The agency wants to get a good grasp on how competitive and dynamic, or sluggish, the market is. But if the agency goes to court it will probably take advantage of the presumption.

If the theory of harm is a unilateral effects story (increase of single-firm market power), the agencies might not travel the above route at all. Suppose that Coca–Cola proposes to buy Pepsi. The theory is that Pepsi is the first next choice of Coke lovers and no other drink comes close. If Coke buys Pepsi, it may be able to raise the price of Coke and capture the lost Coke profits on the sales diverted to Pepsi. If this is the theory, the agency might not even define a market (and thus it would have no need to calculate Herfindahls). It might, however, "back into" a market definition. In a unilateral effects case, the agency is likely to estimate a diversion ratio. In our hypothetical case, this will be the diversion of sales from Coke to Pepsi in the event of higher prices for Coke. One assumes that Coke raises its price, and calculates what part of the unit sales lost by reason of the price increase would be diverted to Pepsi. This fraction is the diversion ratio. The value of the sales diverted to Pepsi equals the number of units diverted divided by the difference between the price and incremental cost of Pepsi.

The value of the sales diverted to Pepsi indicates the release of pressure on Coke by Pepsi as a result of the disappearance of Pepsi's competition. This is called "upward pricing pressure" or "UPP". More accurately, it signifies the release of downward pricing pressure.

The agencies will also take account of incentives of the merged firm to reduce price after a unilateral-effects merger if there are expected cost savings from the merger. Efficiencies could be seen as a discount from the UPP harm.

The value of diverted sales to Pepsi divided by the lost revenues attributed to the increase in the price of a bottle of Coke is called "Gross Upward Pricing Pressure," or GUPPI.

GUPPI

lost revenue) value of diverted sales to Pepsi
to Coke

The higher the GUPPI, the greater the freedom and incentive of Coke to raise its prices without negative consequences (lost profits), and thus the greater the likelihood that the merger will harm consumers and is anticompetitive.

Whether the story is one of coordinated effects (the firms in the whole market will behave like a cartel) or unilateral effects (the merged firm gets power simply by eliminating the competition between the merger partners), conditions of entry matter. If, in the event of a price increase, entry can be expected to be timely, likely, and sufficient to fully counter a price rise, the merger is not likely to be anticompetitive.

As for efficiencies, they are part of the competitive analysis. The agencies will not challenge a merger if cognizable efficiencies (merger specific, substantiated, not likely to be accomplished without the merger) "are of a character and magnitude such that the merger is not likely to be anticompetitive in any relevant market."

There is a possibility of a failing firm or even a failing division defense, but the requirements to prove the defense are so hard to meet that this is almost never an issue.

All of these concepts are explained in the horizontal merger guidelines (App. C). Read and study the horizontal merger guidelines.

2. HHI PRACTICE

We mentioned above a set of Herfindahl numbers, but unless you have used this measure of concentration before, you will need orientation and practice to get a sense of the numbers' meaning. Remember that the HHIs are derived from market shares, which are derived from the market definition. If the market definition is wrong, the HHIs are meaningless. Sometimes, market definition is ambiguous and alternative definitions are equally plausible, and you may want to consider HHIs based on alternative market definitions. In any event, for a possibly underinclusive but plausible market definition (colas?), you will want to give serious consideration to the competitive force of the next best substitute (non-cola carbonated beverages). The case should turn on the true picture of the market, not the HHI numbers, when you analyze the realities of competition in the market.

First, computing deltas:

For reference: A merger of a 7% firm and an 8% firm would produce an increase in the HHI ("delta") by more than 100. The increase resulting from a merger can be calculated by multiplying the shares of the two firms and multiplying the product by 2. Thus, 7 × 8 × 2 = 112 delta. Five equal-sized firms have an HHI of 2000; six equal-sized firms have an HHI of 1666.6. A merger of a 5% firm and a 10% firm would produce a delta of 100.

Computing the HHI: Assume a four-firm market with firm shares of 40%, 30%, 20%, and 10%. The 20% and 10% firms merge.

a. Post-merger HHI

40^2	1600
30^2	900
30^2	900
	3400 HHI

b. The increase in the HHI as a result of the merger:

Compute the premerger HHI and subtract this figure from the post-merger HHI.

40^2	1600		
30^2	900		
20^2	400		
10^2	100		
	3000 HHI	3400	post merger HHI
		− 3000	premerger HHI
		400	increase, or "delta"

For a short cut: multiply the shares of the merging firms, and multiply the product by 2.

20 × 10 × 2 = 400

c. Note the limiting cases:

i. The highest possible HHI is the monopoly situation:

Single firm market: 100^2 = 10,000 HHI

ii. A highly fragmented market has an insignificant HHI.

Assume a 200–firm market, each firm with .5%:

(a) $.5^2$ = .25 × 200 = 50 HHI

(b) Because the square of any number less than one is always lower than the number being squared, if no firm in a market has one percent or more, the HHI will be less than 100.

d. Note that the HHI differs from the 4–, 8–, or 10–firm concentration ratio in that the HHI gives significance to the size-distribution of firms in the market, since firms are weighted by their market share. The following three markets all yield a four-firm concentration ratio of 85%:

i. A 65% firm, a 10% firm, two 5% firms, and a fringe of very small firms;

ii. A 40% firm, three 15% firms, and a fringe of very small firms;

iii. A 25% firm, three 20% firms, and a fringe of very small firms.

However, they yield very different HHIs:

i.	65^2	=	4225
	10^2	=	100
	5^2	=	25
	5^2	=	25
			4375 HHI
ii.	40^2	=	1600
	15^2	=	225
	15^2	=	225
	15^2	=	225
			2275 HHI
iii.	25^2	=	625
	20^2	=	400
	20^2	=	400
	20^2	=	400
			1825 HHI

Very small firms are normally not reflected in the calculations because they yield insignificant numbers. One squared is only one.

3. THE CASE LAW

a. Market definition

The agencies have softened their reliance on market definition. See Horizontal Merger Guidelines (App. C), § 4. Scholarly work also has challenged the usefulness of market definition. See Louis Kaplow, *Why (Ever) Define Markets?*, 124 HARV. L. REV. 437 (2010) (observing that we form market hypotheses and then proceed to confirm these hypotheses, and arguing that we should be trying to measure market power by more direct and less circular means).

Nevertheless, courts are accustomed to defining markets as the first, necessary step in the analysis, and thus far have not accepted the notion that market definition may be a dispensable exercise in merger analysis. Moreover, while market definition can sometimes seem not the best starting point, you are likely to find it helpful in getting a grasp on where anticompetitive effects might be expected. Ask yourself, as you read the materials in this chapter, how important was the definition of the market in understanding whether the merger was anticompetitive.

Here are excerpts from cases in which the market definition seemed critical to the outcome.

NOTE ON ***FTC v. STAPLES, INC.,*** 970 F.Supp. 1066 (D.D.C. 1997)

> "Thomas Stemberg [of Staples] pioneered the office supply superstore concept in 1985. He created a deep discount chain selling a broad array of office supplies primarily to small businesses which theretofore were undeniably "paying through the nose" for office supplies. Staples was to be a high volume chain operating at low gross margins, with higher volume leading to still lower costs for consumers. Staples' pricing as well as the pricing of other office supply superstores which soon followed Staples' lead, revolutionized the office products industry, impacting all channels of office products retailing. By selling office products at 30 to 60% off list price, Staples and the other superstores worked as a catalyst that forced everyone else in the industry to focus on cutting their prices. In a relatively short period of time, the office supply superstores caused a general decrease in the price of office products across the board. That decrease continued as the superstores have increased their buying power, forcing manufacturers and suppliers to implement efficiencies in their own businesses in order to compete in the sale of their products."

Office Depot and Office Max were the two other office supply superstores in the country. Office Depot was number one and Staples was number two. They faced competition from one another as well as, at least to some extent, from mass merchandisers (Kinko's, Kmart, CVS, Wal–Mart), wholesale clubs, and mail order houses.

Office Depot and Staples, which competed in some 42 metropolitan areas, proposed to merge. FTC evidence showed that, where Staples did not compete with other office supply superstores, it charged prices that were well over 5% higher and sometimes 15% higher than in areas where it did compete with other superstores.

To define the market, the court used the *Brown Shoe* "practical indicia" of submarkets (see page 361 supra). It found low cross-elasticity of demand between superstore and non-superstore retailers, and it found that the superstores had unique characteristics—in appearance, size, format, product variety, type of customer, and public recognition. The court found a submarket in consumable office supplies sold through office supply superstores.

In this category, in many local markets post-merger HHIs would be 10,000 (meaning only one superstore) and the average delta would be 2715.

The court determined that the FTC had established a prima facie case of violation, that Staples then had the burden to rebut the prima facie case, and that it did not meet its burden. Staples did not establish, for example, that entry into the office supply superstore market would counter the price effects of the merger, and their evidence of efficiencies—even if legally admissible—was not accepted as a matter of fact.

The court granted a preliminary injunction. It expressed uneasiness in enjoining the merger, both because Staples' founder had pioneered the format and because the finding of a superstore or "category killer" market could in theory have broad ramifications in other cases. The court emphasized that "this case is based strictly on [its] facts" and should not be construed as a broad endorsement of superstore submarkets.

Do you agree with the market definition? Can a mode of delivery be a market? What additional considerations, or hypotheses, would you have entertained in defining the market? Do you suspect that Staples/Office Depot would have earned supracompetitive profits in metropolitan areas that, after the merger, would have only one office supply superstore?

NOTE ON MERGER BETWEEN ***JD GROUP AND ELLERINE HOLDINGS***

Competition Tribunal, South Africa, case 78/LM/Jul00 (2000)

Two of South Africa's best known department stores proposed to merge. One of these enterprises had pioneered a marketing approach that offered generous credit to "some of South Africa's poorest consumers, many of whom do not even have access to a bank account." Because no credit had been available to black South Africans, many of these individuals had not previously been able to buy furniture and appliances. In discussing whether the market was limited to credit purchases of furniture and appliances and also whether it included more upscale sellers, the Tribunal said:

> In this case . . . the parties to the transaction are the final link with the consumers, and, at that, the poorest, least powerful of South African consumers. In other words, the interests directly affected by this merger are represented by millions of atomized, disorganized individuals incapable of defending their economic interests except to the extent that they are able to exercise a preference for one retail outlet over another. This evaluation will seek to assess whether the transaction has the potential to increase the power of the parties over the consumers that they serve and who are the source of their prosperity.

Rejecting defendants' argument that the market included higher-end stores, the Tribunal said:

> The distinction [based on Living Standard categories] informs advertising strategy in very subtle ways as an amusing example alluded to during our proceedings shows. Ellerines in the LSM [Living Standard Measure] 3–5 market offer a free sheep worth R300 if goods above a specified amount are purchased. A graphic of a sheep is depicted in the advert. Bradlow's, the high end JD brand, also offers a free gift for customers purchasing above a specific amount. The gift, however, underlines the difference in social status of the LSM categories–Bradlow's offers not a free sheep, but a coffee table book on 101 ways to cook lamb!

The Tribunal found that the relevant market was the sale of furniture and appliances on credit to consumers in a low-end LSM category through national chains of furniture shops. It enjoined the merger.

NOTE ON ***FTC*** *v.* ***WHOLE FOODS MARKET, INC.***

548 F.3d 1028 (D.C. Cir. 2008)

Whole Foods Market, a supermarket specializing in premium natural and organic foods with some 194 stores, decided to buy Wild Oats Markets, another premium natural and organic supermarket (PNOS) with some 110 stores. Whole Foods and Wild Oats were the only nation-wide operators of PNOSs and they were allegedly one another's closest competitors in 21 geographic markets. The FTC brought proceedings to enjoin the merger and sought a preliminary injunction under Section 13(b) of the Federal Trade Commission Act. The district court denied the injunction, finding that Whole Foods and Wild Oats compete with other supermarkets and do not uniquely compete with one another. Thus, it thought, the relevant market could not be PNOSs, therefore the FTC had not shown a likelihood of success on the merits, and therefore, the court concluded, it need not consider the equities and the public interest which would otherwise be relevant factors in granting a preliminary injunction under Section 13(b). The transaction closed, but meanwhile the FTC appealed, and on appeal the Court of Appeals for the DC Circuit reversed and remanded. The majority stressed that the FTC need not *prove* its case on a motion for preliminary injunction. It "will usually be able to obtain a preliminary injunction blocking a merger by 'rais[ing] questions going to the merits so serious, substantial, difficult[,] and doubtful as to make them grounds for thorough investigation.' " If the FTC raises such serious questions, the merging parties may come forward with evidence in their favor on merits and equities, and if they do so the court must then apply a sliding scale.

On the merits, the appellate court, relying on *Brown Shoe* and *Staples,* held that the district court erred as a matter of law in concluding that the relevant market must comprise all supermarkets. Rather, the merger law should be applied to protect the core customers of PNOSs from exploitation as a result of a merger. The court referred to direct evidence introduced by the FTC that "PNOS competition had a greater effect than conventional supermarkets on PNOS prices." The concurring judge stressed an e-mail from Whole Foods' CEO to the board stating: "[Wild Oats] is the one existing company that has the brand and number of stores to be a meaningful springboard for another player to get into this space. Eliminating them means eliminating this threat forever, or almost forever."

The court reversed the denial of the preliminary injunction, and remanded.

The dissenting judge argued that the majority had made a basic mistake by confusing product differentiation with product markets.

UNITED STATES V. H&R BLOCK, INC.

___ F. Supp. 3d ___ (D.D.C. 2011).

JUDGE HOWELL:

[H&R Block, a leading producer of software for preparation of tax returns, proposed to acquire its competitor TaxAct. There are three principal modes of tax preparation, ranging from hiring an accountant or other specialist to using do-it-yourself digital software (DDIY), to doing it yourself manually, filing the returns with free electronic forms. In the digital do-it-yourself tax-preparation market, Intuit (owner of TurboTax) was number 1 with 62.2%, H&R Block was second with 15.6%, and TaxAct was third with 12.8%. Thus, after the merger H&R/TaxAct would hold 28.4% and the top two firms would hold more than 90%. The next largest firm, TaxHawk, had 3.2%, followed by TaxSlayer with 2.7%. There were a number of very small firms with less than 1%. But if the market included all modes of tax preparation, it appeared highly dispersed.

The Department of Justice sued, alleging that the merger would raise price, lessen innovation, and lessen consumer choice. Its motion for a preliminary injunction was turned into a trial on the merits. The court gave judgment to the DOJ.

Regarding relevant market the court said:]

"Merger analysis begins with defining the relevant product market." *FTC v. Swedish Match*, 131 F. Supp. 2d 151, 156 (D.D.C. 2000) (citing *Brown Shoe*, 370 U.S. 294, 324 (1962)). "Defining the relevant market is critical in an antitrust case because the legality of the proposed merger[] in question almost always depends upon the market power of the parties involved." *Id.* Indeed, the relevant market definition is often "the key to the ultimate resolution of this type of case because of the relative implications of market power." *Id.*

The government argues that the relevant market in this case consists of all DDIY products, but does not include assisted tax preparation or pen-and-paper. Under this view of the market, the acquisition in this case would result in a DDIY market that is dominated by two large players—H&R Block and Intuit—that together control approximately 90 percent of the market share, with the remaining 10 percent of the market divided amongst a plethora of smaller companies. In contrast, the defendants argue for a broader market that includes all tax preparation methods ("all methods"), comprised of DDIY, assisted, and pen-and-paper. Under this view of the market, the market concentration effects of this acquisition would be much smaller and would not lead to a situation in which two firms control 90 percent of the market. This broader view of the market rests primarily on the premise that providers of all methods of tax preparation compete with each other for the patronage of the same pool of customers—U.S. taxpayers. After carefully considering the evidence and arguments presented by all parties, the Court has concluded that the relevant market in this case is, as the DOJ contends, the market for digital do-it-yourself tax preparation products. * * *

An analytical method often used by courts to define a relevant market is to ask hypothetically whether it would be profitable to have a monopoly over a given set of substitutable products. If so, those products may constitute a relevant market. *See* 5C PHILLIP E. AREEDA & HERBERT HOVENKAMP, ANTITRUST LAW (hereinafter, "Areeda & Hovenkamp"), ¶ 530a, at 226 (3d ed. 2007) ("[A] market can be seen as the array of producers of substitute products that could control price if united in a hypothetical cartel or as a hypothetical monopoly."). This approach—sometimes called the "hypothetical monopolist test"—is endorsed by the Horizontal Merger Guidelines issued by the DOJ and Federal Trade Commission. *See Fed. Trade Comm'n & U.S. Dep't of Justice Horizontal Merger Guidelines* (2010) (hereinafter, "Merger Guidelines"), § 4.1.1. In the merger context, this inquiry boils down to whether "a hypothetical profit-maximizing firm, not subject to price regulation, that was the only present and future seller of those products . . . likely would impose at least a small but significant and non-transitory increase in price ("SSNIP") on at least one product in the market, including at least one product sold by one of the merging firms." *Id.* The "small but significant and non-transitory increase in price," or SSNIP, is typically assumed to be five percent or more. *Id.* § 4.1.2.

Thus, the question here is whether it would be hypothetically useful to have a monopoly over all DDIY tax preparation products because the monopolist could then profitably raise prices for those products by five percent or more; or whether, to the contrary, there would be no reason to monopolize all DDIY tax preparation products because substitution and price competition with other methods of tax preparation would restrain any potential DDIY monopolist from profitably raising prices. In other words, would enough DDIY users switch to the assisted or pen-and-paper methods of tax preparation in response to a five-to-ten percent increase in DDIY prices to make such a price increase unprofitable?

In evaluating the relevant product market here, the Court considers business documents from the defendants and others, the testimony of the fact witnesses, and the analyses of the parties' expert economists. This evidence demonstrates that DDIY is the relevant product market in this case.

[The court proceeded to examine relevant business documents of the defendants, which revealed that both of the would-be merger partners viewed the DDIY firms as their primary competitors. It concluded that "DDIY products involve different technology, price, convenience level, time investment, mental effort and type of interaction by the consumer."

As for specialist-assisted products:]

The key question for the Court is whether DDIY and assisted products are sufficiently close substitutes to constrain any anticompetitive DDIY pricing after the proposed merger. Evidence of the absence of close price competition between DDIY and assisted products makes clear that the answer to that question is no—and that DDIY is the relevant product market here.... Significantly, despite some DDIY efforts to capture tax store customers, none of the major DDIY competitors sets their prices based on consideration of assisted prices.... The overall lack of evidence of price competition between

DDIY and assisted products supports the conclusion that DDIY is a separate relevant product market for evaluating this transaction, despite the fact that DDIY and assisted firms target their marketing efforts at the same pool of customers.

[As for manual tax preparation:]

The Court finds that pen-and-paper is not part of the relevant market because it does not believe a sufficient number of consumers would switch to pen-and-paper in response to a small, but significant increase in DDIY prices. The possibility of preparing one's own tax return necessarily constrains the prices of other methods of preparation at some level. For example, if the price of DDIY and assisted products were raised to $1 million per tax return, surely all but the most well-heeled taxpayers would switch to pen-and-paper. Yet, at the more practical price increase levels that trigger antitrust concern—the typical five to ten percent price increase of the SSNIP test—pen-and-paper preparation is unlikely to provide a meaningful restraint for DDIY products, which currently sell for an average price of $44.13.

The government well illustrated the overly broad nature of defendants' proposed relevant market by posing to the defendants' expert the hypothetical question of whether "sitting at home and drinking chicken soup [would be] part of the market for [manufactured] cold remedies?" The defendants' expert responded that the real "question is if the price of cold medicines went up sufficiently, would people turn to chicken soup?" As an initial matter, in contrast to the defendants' expert, the Court doubts that it would ever be legally appropriate to define a relevant product market that included manufactured cold remedies and ordinary chicken soup. This conclusion flows from the deep functional differences between those products...

* * *

The defendants' proposed relevant market of all methods of tax return preparation is so broadly defined that, as the plaintiff's expert testified, there are no conceivable alternatives besides going to jail, fleeing to Canada, or not earning any taxable income. Warren–Boulton, [Testimony]. As the plaintiff's expert put it, "if you're talking about the market for all tax preparation, you're talking about a market where, in economist terms, demand is completely [in]elastic. There are no alternatives." In such circumstances, the usual tools of antitrust analysis—such as the hypothetical monopolist test—cease being useful because it is self-evident that a monopolist of all forms of tax preparation, including self-preparation, could impose a small, but significant price increase. Indeed, a monopolist in that situation could essentially name any price since taxpayers would have no alternative but to pay it.... The Court ... finds the defendants' proposed relevant market to be overbroad.

[The court reviewed the expert testimony at length, including data regarding "critical loss" analysis—how many sales a monopolist can lose before a price increase becomes unprofitable; and whether the hypothetical monopolist of DDIY, trying to raise price, would suffer critical loss. If so, DDIY would not be a market. The court accepted the expert testimony that rebutted defendants' critical loss story.]

QUESTIONS AND COMMENTS

1. The cases above found smaller rather than larger markets, and in these cases the finding of a smaller market greatly advanced the plaintiff's case. In other cases the finding of a larger market diminished the defendant's share, as in *Oracle/PeopleSoft*, below at page 409; and the finding of smaller markets put the merging firms in separate markets and belied their status as competitors. See *FTC v. Lundbeck, Inc.*, 650 F.3d 1236 (8th Cir. 2011), holding to be in separate markets the only two drugs used to treat a life-threatening heart condition found in premature babies. Lundbeck, the owner of one of the drugs, acquired the other drug. Thereupon, prices rose thirteen-fold. At trial, the doctors testified that they never took price into account in choosing to prescribe one or the other drug; they considered only the characteristics of the baby vis-à-vis the qualities of the drug, which differed slightly. The FTC lost the case. (Was this result correct?)

2. Regarding *H&R Block*, chicken soup and cold remedies: Who was correct—the court or the defendants' expert?

3. As to each of the cases above—*Staples*, *JD Group/Ellerine*, *Whole Foods*, and *H&R Block*—were you convinced? What was the strongest argument for a more inclusive market? If you were representing the merging parties, what evidence would you pursue in your attempt to prove a larger market? Remember, you want to include in the market all good price checks on the merging firms.

4. Suppose you were a lawyer with the DOJ or FTC and your agency was suing. Could you have made a convincing case of harm to competition in any of the above cases without defining the market? You will want to revisit this question after we have analyzed the possible harms to competition from mergers.

b. Horizontal Mergers

i. Mergers Likely to Produce Coordinated Effects

We have taken note of the two "stories" of how competition may be harmed by horizontal mergers: coordinated effects and unilateral effects. We turn first to mergers that may produce coordinated effects—which is the same as saying that the merger will produce a change in market structure or environment that will probably lead the firms to behave less rivalrously or more cartel-like. Reread the Agency Horizontal Merger Guidelines, Section 7.

We begin with a classic horizontal case, *Hospital Corporation of America*, decided long before the agencies issued their 2010 Horizontal Merger Guidelines but nonetheless modern in its analysis of factors that facilitate coordinated behavior.

HOSPITAL CORP. OF AMERICA v. FTC

807 F.2d 1381 (7th Cir.1986), *cert. denied,* 481 U.S. 1038 (1987).

JUDGE POSNER: Hospital Corporation of America, the largest proprietary hospital chain in the United States, asks us to set aside the decision by the Federal Trade Commission that it violated section 7 of the Clayton Act by the acquisition in 1981 and 1982 of two corporations, Hospital Affiliates International, Inc. and Health Care Corporation. Before these acquisitions (which cost Hospital Corporation almost $700 million), Hospital Corporation had owned one hospital in Chattanooga, Tennessee. The acquisitions gave it ownership of two more. In addition, pursuant to the terms of the acquisitions it assumed contracts, both with four-year terms, that Hospital Affiliates International had made to manage two other Chattanooga-area hospitals. So after the acquisitions Hospital Corporation owned or managed 5 of the 11 hospitals in the area. . . .

If all the hospitals brought under common ownership or control by the two challenged acquisitions are treated as a single entity, the acquisitions raised Hospital Corporation's market share in the Chattanooga area from 14 percent to 26 percent. This made it the second largest provider of hospital services in a highly concentrated market where the four largest firms together had a 91 percent market share compared to 79 percent before the acquisitions. These are the FTC's figures, and Hospital Corporation thinks they are slightly too high (quite apart from the question what to do with either or both management contracts); but the discrepancy is too slight to make a legal difference. Nor would expressing the market shares in terms of the Herfindahl index alter the impression of a highly concentrated market.

The administrative law judge concluded that the acquisitions violated section 7 because of their probable anticompetitive effects in the Chattanooga hospital market. While modifying some of his findings, the Commission agreed that the acquisitions were unlawful and ordered Hospital Corporation to divest the hospitals acquired in Chattanooga and to notify the Commission, in advance, of any similar acquisitions planned for anywhere in the country. . . . * * *

When an economic approach is taken in a section 7 case, the ultimate issue is whether the challenged acquisition is likely to facilitate collusion. In this perspective the acquisition of a competitor has no economic significance in itself; the worry is that it may enable the acquiring firm to cooperate (or cooperate better) with other leading competitors on reducing or limiting output, thereby pushing up the market price. . . . * * *

The acquisitions reduced the number of competing hospitals in the Chattanooga market from 11 to 7. True, this calculation assumes that the hospitals that came under the management although not ownership of Hospital Corporation should be considered allies rather than competitors of Hospital Corporation; but the Commission was entitled to so conclude. The manager (Hospital Corporation) sets the prices charged by the managed hospitals, just as it sets its own prices. Although the pricing and other decisions that it makes in its management role are subject to the ultimate control of the board of directors of the managed hospital, there is substantial evidence that the board usually defers to the manager's decisions. . . .

The reduction in the number of competitors is significant in assessing the competitive vitality of the Chattanooga hospital market. The fewer competitors there are in a market, the easier it is for them to coordinate their pricing without committing detectable violations of section 1 of the Sherman Act, which forbids price fixing. This would not be very important if the four competitors eliminated by the acquisitions in this case had been insignificant, but they were not; they accounted in the aggregate for 12 percent of the sales of the market. As a result of the acquisitions the four largest firms came to control virtually the whole market, and the problem of coordination was therefore reduced to one of coordination among these four.

Moreover, both the ability of the remaining firms to expand their output should the big four reduce their own output in order to raise the market price (and, by expanding, to offset the leading firms' restriction of their own output), and the ability of outsiders to come in and build completely new hospitals, are reduced by Tennessee's certificate-of-need law. Any addition to hospital capacity must be approved by a state agency. . . .

All this would be of little moment if, in the event that hospital prices in Chattanooga rose above the competitive level, persons desiring hospital services in Chattanooga would switch to hospitals in other cities, or to nonhospital providers of medical care. But this would mean that the Chattanooga hospital market, which is to say the set of hospital-services providers to which consumers in Chattanooga can feasibly turn, includes hospitals in other cities plus nonhospital providers both in Chattanooga and elsewhere; and we do not understand Hospital Corporation to be challenging the Commission's market definition, which is limited to hospital providers in Chattanooga. Anyway, these competitive alternatives are not important enough to deprive the market shares statistics of competitive significance. Going to another city is out of the question in medical emergencies; and even when an operation or some other hospital service can be deferred, the patient's doctor will not (at least not for reasons of price) send the patient to another city, where the doctor is unlikely to have hospital privileges. . . .

In showing that the challenged acquisitions gave four firms control over an entire market so that they would have little reason to fear a competitive reaction if they raised prices above the competitive level, the Commission went far to justify its prediction of probable anticompetitive effects. Maybe it need have gone no further. See *United States v. Philadelphia Nat'l Bank,* 374 U.S. at 362–63. But it did. First it pointed out that the demand for hospital services by patients and their doctors is highly inelastic under competitive conditions. This is not only because people place a high value on their safety and comfort and because many of their treatment decisions are made for them by their doctor, who doesn't pay their hospital bills; it is also because most hospital bills are paid largely by insurance companies or the federal government rather than by the patient. The less elastic the demand for a good or service is, the greater are the profits that providers can make by raising price through collusion. A low elasticity of demand means that raising price will cause a relatively slight fall in demand, with the result that total revenues will rise sharply. For example, if the price elasticity of demand throughout the relevant portion of the demand curve is –.2, meaning that within that area every 1 percent increase in price will result in a two-tenths of 1 percent decrease in the quantity demanded, then a 10 percent increase in price will cause only a 2 percent reduction in quantity sold, and hence an almost 8 percent increase in total revenue. And since less is being produced, costs will fall at the same time that revenue is rising, resulting in an even greater percentage increase in profit than in revenue.

Second, there is a tradition, well documented in the Commission's opinion, of cooperation between competing hospitals in Chattanooga.... [A] market in which competitors are unusually disposed to cooperate is a market prone to collusion. The history of successful cooperation establishes a precondition to effective collusion—mutual trust and forebearance, without which an informal collusive arrangement is unlikely to overcome the temptation to steal a march on a fellow colluder by undercutting him slightly. The temptation is great. A seller who makes a profit of $10 on each sale at the cartel price, and cuts price by $1 and thereby (let us suppose) doubles his output, will increase his total profits by 180 percent.

The management contracts between Hospital Affiliates (itself an owner as well as manager of hospitals) and two other hospitals in Chattanooga—contracts that when taken over by Hospital Corporation gave it virtual control over the pricing and other decisions of two of its competitors, at least for a time—illustrate the unusual degree of cooperation in this industry; imagine Ford's signing a management contract with General Motors whereby General Motors installed one of its officers (who would remain an officer of GM) as Ford's manager. Hospitals routinely exchange intimate information on prices and costs in connection with making joint applications to insurers for higher reimbursement schedules. Such cooperation may be salutary but it facilitates collusion and therefore entitles the Commission to worry even more about large horizontal acquisitions in this industry than in industries where competitors deal with each other at arm's length.

Third, hospitals are under great pressure from the federal government and the insurance companies to cut costs. One way of resisting this pressure is by presenting a united front in negotiations with the third-party payors—which indeed, as we have just said, hospitals in Chattanooga have done. The fewer the independent competitors in a hospital market, the easier they will find it, by presenting an unbroken phalanx of representations and requests, to frustrate efforts to control hospital costs. This too is a form of collusion that the antitrust laws seek to discourage, though within the limitations of the *Noerr–Pennington* doctrine, which insulates some cooperative efforts to obtain government benefits from attack under antitrust law.... [B]ut the doctrine does not forbid enforcement efforts designed to make such efforts less effective by preserving a substantial number of competitors.

All these considerations, taken together, supported—we do not say they compelled—the Commission's conclusion that the challenged acquisitions are likely to foster collusive practices, harmful to consumers, in the Chattanooga hospital market. Section 7 does not require proof that a merger or other acquisition has caused higher prices in the affected market. All that is necessary is that the merger create an appreciable danger of such consequences in the future.... Considering the concentration of the market, the absence of competitive alternatives, the regulatory barrier to entry (the certificate of need law), the low elasticity of demand, the exceptionally severe cost pressures under which American hospitals labor today, the history of collusion in the industry, and the sharp reduction in the number of substantial competitors in this market brought about by the acquisition of four hospitals in a city with only eleven (one already owned by Hospital Corporation), we cannot say that the Commission's prediction is not supported by substantial evidence.

But of course we cannot just consider the evidence that supports the Commission's prediction. We must consider all the evidence in the record. We must therefore consider the significance of the facts, pressed on us by Hospital Corporation, that hospital services are complex and heterogeneous, that the sellers in this market are themselves heterogeneous because of differences in the services provided by the different hospitals and differences in the corporate character of the hospitals (some are publicly owned, some are proprietary, and some are private but nonprofit), that the hospital industry is undergoing rapid technological and economic change, that the payors for most hospital services (Blue Cross and other insurance companies, and the federal government) are large and knowledgeable, and that the FTC's investigation which led to this proceeding was touched off by a complaint from a competitor of Hospital Corporation. Most of these facts do detract from a conclusion that collusion in this market is a serious danger, but it was for the Commission—it is not for us—to determine their weight. * * *

QUESTIONS AND COMMENTS

1. What does Judge Posner mean by "collusion" when he speaks of the predictive judgment to be made in merger cases? Is it the same as the collusion we spoke of in Chapter 2 (Cartels)? Is it the same as coordinated interaction as referenced by the current agency guidelines?

2. Why and how did the reduction in the number of competitors, in the context of the particular features of this market, lead to collusive behavior that would lower output and raise price? Examine each point of Judge Posner's reasoning. How is Judge Posner's analysis consonant with analysis of cartel behavior (see Chapter 2)?

3. Judge Posner does not give us the market shares of all of the leading firms. He tells us that post-acquisition the four largest firms will hold 91% of the market, compared to 79% before the acquisitions. Assume the post-acquisition shares were: 30%, 26%, 20%, 15%. By the acquisitions, HCA raised its share from 14% to 26%. Calculate the post-acquisition HHI. What observations would you make?

4. Look again at the last paragraph in the case excerpt. How would you, as a judge, weigh the considerations urged by HCA? Are there additional facts that you would like to know?

5. Read again the 2010 Agency Horizontal Merger Guildelines, Sec. 7, on coordinated effects. Analyze the hospital consolidations under the guidelines. Would the agencies today find the hospital consolidations anticompetitive?

6. More often than in most other sectors, hospital mergers lie in that fraught area in which competition is lessened but efficiencies are achieved, and are achieved in a way that could not otherwise be easily realized. See the efficiencies provision in the Agency Horizontal Merger Guidelines, Section 10. Do the agencies recognize an efficiencies defense to a price-raising merger?

Courts have found an efficiencies defense in several hospital merger cases. *See, e.g., United States v. Long Island Jewish Med. Ctr.*, 983 F.Supp. 121 (E.D.N.Y. 1997). These cases are exceptional. But are they responding to a felt need?

Another tack taken to approve a competition-lessening hospital merger is to find (on dubious evidence) that it was authorized by the state and immune from antitrust. See *FTC v. Phoebe Putney Health System*, 663 F.3d 1369 (11th Cir. 2011).

Not all mergers of competitors that create high concentration, even very high concentration, produce either coordinated interaction or unilateral effects. The following case involves a merger in an environment of more robust competition.

UNITED STATES v. BAKER HUGHES INC.

908 F.2d 981 (D.C. Cir. 1990).

JUDGE CLARENCE THOMAS: Appellee Oy Tampella AB, a Finnish corporation, through its subsidiary Tamrock AG, manufactures and sells hardrock hydraulic underground drilling rigs (HHUDRs) in the United States and throughout the world. Appellee Baker Hughes Inc., a corporation based in Houston, Texas, owned a French subsidiary, Eimco Secoma, S.A. (Secoma), that was similarly involved in the HHUDR industry. In 1989, Tamrock proposed to acquire Secoma.

The United States challenged the proposed acquisition, charging that it would substantially lessen competition in the United States HHUDR market in violation of section 7 of the Clayton Act.... * * *[2]

By presenting statistics showing that combining the market shares of Tamrock and Secoma would significantly increase concentration in the already highly concentrated United States HHUDR market, the government established a prima facie case of anticompetitive effect.[3] The district court, however, found sufficient evidence that the merger would not substantially lessen competition to conclude that the defendants had rebutted this prima facie case. The government did not produce any additional evidence showing a probability of substantially lessened competition, and thus failed to carry its ultimate burden of persuasion. * * *

I.

... [T]he court gave particular weight to two non-entry factors: the flawed underpinnings of the government's prima facie case and the sophistication of HHUDR consumers. The court's consideration of these factors was not only appropriate, but imperative, because in this case these factors significantly affected the probability that the acquisition would have anticompetitive effects.

With respect to the first factor, the statistical basis of the prima facie case, the court accepted the defendants' argument that the government's statistics were misleading. Because the United States HHUDR market is minuscule, market share statistics are "volatile and shifting," and easily skewed. In 1986, for instance, only 22 HHUDRs were sold in the United States. In 1987, the number rose to 43, and in 1988 it fell to 38. Every HHUDR sold during this period, thus, increased the seller's market share by two to five percent. A contract to provide multiple HHUDRs could catapult a firm from last to first place. The district court found that, in this unusual market, "at any given point in time an individual seller's future competitive strength may not be accurately reflected." While acknowledging that the HHUDR market would be highly concentrated after Tamrock acquired Secoma, the court found that such concentration in and of itself would not doom competition. High concentration has long been the norm in this market. For example, only four firms sold HHUDRs in

2. The parties in this case do not seriously contest the district court's definition of the relevant markets. The court defined the geographic market as the entire United States, and the relevant product as three types of HHUDRs: face drills ("jumbos"), long-hole drills, and roof-bolting drills, as well as associated spare parts, components, and accessories, and used drills....

3. From 1986 through 1988, Tamrock had an average 40.8% share of the United States HHUDR market, while Secoma's share averaged 17.5%. In 1988 alone, the two firms enjoyed a combined share of 76% of the market.... This acquisition has increased the HHI in this market from 2878 to 4303.

the United States between 1986 and 1989. Nor is concentration surprising where, as here, a product is esoteric and its market small. Indeed, the trial judge found that "[c]oncentration has existed for some time [in the United States HHUDR market] but there is no proof of overpricing, excessive profit or any decline in quality, service or diminishing innovation."

The second non-entry factor that the district court considered was the sophistication of HHUDR consumers. HHUDRs currently cost hundreds of thousands of dollars, and orders can exceed $1 million. These products are hardly trinkets sold to small consumers who may possess imperfect information and limited bargaining power. HHUDR buyers closely examine available options and typically insist on receiving multiple, confidential bids for each order. This sophistication, the court found, was likely to promote competition even in a highly concentrated market. * * *

II.

The existence and significance of barriers to entry are frequently, of course, crucial considerations in a rebuttal analysis. In the absence of significant barriers, a company probably cannot maintain supracompetitive pricing for any length of time. . . .

. . . The district court in this case discussed a number of considerations that led it to conclude that entry barriers to the United States HHUDR market were not high enough to impede future entry should Tamrock's acquisition of Secoma lead to supracompetitive pricing. First, the court noted that at least two companies, Cannon and Ingersoll–Rand, had entered the United States HHUDR market in 1989, and were poised for future expansion. Second, the court stressed that a number of firms competing in Canada and other countries had not penetrated the United States market, but could be expected to do so if Tamrock's acquisition of Secoma led to higher prices. Because the market is small, "[i]t is inexpensive to develop a separate sales and service network in the United States." Third, these firms would exert competitive pressure on the United States HHUDR market even if they never actually entered the market. Finally, the court noted that there had been tremendous turnover in the United States HHUDR market in the 1980s. Secoma, for example, did not sell a single HHUDR in the United States in 1983 or 1984, but then lowered its price and improved its service, becoming market leader by 1989. Secoma's growth suggests that competitors not only can, but probably will, enter or expand if this acquisition leads to higher prices. The district court, to be sure, also found some facts suggesting difficulty of entry, but these findings do not negate its ultimate finding to the contrary.

In sum, we see no error—legal or factual—in the district court's determination that entry into the United States HHUDR market would likely avert anticompetitive effects from Tamrock's acquisition of Secoma. The court's determination on entry, considered along with the findings discussed in section I of this opinion, suffices to rebut the government's prima facie case. * * *

QUESTIONS AND COMMENTS

1. As the court said, the buyers were big and sophisticated. In the absence of high transportation costs or trade barriers, one would expect the buyers to search for their best options around the world. If so, the market was world-wide.

Why did the court delineate a U.S. market rather than a world market? Did it matter? Note that the court took account of all competition into or potentially coming into the United States.

2. Is this decision consistent with Judge Posner's decision in *HCA*? Is it consistent with the agencies' 2010 Horizontal Merger Guidelines?

FTC v. H.J. HEINZ CO.

246 F.3d 708 (D.C. Cir. 2001).

[The FTC sought a preliminary injunction against the merger of the baby food divisions of Heinz and Beech–Nut. The district court set out the facts as follows. It denied the preliminary injunction on grounds that the defendant had rebutted the prima facie case and the merger would be procompetitive.]

Excerpt from the district court, 116 F.Supp. 2d 190 (D.D.C. 2000):

Four million infants in the United States consume 80 million cases of jarred baby food annually, representing a domestic market of $865 million to $1 billion. There are only three major manufacturers and distributors of jarred baby food in the United States: Heinz, Beech–Nut, and Gerber Products Company. Gerber is by far the largest domestic manufacturer. It enjoys, and has enjoyed for some 40 years, a dominant market share that has recently grown to between 65 and 70 percent. The Gerber market share is now 65 percent, the Heinz share 17.4 percent, and the Beech–Nut share 15.4 percent.

Heinz manufactures and distributes a variety of food products worldwide, and, despite its relatively low domestic market share, is the largest producer of baby food in the world. Heinz's domestic baby food products are manufactured at its Pittsburgh, Pennsylvania plant, which was recently updated at a cost of $120 million. The Pittsburgh plant now operates at 40 percent of its production capacity and produces 12 million cases of baby food annually.

. . . Beech–Nut's annual sales of baby food are $138.7 million, of which 72 percent is jarred baby food. Beech–Nut manufactures all of its baby food in Canajoharie, New York, at a manufacturing plant that was built in 1907 and began manufacturing baby food in 1931. The plant is not technologically current. Beech–Nut submitted proof that it would be prohibitively expensive to make further improvements in the Canajoharie plant; that management has realized all the cost-savings that can be achieved in Beech–Nut's production and distribution; and that, although

Beech–Nut is currently profitable, its business is stagnant or declining without any realistic prospect of change. The FTC has not disputed this evidence.

Heinz and Beech–Nut both maintain that, despite all their efforts, neither is able to build market share, either against one another or against Gerber. See Tr. 440; 442–43; 859. Gerber, on the other hand, does not aggressively pursue market share, because, given its already dominant position in the market, striving for any further gain in market share "becomes so costly you get no return out of it."

As the dominant firm in the market, Gerber is generally the first company to increase its price. Its prices have increased every year, above levels explainable by the rate of inflation. Heinz has tended to follow Gerber's prices, but it markets its baby food as a "value brand," with a shelf price several cents below Gerber's. Gerber has expressed no desire to compete in the "value priced" sector of the market and has in fact conceded that market sector to Heinz. Beech–Nut strives to maintain price parity with Gerber, marketing its product as a premium brand, and has been able to maintain premium pricing without losing sales volume. Gerber sometimes lowers prices against Beech–Nut, but only if and when Beech–Nut manifests sufficient strength in a particular market.

Gerber enjoys unparalleled brand recognition, and its brand loyalty is greater than that of any [other] product sold in the United States, including Coca–Cola and Nike. Consumers generally view Heinz as being of slightly lower quality than Gerber. Beech Nut's products are generally perceived as comparable in quality to Gerber's.

Nearly all supermarkets stock only two brands of baby food, not three. Gerber is invariably one of the two. The food products industry measures the extent of a particular product's presence in stores across the country by referring to a product's ACV (All Commodity Volume), which is stated as the percentage of stores that carry a certain product or product line. Gerber's ACV for jarred baby food approaches 100 percent, which means that Gerber is sold in virtually every food store in the United States. Heinz has an ACV of approximately 40 percent, and Beech–Nut, approximately 45 percent. Heinz's sales are nationwide but are concentrated in northern New England, the Southeast and Deep South, and the Midwest. Beech–Nut's sales, also nationwide, are concentrated in the Atlantic region (New York and New Jersey), California, and Florida.

In general, witnesses described the baby food market as "boring," and "declining." During the last five years, grocery store sales have fallen more than 15 percent, despite the fact that the birth rate has remained stable. This decline is partially attributable to a shift from jarred baby food to table food. Beech–Nut's sales have either been flat or declining since the early 1990s, and it expects this trend to continue. * * *

It is undisputed that the baby food industry is a highly concentrated market, and the FTC adduced evidence that the proposed merger will significantly increase market concentration. Gerber's 65 percent market share results in a Herfindahl–Hirschman index of 4225. The expert testimony establishes that the total index score for the baby food industry is 4775. The proposed merger would increase the index to 5285, an increase of 510 points. This increase is five times the 100 point threshold established in the Merger Guidelines.

JUDGE HENDERSON: [After noting extraordinarily high concentration, high delta, and high barriers to entry:] As far as we can determine, no court has ever approved a merger to duopoly under similar circumstances.

REBUTTAL ARGUMENTS

In response to the FTC's prima facie showing, the appellees make three rebuttal arguments, which the district court accepted in reaching its conclusion that the merger was not likely to lessen competition substantially. For the reasons discussed below, these arguments fail and thus were not a proper basis for denying the FTC injunctive relief.

1. Extent of Pre–Merger Competition

The appellees first contend, and the district court agreed, that Heinz and Beech–Nut do not really compete against each other at the retail level. Consumers do not regard the products of the two companies as substitutes, the appellees claim, and generally only one of the two brands is available on any given store's shelves. Hence, they argue, there is little competitive loss from the merger.

This argument has a number of flaws which render clearly erroneous the court's finding that Heinz and Beech–Nut have not engaged in significant pre-merger competition. First, in accepting the appellees' argument that Heinz and Beech–Nut do not compete, the district court failed to address the record evidence that the two do in fact price against each other, and that, where both are present in the same areas, they depress each other's prices as well as those of Gerber even though they are virtually never all found in the same store. This evidence undermines the district court's factual finding.

Second, the district court's finding is inconsistent with its conclusion that there is a single, national market for jarred baby food in the United States. . . .

Third, and perhaps most important, the court's conclusion concerning pre-merger competition does not take into account the indisputable fact that the merger will eliminate competition at the wholesale level between the only two competitors for the "second shelf" position. Competition between Heinz and Beech–Nut to gain accounts at the wholesale level is fierce with each contest concluding in a winner-take-all result. The district court regarded this loss of competition as irrelevant because the FTC did not establish to its satisfaction that wholesale competition ultimately benefitted consumers through lower retail prices. The district court concluded that fixed trade spending did not affect consumer prices and that "the FTC's assertion that the proposed merger will affect variable trade spending levels and consumer prices is ... at best, inconclusive."[16] Although the court noted the FTC's examples of consumer benefit through couponing initiatives, the court held that it was "impossible to conclude with any certainty that the consumer benefit from such couponing initiatives would be lost in the merger."

In rejecting the FTC's argument regarding the loss of wholesale competition, the court committed two legal errors. First, as the appellees conceded at oral argument, no court has ever held that a reduction in competition for wholesale purchasers is not relevant unless the plaintiff can prove impact at the consumer level.... Second, it is, in any event, not the FTC's burden to prove such an impact with "certainty." To the contrary, the antitrust laws assume that a retailer faced with an increase in the cost of one of its inventory items "will try so far as competition allows to pass that cost on to its customers in the form of a higher price for its product." *In re Brand Name Prescription Drugs Antitrust Litig.* 123 F.3d 599, 605 (7th Cir.1997)....

2. Post–Merger Efficiencies

The appellees' second attempt to rebut the FTC's prima facie showing is their contention that the anticompetitive effects of the merger will be offset by efficiencies resulting from the union of the two companies, efficiencies which they assert will be used to compete more effectively against Gerber. It is true that a merger's primary benefit to the economy is its potential to generate efficiencies. As the Merger Guidelines [1992] now recognize, efficiencies "can enhance the merged firm's ability and incentive to compete, which may result in lower prices, improved quality, or new products."

Although the Supreme Court has not sanctioned the use of the efficiencies defense in a section 7 case, ... the trend among lower courts is to recognize the defense....

Nevertheless, the high market concentration levels present in this case require, in rebuttal, proof of extraordinary efficiencies, which the appellees failed to supply....

In support of its conclusion that post-merger efficiencies will outweigh the merger's anticompetitive effects, the district court found that the consolidation of baby food production in Heinz's under-utilized Pittsburgh plant "will achieve substantial cost savings in salaries and operating costs." The court also credited the appellees' promise of improved product quality as a result of recipe consolidation.[19] The only cost reduction the

16. Fixed trade spending consists of "slotting fees," "pay-to-stay" arrangements, new store allowances and other payments to retailers in exchange for shelf space and desired product display. *H.J. Heinz,* 116 F.Supp.2d at 197. Variable trade spending includes payments to retailers tied to sales volume and intended to insure a specific sales volume and lower shelf price.

19. In addition, the district court described Heinz's distribution network as much more efficient than Beech–Nut's. *H.J. Heinz,* 116 F.Supp.2d at 199. It failed to find, however, a court quantified as a percentage of pre-merger costs, however, was the so called "variable conversion cost": the cost of processing the volume of baby food now processed by Beech–Nut. The court accepted the appellees' claim that this cost would be reduced by 43% if the Beech–Nut production were shifted to Heinz's plant, a reduction the appellees' expert characterized as "extraordinary."

The district court's analysis falls short of the findings necessary for a successful efficiencies defense in the circumstances of this case. We mention only three of the most important deficiencies here. First, "variable conversion cost" is only a percentage of the total variable manufacturing cost. A large percentage reduction in only a small portion of the company's overall variable manufacturing cost does not necessarily translate into a significant cost advantage to the merger. Thus, for cost reduction to be relevant, we must at least consider the percentage of Beech–Nut's total variable manufacturing cost that would be reduced as a consequence of the merger. At oral argument, the appellees' counsel agreed. This correction immediately cuts the asserted efficiency gain in half since, according to the appellees' evidence, using total variable manufacturing cost as the measure cuts the cost savings from 43% to 22.3%.

Second, the percentage reduction in Beech–Nut's cost is still not the relevant figure. After the merger, the two entities will be combined, and to determine whether the merged entity will be a significantly more efficient competitor, cost reductions must be measured across the new entity's combined production—not just across the pre-merger output of Beech–Nut. The district court, however, did not consider the cost reduction over the merged firm's combined output. At oral argument the appellees' counsel was unable to suggest a formula that could be used for determining that cost reduction.

Finally, and as the district court recognized, the asserted efficiencies must be "merger-specific" to be cognizable as a defense. That is, they must be efficiencies that cannot be achieved by either company alone because, if they can, the merger's asserted benefits can be achieved without the concomitant loss of a competitor. Yet the district court never explained why Heinz could not achieve the kind of efficiencies urged without merger. As noted, the principal merger benefit asserted for Heinz is the acquisition of Beech–Nut's better recipes, which will allegedly make its product more attractive and permit expanded sales at prices lower than those charged by Beech–Nut, which produces at an inefficient plant. Yet, neither the district court nor the appellees addressed the question whether Heinz could obtain the benefit of better recipes by investing more money in product development and promotion—say, by an amount less than the amount Heinz would spend to acquire Beech–Nut. At oral argument, Heinz's counsel agreed that the taste of Heinz's products was

significant diseconomy of scale in distribution from which either Heinz or Beech–Nut suffers. In other words, although Beech–Nut has an inefficient distribution system, it can make that system more efficient without merger. Heinz's own efficient distribution network illustrates that a firm the size of Beech–Nut does not need to merge in order to attain an efficient distribution system.

not so bad that no amount of money could improve the brand's consumer appeal. That being the case, the question is how much Heinz would have to spend to make its product equivalent to the Beech–Nut product and hence whether Heinz could achieve the efficiencies of merger without eliminating Beech–Nut as a competitor. The district court, however, undertook no inquiry in this regard. In short, the district court failed to make the kind of factual determinations necessary to render the appellees' efficiency defense sufficiently concrete to offset the FTC's prima facie showing.

3. Innovation

The appellees claim next that the merger is required to enable Heinz to innovate, and thus to improve its competitive position against Gerber. Heinz and Beech–Nut asserted, and the district court found, that without the merger the two firms are unable to launch new products to compete with Gerber because they lack a sufficient shelf presence or ACV. This kind of defense is often a speculative proposition. *See* 4A Areeda, *et al.,* [Antitrust Law] p 975g (noting "truly formidable" proof problems in determining innovation economies). In this case, given the old-economy nature of the industry as well as Heinz's position as the world's largest baby food manufacturer, it is a particularly difficult defense to prove. The court below accepted the appellees' argument principally on the basis of their expert's testimony that new product launches are cost-effective only when a firm's ACV is 70% or greater (Heinz's is presently 40%; Beech–Nut's is 45%). That testimony, in turn, was based on a graph that plotted revenue against ACV. According to the expert, the graph showed that only four out of 27 new products launched in 1995 had been successful—all for companies with an ACV of 70% or greater.

The chart, however, does not establish this proposition and the court's consequent finding that the merger is necessary for innovation is thus unsupported and clearly erroneous. All the chart plotted was revenue against ACV and hence all it showed was the unsurprising fact that the greater a company's ACV, the greater the revenue it received.... In the absence of reliable and significant evidence that the merger will permit innovation that otherwise could not be accomplished, the district court had no basis to conclude that the FTC's showing was rebutted by an innovation defense.

Moreover, Heinz's insistence on a 70–plus ACV before it brings a new product to market may be largely to persuade the court to recognize promotional economies as a defense. Heinz argues that to profitably launch a new product, it must have nationwide market penetration to recoup the money spent on advertising and promotion. It wants to spread advertising costs out among as many product units as possible, thereby lowering the advertising cost per unit. It does not want to "waste" promotional expenditures in markets where its products are not on the shelf or where they are on only a few shelves. For example, in a metropolitan area in which Heinz has a 75 per cent ACV, every dollar spent on advertising is two or three times more "effective" than in a market in which it has only a 25 per cent ACV. As one authority notes, however, "[t]he case for recognizing a defense based on promotional economies is relatively weak." 4A Areeda, *et al., supra,* p 975f, at 77. The district court accepted Heinz's claim that it could not introduce new products without at least a 70 per cent ACV because it would be unable to adequately diffuse its advertising and promotional expenditures. But the court failed to determine whether substantial promotional scale economies exist now and, if they do, whether Heinz and Beech–Nut "for that reason operate at a substantial competitive disadvantage in the market or markets in which they sell" or whether there are effective alternatives to merger by which the disadvantage can be overcome. *Id.* at p 975f2, at 78.

4. *Structural Barriers to Collusion*

In a footnote the district court dismissed the likelihood of collusion derived from the FTC's market concentration data. "[S]tructural market barriers to collusion" in the retail market for jarred baby food, the court said, rebut the normal presumption that increases in concentration will increase the likelihood of tacit collusion. The court's sole citation, however, was to testimony by the appellees' expert, Jonathan B. Baker, a former Director of the Bureau of Economics at the FTC, who testified that in order to coordinate successfully, firms must solve "cartel problems" such as reaching a consensus on price and market share and deterring each other from deviating from that consensus by either lowering price or increasing production. He opined that after the merger the merged entity would want to expand its market share at Gerber's expense, thereby decreasing the likelihood of consensus on price and market share. In his report, Baker elaborated on his theory, explaining that the efficiencies created by the merger will give the merged firm the ability and incentive to take on Gerber in price and product improvements. He also predicted that policing and monitoring of any agreement would be more difficult than it is now, due in part to a time lag in the ability of one firm to detect price cuts by another. But the district court made no finding that any of these "cartel problems" are so much greater in the baby food industry than in other industries that they rebut the normal presumption. In fact, Baker's testimony about "time lag" is refuted by the record which reflects that supermarket prices are available from industry-wide scanner data within 4–8 weeks.... His testimony is further undermined by the record evidence of past price leadership in the baby food industry.

The combination of a concentrated market and barriers to entry is a recipe for price coordination.... The creation of a durable duopoly affords both the opportunity and incentive for both firms to coordinate to increase prices. The district court recognized this when it questioned Baker on whether the merged entity will, up to a point, expand its market share but "then [with Gerber will] find a nice equilibrium and they'll all get along together." Tacit coordination

> is feared by antitrust policy even more than express collusion, for tacit coordination, even when observed, cannot easily be controlled directly by the antitrust laws. It is a central object of merger policy to obstruct the creation or reinforcement by merger of such oligopolistic market structures in which tacit coordination can occur.

4 Phillip E. Areeda, Herbert Hovenkamp & John L. Solow, *Antitrust Law* p 901b2, at 9 (rev. ed. 1998). Because the district court failed to specify any "structural market barriers to collusion" that are unique to the baby food industry, its conclusion that the ordinary presumption of collusion in a merger to duopoly was rebutted is clearly erroneous. * * *

QUESTIONS AND COMMENTS

1. Both the district and appellate courts, as well as courts in other cases we have read, accepted the *Philadelphia National Bank* presumption. How is the presumption reflected in the current agency guidelines? If no presumption were applicable, would this have made a difference? What should be the future of the presumption?

2. Consider each of defendants' defenses: Lack of price competition between Heinz and Beech–Nut; lack of a collusion scenario; the merger was necessary to compete effectively against the industry giant; the merger would increase innovation and competition; the merger was efficient and would save an enormous amount of resources. Which were most compelling? Should any defense have succeeded? Reflect particularly on the claim of lack-of-collusion scenarios. How would this claim probably fare under the Agency Horizontal Merger Guidelines?

3. Canada specifically allows an efficiency defense if the efficiencies outweigh the competition loss. The defense involves a "balancing weights" approach, according to the Federal Court of Appeal. Under this standard, in the case of a merger proved to be anticompetitive, the Competition Tribunal must consider the effects of the merger based on a range of factors, including deadweight loss, socially adverse effects on consumers, loss of choice and services, and impact on small and medium-sized business. The Tribunal must assign different weights to the factors on a case-by-case basis, quantifying even qualitative factors. The court held that the Tribunal, in considering socially adverse effects of Superior Propane's acquisition of its only competitor, properly counted only the higher prices paid by low income households (thus, not the total consumer welfare loss); and that the Competition Commissioner had not sufficiently proved that the merger would deny small and medium sized businesses an equitable opportunity to participate in the economy. The appellate court remanded the case to the Tribunal to consider all adverse economic effects of the merger, including redistributive effects, and directed the Tribunal to formulate a methodology for determining how the effects should be weighed. *Commissioner of Competition v. Superior Propane*, 2001, 199 DIL.R. (4th) 130. On remand, using a balancing weights approach, the Tribunal again determined that the expected efficiencies outweighed the economic loss. 2000 Comp. Trib. 16, File No. CT1998002 (Apr. 4,

2002). Compare the Canadian efficiencies defense with the U.S. treatment of efficiencies. Which do you find more satisfactory?

ii. Mergers Likely to Produce Unilateral Effects: Monopoly and Dominance

Mergers to monopoly or dominance (near-monopoly) are the quintessential unilateral effects cases. Perhaps surprisingly, since *Standard Oil* (1911), supra page 33 (which also involved many anticompetitive acts), there are relatively few decisions in cases of mergers to dominance.

We present two recent mergers on point, and then an earlier one in a global market with transnational implications.

Sirius–XM

Sirius Satellite Radio proposed a $3.3 billion buyout of XM Satellite Radio Holdings. This would be a merger of the only two satellite radio providers (the only two pay-radio companies) in the country. Critics argued that the merger would raise prices, reduce innovation, and reduce program choices for consumers. The land-based radio industry lobbied against the merger. Why? Opposition came also from consumer groups and state attorneys general.

The Department of Justice Antitrust Division studied the merger and cleared it without imposing any conditions, with the following statement:

STATEMENT OF THE DEPARTMENT OF JUSTICE ANTITRUST DIVISION ON ITS DECISION TO CLOSE ITS INVESTIGATION OF XM SATELLITE RADIO HOLDINGS INC.'S MERGER WITH SIRIUS SATELLITE RADIO INC.

(2008)

Evidence Does Not Establish that Combination of Satellite Radio Providers Would Substantially Reduce Competition

WASHINGTON, March 24, 2008—The Department of Justice's Antitrust Division issued the following statement today after announcing the closing of its investigation into the proposed merger of XM Satellite Radio Holdings Inc. with Sirius Satellite Radio Inc.:

"After a careful and thorough review of the proposed transaction, the Division concluded that the evidence does not demonstrate that the proposed merger of XM and Sirius is likely to substantially lessen competition, and that the transaction therefore is not likely to harm consumers. The Division reached this conclusion because the evidence did not show that the merger would enable the parties to profitably increase prices to satellite radio customers for several reasons, including: a lack of competition between the parties in important segments even without the merger; the competitive alternative services available to consumers; technological change that is expected to make those alternatives increasingly attractive over time; and efficiencies likely to flow from the transaction that could benefit consumers.

"The Division's investigation indicated that the parties are not likely to compete with respect to many segments of the satellite radio business even in the absence of the merger. Because customers must acquire equipment that is specialized to the satellite radio service to which they subscribe, and which cannot receive the other provider's signal, there has never been significant competition for customers who have already subscribed to one or the other service. For potential new subscribers, past competition has resulted in XM and Sirius entering long-term, sole-source contracts that provide incentives to all of the major auto manufacturers to install their radios in new vehicles. The car manufacturer channel accounts for a large and growing share of all satellite radio sales; yet, as a result of these contracts, there is not likely to be significant further competition between the parties for satellite radio equipment and service sold through this channel for many years. In the retail channel, where the parties likely would continue to compete to attract new subscribers absent the merger, the Division found that the evidence did not support defining a market limited to the two satellite radio firms that would exclude various alternative sources for audio entertainment, and similarly did not establish that the combined firm could profitably sustain an increased price to satellite radio consumers. Substantial cost savings likely to flow from the transaction also undermined any inference of competitive harm. Finally, the likely evolution of technology in the future, including the expected introduction in the next several years of mobile broadband Internet devices, made it even more unlikely that the transaction would harm consumers in the longer term. Accordingly, the Division has closed its investigation of the proposed merger."

ANALYSIS

During the course of its investigation, the Division reviewed millions of pages of documents, analyzed large amounts of data related to sales of satellite radios and subscriptions for satellite radio service, and interviewed scores of industry participants.

Extent of Likely Future Competition between XM and Sirius

The Division's analysis considered the extent to which the two satellite radio providers compete with one another. Although the firms in the past competed to attract new subscribers, there has never been significant competition between them for customers who have already subscribed to one or the other service and purchased the requisite equipment. Also, competition for new subscribers is likely to be substantially more limited in the future than it was in the past.

As to existing subscribers, the Division found that satellite radio equipment sold by each company is customized to each network and will not function with the other service. XM and Sirius made some efforts to develop an interoperable radio capable of receiving both sets of satellite signals. Depending on how such a radio would be configured, it could enable consumers to switch between providers without incurring the costs of new equipment. The Division's investigation revealed, however, that no such interoperable radio is on the market and that such a radio likely would not be introduced in the near term. For example, in the important automotive channel, such a radio could not be introduced in the near term due to the engineering required to integrate radios into new vehicles. The need for equipment customized to each network means that in order to switch from XM to Sirius, or vice versa, a subscriber would have to purchase new equipment designed for the other service. In the case of a factory-installed car radio, switching satellite radio providers would have the additional disadvantage of requiring an aftermarket radio that would be less integrated into the vehicle's systems. Data analyzed by the Division confirmed that subscribers rarely switch between XM and Sirius.

As to new subscribers, XM and Sirius sell satellite radios and service primarily through two distribution channels: (1) car manufacturers that install the equipment in new cars and (2) mass-market retailers that sell automobile aftermarket equipment and other stand-alone equipment. Car manufacturers account for an increasingly large portion of XM and Sirius sales, and the parties have focused more and more of their resources on attracting subscribers through the car manufacturer channel. Historically, XM and Sirius engaged in head-to-head competition for the right to distribute their products and services through each car company. As a result of this competitive process, XM and Sirius have provided car manufacturers with subsidies and other payments that indirectly reduce the equipment prices paid by car buyers to obtain a satellite radio. However, XM and Sirius have entered into sole-source contracts with all the major automobile manufacturers that fix the amount of these subsidies and other pertinent terms through 2012 or beyond. Moreover, there was no evidence that competition between XM or Sirius beyond the terms of these contracts would affect customers' choices of which car to buy. As a result, there is not likely to be significant competition between XM and Sirius for satellite radio equipment and service sold through the car manufacturer channel for many years.

The Division's investigation identified the mass-market retail channel as an arena in which XM and Sirius would compete with one another for the foreseeable future. Both XM and Sirius devote substantial effort and expense to attracting subscribers in this arena, with both companies offering discounts, most commonly in the form of equipment rebates, to attract consumers. Retail channel sales have dropped significantly since 2005, and the parties contended that the decline was accelerating. However, retail outlets still account for a large portion of the firms' sales, and the Division was unable to determine with any certainty that this channel would not continue to be important in the future.

Effect on Competition in the Retail Channel

Because XM and Sirius would no longer compete with one another in the retail channel following the merger, the Division examined what alternatives, if any, were available to consumers interested in purchasing satellite radio service, and specifically whether the relevant market was limited to the two satellite radio providers, such that their combination would create a monopoly. The parties contended that they compete with a variety of other sources of audio entertainment, including traditional AM/FM radio, HD Radio, MP3 players (*e.g.*, iPods®), and audio offerings delivered through wireless telephones. Those options, used individually or in combination, offer many consumers attributes of satellite radio service that they may find attractive. The parties further contended that these audio entertainment alternatives were sufficient to prevent the merged company from profitably raising prices to consumers in the retail channel for example, through less discounting of equipment prices, increased subscription prices, or reductions in the quality of equipment or service.

The Division found that evidence developed in the investigation did not support defining a market limited to the two satellite radio firms, and similarly did not establish that the combined firm could profitably sustain an increased price to satellite radio consumers. XM and Sirius seek to attract subscribers in a wide variety of ways, including by offering commercial-free music (with digital sound quality), exclusive programming (such as Howard Stern on Sirius and "Oprah & Friends" on XM), niche music formats, out-of-market sporting events, and a variety of news and talk formats in a service that is accessible nationwide. The variety of these offerings reflects an effort to attract consumers with highly differentiated interests and tastes. Thus, while the satellite radio offerings of XM and Sirius likely are the closest substitutes for some current or potential customers, the two offerings do not appear to be the closest substitutes for other current or potential customers. For example, a potential customer considering purchasing XM service primarily to listen to Major League Baseball games or one considering purchasing Sirius service primarily to listen to Howard Stern may not view the other satellite radio service, which lacks the desired content, as a particularly close substitute. Similarly, many customers buying radios in the retail channel are acquiring an additional receiver to add to an existing XM or Sirius subscription for their car radio, and these customers likely would not respond to a price increase by choosing a radio linked to the other satellite radio provider. The evidence did not demonstrate that the number of current or potential customers that view XM and Sirius as the closest alternatives is large enough to make a price increase profitable. Importantly in this regard, the parties do not appear to have the ability to identify and price discriminate against those actual or potential customers that view XM and Sirius as the closest substitutes.

Likely Efficiencies

To the extent there were some concern that the combined firm might be able profitably to increase prices in the mass-market retail channel, efficiencies flowing from the transaction likely would undermine any such concern. The Division's investigation confirmed that the parties are likely to realize significant variable and fixed cost savings through the merger. It was not possible to estimate the magnitude of the efficiencies with precision due to the lack of evidentiary support provided by XM and Sirius, and many of the efficiencies claimed by the parties were not credited or were discounted because they did not reflect improvements in economic welfare, could have been achieved without the proposed transaction, or were not likely to be realized within the next several years. Nevertheless, the Division estimated the likely variable cost savings those savings most likely to be passed on to consumers in the form of lower prices to be substantial. For example, the merger is likely to allow the parties to consolidate development, production and distribution efforts on a single line of radios and thereby eliminate duplicative costs and realize economies of scale. These efficiencies alone likely would be sufficient to undermine an inference of competitive harm.

Effect of Technological Change

Any inference of a competitive concern was further limited by the fact that a number of technology platforms are under development that are likely to offer new or improved alternatives to satellite radio. Most notable is the expected introduction within several years of next-generation wireless networks capable of streaming Internet radio to mobile devices. While it is difficult to predict which of these alternatives will be successful and the precise timing of their availability as an attractive alternative, a significant number of consumers in the future are likely to consider one or more of these platforms as an attractive alternative to satellite radio. The likely evolution of technology played an important role in the Division's assessment of competitive effects in the longer term because, for example, consumers are likely to have access to new alternatives, including mobile broadband Internet devices, by the time the current long-term contracts between the parties and car manufacturers expire.

QUESTIONS AND COMMENTS

1. After the Department of Justice closed its file, the merger had yet to be approved by the Federal Communications Commission, under a public interest standard. The FCC, after contentious debate, approved the merger by a vote of 3 to 2 along party lines. The FCC accepted the following conditions offered by the companies: The companies would abide by a three-year price cap; they would provide an 8% set aside of full time channels for public interest and minority programming; they would offer a limited à la carte option that would allow listeners to pay only for the channels they chose to receive; and they would introduce an open radio standard that would allow radios to receive both XM and Sirius channels. *http://hraunfoss.fcc.gov/edocs_public/attachmatch/DOC-284108A1.doc.*

Why was a price cap necessary if the competition would keep the prices down?

2. Analyze the DOJ statement. Was this a merger to monopoly, or simply an efficient merger of financially struggling companies that were usually not in head-to-head competition and that were facing increased competition from new technologies that deliver music (iPods, music-enabled cell phones) as well as from the traditional radio stations? Did the fate of this merger turn on market definition? on the environment of fast-changing technologies? on assumptions that competition from alternative technologies were sufficiently close and robust to check any laggard or exploitative performance?

3. The parties merged. Sirius XM raised some prices and levied a royalty fee. Subscribers sued, in a class action, claiming that the merger proved to be anticompetitive. Sirius XM justified the price increases as necessary to cover higher costs. The class action was settled for a package valued at $180 million in which Sirius XM agreed not to increase prices through the end of the year. *Blessing v. Sirius XM Radio Inc.*, 2011 WL 3739024 (S.D.N.Y. 2011).

Google AdMob

High Technology and Nascent Markets

Google proposed to acquire AdMob, the largest mobile advertising network. Mobile advertising networks facilitate transactions between advertisers and software developers on mobile devices. AdMob had about a third of the market. Google owns the world's most popular search engine and was beta-testing an advertising network for mobile applications. Apple had recently acquired another significant mobile advertising network.

The Federal Trade Commission took a close look at the acquisition. The FTC staff was reportedly opposed to the deal, fearful that the merger would remove one of the only three important players from the market. Ultimately, the FTC cleared the transaction, issuing the following closing statement:

STATEMENT OF THE FEDERAL TRADE COMMISSION

Google/AdMob

FTC File No. 101–0031
May 21, 2010

The Federal Trade Commission has voted 5–0 to close its investigation of Google's proposed acquisition of AdMob. The decision was a difficult one because the parties currently are the two leading mobile advertising networks, and the Commission was concerned about the loss of head-to-head competition between them. The Commission reached this decision based on important developments in the mobile advertising marketplace, particularly actions by Apple that should mitigate the anticompetitive effects of Google's AdMob acquisition.

Google and AdMob today are the leading competitors among mobile ad networks, which drive the availability of free or low-cost applications and content for smartphones and other mobile devices. Mobile ad networks "monetize" mobile publishers' content by selling publishers' advertising space; advertising revenues, in turn, fuel the development of mobile applications and Internet content. Mobile application developers and other publishers rely on mobile ad networks to sell advertising space that they cannot effectively sell on their own.

Google's proposed $750 million acquisition of AdMob necessitated close scrutiny because the transaction appeared likely to lead to a substantial lessening of competition in violation of Section 7 of the Clayton Act. Those companies generate the most revenue among mobile advertising networks, and both companies are particularly strong in one segment of the market, namely performance ad networks.[1] The Commission's six-month investigation yielded evidence that each of the merging parties viewed the other as its primary competitor, and that each firm made business decisions in direct response to this perceived competitive threat.

During the investigation, Apple acquired the third largest mobile ad network, Quattro Wireless, in December 2009 and then introduced its own mobile advertising network, iAd, as part of its iPhone applications package. The Commission has reason to believe that Apple quickly will become a strong mobile advertising network competitor. Apple not only has extensive relationships with application developers and users, but also is able to offer targeted ads (heretofore a strength of AdMob) by leveraging proprietary user data gleaned from users of Apple mobile devices. Furthermore, Apple's ownership of the iPhone software development tools, and its control over the developers' license agreement, gives Apple the unique ability to define how competition among ad networks on the iPhone will occur and evolve.

As a result of Apple's entry, AdMob's success to date on the iPhone platform is unlikely to be an accurate predictor of AdMob's competitive significance going forward, whether AdMob is owned by Google or not. This is particularly important given that AdMob's revenue and market share are derived largely from the iPhone platform.

AdMob also competes with Google in the sale of mobile advertising on Google's Android platform. Competitive harm from the acquisition appears unlikely there as well. Android and iPhone compete against each other as platforms, and the availability of free or low-cost applications helps drive that competition. Thus, Google has a strong incentive to encourage the development of applications on Android to maintain the competitiveness of Android against the iPhone. As discussed above, these applications are often made available to consumers in their current low- or no-cost form through advertising provided by mobile ad networks like

1. Both Google and AdMob focus their businesses on performance mobile ad networks, in which advertisers often buy ad space through auction rather than through sales relationships, and pay for the advertising on a "per click" or other direct response basis. Brand advertising, conversely, is typically paid for on a "per impression" basis, as the goal in brand advertising is to put the advertisement in front of the user, not necessarily to generate a click or other immediate action.

AdMob. To the extent Google were to exercise market power on Android after this acquisition, it would risk making Android less competitive against the iPhone and other platforms.

Further, as has been reported in the financial press, a number of firms appear to be developing or acquiring smartphone platforms to better compete against Apple's iPhone and Google's Android. Because of the importance of advertising-supported content to the success of smartphone platforms, these firms would have a strong incentive to facilitate competition among mobile advertising networks, including through self-supply.

In sum, the Commission voted unanimously to close its investigation of Google's acquisition of AdMob because it lacked reason to believe that the transaction would likely result in a substantial lessening of competition, especially in light of marketplace developments that occurred during the course of its investigation, including Apple's acquisition of Quattro and its subsequent introduction of iAd. In any nascent market there will be uncertainty about the path of competition and the durability of early leads in market share. In order to fully protect consumers, however, the Commission must subject mergers in nascent markets to the same level of antitrust scrutiny as mergers in other markets, taking into account all relevant information that becomes available during the course of an investigation. Had the facts supported a challenge here, the Commission would not have hesitated to act to preserve competition in the mobile ad network market.

Though we have determined not to take action today, the Commission will continue to monitor the mobile marketplace to ensure a competitive environment and to protect the interests of consumers.

QUESTIONS AND COMMENTS

1. Neither the FTC nor the DOJ normally issue closing statements. In *Sirius–XM* and *Google/AdMob*, the agencies apparently believed that an explanation was important, given the controversy surrounding both transactions. As for *Google/AdMob*, the FTC apparently welcomed the opportunity to explain its approach to nascent, high-tech markets.

2. In *Google/AdMob*, what was the significance of Apple's competition to the FTC's determination?

3. Does this merger make mobile users and advertisers better off?

BOEING/McDONNELL DOUGLAS

One of the highest profile mergers of the 1990s was Boeing/McDonnell Douglas. This was the first merger vetted by both the U.S. authorities and the European Commission that was cleared by the Americans and nearly prohibited by the European Union. The European Commission finally cleared the merger after imposing strong conditions.

Boeing was the largest manufacturer of commercial jet aircraft in the world, accounting for about 64% of world market sales. Its only competitors were McDonnell Douglas, with about 5%, and Airbus Industrie, with about 30%. Airbus was a consortium of manufacturers in Britain, France, Germany and Spain.

Boeing and McDonnell Douglas were U.S. companies and had no production assets in Europe, although they regularly made sales there. McDonnell Douglas also produced military jets, and its technology portfolio included patents from research and development undertaken with U.S. government financing. In the commercial jet market, McDonnell Douglas had failed to invest in important new-generation developments and was facing financial and competitive difficulties. Its market share of new aircraft sales was withering. Boeing, meanwhile, had recently concluded 20–year exclusive supply agreements with three big American airlines—Delta, American, and Continental. The exclusive supply agreements represented about 11% of all world purchases of big commercial jets.

Commercial jet airplanes are very complex and sell in the range of $32 million to $171 million each. An order from an airline is typically worth billions of dollars. In view of the fact that each sale to an airline is so significant, Airbus and Boeing were fierce competitors for sales around the world.

Boeing and McDonnell Douglas filed premerger notifications in the United States and in the European Union. European Competition Commissioner Karel Van Miert immediately expressed concerns about the proposed merger and the contemporaneous exclusive agreements. The U.S. FTC opened an investigation. The European Commission and the FTC made notifications to one another under their 1991 cooperation agreement, and the European and American officials shared their perspectives. They sharply disagreed on the analysis of anticompetitive effects.

Early on, politicians entered the fray, with Europeans declaring that the merger was blatantly anticompetitive and seriously harmful to competition and to Airbus, and Americans declaring that the merger was good for the American economy. Laura D'Andrea Tyson, former head of the Council of Economic Advisors, was reported as saying that this merger was good for America "even if consumers of airplane seats are somewhat worse off." (Washington Post, May 4, 1997. Commissioner Van Miert threatened that, if the merger should be consummated without European approval, the European Commission would impose prohibitive fines on Boeing and might seize Boeing planes flying into Europe.

On July 1, 1997, the U.S. FTC issued a statement announcing the closing of its investigation.

MATTER OF BOEING COMPANY/McDONNELL DOUGLAS CORPORATION

U.S. Federal Trade Commission, Statement 5 CCH Trade Reg. Rep. (CCH) [Transfer Binder 1997–2001], ¶ 24,295 (July 1, 1997).

After an extensive and exhaustive investigation, the Federal Trade Commission has decided to close the investigation of The Boeing Company's proposed acquisition of McDonnell Douglas Corporation. For reasons discussed below, we have concluded that the acquisition would not substantially lessen competition or tend to create a monopoly in either defense or commercial aircraft markets.

There has been speculation in the press and elsewhere that the United States antitrust authorities might allow this transaction to go forward—particularly the portion of the transaction dealing with the manufacture of commercial aircraft—because aircraft manufacturing occurs in a global market, and the United States, in order to compete in that market, needs a single powerful firm to serve as its "national champion." A powerful United States firm is all the more important, the argument proceeds, because that firm's success contributes much to improving the United States' balance of trade and to providing jobs for U.S. workers. * * *

We do not have the discretion to authorize anticompetitive but "good" mergers because they may be thought to advance the United States' trade interests. If that were thought to be a wise approach, only Congress could implement it. In any event, the "national champion" argument is almost certainly a delusion. In reality, the best way to boost the United States' exports, address concerns about the balance of trade, and create jobs is to require United States' firms to compete vigorously at home and abroad. . . .

On its face, the proposed merger appears to raise serious antitrust concerns. The transaction involves the acquisition by Boeing, a company that accounts for roughly 60% of the sales of large commercial aircraft, of a non-failing direct competitor in a market in which there is only one other significant rival, Airbus Industrie, and extremely high barriers to entry. The merger would also combine two firms in the U.S. defense industry that develop fighter aircraft and other defense products. Nevertheless, for reasons we will now discuss, we do not find that this merger will substantially lessen competition in any relevant market. * * *

The evidence collected during the staff investigation, including the virtually unanimous testimony of forty airlines that staff interviewed, revealed that McDonnell Douglas's commercial aircraft division, Douglas Aircraft Company, can no longer exert a competitive influence in the worldwide market for commercial aircraft. Over the past several decades, McDonnell Douglas has not invested at nearly the rate of its competitors in new product lines, production facilities, company infrastructure, or research and development. As a result, Douglas Aircraft's product line is not only very limited, but lacks the state of the art technology and performance characteristics that Boeing and Airbus have developed. Moreover, Douglas Aircraft's line of aircraft do not have common features such as cockpit design or engine type, and thus cannot generate valuable efficiencies in interchangeable spare parts and pilot training that an airline may obtain from a family of aircraft, such as Boeing's 737 family or Airbus's A–320 family.

In short, the staff investigation revealed that the failure to improve the technology and efficiency of its commercial aircraft products has lead to a deterioration of Douglas Aircraft's product line to the point that the vast majority of airlines will no longer consider purchasing Douglas aircraft and that the company is no longer in a position to influence significantly the competitive dynamics of the commercial aircraft market. * * *

Immediately after the FTC closed its investigation, the Clinton Administration took an active role in defending the merger to Europe. Key White House officials, including the President of the United States, argued to key European officials, including the President of the European Commission, that the merger was not anticompetitive, that it was important to the defense interests of the United States (because the military assets of McDonnell Douglas would be best preserved in the hands of Boeing), and to employment in the United States, and that the United States was "considering how to retaliate against Europe if it makes good on its threat to try and undermine the merger of [the] U.S. aerospace giants...." The Washington Post, July 17, 1997, p. C1. Reportedly, the Administration officials were considering imposing tariffs on European planes, limiting flights between the United States and France (the most adamant objector to the merger), and filing a protest with the World Trade Organization in view of European subsidies to Airbus.

BOEING/McDONNELL DOUGLAS: THE EUROPEAN COMMISSION (1987)

On July 30, 1997, the European Commission issued its decision on the merger. It concluded that the merger would increase Boeing's dominance. It backed away from a prohibition of the merger, and imposed significant conditions. Among other things it found:

Competitive potential of MDC

(i) The competitive influence of MDC was in the past greater than reflected by its market share

58 Although, as outlined above, the market share of MDC has been continuously declining, it appears that the impact of MDC on the conditions of competition in the market for large commercial aircraft was higher than reflected by its market share in 1996.

The Commission has received replies from 31 airlines which have all purchased new large commercial aircraft over the last five years. Two

> of them purchased only MDC aircraft. Out of the remaining 29 airlines, 20 stated that in those cases where they had placed orders with Boeing or Airbus, MDC had been in competition for all or a part of the orders. Out of the 20 airlines, 13 stated that competition from MDC had an influence on the outcome of their negotiations with the winner of the bid in terms of a better price or better purchasing conditions. Two airlines stated that this influence was of major importance and three stated that this influence was of minor importance. Seven airlines stated that the influence of MDC's competition was of significant importance.
>
> This is confirmed by a study conducted by Lexecon Ltd. on behalf of Airbus and presented at the Hearing, in which 52 aircraft-supply competitions between 1994 and 1996 were analysed, comparing those in which MDC participated with those in which it did not participate. In this study, it was found that the MDC presence led to a reduction of over 7% in the realized price as compared with the list price as far as orders placed with Airbus were concerned. * * *

Boeing undertook, among other things: not to enforce its exclusivity rights under the agreements with American, Delta and Continental; not to enter into exclusive agreements with those or other buyers until 2007; not to "use its privileged access to the existing fleet in service of DAC [Douglas] aircraft in order to leverage its opportunities for persuading current DAC operators to purchase Boeing aircraft"; to license to competitors upon request all US-funded patents usable in the manufacture or sale of commercial jet aircraft; and not to leverage its relationship with suppliers to refuse to deal with Boeing's competitors or to grant preferential treatment to Boeing. Boeing/McDonnell Douglas, European Commission Decision Case IV/M.877, O.J. L 336/16 (Dec. 8, 1997).

QUESTIONS AND COMMENTS

1. What is the significance of the facts (which the European Commission found) that: McDonnell Douglas was "no longer a real force in the market for the sale of new aircraft on a stand alone basis" (European Commission decision, para. 58); no one but Boeing wanted to acquire McDonnell Douglas; the presence in the market of McDonnell Douglas had, in the past, caused prices to be 7% lower; and if the merger were prohibited, Boeing probably would have absorbed McDonnell Douglas' share.

2. Comment on the statement by the U.S. Federal Trade Commission. Was the national champion argument irrelevant to the Commissioners in closing the investigation? Should it have been relevant?

3. Was Boeing–McDonnell Douglas purely a competition case? Who had the stronger side of the argument: The Europeans, most of whom seemed to believe that the U.S. green light was industrial policy to promote Boeing as

the U.S. national champion; or the Americans, most of whom seemed to believe that the European opposition was industrial policy to protect Airbus as the European champion?

iii. Mergers Likely to Produce Unilateral Effects in Oligopolistic Markets

As explained in the 2010 Agency Horizontal Merger Guidelines, negative effects can occur without a monopoly scenario and without a coordination scenario. There may be a spectrum of competitors, with the merging parties situated as major alternatives to one another, and it may be that no other competitor is well situated to reposition itself to take up the slack if the merged firm should raise price.

In *Staples/Home Depot*, supra page 375, the FTC's theory of the case was unilateral effects. See Jonathan Baker and Robert Pitofsky, A Turning Point in Merger Enforcement: *Federal Trade Commission v. Staples*, Chapter 11 in ANTITRUST STORIES, at 311 (Fox and Crane, eds., 2007). But, as you saw, the court took a more familiar route: It found consumable retail office supplies to be a submarket authorized by the *Brown Shoe* criteria. How would you have argued *Staples* as a unilateral effects case under the 2010 Merger Guidelines?

We turn now to a recent alleged unilateral effects case where the judge held that the evidence fell short.

UNITED STATES v. ORACLE CORPORATION

331 F. Supp. 2d 1098 (N.D. Cal. 2004).

JUDGE WALKER: The government, acting through the Department of Justice, Antitrust Division [together with a number of U.S. states] seek to enjoin Oracle Corporation from acquiring, directly or indirectly, the whole or any part of the stock of PeopleSoft, Inc. Plaintiffs allege that the acquisition would violate section 7 of the Clayton Act, 15 USC § 18....

INTRODUCTORY FINDINGS: INDUSTRY OVERVIEW

[T]he present case deals with only applications that automate the overall business data processing of business and similar entities; these applications are called "enterprise application software" (EAS).... Plaintiffs focus their claims on the ... intermediate category of EAS—enterprise resource planning (ERP) system software. ERP is packaged software that integrates most of an entity's data across all or most of the entity's activities. Oracle and PeopleSoft develop, produce, market and service ERP software. * * * [They are the #1 and #2 firms, respectively, in the sale of this high function software in the United States, with SAP of Germany being the only other competitor in the high function segment.]

Many ERP programs were developed to address the needs of particular industries, such as banking and finance, insurance, engineering, construction, healthcare, government, legal and so forth (in industry lingo, these are called "verticals"). Vertical-specific ERP programs, although well suited to the needs of firms engaged in a particular industry, often are not well suited to the needs of firms in other verticals. An enterprise that relies on vertical-specific ERP software products, but whose operations embrace more than one vertical faces the task of integrating the programs.

The largest and most complex organizations face particular difficulty. "[O]nly custom-written software or carefully tailored and integrated cross-industry packages [can] handle larger firms' historically idiosyncratic accounting systems and diverse overseas operations." ERP programs have been developed to handle the full range of an enterprise's activities; these include human relations management (HRM), financial management systems (FMS), customer relations management (CRM), supply chain management (SCM), Product Life Cycle Management, Business Intelligence (BI), among many others. These are called "pillars."

Although ERP encompasses many pillars, plaintiffs assert claims with respect to only two pillars, HRM and FMS. Within these two pillars, plaintiffs further limit their claims to only those HRM and FMS products able to meet the needs of large and complex enterprises with "high functional needs." Plaintiffs label HRM and FMS products capable of meeting these high function needs "high function HRM software" and "high function FMS software," respectively. ERP pillars incapable of meeting these high function needs are called "mid-market" software by plaintiffs.

"High function software" is a term adopted by plaintiffs to describe what they contend is the separate and distinct line of commerce in which they contend competition would be lessened by the proposed acquisition. Plaintiffs apply the term "high function" to both HRM and FMS. "High function software," as defined by plaintiffs, has no recognized meaning in the industry. Rather, industry participants and software vendors use the terms "enterprise" software, "up-market" software and "Tier One" software to denote ERP that is capable of executing a wide array of business processes at a superior level of performance. Software vendors use these terms to focus sales and marketing initiatives.

Each ERP pillar consists of "modules" that automate particular processes or functions. HRM and FMS software each consists of numerous modules. HRM modules include such functions as payroll, benefits, sales incentives, time management and many others. FMS modules include such functions as general ledger, accounts receivable, accounts payable, asset management and many others.

"Core" HRM modules are those specific ERP modules that individually or collectively automate payroll, employee tracking and benefits administration. Core FMS modules are those ERP modules that individually or collectively track general ledger, accounts receivable, accounts payable and cash and asset management business processes. Core FMS and HRM modules are offered by all the ERP vendors that have HRM and FMS offerings. Large enterprise customers rarely, if ever, buy core HRM or

FMS modules in isolation. Customarily, FMS and HRM software are purchased in bundles with other products.

Customers purchase a cluster of products such as Oracle's E–Business Suite that provide the customer with a "stack" of software and technology, which may include core HRM or FMS applications, add-on modules, "customer-facing" business applications such as CRM software, and the infrastructure components (application servers and database) on which the applications run.

ERP vendors, including Oracle and PeopleSoft, sell modules individually as well as integrated suite products. Some ERP vendors sell only one or a few modules. Individual modules are referred to as "point solutions" as they address a particular need of the enterprise. ERP vendors that sell products for only one or a limited number pillars are referred to as point solution or "best of breed" providers. A customer licensing a particular module because it fits the specific needs of the enterprise is sometimes said to be seeking a best of breed or point solution. An ERP customer that acquires best of breed or point solutions faces the task of integrating these solutions with one another and with the customer's existing ERP or legacy footprint.

Although the production cost of ERP applications is negligible, vendors bear significant development and marketing expenses and substantial costs of pre- and post-sales support and ongoing maintenance and enhancement. ERP vendors employ and bear substantial costs of account managers, technical sales forces and personnel for user training, product documentation and post-sale support. * * *

Many firms develop, produce, market and maintain ERP software. Some ERP software vendors, notably Oracle, PeopleSoft and a German company, SAP AG, developed cross industry applications or "suites" of "generalized integrated software that could be customized for virtually any large business." It is to the products of these three vendors that plaintiffs direct their allegations. Although not alone in the ERP business, these three firms have the most comprehensive ERP software offerings. * * *

Despite the identity of code in each company's ERP packaged product, ERP product offerings are not homogeneous. While the ERP products offered by Oracle and PeopleSoft and other vendors perform the same or similar functions, these products are not uniform in their architecture, scalability, functionality or performance characteristics. The product of each vendor possesses certain features or qualities so that none is a perfect substitute for any other. As the testimony indicated, and the court finds, no vendor is capable of meeting all of the high function needs, as defined by plaintiffs, of all customers.

Furthermore, because each packaged ERP product must be customized and configured to fit the software footprint of the customer, a packaged ERP product may, as fitted to one customer's information technology footprint, differ significantly from the same packaged ERP product fitted to another customer's footprint. Because of these facts, the court finds the ERP products in suit to be differentiated products. * * *

Customers almost always purchase a cluster of products such as Oracle's E–Business Suite that provide the customer with a stack of software and technology, which may include core HRM or FMS applications, add-on modules, customer-facing business applications such as CRM software and the infrastructure components (application servers and database) on which the applications run. * * *

Plaintiffs' Claim of Threatened Injury to Competition

Plaintiffs allege that the HRM and FMS sold by Oracle, PeopleSoft and SAP are the only HRM and FMS products that can appropriately be deemed "high function HRM and FMS." Plaintiffs allege that these "high function" HRM and FMS products have the "scale and flexibility to support thousands of simultaneous users and many tens of thousands of simultaneous transactions and the ability to integrate seamlessly into bundles or 'suites' of associated HRM and FMS functions." Plaintiffs allege that "high function" HRM and FMS products compete in a market that is separate and distinct from that of all other ERP products, such as SCM, CRM or mid-market HRM and FMS, the latter being HRM or FMS products designed for organizations having less demanding needs. These mid-market products include Oracle's E–Business Suite Special Edition, SAP's MySAP and All-in-One, PeopleSoft's PeopleSoft Enterprise One and the products of ERP vendors such as Lawson and AMS.

Moreover, plaintiffs allege that this competition is geographically confined to the United States. Within this narrowly defined product and geographic market, plaintiffs allege that with limited and specially explained exceptions, only Oracle, PeopleSoft and, to a lesser degree, SAP's United States arm, SAP America, are in effective competition. The proposed merger would therefore, in plaintiffs' view, constrict this highly concentrated oligopoly to a duopoly of SAP America and a merged Oracle/PeopleSoft. * * *

Customer Witnesses * * *

[T]he court found the testimony of the customer witnesses largely unhelpful to plaintiffs' effort to define a narrow market of high function FMS and HRM.

The test of market definition turns on reasonable substitutability. *du Pont*, 351 US 377. This requires the court to determine whether or not products have "reasonable interchangeability" based upon "price, use and qualities...." *Id* at 404. What, instead, these witnesses testified to was, largely, their preferences.

Customer preferences towards one product over another do not negate interchangeability. See *R R Donnelley & Sons Co*, 20 FTC 36, 54 n65 (1995) (citing Robert Pitofsky, New Definitions of the Relevant Market and the Assault on Antitrust, 90 COLUM L REV 1805, 1816 (1990) ("There will almost always be classes of customers with strong preferences . . . but to reason from the existence of such classes to a conclusion that each is entitled to . . . a separate narrow market definition grossly overstates the market power of the sellers.")). The preferences of these customer witnesses for the functional features of PeopleSoft or Oracle products was evident. But the issue is not what solutions the customers would like or prefer for their data processing needs; the issue is what they could do in the event of an anticompetitive price increase by a post-merger Oracle. Although these witnesses speculated on that subject, their speculation was not backed up by serious analysis that they had themselves performed or evidence they presented. There was little, if any, testimony by these witnesses about what they would or could do or not do to avoid a price increase from a post-merger Oracle. To be sure, each testified, with a kind of rote, that they would have no choice but to accept a ten percent price increase by a merged Oracle/PeopleSoft. But none gave testimony about the cost of alternatives to the hypothetical price increase a post-merger Oracle would charge: e.g., how much outsourcing would actually cost, or how much it would cost to adapt other vendors' products to the same functionality that the Oracle and PeopleSoft products afford.

If backed by credible and convincing testimony of this kind or testimony presented by economic experts, customer testimony of the kind plaintiffs offered can put a human perspective or face on the injury to competition that plaintiffs allege. But unsubstantiated customer apprehensions do not substitute for hard evidence. While listening to the testimony of these customer witnesses, it became clear to the court that these witnesses represent a group of extremely sophisticated buyers and users of information technology; they have decades of experience in negotiating in this field. This made more evident the failure of these witnesses to present cost/benefit analyses of the type that surely they employ and would employ in assessing an ERP purchase. The evidence at trial established that ERP customers have choices outside the integrated suites of Oracle, PeopleSoft and SAP.

Indeed, Glover's testimony showed that—as Oracle contends—customers have some leverage by virtue of their existing installed base "to do nothing" and thereby resist anticompetitive price increases by ERP vendors. Although the court is not convinced that this is a long-term option due to the ever changing business and legal environment in which enterprises operate, this option does afford ERP customers some limited protection and leverage. At any rate, plaintiffs' customer witnesses did not, in their testimony, provide the court with data from actual or probable ERP purchases and installations to demonstrate that the witnesses' employers would have had no choice but to submit to a SSNIP imposed by a post-merger Oracle.

The court, therefore, finds that these witnesses did not establish by a preponderance of the evidence that the products offered by Oracle, PeopleSoft and SAP are in a distinct line of commerce or product market from those offered by other ERP vendors. The court finds that these witnesses did not establish that it was more likely than not that customers of a post-merger Oracle would have no choice but to submit to a small but significant non-transitory price increase by the merged entity. These findings do not rest alone on the court's skepticism about the testimony of plaintiffs' customer witnesses. * * *

Findings of Fact: Product Market Definition

In order to sustain plaintiffs' product market definition the court must find, by a preponderance of the evidence, that plaintiffs' have shown an articulable and distinct product market for HRM and FMS sold by Oracle, PeopleSoft and SAP only that does not include mid-market software, outsourcing solutions, best of breed solutions, legacy systems or the infrastructure layer.

Based upon a review of the law and the evidence, the court concludes that the plaintiffs have not met their burden of establishing that the relevant product market is limited to so-called high function FMS and HRM sold by Oracle, PeopleSoft and SAP. The equivocal and vague evidence presented by plaintiffs at trial does not permit the court to exclude mid-market vendors, outsourcing or best of breed solutions from any product market that includes ERP software sold by Oracle, PeopleSoft and SAP.

For reasons discussed above, the court cannot rely upon the testimony of the customer witnesses offered by plaintiffs in determining if plaintiffs have met their burden. Likewise, the testimony of all three industry witnesses offered by plaintiffs affords no reliable or articulable basis to distinguish a high function product market. Ironically, much of plaintiffs' testimony supports a finding of no clear or articulable distinction. Accordingly, the full weight of the plaintiffs' product market burden fell at trial upon [plaintiffs' expert witness] Elzinga.... * * *

Not only does the court find Elzinga's data to be unreliable in establishing a distinct and articulable product market, but Elzinga himself admitted that plaintiffs' product market has no "quantitative metric" that could be used to determine the distinction between a high function product and a mid-market product. Rather, Elzinga kept telling the court that there is "something different" about the products sold by Oracle, SAP and PeopleSoft. But the court cannot delineate product boundaries in multi-billion dollar merger suits based upon the mere notion that there is "something different" about the merging products and all others, especially when that "something different" cannot be expressed in terms to make a judgment of the court have meaning. More is required.

Accordingly, based upon the evidence presented at trial, the court concludes that the following products cannot be excluded from the relevant product market for purposes of analyzing the effects of this merger.

Outsourcing. Professor Hausman presented evidence of over twenty large enterprises that currently outsource all or some of their HRM needs. Furthermore, the testimony of Peters, Bass, Sternklar and Rising all support Hausman's contention that large companies can, and do, have their HRM needs effectively met by outsourcing. Accordingly, outsourcing solutions cannot be excluded. * * *

Mid-market vendors. The court is perplexed about plaintiffs' position that "mid-market solutions" are not part of the product market for high function ERP.... [P]laintiffs' own evidence shows that either (1) Lawson and AMS are a substitute for high function vendors or (2) no substantive demarcation between these two types of vendors exists. This evidence glaringly shows that plaintiffs have failed to prove a distinct relevant product market for this court to analyze. * * *

Microsoft ... Microsoft has the money, the reputation and now, due to the BearingPoint alliance, it has the sales force necessary to become a major competitor for up-market business. Accordingly, the court finds that Microsoft will be a viable substitute for a significant number of consumers should a post-merger Oracle impose a SSNIP in its pricing of ERP software.

Best of breed solutions. The court does not dismiss defendant's bundle argument as an "elaborate distraction" or "economical nonsense" as plaintiffs urge. The reality of this industry is that 90 percent of consumers purchase software "bundles" containing several pillars; rarely does a consumer purchase a single pillar. FMS and HRM pillars typically are sold in a bundle along with additional kinds of EAS, such as CRM or SCM. Further, the discounts that are offered to potential consumers are based on the value of the entire bundle, not simply based upon the presence of an HRM or FMS pillar. Accordingly, when Oracle or PeopleSoft offer a discount on a bundle, they are doing so in order to ensure that the customer purchases all the pillars from Oracle or PeopleSoft, rather than turn to a best of breed vendor.

Incumbent solutions. The court, however, is not persuaded that incumbent solutions would be able to constrain a post-merger Oracle from imposing a SSNIP. Companies can, and apparently do, threaten to "do nothing," in hopes of getting a better price on ERP software. But it is highly unlikely that any monopolist would see this threat as "credible," thereby preventing a SSNIP. Given the ever-changing conditions of both the regulatory and technological aspects of human resources and financial management, it is hard to sustain the idea that large corporations would rather employ an antiquated software system than pay 10 percent more for modern and continuously maintained products. Such a choice in today's business world would be extremely risky and unlikely.

Accordingly, without a relevant market having been established, the court cannot conduct a burden-shifting statistical analysis under Philadelphia National Bank, much less hold that plaintiffs are entitled to such a presumption. Nor, of course, can the court apply the concentration methodology of the Guidelines.... * * *

Findings of Fact: Geographic Market * * *

The court finds that the geographic market in this case is global. * * *

Anticompetitive Effects

Plaintiffs' Evidence of Coordinated Effects

Plaintiffs presented no evidence at trial on coordinated effects. This was a wise decision, as proving the probability of such collusion would definitely be an uphill battle for two reasons. First, the products in the relevant market are not homogeneous. Plaintiffs themselves even argue against homogeneity. Second, there is no price transparency in this market. Prices and discount rates for software are known only to the vendor and the customer, both of whom take great pains to keep such information confidential. Without homogeneity or transparency, the market conditions are not conducive to coordinated effects, either tacit or express ... * * *

Findings of Fact: Unilateral Effects

The court finds that the plaintiffs have wholly failed to prove the fundamental aspect of a unilateral effects case—they have failed to show a "node" or an area of localized competition between Oracle and PeopleSoft. In other words, plaintiffs have failed to prove that there are a significant number of customers (the "node") who regard Oracle and PeopleSoft as their first and second choices. If plaintiffs had made such a showing, then the court could analyze the potential for exercise of monopoly power over this "node" by a post-merger Oracle or the ability of SAP or Lawson to reposition itself within the node in order to constrain such an exercise of monopoly power.

Plaintiffs' attempt to show localized competition based upon customer and expert testimony was flawed and unreliable. Moreover, plaintiffs' evidence was devoid of any thorough econometric analysis such as diversion ratios showing recapture effects. Both the *Kraft Gen Foods* and *Swedish Match* courts, the only other courts explicitly to address unilateral effects, based their rulings in part upon econometric evidence submitted by the parties. *Kraft Gen Foods*, 926 F.Supp. at 356 (relying on econometric evidence of the cross-price elasticity of demand between Post cereal brands and Nabisco brands); *Swedish Match*, 131 F.Supp.2d at 169 (relying upon the diversion ratio between two brands of loose leaf tobacco). * * *

Findings of Fact: Efficiencies

In order for a claimed efficiency to be "cognizable," it must be "substantiate[d]" and "verfi[able]." [1992] *Guidelines* § 4.0. The court finds Oracle's evidence on the claimed cost savings efficiency to be flawed and unverifiable. Catz and Ellison's personal estimations regarding the potential cost savings to Oracle are much too speculative to be afforded credibility. Oracle's efficiency defense based upon future innovations (e g, the superset product) was not verified by internal documents. Oracle presented no evidence regarding the functionality or characteristics the innovative product will contain, nor any evidence regarding its date of availability.

Accordingly, both claimed efficiencies are much too vague and unreliable to rebut a showing of anticompetitive effects. * * *

Conclusions Of Law * * *

Because plaintiffs have failed to meet [the burden of proving the relevant product and geographic market by a preponderance of the evidence], plaintiffs are not entitled to a presumption of illegality under *Philadelphia National Bank* or the *Guidelines*.

Plaintiffs have failed to prove the likelihood that a post-merger Oracle and SAP would tacitly coordinate by allocating customers or markets. Accordingly, the plaintiffs have not met their burden of establishing anticompetitive coordinated effects.

Plaintiffs have failed to prove an area of localized competition between Oracle and PeopleSoft in which a post-merger Oracle could profitably impose a SSNIP. Accordingly, plaintiffs have not met their burden of establishing the likelihood of anticompetitive unilateral effects.

Notwithstanding that plaintiffs have failed to carry their burden to be entitled to relief, Oracle has not proved by a preponderance of the evidence cognizable efficiencies sufficient to rebut any anticompetitive effects of Oracle's acquisition of PeopleSoft.

Because plaintiffs have not shown by a preponderance of the evidence that the merger of Oracle and PeopleSoft is likely substantially to lessen competition in a relevant product and geographic market in violation of 15 USC § 7, the court directs the entry of judgment against plaintiffs and in favor of defendant Oracle Corporation. * * *

QUESTIONS AND COMMENTS

1. Was the court too hard or appropriately hard on the government in its demands for proof?

2. Was the court right to discount the evidence from the customers? Consider the 2010 Horizontal Merger Guidelines advice on customer evidence § 2.2.2. Did the evidence in *Oracle/PeopleSoft* meet the standard of the guidelines?

3. The firms merged in 2006. In 2008 Oracle and SAP raised their prices. As reported by the Wall Street Journal, the price-rise was "a sign that consolidation in the industry may be easing the competition over prices that

has been a hallmark of the last decade." Ben Worthen, SAP, Oracle Boost Software Prices, Wall St. J. July 17, 2008.

NOTE ON UNITED STATES v. H&R BLOCK, INC.

In *H&R Block/TaxAct*, supra page 377, the court found that both coordinated and unilateral effects were probable. The court determined that the government had made out its prima facie case by use of the *Philadelphia National Bank* presumption in view of the high HHI (4291), and that defendants had not rebutted the presumption. Reputation and strong brand names were barriers that kept small competitors and new entrants from challenging the majors. Regarding coordinated effects, the court accepted the government's analysis "that coordination would likely take the form of mutual recognition that neither firm has an interest in an overall 'race to free' in which high-quality tax preparation software is provided for free or very low prices." The court gave credence to evidence that 1) HRB and Intuit had coordinated in the past to lobby the IRS for limits on free offers, and 2) TaxAct had played a special role in constraining price. It "buck[ed] prevailing norms by introducing the free-for-all offer, which others later matched," and was the only significant competitor that offered high quality product free with associated offerings at low prices. Defendants did not rebut plaintiff's case.

The merger was likely to have unilateral effects also, the court found. The evidence showed that HRB and TaxAct were head-to-head competitors. The court rejected defendants' attempt to place HRB and TaxAct in different segments of the market (premium and value). It observed that, even if Intuit is the closest competitor of both HRB and TaxAct, unilateral effects are possible. The government's expert's merger simulation suggested that a unilateral price rise was likely, based in part on the prediction of a diversion rate from TaxAct to HRB of 12% and a diversion rate from HRB to TaxAct of 14%.

Finally, the merger efficiencies claimed were either not merger specific or not verifiable.

MERGERS BETWEEN COMPETITORS

Theory of two effects

Coordinated effects

> By removing a competitive force, mergers can change the competitive environment, creating conditions in which the firms are more likely to behave in cartel-like fashion—albeit without agreement. Prices across the market are likely to rise.

Unilateral effects

> Each of the merging partners puts significant competitive pressure on the other. If one partner raises its prices, it will predictably lose some sales; but a significant part of the lost sales will be diverted to the product of the other partner. The merged firm will thus simultaneously recoup so much of the otherwise lost sales as to make a price rise profitable, and prices of the merged firm will rise. The effect occurs without regard to whether the other firms in the market follow the price rise. But usually the other market participants will adjust their prices upwards under the new umbrella. That is why the European Union calls the phenomenon non-coordinated effects rather than unilateral effects.

iv. Mergers Eliminating Important Potential Competitors

Mergers eliminating potential competitors may be called "potential horizontal mergers." They are often called conglomerate mergers in the caselaw, but they are classified as horizontal by the merger guidelines. They do not increase concentration, but they can possibly change the market dynamics.

The most important Supreme Court case on point is *United States v. Marine Bancorporation*, decided in 1974 on the cusp of the change towards more rigorous microeconomic analysis. The opinion in *Marine Bancorporation* articulates the theories of how a merger between a leading incumbent and a major potential entrant may lessen competition by removing a substantial check against high pricing from the edge of the market or possibly (depending on what counts as lessening competition) remove a player who would have entered the relevant market in a procompetitive way and caused competition to break out in a sluggish market. There are few such cases, and they are seldom won by the plaintiff.

UNITED STATES v. MARINE BANCORPORATION, INC.

418 U.S. 602 (1974).

JUSTICE POWELL: [National Bank of Commerce (NBC), a subsidiary of Marine Bancorporation, was the second largest bank headquartered in the State of Washington. NBC proposed to acquire Washington Trust Bank (WTB), the third largest bank in Spokane. The top three banks in Spokane held 42.1%, 31.6% and 18.6% of deposits, respectively. NBC did not operate in Spokane. The government sued on potential competition theories. The district court dismissed the complaint.] * * *

. . . In developing and applying the [potential competition] doctrine, the Court has recognized that a market extension merger may be unlawful if the target market is substantially concentrated, if the acquiring firm has the characteristics, capabilities, and economic incentive to render it a perceived potential *de novo* entrant, and if the acquiring firm's premerger presence on the fringe of the target market in fact tempered oligopolistic behavior on the part of existing participants in that market. In other words, the Court has interpreted § 7 as encompassing what is commonly known as the "wings effect"—the probability that the acquiring firm prompted premerger procompetitive effects within the target market by being perceived by the existing firms in that market as likely to enter *de novo*.... The elimination of such present procompetitive effects may render a merger unlawful under § 7.

Although the concept of perceived potential entry has been accepted in the Court's prior § 7 cases, the potential-competition theory upon which the Government places principal reliance in the instant case has not. The Court has not previously resolved whether the potential-competition doctrine proscribes a market extension merger solely on the ground that such a merger eliminates the prospect for long-term deconcentration of an oligopolistic market that in theory might result if the acquiring firm were forbidden to enter except through a *de novo* undertaking or through the acquisition of a small existing entrant (a so-called foothold or toehold acquisition).... * * *

C. Potential De Novo or Foothold Entry

... The Government contends that the challenged merger violates § 7 because it eliminates the alleged likelihood that, but for the merger, NBC would enter Spokane *de novo* or through a foothold acquisition. Utilization of one of these methods of entry, it is argued, would be likely to produce deconcentration of the Spokane market over the long run or other procompetitive effects, because NBC would be required to compete vigorously to expand its initially insignificant market share.

Two essential preconditions must exist before it is possible to resolve whether the Government's theory, if proved, establishes a violation of § 7. It must be determined: (i) that in fact NBC has available feasible means for entering the Spokane market other than by acquiring WTB; and (ii) that those means offer a substantial likelihood of ultimately producing deconcentration of that market or other significant procompetitive effects. The parties are in sharp disagreement over the existence of each of these preconditions in this case. There is no dispute that NBC possesses the financial capability and incentive to enter. The controversy turns on what methods of entry are realistically possible and on the likely effect of various methods on the characteristics of the Spokane commercial banking market.

It is undisputed that under state law NBC cannot establish *de novo* branches in Spokane and that its parent holding company cannot hold more than 25% of the stock of any other bank. Entry for NBC into Spokane therefore must be by acquisition of an existing bank. The Government contends that NBC has two distinct alternatives for acquisition of banks smaller than WTB and that either alternative would be likely to benefit the Spokane commercial banking market. [The Court concluded that neither would provide a base for expansion and long term benefits.]

... Accordingly, we cannot hold for the Government on its principal potential-competition theory. Indeed, since the preconditions for that theory are not present, we do not reach it, and therefore we express no view on the appropriate resolution of the question reserved in *Falstaff* [whether a merger that does not worsen existing competitive conditions but eliminates the chance for their improvement can ever violate Section 7]. We reiterate that this case concerns an industry in which new entry is extensively regulated by the State and Federal Governments.

D. Perceived Potential Entry.

The Government's failure to establish that NBC has alternative methods of entry that offer a reasonable likelihood of producing procompetitive effects is determinative of the fourth step of its argument. Rational commercial bankers in Spokane, it must be assumed, are aware of the regulatory barriers that render NBC an unlikely or an insignificant potential entrant except by merger with WTB. In light of those barriers, it is improbable that NBC exerts any meaningful procompetitive influence over Spokane banks by "standing in the wings."

Moreover, the District Court found as a fact that "the threat of entry by NBC into the Spokane market by any means other than the consummation of the merger, to the extent any such threat exists, does not have any significant effect on the competitive practices of commercial banks in that market nor any significant effect on the level of competition therein." . . . Our review of the record indicates that the court's finding was not in error. . . . * * *

Conclusion

In applying the doctrine of potential competition to commercial banking, courts must, as we have noted, take into account the extensive federal and state regulation of banks. Our affirmance of the District Court's judgment in this case rests primarily on state statutory barriers to *de novo* entry and to expansion following entry into a new geographic market. In States where such stringent barriers exist and in the absence of a likelihood of entrenchment, the potential-competition doctrine—grounded as it is on relative freedom of entry on the part of the acquiring firm—will seldom bar a geographic market extension merger by a commercial bank. * * *

QUESTIONS AND COMMENTS

1. Distinguish the two types of potential competition cases—elimination of wings (or moderating) effect and elimination of the probability of actual independent entry but for the merger. What must the plaintiff prove in each case? Why is the Court confident that elimination of a wings effect may lessen competition within the meaning of Section 7 and not confident that elimination of the acquirer's independent entry may violate Section 7?

2. *Marine Bancorporation* is the Supreme Court's last word on mergers that eliminate potential competition. Has it been undercut or confirmed by contemporary Supreme Court antitrust analysis?

NOTE ON GINSBURG v. INBEV, 623 F.3d 1229 (8th Cir. 2010)

Anheuser–Busch, the largest beer brewer in the country with 50% of sales, was acquired by InBev, the largest brewer in the world, which had only a minimal presence in the United States. In *Ginsburg v. InBev*, beer consumers challenged the transaction. The court dismissed the complaint on the pleadings, before significant discovery.

Plaintiffs alleged that the acquisition removed an actual and perceived potential entrant within the parameters of *Marine Bancorporation*. The district court found that plaintiffs had not supported, with sufficient facts, their conclusory allegations either that InBev intended to enter the U.S. market de novo or that any rational market participant had tempered its pricing because it viewed InBev as a potential entrant. The appellate court indicated doubt that plaintiffs could carry their burden. It affirmed dismissal on procedural grounds, but not before commenting on the difficulties of proving that loss of potential competition harms competition. Thus:

> The potential competition theories of § 7 address mergers between firms that are not actual competitors because they produce different products or operate in different geographic markets. Thus, their merger does not reduce the number of competitors or raise concentration in the markets of either. However, their merger *may* reduce competition in two ways—because the threat of new entry by the acquiring firm induced competitors in the acquired firm's market to perform more competitively ("perceived potential competition"), or because the merger forecloses the acquiring firm's future *de novo* entry into the acquired firm's market ("actual potential competition"). Nearly forty years ago, the Supreme Court identified these as plausible theories of § 7 liability but left their parameters undefined; we then upheld the Federal Trade Commission's application of the theories five years later.... Neither court [the Supreme Court nor the Eighth Circuit Court] has applied the theories since [*Marine Bancorporation* and *Yamaha*]. Whatever else may be said, proof of liability under either theory is certain to entail expensive, uncertain litigation, even if, as here, the acquiring firm is rich and powerful and the acquired firm's market highly concentrated. * * *

Is the court appropriately tough on challenges to mergers whose only claimed anticompetitive effect is eliminating potential competition? Does it make any difference if the largest brewer in the world acquires the largest brewer in the United States, there are only a few large and well-known brewers in the country and in the world, and barriers to entry are high in part due to very strong brand names?

c. Non–Horizontal Mergers

Vertical mergers are mergers in the buyer-supplier line. Mergers of firms that are neither competitors nor buyer-suppliers are normally called conglomerate. Often, the firms make complements and therefore their mergers resemble vertical mergers. Vertical and other complementary mergers normally have strong efficiency properties, saving costs and increasing avenues for innovative solutions, and often there is no good anticompetitive story to tell. But not always. The mergers may foreclose competitors from scarce inputs or outlets, increase barriers to entry, and induce collusion. In thinking about all of these properties you may draw lessons from foreclosure analysis and efficiency analysis in the monopoly chapter above and the vertical chapter that follows.

i. Vertical Mergers

For many years, mergers between leading or large buyer-supplier pairs were highly suspect, on grounds that one partner would unfairly get a foot in the door, giving it a preference on the business of the other, all things being equal. This was the rationale for the Supreme Court's condemnation of du Pont's purchase of a large block of General Motors' stock: du Pont gained the privilege of supplying half of GM's needs for automotive fabrics and finishes; GM's needs comprised half of all auto companies' needs. United States v. E.I. du Pont de Nemours & Co., 353 U.S. 586 (1957).

Since the 1980's, the agencies have stressed the efficiency aspects, rather than the foreclosing aspects, of vertical integration. Vertical integration can produce substantial production economies, save substantial transaction costs, and often facilitate innovation. The focus is, first, on whether the merger has consumer-harming properties (not just foreclosure effects), and if so, whether it will produce outbalancing efficiencies that would otherwise be lost to consumers. If the merger conveys market power *and* is efficient, can the efficiency gains be preserved while anticompetitive aspects are substantially cured, for example, by relief that imposes conditions of access?

The FTC entered into several earlier consent orders resolving vertical merger concerns by, among other things, requiring non-discriminatory access by competitors to networks and cable systems. See *AOL/Time Warner*; FTC Dkt. No. C–3989 (consent order to cease and desist, Apr. 17, 2001); *Cadence Design Systems*, Inc., FTC Dkt. No. C–3761 (Aug. 7, 1997). In 2002, the Commission closed its investigation into the acquisition of Avant! by Synopsys, both in the high-tech, network market of electronics design automation, even though Synopsys occupied nearly 90% of the market for front-end tools for chips design and Avant! accounted for about 40% of back end tools.

SYNOPSYS INC. /AVANT! CORPORATION

FTC File No. 021–0049 (2002).

Closing Statement of Commissioner Thomas B. Leary

After an extensive inquiry, the Commission has voted unanimously to close its investigation of the already-consummated acquisition by Synopsys, Inc. of Avant! Corporation. The acquisition was notified under the Hart–Scott–Rodino process on December 28, 2001. The Commission did not choose to seek a preliminary injunction and the transaction closed on June 6, 2002, but the Commission kept the investigation open to consider whether it would be appropriate to bring an administrative complaint for post-closing relief.

Despite the ultimate unanimous vote, resolution of the matter has not been easy. The investigation has generated a small mountain of internal and external commentary, and it has been the subject of intense debate. Not only are the products somewhat exotic but the acquisition is vertical, and analysis of potential effects in vertical mergers is complicated. Like others, I feel an obligation in these circumstances to explain my views, within the constraints imposed by confidentiality obligations.

The products involved in the transaction involve software that is used in the design of computer chips. Synopsys currently enjoys a share of almost 90% in so-called "logical synthesis" or "front-end" tools for chip design and Avant! has a share of about 40% in so-called "place and route" or "back-end" tools. (I am informed that "front-end" tools are roughly analogous to a narrative description of the routes needed to travel between various different destinations and "back-end" tools are roughly analogous to plotted routes on a map.) Traditionally, the front-end tools and the back-end tools have communicated with each other through standard formats that made it possible for tools from one supplier to be used in combination with tools from another.

The first question in this case was whether the acquisition would give Synopsys an incentive to enhance the back-end competitive position of the formerly independent Avant!, by making it harder for competing back-end products to communicate with Synopsys' dominant front-end product. Only if the answer to the first question is affirmative, is it necessary to consider the second question whether any such strategy would adversely affect the competitive process and ultimately injure consumers.

At the risk of over-simplification, it could be said that the early merger cases simply assumed that the answer to both questions should be "yes"—that a vertical merger would create the incentive for the upstream entity to deal exclusively (or on a favored basis) with the downstream affiliate and that this "foreclosure" would adversely affect competition. The so-called "New Learning" or "Chicago–School" theories, which gained widespread acceptance after the late 1970s, challenged both assumptions. It was argued that in many cases a dominant upstream firm could not even theoretically increase its available "single monopoly profit" by foreclosing rivals of a downstream affiliate and that, in any event, a hypothetical foreclosure would not necessarily have an adverse effect on competition.

The 1984 Merger Guidelines [App. D]—which are still authoritative, insofar as they address vertical transactions—specifically mention some circumstances where it was thought that foreclosure could cause competitive harm. Section 4.21, which is potentially pertinent here, states that a merger can raise barriers to entry if the "vertical integration" between the upstream and the downstream markets is so extensive an entrant would have to get into both markets simultaneously, and that this could result in competitive harm if the potential for entry is an important market discipline.

In the intervening years, an extensive "post-Chicago" literature has continued to identify hypothetical situations where an integrated firm may have the incentive to foreclose or disadvantage rivals of its downstream affiliate. Even though it may not be possible to earn more than a single monopoly profit in the short-term, it is argued that conduct of this kind may sufficiently weaken rivals to injure competition and consumers in the long-term. It is, of course, possible that the incentives of a supplier can change if it integrates downstream but an analysis of the factors that will make foreclosure strategies profitable for a single firm is complicated. The further analysis of the factors that will cause these strategies to be anticompetitive (including consideration of offsetting efficiencies) is more complicated still. This complexity may help to explain why the agencies have not revisited the vertical merger guidelines in the last eighteen years.

In light of the economic literature on strategic conduct, however, I believe it is appropriate to broadly interpret the "barriers to entry" language in the 1984 Guidelines. Specifically, I would apply the entry barrier language not only to new competitors but to expanded sales by existing competitors. It still is not enough to show that a foreclosure strategy will benefit the downstream affiliate at the expense of its rivals, but there is concern if these rivals will be so weakened that they are no longer able to discipline a hypothetical price increase through expanded sales of their own.

As the 1984 Guidelines indicate, it is also appropriate to scrutinize with particular care a vertical merger by a company that arguably already enjoys market dominance at one level. Courts are reluctant to pass judgement on aggressive (but non-predatory) strategies of dominant companies, and rightly so. In my view, however, this hands-off policy should not necessarily apply to mergers. I believe we have a statutory obligation to try to sort out and weigh the possible anti-competitive or pro-competitive aspects of a merger transaction, complex though the process may be.

Potential complexities are present here. On the one hand, a merger that could even slightly reinforce the position of an already dominant firm raises serious questions. On the other hand, it is possible that this merger will facilitate an eventual seamless integration between the front-end and the back-end tools. This could result in a vastly improved product, which would be a genuine merger efficiency. We would not want to interfere with this development even if it made life very uncomfortable for competitors at either end.

The point of this discussion is simply to indicate that a full analysis of the potential competitive effects of the Synopsys/Avant! transaction could have been very difficult, particularly since there was a diversity of informed (but not necessarily disinterested) opinions about what the future would hold. Fortunately, the analysis can proceed step-by-step. As my colleagues point out in their own statements, there is good reason to believe that Synopsys has neither the incentive nor the intention to adopt a strategy of total or partial foreclosure (by impeding connections). We can therefore resolve the case at the first step of the analysis. When we decide to close the investigation on this basis, after searching analysis, it does not mean that this is the only important issue. It simply means that right now we do not need to address the even-more complicated issue of the competitive effects of a hypothetical foreclosure.

I also agree that it is prudent to watch this market closely in the future, to see whether our present views about incentives and intentions prove to be accurate....

QUESTIONS AND COMMENTS

1. In *Synopsys*, a real foreclosure could not be expected. But what if the converse had been true? How does the agency or other plaintiff make a convincing story that the merger will increase market power? The most common story in vertical cases is based on foreclosure. For a foreclosure story, rivals of at least one of the merged firms must be foreclosed from a significant percentage of needed inputs or outlets, and it must be the case that the excluded firms cannot efficiently maneuver around the restraint, the market is concentrated, and barriers are high. In some cases, a vertical merger might effectively force two-level entry, if entry is to occur at all. The higher barriers might facilitate collusion by the incumbents. Especially since many vertical mergers entail significant efficiencies, vertical mergers are usually approved, sometimes with conditions requiring nondiscriminatory access.

2. The *AOL/Time Warner* consent order required the merged firm, in its cable and broad band distribution function, to provide non-discriminatory access to Time Warner's content-supplying competitors.

After the FTC's *Synopsys*, the Justice Department faced an important challenge with the announcement by Ticketmaster Entertainment Inc., the largest provider of primary ticketing to major concert venues in the United States and the world with 80% of the U.S. market, that it would merge with Live Nation Worldwide, Inc. Live Nation was the largest promoter of live concerts in the world, owner or operator of 75 live entertainment venues, and the second largest primary ticketing company in the United States.

Live Nation had been a major customer of Ticketmaster. It transformed itself from the only major customer of Ticketmaster to its only major competitive threat, for Live Nation could sell tickets to its own venues, and it began to do so. The merger was apparently a response to the competitive threat, although the companies presented the merger's appeal as efficiencies: The merger would efficiently integrate the production and sale of concerts, reducing costs to concert venue owners and ultimately to consumer/concert-goers.

The Justice Department approved this hotly contested merger, with conditions. To cure the horizontal problem, the judgment required the merged firm, Live Nation International (LNE), to establish two new ticketing entities. But the DOJ was worried also about vertical foreclosure effects—the use of power over performances to foreclose ticketing competitors. The DOJ fashioned conduct remedies with a view to preserving competition by "equally efficient rivals."

JUSTICE DEPARTMENT REQUIRES TICKETMASTER ENTERTAINMENT INC. TO MAKE SIGNIFICANT CHANGES TO ITS MERGER WITH LIVE NATION INC.

(January 25, 2010)

Software Licensing Agreement, Divestiture and Anti–Retaliation Provisions Will Preserve Competition in Ticketing in the United States

The Department of Justice announced today that it will require Ticketmaster Entertainment Inc. to license its ticketing software, divest ticketing assets and subject itself to anti-retaliation provisions in order to proceed with its proposed merger with Live Nation Inc. The department said that the proposed settlement will protect competition for primary ticketing, which will in turn maintain incentives for innovation and discounting. The department said that the merger, as originally proposed, would have substantially lessened competition for primary ticketing in the United States, resulting in higher prices and less innovation for consumers.

The Department of Justice's Antitrust Division, along with 17 state attorneys general, filed a civil antitrust lawsuit today in the U.S. District Court in Washington, D.C., to block the proposed transaction. At the same time, the department and the states' Attorneys General filed a proposed settlement that, if approved by the court, would resolve the competitive concerns in the lawsuit. The state attorneys general offices are: Arizona; Arkansas; California; Florida; Illinois; Iowa; Louisiana; Massachusetts; Nebraska; Nevada; Ohio; Oregon; Pennsylvania; Rhode Island; Tennessee; Texas; and Wisconsin.

The Department of Justice cooperated closely with the Canadian Competition Bureau throughout the course of its investigation, and the two agencies worked together to obtain the same remedy that preserves competition in both the United States and Canada.

Under the proposed settlement, Ticketmaster must license ticket software and divest ticketing assets to two different companies—Anschutz Entertainment Group (AEG) and either Comcast–Spectacor or another buyer suitable to the department, respectively—allowing both companies to compete head-to-head with Ticketmaster. Ticketmaster will also subject itself to court-ordered restrictions on its behavior.

"The Department of Justice's proposed remedy promotes robust competition for primary ticketing services and preserves incentives for competitors to innovate and discount, which will benefit consumers," said Christine Varney, Assistant Attorney General in charge of the Department of Justice's Antitrust Division. "The proposed settlement allows for strong competitors to Ticketmaster, allowing concert venues to have more and better choices for their ticketing needs, and provides for anti-retaliation provisions, which will keep the merged company in check."

As part of the proposed settlement, Ticketmaster must license a copy of its primary ticketing software to AEG, the nation's second-largest concert promoter and operator of some of the most important concert venues in the country. With a copy of the Ticketmaster software, AEG will be able to market a ticketing system that is an attractive choice to venues. AEG will have incentives similar to Live Nation to provide better services at lower prices. Within five years, AEG can purchase the Ticketmaster ticketing software, decide to create its own software, or partner with a ticketing company other than Ticketmaster. The department said that this remedy enhances short and long term competition in the primary ticketing market.

Ticketmaster must divest Paciolan Inc., a ticketing company that it currently owns, within 60 days to either Comcast–Spectacor, which has already signed a letter of intent to purchase the assets, or some other buyer suitable to the department. Comcast–Spectacor is a sports and entertainment company with management relationships with a number of concert venues and ticketing experience with its New Era Tickets company. Paciolan is used by hundreds of venues to sell tickets including major concert venues around the country. Venues that contract with Paciolan have greater flexibility to lower the ticket service fees that are charged to consumers who buy tickets. The department said that divesting Paciolan to Comcast–Spectacor, or another suitable buyer, in conjunction with the AEG license, will replace the competitive pressure on Ticketmaster lost as a result of the merger.

Under the settlement, the merged firm will be forbidden from retaliating against any venue owner that chooses to use another company's ticketing services or another company's promotional services, including restrictions on anticompetitive bundling. The merged firm must also allow any client that leaves and chooses to use another primary ticketing service to take a copy of the ticketing data related to that client's sales. The settlement also sets up firewalls that protect confidential and valuable competitor data by preventing the merged firm from using information gleaned from its ticketing business in its day-to-day operations of its promotions or artist management business. Additionally, the merged firm must provide notice of any other acquisitions of a ticketing company so that the department may investigate the competitive effect of such an acquisition.

Together, these remedies will preserve the competition that Ticketmaster faced from Live Nation, a new ticketing entrant, the department said. Prior to its proposed merger with Ticketmaster, Live Nation had established incentives to reduce service fees to sell more tickets. Today's settlement offers a new competitor comparable incentives to ensure ticket sales are maximized for the benefit of consumers, the department said.

Ticketmaster ... is the world's largest ticketing company. In 2008, Ticketmaster sold more than 141 million tickets valued at more than $8.9 billion on behalf of more than 10,000 clients worldwide and earned approximately $1.4 billion in gross revenues.

Live Nation ... is the world's largest promoter of live concerts, with 2008 worldwide gross revenues of $4 billion. Live Nation also owns or operates more than 75 concert venues of various sizes in the United States.

AEG ... is one of the leading sports and entertainment presenters in the world. AEG ... owns or controls a collection of venues, such as the Staples Center (Los Angeles), Prudential Center (Newark, N.J.), Sprint Center (Kansas City, Mo.) and Citizen's Business Bank Arena (Ontario, Canada). The company's live entertainment division, AEG Live, is one of the world's leading concert promotion and touring companies with 15 regional offices that has recently promoted national tours on behalf of artists such as Prince, Usher, Kenny Chesney, Rod Stewart, Paul McCartney, Yanni, The Eagles, George Strait, Justin Timberlake, Christina Aguilera, Dixie Chicks, Hannah Montana and American Idol. AEG is also a 50 percent owner of Wright Entertainment Group, which manages major artists such as the Jonas Brothers, Justin Timberlake, Janet Jackson and 'N Sync.

Comcast–Spectacor ... has more than $1 billion in annual sales. It is a joint venture between a private investor and Comcast Corp., a leading provider of cable, Internet and phone services in the United States. Comcast–Spectacor owns a national ticketing services company, owns and operates major venues and sport franchises, manages approximately 90 public assembly facilities, and runs a major North American food and beverage concessions company.

* * *

QUESTIONS AND COMMENTS

1. Explain how the vertical aspects of this merger could harm competition. Also explain how the horizontal aspects could do so.

2. Was the final judgment (which was entered on July, 30, 2010) likely to protect competition in concert ticketing and incentivize innovation and discounting? Has it? Are ticket prices higher or lower? Has ticketing competition broken out?

3. Is the final judgment hard or easy to police?
4. Why didn't the DOJ try to enjoin the deal?

ii. Conglomerate Mergers

GE/Honeywell

The European Union courts have more recent experience than U.S. courts with conglomerate mergers. GE/Honeywell—the one "American" merger that was cleared by the American authorities but prohibited by the EU—was conceptualized largely as a conglomerate case, although it had horizontal aspects. A study of the case and particularly the court's judgment shows just how difficult it is to prove that a merger of leading firms that produce complements (different parts and parts systems that go into the same aircraft) is likely to harm consumers and the market.

General Electric Company was the world's largest producer of large and small jet engines for commercial and military aircraft. It and its 50–50 joint venture supplied more than half of all engines for large commercial jets. The engine market was concentrated, with Pratt & Whitney and Rolls–Royce being GE's principal competitors. GE Commercial Aviation Services (GECAS) was one of the world's largest aircraft leasing companies and one of the largest buyers of planes. It bought about 10% of aircraft, it and a sister corporation financed the purchase of airplanes, and it was an important launch customer for airplanes. Once an aircraft manufacturer chooses to incorporate a particular supplier's engine and other elements, the manufacturer normally prefers to continue purchasing the same brand because of efficiencies such as acquired knowledge and training, and replaceability of parts across a fleet. GE had in the past made known its policy or preference to buy only aircraft that incorporated GE engines.

Honeywell International was a leading firm in the production of avionics including navigating equipment, certain nonavionic products, engines for corporate jets, and engine starters.

GE and Honeywell agreed to merge, in what would then have been the largest industrial merger in history. They filed their merger notifications with the U.S. authorities, who cleared the deal after requiring a spinoff of competitively overlapping engine assets, and they filed with the European Commission (among others).

The European Commission expressed concerns on several fronts, including the predictions that: 1) The merged firm, having a large line of complementary products, would probably engage in product bundling. It was likely to lower the price of the bundle. The competitors would be unable to lower their prices to the same extent and would eventually be squeezed from the market, at which time the merged firm would be in a position to raise its prices. 2) GECAS would use its buying and launching platform leverage to induce aircraft makers to shift their business to

Honeywell as well as to GE products, causing a significant shift of business to GE, a weakening of the deserted competitors, and their eventual exit from the market, at which time prices would rise.

On July 3, 2001, the European Commission blocked the merger. General Electric/Honeywell, Case COMP/M2220, July 3, 2001. The Commission declared:

> The combination of the two companies' activities would have resulted in the creation of dominant positions in the markets for the supply of avionics, non-avionics and corporate jet engines, as well as [in] the strengthening of GE's existing dominant positions in jet engines for large commercial and large regional jets. The dominance would have been created or strengthened as a result of horizontal overlaps in some markets as well as through the extension of GE's financial power and vertical integration to Honeywell activities and of the combination of their respective complementary products. Such integration would enable the merged entity to leverage the respective market power of the two companies into the products of one another. This would have the effect of foreclosing competitors, thereby eliminating competition in these markets, ultimately affecting adversely product quality, service and consumers' prices.

Press Release, European Commission, IP/01/939, Brussels, 3 July 2001.

U.S. Assistant Attorney General Charles James issued a press release declaring that the merger "would have been procompetitive and beneficial to consumers.... [The European Commission] apparently concluded that a more diversified, and thus more competitive GE, could somehow disadvantage other market participants." Press release, July 3, 2001.

The prohibition against the GE/Honeywell merger was affirmed by the European General Court on the basis of three horizontal overlaps in engines. As for the Commission's findings that the vertical and conglomerate effects of that merger were anticompetitive, the court reversed. It held that the Commission did not introduce sufficient evidence that the combined firm would have used its leverage; e.g., to cause Honeywell's customers of avionics equipment to buy GE engines or vice versa. The Commission had not proved that the merged firm would have tied products or sold them in bundles. Moreover, the court thought that the abuse of dominance law might have deterred uses of leverage and faulted the Commission for failing to consider whether this would have been the case. *General Electric v. Commission*, Case T–210/01, [2005] ECR–II 5575.

Even if the merged firm would probably have sold its products in bundles, would competition have been harmed? This was a contentious issue that the court did not reach.

What facts would it have taken to establish that the merger of GE and Honeywell was likely to be price-raising? What facts would it have taken to prove that the merger was probably price-lowering? If price effects were too speculative to predict, should we have feared the merger on grounds that the merged firm was likely to use its leverage to shift market share to itself from competitors in both markets—avionics and engines? or, on the contrary, should we have welcomed it on the grounds that the merged firm could offer lower-priced bundles?

In any event, after making the deal, Honeywell's performance deteriorated, and GE, by its chief executive Jack Welch, was no longer happy with the planned merger. The European prohibition was a boon to Welch and GE. See E. Fox, *GE/Honeywell*: The U.S. Merger that Europe Stopped—A Story of the Politics of Convergence, Chap. 12 in ANTITRUST STORIES at 331 (in D. Crane and E. Fox, eds, 2007).

In the years after *GE/Honeywell*, U.S. and EU merger law has come closer and closer together, although the EU remains more concerned than the U.S. about vertical and other foreclosing restraints that tend to increase the market share of firms with significant economic power—as reflected also in EU law on abuse of dominance. Case teams from the U.S. and the EU normally work closely together in vetting mergers of common interest to the extent they can do so consistently with obligations of confidentiality, and usually they reach common assessments.

C. MERGERS AND THE PUBLIC INTEREST

South Africa. The South African Competition Law prohibits mergers likely to substantially prevent or lessen competition, except that the Commission and Tribunal must also examine the transaction's impact on the public interest and it may allow or disallow a merger on public interest grounds whether or not the merger is anticompetitive. The statute says:

> When determining whether a merger can or cannot be justified on public interest grounds, the Competition Commission or the Competition Tribunal must consider the effect that the merger will have on—
>
> "a) a particular industrial sector or industry;
>
> b) employment;
>
> c) the ability of small businesses, or firms controlled or owned by historically disadvantaged persons, to become competitive; and
>
> d) the ability of national industries to compete in international markets." § 12A(3).

Wal–Mart stores, the largest retailer in the world, with a reputation for low prices, low wages, hostility to unions and a global-sourcing chain, sought to enter the South African market by acquiring Massmart Holdings. The Competition Commission—charged with investigating large mergers and presenting them to the Tribunal for action—found no competition problems. After assessing the public interest, including the likelihood that Wal–Mart would create a significant number of jobs, it asked the Tribunal to approve the transaction unconditionally. The unions and the Small Enterprise Forum intervened and asked the Competition Tribunal to block the transaction or, in the alternative, to impose conditions.

Meanwhile, Wal–Mart volunteered to adopt several undertakings, including a moratorium on retrenchments of employees, except for unreasonable refusals of individuals to be redeployed, and hiring preferences for the 503 employees who had been recently laid off by Massmart. Also, it agreed to make an investment in the amount of 100 million Rands (equivalent to approximately US $12 million) to develop South African suppliers' capability to supply Wal–Mart over the next three years, and it agreed to honor collective bargaining rights and the status of the largest retail workers union.

Here is the Competition Tribunal's statement on the conditional approval of the merger, which is a summary of the much longer "Reasons for Decision," which it issued the following month.

WAL–MART AND MASSMART– SOUTH AFRICAN COMPETITION TRIBUNAL

Statement on Conditional Approval of the Merger

(May 31, 2011)
(substantially aff'd, modified in part, by Court of Appeal; see below)
http://www.comptrib.co.za/publications/press-releases/wal-mart-and-massmart-31-may-2011

Introduction

The Competition Tribunal has today approved the merger between Wal–Mart Stores Inc. of the United States ("Walmart") and South African retailer Massmart Holdings Limited ("Massmart"), subject to conditions which are contained in the attached annexure.

The merging parties had initially argued for unconditional approval of the merger, a position initially supported by the Competition Commission. Opposed to this view were three government departments, Economic Development, Trade and Industry and Agriculture, Forestry and Fisheries, who had proposed that the merger be approved, but subject to conditions to protect the public interest. Also intervening were the South African Commercial, Catering and Allied Workers' Union ("SACCAWU") which is recognised by Massmart, the South African Clothing & Textile Workers' Union ("SACTWU"), other unions organising workers in industries which sell products into the retail sector and their federation Congress of South African Trade Unions ("COSATU"). The unions had proposed that the merger be approved subject to a wide range of public interest conditions, but that if this was not possible, that the merger should be prohibited.

The evidence that the Tribunal considered differed in important respects from that considered by the Competition Commission during its earlier investigative process. In our proceedings we have had the benefit of further discovery of documents at the instance of the government departments' team, and the testimony and examination of witnesses brought by the intervenors.

This explains why the Commission changed its recommendation in argument at the end of the hearing, from one of unconditional approval to one with suggested conditions to meet the retrenchment dispute and the concerns over collective bargaining rights. We commend the Commission for not taking a static approach to the proceedings, but we believe that the undertakings furnished by the merging parties largely address the Commission's concerns.

The Tribunal process has also been instrumental in raising issues of concern that, as we consider more fully below, the merging parties have seen fit to react to by making certain undertakings, albeit that they do not concede that they were legally obliged to do so. We appreciate the testimony of witnesses and experts put up by all the parties in these proceedings.

Outcome

It is common cause that this merger raises no competition concerns. Walmart does not compete with Massmart in South Africa and its only presence in the country is a small procurement arm that sources local products for its stores globally. The merging parties contend that the merger will indeed be good for competition by bringing lower prices and additional choice to South African consumers. We accept that this is a likely outcome of the merger based on Walmart's history in bringing about lower prices. However the extent of this consumer benefit is by no means clear—Walmart itself has not been able to put a number to this claim, only that it is likely.

Given our highly concentrated retail market, the strengthening of Massmart, which is in some product categories only a number four or five size retailer, measured in terms of sales, is likely to benefit consumers by strengthening rivalry and improving choice.

This merger will also likely have certain losers. Walmart's proposed entry into areas presently under served by large retailers may displace certain small businesses and in others, reduce the market share of some of the major retailers. That is an inevitable consequence of the competitive process.

We are however required by the Act not to be indifferent to certain public interest concerns caused by a merger, if they are substantial. The purpose of public interest concerns is not to protect firms from losing out to market forces, but to protect a substantial public interest. However the Act does limit our ability to remedy public interest concerns in two ways. First, the Act recognises only a limited set of public interest concerns as specified in the Act. Second, the public interest concerns must be merger specific. Expressed in less technical language, unless the merger is the cause of the public interest concerns, we have no remit to do anything about them. Our job in merger control is not to make the world a better place, only to prevent it becoming worse as a result of a transaction. This narrow construction of our jurisdiction has not always been appreciated by some of the intervenors who have sought remedies whose ambition lies beyond our purpose. It is not our task to determine whether those ambitions are legitimate public policy goals; only whether they lie within our powers.

On the final day of this hearing the merging parties offered certain undertakings to the Tribunal which they agreed might be imposed as conditions for the approval of the merger. These undertakings were made to address certain labour and local procurement concerns raised by intervening parties during the course of the hearing process. The merging parties made it clear that in their view the undertakings were not required legally in order for the merger to be approved, but were offered to meet adverse perceptions about the effect of the merger on the public interest.

Given that the merging parties have tendered certain conditions, our task in assessing the merger has changed in emphasis.

The Tribunal will thus take the approach that it must examine if the undertakings adequately remedy the merger specific public interests concerns raised, on the assumption that they have been established, and provided that their remit is within our jurisdiction. We have come to the conclusion that they are adequate.

Conditions

One of the concerns raised by the intervenors relates to the effect of the merger on employment. The effect on employment may not be confined to the jobs of those employed by the merged firm—it may extend to those not employed by the firm, but whose jobs may be threatened as a result of the merger. Further, employment concerns may not only relate to jobs lost, but also, as we will explain in our reasons, an adverse effect on conditions of employment. The remit of how far we can go in addressing these concerns is controversial and we will address this in our reasons. On the assumption that the merger will have certain adverse affects on employment and conditions of employment, we have examined whether the undertakings adequately remedy them.

Whilst Walmart's expansion plans suggest that retrenchments of the existing workforce are unlikely and that increased employment is more likely, the parties have given an undertaking that there will be no retrenchments at Massmart for two years for merger specific reasons. Although the undertaking is diluted by a redeployment exception, we find that as post merger retrenchments are not likely, the undertaking is adequate.

A hotly contested issue during the merger was whether certain retrenchments that took place in June 2010 affecting certain Massmart employees were merger specific. Whilst the retrenchments coincided with the commencement of the merger negotiations there is no conclusive evidence that it was the cause. Despite this the merging parties agreed during the proceedings to make an undertaking that they will give preference to re-employing these retrenched workers if vacancies arise and to recognise past seniority for this purpose.

A major concern articulated by the union intervenors was that the merger would likely lead to a diminution of their collective bargaining rights. The undertaking to honour collective bargaining rights presently enjoyed addresses this concern. It goes further in undertaking not to challenge the status of SACCAWU as the largest representative of workers in its divisions and invites us to determine the appropriate period for which this condition should hold. We have determined that it should operate for three years.

Finally the parties offered an undertaking to address the local procurement concern raised by the intervenors. Intervenors were concerned that as a result of Walmart's global purchasing powers, which dwarf those of Massmart, the merged firm would be able to source cheaper imports and hence switch some of Massmart's procurement away from local manufacturers to imports, with adverse effects on those employed in these sectors. No specific figure could be given to this apprehended substitution by the intervenors, and the merging parties have contested this, alleging that at worst local importers would be replaced by direct imports and that there would not be a significant decrease in net procurement from local manufacturers. Again this concern is the subject of indeterminate evidence from either side. However, even if the concern is valid, the undertaking for an investment remedy as suggested by the merging parties is in our view appropriate, proportional and enforceable. It avoids concerns that the conditions suggested by some intervenors to impose a form of quota of mandatory domestic purchases on the merged entity, could violate the country's trade obligations, be anti-competitive or be incapable of practical implementation.

Furthermore the investment undertaking is a more positive response to the procurement concern. Instead of insulating local industry from international competition for a period, it seeks to make local industry more competitive to meet international competition. Whilst at a macroeconomic level the remedy is modest, at the level of a single firm commitment it is not. Expenditure of R 100 million over a three year period is significant. Further the remedy seeks to engage those very critics of Walmart in the decision making process over the disbursement of the funds, including representatives of small, medium and micro enterprises ("SMMEs").

We note that the conditions have met some, but not all, the intervenors' expectations of what conditions should be imposed. We will explain in our reasons why some of these expectations are misplaced.

Because the undertakings are made as conditions for the approval of the merger they are enforceable. Non-adherence can lead to serious consequences for the merged firm, including the risk that the merger could be undone. This illustrates that the parties view the undertakings as a serious commitment and not a public relations gesture.

For this reason we have decided to approve the merger subject to the undertakings made by the parties becoming conditions for the approval.

After the Tribunal issued its decision, the Ministers filed a petition for review with the Competition Appeal Court challenging certain discovery procedures and scheduling decisions that limited their interventions. The review was denied.

The South African Commercial Catering and Allied Workers Union (SACCAWU) appealed on the merits. The court permitted the merger and largely affirmed the conditions. However, it reversed as to the retrenched workers and the sufficiency of the investment-fund conditions agreed to by the merging parties. It ordered a study of the effects of global procurement on South African small-and medium-sized businesses.

SOUTH AFRICAN COMMERCIAL CATERING & ALLIED WORKERS UNION v. WAL-MART STORES INC.

Competition Appeal Court of South Africa, 111/CAC/Jun11 (March 9, 2012)

* * *[91] SACCAWU based the foundation of its appeal upon a criticism of the normative approach adopted by the Tribunal to the application of the Act. Thus, it contends that the approach adopted by the Tribunal and further contended for by the merging parties ignored the express language of the Act. It argues that the South African competition regime is concerned with economic or market power, its creation, extension, distribution and (ab)use, and that the entry of a firm with the scale of operations and consequent economic power of Wal-Mart into the South African economy will disrupt the competitive equilibrium and processes in the retail sector, as well as alter competition for suppliers in the retail supply chain.

[92] SACCAWU therefore contends that the merging parties' uncritical adoption of the perspective of a consumer welfare standard ignores its explicit rejection by the Act. SACCAWU suggests that § 12 A [see p. 432 supra] enjoins the competition authorities to take account of factors which do not play a role in terms of the consumer welfare approach to competition policy .... [W]e did not take SACCAWU to be arguing in favour of a total welfare standard which would take account only of consumer and producer surplus, but rather that the Act supported a more nuanced test than that of a consumer welfare standard.

[93] Mr Kennedy, who appeared together with Ms Le Roux on behalf of SACCAWU, contended that a new paradigm was established in terms of the Act, particularly as a result of § 12 A (1) and (3). The articulated public interest concerns incorporated a legislative commitment to a com-

petitive process which seeks to correct socio-economic disadvantage and distortion which arose as result of South Africa's discriminatory past. Accordingly, competition law and policy, as set out in the Act, includes instruments for South Africa's economic development and complement other policy instruments, including trade and industrial policy. In short, § 12 A makes it clear that the analysis, as required by the Act, enjoins the competition authority to undertake an examination of factors beyond standard questions of a contemplated transaction's impact on price and output. * * *

97 While the Tribunal's decision and SACCAWU's argument appear to make common cause that public interest considerations are both part of the overall inquiry into competition concerns, the Act would appear to enjoin the Tribunal to initially examine the transaction within a traditional consumer welfare standard and, thereafter, to test its initial finding further in terms of the broader inquiry as mandated in terms of § 12 A (2) read with § 12 A (3). In other words, having examined whether the merger is likely to substantially prevent or lessen competition by a consideration of factors set out in § 12 A (2), a further inquiry must then take place in terms of a justification on the substantial public interest grounds as set out in subsection (3).

98 Viewed holistically, there is merit in the argument that the Act should be read in terms of an economic perspective that extends beyond a standard consumer welfare approach. By virtue of an embrace of the goals of a free market and effective competition together with an incorporation of uniquely South African elements, including the need to address our exclusionary past, which need is reflected expressly in the preamble together with § 2 of the Act, the legislature imposed ambitious goals upon the competition authorities created in terms of the Act. Within the context of the present dispute, this ambition is further captured in § 12 A which mandates an enquiry into substantial public interest grounds.

99 Correctly, Mr Unterhalter contended on behalf of the merging parties, that the adoption of a standard other than that of consumer welfare would significantly complicate the implementation of the Act, particularly owing to the complexity of the economic calculation of total welfare of a particular transaction, particularly if total welfare extended beyond an exclusive calculation of consumer and producer surplus alone.... An evaluation of whether societal welfare, as envisaged in the Act increases in circumstances where the price of a product reduces to realise a benefit for consumers but takes place at the expense of job losses is extremely difficult to determine; even more so within the context of South African competition law and the scarce technical resources available to the competition authorities, let alone the broader economic tools available. Expressed differently, what weight is to be given to the factors set out in § 12 A (3) in order to determine whether these should trump a finding based on more traditional considerations of consumer welfare as captured in § 12 A (2)?

100 This question does, within the context of the dispute and the wording of the Act as employed in the preamble, read together with sections 2 and 12 A require an answer. From the structure of § 12 A, the Tribunal or this court may be faced with arguments that go to consumer welfare and those that then extend to employment and the interest of small business. An engagement with an exercise of proportionality is then required to determine how to balance the competing arguments. While this exercise may, by its nature and for the reasons set out above, never be precise, it is what the Act appears to require in respect of mergers. En passant, this should not be interpreted to mean that the Act mandates a narrow view of consumer welfare determined exclusively in terms of affects upon price and output. However, a proportionality exercise requires evidence which would enable the exercise, justify the calculation which flows therefrom and permit a balance to be struck between the competing issues of consumer welfare[,] employment and small business. * * *

[The court then examined the economic evidence presented to the Tribunal which demonstrated an ambiguity in the tension between consumer welfare and employment: Namely, even as shifted procurement to overseas sources would clearly eliminate many domestic jobs, lower prices would increase the purchasing power of consumers. Their additional spending in other areas would then create additional jobs. Assessing this offset is a serious problem for the appellants.]

118 These positive factors [lower prices, access to Wal–Mart's global supply chains] would need to be weighed against any losses which will be experienced by small and medium sized businesses, as well as the consequences for employment, when the transaction is viewed holistically. But, as we have noted, in dealing with a standard that seeks to balance consumer and other forms of societal welfare as set out in the Act, it is highly unlikely that, even with further information as sought by the Ministers, a set of calculations could have been produced which would ultimately have justified the conclusion based on such a standard, that the merger should not have b[e]en approved. The available evidence, together with inferences that could reasonably be drawn, particularly from uncontested evidence, supports this conclusion. * * *

[The court proceeded to analyze the evidence of Wal–Mart's anti-union practices, concluding:]

136 But is it the role of competition law to provide the specific safeguards sought by SACCAWU? Viewed within the prevailing analytical discourse of labour law, SACCAWU has raised a series of disputes of interest which must ultimately be determined by way of an exercise of collective power. The conceptual distinction between interest and rights disputes is fundamental to existing South African labour law. The law deals with rights and not interests, which are to be resolved by the exercise of collective power. The negative evidence concerning the 'Wal–Mart model' notwithstanding, this principle should still apply within the context of the merger,

even when the considerations of § 12 A (3) read together with the balance of § 12 A are taken into account. In terms of the conditions set out in the Tribunal's order, no retrenchments for operational reasons can take place for two years and SACCAWU's current position in Massmart is guaranteed for 3 years. Beyond these protections, SACCAWU must use either its bargaining power or, where applicable, rights guaranteed to workers under existing labour law, to protect its members. In summary, it is not the role of competition law to provide legal protections to potential disputes of interest which stand to be resolved by the exercise of collective power. To the extent that the merging parties would seek to erode union or employee rights guaranteed under existing law, these will be protected by the labour courts, which are set up to deal with disputes of rights. * * *

148 The Tribunal accepted the proposal [see the conditions agreed to by the parties in the Tribunal's decision above] and made it part of its order. Unfortunately, as it appears from its determination, it did so without any sustained engagement as to how the remedy would operate, whether an amount of R 100 million was excessive or too little and, further, what effect the proposal would have in dealing with the concern that, at the very least, post the merger there would be some substitution of local procurement for import. The merging parties' proposal received no more than three paragraphs of explanation in the determination of the Tribunal. Accordingly, in our view, there was an inadequate interrogation of this proposal in relation to the arguments that have been put up by the intervening parties concerning the possible problem of increased procurement by way of imports and, in turn, the potential for a negative effect upon the South African economy, in terms of factors which fell within the scope of § 12 A (3); in particular the effect on small producers, as it emerged from the evidence, and employment. * * *

154 That there is insufficient evidence to refuse the approval of the merger does not mean that the case made out by the intervening parties stands to be rejected completely and hence the concerns raised regarding the effect of the merger on small and medium sized producers and employment have no justification. The fact that conditions were imposed by the Tribunal, no matter the criticism of its reasoning, is reflective of this concern. Manifestly, competition law cannot be a substitute for industrial or trade policy; hence this court cannot construct a holistic policy to address the challenges which are posed by globalisation. But the public interest concerns set out in § 12 A demands that this court gives tangible effect to the legislative ambition.

155 Within this context a key issue with regard to this merger and its effect on both the South African consumer and small producer turns on an understanding of the development of global value chains, viewed within the broader context of economic globalisation. Only within this framework can the effect on South African small and medium sized business be adequately assessed.... This exercise would greatly have assisted this Court to tease out the comprehensive implications of the development of

global value chains and the consequences of the introduction of the Wal–Mart model into South Africa. * * *

158 Even this brief reference to the nature of global value chains reveals that the introduction of the largest retailer in the world to the South African economy may pose significant challenges for the participation of South African producers in global value chains which, as the evidence indicates within the retailing sector, is dominated by Wal–Mart. Failure to engage meaningfully with the implications of this challenge posed by globalisation can well have detrimental economic and social effects for the South African economy in general and small and medium sized business in particular. * * *

[The court held that the Tribunal insufficiently investigated the impact of a global procurement model on small-and medium-sized South African businesses and that a much more expansive consideration of proposals to remedy that impact was necessary.]

170 For these reasons, a dialogic model in which this court can engage with the parties to resolve the outstanding disputes is, in our view, suitable for adjudication in these kind of matters and thus justifies an order that the court benefit from expert advice, further responses from the parties, all of which must be made available in the shortest possible time. * * *

The Court of Appeal affirmed the Tribunal as to approval of the merger. It ordered a study of the potential consequences of the merger to South African suppliers. It set a three month deadline for the study, which is to be paid for by the merged entity and conducted by representatives of the merged entity, the union, and the Ministers. Additionally, it replaced the commitment to preferrential hiring of the 503 retrenched workers in the event of job openings with required reinstatement. There must be no future merger-related retrenchments for two years. The merger must honor existing labor agreements for at least three years.

QUESTIONS AND COMMENTS

1. Wal–Mart's annual revenue is more than US $400 billion—larger than South Africa's GDP. "In 2004, Wal–Mart, if it was measured as a country, would have been China's 8th largest trade partner and would have a GDP larger than 75 percent of countries worldwide." Joint statement of the government departments explaining their decision to seek review, available at *http://www.thedti.gov.za/editmedia.jsp?id=2255*. Are these facts relevant?

2. Compare the differences in approach, and therefore differences in the conditions imposed, by the Tribunal and by the Court of Appeal. Is one perspective wiser or truer to the law or its spirit than the other?

3. Describe how the Tribunal and Court grapple with the tensions between protecting workers, protecting small suppliers, and protecting con-

sumers. To what extent are the harms static rather than dynamic (i.e. harms to existing workers as opposed to future jobs in South Africa)? Does a formula or methodology emerge for assessing the harms and making the trade-offs? Can you suggest a better formula or methodology?

4. What is the threshold, and what should it be, for finding that a merger raises substantial public interest problems and therefore should be enjoined or conditioned? Note that both judicial bodies find that substantial public interest issues are raised; the merger should not be prohibited; but it should be conditioned. (Do you agree?) The Court declares that the conditions should be proportionate to the harm. Thus, the fund itself, which is meant to enable South African suppliers, should be sufficiently well financed and the monies appropriately distributed to cure the harm that would befall South African suppliers by reason of the merger. (Or is it: by reason of Wal–Mart's entry into South Africa?) Advise the lawyers preparing the report to the Court on how to determine the level of funding necessary and the modus operandi suited for distribution of the funds.

Similar job and supplier issues arose in a U.S. court, but, of course, under a different statute. Following are excerpts from the Federal District Court in Puerto Rico. After the decision issued, the parties settled the case on the basis of undisclosed commitments by Wal–Mart, and the court accepted the entreaty of the parties (obviously motivated by Puerto Rico) to vacate the opinion and judgment particularly in view of a controversy whether the U.S. federal court has the power to enjoin an act of a Puerto Rican Minister.

Wal–Mart–United States

Wal–Mart Stores, Inc. v. Rodriguez, 238 F.Supp.2d 423 (D.P.R. 2003), settled and decision vacated on unrelated grounds, 322 F.3d 747 (1st Cir. 2003). (Therefore this is not legal authority; it is included for its perspective and reasoning.)

Wal–Mart sought to buy Supermercados Amigo, a supermarket chain in Puerto Rico. The parties notified both the federal and commonwealth antitrust authorities. The FTC approved the acquisition subject to divestiture of four stores at locations where there were competitive overlaps. Meanwhile, local interests were pressuring the Puerto Rico Department of Justice and Anabelle Rodriguez, Secretary of Justice, to stop the merger under the Puerto Rico Anti–Monopoly Act, or at least to protect the public interest in jobs and local sales. Rodriguez believed that she was at liberty to negotiate for concessions on these points for the good of the people of the Commonwealth of Puerto Rico. "[T]he protection and preservation of existing jobs, as well as the creation of new ones, [was] the highest priority of the current administration." Rodriguez demanded that Wal–Mart agree not to "reduce or suspend its current volume of local agricultural and/or food products" and that Wal–Mart guarantee that it would continue to employ the current work force. Wal–Mart was willing to commit to buy as much locally as "it could" and submitted evidence that its purchases were increasing; and it was willing even to maintain the *level* of its current workforce, but not to retain all existing employees. When the negotiations faltered, Rodriguez sued to enjoin the "monopolistic" merger.

In turn, Wal–Mart sued Rodriguez to block her from prohibiting the merger. The court granted Wal–Mart a preliminary injunction on grounds that Rodriguez had evidenced a pattern of bad faith in the negotiations and that the imposition of the conditions guaranteeing jobs and local purchases violated the Commerce Clause and Equal Protection Clause of the U.S. Constitution.

In the course of its analysis, the court noted these effects of the "public policy" clauses:

> *Labor*
>
> The controversy in the language of the agreements with regards to [the] labor issue can be best summarized as follows: while the PRDOJ wanted to get Wal–Mart to agree not to alter the current labor force, that is, the employees that are currently working at the Amigo stores, Wal–Mart was willing to agree to maintain the current number of employees, leaving open the possibility that current employees could be terminated as long as their positions were not eliminated. But despite their lack of intention to downsize their current work force, Plaintiffs could not agree to maintain the current employees and forego the possibility of ever letting go of anyone who currently works at Amigo. Wal–Mart anticipated that just like in any other acquisition, there was a possibility that the integration process would reveal deficiencies in the labor force that would need to be remedied. Moreover, no layoffs in the stores were anticipated, but Wal–Mart could not make the same commitment with regards to positions in their administrative and home offices. The phenomenon of attrition, over which they have no control, was also raised as a concern for Wal–Mart. Finally, as with the levels of purchase condition, Wal–Mart would be at a disadvantage with competitors if forced to maintain the current labor work force.
>
> *"Buy-local"*
>
> ... Defendant suggested in her various press releases that the people of Puerto Rico would be negatively affected by the merger of

Wal–Mart and Amigo since there was no guarantee that they would buy the same level of merchandise and agricultural goods from local suppliers and distributors as Amigo had in the past. But Wal–Mart understood that these requests were not only unfair but contrary to the interest of the people of Puerto Rico. Knowledge of imposed quotas on Wal–Mart would limit its bargaining power with suppliers, who would end up selling goods at higher prices in light of the quotas, and that increment would have to be passed on to consumers, of course, the people of Puerto Rico.

* * *

... In both its effect and purpose, the requirement differentiates between local Puerto Rico growers and out-of-state producers by mandating a quota of local products to be purchased annually. This differential treatment favors the interests of Puerto Rico growers, who are given a guaranteed market for the products sheltered from the usual perils of the market, while shutting out out-of-state growers from the potentially lucrative business relationship with Wal–Mart. Regardless of the quality of their products, the consistency of their supply, or the prices they offer, local growers would have a guaranteed and insurmountable advantage over out-of-state growers. This, in part, violates Wal–Mart's right to engage in interstate commerce, which is now reduced to "exclusivity contracts" with local growers, despite the myriad alternatives in interstate commerce.

In the face of this direct and discriminatory interference with interstate commerce, the Secretary of Justice offers no legitimate purpose. As has been suggested throughout this opinion, she invokes the public policy of the administration she currently works with as her source of authority that allows her to make these demands from Plaintiffs during their negotiations. She stated in a press release that "the public policy is directed at protecting the necessary balance that should exist between Puerto Rican and foreign capital and the benefits that it entails for the consumers." Whether or not Wal–Mart *should* attempt to strike that balance is not for this Court nor any other to determine for as long as it engages as a free market participant within the boundaries of the law, it is to make its own business decisions without governmental interference. But confronted with facially discriminatory remarks such as this one, we can and do determine that the Secretary is engaging in state protectionism prohibited by the federal constitution.

QUESTIONS AND COMMENTS

1. Is there a "Wal–Mart problem"? If so, how do you define it? Should it be addressable within the discipline of antitrust? Is there a "law of Wal–Mart"? See L. Backer. Economic Globalisation and the Rise of Efficient Systems of Global Private Lawmaking: Wal–Mart as a Global Legislator, 39 U. Conn. L. Rev. 39 (2007).

2. Take stock now of the few alleged public interest antitrust cases we have met. *Boeing*—national champion (page 404 supra); *International Shoe* and *Citizens Publishing Company*—failing company (pages 367 supra). In the next chapter we will deal with education (distributing college financial aid to more students, *Brown/MIT*, page 533 infra), and defense, *United Launch Alliance* (page 584 infra). We have also dealt with many exemptions and exceptions including state action and labor exemptions, and there are also exemptions in agriculture and insurance, among others. We have dealt with cases in which non-competition public interest defenses have been denied: *Standard Oil* (supra, page 33), *National Society of Professional Engineers* (supra page 77), *Superior Court Trial Lawyers* (supra page 102.

Other jurisdictions have allowed a public interest override for bank mergers in times of financial crisis to save the bank and financial system, as in UK's approval of Lloyds/HBOS in 2008 after the UK Office of Fair Trading had found the merger anticompetitive. Two years later John Vickers, the Chairman of the UK's Independent Commission on Banking, said the government's decision to waive normal merger law "would appear to have been a mistake." Paper prepared for Bank of International Settlement; see The Guardian, Nov. 26, 2010. The UK Parliament Treasury Committee also acknowledged the need for more competition in banking and regretted that "it may be too late to unwind" Lloyds/HBOS. See George Parker and Charlene Goff, Too Late for an 'Unbundling' of Lloyds–HBOS, Financial Times, April 8, 2011.

South Africa's public interest component has had greatest play in attempts to improve the competitive opportunities of historically discriminated-against persons as well as to improve employment conditions that particularly affect historically discriminated-against persons. See, for example, the Tribunal's consideration and rejection of a public interest override in *Shell South Africa and Tepco Petroleum Ltd.*, Case 66 /LM/Oct01, Feb. 22, 2002 (requiring an acquiring company to keep alive a "black" brand, where imposing such conditions would have decreased the sales value of the selling companies and would have hurt, not helped, historically disadvantaged persons).

3. Comment on the U.S. stance on antitrust and non-competition public interests. Has U.S. antitrust law taken the right approach for the United States? Has South Africa taken the right approach for South Africa?

D. PROCEDURE: PRE-MERGER NOTIFICATION

Much of antitrust merger practice is devoted to premerger filings and attendant analyses and meetings with government officials. Large international mergers may require filings in some 30 to 40 jurisdictions. Before Exxon and Mobil merged in 1999 they were required to vet their merger in more than 30 jurisdictions, including, in addition to the United States: Australia, Canada, the European Union, Japan, and countries in Africa, Central and Eastern Europe, Latin America, and the former Soviet Union.

The agencies normally want to know the same basic facts from the hopeful merger partners, and often the regulating countries' markets present identical problems. Yet each of the jurisdictions has its separate forms, timetables, and filing fees. The overlaps and burdens have led to serious efforts for harmonization some of which has been accomplished in the context of the International Competition Network.

Here is a skeletal view of the U.S. system, under the Hart–Scott–Rodino Antitrust Improvements Act of 1976, as amended:

Merger parties must file premerger notification, along with a significant amount of information, for mergers above a threshold size. They must then wait (not close the transaction) for 30 days (15 days for cash tender offers). Within the waiting period the government may require further information by way of a "second request." The second request typically requires an extensive amount of information. The waiting period may be extended for 30 days (10 days for cash tender offers) from the time of compliance with the second request. If within the waiting period the government sues and moves for preliminary relief, its motion is entitled to expedited treatment in the courts.

In general, notification is required where (for 2012), as the result of the acquisition, the acquiring person would hold aggregate stock or assets of the acquired person:

(A) in excess of $272.8 million; or if less:

(B) (i) in excess of $68.2 million and

(ii) (I) any voting securities or assets of a manufacturer having sales or assets of $13.6 million or more are being acquired by a person with sales or assets of $136.4 million or more,

(II) any voting securities or assets of a non-manufacturer which has assets of $13.6 million or more are being acquired by a person with sales or assets of $136.4 million or more, or

(III) any voting securities or assets of a person with sales or assets of $136.4 million or more are being acquired by a person with sales or assets of $13.6 million or more.

These figures are adjusted annually.

E. ENFORCEMENT

In the United States, if a merger passes successfully through the Hart–Scott–Rodino process without challenge, the legal effect is merely that the federal government has waived its right to seek a preliminary injunction before the closing. The merger may still be challenged by the federal government if it is deemed anticompetitive, although subsequent federal challenge is rare. Also, private parties and state attorneys general can still sue. In *California v. American Stores Co.*, after American Stores had acquired Von's and had disposed of certain overlapping supermarkets pursuant to an FTC consent order, the State of California, on behalf of natural persons in the state, sued for further divestiture. The Supreme Court upheld California's right to proceed. 495 U.S. 271 (1990).

In Europe, a merger is of "Community dimension" if it passes the size and geographic thresholds of the European Merger Regulation. A merger of Community dimensions must be vetted by the European Commission and not by any of the Member States, unless it is "handed back" to a specially interested state or is necessary to protect legitimate interests of the Member State such as in public security, plurality of the media, or prudential rules. If the Commission clears the merger, with or without conditions, the merger may not be challenged by any state or person within the European Union or the broader European Economic Area. Thus, there is a one-stop shop.

Compare the two systems: one-stop shop versus diversity of enforcement centers. Is one system superior? For international mergers, should there be a one-stop shop for the world?

F. PRIVATE STANDING TO SUE

Sections 4 and 16 of the Clayton Act created an enforcement role for private attorneys general. Private persons injured by or threatened with injury from antitrust violations are empowered to sue. Under Section 4 they can get treble damages. Under Section 16 they can get injunctive relief. But how robust is the private right of action against mergers, which may be held illegal, if at all, for a prospective harm? And what must be the relation of the plaintiff to the violation?

In *Brunswick v. Pueblo Bowl–O–Mat, Inc.*, 429 U.S. 477 (1977), a small operator of bowling alleys challenged Brunswick's acquisition of several failing bowling alleys, some of which competed directly with plaintiff. Plaintiff alleged that the acquisitions were anticompetitive and that it was injured by the antitrust violation; but for the acquisitions the acquired alleys would have failed and the plaintiff would have won the "extra" business available. The Supreme Court took the opportunity to clarify the limits of Section 4 of the Clayton Act. A damage claimant must prove "antitrust injury"—injury by reason of that which the antitrust laws forbid. Pueblo Bowl–O–Mat was injured not by restrained competition but by competition itself. Brunswick had kept alive the faltering alleys; as a result of its acquisitions the failing bowling alleys became competitive factors in the marketplace. Injury from competition itself cannot be antitrust injury.

Most private antimerger actions have not been damage actions. Private plaintiffs—usually competitors or targets—may want to prevent a merger or takeover from occurring. For many years, in most cases, these plaintiffs were accorded standing without challenge.

In the early 1980s the Justice Department embarked on an effort, through speeches and amicus briefs, to stop private competitor and takeover target lawsuits. For competitor lawsuits, the Justice Department presented a simple paradigm: If a merger is anticompetitive, that is so because it is price-raising and output-limiting. If a merger raises price the competitors will come under the price umbrella and stand to profit. They will be happy and they will not sue. But if the merger is efficiency-creating the merged firm is likely to become a fierce rival. The competitors will be unhappy and will try to block the merger. Therefore, if competitors sue, the merger must be efficient and good. Does this make sense? Does the proposition always hold true? Does your answer depend upon whether strategic behavior can hurt both targeted competitors and consumers? See O. Williamson, Delimiting Antitrust, 76 Geo.L.J. 271 (1987), for an economic explanation as to how a merger of competitors can threaten antitrust injury to smaller rivals as well as to consumers.

In the mid–1980s, Monfort of Colorado, a beef packer, challenged the merger of two of its big competitors, Cargill (Excel) and Spencer. The district court found a violation of Section 7 of the Clayton Act and ordered divestiture. When the case reached the Supreme Court the Justice Department filed an amicus brief, arguing among other things that Monfort did not have standing to sue. The Supreme Court dealt only with the standing issue.

CARGILL, INC. v. MONFORT OF COLORADO, INC.

479 U.S. 104 (1986).

JUSTICE BRENNAN: Under § 16 of the Clayton Act, private parties "threatened [with] loss or damage by a violation of the antitrust laws" may seek injunctive relief. This case presents two questions: whether a plaintiff seeking relief under § 16 must prove a threat of antitrust injury, and, if so, whether loss or damage due to increased competition constitutes such injury.

I

Respondent Monfort of Colorado, Inc. (Monfort), the plaintiff below, owns and operates three integrated beef-packing plants, that is, plants for both the slaughter of cattle and the fabrication of beef.[1] Monfort operates in both the market for fed cattle (the input market) and the market for fabricated beef (the output market). These markets are highly competi-

1. As the District Court explained, " '[f]abrication' is the process whereby the carcass is broken down into either whole cuts (referred to as 'primals', 'subprimals' and 'portions') or ground beef." 591 F.Supp. 683, 690 (D.Colo.1983). Whole cuts that are then vacuum-packed before shipment are called "boxed beef"; the District Court found that "80% of all beef received at the retail supermarket level and at the hotel, restaurant, and institutional ('HRI') level" is boxed beef. *Ibid.*

tive, and the profit margins of the major beef packers are low. The current markets are a product of two decades of intense competition, during which time packers with modern integrated plants have gradually displaced packers with separate slaughter and fabrication plants.

Monfort is the country's fifth-largest beef packer. Petitioner Excel Corporation (Excel), one of the two defendants below, is the second-largest packer. Excel operates five integrated plants and one fabrication plant. It is a wholly owned subsidiary of Cargill, Inc., the other defendant below, a large privately owned corporation with more than 150 subsidiaries in at least 35 countries.

On June 17, 1983, Excel signed an agreement to acquire the third-largest packer in the market, Spencer Beef, a division of the Land O'Lakes agricultural cooperative. Spencer Beef owned two integrated plants and one slaughtering plant. After the acquisition, Excel would still be the second-largest packer, but would command a market share almost equal to that of the largest packer, IBP, Inc. (IBP).[2]

Monfort brought an action under § 16 of the Clayton Act, 15 U.S.C. § 26, to enjoin the prospective merger. Its complaint alleged that the acquisition would "violat[e] Section 7 of the Clayton Act because the effect of the proposed acquisition may be substantially to lessen competition or tend to create a monopoly in several different ways...." Monfort described the injury that it allegedly would suffer in this way:

> "(f) *Impairment of plaintiff's ability to compete.* The proposed acquisition will result in a concentration of economic power in the relevant markets which threatens Monfort's supply of fed cattle and its ability to compete in the boxed beef market." *Id.,* at 20.

... After the trial, the court entered a memorandum opinion and order enjoining the proposed merger. The court held that Monfort's allegation of "price-cost 'squeeze'" that would "severely narro[w]" Monfort's profit margins constituted an allegation of antitrust injury. It also held that Monfort had shown that the proposed merger would cause this profit-squeeze to occur, and that the merger violated § 7 of the Clayton Act.

On appeal, Excel argued that an allegation of lost profits due to a "price-cost squeeze" was nothing more than an allegation of losses due to vigorous competition, and that losses from competition do not constitute antitrust injury. It also argued that the District Court erred in analyzing the facts relevant to the § 7 inquiry. The Court of Appeals affirmed the judgment in all respects. It held that Monfort's allegation of a "price-cost squeeze" was not simply an allegation of injury from competition; in its view, the alleged "price-cost squeeze" was a claim that Monfort would be injured by what the Court of Appeals "consider[ed] to be a form of

---

2. ... According to the testimony, Monfort's share of the cattle slaughter market was 5.5%, Excel's share was 13.3%, and IBP's was 24.4%. Monfort's share of the production market was 5.7%, Excel's share was 14.1%, and IBP's share was 27.3%. After the merger, Excel's share of each market would increase to 20.4%.

predatory pricing in which Excel will drive other companies out of the market by paying more to its cattle suppliers and charging less for boxed beef that it sells to institutional buyers and consumers." 761 F.2d 570, 575 (CA10 1985). On the § 7 issue, the Court of Appeals held that the District Court's decision was not clearly erroneous. We granted certiorari.

II

This case requires us to decide, at the outset, a question we have not previously addressed: whether a private plaintiff seeking an injunction under § 16 of the Clayton Act must show a threat of antitrust injury. To decide the question, we must look first to the source of the antitrust injury requirement, which lies in a related provision of the Clayton Act, § 4.

Like § 16, § 4 provides a vehicle for private enforcement of the antitrust laws. Under § 4, "any person who shall be injured in his business or property by reason of anything forbidden in the antitrust laws may sue therefor in any district court of the United States . . ., and shall recover threefold the damages by him sustained, and the cost of suit, including a reasonable attorney's fee." In *Brunswick Corp. v. Pueblo Bowl–O–Mat, Inc.,* [429 U.S. 477 (1977)] we held that plaintiffs seeking treble damages under § 4 must show more than simply an "injury causally linked" to a particular merger; instead, "plaintiffs must prove *antitrust* injury, which is to say injury of the type the antitrust laws were intended to prevent and that flows from that which makes the defendants' acts unlawful." *Id.,* at 489 (emphasis in original). The plaintiffs in *Brunswick* did not prove such injury. The plaintiffs were 3 of the 10 bowling centers owned by a relatively small bowling chain. The defendant, one of the two largest bowling chains in the country, acquired several bowling centers located in the plaintiffs' market that would have gone out of business but for the acquisition. The plaintiffs sought treble damages under § 4, alleging as injury "the loss of income that would have accrued had the acquired centers gone bankrupt" and had competition in their markets consequently been reduced. *Id.,* at 487. We held that this injury, although causally related to a merger alleged to violate § 7, was not an antitrust injury, since "[i]t is inimical to [the antitrust] laws to award damages" for losses stemming from continued competition. *Id.,* at 488. This reasoning in *Brunswick* was consistent with the principle that "the antitrust laws . . . were enacted for 'the protection of *competition,* not *competitors.*' " *Ibid.,* quoting *Brown Shoe Co. v. United States,* 370 U.S. 294, 320 (1962) (emphasis in original).

Subsequent decisions confirmed the importance of showing antitrust injury under § 4. In *Blue Shield of Virginia v. McCready,* 457 U.S. 465 (1982), we found that a health-plan subscriber suffered antitrust injury as a result of the plan's "purposefully *anticompetitive scheme*" to reduce competition for psychotherapeutic services by reimbursing subscribers for services provided by psychiatrists but not for services provided by psychologists. *Id.,* at 483. We noted that antitrust injury, "as analyzed in *Brunswick,* is one factor to be considered in determining the redressability of a particular form of injury under § 4," *id.,* at 483, n. 19, and found it "plain that McCready's injury was of a type that Congress sought to redress in providing a private remedy for violations of the antitrust laws." *Id.,* at 483. Similarly, in *Associated General Contractors of California, Inc. v. Carpenters,* 459 U.S. 519 (1983), we applied "the *Brunswick* test," and found that the petitioner had failed to allege antitrust injury. *Id.,* at 539–540.[5]

Section 16 of the Clayton Act provides in part that "[a]ny person, firm, corporation, or association shall be entitled to sue for and have injunctive relief ... against threatened loss or damage by a violation of the antitrust laws...." It is plain that § 16 and § 4 do differ in various ways. For example, § 4 requires a plaintiff to show actual injury, but § 16 requires a showing only of "threatened" loss or damage; similarly, § 4 requires a showing of injury to "business or property," cf. *Hawaii v. Standard Oil Co.,* 405 U.S. 251 (1972), while § 16 contains no such limitation.[6] Although these differences do affect the nature of the injury cognizable under each section, the lower courts, including the courts below, have found that under both § 16 and § 4 the plaintiff must still allege an injury of the type the antitrust laws were designed to prevent. We agree.

The wording concerning the relationship of the injury to the violation of the antitrust laws in each section is comparable. Section 4 requires proof of injury "by reason of anything forbidden in the antitrust laws"; § 16 requires proof of "threatened loss or damage by a violation of the antitrust laws." It would be anomalous, we think, to read the Clayton Act to authorize a private plaintiff to secure an injunction against a threatened injury for which he would not be entitled to compensation if the injury actually occurred.

---

5. A showing of antitrust injury is necessary, but not always sufficient, to establish standing under § 4, because a party may have suffered antitrust injury but may not be a proper plaintiff under § 4 for other reasons.... Thus, in *Associated General Contractors* we considered other factors in addition to antitrust injury to determine whether the petitioner was a proper plaintiff under § 4. 459 U.S., at 540. As we explain *infra,* n. 6, however, many of these other factors are not relevant to the standing inquiry under § 16.

6. Standing analysis under § 16 will not always be identical to standing analysis under § 4. For example, the difference in the remedy each section provides means that certain considerations relevant to a determination of standing under § 4 are not relevant under § 16. The treble-damages remedy, if afforded to "every person tangentially affected by an antitrust violation," *Blue Shield of Virginia v. McCready,* 457 U.S. 465, 476–477 (1982), or for "all injuries that might conceivably be traced to an antitrust violation," *Hawaii v. Standard Oil Co.,* 405 U.S., at 263, n. 14, would "open the door to duplicative recoveries," *id.,* at 264, and to multiple lawsuits. In order to protect against multiple lawsuits and duplicative recoveries, courts should examine other factors in addition to antitrust injury, such as the potential for duplicative recovery, the complexity of apportioning damages, and the existence of other parties that have been more directly harmed, to determine whether a party is a proper plaintiff under § 4. See *Associated General Contractors,* 459 U.S., at 544–545; *Illinois Brick Co. v. Illinois,* 431 U.S. 720 (1977). Conversely, under § 16, the only remedy available is equitable in nature, and, as we recognized in *Hawaii v. Standard Oil Co.,* "the fact is that one injunction is as effective as 100, and, concomitantly, that 100 injunctions are no more effective than one." 405 U.S., at 261. Thus, because standing under § 16 raises no threat of multiple lawsuits or duplicative recoveries, some of the factors other than antitrust injury that are appropriate to a determination of standing under § 4 are not relevant under § 16.

There is no indication that Congress intended such a result. Indeed, the legislative history of § 16 is consistent with the view that § 16 affords private plaintiffs injunctive relief only for those injuries cognizable under § 4....[8] Sections 4 and 16 are thus best understood as providing complementary remedies for a single set of injuries. Accordingly, we conclude that in order to seek injunctive relief under § 16, a private plaintiff must allege threatened loss or damage "of the type the antitrust laws were designed to prevent and that flows from that which makes defendants' acts unlawful." *Brunswick,* 429 U.S., at 489. We therefore turn to the question of whether the proposed merger in this case threatened respondent with antitrust injury.

III

... Monfort did present testimony and other evidence that helped define the threatened loss. Monfort alleged that after the merger, Excel would attempt to increase its market share at the expense of smaller rivals, such as Monfort. To that end, Monfort claimed, Excel would bid up the price it would pay for cattle, and reduce the price at which it sold boxed beef. Although such a strategy, which Monfort labeled a "cost-price squeeze," would reduce Excel's profits, Excel's parent corporation had the financial reserves to enable Excel to pursue such a strategy. Eventually, according to Monfort, smaller competitors lacking significant reserves and unable to match Excel's prices would be driven from the market; at this point Excel would raise the price of its boxed beef to supracompetitive levels, and would more than recoup the profits it lost during the initial phase.

From this scenario two theories of injury to Monfort emerge: (1) a threat of a loss of profits stemming from the possibility that Excel, after the merger, would lower its prices to a level at or only slightly above its costs; (2) a threat of being driven out of business by the possibility that Excel, after the merger, would lower its prices to a level below its costs. We discuss each theory in turn.

A

Monfort's first claim is that after the merger, Excel would lower its prices to some level at or slightly above its costs in order to compete with other packers for market share. Excel would be in a position to do this

8. See also S.Rep. No. 698, 63d Cong., 2d Sess., 17–18, 50 (1914). Although the references to § 16 in the debates on the passage of the Clayton Act are scarce, those that were made are consistent with the House and Senate Reports. For example, in this excerpt from a provision-by-provision description of the bill, Representative McGillicuddy (a member of the House Judiciary Committee) stated:

> "Under the present law any person injured in his business or property by acts in violation of the Sherman antitrust law may recover his damage. In fact, under the provisions of the law he is entitled to recover threefold damage whenever he is able to prove his case. There is no provision under the present law, however, to prevent threatened loss or damage even though it be irreparable. The practical effect of this is that a man would have to sit by and see his business ruined before he could take advantage of his remedy. In what condition is such a man to take up a long and costly lawsuit to defend his rights? ..."

because of the multiplant efficiencies its acquisition of Spencer would provide. To remain competitive, Monfort would have to lower its prices; as a result, Monfort would suffer a loss in profitability, but would not be driven out of business.[10] The question is whether Monfort's loss of profits in such circumstances constitutes antitrust injury.

To resolve the question, we look again to *Brunswick v. Pueblo Bowl–O–Mat, supra.* In *Brunswick,* we evaluated the antitrust significance of several competitors' loss of profits resulting from the entry of a large firm into its market. We concluded:

> "[T]he antitrust laws are not merely indifferent to the injury claimed here. At base, respondents complain that by acquiring the failing centers petitioner preserved competition, thereby depriving respondents of the benefits of increased concentration. The damages respondents obtained are designed to provide them with the profits they would have realized had competition been reduced. The antitrust laws, however, were enacted for 'the protection of *competition,* not *competitors,*' *Brown Shoe Co. v. United States,* 370 U.S., at 320. It is inimical to the purposes of these laws to award damages for the type of injury claimed here." *Id.,* at 488.

The loss of profits to the competitors in *Brunswick* was not of concern under the antitrust laws, since it resulted only from continued competition. Respondent argues that the losses in *Brunswick* can be distinguished from the losses alleged here, since the latter will result from an increase, rather than from a mere continuation, of competition. The range of actions unlawful under § 7 of the Clayton Act is broad enough, respondent claims, to support a finding of antitrust injury whenever a competitor is faced with a threat of losses from increased competition. We find respondent's proposed construction of § 7 too broad, for reasons that *Brunswick* illustrates. *Brunswick* holds that the antitrust laws do not require the courts to protect small businesses from the loss of profits due to continued competition, but only against the loss of profits from practices forbidden by the antitrust laws. The kind of competition that Monfort alleges here, competition for increased market share, is not activity forbidden by the antitrust laws. It is simply, as petitioners claim, vigorous competition. To hold that the antitrust laws protect competitors from the loss of profits due to such price competition would, in effect, render illegal any decision by a firm to cut prices in order to increase market share. The antitrust laws require no such perverse result.... The logic of *Brunswick* compels the conclusion that the threat of loss of profits due to possible price competition following a merger does not constitute a threat of antitrust injury.

B

The second theory of injury argued here is that after the merger Excel would attempt to drive Monfort out of business by engaging in sustained

10. In this case, Monfort has conceded that its viability would not be threatened by Excel's decision to lower prices: "Because Monfort's operations were as efficient as those of Excel, only below-cost pricing could remove Monfort as an obstacle."

predatory pricing. Predatory pricing may be defined as pricing below an appropriate measure of cost for the purpose of eliminating competitors in the short run and reducing competition in the long run. It is a practice that harms both competitors *and* competition. In contrast to price cutting aimed simply at increasing market share, predatory pricing has as its aim the elimination of competition. Predatory pricing is thus a practice "inimical to the purposes of [the antitrust] laws," *Brunswick,* 429 U.S., at 488, and one capable of inflicting antitrust injury.[13]

The Court of Appeals held that Monfort had alleged "what we consider to be a form of predatory pricing...." 761 F.2d, at 575. The court also found that Monfort "could only be harmed by sustained predatory pricing," and that "it is impossible to tell in advance of the acquisition" whether Excel would in fact engage in such a course of conduct; because it could not rule out the possibility that Excel would engage in predatory pricing, it found that Monfort was threatened with antitrust injury. *Id.,* at 576.

Although the Court of Appeals did not explicitly define what it meant by predatory pricing, two interpretations are plausible. First, the court can be understood to mean that Monfort's allegation of losses from the above-cost "cost-price squeeze" was equivalent to an allegation of injury from predatory conduct. If this is the proper interpretation, then the court's judgment is clearly erroneous because (a) Monfort made no allegation that Excel would act with predatory intent after the merger, and (b) price competition is not predatory activity.

Second, the Court of Appeals can be understood to mean that Monfort had shown a credible threat of injury from below-cost pricing. To the extent the judgment rests on this ground, however, it must also be reversed, because Monfort did not allege injury from below-cost pricing before the District Court. The District Court twice noted that Monfort had made no assertion that Excel would engage in predatory pricing. Monfort argues that there is evidence in the record to support its view that it did raise a claim of predatory pricing below. This evidence, however, consists only of four passing references, three in deposition testimony, to the possibility that Excel's prices might dip below costs. Such references fall far short of establishing an allegation of injury from predatory pricing. We conclude that Monfort neither raised nor proved any claim of predatory pricing before the District Court.

IV

In its *amicus* brief, the United States argues that the "danger of allowing a competitor to challenge an acquisition on the basis of necessarily speculative claims of post-acquisition predatory pricing far outweighs the danger that any anticompetitive merger will go unchallenged." On

13. See also *Brunswick,* 429 U.S., at 489, n. 14 ("The short-term effect of certain anticompetitive behavior—predatory below-cost pricing, for example—may be to stimulate price competition. But competitors may be able to prove antitrust injury before they actually are driven from the market and competition is thereby lessened").

this basis, the United States invites the Court to adopt in effect a *per se* rule "denying competitors standing to challenge acquisitions on the basis of predatory pricing theories."

We decline the invitation. As the foregoing discussion makes plain, predatory pricing is an anticompetitive practice forbidden by the antitrust laws. While firms may engage in the practice only infrequently, there is ample evidence suggesting that the practice does occur. It would be novel indeed for a court to deny standing to a party seeking an injunction against threatened injury merely because such injuries rarely occur. In any case, nothing in the language or legislative history of the Clayton Act suggests that Congress intended this Court to ignore injuries caused by such anticompetitive practices as predatory pricing.

V

We hold that a plaintiff seeking injunctive relief under § 16 of the Clayton Act must show a threat of antitrust injury, and that a showing of loss or damage due merely to increased competition does not constitute such injury. The record below does not support a finding of antitrust injury, but only of threatened loss from increased competition. Because respondent has therefore failed to make the showing § 16 requires, we need not reach the question of whether the proposed merger violates § 7. The judgment of the Court of Appeals is reversed, and the case is remanded for further proceedings consistent with this opinion.

JUSTICE STEVENS, joined by JUSTICE WHITE, dissenting: This case presents the question whether the antitrust laws provide a remedy for a private party that challenges a horizontal merger between two of its largest competitors. The issue may be approached along two fundamentally different paths. First, the Court might focus its attention entirely on the postmerger conduct of the merging firms and deny relief unless the plaintiff can prove a violation of the Sherman Act. Second, the Court might concentrate on the merger itself and grant relief if there is a significant probability that the merger will adversely affect competition in the market in which the plaintiff must compete. Today the Court takes a step down the former path; I believe that Congress has directed us to follow the latter path.

In this case, one of the major firms in the beef-packing market has proved to the satisfaction of the District Court and the Court of Appeals that the merger between Excel and Spencer Beef is illegal. This Court holds, however, that the merger should not be set aside because the adverse impact of the merger on respondent's profit margins does not constitute the kind of "antitrust injury" that the Court described in *Brunswick Corp. v. Pueblo Bowl–O–Mat, Inc.*, 429 U.S. 477 (1977).... *Brunswick* merely rejected a "novel damages theory," *id.*, at 490; the Court's implicit determination that *Brunswick* forecloses the appropriate line of inquiry in this quite different case is therefore misguided. In my view, a competitor in Monfort's position has standing to seek an injunction against the merger. Because Monfort must compete in the relevant market, proof establishing that the merger will have a sufficient probability of an adverse effect on competition to violate § 7 is also sufficient to authorize equitable relief.

* * *

QUESTIONS AND COMMENTS

1. Should this case have been dismissed for lack of standing? Is there no way for Monfort to prove antitrust injury other than by proof of probable predatory pricing—which the Court has made extremely difficult to prove even when defendants are engaging in a below-cost pricing siege? See *Brooke Group*, supra at 267.

2. Could/should Monfort have been able to establish its standing by proof of a threatened price squeeze? But has such a claim been decimated by *linkLine*, supra at page 277?

3. In view of *Monfort*, could one of the small hospitals have challenged the acquisitions in *Hospital Corporation of America*, supra at 382? Would it have had the incentive to do so? Would Airbus have had standing to challenge the merger of Boeing and McDonnell Douglas?

4. Recall that in *In–Bev*, Anheuser–Busch, the largest beer brewer in the country, was acquired by the largest brewer in the world, and plaintiff beer consumers alleged that the acquisition removed an actual and perceived potential entrant within the parameters of *Marine Bancoporation*, supra at page 419. The district court found that the complaint failed on *Twombly* grounds because plaintiffs had not supported its allegations of lost competition with sufficient facts. The appellate court sidestepped the *Twombly* issue and affirmed the district court on the following grounds: Plaintiffs were indirect purchasers and could not sue for damages. Having not sued before the merger closed, they could not seek a preliminary injunction. Divestiture would be their only remedy. Divestiture can in theory be granted where it is appropriate in view of equitable principles, but plaintiffs were dilatory in not seeking an injunction before the transaction closed. Their substantive claims were speculative, and the merging parties would suffer hardship and competitive disadvantage from forced divestiture. *Ginsburg v. InBev*, 623 F.3d 1229 (8th Cir. 2010).

Does *InBev* illustrate how *Twombly*, *Illinois Brick*, *Monfort*, and related doctrines seriously limit private anti-merger actions? Or is *InBev* merely a case of a dilatory plaintiff?

5. In the EU, only the European Commission may challenge a merger of Community dimension, unless it cedes authority to a Member State. But competitors or any other directly affected person can seek to annul a Commission decision allowing, disallowing or conditioning a merger. See, e.g., *British American Tobacco Co. v. Commission (Rothman's)*, [1987] ECR 4487. The party seeking annulment need not be in the line of antitrust injury. Is this a good or bad alternative to the U.S. institutional arrangement?

6. What should be the role of private parties in merger control? Does internationalization and the proliferation of overlapping merger systems call for a greater or lesser role for private enforcement?

7. Recall *Empagran S.A. v. F. Hoffmann–LaRoche*, supra p. 180, limiting access of foreign victims of world cartels to Sherman Act damages. Should a U.S. purchaser from foreign merger partners have standing to invoke U.S. law to enjoin the merger?

In 2011, AT&T announced it was merging with T–Mobile, a subsidiary of Deutsche Telekom. Had the merger been consummated, it would have combined the second and fourth largest US wireless carriers to form the largest. The Department of Justice sued to block the merger. AT&T argued that markets were local, competition was vibrant, and the merger was necessary to roll out 4G service and improve the nation's cellular networks. The company was so confident that the merger would overcome regulatory hurdles on the strength of its efficiency benefits to the American economy that it agreed to pay a three billion dollar breakup fee to T–Mobile, plus billions in contract benefits, in the event the merger was called off.

Competitors Sprint Nextel, the nation's third largest wireless carrier, and Cellular South filed suit for injunctive relief under § 16 of the Clayton Act. AT&T moved to dismiss the private action on grounds that the complaint failed to allege antitrust injury and that plaintiffs lacked standing.

SPRINT NEXTEL CORP. v. AT&T INC.

___ F.Supp.2d ___, 2011 WL 5188081 (D.D.C. 2011)

JUDGE HUVELLE: These are antitrust cases between competing mobile wireless carriers. Before the Court are motions to dismiss lawsuits which Sprint and Cellular South brought to enjoin AT&T's proposed acquisition of T–Mobile. AT&T and T–Mobile move for dismissal pursuant to Federal Rule of Civil Procedure 12(b)(6), arguing that Sprint's and Cellular South's complaints fail to adequately allege that the merger would cause them "antitrust injury," and therefore that they lack the "antitrust standing" required to seek injunctive relief under § 16 of the Clayton Act.

Plaintiff Sprint Nextel Corporation ("Sprint") is the third largest national provider of mobile wireless services, with 50 million wireless customers. In 2010, Sprint "accounted for 15 percent of all mobile wireless services revenues." Plaintiffs Cellular South, Inc., and its wholly owned subsidiary Corr Wireless Communications, L.L.C. (collectively, "Cellular South" unless otherwise stated), are regional carriers operating a wireless network that "serves more than 887,000 customers located in Mississippi, Tennessee, Alabama, Florida, and other surrounding states."

Defendant AT&T Mobility, L.L.C. ("AT&T"), the wholly owned subsidiary of defendant AT&T, Inc., is the second largest national carrier, with 95 million customers. In 2010, AT&T "accounted for 32 percent of all mobile wireless services revenues." Defendant T–Mobile USA, Inc. (T–Mobile), the wholly owned subsidiary of defendant Deutsche Telekom AG, is the fourth largest national carrier, with 34 million customers. In 2010, T–Mobile "accounted for 12 percent of all mobile wireless services revenues."

On March 20, 2011, AT&T entered into a stock purchase agreement to acquire T–Mobile and to merge the two companies' mobile wireless services businesses. Five months later, the United States brought suit to enjoin the acquisition, alleging that its effect would "be substantially to lessen competition, or to tend to create a monopoly" in violation of § 7 of the Clayton Act. 15 U.S.C. § 18.3. Sprint and Cellular South filed the present suits in the subsequent weeks, and defendants moved to dismiss both.

. . . [T]he Court will grant the motions except as to plaintiffs' claims regarding mobile wireless devices, and Cellular South's roaming claim insofar as it relates to Corr Wireless.

ANALYSIS

I. GOVERNING LEGAL PRINCIPLES

Section 16 of the Clayton Act authorizes private parties to seek injunctive relief to protect "against threatened loss or damage by a violation of the antitrust laws." While the statute's text is broad, providing for suits by "[a]ny person, firm, corporation, or association," courts have limited its reach to those plaintiffs that allege a threat of "antitrust injury." *Cargill, Inc. v. Monfort of Colo., Inc.*, 479 U.S. 104, 113 (1986).

Antitrust injury is injury "of the type the antitrust laws were designed to prevent and that flows from that which makes the defendants' acts unlawful." *Brunswick Corp. v. Pueblo Bowl–O–Mat, Inc.*, 429 U.S. 477, 489 (1977). Accordingly, a private antitrust plaintiff must allege more than threatened loss or damage that is merely "causally linked" to the defendant's anticompetitive behavior. The plaintiff must additionally allege that its threatened injury "reflect[s] the anticompetitive effect either of the [antitrust] violation or of anticompetitive acts made possible by the violation." Thus, even if a threatened injury is "causally related to an antitrust violation," it "will not qualify as 'antitrust injury' unless it is attributable to an anticompetitive aspect of the practice under scrutiny." *Atl. Richfield Co. v. USA Petroleum Co.*, 495 U.S. 328, 334 (1990).

The antitrust injury requirement aligns antitrust suits brought by private parties " 'with the purposes of the antitrust laws, and prevents abuses of those laws' by claimants seeking to halt the strategic behavior of rivals that increases, rather than reduces competition." *NicSand*, 507 F.3d at 449–50 (quoting *HyPoint Tech., Inc. v. Hewlett–Packard Co.*, 949 F.2d 874, 877 (6th Cir.1991)). "It ensures that the harm claimed by the plaintiff corresponds to the rationale for finding a violation of the antitrust laws in the first place, and it prevents losses that stem from competition from supporting suits by private plaintiffs. . . ." *Atl. Richfield Co.*, 495 U.S. at 342.

. . . Methodologically, then, assessing antitrust injury at the pleadings stage of a § 16 suit requires two distinct inquiries. First, does plaintiff's complaint allege a threatened injury-in-fact? Second, does the threatened injury result from an anticompetitive aspect of defendant's proposed conduct, *i.e.*, that which would make the transaction illegal under the antitrust laws? A plaintiff has sufficiently pleaded a claim to antitrust injury only if its complaint satisfies both inquiries under the conventional Federal Rule of Civil Procedure 8(a) pleading standards that govern " 'in all civil actions.' " *Ashcroft v. Iqbal*, 556 U.S. 662, 129 S.Ct. 1937, 1953, 173 L.Ed.2d 868 (2009) (quoting Fed.R.Civ.P. 1); *see Bell Atl. Corp. v. Twombly*, 550 U.S. 544, 554–58, 570 (2007).

The Court's analysis, however, is not confined to the discrete question of whether Sprint and Cellular South have sufficiently alleged antitrust injuries. Antitrust injury is but one factor to be considered in assessing whether private plaintiffs have standing to sue under the antitrust laws. In *Associated General Contractors of California, Inc. v. California State Council of Carpenters*, 459 U.S. 519 (1983), the Supreme Court described other factors relevant to determining whether a plaintiff seeking treble damages pursuant to § 4 of the Clayton Act has antitrust standing: "the directness of the injury, whether the claim for damages is 'speculative,' the existence of more direct victims, the potential for duplicative recovery and the complexity of apportioning damages." *Andrx Pharm.*, 256 F.3d at 806 (citing *Associated Gen. Contractors*, 459 U.S. at 542–45).

To be sure, "many of these other factors are not relevant to the standing inquiry under § 16," *Cargill*, 479 U.S. at 110 n. 5, and therefore have no application here. The antitrust standing inquiry under § 16 is "less demanding" than that under § 4 because § 16 "provides for injunctive relief, not treble damages," and therefore "the risk of duplicative recovery or the danger of complex apportionment that pervades the analysis of standing under [§]4 is not relevant to the issue of standing under [§]16." *Palmyra Park Hosp.*, 604 F.3d at 1299–1300. . . .

Ultimately, "[t]he extent to which [factors other than antitrust injury] apply when plaintiffs sue for injunctive relief depends on the circumstances of the case," and "the weight to be given the various factors will [also] necessarily vary" depending on the context. *Daniel*, 428 F.3d at 443. Of particular relevance here is the fact that courts assessing the viability of a § 16 plaintiff's claim to antitrust injury on the pleadings have considered whether the plaintiff's allegations are too speculative to be allowed to proceed. Indeed, "Section 16's requirement of 'threatened injury,' dovetails with Article III's requirement that in order to obtain forward-looking relief, a plaintiff must face a threat of injury that is both 'real and immediate, not conjectural or hypothetical.'" *In re New Motor Vehicles Canadian Exp. Antitrust Litig.*, 522 F.3d 6, 14 (1st Cir.2008). Thus, although § 16 of the Clayton Act protects "against *threatened* loss or damage by a violation of the antitrust laws" (emphasis added), and although § 7 "was intended to arrest the anticompetitive effects of market power in their incipiency," *FTC v. Procter & Gamble Co.*, 386 U.S. 568, 577 (1967), the Act does not authorize suits by those whose allegations of threatened injury amount to little more than conjecture.

With these principles in mind, the Court turns to Sprint's and Cellular South's claims to antitrust standing and, in particular, antitrust injury. For purposes of this inquiry only, the Court assumes that AT&T's proposed acquisition of T–Mobile would violate § 7 of the Clayton Act, and focuses instead on whether plaintiffs have sufficiently alleged a threatened loss or damage stemming from an aspect or effect of the proposed acquisition that would make it illegal.

II. PLAINTIFFS' CLAIMS

Sprint and Cellular South allege threatened injuries that stem from both horizontal and vertical aspects of AT&T's proposed acquisition of T–Mobile. That is to say: as participants in a number of different markets, wireless carriers are related both horizontally and vertically. In certain markets, the carriers compete with each other to sell outputs, and in other markets, they compete to purchase inputs. Such relationships are deemed horizontal in that they pit carriers against carriers, acting in parallel as either sellers or buyers. (Where the carriers compete as sellers, the proposed acquisition raises monopoly concerns. Where they compete as buyers of inputs, the anticompetitive form is monopsony.) In yet other markets, the wireless carriers buy and sell services to and from each other, and are therefore vertically related. In this complex and constantly evolving industry, markets are interconnected and the carriers play multiple roles simultaneously. * * *

A. Horizontal Effects

AT&T, T–Mobile, Sprint, and Cellular South are primarily competing wireless carriers: they compete horizontally to sell wireless services and a broad array of wireless devices, including basic mobile phones, smartphones (*e.g.*, Android phones, BlackBerry phones, the Apple iPhone), tablets (*e.g.*, the Samsung Galaxy Tab, the BlackBerry PlayBook, the Apple iPad), and other products that access their voice and data networks. In addition to competing horizontally in the output market, the carriers compete horizontally in the input market, as purchasers of wireless devices: they attempt to secure the most desirable devices for their respective networks so they can sell them to customers. The carriers also compete horizontally as purchasers in the market for wireless spectrum, as they acquire new frequency bands and as they work to develop and buy network equipment, chipsets, and device antennae that operate on them.

1. The Market for Wireless Services

Sprint and Cellular South compete with AT&T, T–Mobile, and other wireless carriers—most prominently, Verizon—to sell wireless services. In the market that is of primary concern here, that for postpaid wireless services, the "goods" in question consist of retail consumer plans and corporate and government plans that customers purchase so that they can use their wireless devices for voice calls, text messaging, and data delivery (*e.g.*, email and the internet). The relevant market prices are the monthly fees that consumers pay for postpaid wireless services and the bulk fee corporate and government entities negotiate for the same.

Sprint and Cellular South allege that AT&T's acquisition of T–Mobile would affect an illegal concentration of market power and lead to higher retail wireless rates. * * *

. . . Standing alone, however, such allegations do not help to resolve the question of whether these competitor plaintiffs have pleaded antitrust injury. At issue here are Sprint's and Cellular South's allegations regarding the injuries that *they* will suffer if the merger is consummated. Alleging harm to consumers, while relevant to showing an antitrust violation, is not sufficient to demonstrate antitrust injury; harm to *consumers* by way of increased prices is the type of injury the antitrust laws were designed to prevent, but it is not an injury-in-fact that *competitors* suffer. When allegedly anticompetitive behavior "[has] the effect of either raising market price or limiting output" and is therefore "harmful to competition," it "actually *benefit[s]* competitors by making supracompetitive pricing more attractive." *Matsushita Elec. Indus. Co., Ltd. v. Zenith Radio Corp.*, 475 U.S. 574, 583 (1986) . . .

. . . That remains the case even if, as Sprint and Cellular South allege, the proposed acquisition will incentivize Verizon, "AT&T's most significant competitor post-merger, . . . to coordinate with AT&T rather than compete." In *Matsushita Electrical Industrial Co.*, the Supreme Court addressed allegations by American television manufacturers that their Japanese rivals "had illegally conspired to drive American firms from the . . . market." 475 U.S. at 577–78. The Court began its analysis "by emphasizing what [plaintiffs'] claim is *not*:"

> Nor can [plaintiffs] recover damages for any conspiracy by [defendants] to charge higher than competitive prices in the American market. Such conduct would indeed violate the [antitrust laws], but it could not injure [plaintiffs]: as [defendants'] competitors, [plaintiffs] stand to gain from any conspiracy to raise the market price in [televisions].

Id. at 582–83. The Court's logic is directly applicable here. Whether the result of an increase in market concentration by itself, or "the oligopolistic price coordination" that "excessive concentration . . . portends," *Brooke*

Group Ltd., 509 U.S. at 229–30, an increase in market prices alone does not harm competitors. To the contrary, "You want your competitors to charge high prices." *JTC Petroleum Co. v. Piasa Motor Fuels, Inc.*, 190 F.3d 775, 778 (7th Cir.1999) (Posner, J.). The possibility that a post-merger AT&T could raise market prices does not, without more, threaten injury-in-fact to Sprint and Cellular South. It therefore does not confer antitrust standing on them.

2. The Market for Wireless Devices

Plaintiffs claim that wireless devices "are becoming the primary driver in selection of wireless service." "Device preference increasingly drives customer choice of wireless carriers." As such, wireless carriers compete with each other to secure the most desirable devices for their own networks, sometimes leveraging exclusivity deals with device manufacturers to aid their efforts. Sprint and Cellular South allege that, together with Verizon, a post-merger AT&T would "foreclose their ... access to the most innovative handsets and raise their costs," such that their "offers to [their] customers would be less attractive and [their] business would be injured." The increased market concentration brought about by the proposed acquisition would, according to Sprint, "enable both AT&T and Verizon to coerce exclusionary handset deals ... without AT&T having gained that advantage through competition on the merits."

Where a defendant, by means of anticompetitive conduct, restricts or forecloses a competitor plaintiff's access to a necessary input, courts have found that the resulting loss is injury of the type that the antitrust laws were designed to prevent. *See Eastman Kodak Co. v. Image Technical Servs., Inc.*, 504 U.S. 451 (1992). Indeed, defendants concede that a plaintiff has stated a "theory of competitor harm that is cognizable under the antitrust laws" when it has alleged that its rival's anticompetitive acts will result in its paying more for necessary inputs.

* * *

What distinguishes the present case from *Eastman Kodak*, however, is the alleged source of the defendants' power to impair plaintiffs' ability to compete in the input market. In *Eastman Kodak*, the defendant was both the plaintiffs' competitor and their supplier. Here, the wireless carriers—plaintiffs, defendants, Verizon, and all the rest, national and regional alike—compete against each other as fellow purchasers of wireless devices, which they procure from manufacturers in order to sell to consumers. It would not be the alleged antitrust violation—AT&T's acquisition of T–Mobile—but rather the "anticompetitive acts made possible by the violation" that plaintiffs claim would injure them. *Brunswick Corp.*, 429 U.S. at 489. Theirs is a threatened injury of the type the antitrust laws were intended to prevent, *id.*, but because their theory depends on the merged entity's monopsony power, and not its simple ability to refuse to sell to them, alleging a plausible threat of loss or damage is a more complex task for Sprint and Cellular South than it was for the *Eastman Kodak* plaintiffs.

Yet, other plaintiffs have succeeded on similar theories in the past.

* * *

Finally, in *Tasty Baking*, the manufacturer of Tastykake snack cakes sued to unravel the merger of the manufacturers of the Hostess and Drake snack cake brands. 653 F.Supp. at 1254. The plaintiff alleged that the transaction would "impair [its] ability to enter new markets and develop business, by facilitating [defendants'] negotiations with retailers for better store shelf space and promotional time slots in markets where [plaintiff] does compete and by" enabling the merged entity to engage in predatory pricing. *Id.* at 1255. The Court concluded that the plaintiff had "alleged antitrust injury," and rejected defendants' argument that plaintiff's harm stemmed from defendants' "increased operating efficiencies" as stating "a factual dispute" but not "demonstrat[ing] any inadequacy" in the pleading. *Id.* Turning to the evidence adduced at the hearing on the preliminary injunction, the Court paid particular attention to the plaintiff's allegations of "threatened predatory non-pricing actions." *Id.* at 1276. The Court found support in the record for plaintiff's claims that defendants could "successfully pressure retailers" to stop carrying its products, to place them in less desirable locations in stores, and to allot them less promotional time. *Id.* at 1273. The Court concluded that because plaintiff's "entry into, expansion within, and preservation of share in relevant markets could be frustrated by defendants'" anticompetitive strategies, *id.*, plaintiff had standing to sue. *Id.* at 1274.

Mobile wireless devices, and smartphones in particular, are Sprint's and Cellular South's ... shelf space and promotional time, for they are necessary inputs for plaintiffs' businesses.... As a general matter, plaintiffs' threatened injuries are those of the type the antitrust laws were designed to prevent, and courts have approved claims similar to those specifically raised here.

Nonetheless, the Court must still determine the sufficiency of plaintiffs' pleadings, and in particular the plausibility of their threat to injury-in-fact arising from the monopsony power AT&T would gain in the market for mobile wireless devices with the acquisition of T–Mobile. Defendants argue that, because plaintiffs' complaints do not describe the state of competition among device manufacturers, their claims must fail. The Court disagrees. Where monopsony power is the concern, what matters is market concentration on the buying side of the market, not the selling side. *Weyerhaeuser Co.*, 549 U.S. at 320, 127 S.Ct. 1069 ("Monopsony power is market power on the buy side of the market."); *see also Todd v. Exxon Corp.*, 275 F.3d 191, 202 (2d Cir.2001) (Sotomayor, J.) (Because "the equation for measuring market power in monopsony is a mirror image of the relationships that create market power in a seller[,] ... [a] greater availability of substitute buyers indicates a smaller quantum of market power on the part of the buyers in question." (citation and internal quotation marks omitted)). That there may be and, indeed, by all accounts is, healthy competition among firms that *sell* mobile wireless devices is irrelevant to understanding whether, by acquiring T–Mobile, AT&T could so increase its *buying* power as to dictate terms to device manufacturers and otherwise impair plaintiffs' access to these necessary inputs. Judged against these standards, the Court concludes that plaintiffs' complaints contain sufficient facts, which must at this stage be accepted as true, to state a plausible claim to threatened loss or damage in the market for mobile wireless devices.

Sprint's and Cellular South's complaints provide factual support for the allegation that AT&T already possesses significant market power as a purchaser of mobile wireless devices, and that the acquisition of T–Mobile threatens them with harm. Sprint alleges that the proposed transaction would add T–Mobile's 34 million customers to AT&T's 95 million customers, leaving the merged entity with 129 million customers (a 37 percent increase) and controlling "in excess of 40 percent of the national markets."

Crucially, Sprint then alleges two links between a carrier's power as a seller in the output market and a carrier's power as a buyer in the input market. The first regards volume commitments:

> Given the expense of developing new handsets, [manufacturers] commonly require volume commitments from carriers in order to spread R&D and production costs over a large volume of unit sales. Because of these volume commitments, carriers with smaller subscriber bases are at a significant disadvantage in attracting [manufacturers] to develop new devices or technology for their networks. For example, while regional carriers now offer some smartphones, [manufacturers] developing handsets with the latest technology tend to design them for the large national carriers because they have the ability to sell the most phones, thus spreading R&D costs over a larger number of units.

Sprint's second alleged connection between concentration in the selling and buying markets relates to "exclusivity arrangements or 'time-to-market' advantages" through which larger carriers secure exclusive access to certain devices—typically "cutting-edge smartphones"—for a specific period of time. Sprint alleges that the Federal Communications Commission ("FCC") has found that while larger carriers can negotiate handset exclusivity agreements, smaller carriers such as Sprint cannot. Sprint cites Apple's iPhone as an example. AT&T was the exclusive provider of the "iconic" iPhone from 2007 until early 2011, when Apple "gave Verizon a time-to-market advantage . . . most likely because Verizon had the largest subscriber base in the United States." Accordingly, Sprint "had to compete without access to the iPhone for nearly five years." That AT&T and Verizon thus wielded their purchasing power in the past substantiates Sprint's claim to threatened injury-in-fact from the merger.

* * *

Cellular South's claims to antitrust injury from the proposed transaction's effect on the market for wireless devices are, if anything, even more plausible. Cellular South adds narrative to the numbers and market logic alleged by Sprint:

> Cellular South and other carriers have often been refused access to current devices and given access only when the device is no longer the most current model. Cellular South and other carriers receive older phones at higher prices. The proposed merger will continue and exacerbate that conduct.

Cellular South also focuses on the proposed acquisition's elimination of "T–Mobile as an independent source of demand for wireless devices," thus squarely stating a monopsony concern. * * * ... But Cellular South worries about more than the mere fact of the post-merger AT&T's enhanced buying power in the market for devices. It alleges that the proposed transaction would exacerbate its network interoperability woes. As will be discussed in more detail below, not all carriers' networks are compatible with each other: phones designed for one network cannot be used on many others. Cellular South claims that AT&T and Verizon have exercised their purchasing power in the markets for devices and network equipment to propagate "their own separate 'ecosystems' of compatible infrastructure ... that cannot be utilized by other competitors," and that the proposed acquisition would increase the big carriers' "incentive and power to exclude competitors from those ecosystems." Accordingly, "Without T–Mobile's independent demand for devices, device manufacturers will be even less willing to design or build devices for any carrier, like Cellular South, which is operating outside of the ecosystem of one or the other of [Verizon and AT&T]." In other words, Cellular South alleges that the proposed acquisition threatens its access not only to handsets that are particularly desirable, but also, more fundamentally, to whole "ecosystems" of devices and network infrastructure—and customers. Based on these allegations, the Court concludes that Cellular South's complaint also satisfies *Twombly* as regards its claim of threatened injury-in-fact from an anticompetitive aspect of the proposed merger—AT&T's acquisition of monopsony power in the market for mobile wireless devices.

By contrast, certain of the plaintiffs' seemingly device-related claims do not plausibly allege threatened injury-in-fact. Sprint states that the post-merger AT&T would, with Verizon, compose a "Twin Bell duopoly" gatekeeper, controlling "access to the wireless bridge between upstream developers and the consumers they seek to connect with via wireless communications." This may be a plausible allegation, but it does not describe a threatened loss or damage to *Sprint*, as opposed to one faced by the upstream producers.

Sprint's claim to threatened injury arising from the potential loss of T–Mobile as a partner in ventures "to create substantial scale for the creation of new handsets and to compete with [AT&T and Verizon] for such handsets" also fails. Sprint frames this allegation in terms of "innovation in handsets," but in order to state a claim to antitrust injury it must do more—again, it must allege its own injury-in-fact stemming from defendants' allegedly anticompetitive behavior. * * *

3. The Market for Wireless Spectrum and Network Development

* * *

[Mobile wireless devices depend upon radio spectrum to broadcast data. Bands of spectrum, which vary in strength, are auctioned off to wireless providers by the FCC. Each band requires compatible infrastructure, equipment, and handsets, and the development of new bands (such as 700 MHz) requires considerable investment.]

To the extent that Cellular South's claims regarding wireless spectrum relate to cutting-edge wireless devices, these allegations have been addressed above. Sprint, on the other hand, focuses on the fact that the merger "would add T–Mobile's spectrum to AT&T's already substantial spectrum holdings." Sprint also claims that, "[a]bsent the acquisition of T–Mobile, all of the national wireless carriers, with the possible exception of Verizon, likely would seek spectrum in 'new' bands for which the research and development costs for new equipment have not yet been incurred." Thus, "[b]y acquiring developed spectrum through the T–Mobile acquisition, AT&T would effectively and improperly shift the costs of spectrum development to Sprint and other carriers" and "further weaken their ability to compete on the merits by increasing their costs and delaying their access to new equipment."

What differentiates this claim from plaintiffs' devices claims is that here, Sprint has not alleged that the proposed transaction would be a merger-to-monopsony. Sprint does not claim that the acquisition would enable AT&T to muscle other carriers out of FCC auctions for wireless spectrum, but rather, that the transaction would add to AT&T's inventory of spectrum and reduce its network development costs. To the extent Sprint challenges the mere fact that, if AT&T acquires T–Mobile, it will also acquire some additional amount of spectrum, Sprint does not allege injury-in-fact. Without additional guidance as to this claim, the Court is left to assume that AT&T's acquisition of T–Mobile's spectrum would threaten Sprint with injury-in-fact only if the acquisition would curtail Sprint's access to a supply of spectrum that it demonstrably needed. The parties differ significantly as to the sufficiency of AT&T's spectrum holdings, but Sprint neither alleges facts about T–Mobile's holdings nor describes its own holdings. Without more, Sprint has not alleged facts sufficient to state a claim to antitrust injury arising from AT&T's acquisition of T–Mobile's unknown stock of spectrum. * * *

B. Vertical Effects

AT&T, T–Mobile, Sprint, and Cellular South also buy and sell services and products among themselves, such that Sprint and Cellular South challenge two vertical effects of the proposed acquisition—effects that alter the dynamics of their relationship with AT&T as purchasers of services that AT&T sells or that are allegedly related to services that AT&T sells.

Plaintiffs' first allegation of a vertical effect regards the market for roaming. "Roaming agreements between carriers can be used to add coverage for subscribers beyond the carrier's network, or supplement its capacity." Regional carriers such as Cellular South are particularly dependent on roaming agreements: because they do not have nationwide networks, they rely on their contracts with the national carriers to provide their subscribers with coast-to-coast access to wireless networks. Both Sprint and Cellular South allege that the proposed acquisition threatens them harm because it will result in their paying higher prices for roaming. Sprint alone raises a second claim regarding the proposed acquisition's vertical effects, this with regard to the market for "backhaul." Backhaul is also a necessary input in the market for mobile wireless services in that it connects cell sites to the traditional wireline networks where calls are routed. In addition to acting as wireless carriers themselves, AT&T and Verizon also supply the lion's share of backhaul to other wireless carriers, including Sprint and, at the present, T–Mobile. Sprint alleges that by eliminating T–Mobile as an independent purchaser of backhaul, the proposed acquisition will enable AT&T and Verizon to charge Sprint and other carriers higher prices for the service.

What plaintiffs' claims regarding roaming and backhaul share in common is the general allegation that AT&T's purchase of T–Mobile will result in plaintiffs paying more to procure necessary inputs. Accordingly, as it did with regard to plaintiffs' allegations about the proposed acquisition's effect on the market for wireless devices, the Court concludes that plaintiffs' alleged injuries are of the type that the antitrust laws were designed to prevent. The inquiry focuses instead on the other component of antitrust injury: have plaintiffs alleged, with the requisite specificity, a threatened injury-in-fact?

At the outset, it is important to note one critical difference between plaintiffs' devices allegations addressed above, on the one hand, and their roaming and backhaul allegations on the other. In the market for devices, plaintiffs allege that AT&T's acquisition of T–Mobile would be a merger-to-monopsony. Their allegations of loss or damage stem from the post-merger AT&T's purchasing power in the market for devices—an input market for all carriers. Because plaintiffs have alleged facts about the proposed transaction's effects on the output market (the market for mobile wireless services), and because they posited links between AT&T's increased selling power in the output market and its increased purchasing power in the input market, they have stated a plausible claim to antitrust injury in the market for wireless devices.

In the markets for roaming and backhaul, however, plaintiffs do not raise monopsony claims. Rather, plaintiffs allege that they, along with T–

Mobile, purchase roaming and backhaul from AT&T and Verizon in various configurations. Plaintiffs' roaming and backhaul claims relate not to the merged entity's purchasing power, but rather to its selling power, for they allege the proposed acquisition will increase concentration among sellers of roaming and backhaul (and that they will be affected *as purchasers* in those markets). The economic analysis does not differ and the antitrust laws are concerned with both monopsony and monopoly power. But whereas factual allegations about the output market (for mobile wireless services), combined with descriptions of the links between the merged entity's power as a seller in the output market and its power as a buyer in the input market (for mobile wireless devices), sufficed to support plaintiffs' claims regarding devices, those allegations are less directly relevant to plaintiffs' claims regarding roaming and backhaul. In order to successfully allege that the proposed transaction threatens them with injuries-in-fact in the markets for roaming and backhaul, plaintiffs must describe those markets with greater specificity than they have done if *Twombly* is to be satisfied.

1. The Market for Roaming

Roaming allows one carrier's subscribers to access another carrier's network when they are outside of their own network's range, as long as the two carriers' networks are compatible and as long as the carriers have a roaming agreement. * * *

Thus, carriers sign roaming agreements to supplement their networks' capacities and so their customers do not lose service when traveling outside their service areas. "Verizon and AT&T have large wireless network footprints in the United States," and "therefore have a higher percentage of on-network calls than other carriers" so "their subscribers have less need for roaming. AT&T and Verizon realize revenue from carriers who contract for roaming services over their networks." Implicit in the fact that Verizon and AT&T have *less* need is the fact that they both buy and sell roaming, but Sprint's complaint says nothing more about their purchasing activities. Nor does Sprint provide any description of its own roaming contracts.

Rather, Sprint merely alleges that "[t]he merger would raise [its] input costs for roaming." Because Sprint is a CDMA carrier and AT&T and T–Mobile are GSM carriers [CDMA and GSM are two distinct types of transmission technology], however, Sprint cannot purchase roaming from defendants. In order to justify its allegation of threatened harm, Sprint posits the following sequence: After the merger, AT&T will increase its retail wireless rates.

> Increasing its retail wireless rates would give AT&T an incentive to increase its roaming prices, and increasing its roaming prices to its rivals would support higher retail prices. With AT&T setting higher prices, Verizon would have an incentive to increase its retail prices and also to raise its roaming fees to CDMA carriers, including Sprint.

Even accepting for the moment that the acquisition will prompt AT&T to raise its retail rates, there remain three assumptions that underlie this scenario for which Sprint alleges *no* factual basis: First, that AT&T's increased retail wireless rates would give it "an incentive to increase" the rates it charges its competitors for roaming; second, that Verizon would match AT&T's increase in retail rates rather than keep its prices low to attract new customers; and third, similar to the first, that Verizon's increased retail wireless rates would prompt it to raise its roaming fees to Sprint. * * *

Cellular South, on the other hand, presents more concrete claims to antitrust injury in the market for roaming when it alleges that, "[b]y reducing the number of potential roaming partners, the merger threatens" it with "pay [ing] higher roaming prices." The crucial difference is that Cellular South's Corr Wireless subsidiary, which uses the GSM transmission technology, has been a roaming customer of T–Mobile and is currently a roaming customer of AT&T. As such, given that roaming is a necessary input for Cellular South, the fact that "the removal of T–Mobile from the marketplace would leave only AT&T as a potential GSM roaming partner," might be enough to demonstrate Cellular South's antitrust standing.

Defendants protest that only "a small fraction of Cellular South's customer base relies on roaming technology compatible with AT&T's and T–Mobile's networks." This is certainly true, and defendants are correct that "Cellular South's assertion that AT&T and T–Mobile's merger will nevertheless somehow result in Cellular South paying higher roaming rates for its CDMA technology to Verizon has no greater factual support than the parallel allegation in Sprint's complaint." . . . Accordingly, defendants' Motion to Dismiss Cellular South is granted as to Cellular South's CDMA roaming claims.

Defendants' Motion is denied, however, as to Cellular South's GSM roaming claims. Defendants have cited no case establishing a *de minimis* exception to antitrust injury. Even if Corr Wireless represents only a small part of Cellular South's business, Cellular South's allegations suggest that its threatened loss from the merger is plausible. * * *

2. The Market for Backhaul

Backhaul comprises the physical infrastructure—dedicated copper, microwave, or fiber optic circuits—that connects cell sites to the wireline network to which wireless calls are routed. "Wireless carriers, including Sprint, depend on backhaul to connect their cell sites to their networks and to the public switched telephone network." * * *

The contemporary market for backhaul reflects the recent history of the telecommunications industry. "For decades" prior to its breakup in 1984, "the Bell System controlled wireline monopolies across the country." Since then, Sprint alleges that "the 'Ma Bell' descendants, AT&T and Verizon, have largely reassembled the Bell monopolies under their joint control." Therefore, AT&T and Verizon own wires—both the wireline networks, which they control as "[t]he two remaining [incumbent local exchange carriers ("ILECs")] of the old Bell System," and the backhaul that connects cell sites to those networks. Indeed, Sprint claims that AT&T and Verizon "are the predominant providers of [backhaul]," although, crucially, they compete with "some independent telecommunications firms" that also provide backhaul. Specifically, Sprint alleges that "[o]ver 90 percent of all special access services in the United States, including backhaul, are provided by the ILECs, primarily AT&T and Verizon."

Because it reflects the initial inheritances from the Bell System and the subsequent mergers among the Baby Bells, the market for backhaul is geographically bifurcated. AT&T and Verizon have distinct traditional service territories, such that they rarely compete with each other as backhaul providers. AT&T's ILEC territory comprises twenty-two states. Sprint alleges that "AT&T has market or monopoly power for backhaul in a number of relevant geographic markets ... in its traditional service territor[y]."

Like Sprint's claims to antitrust injury in the markets for mobile wireless devices and roaming, Sprint's claim to antitrust injury in the market for backhaul alleges that the proposed acquisition would increase Sprint's costs for a necessary input. Sprint purchases backhaul from AT&T. Where these claims differ, however, is with regard to T–Mobile's current role in the market. T–Mobile, while not a potential roaming partner for Sprint due to the incompatibility of their networks, both buys and sells roaming. With regard to backhaul, by contrast, T–Mobile is only a fellow purchaser.

Sprint cannot allege, therefore, that the proposed transaction would be a merger-to-monopoly. By acquiring T–Mobile, AT&T will not gain any backhaul infrastructure, and the merger would not lead immediately to increased concentration among backhaul *suppliers*. Sprint gets there in a roundabout way, though, by alleging first that the acquisition will decrease the number of backhaul *purchasers*. Sprint quotes an industry association filing before the FCC stating that " 'AT&T has indicated that it will move T–Mobile's backhaul traffic on to its own transport network wherever possible.' " The same filing states that T–Mobile currently sources backhaul " 'for approximately 20 percent of its cell sites' " from independent providers, *i.e.*, not AT&T and not Verizon. When the merger eliminates that demand, Sprint's theory goes, independent providers will exit the market and the incentives for entry by new providers will be diminished. At the end of this chain of events, the market for backhaul is more concentrated and Sprint will suffer harm when AT&T and Verizon, no longer checked by rival suppliers, are able to raise their rates.

It bears repeating that, as has been established and as defendants concede, such an injury would be of the type that the antitrust laws are designed to prevent. Having satisfied the second component of antitrust injury, if Sprint stated a claim to threatened injury-in-fact in the backhaul market that was plausible on its face, Sprint would succeed.

As it stands, Sprint's claims fail. Sprint alleges no facts to support its theory that the elimination of T–Mobile as a purchaser of backhaul will increase concentration among backhaul sellers by putting the independent providers out of business. Sprint might have described the independent providers by more than just name and the local markets where T–Mobile's presence as an independent purchaser ensures their survival. Crucially, Sprint might have provided even rough estimates of the percentage of the independent purchasers' business that T–Mobile represents. Sprint's complaint, however, says nothing about the sell side of the market apart from its statements regarding AT&T's and Verizon's present market power and its claims about barriers to entry and expansion. The Court therefore has no means by which to assess the plausibility of the scenario Sprint suggests. That the scenario is extreme—positing that the decrease in demand after T–Mobile's elimination as a purchaser will be so significant as to be lethal to the independent providers, leading to a price *increase*, whereas demand decreases usually coincide with price *decreases*—only makes the Court's task more difficult. At the pleadings stage, Sprint need not supply "detailed factual allegations," and yet it must state facts sufficient to "raise a right to relief above the speculative level." *Twombly*, 550 U.S. at 555. . . .

CONCLUSION

* * *

While perhaps "elusive," the antitrust injury requirement not only aligns private antitrust enforcement to the aims of the antitrust laws; it also performs the more conventional function of only allowing plaintiffs to proceed on claims made facially plausible by the allegation of sufficient facts. *Id.* at 570, 103 S.Ct. 897; *see NicSand*, 507 F.3d at 451. It is unsurprising, therefore, that established precedent forecloses competitors' claims that challenge a proposed transaction's effect on competition without sufficiently alleging the threat of an injury-in-fact that they face and that is " 'of the type the antitrust laws were designed to prevent.' " *Cargill*, 479 U.S. at 113, 107 S.Ct. 484 (quoting *Brunswick Corp.*, 429 U.S. at 489, 97 S.Ct. 690). Such claims belong to the government. But where private plaintiffs have successfully pleaded antitrust injury, the fact that they are defendants' competitors is no bar. *Cf. id.* at 120–22, 107 S.Ct. 484 (rejecting the government's proposed per se rule denying competitors standing to challenge acquisitions on the basis of predatory pricing theories).

QUESTIONS AND COMMENTS

1. The district court assumed that the merger violated the Clayton Act for the purpose of assessing a Rule 12(b)(6) motion to dismiss. It nevertheless

dismissed all but one of Sprint's claims. Why couldn't Sprint claim that the merger was price-raising to consumers of wireless service?

2. What distinguishes the claims the court rejected from the claim that the merger would cement AT&T's clout in the buying market for cellular handsets, which the court found plausible? How important was the history of exclusive and time-to-market contracts in the buying market for handsets?

3. Was the court correct to hold that plaintiffs had standing to assert AT&T's monopsony power over cellular handsets? Why was this not simply a complaint that AT&T would gain economies of scale or scope that would make it an especially valuable partner to handset manufacturers? Why couldn't Section 1 of the Sherman Act take care of any anticompetitive agreements between the handset manufacturers and the service suppliers?

4. The district court dismissed vertical effects claims—that the merger would concentrate the markets for roaming and backhaul—superficially similar to the handset claim. What is the crucial difference? Is it factual or conceptual? Both? What does the surviving Cellular South roaming claim suggest? Are Sprint's theories of injury simply too attenuated?

5. Compare the Supreme Court's fact-heavy analysis in *Monfort* to the district court's face-heavy analysis here. It is worth noting that, while *Monfort* was an appeal from a judgment after trial and *Sprint* is a Rule 12(b)(6) motion to dismiss, the district court's scrutiny of the Sprint/AT&T facts is more rigorous. This is *Twombly* in action.

6. AT&T and T–Mobile called off their merger three months after this decision, one month after a critical report by the staff of the FCC was leaked, and one month before the trial of the Justice Department's action challenging the merger was due to begin.

Thus, we complete our study of U.S. antitrust merger law—from the emergence of modern substantive analysis, which is tracked more or less by many other jurisdictions in the world, to private actions, which are not so commonly replicated. The private action, as we have seen, is often a good vehicle for testing theories of antitrust harm.

G. INTERNATIONAL DIMENSIONS OF MERGER LAW

A large percentage of significant mergers today are international, either in the sense that the merger partners are based in different nations or in the sense that the firms operate across national borders.

Any one or more of some 75 jurisdictions may vet the merger. The jurisdictions may have different procedures and different standards, or different applications of the same standard. And jurisdictions may impose different remedies, either because of different standards or because the merger harms nations in different ways.

Antitrust agencies in many countries cooperate with one another today. They may share analyses, to the extent possible in view of the companies' privilege of confidentiality, which they sometimes but do not always waive. Many agencies try to coordinate their merger review processes. But even so, there are persistent issues regarding and high costs of multi-jurisdictional review. The International Competition Network has adopted guiding principles and recommended practices that have resulted in significant convergence of the pre-merger procedures of the various nations. The Merger Working Group of the ICN has developed recommended practices for merger analysis. These documents may be found at *http://www.internationalcompetitionnetwork.org*. Select: Merger Working Group.

On a grander scale, we confront questions of political economy and sovereignty. Do mergers "belong" to a country? Did Boeing/McDonnell Douglas "belong" to the United States? Is there a reason why the United States should have had paramount say as to the fate of the merger? Or should nations and authorities prefer a cosmopolitan view? Antitrust authorities tend to take a non-nationalistic view; but this is not so for legislators.

What is the cosmopolitan view? Is any multinational merger fair game for prohibition by any antitrust agency in a jurisdiction in the line of harm? Should national agencies be authorized or even required to take account of harms beyond their borders? What are the limitations to applying national law to mergers in global markets? Are limitations best addressed through horizontal cooperation? At the end of the next half century, will we still see multinational mergers vetted by numerous national bodies or will there be a global merger review procedure for mergers with a world dimension? See Eleanor Fox, *Antitrust Without Borders: From Roots to Codes to Networks, in* COOPERATION, COMITY AND COMPETITION POLICY 265, 283 (Andrew T. Guzman ed., 2011) (recommending an opt-in international clearing house system); ANTITRUST MODERNIZATION COMMISSION, REPORT AND RECOMMENDATIONS: INTERNATIONAL ANTITRUST ENFORCEMENT 217 (2007), Recommendation 38 (recommending study of the possibility of a centralized international pre-merger notification system).

CHAPTER 5

COLLABORATION AMONG COMPETITORS OTHER THAN CARTELS

■ ■ ■

A. INTRODUCTION

We now have a foundation for analyzing competitor collaborations and determining when they are anticompetitive in violation of Section 1 of the Sherman Act. The characterization cases (Chapter 2) have alerted us to essential questions: Is the agreement a response to buyers and the market, or is it an attempt to suppress competition and get a higher price? Is it a conspiracy against consumers,[1] or is it a normal, competitive business transaction? If the transaction is not a cartel, the collaborators get the benefit of a fuller analysis. Sometimes a quick look will suffice to assure a court that the transaction has overwhelming cartel-like or market-degrading characteristics and should be condemned. Other times the first look will lead to a longer look; perhaps a full market analysis, much like we have done in merger cases.

Anything beyond per se condemnation is called "rule of reason" analysis. But the rule of reason is not a potpourri. The plaintiff must tell a convincing story of how the agreement increases (or preserves) market power and thus is against the interests of (in the usual case) buyers and other consumers. The defendant may deny the facts and/or show that the agreement will produce efficiencies or innovation that would prevent the consumer harm and indeed benefit consumers. Sometimes the plaintiff's story virtually speaks for itself and little additional flesh need be put on the skeletal bones before defendant is called upon to explain. Other times, making out the plaintiff's case is a complex exercise. The inquiry is made simpler by the fact that U.S. antitrust law does not weigh social virtues or industrial policy in antitrust analysis (recall *National Society of Professional Engineers*, supra at 77), except in the rare rogue case.

The concepts learned in merger analysis are helpful. The merger cases and guidelines provide excellent instruction on how to think about markets, analyze market power and competition, and predict anticompetitive (or procompetitive) effects.

1. Or suppliers, if the arrangement might be a buyers' cartel.

Also, the monopoly cases have added to our tool chest for analysis. Recall, in the *Microsoft* case (D.C.Cir. 2001), p. 310 supra, the court's statement that Section 2 rule-of-reason analysis mirrors Section 1 rule-of-reason analysis.

In this chapter we deal with two types of collaborations. One is loose knit; the competitors do not integrate their businesses, even in part; but they have common objectives. Many of these cases are trade association cases. Competitors may be sharing information, setting standards, policing fraud, or pooling patents that block one another. The second type of collaboration is tighter knit. It involves a degree of business integration normally undertaken to realize synergies and solve market problems. This class of cases includes joint ventures and alliances.

Cases that have prepared us for this chapter include *BMI*, supra page 83, as an example of an integrated enterprise, and *California Dental Association*, supra page 105, as an example of an unintegrated collaboration. In both cases plaintiffs unsuccessfully alleged a per se or near per se violation. A question in this chapter is how to apply deeper competitive analysis to the facts.

B. CONTEMPORARY CASES

Touchstones for Analysis

In Chapter 2 we reviewed contemporary U.S. Supreme Court cases to determine: When is conduct properly characterized as price fixing, and when does competitor collaboration so directly tamper with the market mechanism as to be illegal per se? In this chapter we look through the other end of the telescope: When an agreement is not facially illegal, how is it analyzed under the rule of reason? When is the matter relatively quickly disposed of, for plaintiff or defendant; when is a full-blown competitive analysis required? When do the exigencies of modern day global competition mean that the antitrust agencies should defer to the market and simply let the competition—and innovation—happen?

Many cases fall into specialized categories, such as trade association by-laws or joint venture agreements. We begin not with the categories but with a kaleidoscope of modern or forward-looking cases and authorities, for contemporary problems must be solved under the "modern" umbrella—the forms of analysis and the vocabulary accepted by the courts today.

Beginning in the mid–1980s, the Supreme Court dealt with a series of cases on the border line between a per se rule and a rule of reason. We present here two such cases, both involving loose combinations. We present a third case, from an appellate court, where the collaboration was somewhat but minimally integrative. Next, we build upon the Supreme Court decision in *BMI*, supra p. 83, which involves integration. Finally, we present two excerpts, one from the Supreme Court and one from the FTC, exemplary of pragmatic, contemporary analysis in more integrative cases.

Here is a roadmap of the five touchstones:

Indiana Federation of Dentists (IFD) affirms a quick rule-of-reason analysis in the case of a restraint that is worrisome on its face because it is concerted action that resembles a boycott and is coercive of the consumer/customers. This case was brought by the Federal Trade Commission. Note that the FTC did not by-pass rule of reason analysis—it introduced *some* proof of the market, market power, and effect of the restraint, and it paid attention to the defendants' claimed justifications. But it did the rule of reason analysis quickly by the use of a presumption and shift of the burden.

California Dental Association, more than a decade later and strikingly also a case against a dentists' association, reversed an FTC decision. This time the Court was worried about the dental association's advertising restraints including limits on discount advertising. See if you detect a shift in the inner compass of the Court between *IFD* and *California Dental Association*. Is the Court now more deferent to decisions of professionals? Is it more demanding of the plaintiff to prove output effects? more skeptical of quicker looks? Is the case explainable as involving, and might it be limited to, professional associations, on the theory that professionals might be entrusted with self-regulation? (But how to explain *Indiana Federation of Dentists*? *Maricopa*? *National Society of Professional Engineers*?) You should draw distinct lessons from *California Dental Association* about the Court's current skepticism towards quick-look approaches; about the "continuum" nature of rule-of-reason analysis (the less worrisome the restraint the heavier burden on the plaintiff); and about the sympathetic ear lent to efficiency and pro-market stories of defendants.

Next we pick up a small sampling of authorities attuned to the current dominant perceptions. The cases selected involve increasingly more integration. More integration is likely to entail more deference to the collaborators, who may need restrictions to make their collaboration work efficiently. *Rothery*, from the Court of Appeals of the D.C. Circuit, analyzes a covenant not to compete in a situation rife with free rider problems. *BMI*, which we revisit, involves more significant integration and a package offering with strong efficiency properties. *Credit Suisse* shows how securities underwriters come together to launch initial public offerings entailing various restraints that look at first blush like manipulative practices (maybe some of them are). The Court finds the subject matter preempted by the Securities and Exchange Act, while Justice Stevens, concurring, provides a modern rule-of-reason analysis as to why these arrangements "should be treated as procompetitive joint ventures."

As a last touchstone, we refer to *Google/AdMob* (supra page 402), which you will recall was an acquisition. We invoke it here for two reasons. First, the most tightly integrated joint ventures are in many senses equivalent to a merger, and indeed notification must be filed under Hart–Scott–Rodino pre-merger process if they meet threshold size. Such tight joint ventures stand at the other end of the continuum from the loosest collaborations among competitors. Second, *Google/AdMob* was a new economy, high technology collaboration. One of the lessons of the FTC's closing statement is that high tech collaborations may be more likely to take place in dynamic, changing markets in which the market will work to protect consumers, and the collaboration itself might lead to dynamic pro-competitive change. Not always, as the FTC statement reminds us; but this is a possibility that the analyst must take seriously.

These, then, are our touchstones—the loose collaboration in *IFD*, which coerced consumers and was suspect; the loose collaboration in *California Dental*, which regulated deception and required a longer look; the more integrated projects of Atlas Moving Company and its agent, and of risk-sharing investment bankers launching an IPO (*Rothery* and *Credit Suisse*); and a fully integrated collaboration of Google in a new economy market. All that follows falls under the dome of the touchstones.

We start with conduct near the border line but not challenged as per se illegal. Pay attention to why the agreement is treated as suspect and deserves a shift of the burden.

FTC v. INDIANA FEDERATION OF DENTISTS

476 U.S. 447 (1986).

JUSTICE WHITE: This case concerns commercial relations among certain Indiana dentists, their patients, and the patients' dental health care insurers. The question presented is whether the Federal Trade Commission correctly concluded that a conspiracy among dentists to refuse to submit x rays to dental insurers for use in benefits determinations constituted an "unfair method of competition" in violation of § 5 of the Federal Trade Commission Act.

I

Since the 1970's, dental health insurers, responding to the demands of their policyholders, have attempted to contain the cost of dental treatment by, among other devices, limiting payment of benefits to the cost of the "least expensive yet adequate treatment" suitable to the needs of individual patients. Implementation of such cost-containment measures, known as "alternative benefits" plans, requires evaluation by the insurer of the diagnosis and recommendation of the treating dentist, either in advance of or following the provision of care. In order to carry out such evaluation, insurers frequently request dentists to submit, along with insurance claim forms requesting payment of benefits, any dental x rays that have been used by the dentist in examining the patient as well as other information concerning their diagnoses and treatment recommendations. Typically, claim forms and accompanying x rays are reviewed by lay claims examiners, who either approve payment of claims or, if the materials submitted raise a question whether the recommended course of treatment is in fact necessary, refer claims to dental consultants, who are licensed dentists, for further review. On the basis of the materials available, supplemented where appropriate by further diagnostic aids, the dental consultant may recommend that the insurer approve a claim, deny it, or pay only for a less expensive course of treatment.

Such review of diagnostic and treatment decisions has been viewed by some dentists as a threat to their professional independence and economic well-being. In the early 1970's, the Indiana Dental Association, a professional organization comprising some 85% of practicing dentists in the State of Indiana, initiated an aggressive effort to hinder insurers' efforts to implement alternative benefits plans by enlisting member dentists to pledge not to submit x rays in conjunction with claim forms.[2] The Association's efforts met considerable success: large numbers of dentists signed the pledge, and insurers operating in Indiana found it difficult to obtain compliance with their requests for x rays and accordingly had to choose either to employ more expensive means of making alternative benefits determinations (for example, visiting the office of the treating dentist or conducting an independent oral examination) or to abandon such efforts altogether.

By the mid–1970's, fears of possible antitrust liability had dampened the Association's enthusiasm for opposing the submission of x rays to insurers. In 1979, the Association and a number of its constituent societies consented to a Federal Trade Commission order requiring them to cease and desist from further efforts to prevent member dentists from submitting x rays. *In re Indiana Dental Assn.,* 93 F.T.C. 392 (1979). Not all Indiana dentists were content to leave the matter of submitting x rays to the individual dentist. In 1976, a group of such dentists formed the Indiana Federation of Dentists, respondent in this case, in order to continue to pursue the Association's policy of resisting insurers' requests for x rays. The Federation, which styled itself a "union" in the belief that this label would stave off antitrust liability,[3] immediately promulgated a "work rule" forbidding its members to submit x rays to dental insurers in conjunction with claim forms. Although the Federation's membership was

---

2. A presentation made in 1974 by Dr. David McClure, an Association official and later one of the founders of respondent Indiana Federation of Dentists, is revealing as to the motives underlying the dentists' resistance to the provision of x rays for use by insurers in making alternative benefits determinations:

"The problems associated with third party programs are many, but I believe the 'Indiana Plan' [*i.e.,* the policy of refusing to submit x rays] to be sound and if we work together, we can win this battle. We are fighting an economic war where the very survival of our profession is at stake.

"How long can some of the leaders of dentistry in other states be so complacent and willing to fall into the trap that is being set for us. If only they would take the time, to see from whence come the arrows that are heading in our direction. The Delta Dental Plans have bedded down with the unions and have been a party to setting up the greatest controls that any profession has ever known in a free society....

"The name of the game is money. The government and labor are determined to reduce the cost of the dental health dollar at the expense of the dentist. There is no way a dental service can be rendered cheaper when the third party has to have its share of the dollar.

"Already we are locked into a fee freeze that could completely control the quality of dental care, if left on long enough." FTC Complaint Counsel's Trial Exhibit ....

3. Respondent no longer makes any pretense of arguing that it is immune from antitrust liability as a labor organization.

small, numbering less than 100, its members were highly concentrated in and around three Indiana communities: Anderson, Lafayette, and Fort Wayne. The Federation succeeded in enlisting nearly 100% of the dental specialists in the Anderson area, and approximately 67% of the dentists in and around Lafayette. In the areas of its strength, the Federation was successful in continuing to enforce the Association's prior policy of refusal to submit x rays to dental insurers.

In 1978, the Federal Trade Commission issued a complaint against the Federation, alleging in substance that its efforts to prevent its members from complying with insurers' requests for x rays constituted an unfair method of competition in violation of § 5 of the Federal Trade Commission Act. Following lengthy proceedings including a full evidentiary hearing before an Administrative Law Judge, the Commission ruled that the Federation's policy constituted a violation of § 5 and issued an order requiring the Federation to cease and desist from further efforts to organize dentists to refuse to submit x rays to insurers. . . .

. . . [T]he United States Court of Appeals for the Seventh Circuit . . . vacated the order. . . . Accepting the Federation's characterization of its rule against submission of x rays as merely an ethical and moral policy designed to enhance the welfare of dental patients [on grounds that the provision of x rays might lead the insurers to make inaccurate determinations of the proper level of care and thus injure the health of the insured patients], the majority concluded that the Commission's findings that the policy was anticompetitive were erroneous. . . . Further, the court held that the Commission's findings were inadequate because of its failure both to offer a precise definition of the market in which the Federation was alleged to have restrained competition and to establish that the Federation had the power to restrain competition in that market. Finally, the majority faulted the Commission for not finding that the alleged restraint on competition among dentists had actually resulted in higher dental costs to patients and insurers. The third member of the Court of Appeals panel concurred in the judgment solely on the ground that there was insufficient proof that cooperation with insurers was an element of dental services as to which dentists would tend to compete. . . .

. . . We now reverse. * * *

III

The relevant factual findings are that the members of the Federation conspired among themselves to withhold x rays requested by dental insurers for use in evaluating claims for benefits, and that this conspiracy had the effect of suppressing competition among dentists with respect to cooperation with the requests of the insurance companies. As to the first of these findings there can be no serious dispute: abundant evidence in the record reveals that one of the primary reasons—if not *the* primary reason—for the Federation's existence was the promulgation and enforcement of the so-called "work rule" against submission of x rays in conjunction with insurance claim forms.

As for the second crucial finding—that competition was actually suppressed—the Seventh Circuit held it to be unsupported by the evidence, on two theories. First, the court stated that the evidence did not establish that cooperation with requests for information by patients' insurance companies was an aspect of the provision of dental services with respect to which dentists would, in the absence of some restraint, compete. Second, the court found that even assuming that dentists would otherwise compete with respect to policies of cooperating or not cooperating with insurance companies, the Federation's policy did not impair that competition, for the member dentists continued to allow insurance companies to use other means of evaluating their diagnoses when reviewing claims for benefits: specifically, "the IFD member dentists allowed insurers to visit the dental office to review and examine the patient's x rays along with all of the other diagnostic and clinical aids used in formulating a proper course of dental treatment." 745 F.2d, at 1143.

Neither of these criticisms of the Commission's findings is well founded. The Commission's finding that "[i]n the absence of . . . concerted behavior, individual dentists would have been subject to market forces of competition, creating incentives for them to . . . comply with the requests of patients' third-party insurers," 101 F.T.C., at 173, finds support not only in common sense and economic theory, upon both of which the FTC may reasonably rely, but also in record documents, including newsletters circulated among Indiana dentists, revealing that Indiana dentists themselves perceived that unrestrained competition tended to lead their colleagues to comply with insurers' requests for x rays. Moreover, there was evidence that outside of Indiana, in States where dentists had not collectively refused to submit x rays, insurance companies found little difficulty in obtaining compliance by dentists with their requests. A "reasonable mind" could conclude on the basis of this evidence that competition for patients, who have obvious incentives for seeking dentists who will cooperate with their insurers, would tend to lead dentists in Indiana (and elsewhere) to cooperate with requests for information by their patients' insurers.

The Commission's finding that such competition was actually diminished where the Federation held sway also finds adequate support in the record. The Commission found that in the areas where Federation membership among dentists was most significant (that is, in the vicinity of Anderson and Lafayette) insurance companies were unable to obtain compliance with their requests for submission of x rays in conjunction with claim forms and were forced to resort to other, more costly, means of reviewing diagnoses for the purpose of benefit determination. Neither the opinion of the Court of Appeals nor the brief of respondent identifies any evidence suggesting that the Commission's finding that the Federation's policy had an actual impact on the ability of insurers to obtain the x rays they requested was incorrect. . . .

IV

[The agreement is anticompetitive and needs justification]

The question remains whether these findings are legally sufficient to establish a violation of § 1 of the Sherman Act—that is, whether the Federation's collective refusal to cooperate with insurers' requests for x rays constitutes an "unreasonable" restraint of trade. Under our precedents, a restraint may be adjudged unreasonable either because it fits within a class of restraints that has been held to be *per se* "unreasonable," or because it violates what has come to be known as the "Rule of Reason," under which the "test of legality is whether the restraint imposed is such as merely regulates and perhaps thereby promotes competition or whether it is such as may suppress or even destroy competition." *Chicago Board of Trade v. United States,* 246 U.S., at 238.

The policy of the Federation with respect to its members' dealings with third-party insurers resembles practices that have been labeled "group boycotts": the policy constitutes a concerted refusal to deal on particular terms with patients covered by group dental insurance. Although this Court has in the past stated that group boycotts are unlawful *per se,* we decline to resolve this case by forcing the Federation's policy into the "boycott" pigeonhole and invoking the *per se* rule. . . .

Application of the Rule of Reason to these facts is not a matter of any great difficulty. The Federation's policy takes the form of a horizontal agreement among the participating dentists to withhold from their customers a particular service that they desire—the forwarding of x rays to insurance companies along with claim forms. "While this is not price fixing as such, no elaborate industry analysis is required to demonstrate the anticompetitive character of such an agreement." *Society of Professional Engineers, supra,* 435 U.S. at 692. A refusal to compete with respect to the package of services offered to customers, no less than a refusal to compete with respect to the price term of an agreement, impairs the ability of the market to advance social welfare by ensuring the provision of desired goods and services to consumers at a price approximating the marginal cost of providing them. Absent some countervailing procompetitive virtue—such as, for example, the creation of efficiencies in the operation of a market or the provision of goods and services, . . . such an agreement limiting consumer choice by impeding the "ordinary give and take of the market place," *Society of Professional Engineers, supra,* 435 U.S. at 692, cannot be sustained under the Rule of Reason. No credible argument has been advanced for the proposition that making it more costly for the insurers and patients who are the dentists' customers to obtain information needed for evaluating the dentists' diagnoses has any such procompetitive effect.

[IFD's arguments]

The Federation advances three principal arguments for the proposition that, notwithstanding its lack of competitive virtue, the Federation's policy of withholding x rays should not be deemed an unreasonable restraint of trade. First, . . . the Federation suggests that in the absence of specific findings by the Commission concerning the definition of the market in which the Federation allegedly restrained trade and the power of the Federation's members in that market, the conclusion that the Federation unreasonably restrained trade is erroneous as a matter of law, regardless of whether the challenged practices might be impermissibly anticompetitive if engaged in by persons who together possessed power in a specifically defined market. This contention, however, runs counter to the Court's holding in *NCAA v. Board of Regents* that "[a]s a matter of law, the absence of proof of market power does not justify a naked restriction on price or output," and that such a restriction "requires some competitive justification even in the absence of a detailed market analysis." 468 U.S., at 109–110. Moreover, even if the restriction imposed by the Federation is not sufficiently "naked" to call this principle into play, the Commission's failure to engage in detailed market analysis is not fatal to its finding of a violation of the Rule of Reason. The Commission found that in two localities in the State of Indiana (the Anderson and Lafayette areas), Federation dentists constituted heavy majorities of the practicing dentists and that as a result of the efforts of the Federation, insurers in those areas were, over a period of years, actually unable to obtain compliance with their requests for submission of x rays. Since the purpose of the inquiries into market definition and market power is to determine whether an arrangement has the potential for genuine adverse effects on competition, "proof of actual detrimental effects, such as a reduction of output" can obviate the need for an inquiry into market power, which is but a "surrogate for detrimental effects." 7 P. Areeda, Antitrust Law ¶ 1511, p. 429 (1986). In this case, we conclude that the finding of actual, sustained adverse effects on competition in those areas where IFD dentists predominated, viewed in light of the reality that markets for dental services tend to be relatively localized, is legally sufficient to support a finding that the challenged restraint was unreasonable even in the absence of elaborate market analysis.

Second, the Federation, again following the lead of the Court of Appeals, argues that a holding that its policy of withholding x rays constituted an unreasonable restraint of trade is precluded by the Commission's failure to make any finding that the policy resulted in the provision of dental services that were more costly than those that the patients and their insurers would have chosen were they able to evaluate x rays in conjunction with claim forms. This argument, too, is unpersuasive. Although it is true that the goal of the insurers in seeking submission of x rays for use in their review of benefits claims was to minimize costs by choosing the least expensive adequate course of dental treatment, a showing that this goal was actually achieved through the means chosen is not an essential step in establishing that the dentists' attempt to thwart its achievement by collectively refusing to supply the requested information was an unreasonable restraint of trade. A concerted and effective effort to withhold (or make more costly) information desired by consumers for the purpose of determining whether a particular purchase is cost-justified is likely enough to disrupt the proper functioning of the price-setting mechanism of the market that it may be condemned even absent proof that it resulted in higher prices or, as here, the purchase of higher-priced services, than would occur in its absence. Moreover, even if the desired information were in fact completely useless to the insurers and their patients in making an informed choice regarding the least costly adequate course of treatment—or, to put it another way, if the costs of evaluating the information were far greater than the cost savings resulting from its use—the Federation would still not be justified in deciding on behalf of its members' customers that they did not need the information: presumably, if that were the case, the discipline of the market would itself soon result in the insurers' abandoning their requests for x rays. The Federation is not entitled to pre-empt the working of the market by deciding for itself that its customers do not need that which they demand.

Third, the Federation complains that the Commission erred in failing to consider, as relevant to its Rule of Reason analysis, noncompetitive "quality of care" justifications for the prohibition on provision of x rays to insurers in conjunction with claim forms. This claim reflects the Court of Appeals' repeated characterization of the Federation's policy as a "legal, moral, and ethical policy of quality dental care, requiring that insurers examine and review all diagnostic and clinical aids before formulating a proper course of dental treatment." The gist of the claim is that x rays, standing alone, are not adequate bases for diagnosis of dental problems or for the formulation of an acceptable course of treatment. Accordingly, if insurance companies are permitted to determine whether they will pay a claim for dental treatment on the basis of x rays as opposed to a full examination of all the diagnostic aids available to the examining dentist, there is a danger that they will erroneously decline to pay for treatment that is in fact in the interest of the patient, and that the patient will as a result be deprived of fully adequate care.

The Federation's argument is flawed both legally and factually. The premise of the argument is that, far from having no effect on the cost of dental services chosen by patients and their insurers, the provision of x rays will have too great an impact: it will lead to the reduction of costs through the selection of inadequate treatment. Precisely such a justification for withholding information from customers was rejected as illegitimate in the *Society of Professional Engineers* case. The argument is, in essence, that an unrestrained market in which consumers are given access to the information they believe to be relevant to their choices will lead them to make unwise and even dangerous choices. Such an argument amounts to "nothing less than a frontal assault on the basic policy of the Sherman Act." *Society of Professional Engineers, supra,* 435 U.S. at 695. Moreover, there is no particular reason to believe that the provision of information will be more harmful to consumers in the market for dental services than in other markets. Insurers deciding what level of care to pay for are not themselves the recipients of those services, but it is by no means clear that they lack incentives to consider the welfare of the patient as well as the minimization of costs. They are themselves in competition for the patronage of the patients—or, in most cases, the unions or businesses that contract on their behalf for group insurance coverage—and must satisfy their potential customers not only that they will provide coverage at a reasonable cost, but also that that coverage will be adequate to meet their customers' dental needs. There is thus no more reason to expect dental insurance companies to sacrifice quality in return for cost savings than to believe this of consumers in, say, the market for engineering services. Accordingly, if noncompetitive quality-of-service justifications are inadmissible to justify the denial of information to consumers in the latter market, there is little reason to credit such justifications here.

In any event, the Commission did not, as the Federation suggests, refuse even to consider the quality of care justification for the withholding of x rays. Rather, the Commission held that the Federation had failed to introduce sufficient evidence to establish such a justification.... The Commission was amply justified in concluding on the basis of this conflicting evidence that even if concern for the quality of patient care could under some circumstances serve as a justification for a restraint of the sort imposed here, the evidence did not support a finding that the careful use of x rays as a basis for evaluating insurance claims is in fact destructive of proper standards of dental care. * * * *Reversed.*

QUESTIONS AND COMMENTS

1. The FTC argued that the dentists' agreement was so close to a naked restraint of trade that it should be presumptively unlawful, and that a quick-look rule of reason would suffice. Did the Court agree? Presumptions are very important in litigation; they can be determinative of outcomes.

2. To qualify for a quick look, must the agreement appear to be output limiting and price raising, creating market power to the detriment of the consumer? Does this agreement meet that test?

3. In this case the analysis was truncated. The Court demanded less than full-blown evidence, given defendants' interference with the central nervous system of the market. Even so, note the steps taken, or that the Court acknowledges must usually be taken, in rule-of-reason analysis: 1) What is the market? 2) Do defendants occupy a sufficient share of the market to indicate market power? 3) What is the anticompetitive nature of the agreement and how does/might it harm competition? 4) Does the agreement have procompetitive virtues?

On which of these steps did the Court allow short cuts? Why? Were the short cuts warranted? Did the FTC prove competitive harm?

4. Note that the anticompetitive effect of the dentists' agreement was a dynamic effect—"consumers" (through the agency of the insurance companies) could not get the information they demanded. Consumer sovereignty was directly affronted. In most rule-of-reason cases, proof of anticompetitive

effects involves evidence that, as a result of the agreement, competitors in the market as a whole behave less rivalrously and prices are likely to rise.

5. Was the Court correct to rule out quality of care issues—i.e., the dentists' argument that if they did not collaborate to hold the line, dentists would not be able to resist the insurance companies' demands for x-rays, and compliance with the demands would give the insurance companies false information and stand in the way of good health care? Is this defense a frontal assault on the Sherman Act?

CALIFORNIA DENTAL ASSOCIATION v. FTC

526 U.S. 756 (1999).

Reread the case at page 105 supra.

[Recall that the Dental Association Bylaws greatly restricted the dentists' rights to advertise. For example, it prohibited simple across-the-board price advertising. The Court rejected quick-look analysis and remanded for a fuller inquiry. In Chapter 2 we asked whether the by-laws were or should have been illegal on their face. The Court said, No. Here, we ask: How do you analyze this case under the rule of reason?]

QUESTIONS AND COMMENTS

1. To perform the deeper analysis mandated by the Court, what must the FTC prove? Must it prove that the dentists had market power and used this power to increase price, decrease quality and/or decrease output of dental services? If the dentists prove that the rules increase trust in dentists by limiting deceptive advertising and they therefore increase trust in honest dentists, do they win? After *California Dental*, how would you deal with the Indiana dentists' argument that their action (refusing to supply x-rays to insurers allegedly because the x-rays might mislead the insurers to deny coverage for needed services) was important to promote quality dental care? Is *Indiana Federation of Dentists* distinguishable from *California Dental*?

2. Was the Court properly critical of the FTC's conclusion that the restrictions on advertising and promotion were a form of output limitation?

3. The Court shows distinct reluctance towards finding the restraints inherently suspect and subject to condemnation in the absence of a plausible pro-market or efficiency justification. Also, it shows receptivity to defendants' claim of no market harm. How dependent was this approach on the fact that the subject of the case was professional advertising? How linked was the approach to the fact that the market was "characterized by striking disparities between the information available to the professional and the patient"? The Federal Trade Commission (2003) believes that these two facts were critical. See *Matter of PolyGram Holding, Inc. (Three Tenors)*, 5 Trade Reg. Rep. (CCH) ¶ 15,453 (FTC 2003), substantially affirmed, 416 F.3d 29 (D.C. Cir.2005), page 111 supra.

4. See the FTC and DOJ Antitrust Guidelines for Collaborations Among Competitors (2000) for a structural approach to the rule of reason. *http://www.ftc.gov/os/2000/04/ftcdojguidelines.pdf*.

The next case involves a covenant not to compete. The court treats the agreement as one pursuant to an integrated enterprise, and therefore entitled to more deference than a loose-knit agreement. The "integration" was, however, modest.

ROTHERY STORAGE & VAN CO. v. ATLAS VAN LINES, INC.

792 F.2d 210 (D.C. Cir. 1986), cert. denied, 479 U.S. 1033 (1987).

JUDGE BORK: Appellants, plaintiffs below [Rothery et al.], seek review of the district court's decision dismissing their antitrust action against Atlas Van Lines, Inc. ("Atlas"). Appellants are five present and three former agents of Atlas. For convenience, we will frequently refer to them by the name of the first-named appellant, Rothery Storage & Van Co. ("Rothery"). Rothery claims that Atlas and several of the carrier agents affiliated with Atlas adopted a policy constituting a "group boycott" in violation of section 1 of the Sherman Act.... The trial court granted Atlas' motion for summary judgment on several alternative grounds. Because we find that Atlas' policy is designed to make the van line more efficient rather than to decrease the output of its services and raise rates, we affirm.

Atlas operates as a nationwide common carrier of used household goods under authority granted by the Interstate Commerce Commission. It contracts to provide moving services to individuals and to businesses transferring employees. Like most national moving companies, Atlas exercises its interstate authority by employing independent moving companies throughout the country as its agents....

The deregulation of the moving industry, beginning in 1979, produced changes that had a profound impact on the relationship between van lines and their agents. Prior to the regulatory changes, independent moving companies had little ability to obtain their own interstate transportation authority. The ICC's Policy Statement on Motor Carrier Regulation (1979), and the Motor Carrier Act of 1980, greatly increased the ability of common carriers to obtain interstate moving authority. In 1981, moreover, the ICC repealed its requirement that carrier agents [agents with their own interstate authority] charge the same rate for agency shipments and shipments carried on their own accounts. Thus, agents could obtain interstate authority and could cut prices to attract business for their own accounts that otherwise might have constituted agency shipments for the van line's account.

This increased potential for the diversion of interstate business to its carrier agents posed free-rider problems for Atlas....

To meet these problems ... Atlas announced that it would terminate the agency contract of any affiliated company that persisted in handling interstate carriage on its own account as well as for Atlas. Under the new policy, any carrier agent already affiliated with Atlas could continue to exercise independent interstate authority only by transferring its independent interstate authority to a separate corporation with a new name. These new entities could not use the facilities or services of Atlas or any of its affiliates.

Because Atlas and its affiliates refuse to deal with any carrier agent that does not comply, several Atlas carrier agents, appellants here, charged that Atlas' new policy constitutes a "group boycott." They filed this action, and after the completion of discovery on the issue of liability, both sides filed cross motions for summary judgment.

The district court granted summary judgment to Atlas. . . .

While we do not agree that the challenged arrangement lacks the elements of a horizontal agreement, we uphold the trial judge's conclusion that Atlas' new policy does not offend the antitrust laws. The challenged restraint is ancillary to the economic integration of Atlas and its agents so that the rule of per se illegality does not apply. Neither are the other tests of the rule of reason offended since Atlas' market share is far too small for the restraint to threaten competition or to have been intended to do so. . . .

* * *

Atlas has required that any moving company doing business as its agent must not conduct independent interstate carrier operations. Thus, a carrier agent, in order to continue as an Atlas agent, must either abandon its independent interstate authority and operate only under Atlas' authority or create a new corporation (a "carrier affiliate") to conduct interstate carriage separate from its operation as an Atlas agent. Atlas' agents may deal only with Atlas or other Atlas agents.

The result of this is an interstate system for the carriage of household goods in which legally separate companies integrate their activities by contract. In this way the participants achieve many of the same benefits or efficiencies that would be available if they were integrated through ownership by Atlas. At the outset of this opinion, we set out the functions performed by Atlas and by the agents and stated that the system is a contract integration, one identical, in economic terms, to a partnership formed by agreement. Analysis might begin and end with the observation that Atlas and its agents command between 5.1 and 6% of the relevant market, which is the interstate carriage of used household goods. It is impossible to believe that an agreement to eliminate competition within a group of that size can produce any of the evils of monopoly. A monopolist (or those acting together to achieve monopoly results) enhances its revenues by raising the market price. It can do that only if its share of the market is so large that by reducing its output of goods or services the amount offered by the industry is substantially reduced so that the price is bid up. If a group of Atlas' size reduced its output of services, there would be no effect upon market price because firms making up the other 94% of the market would simply take over the abandoned business. The only effect would be a loss of revenues to Atlas. Indeed, so impotent to raise prices is a firm with a market share of 5 or 6% that any attempt by it to engage in a monopolistic restriction of output would be little short of suicidal.

Appellants argue that Atlas' 6% national market share understates the market power of Atlas and its agents to impose an anticompetitive result because appellants introduced evidence of the existence of distinct product geographic submarkets and because of evidence that the national market "approximates a tight oligopoly." Each of these propositions is wrong. With respect to the existence of submarkets, plaintiffs conceded the existence of a nationwide market and did not offer the district court any evidence that created a genuine issue of material fact as to the existence of submarkets. The district judge, therefore, had only the national market before him. Indeed, so clear is the state of the evidence that we would affirm on this basis even if we thought it was not the rationale of the district court's decision. * * *

All that was before the district court, and all that is before us, therefore, is a nationwide market. Atlas, it is agreed, did 6% of the business in that market. And the relevance of this figure as a measure of market power is in no way diminished by appellants' fanciful claims of "tight oligopoly" in the national market.

Given the fact that this industry consists of 1100 to 1300 interstate carriers, employing about 8000 agents, it would seem to be impossible to entertain any notion of market power. What plaintiffs offered to support their theory of "tight oligopoly" was a list of van lines and market shares that affirmatively proved their market power contention to be chimerical.... * * *

We might well rest, therefore, upon the absence of market power as demonstrated both by Atlas' 6% national market share and by the structure of the market. If it is clear that Atlas and its agents by eliminating competition among themselves are not attempting to restrict industry output, then their agreement must be designed to make the conduct of their business more effective. No third possibility suggests itself. But we need not rely entirely upon that inference because the record made in the district court demonstrates that the challenged agreement enhances the efficiency of the van line. The chief efficiency, as already noted, is the elimination of the problem of the free ride.

A carrier agent can attract customers because of Atlas' "national image" and can use Atlas' equipment and order forms when undertaking carriage for its own account. The carrier agents "benefit from use of the services of moving and storage firms affiliated with Atlas, for origin or destination work at remote locations, when operating independently of Atlas." This benefit involves not only the availability of a reliable network of firms providing such services, but also includes the benefit of Atlas' "mediating collection matters" among its affiliates. To the degree that a carrier agent uses Atlas' reputation, equipment, facilities, and services in conducting business for its own profit, the agent enjoys a free ride at Atlas' expense. The problem is that the van line's incentive to spend for reputation, equipment, facilities, and services declines as it receives less of the benefit from them. That produces a deterioration of the system's efficiency because the things consumers desire are not provided in the amounts they are willing to pay for. In the extreme case, the system as a whole could collapse.

... We find the district court's conclusion that free riding existed to be amply supported and by no means clearly erroneous.

A few examples will suffice. Plaintiff-appellants conceded below that the carrier agents "benefited" from their association with Atlas' "national image." We cannot rationally infer that this consumer identification advantage did not benefit the carrier agents in operating on their own accounts while using Atlas equipment and personnel trained by Atlas. Rothery also allowed that, while the carrier agents bore the bulk of costs associated with their operations, Atlas did make "some small contributions" to the group advertising programs and "some contributions" to the painting of trucks on which the Atlas logo appeared.

Rothery also credited Atlas with providing a dispatching service, a clearinghouse service for the settlement of accounts among its affiliates, assistance in settling claims among affiliates, certain written forms, sales meetings to provide exposure to national customers, driver and employee training programs, and the screening of the quality and reliability of affiliated firms that provided origin and destination services for the carrier agents.

Rothery did not assert in its Statement of Material Undisputed Facts, nor may we infer, that the carrier agents could not avail themselves of the benefits derived from these services when operating for their own accounts. Many of these services confer intangible advantages that redound to the benefit of the carrier agent as a whole, and do not admit of easy segregation as between shipments on Atlas' interstate authority and shipments on the carrier agent's authority. For example, if Atlas provides superior training to the employees of its carrier agents, that training improves the quality of work not only on shipments undertaken for Atlas but also on shipments made on the carrier agent's own interstate authority. And because carrier agents may elect to use their own or Atlas' interstate authority for a given shipment, exposure to national clients at Atlas' sales meetings can provide them with interstate customers for their own, as well as for Atlas', accounts.

... [B]ecause the plaintiff-appellants asserted that the carrier agents paid Atlas only for its clearinghouse service and for the provision of written forms, we agree with the district court's finding that many of the services supplied as part of Atlas' arrangement with the carrier agents' arrangement resulted in Atlas subsidizing its competitors.

If the carrier agents could persist in competing with Atlas while deriving the advantages of their Atlas affiliation, Atlas might well have found it desirable, or even essential, to decrease or abandon many such services.... Of that tendency there can be no doubt. When a person or business providing goods or services begins to receive declining revenues, then, other things being equal, that person or firm will provide fewer goods or services. As marginal revenue drops, so does output. Thus, when Atlas' centralized services, equipment, and national image amount to a subsidy of competing carrier agents, this cuts down the marginal revenue derived from the provision of such things so that less will be offered than the market would reward.

On the other side, the firm receiving a subsidized good or service will take more of it. As cost declines, then, other things being equal, demand increases. Carrier agents, that is, will increase the use of Atlas' services, etc., on interstate carriage for their own accounts, over-consuming that which they can obtain at less than its true cost. In this way, free riding distorts the economic signals within the system so that the van line loses effectiveness in serving consumers. The restraint at issue in this case, therefore, is a classic attempt to counter the perceived menace that free riding poses. By compelling carrier agents to transfer their interstate authority to a separate entity, Atlas can continue providing services at optimal levels, confident that it will be paid for those services.

The Atlas agreements thus produce none of the evils of monopoly but enhance consumer welfare by creating efficiency. There seems no reason in the rationale of the Sherman Act, or in any comprehensible policy, to invalidate such agreements....

... [In recent decisions, the Supreme Court has adopted the formulation] of Judge Taft in *Addyston Pipe & Steel:* a naked horizontal restraint, one that does not accompany a contract integration, can have no purpose other than restricting output and raising prices, and so is illegal per se; an ancillary horizontal restraint, one that is part of an integration of the economic activities of the parties and appears capable of enhancing the group's efficiency, is to be judged according to its purpose and effect....

The application of these principles to Atlas' restraints is obvious because, as we have seen, these restraints are ancillary to the contract integration or joint venture that constitutes the Atlas van line. The restraints preserve the efficiencies of the nationwide van line by eliminating the problem of the free ride. There is, on the other hand, no possibility that the restraints can suppress market competition and so decrease output. Atlas has 6% or less of the relevant market, far too little to make even conceivable an adverse effect upon output. If Atlas should reduce its output, it would merely shrink in size without having any impact upon market price. Under the rule of *Addyston Pipe & Steel* [as adopted in recent Supreme Court doctrine] therefore, it follows that the Atlas agreements do not violate section 1 of the Sherman Act.[11]

---

11. Two additional points should be made. First, we do not think it significant to the outcome that Atlas' policy allowed agents to exercise their own interstate authority through separate corporations. Once it is clear that restraints can only be intended to enhance efficiency rather

A joint venture made more efficient by ancillary restraints, is a fusion of the productive capacities of the members of the venture. That, in economic terms, is the same thing as a corporate merger. Merger policy has always proceeded by drawing lines about allowable market shares and these lines are based on rough estimates of effects because that is all the nature of the problem allows. If Atlas bought the stock of all its carrier agents, the merger would not even be challenged under the Department of Justice Merger Guidelines because of inferences drawn from Atlas' market share and the structure of the market. We can think of no good reason not to apply the same inferences to Atlas' ancillary restraints. * * *

QUESTIONS AND COMMENTS

1. *Rothery* (1986) is the earliest contemporary Section 1 rule-of-reason analysis we have presented in which plaintiff did not get a presumption of anticompetitive effects. Also, it is the fullest explanation we have seen of the free rider effect.

From 1911 (*Dr. Miles*, infra p. 615, now overruled) until the mid 1970s, a main concern of the antitrust law was impairing the freedom of firms without power to compete on the merits (the "free trader" concern). From the late 1970s to the present, the antitrust law has expressed and expresses a paramount concern with the "free rider problem." Is free riding as serious and pervasive a problem as Judge Bork supposes? Regard for the "free rider problem" has revolutionized the law on vertical restraints. See Chapter 6, infra.

2. Suppose Atlas had market power. Allegedly it had a 40% market share in one region and a 60% share in another. Suppose, as Judge Bork invites us to assume (see his note 11), that Atlas forbade its agents from competing in any form, including through separate corporations. What would be the next step in analysis? Consider the following questions: Are there significant barriers to entry into the household moving market on an efficient region-wide scale, and are prices in the market higher than competitive? Are the agents, themselves or through networks they might establish, the most likely entrants into the market? Suppose the answers are affirmative. Are Atlas' restraints on its agents pro-competitive and efficient, or anti-competitive? If the latter, is there an obvious less restrictive alternative that will allow the efficiencies to be realized? (You may not tightly second-guess business judgment.)

3. Do you agree with Judge Bork's statement: If Atlas and its agents "are not attempting to restrict industry output, then their agreement must be

---

than to restrict output, the degree of restraint is a matter of business rather than legal judgment. Second, though it is sometimes said that, in the case of restraints like these, it is necessary to weigh procompetitive effects against anticompetitive effects, we do not think that a useable formula if it implies an ability to quantify the two effects and compare the values found. Here, there are no anticompetitive effects and so there is nothing to place on that side of the scale. If the underlying contract integration is lawful, *i.e.*, not of such size as to violate the Sherman Act, restraints ancillary to the integration, in the sense we have described, should be lawful. Weighing effects in any direct sense will usually be beyond judicial capabilities. . . .

designed to make the conduct of their business more effective. No third possibility suggests itself." Is there a third possibility?

Now we revisit a case that more decidedly involved business integration. In *BMI*, at the cusp of the modern era, the Supreme Court declared that per se treatment of the case was inappropriate. We will ask you to do the rule-of-reason analysis.

BROADCAST MUSIC INC. v. COLUMBIA BROADCASTING SYSTEM, INC.

441 U.S. 1 (1979).

Reread the case at page 83 supra.

[In *BMI*, the Court held not illegal on its face the agreement imposed by BMI that denied its customers (TV networks and stations) the right to pay only for the musical compositions that they used. The Court denied per se treatment. Now, we ask you to apply the rule of reason.]

QUESTIONS AND COMMENTS

1. BMI (and separately ASCAP) was a business venture that "made the market" for broadcast and TV use of musical compositions. The venture necessarily involved a combination of composers, and it required a single agent for the group to market the product and police copyright infringements. The venture was reasonable in essence. The question was whether the blanket license was unduly restrictive; i.e., whether users (licensees) were entitled to per use licenses; whether CBS was entitled to pay BMI only for the musical compositions it chose to use, rather than a blanket fee calculated as a percentage of CBS' advertising revenues. Recall that CBS was free to license compositions directly from the composers. CBS claimed that the blanket license restricted competition and that a system that allowed buyers' choice of a per use license was an available less restrictive alternative.

2. For a rule of reason analysis, you will need to ask the following questions: Did BMI have market power? Did the blanket license, as compared with per use options, tend to raise license fees? What competitive forces would tend to keep blanket license fees down to a competitive price? If there were price-raising aspects of the mandatory blanket license, were there also pro-competitive or efficiency aspects that could not otherwise easily be achieved? Even if the joint venture itself was reasonable, were there unnecessary and unreasonably restrictive ancillary restraints?

Justice Stevens thought that he could answer these questions without any further detailed inquiry; but he was in the minority. Here is his analysis. It is, in effect, a quick-look analysis. Consider, as you read it, where are the vulnerable points and why the majority disagreed.

JUSTICE STEVENS, dissenting: The Court holds that ASCAP's blanket license is not a species of price fixing categorically forbidden by the Sherman Act. I agree with that holding. The Court remands the case to the Court of Appeals, leaving open the question whether the blanket license as employed by ASCAP and BMI is unlawful under a rule-of-reason inquiry. I think that question is properly before us now and should be answered affirmatively. * * *

... In my judgment, a remand is not necessary. The record before this Court is a full one, reflecting extensive discovery and eight weeks of trial. The District Court's findings of fact are thorough and well supported. They clearly reveal that the challenged policy does have a significant adverse impact on competition. I would therefore affirm the judgment of the Court of Appeals.

II

Under our prior cases, there would be no question about the illegality of the blanket-only licensing policy if ASCAP and BMI were the exclusive sources of all licenses. A copyright, like a patent, is a statutory grant of monopoly privileges. The rules which prohibit a patentee from enlarging his statutory monopoly by conditioning a license on the purchase of unpatented goods, or by refusing to grant a license under one patent unless the licensee also takes a license under another, are equally applicable to copyrights. * * *

... ASCAP does not have exclusive control of the copyrights in its portfolio, and it is perfectly possible—at least as a legal matter—for a user of music to negotiate directly with composers and publishers for whatever rights he may desire. The availability of a practical alternative alters the competitive effect of a blockbooking or blanket-licensing policy. ASCAP is therefore quite correct in its insistence that its blanket license cannot be categorically condemned on the authority of the blockbooking and package-licensing cases. While these cases are instructive, they do not directly answer the question whether the ASCAP practice is unlawful.

The answer to that question depends on an evaluation of the effect of the practice on competition in the relevant market. And, of course, it is well settled that a sales practice that is permissible for a small vendor, at least when no coercion is present, may be unreasonable when employed by a company that dominates the market. We therefore must consider what the record tells us about the competitive character of this market.

III

The market for music at issue here is wholly dominated by ASCAP-issued blanket licenses. Virtually every domestic copyrighted composition is in the repertoire of either ASCAP or BMI. And again, virtually without exception, the only means that has been used to secure authority to perform such compositions is the blanket license.

The blanket all-or-nothing license is patently discriminatory. The user purchases full access to ASCAP's entire repertoire, even though his needs could be satisfied by a far more limited selection. The price he pays for this access is unrelated either to the quantity or the quality of the music he actually uses, or, indeed, to what he would probably use in a competitive system. Rather, in this unique all-or-nothing system, the price is based on a percentage of the user's advertising revenues, a measure that reflects the customer's ability to pay but is totally unrelated to factors—such as the cost, quality, or quantity of the product—that normally affect price in a competitive market. The ASCAP system requires users to buy more music than they want at a price which, while not beyond their ability to pay and perhaps not even beyond what is "reasonable" for the access they are getting, may well be far higher than what they would choose to spend for music in a competitive system. It is a classic example of economic discrimination.

The record plainly establishes that there is no price competition between separate musical compositions. Under a blanket license, it is no more expensive for a network to play the most popular current hit in prime time than it is to use an unknown composition as background music in a soap opera. Because the cost to the user is unaffected by the amount used on any program or on all programs, the user has no incentive to economize by, for example, substituting what would otherwise be less expensive songs for established favorites or by reducing the quantity of music used on a program. The blanket license thereby tends to encourage the use of more music, and also of a larger share of what is really more valuable music, than would be expected in a competitive system characterized by separate licenses. And since revenues are passed on to composers on a basis reflecting the character and frequency of the use of their music, the tendency is to increase the rewards of the established composers at the expense of those less well known. Perhaps the prospect is in any event unlikely, but the blanket license does not present a new songwriter with any opportunity to try to break into the market by offering his product for sale at an unusually low price. The absence of that opportunity, however unlikely it may be, is characteristic of a cartelized rather than a competitive market. * * *

IV

Since the record describes a market that could be competitive and is not, and since that market is dominated by two firms engaged in a single, blanket method of dealing, it surely seems logical to conclude that trade has been restrained unreasonably. ASCAP argues, however, that at least as to CBS, there has been no restraint at all since the network is free to deal directly with copyright holders.

The District Court found that CBS had failed to establish that it was compelled to take a blanket license from ASCAP. While CBS introduced evidence suggesting that a significant number of composers and publishers, satisfied as they are with the ASCAP system, would be "disinclined" to deal directly with the network, the court found such evidence unpersuasive in light of CBS's substantial market power in the music industry and the importance to copyright holders of network television exposure. Moreover, it is arguable that CBS could go further and, along with the other television networks, use its economic resources to exploit destructive competition among purveyors of music by driving the price of performance rights down to a far lower level. But none of this demonstrates that ASCAP's practices are lawful, or that ASCAP cannot be held liable for injunctive relief at CBS's request.

The fact that CBS has substantial market power does not deprive it of the right to complain when trade is restrained. Large buyers, as well as small, are protected by the antitrust laws. Indeed, even if the victim of a conspiracy is himself a wrongdoer, he has not forfeited the protection of the law.... * * *

QUESTIONS AND COMMENTS

1. Evaluate Justice Stevens' dissenting opinion. State the case to the contrary, including significant factual issues to be explored. You would not be wrong to conclude that the difference is one of perspective, with the majority more concerned with liberating the discretion of business to reach its audience efficiently and trusting in the market to overcome "little" restraints. The majority perspective is in the ascendancy.

2. The trial court in a companion case found the agreements reasonable. See *Buffalo Broadcasting Co. v. ASCAP*, 744 F.2d 917 (2d Cir. 1984), cert. denied, 469 U.S. 1211 (1985).

CREDIT SUISSE SECURITIES v. BILLING

551 U.S. 264 (2007).

[Investors in initial public offerings sued underwriters for various practices including tying and "laddering" in the course of launching initial public stock offerings for hundreds of technology companies (buyers in the IPO were required to buy more stock in successive stages to stabilize the launch). Allegedly, these practices violated the antitrust laws. The Supreme Court held that the Securities and Exchange Act preempted the antitrust laws. Justice Stevens agreed that the case was properly dismissed, but on grounds that the practices were not unreasonable under the rule of reason.]

JUSTICE STEVENS, concurring in the judgment.

When investment bankers cooperate in underwriting an initial public offering (IPO), they increase the amount of capital available to firms producing goods and services and make additional securities available for purchase. By agglomerating networks of investors and spreading the risk of overvaluation, syndicates make positive contributions to the economy that could not be achieved through independent action. In my view, agreements among underwriters on how best to market IPOs, including agreements on price and other terms of sale to initial investors, should be treated as procompetitive joint ventures for purposes of antitrust analysis. In all but the rarest of cases, they cannot be conspiracies in restraint of trade within the meaning of § 1 of the Sherman Act.

After the initial purchase, the prices of newly issued stocks or bonds are determined by competition among the vast multitude of other securities traded in a free market. To suggest that an underwriting syndicate can restrain trade in that market by manipulating the terms of IPOs is frivolous. See *United States v. Morgan,* 118 F.Supp. 621, 689 (S.D.N.Y. 1953) (Medina, J.) ("[T]he syndicate system has no effect whatever on general market prices, nor do the participating underwriters and dealers intend it to have any. On the contrary, it is the general market prices of securities of comparable rating and quality which control the public offering price.... The particular issue, even if a large one, is but an infinitesimal unit of trade in the ocean of security issues running into the billions, which constitutes the general market"). It is possible of course that the practices described in the complaints in these two cases may have enabled the underwriters to divert some of the benefits of the offerings from the issuers to themselves, thus breaching the agents' fiduciary obligations to their principals. But if such an injury did occur, it is not an "antitrust injury" giving rise to a damages claim by investors. See *Brunswick Corp. v. Pueblo Bowl–O–Mat, Inc.,* 429 U.S. 477, 489 (1977).

Nor do I believe that the so-called "laddering" and "tying" described in the complaints constitute vertical restraints that violate either the Sherman Act or § 2(c) of the Robinson–Patman Act. Given the magnitude of the market these practices are alleged to have influenced, I think it obvious as a matter of law that there has been no injury to any relevant competition....

The defendants moved to dismiss for failure to state a claim on the ground, among others, that the plaintiffs' claims challenge "the ordinary activities of participants in underwriting syndicates, which are recognized to be completely lawful and pro-competitive." I agree and would hold ... that the defendants' alleged conduct does not violate the antitrust laws, rather than holding [as the Court did] that Congress has implicitly granted them immunity from those laws....

GOOGLE/AdMOB

(FTC statement closing the investigation, 2010)

Reread FTC statement at p. 402 supra

QUESTIONS AND COMMENTS

1. Suppose Google/AdMob were a fully integrated 50–50 joint venture for an indefinite term, cancellable by either party on six months' notice; the parents agreed to place all of their mobile advertising functions in the joint venture and not to compete in mobile advertising against the joint venture; and the parents continued to operate in their other markets.

Would the case for antitrust legality be clearer, or more difficult? What additional inquiries would you want to make?

For additional lines of inquiry, consider: Do the terms of the joint venture include any unreasonable ancillary covenants? Does the joint venture tend to facilitate cartel-like behavior of the parents in other markets in which they both compete?

Note that a joint venture may add a new competitive force to the market, sometimes—although not in this case—without taking any competition off the market, and that a joint venture is less permanent than a merger and therefore any harmful aspects are more readily reversible than in the case of a merger.

With the touchstones in place, we turn to specific subject areas.

First, loose combinations: concerted refusal to deal, information exchange, limited agreements not to compete, intellectual property licensing, standard setting. Second, tighter combinations—joint ventures and alliances.

C. LOOSE KNIT AGREEMENTS

1. CONCERTED REFUSALS TO DEAL WITH OUTSIDERS

Is it a boycott or a good business cooperation?

By one metric there are two types of restraints: exploitative (e.g. price fixing and other collaborations that push price up and exploit consumers), and exclusionary. Boycotts are, centrally and directly, exclusionary. Exclusionary restraints might eliminate or marginalize competitors, and by disabling the competition the defendant firm might protect or increase its own power at the expense of consumers. In that sense, exclusionary restraints might be en route to exploitation.

There are many agreements among competitors that have an effect of excluding other competitors, ranging from "naked" agreements to exclude and thereby to protect market power, as in *Fashion Originators' Guild* (1941), *supra* page 73 (a boycott by the fabric and dress designers of the design copiers), to agreements that exclude others for good business purposes and that will probably enhance competition, as in *Rothery*, above (a restraint on a party to a contract). Moreover, any joint venture that is closed to outsiders is in that sense exclusionary.

During the years of expansive antitrust, duties not to exclude expanded, giving rise to the litigation in *Northwest Wholesale Stationers v. Pacific Stationery & Printing Co.* A buying cooperative of small retailers of stationery ousted a dual distributor (wholesaler-retailer) without notice and apparently based on a pretext. The dual distributor claimed, unsuccessfully, that its expulsion was a concerted refusal to deal, illegal per se. It relied on a now antiquated case that accorded per se treatment to the cut-off of a broker-dealer from access to stock exchange lines without notice or hearing. In *Northwest Wholesale Stationers*, the Court narrowed per se treatment.

NORTHWEST WHOLESALE STATIONERS v. PACIFIC STATIONERY & PRINTING CO.

472 U.S. 284 (1985).

JUSTICE BRENNAN:

* * *

Cases to which this Court has applied the *per se* approach have generally involved joint efforts by a firm or firms to disadvantage competitors by "either directly denying or persuading or coercing suppliers or customers to deny relationships the competitors need in the competitive struggle." In these cases, the boycott often cut off access to a supply, facility, or market necessary to enable the boycotted firm to compete, and frequently the boycotting firms possessed a dominant position in the relevant market. In addition, the practices were generally not justified by plausible arguments that they were intended to enhance overall efficiency and make markets more competitive. Under such circumstances the likelihood of anticompetitive effects is clear and the possibility of countervailing procompetitive effects is remote.

Although a concerted refusal to deal need not necessarily possess all of these traits to merit *per se* treatment, not every cooperative activity involving a restraint or exclusion will share with the *per se* forbidden boycotts the likelihood of predominantly anticompetitive consequences....

Wholesale purchasing cooperatives such as Northwest are not a form of concerted activity characteristically likely to result in predominantly anticompetitive effects....

... The mere allegation of a concerted refusal to deal does not suffice because not all concerted refusals to deal are predominantly anticompetitive. When the plaintiff challenges expulsion from a joint buying cooperative, some showing must be made that the cooperative possesses market power or unique access to a business element necessary for effective competition.... * * *

Questions and Comments

React to the following proposition. Pacific could not win its case under a rule of reason. There was no story by which the cooperative was acquiring market power by booting the dual distributor out of its organization.

Pacific's complaint was a vestige of a prior era. But what about the modern day credit card system, in which the two leaders, Visa and MasterCard, are (each) joint ventures owned by their member banks. The banks are the issuers of the cards. Can they each (Visa, and MasterCard) maintain rules that prohibit their member banks from issuing American Express or Discover cards? Should Visa and MasterCard be seen more as vertical organizations waging systems competition against other-brand cards? Did the exclusion harm only competitors—who were free to wage their own interbrand competition—or also consumers?

UNITED STATES v. VISA AND MASTERCARD

344 F.3d 229 (2d Cir. 2003).

JUDGE LEVAL:

* * *

I Relevant Markets and Market Power

The district court determined, and we agree, that this case involves two interrelated, but separate, product markets: (1) what the court called the general purpose card market, consisting of the market for charge cards and credit cards, and (2) the network services market for general purpose cards.

A distinct product market comprises products that are considered by consumers to be "reasonabl[y] interchangeab[le]" with what the defendant sells. *Eastman Kodak Co. v. Image Tech'l Servs., Inc.*,[504 U.S. 451, 482 (1992).] After hearing substantial expert testimony, the district court found as a matter of fact that other forms of payment—such as cash, checks, debit cards, and proprietary cards (e.g. the Sears or Macy's cards)—are not considered by most consumers to be reasonable substitutes for general purpose credit or charge cards. As the government's expert witness explained, based on empirical analysis of consumer preferences, if prices for general purpose payment cards were to rise significantly, cardholders would likely pay the increased fees, rather than abandon their cards in favor of other forms of payment. *Id.* Thus, general purpose payment cards constitute a distinct market, separate from the market for such other payment alternatives. We find no reason to doubt the court's conclusion.

Further, we agree with the district court that the four payment card networks compete with one another in a market for "network services." *Id.* at 338–39. General purpose card networks, Judge Jones explained, "provide the infrastructure and mechanisms through which general purpose card transactions are conducted, including the authorization, settlement, and clearance of transactions." *Id.* at 338. Whereas in the market for general purpose *cards,* the issuers are the sellers, and cardholders are the buyers, in the market for general purpose card *network services,* the four networks themselves are the sellers, and the issuers of cards and merchants are the buyers. Issuing banks purchase network services from MasterCard and/or Visa U.S.A., and those two brands compete with Amex and Discover for the banks' business. Networks also compete for merchants, because the price merchants pay for acceptance of payment cards (the merchant discount) is affected by the size of the interchange fee, which is set by the network.

The district court found, on the basis of expert testimony, that there are no products reasonably interchangeable, in the eyes of issuers or merchants, with the network services provided by the four major brands. *Id.* This was a reasonable finding: (1) Network-level costs are so high that banks and merchants cannot provide these services for themselves, and (2) issuance and acceptance of credit and charge cards is so profitable (and network service fees so negligible in comparison) that even a large increase in network fees would not provide a rational financial incentive to abandon the business of issuing or accepting payment cards.

We agree with the district court's finding that Visa U.S.A. and MasterCard, jointly and separately, have power within the market for network services. Market "power has been defined by the Supreme Court to mean the power to control prices or exclude competition." *du Pont,* 351 U.S. at 391, *NCAA,* at 109 n. 38. Such power may be proven through evidence of specific conduct undertaken by the defendant that indicates he has the power to affect price or exclude competition. *KMB Warehouse Distribs., Inc. v. Walker Mfg. Co.,* 61 F.3d 123, 129 (2d Cir.1995). Alternatively, market power may be presumed if the defendant controls a large enough share of the relevant market. Jones based her finding of market power first on the fact that merchants testified that they could not refuse to accept payment by Visa or MasterCard, even if faced with significant price increases, because of customer preference. Indeed, despite recent increases in both networks' interchange fees, no merchant had discontinued acceptance of their cards. In addition, the court inferred market power from the defendants' large shares of a highly concentrated market: In 1999, Visa U.S.A. members accounted for approximately 47% of the dollar volume of credit and charge card transactions, while MasterCard members accounted for approximately 26%. (American Express accounted for 20%; Discover, for 6%.)

The evidence relied on by the district court was sufficient to sustain a finding of market power. In addition, Amex, despite repeated recent attempts, has been unable to persuade any issuing banks in the continental United States to utilize its network services because the exclusivity rule would require such issuing banks to give up membership in the Visa and MasterCard consortiums, and banks are unwilling to do so. In short, Visa U.S.A. and MasterCard have demonstrated their power in the network services market by effectively precluding their largest competitor from successfully soliciting any bank as a customer for its network services and brand.

II Harms to Competition

As noted, to sustain a challenge under 1 of the Sherman Act, the government must prove that the defendants' conduct has adversely affected competition. The district court found that Visa U.S.A. and MasterCard's exclusionary rules harm competition by "reducing overall card output and available card features," as well as by decreasing network services output and stunting price competition. We cannot say that these conclusions were erroneous.

The most persuasive evidence of harm to competition is the total exclusion of American Express and Discover from a segment of the market for network services. As noted, there are only four major payment card network providers in the United States. While competition among (and within) these networks is robust at the issuing level (where 20,000 separate issuers compete to provide products to consumers), at the network level (where four major networks seek to sell their technical, infrastructure, and financial services to issuer banks) competition has been seriously damaged by the defendants' exclusionary rules. As the district court noted, "[i]t is largely undisputed that the exclusionary rules have resulted in the failure of Visa and MasterCard member banks to become issuers of American Express and Discover-branded cards." *Id.* at 383. The district court cited evidence that three major U.S. issuer banks-Banco Popular, Advanta, and Bank One-would have contracted with American Express to issue Amex cards in the United States but for the exclusionary rules. *Id.* at 383–87. In addition, Banco Popular has contracted with Amex to issue its cards in Puerto Rico, where no exclusionary rules apply. *Id.* at 383–84.

As a result, then, of the challenged policies, only two rival networks are effectively able to compete for the business of issuer banks. Testimony at trial revealed that Visa U.S.A. and MasterCard "pay millions of dollars in incentive payments in the form of discounts from the price for network services to selected issuing banks to compete for their business and [that] the banks play Visa and MasterCard against [each] other to obtain lower net prices and higher value for card network services." *Id.* at 382. With only two viable competitors, however, such price and product competition is necessarily limited. Trial testimony strongly indicated that price competition and innovation in services would be enhanced if four competitors, rather than only two, were able to compete in this manner for issuing banks. Indeed, the district court found, based on testimony from Visa U.S.A. and MasterCard executives, that both defendants would "respond to ... greater network competition by offering new and better products and services." MasterCard's former CEO, for example, testified that MasterCard would be forced to "speed up" development of a premium card product were Amex cards issued through MasterCard member banks.

In foreign countries, where Visa International rather than Visa U.S.A. operates the Visa network, and no exclusionary rule applies, Amex has succeeded in convincing banks that issue Visa cards also to issue Amex cards. This has caused Visa International to "proactively strengthen" its product offerings to member banks abroad. In addition, an internal Visa International memorandum cautions that Visa U.S.A. would have to compete more vigorously for market share if Amex were permitted to partner with its member banks: "To date, AmEx has been precluded from partnering with U.S. banks, although that situation could change. Since bank partners could significantly increase [Amex's] acceptance and cards, Visa needs to monitor the situation and counter with competitive products that meet banks['] needs."

The district court also found that product innovation and output has been stunted by the challenged policies. By excluding Amex and Discover from the market for outside card issuers, Visa U.S.A. and MasterCard effectively deny consumers access to products that could be offered only by a network in partnership with individual banks. Such products include cards that are able to link "to transaction accounts, to asset management accounts, to sale of mortgages or other financial products that [banks] offer[ ]."

We find no error in the district court's finding that competition has been harmed by the defendants' exclusionary rules.

III The Defendants' Arguments

Defendants argue on appeal that the district court erred in two ways: (1) by finding that the exclusionary rules harm *competition,* when they in fact disadvantage only individual *competitors;* and (2) by failing to recognize that any adverse effects on competition are outweighed by the substantial procompetitive benefits of exclusivity.

A Harms to Competition

First, the defendants argue that the district court erred by mistaking harm to a *competitor* for harm to *competition.* They cite the familiar formula that the "antitrust laws protect competition, not competitors." *Clorox Co. v. Sterling Winthrop, Inc.,* 117 F.3d 50, 57 (2d Cir.1997). Visa U.S.A. contends, for example, that "[t]he decision and remedy in this case will not benefit consumer welfare. Instead, virtually the sole beneficiary will be AmEx which hopes to gain not by offering lower prices or better products but largely by undermining its major brand competitors." Brief for Appellant Visa U.S.A.

Defendants contend the exclusionary rules are akin to "exclusive distributorship" arrangements, which we have held are "presumptively legal." *Elec. Communications Corp. v. Toshiba Am. Consumer Prods., Inc.,* 129 F.3d 240, 245 (2d Cir.1997) (citing *Oreck Corp. v. Whirlpool Corp.,* 579 F.2d 126, 131 (2d Cir.1978) (in banc)). We find this argument unpersuasive.

Defendants are certainly correct that the proper inquiry is whether there has been an "*actual* adverse effect on competition as a whole in the relevant market." *KMB Warehouse,* 61 F.3d at 127. We have held that competition is not adversely affected if, despite an exclusive dealership arrangement, "competitors can reach the ultimate consumer of the product by employing existing or potential alternative channels of distribution." *CDC Techs., Inc. v. IDEXX Labs., Inc.,* 186 F.3d 74, 80 (2d Cir.1999) (quoting *Omega Envt'l, Inc. v. Gilbarco, Inc.,* 127 F.3d 1157, 1163 (9th Cir.1997)).

The defendants argue that the harms identified by the district court as stemming from their exclusionary rules—that the types of cards that consumers can get from their banks are limited and [that] banks are prevented from combining their particular issuing skills with the AmEx brand-are not harms to Amex's ability to compete as a network (or Discover's), but rather harms to its distributive capacity, in much the same way Pepsi–Cola's distributive capacity might be limited by an exclusive arrangement between Coca–Cola and its truckers. For an exclusive dealership arrangement to cause a harm to competition (and overcome the presumption of legality), it must prevent competitors from getting their products to consumers at all. *CDC Techs.,* 186 F.3d at 80 (citing *Gilbarco,* 127 F.3d at 1163). There is no question, the defendants argue, that Amex and Discover can get their products to consumers, as evidenced by the fact that they are respectively the largest and fifth largest issuers of payment cards in the United States.

The analogy to an exclusive arrangement between Coca–Cola and its truckers is not persuasive. The basic flaw in the analogy is that it depicts Visa U.S.A. (or MasterCard) as a single entity (like Coca–Cola) demanding a restrictive provision in its contract with a supplier of services to it. Visa U.S.A. and MasterCard, however, are not single entities; they are consortiums of competitors. They are owned and effectively operated by some 20,000 banks, which compete with one another in the issuance of payment cards and the acquiring of merchants' transactions. These 20,000 banks set the policies of Visa U.S.A. and MasterCard. These competitors have agreed to abide by a restrictive exclusivity provision to the effect that in order to share the benefits of their association by having the right to issue Visa or MasterCard cards, they must agree not to compete by issuing cards of Amex or Discover. The restrictive provision is a horizontal restraint adopted by 20,000 competitors.

The analogy proposed by the defendants would be more pertinent if Coca–Cola, Pepsi–Cola, and several other leading sellers of soft drinks joined together to form an association to contract for trucking services and exacted of contracting truckers a commitment not to carry for any soft drink maker that was not a part of the consortium. Even then the analogy would lack the feature here presented that the restraint imposed by the consortium members is on themselves. Each has agreed not to compete with the others in a manner which the consortium considers harmful to its combined interests. Far from being "presumptively legal," such arrangements are exemplars of the type of anticompetitive behavior prohibited by the Sherman Act....

In the market for *network services,* where the four networks are sellers and issuing banks and merchants are buyers, the exclusionary rules enforced by Visa U.S.A. and MasterCard have absolutely prevented Amex and Discover from selling their products at all.

Without doubt the exclusionary rules in question harm competitors. The fact that they harm competitors does not, however, mean that they do not also harm competition. We find no fault with the district court's finding that the exclusion of Amex and Discover from the ability to market their cards and programs to banks has harmed competition in the market for network services, and that Visa U.S.A. and MasterCard would be impelled to design and market their products more competitively if the banks to which they sell their services were free to purchase network services from Amex and Discover. Nor do we fault the district court's determination that certain types of products combining unique features of cards offered by Amex and Discover with the advantages of linkage to cardholders' bank accounts would likely become available. The district court was justified in finding harm to competition.

B Procompetitive Justifications

The defendants argue that even if the exclusionary rules do harm competition, those harms are outweighed by the policies' substantial procompetitive effects. The defendants assert that the principal benefit of the exclusionary rules is to promote "cohesion" within the MasterCard and Visa U.S.A. networks, so that those networks may compete effectively in the marketplace. Thus, the defendants argue, the exclusionary rules are ancillary to legitimate, procompetitive business strategies. The district court found that the exclusionary rules are not necessary to accomplish that goal, and that in any event the anticompetitive effects outweigh the procompetitive. We believe the court's finding was reasonable.

The district court found no evidence to suggest that allowing member banks to issue cards of rival networks would endanger cohesion in a manner adverse to the competitive process. *Visa U.S.A.,* 163 F.Supp.2d at 402–06. MasterCard members have long been permitted to issue Visa cards, and vice versa, without such consequences. Moreover, as the district court noted, there is no evidence that the defendants' network cohesion has been harmed overseas, where, in the absence of exclusionary rules, Amex has contracted with Visa and MasterCard member banks to issue Amex-branded payment cards. *Id.* at 407.

In sum, the defendants have failed to show that the anticompetitive effects of their exclusionary rules are outweighed by procompetitive benefits. * * * [*Affirmed*]

QUESTIONS AND COMMENTS

1. Explain why the Northwest Stationary cooperative had the right to exclude competitors but Visa, and separately, MasterCard, had no right to exclude competitors.

2. Is there any sense in which the VISA/MasterCard claim of right was stronger than the stationary coop's claim of right? *Trinko* was decided the following year. Might *Trinko* have helped VISA and MasterCard, had that case been decided earlier?

3. Note that Visa and MasterCard were not accused of agreeing with one another. Who are the competitors who agreed with one another not to deal with others?

4. Do you agree that the Visa network had sufficient market power? that the MasterCard network had sufficient market power? What is the argument that Visa and especially MasterCard did not have market power?

5. Do you agree that the challenged arrangements were more like a horizontal agreement than a vertical agreement? How much turned on this characterization?

6. If the VISA network had excluded MasterCard banks and vice-versa, would defendants' justification—and theory of the case—have been more persuasive?

7. Look back at the naked boycott cases in Chapter 2, pages 73–74, 102–104. Is each of the above cases (in this chapter) different in quality? Does each of the above cases entail a possibly procompetitive justification or a competitively harmless restraint?

2. COMPETITORS' EXCHANGES OF INFORMATION

We move now to another category—information exchanges. This is also, potentially, a complex category, because information exchanges can induce cartel-like behavior, and they can also be the tip of the iceberg underlying a cartel.

Competitors have exchanged information—for salutary and for conspiratorial ends—since the beginning of market economies. For purposes of antitrust, the ambiguities are poignant. Knowledge and information are good. Firms must have reliable market information to compete effectively.

But recall: Collecting the most sensitive market information about the competitors is one of the major tasks of cartelists; they need this information to set the joint profit-maximizing price and to police cheating on the cartel. Moreover, in highly concentrated markets susceptible to lock-step oligopoly behavior, perfect information even without conspiracy can entrench interdependence and cause prices to rise. How to distinguish the good from the bad?

Historically, most exchanges of price and related data took place under the aegis of trade associations. Accordingly, we start this section with a historical note on the American trade association movement.

"Associationalism," as it was sometimes called, had its roots prior to World War I. The movement stemmed in part from an ideal of cooperation and community. As President Theodore Roosevelt once said, no man should be so mean spirited as to refuse to devote some time to the uplift of his trade.

The movement stemmed also from profit-conscious traders; prominently, Jerome Eddy. Eddy had observed that businesses in the same industry often announced prices at levels that would yield "fair" profits (i.e., price comfortably above costs), but that a major hindrance to such profitable cooperation was secret price shading. A firm might follow the industry price on most sales but secretly cut prices to get additional business. Once the process started, firm after firm would cut and, doing so, increase output. Price levels would erode all along the line. Eddy had a solution. Transparency. If every sale were immediately publicized, no one would cut prices. Each seller would know that if it did, retaliation would be swift.

Eddy's 1912 book, The New Competition, became classic. It proposed "open price associations"—trade associations that would supply members with complete information on production, inventories and sales of all members of the industry. Eddy preached this message to responsive audiences. Soon, open price associations became a significant features of American business.

During the 1920s, the association movement gained new champions, the most notable being Herbert Hoover. Hoover, a war time production bureaucrat, became Secretary of Commerce under Harding and Coolidge. Hoover disliked old time cartels but he found associations useful. He was an engineer by training, and a technocrat. He saw the new associations as expressive of the dynamic elements in industrial society. They were, he thought, a way to assure greater efficiency, more orderly growth, better social integration, and a higher degree of American competitiveness in world markets. The small town foundry and backwoods mill would remain moribund unless they could be brought into the modern industrial age. By disseminating technical information about both production and management, the industry association might save them. In Hoover's vision, trade associations should be encouraged by government and would maintain links both to the Department of Commerce and the Chamber of Commerce. The Department would give them status and would help disseminate information they generated, and the Chamber would serve as a kind of Congress of Associations. Such a system would assure that industrial policy was made by enlightened business people and policy makers.

In this environment, the American Hardwood Manufacturers' Association flourished. It became, however, the target of an antitrust attack that threatened the whole association movement.

The American hardwood case (*American Column & Lumber*) and the cases that follow show the evolution of the law from deep suspicion regarding intricate exchanges of competitive information, at first without rigorous analysis as to whether a cartel existed or in the alternative whether the structure of the industry would probably lead to a price-raising effect, to a more nuanced approach that makes both inquiries. Moreover, you will see in this section intuitive applications of behavioral economics: How is a salesperson likely to behave when he or she receives a phone call from her counterpart at a competitor and the caller asks: At what price did you just offer to sell your cardboard boxes to *X*?

AMERICAN COLUMN & LUMBER CO. v. UNITED STATES

257 U.S. 377 (1921).

JUSTICE CLARKE: ... The unincorporated "American Hardwood Manufacturers' Association" was formed in December, 1918 [and administered] the "Open Competition Plan" ... [hereinafter] the "Plan."

Participation in the "Plan" was optional with the members of the Association, but, at the time this suit was commenced, of its 400 members, 365, operating 465 mills, were members of the "Plan." The importance and strength of the Association are shown by the admission in the joint answer that while the defendants operated only five per cent. of the number of mills engaged in hardwood manufacture in the country, they produced one-third of the total production of the United States.... * * *

The record shows that the "Plan" was evolved by a committee, which, in recommending its adoption, said:

> "The purpose of this plan is to disseminate among members accurate knowledge of production and market conditions so that each member may gauge the market intelligently instead of guessing at it; to make competition open and above board instead of secret and concealed; to substitute, in estimating market conditions, frank and full statements of our competitors for the frequently misleading and colored statements of the buyer."....

... [A] further explanation of ... the "Plan" was made in an appeal to members to join it ...:

> "The theoretical proposition at the basis of the Open Competition plan is that,

"*Knowledge regarding prices actually made is all that is necessary to keep prices at reasonably stable and normal levels.*

"The Open Competition plan is a central clearing house for information on prices, trade statistics and practices. By keeping all members fully and quickly informed of what the others have done, the work of the plan results in *a certain uniformity of trade practice.* There is no agreement to follow the practice of others, *although members do naturally follow their most intelligent competitors,* if they know what these competitors have been actually doing. . . ."

And in another later, and somewhat similar, appeal sent to all the members, this is found:

"Competition, blind, vicious, unreasoning, may stimulate trade to abnormal activity but such condition is no more sound than that medieval spirit some still cling to of taking a club and going out and knocking the other fellow and taking away his bone. . . .

"Co-operation will only replace *undesirable competition* as you develop a co-operative spirit. For the first time in the history of the industry, the hardwood manufacturers are organized into one compact, comprehensive body, equipped to serve the whole trade in a thorough and efficient manner. . . . More members mean more power to do more good for the industry. With co-operation of this kind we will very soon have enlisted in our efforts practically every producing interest, *and you know what that means.*" * * *

. . . [The Plan] required each member to make six reports to the Secretary, viz: [detailed daily sales and shipping reports, monthly production and stock reports, price lists, and inspection reports.]

All of these reports by members are subject to complete audit by representatives of the association. . . . * * *

The secretary is required to send to each member [weekly and monthly reports with detailed information on each member's production, sales, shipments and inventory]. . . .

This extensive interchange of reports, supplemented as it was by monthly meetings at which an opportunity was afforded for discussion "of all subjects of interest to the members," very certainly constituted an organization through which agreements, actual or implied, could readily be arrived at and maintained, if the members desired to make them.

Such, in outline, was the paper plan adopted by the association, but elaborate though it was, in practice three important additions were made to it.

First of all, . . . forty-nine of these meetings were held between January 31, 1919, and February 19, 1920,—approximately one for each week, in some part of the territory.

Second. Before each of these meetings a questionnaire was sent out to the members, and from the replies received, supplementing the other reports, the statistician compiled an estimate of the condition of the market, actual and prospective, which was distributed to the members attending each meeting, and was mailed to those not present. There were eleven questions on this list of which the most important were:

"4th. What was your total production of hardwoods during the last month? What do you estimate your production will probably be for the next two months?"

"10th. Do you expect to shut down within the next few months on account of shortage of logs or for any other reason? If so, please state how long mill will be idle?"

"11th. What is your view of market conditions for the next few months? What is the general outlook for business? State all reasons for your conclusions."

The "Plan" on paper provided only for reports of past transactions and much is made of this in the record and in argument—that reporting to one another past transactions cannot fix prices for the future. But each of these three questions plainly invited an estimate and discussion of future market conditions by each member, and a coordination of them by an expert analyst could readily evolve an attractive basis for cooperative, even if unexpressed, "harmony" with respect to future prices.

Third. The "Plan" provided for a monthly "market report letter" to go to all members of the association.... [These] were discussed at all but one or two of the forty-nine meetings which were held....

This elaborate plan ... not only furnishes ... information, with respect to stock, sales and prices, but also reports, giving the views of each member as to "market conditions for the next few months"; what the production of each will be for the next "two months"; frequent analyses of the reports by an expert, with, we shall see, significant suggestions as to both future prices and production; and opportunities for future meetings for the interchange of views, which the record shows were very important. It is plain that the only element lacking in this scheme to make it a familiar type of the competition suppressing organization is a definite agreement as to production and prices. But this is supplied: by the disposition of men "to follow their most intelligent competitors," especially when powerful; by the inherent disposition to make all the money possible, joined with the steady cultivation of the value of "harmony" of action; and by the system of reports, which makes the discovery of price reductions inevitable and immediate. The sanctions of the plan obviously are, financial interest, intimate personal contact, and business honor, all operating under the restraint of exposure of what would be deemed bad faith and of trade punishment by powerful rivals....

Thus, at the meeting held at Cincinnati, on January 21, 1919, in the discussion of business conditions, the chairman said:

> "If there is *no increase in production,* particularly in oak, there is going to be good business." "*No man is safe in increasing his*

> *production.* If he does, he will be in bad shape, as the demand won't come."

Again, at the meeting held on May 9th, at Memphis, in the discussion of market conditions, appears this paragraph:

> "Reference was made to members who contemplate running day and night, and it was stated that the lumber industry had seen these unusual market conditions before and that we ought to be very sure that the market is capable of taking care of night and day lumber."

This warning of May 9th against producing too much lumber was followed, on May 17th, by a sales report sent out by the Manager of Statistics to all members, which was headed, "Stop, Look and Listen." After saying that the hardwood market had assumed a decidedly better tone, with a tendency in quotations upward, with the demand on the increase and with stocks below normal, the writer continues:

> "The lumbermen have gone through several lean years, but we are confronted with the possibility of killing the goose that laid the golden egg. *Overproduction will spell disaster,* as it should always be borne in mind that the maximum productive capacity of the sawmills of the country is much in excess of any demand the country has ever known." ...

Again, a week later, ... one of the members declared: that in his opinion it was "*suicidal to run mills night and day;* that the pine mills had done it, but he hoped they [we] would profit by their past experience and not do it this year." * * *

The "Plan" is, essentially, simply an expansion of the gentlemen's agreement of former days, skillfully devised to evade the law. To call it open competition because the meetings were nominally open to the public, or because some voluminous reports were transmitted to the Department of Justice, or because no specific agreement to restrict trade or fix prices is proved, cannot conceal the fact that the fundamental purpose of the "Plan" was to procure "harmonious" individual action among a large number of naturally competing dealers with respect to the volume of production and prices, without having any specific agreement with respect to them, and to rely for maintenance of concerted action in both respects, not upon fines and forfeitures as in earlier days, but upon what experience has shown to be the more potent and dependable restraints, of business honor and social penalties,—cautiously reinforced by many and elaborate reports, which would promptly expose to his associates any disposition in any member to deviate from the tacit understanding that all were to act together under the subtle direction of a single interpreter of their common purposes, as evidenced in the minute reports of what they had done and in their expressed purposes as to what they intended to do.... Affirmed.

JUSTICE HOLMES, dissenting: ... I should have supposed that the Sherman Act did not set itself against knowledge—did not aim at a transitory cheapness unprofitable to the community as a whole because not corresponding to the actual conditions of the country. I should have thought that the ideal of commerce was an intelligent interchange made with full knowledge of the facts as a basis for a forecast of the future on both sides. A combination to get and distribute such knowledge, notwithstanding its tendency to equalize, not necessarily to raise, prices, is very far from a combination in unreasonable restraint of trade. It is true that it is a combination of sellers only, but the knowledge acquired is not secret, it is public, and the buyers, I think I may assume, are not less active in their efforts to know the facts....

JUSTICE BRANDEIS, dissenting, with whom JUSTICE MCKENNA concurs: ... In the case before us there was clearly no coercion. There is no claim that a monopoly was sought or created. There is no claim that a division of territory was planned or secured. There is no claim that uniform prices were established or desired. There is no claim that by agreement, force, or fraud, any producer, dealer or consumer was to be or has in fact been controlled or coerced. The Plan is a voluntary system for collecting from these independent concerns detailed information concerning the business operations of each, and its opinions as to trade conditions, prospects and policy; and of collating, interpreting, and distributing the data so received among the members of the association and others. No information gathered under the Plan was kept secret from any producer, any buyer or the public. Ever since its inception in 1917, a copy of every report made and of every market letter published has been filed with the Department of Justice, and with the Federal Trade Commission. The district meetings were open to the public. Dealers and consumers were invited to participate in the discussions and to some extent have done so....

It is insisted that there was a purpose to curtail production. No evidence of any such purpose was introduced. There was at no time uniformity in the percentage of production to capacity.... There were, it is true, from time to time, warnings in the "Market Letters" and otherwise, against overproduction—warnings which seem not to have been heeded. But surely Congress did not intend by the Sherman Act to prohibit self-restraint—and it was for self-restraint that the only appeal was made....

It is urged that this was a concerted effort to enhance prices. There was at no time uniformity in prices. So far as appears every mill charged for its product as much as it could get. There is evidence that the hardwood mills expected, by adopting the Plan, to earn more in profits; and to do so, at least in part, by getting higher prices for their product. It may be that the distribution of the trade data, the editorial comment and the conferences enabled the producers to obtain, on the average, higher prices than would otherwise have been possible. But there is nothing in the Sherman Law to indicate that Congress intended to condemn cooperative action in the exchange of information, merely because prophecy resulting from comment on the data collected may lead, for a period, to higher market prices....

The cooperation which is incident to this Plan does not suppress competition. On the contrary it tends to promote all in competition which is desirable. By substituting knowledge for ignorance, rumor, guess and suspicion, it tends also to substitute research and reasoning for gambling and piracy, without closing the door to adventure or lessening the value of prophetic wisdom....

QUESTIONS AND COMMENTS

1. Was Justice Clarke right that the Plan was a cover for a cartel; a hope [or plan?] of the industry to procure harmonious action? Were Justices Holmes and Brandeis right that the Plan was a means to get knowledge? Might they all have been right—and should the plan have been allowed if the hardwood companies had no power to cartelize?

2. Does *American Column & Lumber* condemn the mere exchange of information, or only that plus something more? Does it require, also, a detailed exchange and an intent to harmonize (at least by the ring leader)?

Was the exchange of past prices and current supply and demand data good for competition in this industry? Suppose the information tended to "stabilize" price by bringing prices closer to the average price without causing any change in the average price. Would that impact be anticompetitive or efficient? If the information tended to raise prices because small, scattered sellers learned more accurately what the market would bear, would that impact be anticompetitive or efficient?

Should the Plan be called anticompetitive if it tended to raise prices by developing a camaraderie among producers and a shared attitude that producers should hold production down and refrain from undercutting one another? But how would 365 producers coordinate their pricing and output decisions? Why would an efficient producer hold back its production? If the members did cooperate, how could they achieve a supracompetitive price, given that there were hundreds of them and they represented less than one-third of industry production?

3. Justice Brandeis was not a technocrat like Herbert Hoover. Brandeis was hospitable to trade associations because of their benefits to small business and because he saw them as a counterweight to the consolidation movement, which was bureaucratizing industry. He was more focused on the social and political goals of competition policy in clearing the path for entrepreneurs than on the interests of consumers. He thought a healthy polity required a wide dispersion of economic power and a large number of people with investments in the economy and independent decisionmaking roles. See T. McCraw, the Prophets of Regulation 133–35 (1984).

A few years later another trade association case came before the Court. Hoover encouraged the Justice Department, under recently appointed Attorney General Harlan Fiske Stone, to litigate a second lumber industry case in order to revive the association movement after the blow struck by *American*

Column & Lumber. Historian Ellis Hawley has described Hoover's efforts and President Calvin Coolidge's subsequent appointment of Stone to the Supreme Court. Hawley, *Herbert Hoover and the Sherman Act, 1921–1933: An Early Phase of a Continuing Issue*, 74 Iowa L. Rev. 1067 (1989). As the fates would have it, Justice Stone wrote the opinion.

MAPLE FLOORING MANUFACTURERS' ASS'N v. UNITED STATES

268 U.S. 563 (1925).

JUSTICE STONE: ... The defendants are the Maple Flooring Manufacturers Association, an unincorporated "trade association"; twenty-two corporate defendants, members of the Association, engaged in the business of selling and shipping maple, beech and birch flooring in interstate commerce.

... The activities of the present Association of which the Government complains may be summarized as follows:

(1) The computation and distribution among the members of the association of the average cost to association members of all dimensions and grades of flooring.

(2) The compilation and distribution among members of a booklet showing freight rates on flooring from Cadillac, Michigan [the principal point of shipment], to between five and six thousand points of shipment in the United States.

(3) The gathering of statistics which at frequent intervals are supplied by each member of the Association to the Secretary of the Association giving complete information as to the quantity and kind of flooring sold and prices received by the reporting members, and the amount of stock on hand, which information is summarized by the Secretary and transmitted to members without, however, revealing the identity of the members in connection with any specific information thus transmitted.

(4) Meetings at which the representatives of members congregate and discuss the industry and exchange views as to its problems.

... [I]t is neither alleged nor proved that there was any agreement among the members of the Association either affecting production, fixing prices or for price maintenance.... Nor was there any direct proof that the activities of the Association had affected prices adversely to consumers. On the contrary, the defendants offered a great volume of evidence tending to show that the trend of prices of the product of the defendants corresponded to the law of supply and demand....

[The district court gave judgment to the Government and ordered dissolution of the defendants' association.]

The contention of the Government is that there is a combination among the defendants, which is admitted; that the effect of the activities of the defendants carried on under the plan of the Association must necessarily be to bring about a concerted effort on the part of members of the Association to maintain prices at levels having a close relation to the average cost of flooring reported to members and that consequently there is a necessary and inevitable restraint of interstate commerce.... * * *

The Government [criticized] the use of [a] freight-rate book....

It cannot, we think, be questioned that data as to the average cost of flooring circulated among the members of the Association when combined with a calculated freight rate which is either exactly or approximately the freight rate from the point of shipment, plus an arbitrary percentage of profit, could be made the basis for fixing prices.... But, ... the record is barren of evidence that the published list of costs and the freight-rate book have been so used....

It is contended by the Government that an analysis of the reporting system adopted by the defendants shows that there is no information withheld by one member from another, and that every member is perfectly familiar not only with the summaries which show the exact market condition generally, but also with the exact condition of the business of each of his fellow members. An examination of the record discloses that this is not an accurate statement of the statistical information distributed.... At the time of the filing of the bill, members reported weekly to the Secretary of the Association on forms showing dates of sales made by the reporting member, the quantity, the thickness and face, the grade, the kind of wood, the delivery, the prices at which sold, the average freight rate to destination and the rate of commission paid, if any. Members also reported monthly the amount of flooring on hand of each dimension and grade and the amount of unfilled orders. Monthly reports were also required showing the amount of production for each period and the new orders booked for each variety of flooring. The Association promptly reported back to the members statistics compiled from the reports of members including the identifying numbers of the mills making the reports, and information as to quantities, grades, prices, freight rates, etc., with respect to each sale. The names of purchasers were not reported and from and after July 19, 1923, the identifying number of the mill making the report was omitted....

... During the year in which the bill of complaint was filed meetings appear to have been held monthly.... Trade conditions generally, as reflected by the statistical information disseminated among members, were discussed.... [T]here was no discussion of prices in meetings. There was no occasion to discuss past prices, as those were fully detailed in the statistical reports, and the Association was advised by counsel that future prices were not a proper subject of discussion. It was admitted by several witnesses, however, that upon occasion the trend of prices and future prices became the subject of discussion outside the meeting among individual representatives of the defendants attending the meeting. The Government, however, does not charge, nor is it contended, that there was any understanding or agreement, either express or implied, at the meetings or elsewhere, with respect to prices....

It is not, we think, open to question that the dissemination of pertinent information concerning any trade or business tends to stabilize that trade or business and to produce uniformity of price and trade practice. Exchange of price quotations of market commodities tends to produce uniformity of prices in the markets of the world. Knowledge of the supplies of available merchandise tends to prevent over-production and to avoid the economic disturbances produced by business crises resulting from over-production. But the natural effect of the acquisition of wider and more scientific knowledge of business conditions, on the minds of the individuals engaged in commerce, and its consequent effect in stabilizing production and price, can hardly be deemed a restraint of commerce or if so it cannot, we think, be said to be an unreasonable restraint, or in any respect unlawful.

It is the consensus of opinion [sic] of economists and of many of the most important agencies of Government that the public interest is served by the gathering and dissemination, in the widest possible manner, of information with respect to the production and distribution, cost and prices in actual sales, of market commodities, because the making available of such information tends to stabilize trade and industry, to produce fairer price levels and to avoid the waste which inevitably attends the unintelligent conduct of economic enterprise. Free competition means a free and open market among both buyers and sellers for the sale and distribution of commodities. Competition does not become less free merely because the conduct of commercial operations becomes more intelligent through the free distribution of knowledge of all the essential factors entering into the commercial transaction. General knowledge that there is an accumulation of surplus of any market commodity would undoubtedly tend to diminish production, but the dissemination of that information cannot in itself be said to be restraint upon commerce in any legal sense. The manufacturer is free to produce, but prudence and business foresight based on that knowledge influence free choice in favor of more limited production. Restraint upon free competition begins when improper use is made of that information through any concerted action which operates to restrain the freedom of action of those who buy and sell....

We do not ... think that the proper application of the principles of decision of ... *American Column & Lumber Co. v. United States* ... leads to ... [a different] result. The court held that the defendants ... were engaged in conspiracies against interstate trade and commerce because it was found that the character of the information which had been gathered and the use which was made of it led irresistibly to the conclusion that they had resulted, or would necessarily result, in a concerted effort of the defendants to curtail production.... *reversed.*

Chief Justice Taft and Justices McReynolds and Sanford dissented.

QUESTIONS AND COMMENTS

1. What is the effect of *Maple Flooring* on *American Column & Lumber?* What are the factual differences? Is there any reason to think that the association in *Maple Flooring* had less power than the association had in *American Column & Lumber?* Was its purpose more benign? Did one association behave more offensively than the other?

2. A few years later the Great Depression began. The country sought economic stability with the aid of the National Industrial Recovery Act of 1933. Industries were encouraged to develop codes of ethics; "fair competition" rather than hard competition was encouraged. "Chislers" who cut prices below fair levels and those who paid low wages became objects of public disdain. You will recall that in 1933 the Supreme Court decided *Appalachian Coals*, supra page 65, which gave considerable scope for cooperative activity to an industry plagued with overproduction. But by 1940, the Court had limited that scope and had held in *Socony–Vacuum* that a cooperative effort to stabilize an unruly market was illegal.

Changing political and economic conditions during the twenties and thirties also affected attitudes toward the trade association movement. In the depth of the depression the Court decided *Sugar Institute v. United States,* 297 U.S. 553 (1936). Following the philosophy of *Appalachian Coals,* the Court ruled that an industry "plagued" by secret price concessions granted by "unethical" refiners in a market of declining demand for a standardized product could lawfully agree to make, advance announcement of price changes, along with exchanges of statistical information. Defendants were enjoined only from one phase of their activity: agreeing with each other to adhere to their announced prices. As long as the producers each maintained ultimate freedom of pricing action, they were allowed to act cooperatively "to end abuses and to foster fair competitive opportunities. . . ." 297 U.S. at 598. The Court said:

> Nor does the fact that the correction of abuses may tend to stabilize a business, or to produce fairer price levels, require that abuses should go uncorrected or that an effort to correct them should for that reason alone be stamped as an unreasonable restraint of trade. Id.

The *Sugar Institute* defendants admitted that they wanted to end abuses, including secret price shading. What does this purpose imply about the probable competitive effect of their agreement?

In *Sugar Institute,* the district court and the Supreme Court applied different economic templates. Apparently informed by oligopoly theory developed a few years earlier by Harvard economics professor Edward Chamberlin, the trial judge saw the competitors' advance price announcements as facilitating price restraints. 15 F.Supp. 817, 904 (S.D.N.Y. 1934). In the trial judge's view, the cooperative spirit motivated rivals to treat advance announcements as signals for tacit agreement about prices and terms. But for Justice Hughes, who wrote the opinion for the Supreme Court, the only possible problem could be "steps taken to secure adherence . . . to prices and terms." Id. at 601. The advance announcement of prices and terms introduced valuable information to competitors and buyers. It would, he thought, make the market more competitive.

Trade associations continued to flourish but by mid-century their leaders became more cautious, lest they run afoul of the antitrust laws. The next case is not a trade association case but rather a competitor-to-competitor "loose" exchange of certain data.

UNITED STATES v. CONTAINER CORPORATION OF AMERICA

393 U.S. 333 (1969).

JUSTICE DOUGLAS: This is a civil antitrust action charging a price-fixing agreement in violation of § 1 of the Sherman Act as amended, 15 U.S.C. § 1. The District Court dismissed the complaint....

The case as proved is unlike any other price decisions we have rendered. There was here an exchange of price information but no agreement to adhere to a price schedule as in *Sugar Institute v. United States,* 297 U.S. 553, or *United States v. Socony–Vacuum Oil Co.,* 310 U.S. 150. There was here an exchange of information concerning specific sales to identified customers, not a statistical report on the average cost to all members, without identifying the parties to specific transactions, as in *Maple Flooring Mfrs.' Assn. v. United States,* 268 U.S. 563. While there was present here, as in *Cement Mfrs.' Protective Assn. v. United States,* 268 U.S. 588, an exchange of prices to specific customers, there was absent the controlling circumstance, *viz.,* that cement manufacturers, to protect themselves from delivering to contractors more cement than was needed for a specific job and thus receiving a lower price, exchanged price information as a means of protecting their legal rights from fraudulent inducements to deliver more cement than needed for a specific job.

Here all that was present was a request by each defendant of its competitor for information as to the most recent price charged or quoted, whenever it needed such information and whenever it was not available from another source. Each defendant on receiving that request usually furnished the data with the expectation that it would be furnished reciprocal information when it wanted it. That concerted action is of course sufficient to establish the combination or conspiracy, the initial ingredient of a violation of § 1 of the Sherman Act.

There was of course freedom to withdraw from the agreement. But the fact remains that when a defendant requested and received price information it was affirming its willingness to furnish such information in return.

There was to be sure an infrequency and irregularity of price exchanges between the defendants; and often the data were available from the records of the defendants or from the the customers themselves. Yet the essence of the agreement was to furnish price information whenever requested....

The defendants account for about 90% of the shipment of corrugated containers from plants in the Southeastern United States. While containers vary as to dimensions, weight, color, and so on, they are substantially identical, no matter who produces them, when made to particular specifications.... Suppliers ... do not exceed a competitor's price. It is common for purchasers to buy from two or more suppliers concurrently. A defendant supplying a customer with containers would usually quote the same price on additional orders, unless costs had changed. Yet where a competitor was charging a particular price, a defendant would normally quote the same price or even a lower price.

... Capacity has exceeded the demand from 1955 to 1963, the period covered by the complaint, and the trend of corrugated container prices has been downward. Yet despite this excess capacity and the downward trend of prices, the industry has expanded in the Southeast from 30 manufacturers with 49 plants to 51 manufacturers with 98 plants. An abundance of raw materials and machinery makes entry into the industry easy with an investment of $50,000 to $75,000.

The result of this reciprocal exchange of prices was to stabilize prices though at a downward level. Knowledge of a competitor's price usually meant matching that price. The continuation of some price competition is not fatal to the Government's case. The limitation or reduction of price competition brings the case within the ban, for as we held in *United States v. Socony–Vacuum Oil Co., supra,* at 224, n. 59, interference with the setting of price by free market forces is unlawful *per se.* Price information exchanged in some markets may have no effect on a truly competitive price. But the corrugated container industry is dominated by relatively few sellers. The product is fungible and the competition for sales is price. The demand is inelastic, as buyers place orders only for immediate, short-run needs. The exchange of price data tends toward price uniformity. For a lower price does not mean a larger share of the available business but a sharing of the existing business at a lower return. Stabilizing prices as well as raising them is within the ban of § 1 of the Sherman Act....

Price is too critical, too sensitive a control to allow it to be used even in an informal manner to restrain competition. *Reversed.*

JUSTICE FORTAS, concurring: I join in the judgment and opinion of the Court. I do not understand the Court's opinion to hold that the exchange of specific information among sellers as to prices charged to individual customers, pursuant to mutual arrangement, is a *per se* violation of the Sherman Act....

In summary, the record shows that the defendants sought and obtained from competitors who were part of the arrangement information about the competitors' prices to specific customers. "[I]n the majority of instances," the District Court found that once a defendant had this information he quoted substantially the same price as the competitor, although a higher or lower price would "occasionally" be quoted. Thus the exchange of prices made it possible for individual defendants confidently to name a price equal to that which their competitors were asking. The obvious effect was to "stabilize" prices by joint arrangement—at least to limit any price cuts to the minimum necessary to meet competition....

JUSTICE MARSHALL, with whom JUSTICES HARLAN, and STEWART, joined, dissenting: I agree with the Court's holding that there existed an agreement among the defendants to exchange price information whenever requested. However, I cannot agree that that agreement should be condemned, either as illegal *per se,* or as having had the purpose or effect of restricting price competition in the corrugated container industry in the Southeastern United States....

Complete market knowledge is certainly not an evil in perfectly competitive markets. This is not, however, such a market, and there is admittedly some danger that price information will be used for anticompetitive purposes, particularly the maintenance of prices at a high level. If the danger that price information will be so used is particularly high in a given situation, then perhaps exchange of information should be condemned....

In a competitive situation, each seller will cut his price in order to increase his share of the market, and prices will ultimately stabilize at a competitive level—*i.e.,* price will equal cost, including a reasonable return on capital. Obviously, it would be to a seller's benefit to avoid such price competition and maintain prices at a higher level, with a corresponding increase in profit. In a market with very few sellers, and detailed knowledge of each other's price, such action is possible. However, I do not think it can be concluded that this particular market is sufficiently oligopolistic, especially in light of the ease of entry, to justify the inference that price information will necessarily be used to stabilize prices. Nor do I think that the danger of such a result is sufficiently high to justify imposing a *per se* rule without actual proof.

In this market, we have a few sellers presently controlling a substantial share of the market. We have a large number competing for the remainder of the market, also quite substantial. And total demand is increasing. In such a case, I think it just as logical to assume that the sellers, especially the smaller and newer ones, will desire to capture a larger market share by cutting prices as it is that they will acquiesce in oligopolistic behavior. The likelihood that prices will be cut and that those lower prices will have to be met acts as a deterrent to setting prices at an artificially high level in the first place. Given the uncertainty about the probable effect of an exchange of price information in this context, I would require that the Government prove that the exchange was entered into for the purpose of, or that it had the effect of, restraining price competition.... * * *

QUESTIONS AND COMMENTS

1. Did the government prove the existence of an agreement to exchange information? (The parties stipulated that there was no agreement to fix price.)

Did the government prove facts from which the fact-finder could infer an anticompetitive effect?

Does Justice Douglas lay down a qualified per se rule—a rule invalidating any agreement among competitors to exchange price information under specified structural circumstances? What circumstances? How important is the mode of exchange of information? The structure of the market? The characteristics of the product? Defendants' purpose?

2. Suppose that you are a salesperson for a container manufacturer. A competitor calls you and says: a) "I am trying to sell my cartons to Joe Jones. He says he might buy from you instead. What are you quoting him?" b) "I was just trying to sell my cartons to Joe Jones at Procter & Gamble for $10 a dozen. He tells me he can get cartons from you at $9.50 a dozen. Is that true?" If it is true, will you say so?

What will you (a strategic business person) tell your counterpart?

3. In his dissent, Justice Marshall takes issue less with the Court's legal doctrine than with its characterization of the market. Do you agree with Justice Douglas or with Justice Marshall about whether the structure of and conditions in this market facilitate collaborative price behavior? If the hardwood companies in *American Column & Lumber* had exchanged price information in the *Container* manner, would their exchange have pushed price upward? What about the flooring companies in *Maple Flooring?* the *Sugar Institute* members?

After *Container,* what is the test for the legality of direct exchanges of price information among competing sellers?

4. Note Justice Douglas's reference to a "controlling circumstance." Is there a "controlling circumstance defense" to price information exchanges? Would the need of sellers to protect themselves from buyer fraud constitute a controlling circumstance and justify an interseller price exchange even if it is likely to have a price-raising effect? The next case, *United States v. United States Gypsum Company,* 438 U.S. 422 (1978), will help you to answer these questions.

5. Unlike antitrust law in the United States and numerous other jurisdictions, China's recently-enacted Anti–Monopoly Law (AML) may not require an *agreement* to exchange information in cases of price-signalling. One of China's three antitrust agencies, NDRC (National Development and Reform Commission) fined Unilever the equivalent of U.S. $308,000 for "spreading information" via the media regarding a planned price increase. Although the fine was imposed under the Price Law, which clearly prohibits the conduct, press releases suggest that the price announcement may have violated the AML too. *http://www.ndrc.gov.cn/xwfb/t20110506_410542.htm* (in Chinese). See Bloomberg News, China to Fine Unilever for Telling Media It May Raise Prices, May 6, 2011.

In the 1970s, the major manufacturers of gypsum board were indicted for a criminal price-fixing conspiracy. The government alleged that the companies agreed to fix prices and that one way in which they carried out their conspiracy was by telephoning their competitors to find out what they were currently charging a specific customer. The defendants denied that they fixed prices. They admitted that they telephoned competitors to get information about prices to specific customers, but asserted that they did so because of the "lying buyer" problem. Allegedly, a buyer of gypsum board, negotiating with a major manufacturer, would tell the manufacturer that it had a lower-price offer from another manufacturer. Subject as it was to the Robinson–Patman Act, the manufacturer could not generally offer a discriminatorily low price to one buyer and not to that buyer's competitors. If, however, the lower price was necessary to meet competition from another manufacturer, the selling company would have a Robinson–Patman defense: the good faith meeting of competition. (Robinson–Patman Act, § 2(b).) The gypsum manufacturers asserted that their telephone conversations were necessary to verify whether the buyer had really been offered a lower price by a competitor and thus to establish a meeting-competition defense to the Robinson–Patman Act.

The gypsum board industry had the following characteristics:

Gypsum board is a laminated type of wallboard composed of paper, vinyl, or other specially treated coverings over a gypsum core. The product is essentially fungible; differences in price, credit terms, and delivery services largely dictate the purchasers' choice between competing suppliers. Overall demand, however, is governed by the level of construction activity and is only marginally affected by price fluctuations.

The number of producers in the gypsum board industry ranged from 9 to 15 in the period 1960 to 1973. The eight largest companies accounted for some 94% of the national sales with the seven single-plant producers accounting for the remaining 6%. Most of the major producers and a large number of the single-plant producers were members of the Gypsum Association, which was the trade association of gypsum board manufacturers.

At the trial the judge charged the jury as follows: To return a verdict of guilty, the jury must find that the defendants had a purpose to fix prices; that an information exchange made in good faith to comply with the Robinson–Patman Act was not sufficient by itself to establish an agreement to fix prices. If the jury found that the effect of the exchange was to raise, fix, or stabilize price, they could infer the forbidden purpose from that effect, since people are presumed to intend the necessary consequences of their acts.

The jury returned a verdict of guilty. The court of appeals reversed. The Supreme Court affirmed the appellate court. The Supreme Court held, first, that the trial judge's charge was reversible error. The charge allowed, and may have required, the jury to find criminal liability if it found that defendants' activity had an effect on prices, regardless of whether defendants intended or even were aware of the price effect.

Although reversing on *mens rea* grounds, the Court rejected defendants' "controlling circumstance" defense on the facts.

Here are excerpts.

Note that the Justice Department has the power to bring suits civilly or criminally. It normally reserves criminal prosecution for hard core violations.

UNITED STATES v. UNITED STATES GYPSUM CO.

438 U.S. 422 (1978).

JUSTICE BURGER: ... We are unwilling to construe the Sherman Act as mandating a regime of strict-liability criminal offenses .....

Close attention to the type of conduct regulated by the Sherman Act buttresses [the] conclusion [that *mens rea* is an element of the criminal violation]. With certain exceptions for conduct regarded as *per se* illegal because of its unquestionably anticompetitive effects, ... the behavior proscribed by the Act is often difficult to distinguish from the gray zone of socially acceptable and economically justifiable business conduct. Indeed, the type of conduct charged in the indictment in this case—the exchange of price information among competitors—is illustrative in this regard.[16] The imposition of criminal liability on a corporate official, or for that matter on a corporation directly, for engaging in such conduct which only after the fact is determined to violate the statute because of anticompetitive effects, without inquiring into the intent with which it was undertaken, holds out the distinct possibility of overdeterrence; salutary and procompetitive conduct lying close to the borderline of impermissible conduct might be shunned by businessmen who chose to be excessively cautious in the face of uncertainty regarding possible exposure to criminal punishment for even a good-faith error of judgment.[17] ...[21]

[In civil cases, however, the government need not prove *mens rea;* proof of the effect on price of conduct deliberately entered into is enough to prove the violation.]

---

16. The exchange of price data and other information among competitors does not invariably have anticompetitive effects; indeed such practices can in certain circumstances increase economic efficiency and render markets more, rather than less, competitive. For this reason, we have held that such exchanges of information do not constitute a *per se* violation of the Sherman Act. See, *e.g.,* ... *United States v. Container Corp.*, 393 U.S., at 338 (Fortas, J., concurring). A number of factors including most prominently the structure of the industry involved and the nature of the information exchanged are generally considered in divining the procompetitive or anticompetitive effects of this type of interseller communication.... Exchanges of current price information, of course, have the greatest potential for generating anticompetitive effects and although not *per se* unlawful have consistently been held to violate the Sherman Act. See *American Column & Lumber Co. v. United States*, 257 U.S. 377 (1921); ... *United States v. Container Corp.*, supra.

17. The possibility that those subjected to strict liability will take extraordinary care in their dealings is frequently regarded as one advantage of a rule of strict liability. However, where the conduct proscribed is difficult to distinguish from conduct permitted and indeed encouraged, as in the antitrust context, the excessive caution spawned by a regime of strict liability will not necessarily redound to the public's benefit....

21. ... [P]roof that the defendant's conduct was undertaken with knowledge of its probable consequences will satisfy the Government's burden [to prove criminal intent].

There remains the possibility that in a limited number of situations a seller may have substantial reasons to doubt the accuracy of reports of a competing offer and may be unable to corroborate such reports in any of the generally accepted ways. . . .

[Price verification for the purpose of taking advantage of the Robinson–Patman meeting-competition defense is not a "controlling circumstance" within the meaning of *Container Corporation.* The Robinson–Patman requirement can usually "be satisfied by efforts falling short of interseller verification."]

. . . As an abstract proposition, resort to interseller verification as a means of checking the buyer's reliability seems a possible solution to the seller's plight, but careful examination reveals serious problems with the practice.

Both economic theory and common human experience suggest that interseller verification—if undertaken on an isolated and infrequent basis with no provision for reciprocity or cooperation—will not serve its putative function of corroborating the representations of unreliable buyers regarding the existence of competing offers. Price concessions by oligopolists generally yield competitive advantages only if secrecy can be maintained; when the terms of the concession are made publicly known, other competitors are likely to follow and any advantage to the initiator is lost in the process. Thus, if one seller offers a price concession for the purpose of winning over one of his competitor's customers, it is unlikely that the same seller will freely inform its competitor of the details of the concession so that it can be promptly matched and diffused. Instead, such a seller would appear to have at least as great an incentive to misrepresent the existence or size of the discount as would the buyer who received it. Thus verification, if undertaken on a one-shot basis for the sole purpose of complying with the § 2(b) defense, does not hold out much promise as a means of shoring up buyers' representations.

The other variety of interseller verification is, like the conduct charged in the instant case, undertaken pursuant to an agreement, either tacit or express, providing for reciprocity among competitors in the exchange of price information. Such an agreement would make little economic sense, in our view, if its sole purpose were to guarantee all participants the opportunity to match the secret price concessions of other participants under § 2(b). For in such circumstances, each seller would know that his price concession could not be kept from his competitors and no seller participating in the information exchange arrangement would, therefore, have any incentive for deviating from the prevailing price level in the industry. Regardless of its putative purpose, the most likely consequence of any such agreement to exchange price information would be the stabilization of industry prices. Instead of facilitating use of the § 2(b) defense, such an agreement would have the effect of eliminating the very price concessions which provide the main element of competition in oligopolistic industries and the primary occasion for resort to the meeting-competition defense.

Especially in oligopolistic industries such as the gypsum board industry, the exchange of price information among competitors carries with it the added potential for the development of concerted price-fixing arrangements which lie at the core of the Sherman Act's prohibitions....

We are left, therefore, on the one hand, with doubts about both the need for and the efficacy of interseller verification as a means of facilitating compliance with § 2(b), and, on the other, with recognition of the tendency for price discussions between competitors to contribute to the stability of oligopolistic prices and open the way for the growth of prohibited anticompetitive activity. To recognize even a limited "controlling circumstance" exception for interseller verification in such circumstances would be to remove from scrutiny under the Sherman Act conduct falling near its core with no assurance, and indeed with serious doubts, that competing antitrust policies would be served thereby. In *Automatic Canteen Co. v. FTC,* 346 U.S. 61, 74 (1953), the Court suggested that as a general rule the Robinson–Patman Act should be construed so as to insure its coherence with "the broader antitrust policies that have been laid down by Congress"; that observation buttresses our conclusion that exchanges of price information—even when putatively for purposes of Robinson–Patman Act compliance—must remain subject to close scrutiny under the Sherman Act.... * * *

QUESTIONS AND COMMENTS

1. *Gypsum* was decided in 1978, after Chief Justice Earl Warren had retired, Warren Burger had been appointed Chief Justice, and a new antitrust majority had emerged. Prior to *Gypsum,* the Court generally assumed a broad margin between anticompetitive and procompetitive behavior; the Court had not expressed concern about over-deterrence. In *Gypsum,* for the first time, we see a strong statement of concern that overly aggressive antitrust rules will deter procompetitive conduct.

2. In ruling out a Robinson–Patman defense, how does the Chief Justice carry forward the argument that interseller verification under certain market conditions normally holds more dangers than benefits? To what market conditions does he refer?

Suppose that interseller verification of the sort found in *Container* occurred in the gypsum board industry and the United States filed a civil suit to enjoin it. What, in light of *Gypsum,* would the government have to prove to make out a prima facie case?

3. European law more aggressively proscribes information exchanges than does U.S. law. In *John Deere Ltd. v. Commission*, case C–7/95 P, [1998] ECR I–3111, the Agricultural Tractor Makers Association organized among its members an exchange of information. The information was derived from registration forms required to be filed in the UK. The four largest firms in the market accounted for 80% of sales. There were some 200 other members of

the association. The association was open to membership by all agricultural tractor companies. Barriers to entry into the market were high.

The data exchanged revealed great detail of sales and market shares, broken down by year, quarter, month and week, and by country, region, county, and dealer territory, and made it possible to identify not only the sales of each producer but also the imports and exports between dealer territories. The information exchanged did not directly concern prices, and there was no evidence that the information exchange was designed in support of a cartel. Indeed, there was no claim that the *object* of the agreement was to harm trade or competition; and the European Commission was unable to establish that the agreement, which was in force for 20 years, produced an actual anticompetitive effect (higher prices). The Commission found that the information exchange agreement was caught by (then) Article 85(1) of the Treaty (now Article 101) and was not entitled to an exemption under (then) Article 85(3). [The exemption is available for agreements that are generally efficient or technologically progressive and from which consumers get a fair share of benefits.] The European Court of First Instance agreed. It upheld Commission findings that the data exchange (1) disadvantaged non-members, who would forgo the information exchanged; (2) produced *potential* anticompetitive effects among members, by providing a forum for facilitating a high price policy; and (3) made it possible for each participating manufacturer to monitor *its* dealers' sales and thus made "it possible for [manufacturers] to confer absolute territorial protection on each of their dealers." para. 96. The association did not show that the restrictions on competition resulting from the agreement were indispensable, "particularly with regard to the objectives of contributing to economic progress and equitable distribution of the benefits." para. 105. *John Deere*, Case T–35/92, [1995] ECR II–957. The European Court of Justice affirmed. (see citation above). As to each of the three concerns, would it have been a concern under U.S. law?

In *T–Mobile Netherlands*, Case C–8/08, 2009 ECR I–04529, ECJ, representatives of the five big mobile telephone operators "held a meeting ... [on 13 June 2001 at which] they discussed ... the reduction of standard dealer renumerations for postpaid subscriptions [commissions to their agents for distributing their product to consumers], which was to take effect on or about 1 September 2001." They shared confidential information in their discussions. para. 12. When challenged, the firms argued that they had not made an agreement (the Dutch court found to the contrary) and that their conversations had no effect on consumer prices. The Dutch court made a preliminary reference—asked a question—to the European Court of Justice. The Court of Justice held that, for a concerted practice to have an anticompetitive object, "it is sufficient that it has the potential to have a negative impact on competition." In the case of an anticompetitive object, it is not necessary that there be an anticompetitive effect, which "can only be of relevance for determining the amount of any fine and assessing any claim for damages." paras. 30, 31. "Article [101] ... is designed to protect not only the immediate interests of individual competitors or consumers but also to protect the structure of the market and thus competition as such." para. 38

Does this mean that the information exchange agreement was automatically caught by Article 101(1)? Do you think that it was merely a benign agreement to exchange information and thus get knowledge? Or did the agreement reflect a thinly veiled attempt to ratchet down commissions payable to the agents?

4. Exchange of non-price information can also pose risks when it is not meant to be a cartel. The Electric Power Research Institute, a non-profit organization created to develop solutions to energy industry problems, proposed to exchange information to improve security against cyber-threats. The Justice Department approved the exchange, but only on condition that members do not discuss specific prices for products and systems or other company-specific information, lest the Institute become "a conduit for discussions or negotiations ... [of] price, purchase and future product innovation." Justice Department Approves Information Exchange Proposed by the Electric Power Research Institute (October 2, 2000), available at *http://www.usdoj.gov/atr/public/press_releases/2000/6619.htm.*

5. Many industry organizations that propose information exchanges consult the Justice Department, and many of these get a business review letter (stating that the Department does not presently plan to sue), or assurance that a business review letter will follow if certain protections are imposed.

The next case involved the exchange of salary information among "buyers" of workers' services; that is, employers. As buyers, the collaborators apparently had a lower consciousness of the antitrust pitfalls.

TODD v. EXXON CORPORATION

275 F.3d 191 (2d Cir. 2001).

JUDGE SOTOMAYOR: Plaintiff-appellant Roberta Todd appeals from an order ... granting defendants-appellees' motion to dismiss the complaint for failure to state a claim pursuant to Fed. R. Civ. P. 12(b)(6). We hold that plaintiff adequately alleges a § 1 Sherman Act violation for an unlawful information exchange. Plaintiff's complaint alleges a plausible product market, a market structure that is susceptible to collusive activity, a data exchange with anticompetitive potential, and antitrust injury. We therefore vacate and remand.

Plaintiff brought this action against fourteen major companies in the integrated oil and petrochemical industry, collectively accounting for 80–90% of the industry's revenues and employing approximately the same percentage of the industry's workforce. On behalf of herself and ... the putative class, plaintiff alleges that defendants violated § 1 of the Sherman Act by regularly sharing detailed information regarding compensation paid to nonunion managerial, professional, and technical ("MPT") employees and using this information in setting the salaries of these employees at artificially low levels. Plaintiff seeks money damages and equitable relief pursuant to § 1 of the Sherman Act.

Accepting the allegations in the complaint as true, as we must on this motion to dismiss, the facts of this case are as follows. Defendants instituted a system whereby they periodically conducted surveys comparing past and current MPT salary information and participated in regular meetings at which current and future salary budgets were discussed. The data exchanges were also accompanied by assurances that the information would be used in setting the salaries of MPT employees. Defendants' "Job Match Survey" created a common denominator to facilitate the comparison of MPT salaries. The survey used certain jobs at defendant Chevron as benchmarks. The other defendants would submit detailed information regarding the jobs at their companies that were most comparable to the Chevron benchmark jobs so that they could be matched. [A] third-party consultant, Towers Perrin ... compiled the information, then analyzed, refined, and distributed it to the defendants on diskettes and in the form of hard copies. The Job Match Survey was performed every two years and was supplemented in the "off years" by the "Grade Average Update," which would calculate the change in grade average salaries since the last Job Match Survey and then adjust the salary level from the previous year's survey by the amount of the change ..... The information gathered in the survey was updated and distributed to the participants several times per year....

Although these were the primary forms of salary information exchange, defendants supplemented this information with data from other sources.... In addition to the data exchange surveys, human resource personnel at defendant companies held regular meetings—at least three times per year—to discuss and exchange salary and salary-related information. These meetings included discussions of individual defendants' current and future salary budgets for MPT employees....

Plaintiff contends that defendants' arrangement violated § 1 of the Sherman Act ... [and that] these violations had the purpose and effect of depressing MPT salaries paid by defendants. The arrangement reduced the incentive for defendants to bid up salaries in order to attract experienced MPT employees or to retain employees who might be lured to other firms. As a result, the plaintiffs in the putative class received compensation that was materially lower than what they would have received but for defendants' anticompetitive practices....

.... Traditional "hard-core" price fixing remains *per se* unlawful under the seminal case *United States v. Socony–Vacuum Oil Co.* (1940), and its progeny. If the plaintiff in this case could allege that defendants actually formed an agreement to fix MPT salaries, this *per se* rule would likely apply. Furthermore, even in the absence of direct "smoking gun" evidence, a horizontal price-fixing agreement may be inferred on the basis of conscious parallelism, when such interdependent conduct is accompanied by circumstantial evidence and plus factors such as defendants' use of facilitating practices.... Information exchange is an example of a facilitating practice that can help support an inference of a price-fixing agreement.

There is a closely related but analytically distinct type of claim, also based on § 1 of the Sherman Act, where the violation lies in the information exchange itself—as opposed to merely using the information exchange as evidence upon which to infer a price-fixing agreement. This exchange of information is not illegal *per se*, but can be found unlawful under a rule of reason analysis.... * * *

As plaintiff does not allege an actual agreement among defendants to fix salaries, we analyze plaintiff's complaint solely as to whether it alleges unlawful information exchange pursuant to this rule of reason.... * * *

The traditional horizontal conspiracy case involves an agreement among sellers with the purpose of raising prices to supracompetitive levels. The Sherman Act, however, also applies to abuse of market power on the buyer side-often taking the form of monopsony or oligopsony.... * * *

At issue is the interchangeability, from the perspective of an MPT employee, of a job opportunity in the oil industry with, for example, one in the pharmaceutical industry....

In finding that plaintiff's allegation[s] support[ ] a plausible product market, we do not indicate whether plaintiff will succeed in proving the alleged market.... We find only that the allegation of a market limited to employers in the oil and petrochemical industry [on grounds that other jobs are not good substitutes for the employees] is plausible on its face ... * * *

Plaintiff's alleged product market would support the 80–90% market share figure for defendants. Market power defined as a percentage market share, however, is not the only way to demonstrate defendants' ability to depress salaries.... If a plaintiff can show that a defendant's conduct exerted an actual adverse effect on competition, this is a strong indicator of market power. In fact, this arguably is more direct evidence of market power than calculations of elusive market share figures....

If, for example, the plaintiff in this case could prove that (1) defendants engaged in information exchanges that would be deemed anticompetitive under *Gypsum* and (2) such activities did in fact have an anticompetitive effect on the market for MPT labor in the oil and petrochemical industry, we would not deny relief on the basis of market share figures. On remand, therefore, the court should consider whether plaintiff has demonstrated anticompetitive effects as part of the court's assessment of defendants' market power....

[Susceptibility of the market to coordination]

The Supreme Court in *Gypsum* explained that one of the two "most prominent[]" factors in the rule of reason analysis of a data exchange is "the structure of the industry involved." Therefore, once the relevant market is defined, a court must analyze the structure of that market to determine whether it is "susceptible to the exercise of market power through tacit coordination." ... As the district court explained, "[s]usceptible markets tend to be highly concentrated—that is, oligopolistic—and to have fungible products subject to inelastic demand."

Generally speaking, the possibility of anticompetitive collusive practices is most realistic in concentrated industries. If the relevant market in this case is defined as the plaintiff contends, the defendants would control collectively a 80–90% market share. While this is an extremely high market share by any measure, . . . the district court points out that there are fourteen defendants in this case, and that this is not a concentrated market under the Department of Justice Merger Guidelines. That the market would not be deemed highly concentrated by this measure, however, does not preclude the possibility of collusive activity.

. . . We . . . find it unsurprising that data exchange cases may involve a number of participants that begins to push the boundaries of oligopoly. These players are *most* in need of such data exchange arrangements in order to facilitate price coordination; a very small handful of firms in a more highly concentrated market may be less likely to require the kind of sophisticated data dissemination alleged in this case. . . .

Concluding its discussion of the susceptibility of the market to tacit coordination, the district court stated that "plaintiff has pleaded no facts tending to establish that the demand for these 'products' is inelastic." We disagree. . . .

Here again, we reverse the equation in the context of an oligopsony. Where market power is exercised by buyers, it is the elasticity of the sellers' *supply* that is at issue. Sellers' supply could be elastic if, for example, they have "the option of withholding some output from the market in hopes of higher prices in future years." If, however, the goods are perishable, short-run supply may be quite inelastic. In this case, the supply at issue is the labor of the MPT employees. "Labor is an extremely perishable commodity—an hour not worked today can never be recovered." . . . As labor is a classic example of inelastic supply flow, it is unclear what additional facts plaintiffs would have to allege with regard to this aspect of the inquiry.

In sum, the pleadings support the contention that the market was susceptible to tacit coordination by the defendant companies: The market is sufficiently concentrated under *Container Corp.*; the defendants have in effect manufactured a form of fungibility through sophisticated comparison techniques; and the supply of labor has an inherently inelastic quality.

[Nature of the data, who has access, how it is exchanged]

Alongside the "structure of the industry involved," the other major factor for courts to consider in a data exchange case is the "nature of the information exchanged." There are certain well-established criteria used to help ascertain the anticompetitive potential of information exchanges. . . . Applying the relevant criteria reveals anticompetitive potential in this case. . . .

The first factor to consider is the time frame of the data. The Supreme Court has made clear that "[e]xchanges of current price information, of course, have the greatest potential for generating anti-competitive effects and although not *per se* unlawful have consistently been held to violate the Sherman Act." The exchange of past price data is greatly preferred because current data have greater potential to affect future prices and facilitate price conspiracies. By the same reasoning, exchanges of future price information are considered especially anticompetitive.

Plaintiff's complaint alleges that defendants exchanged past and current salary information, as well as future salary budget information....

[A]nother factor courts look to is the specificity of the information. Price exchanges that identify particular parties, transactions, and prices are seen as potentially anticompetitive because they may be used to police a secret or tacit conspiracy to stabilize prices....

Another important factor to consider in evaluating an information exchange is whether the data are made publicly available. Public dissemination is a primary way for data exchange to realize its procompetitive potential. For example, in the traditional oligopoly (seller-side) context, access to information may better equip buyers to compare products, rendering the market more efficient while diminishing the anticompetitive effects of the exchange....

In the instant case, dissemination of the information to the employees could have helped mitigate any anticompetitive effects of the exchange and possibly enhanced market efficiency by making employees more sensitive to salary increases. No such dissemination occurred, however. The information was not disclosed to the public nor to the employees whose salaries were the subject of the exchange. Plaintiff alleges that "[t]he confidential treatment of the information exchanged impedes the ability of employees to bargain intelligently and competitively with the members of the information exchange." ...

A final troubling aspect of the arrangement at issue is the fact that the defendants allegedly participated in frequent meetings to discuss the salary information, accompanied by assurances that the participants would primarily use the exchanged data in setting their MPT salaries. Meetings, of course, are not inherently unlawful but in this context they have the potential to enhance the anticompetitive effects and "likelihood of ... uniformity" caused by information exchange....

In sum, the "nature of the information exchanged" weighs against the motion to dismiss. The characteristics of the data exchange in this case are precisely those that arouse suspicion of anticompetitive activity under the rule of reason....

An antitrust plaintiff must allege not only cognizable harm to herself, but an adverse effect on competition market-wide. In the traditional oligopoly case, horizontal coordination may inflate prices to supracompetitive levels. In an oligopsony, the risk is that buyers will collude to depress prices, causing harm to sellers....

In all, plaintiff alleges that with Exxon's total salary budget at $800 million, the conduct described in the complaint had the effect of lowering Exxon's MPT salaries by a total of $20 million per year. . . .

For the reasons stated, we vacate the district court's grant of defendants' Rule 12(b)(6) motion to dismiss and remand for proceedings consistent with this opinion.

QUESTIONS AND COMMENTS

1. Note that this arrangement would not be exempted by the labor exemption, Clayton Act § 6. Clayton § 6 exempts workers' collective bargaining and their collective pursuit of legitimate labor interests. A non-statutory exemption extends to employees or their organizations bargaining with employers, and corresponding management collective bargaining.

2. Was the information exchange likely to depress the salaries of the MPT workers? If you represented the plaintiffs, what additional market facts would you try to develop? Consider: scarcity of jobs, mobility of workers, competitive characteristics of the employers.

3. If you were Exxon, why would you exchange this information? Would your information exchange agreement deter you from bidding more than an average wage for a talented MPT worker who would enhance your business? If not, what are the implications for the plaintiffs' case?

Rules of Thumb to Avoid Illegality

When information exchanges involve certain kinds of data, and certain modes of exchanging it, the dangers of oligopolistic price coordination and ultimately a real price-fixing conspiracy may be high. Risky subjects of data exchange include: current prices, costs and output; plans for future prices and output; predictions or advice for future prices and output for one's firm or for the industry. The riskiest mode of exchange is direct personal contact with competitors.

Because of the anticompetitive dangers, antitrust lawyers frequently advise that competitors should never exchange facts or predictions about current or prospective price, cost and output. Further, they should never exchange industry information by direct personal contact with competitors, except that they may discuss common economic problems and trends. Discussion of economic problems common to the industry frequently takes place at trade association meetings. Are there important benefits of such discussions? How great are the anticompetitive dangers? What would you advise your client before she or he participates in such discussions? Would a well advised association have a lawyer present at all such meetings? Would it keep an accurate and reasonably complete record of the proceedings?

Trade associations frequently compile industry data, including price and production information, and distribute it to their members. Antitrust precautions include the following:

1. Gather information as to past transactions only.

2. Use an independent person (not an employee of any of the members) to receive and compile the data, so that no member sees the raw data of its competitor.

3. Disseminate the information in aggregate form only, so that members cannot attribute information to individual firms.

If the industry is highly concentrated, would you suggest other precautions? Would providing the information to all interested persons, including buyers and non-members, help your client's antitrust posture? Is there a level of concentration at which you would advise against any exchange of price and production data (e.g., three firms in a high-barrier market with a standardized product)?

3. AGREEMENTS OF COMPETITORS TO RESTRAIN THEIR OWN COMPETITION

Competitors often agree with one another to restrict their own competition. Cartels are, of course, the prime example—a strategy to increase or maintain prices, which works only if no one on the inside cheats (too much) and no one on the outside can quickly fill the slack. But there are many other agreements among competitors for ostensibly good reasons. The firms may be trying to increase the safety of their products, to maintain high professional standards, to differentiate a product, or to safeguard the efficiency of their joint activity by protecting against free rider problems. Our touchstones *California Dental Association* and *Rothery* fall into these categories. In other cases you have read, defendants invoked one of these categories, but not convincingly; for example, *Polygram*, supra p. 111, and *National Society of Professional Engineers*, supra p. 77.

From these cases we can already draw important analytical lessons: Some competitors' agreements to restrain themselves are so clearly harmful to competition and so clearly unnecessary for efficient competition that courts will condemn them with little inquiry (*Polygram*); some have anticompetitive aspects on their face but are not so clearly harmful or have credible good justifications so that the courts will take a longer look; and some are simply complex arrangements that require a full analysis.

We divide this section into three parts. In the first part we revisit professional restraints—very briefly because we have treated this subject above. The second part examines a case about college admissions, financial aid, and public interest. The third involves the real estate broker market.

a. Professional Restraints and By-Laws

The professions have imposed restraints on themselves since early times, virtually always in the name of professionalism, safety, or other "high" standards. For many years, these restraints in the name of self regulation were respected and deferred to, as if the profession knew what was in the best interests of the public and would safeguard public welfare.

It was not until the late 1960s that the antitrust authorities began to call attention to the self-interested motivations (as well as the effect) of the "club" to preserve the mystique and to keep fees, amenities and barriers high—even while many of the same individuals who guarded the club doors were highly "public-interested." The new focus by the antitrust enforcers gave rise to a string of cases—*Goldfarb*, *Bates*, *Indiana Federation of Dentists*, and *National Society of Professional Engineers*—in some of which the professionals' by-laws themselves tipped their hands and revealed their strategies to keep prices high. See footnote 4 at 76 (*Goldfarb*), footnote 3 at 77 (*Professional Engineers*). Not until the new millennium did the Court revert to a stance more sympathetic to professional restraints, crediting self-regulation as a means to rout out deceptive advertising, as it did in *California Dental Association*, and raising the bar on proof of anticompetitive effects.

Still, professional by-laws and rules are not exempt from U.S. antitrust. Can lawyers (the "bar") decide that law firm partnerships may not include accountants and economists? Would not such a partnership involve significant efficiencies including delivery to clients of full-line services that they want? Is not such an agreement to exclude clearly anticompetitive on its face? Can it be defended as good for the public nonetheless? The answers to the last three questions are yes, yes, no. But—recall the state action doctrine. Lawyers' by-laws are subject to authorization and approval by the courts in numerous states. The judges (lawyers themselves) approve the by-laws. Once approved, the by-laws are a public restraint, not a private one.

b. Higher Education—Brown/MIT

UNITED STATES v. BROWN UNIVERSITY

5 F.3d 658 (3d Cir. 1993).

JUDGE COWEN: [The eight colleges and universities in the Ivy League—Brown, Columbia, Cornell, Dartmouth, Harvard, Princeton, University of Pennsylvania, Yale—and MIT agreed to base all financial aid awards solely on need; thus, not to give merit scholarships. They held annual meetings at which they and 15 other prestigious colleges in the Northeast discussed the financial aid applications of the 10,000 students who had been accepted by more than one school in the group. At these "overlap" meetings they shared information regarding how much the overlap applicants and their families could afford to pay, and they agreed on the amount of the family contribution that each school would require from each applicant. In effect, they agreed on the amount of financial aid (or the discount from tuition) that they would give to each applicant that had been accepted by more than one of the schools. As a result of this agreement, the schools said, they would be able to "spread out" their financial aid moneys to more students, and the students would be able to select a school on the basis of its merits, not on the basis of price. The schools called financial aid charity, not commerce.

Tuition and the time and amount of increases in tuition at the collaborating schools were quite similar. For 1990–91, tuition, room and board ranged from $20,164 for Cornell to $20,820 for Yale.

The Justice Department sued. All of the universities settled except MIT, which went to trial. The district court held the agreement illegal. It found that the agreement was a direct interference with free market competition and that MIT did not meet the heavy burden of justification by proof of offsetting procompetitive effects. Indeed, according to the district court, the schools had no procompetitive justification.]

MIT does not dispute that the stated purpose of Overlap is to eliminate price competition for talented students among member institutions. Indeed, the intent to eliminate price competition among the Overlap schools for commonly admitted students appears on the face of the Agreement itself. In addition to agreeing to offer financial aid solely on the basis of need and to develop a common system of needs analysis, the Overlap members agreed to meet each spring to compare data and to conform one another's aid packages to the greatest possible extent. Because the Overlap Agreement aims to restrain "competitive bidding" and deprive prospective students of "the ability to utilize and compare prices" in selecting among schools, it is anticompetitive "on its face." *Professional Engineers,* 435 U.S. at 693.... We therefore agree that Overlap initially "requires some competitive justification even in the absence of a detailed market analysis." *Indiana Dentists,* 476 U.S. at 460 quoting *NCAA,* 468 U.S. at 109–10....

* * *

Since the Overlap Agreement is a price fixing mechanism impeding the ordinary functioning of the free market, MIT is obliged to provide justification for the arrangement. In *NCAA,* the Supreme Court credited the district court's findings that the NCAA's television agreements actually increased prices and restricted output. "Price is higher and output lower than they would otherwise be, and both are unresponsive to consumer preference." *NCAA,* 468 U.S. at 107. According to the Court, "these hallmarks of anticompetitive behavior place[d] upon [the NCAA] a *heavy burden* of establishing an affirmative defense." *Id.* at 113 (emphasis added).

The district court did not make any conclusive findings with regard to these "hallmark" consequences of price fixing in the present case. First, the district court did not find, and we do not understand the Division to suggest, that Overlap has caused or is even likely to cause any reduction of output. Second, while the parties sharply dispute the effect of Overlap on the price of education at the member colleges, the district court expressed doubt as to whether price effects could be determined to a reasonable degree of economic certainty. The court therefore assumed without deciding that the cooperation among the schools had no aggregate effect on the price of an MIT education. Thus, while MIT bears the burden of establishing an affirmative justification for Overlap, ... the absence of any finding of adverse effects such as higher price or lower output is relevant, albeit not dispositive, when the district court considers whether MIT has met this burden. Nevertheless, the absence or inconclusivity of a finding of actual adverse effects does not mitigate MIT's burden to justify price fixing with some procompetitive virtue, or with a showing of Overlap's reasonable necessity to its institutional purpose, because actual dollar amount effects do not necessarily reflect the harm to competition which Congress intended to eliminate in enacting the Sherman Act. * * *

At trial, MIT maintained that Overlap had the following procompetitive effects: (1) it improved the quality of the educational program at the Overlap schools; (2) it increased consumer choice by making an Overlap education more accessible to a greater number of students; and (3) it promoted competition for students among Overlap schools in areas other than price. The district court rejected each of these alleged competitive virtues, summarily concluding that they amounted to no more than non-economic social welfare justifications.

On appeal, MIT first contends that by promoting socio-economic diversity at member institutions, Overlap improved the quality of the education offered by the schools and therefore enhanced the consumer appeal of an Overlap education. The Supreme Court has recognized improvement in the quality of a product or service that enhances the public's desire for that product or service as one possible procompetitive virtue. See *NCAA,* 468 U.S. at 114–15. The district court itself noted that it cannot be denied "that cultural and economic diversity contributes to the quality of education and enhances the vitality of student life." *Brown University,* 805 F.Supp. at 306. Albeit in a different context, the Supreme Court also has recognized that "the atmosphere of 'speculation, experiment and creation'—so essential to the quality of higher education—is widely believed to be promoted by a diverse student body." *Regents of the Univ. of California v. Bakke*, 438 U.S. 265, 312 (1978) (opinion of Powell, J.) (use of race as a factor in medical school admissions survives equal protection challenge).

MIT also contends that by increasing the financial aid available to needy students, Overlap provided some students who otherwise would not have been able to afford an Overlap education the opportunity to have one. In this respect, MIT argues, Overlap enhanced consumer choice. The policy of allocating financial aid solely on the basis of demonstrated need has two obvious consequences. First, available resources are spread among more needy students than would be the case if some students received aid in excess of their need. Second, as a consequence of the fact that more students receive the aid they require, the number of students able to afford an Overlap education is maximized. In short, removing financial obstacles for the greatest number of talented but needy students increases educational access, thereby widening consumer choice. Enhancement of consumer choice is a traditional objective of the antitrust laws and has also been acknowledged as a procompetitive benefit. *See NCAA*, 468 U.S. at 102.

Finally, MIT argues that by eliminating price competition among participating schools, Overlap channelled competition into areas such as curriculum, campus activities, and student-faculty interaction. As the Division correctly notes, however, any competition that survives a horizontal price restraint naturally will focus on attributes other than price. This is not the kind of procompetitive virtue contemplated under the Act, but rather one mere consequence of limiting price competition.

MIT next claims that beyond ignoring the procompetitive effects of Overlap, the district court erroneously refused to consider compelling social welfare justifications. MIT argues that by enabling member schools to maintain a steadfast policy of need-blind admissions and full need-based aid, Overlap promoted the social ideal of equality of educational access and opportunity. * * *

The district court was not persuaded by the alleged social welfare values proffered for Overlap because it believed the Supreme Court's decisions in *Professional Engineers* and *Indiana Dentists* required a persuasive procompetitive justification, or a showing of necessity, neither of which it believed that MIT demonstrated.... * * *

Both the public safety justification rejected by the Supreme Court in *Professional Engineers* and the public health justification rejected by the Court in *Indiana Dentists* were based on the defendants' faulty premise that consumer choices made under competitive market conditions are "unwise" or "dangerous." Here MIT argues that participation in the Overlap arrangement provided some consumers, the needy, with additional choices which an entirely free market would deny them. The facts and arguments before us may suggest some significant areas of distinction from those in *Professional Engineers* and *Indiana Dentists* in that MIT is asserting that Overlap not only serves a social benefit, but actually enhances consumer choice. Overlap is not an attempt to withhold a particular desirable service from customers, as was the professional combination in *Indiana Dentists,* but rather it purports only to seek to extend a service to qualified students who are financially "needy" and would not otherwise be able to afford the high cost of education at MIT. Further, while Overlap resembles the ban on competitive bidding at issue in *Professional Engineers,* MIT alleges that Overlap enhances competition by broadening the socio-economic sphere of its potential student body. Thus, rather than suppress competition, Overlap may in fact merely regulate competition in order to enhance it, while also deriving certain social benefits. If the rule of reason analysis leads to this conclusion, then indeed Overlap will be beyond the scope of the prohibitions of the Sherman Act.

We note the unfortunate fact that financial aid resources are limited even at the Ivy League schools. A trade-off may need to be made between providing some financial aid to a large number of the most needy students or allowing the free market to bestow the limited financial aid on the very few most talented who may not need financial aid to attain their academic goals. Under such circumstances, if this trade-off is proven to be worthy in terms of obtaining a more diverse student body (or other legitimate institutional goals), the limitation on the choices of the most talented students might not be so egregious as to trigger the obvious concerns which led the Court to reject the "public interest" justifications in *Professional Engineers* and *Indiana Dentists.* However, we leave it for the district court to decide whether full funding of need may be continued on an individual institutional basis, absent Overlap, whether tuition could be lowered as a way to compete for qualified "needy" students, or whether there are other imaginable creative alternatives to implement MIT's professed social welfare goal.

We note too, however, that another aspect of the agreements condemned in *Professional Engineers* and *Indiana Dentists* was that those agreements embodied a strong economic self-interest of the parties to them....

The role that economic self-interest plays in evaluating affirmative defenses to a Sherman Act claim was made clear by the Court in *FTC v. Superior Court Trial Lawyers Ass'n,* 493 U.S. 411 (1990), where the Court condemned as *per se* illegal the trial lawyers' concerted refusal to accept further assignments to defend indigents until they receive an increase in compensation.... The Court distinguished *Claiborne Hardware,* where a boycott was aimed at promoting equal respect and equal treatment instead of naked economic self-interest. The justification based on the First Amendment rights as in *Claiborne Hardware* does not apply, the Court emphasized, to a boycott conducted by business competitors who "stand to profit financially from a lessening of competition in the boycotted market." *Trial Lawyers,* 493 U.S. at 427. In the case *sub judice,* the quest for economic self-interest is professed to be absent, as it is alleged that the Overlap agreement was intended, not to obtain an economic profit in the form of greater revenue for the participating schools, but rather to benefit talented but needy prospective students who otherwise could not attend the school of their choice.

The nature of higher education, and the asserted procompetitive and pro-consumer features of the Overlap, convince us that a full rule of reason analysis is in order here. It may be that institutions of higher education "require that a particular practice, which could properly be viewed as a violation of the Sherman Act in another context, be treated differently." *Goldfarb v. Virginia*, 421 U.S. 773, 788 n. 17....

It is most desirable that schools achieve equality of educational access and opportunity in order that more people enjoy the benefits of a worthy higher education. There is no doubt, too, that enhancing the quality of our educational system redounds to the general good. To the extent that higher education endeavors to foster vitality of the mind, to promote free exchange between bodies of thought and truths, and better communication among a broad spectrum of individuals, as well as prepares individuals for the intellectual demands of responsible citizenship, it is a common good that should be extended to as wide a range of individuals from as broad a range of socio-economic backgrounds as possible. It is with this in mind that the Overlap Agreement should be submitted to the rule of reason scrutiny under the Sherman Act.

We conclude that the district court was obliged to more fully investigate the procompetitive and noneconomic justifications proffered by MIT than it did when it performed the truncated rule of reason analysis. Accordingly, we will remand this case to the district court with instructions to evaluate Overlap using the full-scale rule of reason analysis outlined above.

The final step of the rule of reason involves determining whether the challenged agreement is necessary to achieve its purported goals. The district court alternatively rejected MIT's social welfare justifications because it "questioned" whether Overlap was necessary to achieve egalitarian educational access. Even if an anticompetitive restraint is intended to achieve a legitimate objective, the restraint only survives a rule of reason analysis if it is reasonably necessary to achieve the legitimate objectives proffered by the defendant. . . . To determine if a restraint is reasonably necessary, courts must examine first whether the restraint furthers the legitimate objectives, and then whether comparable benefits could be achieved through a substantially less restrictive alternative. Once a defendant demonstrates that its conduct promotes a legitimate goal, the plaintiff, in order to prevail, bears the burden of proving that there exists a viable less restrictive alternative. . . .

On remand if the district court, under a full scale rule of reason analysis, finds that MIT has proffered a persuasive justification for the Overlap Agreement, then the Antitrust Division of the Justice Department, the plaintiff in this case, must prove that a reasonable less restrictive alternative exists. The district court should consider, if and when the issue arises, whether the Antitrust Division has shown, by a preponderance of the evidence, that another viable option, perhaps the free market, can achieve the same benefits as Overlap. * * *

QUESTIONS AND COMMENTS

1. A 1993 settlement between MIT and the Justice Department ended the litigation. Under its terms (which tracked a 1991 consent decree settling the case with the Ivy League defendants), the schools were barred from meeting annually to fix tuition, faculty salaries, or aid. However, the schools were permitted to exchange data on principles of student aid. This settlement agreement was codified in § 568(d) of the Improving America's Schools Act (1994), extended to 2015 by Need–Based Educational Aid Act of 2008. Pub. L. No. 110–327 (2008).

2. Who was the biggest loser from the colleges' agreement not to compete on financial aid?

3. Do you agree with the court that promoting socioeconomic diversity is a procompetitive as well as social value? Is suppressing competition for financial aid to enable administrators to allocate it in their view of the public interest an antitrust value?

4. Comment on the court's treatment regarding absence of evidence of lower output and higher price, and the legal effect of this absence in raising plaintiffs' burden. Do you agree? If there is no reduction of output, i.e., no fewer college students admitted, is that because of inelasticity of demand? Does that mean that the plan gives MIT and its competitors power to raise the price (offer less of a discount) for their educational product?

Might competition for students on the basis of competitive financial aid packages help universities raise *more* money for financial aid? Is it possible that the social welfare interest is aligned with the competition interest?

5. Was *Professional Engineers* wrong? Should the rule of reason permit the claim that agreements with anticompetitive effects might be justified by important public interests? Some jurisdictions allow a gateway, more or less narrow, for such justifications. See European Union cases on the environment and labor, ELEANOR FOX, THE COMPETITION LAW OF THE EUROPEAN UNION 180–91 (2009). South Africa's antitrust law provides: A firm may apply to the Competition Commission to exempt an agreement ... that contributes to promotion of the ability of small businesses, or firms controlled or owned by historically disadvantaged persons, to become competitive.... § 10(1), (3), Competition Act (1998). The South African law requires the Tribunal to examine public interest considerations in mergers. Was the decision in *United States v. Brown University* hidden public policy? If courts are constrained by rigid rules they think wrong, will they find a way to soften the rules?

What would be the consequences of allowing a narrowly-tailored social welfare or public interest defense? Would the costs of such a defense to clarity, and thus the deterrent effect of the law, be greater or lesser than its benefits? Is a social welfare defense, much like a ruinous competition defense or a reasonableness-of-fixed-prices defense, "setting sail on the seas of doubt" of Judge Taft?

c. Real Estate Brokers' Multi–List Services and Restrictions on Web Discount Listings

Real estate brokers' multi-listing services have not infrequently met antitrust problems. In *United States v. Realty Multi–List*, 629 F.2d 1351 (5th Cir. 1980), the MLS rules denied membership to brokers who did not keep regular business hours or maintain a favorable credit report or business reputation. The court held the restrictions illegal because they were not narrowly tailored to serve a legitimate purpose of the multi-list and could be used to exclude competitors.

In the following case, the Federal Trade Commission challenged an MLS web policy of the National Association of Retailers. The policy prohibited members from distributing information on public real estate advertising websites about discount listings that consumers could search. With respect to these discount listings, only limited compensation would be paid to the broker if the homeowner should sell the property without further assistance.

REALCOMP II, LTD. v. FTC

635 F.3d 815 (6th Cir. 2011).

JUDGE MOORE:

* * *

The FTC as a party and the Commission in its decision below both assert that the Realcomp website policy is "inherently suspect" and therefore subject to an abbreviated or quick-look review. Because the Commission found that the website policy was inherently suspect, the Commission concluded that anticompetitive effects could be inferred without proof of Realcomp's market power or a demonstration of actual adverse impact. But, notwithstanding its initial quick-look analysis, the Commission alternatively invalidated the challenged restraints under a more searching inquiry, which included an assessment of Realcomp's market power and the actual, as well as likely, anticompetitive effects of its policies. Realcomp objects that the website policy should not be treated as inherently suspect, and that under any test, the website policy is not an unreasonable restraint of trade.

We uphold the Commission on the basis of the more extended rule-of-reason analysis without reaching the question of whether to apply quick-look analysis. "The object" in determining whether to apply an abbreviated quick-look analysis "is to see whether the experience of the market has been so clear, or necessarily will be, that a confident conclusion about the principal tendency of a restriction will follow from a quick (or at least quicker) look, in place of a more sedulous one." *Cal. Dental Assn,* 526 U.S. at 781. Courts have found potential antitrust violations when MLS [Multi Listing Services] rules deny MLS membership to some brokers ... and when dealers have excluded discount brokers altogether from a venue.... Here, in comparison, the challenged restraint is an internal rule within an MLS regarding its distribution of certain types of real-estate listings to the public. We need not and do not decide whether this policy is sufficiently analogous to practices already deemed by courts to be anticompetitive for it to qualify as a facially anticompetitive restraint....

Rule of Reason

Applying the rule of reason, we first look to see "whether [the] FTC has demonstrated 'actual detrimental effects' or 'the potential for genuine adverse effects on competition.'" *In re Detroit Auto Dealers Assn,* 955 F.2d at 469 (quoting *Ind. Fedn,* 476 U.S. at 460.) Market power and the anticompetitive nature of the restraint are sufficient to show the potential for anticompetitive effects under a rule-of-reason analysis, and once this showing has been made, Realcomp must offer procompetitive justifications. Realcomp contends that, to the contrary, "the requirement for proof of market power can be obviated by evidence of actual anticompetitive effects, not the other way around," and so Realcomp urges that actual anticompetitive effects must be proven....

* * *

. . . Similarly to *Indiana Federal of Dentists*, the website policy is alleged to be an "effort to withhold (or make more costly) information desired by consumers" that would result in "the purchase of higher priced [brokerage] services, than would occur in its absence." Thus, we next assess whether Realcomp's website policy resulted in " 'actual detrimental effects' or 'the *potential* for genuine adverse effects on competition.' " . . . Under either inquiry, substantial evidence supports the Commission's findings.

1. Potential Adverse Effects

a. Market Power

The Commission adopted the ALJ's findings that Realcomp possessed substantial market power in the relevant markets, and Realcomp does not dispute those findings. The ALJ defined the relevant product market as real-estate-brokerage services and found that, for most home sellers and buyers, no reasonable substitutes for such services exist because of the significant advantages of using a real-estate broker to sell a home. Because of the local nature of real-estate markets, the ALJ found that counties in southeastern Michigan define the geographic scope of competition for real-estate-brokerage services. Because of the lack of substitutes for brokerage services, the ALJ found that a broker monopolist could profitably increase commissions significantly above competitive levels.

Defining the relevant input market as the supply of multiple listing services to real-estate brokers, the ALJ found that an MLS like Realcomp exhibits network effects, meaning that the value of the MLS increases as the number of other users of the service increases. The value of an MLS to home sellers (or their representatives) increases with the number of home buyers (or their representatives) using the site, and, similarly, the value to home buyers increases as more home sellers list their properties on the MLS. "Brokers without full access to an MLS would . . . be at a significant competitive disadvantage," "listing services with fewer users are not economically viable substitutes," and barriers to entry make it "improbable" for a rival MLS successfully to enter the market. . . . Because the value of an MLS depends on the number of users, the ALJ observed that "market share is a good indicator of market power," and found that Realcomp possessed a large market share in each relevant county. In light of Realcomp MLS's market share, network effects, and barriers to entry, the ALJ concluded that Realcomp possessed substantial market power in the relevant markets.

Adopting these findings, the Commission agreed that "Realcomp possessed substantial market power in two relevant markets in Southeastern Michigan: the market for residential real estate brokerage services and the market for multiple listing services, which is a vital input into the brokerage services market." Given the extensive and undisputed market analysis undertaken by the ALJ and adopted by the Commission, substantial evidence supports the Commission's findings that Realcomp possessed substantial market power.

b. Anticompetitive Nature

Because Realcomp possesses substantial market power, we next evaluate the anticompetitive tendencies of the Realcomp website policy. Realcomp does not regulate rates of commission, offers of compensation, or other price terms; thus, we examine the effect of Realcomp's restrictions on consumer choice, specifically, the reduction in competitive brokerage options available to home sellers. The relevant output to be measured, therefore, is the share of non-ERTS [Exclusive Right to Sell] listings in the Realcomp MLS, the exposure of these listings to consumers, and the relationship of these outcomes to the Realcomp website policy.

In establishing that Realcomp's policies narrow consumer choice and hinder the competitive process, the Commission made the following relevant findings:

> (1) because of its database of listings, the Realcomp MLS is the most effective tool for the sale of residential real estate in Southeastern Michigan; (2) brokers offering limited service and brokers offering traditional, full-service brokers' services compete with one another for new listings; (3) limited service brokers' services potentially cost less than the services of brokers offering only full-service listings (they not only unbundle the services offered but also unbundle the commission structure); (4) limited service brokers' listings consequently exert 'price pressure' on full-service brokers' listings; (5) Realcomp's Website Policy, coupled with its Minimum Service Requirement, severely restricted consumers' access to limited service listings because, as a result of those policies, the listings were not available on the most popular websites.

These findings are supported by the evidence before the ALJ and the Commission that the website policy created barriers to the dissemination of discount listings to public websites—the entry point for many consumers in their online real-estate searches. This evidence showed that EA listings can be posted on some public websites, despite Realcomp's policies, but only by dual-listing with another MLS that does not impose similar restrictions. Moreover, such dual-listing raises costs for offering and advertising such discount services, and limited-service brokers testified that Realcomp's policies placed them at a competitive disadvantage. In addition, two of the top four public websites used by consumers in the relevant market can be accessed only through the Realcomp MLS; therefore, due to the website policy, EA [Exclusive Agency] listings cannot be placed on these websites. Consumers using these websites are not informed that the websites display only ERTS listings. Realcomp's website policy thus limited access to internet marketing and imposed additional costs on the marketing of discount listings.

Furthermore, the ALJ and Commission both found that limited-service listings exert price pressure on the full-service brokerage model; and brokers testified that discounted online and limited-service models have led to customers asking agents to reduce their commissions. Evidence that the website policy limited exposure of discount listings thus reveals "a concerted refusal to deal with [EA listings] on substantially equal terms" and establishes that the website policy is likely to protect its full-service brokers from competitive pricing pressure.... Combining these findings with Realcomp's substantial market power, the Commission reasonably concluded that Realcomp's website policy is likely to be anti-competitive.

The ALJ observed that the Realcomp MLS alone reached about 80% of home buyers, and brokers could place EA listings on Realtor.com and reach approximately 90% of home buyers. The ALJ concluded that, consequently, the website policy prevented EA listings from reaching "only a relatively small additional percentage of home buyers"—the 10% who perused home listings on the inaccessible websites. To the contrary, however, by reducing by 10% the number of home buyers that are exposed to discount listings, the website policy may very well constitute an unreasonable restraint. Restricting the online dissemination of home listings is especially pernicious because of the emerging competitive impact of the internet and of discounted brokerage services on the residential real-estate market. As the D.C. Circuit observed, "the exclusion of nascent threats is the type of conduct that is reasonably capable of contributing significantly to a defendant's continued monopoly power." *United States v. Microsoft Corp.*, 253 F.3d 34, 79 (D.C.Cir.2001). The D.C. Circuit was analyzing a monopolization claim under Section 2 of the Sherman Act, rather than a horizontal restraint under Section 1. Substantial evidence shows, though, that "the exclusion of nascent threats" such as discount brokerage services and consumer access to online listings "is reasonably capable of contributing significantly" to anticompetitive effects.

... [C]ourts have found potential antitrust violations when MLS rules deny MLS membership to some brokers, *see, e.g., Realty Multi–List, Inc.*, 629 F.2d at 1388–89, and when dealers have excluded discount brokers altogether from a venue, *see, e.g., Dennys Marina, Inc.*, 8 F.3d at 1220–22. At issue here is a different sort of restriction than membership exclusion—internal rules within an MLS regarding its distribution of certain types of real-estate listings to the public. There is no rule of complete exclusion from the MLS, and evidence shows that brokers are allowed to and do place limited-service listings on the Realcomp MLS.

Nonetheless, similar to excluding discount brokers from the MLS altogether, the website policy limits exposure of discount listings. "[L]istings [are] not ... distributed as widely as possible" due to the website policy, "resulting in inefficient sales prices," which is the same kind of economic harm caused by MLS exclusions....

It is undisputed that the website policy restricted the public dissemination of Realcomp real-estate listings tending to offer consumers limited-brokerage services at reduced costs. The Commission concluded that "[the] finding of market power, coupled with [the] ... determination that the tendency of the challenged policies was to suppress competition, provide 'indirect' evidence that those policies have or likely will have anticompetitive effects." Evaluating the website policy, the ALJ also notably found that "the nature of the restraint is such that it is likely to be anticompetitive." Given the significance of the Realcomp MLS to the advertising of real-estate listings, and given the role of the internet in providing consumers with the ability to self-provide certain real-estate services, substantial evidence supports the Commission's conclusion that Realcomp's website policy is likely to have an adverse impact on competition by restricting consumer access to discount listings.

2. Actual Adverse Effects

The Commission also examined direct evidence of competitive effects and concluded that Realcomp's policies adversely affected competition. We conclude that the Commission's findings of actual adverse effects are supported by "relevant evidence that a reasonable mind might accept as adequate to support [its] conclusion." *In re Detroit Auto Dealers Assn,* 955 F.2d at 469. Evidence ... demonstrates that the website policy in fact limited access to internet marketing and imposed financial and administrative costs on brokers seeking to dual-list with other MLSs. Three quantitative analyses conducted by the Commission's economic expert, Dr. Darrell Williams, corroborated other record evidence showing substantial consumer harm—specifically, a reduction of the share of discount listings in the southeastern Michigan real-estate market.

* * *

Dr. Williams's time-series, benchmark, and statistical-regression analyses thus provide substantial evidence in support of the Commission's findings of anticompetitive effects. And, even if the evidence of actual effects is inconclusive, the Commission also demonstrated the adverse potential of Realcomp's website policy by establishing Realcomp's market power and the anticompetitive tendencies of the website policy.

3. Procompetitive Justifications

Realcomp might still prevail, despite evidence of actual or likely anticompetitive effects, by demonstrating "some countervailing procompetitive virtue—such as, for example, the creation of efficiencies in the operation of a market or the provision of goods and services." *Ind. Fedn,* 476 U.S. at 459. Giving "some deference" to the Commission's conclusion, *In re Detroit Auto Dealers,* 955 F.2d at 469, we conclude that the Commission properly rejected Realcomp's proffered justifications as not "legitimate, plausible, substantial and reasonable."

The ALJ concluded that, without the website restrictions, home sellers with EA agreements "would free ride on the Realcomp members who invest and participate in the MLS through the payment of dues and who otherwise undertake to support the cooperative endeavor of the MLS." However, as the Commission found, the circumstances of this case do not establish free-riding. EA home sellers making use of the Realcomp MLS still must employ a listing broker who is a paying Realcomp member. Realcomp charges equal membership fees to all users. Therefore, Realcomp's services to EA home sellers are compensated through payments of the EA seller to her listing broker, who in turn pays Realcomp for the benefit of participation in the MLS.

Realcomp also erroneously argues that the EA home seller free-rides specifically on Realcomp cooperating agents because the EA home seller may act as her own cooperating broker. By not employing a cooperating broker, the argument goes, the EA home seller compensates Realcomp only through her payment to the listing broker, which does not cover all of Realcomp's costs. These costs are shared by cooperating brokers who pay dues to Realcomp in order to benefit from the business generated by the MLS. Thus, Realcomp asserts, cooperating brokers "subsidize the cost that property owners would otherwise incur to procure buyers who do not use cooperating brokers."

Cooperating brokers are compensated, however, for whatever services they do provide to the EA home seller, and the EA home seller receives no free services. If an EA home seller does choose to transact with a cooperating buyer, which the EA home seller does in 80% of EA listing transactions, compensation is provided for the cooperating broker by the terms of the EA listing contract, of which the cooperating broker is aware before the sale.

Moreover, the free-riding justification fails because a home seller may contract with an unrepresented buyer regardless of the type of listing contract, and under either EA or ERTS listing agreements, there is no compensation provided to cooperating brokers when the home seller chooses not to employ their services....

The website policy also purportedly eliminates a "bidding disadvantage" faced by a buyer represented by a cooperating broker when bidding against an unrepresented buyer in an EA transaction. But rather than enhance competition, such a policy insulates cooperating brokers' commissions from competitive pricing pressure. As the Commission found, the bidding-disadvantage justification "reinforces the conclusion that [the policies] have an anti-competitive effect" by deliberately protecting established commissions and preventing the reduction in the cost of selling a home. Even if there are financial incentives for a home seller to contract with an unrepresented buyer over a cooperating broker, Realcomp offers no meritorious procompetitive justification for protecting cooperating brokers from pressure to lower costs. And, as with the free-riding justification, Realcomp fails to demonstrate how EA listings give rise to a greater "bidding disadvantage" than do ERTS listings given that a listing broker in an ERTS agreement presumably prefers to retain the cooperating broker's commission for herself by transacting with an unrepresented buyer.

Conclusion

Under a full rule-of-reason analysis, we conclude that substantial evidence supports the Commission's findings that: 1) Realcomp's website policy gave rise to potential genuine adverse effects on competition due to Realcomp's substantial market power and the website policy's anticompetitive nature; 2) the website policy in fact caused actual anticompetitive effects; and 3) Realcomp's proffered procompetitive justifications were insufficient to overcome a prima facie case of adverse impact. These findings establish that Realcomp's website policy unreasonably restrained competition in the market for the provision of residential real-estate-brokerage services in southeastern Michigan and the Realcomp MLS area. . . .

QUESTIONS AND COMMENTS

1. What was Realcomp's best argument? Do you think the Supreme Court (in *Cal Dental*) would agree with the *Realcomp* court's analysis? Do you agree with it?

2. Thus concludes our study of loose knit agreements other than those involving intellectual property, to which we turn. Note, in all of these cases, how much the characterization and initial assessment of the restraint influences the apportionment of the burden of proof or production of evidence; and that who has the burden may heavily influence the outcome of the case.

4. INTELLECTUAL PROPERTY

a. Introduction

Antitrust issues frequently involve intellectual property. Intellectual property includes patents, copyrights, trademarks and trade secrets. Intellectual property protection normally involves the exclusive right to make use and sell or license the product or process. See Agency Intellectual Property Guidelines, Appendix G § 1. The term of a patent is 20 years from time of filing. If a patent is commensurate with a market (it often is not), the patent law grants a monopoly for those years, and patent law could be in tension with the policy of competition. But the very availability of patents and other IP protection is meant to inspire innovation, and the innovation and even the description of how to make or do it are meant to be disseminated widely when the protection expires. Therefore IP and antitrust are regarded as largely in harmony, working to achieve the same goals of promoting innovation and dynamic markets.

We have already seen, in the Monopoly chapter, that intellectual property rights are not absolute. Abusive exercises of intellectual property may be trumped by antitrust. But the antitrust analysis will, or usually will, take into account the question of how best to enhance innovation. You saw examples of this in the merger cases.

b. Licensing and Cross–Licensing of Intellectual Property; Pooling of Patents

Licensing and cross-licensing of intellectual property and pooling of patents are subject of immense current interest. They are largely a subject of specialized interest; but the extent to which antitrust law may reprehend uses (abuses?) of IP is obviously a subject of antitrust. For much of the last century, antitrust prohibitions in matters involving intellectual property were easily triggered. Beginning notably with 1995 guidelines, printed in Appendix G, the tide turned in favor of a more deferent view of protection of intellectual property rights as critical to fostering incentives to innovate. We begin this section with an excerpt from remarks introducing the 1995 guidelines and identifying some changes in appreciation from an earlier day; then, an excerpt from the guidelines' section on cross-licensing and pooling, and, finally, advice of the Department of Justice on IP and standard-setting.

i. Licensing: General Principles

Licensing of intellectual property covers a broad field. Normally, antitrust problems are not raised if the licensee is neither a competitor nor a potential competitor. When problems are raised, often it is because there is an underlying cartel (see Chapter 2), or the licensing conduct is a part of a strategy of monopolization. See Chapter 3; in particular, *Microsoft*, *Kodak*, and *CSU*.

Richard Gilbert, then Deputy Assistant Attorney General in the Antitrust Division of the Justice Department, made these still timely remarks upon the introduction of the 1995 guidelines:

THE 1995 ANTITRUST GUIDELINES FOR THE LICENSING OF INTELLECTUAL PROPERTY: NEW SIGNPOSTS FOR THE INTERSECTION OF INTELLECTUAL PROPERTY AND THE ANTITRUST LAWS

April 6, 1995

* * *

The new Guidelines share the core principles expressed in [earlier (1988) international guidelines]. These include the generally procompetitive nature of licensing arrangements, the absence of a presumption that intellectual property necessarily creates market power in the antitrust context, and the validity of applying the same general antitrust approach to the analysis of conduct involving intellectual property that the Agencies apply to conduct involving other forms of tangible or intangible property.

These three core principles provide a foundation for the policy statements in the Guidelines. Because licensing often has significant efficiency benefits (for example, by facilitating the integration of the licensed property with complementary factors of production), antitrust concerns that may arise in licensing arrangements normally will be evaluated under the rule of reason. The absence of a presumption that intellectual property necessarily creates market power implies that an antitrust evaluation of licensing restraints such as tying arrangements normally will require investigation of market circumstances to establish anticompetitive effects. The principles that the Agencies will apply the same general antitrust approach to intellectual property does not mean that intellectual property is the same as other forms of property. There are important differences, but the antitrust laws are sufficiently flexible to take these differences into account and should not impose greater or lesser scrutiny for intellectual property than for other forms of property.

Key changes from the 1988 Guidelines

... The new Guidelines include a safe harbor for licensing transactions. "Absent extraordinary circumstances, the Agencies will not challenge a restraint in a licensing arrangement if (1) the restraint is not facially anticompetitive and (2) the licensor and its licensees collectively account for no more than twenty percent of each relevant market significantly affected by the restraint." Facially anticompetitive restraints include those that would normally warrant per se treatment under the antitrust laws, such as price fixing and market division, and also agreements not to compete in terms of price or output that the Supreme Court said could be condemned as anticompetitive without an elaborate inquiry into market circumstances.

The new Intellectual Property Guidelines include a section on analysis of competitive effects in research and development and on the use of innovation markets to address such effects.... The discussion of innovation markets in the 1995 Intellectual Property Guidelines ... is a refinement of a concept already familiar in antitrust analysis.

Using an innovation market to analyze competitive effects is appropriate if the competitive effects of an arrangement cannot be adequately analyzed in conventional product markets. This threshold condition also applies to the use of technology markets. The 1995 Intellectual Property Guidelines state that "[T]he competitive effects of licensing arrangements often can be adequately assessed within the relevant markets for the goods affected by the arrangements. In such instances, the Agencies will delineate and analyze only goods markets. In other cases, however, the analysis may require the delineation of markets for technology or markets for research and development (innovation markets)."

An innovation market can be useful to identify competitive effects that cannot be adequately analyzed in markets for goods and services when the arrangement may affect the quantities, availabilities or prices of products that do not presently exist, as in a research and development joint venture. Innovation markets also may be useful when an arrangement has competitive effects from research and development in geographic markets where product market competition is limited or non-existent. That situation occurred in the proposed acquisition of the Allison Division of General Motors by ZF Friedrichshafen. General Motors and ZF compete in Europe in the supply of automatic transmissions for large trucks and buses and in some but not all relevant product markets in the U.S. The acquisition would have likely affected the development of new transmissions worldwide. In particular, the acquisition would have affected the development of new transmission models for sale in the U.S. by both General Motors and ZF, even if they are neither actual or likely potential competitors in the relevant product markets. The Department of Justice challenged the acquisition, alleging likely adverse effects on competition in the product markets in which General Motors and ZF compete in the U.S., and also in a worldwide innovation market for the design and development of new and improved heavy-duty transmissions for trucks and buses.

When does a licensing arrangement warrant antitrust scrutiny?

The 1995 Intellectual Property Guidelines differ from the 1988 Guidelines for International Operations in their approach to identifying when a licensing arrangement may warrant antitrust scrutiny. The 1988 Guidelines focused on the scope of the intellectual property right and stated that "[T]he owner of intellectual property is entitled to enjoy whatever market power the property itself may confer." The 1988 Guidelines did not provide clear signposts to distinguish market power that is conferred by the intellectual property from market power that is not. As former Assistant Attorney General William Baxter once said, intellectual property may confer the power to license under the condition that the licensee eliminate the licensor's mother-in-law, but that does not cause such power to be [il]legal.

In place of the condition that "[T]he owner of intellectual property is entitled to enjoy whatever market power the property itself may confer," the 1995 Intellectual Property Guidelines state the principle that "antitrust concerns may arise when a licensing arrangement harms competition among entities that would have been actual or likely potential competitors in a relevant market in the absence of the license." This principle is offered as a way to identify when antitrust concerns may arise in a licensing arrangement. It should not be interpreted as a "baseline" against which to measure the economic effects of a licensing arrangement. Specifically, it does not mean that in assessing the legality of a licensing arrangement, the antitrust authorities will compare the benefits of the licensing arrangement to a hypothetical baseline in which the intellectual property is not licensed at all.

If entities affected by a licensing arrangement would not have been actual or likely potential competitors in a relevant market in the absence of the license, the arrangement generally cannot result in harm to the economy and therefore should not be considered to have an adverse effect on competition. This is so even if an alternative licensing arrangement could have created more competition. The principle of "harm to competition among entities that would have been actual or likely potential competitors in a relevant market in the absence of the license" parallels the Agencies' approach to the evaluation of a joint venture. If the parties to a joint venture would not have been competitors in the absence of the joint venture, it is unlikely that the joint venture could adversely affect competition among those parties, although it is conceivable that collateral restraints could harm competition with others who are horizontal competitors to one of the parties, or in other markets.

As an example, suppose a manufacturer of jet engines and a firm that develops advanced composite materials enter into a joint venture to produce a new type of turbine blade. The joint venture could include a cross-licensing arrangement in which the parties agree to exchange rights to relevant intellectual property with the objective of developing the new product. In this hypothetical, the parties to the joint venture are not competitors in any relevant market. Normally, the antitrust authorities would not scrutinize the specific arrangement between the parties to this joint venture, because it does not harm competition that would have existed in its absence. For example, the antitrust authorities normally would not be concerned about the particular structure of the joint venture, such as the number of jet engine facilities in which the composite materials may be used.

Concerns about possible adverse impacts on competition may arise if the joint venture included restraints that harmed competition with rivals who are not parties to the joint venture or that harmed competition in other markets. A plausible example of such a restraint is a requirement that the suppliers of composite materials to the joint venture refrain from supplying similar materials to competing jet engine manufacturers. The Agencies likely would examine such a restraint to determine whether it is likely to have an anticompetitive effect and, if so, would assess whether it is reasonably necessary to achieve the benefits of the joint venture. * * *

. . . [T]he 1995 Intellectual Property Guidelines affirm that the Agencies' approach to technology licensing arrangements is, in most cases, a standard application of the rule of reason. Section 3.4 of the Guidelines state that "[T]he Agencies general approach in analyzing a licensing restraint under the rule of reason is to inquire whether the restraint is likely to have anticompetitive effects and, if so, whether the restraint is reasonably necessary to achieve procompetitive benefits that outweigh those anticompetitive effects." (p. 16) In making this assessment, the Agencies will not engage in a search for a theoretically least restrictive alternative that is not realistic in the practical prospective business situation faced by the parties. As in the Agencies' approach to the evaluation of a joint venture, if a proposed licensing arrangement includes restraints that have adverse effects on competition that would have occurred in the absence of the license, the Agencies would evaluate whether those restraints are reasonably necessary to achieve the procompetitive benefits of the arrangement. If not, the Agencies would be likely to challenge such restraints. If they are reasonably necessary, the Agencies would inquire whether the procompetitive benefits of the arrangement outweigh any harm to competition. * * *

The 1995 Intellectual Property Guidelines include a ... statement of the likely absence of anticompetitive effects from non-exclusive licensing arrangements. They recognize that non-exclusive licenses of intellectual property that do not contain any restraints on the competitive conduct of the licensor or the licensee generally do not present antitrust concerns even if the parties to the license are in a horizontal arrangement. In such a non-exclusive license, each party to the arrangement is free to compete using the licensed intellectual property and therefore the non-exclusive license normally does not diminish competition that would occur in its absence. Note, however, that agreements to cross-license technology prospectively (even if non-exclusive) may reduce incentives to develop a new technology because each party to the agreement can free ride on the accomplishments of others. Moreover, certain types of cross-licensing arrangements, even if non-exclusive, may reduce competition that would occur in the absence of the arrangement, for example by levying royalties that increase rivals' costs or by promoting price coordination.

The Intellectual Property Guidelines recognize that a grantback provision in an intellectual property license may have procompetitive effects by promoting the dissemination of new technology, sharing risks, and rewarding the licensor for making possible further innovation based on or informed by the licensed technology, and may be necessary to ensure that the licensor is not prevented from effectively competing because it is denied access to improvements developed with the aid of its own technology. Grantback provisions in licensing arrangements may have anticompetitive effects on total industry innovative effort, however, by reducing incentives to engage in research and development. The new Guidelines note that compared with an exclusive grantback, a non-exclusive grantback, which leaves the licensee free to license improvements technology to others, is less likely to have anticompetitive effects. * * *

ii. Cross Licensing and Pooling

At mid twentieth century, patent pooling was often used as a pejorative term. It connoted cartelizing in the guise of eliminating the blocking effect of patents, such as in United States v. National Lead Co., 63 F. Supp. 513 (S.D.N.Y. 1945), modified and aff'd, 332 U.S. 319 (1947).

Today it is well recognized that patent pooling may be a way for inventors and producers to use common standards that serve consumers, e.g., standard DVD technology. The U.S. antitrust agencies have given this advice:

ANTITRUST GUIDELINES FOR THE LICENSING OF INTELLECTUAL PROPERTY

Department of Justice and Federal Trade Commission, April 1995.

5.5 Cross–Licensing and Pooling Arrangements

Cross-licensing and pooling arrangements are agreements of two or more owners of different items of intellectual property to license one another or third parties. These arrangements may provide procompetitive benefits by integrating complementary technologies, reducing transaction costs, clearing blocking positions, and avoiding costly infringement litigation. By promoting the dissemination of technology, cross-licensing and pooling arrangements are often procompetitive.

Cross-licensing and pooling arrangements can have anticompetitive effects in certain circumstances. For example, collective price or output restraints in pooling arrangements, such as the joint marketing of pooled intellectual property rights with collective price setting or coordinated output restrictions, may be deemed unlawful if they do not contribute to an efficiency-enhancing integration of economic activity among the participants. Compare NCAA, 468 U.S. at 114 (output restriction on college football broadcasting held unlawful because it was not reasonably related to any purported justification) with Broadcast Music, 441 U.S. at 23 (blanket license for music copyrights found not per se illegal because the cooperative price was necessary to the creation of a new product). When cross-licensing or pooling arrangements are mechanisms to accomplish naked price fixing or market division, they are subject to challenge under the per se rule. . . .

Settlements involving the cross-licensing of intellectual property rights can be an efficient means to avoid litigation and, in general, courts favor such settlements. When such cross-licensing involves horizontal competitors, however, the Agencies will consider whether the effect of the settlement is to diminish competition among entities that would have been actual or likely potential competitors in a relevant market in the absence of the cross-license. In the absence of offsetting efficiencies, such settlements may be challenged as unlawful restraints of trade. . . .

Pooling arrangements generally need not be open to all who would like to join. However, exclusion from cross-licensing and pooling arrangements among parties that collectively possess market power may, under some circumstances, harm competition. . . . In general, exclusion from a pooling or cross-licensing arrangement among competing technologies is unlikely to have anticompetitive effects unless (1) excluded firms cannot effectively compete in the relevant market for the good incorporating the licensed technologies and (2) the pool participants collectively possess market power in the relevant market. If these circumstances exist, the Agencies will evaluate whether the arrangement's limitations on participation are reasonably related to the efficient development and exploitation of the pooled technologies and will assess the net effect of those limitations in the relevant market. . . .

Another possible anticompetitive effect of pooling arrangements may occur if the arrangement deters or discourages participants from engaging in research and development, thus retarding innovation. For example, a pooling arrangement that requires members to grant licenses to each other for current and future technology at minimal cost may reduce the incentives of its members to engage in research and development because members of the pool have to share their successful research and development and each of the members can free ride on the accomplishments of other pool members. . . . However, such an arrangement can have procompetitive benefits, for example, by exploiting economies of scale and integrating complementary capabilities of the pool members (including the clearing of blocking positions), and is likely to cause competitive problems only when the arrangement includes a large fraction of the potential research and development in an innovation market. . . .

---

c. Standard–Setting and FRAND Obligations: Avoiding Patent Ambush

Standard setting organizations sponsor the development of standards for performance and interoperability in a number of industries, notably Internet and computer technologies, electronics, and telecommunications. The standard they set may reflect market power; once the standard is set, competitors and consumers are normally locked in. Owners of technology necessary to practice the standard may try to capitalize on their advantage, demanding super-high royalties for a license. This is called "patent ambush"—a tactic of which the FTC accused Rambus in a famously unsuccessful monopolization suit against it. See Chapter 3, supra p. 304. To avoid the ambush problem, SSOs now generally require that their members disclose in advance all patents that may be infringed by the standard and agree to license their relevant technology on reasonable and non-discriminatory terms (RAND terms). To avoid opportunists' insisting on high royalty rates nonetheless, one group, VITA, devised FRAND: fair, reasonable and non-discriminatory terms. See *http://www.usdoj.gov/atr/public/busreview/219380.pdf*. Under FRAND, each member agrees to declare, in advance, the maximum royalty rates and the most restrictive other terms that it will require in licensing its technology to users of the standard.

Here are remarks of the then Deputy Assistant Attorney General.

ANTITRUST ENFORCEMENT AND STANDARD SETTING: THE VITA AND IEEE LETTERS AND THE IP2 REPORT*

Gerald F. Masoudi
Deputy Assistant Attorney General

May 10, 2007

I. Introduction

In October 2006, the Department of Justice (DOJ) issued a business review letter to the VMEbus International Trade Association (VITA), a standards development organization (SDO) that develops standards for certain computer bus architecture. On April 17, 2007, DOJ and the Federal Trade Commission (FTC) issued a joint report known as the "IP2" Report, covering six topics at the intersection of intellectual property law and antitrust, one of which is standard setting. And on April 30, 2007, DOJ issued a business review letter to the Institute of Electrical and Electronics Engineers, Inc. (IEEE), which develops a wide range of technology standards....

I will spend some time discussing each of these documents. My more important message, however, is a general one concerning the broader policy that underlies the letters, the report, and recent statements by officials in the Antitrust Division and the FTC. The message is that United States enforcers see antitrust and intellectual property as complementary forces, not forces in tension, and we support a high degree of licensing freedom. DOJ and the FTC are not in the business of endorsing particular approaches to intellectual property licensing; instead, in standard setting as in any other area, we leave the marketplace to pick winners and losers, and we intervene only where a practice imposes a restraint on competition *and* is likely to harm long-term efficiency and the competitive process itself. Businesses should be confident that antitrust enforcement will not stand in the way of competition related to intellectual property. Businesses also should know that if they are on the losing end of competition, a petition to the U.S. antitrust authorities will not save them.

II. The VITA and IEEE Business Review Letters

A. Background

Turning now to the two business review letters, it is necessary first to understand the DOJ business review process. The business review process begins when a firm submits a formal written request. DOJ opens an investigation and may research market conditions, conduct party interviews, and perform interviews of customers and competitors. Typically, however, DOJ relies heavily on the factual representations of the firm

* (footnotes omitted)

requesting the review, for three reasons: (1) conducting a full investigation is costly; (2) DOJ reviews only proposed conduct (not conduct that has already occurred), so many facts will be largely within the control of the requesting firm; and (3) any guidance issued will be valid only for the facts explained in the letter, so there is little incentive to withhold information—doing so could render the letter worthless. The process concludes when DOJ issues a letter stating that it has no intention to challenge the proposed conduct, that it does have an intention to challenge, or that it cannot make a decision based on the facts in the request or the conditions of the market. Information about DOJ's enforcement intentions is useful on its own merits and can also have value in persuading private litigants not to sue, or courts to be skeptical of claims, under the Sherman Act. Note, however, that due to the narrow format of the request and answer, this is not a vehicle for DOJ to endorse a particular practice as the best or only solution for an industry.

For purposes of antitrust analysis in standard setting, it is also helpful to understand patent hold up. Patent hold up can be defined to involve a situation where all the following conditions exist:

- after the standard is set, the holder of a patent essential to that standard identifies a patent, or attempts to impose licensing terms, that SDO members could not reasonably have anticipated;
- it is not a commercially reasonable option to abandon the standard and attempt to create an alternative, due to the cost of the standard setting process itself or the cost of developing products incorporating the alternative standard;
- and—most importantly—if the other SDO members *had* anticipated the patent holder's demands, those SDO members could have chosen a different technology that avoided this patent.

Thus, one of two results likely would have occurred if the SDO members had known of the patent and the patent holder's demands: the SDO (1) actually would have chosen the alternative technology, or (2) the patent holder might seek to induce SDO members to adopt its patented technology by offering a license with a competitive royalty rate. This definition is important because it makes clear that hold up involves the loss of the opportunity to pursue a meaningful competitive alternative. Hold up involves market power that is created by a standard itself, *not* market power that would have existed regardless of the standard. Hold up, as I use the term, does not exist merely because a group of licensors is upset that a patentee holds the key to an essential technology. Hold up certainly does not exist merely by the fact that a patentee charges a particular rate for its royalty when licensees would prefer to pay a lower rate.

B. The VITA Letter

VITA described its proposed policy as an effort to avoid hold up as I have defined it. The VITA policy contains a number of provisions, including these five:

- *Disclosure.* Each member of a standards working group must disclose all patents or patent applications that it knows about and that it believes may become essential to implementation of the future standard. Members must do this on three occasions: before a working group is formed to create a standard; within sixty days after the working group is formed; and within fifteen days after the draft standard is published. In addition, any member must disclose any previously undisclosed essential patents at any meeting, and must follow that disclosure with a formal declaration within thirty days.
- *Maximum terms.* Members must disclose maximum royalty rates, whether in terms of dollars or as a percentage of a device sale price, and also the most restrictive non-royalty terms they will demand for essential rights. The commitments are irrevocable; however, patent holders are free to submit subsequent declarations with lower rates and less restrictive terms.
- *Limited application.* These commitments apply to implementation of the VITA standard being developed, and any revisions to that standard, but they do not apply to any other uses of the technology.
- *No horizontal negotiations.* Working group members may consider the various declared licensing terms when deciding which technology to support for the standard, but cannot negotiate or discuss specific licensing terms among working group members or with third parties.
- *Arbitration and consequences.* The policy creates an arbitration procedure to resolve any disputes over members' compliance. There are a number of specified consequences for non-compliance, including that failure to disclose an essential patent will lead to that patent being licensed on a royalty-free basis within the standard.

In its response to the request from VITA, the Department of Justice concluded that this policy was not likely to harm competition. DOJ found that the policy should not lead to depression of the price for licenses through joint, anticompetitive actions because it prohibits any joint negotiation of licensing terms. Working group members do not set actual licensing terms: the patent holders propose their terms, balancing their interest in higher royalties against the possibility that too high a "price" ex ante would prevent their technology from being chosen for the standard because of competitive alternatives. Before or after the standard is set, the patent holder and each prospective licensee will negotiate separately, subject only to the maximum terms set forth in the patent holder's original, unilateral declaration. Any attempt to use this process as a sham to cover horizontal price fixing likely would result in antitrust liability, as an illegal agreement under Section 1 of the Sherman Act, but the restrictions put in place by VITA appear to promote efficiency if they are followed and enforced.

C. The IEEE Letter

The IEEE request differs from VITA's policy chiefly in that it gives patent holders more options. Under the IEEE proposal, if the chair of an IEEE standards working group believes that a patent holder has a patent that potentially will be essential to the proposed standard, the chair may ask the patent holder to disclose relevant patent rights and to provide IEEE a letter of assurance (LOA) about licensing terms. The patent holder then has five options:

- provide no assurance;
- state that it does not hold essential patents;
- commit not to assert its patents against implementers of the standard;
- commit to license on RAND terms; or
- commit to maximum price terms or most restrictive non-price terms.

The IEEE will then post the licensing assurances, or lack thereof, on its website. If a patent holder chooses the fifth option, the IEEE working groups may then use this information to assess the relative costs of alternative technologies. The explicit consideration of relative costs makes IEEE's policy somewhat different from VITA's. In addition, unlike VITA, IEEE has not created a consequences provision that could impose arbitration and royalty-free licenses. If a patent holder were to choose IEEE's fifth option and then fail to adhere to its assurances, any party that claims injury would be left to seek redress in a civil court action. IEEE has no obligation to become directly involved in enforcing the policy.

DOJ concluded that IEEE's policy offered potential benefits comparable to VITA's, and did not merit an enforcement challenge. DOJ stated:

The proposed IEEE policy ... could generate similar benefits as patent holders may compete to offer the most attractive combination of technology and licensing terms ... members may make better informed decisions by considering potential licensing fees when weighing the relative costs of technological alternatives in addition to their technological merits."

DOJ did not object to IEEE's desire to permit its members to consider the relative costs of alternative technologies. This strikes me as not particularly controversial. Former AAG Hew Pate said as early as 2005 that "[i]t would be a strange result if antitrust policy [were] used to prevent price competition," which perfectly encapsulates the issue. FTC Chairman Deborah Majoras has made similar statements. But note that, in essence, the IEEE policy permits its members to consider such costs only in generalized or non-collaborative ways. The policy "prohibits discussion of specific licensing terms within ... standards development meetings" and, based on statements by IEEE's counsel, DOJ understood that "this prohibition extends to joint negotiations of licensing terms within standards development meetings." IEEE did not request, and DOJ did not provide, "views on joint negotiations that might take place inside or outside such standards development meetings or IEEE sponsored meetings," but DOJ noted in a footnote that it would "typically apply a rule-of-reason analysis to joint negotiations of licensing terms in the standard setting context."

III. The IP2 Report and Standard Setting

The IP2 Report consists of six chapters devoted to particular IP-related practices, and states conclusions for each chapter. Briefly, those conclusions are:

- *Chapter 1:* Antitrust liability for mere unilateral, unconditional refusals to license patents will not play a meaningful part in the interface between patent rights and antitrust protections. Conditional refusals to license, however, can be subject to antitrust liability if they cause competitive harm.
- *Chapter 2:* Ex ante consideration of licensing terms by SDO participants is likely to be procompetitive. Such joint action might pose problems in some contexts but is most likely to be reasonable where adoption of a standard would create or enhance market power in a patent holder. Such joint negotiations, therefore, are likely to be analyzed under the rule of reason, not considered as per se violations (buyer price fixing) under the Sherman Act.
- *Chapter 3:* Combining complementary patents in cross licenses or patent pools is generally procompetitive. Combining substitute patents in a pool can raise concerns but is not presumptively anticompetitive. Cross licenses and patent pools, whatever their design, typically will be analyzed on a rule-of-reason basis, and the Agencies generally will not inquire into the reasonableness of royalties set as a result.
- *Chapter 4:* The flexible rule of reason approach set forth in the Agencies' 1995 *Antitrust–IP Guidelines* is fundamentally sound. The Agencies will continue to use it to assess the competitive effects of a range of licensing restraints, including non-assertion clauses, grantbacks, and reach-through royalty agreements.
- *Chapter 5:* Regarding IP-related bundling and tying, the *Antitrust–IP Guidelines* will continue to govern the Agencies' analysis, meaning that the Agencies will focus on seller market power, competitive effects in the tied product market, and efficiency justifications proffered in favor of the bundle or tie.
- *Chapter 6:* When licensing practices are alleged to extend a patent beyond its statutory term, the Agencies will apply standard antitrust analysis, including consideration of whether the patent confers market power, which generally will lead to analysis under the rule of reason. In particular, the Agencies recognize that it may be efficient to collect royalties—or perhaps more accurately, to collect

payments related to use of the formerly-patented invention—beyond the patent's term.

So from an SDO's perspective, the IP2 Report is an interesting addition to the VITA and IEEE business reviews. The report's Chapter 2 considers standard setting as a whole, rather than just the two specific VITA and IEEE proposals, and unlike those proposals it does consider the issue of joint license negotiations in depth. And the report as a whole places standards setting questions within a much larger, and instructive, context of intellectual property and antitrust policy. That larger context shows that antitrust analysis of SDO practices properly focuses not on the effects to individual competitors—or on the individual participants in a standard setting process, regardless of whether they are in a horizontal or vertical relationship—but on competition as a whole. That means focusing on three items in particular: market power, competitive effects, and dynamic efficiencies. . . .

IV. Observations About Antitrust and Standard Setting

I considered writing out a hypothetical regarding an SDO evaluating different approaches to a patent disclosure policy, so that I could walk you down the various branches of the decision tree and identify the antitrust inflection points. When I started to do this, however, I did not produce a tree—I produced a fractal. There are potentially infinite problems, solutions, and practical and legal questions facing SDOs. Sham or otherwise marginal cases aside, there is simply no way to make definitive statements about these issues without analyzing a specific SDO policy, on a case-by-case basis. But that is hardly a reason for despair. Case-by-case, effects-based analysis is familiar to all of us who practice U.S. antitrust law. In fact, the clearest message of the IP2 Report, like the *Antitrust–IP Guidelines* before it, is that intellectual property is not really a special antitrust case. Neither is standard setting.

Allow me to make some general observations. First, you will go a long way toward answering your antitrust questions if you focus on how a practice affects the exercise of market power, and in the SDO context it is particularly helpful to start by distinguishing market power created by a standard from market power, if any, that exists in the IP rights, independent of the standard. It might well be reasonable for SDO members, ex ante, to engage in joint licensing negotiations with the owners of several roughly equivalent patents, since no one invention would have market power ex ante and the SDO members may be attempting merely to prevent the creation of a patent blocking position that would not exist absent the SDO members' own standard-setting efforts. In contrast, if SDO members ex ante already know that a particular patent is essential, and their joint negotiations are just an attempt to drive down the price via a buyer-side agreement not to compete for this necessary input, we would need to ask more questions, such as whether the "buyers" have inappropriately created market power for use against the patent license "seller."

Second, harm to a particular faction does not necessarily equate to harm to competition. If a particular SDO's policy would reduce the royalties obtained by a particular patentee, that is not necessarily a violation of the antitrust laws. The antitrust laws may not be violated even if such an SDO policy reduces innovation incentives to that particular patentee; antitrust policy may ask broader questions, such as whether the combined innovation incentives of *all* patentees and SDO creators, or an economically significant number, will suffer. Similarly, harm to short-term efficiency does not necessarily equate to harm to competition. If a patentee and an SDO cannot agree about disclosure policies or royalty rates, and end up with competing standards backed by each camp, this may be costly to efficiency in the short run; however, if the credible threat to set up competing standards causes parties to bargain, innovate, or otherwise compete harder, long-term efficiency may benefit. There is always a temptation to focus on short-term, party-specific harm, since that is the easiest to measure, but the proper focus is on the competitive process and the long-term efficiency of standard setting. Measuring long-term efficiency is difficult but we need to remind ourselves constantly that this is the goal. * * *

I previously stated, and it bears repeating, that antitrust enforcers need to act with caution in the standard setting area. Antitrust has a role to play, but we need to bear in mind that where an unsound rule is proposed by a government enforcer, there is often no way to contract around it, and worse, there may be no way to conduct a natural experiment without the rule that can prove it should be abandoned. The standard setting community should continue to bring us its concerns whenever it believes a practice harms competition, and should particularly come to us if our position as neutral entities could lend special force to competition advocacy. The standards community should remember, however, that the first solution to any competitive problem is more and harder competition, and we will be reluctant to intervene against practices by either side to an SDO licensing discussion if those practices can be characterized merely as hard bargaining over terms and price.

QUESTIONS AND COMMENTS

1. What are the principal competitive fears about SDO standard-setting and FRAND obligations? That is, if competition may be hurt, how? What are the principal procompetitive benefits? As between the VITA and the IEEE programs, which poses more competitive concerns? Which offers more competitive benefits?

2. How would you characterize the DOJ's perspective on SDO standard-setting and FRAND obligations? (hospitable, hostile?)

d. Settlement of Infringement Actions Against First-Filing Generics

The Hatch–Waxman Act of 1984 provides an expedited process for approval by the Food and Drug Administration of generic versions of an approved branded drug. The generic firm may file a pre-expiration challenge ("ANDA IV"). The ANDA IV certificate constitutes an act of infringement of the patent, giving the branded manufacturer the right to sue. The first generic to file an ANDA IV gets a 180–day exclusive right to market a generic version of the drug.

A practice has developed wherein the patent holder sues the generic ANDA–IV filer for infringement; the parties settle the suit with an agreement of the patent holder to pay the generic a huge sum—usually hundreds of millions of dollars—and the generic agrees not to sell its product for a period usually up to the expiration date of the patent. This is called "reverse payment." One would usually expect a payment running in the other direction. If the patent were found valid and infringed, the infringer would normally pay the patentee damages (although here, no damages would yet have been incurred). If the patent were found invalid or otherwise not infringed, the generic would owe nothing and would enter the market or would continue selling. But why would the patentee pay the generic—and why would it agree to pay millions of dollars? The Federal Trade Commission, by its Chairman Jon Liebowitz, has called the settlements sweetheart deals to "game" Hatch–Waxman. The generic company makes more profits from pay-to-delay agreements than if it had entered the market. The patent holder gets protection from all generic competition up to the end of the patent term even if its patent is vulnerable. The FTC calculates that reverse-payment settlements cost American consumers $3.5 billion a year. FTC Press Release, June 23, 2009, *http://www.ftc.gov/opa/2009/06/capspeech.shtm*. (Generic drugs sell at only a fraction of the price of branded drugs.) The European Commission's Competition Directorate made a similar calculation regarding the costs of reverse payment settlements in Europe even without a Hatch–Waxman Act. See *http://ec.europa.eu/competition/sectors/pharmaceuticals/inquiry/comm unication_en.pdf*.

However, the FTC has not fared well in the courts on its challenges to the reverse-payment settlements. Here are excerpts from the case commonly known as "*Cipro*."

ARKANSAS CARPENTERS HEALTH AND WELFARE FUND v. BAYER AG (CIPRO III)

604 F.3d 98 (2d Cir. 2010), rehearing en banc denied, 625 F.3d 779 (2d Cir. 2010), 131 S.Ct. 1606 (2011).

PER CURIAM

* * *

In 2000, direct and indirect purchasers of Cipro filed over thirty antitrust lawsuits against Bayer under federal and state law. These cases were consolidated by the Multi–District Litigation Panel in the Eastern District of New York. ("*Cipro I*"). Plaintiffs allege that defendants' settlement [for more than $50 million] exceeded the scope of Bayer's patent rights because Bayer effectively paid its potential competitors hundreds of millions of dollars not to challenge its patent. Plaintiffs also allege that the agreements were unlawful because Barr was permitted to reclaim the 180–day market exclusivity period if a subsequent challenger was successful in having the patent invalidated, and because the generic manufacturers agreed not to file any ANDA–IV certifications for products that relate to Cipro. But for the challenged agreements, plaintiffs assert that (1) Barr would have entered the market pending resolution of the patent litigation; (2) Barr would have prevailed in the litigation and entered the market; or (3) Bayer would have granted Barr a license to market a generic version of Cipro to avoid a trial on the patent's validity. On cross-motions for summary judgment, the district court granted summary judgment for the defendants. *In re Ciprofloxacin Hydrochloride Antitrust Litig.*, 363 F.Supp.2d 514, 548 (E.D.N.Y.2005) ("*Cipro III*"). The court stated:

> The ultimate question—and this is the crux of the matter—is not whether Bayer and Barr had the power to adversely affect competition for ciprofloxacin as a whole, but whether any adverse effects on competition stemming from the Agreements were outside the exclusionary zone of the § 444 Patent. It goes without saying that patents have adverse effects on competition. However, any adverse effects within the scope of a patent cannot be redressed by antitrust law.

Id. at 523–24. In eschewing a "*post hoc* determination of the potential validity of the underlying patent," the court reasoned that "such an approach would undermine the presumption of validity of patents in all cases, as it could not logically be limited to drug patents, and would work a revolution in patent law." *Id.* at 529. . . .

. . . The court summarized as follows:

> [I]n the absence of any evidence that the Agreements created a bottleneck on challenges to the § 444 Patent, or that they otherwise restrained competition beyond the scope of the claims of the § 444

> Patent, the Agreements have not had any anti-competitive effects on the market for ciprofloxacin beyond that which are permitted under the § 444 Patent. The fact that Bayer paid what in absolute numbers is a handsome sum to Barr to settle its lawsuit does not necessarily reflect a lack of confidence in the § 444 Patent, but rather the economic realities of what was at risk. There is simply no precedent for plaintiffs' argument that the parties to a settlement are required to preserve the public's interest in lower prices. Such a rule would only result in parties being less likely to reach settlements, aside from undermining well-settled principles of patent law. Finally, to even attempt to quantify the public's interest in a patent settlement between private parties would require devaluing patents across the board, a result that would contravene the presumption of validity afforded by Congress and impact the very way patent licenses are handled in countless daily transactions.

Cipro III, 363 F.Supp.2d at 540–41.

Plaintiffs timely appealed.... * * *

Reverse Exclusionary Payment Settlements, Antitrust Law, and *Tamoxifen*

Plaintiffs argue that when Bayer paid Barr to withdraw its challenge to the Cipro patent, defendants effectively entered into a market-sharing agreement in restraint of trade. Patent settlements, like all private contracts, are subject to antitrust scrutiny. *Cf. Standard Oil Co. v. United States,* 283 U.S. 163, 169 (1931) ("The limited monopolies granted to patent owners do not exempt them from the prohibitions of the Sherman Act...."); (the Sherman Act prevents patentees from obtaining a greater monopoly than was inherent in the relevant patent grant). Thus, like ordinary contracts, patent settlements cannot take the form of "market-sharing agreements." *See Palmer v. BRG of Georgia, Inc.*, 498 U.S. 46, 49 (1990) (per curiam) (market-sharing agreement is unlawful on its face)....

The question, therefore, is whether patent settlements in which the generic firm agrees to delay entry into the market in exchange for payment fall within the scope of the patent holder's property rights, or whether such settlements are properly characterized as illegal market-sharing agreements. Authorities are divided on this question. The Federal Trade Commission ("FTC"), the U.S. antitrust enforcement agency charged with supervising the pharmaceutical industry, has long insisted that reverse exclusionary payment settlements violate antitrust law and has challenged numerous agreements as unreasonable restraints of trade. Although it initially took a different view, the United States has since maintained that reverse exclusionary payment settlements may violate antitrust laws.... Many academic commentators share the United States's view.

Most courts, by contrast, including this Court, *Joblove v. Barr Labs. Inc, (In re Tamoxifen Citrate Antitrust Litig.),* 466 F.3d 187, 216 (2d Cir.2006) ("*Tamoxifen*"), have held that the right to enter into reverse exclusionary payment agreements falls within the terms of the exclusionary grant conferred by the branded manufacturer's patent. *See In re Ciprofloxacin Antitrust Litig.,* 544 F.3d at 1333; *Schering–Plough Corp. v. FTC,* 402 F.3d 1056, 1076 (11th Cir.2005). *But see La. Wholesale Drug Co. v. Hoechst Marion Roussel, Inc. (In re Cardizem CD Antitrust Litig.),* 332 F.3d 896, 908 (6th Cir.2003) (holding such agreements to be per se illegal); *In re Terazosin Hydrochloride Antitrust Litig.,* 352 F.Supp.2d 1279 (S.D.Fla.2005) (same).

Particularly relevant here is this Court's decision in *Tamoxifen*. The plaintiffs in *Tamoxifen* challenged a reverse exclusionary payment settlement between Zeneca and Barr that the parties entered into after a district court had declared Zeneca's patent invalid. At the 12(b)(6) stage, *Tamoxifen* rejected as speculative plaintiffs' allegation that Barr would have prevailed on appeal but for the settlement agreement. *Id.* at 203–04. Assuming the truth of plaintiffs' allegation that the exclusion payments exceeded the profits Barr would have obtained upon entering the market as a generic competitor, the *Tamoxifen* court determined that the plaintiffs had no antitrust claim because a patent holder is entitled to protect its "lawful monopoly over the manufacture and distribution of the patented product." *Id.* at 205, 208–09.

Notably, *Tamoxifen* expressly adopted aspects of the lower court's summary judgment decision in this case, holding:

> Unless and until the patent is shown to have been procured by fraud, or a suit for its enforcement is shown to be objectively baseless, there is no injury to the market cognizable under existing antitrust law, as long as competition is restrained only within the scope of the patent.

Id. at 213.... The *Tamoxifen* court ruled that the settlement agreement did not exceed the scope of the patent where (1) there was no restriction on marketing non-infringing products; (2) a generic version of the branded drug would necessarily infringe the branded firm's patent; and (3) the agreement did not bar other generic manufacturers from challenging the patent.

Since *Tamoxifen* rejected antitrust challenges to reverse payments as a matter of law, we are bound to review the *Cipro* court's rulings under the standard adopted in *Tamoxifen*. ... Plaintiffs do not argue that the patent infringement lawsuit was a sham or that the Cipro patent was procured by fraud. Thus, the only reasonable basis for distinguishing *Tamoxifen* would be if plaintiffs demonstrated that the settlement agreement here, unlike in *Tamoxifen,* exceeded the scope of the Cipro patent. Plaintiffs cannot establish this because a generic version of Cipro would necessarily infringe Bayer's patent.... * * *

... As defendants note, this panel is bound by *Tamoxifen* "absent a change in law by higher authority or by way of an in banc proceeding."

... However, there are several reasons why this case might be appropriate for reexamination by our full Court.

First, the United States has itself urged us to repudiate *Tamoxifen,* arguing that *Tamoxifen* adopted an improper standard that fails to subject reverse exclusionary payment settlements to appropriate antitrust scrutiny.... In the pending case, the United States argues:

> This Court's *Tamoxifen* standard inappropriately permits patent holders to contract their way out of the statutorily imposed risk that patent litigation could lead to invalidation of the patent while claiming antitrust immunity for that private contract.... [T]his standard effectively bars considering whether the agreement might violate the antitrust laws, and so offers no protection to the public interest in eliminating undeserved patents.

Brief for the United States as Amicus at 14–15. While acknowledging that patent-holders are entitled to settle disputes over the validity of their patent, the United States proposes that excessive reverse payment settlements be deemed presumptively unlawful unless a patent-holder can show that settlement payments do not greatly exceed anticipated litigation costs.

Second, there is evidence that the practice of entering into reverse exclusionary payment settlements has increased since we decided *Tamoxifen.* Prior to our *Tamoxifen* decision, there were fourteen settlements of Hatch–Waxman lawsuits, none of which involved reverse payments to a generic manufacturer.... After *Tamoxifen,* however, plaintiffs represent that twenty of twenty-seven Hatch–Waxman settlements have involved reverse payments.

Third, after *Tamoxifen* was decided, a principal drafter of the Hatch–Waxman Act criticized the settlement practice at issue here. *See* 148 Cong. Rec. S7565 (July 30, 2002) (remarks of Sen. Hatch) ("As coauthor of the [Hatch–Waxman Act], I can tell you that I find these type[s] of reverse payment collusive arrangements appalling")....

Fourth and finally, the *Tamoxifen* panel appears to have relied on an erroneous characterization of the Hatch–Waxman Act. *Tamoxifen* was based in no small part on the panel majority's statement that reverse exclusionary settlements "open[ ] the [relevant] patent to immediate challenge by other potential generic manufacturers which did indeed follow—spurred by the additional incentive (at the time) of potentially securing the 180–day exclusivity period available upon a victory in a subsequent infringement lawsuit ..." 466 F.3d at 214. If understood as a legal conclusion this remark that the statutory exclusivity period cedes to the first ANDA filer to successfully defend, was erroneous. *See* Scott Hemphill, *Paying for Delay: Pharmaceutical Patent Settlement As a Regulatory* 81 N.Y.U. L.Rev. 1553, 1583–86 (2006)....

In addition, unlike *Tamoxifen,* which was decided at the 12(b)(6) [motion to dismiss] stage, this case involves a summary judgment decision based on a full record. This case could provide our full Court with an opportunity to revisit the issues in play in *Tamoxifen* and to analyze the competing interests that underlie antitrust challenges to reverse payment settlements in light of the full record and the arguments of the parties and amici, including the United States, that have been raised in this appeal. We therefore invite plaintiffs-appellants to petition for in banc rehearing. * * * [The District Court opinion is affirmed.]

[Plaintiffs sought rehearing en banc, which the full court denied. Plaintiffs applied for certiorari, which the Supreme Court denied.]

QUESTIONS AND COMMENTS

1. What are the principal points of disagreement between the U.S. antitrust agencies and the court?

2. Which analysis persuades you?

3. The FTC has triggered the introduction of a bill in Congress to declare reverse payments illegal. Should the bill pass?

4. Comment on how the existence of IP rights changes the antitrust analysis.

D. MORE INTEGRATION: JOINT BUYING, SELLING, MARKETING, RESEARCHING—SHARING RISKS AND SAVING COSTS, OR GETTING POWER?

1. INTRODUCTION

We have drawn a continuum from loose-knit collaborations (more likely to offend the law, see *Indiana Federation of Dentists*), to more integration (more likely to entail efficient production or delivery of goods or services, see *BMI)* to full integration (most likely to entail efficient production or delivery of goods or services, see *Google/AdMob*); all touchstones.

The category of "more integration" includes joint selling, where, for example, the collaborating firms achieve significant economies of scale or scope and do not get market power. Was *Appalachian Coals*, supra page 65, such a case? Or was the Appalachian Coals venture only a device to keep the troubled coal producers of Appalachia from competing with one another and worsening a deteriorating market?

Consider also the facts of *American Needle*—the NFL teams combined (in a single corporation) to jointly license their trademarks—the right to affix the name and logos of each team to caps and T-shirts. Did the teams get market power by banding together? How? Did they get efficiencies? Would their joint licensing to a single licensee tend to raise the price of the license and thus the price of the caps and T-shirts to consumers? How could this happen?

Another prominent joint selling and marketing arrangement was a collaboration of the Hollywood movie studios, United International Pictures, to distribute the American movies in Europe. The collaboration was vetted in the European Commission and approved on the grounds that it produced economic benefits for the audio-visual sector in Europe. The Commission recognized the substantial efficiencies of the venture, but was concerned by the potential for collusion. As such, it set certain conditions on collaboration including information sharing among the studios, and record-keeping to measure what, if any, positive impact the venture had on European producers. Commission Decision Relating to a Proceeding Pursuant to Article 85 of the EEC Treaty Against United International Pictures 89/467/EEC, 1989 O.J. (L 226) 25–34.

Another type of collaboration or alliance is one commonly adopted by airlines—code sharing. Code sharing—especially between airlines serving different geographic markets—may have great efficiencies but also can take competition or potential competition off the market. Congress has given the Federal Aviation Authority the power to immunize these alliances. The Department of Justice normally provides advice beforehand, which the FAA usually—but does not always—accept. Pub. L. No. 95–504, 92 Stat. 1705 (1978).

Finally, before we turn to the important subject of cooperation among health care institutions and professionals, we mention cooperative research. In the 1980s, against the background of then aggressive use of per se rules, Congress was concerned that antitrust law would peremptorily condemn research and development joint ventures. Accordingly, it passed the National Cooperative Research Act, 15 U.S.C. §§ 4301–05 (1984), assuring that research and development joint ventures would be judged under a rule of reason. The law also provides freedom from treble damages for ventures operating from domestic facilities (a nationalistic twist). The law was amended in 1993 to include production joint ventures.

The Justice Department and the FTC are active in monitoring competitor collaborations. They have published guidelines for the health care industry, available at *http://www.ftc.gov/bc/ healthcare/industryguide/policy/index.htm,* and for licensing of intellectual property, available at *http://www.justice.gov/atr/public/guidelines/0558.htm* and Appendix G. In 2000 they published Antitrust Guidelines for Collaborations among Competitors, *http://www.ftc.gov/os/2000/04/ftc dojguidelines.pdf.* The preamble states that competitor collaborations "often are not only benign but procompetitive." The Guidelines' structured approach and the examples used provide a useful framework for considering the initial question of per se illegality (Is this arrangement really a cartel?), as well as a framework for analyzing collaborations that pass the cartel test.

Note that in some of these cases the question is whether the cooperation itself is anticompetitive. In other cases, as in our touchstone *Rothery*, the essence of the cooperation is not questioned but an ancillary restraint (e.g., covenant not to compete) is questioned, and the issue is whether this ancillary restraint itself creates or maintains market power and, if so, is it reasonably necessary or important to make the cooperation work. If the answer to both questions is affirmative the court might ask whether there was an obviously less restrictive alternative—without closely second-guessing the firm. This was the tack that Justice Stevens proposed in *BMI* (BMI could have charged CBS for each musical composition separately on request of the broadcaster); but his fellow Justices and later lower courts were more sympathetic to the argument that the restraint was reasonable.

We turn to cooperation in health care.

2. HEALTH CARE—AGENCY GUIDANCE

In 1996 the agencies issued guidance statements on health care collaborations, such as hospital joint purchasing, which delineates requirements for safety zones and warns of risk areas. Department of Justice/FTC HealthCare Policy Statements, *available at http:/www.ftc.gov/bc/healthcare/industryguide/policy/statement2.htm.*

More recently, the problem of unaffordable health care reached the top of the national agenda. In 2010 Congress passed the Patient Protection and Affordable Care Act. The act encourages health care providers to form integrated organizations of doctors, hospitals and other providers (Affordable Care Organizations or ACOs) to offer their services jointly to reduce costs and increase quality of health care in the United States.

Noting that the ACOs may cause competitive concerns, the agencies jointly issued a policy statement, giving guidance on what to avoid and on parameters of a safety zone, and promising an expedited antitrust review. THE DEPARTMENT OF JUSTICE AND THE FEDERAL TRADE COMMISSION, STATEMENT OF ANTITRUST ENFORCEMENT POLICY REGARDING ACCOUNTABLE CARE ORGANIZATIONS PARTICIPATING IN THE MEDICARE SHARED SAVINGS PROGRAM (2011). The statement is printed in Appendix E. Read the statement. The policy would apply to ACOs treating commercially-insured as well as Medicare-insured patients as long as the ACO supplies essentially the same services to both.

The proposed guidance recognizes that joint pricing may be necessary or justified. This is especially so where the network's providers share financial risk; for example, capitated pricing, and complex treatment requiring coordination among multiple providers. Even where the providers do not share the risks, pricing arrangements may be permissible in the case of sufficient clinical integration that creates efficiencies; for example, in promoting financial incentives for practice patterns that control costs and improve quality of care.

The guidance recognizes that exclusive dealing—e.g. with a particular health plan—may be important (from the buyer's perspective) to assure supply and afford protection against price rises, and (from the seller's perspective) to reduce selling expenses and protect against price fluctuations, although exclusivity clauses have risks. For exclusivity clauses, the agencies propose an antitrust safety zone where providers' market share is less than 30%, and no safety zone if any hospital, ambulatory surgery center, or dominant provider (more than 50%) is exclusive to the ACO.

Should the agencies relax antitrust enforcement to promote ACOs? Is health care an area in which efficiencies of collaboration tend to outweigh the loss from lessened competition? or is it the other way around? Is competition the most vital force likely to contain the costs and improve the quality of health care?

Consider the following advisory opinion of the FTC, pre-ACOs, opining on a proposed physician independent practice association that would partially integrate the member doctors' practices and provide for joint negotiations with third-party payers.

MED SOUTH

Advisory Opinion of FTC Bureau of Competition.
Feb. 19, 2002.

John J. Miles

Dear Mr. Miles:

You have requested an advisory opinion relating to the proposal of MedSouth, Inc., a physician independent practice association located in Denver, Colorado, to integrate partially its member physicians' practices in the ways discussed below, and to enter into contracts with third-party payers for the sale of those physicians' services on a fee-for-service basis. Specifically, you request a statement whether the Commission staff would recommend a challenge to the proposed activities as a violation of Section 5 of the Federal Trade Commission Act.

Based on the information you provided as well as our independent inquiry, we have concluded that *per se* analysis would not be appropriate in evaluating MedSouth's proposed course of conduct, including its proposed joint negotiation of payer contracts. The program you have described appears to involve partial integration among MedSouth physicians that has the potential to increase the quality and reduce the cost of medical care that the physicians provide to patients. In addition, we have concluded that the joint contracting appears to be sufficiently related to, and reasonably necessary for, the achievement of the potential benefits to be regarded as ancillary to the operation of the venture.

... [W]e have concluded that we would not recommend at this time that the Commission bring an enforcement action against MedSouth if it engages in the proposed conduct. As long as MedSouth's physician members actually are available and willing to contract individually with payers who prefer not to contract with the network, at prices that do not reflect the aggregate power of the group, or its membership is at a level where the network physicians are unable to exercise significant market power, implementation of the arrangement is not likely to endanger competition unreasonably. We will, however, closely monitor MedSouth's activities, and will recommend that the Commission take appropriate action if the proposed conduct appears to result in actual anticompetitive effects.

Description

MedSouth is an independent practice association (IPA) that includes competing primary care and specialist physicians who practice in the "South Denver/Arapahoe County" area of Denver, Colorado. It is a for-profit corporation owned by the physician practices of its members. All MedSouth physicians have a practice location in South Denver, and staff privileges at one of the three hospitals located in that area.

As we understand the facts based on the information you have submitted, MedSouth currently includes approximately 432 physicians in 216 practices. One hundred one of the physicians are primary care practitioners (PCPs) (family practitioners, general internists, and pediatricians); and 331 are specialists in 39 specialties and subspecialties. In general, the specialists in MedSouth are those to whom MedSouth PCPs most frequently refer. Until the year 2000, MedSouth had capitated risk contracts with payers that required most referrals to be made to other physicians in MedSouth. The referral patterns established under those contracts largely have continued. MedSouth estimates that its PCPs make 90% to 95% of their referrals to specialty physicians in MedSouth. MedSouth's specialists, however, also receive a large number of referrals from doctors outside the IPA.

MedSouth expects that a number of its current members will terminate their membership in the organization before it fully implements the proposed program and attempts to negotiate contracts, so that it will represent fewer physicians in negotiations with payers than currently are members. The IPA is not currently accepting new member practices, and it does not intend to do so in the future, except perhaps in practice areas where it has no or few members and has a definite need for the services in question. It does permit physicians who join practices whose members already are MedSouth participants to become participating physicians, but few practices have taken on new members recently.

Contractual relationships between physicians and payers in the Denver area have undergone significant change in the past several years. Beginning in 1998 or 1999, Denver physicians established a number of financially-integrated IPAs that entered into capitated contracts with local HMOs. Many of these groups experienced significant financial difficulties under those contracts, and a number of the organizations declared bankruptcy. In the wake of this experience, payers and most physician groups, including MedSouth, terminated their capitated contracts. Some MedSouth physicians, however, wish to continue to practice on a partially-integrated basis with other members of the IPA.

The Proposed Integration Program

MedSouth proposes to implement a program that it believes will result in lower costs, higher quality, and more efficient delivery of its members' services. MedSouth has not yet placed the program into operation, or engaged in negotiation or contracting with insurance plans concerning the provision of physician services under the program. The essential features of the program, however, have been determined, and MedSouth has developed or is in the process of developing its various components. According to your letter, the proposed program has three major goals:

1. to integrate the provision of primary and specialty services so they are delivered in a coordinated fashion;

2. to integrate these coordinated physician services with a clinical resource management program that involves sharing of patient clinical information, development and implementation of practice protocols, and oversight and reporting of physicians' performance relative to preestablished benchmarks, so as to improve patient outcomes, decrease use of physician resources, and provide MedSouth with a competitive advantage with respect to other physician practices in the area; and

3. to offer payers a network in which all physicians have agreed to participate and in which the physicians will work together to improve care and to compete with other physicians and physician groups. * * *

Negotiation of Contracts

MedSouth proposes to offer the medical services of its participating members pursuant to this program to commercial third-party payers, and to negotiate and execute contracts under which MedSouth members would provide services to health plan enrollees. Thus, the IPA will seek to negotiate price and other contract terms on behalf of physician members of the network. It will retain a consultant to develop fee proposals for use in contract negotiations and, if necessary, to gather information from MedSouth physicians. The consultant will not disclose competitively sensitive information received from MedSouth physicians to other physicians in the network. Physician services will be paid for on a fee-for service basis. In addition, MedSouth intends to charge a network access fee to payers purchasing the package of services, that will support its operating and administrative costs. MedSouth will not be involved in claims processing or payment. Claims will be submitted by the physicians directly to the payers, and payment will be made directly to the physician providing the service. All MedSouth members will be required to provide services under those contracts, and to participate fully in MedSouth activities. MedSouth will not negotiate or execute such contracts on behalf of its members until all parts of the program are operational.

While MedSouth seeks to offer its members' services to payers as a package, you represent that it is intended to be, and will actually be, a non-exclusive network. The MedSouth Physician Participation Agreement will specifically state that physicians are not precluded from participating in other physician contracting organizations, or from contracting with payers independently. You have represented that customers not wishing to purchase the network services will be able to negotiate and contract with MedSouth physicians individually, and that MedSouth members will be advised by counsel that they may not reach agreements or understandings with competing physicians in the IPA to contract only through MedSouth, or exchange information about their prices or contracting strategies other than as they relate to MedSouth . . .

Analysis

Form of Analysis

The first question to be addressed is how MedSouth's proposed negotiation of fee-for-service contracts on behalf of its participating physicians should be analyzed. The information sharing and guidelines activities that MedSouth proposes to undertake, by themselves, are not inherently anticompetitive. Agreement by a group of physicians jointly to adopt an electronic patient record system that permits them more easily to communicate and share information about their patients, or to adopt and promote adherence to recognized, evidence-based practice guidelines or clinical protocols, would not normally raise serious concerns about anticompetitive effects.

Standing alone, however, joint negotiation of price terms by non-integrated, competing physicians would constitute an agreement among the physicians not to compete on price, and would be illegal *per se*. *Per se* treatment is inappropriate, however, and more elaborate analysis under the rule of reason is warranted, when the joint negotiation of price is reasonably related to an efficiency-enhancing integration of the participants' economic activity and is reasonably necessary to achieve the procompetitive benefits of that integration . . .

Efficiency-enhancing integration typically involves joint performance of one or more business functions of the participants in a way that potentially benefits consumers by expanding output, reducing price, or enhancing quality, service or innovation, and that could not reasonably be achieved by the participants individually. The integration must likely generate procompetitive benefits that enhance the participants' ability or incentives to compete, and thus offset any anticompetitive tendencies of the arrangement. Joint negotiation of prices is not "reasonably necessary" if the participants could achieve an equivalent or comparable efficiency-enhancing integration through practical means that provide significantly less restriction on competition.

We conclude that MedSouth's overall proposed course of conduct, as described in the information you have supplied, should not be accorded *per se* treatment. The program in which MedSouth proposes to engage appears to be capable of creating substantial partial integration of the participating physicians' practices, and to have the potential to produce efficiencies in the form of higher quality or reduced costs for patient care services rendered by network physicians. More elaborate analysis under the rule of reason, therefore, is warranted.

Integration and Likely Efficiencies

Taken as whole, the proposed program is designed to facilitate and increase communication and cooperation among MedSouth physicians, both in the treatment of individual patients and in modifying the regular practice patterns of members of the IPA. The collective development and implementation of the protocols and benchmarks has the potential to create significant integration and interdependence among the physicians in their rendering of medical services. The physicians have pooled their resources and expertise to identify common standards of care. Through their agreement to abide by those standards, the physicians have subjected themselves, to some extent, to the collective judgment of the group with respect to their patterns of practice; and they have agreed to make themselves individually and collectively accountable for their performance by making information about their achievement of goals, which are linked to those standards, available to customers.

Wide-spread attention has been given to the prospect that greater adherence to practice guidelines based on solid evidence can improve the quality, and in many cases reduce the cost, of medical care. Rigorous and effective implementation of the program proposed by MedSouth appears to have the potential to help the doctors render more appropriate, high-quality, and cost-effective care. Individual physicians acting independently do not appear capable of creating comparable efficiencies. A group of physicians who practice in different specialty areas is better able than would be an individual physician to select and implement practice protocols that are broadly applicable to a wide range of patient conditions. It would be much more costly for individual doctors to research protocols and to identify other doctors who would agree to abide by the same standards with whom to collaborate. The common adoption of these standards by doctors who refer patients to one another creates a pool of physicians offering a wide range of services who have undertaken to abide by disclosed standards, and who are accountable for their performance with respect to predetermined measures. The establishment of such a group to compete for patients and for health plan contracts should, in principle, stimulate competition with other physicians and physician groups.

The computer system facilitates both dissemination and implementation of these common standards and communications among MedSouth doctors relating to the care of particular patients. The system is intended thereby to reduce duplicative tests and procedures, promote better coordination of treatment, and speed up provision of referral services. Computerized prescribing and other data entry systems have the potential to reduce errors and adverse events. While any physician could achieve some of these benefits by investing in his/her own information system, adoption of the same system by a group of physicians who maintain referral relationships with one another can provide a number of additional benefits. Having compatible systems permits physicians in different practices who are caring for the same patients to communicate and share clinical information more easily. The cost of developing the system is spread over a larger number of practices, and those physicians who are less knowledgeable about information technology can benefit from the experience and interest of those who are more conversant with it. The existence of the system is likely to further cement referral relationships within the network and lead to closer working relationships among network physicians in the future, thus amplifying the benefits that result from the physicians' participation in the program. We note, however, that mere adoption of a common clinical information system by itself, without the other programs that MedSouth intends to implement, would not suffice to establish that otherwise competing members of a physician network have integrated their practices in a manner or to an extent that joint negotiation of prices could be deemed ancillary to an efficiency-enhancing joint venture.

The Relationship of Joint Contracting to the Production of Efficiencies

The extent to which collective negotiation of prices is ancillary to this integration is a crucial question. Generally speaking, an agreement is ancillary to a competitor collaboration to the extent that it is subordinate to and reasonably necessary to accomplish the goals of the integration, unless the parties could have achieved similar efficiencies by practical, significantly less restrictive means. It may be possible to develop an arrangement, apart from payment for the professional services of the network physicians, under which those physicians could be appropriately compensated for the costs entailed in providing programs of the type MedSouth intends to undertake. In this instance, however, we conclude that the price agreement embodied in joint negotiation of contracts for services to be provided subject to the entire proposed program appears to be reasonably related to the integration among MedSouth members, and reasonably necessary for MedSouth to achieve the procompetitive benefits it seeks.

In order to establish and maintain the on-going collaboration and interdependence among physicians from which the projected efficiencies flow, the doctors need to be able to rely on the participation of other members of the group in the network and its activities on a continuing basis. This does not appear to be possible if contracting for the sale of services is done individually. The price for professional services rendered under health plan contracts needs to be established, and if it is done through individual negotiation and contracting, then no one can count on the full participation of the group's members. Whatever value the program has for consumers, beyond what would result from individual doctors computerizing their records and determining to follow particular guidelines, is significantly dependent on the doctors being able to function as a group within which patients are commonly referred. In the absence of the group being able to assure continuing participation of its members in its contracts, some of the benefits are likely to go unrealized.

In addition, joint contracting may permit the network to allocate the returns among members of the network in a way that creates incentives for the physicians to make appropriate investments of time and effort in setting up and implementing the proposed program. According to your letter, it is important for MedSouth to be able to assure that the rewards from the program flow to the doctors in an equitable manner, so that some are not able to charge disproportionately high prices relative to other members, and thereby capture an excessive proportion of the value of the network's programs.

It is unclear whether the proposed arrangement creates a level of interdependence and integration among each and every physician who currently is a member of MedSouth so as to make joint negotiation of their fees ancillary to operation of the venture. For example, MedSouth contains certain subspecialists who may or may not have enough patients referred by other MedSouth members to cause them either to be significantly involved in the design or implementation of protocols, or to have their practice patterns significantly affected by them. Because it is not clear at present how many of these physicians will remain members of the network when the program is fully operational, however, we have not attempted in this opinion to delineate more precisely which physician practices are integrated through the proposed program. Both MedSouth and the affected physicians would face significant antitrust risk if MedSouth negotiated prices on behalf of physicians who are not sufficiently integrated with the venture through their participation in the activities that are expected to give rise to the efficiencies.

Competitive Effects

The fundamental concern of antitrust analysis is whether a given arrangement may have a substantial anticompetitive effect and, if so, whether that potential effect is offset by any procompetitive efficiencies resulting from the conduct. The central question is whether, taking into account both potential procompetitive and anticompetitive effects, the arrangement is likely to harm competition by increasing the ability or incentive of the participants to raise price above—or reduce output, quality, service, or innovation below—the level that likely would prevail in the absence of the agreement. The ability and incentive of the participants to compete individually with one another and with their joint undertaking is an important part of the analysis.

. . . [T]he information available to us indicates that the MedSouth membership as presently constituted likely would be able to exercise significant market power, and thus to extract higher prices, if the doctors coordinate their actions outside the integrated group.

MedSouth currently has a large number of participating doctors who are concentrated in a distinct area of the city. In a number of specialties, they constitute half or more of the physicians with admitting privileges at the three hospitals in south Denver. Of particular significance with respect to the needs of local health plans that contract for physician services, MedSouth contains a substantial proportion of the internists and family practitioners in the south Denver area. For example, MedSouth's current members are 51% of the internists and 33% of the family practitioners at Swedish Hospital, and from 50% to 100% of the specialists in 19 other practice areas at that hospital (allergy/immunology, cardiology, endocrinology, hematology/oncology, infectious disease, nephrology, neurology, oncology, pulmonary medicine, radiology, rheumatology, hand surgery, neurosurgery, pathology, podiatric surgery, urology, vascular surgery, pediatric cardiology, and pediatric neurology). They are 44% of the family practice physicians and 48% of the internists at the two Adventist hospitals, and from 50% to 100% of the specialists in 21 other fields at those two hospitals (allergy, cardiology, cardiovascular surgery, endocrinology, gastroenterology, gynecology. infectious diseases, nephrology, neurology, neurosurgery, oncology, otolaryngology, otology, pathology, podiatry, pulmonology, radiation oncology, radiology, rheumatology, hand surgery, and urology). As noted above, however, we do not know how many of these physicians will remain members of MedSouth after the venture is launched. A significant decrease in the number of MedSouth participating physicians would lessen the risk of anticompetitive harm.

It appears that access to some significant number of MedSouth doctors is necessary for health plans to have adequate networks to support a marketable product and to have enough conveniently located doctors to care for their current enrollees. The area south of Denver is undergoing rapid population growth. The number of physicians in the Denver area is not growing and may have declined, and existing physicians have not relocated their practices into the area where the most rapid population growth is occurring. Consequently, there may be a shortage of doctors in that area. The doctors in the south Denver area where MedSouth members have their offices are the closest to this area of rapid population growth. As a result, as MedSouth representatives confirmed, many practices in that area are full and some are closed to new patients. We have heard some evidence that waiting times for doctor appointments can be long and that it can be hard to find a doctor, particularly a primary care doctor. To date, however, in spite of that shortage, there appears to have been little new entry by physicians.

Doctors in other areas of the city do not appear to be realistic alternatives to many of the doctors located in south Denver, especially the PCPs. Many patients already travel a long way to reach the offices of the south Denver doctors, and are not willing to travel further north into the city. Traffic patterns and congestion make travel to other areas of Denver slow and difficult. Moreover, health plans need contracts with a sufficient number of doctors at each of the South Denver hospitals, because many patients are admitted through the emergency room, and then must be treated in that hospital. Consequently, individual contracts with MedSouth members appear to be a principal alternative to a contract with the group as a whole. Health plans appear to be vulnerable to a threat by the group's members not to contract outside the group unless the plans pay higher than prevailing fees. Our experience in a number of markets suggests that actions of even relatively small groups of doctors can sometimes produce significant anticompetitive effects and consumer injury in the form of higher prices, fewer services, or reduced access to care.

In spite of MedSouth's explicit policy of "nonexclusivity," MedSouth members may have the incentive and the ability to agree not to contract independently of the venture. They have incentives to seek higher fees to recoup their investments in developing and implementing the proposed program. Negotiation of fee-for-service rates for the group will involve identification of price levels that could become the focal point for collusion on individual contracts. To the extent that the program creates greater communication and interdependence among the doctors, the easier it likely would be for them to coordinate their activities. Particularly in light of the doctors' existing referral arrangements, MedSouth members may be able to discipline members of the IPA who might be inclined to break ranks and contract independently. We cannot conclude with certainty that MedSouth's physicians actually will contract outside the IPA; nor can we conclude, at this early stage, that MedSouth's operation will restrict competition unreasonably. MedSouth plans to take steps to ensure that its physicians will in fact be available to contract independently with health plans . . .

In addition, we cannot now determine the extent to which the group will achieve the efficiencies that it expects. We are aware, however, that electronic record keeping and prescribing, and the application of evidence-based practice guidelines to regular clinical practice, are widely seen as potentially effective ways to increase the quality and efficiency of medical care. These practices may reduce errors, reduce the use of ineffective or counterproductive treatments, and increase the use of interventions that have been shown to be effective. We recognize the intention of MedSouth's leadership to achieve the goals they have established for the network, and the potential value of the means they have chosen to employ.

The information we have obtained in analyzing physician markets suggests that, in actual practice, it is often difficult to change physicians' established patterns of practice. Doing so does not result simply from the adoption of guidelines and benchmarks. Rather, the effectiveness of such programs depends upon a number of intangible factors, including the degree of commitment to the process by the members of the group and the effectiveness of its leadership . . .

The ultimate conclusion we draw in this advisory opinion turns in substantial measure on your representations concerning MedSouth's determination and ability to overcome these challenges. MedSouth has established efficiency goals and developed concrete plans to achieve them.

We think a conclusion at this stage that MedSouth is unlikely to achieve the efficiencies it seeks is unwarranted. Nonetheless, the extent to which efficiencies actually are achieved would be an important factor in assessing the overall competitive effects of the proposed conduct.

Conclusions

Based on all the factors discussed above, we have concluded that we would not recommend a challenge to MedSouth fully implementing the program and then offering it to payers on a collective basis. This office will monitor MedSouth's operations and the behavior of its physician members for indications that the proposed conduct is resulting in significant anticompetitive effects.

This letter sets out the views of the staff of the Bureau of Competition.... [T]he Commission is not bound by this staff opinion and reserves the right to rescind it at a later time.

Sincerely yours,
Jeffrey W. Brennan
Assistant Director

QUESTIONS AND COMMENTS

1. Does *MedSouth* accord with the spirit of the agencies' guidance on ACOs? Would the agency guidance cause a new MedSouth to be more or less confident of antitrust compliance in collective price negotiations or other aspects of collaboration?

2. Would MedSouth, or parts of it, fall into the "antitrust safety-zone" defined by the agencies' guidance on ACOs? What does market share tell you? What is the relevance of its degree of integration? of non-exclusivity? Do any of the concerns expressed by the Bureau of Competition fade in the light of the agencies' guidance?

3. Under the agencies' guidelines, what are the pitfalls to be avoided? Are they limited to certain circumstances (e.g., high market share) or kinds of restraints (e.g. exclusivity)? What would you advise your client ACO that includes doctors with more than 50% market shares in their specialties? Will they be able to be part of a group that jointly negotiates with payers? that jointly sets fees? Does it matter what kind of innovation and cost-savings they can provide? Does everything fall under a rule of reason?

In sum, in the case of more highly integrated collaborations, the analyst assesses the anticompetitive risks and the procompetitive, pro-efficiency benefits, determines whether the risks are inherent in the activity that produces the benefits, and makes a decision as to whether the benefits outweigh the risks. When the bona fides of the collaborators are clear and the hoped-for benefits are important, as in health care, we are likely to see an approach sympathetic to the collaboration.

E. TIGHTER ALLIANCES AND TIGHT JOINT VENTURES

1. INTRODUCTION

Joint ventures frequently combine competitively overlapping or complementary functions of two firms. In the latter case they may add a new player to the market. In the former case they resemble mergers of competitors except that they are less permanent.

Virtually all of the analysis that we encountered in the study of mergers is applicable to joint ventures. Does the collaboration increase market power and probably lead to an increase in price or undermine incentives to invent? Or does it produce a more efficient competitor and more competition? If the transaction has both procompetitive and anticompetitive properties, are there ways to preserve the former while eliminating the latter?

In some cases the transaction takes the form of a joint venture rather than a merger for extraneous reasons. For example, a hostile takeover might have failed but a looser collaboration wins the support of the target—as in both Microsoft–Yahoo, below, and BHP Billiton–Rio Tinto, a joint venture for iron ore recovery and production in Australia with worldwide markets.

In some cases joint ventures have so many indicia of mergers that they are subject to pre-merger notification under the Hart–Scott–Rodino Act.

We refer here to three joint ventures—Texaco/Shell Oil (recall the *Dagher* case), Microsoft/Yahoo, and Boeing/Lockheed Martin.

2. TEXACO/SHELL OIL

Recall in *Texaco v. Dagher*, supra page 118, Texaco and Shell Oil, two of the leading competitors in the production/refining of oil and sale of gasoline, formed the joint venture Equilon to refine and sell gasoline in Western United States under the Texaco and Shell Oil brand names; the Supreme Court held that it was not illegal per se (and presumably not illegal) for Equilon to make a "pricing decision" to sell the two brands at the same price.

But what were the circumstances and conditions pursuant to which the joint venture itself was approved? Attached is the FTC's press release announcing the consent order.

SHELL, TEXACO TO DIVEST ASSETS TO SETTLE FTC CHARGES

Federal Trade Commission
Press Release, December 19, 1997.

Shell Oil Company and Texaco, Inc., have agreed to divest a package of assets, including Shell's Anacortes, Washington, refinery; a Hawaiian terminal; and retail gasoline stations in Hawaii and in California, to settle Federal Trade Commission charges that their proposed joint venture could raise gasoline prices by tens of millions of dollars and would violate federal antitrust laws. The assets would be divested to Commission-approved buyers and the sales would be consummated within six months of final approval of the settlement.

"This settlement is a victory for motorists," said William J. Baer, Director of the FTC's Bureau of Competition. "It preserves competition and assures that consumers will not pay more for gasoline and other petroleum products, especially on the West Coast."

In investigating this joint venture, the Commission worked closely with the staffs of the Attorneys General of California, Washington, Oregon and Hawaii, and those Attorneys General also are commencing actions and entering into consent decrees with Shell and Texaco, seeking similar relief.

According to the complaint detailing the charges, the proposed joint venture would violate federal antitrust laws by lessening competition in:

- the market for gasoline and jet fuel in the states of Washington and Oregon, west of the Cascade mountains, including the Washington cities of Seattle, Tacoma, Olympia, and Bremerton, and the Oregon cities of Portland, Salem, and Eugene;
- the market for the specially formulated, cleaner burning gasoline (CARB) required in the state of California, and the wholesale and retail markets for CARB in San Diego County;
- the markets for gasoline and diesel fuel on the island of Oahu, Hawaii;
- the transportation of refined light petroleum products to portions of the states of Mississippi, Alabama, Georgia, South Carolina, North Carolina, Virginia and Tennessee; and
- the market for asphalt in the northern portion of the state of California.

Texaco and Shell would be required to divest assets or make other commitments in each of the affected geographic areas to restore competition as part of the settlement.

Both Shell and Texaco own refineries in Puget Sound. Between them, they make about 50 percent of the gasoline refined in the Puget Sound area. The FTC complaint alleges that eliminating that direct competition could raise prices for gasoline and jet fuel in the Pacific Northwest and CARB in California by more than $150 million a year. To settle the FTC charges Shell would divest its Anacortes, Washington, refinery and would allow its dealers and jobbers in Washington and Oregon to affiliate with the new owner if they choose to do so.

Shell and Texaco are two of the six oil companies that control approximately 90 percent of the wholesale and retail gasoline market in San Diego County. According to the FTC complaint, the proposed joint venture would enhance prospects of collusion by the existing competitors and could increase prices for San Diego consumers by more than $10 million a year. To settle the FTC charges, Shell and Texaco would be required to divest a sufficient number of gasoline stations to a single new entrant to create a viable new competitor.

Both companies also own oil terminals and retail operations on Oahu. According to the FTC complaint, the competition lost through the proposed joint venture could increase costs of petroleum products for Hawaiian consumers by more than $2 million a year. To settle charges that the joint venture could increase prices of gasoline and diesel fuel on the island, the agreement would require divestiture of Shell's or Texaco's Oahu terminal and retail assets.

Shell and Huntway Refining Company make about 85 percent of the asphalt used in northern California and both buy the undiluted heavy crude used to make it from Texaco, which transports it through its heated pipeline. As a result of the joint venture, Texaco could raise Huntway's cost for the undiluted heavy crude, raising its prices for asphalt and allowing Shell to increase its asphalt prices as well. The joint venture could result in an increase in asphalt prices for northern California consumers of nearly $1 million a year, the FTC alleges. Under the terms of the settlement, the joint venture would enter into a Commission-approved, 10–year supply agreement with Huntway to prevent price increases and assure adequate supply.

Two pipelines—Colonial and Plantation—compete in transporting light petroleum products (including gasoline, diesel fuel and jet fuel) from Gulf Coast refineries to the Southeast and Northeast, and provide virtually all light petroleum products, including gasoline, diesel fuel and jet fuel, used in inland portions of seven southeastern states. Shell owns approximately 24 percent of the Plantation pipeline and Texaco owns approximately 14 percent of Colonial. The joint venture would give both companies access to sensitive competitive information about the other pipeline and would put them in a position to influence the decisions of both pipelines, thereby threatening to reduce competition and raise prices. To prevent those threats to the competition between the pipelines, the settlement would require divestiture of either Texaco's interest in the Colonial pipeline or Shell's interest in the Plantation pipeline.

The agreement would require prior Commission notification, for ten years, of the acquisition of any petroleum refining assets in Alaska, California, Oregon or Washington valued at $100 million or more.

Divestiture of all assets would have to take place within six months of the date of final approval of the agreement.

Shell and Texaco are among the world's largest integrated oil companies, with refinery, distribution and retail operations nationwide. Shell operates 3,400 retail outlets across the country and Texaco and its affiliates operate approximately 14,000 retail outlets that sell Texaco-brand gasoline. The companies have proposed a $17 billion joint venture to combine their U.S. refining, transportation and marketing operations. The venture would create the single largest refiner and marketer of petroleum products in the United States.

QUESTIONS AND COMMENTS

1. This settlement is rather typical for joint ventures and mergers that raise antitrust concerns where the concerns can be alleviated by structural or behavioral obligations.

2. Is the relief likely to cure all of the problems? If the parties were vibrant competitors before the transaction, is the relief likely to replace or enhance the lost forces of competition while preserving the efficiencies of the deal? Is there any aspect of the order that you think especially hard to carry out successfully?

In *Texaco/Shell* the market was relatively unconcentrated and the FTC assessed the competition as strong. With the divestitures of the directly overlapping assets, is it correct to say that one would not anticipate either coordinated or unilateral effects?

In all of the next three cases, concentration was very high. Two of the transactions were approved nonetheless, and one was disbanded under the serious threat of challenge from at least two jurisdictions.

3. MICROSOFT/YAHOO

Google, Microsoft and Yahoo were the only significant Internet search companies. Google had the lion's share, with close to 80% of the market. Yahoo had about 14% of the search market, and Microsoft was the newest and smallest with about 6%. Google had tried to court Yahoo, but its bid was stymied by a concerned Department of Justice. Microsoft pursued a hostile takeover of Yahoo, which Yahoo successfully resisted; but then, after a change of management, Microsoft and Yahoo agreed to a partnership. Microsoft would power Yahoo's search engine. Microsoft would acquire a 10–year exclusive license to Yahoo's search technologies and accordingly Yahoo would cease using its own technologies. Yahoo would provide the worldwide relationship sales force for the premium search advertisers for both companies. Microsoft would retain 12% of the search revenues generated on Yahoo's websites for the first five years of the agreement, paying 88% to Yahoo, with reapportionment thereafter. The partnership would last for 10 years.

Would this joint venture increase competition and innovation by providing a stronger number 2 to Google? Or was it predominantly anticompetitive by reducing the small cast of characters from three to two? What would be the theory of harm to competition and the consumer?

Here is the DOJ's press release.

STATEMENT OF THE DEPARTMENT OF JUSTICE ANTITRUST DIVISION ON ITS DECISION TO CLOSE ITS INVESTIGATION OF THE INTERNET SEARCH AND PAID SEARCH ADVERTISING AGREEMENT BETWEEN MICROSOFT CORPORATION AND YAHOO! INC.

Investigation Shows That Agreement Not Likely to Reduce Competition

(February 18, 2010)

The Department of Justice's Antitrust Division issued the following statement today after announcing the closing of its investigation into the proposed Internet search and paid search advertising agreement between Microsoft Corporation and Yahoo! Inc.:

The Antitrust Division obtained extensive information from Microsoft, Yahoo! and a wide range of market participants. Experience and expertise developed during our 2008 investigation of the proposed Google/Yahoo! search advertising agreement also informed our analysis. After a thorough review of the evidence, the division has determined that the proposed transaction is not likely to substantially lessen competition in the United States, and therefore is not likely to harm the users of Internet search, paid search advertisers, Internet publishers, or distributors of search and paid search advertising technology. In addition, the proposed agreement likely will enable more rapid improvements in the performance of Microsoft's search and paid search advertising technology than would occur if Microsoft and Yahoo! were to remain separate.

The proposed transaction will combine the back-end search and paid search advertising technology of both parties. U.S. market participants express support for the transaction and believe that combining the parties' technology would be likely to increase competition by creating a more viable competitive alternative to Google, the firm that now dominates these markets. Most customers view Google as posing the most significant competitive constraint on both Microsoft and Yahoo!, and the competitive focus of both Microsoft and Yahoo! is predominately on Google and not on each other.

The search and paid search advertising industry is characterized by an unusual relationship between scale and competitive performance. The transaction will enhance Microsoft's competitive performance because it will have access to a larger set of queries, which should accelerate the automated learning of Microsoft's search and paid search algorithms and enhance Microsoft's ability to serve more relevant search results and paid search listings, particularly with respect to rare or "tail" queries. The increased queries received by the combined operation will further provide Microsoft with a much larger pool of data than it currently has or is likely to obtain without this transaction. This larger data pool may enable more effective testing and thus more rapid innovation of potential new search-related products, changes in the presentation of search results and paid search listings, other changes in the user interface, and changes in the search or paid search algorithms. This enhanced performance, if realized, should exert correspondingly greater competitive pressure in the marketplace.

Although this particular transaction is not likely to cause harm, the department will continue to be vigilant in our enforcement of the antitrust laws in the search and paid search advertising industry.

The offices of the attorneys general from California and Washington actively participated in the division's investigation of the proposed transaction.

* * *

QUESTIONS AND COMMENTS

1. Did the DOJ make the right choice?

2. Has Microsoft/Yahoo become a more formidable competitor to Google?

3. After *Google/AdMob* (see Mergers, supra page 402) and *Microsoft/Yahoo*, what generalizations can you make about antitrust, concentration, competition and innovation in new economy markets? Does the *Microsoft* monopoly case, supra page 310, help?

4. BOEING/LOCKHEED MARTIN—UNITED LAUNCH ALLIANCE

Boeing and Lockheed Martin both (and these two firms alone) made expendable launch vehicles (rockets) that were used to launch medium to heavy satellites and other space vehicles. Their customer was the U.S. government. They wished to combine these capabilities in a joint venture, United Launch Alliance. This would be a joint venture monopoly. But the Department of Defense supported the venture as efficient and important to U.S. security. Given the small number of launches, the DOD said, combining the launch teams and technologies of Boeing and Lockheed would assure the most reliable access to space for U.S. military and government spacecraft.

Here is the FTC's analysis of the proposed consent order, which order was adopted on May 1, 2007. C–4188, 2007 WL 1406411 (FTC 2007).

IN THE MATTER OF THE BOEING COMPANY, LOCKHEED MARTIN CORPORATION, AND UNITED LAUNCH ALLIANCE

Analysis of Agreement Containing Consent Order to Aid Public Comment

File No. 051–0165 (FTC, October 12, 2006).

I. Introduction

The Federal Trade Commission ("Commission") has accepted, subject to final approval, an Agreement Containing Consent Order ("Consent Agreement") from The Boeing Company ("Boeing"), Lockheed Martin Corporation ("Lockheed"), and United Launch Alliance L.L.C. ("ULA"). The purpose of the proposed Consent Agreement is to remedy the anti-competitive effects resulting from the formation of ULA, a joint venture of Boeing and Lockheed that will provide launch services to the Department of Defense ("DoD") and other U.S. government customers, that are not necessary to achieve the national security benefits that DoD believes will flow from the creation of ULA. The proposed Consent Agreement requires that: (1) ULA cooperate on equivalent terms with all providers of government space vehicles; (2) the space vehicle businesses of Boeing and Lockheed provide equal consideration and support to all launch services providers when seeking any U.S. government delivery in orbit contract; and (3) Boeing, Lockheed, and ULA safeguard competitively sensitive information obtained from other providers of space vehicles and launch services.

The Consent Agreement has been placed on the public record for 30 days for receipt of comments by interested persons. Comments received during this period will become part of the public record. After 30 days, the Commission will again review the Consent Agreement and the comments received, and will decide whether it should withdraw from the proposed Consent Agreement or make it final.

Pursuant to a Joint Venture Master Agreement, dated May 2, 2005, Boeing and Lockheed agreed to form a joint venture to be called ULA ("Proposed Joint Venture"). The Proposed Joint Venture would consolidate manufacturing and development of Boeing and Lockheed's Expendable Launch Vehicles ("ELV"). Sales of launch services to the U.S. government will also be merged into ULA. Boeing and Lockheed will not exchange any cash in the transaction, but each party's contributed businesses are valued in excess of $530.7 million. The Commission's complaint alleges that the Proposed Joint Venture would violate Section 7 of the Clayton Act, as amended, 15 U.S.C. § 18, and Section 5 of the Federal Trade Commission Act, as amended, 15 U.S.C. § 45, by substantially lessening competition in the U.S. markets for government medium to heavy ("MTH") launch services and government space vehicles.

II. The Parties

Boeing maintains its headquarters in Chicago, Illinois. It is the world's largest aerospace company and the second largest supplier to the Department of Defense. Boeing manufactures and sells MTH launch services to the U.S. government on its two ELVs, the Delta II and Delta IV. Delta II provides medium lift capability; Delta IV provides heavy lift capability. Boeing is the third largest supplier of government space vehicles.

Lockheed, based in Bethesda, Maryland, is the largest defense contractor in the United States. Lockheed provides MTH launch services to the U.S. government with its Atlas V ELV. Lockheed is the largest supplier of government space vehicles.

III. Government MTH Launch Services and Space Vehicles

Government MTH launch services are a relevant product market for the purposes of assessing the likely competitive effects of the Proposed Joint Venture. Launch service providers deliver space vehicles (i.e., satellites, interplanetary spacecraft, and other payloads) into earth orbit or beyond into outer space. Payloads in excess of 4,150 pounds require, at minimum, a medium lift launch vehicle to attain low earth orbit, the lowest sustainable orbit. MTH launch vehicles are generally based on a common vehicle configuration, i.e., the Delta IV and Atlas V, and are customized to adjust lift capability by adding "strap-on" motors or additional booster engines. There is no alternative technology currently available to deliver satellites and other payloads to space in the medium and heavy weight classes. Light launch vehicles cannot be "scaled-up" with strap-on motors or booster engines to increase lift capability. Further, with the U.S. government's demand for communication and reconnaissance capabilities increasing, space vehicles are not expected to become lighter in the future. Accordingly, the U.S. government has no alternatives for the functions performed by space vehicles and no alternative technology to deliver MTH payloads to space.

Government space vehicles are a second relevant product market for the purposes of analyzing the competitive effects of the Proposed Joint Venture. The United States government purchases space vehicles for a multitude of unique (and often classified) applications, including military communications and navigation, reconnaissance, atmospheric observation, and scientific exploratory missions, among other things. Other forms of communication, navigation, reconnaissance, and scientific observation are not substitutes for the unique capabilities of government space vehicles.

The relevant geographic market is the United States. Federal law and national security imperatives require that the U.S. government purchase MTH launch services and space vehicles from domestic companies.

The U.S. markets for government MTH launch services and government space vehicles are highly concentrated. In the U.S. government MTH launch services market, Boeing and Lockheed are the only competitors, and their consolidation will result in a monopoly. Space Exploration Technologies Corp. ("SpaceX") is attempting to enter the MTH launch services market, but the timing of its possible entry and the reliability of its MTH launch vehicles is uncertain. Additionally, DoD and other government customers would require several validation launches before purchasing MTH launch services from SpaceX, further postponing the market impact of SpaceX's potential entry. In the U.S. market for government space vehicles, three firms, Boeing, Lockheed, and Northrop Grumman ("Northrop"), account for the large majority of sales.

IV. Entry

Entry into the government MTH launch services market and the government space vehicle market is extremely difficult. For MTH launch vehicles and government space vehicles alike, design and development alone require many years and cost in excess of a billion dollars. Government space vehicles cost approximately $1 billion and take approximately five years to produce. Moreover, because the costs of a launch failure or a space vehicle malfunction are extremely high in terms of dollars and delays in vital national security or scientific services, the U.S. government only procures MTH launch services and space vehicles from firms with an established track record for success. As a result, new entry is unlikely to reverse the anticompetitive effects of the Proposed Joint Venture.

V. Competitive Effects

DoD has contracted with both Boeing and Lockheed to provide MTH launch services through 2011. Under the current procurement program—known as "Buy III"—Boeing's and Lockheed's fixed costs are covered by DoD, and launch services are purchased at variable cost. The rationale for this program is grounded in a Presidential Decision Directive requiring the U.S. Government to maintain "assured access to space," which is interpreted to require maintaining at least two independent MTH launch vehicle providers.

Despite the absence of current price competition under Buy III, significant anticompetitive effects, including the loss of non-price competition and the loss of potential future price competition, are likely to occur if the proposed transaction is consummated. Under Buy III, launches that are more than two years away may be awarded to either Boeing or Lockheed. As a result, each has an incentive to improve the capability and reliability of its launch services to increase the likelihood that DoD will award it future launches. In addition, Buy III expires in 2011, after which full price and non-price competition pursuant to DoD's usual procurement process may be reinstated. Finally, the creation of the Proposed Joint Venture would deny the government the benefits of a competitive "down select" to either the Delta or Atlas ELV if assured access to space is later determined not to require two separate families of launch vehicles.

National security issues, however, are also a vital element of an analysis of the Proposed Joint Venture. To understand the unique national security implications of the Proposed Joint Venture, the Commission has consulted closely with the DoD and other federal agencies. Indeed, as the primary customer of government MTH launch services and space vehicles and the government agency ultimately responsible for the security of the United States, DoD's views on ULA were particularly significant. Under these unique circumstances, the Commission placed a great deal of weight on DoD's position as to whether ULA would benefit national security and whether the Commission should challenge the Proposed Joint Venture.

DoD has informed the Commission that the creation of ULA will advance U.S. national security interests by improving the United States' ability to access space reliably. DoD considers access to space "essential" given the military's increasing dependence on space-based reconnaissance, communication, and munitions-guidance systems. Maximizing the reliability of launch vehicles that provide access to space is of paramount importance to DoD. A single launch failure can result in the loss of a mission-critical payload and threaten military programs by delaying future launches until the cause of the failure is discovered and remedied.

ULA will improve launch vehicle reliability in several ways. First, the single ULA workforce will benefit from a launch tempo (the number of vehicles assembled and launched per year) greater than could be expected from the two separate Lockheed and Boeing workforces. A single workforce with more launch experience will be critical in minimizing mistakes and malfunctions that jeopardize mission success. In addition, integrating the two firms' complementary technologies will infuse each firm's launch vehicles with the technical improvements and innovations of its competitor, further enhancing the reliability of Atlas V and Delta IV. Under these unique circumstances, the increase in reliability can be recognized as an efficiency flowing from the joint venture.

After thorough review, DoD has determined that the national security benefits flowing from ULA would exceed any anticompetitive harm caused by the proposed transaction. DoD has expressed three competitive concerns, however, that are not intrinsically linked to ULA's national security benefits. These vertical issues are competitively significant because ULA's pricing will be regulated, rather than competitive, giving ULA the incentive to exert its monopoly power in related, but unregulated, markets. The first of DoD's concerns is that ULA will favor its parents' space vehicle businesses to the detriment of other space vehicle manufacturers, such as Northrop. Today, competition between Boeing and Lockheed for launch services induces the companies to cooperate with other space vehicle suppliers, notwithstanding the fact that each has incentives to favor its own space vehicle business, out of fear that the other would cooperate and win the launch. The proposed transaction eliminates that threat, and, as a result, reduces the incentives for ULA to optimize its launch vehicles for use with Northrop space vehicles, to the detriment of Northrop and the government.

Second, DoD believes that Boeing and Lockheed may utilize their positions in the space vehicle market to raise barriers to entry in the government MTH launch services market. In this regard, one type of space vehicle procurement presents a problem. Occasionally, DoD requires a space vehicle supplier to select a launch service and provide one price for the space vehicle as well as the launch. In these so-called "delivery in orbit" procurements, DoD is concerned that Boeing and Lockheed will have an incentive to defend ULA's monopoly by refusing to consider on equal terms any other launch service competitors that may emerge, such as SpaceX.

Third, the creation of ULA increases the likelihood that competitively sensitive information from third parties will be disclosed among ULA, Boeing, and Lockheed in a manner that harms competition. For example, as vertically integrated suppliers, Boeing and Lockheed may have incentives to share confidential Northrop information obtained as a launch vehicle services suppler with their respective space vehicle businesses. Similarly, Boeing and Lockheed may have an incentive to share with ULA confidential information that their space vehicle businesses may learn from any future launch vehicle service competitors. This concern arises because third parties, such as Northrop, will no longer be able to utilize competition between Boeing and Lockheed in the MTH launch services market to negotiate the creation of firewalls and other protections for their confidential information.

VI. The Proposed Consent Agreement

To allow the United States to obtain the national security enhancements offered by ULA, the proposed Consent Agreement does not attempt to remedy the loss of direct competition between Boeing and Lockheed Martin under these unique circumstances. Instead, the purpose of the proposed Consent Agreement is to address ancillary competitive harms that DoD has identified as not inextricably tied to the national security benefits associated with the creation of ULA. To ensure that the provisions of the proposed Consent Agreement are followed, it provides for a compliance officer who will be appointed by the Secretary of Defense. The compliance officer will have broad investigative and remedial powers and may interview respondents' personnel, inspect respondents' facilities, and require respondents to provide documents, data, and other information.

To alleviate DoD's concerns in the government space vehicle market, the proposed Consent Agreement requires ULA to cooperate on equivalent terms with all government space vehicle providers seeking to win U.S. government procurement contracts. Because a space vehicle and launch vehicle require significant integration to achieve successful placement of a space vehicle into orbit, space vehicle and launch services providers work closely together pursuant to teaming arrangements when seeking to win government contracts. Pursuant to the proposed agreement, ULA must provide all space vehicle suppliers with equal access to engineering resources, personnel, and technical information. These provisions ensure that ULA cannot give an unfair advantage to the space vehicle businesses of its parents during DoD's space vehicle procurement process.

The proposed Consent Agreement addresses DoD's concern that Boeing and Lockheed will refuse to support or deal with future competitors to ULA by requiring Boeing and Lockheed to provide equal consideration, information, and resources to any launch services competitors of ULA when bidding on a delivery in orbit contract. These provisions prevent Boeing and Lockheed from slowing or deterring entry into the MTH launch services businesses in order to protect ULA's monopoly status. To ensure the parties' compliance with this requirement, Boeing and Lockheed must create selection criteria and have those criteria approved by the compliance officer. Further, the proposed Consent Agreement prohibits Boeing and Lockheed from selecting ULA as a launch services supplier without the prior approval of the compliance officer.

To address DoD's concern that competitive harm may occur as the result of the exchange of confidential information, the proposed agreement forbids ULA, Boeing, and Lockheed from sharing third parties' competitively sensitive information. ULA must establish separate teams to support each space vehicle supplier's efforts to win government contracts and implement procedures, pursuant to the compliance officer's oversight, that will ensure that confidential information is not exchanged among the teams. Additionally, the order requires a number of prophylactic measures designed to ensure that confidential information is not exchanged between ULA and its parents. Pursuant to these provisions, ULA's facilities must be physically separate from those of Boeing and Lockheed, and employees must be able to access only the facilities of their respective employer. If ULA requires technical support from Boeing or Lockheed employees, these employees must sign confidentiality agreements, which must be provided to the compliance officer, agreeing not to disclose the confidential information of any space vehicle supplier teaming with ULA. In addition, for a one-year period, any such employee may not join or assist a Boeing or Lockheed project that is competing with a space vehicle supplier whose confidential information was obtained by the employee during work at ULA.

The purpose of this analysis is to facilitate public comment on the proposed Consent Agreement, and it is not intended to constitute an official interpretation of the proposed Consent Agreement or to modify its terms in any way.

QUESTIONS AND COMMENTS

1. The following observations are from the statement of Commissioner Kovacic, joined by Commissioners Majoras and Rosch, accompanying the proposed consent order and the above analysis of the Commission.

> In reviewing defense industry mergers, competition authorities and the DOD generally should apply a presumption that favors the maintenance of at least two suppliers for every weapon system or subsystem. *See* William E. Kovacic & Dennis E. Smallwood, *Competition Policy, Rivalries, and Defense Industry Consolidation*, 8 J. Econ. Persp. 91, 101–02 (1994). The decisive factor that overrides this presumption and supports the settlement approved today is the cost of subdividing a small number of launches in the face of a national policy that mandates the maintenance of two families of launch vehicles. The capability of a launch vehicle producer resides chiefly in three places: in teams of engineers who develop designs, in teams of production workers who translate the designs into working hardware, and in teams of launch site personnel who prepare vehicles for launch. Experience increases the ability of these teams to execute their tasks skillfully. There comes a point at which subdividing a relatively small number of design, production, or launch events between two firms denies each firm the experience it needs to remain proficient. The compelling justification for permitting the ULA transaction to proceed, subject to conditions, is its capacity to improve quality in the performance of design, production, and launch preparation tasks in a discipline in which operational reliability is a paramount objective.

2. What was the principle by which the Commission allowed national defense to trump antitrust?

3. Does the consent agreement ensure appropriate protection to competition, given the DoD's objectives?

4. Does *United Launch Alliance* entail a big or a small exception from pro-competition policy? Did the Commission do the right thing?

We have now run the gamut of our touchstones, from a suspect restraint in a loose-knit collaboration to deep integration that appears to advance innovation and promise substantial efficiencies; and we have seen permutations in between. Have we seen "flexibility" in matters of higher education, health care, and national defense?

F. IS THERE AN OLIGOPOLY PROBLEM?—NON-COMPETITIVE BEHAVIOR WITHOUT COLLABORATION

We have studied the jurisprudence on anticompetitive collaborations, and we have studied the jurisprudence prohibiting mergers that are likely to induce non-competitive patterns of behavior even without collusion.

Indeed, oligopolistic mergers are prevented precisely because the resulting non-competitive behavior cannot be caught by Section 1 of the Sherman Act. Does this suggest a residual problem that evades antitrust? We present two sets of cases below. The first set presents the question whether the major firms in non-competitive highly-concentrated markets should be broken up to create better incentives to compete. The second set asks whether and when certain conduct remedies might be appropriate. We alert you, at the start, that the "oligopoly problem" has attracted little attention in these early years of the twenty-first century. Have the problems gone away? Are open world markets the best check against oligopolistic behavior? Or might concerns with unaccountable concentrated industries re-emerge as major competitors consolidate within nations and across the world?

We begin with some basics; indeed, a little review. As we have repeatedly seen, in markets of few firms, the sellers may have market power. This is more likely to be the case where barriers to entry and to expansion by fringe firms are high, the product is homogeneous and simple, buyers are numerous and have no acceptable substitutes, and there are many, continuous and open sales. Where most of these circumstances are present, the few sellers may be able to avoid price competition and to achieve a higher than competitive price without entering into an agreement proscribed by Section 1 of the Sherman Act. Indeed it may be easier for firms in an oligopoly to achieve a supracompetitive price without any agreement than it is for firms in more fragmented markets to achieve a supracompetitive price through an explicit cartel.

In oligopoly markets, the same phenomena that facilitate cooperative pricing may also produce less aggressive technological competition (although sometimes the incentives are the other way around; the firms might compete on innovation but not price). Research and development initiatives may be directed more towards style changes than breakthroughs that could obsolete existing stocks, plants, and modes of doing business. Moreover, in such markets x-inefficiencies may abound. Firm managers may not work as hard at cutting costs as they would under competitive pressure. Advertising expenditures may be high and may emphasize image or trivial product differences, and may not provide price or other information of significant value to consumers. Firms in these markets may earn only normal profits for stockholders, yet they may buy peace with unions at the cost of excessive wage rates; they may split orders for inputs among oligopolistic sellers and buy at going prices rather than shopping aggressively; and they may provide executives with costly amenities.

Of course, in different settings, market forces can push firms to be always on their toes. This is especially true of global-economy high-tech firms.

At various times when there has been a perceived oligopoly problem, enforcers have sought to stretch the law to deal with it. These initiatives have taken two forms. First, the Department of Justice and the Federal Trade Commission have targeted "facilitating practices"—practices that foster oligopolistic coordination. Second, the Federal Trade Commission sought to break up a tight oligopoly in the cereals market under Section 5 of the Federal Trade Commission Act, which we deal with below; and it considered such proceedings in the auto and other industries. The effort failed, and is a cautionary tale of the rocks and shoals of a policy of break-ups. Here is the story of breakfast cereal:

In the 1960s the staff of the FTC attempted to identify a test oligopoly case. That endeavor is described in the following headnote, printed in The Antitrust Law and Economics Review, along with a 1969 memorandum by FTC Bureau Chief Rufus E. Wilson asking the Commission to open an investigation of the cereals industry.

THE FTC'S DECONCENTRATION CASE AGAINST THE BREAKFAST-CEREAL INDUSTRY: A NEW 'BALLGAME' IN ANTITRUST?

(excerpt)

Knowledgeable antitrust-watchers in Washington have known for some time now that a policy debate of fairly heroic proportions was in progress at the FTC and that the breakfast-cereal industry was very much in the eye of this particular storm. Unimpressed by the progress antitrust had made in reducing industrial concentration during the eight decades since the passage of the Sherman Act in 1890, a number of attorneys in FTC's then Bureau of Restraint of Trade (now called the Bureau of Competition) reportedly began "lobbying" their superiors for permission to bring a series of lawsuits aimed at deconcentrating a number of the country's major oligopolies in the mid–1960s. Finally, on June 4, 1969, one of the Bureau's division chiefs, Rufus E. Wilson, signed and forwarded to the five FTC commissioners one of these proposals, a request by his staff attorneys for permission to investigate the breakfast-cereal industry with an eye toward requiring its larger firms—Kellogg, General Mills, and General Foods—to separate themselves (by "spin-off") into several cereal firms each. Various newspaper accounts of this proposed "investigation" have appeared since that time but few knowledgeable students of the FTC, and certainly not the country's antitrust lawyers, have suspected that anything significant was going to come of the matter. The members of that agency, as we have emphasized in these pages a number of times during the past four years, are for the most part constrained by political and intellectual limitations to much shallower waters than these.

Now, however, we are being assured that the FTC's new reform Chairman might well be for real; that his new head of the agency's Bureau of Economics is seriously studying a number of major American oligopolies with an eye toward deconcentrating them; that the heads of his two legal bureaus are serious about reducing concentration and product differentiation in the more important oligopoly industries; that his new policy-planning chief is actually attempting to introduce the FTC to structural economic analysis and cost-benefit concepts; and that, as proof of all this, the agency has completed its investigation of the breakfast-cereal industry and is on the very eve of filing the first case in antitrust history that seeks to (1) declare high concentration (oligopoly) and its accompanying super-competitive prices illegal and (2) actually do something about the structure of such an industry, namely, deconcentrate it.

If such a case is in fact filed by the FTC, it would easily be the most important antitrust action in the nation's history, one that, by its mere filing, would amount to nothing less than a challenge to the legality of perhaps a third of the country's manufacturing sector, the third that, in Professor Galbraith's phrase, constitutes the country's "industrial heartland." The notion that America is about to seriously address itself to its long festering monopoly problem—and, what is more, that it is about to do so through so unlikely an instrument as the "little old lady of Pennsylvania Avenue" (as the droller members of the antitrust bar have always referred to the FTC)—is not, to put it conservatively, one that enjoys wide currency among the more cynical students of such matters. If a complaint should actually issue against the cereal producers, this group maintains, it will either be (a) focused on some economically insignificant aspects of the industry's "conduct"—e.g., false advertising, price discrimination, or the like—or (b) accompanied by a meaningless consent-order "settlement" under which the cereal producers will agree, as the quid pro quo for being allowed to retain their concentrated industry structure and thus their power to charge super-competitive prices, to "cease and desist" doing something that has nothing to do with their monopoly power anyway, the economic equivalent of an order to stop spitting on the sidewalks in Battle Creek.*

In 1972 the complaint issued. The Federal Trade Commission sued the four largest manufacturers of ready-to-eat (RTE) cereals, alleging that their actions and non-actions for at least the past 30 years resulted in maintenance of a highly concentrated, noncompetitive market structure in violation of Section 5 of the Federal Trade Commission Act. The four firms and their approximate market shares prior to suit were:

Kellogg Co.	–	45%
General Mills, Inc.	–	21%
General Foods Corp.	–	16%
Quaker Oats Co.[1]	–	9%

The complaint alleged, among other things, that respondents proliferated brands; artificially differentiated products through promotion of trademarks and intensive advertising; made numerous acquisitions during

* 4 Antitrust Law & Econ. Rev. 57 (1971).

1. Quaker Oats was dropped from the case before trial.

the prior 70 years, eliminating sources of private label RTE cereals; refused to make private label products, although they had unused capacity; and, through Kellogg's services in providing shelf space in supermarkets and placing cereals on it, perpetuated their market shares and limited the exposure of other producers' product. Complaint counsel's brand proliferation theory was highly developed: RTE cereal can be differentiated in several ways: grain used; shape; texture; sweetness. Some buyers may like sweet, soggy wheat, others bland, crunchy oats. Although in some segments (e.g., those filled by corn flakes, wheaties, shredded wheat) the popularity of particular products was stable, in other segments products introduced tended to have relatively short life cycles. The essence of the FTC's brand proliferation theory was that possible grain, texture, shape and sweetness variations were finite and that the cumulative result of the strategies of the RTE companies was to keep every plausible product nitch filled by repeatedly and promptly introducing and promoting new brands in each nitch where the popularity of an existing brand was falling and its producer could be expected to let it lapse. Thus, as predicted, the complaint did not attack structure alone; but on the other hand, it did not rest either on collusion or on conduct that, if engaged in by one firm only, would have been subject to challenge.

Respondents and critics of the FTC's theory used the phrase "shared monopoly" in an effort to discredit the theory of the case; the term suggested something radical and untested. Meanwhile, government lawyers and others tried to make a virtue of the terminology. They used it descriptively to identify a structural condition involving oligopoly so tight that the participating sellers are able to approximate the monopoly result by interdependent behavior.

Perhaps because of the ambiguities of the phrase, some who criticized prosecution of the case as well as some who approved it shied away from the shared monopoly label. Many who did so emphasized the similarity of tight oligopoly with collusion, not monopoly. This partly semantic controversy was not adequately resolved.

The case was tried before an administrative law judge, who stressed the FTC staff's failure of proof and decided in favor of the cereal companies. The then director of the Bureau of Competition filed a notice of intent to appeal. At about that time, administrations changed from that of President Jimmy Carter to that of President Ronald Reagan. Reagan appointed James C. Miller III as head of the Federal Trade Commission. Miller's FTC withdrew the earlier notice of intent to appeal. The Commission took the unusual step of reviewing the record to determine whether the case should continue. Statements of three commissioners follow.

IN THE MATTER OF KELLOGG CO.

99 F.T.C. 8 (1982).

STATEMENT OF COMMISSIONER CLANTON: This case raises important issues concerning the application of Section 5 of the FTC Act to oligopolistic conduct. Because of these issues and the present posture of this case—Administrative Law Judge Berman's decision in favor of respondents coupled with the Bureau Director's decision not to appeal—it seems highly desirable for the Commission to determine now whether a full briefing on the merits is warranted. * * *

... I cannot find a basis for continuing the case. In its most succinct form, complaint counsel urge that liability be premised on the basis of two related but distinct theories. The first is a traditional conspiracy to monopolize based upon principles contained in Section 2 of the Sherman Act; the second is a shared monopoly theory under Section 5 of the FTC Act, a theory which does not depend upon a showing of collusion. Under either of these theories, complaint counsel argue that the only effective form of relief would be a divestiture order, including royalty-free licensing of respondents' cereal trademarks.

... [A] conspiracy to monopolize was not properly pled. As for the separate shared monopoly theory, I do not believe such a theory, however characterized, can serve as a predicate for the Commission to restructure an industry, at least in the absence of clear predatory behavior, which is not claimed here.

I do want to emphasize, however, that Section 5 may well provide the Commission with sufficient authority to attack noncollusive behavior that contributes to or enhances anticompetitive conduct, and which is without compelling business justification. In such circumstances, the principal remedial tool for dealing with this kind of behavior would be a conduct order.

Before elaborating further on these points, I would offer a comment about the characterizations, or mischaracterizations, that have been advanced in the past by critics of this case. An awful lot of rhetoric has been spilled on this subject, with some critics claiming that the case is just the first step in a broad-based attack on concentrated industries. Others have accused the agency of attacking competitive forms of behavior, such as product differentiation and brand proliferation; while still others have derided the "shared monopoly" concept, suggesting that this is evidence alone of the Commission's confused thinking since the description itself is a contradiction in terms.

Suffice it to say, I do not share all of the views of the critics of this case. In issuing the complaint, I think the Commission sought to address a legitimate concern, not about oligopolies per se, but rather about oligopolistic behavior that is uniquely anticompetitive. Respected antitrust commentators of different persuasions—such as Professor Posner and Professors Areeda and Turner—have advocated different approaches for dealing with collusive-type behavior among oligopolists. Whether the theories of relief proposed by complaint counsel are proper is one thing, but it is clear to me that the Commission was not attempting through this case to challenge structure or bigness *per se*. * * *

Section 5—Shared Monopoly

... Complaint counsel ... argue that even absent a conspiracy the conduct is sufficiently like one to justify a finding of liability under Section 5 of the FTC Act. It is quite clear, of course, that Section 5 can reach anticompetitive behavior that is not covered by the Clayton or Sherman Acts. And, I believe such authority extends to non-collusive, marketwide behavior that may not involve traditional forms of predation. Presumably, this could include behavior that would not be illegal for a single firm to engage in but, due to the industrywide nature of the practice, could lead to significant anticompetitive effects.

Various commentators have also urged that the antitrust laws are flexible enough to deal with shared monopolies or oligopolistic behavior outside the context of a traditional conspiracy. In highly concentrated industries competitors may learn to react to each others' moves in a fashion that is closely analogous to the workings of a cartel. Firms will recognize that it is not in their self-interest to chart an independent course because other competitors will be able to quickly detect and match their moves, thereby leading to lower profits for the industry as a whole. The degree to which this phenomena occurs, and its success, are obviously subjects of great debate and the identification of markets in which firms are operating in a closely interdependent fashion is admittedly complex.

Because of the difficulties in proving collusion, Professors Areeda and Turner have advocated a different approach to the problem of single firm monopolization and shared monopolies. In their recent treatise, they suggest that evidence of persistent monopoly performance in a market, whether exhibited by a single firm or a small group of firms, should be sufficient to justify sweeping relief in the form of divestiture or other like remedies. Of course, they would require fairly strong evidence that the market is performing badly and that structural remedies would not lead to inefficiencies. They also believe that such actions should be limited to government initiatives and not allowed in private suits. In essence, their proposal does not depend on improper conduct for establishing liability and is akin to various no-fault monopoly proposals that have been advanced in the past.

But even Areeda and Turner recognize that the kinds of markets that might warrant intervention under such an approach are limited, even more so in the shared monopoly area than for single firm monopolies.

Complaint counsel, of course, are not advocating a no-fault approach in this case. Instead, they have attempted to develop their case in a way that focuses on the extent to which respondents' interrelated behavior has exacerbated competitive problems in the RTE cereal industry. Their theory depends less on the unreasonableness of specific forms of behavior than it does on the totality of the conduct.

Nevertheless, even under complaint counsel's theory, one must recognize the implications of using such an approach to restructure an entire industry. As complaint counsel acknowledge, the kind of theory and relief they are seeking require extensive proof of industry structure, performance and conduct. While that kind of analysis is highly commendable, it provides a less than certain guide as to what kinds of conduct or market conditions would be subjected to antitrust attack. In addition, such an approach, of necessity, dramatically limits the number of instances where market intervention is warranted and, even then, it does not fully remove the risks associated with developing a structural remedy for an industry.

Thus, absent collusion or clear evidence of predatory behavior, I believe it would be unwise for the Commission to seek dissolution of an industry on the basis of the cumulative effects of multi-firm behavior. That does not mean, however, that such behavior would go unaddressed. Rather, it means that the kind of relief sought—namely, conduct remedies—would reflect two realities about the oligopolistic market context: (1) the lower probability that serious anticompetitive problems will exist for long, and (2) the potentially greater costs of attempting to restructure an industry. Because of the complexity involved, it may take many years to recover the costs of obtaining and implementing a successful dissolution order. Those costs may be worth incurring where we can be fairly confident that the market behavior under attack cannot be justified. The rigor of conspiracy analysis can help to provide that assurance, and strong evidence of predatory behavior may also provide the necessary predicate for divestiture.

But to pursue structural relief in less compelling circumstances carries with it too great a risk of wrong or imperfect judgments. The alternative, conduct relief, obviously has its limitations. Such a focus, however, enables more precise judgments to be made about the reasonableness of particular behavior without the risk of overkill. . . .

Although I am opposed to structural remedies, I reiterate my belief that the Commission can reach non-collusive, industrywide behavior under Section 5 of the FTC Act. An example of such an approach is the Commission's decision in *Boise Cascade,* 91 F.T.C. 1 (1978), rev'd, *Boise Cascade Corp. v. FTC*, 637 F.2d 573 (9th Cir.1980). There, the Commission found that the industrywide use of an artificial freight factor contributed to price stability and could not be justified by market exigencies. Although the Ninth Circuit Court of Appeals felt that the Commission did not make a satisfactory showing of anticompetitive effect, the appellate decision did not foreclose the possibility that the Commission could employ Section 5 to reach unjustified forms of noncollusive behavior which are practiced on a marketwide basis. It should also be emphasized that the Commission in *Boise Cascade* believed that it could fashion an effective conduct order that would not be highly regulatory in nature. * * *

. . . . While we might desire a better mix of price and nonprice competition in the RTE cereal industry, the potential costs associated with a divestiture order, not to mention the difficulty in getting a court to approve such an exercise of our remedial discretion, lead me to reject this approach. . . . * * *

COMMISSIONER PERTSCHUK, dissenting: ... The Commission today takes an unprecedented step in refusing to hear the appeal of this matter. This decision raises serious implications for the integrity and propriety of Commission adjudicatory procedures.

[Commissioner Pertschuk noted respondents' "aggressive legal and political maneuver," intensive lobbying, and Congressional intervention.] * * *

The shared monopoly theory, as reflected in the Commission's complaint in this matter, was predicated upon an allegation of high concentration, as evidenced by a three-firm concentration exceeding 80%; poor competitive performance, as measured, for example, by sustained high profits and the absence of price competition; and high barriers to entry caused by exclusionary conduct of industry members, as evidenced, for example, by the absence of significant new entry since 1950. Thus, the theory of the case does not "condemn the [industry] structure itself" as the Bureau Director's statement of December 11 supposes.

Such a theory is supported by scholarly commentary, including that of Professors Areeda and Turner, Professor Sullivan and others. Thus, it is not the case that "the theory has ... utterly failed to enter the mainstream of economic thought," as the respondents claim. Rather, this case represents a serious, carefully thought out attempt by a no-nonsense Republican-led Commission in 1972 to deal with the problem of a tight oligopoly and a poorly performing industry.

Today, the Commission turns its back on this attempt, not wishing to deal with the difficult but necessary task of spelling out whether and under what circumstances the antitrust laws reach this problem. Such a step by the Commission is a significant one, with major ramifications for government antitrust policy. We should make no mistake about it: the problem of high concentration—industries operated by a few giant companies with poor competitive performance, as indicated by the absence of meaningful price competition and the absence of significant entry of new competitors over a long period—is not going to disappear from our economy in the coming decades. Our economy is now made up of a number of highly concentrated industries without meaningful price competition and, if the merger laws are not to be enforced vigorously, this situation will become more frequent, not less.

I for one believe that § 5 of the Federal Trade Commission Act does reach a situation where an industry is highly concentrated; the performance of the industry as measured by profit levels, lack of price competition or other factors, is poor; effective barriers to entry are created by exclusionary conduct on the part of the firms; and a government-ordered remedy can be shown to be likely to improve competition. I also believe that it is possible for this Commission and for the courts to identify, after careful study, which industries are appropriate for restructuring in order to deal with this problem, and which industries are not....

. . . [This] is a problem which is destined to become more, rather than less, significant for our society.

STATEMENT OF COMMISSIONER BAILEY: . . . [T]he paramount difficulty with [the shared monopoly] case has always been the question of remedy. For whatever it is that Kellogg and the other respondents may have done, the proposed solution—to carve new cereal companies from the hides of existing ones and to force the licensing of successful trade names to the newly created competitors—is both draconian and manifestly uncertain to achieve the relief complaint counsel postulates that it will. * * *

QUESTIONS AND COMMENTS

1. Is non-competitive performance of oligopolists that blocks procompetitive entry a problem of the past?

Has globalization, with lower barriers to entry and new technologies, made the phenomenon less likely to occur?

2. South Africa passed a law to condemn and correct non-competitive markets. It is subject to presidential proclamation of the date of effectiveness. Competition Amendment Act 1 of 2009. If proclaimed (which is not sure to occur), the act would add as a violation situations in which 75% or more of goods or services are supplied by five or fewer firms and those firms conduct their business in a consciously parallel or coordinated manner.

In Germany, legislation was introduced in 2011 to allow the break-up of firms whose dominance hinders competition. The bill was amended, however, to authorize break-up of dominant firms only if they have engaged in anticompetitive conduct. See Stefan Thomas, *De–Merger Regimes in Europe*, 2 J. OF EUR. COMPETITION L. AND PRAC. 201 (2011).

In the UK, the Competition Commission has the power to break up nonperforming industries where features of the market prevent, restrict or distort competition and the industry is not likely to correct its behavior without intervention. Under this power the Commission has required British Airways to divest itself of slots at Heathrow airport, and the Office of Fair Trading has announced to the concentrated banking industry that it will refer their case to the Commission for a potential breakup unless they show rapid change in curing the problems—e.g., consumers' difficulty in switching current accounts, lack of competition in the small business market, and lack of competition in payment systems that are under bank control. See John Fingleton, Competition in UK Banking, available at *http://www.oft.gov.uk/news-and-updates/speeches/2012/0212*.

But from the vantage of twenty-first century America, a Kellogg-type initiative to deconcentrate poorly-performing markets is far from the public imagination.

Oligopolistic interdependence: Should non-collusive facilitating practices be enjoined?

There may be circumstances of tight oligopoly where strong interdependence, far from supporting the inference of agreement, may negate that inference because it convincingly shows that consciously parallel, non-competitive behavior occurs without agreement. See *Twombly*, page 154 supra. What should the law do when firms do not behave like rivals because forces facilitate or even lead them into collaborative patterns? Should clearly interdependent conduct having anticompetitive consequences be treated as a violation of Section 1, or of Section 5 of the Federal Trade Commission Act? Is there any satisfactory remedy? Some years ago there were initiatives to catch price-raising interdependent action, possibly by expanding the scope of the word "combination." In general these initiatives did not succeed. But did courts, trying to fill the gap, sometimes take liberties in inferring combinations?

BOGOSIAN v. GULF OIL CORP.

561 F.2d 434 (3d Cir.1977), cert. denied, 434 U.S. 1086 (1978).

CHIEF JUDGE SEITZ: In separate lawsuits, two independent service station dealers, Bogosian and Parisi, sued their respective lessors, Gulf and Exxon, alleging that the lease contracts imposed a tie-in in violation of § 1 of the Sherman Act. Each plaintiff also joined as party defendants fourteen other major oil companies whom they alleged, together with Gulf and Exxon, engaged in what they now argue was concerted action to unlawfully tie the leasing and subleasing of gas station sites to the purchase of gasoline supplied by each dealer's lessor. More specifically, plaintiffs alleged that, at least since 1957, and continuing to the present, "defendants, through a course of interdependent consciously parallel action, have required all dealers who lease, sublease, or renew such leases or subleases for one or more of defendants' service stations to:

(a) license the use of the lessor's trademark;

(b) sell only the lessor's gasoline; and

(c) not sell gasoline purchased from any other source under the licensed trademark."

Plaintiffs alleged that these restrictions forced them to buy gasoline at whatever price their lessor offered and prevented them from selling other brands of gasoline.... * * *

The district court held that the complaint failed to allege either a "contract or conspiracy," and that the allegation of "interdependent consciously parallel action" did not plead the concerted action required to state a claim under § 1. Although the court recognized that, together with other evidence, consciously parallel business behavior may support an inference of conspiracy, it thought that an allegation of contract, conspiracy or combination is essential to state a claim. The court regarded the omission of the word "conspiracy" for the complaint to be a "deliberately employed strategy" by "experienced and learned attorneys in the field of antitrust litigation." Thus, it reasoned that although it terminated plaintiffs' actions for failure to plead the word "conspiracy" it was not resurrecting the requirement of pleading "magic words" which characterized common law pleading.

Plaintiffs argue that the complaint fairly read as a whole alleges a "combination," and that such an allegation combined with a statement of the specific course of conduct alleged to be unlawful clearly states a claim. We agree.

Paragraphs 16, 17, and 19 of the second amended complaint [hereinafter complaint] expressly refer to an unlawful combination. It is unnecessary to restate defendants' linguistic arguments to the effect that the word "combination" was not used to refer to an actual combination. Suffice it to say that their acceptance would hardly be consistent with the precept that the complaint be liberally construed.

Even if we had no doubt that plaintiffs' substitution of "combination" for "conspiracy" was deliberate and purposeful, we would be unwilling to speculate at this stage as to plaintiffs' theory. Plaintiffs' complaint alleges an unlawful combination and their briefs have not sought to explain that allegation in terms other than that of a classic combination or conspiracy. We perceive no distinction between the terms combination and conspiracy which would distinguish the two complaints. Our reading of § 1 cases indicates that the two terms are used interchangeably. As one commentator has noted, the cases have interpreted the statute as "present[ing] a single concept about common action, not three separate ones: 'contract ... combination or conspiracy' becomes an alliterative compound noun, roughly translated to mean 'concerted action.' There is little need to grapple with issues about the meanings of the particular words of the statute nor to mark nice distinctions among them." L. Sullivan, *Law of Antitrust* 312 (1977). We therefore consider the sufficiency of a complaint which fairly read alleges a combination or conspiracy based upon interdependent consciously parallel action among defendants to impose allegedly unlawful tie-in agreements upon defendants' respective lessees.

The law is settled that proof of consciously parallel business behavior is circumstantial evidence from which an agreement, tacit or express, can be inferred but that such evidence, without more, is insufficient unless the circumstances under which it occurred make the inference of rational, independent choice less attractive than that of concerted action. We recently articulated those circumstances in *Venzie Corp. v. United States Mineral Products Co.*, 521 F.2d 1309[, 1314] (3d Cir.1975):

> "(1) a showing of acts by defendants in contradiction of their own economic interests ...; and
>
> "(2) satisfactory demonstration of a motivation to enter an agreement ..."

Plaintiffs argue that, given an opportunity to conduct discovery, they will prove that both of these circumstances are present. They contend that independent self interest would indicate that each oil company seek to market gasoline to their competitors' lessees, and that the failure to so compete can be explained only by a mutual understanding, tacit or expressed, that gasoline be marketed to lessee-dealers on an exclusive basis. The motivation to participate in such an agreement, of course, is the elimination of price competition among oil companies at the wholesale level. We need not, at this time, consider whether this theory would necessarily carry the day, for we are satisfied that, at the least, it does not appear to a certainty that plaintiffs can prove no set of facts which under *Venzie* would entitle them to reach the jury. * * *

Plaintiffs also contend that even if their complaints are construed not to allege a combination, that an allegation of interdependent consciously parallel action states a § 1 claim. Neither plaintiffs nor defendants offer a definition of interdependence, however. A situation of interdependence has been said to exist when, in a highly concentrated market, there is an awareness that, because of the limited number of sellers, any variation in price or price-related structures will necessarily have a demonstrable effect on the sales of others such that each firm bases its decisions, at least in part, on the anticipated reactions of the others to its initiative. *See Sullivan, supra,* § 116.

There is a lively debate, however, concerning the relationship of interdependence to collusion. On the one hand, Professor Posner, for example, has said that interdependence cannot occur without, and hence is a product of, collusion. *See* Posner, *Oligopoly and the Antitrust Laws: A Suggested Approach,* 21 Stan.L.Rev. 1562–76; 1591–92 (1969). On the other hand, Professor Sullivan has said that interdependence can exist apart from collusion, but that noncollusive interdependent activity can, under certain circumstances, amount to an unlawful combination. *Sullivan, supra* § 122; *See* Turner, *The Definition of Agreement Under the Sherman Act: Conscious Parallelism and Refusals to Deal,* 75 Harv.L.Rev. 655, 660–81 (1962).

If these theories are to be tested, it should be done on a fully developed factual record which probes the conflicting economic facts on which they are premised. The complaint is much too blunt an instrument with which to forge fundamental policies regarding the meaning of competition in concentrated industries. We conclude that the ruling that the specific allegation of interdependent consciously parallel action made here fails to state a claim should be vacated so that the issue can be decided, if necessary, after the relevant facts are fully developed....

Judge Aldisert dissented on grounds that "an allegation of consciously parallel behavior, without more, does not state a Sherman Act claim."

QUESTIONS AND COMMENTS

1. Note the remedial problems: if interdependent, supra-competitive pricing in a three firm industry were an unlawful "contract, combination or conspiracy," would enjoining that contract, combination or conspiracy be meaningful? Could the injunction be more specific—e.g., do not price [excessively] above cost? Courts would become price regulators. If interdependent

pricing was found unlawful, could a court order a structural remedy—e.g., break up the oligopoly?

Note the anomalies in holding non-collusive, interdependent pricing by oligopolists to be a violation while recognizing that monopoly pricing by a monopolist is lawful.

2. Are there some forms of interdependence (e.g., price leadership) that are or should be beyond the reach of Section 1 as a matter of law, while other forms (e.g., restrictive clauses) should be within the reach of the law?

The Federal Trade Commission attempted to deal with interdependence under Section 5 in the market for lead antiknock additives to gasoline. The FTC sued the four producers for using four facilitating practices to lessen competition. The Commission found a violation, after finding the market highly concentrated, sluggish and unresponsive, and entry unlikely. Chairman Miller dissented. Miller saw the market as highly competitive. He thought entry was easy, and that each challenged practice was employed for a good business purpose that was responsive to consumers. The case was appealed to the Court of Appeals for the Second Circuit. The appellate court adopted the Miller version of the facts.

E.I. Du PONT De NEMOURS CO. v. FEDERAL TRADE COMMISSION

729 F.2d 128 (2d Cir.1984).

JUDGE MANSFIELD: E.I. Du Pont De Nemours and Company ("Du Pont") and Ethyl Corporation ("Ethyl"), the nation's two largest manufacturers of lead antiknock gasoline additives, petition this court to review and set aside a final order of the Federal Trade Commission ("FTC") entered with an accompanying opinion on April 1, 1983. The FTC held that Du Pont, Ethyl and two other antiknock compound manufacturers, PPG Industries, Inc. ("PPG") and Nalco Chemical Company ("Nalco"), had engaged in unfair methods of competition in violation of § 5(a)(1) of the Federal Trade Commission Act when each firm independently and unilaterally adopted at different times some or all of three business practices that were neither restrictive, predatory, nor adopted for the purpose of restraining competition. These challenged practices were: (1) the sale of the product by all four firms at a delivered price which included transportation costs, (2) the giving by Du Pont and Ethyl of extra advance notice of price increases, over and above the 30 days provided by contract, and (3) the use by Du Pont and Ethyl (and infrequently by PPG) of a "most favored nation" clause under which the seller promised that no customer would be charged a higher price than other customers. The Commission reasoned that, although the petitioners' adoption of these practices was non-collusive, they collectively had the effect, by removing some of the uncertainties about price determination, of substantially lessening competition by facilitating price parallelism at non-competitive levels higher than might have otherwise existed. The order is set aside.

Lead-based antiknock compounds have been used in the refining of gasoline since the 1920s. The compounds are essentially homogeneous, consisting in part of tetraethyl lead (TEL), originally produced in the 1920s, and tetramethyl lead (TML), first produced in 1960. They are now usually sold as mixtures, sometimes with additives. The compounds are added to gasoline to prevent "knock," i.e., premature detonation in a gasoline engine's cylinders. Resistance to knock is measured by octane ratings; for a gasoline refiner use of lead-based antiknock mixtures is the most economical way to raise the octane rating of gasoline for vehicles that take leaded gas. Since the compounds are highly toxic and volatile, great care must be taken in transporting and storing them. Refiners therefore maintain only limited inventories. Since an uninterrupted supply is important, the refiner usually purchases the compounds periodically from at least two antiknock producers pursuant to one-year contracts.

From the 1920s until 1948, Ethyl was the sole domestic producer of antiknock compounds. Demand for the compounds increased with the increase in gasoline use, however, and in 1948 Du Pont entered the industry and captured a substantial market share. In 1961 PPG (then known as Houston Chemical Company) began to manufacture and sell the compounds; and in 1964 Nalco followed suit. By 1974, Du Pont had 38.4% of the market; Ethyl 33.5%; PPG 16.2%; and Nalco 11.8%. During 1974–1979, the period of the alleged violations, these were the only four domestic producers and sellers of the compounds. No other firm has ever made or sold the compounds in this country. Thus the industry has always been highly concentrated. However, there are no technological or financial barriers to new entries.

The only purchasers of lead antiknocks are the gasoline refining companies which are large, aggressive and sophisticated buyers. Indeed, several are among the largest industrial corporations in the world. If prospective profits from the sale of antiknock compounds were sufficiently attractive, nothing would prevent them from integrating backwards into the antiknock industry. Of the 154 refiners who purchase the product, the ten largest buy about 30% of the total amount produced in this country. * * *

Following extensive hearings before the ALJ, the ALJ [found] . . . that the alleged practices, which were not disputed, constituted both "unfair methods of competition" and "unfair acts and practices" in violation of § 5. He entered an order prohibiting advance notice of price increases, uniform delivered prices, use of "most favored nation" clauses by Du Pont and Ethyl, and limiting announcements of price increases to the press and others.

Upon appeal the FTC, by a 3–1 margin with Chairman Miller dissenting, on March 22, 1983, issued a 119–page Final Order and Opinion finding that Du Pont and Ethyl had engaged in "unfair methods of competition" through the combined use of the "most favored nation" contractual clauses, uniform delivered pricing, and extra advance notice to customers of price increases beyond the 30–day contractual period. PPG and Nalco were found to have violated § 5 only with regard to the use of uniform delivered pricing. The Commission acknowledged that § 5 of the Act does not prohibit independent pricing by individual firms, even at high levels, in an oligopolistic industry. Yet, the Commission took the view that because § 5 is not confined to the strictures of the Sherman and Clayton Acts but prohibits a broader range of conduct, it can be violated even in the absence of agreement if the firms engage in interdependent conduct that, because of the market structure and conditions, facilitates price coordination in a way that substantially lessens competition in the industry.

As support for its theory the Commission relied upon the legislative history of § 5, certain prior decisions dealing with its challenges to basing point pricing schemes, and general statements of the Supreme Court and commentators regarding the reach of § 5. Rejecting petitioners' contention that § 5 liability requires a showing of at least a tacit agreement, the Commission articulated what it called a "rule of reason" test whereby unilateral business practices could violate the Act if the structure of the industry rendered it susceptible to anticompetitive price coordination, if there was substantial evidence of actual noncompetitive performance, and if there was no "pro-competitive" justification offsetting the harmful effect of the practices.

The Commission concluded from its examination of the record that the structure of the antiknock industry—high concentration, high barriers to entry, a homogeneous product, and inelastic demand—rendered it susceptible to unilateral but interdependent conduct which lessened competition. The Commission further decided that the record contained substantial evidence of noncompetitive performance in the industry: highly uniform prices and price changes, limited price discounting, stable market shares, relatively high profits, prices in excess of marginal cost, and rising prices despite excess capacity and sluggish demand. On such a record, the FTC held that unilateral but interdependent practices engaged in by the petitioners constituted an unfair method of competition in violation of § 5. Conceding that the challenged practices each had a legitimate business purpose, the Commission concluded nevertheless that the anticompetitive effect of those practices rendered them unlawful. Specifically rejected by the majority were the ALJ's findings that the practices also constituted "unfair acts and practices" under § 5 and that the contractual requirement of 30 days advance notice to buyers of price increases and the press announcements of such price increases were unlawful. Thus, the Commission found that giving buyers 30 days advance notice of price increases was not unlawful but giving buyers a few more days advance notice of price increases was an unfair method of competition. Furthermore, even though none of the practices by itself was an unfair method of competition, and none of the practices was undertaken in agreement with the other manufacturers, the FTC concluded that their cumulative effect was to reduce competition and that the practices thus constituted unfair methods of competition in violation of the Act.

The FTC issued a cease and desist order only against Ethyl and Du Pont, prohibiting them from announcing price changes prior to the 30day contractual period and from using "most favored nation" clauses in their sales contracts. The order also required Ethyl and Du Pont to afford their customers the option of purchasing antiknock additives at a "point of origin" price. The Commission did not prohibit the use of press releases or the 30–day advance notice of price increases. No order was entered against PPG because that company has withdrawn from the industry and no order was entered against Nalco because of the Commission's conclusion that Nalco was unlikely to be an initiator of price increases.

DISCUSSION

The essential question is whether, given the characteristics of the antiknock industry, the Commission erred in holding that the challenged business practices constitute "unfair methods of competition" in violation of § 5 simply because they "facilitate" consciously parallel pricing at identical levels. The question goes to the scope of the Commission's power. Although its interpretation of § 5 is entitled to great weight, and its power to declare trade practices unfair is broad, it is the function of the court ultimately to determine the scope of the statute upon which the Commission's jurisdiction depends.

Congress' use of the vague general term "unfair methods of competition" in § 5 without defining what is "unfair" was deliberate. The statute's legislative history reveals that, in reaction to the relatively narrow terms of the Sherman Act as limited by the Supreme Court's adoption of the Rule of Reason in *Standard Oil Co. v. United States,* 221 U.S. 1 (1911), Congress sought to provide broad and flexible authority to the Commission as an administrative body of presumably practical men with broad business and economic expertise in order that they might preserve business' freedom to compete from restraints. Congress' aim was to protect society against oppressive anti-competitive conduct and thus assure that the conduct prohibited by the Sherman and Clayton Acts would be supplemented as necessary and any interstices filled. Indeed, Congress, in the process of drafting § 5, gave up efforts to define specifically which methods of competition and practices are competitively harmful and abandoned a proposed laundry list of prohibited practices for the reason that there were too many practices to define and many more unforeseeable ones were yet to be created by ingenious business minds. The specific practices that might be barred were left to be defined by the Commission, applying its expertise, subject to judicial review. Congress did not, however, authorize the Commission under § 5 to bar any business practice found to have an adverse effect on competition. Instead, the Commission could proscribe only "unfair" practices or methods of competition. Review by the courts was essential to assure that the Commission would not act arbitrarily or without explication but according to definable standards that would be properly applied.

During the period since the enactment of the Federal Trade Commission Act the courts have established certain principles bearing on the scope of the Commission's powers. Although the Commission may under § 5 enforce the antitrust laws, including the Sherman and Clayton Acts, it is not confined to their letter. It may bar incipient violations of those statutes, and conduct which, although not a violation of the letter of the antitrust laws, is close to a violation or is contrary to their spirit. In prosecuting violations of the spirit of the antitrust laws, the Commission has, with one or two exceptions, confined itself to attacking collusive, predatory, restrictive or deceitful conduct that substantially lessens competition.

The Commission here asks us to go further and to hold that the "unfair methods of competition" provision of § 5 can be violated by non-collusive, non-predatory and independent conduct of a non-artificial nature, at least when it results in a substantial lessening of competition. We recognize that § 5 invests the Commission with broad powers designed to enable it to cope with new threats to competition as they arise.... However, appropriate standards must be adopted and applied to protect a respondent against abuse of power. As the Commission moves away from attacking conduct that is either a violation of the antitrust laws or collusive, coercive, predatory, restrictive or deceitful, and seeks to break new ground by enjoining otherwise legitimate practices, the closer must be our scrutiny upon judicial review. A test based solely upon restraint of competition, even if qualified by the requirement that the conduct be "analogous" to an antitrust violation, is so vague as to permit arbitrary or undue government interference with the reasonable freedom of action that has marked our country's competitive system....

The term "unfair" is an elusive concept, often dependent upon the eye of the beholder. A line must therefore be drawn between conduct that is anticompetitive and legitimate conduct that has an impact on competition. Lessening of competition is not the substantial equivalent of "unfair methods" of competition. Section 5 is aimed at conduct, not at the result of such conduct, even though the latter is usually a relevant factor in determining whether the challenged conduct is "unfair." Nor does the statute obligate a business to engage in competition; if that were the case, many acceptable pricing and market decisions would be barred. A manufacturer, for instance, would be prevented from making a concededly lawful change in its distribution system, designed to increase sales efficiency, by unilaterally reducing the number of its wholesalers, since the effect would be to diminish substantial competition at the wholesaler level. Similarly, if anticompetitive impact were the sole test, the admittedly lawful unilateral closing of a plant or refusal to expand capacity could be found to be "unfair." The holder of a valid product patent could be prevented from exercising its lawful monopoly to charge whatever the traffic would bear, even though "a monopolist, as long as he has no purpose to restrain competition or to enhance or expand his monopoly, and does not act coercively, retains [the right to trade with whom he wishes]." *Official Airline Guides, Inc. v. FTC,* 630 F.2d 920, 927–28 (2d Cir.1980), *cert. denied,* 450 U.S. 917 (1981).

When a business practice is challenged by the Commission, even though, as here, it does not violate the antitrust or other laws and is not collusive, coercive, predatory or exclusionary in character, standards for determining whether it is "unfair" within the meaning of § 5 must be formulated to discriminate between normally acceptable business behavior and conduct that is unreasonable or unacceptable. Otherwise the door would be open to arbitrary or capricious administration of § 5; the FTC could, whenever it believed that an industry was not achieving its maximum competitive potential, ban certain practices in the hope that its action would increase competition. The mere existence of an oligopolistic market structure in which a small group of manufacturers engage in consciously parallel pricing of an identical product does not violate the antitrust laws. It represents a condition, not a "method;" indeed it could be consistent with intense competition. Labelling one producer's price change in such a market as a "signal," parallel price changes as "lock-step," or prices as "supracompetitive," hardly converts its pricing into an "unfair" method of competition. To so hold would be to condemn any such price increase or moves, however independent; yet the FTC has not suggested that § 5 authorizes it to ban all price increases in an oligopolistic market. On the contrary, it states that "Section 5 should not prohibit oligopolistic pricing *alone,* even supracompetitive parallel prices, in the absence of specific conduct which promotes such a result." (Emphasis in original). This fine distinction creates doubt as to the types of otherwise legitimate conduct that are lawful and those that are not. The doubt is increased by the Commission's concession that price uniformity is normal in a market with few sellers and homogeneous products, such as that in the antiknock compound industry. * * *

In our view, before business conduct in an oligopolistic industry may be labelled "unfair" within the meaning of § 5 a minimum standard demands that, absent a tacit agreement, at least some indicia of oppressiveness must exist such as (1) evidence of anticompetitive intent or purpose on the part of the producer charged, or (2) the absence of an independent legitimate business reason for its conduct. If, for instance, a seller's conduct, even absent identical behavior on the part of its competitors, is contrary to its independent self-interest, that circumstance would indicate that the business practice is "unfair" within the meaning of § 5. In short, in the absence of proof of a violation of the antitrust laws or evidence of collusive, coercive, predatory, or exclusionary conduct, business practices are not "unfair" in violation of § 5 unless those practices either have an anticompetitive purpose or cannot be supported by an independent legitimate reason. To suggest, as does the Commission in its opinion, that the defendant can escape violating § 5 only by showing that there are "countervailing procompetitive justifications" for the challenged business practices goes too far.

In the present case the FTC concedes that the petitioners did not engage in the challenged practices by agreement or collusively. Each acted independently and unilaterally. There is no evidence of coercive or predatory conduct. If the petitioners nevertheless were unable to come forward with some independent legitimate reason for their adoption of these practices, the Commission's argument that they must be barred as "unfair" when they have the effect of facilitating conscious price parallelism and interdependence might have some merit. But the evidence is overwhelming and undisputed, as the ALJ found, that each petitioner independently adopted its practices for legitimate business reasons which we have described. * * *

The Commission contends that although the business practices at issue here might not be unfair under other market conditions, they assume that unlawful character when adopted in a concentrated or oligopolistic market in which a few producers sell a homogenous product, demand is inelastic, prices are "supracompetitive," and barriers to entry are high. It is argued that in such a milieu the practices assist the producers in independently maintaining prices at higher levels than would otherwise be the case. Perhaps this argument would be acceptable if the market were clearly as so described and a causal connection could be shown between the practices and the level of prices. Indeed the Commission majority concedes that "facilitating practices will be found to violate § 5 as unfair methods of competition only if the weight of the evidence shows that competition has been substantially lessened" and that it was required to "establish a *clear nexus* between the challenged conduct and adverse competitive effects before invoking our authority in this regard." But the record does not contain substantial evidence supporting many of the Commission's conclusions or showing a causal connection between the challenged practices and market prices. Indeed, it appears to be riddled with deficiencies and inconsistencies, many of which are noted by Chairman Miller in his dissent.

In the first place, price uniformity and parallelism was much more limited than the FTC would have it. During the relevant period (1974–1979) Nalco extended price discounts on more than 80% of its sales and PPG on more than one-third of its sales, the latter increasing to 58% of its sales in 1979 as the sellers competed for fewer buyers in a diminishing market. Although there was for the most part price parallelism on the part of Du Pont and Ethyl, they effectively met the price discounts of the other two producers by providing competition in the form of extensive services which had the effect of retaining old customers or luring away new ones. Thus the total package, including free valuable services and discounts, presents a picture of a competitive market in which large, sophisticated and aggressive buyers were making demands and were satisfied with the results. To the extent that there was price uniformity, that condition is as consistent with competitive as with anticompetitive behavior.

The problems faced by anyone thinking of entering the market were not "barriers" in the usual sense used by economists, such as requirements for high capital investment or advanced technological know-how. The main problem has been that market demand, due to factors uncontrolled by petitioners, is sharply declining. A dying market, which will soon dry up altogether, does not attract new entries. Absent some reasonable prospect that a price reduction would increase demand—and there is none—it is not surprising that existing producers have not engaged in as much price competition as might exist under other conditions. To suggest that industry-wide use of delivered instead of f.o.b. pricing restrained price competition in such a market ignores the de minimis part freight charges played in the price paid by customers. It also overlooks the fact that f.o.b. pricing is not necessarily more competitive than delivered pricing.

In short, we do not find substantial evidence in this record as a whole that the challenged practices significantly lessened competition in the antiknock industry or that the elimination of those practices would improve competition. The Commission's expert, Dr. George Hay, stated merely that "the market would have operated differently absent these practices"; he could not estimate the extent of that difference. All four of the petitioners' experts, however, who had impressive credentials and experience, stated conclusively that the lack of perfect competition in the antiknock industry was due to the structure of the industry and that the challenged practices had little if any effect on competition. The Commission contends that the practices reduced uncertainty about prices in the industry; the petitioners' experts convincingly argued, on the other hand, that regardless of the practices, competitors learned of each other's prices anyway within hours and that most of the significant competition within the industry occurred on non-price terms. Thus, even if the Commission has authority under § 5 to forbid legitimate, non-collusive business practices which substantially lessen competition, there has not been a sufficient showing of lessening of competition in the instant case to permit the exercise of that power.

The Federal Trade Commission's order is vacated.

JUDGE LUMBARD, concurring and dissenting: In propounding a more flexible standard for § 5 violations, the FTC has imposed on itself the heightened requirement of showing that challenged practices have had a substantial adverse effect on competition. As I agree with Judge Mansfield that the record does not support the FTC's finding of substantial effect here, I concur in denying enforcement of the FTC's proposed order.

As this failure alone requires us to deny enforcement, it is unnecessary for us to reach the broader question raised by the FTC's order: whether, as my colleagues hold, the FTC's authority under § 5 is limited to conduct that is either *per se* pernicious (i.e., collusive, coercive, predatory or exclusionary) or could not have been adopted for other than pernicious reasons; or whether, as the FTC now argues, it extends also to conduct that may be acceptable in some situations but not in others, in light of poor industry structure and performance, substantial anticompetitive effects, and lack of offsetting procompetitive justification. I would prefer to leave that question to another day, when the FTC has developed a record that more strongly supports the power it now seeks, and has better defined the standards for its exercise. . . .

QUESTIONS AND COMMENTS

1. If the FTC's factual conclusions were correct, would the antiknock makers have violated the law? Would there have been a violation under Judge Lumbard's standard? Under Judge Mansfield's? Should there be a violation? Assuming that we do not want to enjoin practices that are procompetitive or at least are in good faith responsive to consumers' needs or wishes, and that we do want to enjoin practices that are anticompetitive as long as the injunction does not work perversely to harm consumers, would you condemn facilitating practices? By what test?

2. Computers and the Internet have greatly increased transparency of price information such as airline ticket fares. In one episode the Department of Justice accused six airlines and their service for the collection and dissemination of fare information of signalling the threat of punishment (punitive low prices) to any airline that deviated from certain published fares. Could the DOJ have proved an agreement? The parties settled. See United States v. Airline Tariff Pub. Co., 1994–2 Trade Cas. (CCH) ¶ 70,687 (D.D.C. 1994) (consent decree). In the consent agreement, the six airlines and their service agreed not to use their computerized fare exchange system in certain ways; e.g.: "making visible or disseminating to any other airline any fare that is intended solely to communicate a defendant's planned or contemplated fares or changes to fares."

G. CONCLUSION

We have now explored the full set of collaboration problems ranging from loose and suspicious agreements (*IFD. Polygram*) to loose and not so suspicious agreements (*California Dental*) to moderate integrations that presumptively hold benefits for consumers and markets (ACOs) to tight integrations whose benefits are even more obvious—all of which might nonetheless hold anticompetitive dangers. As the Supreme Court said in *California Dental*, the level of analysis should be one meet for the occasion. (Reasonable minds can differ on what is "meet.") At the end of the chapter we asked whether there is an oligopoly problem that can and should be addressed even in the absence of (provable) collusion. The answer, at least in America in the twenty-first century, seems to be, No.

As we conclude this chapter we add a thought question with an international dimension. Collaborations often have cross-border effects. An example is the reinsurance industry agreements in the early 1990s. Lloyds of London consortia agreed not to cover U.S. primary insurers' pollution risks and "long-tail" harms—those occurring beyond the term of the contract. Was this a cartel and boycott, illegal under U.S. law? Or was it a benign or efficient agreement based on sharing of portfolio risks? What if the United States condemns the consortia outright while the UK regards it as a collaboration important to the financial stability of the Lloyds of London market? See *Hartford Fire Insurance Co. v. California*, 509 U.S. 764 (1993), p. 178 supra. How would you, for the international community, solve the problem?

CHAPTER 6

VERTICAL RESTRAINTS: RESTRAINTS IN THE COURSE OF BUYING AND SELLING

■ ■ ■

Introduction

Verticality, in industry organization and in antitrust, refers to the imaginary vertical line from extraction of raw materials through the stages of production and marketing to the ultimate consumer. Thus, vertical restraints are those imposed by one participant along the vertical chain on another participant, or mutually agreed to by them. An example is a resale price-fixing agreement; the manufacturer may extract from the retailer a promise to resell widgets at no more than $10, or a reseller may demand that the manufacturer impose a $10 floor on its dealers' resale price. Other examples are requirements contracts, exclusive dealing contracts, tying, and customer and territorial restraints. A more permanent form of vertical arrangement is corporate integration; a single firm may bring successive functions under one roof.

For many years vertical contractual restraints were seriously suspect and often condemned outright under the U.S. antitrust laws. Analyzed most commonly under Section 1 of the Sherman Act and Section 3 of the Clayton Act, and, if monopolistic, under Section 2 of the Sherman Act, vertical restraints were condemned as instruments for limiting entrepreneurial freedom, exploiting customers, and blocking small or less advantaged sellers from free and open access to markets. But in the mid to late 1970s, and more dramatically in the early 1980s, the tide turned. Indeed, in the early 1980s, the antitrust agencies advised that if a restraint is vertical it must be efficient and good for competition, because each manufacturer tries to minimize its costs of distribution in order to get its product to consumers at the lowest possible cost, given the price it sets for the first sale. Vertical restraints began to be seen as particularly useful to protect a seller from free riding by discount dealers on their full-service competitors. But it is also the case that vertical strategic behavior can harm competition and consumers, as we shall see.

To understand modern law, you will want to understand its evolution. You will need to read the earlier cases with some skepticism. Caselaw that would tend to harm consumers is no longer good law.

Vertical restraints fall in two categories: Restraints that limit the freedom of a party to the contract; typically, restraints in the course of distributing a product; and restraints that also foreclose outsiders; typically, tying and exclusive dealing. We begin here with the first category: restraints that limit the freedom of resellers as to the price at which, persons to whom, or territory in which they may deal. We include the legislative response to caselaw prohibiting resale price-fixing, and the important state-action jurisprudence to which it led. Thereafter we approach the main contemporary vertical restraints case—*Leegin* (page 630 infra), which emphasizes the role of vertical restraints in achieving efficiences. We proceed to cover other distribution restraints, and then the foreclosing restraints such as tie-ins.

A. RESTRAINTS IN THE COURSE OF DISTRIBUTION

1. FORMATIVE LAW: RESALE PRICE MAINTENANCE

a. The Basic Rule for the First Century—Dr. Miles

Vertical price-fixing is also called resale price maintenance, or RPM. Most commonly, it refers to the situation in which the manufacturer dictates the price at which its buyers, who are intermediaries in the vertical chain, may resell.

Dr. Miles Medical Co. v. John D. Park & Sons Co., 220 U.S. 373 (1911), established the principle, for nearly a century, that resale price maintenance agreements were illegal per se. These were the facts of *Dr. Miles*:

Dr. Miles established a network of some 400 jobbers and wholesalers and 25,000 retailers to sell its medicines. Each entered into a contract with Dr. Miles specifying the price at which it would resell. The jobbers and wholesalers agreed to sell only to authorized dealers. John D. Park, knowing of the contracts, nonetheless procured the medicines "cheap" through authorized dealers and resold them at discounts. Dr. Miles sued for interference with contracts. Park defended that the contracts were illegal restraints and void under the antitrust laws. Dr. Miles responded that the restrictions were valid because they related to proprietary medicines manufactured under a secret process, and also that a manufacturer is entitled to control the prices on all sales of its own products.

Dr. Miles lost on both grounds. The Court said that liberty of the producer is not unqualified; it is against principles of free trade and commerce for a seller to restrict the alienation of things it no longer owns; and in any event the advantage of the resale price restriction would go to the dealers, who would get extra profits by the elimination of price competition against one another.

The Court said:

> [A]greements or combinations between dealers, having for their sole purpose the destruction of competition and the fixing of prices, are injurious to the public interest and void. They are not saved by the advantages which the participants expect to derive from the enhanced price to the consumer.
>
> . . . The complainant having sold its product at prices satisfactory to itself, the public is entitled to whatever advantage may be derived from competition in the subsequent traffic.

JUSTICE HOLMES wrote, in his famous dissenting opinion:

> . . . [T]he only question is whether the law forbids a purchaser to contract with his vendor that he will not sell below a certain price. * * *
>
> . . . [T]he most enlightened judicial policy is to let people manage their own business in their own way, unless the ground for interference is very clear. What then is the ground upon which we interfere in the present case? . . . Perhaps it may be assumed to be the interest of the consumers and the public. On that point I confess that I am in a minority as to larger issues than are concerned here. I think that we greatly exaggerate the value and importance to the public of competition in the production or distribution of an article (here it is only distribution), as fixing a fair price. What really fixes that is the competition of conflicting desires. We, none of us, can have as much as we want of all the things that we want. Therefore, we have to choose. As soon as the price of something that we want goes above the point at which we are willing to give up other things to have that, we cease to buy it and buy something else. Of course, I am speaking of things that we can get along without. There may be necessaries that sooner or later must be dealt with like short rations in a shipwreck, but they are not Dr. Miles's medicines. With regard to things like the latter it seems to me that the point of most profitable returns marks the equilibrium of social desires and determines the fair price in the only sense in which I can find meaning in those words. The Dr. Miles Medical Company knows better than we do what will enable it to do the best business. We must assume its retail price to be reasonable, for it is so alleged and the case is here on demurrer; so I see nothing to warrant my assuming that the public will not be served best by the company being allowed to carry out its plan. I cannot believe that in the long run the public will profit by this court permitting knaves to cut reasonable prices for some ulterior purpose of their own and thus to impair, if not to destroy, the production and sale of articles which it is assumed to be desirable that the public should be able to get. . . .

COMMENTS

While the reasoning of the Court was surely arcane from the vantage of modern antitrust analysis, the bright-line rule of the case held firm for many years and was normally explained by the fact that, when firms adopted resale price maintenance, consumer prices usually rose.

In the years that followed, the Supreme Court adopted more rules of per se illegality in vertical cases, all supported by a now jettisoned principle of freedom of trade. In the per se rules adopted after *Dr. Miles* (e.g., for vertical territorial restraints), one could observe the tension between free trader benefits and consumer harm, whereas the *Dr. Miles* rule against resale price fixing appeared to be unambiguously pro-consumer. But was it?

The vertical per se rules were eventually overturned. *Dr. Miles* was overruled by the Supreme Court in 2007 in *Leegin Creative Leather Products*, page 630 *infra*, wherein the Supreme Court catalogues the costs and benefits of RPM.

Before we study *Leegin*, we trace the legislative and judicial history in the aftermath of *Dr. Miles*, a period that brought important pronouncements on the state action doctrine. Also, as firms tried to evade *Dr. Miles* by "unilaterally imposing" rather than jointly agreeing to RPM, the Court made important judicial declarations on what it takes to prove an "agreement."

b. The Legislative Response: Fair Trade; The Limits of State Action Protection

The rule of *Dr. Miles* was not entirely popular. Opposition heightened during the depression of 1929. Small retailers and their trade associations complained that "monopolistic" dealers adopted loss-leader selling and price cutting to crush small business, and the small dealers wanted Congress to authorize agreements that would keep prices up. State legislators responded. In 1931 California passed the first "fair trade" law. 1931 Cal.Stat. 583. The California law permitted producers and owners of trademarked goods to enter into contracts with buyers that forbade resale "except at the price stipulated by the vendor," as long as the goods were in "fair and open competition with commodities of the same general class" produced by others. The statute proved ineffective, however, from the small retailers' point of view. As long as retailers were not required to charge the fair trade price, discounters would erode the price structure. California, therefore, amended its statute to provide that all nonsigners having notice of a fair trade contract for goods of a certain manufacturer would be bound by the contract price. 1933 Cal.Stat. 793. By 1937, more than half of the states had passed fair trade laws with nonsigner clauses. By 1945 all but three states had done so. Justice Frankfurter elaborately details this history in his dissenting opinion in Schwegmann Bros. v. Calvert Distillers Corp., 341 U.S. 384, 397–98 (1951).

Still, for those who supported states' rights to adopt "price-protection" systems, one problem remained. It was a problem of federalism.

Under *Dr. Miles,* resale price maintenance was illegal *per se.* Could a state, by authorizing RPM contracts, grant immunity from federal law to private price fixers? Uncertainty about the answer to this question produced the 1937 Miller–Tydings Amendment to Section 1 of the Sherman Act. The Miller–Tydings Act declared that nothing in Section 1 of the Sherman Act shall render illegal "contracts or agreements prescribing minimum prices for the resale of trademarked goods that are in free and open competition with goods of the same general class produced by others when under state law contracts or agreements of that description are lawful as applied to intrastate transactions."

But the Miller–Tydings Act was silent as to nonsigners. Could a state require adherence to RPM by nonsigners and give them and their suppliers immunity from the Sherman Act? The Supreme Court was soon to answer, No. "[W]hen a state compels retailers to follow a parallel price policy, it demands private conduct which the Sherman Act forbids." *Schwegmann Bros. v. Calvert Distillers Corp.*, 341 U.S. 384, 389 (1951). (This is still the law—subject to the hiatus below—and is an important limitation on state-action immunity.)

Retailers lobbied vigorously for a federal law to overrule *Schwegmann.* In 1952 Congress obliged by passing the McGuire Act. The McGuire Act amended Miller–Tydings to extend Sherman Act immunity to RPM systems embracing nonsigners in cases in which state law endorsed nonsigner clauses.

Within the next decade, RPM inflated prices. Studies showed that prices of fair traded goods were between 10 to 23 percent higher than prices of goods of the same brand in states that did not authorize fair trade contracts. F.M. Scherer and David Ross, Industrial Market Structure and Economic Performance 555–56 (3rd ed. 1990). Consumers lobbied against the state statutes. Several states responded by withdrawing their statutory exemptions, thus reinstating the rule of *Dr. Miles.* Some state courts held their states' statutory nonsigner clauses invalid under state constitutions. Other states tried to hold course, standing by their RPM systems.

In 1975, despite claims by small retailers that they feared for their survival, pro-consumer and pro-competition forces coalesced to secure passage of the Consumer Goods Pricing Act, Pub.L. 94–145, 89 Stat. 801 (1975). The act was passed; it repealed the Miller–Tydings and McGuire Acts.

Repeal of the federal authorization for state fair trade laws still left open questions of federalism and preemption. If a state had a fair trade law *requiring* RPM (e.g., for wine and liquor), did the state law oust the federal law—and thus provide a defense to RPM agreements—even without a specific federal exemption from the antitrust laws? See Parker v. Brown, 317 U.S. 341 (1943) *supra* at p. 159. Or did *Schwegmann* signal that the states had no such power?

The point was soon to be tested. In the 1970s, a California statute required all producers and wholesalers of wine sold in the state to post a resale price schedule, and it prohibited wholesalers from selling below the posted prices. Violations were punishable by fine and by suspension or revocation of the violator's license. A California wholesaler challenged the law. It sold 27 cases of Gallo wine below the posted prices. Charged with violating the statute, the wholesaler took the initiative and sued the State Department of Alcoholic Beverage Control, in the California courts, for an injunction against enforcement of the state liquor RPM system. The California Court of Appeals granted the injunction, holding that the state's scheme violated the Sherman Act, was not immune under the state action doctrine of *Parker v. Brown,* and was not protected by the Twenty–First Amendment to the Constitution (which gives states control over the transportation and importation of liquor into their territory). The Department of Alcoholic Beverage Control, apparently not unhappy with the result, demurred; it did not appeal. The retailers, however, were not happy. The California Retail Liquor Dealers Association intervened and took the case to the Supreme Court of the United States.

CALIFORNIA RETAIL LIQUOR DEALERS ASS'N v. MIDCAL ALUMINUM, INC.

445 U.S. 97 (1980).

JUSTICE POWELL: * * * California's system for wine pricing plainly constitutes resale price maintenance in violation of the Sherman Act. The wine producer holds the power to prevent price competition by dictating the prices charged by wholesalers. As Mr. Justice Hughes pointed out in *Dr. Miles,* such vertical control destroys horizontal competition as effectively as if wholesalers "formed a combination and endeavored to establish the same restrictions ... by agreement with each other." 220 U.S., at 408....

Thus, we must consider whether the State's involvement in the price-setting program is sufficient to establish antitrust immunity under *Parker v. Brown,* 317 U.S. 341 (1943) [see supra at p. 159]. That immunity for state regulatory programs is grounded in our federal structure. "In a dual system of government in which, under the Constitution, the states are sovereign, save only as Congress may constitutionally subtract from their authority, an unexpressed purpose to nullify a state's control over its officers and agents is not lightly to be attributed to Congress." *Id.,* at 351. In *Parker v. Brown,* this Court found in the Sherman Act no purpose to nullify state powers. Because the Act is directed against "individual and not state action," the Court concluded that state regulatory programs could not violate it. *Id.,* at 352. * * *

The decisions establish two standards for antitrust immunity under *Parker v. Brown.* First, the challenged restraint must be "one clearly articulated and affirmatively expressed as state policy"; second, the policy must be "actively supervised" by the State itself. *City of Lafayette v.*

Louisiana Power & Light Co., 435 U.S. 389, 410 (1978) (opinion of BRENNAN, J.). The California system for wine pricing satisfies the first standard. The legislative policy is forthrightly stated and clear in its purpose to permit resale price maintenance. The program, however, does not meet the second requirement for *Parker* immunity. The State simply authorizes price setting and enforces the prices established by private parties. The State neither establishes prices nor reviews the reasonableness of the price schedules; nor does it regulate the terms of fair trade contracts. The State does not monitor market conditions or engage in any "pointed reexamination" of the program. The national policy in favor of competition cannot be thwarted by casting such a gauzy cloak of state involvement over what is essentially a private price-fixing arrangement....

Petitioner contends that even if California's system of wine pricing is not protected state action, the Twenty-first Amendment bars application of the Sherman Act in this case. * * *

... The Twenty-first Amendment grants the States virtually complete control over whether to permit importation or sale of liquor and how to structure the liquor distribution system. Although States retain substantial discretion to establish other liquor regulations, those controls may be subject to the federal commerce power in appropriate situations. The competing state and federal interests can be reconciled only after careful scrutiny of those concerns in a "concrete case." * * *

We have no basis for disagreeing with the view of the California courts that the asserted state interests [in temperance and protecting small retailers' interests] are less substantial than the national policy in favor of competition.... Nothing in the record in this case suggests that the wine pricing system helps sustain small retail establishments. Neither the petitioner nor the State Attorney General in his *amicus* brief has demonstrated that the program inhibits the consumption of alcohol by Californians. We need not consider whether the legitimate state interests in temperance and the protection of small retailers ever could prevail against the undoubted federal interest in a competitive economy. The unsubstantiated state concerns put forward in this case simply are not of the same stature as the goals of the Sherman Act. * * *

QUESTIONS AND COMMENTS

1. The California statute authorized and ordered "only" vertical restraints. Why didn't competition from other brands drive Gallo to post a competitively low price? Do you suspect that the statute facilitated a wine producers' cartel?

2. Did the Court strike the right balance between protected state action and non-protected private action? Should the state be able to protect some of its citizens (wine dealers) from competition? On what should the answer depend: federal versus state power to regulate? consumer effects? The extent

of anticompetitive spillovers to other states? the relationship between the means chosen by the state to the end likely to be achieved? What was the answer of the Court?

3. After *Midcal,* states had to recognize that their wine and liquor resale price laws were void. As the states repealed their laws, prices fell by approximately 20%. See Waldon, Foes Map Liquor War Tactics, New York Times, Sun. Jan. 14, 1979, § XI, 1, col. 1; Sullivan, Jersey Will Remove Liquor Price Rules, New York Times, Jan. 3, 1979, p. 1, col. 1.

c. Refusal to Deal and Resale Prices: When is RPM unilateral? When is It Undertaken by Agreement?

Section 1 of the Sherman Act prohibits only anticompetitive contracts, combinations, and conspiracies. It does not prohibit a firm's unilateral policy of RPM. A firm and its wholly-owned subsidiaries are treated as one firm, whose parts cannot conspire or agree. *Copperweld Corp. v. Independence Tube Corp.*, 467 U.S. 752 (1984). A supplier may choose to deal only with firms that adhere to its schedule of resale prices without triggering examination under Section 1 of the Sherman Act. When is there a contract, combination or conspiracy (terms that are treated as interchangeable) to set resale prices, sufficient to bring the case within Section 1?

In the period between *Dr. Miles* and *Leegin*, numerous manufacturers tried to maintain RPM programs "unilaterally," since unilateral RPM would not be caught by the Sherman Act. There was much legal sparring to determine when a firm—usually the manufacturer—crossed the line from unilateral action to agreement. The law itself took distinct turns from limiting the scope of what would qualify as "agreement" (see *Colgate* below) to expanding the scope (see *Parke Davis*, below) and back again (as it stands now) to a tightly limited space (see *Monsanto* below, and, implicitly, *Twombly*).

UNITED STATES v. COLGATE & CO.

250 U.S. 300 (1919).

JUSTICE MCREYNOLDS: [Upon writ of error from a district court judgment quashing an indictment] ... The indictment runs only against Colgate & Company, a corporation engaged in manufacturing soap and toilet articles and selling them throughout the Union. It makes no reference to monopoly, and proceeds solely upon the theory of an unlawful combination.... [I]t alleges—

> "... the defendant knowingly and unlawfully created and engaged in a combination with said wholesale and retail dealers, in the eastern district of Virginia and throughout the United States, for the purpose and with the effect of procuring adherence on the part of such dealers (in reselling such products sold to them as aforesaid) to resale prices fixed by the defendant, and of preventing such dealers from reselling

such products at lower prices, thus suppressing competition amongst such wholesale dealers, and amongst such retail dealers. . . ."

Following this is a summary of things done to carry out the purposes of the combination: Distribution among dealers of letters, telegrams, circulars and lists showing uniform prices to be charged; urging them to adhere to such prices and notices, stating that no sales would be made to those who did not; requests, often complied with, for information concerning dealers who had departed from specified prices; investigation and discovery of those not adhering thereto and placing their names upon "suspended lists"; requests to offending dealers for assurances and promises of future adherence to prices, which were often given; uniform refusals to sell to any who failed to give the same; sales to those who did; similar assurances and promises required of, and given by, other dealers followed by sales to them; unrestricted sales to dealers with established accounts who had observed specified prices, etc. * * *

Our problem is to ascertain, as accurately as may be, what interpretation the trial court placed upon the indictment—not to interpret it ourselves. . . .

Considering all said in the opinion (notwithstanding some serious doubts) we are unable to accept the construction placed upon it by the Government. We cannot, *e.g.*, wholly disregard the statement [also made by the district court] that "The retailer, after buying, could, if he chose, give away his purchase, or sell it at any price he saw fit, or not sell it at all; his course in these respects being affected only by the fact that he might by his action incur the displeasure of the manufacturer, who could refuse to make further sales to him, as he had the undoubted right to do." And we must conclude that, as interpreted below, the indictment does not charge Colgate & Company with selling its products to dealers under agreements which obligated the latter not to resell except at prices fixed by the company.

* * *

The purpose of the Sherman Act is to prohibit monopolies, contracts and combinations which probably would unduly interfere with the free exercise of their rights by those engaged, or who wish to engage, in trade and commerce—in a word to preserve the right of freedom to trade. In the absence of any purpose to create or maintain a monopoly, the act does not restrict the long recognized right of trader or manufacturer engaged in an entirely private business, freely to exercise his own independent discretion as to parties with whom he will deal. And, of course, he may announce in advance the circumstances under which he will refuse to sell. . . .

QUESTIONS AND COMMENTS

1. Under the rule of *Colgate,* could any well informed manufacturer effectively control downstream prices and evade *Dr. Miles*? Could it do so without fear of crossing over the line to "agreement"? The safe harbor of

Colgate was not as safe as it appeared. In *United States v. Parke, Davis & Co.*, 362 U.S. 29 (1960), Parke Davis produced some 600 pharmaceutical products and marketed them nationally through drug wholesalers and retailers. Its wholesalers' and retailers' catalogues specified suggested minimum resale prices. The wholesalers' catalogue stated that it was Parke Davis' policy to deal only with drug wholesalers that observed the schedule. In spring and early summer 1956, drug retailers in Richmond, Virginia and Washington, D.C. advertised and sold Parke Davis drugs at substantially below the suggested minimum retail prices. Thereupon, Parke Davis put into effect a program to promote compliance with its RPM policy. With the help of its wholesalers, who identified discounting retailers, it cut off the discounters. A large chain, Peoples Drug, said it would abide by the price policy, and it was not cut off. Parke Davis procured Dart Drugs' "willingness" to stop advertising discounts, used this acquiescence to obtain the cooperation of others, and reported back its success to Dart Drugs. The Court held that Parke Davis "plainly exceeded the limits of the *Colgate* doctrine . . .":

> [I]f a manufacturer is unwilling to rely on individual self-interest to bring about general voluntary acquiescence which has the collateral effect of eliminating price competition, and takes affirmative action to achieve uniform adherence by inducing each customer to adhere to avoid such price competition, the customers' acquiescence is not then a matter of individual free choice prompted alone by the desirability of the product. The product then comes packaged in a competition-free wrapping—a valuable feature in itself—by virtue of concerted action induced by the manufacturer. The manufacturer is thus the organizer of a price-maintenance combination or conspiracy in violation of the Sherman Act.

After *Parke Davis,* some antitrust lawyers advised their clients that *Colgate* was substantially dead. In theory manufacturers could lawfully announce their price policy and refuse to deal with violators, but they must do nothing more to induce conformance. A unilateral refusal to deal would quickly spill over into a combination or conspiracy. Non-discounters would complain about discounters and manufacturers would respond with some action to enforce RPM. Shortly after *Parke Davis,* the Court of Appeals for the Second Circuit described the remnants of *Colgate* as follows:

> The Supreme Court has left a narrow channel through which a manufacturer may pass even though the facts would have to be of such Doric simplicity as to be somewhat rare in this day of complex business enterprise.

George W. Warner & Co. v. Black & Decker Mfg. Co., 277 F.2d 787, 790 (2d Cir.1960).

In the mid 1980s the Reagan Justice Department sought to expand *Colgate* and overturn *Dr. Miles.* It believed that, if a producer desires RPM, RPM is probably efficient and good for consumers. RPM is vertical. If the market is competitive, each producer, acting without collusion with competitors, must be choosing the route it believes is the most efficient route to get to market. Therefore the producers can be trusted to do what is good for consumers. If a producer chooses RPM, this choice must be designed to prevent lazy or cream-skimming distributors from free riding on services provided by well-performing distributors. By this view, RPM was generally not anticompetitive and was surely not the proper subject of per se condemnation.

The Justice Department sought a vehicle to argue its case to the Supreme Court. It found this vehicle in *Monsanto v. Spray–Rite,* participating as friend of the court. However, when the Justice Department advocated in its brief that the Supreme Court overrule *Dr. Miles* and abolish the per se rule against RPM agreements, Congress was angered. It viewed the move as part of a Reagan-administration strategy to undermine the antitrust laws. It refused to allow the Department of Justice to spend a penny of its authorized budget to urge repeal of the *Dr. Miles* rule. Pub.L. No. 98–166 § 510, 97 Stat. 1102 (1983). See *Monsanto's* footnote 7, below, noting the DOJ argument. The argument was made by brief only because, by the time of the oral argument, Congress had forbidden the DOJ to argue for repeal of *Dr. Miles*. The *Monsanto* case itself is a major, modern authority on sufficiency of evidence to infer contract, combination, or conspiracy, and on the proposition that, in vertical cases, such inferences should not be lightly drawn.

Monsanto came at a time when, virtually whenever a manufacturer cut off a discounting distributor, the terminated distributor would sue the manufacturer, alleging that the cut-off was pursuant to an RPM agreement with the complaining full-pricers. In several circuits the plaintiff could get easily and quickly to a jury, and often won—despite the manufacturer's insistence that it terminated the distributor for its sub-standard performance. Manufacturers regarded many of these lawsuits as nuisance suits, and settled many. A split of the circuits emerged as to whether the terminated discounter could get to the jury (survive a motion to dismiss) on the "RPM *agreement*" question merely by evidence that plaintiff was a discounter, full-pricers complained, and the manufacturer cut off the discounter. The Court of Appeals in *Monsanto*, the Seventh Circuit, had held in the affirmative.

MONSANTO CO. v. SPRAY–RITE SERVICE CORP.

465 U.S. 752 (1984).

JUSTICE POWELL: This case presents a question as to the standard of proof required to find a vertical price-fixing conspiracy in violation of § 1 of the Sherman Act.

I.

Petitioner Monsanto Co. manufactures chemical products, including agricultural herbicides. By the late 1960's, the time at issue in this case, its sales accounted for approximately 15% of the corn herbicide market and 3% of the soybean herbicide market. In the corn herbicide market, the market leader commanded a 70% share. In the soybean herbicide market, two other competitors each had between 30% and 40% of the market. Respondent Spray–Rite Service Corp. was engaged in the wholesale distribution of agricultural chemicals from 1955 to 1972. Spray–Rite was essentially a family business, whose owner and president, Donald Yapp, was also its sole salaried salesman. Spray–Rite was a discount operation, buying in large quantities and selling at a low margin.

Spray–Rite was an authorized distributor of Monsanto herbicides from 1957 to 1968. In October 1967, Monsanto announced that it would appoint distributors for 1–year terms, and that it would renew distributorships according to several new criteria. Among the criteria were: (i) whether the distributor's primary activity was soliciting sales to retail dealers; (ii) whether the distributor employed trained salesmen capable of educating its customers on the technical aspects of Monsanto's herbicides; and (iii) whether the distributor could be expected "to exploit fully" the market in its geographical area of primary responsibility. Shortly thereafter, Monsanto also introduced a number of incentive programs, such as making cash payments to distributors that sent salesmen to training classes, and providing free deliveries of products to customers within a distributor's area of primary responsibility.

In October 1968, Monsanto declined to renew Spray–Rite's distributorship. At that time, Spray–Rite was the 10th largest out of approximately 100 distributors of Monsanto's primary corn herbicide. Ninety percent of Spray–Rite's sales volume was devoted to herbicide sales, and 16% of its sales were of Monsanto products. After Monsanto's termination, Spray–Rite continued as a herbicide dealer until 1972. It was able to purchase some of Monsanto's products from other distributors, but not as much as it desired or as early in the season as it needed. Monsanto introduced a new corn herbicide in 1969. By 1972, its share of the corn herbicide market had increased to approximately 28%. Its share of the soybean herbicide market had grown to approximately 19%.

Spray–Rite brought this action under § 1 of the Sherman Act. It alleged that Monsanto and some of its distributors conspired to fix the resale prices of Monsanto herbicides. Its complaint further alleged that Monsanto terminated Spray–Rite's distributorship, adopted compensation programs and shipping policies, and encouraged distributors to boycott Spray–Rite in furtherance of this conspiracy. Monsanto denied the allegations of conspiracy, and asserted that Spray–Rite's distributorship had been terminated because of its failure to hire trained salesmen and promote sales to dealers adequately.

The case was tried to a jury. The District Court instructed the jury that Monsanto's conduct was *per se* unlawful if it was in furtherance of a conspiracy to fix prices. In answers to special interrogatories, the jury found that (i) the termination of Spray–Rite was pursuant to a conspiracy between Monsanto and one or more of its distributors to set resale prices, (ii) the compensation programs, areas of primary responsibility, and/or shipping policies were created by Monsanto pursuant to such a conspiracy, and (iii) Monsanto conspired with one or more distributors to limit Spray–Rite's access to Monsanto herbicides after 1968.[2]

2. The three special interrogatories were as follows:

The jury awarded $3.5 million in damages, which was trebled to $10.5 million. Only the first of the jury's findings is before us today.

The Court of Appeals for the Seventh Circuit affirmed....

In substance, the Court of Appeals held that an antitrust plaintiff can survive a motion for a directed verdict if it shows that a manufacturer terminated a price-cutting distributor in response to or following complaints by other distributors. This view brought the Seventh Circuit into direct conflict with a number of other Courts of Appeals. We granted certiorari to resolve the conflict. We reject the statement by the Court of Appeals for the Seventh Circuit of the standard of proof required to submit a case to the jury in distributor-termination litigation, but affirm the judgment under the standard we announce today.

II.

This Court has drawn two important distinctions that are at the center of this and any other distributor-termination case. First, there is the basic distinction between concerted and independent action.... Under *Colgate,* the manufacturer can announce its resale prices in advance and refuse to deal with those who fail to comply. And a distributor is free to acquiesce in the manufacturer's demand in order to avoid termination.

The second important distinction in distributor-termination cases is that between concerted action to set prices and concerted action on nonprice restrictions. The former have been *per se* illegal since the early years of national antitrust enforcement. See *Dr. Miles Medical Co. v. John D. Park & Sons Co.,* 220 U.S. 373, 404–409 (1911) [overruled by *Leegin*, infra]. The latter are judged under the rule of reason....[7]

While these distinctions in theory are reasonably clear, often they are difficult to apply in practice.... [T]he economic effect of all of the conduct

"1. Was the decision by Monsanto not to offer a new contract to plaintiff for 1969 made by Monsanto pursuant to a conspiracy or combination with one or more of its distributors to fix, maintain or stabilize resale prices of Monsanto herbicides?

"2. Were the compensation programs and/or areas of primary responsibility, and/or shipping policy created by Monsanto pursuant to a conspiracy to fix, maintain or stabilize resale prices on Monsanto herbicides?

"3. Did Monsanto conspire or combine with one or more of its distributors so that one or more of those distributors would limit plaintiff's access to Monsanto herbicides after 1968?"

The jury answered "Yes" to each of the interrogatories.

7. The Solicitor General (by brief only) and several other *amici* suggest that we take this opportunity to reconsider whether "contract[s], combination[s] ... or conspirac[ies]" to fix resale prices should always be unlawful. They argue that the economic effect of resale price maintenance is little different from agreements on nonprice restrictions. See generally *Continental T.V., Inc. v. GTE Sylvania Inc.*, 433 U.S., at 69–70 (White, J., concurring in judgment).... They say that the economic objections to resale price maintenance that we discussed in *Sylvania* ... such as that it facilitates horizontal cartels—can be met easily in the context of rule-of-reason analysis.

Certainly in this case we have no occasion to consider the merits of this argument. This case was tried on *per se* instructions to the jury. Neither party argued in the District Court that the rule of reason should apply to a vertical price-fixing conspiracy, nor raised the point on appeal. In fact, neither party before this Court presses the argument advanced by *amici*. We therefore decline to reach the question, and we decide the case in the context in which it was decided below and argued here.

described above—unilateral and concerted vertical price setting, agreements on price and nonprice restrictions—is in many, but not all, cases similar or identical. And judged from a distance, the conduct of the parties in the various situations can be indistinguishable. For example, the fact that a manufacturer and its distributors are in constant communication about prices and marketing strategy does not alone show that the distributors are not making independent pricing decisions. A manufacturer and its distributors have legitimate reasons to exchange information about the prices and the reception of their products in the market. Moreover, it is precisely in cases in which the manufacturer attempts to further a particular marketing strategy by means of agreements on often costly nonprice restrictions that it will have the most interest in the distributors' resale prices. The manufacturer often will want to ensure that its distributors earn sufficient profit to pay for programs such as hiring and training additional salesmen or demonstrating the technical features of the product, and will want to see that "freeriders" do not interfere. Thus, the manufacturer's strongly felt concern about resale prices does not necessarily mean that it has done more than the *Colgate* doctrine allows.

Nevertheless, it is of considerable importance that independent action by the manufacturer, and concerted action on nonprice restrictions, be distinguished from price-fixing agreements, since under present law the latter are subject to *per se* treatment and treble damages. On a claim of concerted price fixing, the antitrust plaintiff must present evidence sufficient to carry its burden of proving that there was such an agreement. If an inference of such an agreement may be drawn from highly ambiguous evidence, there is a considerable danger that the doctrines enunciated in *Sylvania* and *Colgate* will be seriously eroded.

The flaw in the evidentiary standard adopted by the Court of Appeals in this case is that it disregards this danger. Permitting an agreement to be inferred merely from the existence of complaints, or even from the fact that termination came about "in response to" complaints, could deter or penalize perfectly legitimate conduct. As Monsanto points out, complaints about price cutters "are natural—and from the manufacturer's perspective, unavoidable—reactions by distributors to the activities of their rivals." Such complaints, particularly where the manufacturer has imposed a costly set of nonprice restrictions, "arise in the normal course of business and do not indicate illegal concerted action." Moreover, distributors are an important source of information for manufacturers. In order to assure an efficient distribution system, manufacturers and distributors constantly must coordinate their activities to assure that their product will reach the consumer persuasively and efficiently. To bar a manufacturer from acting solely because the information upon which it acts originated as a price complaint would create an irrational dislocation in the market....

Thus, something more than evidence of complaints is needed. There must be evidence that tends to exclude the possibility that the manufacturer and nonterminated distributors were acting independently. As Judge

Aldisert has written, the antitrust plaintiff should present direct or circumstantial evidence that reasonably tends to prove that the manufacturer and others "had a conscious commitment to a common scheme designed to achieve an unlawful objective." *Edward J. Sweeney & Sons, supra,* [637 F.2d] at 111. . . .

III.

A.

Applying this standard to the facts of this case, we believe there was sufficient evidence for the jury reasonably to have concluded that Monsanto and some of its distributors were parties to an "agreement" or "conspiracy" to maintain resale prices and terminate price cutters. In fact there was substantial *direct* evidence of agreements to maintain prices. There was testimony from a Monsanto district manager, for example, that Monsanto on at least two occasions in early 1969, about five months after Spray–Rite was terminated, approached price-cutting distributors and advised that if they did not maintain the suggested resale price, they would not receive adequate supplies of Monsanto's new corn herbicide. When one of the distributors did not assent, this information was referred to the Monsanto regional office, and it complained to the distributor's parent company. There was evidence that the parent instructed its subsidiary to comply, and the distributor informed Monsanto that it would charge the suggested price. Evidence of this kind plainly is relevant and persuasive as to a meeting of minds.

An arguably more ambiguous example is a newsletter from one of the distributors to his dealer-customers. The newsletter is dated October 1, 1968, just four weeks before Spray–Rite was terminated. It was written after a meeting between the author and several Monsanto officials, and discusses Monsanto's efforts to "ge[t] the 'market place in order.'" The newsletter reviews some of Monsanto's incentive and shipping policies, and then states that in addition "every effort will be made to maintain a minimum market price level." The newsletter relates these efforts as follows:

> "In other words, we are assured that Monsanto's company-owned outlets will not retail at less than their suggested retail price to the trade as a whole. Furthermore, those of us on the distributor level are not likely to deviate downward on price to anyone as the idea is implied that doing this possibly could discolor the outlook for continuity as one of the approved distributors during the future upcoming seasons. So, none interested in the retention of this arrangement is likely to risk being deleted from this customer service opportunity. Also, as far as the national accounts are concerned, they are sure to recognize the desirability of retaining Monsanto's favor on a continuing basis by respecting the wisdom of participating in the suggested program in a manner assuring order on the retail level 'playground' throughout the entire country. It is elementary that harmony can

only come from following the rules of the game and that in case of dispute, the decision of the umpire is final."

It is reasonable to interpret this newsletter as referring to an agreement or understanding that distributors and retailers would maintain prices, and Monsanto would not undercut those prices on the retail level and would terminate competitors who sold at prices below those of complying distributors; these were "the rules of the game."

B.

If, as the courts below reasonably could have found, there was evidence of an agreement with one or more distributors to maintain prices, the remaining question is whether the termination of Spray–Rite was part of or pursuant to that agreement. It would be reasonable to find that it was, since it is necessary for competing distributors contemplating compliance with suggested prices to know that those who do not comply will be terminated. Moreover, there is some circumstantial evidence of such a link. Following the termination, there was a meeting between Spray–Rite's president and a Monsanto official. There was testimony that the first thing the official mentioned was the many complaints Monsanto had received about Spray–Rite's prices. In addition, there was reliable testimony that Monsanto never discussed with Spray–Rite prior to the termination the distributorship criteria that were the alleged basis for the action. By contrast, a former Monsanto salesman for Spray–Rite's area testified that Monsanto representatives on several occasions in 1965–1966 approached Spray–Rite, informed the distributor of complaints from other distributors—including one major and influential one—and requested that prices be maintained. Later that same year, Spray–Rite's president testified, Monsanto officials made explicit threats to terminate Spray–Rite unless it raised its prices.

IV.

We conclude that the Court of Appeals applied an incorrect standard to the evidence in this case. The correct standard is that there must be evidence that tends to exclude the possibility of independent action by the manufacturer and distributor. That is, there must be direct or circumstantial evidence that reasonably tends to prove that the manufacturer and others had a conscious commitment to a common scheme designed to achieve an unlawful objective. Under this standard, the evidence in this case created a jury issue as to whether Spray–Rite was terminated pursuant to a price-fixing conspiracy between Monsanto and its distributors. The judgment of the court below is affirmed.

QUESTIONS AND COMMENTS

1. Why did the Court take pains to make proof of concerted action not easy? Why did the Court fear that non-discounters' complaints about the low prices of a discounter might be misconstrued?

2. Look hard at the evidence on which the Court affirmed the verdict for plaintiff: (1) Up to and through the time Monsanto terminated Spray–Rite, it never expressed any unhappiness with its performance. (2) After Spray–Rite's termination, Monsanto approached other price cutters and told them that if they did not maintain prices they would not receive supplies of a new product. (3) Monsanto made the same statement of its intention to the parent of a price cutter. The parent then told its subsidiary to "comply" (i.e., to follow Monsanto's suggested prices). (4) A distributor informed dealers through an "ambiguous" newsletter about what steps Monsanto was taking in order to maintain an orderly market. How does each set of facts tend to prove that there was an RPM agreement and that Spray–Rite was terminated pursuant to it? Which sets of facts are at least as consistent with Monsanto's claim of independent action as with Spray–Rite's claim of concert?

During many of the interim years, the Department of Justice continued to advocate for repeal of *Dr. Miles*, on grounds that it handicapped firms from adopting strategies that could be efficient—especially to control free riders and thereby assure the level of service they chose. Often taking its lead from DOJ amicus briefs, the Court, in case after case, qualified the circumstances under which a per se rule would be appropriate. *California Dental Association*, supra at 105, is an example of the Court's distancing itself from per se analysis. Finally, in the early 2000s, a women's clothing store in Lewisville, Texas, was cut off from the supply of an obscure brand of fine leather belts as the result of its discounting the belts to compete with competitors. The retailer sued the producer/designer, Leegin, and Leegin took the case to the Supreme Court. "Agreement" was not in issue; Leegin had procured pledges from its retailers to follow its designated prices. The wisdom of the per se rule against RPM was the issue. The Department of Justice wrote an amicus brief supporting *Leegin*.

d. RPM: The New Rule of Law

LEEGIN CREATIVE LEATHER PRODUCTS, INC. v. PSKS, INC.

551 U.S. 877 (2007).

JUSTICE KENNEDY:

[Leegin was a designer, producer and distributor of leather accessories, including belts it sold under the brand name "Brighton." It sold its products across the United States in more than 5000 retail stores.

PSKS, which operates Kay's Kloset, was a women's apparel store in Lewisville, Texas. It bought Brighton brand from Leegin since 1995. While it bought from many other manufacturers as well, Brighton was its most important brand.

In 1997 Leegin established a policy of not selling to retailers who sold Brighton goods below its suggested prices. It explained that it thought consumers were "perplexed by promises of product quality and support of product which we believe is lacking in . . . larger stores. Consumers are further confused by the ever popular sale, sale, sale, etc." Leegin wanted to "break away from the pack by selling [at] specialty stores" that offer consistently great quality merchandise and support.

PSKS pledged to adhere to the suggested prices, but later marked down its Brighton line by 20% to compete with nearby retailers. Leegin demanded that PSKS stop discounting, and when PSKS refused, Leegin stopped supplying PSKS. PSKS sued. At trial, in view of *Dr. Miles*, the district court excluded Leegin's proffer of testimony regarding the procompetitive effect of its pricing policy. The jury found that Leegin had entered into vertical resale price agreements, and returned a verdict for PSKS, amounting as trebled to a judgment of nearly $4 million.

The Court granted certiorari to determine whether resale price maintenance should continue to be per se illegal.] * * *

Resort to *per se* rules is confined to restraints, like those mentioned [competitor price-fixing or market division], "that would always or almost always tend to restrict competition and decrease output." *Business Electronics*, [485 U.S.] at 723. To justify a *per se* prohibition a restraint must have "manifestly anticompetitive" effects, *GTE Sylvania*, [433 U.S.] at 50, and "lack . . . any redeeming virtue," *Northwest Wholesale Stationers, Inc. v. Pacific Stationery & Printing Co.*, 472 U.S. 284, 289 (1985). . . . * * *

The reasons upon which *Dr. Miles* relied do not justify a *per se* rule. As a consequence, it is necessary to examine, in the first instance, the economic effects of vertical agreements to fix minimum resale prices, and to determine whether the *per se* rule is nonetheless appropriate.

A. * * *

The justifications for vertical price restraints are similar to those for other vertical restraints. Minimum resale price maintenance can stimulate interbrand competition—the competition among manufacturers selling different brands of the same type of product—by reducing intrabrand competition—the competition among retailers selling the same brand. The promotion of interbrand competition is important because "the primary purpose of the antitrust laws is to protect [this type of] competition." *Khan*, 522 U.S., at 15. A single manufacturer's use of vertical price restraints tends to eliminate intrabrand price competition; this in turn encourages retailers to invest in tangible or intangible services or promotional efforts that aid the manufacturer's position as against rival manufacturers. Resale price maintenance also has the potential to give consumers more options so that they can choose among low-price, low-service brands; high-price, high-service brands; and brands that fall in between.

Absent vertical price restraints, the retail services that enhance interbrand competition might be underprovided. This is because discounting retailers can free ride on retailers who furnish services and then capture some of the increased demand those services generate. Consumers might learn, for example, about the benefits of a manufacturer's product from a retailer that invests in fine showrooms, offers product demonstrations, or hires and trains knowledgeable employees. R. Posner, Antitrust Law 172–173 (2d ed. 2001) (hereinafter Posner). Or consumers might decide to buy the product because they see it in a retail establishment that has a reputation for selling high-quality merchandise. Marvel & McCafferty, Resale Price Maintenance and Quality Certification, 15 Rand J. Econ. 346, 347–349 (1984) (hereinafter Marvel & McCafferty). If the consumer can then buy the product from a retailer that discounts because it has not spent capital providing services or developing a quality reputation, the high-service retailer will lose sales to the discounter, forcing it to cut back its services to a level lower than consumers would otherwise prefer. Minimum resale price maintenance alleviates the problem because it prevents the discounter from undercutting the service provider. With price competition decreased, the manufacturer's retailers compete among themselves over services.

Resale price maintenance, in addition, can increase interbrand competition by facilitating market entry for new firms and brands. "[N]ew manufacturers and manufacturers entering new markets can use the restrictions in order to induce competent and aggressive retailers to make the kind of investment of capital and labor that is often required in the distribution of products unknown to the consumer." GTE Sylvania, supra, at 55.... New products and new brands are essential to a dynamic economy, and if markets can be penetrated by using resale price maintenance there is a procompetitive effect.

Resale price maintenance can also increase interbrand competition by encouraging retailer services that would not be provided even absent free riding. It may be difficult and inefficient for a manufacturer to make and enforce a contract with a retailer specifying the different services the retailer must perform. Offering the retailer a guaranteed margin and threatening termination if it does not live up to expectations may be the most efficient way to expand the manufacturer's market share by inducing the retailer's performance and allowing it to use its own initiative and experience in providing valuable services....

B.

While vertical agreements setting minimum resale prices can have procompetitive justifications, they may have anticompetitive effects in other cases; and unlawful price fixing, designed solely to obtain monopoly profits, is an ever present temptation. Resale price maintenance may, for example, facilitate a manufacturer cartel. An unlawful cartel will seek to discover if some manufacturers are undercutting the cartel's fixed prices. Resale price maintenance could assist the cartel in identifying price-cutting manufacturers who benefit from the lower prices they offer. Resale price maintenance, furthermore, could discourage a manufacturer from cutting prices to retailers with the concomitant benefit of cheaper prices to consumers.

Vertical price restraints also "might be used to organize cartels at the retailer level." A group of retailers might collude to fix prices to consumers and then compel a manufacturer to aid the unlawful arrangement with resale price maintenance. In that instance the manufacturer does not establish the practice to stimulate services or to promote its brand but to give inefficient retailers higher profits. Retailers with better distribution systems and lower cost structures would be prevented from charging lower prices by the agreement....

A horizontal cartel among competing manufacturers or competing retailers that decreases output or reduces competition in order to increase price is, and ought to be, *per se* unlawful. To the extent a vertical agreement setting minimum resale prices is entered upon to facilitate either type of cartel, it, too, would need to be held unlawful under the rule of reason. This type of agreement may also be useful evidence for a plaintiff attempting to prove the existence of a horizontal cartel.

Resale price maintenance, furthermore, can be abused by a powerful manufacturer or retailer. A dominant retailer, for example, might request resale price maintenance to forestall innovation in distribution that decreases costs. A manufacturer might consider it has little choice but to accommodate the retailer's demands for vertical price restraints if the manufacturer believes it needs access to the retailer's distribution network.... cf. *Toys "R" Us, Inc. v. FTC*, 221 F.3d 928, 937–938 (C.A.7 2000). A manufacturer with market power, by comparison, might use resale price maintenance to give retailers an incentive not to sell the products of smaller rivals or new entrants. As should be evident, the potential anticompetitive consequences of vertical price restraints must not be ignored or underestimated.

C.

Notwithstanding the risks of unlawful conduct, it cannot be stated with any degree of confidence that resale price maintenance "always or almost always tend[s] to restrict competition and decrease output." *Business Electronics*.... As the [*per se*] rule would proscribe a significant amount of procompetitive conduct, these agreements appear ill suited for *per se* condemnation.

[The Court rejects the argument that administrative convenience can justify the *per se* rule, noting:] Those rules can be counterproductive. They can increase the total cost of the antitrust system by prohibiting procompetitive conduct the antitrust laws should encourage.... They also may increase litigation costs by promoting frivolous suits against legitimate practices....

Respondent also argues the *per se* rule is justified because a vertical price restraint can lead to higher prices for the manufacturer's goods. See also Overstreet 160 (noting that "price surveys indicate that [resale price maintenance] in most cases increased the prices of products sold"). Respondent is mistaken in relying on pricing effects absent a further showing of anticompetitive conduct.... For, as has been indicated already, the antitrust laws are designed primarily to protect interbrand competition, from which lower prices can later result. The Court, moreover, has evaluated other vertical restraints under the rule of reason even though prices can be increased in the course of promoting procompetitive effects. And resale price maintenance may reduce prices if manufacturers have resorted to costlier alternatives of controlling resale prices that are not *per se* unlawful.

Respondent's argument, furthermore, overlooks that, in general, the interests of manufacturers and consumers are aligned with respect to retailer profit margins. The difference between the price a manufacturer charges retailers and the price retailers charge consumers represents part of the manufacturer's cost of distribution, which, like any other cost, the manufacturer usually desires to minimize.... A manufacturer has no incentive to overcompensate retailers with unjustified margins. The retailers, not the manufacturer, gain from higher retail prices.... As a general matter, therefore, a single manufacturer will desire to set minimum resale prices only if the "increase in demand resulting from enhanced service ... will more than offset a negative impact on demand of a higher retail price." Mathewson & Winter 67.

The implications of respondent's position are far reaching. Many decisions a manufacturer makes and carries out through concerted action can lead to higher prices. A manufacturer might, for example, contract with different suppliers to obtain better inputs that improve product quality. Or it might hire an advertising agency to promote awareness of its goods. Yet no one would think these actions violate the Sherman Act because they lead to higher prices. The antitrust laws do not require manufacturers to produce generic goods that consumers do not know about or want. The manufacturer strives to improve its product quality or to promote its brand because it believes this conduct will lead to increased demand despite higher prices. The same can hold true for resale price maintenance.

Resale price maintenance, it is true, does have economic dangers. If the rule of reason were to apply to vertical price restraints, courts would have to be diligent in eliminating their anticompetitive uses from the market. This is a realistic objective, and certain factors are relevant to the inquiry. For example, the number of manufacturers that make use of the practice in a given industry can provide important instruction. When only a few manufacturers lacking market power adopt the practice, there is little likelihood it is facilitating a manufacturer cartel, for a cartel then can be undercut by rival manufacturers. Likewise, a retailer cartel is unlikely when only a single manufacturer in a competitive market uses resale price maintenance. Interbrand competition would divert consumers to lower priced substitutes and eliminate any gains to retailers from their price-fixing agreement over a single brand. Resale price maintenance should be subject to more careful scrutiny, by contrast, if many competing manufacturers adopt the practice....

The source of the restraint may also be an important consideration. If there is evidence retailers were the impetus for a vertical price restraint, there is a greater likelihood that the restraint facilitates a retailer cartel or supports a dominant, inefficient retailer. If, by contrast, a manufacturer adopted the policy independent of retailer pressure, the restraint is less likely to promote anticompetitive conduct. Cf. Posner 177 ("It makes all the difference whether minimum retail prices are imposed by the manufacturer in order to evoke point-of-sale services or by the dealers in order to obtain monopoly profits")....

As a final matter, that a dominant manufacturer or retailer can abuse resale price maintenance for anticompetitive purposes may not be a serious concern unless the relevant entity has market power. If a retailer lacks market power, manufacturers likely can sell their goods through rival retailers. See also *Business Electronics, supra,* at 727, n. 2 (noting "[r]etail market power is rare, because of the usual presence of interbrand competition and other dealers"). And if a manufacturer lacks market power, there is less likelihood it can use the practice to keep competitors away from distribution outlets.

The rule of reason is designed and used to eliminate anticompetitive transactions from the market. This standard principle applies to vertical price restraints. A party alleging injury from a vertical agreement setting minimum resale prices will have, as a general matter, the information and resources available to show the existence of the agreement and its scope of operation. As courts gain experience considering the effects of these restraints by applying the rule of reason over the course of decisions, they can establish the litigation structure to ensure the rule operates to eliminate anticompetitive restraints from the market and to provide more guidance to businesses. Courts can, for example, devise rules over time for offering proof, or even presumptions where justified, to make the rule of reason a fair and efficient way to prohibit anticompetitive restraints and to promote procompetitive ones. * * *

IV.

We do not write on a clean slate, for the decision in *Dr. Miles* is almost a century old. So there is an argument for its retention on the basis of *stare decisis* alone. Even if *Dr. Miles* established an erroneous rule, "*[s]tare decisis* reflects a policy judgment that in most matters it is more important that the applicable rule of law be settled than that it be settled right." *Khan,* 522 U.S., at 20. And concerns about maintaining settled law are strong when the question is one of statutory interpretation.

Stare decisis is not as significant in this case, however, because the issue before us is the scope of the Sherman Act.... From the beginning the Court has treated the Sherman Act as a common-law statute.... Just as the common law adapts to modern understanding and greater experience, so too does the Sherman Act's prohibition on "restraint[s] of trade" evolve to meet the dynamics of present economic conditions. The case-by-case adjudication contemplated by the rule of reason has implemented this common-law approach. Likewise, the boundaries of the doctrine of *per se* illegality should not be immovable. For "[i]t would make no sense to create out of the single term 'restraint of trade' a chronologically schizoid statute, in which a 'rule of reason' evolves with new circumstance and new wisdom, but a line of *per se* illegality remains forever fixed where it was." *Business Electronics,* 485 U.S., at 732. * * *

JUSTICE BREYER, joined by JUSTICES STEVENS, SOUTER and GINSBURG, dissenting: [After noting information that prices go up when minimum resale pricing is allowed, citing a study showing a 19% to 27% price rise during the period of fair trading laws, and cataloging the possible harms and benefits of resale price maintenance:]

I.

The Sherman Act seeks to maintain a marketplace free of anticompetitive practices, in particular those enforced by agreement among private firms. The law assumes that such a marketplace, free of private restrictions, will tend to bring about the lower prices, better products, and more efficient production processes that consumers typically desire. In determining the lawfulness of particular practices, courts often apply a "rule of reason." They examine both a practice's likely anticompetitive effects and its beneficial business justifications.

Nonetheless, sometimes the likely anticompetitive consequences of a particular practice are so serious and the potential justifications so few (or, e.g., so difficult to prove) that courts have departed from a pure "rule of reason" approach. And sometimes this Court has imposed a rule of per se unlawfulness—a rule that instructs courts to find the practice unlawful all (or nearly all) the time.

The case before us asks which kind of approach the courts should follow where minimum resale price maintenance is at issue. Should they apply a per se rule (or a variation) that would make minimum resale price maintenance always (or almost always) unlawful? Should they apply a "rule of reason"? Were the Court writing on a blank slate, I would find these questions difficult. But, of course, the Court is not writing on a blank slate, and that fact makes a considerable legal difference. * * *

The upshot is, as many economists suggest, sometimes resale price maintenance can prove harmful; sometimes it can bring benefits.... But before concluding that courts should consequently apply a rule of reason, I would ask such questions as, how often are harms or benefits likely to occur? How easy is it to separate the beneficial sheep from the antitrust goats?

Economic discussion, such as the studies the Court relies upon, can *help* provide answers to these questions, and in doing so, economics can, and should, inform antitrust law. But antitrust law cannot, and should not, precisely replicate economists' (sometimes conflicting) views. That is because law, unlike economics, is an administrative system the effects of which depend upon the content of rules and precedents only as they are applied by judges and juries in courts and by lawyers advising their clients. And that fact means that courts will often bring their own administrative judgment to bear, sometimes applying rules of *per se* unlawfulness to business practices even when those practices sometimes produce benefits. . . .

I have already described studies and analyses that suggest (though they cannot prove) that resale price maintenance can cause harms with some regularity—and certainly when dealers are the driving force. But what about benefits? How often, for example, will the benefits to which the Court points occur in practice? I can find no economic consensus on this point. There is a consensus in the literature that "free riding" takes place. But "free riding" often takes place in the economy without any legal effort to stop it. Many visitors to California take free rides on the Pacific Coast Highway. We all benefit freely from ideas, such as that of creating the first supermarket. Dealers often take a "free ride" on investments that others have made in building a product's name and reputation. The question is how often the "free riding" problem is serious enough significantly to deter dealer investment.

To be more specific, one can easily *imagine* a dealer who refuses to provide important presale services, say a detailed explanation of how a product works (or who fails to provide a proper atmosphere in which to sell expensive perfume or alligator billfolds), lest customers use that "free" service (or enjoy the psychological benefit arising when a high-priced retailer stocks a particular brand of billfold or handbag) and then buy from another dealer at a lower price. Sometimes this must happen in reality. But does it happen often? We do, after all, live in an economy where firms, despite *Dr. Miles' per se* rule, still sell complex technical equipment (as well as expensive perfume and alligator billfolds) to consumers.

All this is to say that the ultimate question is not whether, but *how much*, "free riding" of this sort takes place. And, after reading the briefs, I must answer that question with an uncertain "sometimes." See, *e.g.*, Brief for William S. Comanor and Frederic M. Scherer as *Amici Curiae* 6–7 (noting "skepticism in the economic literature about how often [free riding] actually occurs"); Scherer & Ross 551–555 (explaining the "severe limitations" of the free-rider justification for resale price maintenance); Pitofsky, Why *Dr. Miles* Was Right, 8 Regulation, No. 1, pp. 27, 29–30 (Jan./Feb.1984) (similar analysis).

How easily can courts identify instances in which the benefits are likely to outweigh potential harms? My own answer is, *not very easily*. For one thing, it is often difficult to identify *who*—producer or dealer—is the moving force behind any given resale price maintenance agreement. Suppose, for example, several large multibrand retailers all sell resale-price-maintained products. Suppose further that small producers set retail prices because they fear that, otherwise, the large retailers will favor (say, by allocating better shelf-space) the goods of other producers who practice resale price maintenance. Who "initiated" this practice, the retailers hoping for considerable insulation from retail competition, or the producers, who simply seek to deal best with the circumstances they find? For another thing, as I just said, it is difficult to determine just when, and where, the "free riding" problem is serious enough to warrant legal protection.

I recognize that scholars have sought to develop check lists and sets of questions that will help courts separate instances where anticompetitive harms are more likely from instances where only benefits are likely to be found. But applying these criteria in court is often easier said than done. The Court's invitation to consider the existence of "market power," for example, invites lengthy time-consuming argument among competing experts, as they seek to apply abstract, highly technical, criteria to often ill-defined markets. And resale price maintenance cases, unlike a major merger or monopoly case, are likely to prove numerous and involve only private parties. One cannot fairly expect judges and juries in such cases to apply complex economic criteria without making a considerable number of mistakes, which themselves may impose serious costs. . . .

Are there special advantages to a bright-line rule? Without such a rule, it is often unfair, and consequently impractical, for enforcement officials to bring criminal proceedings. And since enforcement resources are limited, that loss may tempt some producers or dealers to enter into agreements that are, on balance, anticompetitive.

Given the uncertainties that surround key items in the overall balance sheet, particularly in respect to the "administrative" questions, I can concede to the majority that the problem is difficult. And, if forced to decide now, at most I might agree that the *per se* rule should be slightly modified to allow an exception for the more easily identifiable and temporary condition of "new entry." See Pitofsky 1495. But I am not now forced to decide this question. The question before us is not what should be the rule, starting from scratch. We here must decide whether to change a clear and simple price-related antitrust rule that the courts have applied for nearly a century. * * *

. . . [W]e cannot conclude with confidence that the gains from eliminating the *per se* rule will outweigh the costs. * * *

QUESTIONS AND COMMENTS

1. On remand, the court dismissed the case for failure of plaintiff to prove a proper relevant market in which competition may have been harmed. 615 F.3d 412 (5th Cir. 2010), cert. denied, ___ U.S. ___, 131 S.Ct. 1476 (2011).

2. Which rule is better for consumers: The per se rule subject to narrow gateway exceptions, as suggested by Justice Breyer, or a fuller rule of reason, as decided by the Court?

3. Suggest a structured rule of reason for courts to apply after *Leegin*.

4. Many states of the United States and many foreign jurisdictions condemn RPM agreements on their face or have very strong presumptions against them. This means that businesses must still be advised to exercise caution in implementing RPM programs, even if there is no good story that the programs are in aid of a cartel and even if the firm has no market power.

2. RESTRAINTS ON DISTRIBUTORS OTHER THAN MINIMUM RESALE PRICING— FREE TRADERS TO FREE RIDERS

a. Customer and Territorial Restraints and Maximum Resale Price–Fixing (Earlier Law)

The free-trader freedom-of-alienation principle that evolved from *Dr. Miles* fed smoothly into U.S. antitrust law of the 1960s. It favored opportunity and autonomy for entrepreneurs and people without power and assumed that the owner of goods could respond best to the forces of competition. The most important antitrust case for a decade was *Schwinn*, which set the law and tone for non-price distribution restraints. While *Schwinn* was overruled, its legacy lingers on in some jurisdictions. For example, *Schwinn* has resonances in European Union law, which has adopted a similar principle in order to promote integration of the Member States of the European Union. *Consten and Grundig v. Commission*, cases 56, 58/64, [1966] ECR 299. A tight territorial restraint at Member State borders continues to be a hard core offense against EU law, even though theoretically subject to justification.

In *United States v. Arnold, Schwinn & Co.*, 388 U.S. 365 (1967), overruled by *Continental T.V. v. GTE Sylvania*, infra, Arnold, Schwinn and Company was a major manufacturer of bicycles. In 1951 it was the largest seller in the United States bicycle market, accounting for 22.5% of sales. In the next 10 years, its market share fell to 12.8%. Importers, and mass marketers carrying private label brands, had eroded its share and were powerful competitors. Schwinn sold about 75% of its bicycles directly to retailers under an agency or consignment plan. It sold the rest to independent distributors. Each of its 22 distributors was the exclusive wholesaler within an assigned territory. Each was forbidden to sell outside of its territory, and within its territory could sell only to retailers franchised by Schwinn. These franchised retailers could sell only at designated locations. They could sell only to consumers, not to nonfranchised retailers, and thus not to discounters.

The Supreme Court distinguished sales and consignments. Restraints regarding *consigned* bicycles were deemed reasonable in view of the competition from mass merchandisers of other brands of bicycles and because of reluctance to interfere with intra-enterprise restraints, especially those imposed by small firms. By contrast, all such post-sale restraints on independent distributors and retailers were held illegal per se.

The Court said:

> [W]here a manufacturer *sells* products to his distributor subject to territorial restrictions upon resale, a per se violation of the Sherman Act results. And, as we have held, the same principle applies to restrictions of outlets with which the distributors may deal and to restraints upon retailers to whom the goods are sold. Under the Sherman Act, it is unreasonable without more for a manufacturer to seek to restrict and confine areas or persons with whom an article may be traded after the manufacturer has parted with dominion over it. ... *Dr. Miles*. Such restraints are so obviously destructive of competition that their mere existence is enough. If the manufacturer parts with dominion over his product or transfers risk of loss to another, he may not reserve control over its destiny or the conditions of its resale. ...On the other hand, ... we are not prepared to introduce the inflexibility which a per se rule might bring if it were applied to prohibit all vertical restrictions of territory and all franchising, in the sense of designating specified distributors and retailers as the chosen instruments through which the manufacturer, retaining ownership of the goods, will distribute them to the public. Such a rule might severely hamper smaller enterprises resorting to reasonable methods of meeting the competition of giants and of merchandising through independent dealers, and it might sharply accelerate the trend towards vertical integration of the distribution process. But to allow this freedom where the manufacturer has parted with dominion over the goods—the usual marketing situation—would violate the ancient rule against restraints on alienation and open the door to exclusivity of outlets and limitation of territory further than prudence permits. * * *

The spirit of *Schwinn* (autonomy for the owner) was followed a year later in *Albrecht v. Herald Co.*, 390 U.S. 145 (1968) (overruled by *State Oil Co. v. Khan*, infra, p. 652). In *Albrecht*, the Herald Company, which published the dominant morning newspaper in St. Louis, distributed its paper through independent carriers, each of which was assigned an exclusive territory. The Herald Company advertised a suggested maximum price, and made the exclusive territories subject to termination if its carriers' prices exceeded the suggested maximum price. Albrecht, one of the carriers, persistently exceeded the suggested maximum. The Herald thereupon warned Albrecht to stop over-charging. It contracted with one individual to solicit Albrecht's customers, and another to take over the route until Albrecht got its pricing back into line. Albrecht sued the Herald. The Supreme Court held that vertical resale price agreements, maximum as well as minimum, were illegal per se. The Court said:

> [S]chemes to fix maximum prices, by substituting the perhaps erroneous judgment of a seller for the forces of the competitive market, may severely intrude upon the ability of buyers to compete and survive in that market. Competition, even in a single product, is not cast in a single mold. Maximum prices may be fixed too low for the dealer to furnish services essential to the value which goods have for the

consumer or to furnish services and conveniences which consumers desire and for which they are willing to pay. Maximum price fixing may channel distribution through a few large or specifically advantaged dealers who otherwise would be subject to significant nonprice competition. Moreover, if the actual price charged under a maximum price scheme is nearly always the fixed maximum price, which is increasingly likely as the maximum price approaches the actual cost of the dealer, the scheme tends to acquire all the attributes of an arrangement fixing minimum prices. It is our view, therefore, that the combination formed by the respondent in this case to force petitioner to maintain a specified price for the resale of the newspapers which he had purchased from respondent constituted, without more, an illegal restraint of trade under § 1 of the Sherman Act.

Both *Schwinn* and *Albrecht* were overruled well before *Leegin*. For Schwinn, the per se rule prevented it from protecting its service-providing dealers from free riders. If Schwinn could protect its service-providing dealers from the competition of other Schwinn dealers, it could encourage promotion and service at the point of sale. Without intrabrand restraints, "shoe string" dealers and their customers might free ride on service-giving dealers' investments, filling the demand primed by the loyal service providers. Having lower costs, the no-frills operations could discount their product, capturing market share at the expense of the service providers. The service providers would soon learn that they could not reap the benefits of their investment in service and promotion; they would cut back their investment, and the manufacturer would lose image, reputation, and sales to another brand.

While the next step of the story has already been telegraphed by *Leegin*, it is important to be familiar with the case that overruled *Schwinn*, namely *GTE Sylvania*, and later the case that overruled *Albrecht*, namely *Khan*, for both *Sylvania* and *Khan* have landmark status in U.S. antitrust. *GTE Sylvania* was the first Supreme Court precedent that highlighted the importance of interbrand competition.

b. The Turning of the Tide

i. Non–Price restraints

CONTINENTAL T.V., INC. v. GTE SYLVANIA INC.

433 U.S. 36 (1977).

JUSTICE POWELL: * * * Respondent GTE Sylvania, Inc. (Sylvania) manufactures and sells television sets through its Home Entertainment Products Division. Prior to 1962, like most other television manufacturers, Sylvania sold its televisions to independent or company-owned distributors who in turn resold to a large and diverse group of retailers. Prompted by a decline in its market share to a relatively insignificant 1% to 2% of national television sales,[1] Sylvania conducted an intensive reassessment of its marketing strategy, and in 1962 adopted the franchise plan challenged here. Sylvania phased out its wholesale distributors and began to sell its televisions directly to a smaller and more select group of franchised retailers. An acknowledged purpose of the change was to decrease the number of competing Sylvania retailers in the hope of attracting the more aggressive and competent retailers thought necessary to the improvement of the company's market position. To this end, Sylvania limited the number of franchises granted for any given area and required each franchisee to sell his Sylvania products only from the location or locations at which he was franchised. A franchise did not constitute an exclusive territory, and Sylvania retained sole discretion to increase the number of retailers in an area in light of the success or failure of existing retailers in developing their market. The revised marketing strategy appears to have been successful during the period at issue here, for by 1965 Sylvania's share of national television sales had increased to approximately 5%, and the company ranked as the Nation's eighth largest manufacturer of color television sets.

This suit is the result of the rupture of a franchiser-franchisee relationship that had previously prospered under the revised Sylvania plan. Dissatisfied with its sales in the city of San Francisco, Sylvania decided in the spring of 1965 to franchise Young Brothers, an established San Francisco retailer of televisions, as an additional San Francisco retailer. The proposed location of the new franchise was approximately a mile from a retail outlet operated by petitioner Continental T.V., Inc. (Continental), one of the most successful Sylvania franchisees. Continental protested that the location of the new franchise violated Sylvania's marketing policy, but Sylvania persisted in its plans. Continental then canceled a large Sylvania order and placed a large order with Phillips, one of Sylvania's competitors.

During this same period, Continental expressed a desire to open a store in Sacramento, Cal., a desire Sylvania attributed at least in part to Continental's displeasure over the Young Brothers decision. Sylvania believed that the Sacramento market was adequately served by the existing Sylvania retailers and denied the request. In the face of this denial, Continental advised Sylvania in early September 1965, that it was in the process of moving Sylvania merchandise from its San Jose, Cal., warehouse to a new retail location that it had leased in Sacramento. Two weeks later, allegedly for unrelated reasons, Sylvania's credit department reduced Continental's credit line from $300,000 to $50,000. In response to the reduction in credit and the generally deteriorating relations with Sylvania, Continental withheld all payments owed to John P. Maguire & Co., Inc. (Maguire), the finance company that handled the credit arrangements between Sylvania and its retailers. Shortly thereafter, Sylvania terminated Continental's franchises, and Maguire filed this diversity ac-

1. RCA at that time was the dominant firm with as much as 60% to 70% of national television sales in an industry with more than 100 manufacturers.

tion in the United States District Court for the Northern District of California seeking recovery of money owed and of secured merchandise held by Continental.

The antitrust issues before us originated in cross-claims brought by Continental against Sylvania and Maguire. Most important for our purposes was the claim that Sylvania had violated § 1 of the Sherman Act by entering into and enforcing franchise agreements that prohibited the sale of Sylvania products other than from specified locations. At the close of evidence in the jury trial of Continental's claims, Sylvania requested the District Court to instruct the jury that its location restriction was illegal only if it unreasonably restrained or suppressed competition. Relying on this Court's decision in *United States v. Arnold, Schwinn & Co.,* [388 U.S. 365 (1967)] the District Court rejected the proffered instruction in favor of the following one:

> Therefore, if you find by a preponderance of the evidence that Sylvania entered into a contract, combination or conspiracy with one or more of its dealers pursuant to which Sylvania exercised dominion or control over the products sold to the dealer, after having parted with title and risk to the products, you must find any effort thereafter to restrict outlets or store locations from which its dealers resold the merchandise which they had purchased from Sylvania to be a violation of Section 1 of the Sherman Act, regardless of the reasonableness of the location restrictions.

In answers to special interrogatories, the jury found that Sylvania had engaged "in a contract, combination or conspiracy in restraint of trade in violation of the antitrust laws with respect to location restrictions alone," and assessed Continental's damages at $591,506, which was trebled pursuant to 15 U.S.C. § 15 to produce an award of $1,774,515.

On appeal, the Court of Appeals for the Ninth Circuit, sitting en banc, reversed by a divided vote.... [10] * * *

II.

B. * * *

... In intent and competitive impact, the retail-customer restriction in *Schwinn* is indistinguishable from the location restriction in the present case. In both cases the restrictions limited the freedom of the retailer to dispose of the purchased products as he desired. The fact that one restriction was addressed to territory and the other to customers is irrelevant to functional antitrust analysis and, indeed, to the language and broad thrust of the opinion in *Schwinn.*

III. * * *

... *Per se* rules of illegality are appropriate only when they relate to conduct that is manifestly anticompetitive.... * * *

---

10. ... [Dissenting,] Judge Browning stated that he found the interpretation responsive to and justified by the need to protect " 'individual traders from unnecessary restrictions upon their freedom of action.' "

The market impact of vertical restrictions is complex[18] because of their potential for a simultaneous reduction of intrabrand competition and stimulation of interbrand competition.[19] Significantly, the Court in *Schwinn* did not distinguish among the challenged restrictions on the basis of their individual potential for intrabrand harm or interbrand benefit. Restrictions that completely eliminated intrabrand competition among Schwinn distributors were analyzed no differently from those that merely moderated intrabrand competition among retailers. The pivotal factor was the passage of title: All restrictions were held to be *per se* illegal where title had passed, and all were evaluated and sustained under the rule of reason where it had not. The location restriction at issue here would be subject to the same pattern of analysis under *Schwinn*.

It appears that this distinction between sale and nonsale transactions resulted from the Court's effort to accommodate the perceived intrabrand harm and interbrand benefit of vertical restrictions. The *per se* rule for sale transactions reflected the view that vertical restrictions are "so obviously destructive" of intrabrand competition that their use would "open the door to exclusivity of outlets and limitation of territory further than prudence permits." 388 U.S., at 379–380.[21] Conversely, the continued

18. As in *Schwinn*, we are concerned here only with nonprice vertical restrictions. The *per se* illegality of price resrictions has been established firmly for many years and involves significantly different questions of analysis and policy. [Resale price maintenance may facilitate cartelizing.] ... Furthermore, Congress recently has expressed its approval of a *per se* analysis of vertical price restrictions by repealing those provisions of the Miller–Tydings and McGuire Acts allowing fair trade pricing at the option of the individual States.... No similar expression of congressional intent exists for non-price restrictions.

19. Interbrand competition is the competition among the manufacturers of the same generic product—television sets in this case—and is the primary concern of antitrust law. The extreme example of a deficiency of interbrand competition is monopoly, where there is only one manufacturer. In contrast, intrabrand competition is the competition between the distributors—wholesale or retail—of the product of a particular manufacturer.

The degree of intrabrand competition is wholly independent of the level of interbrand competition confronting the manufacturer. Thus, there may be fierce intrabrand competition among the distributors of a product produced by a monopolist and no intrabrand competition among the distributors of a product produced by a firm in a highly competitive industry. But when interbrand competition exists, as it does among television manufacturers, it provides a significant check on the exploitation of intrabrand market power because of the ability of consumers to substitute a different brand of the same product.

21. The Court also stated that to impose vertical restrictions in sale transactions would "violate the ancient rule against restraints on alienation." 388 U.S., at 380. This isolated reference has provoked sharp criticism from virtually all of the commentators on the decision, most of whom have regarded the Court's apparent reliance on the "ancient rule" as both a misreading of legal history and a perversion of antitrust analysis.... We quite agree with MR. JUSTICE STEWART's dissenting comment in *Schwinn* that "the state of the common law 400 or even 100 years ago is irrelevant to the issue before us: the effect of the antitrust laws upon vertical distributional restraints in the American economy today." 388 U.S., at 392.

We are similarly unable to accept Judge Browning's interpretation of *Schwinn*. In his dissent below he argued that the decision reflects the view that the Sherman Act was intended to prohibit restrictions on the autonomy of independent businessmen even though they have no impact on "price, quality, and quantity of goods and services," 537 F. 2d, at 1019. This view is certainly not explicit in *Schwinn*, which purports to be based on an examination of the "impact [of the restrictions] upon the marketplace." 388 U.S., at 374. Competitive economies have social and political as well as economic advantages, see *e.g.*, *Northern Pac. R. Co. v. United States*, 356 U.S., at 4, but an antitrust policy divorced from market considerations would lack any objective benchmarks. As Mr. Justice Brandeis reminded us: "Every agreement concerning trade, every regulation of trade, restrains. To bind, to restrain, is of their very essence." *Chicago Bd. of Trade* adherence to the traditional rule of reason for nonsale transactions reflected the view that the restrictions have too great a potential for the promotion of interbrand competition to justify complete prohibition. The Court's opinion provides no analytical support for these contrasting positions. Nor is there even an assertion in the opinion that the competitive impact of vertical restrictions is significantly affected by the form of the transaction. Nonsale transactions appear to be excluded from the *per se* rule, not because of a greater danger of intrabrand harm or a greater promise of interbrand benefit, but rather because of the Court's unexplained belief that a complete *per se* prohibition would be too "inflexibl[e]." *Id.*, at 379.

Vertical restrictions reduce intrabrand competition by limiting the number of sellers of a particular product competing for the business of a given group of buyers. . . .

Vertical restrictions promote interbrand competition by allowing the manufacturer to achieve certain efficiencies in the distribution of his products. These "redeeming virtues" are implicit in every decision sustaining vertical restrictions under the rule of reason. Economists have identified a number of ways in which manufacturers can use such restrictions to compete more effectively against other manufacturers. . . . For example, new manufacturers and manufacturers entering new markets can use the restrictions in order to induce competent and aggressive retailers to make the kind of investment of capital and labor that is often required in the distribution of products unknown to the consumer. Established manufacturers can use them to induce retailers to engage in promotional activities or to provide service and repair facilities necessary to the efficient marketing of their products. Service and repair are vital for many products, such as automobiles and major household appliances. The availability and quality of such services affect a manufacturer's goodwill and the competitiveness of his product. Because of market imperfections such as the so-called "free rider" effect, these services might not be provided by retailers in a purely competitive situation, despite the fact that each retailer's benefit would be greater if all provided the services than if none did.

Economists also have argued that manufacturers have an economic interest in maintaining as much intrabrand competition as is consistent with the efficient distribution of their products. Bork, The Rule of Reason and the Per Se Concept: Price Fixing and Market Division [II], 75 Yale L.J. 373, 403 (1966); Posner, *supra,* n. [18], at 283, 287–288.[24] * * *

---

v. United States, 246 U.S., at 238. Although MR. JUSTICE WHITE's opinion endorses Judge Browning's interpretation, it purports to distinguish *Schwinn* on grounds inconsistent with that interpretation.

24. "Generally a manufacturer would prefer the lowest retail price possible, once its price to dealers has been set, because a lower retail price means increased sales and higher manufacturer revenues." Note, 88 Harv.L.Rev. 636, 641 (1975). In this context, a manufacturer is likely to view the difference between the price at which it sells to its retailers and their price to the consumer as its "cost of distribution," which it would prefer to minimize. Posner, [Restricted Distribution, 75 Colum. L. Rev.] at 283.

. . . [Vertical] restrictions, in varying forms, are widely used in our free market economy. As indicated above, there is substantial scholarly and judicial authority supporting their economic utility. There is relatively little authority to the contrary. Certainly, there has been no showing in this case, either generally or with respect to Sylvania's agreements, that vertical restrictions have or are likely to have a "pernicious effect on competition" or that they "lack . . . any redeeming virtue." Accordingly, we conclude that the *per se* rule stated in *Schwinn* must be overruled. In so holding we do not foreclose the possibility that particular applications of vertical restrictions might justify *per se* prohibition under *Northern Pac. R. Co.* But we do make clear that departure from the rule-of-reason standard must be based upon demonstrable economic effect rather than—as in *Schwinn*—upon formalistic line drawing [between sale and nonsale transactions.] * * *

JUSTICE WHITE, concurring in the judgment. Although I agree with the majority that the location clause at issue in this case is not a *per se* violation of the Sherman Act and should be judged under the rule of reason, I cannot agree that this result requires the overruling of *United States v. Arnold, Schwinn & Co.,* 388 U.S. 365 (1967). In my view this case is distinguishable from *Schwinn* because there is less potential for restraint of intrabrand competition and more potential for stimulating interbrand competition. As to intrabrand competition, Sylvania, unlike Schwinn, did not restrict the customers to whom or the territories where its purchasers could sell. As to interbrand competition, Sylvania, unlike Schwinn, had an insignificant market share at the time it adopted its challenged distribution practice and enjoyed no consumer preference that would allow its retailers to charge a premium over other brands. * * *

I have, moreover, substantial misgivings about the approach the majority takes to overruling *Schwinn.* The reason for the distinction in *Schwinn* between sale and nonsale transactions was not, as the majority would have it, "the Court's effort to accommodate the perceived intrabrand harm and interbrand benefit of vertical restrictions"; the reason was rather, as Judge Browning argued in dissent below, the notion in many of our cases involving vertical restraints that independent businessmen should have the freedom to dispose of the goods they own as they see fit. . . . * * *

After summarily rejecting this concern, reflected in our interpretations of the Sherman Act, for "the autonomy of independent businessmen," the majority not surprisingly finds "no justification" for *Schwinn*'s distinction between sale and nonsale transactions because the distinction is "essentially unrelated to any relevant economic impact." But while according some weight to the businessman's interest in controlling the terms on which he trades in his own goods may be anathema to those who view the Sherman Act as directed solely to economic efficiency, this principle is without question more deeply embedded in our cases than the notions of "free rider" effects and distributional efficiencies borrowed by the majority from the "new economics of vertical relationships." Perhaps the Court is right in partially abandoning this principle and in judging the instant nonprice vertical restraints solely by their "relevant economic impact"; but the precedents which reflect this principle should not be so lightly rejected by the Court....

I have a further reservation about the majority's reliance on "relevant economic impact" as the test for retaining *per se* rules regarding vertical restraints. It is common ground among the leading advocates of a purely economic approach to the question of distribution restraints that the economic arguments in favor of allowing vertical nonprice restraints generally apply to vertical price restraints as well. Although the majority asserts that "the *per se* illegality of price restrictions ... involves significantly different questions of analysis and policy," I suspect this purported distinction may be as difficult to justify as that of *Schwinn* under the terms of the majority's analysis. Thus Professor Posner, in an article cited five times by the majority, concludes: "I believe that the law should treat price and nonprice restrictions the same and that it should make no distinction between the imposition of restrictions in a sale contract and their imposition in an agency contract." Posner, *supra,* [Opinion of Court, n. 18], at 298.... The effect, if not the intention, of the Court's opinion is necessarily to call into question the firmly established *per se* rule against price restraints. * * *

QUESTIONS AND COMMENTS

1. Justice White was prescient. If vertical territorial restraints would not withstand a per se prohibition because, among other things, they may be used to induce retailers to provide more service, then resale price maintenance would not withstand a per se prohibition for the same reason. *Leegin,* supra at 630.

2. On remand in *Sylvania,* the district court found that Sylvania's location clauses were reasonable as a matter of law. The Court of Appeals affirmed, holding that the plaintiff has the burden of proving that a non-price vertical restraint is unreasonable, given its overall effect on intrabrand and interbrand competition. Merely proving a lessening of *intra*brand competition does not shift the burden of justification to defendant. *Continental T.V., Inc. v. GTE Sylvania Inc.*, 694 F.2d 1132 (9th Cir.1982).

3. The Court's opinion in *Sylvania* gave little content or structure to the rule of reason that would thenceforth be applicable. In the aftermath of *Sylvania* and later *Leegin*, vertical customer and territorial restraints, including location clauses, raise no red flags unless they happen to fit an anticompetitive story; e.g., that the interbrand competitors were each suppressing intrabrand competition in similar ways as a means to keep the market orderly and prevent competition from breaking out.

Business Electronics v. Sharp

When vertical restraints are used, is a cartel story likely? The answer depends on the facts, but a cartel is surely more likely in the event of vertical price restraints than vertical non-price restraints. This was in part the message of the Court in *Business Electronics Corp. v. Sharp Electronics Corp.*, 485 U.S. 717 (1988), where discounting distributor BEC sued calculator-maker Sharp for cutting it off after complaints by full-pricer Hartwell. Hartwell had given Sharp an ultimatum that it would terminate its relationship with Sharp unless Sharp terminated BEC. Sharp agreed and terminated BEC, but the two firms made no agreement on price. The Court held (this being pre *Leegin*) that the agreement to terminate the discounter was not illegal per se. While the holding of *Sharp* is mooted by *Leegin* (for, at present, neither is an agreement to impose RPM illegal per se), *Sharp* is noteworthy as a reflection of the Court's doubt that vertical restraints tend to facilitate cartels, that agreements to cut off discounters will hurt consumers, and that intrabrand competition matters to consumers.

The Court, by JUSTICE SCALIA, said:

[In *GTE Sylvania*] there was support for the proposition that vertical price restraints reduce inter brand price competition because they " 'facilitate cartelizing.' " The authorities cited by the Court suggested how vertical price agreements might assist horizontal price fixing at the manufacturer level (by reducing the manufacturer's incentive to cheat on a cartel, since its retailers could not pass on lower prices to consumers) or might be used to organize cartels at the retailer level.... Similar support for the cartel-facilitating effect of vertical non-price restraints was and remains lacking.

* * *

There has been no showing here that an agreement between a manufacturer and a dealer to terminate a "price cutter," without a further agreement on the price or price levels to be charged by the remaining dealer, almost always tends to restrict competition and reduce output. Any assistance to cartelizing that such an agreement might provide cannot be distinguished from the sort of minimal assistance that might be provided by vertical nonprice agreements like the exclusive territory agreement in *GTE Sylvania*, and is insufficient to justify a per se rule. Cartels are neither easy to form nor easy to maintain. Uncertainty over the terms of the cartel, particularly the prices to be charged in the future, obstructs both formation and adherence by making cheating easier. Without an agreement with the remaining dealer on price, the manufacturer both retains its incentive to cheat on any manufacturer-level cartel (since lower prices can still be passed on to consumers) and cannot as easily be used to organize and hold together a retailer-level cartel.[2]

* * *

JUSTICE STEVENS, with whom JUSTICE WHITE joins, dissenting: * * *

... What the jury found was a simple and naked " 'agreement between Sharp and Hartwell to terminate Business Electronics because of Business Electronics' price cutting.' " * * *

2. The dissent's principal fear appears to be not cartelization at either level, but Hartwell's assertion of dominant retail power. This fear does not possibly justify adopting a rule of *per se* illegality. Retail market power is rare, because of the usual presence of interbrand competition and other dealers, and it should therefore not be assumed but rather must be proved.

. . . [I]f . . . we focus on the precise character of the agreement before us, we can readily identify its anticompetitive nature. Before the agreement was made, there was price competition in the Houston retail market for respondent's products. The stronger of the two competitors was unhappy about that competition; it wanted to have the power to set the price level in the market and therefore it "complained to respondent on a number of occasions about petitioner's prices." Quite obviously, if petitioner had agreed with either Hartwell or respondent to discontinue its competitive pricing, there would have been no ultimatum from Hartwell and no termination by respondent. . . .

* * *

. . . [W]hile Hartwell may indeed be able to provide better services under the sales franchise agreement with petitioner out of the way, one would not have thought, until today, that the mere possibility of such a result—at the expense of the elimination of price competition and absent the salutary overlay of a manufacturer's distribution decision with the entire product line in mind—would be sufficient to legitimate an otherwise purely anticompetitive restraint. In fact, given the majority's total reliance on "economic analysis," it is hard to understand why, if such a purpose were sufficient to avoid the application of a per se rule in this context, the same purpose should not also be sufficient to trump the per se rule in all other price-fixing cases that arguably permit cartel members to "provide better services." * * *

QUESTIONS AND COMMENTS

1. Consider Justice Scalia's assumptions about markets and restraints: "cartels are neither easy to form nor easy to maintain"; "[r]etail market power is rare." Do you agree with them?

2. Was the dissent just a cry in the wilderness that can be heard no more? What do you make of the *Leegin* Court's dictum that vertical restraints originating from the dealer might be of greater concern than restraints originating from the manufacturer? If Sharp was a market leader in calculators, interbrand competition was sluggish, and BEC was a good performer, can you make an argument that the agreement between Sharp and Hartwell to terminate BEC was anticompetitive under the rule of reason? Which side has the better of the argument?

The limits of the free rider justification. Not all jurists, like Justice Scalia, support prophylactic pro-defendant rules on the assumption that the defendant must be trying to contain free riding. In *Eastman Kodak Co. v. Image Technical Services, Inc.*, 504 U.S. 451 (1992) (see pp. 299, 671 supra), Kodak invoked free riding as a reason to dismiss the monopoly suit against it. It claimed that it cut off the independent service providers from the parts they needed to repair the Kodak equipment in order to prevent the ISOs "from exploit[ing] the investment Kodak has made in product development, manufacturing and equipment sales in order to take away Kodak's service revenues." The Court said:

> According to Kodak, the ISOs are free riding because they have failed to enter the equipment and parts markets. This understanding of free-riding has no support in our caselaw. To the contrary, as the Court of Appeals noted, one of the evils proscribed by the antitrust laws is the creation of entry barriers to potential competitors by requiring them to enter two markets simultaneously.

In *Toys R Us, Inc. (TRU) v. FTC*, 221 F.3d 928 (7th Cir. 2000), TRU, the large retail toy chain, helped popularize "hot" toys for manufacturers such as Mattel (Barbie dolls) and Hasbro (GI Joe), and offered a wide variety of these toys. Toys R Us found itself in intense competition with warehouse clubs. The clubs required modest membership fees (e.g. $30), and then offered brand-name merchandise at "warehouse" style and prices. TRU prevailed upon the manufacturers to restrict sales to the warehouse clubs so that the clubs would not get the same toys or in the same packages sold by TRU. The FTC brought proceedings. It found that TRU had imposed illegal vertical restraints on its suppliers and had coordinated a horizontal manufacturer conspiracy. TRU denied the horizontal conspiracy (unsuccessfully), and alleged, in justification of the individual vertical agreements with each manufacturer that it, TRU, was trying to protect itself from free riding. The court, by Judge Diane Wood, said:

> TRU next urges that its policy was a legitimate business response to combat free riding by the warehouse clubs. We think, however, that it has fundamentally misunderstood the theory of free riding. Briefly, that theory is as follows. The manufacturer of a product, say widgets, has an incentive to distribute as many widgets as it can, while keeping its costs of distribution down as low as possible. In many instances, this means that the manufacturer will want to sell its widgets for a particular wholesale price and it will want its retailer to apply as low a mark-up as possible (*i.e.* put the product on the market for as little extra expense as possible). Sometimes, however, the manufacturer will want the retailer to provide special services or amenities that cost money, such as attractive premises, trained salespeople, long business hours, full-line stocking, or fast warranty service. But the costs of providing some of those amenities (usually pre-sale services) are hard to pass on to customers unless some form of restricted distribution is available. What the manufacturer does *not* want is for the shopper to visit the attractive store with highly paid, intelligent sales help, learn all about the product, and then go home and order it from a discount warehouse or (today) on-line discounters. The shopper in that situation has taken a "free ride" on the retailer's efforts; the retailer never gets paid for them, and eventually it stops offering the services. *If* those services were genuinely useful, in the sense that the product plus service package resulted in greater sales for the manufacturer than the product alone would have enjoyed,

there is a loss both for the manufacturer and the consumer. Hence, antitrust law permits nonprice vertical restraints that are designed to facilitate the provision of extra services, recognizing that a manufacturer in a competitive market who has guessed wrong will eventually be forced by the market to abandon the restrictions.

Here, the evidence shows that the free-riding story is inverted. The manufacturers wanted a business strategy under which they distributed their toys to as many different kinds of outlets as would accept them: exclusive toy shops, TRU, discount department stores, and warehouse clubs. Rightly or wrongly, this was the distribution strategy that each one believed would maximize its individual output and profits. The *manufacturers* did not think that the alleged "extra services" TRU might have been providing were necessary. This is crucial, because the most important insight behind the free rider concept is the fact that, with respect to the cost of distribution services, the interests of the manufacturer and the *consumer* are aligned, and are basically adverse to the interests of the retailer (who would presumably like to charge as much as possible for its part in the process)....

... [TRU's] economic interest was in maximizing its own profits, not in keeping down its suppliers' cost of doing business. Furthermore, we note that the Commission made a plausible argument for the proposition that there was little or no opportunity to "free" ride on anything here in any event ...

ii. Price Restraints: Maximum Price–Fixing

As we have signaled, the rule of *Albrecht* (maximum price-fixing is illegal per se) was overruled. This was inevitable as antitrust became a pro-consumer prescription, for a cap on prices holds prices down. The first relevant case to reach the Supreme Court in the modern era was dismissed for lack of antitrust injury. A gas station had complained about the low prices of its neighbor, a distributor for Atlantic Richfield (ARCO), whose low prices were mandated by agreement with ARCO. The Court said:

... [A] plaintiff must prove the existence of "antitrust injury, which is to say injury of the type the antitrust laws were intended to prevent and that flows from that which makes defendants' acts unlawful." Ibid. (emphasis in original). In Cargill, Inc. v. Monfort of Colorado, Inc., 479 U.S. 104 (1986), we reaffirmed that injury, although causally related to an antitrust violation, nevertheless will not qualify as "antitrust injury" unless it is attributable to an anticompetitive aspect of the practice under scrutiny, "since '[i]t is inimical to [the antitrust] laws to award damages' for losses stemming from continued competition." Id., at 109–110 (quoting Brunswick). * * *

... [A] vertical, maximum price-fixing agreement does not cause a competitor antitrust injury unless it results in predatory pricing.

Low prices benefit consumers regardless of how those prices are set, and so long as they are above predatory levels, they do not threaten competition. Hence, they cannot give rise to antitrust injury.

Finally, a maximum resale price fixing case came to the Supreme Court on the merits.

STATE OIL COMPANY v. KHAN

522 U.S. 3 (1997).

JUSTICE O'CONNOR: [State Oil Company distributed gasoline under the brand name "Union 76." It entered into a contract with gas station owner Khan providing that State Oil would establish a suggested resale price and sell gas to Khan for 3.25 cents less than that price. Khan could charge below the suggested resale price, but his profit margin would decline unless State Oil agreed to lower its price to Khan. Khan could charge above the suggested resale price, but, unless State Oil consented to the price rise, Khan would be required to rebate the entire profit resulting from the price rise. [Is this arrangement minimum price fixing, maximum price fixing, or both?]

Khan failed to pay his rent. State Oil terminated the contract. Khan sued for contract and antitrust damages. The district court granted summary judgment for State Oil, holding that the antitrust case was governed by the rule of reason and noting that the plaintiff had presented no evidence on market definition.

The court of appeals, by Judge Posner, reversed the dismissal on the basis of the rule of *Albrecht*, while giving a complete argument as to why *Albrecht* was wrongly decided. The Supreme Court reversed the decision by Judge Posner on the basis of Judge Posner's arguments].

... [O]ur reconsideration of *Albrecht*'s continuing validity is informed by several of our decisions, as well as a considerable body of scholarship discussing the effects of vertical restraints. Our analysis is also guided by our general view that the primary purpose of the antitrust laws is to protect interbrand competition. See, *e.g., Business Electronics Corp. v. Sharp Electronics Corp.,* 485 U.S. 717, 726 (1988). "Low prices," we have explained, "benefit consumers regardless of how those prices are set, and so long as they are above predatory levels, they do not threaten competition." *ARCO,* [495 U.S. 328, 340 (1990)]. Our interpretation of the Sherman Act also incorporates the notion that condemnation of practices resulting in lower prices to consumers is "especially costly" because "cutting prices in order to increase business often is the very essence of competition." *Matsushita Elec. Industrial Co. v. Zenith Radio Corp.,* 475 U.S. 574, 594 (1986).

So informed, we find it difficult to maintain that vertically imposed maximum prices could harm consumers or competition to the extent necessary to justify their *per se* invalidation. As Chief Judge Posner wrote for the Court of Appeals in this case:

"As for maximum resale price fixing, unless the supplier is a monopsonist he cannot squeeze his dealers' margins below a competitive level; the attempt to do so would just drive the dealers into the arms of a competing supplier. A supplier might, however, fix a maximum resale price in order to prevent his dealers from exploiting a monopoly position.... [S]uppose that State Oil, perhaps to encourage ... dealer services ... has spaced its dealers sufficiently far apart to limit competition among them (or even given each of them an exclusive territory); and suppose further that Union 76 is a sufficiently distinctive and popular brand to give the dealers in it at least a modicum of monopoly power. Then State Oil might want to place a ceiling on the dealers' resale prices in order to prevent them from exploiting that monopoly power fully. It would do this not out of disinterested malice, but in its commercial self-interest. The higher the price at which gasoline is resold, the smaller the volume sold, and so the lower the profit to the supplier if the higher profit per gallon at the higher price is being snared by the dealer."

See also R. Bork, The Antitrust Paradox 281–282 (1978) ("There could, of course, be no anticonsumer effect from [the type of price fixing considered in *Albrecht*], and one suspects that the paper has a legitimate interest in keeping subscriber prices down in order to increase circulation and maximize revenues from advertising"). * * *

In overruling *Albrecht,* we of course do not hold that all vertical maximum price fixing is *per se* lawful. Instead, vertical maximum price fixing, like the majority of commercial arrangements subject to the antitrust laws, should be evaluated under the rule of reason. In our view, rule-of-reason analysis will effectively identify those situations in which vertical maximum price fixing amounts to anticompetitive conduct.

QUESTION

After *Khan*, can you postulate any circumstance other than price predation in which a plaintiff can win a vertical maximum resale pricing case?

In the following term, the Court heard another vertical pricing case. The plaintiff supplier was cut off because of a fraudulent agreement between its customer and its competitor—a vertical restraint that raised consumer prices. Could the antitrust laws be stretched to condemn this fraudulent, anti-consumer agreement?

NYNEX CORP. v. DISCON, INC.

525 U.S. 128 (1998).

JUSTICE BREYER: [In the wake of the AT&T breakup, a market developed for the removal of obsolete telephone equipment. Discon sold removal services to Material Enterprises, a subsidiary of NYNEX, the largest buyer of removal services in the State of New York. Meanwhile, AT&T Technologies, a competitor for the business of NYNEX, made a deal with NYNEX that resulted in NYNEX/Material's replacement of Discon with AT&T Technologies and resulted as well in an artificial price rise to telephone users (NYNEX's customers). As a result, Discon went out of business. The deal was simple—and fraudulent: AT&T Technologies would bill NYNEX more than Discon's price for removal services, the higher price would be incorporated into the cost base of NYNEX as presented to the regulators, the higher price would automatically be passed on to New York Telephone and its customers, and NYNEX and AT&T Technologies would share the gains.

The transaction was, according to Discon, the termination of a supplier pursuant to a conspiracy to raise price, and a per se illegal boycott under *Klors* (see page 74 supra).

In *Klor*'s the Court also applied the *per se* rule. The Court considered a boycott created when a retail store, Broadway–Hale, and 10 household appliance manufacturers and their distributors agreed that the distributors would not sell, or would sell only at discriminatory prices, household appliances to Broadway–Hale's small, nearby competitor, namely, Klor's. The defendants had submitted undisputed evidence that their agreement hurt only one competitor (Klor's) and that so many other nearby appliance-selling competitors remained that competition in the marketplace continued to thrive. The Court held that this evidence was beside the point. [The Court distinguished *Klors* as horizontal as well as vertical.] * * *

To apply the *per se* rule here—where the buyer's decision, though not made for competitive reasons, composes part of a regulatory fraud—would transform cases involving business behavior that is improper for various reasons, say, cases involving nepotism or personal pique, into treble-damages antitrust cases. And that *per se* rule would discourage firms from changing suppliers—even where the competitive process itself does not suffer harm. * * *

The freedom to switch suppliers lies close to the heart of the competitive process that the antitrust laws seek to encourage. Cf. *Standard Oil,* 221 U.S., at 62 (noting "the freedom of the individual right to contract when not unduly or improperly exercised [is] the most efficient means for the prevention of monopoly"). At the same time, other laws, for example, "unfair competition" laws, business tort laws, or regulatory laws, provide remedies for various "competitive practices thought to be offensive to proper standards of business morality." 3 P. Areeda & H. Hovenkamp, Antitrust Law 651d, p. 78 (1996). Thus, this Court has refused to apply *per se* reasoning in cases involving that kind of activity. See *Brooke Group Ltd. v. Brown & Williamson Tobacco Corp.,* 509 U.S. 209, 225, (1993)

("Even an act of pure malice by one business competitor against another does not, without more, state a claim under the federal antitrust laws").

After *Khan* and *NYNEX*, the rule of *Dr. Miles* was the main unfinished business of reform of the law on vertical distribution restraints. *Leegin*, overruling *Dr. Miles*, completed the circle. See page 630 supra.

B. EXCLUSIONARY RESTRAINTS

1. INTRODUCTION

Arrangements between buyers and sellers may have the effect of excluding outsiders, closing so much of the market to competitors that they cannot compete effectively. Tying arrangements, exclusive dealing, requirements contracts, and reciprocity agreements may have foreclosing effects.

In the early 1900s, large sellers often required their customers to deal exclusively with them, blocking opportunities for sales by their rivals and limiting the freedom of their customers to choose alternative sources of supply. These requirements were widely perceived as oppressive. By the time of the election of 1912 reformers were calling for a law against them. Representative Henry D. Clayton, Chairman of the House Judicial Committee, proposed a bill to declare illegal all sales or leases of goods on condition that the buyer not use the goods of a competitor. Section 3 of the Clayton Bill was at first designed to prohibit these practices outright, but as a result of legislative compromise the Act prohibits the enumerated practices where the "effect . . . may be to substantially lessen competition or tend to create a monopoly in any line of commerce."

Section 3 of the Clayton Act was intended to supplement the Sherman Act by reaching certain harmful agreements in their incipiency. In particular, it was intended to overrule *Henry v. A.B. Dick Co.*, 224 U.S. 1 (1912), in which the Court allowed a manufacturer to tie stencil paper and ink to a patented stencil-duplicating machine.

Up to the early 1970s, the Supreme Court applied strong rules against foreclosing restraints. Tying, in particular, was condemned, on the belief that "[t]ying arrangements serve hardly any purpose beyond the suppression of competition." Standard Oil Co., 337 U.S. at 305–06.

In the early 1970s, the Court began to qualify the law, slowly shifting from hostility to hospitality to tie-ins, up to, most recently, *Illinois Tool Works Inc. v. Independent Ink, Inc.*, 547 U.S. 28 (2006), *infra* page 684. You are already well aware of these currents, for we dealt with exclusionary restraints in the chapter on monopolization and the analysis is essentially the same. You will want to know whether the firm has market power, why it imposed the restraint (for efficiencies? to raise rivals' costs?), did the restraint create, enhance or maintain market power? Even if so, were there offsetting benefits to consumers and the market? We turn now to specific rules and their evolution.

2. TYING

Tying entails selling (or licensing) one product on the condition that the buyer buy another. Presumably, the buyer may not want the second product or may prefer to get it from another seller. The buyer must want the tying product enough, or the package enough, at the price the package is offered, to accept the bargain.

Why would the seller impose the tie? It may be that the two products "go" together and the tie ensures that the tied-in-product will work well and safely with the tying product (which might be a machine). It may be that the seller is price-discriminating by use of metering. By putting a premium on the tied product, it can charge more to heavy users of the tying product, who, by definition, are willing and able to pay more. (Carvel soft ice cream might require its franchisees to buy their paper cups from Carvel—at a premium price; those stores with the highest volume of sales would thus pay a higher total franchise fee to Carvel.) Perhaps the seller of the tying product (which is by definition desirable) is using its power and leverage in the tying market to monopolize the tied market (in which case the sales subject to tying must amount to a monopoly share of the tied market; notice that Carvel could never monopolize the paper cup market by its tie). Maybe the seller of the tying product simply wants to expand its sales in the tied market without having to compete for them. Maybe the seller wants to evade price regulation in the tying market (for example, a railroad monopoly) and does so by putting the premium on the tied product (surrounding corridors of land—as in *Northern Pacific Railway*, infra at page 659). Maybe the seller of the tying product wants to protect its monopoly in that product by raising barriers into the tying product market (by forcing two-tiered entry, entrants would have to make both products and they may not be able to do so); or, where the tied product is a potential springboard into the tying market (think of the Netscape browser with Java language as springboard to enter the PC operating system market), tying might preserve market power in the tying (operating system) market by disabling the springboard. See *Microsoft*.

Which of the above possible motivations or strategies are anticompetitive? procompetitive? neutral?

In the early tying cases, the defendants often defended that they needed to police the quality and safety of the tied product. Their justification was usually shown to be a pretext.

Many of these cases were brought under both Sherman Act Section 1 and Clayton Act Section 3. The Sherman Act interpretation gravitated toward the Clayton Act standard, which has a lower threshold; the Clayton Act has an incipiency standard.

Here are several landmark formative cases, which built a strong foundation against tying largely because, it was feared, tying would fence out competitors from the right to compete for significant segments of the market and thus "clog" competition.

International Business Machines Corporation v. United States, 298 U.S. 131 (1936). IBM leased its tabulating machines on condition that lessees use only IBM-manufactured tabulating cards. IBM claimed that the condition was warranted by IBM's patents on both the machines and the cards and by IBM's interest in assuring quality so as not to undermine the performance of the machines. The Supreme Court held the tie in illegal. The Court said:

> There is no contention that others than appellant cannot meet these [quality] requirements. It affirmatively appears, by stipulation, that others are capable of manufacturing cards suitable for use in appellant's machines, and that paper required for that purpose may be obtained from the manufacturers who supply appellant.... The Government, under the provisions of its lease, following its own methods, has made large quantities of the cards, which are in successful use with appellant's machines. The suggestion that without the tying clause an adequate supply of cards would not be forthcoming from competitive sources is not supported by the evidence. "The very existence of such restrictions suggests that in its absence a competing article of equal or better quality would be offered at the same or at a lower price." *Carbice Corporation v. American Patents Development Corp.* [283 U.S. 27]. Appellant's sales of cards return a substantial profit and the Government's payment of 15% increase in rental to secure the privilege of making its own cards is profitable only if it produces the cards at a cost less than 55% of the price charged by appellant.
>
> Appellant is not prevented from proclaiming the virtues of its own cards or warning against the danger of using, in its machines, cards which do not conform to the necessary specifications, or even from making its leases conditional upon the use of cards which conform to them. For aught that appears such measures would protect its good will, without the creation of monopoly or resort to the suppression of competition.
>
> The Clayton Act names no exception to its prohibition of monopolistic tying clauses. Even if we are free to make an exception to its unambiguous command, we can perceive no tenable basis for an exception in favor of a condition whose substantial benefit to the lessor is the elimination of business competition and the creation of monopoly, rather than the protection of its good will, and where it does not appear that the latter can not be achieved by methods which

> do not tend to monopoly and are not otherwise unlawful. (298 U.S. at 139–40)

IBM *created* the IBM-card market. Why did IBM have a duty to share that market with competitors? In contemporary analysis, is *Trinko* relevant?

Would the tie create a second monopoly for IBM? Is the Court using the word "monopoly" loosely, or are IBM cards for IBM tabulating machines a market? Could IBM get a second monopoly profit by being the sole producer of IBM cards? Alternatively, is there a price discrimination story: Could IBM have been charging a premium for the card and using the tie as a metering device, so that heavy users of the tabulators would pay more (ostensibly for the card, but really for the tabulator) than light users? Did any of this matter to the Court?

International Salt Company v. United States, 332 U.S. 392 (1947). The International Salt Company leased patented machines that injected salt into canned products during the canning process (the Saltomat)—and machines that dissolved rock salt into brine for industrial processes (the Lixator) on condition that the lessees bought the salt they would use in the leased machines from International Salt. But there were exceptions. Lessees of the Lixator were given the right to buy salt on the open market if there was a general reduction in market prices and if International Salt declined to meet the price reduction. Lessees of the Saltomat were given a most favored nation's clause on the price of salt; if International Salt generally reduced the price of salt tablets for use in its machine, the lessee would get the benefit of the reduction.

Like IBM, International Salt did not prove the necessity of a tie in to protect good will in its machines. Despite the "exception" clauses, the Supreme Court ruled against the company. Thus:

> Appellant contends, however, that summary judgment was unauthorized because it precluded trial of alleged issues of fact as to whether the restraint was unreasonable within the Sherman Act or substantially lessened competition or tended to create a monopoly in salt within the Clayton Act. We think the admitted facts left no genuine issue. Not only is price-fixing unreasonable, *per se*, but also it is unreasonable, *per se*, to foreclose competitors from any substantial market. The volume of business affected by these contracts cannot be said to be insignificant or insubstantial and the tendency of the arrangement to accomplishment of monopoly seems obvious. Under the law, agreements are forbidden which "tend to create a monopoly," and it is immaterial that the tendency is a creeping one rather than one that proceeds at full gallop; nor does the law await arrival at the goal before condemning the direction of the movement. . . .

The "Lixator" provision does, of course, afford a measure of protection to the lessee, but it does not avoid the stifling effect of the agreement on competition. The appellant had at all times a priority on the business at equal prices. A competitor would have to undercut appellant's price to have any hope of capturing the market, while appellant could hold that market by merely meeting competition. We do not think this concession relieves the contract of being a restraint of trade, albeit a less harsh one than would result in the absence of such a provision. The "Saltomat" provision obviously has no effect of legal significance since it gives the lessee nothing more than a right to buy appellant's salt tablets at appellant's going price.

Why did International Salt tie? Would the Lixator clause keep International Salt's price of salt down to market price, and thus prevent International Salt from following a price discrimination (metering) strategy? Note that International Salt's principal business was salt, and it was one of the few big salt companies. Might the Saltomat and Lixator clauses have been devices to facilitate a salt cartel by policing cheating? Might International Salt have simply wanted to appropriate a market segment without competing for it?

Meanwhile, Congress had granted the predecessor to the Northern Pacific Railway 40 million acres of land to facilitate its construction of a railroad. After the construction the railroad had millions of acres to lease or sell. In many of its sales contracts and most of its leases the railroad extracted preferential routing clauses, requiring the buyer or lessee to ship all goods produced on the land on the Northern Pacific Railway provided that Northern Pacific's rates and in some cases its service were equal to those of competing carriers. (Is this like the Lixator clause?) The Court held the preferential routing clauses per se illegal under Section 1 of the Sherman Act. Justice Black wrote, for the Court, an opinion that is much quoted, even today, although not always with approval (see *Illinois Tool*, infra page 684).

NORTHERN PACIFIC RAILWAY CO. v. UNITED STATES

356 U.S. 1 (1958).

JUSTICE BLACK: * * * The Sherman Act was designed to be a comprehensive charter of economic liberty aimed at preserving free and unfettered competition as the rule of trade. It rests on the premise that the unrestrained interaction of competitive forces will yield the best allocation of our economic resources, the lowest prices, the highest quality and the greatest material progress, while at the same time providing an environment conducive to the preservation of our democratic political and social institutions. But even were that premise open to question, the policy unequivocally laid down by the Act is competition. . . .

... [T]here are certain agreements or practices which because of their pernicious effect on competition and lack of any redeeming virtue are conclusively presumed to be unreasonable and therefore illegal without elaborate inquiry as to the precise harm they have caused or the business excuse for their use. This principle of per se unreasonableness not only makes the type of restraints which are proscribed by the Sherman Act more certain to the benefit of everyone concerned, but it also avoids the necessity for an incredibly complicated and prolonged economic investigation into the entire history of the industry involved, as well as related industries, in an effort to determine at large whether a particular restraint has been unreasonable—an inquiry so often wholly fruitless when undertaken. Among the practices which the courts have heretofore deemed to be unlawful in and of themselves are price fixing; division of markets; group boycotts; and tying arrangements.

... Indeed "tying agreements serve hardly any purpose beyond the suppression of competition." *Standard Oil Co. of California* v. *United States*, 337 U.S. 293, 305–306.[5] They deny competitors free access to the market for the tied product, not because the party imposing the tying requirements has a better product or a lower price but because of his power or leverage in another market. At the same time buyers are forced to forego their free choice between competing products. For these reasons "tying agreements fare harshly under the laws forbidding restraints of trade." *Times–Picayune Publishing Co.* v. *United States*, 345 U.S. 594, 606. They are unreasonable in and of themselves whenever a party has sufficient economic power with respect to the tying product to appreciably restrain free competition in the market for the tied product and a "not insubstantial" amount of interstate commerce is affected. *International Salt Co.* v. *United States*, 332 U.S. 392 [$500,000 held not insubstantial]. Of course where the seller has no control or dominance over the tying product so that it does not represent an effectual weapon to pressure buyers into taking the tied item any restraint of trade attributable to such tying arrangements would obviously be insignificant at most. As a simple example, if one of a dozen food stores in a community were to refuse to sell flour unless the buyer also took sugar it would hardly tend to restrain competition in sugar if its competitors were ready and able to sell flour by itself.

In this case we believe the district judge was clearly correct in entering summary judgment declaring the defendant's "preferential routing" clauses unlawful restraints of trade....

... The very existence of this host of tying arrangements is itself compelling evidence of the defendant's great power, at least where, as here, no other explanation has been offered for the existence of these restraints. The "preferential routing" clauses conferred no benefit on the purchasers or lessees. While they got the land they wanted by yielding

5. As this Court has previously pointed out such nonanticompetitive purposes as these arrangements have been asserted to possess can be adequately accomplished by other means much less inimical to competition.

their freedom to deal with competing carriers, the defendant makes no claim that it came any cheaper than if the restrictive clauses had been omitted. In fact any such price reduction in return for rail shipments would have quite plainly constituted an unlawful rebate to the shipper. So far as the Railroad was concerned its purpose obviously was to fence out competitors, to stifle competition. While this may have been exceedingly beneficial to its business, it is the very type of thing the Sherman Act condemns.... * * *

QUESTIONS AND COMMENTS

1. *Northern Pacific* thus articulated a qualified per se rule against tying. It is still the law today; it has not (yet) been overruled, at least not expressly. Note the qualifications (or conditions precedent) to per se application:

1) Defendant must have sufficient economic power (later developed into "market power").

2) Implicitly: There are two products and the tied product is forced on the buyer.

3) A not insubstantial amount of commerce is affected.

Point 3 entails: Effect on competition need not be proved. Stated differently, where the three conditions are met, the fencing out of competitors and/or the coercion of the buyers *is* the harm to competition. (This was accepted in the 1950s, '60s, and '70s, but not so today.)

2. Major motion picture producer/distributors developed a practice of block-booking (selling or licensing in packages) pre–1948 copyrighted motion picture feature films to television stations. Television stations complained that they had to accept "cabooses" with "engines." To get *Casablanca* they had to accept *Getting Gertie's Garter*. In fact, the movie companies offered the TV stations packages that contained an array of films. Each package typically included a small number of "A" films (outstanding quality), some 50 to 60 "B" films, and perhaps 20 not very desirable or totally undesirable ("C") films. The movie companies argued that the packages resulted from negotiation, not coercion. Moreover, they maintained that there was no tying product; there was no particularly unique product that was the "engine." Rather, they said, the pre–1948 feature films were just a small part of television programming and were largely interchangeable with one another and with other types of television programming.

The Supreme Court rejected defendants' arguments and condemned block booking per se. It repeated the antitrust concerns regarding tie ins: "they may force buyers into giving up the purchase of substitutes for the tied product, ... and they may destroy the free access of competing suppliers of the tied product to the consuming market." *United States* v. *Loew's Inc.*, 371 U.S. 38, 45 (1962). The Court then weakened the market power requirement, saying: "Even absent a showing of market dominance, the crucial economic power may be inferred from the tying product's desirability to consumers or from uniqueness of its attributes.... The requisite economic power is presumed when the tying product is patented or copyrighted." *Id.* (footnote omitted).

The Court emphasized the public interest in limiting the rewards of a patent or copyright grant to the object of the grant.

3. A few years after *Loew's* in a patent tie-in case, the Court clarified the concept of conditioning. Hazeltine Research had a portfolio of some 500 U.S. patents relating to the manufacture of radios and television sets. Zenith wanted to license from Hazeltine nine of the patents for color TV. Hazeltine offered to grant a license for the nine color patents for $275,000 per year, or to grant a license for all of its present and future color and monochrome patents for $200,000 per year.

Zenith contracted for the entire package, and then sued. The district court held that Zenith was coerced to accept the package license. Finding patent misuse and an antitrust violation, the court enjoined Hazeltine from forcing acceptance of a package license by offering a much lower rate for the package than for the license of a few patents. The court of appeals substantially affirmed. The Supreme Court affirmed. *Hazeltine Research, Inc. v. Zenith Radio Corp.*, 388 F.2d 25, 39 (7th Cir.1967), aff'd, 395 U.S. 100 (1969).

Fortner Enterprises, Inc. v. United States Steel Corp., 394 U.S. 495 (1969); 429 U.S. 610 (1977). Soon thereafter the saga of Fortner Enterprises and United States Steel unfolded. United States Steel Homes Credit Corporation was a subsidiary of United States Steel Corporation. It made secured loans to contractors to cover the purchase and subdivision of land and the purchase and construction on the land of prefabricated homes manufactured and sold by U.S. Steel. Fortner obtained such a loan for $2,000,000, purchased and subdivided land, purchased some U.S. Steel houses, and started building. Dissatisfied with the quality of U.S. Steel's houses, Fortner sued to enjoin U.S. Steel from enforcing the loan requirement that Fortner buy only U.S. Steel houses with the proceeds of the loan, and it sought treble damages. The district court entered summary judgment for U.S. Steel but the Supreme Court reversed the dismissal, saying: the fact that U.S. Steel was able to impose the condition on so many buyers proved its sufficient economic power (*Fortner I*). Later, however, in *Fortner II*, in an opinion quite different in tone and spirit, the Court held that the plaintiff had not proved U.S. Steel's economic power over credit. "The unusual credit bargain offered to Fortner proves nothing more than a willingness to provide cheap financing in order to sell expensive houses." Thus, the so-called tie was not a tie; it was merely a strategy to compete in the prefabricated house market. *Fortner II* underlined the seriousness with which market power henceforth had to be proved.

3. TYING—MODERN ANALYSIS

The next decade saw a withering of the inhospitality towards tie-ins, based on the observation that tie-ins may often be used for efficiency ends. *Jefferson Parish*, below, is the most recent Supreme Court case fully addressing tying analysis. The concurring opinion of Justice O'Connor must be given at least equal regard in predicting the direction of the law. *Kodak/ITS* (p. 671 infra), while more recent, contains a sketchier analysis of the tying violation. It concentrates on the narrower question of whether plaintiffs were entitled to a trial. *Microsoft* (p. 680 infra) is important to show the limitations of the *Northern Pacific* rule in software platform cases—and maybe beyond; while *Illinois Tool* (p. 684 infra), nominally dealing only with the question whether ownership of a patent gives rise to a presumption of market power, manages to launch a head-on assault on the historic rule against tying.

Meanwhile, subject to the gathering clouds, *Jefferson Parish* is still a controlling authority.

JEFFERSON PARISH HOSPITAL DISTRICT NO. 2 v. HYDE

466 U.S. 2 (1984).

JUSTICE STEVENS: At issue in this case is the validity of an exclusive contract between a hospital and a firm of anesthesiologists. We must decide whether the contract gives rise to a *per se* violation of § 1 of the Sherman Act because every patient undergoing surgery at the hospital must use the services of one firm of anesthesiologists, and, if not, whether the contract is nevertheless illegal because it unreasonably restrains competition among anesthesiologists.

In July 1977, respondent Edwin G. Hyde, a board-certified anesthesiologist, applied for admission to the medical staff of East Jefferson Hospital. The credentials committee and the medical staff executive committee recommended approval, but the hospital board denied the application because the hospital was a party to a contract providing that all anesthesiological services required by the hospital's patients would be performed by Roux & Associates, a professional medical corporation. Respondent then commenced this action seeking a declaratory judgment that the contract is unlawful and an injunction ordering petitioners to appoint him to the hospital staff. After trial, the District Court denied relief, finding that the anticompetitive consequences of the Roux contract were minimal and outweighed by benefits in the form of improved patient care. The Court of Appeals reversed because it was persuaded that the contract was illegal *"per se."* We granted certiorari, and now reverse.

I.

In February 1971, shortly before East Jefferson Hospital opened, it entered into an "Anesthesiology Agreement" with Roux & Associates (Roux), a firm that had recently been organized by Dr. Kermit Roux. The contract provided that any anesthesiologist designated by Roux would be admitted to the hospital's medical staff. The hospital agreed to provide the space, equipment, maintenance, and other supporting services necessary to operate the anesthesiology department. It also agreed to purchase all necessary drugs and other supplies. All nursing personnel required by the anesthesia department were to be supplied by the hospital, but Roux had the right to approve their selection and retention. The hospital agreed to "restrict the use of its anesthesia department to Roux & Associates and [that] no other persons, parties or entities shall perform such services within the Hospital for the ter[m] of this contract."

... Only Roux was permitted to practice anesthesiology at the hospital. At the time of trial the department included four anesthesiologists. The hospital usually employed 13 or 14 certified registered nurse anesthetists.

... Any consumer of medical services who elects to have an operation performed at East Jefferson Hospital may not employ any anesthesiologist not associated with Roux. No anesthesiologists except those employed by Roux may practice at East Jefferson.

There are at least 20 hospitals in the New Orleans metropolitan area and about 70 percent of the patients living in Jefferson Parish go to hospitals other than East Jefferson.... Noting that 30 percent of the residents of the parish go to East Jefferson Hospital, and that in fact "patients tend to choose hospitals by location rather than price or quality," the Court of Appeals concluded that the relevant geographic market was the East Bank of Jefferson Parish. The conclusion that East Jefferson Hospital possessed market power in that area was buttressed by the facts that the prevalence of health insurance eliminates a patient's incentive to compare costs, that the patient is not sufficiently informed to compare quality, and that family convenience tends to magnify the importance of location.

The Court of Appeals held that the case involves a "tying arrangement" because the "users of the hospital's operating rooms (the tying product) are also compelled to purchase the hospital's chosen anesthesia service (the tied product)." [686 F.2d] at 289. Having defined the relevant geographic market for the tying product as the East Bank of Jefferson Parish, the court held that the hospital possessed "sufficient market power in the tying market to coerce purchasers of the tied product." *Id.*, at 291. Since the purchase of the tied product constituted a "not insubstantial amount of interstate commerce," under the Court of Appeals' reading of our decision in *Northern Pacific R. Co. v. United States*, 356 U.S. 1, 11 (1958), the tying arrangement was therefore illegal *"per se."*

II.

Certain types of contractual arrangements are deemed unreasonable as a matter of law. The character of the restraint produced by such an arrangement is considered a sufficient basis for presuming unreasonableness without the necessity of any analysis of the market context in which the arrangement may be found.... It is far too late in the history of our antitrust jurisprudence to question the proposition that certain tying arrangements pose an unacceptable risk of stifling competition and therefore are unreasonable *"per se."* The rule was first enunciated in *Interna-*

tional Salt Co. v. United States, 332 U.S. 392, 396 (1947), and has been endorsed by this Court many times since. The rule also reflects congressional policies underlying the antitrust laws. In enacting § 3 of the Clayton Act, Congress expressed great concern about the anti-competitive character of tying arrangements. See H.R.Rep. No. 627, 63d Cong., 2d Sess., 10–13 (1914); S.Rep. No. 698, 63d Cong., 2d Sess., 6–9 (1914).[15] While this case does not arise under the Clayton Act, the congressional finding made therein concerning the competitive consequences of tying is illuminating, and must be respected.

It is clear, however, that not every refusal to sell two products separately can be said to restrain competition.... Buyers often find package sales attractive; a seller's decision to offer such packages can merely be an attempt to compete effectively—conduct that is entirely consistent with the Sherman Act.

Our cases have concluded that the essential characteristic of an invalid tying arrangement lies in the seller's exploitation of its control over the tying product to force the buyer into the purchase of a tied product that the buyer either did not want at all, or might have preferred to purchase elsewhere on different terms. When such "forcing" is present, competition on the merits in the market for the tied item is restrained and the Sherman Act is violated. * * *

Thus, the law draws a distinction between the exploitation of market power by merely enhancing the price of the tying product, on the one hand, and by attempting to impose restraints on competition in the market for a tied product, on the other. When the seller's power is just used to maximize its return in the tying product market, where presumably its product enjoys some justifiable advantage over its competitors, the competitive ideal of the Sherman Act is not necessarily compromised. But if that power is used to impair competition on the merits in another market, a potentially inferior product may be insulated from competitive pressures.[17] This impairment could either harm existing competitors or create barriers to entry of new competitors in the market for the tied

---

15. See ... Spivack, The Chicago School Approach to Single Firm Exercises of Monopoly Power: A Response, 52 Antitrust L.J. 651, 664–665 (1983). For example, the House Report on the Clayton Act stated:

> Where the concern making these contracts is already great and powerful, such as the United Shoe Machinery Co., the American Tobacco Co., and the General Film Co., the exclusive or 'tying' contract made with local dealers becomes one of the greatest agencies and instrumentalities of monopoly ever devised by the brain of man. It completely shuts out competitors, not only from trade in which they are already engaged, but from the opportunities to build up trade in any community where these great and powerful combinations are operating under this system and practice.... H.R.Rep. No. 627, 63d Cong., 2d Sess., 12–13 (1914).

Similarly, Representative Mitchell said: "No situation cries more urgently for relief than does this situation, and this bill seeks to prevent exclusive 'tying' contracts that have brought about a monopoly, alike injurious to the small dealers, to the manufacturers, and grossly unfair to those who seek to enter the field of competition and to the millions of consumers." 51 Cong.Rec. 9090 (1914).

17. See Report of the Attorney General's National Committee to Study the Antitrust Laws 145 (1955); Turner, The Validity of Tying Arrangements under the Antitrust Laws, 72 Harv. L.Rev. 50, 60–62 (1958).

product, *Fortner I,* 394 U.S., at 509, and can increase the social costs of market power by facilitating price discrimination, thereby increasing monopoly profits over what they would be absent the tie, *Fortner II,* 429 U.S., at 617. And from the standpoint of the consumer—whose interests the statute was especially intended to serve—the freedom to select the best bargain in the second market is impaired by his need to purchase the tying product, and perhaps by an inability to evaluate the true cost of either product when they are available only as a package.* * *

... [A]ny inquiry into the validity of a tying arrangement must focus on the market or markets in which the two products are sold, for that is where the anticompetitive forcing has its impact. Thus, in this case our analysis of the tying issue must focus on the hospital's sale of services to its patients, rather than its contractual arrangements with the providers of anesthesiological services. In making that analysis, we must consider whether petitioners are selling two separate products that may be tied together, and, if so, whether they have used their market power to force their patients to accept the tying arrangement.

III.

The hospital has provided its patients with a package that includes the range of facilities and services required for a variety of surgical operations. At East Jefferson Hospital the package includes the services of the anesthesiologist. Petitioners argue that the package does not involve a tying arrangement at all—that they are merely providing a functionally integrated package of services. Therefore, petitioners contend that it is inappropriate to apply principles concerning tying arrangements to this case.

Our cases indicate, however, that the answer to the question whether one or two products are involved turns not on the functional relation between them, but rather on the character of the demand for the two items. * * *

Unquestionably, the anesthesiological component of the package offered by the hospital could be provided separately and could be selected either by the individual patient or by one of the patient's doctors if the hospital did not insist on including anesthesiological services in the package it offers to its customers. As a matter of actual practice, anesthesiological services are billed separately from the hospital services petitioners provide. There was ample and uncontroverted testimony that patients or surgeons often request specific anesthesiologists to come to a hospital and provide anesthesia, and that the choice of an individual anesthesiologist separate from the choice of a hospital is particularly frequent in respondent's specialty, obstetric anesthesiology. The District Court found that "[t]he provision of anesthesia services is a medical service separate from the other services provided by the hospital." The record amply supports the conclusion that consumers differentiate between anesthesiological services and the other hospital services provided by petitioners.

Thus, the hospital's requirement that its patients obtain necessary anesthesiological services from Roux combined the purchase of two distinguishable services in a single transaction....

IV.

The question remains whether this arrangement involves the use of market power to force patients to buy services they would not otherwise purchase. Respondent's only basis for invoking the *per se* rule against tying and thereby avoiding analysis of actual market conditions is by relying on the preference of persons residing in Jefferson Parish to go to East Jefferson, the closest hospital. A preference of this kind, however, is not necessarily probative of significant market power.

Seventy percent of the patients residing in Jefferson Parish enter hospitals other than East Jefferson. Thus East Jefferson's "dominance" over persons residing in Jefferson Parish is far from overwhelming. The fact that a substantial majority of the parish's residents elect not to enter East Jefferson means that the geographic data do not establish the kind of dominant market position that obviates the need for further inquiry into actual competitive conditions. * * *

V.

In order to prevail in the absence of *per se* liability, respondent has the burden of proving that the Roux contract violated the Sherman Act because it unreasonably restrained competition. That burden necessarily involves an inquiry into the actual effect of the exclusive contract on competition among anesthesiologists. This competition takes place in a market that has not been defined. The market is not necessarily the same as the market in which hospitals compete in offering services to patients; it may encompass competition among anesthesiologists for exclusive contracts such as the Roux contract and might be statewide or merely local. There is, however, insufficient evidence in this record to provide a basis for finding that the Roux contract, as it actually operates in the market, has unreasonably restrained competition. * * * [Reversed]

JUSTICE O'CONNOR, with whom CHIEF JUSTICE BURGER and JUSTICES POWELL and REHNQUIST join, concurring in the judgment.... I concur in the Court's decision to reverse but write separately to explain why I believe the hospital-Roux contract, whether treated as effecting a tie between services provided to patients, or as an exclusive dealing arrangement between the hospital and certain anesthesiologists, is properly analyzed under the rule of reason.

I. * * *

The time has therefore come to abandon the "*per se*" label and refocus the inquiry on the adverse economic effects, and the potential economic benefits, that the tie may have. The law of tie-ins will thus be brought into accord with the law applicable to all other allegedly anticompetitive economic arrangements, except those few horizontal or quasi-horizontal restraints that can be said to have no economic justification whatsoever. This change will rationalize rather than abandon tie-in doctrine as it is already applied.

II.

Our prior opinions indicate that the purpose of tying law has been to identify and control those tie-ins that have a demonstrable exclusionary impact in the tied-product market, or that abet the harmful exercise of market power that the seller possesses in the tying product market. Under the rule of reason tying arrangements should be disapproved only in such instances.

Market power in the *tying* product may be acquired legitimately (*e.g.*, through the grant of a patent) or illegitimately (*e.g.*, as a result of unlawful monopolization). In either event, exploitation of consumers in the market for the tying product is a possibility that exists and that may be regulated under § 2 of the Sherman Act without reference to any tying arrangements that the seller may have developed. The existence of a tied product normally does not increase the profit that the seller with market power can extract from sales of the *tying* product. A seller with a monopoly on flour, for example, cannot increase the profit it can extract from flour consumers simply by forcing them to buy sugar along with their flour. . . .

Tying may be economically harmful primarily in the rare cases where power in the market for the tying product is used to create *additional* market power in the market for the *tied* product.[4] The antitrust law is properly concerned with tying when, for example, the flour monopolist threatens to use its market power to acquire additional power in the sugar market, perhaps by driving out competing sellers of sugar, or by making it more difficult for new sellers to enter the sugar market. But such extension of market power is unlikely, or poses no threat of economic harm, unless the two markets in question and the nature of the two products tied satisfy three threshold criteria.

First, the seller must have power in the tying-product market. . . .

Second, there must be a substantial threat that the tying seller will acquire market power in the tied-product market. No such threat exists if the tied-product market is occupied by many stable sellers who are not likely to be driven out by the tying, or if entry barriers in the tied-product market are low. . . .

---

4. Tying might be undesirable in two other instances, but the hospital-Roux arrangement involves neither one.

In a regulated industry a firm with market power may be unable to extract a supercompetitive profit because it lacks control over the prices it charges for regulated products or services. Tying may then be used to extract that profit from sale of the unregulated, tied products or services.

Tying may also help the seller engage in price discrimination by "metering" the buyer's use of the tying product. Price discrimination may be independently unlawful, see 15 U.S.C. § 13. Price discrimination may, however, *decrease* rather than increase the economic costs of a seller's market power.

Third, there must be a coherent economic basis for treating the tying and tied products as distinct. All but the simplest products can be broken down into two or more components that are "tied together" in the final sale. Unless it is to be illegal to sell cars with engines or cameras with lenses, this analysis must be guided by some limiting principle. For products to be treated as distinct, the tied product must, at a minimum, be one that some consumers might wish to purchase separately *without also purchasing the tying product.* When the tied product has no use other than in conjunction with the tying product, a seller of the tying product can acquire no *additional* market power by selling the two products together....

Even when the tied product does have a use separate from the tying product, it makes little sense to label a package as two products without also considering the economic justifications for the sale of the package as a unit. When the economic advantages of joint packaging are substantial the package is not appropriately viewed as two products, and that should be the end of the tying inquiry....

These three conditions—market power in the tying product, a substantial threat of market power in the tied product, and a coherent economic basis for treating the products as distinct—are only threshold requirements. Under the rule of reason a tie-in may prove acceptable even when all three are met. Tie-ins may entail economic benefits as well as economic harms, and if the threshold requirements are met these benefits should enter the rule-of-reason balance. * * *

... A tie-in should be condemned only when its anticompetitive impact outweighs its contribution to efficiency.

III.

Application of these criteria to the case at hand is straightforward.

Although the issue is in doubt, we may assume that the hospital does have market power in the provision of hospital services in its area....

Second, in light of the hospital's presumed market power, we may also assume that there is a substantial threat that East Jefferson will acquire market power over the provision of anesthesiological services in its market....

But the third threshold condition for giving closer scrutiny to a tying arrangement is not satisfied here: there is no sound economic reason for treating surgery and anesthesia as separate services. Patients are interested in purchasing anesthesia only in conjunction with hospital services, so the hospital can acquire no *additional* market power by selling the two services together. Accordingly, the link between the hospital's services and anesthesia administered by Roux will affect neither the amount of anesthesia provided nor the combined price of anesthesia and surgery for those who choose to become the hospital's patients. In these circumstances, anesthesia and surgical services should probably not be characterized as distinct products for tying purposes.

Even if they are, the tying should not be considered a violation of § 1 of the Sherman Act because tying here cannot increase the seller's already absolute power over the volume of production of the tied product, which is an inevitable consequence of the fact that very few patients will choose to undergo surgery without receiving anesthesia. The hospital-Roux contract therefore has little potential to harm the patients. On the other side of the balance, . . . the tie-in conferred significant benefits upon the hospital and the patients that it served.

The tie-in improves patient care and permits more efficient hospital operation in a number of ways. From the viewpoint of hospital management, the tie-in ensures 24–hour anesthesiology coverage, aids in standardization of procedures and efficient use of equipment, facilitates flexible scheduling of operations, and permits the hospital more effectively to monitor the quality of anesthesiological services. . . .

IV.

[As to exclusive dealing:] . . . Even without engaging in a detailed analysis of the size of the relevant markets we may readily conclude that there is no likelihood that the exclusive-dealing arrangement challenged here will either unreasonably enhance the hospital's market position relative to other hospitals, or unreasonably permit Roux to acquire power relative to other anesthesiologists. Accordingly, this exclusive-dealing arrangement must be sustained under the rule of reason. * * *

QUESTIONS AND COMMENTS

1. Did Justice Stevens make a convincing case that 1) firms with market power that force a second product or service on their buyers presumptively harm competition? 2) that two products (services) were at issue in this case? 3) that East Jefferson did not "force" the Roux anesthesiologists on its patients?

2. What does the Court mean by the words "impair competition on the merits"? Does reduced choice of consumers and reduced freedom of the firms that would serve them impair competition? or is a probable output effect necessary?

3. What is the significance of East Jefferson's "mere" 30% of the market? Does *Jefferson Parish* hold that a firm with no more than 30% of the market, even if it has market power, presumptively does not have sufficient power to force customers to buy a second product? See part IV of the opinion of the Court. Do you agree?

4. What are the major differences between Justice Stevens' approach and Justice O'Connor's approach to the analysis of tie-ins? Consider their perspectives on harm to competition and on efficiencies, and whether "mere" *use* of market power must be distinguished from conduct that *increases* market power. Why might we want antitrust to ignore *mere use* of market power and to intervene only against conduct that *increases* market power? Consider the evolution of the law of monopolization in Chapter 3.

5. While Justice Stevens' view of "two products" has largely prevailed, Justice O'Connor's analysis of why plaintiffs should be required to prove anticompetitive effects enjoys increasing traction.

EASTMAN KODAK CO. v. IMAGE TECHNICAL SERVICES, INC.

504 U.S. 451 (1992)
(tying).

(See relevant market portion of the case at page 214 supra, and monopolization portion at page 246 supra).

JUSTICE BLACKMUN: * * * [Eastman Kodak entered the market for manufacturing copying and micrographic equipment. There were several other important producers in this field. At first Kodak encouraged independent service companies to enter the business of servicing and repairing Kodak machines for Kodak's customers. Later it changed course. It stopped selling replacement parts to the independent service organizations (ISOs), and it announced to its customers that it would provide replacement parts to them only if they bought repair services from Kodak or performed the repairs themselves. The ISOs, squeezed from the business, sued for monopolization and tying violations. They did not assert (until much later in the litigation) that Kodak had market power in the interbrand machine market. Kodak moved for summary judgment. The district court granted its motion. The appellate court reversed.]

II. A.

For the respondents to defeat a motion for summary judgment on their claim of a tying arrangement, a reasonable trier of fact must be able to find, first, that service and parts are two distinct products, and, second, that Kodak has tied the sale of the two products.

For service and parts to be considered two distinct products, there must be sufficient consumer demand so that it is efficient for a firm to provide service separately from parts. *Jefferson Parish Hospital Dist. No. 2 v. Hyde,* 466 U.S. 2, 21–22 (1984). Evidence in the record indicates that service and parts have been sold separately in the past and still are sold separately to self-service equipment owners. Indeed, the development of the entire high-technology service industry is evidence of the efficiency of a separate market for service.

Kodak insists that because there is no demand for parts separate from service, there cannot be separate markets for service and parts. By that logic, we would be forced to conclude that there can never be separate markets, for example, for cameras and film, computers and software, or automobiles and tires. That is an assumption we are unwilling to make. "We have often found arrangements involving functionally linked products at least one of which is useless without the other to be prohibited tying devices." *Jefferson Parish*, 466 U.S., at 19, n. 30. * * *

Finally, respondents have presented sufficient evidence of a tie between service and parts. The record indicates that Kodak would sell parts to third parties only if they agreed not to buy service from ISOs.

B.

Having found sufficient evidence of a tying arrangement, we consider the other necessary feature of an illegal tying arrangement: appreciable economic power in the tying market. Market power is the power "to force a purchaser to do something that he would not do in a competitive market." *Jefferson Parish*, 466 U.S., at 14. It has been defined as "the ability of a single seller to raise price and restrict output." *Fortner Inc.*, 394 U.S., at 503. The existence of such power ordinarily is inferred from the seller's possession of a predominant share of the market.

1.

Respondents contend that Kodak has more than sufficient power in the parts market to force unwanted purchases of the tied market service. Respondents provide evidence that certain parts are available exclusively through Kodak. Respondents also assert that Kodak has control over the availability of parts it does not manufacture. According to respondents' evidence, Kodak has prohibited independent manufacturers from selling Kodak parts to ISOs, pressured Kodak equipment owners and independent parts distributors to deny ISOs the purchase of Kodak parts, and taken steps to restrict the availability of used machines.

Respondents also allege that Kodak's control over the parts market has excluded service competition, boosted service prices, and forced unwilling consumption of Kodak service. Respondents offer evidence that consumers have switched to Kodak service even though they preferred ISO service, that Kodak service was of higher price and lower quality than the preferred ISO service, and that ISOs were driven out of business by Kodak's policies. Under our prior precedents, this evidence would be sufficient to entitle respondents to a trial on their claim of market power.

2.

Kodak counters that even if it concedes monopoly share of the relevant parts market, it cannot actually exercise the necessary market power for a Sherman Act violation. This is so, according to Kodak, because competition exists in the equipment market. Kodak argues that it could not have the ability to raise prices of service and parts above the level that would be charged in a competitive market because any increase in profits from a higher price in the aftermarkets at least would be offset by a corresponding loss in profits from lower equipment sales as consumers began purchasing equipment with more attractive service costs.

Kodak does not present any actual data on the equipment, service, or parts markets. Instead, it urges the adoption of a substantive legal rule that "equipment competition precludes any finding of monopoly power in derivative aftermarkets." . . .

Legal presumptions that rest on formalistic distinctions rather than actual market realities are generally disfavored in antitrust law. This Court has preferred to resolve antitrust claims on a case-by-case basis, focusing on the "particular facts disclosed by the record." *Maple Flooring Mfrs.' Assn. v. United States*, 268 U.S. 563, 579 (1925)....

Kodak contends that there is no need to examine the facts when the issue is market power in the aftermarkets. A legal presumption against a finding of market power is warranted in this situation, according to Kodak, because the existence of market power in the service and parts markets absent power in the equipment market "simply makes no economic sense," and the absence of a legal presumption would deter procompetitive behavior. *Matsushita*, 475 U.S., at 587. * * *

Kodak, then, bears a substantial burden in showing that it is entitled to summary judgment. It must show that despite evidence of increased prices and excluded competition, an inference of market power is unreasonable. To determine whether Kodak has met that burden, we must unravel the factual assumptions underlying its proposed rule that lack of power in the equipment market necessarily precludes power in the aftermarkets.

The extent to which one market prevents exploitation of another market depends on the extent to which consumers will change their consumption of one product in response to a price change in another, *i.e.*, the "cross-elasticity of demand." Kodak's proposed rule rests on a factual assumption about the cross-elasticity of demand in the equipment and aftermarkets: "If Kodak raised its parts or service prices above competitive levels, potential customers would simply stop buying Kodak equipment. Perhaps Kodak would be able to increase short term profits through such a strategy, but at a devastating cost to its long term interests." Brief for Petitioner. Kodak argues that the Court should accept, as a matter of law, this "basic economic realit[y]," *id.*, that competition in the equipment market necessarily prevents market power in the aftermarkets.

Even if Kodak could not raise the price of service and parts one cent without losing equipment sales, that fact would not disprove market power in the aftermarkets. The sales of even a monopolist are reduced when it sells goods at a monopoly price, but the higher price more than compensates for the loss in sales. Kodak's claim that charging more for service and parts would be "a short-run game" ... is based on the false dichotomy that there are only two prices that can be charged—a competitive price or a ruinous one. But there could easily be a middle, optimum price at which the increased revenues from the higher-priced sales of service and parts would more than compensate for the lower revenues from lost equipment sales. The fact that the equipment market imposes a restraint on prices in the aftermarkets by no means disproves the existence of power in those markets.... Thus, contrary to Kodak's assertion, there is no immutable physical law—no "basic economic reality"—insisting that competition in the equipment market cannot coexist with market power in the aftermarkets.

We next consider the more narrowly drawn question: Does Kodak's theory describe actual market behavior so accurately that respondents' assertion of Kodak market power in the aftermarkets, if not impossible, is at least unreasonable?

To review Kodak's theory, it contends that higher service prices will lead to a disastrous drop in equipment sales. Presumably, the theory's corollary is to the effect that low service prices lead to a dramatic increase in equipment sales. According to the theory, one would have expected Kodak to take advantage of lower-priced ISO service as an opportunity to expand equipment sales. Instead, Kodak adopted a restrictive sales policy consciously designed to eliminate the lower-priced ISO service, an act that would be expected to devastate either Kodak's equipment sales or Kodak's faith in its theory. Yet, according to the record, it has done neither. Service prices have risen for Kodak customers, but there is no evidence or assertion that Kodak equipment sales have dropped.

Kodak and the United States attempt to reconcile Kodak's theory with the contrary actual results by describing a "marketing strategy of spreading over time the total cost to the buyer of Kodak equipment." In other words, Kodak could charge subcompetitive prices for equipment and make up the difference with supra-competitive prices for service, resulting in an overall competitive price. This pricing strategy would provide an explanation for the theory's descriptive failings—if Kodak in fact had adopted it. But Kodak never has asserted that it prices its equipment or parts subcompetitively and recoups its profits through service. Instead, it claims that it prices its equipment comparably to its competitors, and intends that both its equipment sales and service divisions be profitable. Moreover, this hypothetical pricing strategy is inconsistent with Kodak's policy toward its self-service customers. If Kodak were underpricing its equipment, hoping to lock in customers and recover its losses in the service market, it could not afford to sell customers parts without service. In sum, Kodak's theory does not explain the actual market behavior revealed in the record.

Respondents offer a forceful reason why Kodak's theory, although perhaps intuitively appealing, may not accurately explain the behavior of the primary and derivative markets for complex durable goods: the existence of significant information and switching costs. These costs could create a less responsive connection between service and parts prices and equipment sales.

For the service-market price to affect equipment demand, consumers must inform themselves of the total cost of the "package"—equipment, service and parts—at the time of purchase; that is, consumers must engage in accurate lifecycle pricing. Lifecycle pricing of complex, durable equipment is difficult and costly. In order to arrive at an accurate price, a consumer must acquire a substantial amount of raw data and undertake sophisticated analysis. The necessary information would include data on price, quality, and availability of products needed to operate, upgrade, or enhance the initial equipment, as well as service and repair costs, including estimates of breakdown frequency, nature of repairs, price of service and parts, length of "down-time" and losses incurred from down-time.

Much of this information is difficult—some of it impossible—to acquire at the time of purchase. During the life of a product, companies may change the service and parts prices, and develop products with more advanced features, a decreased need for repair, or new warranties. In addition, the information is likely to be customer specific; lifecycle costs will vary from customer to customer with the type of equipment, degrees of equipment use, and costs of down-time.

Kodak acknowledges the cost of information, but suggests, again without evidentiary support, that customer information needs will be satisfied by competitors in the equipment markets. It is a question of fact, however, whether competitors would provide the necessary information. A competitor in the equipment market may not have reliable information about the lifecycle costs of complex equipment it does not service or the needs of customers it does not serve. Even if competitors had the relevant information, it is not clear that their interests would be advanced by providing such information to consumers. * * *

As Kodak notes, there likely will be some large-volume, sophisticated purchasers who will undertake the comparative studies and insist, in return for their patronage, that Kodak charge them competitive lifecycle prices. Kodak contends that these knowledgeable customers will hold down the package price for all other customers. There are reasons, however, to doubt that sophisticated purchasers will ensure that competitive prices are charged to unsophisticated purchasers, too. As an initial matter, if the number of sophisticated customers is relatively small, the amount of profits to be gained by supracompetitive pricing in the service market could make it profitable to let the knowledgeable consumers take their business elsewhere. More importantly, if a company is able to price-discriminate between sophisticated and unsophisticated consumers, the sophisticated will be unable to prevent the exploitation of the uninformed. A seller could easily price discriminate by varying the equipment/parts/service package, developing different warranties, or offering price discounts on different components.

Given the potentially high cost of information and the possibility a seller may be able to price-discriminate between knowledgeable and unsophisticated consumers, it makes little sense to assume, in the absence of any evidentiary support, that equipment-purchasing decisions are based on an accurate assessment of the total cost of equipment, service, and parts over the lifetime of the machine.

Indeed, respondents have presented evidence that Kodak practices price-discrimination by selling parts to customers who service their own equipment, but refusing to sell parts to customers who hire third-party service companies. Companies that have their own service staff are likely to be high-volume users, the same companies for whom it is most likely to be economically worthwhile to acquire the complex information needed for comparative lifecycle pricing.

A second factor undermining Kodak's claim that supracompetitive prices in the service market lead to ruinous losses in equipment sales is the cost to current owners of switching to a different product. If the cost of switching is high, consumers who already have purchased the equipment, and are thus "locked-in," will tolerate some level of service-price increases before changing equipment brands. Under this scenario, a seller profitably could maintain supracompetitive prices in the aftermarket if the switching costs were high relative to the increase in service prices, and the number of locked-in customers were high relative to the number of new purchasers.

Moreover, if the seller can price-discriminate between its locked-in customers and potential new customers, this strategy is even more likely to prove profitable. The seller could simply charge new customers below-marginal cost on the equipment and recoup the charges in service, or offer packages with life-time warranties or long-term service agreements that are not available to locked-in customers.

Respondents have offered evidence that the heavy initial outlay for Kodak equipment, combined with the required support material that works only with Kodak equipment, makes switching costs very high for existing Kodak customers. And Kodak's own evidence confirms that it varies the package price of equipment/parts/service for different customers.

In sum, there is a question of fact whether information costs and switching costs foil the simple assumption that the equipment and service markets act as pure complements to one another.

We conclude, then, that Kodak has failed to demonstrate that respondents' inference of market power in the service and parts markets is unreasonable, and that, consequently, Kodak is entitled to summary judgment. It is clearly reasonable to infer that Kodak has market power to raise prices and drive out competition in the aftermarkets, since respondents offer direct evidence that Kodak did so. It is also plausible, as discussed above, to infer that Kodak chose to gain immediate profits by exerting that market power where locked-in customers, high information costs, and discriminatory pricing limited and perhaps eliminated any long-term loss. Viewing the evidence in the light most favorable to respondents, their allegations of market power "mak[e].... economic sense." Cf. *Matsushita*, 475 U.S., at 587. * * *

We need not decide whether Kodak's behavior has any procompetitive effects and, if so, whether they outweigh the anticompetitive effects. We note only that Kodak's service and parts policy is simply not one that appears always or almost always to enhance competition, and therefore to warrant a legal presumption without any evidence of its actual economic impact. In this case, when we weigh the risk of deterring procompetitive behavior by proceeding to trial against the risk that illegal behavior will go unpunished, the balance tips against summary judgment.

... We ... affirm the denial of summary judgment on respondents' § 1 claim. * * *

JUSTICE SCALIA, joined by JUSTICES O'CONNOR and THOMAS, dissenting: * * * The Court today finds in the typical manufacturer's inherent power over its own brand of equipment—over the sale of distinctive repair parts for that equipment, for example—the sort of "monopoly power" sufficient to bring the sledgehammer of § 2 into play. And, not surprisingly in light of that insight, it readily labels single-brand power over aftermarket products "market power" sufficient to permit an antitrust plaintiff to invoke the *per se* rule against tying. In my opinion, this makes no economic sense. The holding that market power can be found on the present record causes these venerable rules of selective proscription to extend well beyond the point where the reasoning that supports them leaves off. Moreover, because the sort of power condemned by the Court today is possessed by every manufacturer of durable goods with distinctive parts, the Court's opinion threatens to release a torrent of litigation and a flood of commercial intimidation that will do much more harm than good to enforcement of the antitrust laws and to genuine competition.... [N]either logic nor experience suggests, let alone compels, application of the *per se* tying prohibition and monopolization doctrine to a seller's behavior in its single-brand aftermarkets, when that seller is without power at the interbrand level. * * *

In the absence of interbrand power, a seller's predominant or monopoly share of its single-brand derivative markets does not connote the power to raise derivative market prices *generally* by reducing quantity. As Kodak and its principal *amicus*, the United States, point out, a rational consumer considering the purchase of Kodak equipment will inevitably factor into his purchasing decision the expected cost of aftermarket support. "[B]oth the price of the equipment and the price of parts and service over the life of the equipment are expenditures that are necessary to obtain copying and micrographic services." Brief for United States as *Amicus Curiae* 13. If Kodak set generally supracompetitive prices for either spare parts or repair services without making an offsetting reduction in the price of its machines, rational consumers would simply turn to Kodak's competitors for photocopying and micrographic systems. True, there are—as the Court notes—the occasional irrational consumers that consider only the hardware cost at the time of purchase (a category that regrettably includes the Federal Government, whose "purchasing system," we are told, assigns foremarket purchases and aftermarket purchases to different entities). But we have never before premised the application of antitrust doctrine on the lowest common denominator of consumer.

The Court attempts to counter this theoretical point with theory of its own. It says that there are "information costs"—the costs and inconvenience to the consumer of acquiring and processing life-cycle pricing data for Kodak machines—that "could create a less responsive connection between service and parts prices and equipment sales." But this truism about the functioning of markets for sophisticated equipment cannot create "market power" of concern to the antitrust laws where otherwise there is none. "Information costs," or, more accurately, gaps in the availability and quality of consumer information, pervade real-world markets; and because consumers generally make do with "rough cut" judgments about price in such circumstances, in virtually any market there are zones within which otherwise competitive suppliers may overprice their products without losing appreciable market share. We have never suggested that the principal players in a market with such commonplace informational deficiencies (and, thus, bands of apparent consumer pricing indifference) exercise market power in any sense relevant to the antitrust laws. "While [such] factors may generate 'market power' in some abstract sense, they do not generate the kind of market power that justifies condemnation of tying." *Jefferson Parish Hospital Dist. No. 2* v. *Hyde*, 466 U.S., at 27.

Respondents suggest that, even if the existence of interbrand competition prevents Kodak from raising prices generally in its single-brand aftermarkets, there remain certain consumers who are necessarily subject to abusive Kodak pricing behavior by reason of their being "locked in" to their investments in Kodak machines. The Court agrees; indeed, it goes further by suggesting that even a *general* policy of supracompetitive aftermarket prices might be profitable over the long run because of the "lock-in" phenomenon. "[A] seller profitably could maintain supracompetitive prices in the aftermarket," the Court explains, "if the switching costs were high relative to the increase in service prices, and the number of locked-in customers were high relative to the number of new purchasers." In speculating about this latter possibility, the Court is essentially repudiating the assumption on which we are bound to decide this case, viz., Kodak's lack of any power whatsoever in the interbrand market. If Kodak's *general* increase in aftermarket prices were to bring the total "system" price above competitive levels in the interbrand market, Kodak would be wholly unable to make further foremarket sales—and would find itself exploiting an ever-dwindling aftermarket, as those Kodak micrographic and photocopying machines already in circulation passed into disuse.

The Court's narrower point, however, is undeniably true. There will be consumers who, because of their capital investment in Kodak equipment, "will tolerate some level of service-price increases before changing equipment brands;" ... this is *necessarily* true for "every maker of unique parts for its own product." Areeda & Hovenkamp, Antitrust Law ¶ 525.1b, at 563. But this "circumstantial" leverage created by consumer investment regularly crops up in smoothly functioning, even perfectly competitive, markets, and in most—if not all—of its manifestations, it is of no concern to the antitrust laws. The leverage held by the manufacturer of a malfunctioning refrigerator (which is measured by the consumer's reluctance to walk away from his initial investment in that device) is no different in kind or degree from the leverage held by . . . a mobile home park owner over his tenants, who are unable to transfer their homes to a different park except at great expense. Leverage, in the form of circumstantial power, plays a role in each of these relationships; but in none of them is the leverage attributable to the dominant party's market power in any relevant sense. Though that power can plainly work to the injury of certain consumers, it produces only "a brief perturbation in competitive conditions—not the sort of thing the antitrust laws do or should worry about." *Parts & Elec. Motors, Inc.* v. *Sterling Elec., Inc.*, 866 F.2d 228, 236 (CA7 1988) (Posner, J., dissenting). * * *

. . . Because the interbrand market will generally punish intrabrand restraints that consumers do not find in their interest, we should not—under the guise of a per se rule—condemn such potentially procompetitive arrangements simply because of the antitrust defendant's inherent power over the unique parts for its own brand. * * *

QUESTIONS AND COMMENTS

1. Kodak argued, as a matter of law, that the complaint should be dismissed because Kodak did not have sufficient market power in the Kodak parts aftermarket. How strong was this argument, and why did the Court reject it?

2. How important to the Court was the role of asymmetrical information? lock-in effect? If the information available to buyers and sellers had been symmetrical or if there had been no substantial switching costs, would the Court have granted Kodak's motion for summary judgment?

3. Why were *GTE Sylvania, Jefferson Parish,* and *Matsushita* not controlling authorities favoring Kodak? Should they have been?

4. What are the essential differences between the majority and the dissent? Consider the role of assumptions about how well markets work, the appropriate limits of government intervention, and the purpose of antitrust.

5. Despite the Court's protestations, do you think the *possibility* that Kodak had market power in the interbrand market influenced the Court? If this were a household vacuum machine market with 20 sellers, all at the same level of technology, some supplying machines plus service and parts as a package and some offering all goods and services separately, would the outcome have been the same? Would a seller in a highly competitive original equipment market have any power or incentive to steer its customers away from the service providers of their choice?—especially where it appeared that the ISOs were providing good service at lower cost?

6. Suppose Kodak had always supplied aftersales services and parts as a package and had never sold parts to independents. Could an independent service organization that wished to service Kodak machines, and was ready

and able, successfully claim a right to do so? Make your best argument to justify a rule of law that prohibits exclusionary *cut-offs* by dominant firms but does not necessarily impose duties to deal with strangers. The European Union and a number of European countries have such a rule. See, e.g., *United Brands Co v. Commission*, case 27/76, [1978] ECR 207. Is your argument supported by concerns of equity? of competition? of efficiency?

In the next case, Microsoft tested the limits of the qualified per se rule against tying, this time from a different perspective and with greater success than Kodak.

UNITED STATES v. MICROSOFT CORPORATION

253 F.3d 34 (D.C.Cir.), cert. denied, 534 U.S. 952 (2001).

(tying; see also pp. 216 and 310 supra).

PER CURIAM. * * * The District Court concluded that Microsoft's contractual and technological bundling of the IE web browser (the "tied" product) with its Windows operating system (AOS) (the "tying" product) resulted in a tying arrangement that was per se unlawful. We hold that the rule of reason, rather than per se analysis, should govern the legality of tying arrangements involving platform software products. * * *

A. SEPARATE-PRODUCTS INQUIRY UNDER THE PER SE TEST

Recognizing the potential benefits from tying, the Court in *Jefferson Parish* forged a separate-products test that, like those of market power and substantial foreclosure, attempts to screen out false positives under per se analysis. The consumer demand test is a rough proxy for whether a tying arrangement may, on balance, be welfare-enhancing, and unsuited to per se condemnation. In the abstract, of course, there is always direct separate demand for products: assuming choice is available at zero cost, consumers will prefer it to no choice. Only when the efficiencies from bundling are dominated by the benefits to choice for enough consumers, however, will we actually observe consumers making independent purchases. In other words, perceptible separate demand is inversely proportional to net efficiencies. On the supply side, firms without market power will bundle two goods only when the cost savings from joint sale outweigh the value consumers place on separate choice. So bundling by all competitive firms implies strong net efficiencies. If a court finds either that there is no noticeable separate demand for the tied product or, there being no convincing direct evidence of separate demand, that the entire "competitive fringe" engages in the same behavior as the defendant, then the tying and tied products should be declared one product and per se liability should be rejected. * * *

In fact there is merit to Microsoft's broader argument that *Jefferson Parish*'s consumer demand test would "chill innovation to the detriment of consumers by preventing firms from integrating into their products new functionality previously provided by standalone products—and hence, by definition, subject to separate consumer demand." The per se rule's direct consumer demand and indirect industry custom inquiries are, as a general matter, backward-looking and therefore systematically poor proxies for overall efficiency in the presence of new and innovative integration. . . . If integration has efficiency benefits, these may be ignored by the *Jefferson Parish* proxies. Because one cannot be sure beneficial integration will be protected by the other elements of the per se rule, simple application of that rule's separate-products test may make consumers worse off.

In light of the monopoly maintenance section [holding some of the same conduct illegal, see p. 256 supra], obviously, we do not find that Microsoft's integration is welfare-enhancing or that it should be absolved of tying liability. Rather, we heed Microsoft's warning that the separate-products element of the per se rule may not give newly integrated products a fair shake.

B. PER SE ANALYSIS INAPPROPRIATE FOR THIS CASE. * * *

In none of [the Supreme Court tying] cases was the tied good physically and technologically integrated with the tying good. Nor did the defendants ever argue that their tie improved the value of the tying product to users *and* to makers of complementary goods. In those cases where the defendant claimed that use of the tied good made the tying good more valuable to users, the Court ruled that the same result could be achieved via quality standards for substitutes of the tied good. Here Microsoft argues that IE [the Internet Explorer browser] and Windows are an integrated physical product and that the bundling of IE APIs [applications programming interfaces] with Windows makes the latter a better applications platform for third-party software. It is unclear how the benefits from IE APIs could be achieved by quality standards for different browser manufacturers. We do not pass judgment on Microsoft's claims regarding the benefits from integration of its APIs. We merely note that these and other novel, purported efficiencies suggest that judicial "experience" provides little basis for believing that, "because of their pernicious effect on competition and lack of *any* redeeming virtue," a software firm's decisions to sell multiple functionalities as a package should be "conclusively presumed to be unreasonable and therefore illegal without elaborate inquiry as to the precise harm they have caused or the business excuse for their use." *N. Pac. Ry.,* 356 U.S. at 5, 78 S.Ct. 514 (emphasis added). * * *

While the paucity of cases examining platform software bundling suggests a high risk that per se analysis may produce inaccurate results, the nature of the platform software market affirmatively suggests that per se rules might stunt valuable innovation. We have in mind two reasons.

First, as we explained in the previous section, the separate-products test is a poor proxy for net efficiency from newly integrated products. Under per se analysis the first firm to merge previously distinct functionalities (*e.g.*, the inclusion of starter motors in automobiles) or to eliminate entirely the need for a second function (*e.g.*, the invention of the stain-resistant carpet) risks being condemned as having tied two separate products because at the moment of integration there will appear to be a robust "distinct" market for the tied product. . . .

The failure of the separate-products test to screen out certain cases of productive integration is particularly troubling in platform software markets such as that in which the defendant competes. Not only is integration common in such markets, but it is common among firms without market power. We have already reviewed evidence that nearly all competitive OS vendors also bundle browsers. Moreover, plaintiffs do not dispute that OS vendors can and do incorporate basic internet plumbing and other useful functionality into their OSs. . . . Firms without market power have no incentive to package different pieces of software together unless there are efficiency gains from doing so. The ubiquity of bundling in competitive platform software markets should give courts reason to pause before condemning such behavior in less competitive markets.

Second, because of the pervasively innovative character of platform software markets, tying in such markets may produce efficiencies that courts have not previously encountered and thus the Supreme Court had not factored into the per se rule as originally conceived. For example, the bundling of a browser with OSs enables an independent software developer to count on the presence of the browser's APIs, if any, on consumers' machines and thus to omit them from its own package. . . . [O]ur qualms about redefining the boundaries of a defendant's product and the possibility of consumer gains from simplifying the work of applications developers makes us question any hard and fast approach to tying in OS software markets.

There may also be a number of efficiencies that, although very real, have been ignored in the calculations underlying the adoption of a per se rule for tying. We fear that these efficiencies are common in technologically dynamic markets where product development is especially unlikely to follow an easily foreseen linear pattern. . . .

These arguments all point to one conclusion: we cannot comfortably say that bundling in platform software markets has so little "redeeming virtue," *N. Pac. Ry.*, 356 U.S. at 5, and that there would be so "very little loss to society" from its ban, that "an inquiry into its costs in the individual case [can be] considered [ ] unnecessary." *Jefferson Parish,* 466 U.S. at 33–34 (O'Connor, J., concurring). We do not have enough empirical evidence regarding the effect of Microsoft's practice on the amount of consumer surplus created or consumer choice foreclosed by the integration of added functionality into platform software to exercise sensible judgment regarding that entire class of behavior. . . .

Our judgment regarding the comparative merits of the per se rule and the rule of reason is confined to the tying arrangement before us, where the tying product is software whose major purpose is to serve as a platform for third-party applications and the tied product is complementary software functionality. While our reasoning may at times appear to have broader force, we do not have the confidence to speak to facts outside the record, which contains scant discussion of software integration generally. Microsoft's primary justification for bundling IE APIs is that their inclusion with Windows increases the value of third-party software (and Windows) to consumers. Because this claim applies with distinct force when the tying product is *platform* software, we have no present basis for finding the per se rule inapplicable to software markets generally. Nor should we be interpreted as setting a precedent for switching to the rule of reason every time a court identifies an efficiency justification for a tying arrangement. Our reading of the record suggests merely that integration of new functionality into platform software is a common practice and that wooden application of per se rules in this litigation may cast a cloud over platform innovation in the market for PCs, network computers and information appliances....

[Vacated and remanded. Plaintiffs must prove the relevant market and show the actual effect of the tie on competition in the tied product market.]

QUESTIONS AND COMMENTS

1. Microsoft regarded its browser and its operating system as two separate products at the time of the tie. It decided to bind the two together (and disable the function for deleting the browser), allegedly in order to "cut off [the] air supply" of Netscape. See Microsoft, Intel wage war of words, CNET News, Nov. 12, 1998. Should this have been relevant to a consideration of whether the browser and the operating system were one product or two products and whether the per se rule should apply?

2. Do you agree with the Court's explanation of the rationale for the existence of the "two separate products" rule?

3. Despite the court's protestations that it was deciding only the case before it, did the court erode the per se rule? How similar is the analysis, conceptually, to the analysis of Justice O'Connor in *Jefferson Parish*, who at the time failed—but just barely—to muster a majority in favor of abandoning the qualified per se rule against tie-ins and moving to a rule of reason? If you should represent the defendant in a future "*Jefferson Parish*" case, or in the case of a hardware/software tie, what arguments used by the court would you find helpful?

4. On remand, plaintiffs withdrew the tie-in claim and merely pursued the question of relief for the monopolization violations. It was generally acknowledged that it would have been difficult to win the tie-in claim on remand under the rule of reason. Plaintiffs had not proved, and had forfeited their right to prove, that there was a browser market and that there were barriers to entry into such a market "other than what might be implicit in Microsoft's tying arrangement." 253 F.3d at 95. How, then, could plaintiffs have proved harm to competition in a browser market?

In many cases the tying product is protected by a patent. Does a patent presumptively confer market power? Past cases answered in the affirmative, making it quite simple for a plaintiff to prove a prima facie case in a challenge to a patent tie-in. In *Illinois Tool Works*, involving the tie of ink to a patented printer, the Supreme Court disavowed any such presumption. But the case stands for a far larger proposition regarding the appropriate attitude towards tie-ins.

ILLINOIS TOOL WORKS INC. v. INDEPENDENT INK, INC.

547 U.S. 28 (2006).

JUSTICE STEVENS: * * * Over the years, ... this Court's strong disapproval of tying arrangements has substantially diminished. Rather than relying on assumptions, in its more recent opinions the Court has required a showing of market power in the tying product. Our early opinions consistently assumed that "[t]ying arrangements serve hardly any purpose beyond the suppression of competition." *Standard Oil Co.*, 337 U.S., at 305–306. In 1962, in *Loew's*, 371 U.S., at 47–48, the Court relied on this assumption despite evidence of significant competition in the market for the tying product. And as recently as 1969, Justice Black, writing for the majority, relied on the assumption as support for the proposition "that, at least when certain prerequisites are met, arrangements of this kind are illegal in and of themselves, and no specific showing of unreasonable competitive effect is required." *Fortner Enterprises, Inc.* v. *United States Steel Corp.*, 394 U.S. 495, 498–499 *(Fortner I)*. ... [H]e stated that "decisions rejecting the need for proof of truly dominant power over the tying product have all been based on a recognition that because tying arrangements generally serve no legitimate business purpose that cannot be achieved in some less restrictive way, the presence of any appreciable restraint on competition provides a sufficient reason for invalidating the tie." *Id.*, at 503.

Reflecting a changing view of tying arrangements, four Justices dissented in *Fortner I*, arguing that the challenged "tie"—the extension of a $2 million line of credit on condition that the borrower purchase prefabricated houses from the defendant—might well have served a legitimate purpose.... In his opinion, Justice White noted that promotional tie-ins may provide "uniquely advantageous deals" to purchasers. *Id.*, at 519. And Justice Fortas concluded that the arrangement was best characterized as "a sale of a single product with the incidental provision of financing." *Id.*, at 522.

The dissenters' view that tying arrangements may well be procompetitive ultimately prevailed; indeed, it did so in the very same lawsuit. After the Court remanded the suit in *Fortner I*, a bench trial resulted in judgment for the plaintiff, and the case eventually made its way back to this Court. Upon return, we unanimously held that the plaintiff's failure of proof on the issue of market power was fatal to its case—the plaintiff had proved "nothing more than a willingness to provide cheap financing in order to sell expensive houses." *United States Steel Corp.* v. *Fortner Enterprises, Inc.*, 429 U.S. 610, 622 (1977) *(Fortner II).*

The assumption that "[t]ying arrangements serve hardly any purpose beyond the suppression of competition," rejected in *Fortner II*, has not been endorsed in any opinion since. Instead, it was again rejected just seven years later in *Jefferson Parish*, where, as in *Fortner II*, we unanimously reversed a Court of Appeals judgment holding that an alleged tying arrangement constituted a *per se* violation of § 1 of the Sherman Act. 466 U.S., at 5. Like the product at issue in the *Fortner* cases, the tying product in *Jefferson Parish*—hospital services—was unpatented, and our holding again rested on the conclusion that the plaintiff had failed to prove sufficient power in the tying product market to restrain competition in the market for the tied product—services of anesthesiologists. 466 U.S., at 28–29. * * *

Justice O'Connor wrote separately in *Jefferson Parish*, concurring in the judgment on the ground that the case did not involve a true tying arrangement because, in her view, surgical services and anesthesia were not separate products. In her opinion, she questioned not only the propriety of treating any tying arrangement as a *per se* violation of the Sherman Act, *id.*, at 35, but also the validity of the presumption that a patent always gives the patentee significant market power, observing that the presumption was actually a product of our patent misuse cases rather than our antitrust jurisprudence. It is that presumption, a vestige of the Court's historical distrust of tying arrangements, that we address squarely today.

IV.

[In patent misuse cases, the courts equated patents with market power, and this presumption migrated into antitrust; but in 1988 Congress eliminated this presumption and narrowed the patent misuse defense in infringement litigation.] [I]t would be anomalous to preserve the presumption in antitrust after Congress has eliminated its foundation. * * *

After considering the congressional judgment reflected in the 1988 amendment, we conclude that tying arrangements involving patented products should be evaluated under the standards applied in cases like *Fortner II* and *Jefferson Parish* rather than under the *per se* rule applied in *Morton* [sic; *International*?] *Salt* and *Loew's*. While some such arrangements are still unlawful, such as those that are the product of a true monopoly or a marketwide conspiracy, see, *e.g.*, *United States* v. *Paramount Pictures, Inc.*, 334 U.S. 131, 145–146 (1948), that conclusion must be supported by proof of power in the relevant market rather than by a mere presumption thereof.

V.

Rather than arguing that we should retain the rule of *per se* illegality, respondent contends that we should endorse a rebuttable presumption that patentees possess market power when they condition the purchase of the patented product on an agreement to buy unpatented goods exclusively from the patentee. Cf. *supra*, at 7–8. Respondent recognizes that a large number of valid patents have little, if any, commercial significance, but submits that those that are used to impose tying arrangements on unwilling purchasers likely do exert significant market power. Hence, in respondent's view, the presumption would have no impact on patents of only slight value and would be justified, subject to being rebutted by evidence offered by the patentee, in cases in which the patent has sufficient value to enable the patentee to insist on acceptance of the tie.

Respondent also offers a narrower alternative, suggesting that we differentiate between tying arrangements involving the simultaneous purchase of two products that are arguably two components of a single product—such as the provision of surgical services and anesthesiology in the same operation, *Jefferson Parish*, 466 U.S., at 43 (O'Connor, J., concurring in judgment), or the licensing of one copyrighted film on condition that the licensee take a package of several films in the same transaction, *Loew's*, 371 U.S. 38—and a tying arrangement involving the purchase of unpatented goods over a period of time, a so-called "requirements tie." According to respondent, we should recognize a presumption of market power when faced with the latter type of arrangements because they provide a means for charging large volume purchasers a higher royalty for use of the patent than small purchasers must pay, a form of discrimination that "is strong evidence of market power." * * *

As we have already noted, the vast majority of academic literature recognizes that a patent does not necessarily confer market power. Similarly, while price discrimination may provide evidence of market power, particularly if buttressed by evidence that the patentee has charged an above-market price for the tied package, it is generally recognized that it also occurs in fully competitive markets.... We are not persuaded that the combination of these two factors should give rise to a presumption of market power when neither is sufficient to do so standing alone. Rather, the lesson to be learned from *International Salt* and the academic commentary is the same: Many tying arrangements, even those involving patents and requirements ties, are fully consistent with a free, competitive market. For this reason, we reject both respondent's proposed rebuttable presumption and their narrower alternative. * * *

Congress, the antitrust enforcement agencies, and most economists have all reached the conclusion that a patent does not necessarily confer market power upon the patentee. Today, we reach the same conclusion, and therefore hold that, in all cases involving a tying arrangement, the plaintiff must prove that the defendant has market power in the tying product. * * *

[Vacated and remanded.]

QUESTION

What does *Illinois Tool* imply regarding the future of the qualified per se rule on tying?

4. EXCLUSIVE DEALING AND REQUIREMENTS CONTRACTS

a. Earlier Law

Exclusive dealing, partial exclusive dealing, and requirements contracts can (like tie-ins) have a foreclosing effect on competitors; but the efficiencies of such contracts for buyers and sellers are more obvious.

The first landmark case—and the guiding light for half a century—was "*Standard Stations.*" (*Standard Oil of California v. United States*, 337 U.S. 293 (1949).) Standard Stations and its competitors (who were its corporate sisters before the big breakup) sold much of their gasoline through their own outlets and the rest through independent gas stations under one-year exclusive contracts. The one-year contracts were virtually always renewed.

The Justice Department sued Standard Oil, the largest of the competitors in the Western states, which accounted for 23% of Western gasoline sales. Of all retail gas outlets in the Western area, 16% (5,937 operators) had exclusive supply contracts with Standard Oil. Through these outlets, 6.7% of the gasoline in the Western states was sold. The DOJ sued Standard Oil under Section 3 of the Clayton Act and Section 1 of the Sherman Act, relying principally on Section 3 of the Clayton Act, which declares:

> It shall be unlawful for any person . . . to lease or [sell] . . . goods . . . on the condition that the leasee or purchaser thereof shall not use or deal in the goods . . . of a competitor . . ., where the effect may be to substantially lessen competition or tend to create a monopoly. . . .

The DOJ was concerned that the network of exclusive contracts would, as the Supreme Court was to say, "enable the established suppliers individually to maintain their own standing and at the same time collectively, even though not collusively, to prevent a late arrival from wresting away more than an insignificant portion of the market."

En route to this conclusion, the Court took note of the possible efficiencies of exclusive contracts (You, the buyer, buy exclusively from me and not from my competitors) and requirements contracts (You, the seller, promise to fulfill my requirements). Thus:

> Requirements contracts . . . may well be of economic advantage to buyers as well as to sellers, and thus indirectly of advantage to the consuming public. In the case of the buyer, they may assure supply,

> afford protection against rises in price, enable long-term planning on the basis of known costs, and obviate the expense and risk of storage in the quantity necessary for a commodity having a fluctuating demand. From the seller's point of view, requirements contracts may make possible the substantial reduction of selling expenses, give protection against price fluctuations, and—of particular advantage to a newcomer to the field to whom it is important to know what capital expenditures are justified—offer the possibility of a predictable market. They may be useful, moreover, to a seller trying to establish a foothold against the counter-attacks of entrenched competitors.
>
> * * *
>
> We conclude, therefore, that the qualifying clause of § 3 [may be to substantially lessen competition] is satisfied by proof that competition has been foreclosed in a substantial share of the line of commerce affected. It cannot be gainsaid that observance by a dealer of his requirements contract with Standard does effectively foreclose whatever opportunity there might be for competing suppliers to attract his patronage, and it is clear that the affected proportion of retail sales of petroleum products is substantial. In view of the widespread adoption of such contracts by Standard's competitors and the availability of alternative ways of obtaining an assured market, evidence that competitive activity has not actually declined is inconclusive. Standard's use of the contracts creates just such a potential clog on competition as it was the purpose of § 3 to remove wherever, were it to become actual, it would impede a substantial amount of competitive activity.

The *Standard Station* test—an exclusive contract was illegal if it foreclosed a substantial share of the market—was referred to as "quantitative substantiality." This was to distinguish exclusive and requirements contracts from tying contracts, which were thought (until the last few decades) to be designed to clog the market and not necessary or important to serve good business purposes, and therefore appropriately condemned even without proof of substantial foreclosure.

The punitive rule of *Standard Stations* necessarily put weight on market definition. If the share foreclosed was significant, the exclusive contract was illegal. If not, it was probably legal. This state of affairs gave rise to the famous case of *Tampa Electric* (although its fame has been overshadowed by the eclipse of *Standard Stations* as a consequence of modern effects analysis). *Tampa Electric Co. v. Nashville Coal Co.*, 365 U.S. 320 (1961).

Tampa Electric Company, which served peninsular Florida, had been using oil as its source of energy. It planned to construct an additional generating plant for which it decided to use coal. It entered into a contract with Nashville Coal Company, by which the latter agreed to supply the new plant's coal requirements for 20 years at a stated price. After Tampa invested millions of dollars in the new plant, the market price of coal rose.

Nashville reneged on the supply contract, claiming that the contract was illegal under the Clayton and Sherman Acts and thus unenforceable.

Nashville, of course, wanted the Court to find a very narrow market, such as peninsular Florida, for Tampa's new plant would use 18% of all coal sold in peninsular Florida; by this account a significant portion of the market would notionally be foreclosed to competitors of Nashville (a strange argument from the mouth of Nashville that its supply contract was illegal and should be voided because it, Nashville, deprived its coal competitors of the chance to compete to supply the plant of Tampa). Tampa, on the other hand, which wanted to keep the benefit of this good deal (and had economics and reality on its side), wanted the Court to find a large market within which Tampa's needs for coal (or better yet energy) were a drop in the bucket. The Supreme Court agreed with Tampa, found that Tampa's requirements for coal were less than 1% of the total coal supplied by Nashville and its Appalachian area competitors, and dismissed the case. Moreover, the Court suggested in dictum that "substantiality" implies an inquiry into the impact of the contract on effective competition; not just a calculation of market share.

Today, Nashville would not even get to trial. We would ask two preliminary questions. The second is: What is the story by which Nashville's contract to supply Tampa gives Nashville market power or increases or preserves its market power? None can be imagined.

The first is: Why does Nashville have standing to make this claim? What is the antitrust injury that Nashville might suffer from an anticompetitive aspect of this contract? How is it hurt by the (alleged) anticompetitive nature of the contract? We can imagine no credible answer.

b. Modern Law and Analysis

By the 1980s, exclusive dealing was judged by the usual analysis: Does this contract harm competition and consumers? Does it convey market power? Or is it merely a means to compete? Section 3 of the Clayton Act is seldom invoked, and, when it is, it is generally read in conformity with the Sherman Act (although its language of potentiality could give a plaintiff a little more leeway).

The *Barry Wright* case follows. It involves a huge market share and invites us to think about what we mean by foreclosure and by anticompetitive foreclosure. The *Microsoft* and *Dentsply* cases, following *Barry Wright*, are good examples of exclusive dealing that harms competition.

BARRY WRIGHT CORP. v. ITT GRINNELL CORP.

724 F.2d 227 (1st Cir. 1983).

JUDGE BREYER: [Mechanical snubbers are shock absorbers used in building pipe systems for nuclear power plants. Grinnell makes and installs nuclear plant pipe systems and buys more than 50% of all mechanical snubbers used. Grinnell was a customer of Pacific Scientific

Company, the only domestic manufacturer of the snubbers. Foreign-produced snubbers did not satisfy U.S. regulatory standards. Wanting an alternative source of supply, Grinnell contracted with Barry Wright, agreed to help Barry develop a full mechanical snubber line, and agreed to use Barry as its exclusive source in 1977 when Barry was expected to have sufficient production. When Grinnell began to shift some purchases to Barry, Pacific offered Grinnell a 25–30% discount in return for a $5.7 million order that would have met Grinnell's need through 1977. Barry, meanwhile, failed to meet its production schedule. Grinnell and Pacific agreed to further supply deals at discounted prices in a dollar amount that would meet Grinnell's needs for the next two years, and Grinnell cancelled its deal with Barry. Barry abandoned the snubber business and sued for violations of the Sherman and Clayton Acts.] * * *

Barry argues next that Pacific's "requirements contract" with Grinnell was exclusionary, that it was more restrictive of competition than legitimate business considerations could justify. The district court, however, disagreed. And so do we.

The antitrust problem that courts have found lurking in requirements contracts grows out of their tendency to "foreclose" other sellers from the market by "tying up" potential purchases of the buyer. Arguably, under certain circumstances substantial foreclosure might discourage sellers from entering, or seeking to sell in, a market at all, thereby reducing the amount of competition that would otherwise be available. Of course, the connection between "foreclosure" and lessened entry is somewhat distant, since it depends on how potential competitors perceive the foreclosure's likely effects on their opportunities. Moreover, virtually *every* contract to buy "forecloses" or "excludes" alternative sellers from *some* portion of the market, namely the portion consisting of what was bought. It is not surprising, then, that courts have judged the lawfulness of contracts to purchase not under per se rules but under a "rule of reason." *Tampa Electric Co. v. Nashville Coal Co.,* 365 U.S. 320, 333 (1961). And this is so whether those contracts involve a buyer's promise to buy "exclusively" from the seller, a promise to buy all his "requirements" from the seller for a specified time, or a promise to buy a large dollar amount. Thus, in determining "the probable effect of the contract on the relevant area of effective competition," *Tampa Electric Co. v. Nashville Coal Co.,* 365 U.S. at 329, we are to take into account both the extent of the foreclosure and the buyer's and seller's business justifications for the arrangement. *Id.* at 333–34. We must look both to the severity of the foreclosure (a fact which, other things being equal, suggests anticompetitive harm) and the strength of the justifications in determining whether the "size" of the contract to purchase is reasonable.

. . . [I]f Barry correctly describes Grinnell as accounting for half the snubber market, this characterization suggests a three-year "foreclosure" of 50 percent of the relevant market. In terms of the case law, this sounds like a significant foreclosure. But this description considerably overstates the size of the foreclosure and its likely anticompetitive effect for several reasons.

First, Grinnell did not actually promise to buy all its requirements from Pacific; it entered into a contract for a fixed dollar amount. A true requirements contract flatly eliminates the buyer from the market for its duration; a fixed quantity contract leaves open the possibility that the buyer's needs will exceed his contractual commitment; he is free to purchase from others any excess amount that he may want. This flexibility is important here, for it left Grinnell the legal power to buy small (and then in 1979, larger) amounts from Barry should they have become available.

Second, the Grinnell–Pacific contract was not a single three-year agreement. [T]he scope of this agreement's preclusive effect ... extended over something less than Grinnell's expected requirements and lasted about two years.

Third, Grinnell's contract with Barry suggests that a snubber buyer typically places orders for snubbers well in advance of expected delivery.... Under these circumstances, a Grinnell decision to buy a year or two's worth of snubbers from Pacific *at one shot* instead of *from time to time* seems likely, as a practical matter, to have had, at most, limited anticompetitive effects.

At the same time, the record suggests the existence of legitimate business justifications for the agreements from the perspectives of both buyer and seller. For Grinnell, the contracts guaranteed a stable source of supply, and, perhaps, more important, they assured Grinnell a stable, favorable price. For Pacific, they allowed use of considerable excess snubber capacity; and they allowed production planning that was likely to lower costs....

Finally, Grinnell is not a small firm that Pacific could likely bully into accepting a contract that might foreclose new competition. To the contrary, it was Grinnell, not Pacific, that sought the extensions for 1978 and 1979. Moreover, Grinnell had every interest in promoting new competition. It agreed to provide Barry with several hundred thousand dollars expressly to develop a new source of supply. Grinnell could have obtained snubbers without placing such large orders had it given up the "special" extra 5 to 10 percent price discount, a matter of a few hundred thousand dollars per year. Had Grinnell believed that the long-term nature of the contracts significantly interfered with new entry, or inhibited the development of a new source of supply, it is difficult to understand why it would have sought the agreements.

In sum, in light of the nature of the contracts and the market, their fairly short time period, their business justifications, the characteristics of the parties, and their likely motives as revealed by their business interests, we believe that the district court could reasonably have concluded they were not "exclusionary." * * *

If Pacific's challenged conduct is not "exclusionary," for purposes of Sherman Act § 2, then a fortiori, it does not violate the other provisions of law that Barry cites. [e.g. Section 1 of the Sherman Act].

QUESTIONS AND COMMENTS

1. From what percent of the market were mechanical scrubber producers foreclosed as a result of Grinnell's contracts with Pacific?

2. What does "foreclosure" mean in this context? Is it a basis for inferring harm to competition and consumers, or not? Is foreclosure irrelevant when the buyer needs assured supply? or should the court balance the market harm (what harm?) against the efficiency benefits?

UNITED STATES v. MICROSOFT CORP.

253 F.3d 34 (D.C.Cir.), cert. denied, 534 U.S. 952 (2001).

(see also pp. 310, 680 supra) (exclusive dealing).

(Recall the monopoly maintenance and tying parts of the case, above: Microsoft had set upon a strategy to keep Netscape's browser at bay because Netscape's Navigator combined with cross-platform Java language threatened to destroy its market power in the operating system.)

PER CURIAM: * * * [Microsoft made exclusive deals with all leading Internet Access Providers (IAPs); most significantly with AOL, which accounted for a substantial portion of Internet access subscribers. Microsoft agreed to put the AOL icon on the Windows desktop and AOL agreed in return not to promote any non-Microsoft browser nor provide software using any non-Microsoft browser except at the customer's request and even then AOL agreed not to supply more than 15% of its customers with a browser other than Microsoft's.

Plaintiffs challenged this and other exclusionary contracts under Section 1 as well as Section 2 of the Sherman Act. The trial court dismissed the Section 1 claims on grounds that the contracts did not foreclose Netscape's Navigator browser absolutely from access to about 40% of the browser market. (Was this sound?) Plaintiffs did not appeal the dismissal under Section 1, for the trial court held the contracts illegal under Section 2.]

Though what is "significant [foreclosure]" [as required by *Tampa Electric*] may vary depending upon the antitrust provision under which an exclusive deal is challenged, it is clear that in all cases the plaintiff must both define the relevant market and prove the degree of foreclosure. This is a prudential requirement; exclusivity provisions in contracts may serve many useful purposes. *See, e.g., Omega Envtl., Inc. v. Gilbarco, Inc.,* 127 F.3d 1157, 1162 (9th Cir. 1997) ("There are, however, well-recognized economic benefits to exclusive dealing arrangements, including the enhancement of interbrand competition."); *Barry Wright Corp. v. ITT Grinnell Corp.,* 724 F.2d 227, 236 (1st Cir.1983) (Breyer, J.) ("[V]irtually *every* contract to buy 'forecloses' or 'excludes' alternative sellers from *some* portion of the market, namely the portion consisting of what was bought."). Permitting an antitrust action to proceed any time a firm enters into an exclusive deal would both discourage a presumptively legitimate business practice and encourage costly antitrust actions. Because an exclusive deal affecting a small fraction of a market clearly cannot have the requisite harmful effect upon competition, the requirement of a significant degree of foreclosure serves a useful screening function. *Cf.* Frank H. Easterbrook, *The Limits of Antitrust,* 63 TEX. L. REV. 1, 21–23 (1984) (discussing use of presumptions in antitrust law to screen out cases in which loss to consumers and economy is likely outweighed by cost of inquiry and risk of deterring procompetitive behavior). * * *

The basic prudential concerns relevant to §§ 1 and 2 are admittedly the same: exclusive contracts are commonplace—particularly in the field of distribution—in our competitive, market economy, and imposing upon a firm with market power the risk of an antitrust suit every time it enters into such a contract, no matter how small the effect, would create an unacceptable and unjustified burden upon any such firm. At the same time, however, we agree with plaintiffs that a monopolist's use of exclusive contracts, in certain circumstances, may give rise to a § 2 violation even though the contracts foreclose less than the roughly 40% or 50% share usually required in order to establish a § 1 violation. *See generally* Dennis W. Carlton, *A General Analysis of Exclusionary Conduct and Refusal to Deal—Why* Aspen *and* Kodak *Are Misguided,* 68 ANTITRUST L.J. 659 (2001) (explaining various scenarios under which exclusive dealing, particularly by a dominant firm, may raise legitimate concerns about harm to competition).

In this case, plaintiffs allege that, by closing to rivals a substantial percentage of the available opportunities for browser distribution, Microsoft managed to preserve its monopoly in the market for operating systems. The IAPs [Internet access providers] constitute one of the two major channels by which browsers can be distributed. Microsoft has exclusive deals with "fourteen of the top fifteen access providers in North America[, which] account for a large majority of all Internet access subscriptions in this part of the world." By ensuring that the "majority" of all IAP subscribers are offered IE either as the default browser or as the only browser, Microsoft's deals with the IAPs clearly have a significant effect in preserving its monopoly [in the operating system market]; they help keep usage of Navigator below the critical level necessary for Navigator or any other rival to pose a real threat to Microsoft's monopoly....

Plaintiffs having demonstrated a harm to competition, the burden falls upon Microsoft to defend its exclusive dealing contracts with IAPs by providing a procompetitive justification for them. Significantly, Microsoft's only explanation for its exclusive dealing is that it wants to keep developers focused upon its APIs [applications programming interfaces; see *Microsoft*, supra at 312, for the significance of the applications barrier to entry into the operating system market]—which is to say, it wants to preserve its power in the operating system market. That is not an unlawful end, but neither is it a procompetitive justification for the specific means here in question, namely exclusive dealing contracts with IAPs. Accordingly, we affirm the District Court's decision holding that Microsoft's exclusive contracts with IAPs are exclusionary devices, in violation of § 2 of the Sherman Act. * * *

A Note on Dentsply. In *United States v. Dentsply International, Inc.*, 399 F. 3d 181 (3d Cir. 2005), Dentsply was a manufacturer of artificial teeth. It had about 75% to 85% of the market and had a reputation for "aggressive price increases." It distributed its product through 23 authorized dealers. Its distribution contracts were at will. Its dealer criteria stated that, to effectively promote Dentsply product, dealers "may not add further tooth lines to their product offerings." Dentsply enforced this policy, terminating those who took on the product of competitors. However, Dentsply grandfathered those dealers who were already offering competing products, so that they were not subject to its exclusivity policy. Dentsply's justification for exclusivity (more efficient distribution) was a pretext, according to the court; the grandfathered dealers promoted the Dentsply product just as efficiently as did the exclusive dealers.

Dentsply's intent was to choke off its competitors. Its exclusivity policy helped to "keep sales of competing teeth below the critical level necessary for any rival to pose a real threat to Dentsply's market share." A sufficient number of other dealers were not available to competitors, and direct distribution to retailers was not an effective option.

The court found a violation of Section 2 of the Sherman Act.

QUESTIONS AND COMMENTS

1. Critique *Barry Wright*, *Microsoft* and *Dentsply*. Are these essentially fact-based cases? What (plausible) facts might have altered the results in each?

2. Suppose that, in *Jefferson Parish*, supra p. 663, Dr. Hyde had formulated his case as illegal exclusive dealing rather than as illegal tying. What would be the theory of the case? Would Dr. Hyde have been likely to win or lose?

Problem

exclusive licensing

The 32 NFL (professional football) teams formed a corporation, NFLP, to license their trade marks to clothing manufacturers, to be affixed to T-shirts and caps. For many years NFLP granted non-exclusive licenses to licensees including American Needle. At the expiration of existing licenses they shifted course, gave a 10–year exclusive license to Reebok (as you saw in *American Needle, Inc. v. NFLP*, page 122 supra), and accordingly refused to renew the license of American Needle.

American Needle sues for a violation of Section 1 of the Sherman Act, alleging that the contract between Reebok and NFLP is anticompetitive. The lawyers are preparing the case for trial.

Students 1 and 2 (for American Needle):

What is your theory of the case?
On what cases will you rely?
What facts do you hope to prove? Make a list of 5 facts you hope to prove.

Students 3 and 4 (for NFLP and the teams):

What is your theory of defense?
On what cases will you rely?
What alleged facts do you hope to disprove?
What facts will you seek to establish? Make a list of 5 such facts.

The Court has asked you to exchange your proposed fact-finding in advance of trial. Do so. The Court next asks you to try to agree to the facts and to submit a list of agreed facts and those that must be tried. Do this too. On the basis of these documents, argue your case before the Court.

Students 5, 6 and 7: You are the judges.

Litigators, you may make up proposed facts consistent with the problem. Judges, you will be required to find the facts, where there is a disagreement, and apply the law.

As you think about the theory of the case, recall the Supreme Court's decision in *American Needle*. Remember that the case has both horizontal and vertical implications. American Needle team: Remember that you are constructing a story about how the agreement creates market power and ultimately raises the price of NFL-team trade-marked clothing. NFL team: You are constructing a story to the contrary. Both teams and the judges will want to consider the implications of the fact that the NFL teams are acting together, rather than singly.

C. FRANCHISING

Beginning in the 1950s, franchising burgeoned as a way of doing business. Fast food outlets, with uniform and limited menus, grew and flourished. The franchisor would develop a distinctive image or concept, associated with a trademark or trade name, such as Chock Full O'Nuts, Dairy Queen or McDonald's. It would develop plans for a chain of franchised stores, which would sell the product directly to the consumer. It would select individuals or entities—sometimes hundreds or thousands—to be its franchisees and to run the retail operations in the uniform style developed by the franchisor. The franchisor would license each franchisee for a period of years. Sometimes it charged a flat annual fee but usually it charged royalties based on the licensee's revenues. Sometimes the franchisor sought compensation in other ways as well—for example, by tying to the license the supplies that the franchisee would need and by placing a premium on those supplies, or by requiring the franchisee to lease real estate from the franchisor at higher than market rates.

Some franchisors would provide their franchisees with turn-key operations. When the franchisee arrived to begin operations, every table, chair and kitchen facility would be in place (usually on real estate owned by the franchisor and leased to the franchisee). Others would merely license the trade mark, name and logo and provide detailed descriptions of the required structure and design of building, content and quality of the offerings and manner and style of service. Some franchisors would own and operate some of the retail operations in their chain and franchise others; thus, they would be dual distributors. Others would franchise all of the retail operations.

Franchising offered new business opportunities. Entrepreneurial individuals who did not have enough capital, or perhaps imagination, to conceive of a viable business concept and start their own business could nonetheless become "independent" business people. The independence, however, was sometimes illusory because the franchisees were contractually constrained by the franchisor through detailed requirements about business operations and style. Moreover, the profit opportunities, as well as the opportunity to capitalize on the success of their own investment, were limited by the terms of the franchise. Sometimes the franchisor, or extraneous circumstances, gave the franchisee unrealistic expectations of profit, and sometimes the franchisor opportunistically exploited the franchisee—for example, by terminating or squeezing out a franchisee who had invested substantial amounts of money and successfully developed the franchise to the point where its earnings and its capital value were high.

The result was much litigation by franchisees against franchisors. Most of the litigation is for breach of contract, fraud, deception, or violation of the many state statutes or federal regulations adopted to protect franchisees from overreaching by franchisors. Also, the franchisee may allege violations of the antitrust laws.

In some of the cases that arose prior to the advent of franchise regulation, courts were concerned that smaller suppliers were foreclosed from opportunities to sell and that franchisees were foreclosed from the right to negotiate their own deals for supplies or business space. *E.g., Susser v. Carvel Corp.*, 332 F.2d 505 (2d Cir.1964), *cert. denied*, 381 U.S. 125 (1965). But these concerns for autonomy dropped out of the jurisprudence as antitrust values after the Supreme Court decided *GTE Sylvania*. Most antitrust franchise litigation is litigation by the franchisee suing for tying and occasionally for monopolization or attempt to monopolize the franchisor's market. But even these cases are filed with less and less frequency as the Supreme Court raises the bar of illegality.

In the two cases that follow, you will become well acquainted with the key battlegrounds of the franchise antitrust cases: Was the franchisor offering one product or many products? What was the market; was there a market comprised of the particular brand? Did the franchisor have market power? The antitrust laws of some jurisdictions, such as Japan, include provisions against abuse of a superior bargaining position. Consider whether such a provision would be a more natural home than the Sherman Act for the franchisees' complaints.

PRINCIPE v. McDONALD'S CORP.

631 F.2d 303 (4th Cir.1980), cert. denied, 451 U.S. 970 (1981).

JUDGE PHILLIPS: This appeal presents the question of whether a fast food franchisor that requires its licensees to operate their franchises in premises leased from the franchisor is guilty of an illegal tying arrangement in violation of § 1 of the Sherman Act. On the facts of this case, we hold it does not and affirm the directed verdict for the defendants.

I.

The appellants, Frank A. Principe, Ann Principe and Frankie, Inc., a family owned corporation, are franchisees of McDonald's System, Inc. The Principes acquired their first franchise, a McDonald's hamburger restaurant in Hopewell, Virginia, in 1970. At that time, they executed a twenty year franchise license agreement and a store lease of like duration. In consideration for their rights under these agreements, the Principes paid a $10,000 license fee and a $15,000 security deposit, and agreed to remit 2.2 per cent of their gross receipts as royalties under the franchise agreement and 8.0 per cent as rent under the lease. In 1974, Frank Principe and his son, Raymond, acquired a second franchise in Colonial Heights, Virginia, on similar terms. The Colonial Heights franchise subsequently was transferred to Frankie, Inc., a corporation owned jointly by Frank and Raymond Principe.

The Principes sought to purchase a third franchise in 1976 in Petersburg, Virginia. Robert Beavers, McDonald's regional manager, concluded the plaintiffs lacked sufficient management depth and capabilities to take on a third store without impairing the quality of their existing operations. During the next twenty months, the Principes obtained corporate review and reconsideration of the decision to deny them the franchise. They were notified in May 1978 that the Petersburg franchise was being offered to a new franchisee.

They filed this action a few days later alleging violations of federal and state antitrust and securities laws and state franchising laws. Courts I and II alleged McDonald's violated federal antitrust laws by tying store leases and $15,000 security deposit notes to the franchise rights at the Hopewell and Colonial Heights stores. Count XII alleged McDonald's denied the Principes a third franchise in retaliation for their refusal to follow McDonald's pricing guidelines. . . .

Following discovery the district court granted summary judgment for McDonald's on the security deposit note tie in claims. District Judge D. Dortch Warriner found the notes represented deposits against loss and do not constitute a product separate from the store leases to which they pertain.

The court directed a verdict for McDonald's on the store lease tie in counts at the close of all the evidence. . . . Judge Warriner held the Principes had failed to introduce any evidence of McDonald's power in the tying product market, which he held is the food retailing market. The court held, however, McDonald's sells only one product: the license contract and store lease are component parts of the overall package McDonald's offers its prospective franchisees. Accordingly, Judge Warriner held as a matter of law there was no illegal tie in.

The remaining issue, whether McDonald's denied the Principes a third franchise in retaliation for their pricing independence, went to the jury which held for the defendants. The jury returned an unsolicited note stating they felt the Principes had been wronged, although price fixing was not the reason, and should be awarded the Petersburg franchise. The court disregarded the jury's note and entered judgment on the verdict for McDonald's.

The Principes appeal from the summary judgment for McDonald's on the security deposit tying claim, the directed verdict on the lease tying claim, various evidentiary rulings and the refusal of the district court to order a new trial. We affirm.

II.

At the time this suit was filed, McDonald's consisted of at least four separate corporate entities. McDonald's Systems, Inc. controlled franchise rights and licensed franchisees to sell hamburgers under the McDonald's name. Franchise Realty Interstate Corporation (Franchise Realty) acquires real estate, either by purchase or long term lease, builds McDonald's hamburger restaurants, and leases them either to franchisees or to a third corporation, McOpCo. McOpCo, which is not a party to this suit, operates about one-fourth of the McDonald's restaurants in the United States as company stores. Straddling this triad is McDonald's Corporation, the parent, who owns all the stock of the other defendants. Because the various defendants have substantially similar corporate hierarchies and operate in conjunction under the direction and control of the corporate parent, we shall refer to them collectively as McDonald's unless the context requires otherwise.

McDonald's is not primarily a fast food retailer. While it does operate over a thousand stores itself, the vast majority of the stores in its system are operated by franchisees. Nor does McDonald's sell equipment or supplies to its licensees. Instead its primary business is developing and collecting royalties from limited menu fast food restaurants operated by independent business people.

McDonald's develops new restaurants according to master plans that originate at the regional level and must be approved by upper management. Regional administrative staffs meet at least annually to consider new areas into which McDonald's can expand. Once the decision is made to expand into a particular geographic area, specialists begin to search for appropriate restaurant sites.

McDonald's uses demographic data generated by the most recent census and its own research in evaluating potential sites. McDonald's attempts to analyze and predict demographic trends in the geographic area. This process serves a two fold purpose: (1) by analyzing the demographic profile of a given market area, McDonald's hopes to determine whether the residents are likely to buy fast food in sufficient quantities to justify locating a restaurant there; (2) by anticipating future growth, McDonald's seeks to plan its expansion to maximize the number of viable McDonald's restaurants within a given geographic area. Based on a comparison of data for various available sites, the regional staffs select what they believe is the best site in each geographic area. Occasionally no available site suits McDonald's requirements and expansion must be postponed. * * *

After the specifics of each proposed new restaurant are approved, McDonald's decides whether the store will be company operated or franchised. If the decision is to franchise the store McDonald's begins the process of locating a franchisee. This involves offering the store either to an existing franchisee or to an applicant on the franchise waiting list. Applicants need not live near the store in order to be offered the franchise, and they need not accept the first franchise they are offered. The Principes lived in Kenosha, Wisconsin, and rejected eleven separate McDonald's restaurants before accepting their first franchise in Hopewell, Virginia. McDonald's often does not know who will operate a franchised store until it is nearly completed because a new restaurant may be offered to and rejected by several different applicants.

Meanwhile, Franchise Realty acquires the land, either by purchase or long term lease and constructs the store. Acquisition and development costs averaged over $450,000 per store in 1978. All McDonald's restaurants bear the same distinctive features with a few exceptions due to architectural restrictions: the golden arches motif, the brick and glass construction and the distinctive roofline. According to the defendants, these features identify the stores as a McDonald's even where zoning restrictions preclude other advertising or signs.

As constructed, McDonald's restaurants are finished shells; they contain no kitchen or dining room equipment. Furnishing store equipment is the responsibility of the operator, whether a franchisee or McOpCo. McDonald's does provide specifications such equipment must meet, but does not sell the equipment itself.

Having acquired the land, begun construction of the store and selected an operator, McDonald's enters into two contracts with the franchisee. Under the first, the franchise agreement, McDonald's grants the franchisee the rights to use McDonald's food preparation system and to sell food products under the McDonald's name. [Since 1970], [t]he franchisee pays a $12,500 franchise fee and agrees to remit three per cent of his gross sales as a royalty in return. Under the second contract, the lease, McDonald's grants the franchisee the right to use the particular store premises to which his franchise pertains. In return, the franchisee pays a $15,000 refundable security deposit (as evidence of which he receives a twenty year non-negotiable non-interest bearing note) and agrees to pay eight and one half per cent of his gross sales as rent. These payments under the franchise and lease agreements are McDonald's only sources of income from its franchised restaurants. The franchisee also assumes responsibility under the lease for building maintenance, improvements, property taxes and other costs associated with the premises. Both the franchise agreement and the lease generally have twenty year durations, both provide that termination of one terminates the other, and neither is available separately.

III.

The Principes argue McDonald's is selling not one but three distinct products, the franchise, the lease and the security deposit note. The alleged antitrust violation stems from the fact that a prospective franchisee must buy all three in order to obtain the franchise.

As evidence that this is an illegal tying arrangement, the Principes point to the unfavorable terms on which franchisees are required to lease their stores. Not only are franchisees denied the opportunity to build equity and depreciate their property, but they must maintain the building, pay for improvements and taxes, and remit 8.5 per cent of their gross sales as rents. In 1978 the gross sales of the Hopewell store generated about $52,000 in rent. That figure nearly equalled Franchise Realty's original cost for the site and corresponds to more than a fourth of the original cost of the entire Hopewell restaurant complex. At that rate of return, the Principes argue, Franchise Realty will have recouped its entire investment in four years and the remainder of the lease payments will be pure profit. The Principes contend that the fact the store rents are so high proves that McDonald's cannot sell the leaseholds on their own merits.

Nor has McDonald's shown any need to forbid its licensees to own their own stores, the Principes say. Appellants contend that McDonald's is the only fast food franchisor that requires its licensees not only to pay royalties but to lease their stores from the franchisor. Before 1959

McDonald's itself permitted franchisees to own their own stores. McDonald's could maintain its desired level of uniformity by requiring franchisees to locate and construct stores according to company specifications. The Company could even provide planning and design assistance as it apparently does in connection with food purchasing and restaurant management. The Principes argue McDonald's has not shown that the success of its business or the integrity of its trademarks depends on company ownership of all store premises.

A separate tied product is the note that evidences the lessee's $15,000 security deposit, according to the appellants. The Principes argue the security deposit really is a mandatory contribution to McDonald's working capital, not security against damage to the store or breach of the lease contract. By tying the purchase of these $15,000 twenty year non-negotiable non-interest bearing notes to that of the franchise, McDonald's allegedly has generated a capital fund that totalled over $45 million in 1978. It is argued that no one would purchase such notes on their own merits. The Principes assert that only by requiring franchisees to purchase the notes as a condition of obtaining a franchise has McDonald's been able to sell them at all.

McDonald's responds that it is not in the business of licensing use of its name, improving real estate for lease or selling long term notes. Its only business is developing a system of hamburger restaurants and collecting royalties from their sales. The allegedly tied products are but parts of the overall bundle of franchise benefits and obligations. According to McDonald's, the appellants are asking the court to invalidate the way McDonald's does business and to require it to adopt the licensing procedures of its less successful competitors. Federal antitrust laws do not compel such a result, McDonald's contends.

IV.

"There is, at the outset of every tie-in case, including the familiar cases involving physical goods, the problem of determining whether two separate products are in fact involved." *Fortner Enterprises, Inc. v. United States Steel Corp.*, 394 U.S. 495, 507 (1969) (*Fortner I*). Because we agree with McDonald's that the lease, note and license are not separate products but component parts of the overall franchise package, we hold on the facts of this case there was no illegal tie in. Accordingly, we affirm the summary judgment and directed verdict for McDonald's on the tying claims.

As support for their position, the Principes rely primarily on the decision of the Ninth Circuit in *Siegel v. Chicken Delight, Inc.*, 448 F.2d 43 (9th Cir.1971), *cert. denied*, 405 U.S. 955 (1972), one of the first cases to address the problem of franchise tie-ins. Chicken Delight was what McDonald's characterizes as a "rent a name" franchisor: it licensed franchisees to sell chicken under the Chicken Delight name but did not own store premises or fixtures. The company did not even charge franchise fees or royalties. Instead, it required its franchisees to purchase a specified number of cookers and fryers and to purchase certain packaging supplies and mixes exclusively from Chicken Delight. These supplies were priced higher than comparable goods of competing sellers. [The court held that the trademark was a separate product, that the trademark conveyed sufficient market power, that the good will in the trademark could be preserved by specifications regarding the ingredients needed by the franchisees, and that the contractual requirements constituted tying illegal under Section 1 as a matter of law.] * * *

The Principes urge this court to apply the *Chicken Delight* reasoning to invalidate the McDonald's franchise lease note aggregation. They urge that McDonald's can protect the integrity of its trademarks by specifying how its franchisees shall operate, where they may locate their restaurants and what types of buildings they may erect. Customers do not and have no reason to connect the building's owner with the McDonald's operation conducted therein. Since company ownership of store premises is not an essential element of the trademark's goodwill, the Principes argue, the franchise, lease and note are separable products tied together in violation of the antitrust laws. * * *

Without disagreeing with the result in *Chicken Delight,* we conclude that the court's emphasis in that case upon the trademark as the essence of a franchise is too restrictive. Far from merely licensing franchisees to sell products under its trade name, a modern franchisor such as McDonald's offers its franchisees a complete method of doing business. It takes people from all walks of life, sends them to its management school, and teaches them a variety of skills ranging from hamburger grilling to financial planning. It installs them in stores whose market has been researched and whose location has been selected by experts to maximize sales potential. It inspects every facet of every store several times a year and consults with each franchisee about his operation's strengths and weaknesses. Its regime pervades all facets of the business, from the design of the menu board to the amount of catsup on the hamburgers. Nothing is left to chance. This pervasive franchisor supervision and control benefits the franchisee in turn. His business is identified with a network of stores whose very uniformity and predictability attracts customers. In short, the modern franchisee pays not only for the right to use a trademark but for the right to become a part of a system whose business methods virtually guarantee his success. It is often unrealistic to view a franchise agreement as little more than a trademark license.

Given the realities of modern franchising, we think the proper inquiry is not whether the allegedly tied products are associated in the public mind with the franchisor's trademark, but whether they are integral components of the business method being franchised. Where the challenged aggregation is an essential ingredient of the franchised system's formula for success, there is but a single product and no tie in exists as a matter of law.

Applying this standard to the present case, we hold the lease is not separable from the McDonald's franchise to which it pertains. McDonald's practice of developing a system of company owned restaurants operated by franchisees has substantial advantages, both for the company and for franchisees. It is part of what makes a McDonald's franchise uniquely attractive to franchisees. * * *

All of these factors [site selection, ownership of the restaurants by McDonald's, the building of the stores by McDonald's, and substantial investment by both McDonald and its franchisee] contribute significantly to the overall success of the McDonald's system. The formula that produced systemwide success, the formula that promises to make each new McDonald's store successful, that formula is what McDonald's sells its franchisees. To characterize the franchise as an unnecessary aggregation of separate products tied to the McDonald's name is to miss the point entirely. Among would be franchisees, the McDonald's name has come to stand for the formula, including all that it entails. We decline to find that it is an illegal tie in....

* * *

QUESTIONS AND COMMENTS

1. Under the rule of *Jefferson Parish*, are the McDonald's trademark and the land one or two products? How would Justice O'Connor (author of the concurring opinion in *Jefferson Parish*) answer the question? Are your answers the same or different for the Chicken Delight trademark and the ingredients?

2. If the McDonald's trademark is a separate product, does it convey market power? Does the trademark for Chicken Delight do so? In what market? Has the franchisor used its market power to force a tie-in? Is the franchisor likely to have sufficient justifications?

3. Are these the right questions to ask? As a consumer of Big Macs, are you happy with McDonald's prices? Is there any sense in which McDonald's modus operandi has made you worse off?

QUEEN CITY PIZZA, INC. v. DOMINO'S PIZZA, INC.

124 F.3d 430 (3d Cir. 1997), cert. denied, 523 U.S. 1059 (1998).

JUDGE SCIRICA: In this appeal, we must decide whether certain franchise tying restrictions support a claim for violation of federal antitrust laws. Eleven franchisees of Domino's Pizza stores and the International Franchise Advisory Council, Inc. filed suit against Domino's Pizza, Inc., alleging violations of federal antitrust laws, breach of contract, and tortious interference with contract. The district court dismissed the antitrust claims ... for failure to state a claim for which relief can be granted, because the plaintiffs failed to allege a valid relevant market.... We will affirm.

I. Facts and Procedural History

A.

Domino's Pizza, Inc. is a fast-food service company that sells pizza through a national network of over 4200 stores. Domino's Pizza owns and operates approximately 700 of these stores. Independent franchisees own and operate the remaining 3500. Domino's Pizza, Inc. is the second largest pizza company in the United States, with revenues in excess of $1.8 billion per year.

A franchisee joins the Domino's system by executing a standard franchise agreement with Domino's Pizza, Inc. Under the franchise agreement, the franchisee receives the right to sell pizza under the "Domino's" name and format. In return, Domino's Pizza receives franchise fees and royalties.

The essence of a successful nationwide fast-food chain is product uniformity and consistency. Uniformity benefits franchisees because customers can purchase pizza from any Domino's store and be certain the pizza will taste exactly like the Domino's pizza with which they are familiar. This means that individual franchisees need not build up their own good will. Uniformity also benefits the franchisor. It ensures the brand name will continue to attract and hold customers, increasing franchise fees and royalties.

For these reasons, section 12.2 of the Domino's Pizza standard franchise agreement requires that all pizza ingredients, beverages, and packaging materials used by a Domino's franchisee conform to the standards set by Domino's Pizza, Inc. Section 12.2 also provides that Domino's Pizza, Inc. "may in our sole discretion require that ingredients, supplies and materials used in the preparation, packaging, and delivery of pizza be purchased exclusively from us or from approved suppliers or distributors." Domino's Pizza reserves the right "to impose reasonable limitations on the number of approved suppliers or distributors of any product." To enforce these rights, Domino's Pizza, Inc. retains the power to inspect franchisee stores and to test materials and ingredients. Section 12.2 is subject to a reasonableness clause providing that Domino's Pizza, Inc. must "exercise reasonable judgment with respect to all determinations to be made by us under the terms of this Agreement."

Under the standard franchise agreement, Domino's Pizza, Inc. sells approximately 90% of the $500 million in ingredients and supplies used by Domino's franchisees. These sales, worth some $450 million per year, form a significant part of Domino's Pizza, Inc.'s profits. Franchisees purchase only 10% of their ingredients and supplies from outside sources. With the exception of fresh dough, Domino's Pizza, Inc. does not manufacture the products it sells to franchisees. Instead, it purchases these products from approved suppliers and then resells them to the franchisees at a markup.

B.

The plaintiffs in this case are eleven Domino's franchisees and the International Franchise Advisory Council, Inc. ("IFAC"), a Michigan corporation consisting of approximately 40% of the Domino's franchisees in the United States, formed to promote their common interests. The plaintiffs contend that Domino's Pizza, Inc. has a monopoly in "the $500 million aftermarket for sales of supplies to Domino's franchisees" and has used its monopoly power to unreasonably restrain trade, limit competition, and extract supra-competitive profits. Plaintiffs point to several actions by Domino's Pizza, Inc. to support their claims.

First, plaintiffs allege that Domino's Pizza, Inc. has restricted their ability to purchase competitively priced dough. Most franchisees purchase all of their fresh dough from Domino's Pizza, Inc. Plaintiffs here attempted to lower costs by making fresh pizza dough on site. They contend that in response, Domino's Pizza, Inc. increased processing fees and altered quality standards and inspection practices for store-produced dough, which eliminated all potential savings and financial incentives to make their own dough. Plaintiffs also allege Domino's Pizza, Inc. prohibited stores that produce dough from selling their dough to other franchisees, even though the dough-producing stores were willing to sell dough at a price 25% to 40% below Domino's Pizza, Inc.'s price.

Next, plaintiffs object to efforts by Domino's Pizza, Inc. to block IFAC's attempt to buy less expensive ingredients and supplies from other sources. In June 1994, IFAC entered into a purchasing agreement with FoodService Purchasing Cooperative, Inc. (FPC). Under the agreement, FPC was appointed the purchasing agent for IFAC-member Domino's franchisees. FPC was charged with developing a cooperative purchasing plan under which participating franchisees could obtain supplies and ingredients at reduced cost from suppliers other than Domino's Pizza, Inc. Plaintiffs contend that when Domino's Pizza, Inc. became aware of these efforts, it intentionally issued ingredient and supply specifications so vague that potential suppliers could not provide FPC with meaningful price quotations.

Plaintiffs also allege Domino's Pizza entered into exclusive dealing arrangements with several franchisees in order to deny FPC access to a pool of potential buyers sufficiently large to make the alternative purchasing scheme economically feasible. In addition, plaintiffs contend Domino's Pizza, Inc. commenced anti-competitive predatory pricing to shut FPC out of the market. For example, they maintain that Domino's Pizza, Inc. lowered prices on many ingredients and supplies to a level competitive with FPC's prices and then recouped lost profits by raising the price on fresh dough, which FPC could not supply. Further, plaintiffs contend Domino's Pizza, Inc. entered into exclusive dealing arrangements with the only approved suppliers of ready-made deep dish crusts and sauce. Under these agreements, the suppliers were obligated to deliver their entire output to Domino's Pizza, Inc. Plaintiffs allege the purpose of these agreements was to prevent FPC from purchasing these critical pizza components for resale to franchisees.

Finally, plaintiffs allege Domino's Pizza, Inc. refused to sell fresh dough to franchisees unless the franchisees purchased other ingredients and supplies from Domino's Pizza, Inc. As a result of these and other alleged practices, plaintiffs maintain that each franchisee store now pays between $3000 and $10,000 more per year for ingredients and supplies than it would in a competitive market. Plaintiffs allege these costs are passed on to consumers.

C. * * *

The district court granted defendant's motion to dismiss with prejudice plaintiffs' federal antitrust claims.... * * *

III. Discussion

... First, plaintiffs allege Domino's Pizza, Inc. has monopolized the market in pizza supplies and ingredients for use in Domino's stores, in violation of § 2 of the Sherman Act. In support of this contention, plaintiffs allege Domino's Pizza, Inc. has sufficient market power to control prices and exclude competition in this market. Second, plaintiffs contend Domino's Pizza, Inc. has attempted to monopolize the market for Domino's pizza supplies and ingredients, in violation of § 2 of the Sherman Act. Third, plaintiffs allege Domino's Pizza, Inc.'s exclusive dealing arrangements have unreasonably restrained trade in violation of § 1 of the Sherman Act. Fourth, plaintiffs allege Domino's Pizza, Inc. imposed an unlawful tying arrangement by requiring franchisees to buy ingredients and supplies from them as a condition of obtaining fresh dough, in violation of the Sherman Act § 1....

B.

Plaintiffs allege Domino's Pizza, Inc. has willfully acquired and maintained a monopoly in the market for ingredients, supplies, materials and distribution services used in the operation of Domino's stores, in violation of § 2 of the Sherman Act....

... A court making a relevant market determination looks not to the contractual restraints assumed by a particular plaintiff when determining whether a product is interchangeable, but to the uses to which the product is put by consumers in general. Thus, the relevant inquiry here is not whether a Domino's franchisee may reasonably use both approved or non-approved products interchangeably without triggering liability for breach of contract, but whether pizza makers in general might use such products interchangeably. Clearly, they could. Were we to adopt plaintiffs' position that contractual restraints render otherwise identical products non-interchangeable for purposes of relevant market definition, any exclusive dealing arrangement, output or requirement contract, or franchise tying agreement would support a claim for violation of antitrust laws. Perhaps for this reason, no court has defined a relevant product market with reference to the particular contractual restraints of the plaintiff....

Plaintiffs argue that the Supreme Court's decision defining relevant markets in *Eastman Kodak Co. v. Image Technical Services, Inc.,* 504 U.S. 451 (1992) requires a different outcome. We disagree. * * *

Plaintiffs contend that they face information and switching costs that "lock them in" to their position as Domino's franchisees, making it economically impracticable for them to abandon the Domino's system and enter a different line of business. They argue that under *Kodak*, the fact that they are "locked in" supports their claim that an "aftermarket" for Domino's-approved supplies is a relevant market for antitrust purposes. We believe plaintiffs misread *Kodak*. * * *

... *Kodak* does not hold that the existence of information and switching costs alone, such as those faced by the Domino's franchisees, renders an otherwise invalid relevant market valid. In *Kodak,* the repair parts and service were unique and there was a question of fact about cross-elasticity. Judgment as a matter of law was therefore inappropriate. Here, it is uncontroverted that Domino's approved supplies and ingredients are fully interchangeable in all relevant respects with other pizza supplies outside the proposed relevant market....

Kodak is distinguishable from the present appeal in other important respects. The *Kodak* case arose out of concerns about unilateral changes in Kodak's parts and repairs policies. When the copiers were first sold, Kodak relied on purchasers to obtain service from independent service providers. Later, it chose to use its power over the market in unique replacement parts to squeeze the independent service providers out of the repair market and to force copier purchasers to obtain service directly from Kodak, at higher cost. Because this change in policy was not foreseen at the time of sale, buyers had no ability to calculate these higher costs at the time of purchase and incorporate them into their purchase decision. In contrast, plaintiffs here knew that Domino's Pizza retained significant power over their ability to purchase cheaper supplies from alternative sources because that authority was spelled out in detail in ... the standard franchise agreement. Unlike the plaintiffs in *Kodak,* the Domino's franchisees could assess the potential costs and economic risks at the time they signed the franchise agreement. The franchise transaction between Domino's Pizza, Inc. and plaintiffs was subjected to competition at the pre-contract stage. That cannot be said of the conduct challenged in *Kodak* because it was not authorized by contract terms disclosed at the time of the original transaction. Kodak's sale of its product involved no contractual framework for continuing relations with the purchaser. But a franchise agreement regulating supplies, inspections, and quality standards structures an ongoing relationship between franchisor and franchisee designed to maintain good will. These differences between the *Kodak* transaction and franchise transactions are compelling. * * *

Were we to accept plaintiffs' relevant market, virtually all franchise tying agreements requiring the franchisee to purchase inputs such as ingredients and supplies from the franchisor would violate antitrust law.

Courts and legal commentators have long recognized that franchise tying contracts are an essential and important aspect of the franchise form of business organization because they reduce agency costs and prevent franchisees from freeriding—offering products of sub-standard quality insufficient to maintain the reputational value of the franchise product while benefitting from the quality control efforts of other actors in the franchise system. Franchising is a bedrock of the American economy. More than one third of all dollars spent in retailing transactions in the United States are paid to franchise outlets. We do not believe the antitrust laws were designed to erect a serious barrier to this form of business organization.... Here, plaintiffs' acceptance of a franchise package that included purchase requirements and contractual restrictions is consistent with the existence of a competitive market in which franchises are valued, in part, according to the terms of the proposed franchise agreement and the availability of alternative franchise opportunities. Plaintiffs need not have become Domino's franchisees.... Plaintiffs' remedy, if any, is in contract, not under the antitrust laws.... * * *

E.

Plaintiffs allege Domino's Pizza, Inc. imposed an unlawful tying arrangement by requiring franchisees to buy ingredients and supplies from them as a condition of obtaining Domino's Pizza fresh dough, in violation of § 1 of the Sherman Act....

Here, plaintiffs allege Domino's Pizza, Inc. used its power in the purported market for Domino's-approved dough to force plaintiffs to buy unwanted ingredients and supplies from them.... If Domino's had market power in the overall market for pizza dough and forced plaintiffs to purchase other unwanted ingredients to obtain dough, plaintiffs might possess a valid tying claim. But where the defendant's "power" to "force" plaintiffs to purchase the alleged tying product stems not from the market, but from plaintiffs' contractual agreement to purchase the tying product, no claim will lie. For that reason, plaintiffs' claim was properly dismissed. * * *

JUDGE LAY, dissenting.... The plaintiffs allege that DPI [Domino's Pizza, Inc.] has harmed the competitive process by "foreclos[ing] interbrand competition in the market for distributing approved Ingredients and Supplies to Domino's franchisees." The plaintiffs argue that DPI prevented a franchise cooperative and other distributors of ingredients and supplies from entering that market. By stopping any interbrand competition for ingredients and supplies for DPI franchisees, DPI, according to the pleadings, has excluded other potential distributors, and thereby preempted market forces from disciplining the sale of ingredients and supplies. * * *

... The plaintiffs argue that they have experienced information and switching costs which have prevented them from anticipating or responding to the price increases for ingredients and supplies from DPI. They argue that these information and switching costs create a "lock-in" which makes the aftermarket for DPI-approved ingredients and supplies the relevant market. Specifically, the imperfect information they proffer is that the franchisees "could not foresee that Domino's would not follow the policy represented in its Offering Circular and would, instead, commence excluding potential suppliers in order to foreclose competition in the aftermarket." They suggest switching costs arise from sunk costs in the franchise, limits on franchisees' ability to sell their franchise, and noncompetition covenants in the Standard Franchise Agreement.

An important part of the Supreme Court's decision in *Kodak* that the plaintiffs presented a triable claim was that "there is a question of fact whether information costs and switching costs foil the simple assumption that the equipment and service markets act as pure complements to one another." *Kodak,* 504 U.S. at 477. In fact, other circuit courts have held that the presence of these market imperfections was the crucial factor in *Kodak,* and that had Kodak's policy been known at the time businesses bought copiers from Kodak, the result would have been different. ...* * *

Concern is expressed about the possible impact on the franchise industry from adopting plaintiffs' theory of relevant market definition. However, plaintiffs still have to prove the arguments they present for the alleged relevant market, and seek more discovery in order to do so. There are many defenses, which have not been argued, which may be applicable in this case or other franchisor/franchisee antitrust disputes. My main concern with affirming the district court's opinion is the broad rejection of the basis for any antitrust claims by franchisees against franchisors in derivative aftermarkets. *See* Grimes, 65 Antitrust L.J. at 125–26 (describing several types of post-contract franchisor opportunism which may lead to antitrust claims if the franchisor has market power). There may be other problems, which are not before the court, with the plaintiffs' allegations of monopolization and illegal tying in the derivative aftermarkets by a franchisor, but the Supreme Court's clear direction in *Kodak* that information and switching costs are relevant to the ultimate determination of market power is honored by the district court only in the breach. The reality of the aftermarket for ingredients and supplies faced by these plaintiffs, according to the pleadings, is that alternative suppliers do not restrain DPI's ability to increase price, and information and switching costs lock-in the franchisees thereby preventing any competitive response to the price increases from DPI.

* * *

Questions and Comments

1. Do you agree with Judge Scirica or Judge Lay in the interpretation of *Eastman Kodak v. Image Technical Services*? If Judge Lay is correct, is there virtually always a franchisor-brand submarket? If Judge Scirica is correct, what distinguishes Domino's pizza from Kodak's repair parts and services? Can there ever be a franchisee-brand aftermarket?

2. If there is an antitrust problem, what is the main problem: That suppliers of the ingredients lose a critical market outlet (Domino's franchisees), or that the buyers of the ingredients (Domino's franchisees) can be exploited by Domino's; i.e. they pay too much for what they get? Is it possible that the franchisees are merely paying the price of a valuable franchise? Would it be relevant that new franchisees still flock to Domino's after knowing of the high prices for the ingredients?

3. What is the best way to measure market power of a franchisor for purposes of a monopolization, exclusive dealing, or tying inquiry? the strength of the trademark in the goods and services market (power to exploit ultimate customers)? the strength of the franchisor in the franchise market—power to exploit franchisees? Do you expect that McDonald's can and does exploit hamburger eaters? What about Burger King? Do you expect that either one can exploit their franchisees? In each case, do other opportunities for purchasing fast food (or even fast burgers) probably push the price of the burgers down to a competitive price? If either one causes its franchisees to overpay for ingredients, how would this affect price, sales, and competitiveness?

4. To what extent should the facts of *Domino's* be seen as a relational power problem (as opposed to a market problem), and a contract and deception problem? Should a contract or tort solution be an alternative or complement to an antitrust solution?

5. Consider the facts of *Brooke Group*, supra at 267, from the angle of secondary-line discrimination. Recall that Brown & Williamson was giving deep below-cost discounts on its fighting brand of generic cigarettes to wholesalers who could sell large quantities of the fighting brand (Black+Whites), in hopes of pressuring Liggett to raise the price of Liggett's increasingly successful generic cigarette. By doing so it hoped to take the competitive edge off Liggett's challenge. Brown & Williamson was successful in doing exactly that. Why was this not a primary line violation of the Robinson–Patman Act?

6. Is there any change you would make to the Robinson–Patman Act or the Sherman Act (the statute or the caselaw) to bring about convergence? Are there good reasons for divergence?

D. INTERNAL VERTICAL INTEGRATION

Thus far, we have considered loose-knit vertical relationships; we have not focused on tight-knit or corporate integration. Firms may integrate vertically for various reasons and by various means. They may integrate to achieve efficiencies or to gain market power—a subject to which we return. They may integrate loosely, by contract, or more permanently by grass roots entry or merger. Mergers are normally tested under Section 7 of the Clayton Act; we discussed vertical mergers in Chapter 4.

Internal vertical integration (vertical integration by grass roots entry) can in theory be examined under the Sherman Act, although it seldom evokes scrutiny.

When a company enters a new vertical stage by internal expansion, it may be doing so in order to gain efficiencies and thus to reduce the cost of the end product. If significant efficiencies drive vertical integration in an industry, one would expect to see most firms in the industry vertically integrated. For example, if molding and stretching steel into rods is done at lower cost before molten steel hardens, one would expect the companies that make the steel to make the rods. We would think of the performance of these successive functions by one firm as natural and expected integration. Indeed, when the efficiencies are obvious enough, we do not think of the operations as separate stages at all. Pizza ovens could be operated in establishments separate from pizza restaurants, but they are not. We identify single vertical stages with the same intuition with which we identify single products for purposes of tying analysis. We think about efficiencies, observe what the market does, and use common sense.

Many kinds of efficiencies can result from vertical integration. In addition to the most obvious successive-stage efficiencies, a firm might hedge its risks by assuring stable outlets or a stable source of supply, or it might save transaction costs and assure a more tailored fit between the suppliers' product and its own, or it might gain important information to monitor its suppliers and prevent exploitation. The firm might simply want to enter a new field, and might choose a field that it knows something about. Or it might choose to imitate respected competitors.

The integration can also have anticompetitive aspects. First, a firm might invest at a vertically related level in order to increase, protect or exploit market power. If this is not the purpose, it might nevertheless be the effect. If a firm has market power at one level, vertical integration can, under certain conditions, raise barriers to entry at the original level or transfer market power to the newly entered stage, and may tend to raise the price or lessen possibilities for lowering the price of the end product. Second, the integration might enable the firm to exploit market power through price discrimination. Third, the integration might foreclose rivals from an important and limited source of supply or a limited market outlet or might make their supply less dependable, with or without an end-price effect.

Because of the high potential for efficiencies, vertical integration by internal growth rarely presents a serious Sherman Act problem. Problems are more likely to arise from conduct after the integration; for example, a monopolist might refuse to supply necessary inputs to unintegrated competitors, or use other strategies to impose costs on unintegrated competitors. Recall *Otter Tail,* supra at 171. See O. Williamson, Delimiting Antitrust, 76 Geo.L.J. 241 (1987). U.S. caselaw is increasingly deferent to the dominant firm in these respects. EU law, on the other hand, is more aggressive on duties to deal and duties not to price squeeze. See Deutsche Telekom v. Commission, Case C–280/08 P, 2010 ECR I–__ (European Court of Justice); TeliaSonera, Case C–52/09, 2011 ECR I–__ (European Court of Justice).

The Supreme Court addressed internal vertical integration in *United States v. Paramount Pictures, Inc.,* 334 U.S. 131 (1948). *Paramount* involved, also, a number of contracts and conspiracies among competing motion picture producers, distributors and exhibitors, and the Court found these agreements illegal. The Court declined to rule that single-firm integration of production, distribution and exhibition of motion pictures is illegal per se, but said, rather, that the legality of vertical integration involves a rule of reason inquiry. In contemporary terms, we must ask whether the integration helps or hurts consumers. The 1984 Department of Justice Guidelines on vertical mergers (never withdrawn and valid to the extent they are consistent with the current horizontal guidelines) outline the analytical questions. See Appendix D, point 4.2, posing the questions for analysis: Does the integration deter entry into a non-competitive market by imposing on entrants the need to enter two stages at once where entry into the related market is difficult or inefficient; does it facilitate collusion; does it facilitate evasion of regulation? Vertical internal integration is treated much more sympathetically even than vertical mergers because of the high likelihood that the integration is efficient and provides consumers with advantages that they cannot otherwise obtain. Moreover, any remedy is likely to be problematic. Breaking up a firm that grew organically to its size and structure is disfavored, and conduct remedies are poor tools to override incentives (e.g., to discriminate in favor of one's "own") and difficult to police.

Nonetheless, there are limits to the claim that internal integration is pro-competitive.

UNITED STATES v. AMERICAN TELEPHONE & TELEGRAPH CO.

524 F.Supp. 1336 (D.D.C. 1981)
(denying AT&T's motion to dismiss at the close of the Government's case).

JUDGE GREENE: [AT&T owned the local telephone monopolies, which at the time appeared to be natural monopolies; long distance service; the local loop to connect long distance service to the local networks; Western Electric, which made hardware: telephones, wires, lines; and the flagship basic telephony research laboratories, Bell Labs. It engaged in various conduct purportedly to preserve the integrity of its system, which was widely touted as the best telephone system in the world. The United States sued for a violation of Section 2 of the Sherman Act, based on both conduct and market structure. AT&T moved to dismiss the case at the close of the government's evidence at trial. The court denied the motion. See also p. 306 supra.]

IX.

Bell Procurement of Equipment Manufactured by the General Trade

The government's general "procurement" charge is that defendants reinforced and exploited the Bell Operating Companies' structural incentives to purchase equipment, without regard to quality or price, from Western Electric instead of from non-Bell sources (known as the general trade suppliers) and that they thereby anticompetitively foreclosed competition. * * *

This evidence tended to show that the general trade manufacturers encountered a considerable number of obstacles in trying to design equipment for, and to sell this equipment to, the Bell Operating Companies, and that these obstacles perpetuated a buy-Western bias. For example, the competitors had difficulty in locating the employee in Western or the Operating Companies authorized to negotiate a sale; in obtaining from Bell compatibility specifications (without which general trade products could not be designed for interconnection with the Bell network); and in persuading Bell Labs to complete objective evaluations (which were usually required before sales could be effected). The government's evidence further indicated that Bell did not authorize the purchase of the general trade equipment even if no Bell product of equivalent quality, cost, or technical sophistication was available; instead, crash programs were initiated to develop competing Western products (to the extent that, in one instance, Western literally copied the general trade product so that it did not need to wait for the design and development of its own model). Operating Company employees were under pressure from AT&T officials to buy from Western (even when a general trade product was cheaper or of better quality) or to wait until a Western product comparable to the desired general trade equipment was available, and they were required to provide detailed justifications for general trade purchases which were not necessary for the purchase of Western equipment. * * *

The government's evidence has depicted defendants as sole arbiters of what equipment is suitable for use in the Bell System—a role that carries with it a power of subjective judgment that can be and has been used to advance the sale of Western Electric's products at the expense of the general trade. First, AT&T, in conjunction with Bell Labs and Western Electric, sets the technical standards under which the telephone network operates and the compatibility specifications which equipment must meet. Second, Western Electric and Bell Labs . . . serve as counselors to the Operating Companies in their procurement decisions, ostensibly helping them to purchase equipment that meets network standards. Third, Western also produces equipment for sale to the Operating Companies in competition with general trade manufacturers.

The upshot of this "wearing of three hats" is, according to the government's evidence, a rather obviously anticompetitive situation. By setting technical or compatibility standards and by either not communicating these standards to the general trade or changing them in midstream, AT&T has the capacity to remove, and has in fact removed, general trade products from serious consideration by the Operating Companies on "network integrity" grounds. By either refusing to evaluate general trade products for the Operating Companies or producing biased or speculative evaluations, AT&T has been able to influence the Operating

Companies, which lack independent means to evaluate general trade products, to buy Western. And the in-house production and sale of Western equipment provides AT&T with a powerful incentive to exercise its "approval" power to discriminate against Western's competitors.

Defendants' response to all of this is that, in practically every case, the purchasing decision of Western or of the particular Operating Company was made pursuant to reasonable engineering and sound business judgment which should not be second-guessed by the Court. Stating this obviously does not make it so, however. It may well be that defendants will be able to refute the government's procurement evidence and the inferences which may appropriately be drawn therefrom. But the Court holds that on this record a showing has been made which, unless it is rebutted, would support the conclusion that defendants have engaged in anticompetitive conduct in their procurement practices, in violation of the law. * * *

... Defendants argue that the government's evidence shows nothing more than that they took advantage of the efficiencies of their vertically integrated structure, as they are permitted to do under the law. Clearly, vertical integration is not prohibited per se (see United States v. Columbia Steel Co., 334 U.S. 495, 525–26 (1948); and even an alleged monopolist has the right to compete vigorously. But vertical integration may be unlawful under the Sherman Act if it creates monopoly power and is accompanied by an intent to exclude competition. United States v. Paramount Pictures, Inc., [334 U.S. 131 (1948)]. Moreover, when activity among vertically-related affiliates restrains trade it violates the antitrust laws.

The government here did not attempt to prove that vertical integration itself amounts to anticompetitive conduct. Rather, its experts have testified that a combination of vertical integration and rate-of-return regulation has tended to generate decisions by the Operating Companies to purchase equipment produced by Western that is more expensive or of lesser quality than that manufactured by the general trade. The Operating Companies have taken these actions, it is said, because the existence of rate of return regulation removed from them the burden of such additional expense, for the extra cost could simply be absorbed into the rate base or expenses, allowing extra profits from the higher prices to flow upstream to Western rather than to its non-Bell competition.

Operating Company officials—as distinguished from the organizations themselves—likewise have an individual incentive to act to further this goal because, as the testimony shows, promotion decisions within the Bell System tend to create a predisposition within Operating Company managers towards deciding in favor of Western profits and against the general trade competition. It seems that it is helpful to the advancement of an individual's career within an Operating Company to have had a tour of duty at AT&T headquarters in New York, and that it is common for those who occupy high-level positions in the Operating Companies to have had such a tour at some point in their careers. Personnel rotate through

Western Electric, Bell Labs, the Operating Companies, and AT&T central headquarters with some regularity, and they come to acquire a familial attitude towards the different parts of the Bell System as they rise through its ranks. Through this process, those holding management positions in the Bell Operating Companies appear to adopt the objectives, incentives, and prejudices of AT&T and Western top management as their own.

In short, the government has demonstrated that incentives other than those arising from vertical integration per se have underlain the procurement decisions of the Bell Operating Companies.... * * *

Consent decree. By final judgment entered by consent in 1982, a United States District Court ordered American Telephone and Telegraph Company to spin off or divest itself of the local telephone exchange monopolies, all of which would remain regulated by the states. (The local exchanges were called "basic operating companies" or "BOCs.") AT&T would retain the long distance business ("Long Lines"), where it was beginning to face competitors such as MCI and Sprint; and it would retain Western Electric Company, which manufactured telephones, lines, and other telecommunications equipment for the local exchange companies and for the long line business. See *United States v. American Telephone & Telegraph Co.,* 1982–2 (CCH) Trade Cas. ¶ 64,900 (D.D.C.1982).

The theory of the settlement was that the combination of the potentially competitive long distance lines with the natural monopoly local exchanges was inherently inefficient; it encouraged cross-subsidization and the use of power in regulated monopoly markets to foreclose competition in potentially competitive markets. AT&T had the incentive to sell equipment to the BOCs at a monopoly price; and since the price would be a cost to the BOCs that was subject to cost-plus regulation, the premium would get passed on the local telephone user. Another scenario cut in a different direction but would also exacerbate the market imperfections: State authorities put pressure on local exchanges to charge rates too low to cover costs. AT&T's Long Lines division made supra competitive profits and subsidized the local telephone service. Particularly because Long Lines needed the extra revenues in order to be able to subsidize local telephone calls, it suppressed competition in the long line business and consequently suppressed competition by long distance rivals who were offering new low-cost technologies, such as microwave. Moreover, AT&T's vertical integration perpetuated government regulation of the long distance business, although that market was now amenable to effective competition. In short, the integration created all the wrong incentives.

Although Western Electric supplied equipment to Long Lines as well as to the BOCs, the government did not request and the court did not order separation of Long Lines from Western Electric. The government's reasons for this approach are stated in the following paragraphs of the Justice Department's Competitive Impact Statement:

DEPARTMENT OF JUSTICE, COMPETITIVE IMPACT STATEMENT

Proposed Consent Judgment, Feb. 10, 1982.
excerpt

Procurement of Equipment. The divestiture of the BOCs from AT&T will eliminate the incentives of the BOCs to buy from Western Electric regardless of the price or quality of Western's equipment. It will also remove AT&T's ability, through its control of the BOCs, to influence the purchasing decisions of the BOCs unfairly in favor of Western Electric. The injunctive provisions of Paragraph II(B) will reinforce this incentive structure by requiring the BOCs to treat all equipment manufacturers in an evenhanded, non-discriminatory manner. Finally, elimination of the license contracts between the BOCs and AT&T will eliminate the mandatory payments under those contracts as a source of subsidy to AT&T's equipment activities.

Given the divestiture of the operating companies, however, further divestiture of Western Electric or Long Lines is unnecessary to protect competition in equipment markets. While AT&T may retain the technical ability to cause purchases by the expanded Long Lines from Western Electric without regard to price or quality, its incentive to do so will be greatly reduced immediately and ultimately eliminated by divestiture of the BOCs. As explained earlier, because divestiture of the BOCs will remove AT&T's ability to disadvantage its interexchange competitors in access to essential facilities, AT&T will become subject to competition in all of its services. Because excessive transfer prices must be reflected in the cost of AT&T's intercity services, AT&T will have, as it becomes increasingly subject to competition, an incentive to procure inputs as efficiently as possible.

QUESTIONS AND COMMENTS

1. Assistant Attorney General William Baxter was convinced that the incentives emanating from the structure of AT&T were economically perverse, and he ultimately convinced AT&T that the break-up—which would free the long distance function from regulation and relieve it from the political pressures of cross-subsidization—was in the best interests of the company and its shareholders. He was right. Comment on the wisdom of the remedy.

2. Was the Justice Department correct to allow AT&T (Long Lines) to retain Western Electric? Wouldn't AT&T still purchase from Western Electric, all other things being equal? Why didn't Assistant Attorney General Baxter care? If you were a competitor of Western Electric, would you care? If

you were MCI (a purchaser of hardware) would you care? Is this point related to the Supreme Court's admonition that the antitrust laws are for consumers and are not about fairness to competitors? Is it related to the presumption (or not) that even a vertically integrated firm has the incentive to buy the best inputs, whatever the source? (see *Synopsys/Avant!*, supra at 423.) Recall that AT&T virtually always bought from itself even when its product was far inferior to the competitors' products.

A judge cannot rewrite a proposed consent judgment, but can find that the proposed judgment is not in the public interest and can decline to enter the judgment unless modified. Judge Greene followed this procedure in the *AT&T* case, and prevailed upon the parties to accept certain modifications. See *United States v. American Telephone & Telegraph Co., aff'd sub nom. Maryland v. United States*, 460 U.S. 1001 (1983) (Rehnquist, Burger and White dissenting).

3. Recall, now, the structure of Microsoft. Microsoft has monopoly power in the market for PC operating systems. It has extended into the market of various complements (which raise exactly the same issues as vertical integration; inputs are complements). See 310 supra. For example, Microsoft offers browsers, instant messaging, and media players; it bundles them into the system. It also offers low end (work group) servers, which service the network that links all PCs within a single business organization. Is Microsoft's integration similar to or different from AT&T's, in terms of structural incentives to serve consumers versus structural incentives to block competitors from reaching consumers? The district court, like the district court in *AT&T*, found that defendant's structure induced its exclusionary conduct, and ordered that Microsoft be divided into two parts; the operating system and the applications. The appellate court reversed the break-up order, largely for due process reasons. It remanded the relief question, urging caution regarding use of a break-up remedy. See 327 supra. (Microsoft was not broken up.) The alternative to structural relief was conduct relief—much more conservative but very difficult to administer. Consider the costs and benefits of an order breaking up Microsoft. In terms solely of consumer interests, would it have been a good or a bad idea?

E. DISCRIMINATORY PRICING: SECONDARY LINE PRICE DISCRIMINATION—THE ROBINSON–PATMAN ACT

1. INTRODUCTION

Here we treat pricing itself, not pursuant to contract, as a vertical restraint. In Chapter 3 we studied predatory pricing, and saw how pricing strategies can sometimes (although rarely) be predatorily monopolistic and offend Section 2 of the Sherman Act. We then looked briefly at the Robinson–Patman Act and saw how discriminatory pricing by a monopolist or near monopolist can lessen competition on the "primary line" level—competition among the monopolist and its competitors—and can thereby run afoul of the Robinson–Patman Act.

Price discrimination can also cause harm on the secondary line—the level of the disfavored buyer—and even on the tertiary line if there is yet another middleman in the process of distribution. Secondary line effects are thus downstream, or vertical, effects. The legislative history suggests that such effects, with their characteristic impact on small business, were the major concern of the Congress that passed the Robinson–Patman Act. See Hansen, *Robinson–Patman Law: A Review and Analysis*, 51 Fordham L.Rev. 1113 (1983). We look briefly at secondary line impacts in this section.

Downstream impacts, the major concern of Congress, may occur when the seller gives a lower price to one buyer than to other buyers and the disfavored buyer must compete with the favored one in the resale market. The secondary line concern is that large buyers—mainly chains—may use their size and power to extract from sellers prices lower than their small competitors can obtain, and that the discrimination will cause the smaller firms to lose so many sales that they will be hurt, they will be unable to operate effectively, and consumers generally will be hurt. The Robinson–Patman Act limits its proscriptions to price discriminations in interstate commerce. Thus, not only must interstate commerce be affected at the threshold level required by the Sherman Act, but the discriminatory sales must be in interstate commerce.

There are many critics of the Robinson–Patman Act. Critics challenge both of the basic premises of the act; namely, 1) that antitrust law should have concern for small business in order to be fair and to keep small business viable; and 2) that price discrimination threatens harm to downstream competition. See, e.g., E. Kintner & J. Bauer, The Robinson–Patman Act: A Look Backwards, A View Forward, 31 Antitrust Bull. 571 (1986). The criticism is not surprising, for the act was passed principally to protect small business from big-buyer power and for fairness. The Robinson–Patman Act would never have been passed if the goal were to increase output. Critics observe that price discrimination can be used as a method to compete. Depending on the circumstances, a seller who cannot charge dual prices may be more likely to raise the lower price than to lower the higher price. To the extent that the Robinson–Patman Act limits price competition, its enforcement is anticompetitive and harms consumers. Consequently, the Justice Department and the FTC practically never sue to enjoin Robinson–Patman Act violations, and the Antitrust Modernization Commission, a federal task force charged with assessing the state of U.S. competition law and making recommendations, recommended that the Robinson–Patman Act "finally be repealed." ANTITRUST MODERNIZATION COMMISSION, REPORT AND RECOMMENDATIONS (2007), available at *http://govinfo.library.unt.edu/amc/report_recommendation/toc.htm*. Meanwhile, the Robinson–Patman Act generates private treble damage lawsuits, and it engages much attention from in-house counsel, who review marketing programs for legal compliance.

Robinson–Patman cases, whether primary or secondary line, raise a wide range of issues. When is a sale "in commerce"? When is a discrimination "in commerce"? E.g., *Standard Oil v. FTC,* 340 U.S. 231 (1951). What is a "price"? Corn Products Refining Co. v. FTC, 324 U.S. 726 (1945). What is "discrimination"? *FTC v. Anheuser Busch, Inc.,* 363 U.S. 536 (1960). What is a "purchase"? *Naifeh v. Ronson Art Metal Works,* 218 F.2d 202 (10th Cir.1954). When and how must advertising and promotional benefits be made available to competing dealers? "Fred Meyer" Guides for Advertising Allowances and Other Merchandising Payments and Services, 16 C.F.R. § 240 (2001). Cases and commentary treat all of these issues. See ANTITRUST LAW DEVELOPMENTS (SIXTH) CHAPTER 5, (ABA Antitrust Section ed., 2007) and supplements. We do not deal with these and other specific and sometimes technical questions. Rather, we concentrate on the core conceptual issues of requisite anticompetitive effect and antitrust damages in secondary line cases.

Before turning to the cases we set forth relevant portions of the statute. In sum, Section 2(a) prohibits certain price discriminations by sellers, subject to a cost justification defense; Section 2(b) contains a meeting competition defense; and Section 2(f) prohibits buyers from knowingly inducing or receiving prohibited price discriminations.

Section 2(a)

That it shall be unlawful for any person engaged in commerce, in the course of such commerce, either directly or indirectly, to discriminate in price between different purchasers of commodities of like grade and quality, where either or any of the purchases involved in such discrimination are in commerce, where such commodities are sold for use, consumption, or resale within the United States or any Territory thereof or the District of Columbia or any insular possession or other place under the jurisdiction of the United States, and where the effect of such discrimination may be substantially to lessen competition or tend to create a monopoly in any line of commerce, or to injure, destroy, or prevent competition or tend to create a monopoly in any line of commerce, or to injure, destroy, or prevent competition with any person who either grants or knowingly receives the benefit of such discrimination, or with customers of either of them: Provided, That nothing herein contained shall prevent differentials which make only due allowance for differences in the cost of manufacture, sale, or delivery resulting from the differing methods or quantities in which such commodities are to such purchasers sold or delivered....

Section 2(b)

Upon proof being made, at any hearing on a complaint under this section, that there has been discrimination in price or services or facilities furnished, the burden of rebutting the prima-facie case thus made by showing justification shall be upon the person charged with a violation of this section, and unless justification shall be affirmatively shown, the Commission is authorized to issue an order terminating the discrimination: *Provided, however,* That nothing herein contained shall prevent a seller rebutting the prima-facie case thus made by showing that his lower price or the furnishing of services or facilities to any purchaser or purchasers was made in good faith to meet an equally low price of a competitor, or the services or facilities furnished by a competitor.

Section 2(f)

That it shall be unlawful for any person engaged in commerce, in the course of such commerce, knowingly to induce or receive a discrimination in price which is prohibited by this section.

2. LANDMARK CASES

The following cases discuss what is competitive injury under the Robinson–Patman Act, whether it can be inferred, and from what, and what is the appropriate measure of damages. The first case, *Morton Salt*, took an expansive view of the act. In modern times, you will see that the spirit and implications of *Morton Salt* have met resistance.

FEDERAL TRADE COMMISSION v. MORTON SALT CO.

334 U.S. 37 (1948).

JUSTICE BLACK: The Federal Trade Commission, after a hearing, found that the respondent, which manufactures and sells table salt in interstate commerce, had discriminated in price between different purchasers of like grades and qualities, and concluded that such discriminations were in violation of § 2 of the Clayton Act, as amended by the Robinson–Patman Act. It accordingly issued a cease and desist order. Upon petition of the respondent the Circuit Court of Appeals, with one judge dissenting, set aside the Commission's findings and order.... The Court's judgment rested on its construction of the Act, its holding that crucial findings of the Commission were either not supported by evidence or were contrary to the evidence, and its conclusion that the Commission's order was too broad. Since questions of importance in the construction and administration of the Act were presented, we granted certiorari....

Respondent manufactures several different brands of table salt and sells them directly to (1) wholesalers or jobbers, who in turn resell to the retail trade, and (2) large retailers, including chain store retailers. Respondent sells its finest brand of table salt, known as Blue Label, on what it terms a standard quantity discount system available to all customers. Under this system the purchasers pay a delivered price and the cost to both wholesale and retail purchasers of this brand differs according to the quantities bought. These prices are as follows, after making allowance for rebates and discounts:

	Per case
Less-than-carload purchases	$ 1.60
Carload purchases	1.50
5,000–case purchases in any consecutive 12 months	1.40
50,000–case purchases in any consecutive 12 months	1.35

Only five companies have ever bought sufficient quantities of respondent's salt to obtain the $1.35 per case price. These companies could buy in such quantities because they operate large chains of retail stores in various parts of the country.[4] As a result of this low price these five companies have been able to sell Blue Label salt at retail cheaper than wholesale purchasers from respondent could reasonably sell the same brand of salt to independently operated retail stores, many of whom competed with the local outlets of the five chain stores.

Respondent's table salts, other than Blue Label, are also sold under a quantity discount system differing slightly from that used in selling Blue Label. Sales of these other brands in less-than-carload lots are made at list price plus freight from plant to destination. Carload purchasers are granted approximately a 5 per cent discount; approximately a 10 per cent discount is granted to purchasers who buy as much as $50,000 worth of all brands of salt in any consecutive twelve-month period. Respondent's quantity discounts on Blue Label and on other table salts were enjoyed by certain wholesalers and retailers who competed with other wholesalers and retailers to whom these discounts were refused.

In addition to these standard quantity discounts, special allowances were granted certain favored customers who competed with other customers to whom they were denied.

First. Respondent's basic contention, which it argues this case hinges upon, is that its "standard quantity discounts, available to all on equal terms, as contrasted, for example, to hidden or special rebates, allowances, prices or discounts, are not discriminatory within the meaning of the Robinson–Patman Act." Theoretically, these discounts are equally available to all, but functionally they are not. For as the record indicates (if reference to it on this point were necessary) no single independent retail grocery store, and probably no single wholesaler, bought as many as 50,000 cases or as much as $50,000 worth of table salt in one year. Furthermore, the record shows that, while certain purchasers were enjoying one or more of respondent's standard quantity discounts, some of their competitors made purchases in such small quantities that they could not qualify for any of respondent's discounts, even those based on carload shipments. The legislative history of the Robinson–Patman Act makes it abundantly clear that Congress considered it to be an evil that a large buyer could secure a competitive advantage over a small buyer solely because of the large buyer's quantity purchasing ability. The Robinson–Patman Act was passed to deprive a large buyer of such advantages except to the extent that a lower price could be justified by reason of a seller's diminished costs due to quantity manufacture, delivery or sale, or by

4. These chain stores are American Stores Company, National Tea Company, Kroger Grocery Co., Safeway Stores, Inc., and Great Atlantic & Pacific Tea Company.

reason of the seller's good faith effort to meet a competitor's equally low price.

Section 2 of the original Clayton Act had included a proviso that nothing contained in it should prevent "discrimination in price ... on account of differences in the grade, quality, or quantity of the commodity sold, or that makes only due allowance for difference in the cost of selling or transportation...." That section has been construed as permitting quantity discounts, such as those here, without regard to the amount of the seller's actual savings in cost attributable to quantity sales or quantity deliveries. The House Committee Report on the Robinson–Patman Act considered that the Clayton Act's proviso allowing quantity discounts so weakened § 2 "as to render it inadequate, if not almost a nullity." The Committee considered the present Robinson–Patman amendment to § 2 "of great importance." Its purpose was to limit "the use of quantity price differentials to the sphere of actual cost differences. Otherwise," the report continued, "such differentials would become instruments of favor and privilege and weapons of competitive oppression." The Senate Committee reporting the bill emphasized the same purpose, as did the Congressman in charge of the Conference Report when explaining it to the House just before final passage. And it was in furtherance of this avowed purpose—to protect competition from all price differentials except those based in full on cost savings—that § 2(a) of the amendment provided "That nothing herein contained shall prevent differentials which make only due allowance for differences in the cost of manufacture, sale, or delivery resulting from the differing methods or quantities in which such commodities are to such purchasers sold or delivered."

The foregoing references, without regard to others which could be mentioned, establish that respondent's standard quantity discounts are discriminatory within the meaning of the Act, and are prohibited by it whenever they have the defined effect on competition.

Second. The Government interprets the opinion of the Circuit Court of Appeals as having held that in order to establish "discrimination in price" under the Act the burden rested on the Commission to prove that respondent's quantity discount differentials were not justified by its cost savings. Respondent does not so understand the Court of Appeals decision, and furthermore admits that no such burden rests on the Commission. We agree that it does not. First, the general rule of statutory construction that the burden of proving justification or exemption under a special exception to the prohibitions of a statute generally rests on one who claims its benefits, requires that respondent undertake this proof under the proviso of § 2(a). Secondly, § 2(b) of the Act specifically imposes the burden of showing justification upon one who is shown to have discriminated in prices. And the Senate committee report on the bill explained that the provisos of § 2(a) throw "upon any who claim the benefit of those exceptions the burden of showing that their case falls within them." We think that the language of the Act, and the legislative history just cited, show that Congress meant by using the words "discrimination in price" in

§ 2 that in a case involving competitive injury between a seller's customers the Commission need only prove that a seller had charged one purchaser a higher price for like goods than he had charged one or more of the purchaser's competitors. This construction is consistent with the first sentence of § 2(a) in which it is made unlawful "to discriminate in price between different purchasers of commodities of like grade and quality, where either or any of the purchases involved in such discrimination are in commerce ... and where the effect of such discrimination may be ... to injure, destroy, or prevent competition with any person who either grants or knowingly receives the benefit of such discrimination, or with customers of either of them:....

Third. It is argued that the findings fail to show that respondent's discriminatory discounts had in fact caused injury to competition. There are specific findings that such injuries had resulted from respondent's discounts, although the statute does not require the Commission to find that injury has actually resulted. The statute requires no more than that the effect of the prohibited price discriminations "may be substantially to lessen competition ... or to injure, destroy, or prevent competition." After a careful consideration of this provision of the Robinson–Patman Act, we have said that "the statute does not require that the discriminations must in fact have harmed competition, but only that there is a reasonable possibility that they 'may' have such an effect." *Corn Products Co. v. Federal Trade Comm'n,* 324 U.S. 726, 742. Here the Commission found what would appear to be obvious, that the competitive opportunities of certain merchants were injured when they had to pay respondent substantially more for their goods than their competitors had to pay. The findings are adequate.

Fourth. It is urged that the evidence is inadequate to support the Commission's findings of injury to competition. As we have pointed out, however, the Commission is authorized by the Act to bar discriminatory prices upon the "reasonable possibility" that different prices for like goods to competing purchasers may have the defined effect on competition. That respondent's quantity discounts did result in price differentials between competing purchasers sufficient in amount to influence their resale prices of salt was shown by evidence. This showing in itself is adequate to support the Commission's appropriate findings that the effect of such price discriminations "may be substantially to lessen competition ... and to injure, destroy, and prevent competition."

The adequacy of the evidence to support the Commission's findings of reasonably possible injury to competition from respondent's price differentials between competing carload and less-than-carload purchasers is singled out for special attacks here. It is suggested that in considering the adequacy of the evidence to show injury to competition respondent's carload discounts and its other quantity discounts should not be treated alike. The argument is that there is an obvious saving to a seller who delivers goods in carload lots. Assuming this to be true, that fact would not tend to disprove injury to the merchant compelled to pay the less-than-carload price. For a ten-cent carload price differential against a merchant would injure him competitively just as much as a ten-cent differential under any other name. However relevant the separate carload argument might be to the question of justifying a differential by cost savings, it has no relevancy in determining whether the differential works an injury to a competitor....

It is also argued that respondent's less-than-carload sales are very small in comparison with the total volume of its business and for that reason we should reject the Commission's finding that the effect of the carload discrimination may substantially lessen competition and may injure competition between purchasers who are granted and those who are denied this discriminatory discount. To support this argument, reference is made to the fact that salt is a small item in most wholesale and retail businesses and in consumers' budgets. For several reasons we cannot accept this contention.

There are many articles in a grocery store that, considered separately, are comparatively small parts of a merchant's stock. Congress intended to protect a merchant from competitive injury attributable to discriminatory prices on any or all goods sold in interstate commerce, whether the particular goods constituted a major or minor portion of his stock. Since a grocery store consists of many comparatively small articles, there is no possible way effectively to protect a grocer from discriminatory prices except by applying the prohibitions of the Act to each individual article in the store.

Furthermore, in enacting the Robinson–Patman Act, Congress was especially concerned with protecting small businesses which were unable to buy in quantities, such as the merchants here who purchased in less-than-carload lots. To this end it undertook to strengthen this very phase of the old Clayton Act. The committee reports on the Robinson–Patman Act emphasized a belief that § 2 of the Clayton Act had "been too restrictive, in requiring a showing of general injury to competitive conditions...." The new provision, here controlling, was intended to justify a finding of injury to competition by a showing of "injury to the competitor victimized by the discrimination."

Since there was evidence sufficient to show that the less-than-carload purchasers might have been handicapped in competing with the more favored carload purchasers by the differential in price established by respondent, the Commission was justified in finding that competition might have thereby been substantially lessened or have been injured within the meaning of the Act.

Apprehension is expressed in this Court that enforcement of the Commission's order against respondent's continued violations of the Robinson–Patman Act might lead respondent to raise table salt prices to its carload purchasers. Such a conceivable, though, we think, highly improbable, contingency, could afford us no reason for upsetting the Commission's findings and declining to direct compliance with a statute passed by Congress. * * *

[Reversed.]

JUSTICES JACKSON and FRANKFURTER dissented.

QUESTIONS AND COMMENTS

1. Why should the test be "reasonable possibility" of competitive injury, rather than "reasonable probability" as required under the usual Clayton Act incipiency approach? In view of *Morton Salt,* what must plaintiff prove to establish an illegal discrimination? How does the Court conceive of injury to competition? How does the Court relate harm to a small competitor to harm to competition? Is *Brunswick* relevant to consideration of injury to competition under the Robinson–Patman Act? Is there any principled way to distinguish Sherman and Clayton Act (non Robinson–Patman) harm from Robinson–Patman harm?

2. Is the law as formulated in *Morton Salt* likely to produce higher prices? Was the Court correct that this result was doubtful? Is the availability of the cost justification defense sufficient to assure efficient pricing?

3. Consider whether the discriminating firm harms "competitive opportunities" simply because one merchant pays more for goods than another. How significant is the size of the discrimination, absolute and relative ($10 can be 20% of a unit price; $10 can be 1%)? How significant is the relative importance of the product as an input into the downstream process, and the availability of substitutes? Suppose that widgits are an input into the productive process in which B and C compete, that gizmos are a somewhat less desirable substitute, and that widgits have been selling at $100 and gizmos at $85. If A cuts the price on widgits to $90 on sales to B, but keeps selling widgits to C for $100, will competition be hurt? Or suppose that the product in question represents a very small part of the cost of the downstream activity. Morton sells salt to Canner A for 90 cents and to Canner B for $1.00. Both introduce the salt into their competing canned goods. Salt represents less than .25% of the total direct costs of each canner. Is competition hurt?

4. To what extent does the competitive impact of a discrimination depend on how A, the favored buyer, uses the savings, and how B, the disfavored buyer, responds? If A neither lowers its price nor invests the cost savings in promotion but retains the margin of discrimination and pays it out in dividends, is competition hurt in the market for the output? What about the market for new capital? See *McCaskill v. Texaco Inc.,* 351 F.Supp. 1332 (S.D.Ala.1972), *aff'd sub nom. Harrelson v. Texaco Inc.,* 486 F.2d 1400 (5th Cir.1973).

Suppose A, maintaining a constant mark-up, uses the cost savings from the discrimination to cut its price, but B responds with an equivalent price cut, thereby reducing its mark-up. Is competition in the output market injured? Suppose that following its reactive price cut (which reduced its profit margin) B looks around for ways to cut costs, thus to reestablish its old margin. It finds one. By using computers it can better control its inventory and it is able to reduce the amount of its capital that is tied up in inventory. Is competition injured? Suppose A doesn't cut prices but reinvests the benefit of the discrimination in promotion. Is competition injured? To what extent does injury depend on B's response? See *Foremost Dairies Inc. v. FTC,* 348 F.2d 674, 680 (5th Cir.), *cert. denied,* 382 U.S. 959 (1965).

We have thus far focused on competitive injury; and we will return to this issue. But even if we assume that competition has been injured, how can the private plaintiff measure and prove its antitrust damages? For years many antitrust lawyers assumed that in secondary line cases, proof of damages was easy. If defendant charged B $1 per unit more than it charged A, and B purchased 1000 units, B's damages were $1000, the amount of the discrimination. The Supreme Court addressed that issue in *J. Truett Payne.*

J. TRUETT PAYNE CO. v. CHRYSLER MOTORS CORP.

451 U.S. 557 (1981).

JUSTICE REHNQUIST: The question presented in this case is the appropriate measure of damages in a suit brought under § 2(a) of the Clayton Act, as amended by the Robinson–Patman Act.

Petitioner, for several decades a Chrysler–Plymouth dealer in Birmingham, Ala., went out of business in 1974. It subsequently brought suit against respondent in the United States District Court for the Northern District of Alabama, alleging that from January 1970 to May 1974 respondent's various "sales incentive" programs violated § 2(a). Under one type of program, respondent assigned to each participating dealer a sales objective and paid to the dealer a bonus on each car sold in excess of that objective. Under another type of program, respondent required each dealer to purchase from it a certain quota of automobiles before it would pay a bonus on the sale of automobiles sold at retail. The amount of the bonus depended on the number of retail sales (or wholesale purchases) made in excess of the dealer's objective, and could amount to several hundred dollars. Respondent set petitioner's objectives higher than those of its competitors, requiring it to sell (or purchase) more automobiles to obtain a bonus than its competitors. To the extent petitioner failed to meet those objectives and to the extent its competitors met their lower objectives, petitioner received fewer bonuses. The net effect of all this, according to petitioner, was that it paid more money for its automobiles than did its competitors. It contended that the amount of the price discrimination—the amount of the price difference multiplied by the number of petitioner's purchases—was $81,248. It also claimed that the going-concern value of the business as of May 1974 ranged between $50,000 and $170,000.

Respondent maintained that the sales incentive programs were nondiscriminatory, and that they did not injure petitioner or adversely affect competition. The District Court denied respondent's motion for a directed verdict. The jury returned a verdict against respondent and awarded petitioner $111,247.48 in damages, which the District Court trebled.

The Court of Appeals for the Fifth Circuit reversed with instructions to dismiss the complaint. It found that in order to recover treble damages under § 4 of the Clayton Act, a plaintiff must prove (1) a violation of the antitrust laws, (2) cognizable injury attributable to the violation, and (3) at least the approximate amount of damage. It found it unnecessary to consider whether petitioner proved that respondent's incentive programs violated § 2(a) because, in its view, petitioner had "failed to introduce substantial evidence of injury attributable to the programs, much less substantial evidence of the amount of such injury." Rejecting petitioner's theory of "automatic damages," under which mere proof of discrimination establishes the fact and amount of injury, the court held that injury must be proved by more than mere "[c]onclusory statements by the plaintiff, without evidentiary support." The court concluded that the District Court erred in refusing respondent's motion for a directed verdict and in denying its motion for judgment notwithstanding the verdict. We granted certiorari to review the decision of the Court of Appeals.

I.

Petitioner first contends that once it has proved a price discrimination in violation of § 2(a) it is entitled at a minimum to so-called "automatic damages" in the amount of the price discrimination. Petitioner concedes that in order to recover damages it must establish cognizable injury attributable to an antitrust violation and some approximation of damage. It insists, however, that the jury should be permitted to infer the requisite injury and damage from a showing of a substantial price discrimination. Petitioner notes that this Court has consistently permitted such injury to be inferred in injunctive actions brought to enforce § 2(a), *e.g., FTC v. Morton Salt Co.,* 334 U.S. 37 (1948), and argues that private suits for damages under § 4 should be treated no differently. We disagree.

By its terms § 2(a) is a prophylactic statute which is violated merely upon a showing that "the effect of such discrimination *may be* substantially to lessen competition." (Emphasis supplied.) As our cases have recognized, the statute does not "require that the discriminations must in fact have harmed competition." *Corn Products Refining Co. v. FTC,* 324 U.S. 726, 742 (1945); *FTC v. Morton Salt Co., supra,* at 46 ("the statute does not require the Commission to find that injury has actually resulted"). Section 4 of the Clayton Act, in contrast, is essentially a remedial statute. It provides treble damages to "[a]ny person who *shall be injured* in his business or property by reason of anything forbidden in the antitrust laws. . . ." (Emphasis supplied.) To recover treble damages, then, a plaintiff must make some showing of actual injury attributable to something the antitrust laws were designed to prevent.

Our decision here is virtually governed by our reasoning in *Brunswick Corp. v. Pueblo Bowl–O–Mat, Inc.,* 429 U.S. 477 (1977). There we rejected the contention that the mere violation of § 7 of the Clayton Act, which prohibits mergers which *may* substantially lessen competition, gives rise to a damages claim under § 4. We explained that "to recover damages [under § 4] respondents must prove more than that the petitioner violated § 7, since such proof establishes only that injury may result." Likewise in this case, proof of a violation does not mean that a disfavored purchaser has been actually "injured" within the meaning of § 4.

The legislative history buttresses this view....

II.

Petitioner next contends that even though it may not be entitled to "automatic damages" upon a showing of a violation of § 2(a), it produced enough evidence of actual injury to survive a motion for a directed verdict. That evidence consisted primarily of the testimony of petitioner's owner, Mr. Payne, and an expert witness, a professor of economics. Payne testified that the price discrimination was one of the causes of the dealership going out of business. In support of that contention, he testified that his salesmen told him that the dealership lost sales to its competitors, and that its market share of retail Chrysler–Plymouth sales in the Birmingham area was 24% in 1970, 27% in 1971, 23% in 1972, and 25% in 1973. Payne contended that it was proper to infer that the 4% drop in 1972 was a result of the incentive programs. He also testified that the discrimination caused him to "force" business so that he could meet his assigned quotas. That is, his desire to make a sale induced him to "overallow" on trade-ins, thus reducing his profits on his used car operation. Payne adduced evidence showing that his average gross profit on used car sales was below that of his competitors, though that same evidence revealed that his average gross profit on new sales was higher.

Neither Payne nor petitioner's expert witness offered documentary evidence as to the effect of the discrimination on retail prices. Although Payne asserted that his salesmen and customers told him that the dealership was being undersold, he admitted he did not know if his competitors did in fact pass on their lower costs to their customers. Petitioner's expert witness took a somewhat different position. He believed that the discrimination would ultimately cause retail prices to be held at an artificially high level since petitioner's competitors would not reduce their retail prices as much as they would have done if petitioner received an equal bonus from respondent. He also testified that petitioner was harmed by the discrimination even if the favored purchasers did not lower their retail prices, since petitioner in that case would make less money per car.

Even construed most favorably to petitioner, the evidence of injury is weak. Petitioner nevertheless asks us to consider the sufficiency of its evidence in light of our traditional rule excusing antitrust plaintiffs from an unduly rigorous standard of proving antitrust injury. In *Zenith Radio Corp. v. Hazeltine Research, Inc.*, 395 U.S. 100, 123–124 (1969), for example, the Court discussed at some length the fixing of damages in a case involving market exclusion. We accepted the proposition that damages could be awarded on the basis of plaintiff's estimate of sales it could have made absent the violation.... * * *

Applying the foregoing principles to this case is not without difficulty....

But a more fundamental difficulty confronts us in this case. The cases relied upon by petitioner all depend in greater or lesser part on the inequity of a wrongdoer defeating the recovery of damages against him by insisting upon a rigorous standard of proof. In this case, however, we cannot say with assurance that respondent is a "wrongdoer." Because the court below bypassed the issue of liability and went directly to the issue of damages, we simply do not have the benefit of its views as to whether respondent in fact violated § 2(a). Absent such a finding, we decline to apply to this case the lenient damages rules of our previous cases. Had the court below found a violation, we could more confidently consider the adequacy of petitioner's evidence.

Accordingly, we think the proper course is to remand the case so that the Court of Appeals may pass upon respondent's contention that the evidence adduced at trial was insufficient to support a finding of violation of the Robinson–Patman Act.... We emphasize that even if there has been a violation of the Robinson–Patman Act, petitioner is not excused from its burden of proving antitrust injury and damages. It is simply that once a violation has been established, that burden is to some extent lightened. * * *

JUSTICE POWELL, with whom JUSTICES BRENNAN, MARSHALL, and BLACKMUN join, dissenting in part: I concur in Part I of the Court's opinion, but simply would affirm the judgment of the Court of Appeals. * * *

QUESTIONS AND COMMENTS

1. What is the case for "automatic damages"? Should the Court have awarded damages on this basis? What is the probable effect on pricing levels of a rule supporting automatic damages?

2. Did the Court fairly distinguish *Truett Payne* from prior damages cases on grounds that in *Truett Payne* the liability issue was not finally determined? Did the Court leave open the possibility that, where a violation is proved, the discrimination *is* the injury as a matter of law? In spirit, did it leave this question open?

3. If the discrimination is not the measure of injury, what is? Is lost sales or profits caused by the discrimination (which the dissenters suggested)? How can the disfavored purchaser show that sales were lost because of the discrimination? More importantly, how do "mere" (even substantial) lost sales of a competitor equate with harm to competition in the marketplace and thus with antitrust injury under the Sherman Act and the rest of the Clayton Act?

Truett Payne ends an era of "easy" litigation for disfavored buyers. Now plaintiff must gather more information and engage in complex analysis. But what must be proved?

Consider whether the following case, which concerns the problem of the dual distributor, throws light on the answer to this question.

BOISE CASCADE CORP. v. FTC

837 F.2d 1127 (D.C.Cir.1988).

JUDGE STARR: This case comes before us on petition for review of a decision of the Federal Trade Commission holding Boise Cascade Corporation in violation of section 2(f) of the Robinson–Patman Act. The Commission determined that Boise's receipt of price discriminations, in the form of discounts on office products it purchased for resale to consumers, tended to cause competitive injury to dealers in the office products industry with whom Boise competes. In so concluding, the Commission relied upon the "inference" of competitive injury, articulated by the Supreme Court in *FTC v. Morton Salt,* 334 U.S. 37 (1948), that arises when a substantial price discrimination exists over time. . . .

I.

A.

Before examining the facts in this case, we first pause briefly to describe the pertinent statutory framework. Section 2(f) of the Robinson–Patman Act makes it unlawful for any person "knowingly to induce or receive a discrimination in price which is prohibited [under the Robinson–Patman Act]." Since the Act directly proscribes only a *seller's* activities, the liability of a *buyer* under section 2(f) depends on whether the seller discriminated in the buyer's favor in violation of section 2(a) of the Act. See, e.g., *Great Atlantic & Pacific Tea Co. v. FTC,* 440 U.S. 69, 76–77 (1979); *Automatic Canteen Co. v. FTC*, 346 U.S. 61, 70–71 (1953). Section 2(a) prohibits price discrimination between different purchasers "where the effect of such discrimination may be substantially to lessen competition or tend to create a monopoly in any line of commerce, or to injure, destroy, or prevent competition with any person who either grants or knowingly receives the benefit of such discrimination, or with customers of either of them."

To establish a *prima facie* case under section 2(f), the Commission must establish two things: *first,* that the buyer received a lower price than its competitors, and *second,* that the price discrimination caused, or reasonably might cause, competitive injury.

The statute also specifies two defenses to a seller's (and therefore to a buyer's derivative) liability. No violation exists where the discount reflects the lower cost to the seller of selling to the favored customer (the "cost-justification" defense), nor where the seller granted the discount in good faith to meet a competing seller's price (the "meeting competition" defense). *Id.* § 13(a)–(b).... In addition to these statutory defenses, the Commission recognizes a defense, or more precisely, finds an absence of competitive injury, where the discounts are generally and practically available to competitors of the favored customer (the "practical availability" defense).

B.

On April 23, 1980, the Commission issued a complaint, over vigorous dissent, charging that Boise, as a "dual distributor" (both wholesaler and retailer) of office products, had violated section 2(f) of the Robinson–Patman Act. The complaint alleged that Boise's receipt of *wholesale* discounts from manufacturers on products that it then resold in a *retail* capacity to consumers constituted price discrimination for purposes of section 2(a).... The complaint alleged that Boise received these discounts knowingly and that the effect of Boise's receipt of such favorable pricing (and the resulting differential in prices) "has been or may be substantially to lessen, injure, destroy, or prevent competition" with dealers that were ineligible for the wholesale discounts.

In issuing the complaint, the Commission directed the Administrative Law Judge to receive evidence and to make findings of fact sufficient for disposition of the case under the competing standards of two FTC cases, namely *Mueller Co.,* F.T.C. 120 (1962), aff'd, 323 F.2d 44 (7th Cir.1963), cert. denied, 377 U.S. 923 (1964), and an earlier FTC case that *Mueller* had overruled, *Doubleday & Co.,* 52 F.T.C. 169 (1955). *Doubleday,* in brief, had articulated an additional defense under section 2(f) when the amount of the price disparity was reasonably related to the buyer's cost (as distinguished from the seller's cost savings) of providing additional marketing services. As we shall presently see in fuller detail, *Mueller* rejected entirely *Doubleday's* rationale, but both cases nonetheless seemed to live on within FTC chambers as competing strains of Robinson–Patman thought.

II.

* * * B.

In the office products industry, price is typically expressed in the form of a "manufacturer's suggested list price," less a discount, if any. To illustrate by way of a simple example, suppose the manufacturer's suggested list price for a product is $1.00. If the manufacturer offers a buyer a 50% discount, the list price is reduced by 50% and the product is thus sold to that buyer for 50 cents. If the manufacturer offers a 50–20% discount, the list price is reduced first by 50%. A 20% discount is then applied to that amount (50 cents), thus leaving 40 cents as the net price to the buyer.

Manufacturers' discounts take many forms. Perhaps best-known are quantity and volume discounts.... In addition, promotional discounts ... are prevalent in the industry.

To a more limited extent, manufacturers also offer bid discounts ... when large end-users—typically government entities—that need substantial quantities of office products solicit bids from marketing intermediaries.... Manufacturers offer the same "bid" discounts to all distributors submitting bids to these end-users....

Most significant for purposes of this case, however, are functional and trade discounts. A trade discount is one given to purchasers on the basis of the level of trade at which they operate. The discount depends solely on to whom the purchaser resells; it is entirely independent of marketing functions performed by the purchaser. A functional discount, in contrast, is offered by a manufacturer to a purchaser for assuming and performing a function that would otherwise be performed by the manufacturer. The pure functional discount operates independently of the purchaser's level of trade. In other words, any purchaser that performs the required functions would be eligible for the discount regardless of whether it is nominally a wholesaler or retailer.

At issue in this case is the validity of a hybrid discount which partakes of both a trade and functional discount. This discount, which for purposes of clarity and consistency we will call a "wholesale discount," has existed, without change, for many years in the office products industry. Indeed, the wholesale discount has been extended by most manufacturers of office supplies since well before Boise entered the industry. Its purpose is to induce wholesalers to undertake distribution and marketing functions on behalf of manufacturers. Manufacturers therefore extend the discount to *any* company, regardless of size, that meets the objective criteria contained in their respective definitions of "wholesaler."

In defining "wholesaler," all manufacturers in this industry require that the candidate resell products to dealers. Significantly, however, manufacturers do not require that the candidate resell exclusively to dealers (or other non-end-users). Nor do manufacturers limit the availability of the discount to those goods that are resold to dealers.... * * *

III.

A.

Boise is an integrated forest products company. It entered the office products industry in 1964 as a dual distributor through the acquisition of Associated Stationers Company.... Notwithstanding its considerable size, Boise's purchases typically account for less than 5% of any single manufacturer's total sales.... * * *

Although in its capacity as a dealer Boise performs essentially the same marketing functions for manufacturers as do other dealers, Boise is, by virtue of being a dual distributor, able to obtain wholesale discounts unavailable to the 23 dealers selected by the Commission for review in this case. These discounts are received on goods of like grade and quality that Boise sells in competition with those dealers. As we previously indicated, all six manufacturers studied in this case extend to companies (including

Boise) that qualify as wholesalers, wholesale discounts that represent reductions in list prices beyond those offered to dealers. As a result of the difference between dealer and wholesaler discounts, the 23 selected dealers pay between 5% and 33% more for their purchases from manufacturers than does Boise.

... [T]he ALJ did not find that Boise had in any way coerced or pressured the manufacturers into extending it the wholesale discounts. * * *

C.

In addition to this undisputed evidence of competitive health of the selected dealers and in the industry as a whole, there is another aspect of this case that is relevant to resolution of this controversy and unusual in the context of a Robinson–Patman proceeding—a virtually complete absence of sales lost to Boise by the selected dealers traceable to the price differential caused by wholesale discounts to Boise. Although the Commission aggregated 23 dealers, each of which carries hundreds, and in some cases thousands, of accounts, the record shows only 162 specific accounts identified by the dealers as lost to Boise. This stability of dealer accounts is of especial note in an industry where switching of accounts is common. Significantly, none of the selected dealers that lost accounts in whole or in part to Boise was able to conclude that the losses were due to the fact that Boise received a greater discount from the six manufacturers.

To be more specific, the Commission's selected dealers testified that they lost accounts to Boise, in whole or in part, due to Boise's lower prices, better service, or a combination of these factors.... * * *

Further diluting the Commission's attempted showing of diverted sales, Boise introduced considerable evidence of sales that it had lost to the selected dealers.... * * *

IV.

Notwithstanding his findings (1) that the selected dealers were competitively healthy and (2) that "accounts lost to Boise were counterbalanced by accounts which Boise lost to the dealers," the ALJ concluded that that evidence went only to the price discrimination's lack of effect on market structure. By virtue of that characterization, the ALJ determined that market structure evidence was by its nature inadequate to rebut the inference of competitive injury raised by the sustained and substantial price discrimination that Boise received. The ALJ stated his position in the following way: "[I]t is inconceivable that the substantial and sustained price differences documented in this record can have had no substantial effect on the ability of the dealers to compete with Boise."

Having determined that a *prima facie* violation of section 2(f) existed, the ALJ went on to conclude that the discounts were not practically available to the selected dealers, and that Boise knew, or should have known, that the discriminations in price were neither cost-justified nor given in good faith to meet competition. In addition, the ALJ recommended that the Commission adhere to its decision in *Mueller.* On the possibility that the Commission would reembrace the *Doubleday* rule, the ALJ determined that, because Boise did not perform services not performed by the selected dealers, Boise did not qualify for that "defense."

The Commission issued its order and opinion adopting and affirming the ALJ's findings of fact and conclusions of law. In its opinion, the Commission expressly relied on *Morton Salt's* inference that substantial price discrimination between competing purchasers over time causes, or tends to cause, competitive injury. In doing so, the Commission expressly recognized that the inference " 'may be overcome by evidence breaking the causal connection between a price differential and lost sales or profits.' " *Id.* (quoting *Falls City Industries, Inc. v. Vanco Beverage, Inc.,* 460 U.S. 428, 435 (1983)). Specifically, the Commission suggested that the *Morton Salt* inference could be overcome by a showing that market conditions unrelated to the price discrimination explained the lost accounts or shifted sales or the effects on the disfavored competitors (presumably lost profits or market share). * * *

Having found the two essential elements to a *prima facie* case (price discrimination and resulting competitive injury), the Commission concluded that Boise did not satisfy any of the defenses, statutory or Commission-fashioned, to Robinson–Patman liability. In addition, ... the Commission decided that *Doubleday* should not be revitalized and, accordingly, reaffirmed the anti-*Doubleday* holding of *Mueller.*

V.

The Commission's decision confronts us with a difficult issue arising under a statute that does not represent the highwater mark of skillful draftsmanship.... * * *

In recent years, the Supreme Court has reaffirmed the viability of the *Morton Salt* inference of competitive injury arising from a substantial price difference existing over time. It has, moreover, declined to cabin the *Morton Salt* inference to "cases involving 'large buyer preference or seller predation.' " *Falls City,* 460 U.S. at 436. To the contrary, the *Falls City* Court upheld application of *Morton Salt's* rule to a discriminatory pricing system based upon the geographical location of the buyer....

The *Morton Salt* inference is thus alive and well in the law. The case before us, however, presents the Commission's modern-day invocation of that inference in the setting of a pricing system which is entirely different from quantity and regional discounts. For as we have seen, the *Morton Salt* inference has been applied in the case at hand to a system of wholesale discounts. (The Commission uses the term "functional discount" generically to describe the wholesale discounts at issue here. We will therefore proceed to use these terms interchangeably.) ... * * *

... *Mueller* and *Doubleday,* the two warring rules spawned almost a generation ago by the Commission, shared a salient characteristic with

Morton Salt.... In each instance, a manufacturer or supplier's idiosyncratic, non-economically justified pricing regime favored certain identified distributors (big distributors in *Morton Salt, Doubleday* and *Mueller* ...), with nothing but favoritism—the evil sought to be remedied through the Robinson–Patman Act—to explain the disparate treatment.

VI.

* * *

... [T]he Commission (affirming the ALJ) embraced *Mueller*. ... But we see a preliminary difficulty that precludes our declaring in this case whether the champions of *Mueller* or those of *Doubleday* should be the ultimate winners in the long-lived struggle over the application of Robinson–Patman to dual distributors in modern-day distribution systems. And that has to do with the threshold question whether *in this case* competitive injury, even as expansively defined under Robinson–Patman, has been shown. Competitive injury, which no one disputes is the condition precedent for establishing violations of the Act, is a critical element. For, as we have seen, Robinson–Patman is directed to the preservation of competition. Indeed, the terms of the statute itself mandate that, in order for a price differential to be unlawful, it must tend "*to injure, destroy, or prevent competition.*" Injury to competition is thus the name of the Robinson–Patman game.

In its opinion, the FTC waved aside substantial evidence (1) that competition among dealers generally was healthy, (2) that the selected dealers singled out for FTC examination were thriving, and (3) that this happy picture of prosperity was apparently unclouded by instances of diverted sales attributable to the challenged discounts. The Commission flatly concluded that this entire body of evidence was *irrelevant*.... This cannot be. In our view, the Commission's conclusion that Boise's dealer-specific evidence was irrelevant to the inference of competitive injury is wrong as a matter of law.

It is clear that *Morton Salt's* inference of competitive injury "may be overcome by evidence breaking the causal connection between a price differential and lost sales or profits." *Falls City,* 460 U.S. at 435. In reason, *the inference can also be overcome by evidence showing an absence of competitive injury within the meaning of Robinson–Patman.* That is to say, a sustained and substantial price discrimination raises an inference, but it manifestly does not create an irrebuttable presumption of competitive injury. Specific, substantial evidence of absence of competitive injury is, in our view, sufficient to rebut what is, after all, only an inference. The Commission, in effect, employed the *Morton Salt* inference to presume competitive injury conclusively in this case, and would only treat as relevant evidence "breaking the causal connection" between that assumed injury and the price discrimination to rebut the inference. This approach defies both logic and the import of *Morton Salt* that the inference of injury is rebuttable; for if the respondent's evidence demonstrates that there is no competitive injury (or reasonable possibility of competitive injury) to begin with, then evidence breaking the causal connection is obviously impossible to adduce. There is, under those circumstances, no causal connection to break.

As a result of its interpretation of Robinson–Patman, the Commission found it unnecessary to sift and weigh Boise's evidence of absence of injury. All those days of trial before the ALJ were, it seems, largely for naught. In reaching this odd result, the Commission simply failed to determine whether Boise's evidence demonstrated that no injury or "reasonable possibility" of competitive injury existed.

First. Important among the salient facts that the Commission chose to ignore was the ALJ's finding that the selected dealers were not wallowing in a hopeless or deteriorating environment. Quite to the contrary, as we have already recounted, the ALJ found that all selected dealers for which data was available enjoyed an increase in sales and gross profits in excess of 22% annually during the period in question, despite the recessionary condition of the economy.... * * *

In addition, the evidence, as found by the ALJ, failed to demonstrate "displaced sales," another form the *Falls City* Court indicated injury could take. The ALJ found that switches of accounts from one supplier to another were "not uncommon"; to the contrary, they were the order of the day....

Second. To explain its refusal to consider Boise's evidence (and, indeed, the countervailing evidence) of absence of actual competitive injury, the Commission asserted that "the competitive injury requirement of Section 2(a) is satisfied by a showing of 'a reasonable possibility that a price difference may harm competition.' " *Commission Decision,* (quoting *Falls City,* 460 U.S. at 434–35). While true, that principle does not justify abdication of the duty to consider evidence indicating that a "reasonable possibility" of harm does not, in fact, exist in the particular industry. Robinson–Patman has not ushered in a bizarre rule of law that exalts theory "no matter what" in the face of hard, cold facts. That curious rule, if it ever was a rule, has been scotched by *Falls City's* teaching.... * * *

Third. In assuming, without analysis, the existence of competitive injury, we believe that the Commission erred in another way as well. It entirely failed to inform its application of *Morton Salt's* inference of injury with the purposes of the Robinson–Patman Act. As we have previously detailed, it is fairness, as Congress perceives it, that Robinson–Patman is all about. That Act, a legislative monument to smallness in a century which rewards bigness, is aimed at putting a halt to singling out the "Big Fives" and "Big Threes" of the world for disparately favorable treatment (unless, of course, a statutory defense lies).

This is not a case of the "Big Five" retailers (*Morton Salt*), the "Big Three" book distributors (*Doubleday*), the long-established, large jobbers who enjoyed manufacturer protection from uppity newcomers (*Mueller*) or the Hoosier beer distributor which happened to be on the "wrong" side of the Indiana–Kentucky state line (*Falls City*). Quite to the contrary, there is among the six manufacturers selected in this case no regime of favoritism towards Boise. There is not the slightest hint in the ALJ's opinion, or in the Commission's for that matter, that the manufacturers were singling out Boise (and other big fish) for disparately favorable treatment. Rather, in accordance with a practice prevalent well before Boise even entered the industry, *it is undisputed that the six manufacturers in question treated all wholesalers alike and provided the wholesale discount to Boise solely because it met their respective definitions of "wholesaler."* There is simply no cabal between Boise and the six manufacturers to give Boise an additional price break. * * *

Fourth. We note, finally, the irony of the Commission's concept of Robinson–Patman liability, namely that these egalitarian-minded manufacturers with their long-settled commercial practices now stand condemned as price discriminators in violation of federal law. As the Supreme Court has made abundantly clear, a buyer's liability under section 2(f) is entirely derivative in nature. *Great A & P Tea Co.,* 440 U.S. at 76–77. For there to be a guilty buyer, there must be a guilty seller. And thus it cannot pass unnoticed that under the Commission's approach, Bates, Master Products, Boorum & Pease and the other three manufacturers have run afoul of Robinson–Patman even though they have followed neutral, objective criteria in determining what buyers are to be considered wholesalers. . . .

In sum, although the Commission (and the ALJ) correctly took the view that the *Morton Salt* inference is rebuttable, its rejection on relevancy grounds of Boise's evidence of the absence of competitive injury (or reasonable possibility of competitive injury) was in error. The petition for review is therefore granted, and the case is remanded for further proceedings consistent with this opinion.

Questions and Comments

1. Does *Boise Cascade* suggest that plaintiff must prove a reasonable probability of competitive injury? How does the court define injury to competition? Would *Boise Cascade* bring the Robinson–Patman Act into harmony with the Sherman Act?

2. How would a judgment for the FTC have been likely to affect pricing levels?

Two years after *Boise Cascade*, the Supreme Court decided *Texaco Inc. v. Hasbrouck*, 496 U.S. 543 (1990). The Court held that unreasonable functional discounts to dual distributors illegally discriminated against independent retailers, whose sales plummeted. Despite the competitive nature of the market, the Court rejected defendant's argument of no harm to competition. It held that the *Morton Salt* presumption of competitive injury applied, despite the fact that the favored buyers were wholesalers and the complaining buyers were retailers.

Chroma Lighting v. GTE Products Corp., 111 F.3d 653 (9th Cir. 1997). Plaintiff was a distributor of Sylvania lighting products. Sylvania gave discounts to plaintiff's larger competitors, after which, and allegedly because of which, plaintiff went out of business. The case went to trial. After a jury verdict for plaintiff, Sylvania moved for judgment as a matter of law on grounds, among others, that the market was competitive and plaintiff had failed to prove injury to competition. The appellate court, by Judge Norris, affirmed denial of the motion.

> ... We agree with Judge Mikva and the Third Circuit. We are persuaded that the language that the Robinson–Patman Act added to § 2(a) of the Clayton Act—"to injure, destroy, or prevent competition"—expresses Congressional intent to protect individual competitors, not just market competition, from the effects of price discrimination. As we said in Rebel Oil Co. v. Atlantic Richfield Co., 51 F.3d 1421, 1446 n. 18 (9th Cir.1995) (dicta), "[t]he purpose of this passage was to relieve secondary-line plaintiffs—small retailers who are disfavored by discriminating suppliers—from having to prove harm to competition marketwide, allowing them instead to impose liability simply by proving effects to individual competitors." ...
>
> We also agree with the Third Circuit and Judge Mikva that the legislative history confirms that Congress amended the Clayton Act specifically to extend its protection to individual competitors. Congress passed the Robinson–Patman Act primarily out of concern for small retailers who could not compete with large chain-store purchasers because they could not buy in quantity. *See Falls City,* 460 U.S. at 436; *FTC v. Morton Salt Co.,* 334 U.S. at 49. The House Report shows that the Act was animated by concern for "the survival of independent merchants, manufacturers, and other businessmen." H.R.Rep. No. 2287, 74th Cong., 2d Sess. 3 (1936); *see also* Lawrence Anthony Sullivan, Handbook of the Law of Antitrust § 225(a) (finding support in legislative history for construing Robinson–Patman Act to protect individual small competitors irrespective of efficiency concerns). * * *
>
> Finally, Sylvania relies on Brooke Group Ltd. v. Brown & Williamson Tobacco Corp., 509 U.S. 209 (1993). *Brooke Group*, a primary-line price discrimination case, reasons that "[b]y its terms, the Robinson–Patman Act condemns price discrimination only to the extent it threatens to injure *competition*," and therefore holds that the Act must be construed consistently with the broader policies of the antitrust laws to protect competition, not competitors. *Id.* at 219–21. Sylvania claims that the *Brooke Group* reasoning applies with equal force to secondary-line price discrimination claims.
>
> We decline to extend the reasoning of *Brooke Group* to secondary-line cases because of the significant differences between primary- and

secondary-line claims. First and foremost, Congress' concern for the fate of individual competitors, as expressed in the legislative history of the Robinson–Patman Act, focussed on secondary-line, not primary-line competition. *Coastal Fuels of Puerto Rico, Inc. v. Caribbean Petroleum Corp.*, 79 F.3d 182, 191–92 (1st Cir.), *cert. denied*, 519 U.S. 927 (1996).... Since the original Clayton Act addressed only primary-line injury, Congress passed the Robinson–Patman Act to add protection against secondary-line injury, more specifically against injury to small retailers. *Coastal Fuels*, 79 F.3d at 192. Thus, the language added to the Clayton Act by the Robinson–Patman Act, and the legislative history that expresses Congress' solicitude for individual buyers, are still applicable in secondary-line cases, even though they are not applicable in primary-line cases after *Brooke Group*. *See id.* at 191–93 (*Morton Salt's* inference of competitive injury is still good law after *Brooke Group* because *Brooke Group* applies only to primary-line injury cases). Second, *Brooke Group* said that Robinson–Patman protects competition, not competitors, in the context of analogizing primary-line price discrimination claims to Sherman Act predatory pricing claims. The same analogy may not be made to secondary-line price discrimination claims. *Id.* at 193.

CONCLUSION

We hold that in a secondary-line Robinson–Patman case, the *Morton Salt* inference that competitive injury to individual buyers harms competition generally may not be overcome by proof of no harm to competition.

COMMENTS

Professor Hovenkamp writes, of *Chroma Lighting*:

The plaintiff attempted to rebut [the *Morton Salt*] presumption by showing that "competition in the relevant market remains healthy," but the court found such evidence irrelevant, concluding that the Robinson–Patman Act amendments "shift[ed] the focus of the statute from protecting competition to protecting individual disfavored buyers from the loss of business to favored buyers." The court, however, did not explain how Sylvania could profit by injuring the competitiveness of its own distribution system. Instead, without any explanation, the court followed *Morton Salt's* factual supposition that competition itself is presumptively harmed by price differentials among competing resellers of the manufacturer's product. This supposition is not merely false, it is nonsense. Nevertheless, as a proposition of law it continues in full force. H. Hovenkamp, The Robinson–Patman Act and Competition: Unfinished Business, 68 Antitrust L.J. 125, 129 (2000).

The Supreme Court continues to nudge interpretation of the Robinson–Patman Act towards modern interpretations of the Sherman Act, as it does in the following secondary line case.

VOLVO TRUCKS NORTH AMERICA INC. v. REEDER–SIMCO GMC

546 U.S. 164 (2006).

[Volvo Trucks gave discounts to dealers who bid on special orders by retail customers. The practice was: Retail customers would identify their needs and invite bids from dealers. When a Volvo dealer received specifications from a customer, it would ask Volvo for a discount from the wholesale price. The dealer would use the discount in preparing the bid. It would purchase the trucks from Volvo only after its bid was accepted. The plaintiff dealer, Reeder, alleged that it got less favorable concessions than other Volvo dealers. However, it seldom bid against another Volvo dealer. Reeder suspected that its disfavored status was part of a strategy by Volvo to eliminate Reeder as one of its dealers. It sued for unlawful discrimination under the Robinson–Patman Act.

The principal question was whether Volvo's practice constituted a discrimination in price between different purchasers of like commodities where the effect may be substantially to lessen competition or injure competition between a favored and disfavored customer. A jury answered in the affirmative and awarded damages which, as trebled, amounted to $1.3 million. The appellate court affirmed.

The Supreme Court reversed because, in most instances, Reeder had not bid for the business of the same customers as did the Volvo dealers who got the favorable concessions. There were two instances of head-to-head competition between Reeder and other Volvo dealers, but in one of these instances Reeder did not show that it was disfavored, and in the other the loss was trivial.

The general importance of the case lies in its articulation or suggestion of what "competitive injury" means in a Robinson–Patman case.]

JUSTICE GINSBURG: * * *

II.

Section 2, "when originally enacted as part of the Clayton Act in 1914, was born of a desire by Congress to curb the use by financially powerful corporations of localized price-cutting tactics which had gravely impaired the competitive position of other sellers." *FTC* v. *Anheuser–Busch, Inc.*, 363 U. S. 536, 543, and n. 6 (1960) (citing H. R. Rep. No. 627, 63d Cong., 2d Sess., 8 (1914); S. Rep. No. 698, 63d Cong., 2d Sess., 2–4 (1914)). Augmenting that provision in 1936 with the Robinson–Patman Act, Congress sought to target the perceived harm to competition occasioned by powerful buyers, rather than sellers; specifically, Congress responded to the advent of large chain stores, enterprises with the clout to obtain lower prices for goods than smaller buyers could demand. See 14 H. Hovenkamp, Antitrust Law ¶ 2302, p. 11 (2d ed. 2006) (hereinafter Hovenkamp); P. Areeda & L. Kaplow, Antitrust Analysis ¶ 602, pp. 908–909 (5th ed. 1997)....

Mindful of the purposes of the Act and of the antitrust laws generally, we have explained that Robinson–Patman does not "ban all price differences charged to different purchasers of commodities of like grade and quality," *Brooke Group Ltd.* v. *Brown & Williamson Tobacco Corp.*, 509 U. S. 209, 220 (1993); rather, the Act proscribes "price discrimination only to the extent that it threatens to injure competition," *ibid.* Our decisions describe three categories of competitive injury that may give rise to a Robinson–Patman Act claim: primary-line, secondary-line, and tertiary-line. Primary-line cases entail conduct—most conspicuously, predatory pricing—that injures competition at the level of the discriminating seller and its direct competitors. Secondary-line cases, of which this is one, involve price discrimination that injures competition among the discriminating seller's customers (here, Volvo's dealerships); cases in this category typically refer to "favored" and "disfavored" purchasers. See *ibid.; Texaco Inc.* v. *Hasbrouck*, 496 U. S. 543, 558, n. 15 (1990). Tertiary-line cases involve injury to competition at the level of the purchaser's customers.

To establish the secondary-line injury of which it complains, Reeder had to show that (1) the relevant Volvo truck sales were made in interstate commerce; (2) the trucks were of "like grade and quality"; (3) Volvo "discriminate[d] in price between" Reeder and another purchaser of Volvo trucks; and (4) "the effect of such discrimination may be ... to injure, destroy, or prevent competition" to the advantage of a favored purchaser, *i.e.*, one who "receive[d] the benefit of such discrimination." 15 U. S. C. § 13(a). It is undisputed that Reeder has satisfied the first and second requirements. Volvo and the United States, as *amicus curiae*, maintain that Reeder cannot satisfy the third and fourth requirements, because Reeder has not identified any differentially-priced transaction in which it was both a "purchaser" under the Act and "in actual competition" with a favored purchaser for the same customer.

A hallmark of the requisite competitive injury, our decisions indicate, is the diversion of sales or profits from a disfavored purchaser to a favored purchaser. *FTC* v. *Sun Oil Co.*, 371 U.S. 505, 518–519 (1963) (evidence showed patronage shifted from disfavored dealers to favored dealers); *Falls City Industries, Inc.* v. *Vanco Beverage, Inc.*, 460 U. S. 428, 437–438, and n. 8 (1983) (complaint "supported by direct evidence of diverted sales"). We have also recognized that a permissible inference of competitive injury may arise from evidence that a favored competitor received a significant price reduction over a substantial period of time. See *FTC* v. *Morton Salt Co.*, 334 U. S. 37, 49–51 (1948); *Falls City Industries*, 460 U.S., at 435. Absent actual competition with a favored Volvo dealer, however, Reeder cannot establish the competitive injury required under the Act.

III. * * * A.

Both the purchase-to-purchase and the offer-to-purchase comparisons fall short, for in none of the discrete instances on which Reeder relied did

Reeder compete with beneficiaries of the alleged discrimination *for the same customer*. . . .

We decline to permit an inference of competitive injury from evidence of such a mix-and-match, manipulable quality. . . .

Reeder may have competed with other Volvo dealers for the opportunity to bid on potential sales in a broad geographic area. At that initial stage, however, competition is not affected by differential pricing; a dealer in the competitive bidding process here at issue approaches Volvo for a price concession only after it has been selected by a retail customer to submit a bid. Competition for an opportunity to bid, we earlier observed, is based on a variety of factors, including the existence *vel non* of a relationship between the potential bidder and the customer, geography, and reputation. We reiterate in this regard an observation made by Judge Hansen, dissenting from the Eighth Circuit's Robinson–Patman holding: Once a retail customer has chosen the particular dealers from which it will solicit bids, "the relevant market becomes limited to the needs and demands of a particular end user, with only a handful of dealers competing for the ultimate sale." 374 F. 3d, at 719. That Volvo dealers may bid for sales in the same geographic area does not import that they in fact competed for the same customer-tailored sales. In sum, the purchase-to-purchase and offer-to-purchase comparisons fail to show that Volvo sold at a lower price to Reeder's "competitors," hence those comparisons do not support an inference of competitive injury. See *Falls City Industries*, 460 U.S., at 435 (inference of competitive injury under *Morton Salt* arises from "proof of a substantial price discrimination between *competing purchasers* over time" (emphasis added)).

B.

Reeder did offer evidence of two instances in which it competed head to head with another Volvo dealer. . . .

. . . [I]f price discrimination between two purchasers existed at all, it was not of such magnitude as to affect substantially competition between Reeder and the "favored" Volvo dealer.

IV.

Interbrand competition, our opinions affirm, is the "primary concern of antitrust law." *Continental T. V., Inc.* v. *GTE Sylvania, Inc.*, 433 U.S. 36, 51–52, n. 19 (1977). The Robinson–Patman Act signals no large departure from that main concern. Even if the Act's text could be construed in the manner urged by Reeder and embraced by the Court of Appeals, we would resist interpretation geared more to the protection of existing *competitors* than to the stimulation of *competition*. In the case before us, there is no evidence that any favored purchaser possesses market power, the allegedly favored purchasers are dealers with little resemblance to large independent department stores or chain operations, and the supplier's selective price discounting fosters competition among suppliers of different brands. See *id.*, at 51–52 (observing that the market impact of a vertical practice, such as a change in a supplier's distribution system, may be a "simultaneous reduction of intrabrand competition and stimulation of interbrand competition"). By declining to extend Robinson–Patman's governance to such cases, we continue to construe the Act "consistently with broader policies of the antitrust laws." *Brooke Group*, 509 U.S., at 220 (quoting *Great Atlantic & Pacific Tea Co.* v. *FTC*, 440 U.S. 69, 80, n. 13 (1979)); see *Automatic Canteen Co. of America* v. *FTC*, 346 U.S. 61, 63 (1953) (cautioning against Robinson–Patman constructions that "extend beyond the prohibitions of the Act and, in doing so, help give rise to a price uniformity and rigidity in open conflict with the purposes of other antitrust legislation"). * * *

JUSTICE STEVENS, with whom JUSTICE THOMAS joins, dissenting.

Franchised dealers who sell Volvo trucks, like those who sell automobiles, farm equipment, washing machines, and a variety of other expensive items, routinely engage in negotiations with prospective purchasers. Sometimes the prospect is simultaneously negotiating with two Volvo dealers, sometimes with a Volvo dealer and a dealer representing another manufacturer, and still other times a satisfied customer who is generally familiar with the options available in a competitive market may negotiate with only one dealer at a time. Until today, the Robinson–Patman Act's prohibition of price discrimination would have protected the dealer's ability to negotiate in all those situations. Today, however, by adopting a novel, transaction-specific concept of competition, the Court eliminates that statutory protection in all but those rare situations in which a prospective purchaser is negotiating with two Volvo dealers at the same time.

Setting aside for the moment the fact that the case involves goods specially ordered for particular customers rather than goods stocked in inventory, the case is a rather ordinary Robinson–Patman suit. Respondent Reeder alleged a violation of the Act; the parties submitted a good deal of conflicting evidence to the jury; the trial judge properly instructed the jurors on the elements of price discrimination, competitive injury, and damages; and the jury returned a verdict resolving all issues in Reeder's favor. The Court of Appeals found no error in either the instructions or the sufficiency of the evidence. 374 F.3d 701 (C.A.8 2004).

Two issues of fact bear particular mention.

First, Volvo does not challenge the jury's finding of price discrimination. Reeder's theory of the case was that Volvo sought to cut back its number of dealers and deemed Reeder expendable. To avoid possible violations of franchise agreements and state laws, Volvo chose to accomplish this goal by offering Reeder worse prices than other regional dealers.

Reeder introduced substantial evidence of this theory. It showed that Volvo had an explicit business strategy, known as the "Volvo Vision," of "fewer dealers, larger markets." It showed that Volvo could afford to lose sales as it squeezed dealers out, since the boom years of the late 1990's left Volvo with about as many orders as it could fill. And it showed that Volvo frequently gave worse prices to it than to other regional dealers. On at least four occasions, Volvo sold trucks to Reeder at significantly higher prices than to other dealers buying similar trucks around the same time....

Second, the jury found that the favored dealers at issue in these comparisons were competitive players in the same geographic market as Reeder....

For decades, juries have routinely inferred the requisite injury to competition under the Robinson–Patman Act from the fact that a manufacturer sells goods to one retailer at a higher price than to its competitors. This rule dates back to the following discussion of competitive injury in Justice Black's opinion for the Court in *FTC v. Morton Salt Co.*, 334 U.S. 37:

> "It is argued that the findings fail to show that respondent's discriminatory discounts had in fact caused injury to competition. There are specific findings that such injuries had resulted from respondent's discounts, although the statute does not require the Commission to find that injury has actually resulted. The statute requires no more than that the effect of the prohibited price discriminations 'may be substantially to lessen competition ... or to injure, destroy, or prevent competition.' After a careful consideration of this provision of the Robinson–Patman Act, we have said that 'the statute does not require that the discriminations must in fact have harmed competition, but only that there is a reasonable possibility that they "may" have such an effect.' *Corn Products Co. v. Federal Trade Comm'n,* 324 U.S. 726, 742 (1945). Here the Commission found what would appear to be obvious, that the competitive opportunities of certain merchants were injured when they had to pay respondent substantially more for their goods than their competitors had to pay. The findings are adequate." *Id.*,at 4547.

... There is ample evidence that Volvo charged Reeder higher prices than it charged to competing dealers in the same market over a period of many months. That those higher prices impaired Reeder's ability to compete with those dealers is just as obvious as the injury to competition described by the Court in *Morton Salt.*

Volvo nonetheless argues that no competitive injury could have occurred because it never discriminated against Reeder when Reeder and another Volvo dealer were seeking concessions with regard to the same ultimate customer....

Unlike the Court, I cannot accept Volvo's vision. Nothing in the statute or in our precedent suggests that "competition" is evaluated by a transaction-specific inquiry, and such an approach makes little sense. It requires us to ignore the fact that competition among truck dealers is a continuing war waged over time rather than a series of wholly discrete events. Each time Reeder managed to resell trucks it had purchased at discriminatorily high prices, it was forced either to accept lower profit margins than were available to favored Volvo dealers or to pass on the higher costs to its customers (who then might well go to a different dealer the next time). And we have long indicated that lost profits relative to a competitor are a proper basis for permitting the *Morton Salt* inference. See, *e.g., Falls City Industries*, 460 U.S., at 435 (noting that to overcome the *Morton Salt* inference, a defendant needs "evidence breaking the causal connection between a price differential and lost sales *or profits*" (emphasis added)). By ignoring these commonsense points, the Court gives short shrift to the Robinson–Patman Act's prophylactic intent.... * * *

III

As the Court recognizes, the Robinson–Patman Act was primarily intended to protect small retailers from the vigorous competition afforded by chainstores and other large volume purchasers. Whether that statutory mission represented sound economic policy is not merely the subject of serious debate, but may well merit Judge Bork's characterization as "wholly mistaken economic theory." I do not suggest that disagreement with the policy of the Act has played a conscious role in my colleagues' unprecedented decision today. I cannot avoid, however, identifying the irony in a decision refusing to adhere to the text of the Act in a case in which the jury credited evidence that discriminatory prices were employed as means of escaping contractual commitments and eliminating specifically targeted firms from a competitive market. The exceptional quality of this case provides strong reason to enforce the Act's prohibition against discrimination even if Judge Bork's evaluation (with which I happen to agree) is completely accurate.

QUESTIONS AND COMMENTS

1. Why does the Court invoke *Brooke Group*, which was a primary line case?

2. What does the Court mean when it says: "the [Robinson–Patman] Act proscribes 'price discrimination only to the extent that it threatens to injure competition' "? Do the Court's words here and elsewhere suggest reading out of the Robinson–Patman Act the words: "or to injure, destroy, or prevent competition with any person who either grants or knowingly receives the benefit of such discrimination...." [i.e., injuring the competition between the favored and disfavored purchasers]?

3. Since the Robinson–Patman Act focuses on discrimination harming competition between two purchasers of the same brand (intra-brand competition), why does the Court cite *Sylvania*, affirming that "[i]nterbrand competition ... is the 'primary concern of antitrust law' "?

4. Wither the Robinson–Patman Act? Will the Supreme Court, given the opportunity, bring Robinson–Patman Act harm into total conformity with Sherman Act harm? Remember that most Robinson–Patman Act cases are private cases; the agencies seldom enforce the Robinson–Patman Act.

5. What is the obligation and latitude of a judge in interpreting a statute with which he or she disagrees? Does it matter whether advances in economic thinking have made the statute appear obsolete or perverse to the judge? What degree of transparency is required of the judge in giving a statute a construction at odds with its legislative purpose?

Do not assume that you now have a good working knowledge of the Robinson–Patman Act. We have presented only a window into a principal tension—fairness and opportunity for small business, versus efficiency and freedom of action.

---

3. PRICE DISCRIMINATION UNDER FOREIGN LAW

The European Union and various nations. The competition laws of numerous jurisdictions prohibit certain discrimination. Often an objective of the provision is to preserve fair competitive opportunities for small and middle-sized firms. Usually the prohibition applies only to dominant firms. The EU's prohibition, in Article 102 of the Treaty on the Functioning of the European Union, is intended also to overcome "partitioning" of the internal market; to counter different market prices for the same goods in different Member States. See, for example, the Motor Vehicle Block Exemption Regulation, *http://ec.europa.eu/competition/sectors/motor_vehicles/legislation/legislation*.

4. THE UNCTAD MODEL LAW

The United Nations Conference on Trade and Development (UNCTAD) has published a Model Law on Competition (revised 2010), which is particularly influential with developing countries. Under the model law, discriminatory terms may be an abuse of a dominant position of market power.

UNCTAD MODEL LAW ON COMPETITION AND COMMENTARY

CHAPTER IV

Acts or behaviour constituting an abuse of a dominant position of market power

* * *

II. *Acts or behaviour considered as abusive*: * * *

(b) Discriminatory (i.e. unjustifiably differentiated) pricing or terms or conditions in the supply or purchase of goods or services,

including by means of the use of pricing policies in transactions between affiliated enterprises which overcharge or undercharge for goods or services purchased or supplied as compared with prices for similar or comparable transactions outside the affiliated enterprises.... * * *

Commentary

68 Closely related to predatory pricing is the practice of discriminatory pricing. While below cost pricing vis à vis direct competitors may be predatory, discriminatory pricing can also be predatory, as for example in the case of discounts based on quantities, "bonus systems" or "fidelity discounts". In this situation, irrespective of injury to direct competitors, discriminatory pricing can injure competitors of the favoured purchaser. In spite of what has been mentioned, it is also important to point out that in many cases quantity discounts often reflect reduced transaction costs or have the purpose of meeting competition, and should not be discouraged. Injury to competitors of the favoured purchaser should not in and of itself concern competition authorities, because competition laws should protect competition and not competitors.

69 In Peru, although the legislation considers discriminatory pricing as an example of abusive behaviour, discounts and bonuses that correspond to generally accepted commercial practices that are given because of special circumstances such as anticipated payment, quantity, volume, etc., and when they are granted in similar conditions to all consumers, do not constitute a case of abuse of dominant position.

70 Other types of price based discrimination would include "delivered pricing", i.e. selling at uniform price irrespective of location (whatever the transportation costs to the seller), and "base point selling", where one area has been designated as base point (whereby the seller charges transportation fees from that point irrespective of the actual point of shipment and its costs).

71 The proscription of discrimination also includes terms and conditions in the supply or purchase of goods and services. For example, the extension of differentiated credit facilities or ancillary services in the supply of goods and serves can also be discriminatory. In the Australian legislation, the prohibition of discrimination is not limited to price based discriminations, but refers also to credits, provision of services and payment for services provided in respect of the goods. It is also [relevant] to point out that differential terms and conditions should not be considered unlawful if they are related to cost differences. More generally, preventing firms from offering lower prices to some customers may well result in discouraging firms from cutting prices to anyone. However, the Australian Trade Practices Act 1974 was repealed in 1995 and conduct that would have been considered prohibited under Section 49 can instead be addressed by § 45 if it results in a substantial lessening of competition, or under § 46 if it is a result of the misuse of

market power by a corporation. In the Russian Federation, Article (5) of the Law prohibits conduct and agreements by forms that restrict competition.

[72] Undercharging for goods or services in transactions between affiliated enterprises (a case of transfer pricing) can be used as a means of predation against competitors who are not able to obtain supplies at comparable prices.

* * *

QUESTIONS AND COMMENTS

1. Comment on the excerpt from the UNCTAD Model Law and on the commentary. Is the proposed rule wise? Is the commentary helpful? Note that the proposed prohibition, like EU law but unlike U.S. law, requires dominance or market power.

2. Note the concern expressed in the UNCTAD commentary that an integrated firm, perhaps a multinational firm, will discriminate against outsiders in comparison with its intrafirm transactions. Thus, independent buyers in the host country may be "overcharged" as compared with the enterprise's subsidiaries. This is not a concern of U.S. antitrust law. Why, do you suspect, it is a concern in many less developed and developing countries?

3. What observations can you make in recommending or revising a price discrimination law for the United States? for Europe? for developing countries?

F. ARE VERTICAL RESTRAINTS A WORLD PROBLEM? TRADE, COMPETITION AND THE WTO

The law of vertical restraints and the law of monopolization are the areas of greatest divergence among jurisdictions. United States law, post *Sylvania*, *Sharp* and *Leegin* (and apart from Robinson–Patman secondary line discrimination), hesitates to interfere with restraints that are truly vertical; that is, vertical restraints not supportive or reflective of a cartel. Some other jurisdictions are readier to see vertical restraints as exclusionary and exploitative or as unreasonably interfering with the flow of commerce. In the EU, vertical restraint law is a critically important complement to the effort towards internal market integration; vertical restraints that maintain or even reflect different prices for the same goods in different Member States of the European Union are especially condemned. EU law is centrally concerned with the freedom of movement of goods and services across Member State lines and not so concerned with claims that discounters are free riders and will lessen the incentives of full-pricers to invest in services.

It may seem that, of all restraints, vertical restraints would tend to be more localized and therefore less a source of friction in the world. This has turned out not to be the case. Vertical restraints and their cross-border effects have taken center stage in several trade and competition disputes.

In the 1980s the Japanese market seemed closed to outside trade. Although the Japanese Government had negotiated a significant lowering of trade barriers in the context of the GATT/WTO, and it affirmed that it had removed quotas and lowered tariffs as agreed, still, the Japanese market seemed impenetrable. Japanese officials conceded that "structural impediments"—including regulatory law and other non-tariff barriers—remained. Japanese and American officials embarked on trade talks called the Structural Impediments Initiative. The Japanese officials agreed to liberalize certain markets, repealing unnecessary regulation, which would help open those markets to trade and investment. In the course of the talks, American negotiators observed to the Japanese negotiators, in effect: If our firms cannot penetrate your markets, and if government barriers are not the problem, then you must be tolerating private restraints of trade. If you do not enforce your antitrust law to stop these practices, we may sue your firms under *our* antitrust laws. The U.S. officials thereupon revised agency guidelines on international operations, deleting a footnote stating that the Justice Department would sue only to protect American consumers; and later the Justice Department and the FTC issued new guidelines (1995) (see Appendix F) stating the agencies' readiness to use U.S. antitrust law to pry open foreign markets closed by private anticompetitive restraints. *http://www.usdoj.gov/atr/public/guidelines/internat.htm.* See 1995 guidelines, point 3.122.

U.S. antitrust officials used this policy platform to sue Pilkington (UK) for using expired IP rights to block American exporters of float glass from access to European and other markets.[2] The policy position was invoked also in discussions regarding Fuji Film's (near) exclusive dealing arrangements with all of the major film distributors in Japan, allegedly foreclosing Kodak from penetrating the Japanese market; and regarding the three Japanese glass makers' exclusive dealing arrangements with the only established glass distributors in Japan, allegedly foreclosing Guardian Glass; but no U.S. antitrust lawsuits were brought in these matters. (Ultimately, regarding film, the United States brought a *trade* complaint against the Japanese Government in the WTO, but only for barrier-creating regulatory statutes that made market penetration by outsiders difficult. The U.S. trade complaint was rejected because the Japanese laws did not violate GATT rules. They did not discriminate against foreigners and they did not erect new barriers that could have undermined legitimate expectations of Americans at the time that lower tariffs were negotiated. See Panel Report, *Japan—Measures Affecting Consumer Photographic Film and Paper*, WT/DS44/R (Apr. 22, 1998).

2. See United States v. Pilkington plc, 1994–2 Trade Cas. (CCH) ¶ 70,842 (D. Ariz. 1994) (consent decree). The complaint, however, is more traditional. It alleges a competitors' division of world markets, including Pilkington's agreement not to sell float glass into the United States.

Can the United States use its antitrust laws to attack vertical restraints abroad that exclude American exporters and raise prices to foreign consumers? Does *Empagran* (page supra 180) suggest an answer?

If there is a problem of private anticompetitive vertical restraints that block access to foreign markets and undermine competition and efficiency in the world, how should it be handled? Is cooperation among the relevant competition authorities the best answer? Is horizontal cooperation likely to be sufficient? See, for proposals for and against a world competition law system, Andrew T. Guzman, ed., COOPERATION, COMITY, AND COMPETITION POLICY (2011).

AFTERWORD

COMPETITION IN A WORLD OF GLOBAL MARKETS

■ ■ ■

Competition law is a subject of increasing interest in the world. International cartels persist, despite increasingly harsh penalties. Cartel enforcement and merger review remain the staples of antitrust lawyering. Monopolization/abuse of dominance cases maintain a steady flow, as do vertical cases. Cross-border transactions and transnational litigations are increasing in both numbers and profile.

In Europe, competition law has strong links with internal-market trade and related policies. In the United States, antitrust is more isolated from other policies. In developing countries, competition law is embraced as a way to make market players—especially state-owned firms and their progeny—more accountable and markets more efficient, with the promise of deeper integration into world markets and thus a higher standard of living at home; but it is sometimes feared as a cosmopolitan strategy that could override national interests, facilitate multinational takeovers, and exacerbate the woefully unequal distribution of wealth, power and opportunity.

Given the range of interests and approaches in the world, it is perhaps remarkable that so high a degree of convergence of substantive antitrust law has been achieved. Cartels are recognized as a common enemy, except when exempted to serve national industrial policy. Anticompetitive mergers are generally illegal, with public policy exceptions narrow. The understanding of "what is anticompetitive" varies, to be sure, even within the United States, but one metric is becoming clear: transactions and patterns of conduct that create or increase market power at the expense of consumers and without efficiency justification are illegal. The most important technical skill of the antitrust lawyer is to know when these factors exist and align, or to know the questions to ask economists and other experts to determine whether they probably do.

"Know," of course, is a heroic word. We must make estimates and predictions. Even then, we do so on the basis of critical assumptions about markets and power, as the cases and materials show. We hope that this book has prepared you to question assumptions and to ask the right questions.

APPENDIX A

THE FRAMEWORK FOR U.S. ANTITRUST LAW

■ ■ ■

Enforcement, Procedure and the Scope of the Law

Synopsis

I. Introduction: The Statutes

The core antitrust law of the United States is the Sherman Antitrust Act, enacted in 1890 to stem the growth of combinations and monopolies that were gaining control over business in America. The Sherman Act prohibits contracts, combinations and conspiracies in restraint of trade, and monopolization and attempts and conspiracies to monopolize. The Sherman Act is supplemented by the Clayton Act, enacted in 1914 during the Progressive Era, which prohibits potentially anticompetitive acquisitions, exclusive dealing, tie-ins, and interlocking directorates. The Celler–Kefauver Amendment to the merger provision of the Clayton Act was passed in 1950 at a peak of concentration of business power to strengthen the merger law.

The Federal Trade Commission Act, like the Clayton Act, was enacted in 1914. This statute established the Federal Trade Commission and prohibits unfair methods of competition and unfair or deceptive acts or practices. "Unfair" methods of competition is interpreted to mean "anti-competitive."

In 1936, spurred by price discrimination in favor of big buyers, Congress passed the Robinson–Patman Act. The Robinson–Patman Act, which is an amendment to the Clayton Act, prohibits price discrimination in the sale of goods in interstate commerce when it harms or prevents competition and (inter alia) is not cost-justified. The act does not apply to the sale of services.

Congress has passed various specialized qualifications to the antitrust laws, including 1982 amendments that limit antitrust liability in export trade and foreign commerce, and the National Cooperative Research Act of 1984, which declares that research and development joint ventures shall be judged under a rule of reason and that parties who file notification of their research joint ventures are relieved of treble (but not single) damage liability if their joint venture is found to be anticompetitive. This statute was revised in 1993 to include production joint ventures.

Key provisions of these statutes are set forth in Appendix B.

II. Antitrust in the World Today

Antitrust law is a critical element of competition policy. Competition policy includes the laws that establish an environment in which free enterprise can flourish, which limit the growth and exercise of power by private firms, and which set rules of the game that protect the integrity of the competition system. The importance of antitrust law and its symbiotic linkage with democracy and freedom to compete was underscored by the adoption of a market system and an antitrust law by nearly every Central and Eastern European nation upon abolishing Communism and adopting democratic government in or about 1990.

Virtually every industrialized country in the world and most developing countries have an antitrust law. The antitrust "family" includes more than one hundred jurisdictions. Antitrust laws vary in their emphasis. Some, like United States law today, focus on efficiency aspects of competition, particularly consumer welfare. Many newly democratized nations focus also on establishing legitimacy of markets and supporting inclusive growth. Some, like the law of the European Union, focus also on free movement of goods and services and access to and openness of markets. Even within the same nation, the focus of the law may change from time to time as the circumstances and needs of the nation change. The central mission of United States law has shifted over time from preserving pluralism and access to promoting consumer welfare, efficiency, technological progress, and freedom of even dominant firms to pursue those goals.

III. The Enforcement of the Federal Antitrust Laws

A. The Justice Department and the Federal Trade Commission

The federal antitrust laws may be enforced by the government and by private parties. Two arms of the federal government have antitrust enforcement jurisdiction—the Justice Department (DOJ), through its Antitrust Division, and the Federal Trade Commission. The Antitrust Division is headed by the Assistant Attorney General in Charge of the Antitrust Division. When the Justice Department decides to sue, it brings suit in the federal courts. The Federal Trade Commission is an administrative agency and has responsibilities for both consumer protection and antitrust. Within the agency is a Bureau of Competition and a Bureau of Consumer Protection. The Director of the Bureau of Competition generates antitrust complaints. The Commission must approve and issue complaints. The Commission is comprised of five commissioners, each of whom may be appointed for a term of seven years. Both agencies do research, policy work, and advocacy. In an FTC proceeding, the staff tries the case before an Administrative Law Judge. The decision of the ALJ may be appealed to the Commission. If the respondent loses, it may appeal to a federal appellate court. The FTC may seek preliminary relief, e.g. to enjoin a proposed merger, in federal court.

The Department of Justice, through its Antitrust Division, enforces the Sherman Act and the Clayton Act. The Sherman Act is a criminal statute as well as a civil statute. The Justice Department normally chooses to sue criminally only in the event of hard core violations; principally price-fixing, which is a white collar crime. Individuals convicted of a Sherman Act violation may go to jail for up to ten years and may be fined up to one million dollars, or twice the victim's loss or defendant's gain, whichever is larger. Corporations convicted may be fined up to 100 million dollars. A leniency program–waiving fines and jail for the first person to report the details of a cartel–has greatly aided cartel detection and prosecution. In cases that it brings civilly, the Justice Department may seek injunctive and other equitable relief, and it may sue for three times its loss (treble damages) if the government itself is the victim of the violation.

The Federal Trade Commission may sue to enforce the Clayton Act and the Federal Trade Commission Act. It has no criminal jurisdiction. Pre-merger notification filings are made to both agencies, which decide among themselves which agency will investigate the merger.

B. Private Enforcement

The antitrust laws may be enforced by private parties also. To ease the burden of suit faced by victims of violations, the Clayton Act provides that a judgment for the government shall be prima facie evidence of the violation in a later private suit against the same defendants. Successful private plaintiffs are entitled to treble damages, costs, and attorneys' fees. Congress adopted the treble damage remedy in order to enlist the efforts of "private attorneys general" and thus to provide incentives to detect violations and sue. The treble damage remedy is codified in Section 4 of the Clayton Act, which states:

> [A]ny person who shall be injured in his business or property by reason of anything forbidden in the antitrust laws may sue therefor . . . and shall recover threefold the damages by him sustained, and the cost of suit, including a reasonable attorney's fee.

The Supreme Court has put important glosses on the language of Section 4 of the Clayton Act. In Hanover Shoe, Inc. v. United Shoe Machinery Corp., 392 U.S. 481 (1968), the Supreme Court held that an overcharged buyer is entitled to recover the whole artificial price increase charged to it by a seller; the defendant seller may not be relieved of liability or damages by proof that the plaintiff passed on the overcharge to downstream purchasers. In Illinois Brick Company v. Illinois, 431 U.S. 720 (1977), the Supreme Court held that indirect purchasers harmed by a price fix may not affirmatively assert that the direct purchaser passed on the overcharge to them. Accordingly, treble damage suits brought under the Sherman Act by indirect purchasers are normally dismissed for lack of recoverable damages. However, the Supreme Court carved out an exception from the rule of *Illinois Brick.* An indirect purchaser who is party to a preexisting cost-plus contract or other arrangement that does not present the complex problems of tracing who was harmed to what extent may be permitted to prove that overcharges were passed on to it. The exception is narrowly construed. See Kansas v. Utilicorp United, Inc., 497 U.S. 199 (1990). The strength of the "bright line" Illinois Brick rule is reflected in Warren General Hospital v. Amgen, Inc., 643 F.3d 77 (3d Cir. 2011). A hospital that purchased pharmaceutical products through an independent wholesaler sued the manufacturer for illegal tying. The hospital alleged that it was the first party in the line of distribution that was injured; that it bore all of the costs of the illegal act; and that it, the hospital, had direct dealings with the manufacturer. Nonetheless, and even if the wholesaler would not or could not sue, the court denied standing.

Many states authorize suits by indirect purchasers under their state antitrust laws. These state authorizations allow circumvention of the *Illinois Brick* rule.

Brunswick Corporation v. Pueblo Bowl–O–Mat, Inc., 429 U.S. 477 (1977), limited recoverable damages to "antitrust injury." In *Brunswick,* plaintiff bowling alleys sought to recover profits they lost when a big bowling alley bought and revitalized a declining bowling alley that would otherwise have gone out of business. Plaintiffs were injured (they lost profits) not by a lessening of competition, nor by anticompetitive acts en route to the lessening of competition, nor by anticompetitive acts made possible by an antitrust violation. They were injured by competition itself. The Court said, at 429 U.S. 489:

We therefore hold that for plaintiff to recover treble damages on account of [Clayton Act] § 7 [merger] violations, they must prove more than injury causally linked to an illegal presence in the market. Plaintiffs must prove *antitrust* injury, which is to say injury of the type the antitrust laws were intended to prevent and that flows from that which makes defendants' acts unlawful. The injury should reflect the anticompetitive effect either of the violation or of anticompetitive acts made possible by the violation. It should, in short, be "the type of loss that the claimed violations ... would be likely to cause."

While *Brunswick* speaks in terms of antitrust injury, later opinions speak in terms of standing to sue. Standing is determined by application of a balancing test, subject to the *Brunswick* principle that one who is harmed only by competition itself may not recover. The Supreme Court has enumerated five principal factors material to a determination of standing:

(1) The harm should be direct rather than remote.

(2) The harm should be of the sort that the antitrust laws were designed to prevent or inextricably intertwined with it.

(3) Intent to harm plaintiff or those in plaintiff's class weighs in favor of standing.

(4) The prospect that standing will lead to duplicative recovery or difficult questions of apportionment weighs against standing.

(5) The prospect that standing will leave significant violations undetected or unremedied weighs in favor of standing.

Associated General Contractors of California v. California State Council of Carpenters, 459 U.S. 519 (1983); Blue Shield of Virginia v. McCready, 457 U.S. 465 (1982); Verizon Communications v. Law Offices of Curtis V. Trinko, 540 U.S. 398 (2004) (Stevens, J., concurring).

Victims of violations often bring class actions for their aggregate injuries. Often the cases are brought against numerous defendants who are the principal members of an industry charged with price fixing. If plaintiffs prove that defendants violated the law and that the violation caused an antitrust impact upon them, and if they prove the amount of their antitrust injury, they are entitled to judgment for their damages, trebled, against all defendant co-conspirators, jointly and severally. If a defendant settles—which is often at a figure discounted to single damages directly attributable to sales by that defendant—plaintiffs' claim for damages against the remaining defendants is reduced only by the dollar amount of the settlement. Moreover, a defendant who pays more than the share of damages it has caused directly (e.g., the damages attributable to its own sales at the inflated prices) has no recourse against its co-conspirators. Joint tort-feasors have no right to contribution. Texas Indus., Inc. v. Radcliff Materials, Inc., 451 U.S. 630 (1981). However, cooperative amnesty applicants who are given leniency (freedom from fines and jail for supplying detailed information about "their" cartel) are released from liability for the trebled portion of the damages they have caused and from joint and several liability under ACPERA, The Antitrust Criminal Penalties Enhancement and Reform Act of 2004, Pub. L. No. 108–237 (expires in 2020).

This structure of private enforcement can sometimes result in extraordinarily large judgments against a few non-settling defendants, who may be among the few hold-outs from the settlement who decided to go to trial because they believed in the merits of their case (but lost). On the other hand, the prospect of such exposure undoubtedly deters conspiracies. Defendants often control the impact of these rules by agreements among themselves after litigation has been brought.

Private plaintiffs may sue for injunctive relief as well as damages. Under Section 16 of the Clayton Act, "any person" is entitled to an injunction "against threatened loss or damage by a violation of the antitrust laws ... under the same conditions and principles as injunctive relief ... is granted by courts of equity...." To have standing to seek injunctive relief, plaintiffs must be threatened with "antitrust injury," as defined in *Brunswick,* above.

Through a series of cases after *Brunswick,* the courts have defined "antitrust injury" of a sort that will sustain injunctive relief. In Cargill, Inc. v. Monfort of Colorado, Inc., 479 U.S. 104 (1986), the Supreme Court dismissed for lack of standing the plaintiff's suit to enjoin a merger of two of its competitors. The Court said that the plaintiff had failed to show how it might suffer antitrust injury; particularly, it had failed to show that the merged firm was likely to engage in price predation en route to monopolization. If the only effect of the merger was to raise prices, plaintiff competitor would not be injured.

The lawsuit by Sprint and C–Spire to prevent AT&T from acquiring T–Mobile confronted the same problem. Sprint's claims as (merely) a cell phone service competitor were dismissed. But Sprint and C–Spire also made a complaint regarding mobile devices, which are necessary inputs to the supply of cell phone service. They complained that the merger would give AT&T monopsony power to threaten their continued access to mobile devices; AT&T would gain increased power to dictate terms—such as exclusivity—to mobile device manufacturers (such as Apple regarding the iPhone). For this complaint, plaintiffs were in the line of antitrust injury, and the court denied AT&T's motion to dismiss. Sprint Nextel Corp. v. AT&T Inc., ___ F.Supp.3d ___ (D.D.C. Nov. 2, 2011).

Takeover targets are another class of merger-suit plaintiffs. Their standing, too, was called into question by the *Brunswick* principle. The target, like all other antitrust plaintiffs, must show that the challenged act or transaction would cause them antitrust injury. Some courts have denied targets standing, apparently per se, on the theory that the target, becoming part of the merged firm, would be party to and not victim of any anticompetitive advantage gained. See, e.g., Central National Bank v. Rainbolt, 720 F.2d 1183 (10th Cir.1983). But see Consolidated Gold Fields

PLC v. Minorco, S.A., 871 F.2d 252 (2d Cir.1989), cert. dismissed, 492 U.S. 939 (1989).

Two contemporary Supreme Court decisions have narrowed, perhaps substantially, the scope for private enforcement. The first, *Bell Atlantic Corp. v. Twombly*, 550 U.S. 544 (2007), heightened the pleading standard in federal antitrust cases. Under *Twombly*, a claim must be "plausible" at the pleading stage in order to proceed to discovery. Twombly had sued the telecom giants (incumbents) for failing to cross the line into one another's historical territory after the regulatory border-barriers fell. The complaint made the conclusory allegation of a market-division *agreement*, but the alleged facts spoke only of consciously parallel conduct. According to the Court, failure to venture into the territory of one another could rationally be explained as "mere" interdependence: the firms anticipated that, if they stayed out of their neighbor's territory, the neighbor would stay out of theirs. The hypothesis that the firms *agreed* to do so was deemed not sufficiently plausible, and the complaint was dismissed before plaintiffs had an opportunity for discovery.

The second case, *AT&T Mobility LLC v. Concepcion*, 131 S.Ct. 1740 (2011), invalidated a California rule against class action waivers in certain binding arbitration agreements. Each plaintiff's claim in the case was only $30.22; therefore it would pay no victim to arbitrate without a class action, and defendants had closed the door to court litigation by requiring arbitration. Since firms can require arbitration for disputes arising from a contract and can forbid class actions in arbitration, contract-related antitrust claims involving large aggregate but small individual harms may be effectively forestalled.

C. Enforcement of Federal Law by State Attorneys General

State attorneys general may also sue to enforce the federal antitrust laws. They have become major players in federal antitrust litigation, most prominently as co-plaintiffs with the federal government in the *Microsoft* monopolization case. As *parens patriae* on behalf of natural persons residing in their states, they may seek treble damages, along with costs and attorneys fees. The authorizing provisions, Sections 4C to 4H of the Clayton Act, were added to the law by the Hart–Scott–Rodino Antitrust Improvements Act of 1976. This law expressly allows the use of statistical and sampling means to prove aggregate damages, and it authorizes the payment of damages into one fund. The big-fund recovery is called "fluid recovery." For example, if defendants have fixed the price of pencils at one cent higher than the price that would have prevailed without the conspiracy, and the state attorney general can establish by statistical or sampling means that defendants sold ten million pencils in the state at the elevated price during the relevant time period, the state as parens patriae would be awarded $300,000. The state is not put to the burden of calling as witnesses each of the purchasers of the price-fixed pencils.

After the state collects the damages, individuals may come forward to claim their share of the recovery. Money not claimed may be distributed in any manner that the district court may authorize, or the court may declare the money to be a civil penalty and cause it to be deposited with the state as general revenues. Clayton Act, Section 4E.

States may not sue for damages for injury to their general economy. Hawaii v. Standard Oil Co., 405 U.S. 251 (1972). However, states may seek injunctive relief against violations that threaten their economy. Georgia v. Pennsylvania R.R. Co., 324 U.S. 439 (1945).

In the late 1980s when merger enforcement by the federal agencies was at a low level, state attorneys general began to organize a state AG network for merger enforcement. Through the National Association of Attorneys General ("NAAG"), they issued their own merger guidelines, which reflected somewhat more aggressive enforcement than the federal agency merger guidelines. The current NAAG merger guidelines (*http://www.naag.org/assets/files/pdf/at-hmerger_guidelines.pdf*) are largely synchronous with the federal agency merger guidelines. Small differences may be attributable to different default presumptions on questions such as: How robust is potential competition likely to be as a disciplinary force?

Suing under Section 16 of the Clayton Act, the State of California successfully attacked American Stores' acquisition of the stock of one of its major competitors, Lucky Stores, even after the FTC had sued and consented to the acquisition subject to certain minimal divestitures. State of California v. American Stores Co., 495 U.S. 271 (1990). The Supreme Court upheld the district court's grant of a hold-separate order to the state, finding that the state had a reasonable chance of success on the merits and holding that even private parties (and thus states acting on their behalf) may be entitled to divestiture in a merger case if, among other things, they are not barred by laches. A divestiture remedy to private plaintiffs will, however, be very rare if available at all. See Ginsburg v. InBev NV/SA, 623 F.3d 1229 (8th Cir. 2010).

Most famously, 19 states and the District of Columbia joined the federal government in the big monopoly case against Microsoft. See United States v. Microsoft, 253 F.3d 34 (D.C. Cir.), cert. denied, 534 U.S. 952 (2001).

IV. The Reach of the Federal Antitrust Laws—The World, the Nation, the State, the City

Competition policy does not extend to all reaches of United States trade and commerce. State and local governments impose restraints that may lessen competition. The federal government enacts regulatory law and creates exemptions. Foreign government regulation may limit its own firms' competition in the United States. A variety of government granted privileges and government imposed barriers—including licensing statutes and trade restraints—limit the extent to which competitive merit determines success.

With lower barriers to trade in the world, the tension between competition and nationalism, free trade and protected markets, becomes all the more poignant.

A. The Limits of U.S. Antitrust in International Transactions

Transactions that affect American interests increasingly involve foreign commerce. Some challenged acts are directed, authorized, or encouraged by foreign governments. Some are conducted wholly by foreign firms on foreign soil. Some conduct of American firms may cause harm exclusively to foreign interests, and some conduct of foreign firms may harm American interests solely by raising U.S. prices or foreclosing export opportunities. At least two very different sets of facts arise. One, as a matter of statutory construction, how far does the Sherman Act reach? Second, are there other limits to legislative jurisdiction and to the jurisdiction of American courts derived from U.S. foreign relations law or international law in view of the sovereign interests of foreign nations?

The Supreme Court, in an early opinion by Justice Oliver Wendell Holmes, held that the Sherman Act stops at U.S. shores. American Banana Co. v. United Fruit Co., 213 U.S. 347 (1909). Within two decades after *American Banana*, however, this holding was deeply eroded. In United States v. Sisal Sales Corporation, 274 U.S. 268 (1927), the Supreme Court held the Sherman Act applicable to conspiracies and a monopoly in Mexico, involving both private parties and foreign government officials, which threatened to have a direct anticompetitive impact in the United States.

It soon became common ground that the Sherman Act applied even to foreign actors acting abroad when the actors intended to and did affect U.S. commerce and the effects were something more than insubstantial ripples. E.g., United States v. Aluminum Co. of America ("Alcoa"), 148 F.2d 416 (2d Cir.1945); United States v. Watchmakers of Switzerland Info. Center, 133 F.Supp. 40 (S.D.N.Y.1955). This principle became known as the "effects" doctrine. *Alcoa* was often said (somewhat too expansively) to hold that if acts abroad have effects within the United States, they are caught by the Sherman Act.

The effects doctrine always had limits. U.S. courts could not order a foreign firm to do on its home territory that which its home country commanded it not to do, or not to do on its home territory that which its home country ordered it to do. Watchmakers of Switzerland, supra. Moreover, there were (and are) a trio of defenses: (1) Foreign sovereign immunity—The sovereign is immune from suits challenging its sovereign acts (Foreign Sovereign Immunities Act, 28 U.S.C.A. § 1602); (2) Act of State–Courts may not question the validity of the act of a sovereign taken on its own territory; see, for scope and limits, W.S. Kirkpatrick & Co. v. Environmental Tectonics Corp., 493 U.S. 400 (1990); and (3) Foreign sovereign compulsion—If a foreign sovereign compels its own national to do an act, particularly on its own territory, the performance of that act is not a violation of the U.S. law. See Watchmakers of Switzerland, supra.

Within these limits, the U.S. law was very broadly applied in earlier days, but as you will see below, its scope has been narrowed. The law was applied to catch restraints imposed from abroad that hurt American consumers, such as offshore cartels with targeted U.S. effects. U.S. law was also applied to protect American exporters' access to foreign markets. E.g., Continental Ore Co. v. Union Carbide and Carbon Corp., 370 U.S. 690 (1962). Moreover, U.S. law was applied, at least sometimes, to protect foreign firms and foreign consumers from restraints by American firms abroad even when the restraints were permitted by host country law and offended only U.S. law. E.g., Waldbaum v. Worldvision Enterprises, 1978–2 Trade Cas. ¶ 62,378 (S.D.N.Y.1979).

Some lawsuits against foreign firms were class actions for treble damages. In many of these, plaintiffs served extensive American-style discovery requests. The expansive reach of U.S. antitrust law, combined with liberal U.S. discovery practice and the risk of enormous money judgments against losing defendants triggered angry reactions by America's trading partners. Great Britain led the way in objecting to U.S. jurisdiction over British nationals who acted on British territory by acts consistent with British law. See Rio Tinto Zinc Corp. v. Westinghouse Electric Corp., [1978] A.C. 547 (H.L.). Great Britain enacted a "blocking and claw-back" law which blocks discovery of documents located in Britain and entitles British nationals against whom treble damage judgments are entered to "claw-back" in British courts two-thirds of the amount of the judgment paid in the United States. The British Protection of Trading Interests Act of 1980, c. 11 §§ 1–4.

Indirectly at least, pressure was put on U.S. courts to curb their "excesses" in exercising jurisdiction over foreigners. As a result, many U.S. courts retreated from the simple *Alcoa* effects test. They would require that foreign defendants' conduct have a direct, substantial and reasonably foreseeable effect on U.S. commerce, and often purport to balance foreign contacts and interests against U.S. contacts and interests. E.g., Mannington Mills, Inc. v. Congoleum Corp., 595 F.2d 1287 (3d Cir.1979); Timberlane Lumber Co. v. Bank of America, 549 F.2d 597 (9th Cir.1976). See Restatement of Foreign Relations Law (Third) §§ 402, 403, 425 (1987). But see Laker Airways Ltd. v. Sabena, Belgian World Airlines, 731 F.2d 909, 949–50 (D.C.Cir.1984). If U.S. interests were directly and significantly threatened and there was no direct conflict that made compliance with both sets of laws impossible, the balance was virtually always struck in favor of U.S. jurisdiction.

In the early 1980s when the United States faced a serious export deficit, U.S. firms complained that applications of U.S. law to their international transactions handicapped them in their foreign trade and investment. The complaints led Congress to adopt the Export Trading Company Act and the Foreign Trade Antitrust Improvements Act of 1982. The Export Trading Company Act provides a procedure whereby U.S. firms that export or propose to export may seek a certificate of review. To qualify, they must meet certain standards, most notably, that their export activity will not lessen competition within the United States nor create a substantial restraint of the export trade of any competitor. A certificate holder is exempt from the U.S. antitrust laws for activities described in the certificate, except that an injured person may sue for an injunction and single damages if, contrary to predictions, the export activity does lessen competition within the United States or substantially restrain the export trade of a competitor.

The Foreign Trade Antitrust Improvements Act of 1982 (the FTAIA) amends the Sherman Act and the Federal Trade Commission Act. The act is a limitation on the applicability of the Sherman and FTC Acts. The limitation expressly does not apply to conduct involving import trade or commerce. As to conduct involving all other trade or commerce, the Sherman and FTC Acts are declared inapplicable unless the conduct (1) has a "direct, substantial and reasonably foreseeable effect" on U.S. commerce or on the export trade of a person engaged in such trade in the United States, and (2) that effect gives rise to a Sherman or FTC Act offense.

The act thus removed from the scope of the U.S. antitrust laws U.S. firms' acts in foreign commerce where the only persons hurt were foreign competitors or foreign consumers. In other words, as far as the U.S. antitrust laws are concerned, U.S. firms may form export cartels as long as the cartel activity does not spill over into price rises in the United States and does not otherwise harm U.S. competition. In F. Hoffmann–La Roche Ltd. v. Empagran, 542 U.S. 155 (2004), the Supreme Court construed the limits imposed by the FTAIA yet more broadly. It interpreted the act as a sweeping carve-out from the Sherman Act of non-import foreign-related commerce; as restoring to Sherman Act coverage conduct that falls within (1) or (2) above, and as construing (2) as requiring that the particular plaintiff must be injured by the anticompetitive effect within the United States.

While the reach of U.S. law has been limited, other nations may, and many do, apply their own competition laws to imports into their countries. For example, the European Union prohibits importers from implementing a price-fixing conspiracy therein. A. Ahlstrom Osakeyhtio v. Commission (Wood pulp), Cases 89 et al./185, [1988] ECR 5193.

Meanwhile, in the 1990s there were two major sets of developments, one regarding inbound trade and the other regarding U.S. exports. In the first category, the U.S. Supreme Court decided Hartford Fire Ins. Co. v. California, 509 U.S. 764 (1993), which concerned conspiracies of U.S. and London reinsurers to cut back the scope of the reinsurance package that they would offer to insureds in the United States. Refusing to dismiss the London insurers, the Supreme Court held that existence in the UK of an insurance regulatory regime that entrusted self regulation to the industry did not create a conflict that would warrant dismissal on the basis of comity. The Court said: "the Sherman Act applies to foreign conduct that was meant to produce and did in fact produce some substantial effect in the United States.'' *Id.* at 796.

The second set of developments involves U.S. exports. U.S. business had persistently complained that Japan and Japanese business blocked the entry of U.S. firms by tariff and non-tariff barriers. In 1991–1992 the United States was involved in negotiations with Japan called the Structural Impediments Initiative, or SII. While the United States Trade Representative was negotiating with the Japanese government for better terms of trade, the Assistant Attorney General in Charge of the Antitrust Division announced that he was looking for the right case to bring under the Sherman Act against American subsidiaries of Japanese firms that were maintaining an exclusionary cartel in Japan to block access of Americans to the Japanese market. The Clinton Administration incorporated the concept into the 1995 Guidelines on International Operations. (See Appendix (F)).

In addition to extraterritorial limits to the reach of the law, there are defenses or exemptions based on the sovereign status of the defendant, Act of [a foreign] State, and compulsion by a foreign state. OPEC—the Organization of Petroleum Exporting Countries, formed in Iraq in 1960—has maintained an oil producers' cartel for half a century, yet it is commonly understood that the cartel is beyond the reach of U.S. antitrust law. See e.g., Spectrum Stores, Inc. v. Citgo Petroleum Corp., 632 F.3d 938 (5th Cir.2011) (dismissing for lack of jurisdiction). Perennially, Congress entertains a bill, NOPEC (No Oil Producing or Exporting Cartel) that would allow the Justice Department to break up OPEC; but the bill has not had serious traction.

Frequently, foreign defendants raise Act of State, foreign sovereign compulsion, and comity defenses. They have done so, for example, in the case of a vitamin C cartel of Chinese producers supported by the Chinese Ministry of Commerce. Courts have rather consistently rejected such defenses in the absence of real compulsion. E.g., Vitamin C Antitrust Litigation, 810 F.Supp.2d 522 (E.D.N.Y. 2011). See generally E. Fox and D. Crane, GLOBAL ISSUES IN ANTITRUST AND COMPETITION LAW (2010).

B. The Limits of U.S. Antitrust in Domestic Transactions

1. *Interstate and Intrastate Commerce: What is de minimis?*

The Sherman Act covers agreements or acts ''in restraint of trade or commerce among the several States, or with foreign nations.'' The Clayton Act has a similar commerce requirement. The threshold requirement for finding a sufficient impact on interstate commerce is quite low. In Summit Health, Ltd. v. Pinhas, 500 U.S. 322 (1991), the plaintiff, an ophthalmologist on the staff of a Los Angeles hospital, claimed to be the victim of a boycott carried out through a peer review process and resulting in termination of his staff privileges at the hospital. The defendants sought to have the case dismissed for lack of interstate commerce. Defendant relied on the fact there was no allegation and could be no proof that the termination of the doctor's staff privileges affected interstate commerce. The Supreme Court rejected defendants' argument, by a five to four vote. The Court held that effect on commerce must be measured "by a general evaluation of the impact of the restraint on other participants and potential participants in the market from which [the plaintiff] has been excluded." Since the market from which plaintiff was excluded was in interstate commerce and the peer review process was also in interstate commerce, the jurisdictional requirement was satisfied.

Virtually all states have antitrust laws of their own; in most cases the language is quite similar to that of the Sherman Act. State antitrust law governs restraints in intrastate commerce and may apply as well to restraints that have effects both in and out of the state. Thus, in many transactions, both federal and state law apply.

2. *Federal Exemptions*

Federal law contains a series of exemptions from the federal antitrust laws. Some exemptions are explicit; e.g., the labor exemption in Clayton Act § 6, the Capper–Volstead Act's exemption for agricultural cooperatives (7 U.S.C. §§ 291, 292 (1922)), and an exemption for restraints in the business of insurance other than boycotts for companies regulated by the states. 15 U.S.C. §§ 1011, 1012 (1988) (McCarran–Ferguson). The Airline Deregulation Act of 1978, Pub. L. No. 95–504, 92 Stat. 1705 (1978), authorized the Department of Transportation to grant case-by-case antitrust exemptions to the airlines, a power theretofore exercised by the Civil Aeronautics Board. Exemptions have been extended to "open skies" agreements, inter-airline alliances, and, notably, the practice known as "code sharing" whereby airlines sell seats on one another's flights.

Other exemptions are implicit; an exemption is implied where necessary to make a regulatory statute work. United States v. National Ass'n of Securities Dealers, 422 U.S. 694 (1975); Gordon v. New York Stock Exchange, 422 U.S. 659 (1975). It is also implied in cases of clear repugnance. Credit Suisse v. Billing, 551 U.S. 264 (2007). The Supreme Court has stated, "Repeals of the antitrust laws by implication from a regulatory statute are strongly disfavored, and have only been found in cases of plain repugnancy between the antitrust laws and regulatory provisions." United States v. Philadelphia Nat'l Bank, 374 U.S. 321, 350–51 (1963). Accordingly, even in regulated industries such as the telephone industry (pre-breakup), the electric power industry, and the health care industry, the antitrust laws were held to apply. Otter Tail Power Co. v. United States, 410 U.S. 366 (1973); United States v. American Telephone and Telegraph Co., 524 F.Supp. 1336 (D.D.C.1981). But *Credit Suisse*, above, has lowered the bar for clear repugnance.

There are several other exemptions from antitrust law that are simply vestiges of the past. The reserve system of professional baseball is not subject to the federal antitrust laws because, in 1922 when the first antitrust test against baseball came before the Supreme Court, baseball games were likened to exhibitions and were deemed not to be a subject of commerce. Federal Baseball Club v. National League, 259 U.S. 200 (1922). The concept of commerce greatly expanded over the years and now clearly includes professional sports, but Congress never repealed the 1922 precedent despite the repeated introduction of bills to do so. The exemption continues in view of Congress's "positive inaction." See Flood v. Kuhn, 407 U.S. 258, 283 (1972). See also Square D Company v. Niagara Frontier Tariff Bureau, Inc., 476 U.S. 409 (1986), reaffirming the "Keogh" rule which holds that rates filed by carriers with the Interstate Commerce Commission are not a basis for treble damages.

3. State Action

One of the most important exceptions from competition policy is state and local government regulation. In many areas of business, state or local regulation substitutes for market forces. State regulation is an incident of state sovereignty and is not invalidated by reason of its tendency to restrain trade or commerce as long as it does not impose an undue burden on interstate commerce or conflict with the federal antitrust laws. Thus, a Maryland law prohibiting producers and refiners of gasoline from operating retail service stations in the state was held valid and not preempted either by the commerce clause or by the antitrust laws. The Court said: "[I]f an adverse effect on competition were, in and of itself, enough to render a state statute invalid, the State's power to engage in economic regulation would be effectively destroyed." Exxon Corp. v. Governor of Maryland, 437 U.S. 117, 133 (1978)(footnote omitted). On the other hand, the state has no power to authorize or even order private persons to do an act that violates the federal antitrust laws (such as to fix prices) and give the actors immunity from the federal antitrust laws. Schwegmann Bros. v. Calvert Distillers, 341 U.S. 384 (1951). Such state action would create a direct conflict with the federal law and would be preempted. Id. See also California Retail Liquor Dealers Ass'n v. Midcal Aluminum, Inc., 445 U.S. 97 (1980) ("Midcal").

If not preempted and if not an impermissible regulation of commerce (see Section V infra), state action is valid no matter how seriously it restrains competition. E.g., Hoover v. Ronwin, 466 U.S. 558 (1984)(alleged cartel to limit the number of lawyers in Arizona). Moreover, state officials, local governments and private persons carrying out state policy may be accorded some of the benefits of state action immunity.

The case law defining the contours of the state action exemption has been evolving for half a century. We summarize its evolution.

The first and most famous state action case was an action by a California raisin farmer against California state officials to enjoin the officials from carrying out the state's raisin cartel—a stabilization program designed to cure the evils of overproduction of raisins in California. The Supreme Court dismissed the case, holding that the Sherman Act was not intended to prohibit states from exercising control over their own officials in imposing restraints on their domestic commerce. Parker v.

Brown, 317 U.S. 341 (1943). Thus was born the *Parker* doctrine, which, for many years, was thought to shield broadly both public and private acts undertaken pursuant to state and local regulation.

Beginning in the mid 1970s, the Court chipped away at the doctrine. In Goldfarb v. Virginia State Bar, 421 U.S. 773 (1975), in a suit against state and county bar associations for lawyer fee-fixing through minimum fee schedules, the Court upheld liability despite the fact that the state bar, which in one capacity was an arm of the state, approved of and facilitated the fee schedules. The Court said: "It is not enough that ... anticompetitive conduct is 'prompted' by state action; rather, anticompetitive activities must be compelled by direction of the State acting as sovereign." Id. at 790. [But note the later qualification in *Midcal*, below.] Shortly thereafter, in Cantor v. Detroit Edison Company, 428 U.S. 579 (1976), the Supreme Court held that an electric utility's practice of providing its customers with "free" light bulbs along with electricity was not immune from antitrust scrutiny although the tie-in was ordered to be carried out by a state-approved tariff. The Court stressed the fact that Detroit Edison itself had originated the light bulb plan and that the state had no policy regarding light bulbs.

In the following year the Court decided *Midcal*, supra, which remains one of the principal state-action authorities. By statute, California had directed wine producers to fix resale prices in the state, and a discounter had failed to comply with its supplier's price list. The Court held the state statute invalid. The Court ruled that valid state action must meet a two-prong requirement: (1) The state must have a clearly articulated and affirmatively expressed policy to replace competition with regulation, and (2) there must be active supervision by the state. California had failed to meet the first prong.

Meanwhile, there evolved a line of cases involving municipal action. Antitrust cases were brought against cities, and the cities moved to dismiss on grounds that they, the cities, stood in the place of the state and were entitled to assert the state action exemption. In City of Lafayette v. Louisiana Power and Light Company, 435 U.S. 389 (1978), the Supreme Court held that municipal action is not exempt from the federal antitrust laws. Cities are not sovereign; they do not need the freedom to take governmental initiatives that may impair competition, as do the states. Autonomous city regulation (said a plurality of the Court) creates the danger of parochial restraints at the expense of the public. Therefore, exemption must depend upon whether the state authorized the municipality to operate as it did or whether it "contemplated the kind of action complained of." 435 U.S. at 413.

Local officials' fears of litigation were further fueled by the Supreme Court's decision in Community Communications Company v. City of Boulder, 455 U.S. 40 (1982). Boulder was a home rule city. Under the Constitution of the State of Colorado, a home rule city's laws were supreme, even in the event of conflict with laws of the state. Nonetheless,

Boulder's allegedly anticompetitive cable ordinance (which temporarily prevented an incumbent from expanding) was held subject to antitrust scrutiny.

Lafayette and *Boulder* opened the door to a plethora of challenges to cities' social regulation. Claiming that city taxi cab regulation, which limits entry and price, was an unfair method of competition in violation of the Federal Trade Commission Act, the FTC sued two cities—Minneapolis and New Orleans—seeking to dismantle the regulation. 46 BNA Antitrust & Trade Reg. Rep. 970 (May 17, 1984). On the private front, landlords in Berkeley, California sued Berkeley, claiming that its rent stabilization ordinance was both anticompetitive and unconstitutional. The FTC attack on city taxi regulation failed when the states came to the aid of their cities; they specifically authorized the cities' taxi regulation and mooted the suits. In the private attack on rent control, the City of Berkeley won. The Court held that the Sherman Act did not preempt the rent control ordinance because the ordinance did not compel or authorize conduct that was illegal; it did not, for example, compel the landlords to combine and fix prices. Fisher v. City of Berkeley, 475 U.S. 260 (1986).

In 1984, Congress passed the Local Government Antitrust Act, relieving cities and city employees acting in an official capacity of damages for violation of the antitrust laws. The statute does not immunize local governments or officials from injunctive relief.

A remaining question on local government action was clarified in Town of Hallie v. City of Eau Claire, 471 U.S. 34 (1985). Active state supervision is not a requirement where the actor is a municipality. Merely, there must be clear state articulation of a policy to replace competition with regulation. This requirement is satisfied if the state "has delegated to the cities the express authority to take action that foreseeably will result in anticompetitive effects."

Also the Court held that a private party seeking the benefit of the state action defense need not be acting pursuant to *direction* by the state. It is enough that the state has a policy to permit the anticompetitive activity and that the state actively supervises the outcome. Southern Motor Carriers Rate Conference v. United States, 471 U.S. 48 (1985) (carriers combined in rate bureaus to fix proposed tariffs).

In 1992 the Court clarified the second prong of *Midcal:* Active state supervision is a serious and demanding requirement, to assure that the activity is properly attributable to the state. The state must play a substantial role in determining the specifics of the conduct. Thus, a mere negative option of the state to disapprove jointly filed insurance rates does not qualify for state action immunity, absent detailed scrutiny by the state. FTC v. Ticor Title Ins. Co., 504 U.S. 621 (1992).

In short, action that is an act of the state itself is not covered by the antitrust laws. An act of a city that is authorized by the state pursuant to a clearly articulated policy to replace competition with regulation or that is authorized by the state and entails restraints that are foreseeably anticompetitive is exempt. An act of a private party that is directed or permitted by the state (or by an authorized local government) pursuant to such a clearly articulated policy and that is actively supervised by state or local government is exempt. If the scope of these resulting exemptions is unduly broad, recourse lies with Congress.

4. Petitioning Government and Political Boycott

There is a right to petition and lobby for government action, even by competitors in combination with one another and even though the conspirators' sole intent is to kill the competition. This exception is called the *Noerr–Pennington* doctrine, named after Eastern Railroad Presidents Conference v. Noerr Motor Freight, Inc., 365 U.S. 127 (1961) and United Mine Workers v. Pennington, 381 U.S. 657 (1965). The doctrine applies only when government action is seriously invoked and not when the petitioning is mere sham. California Motor Transport Company v. Trucking Unlimited, 404 U.S. 508 (1972).

A lawsuit can qualify as a sham only if it is "objectively baseless" and is " 'an attempt to interfere *directly* with the business relationships of a competitor' " through the use of the government process (the court system) rather than through the outcome of the lawsuit. Professional Real Estate Investors v. Columbia Pictures, 508 U.S. 49 (1993). "Objectively baseless" means no reasonable person would expect a court victory.

What is the effect of defendant's fraud and deceit? The campaign in *Noerr* itself was rife with misstatements, and defendants showered gifts and campaign contributions on government officials to get their anticompetitive legislation. The immunity is available even if the defendant procured the government action by deceit (e.g., Mercatus Group, LLC v. Lake Forest Hosp., 641 F.3d 834 (7th Cir. 2011)) or bribery, if the defendant conspired with legislators to procure the result, or if the outcome was against the "public interest." "[T]he antitrust laws regulate business, not politics.... " City of Columbia v. Omni Outdoor Advertising, Inc., 499 U.S. 365 (1991).

But in judicial and non-legislative administrative proceedings, fraud may disentitle the petitioner to a *Noerr* defense. See Allied Tube & Conduit Corp. v. Indian Head, Inc., 486 U.S. 492, 500 (1988). A party that (1) knowingly misleads a court or other adjudicative body and (2) thereby actually influences its decision forfeits immunity. The courts draw the distinction, somewhat uneasily, between political (legislative) activity, which the First Amendment strongly protects, and adjudicative proceedings, which must be free of misconduct in order to be functional and fair. In *Mercatus Group*, supra, the Seventh Circuit, identified as the crucial question the level of discretion at which a decision-maker operates: If the decision-maker is basically free to choose what it will, the matter is legislative and therefore political; if it is basically confined to reaching conclusions of fact and law, the proceeding is adjudicative.

While the *Noerr-Pennington* doctrine shields conduct designed to hurt competitors by procuring government action, a related concept shields conduct designed to procure political action by hurting traders; i.e., grass-roots boycotts. NAACP v. Claiborne Hardware, 458 U.S. 886 (1982).

The Supreme Court qualified the political boycott exception in FTC v. Superior Court Trial Lawyers Ass'n, 493 U.S. 411 (1990). There, lawyers who regularly accepted appointments by the District of Columbia court to represent indigent criminal defendants ("CJA regulars") lobbied for an increase in their $20 and $30 per hour statutorily-prescribed fees. They claimed that higher fees were necessary to attract sufficient lawyers and to provide proper representation to the indigent defendants. When lobbying failed, almost all of the CJA regulars engaged in a boycott to call attention to their plight. They agreed among themselves to accept no new cases until their fees were raised. The lawyers created a crisis, and the D.C. Council raised their fees. Noting that the lawyers' acts were both a boycott and a price fixing agreement, that the lawyers had restrained trade to get government action rather than seeking government action to restrain trade, and that the lawyers themselves stood to profit financially from their boycott and cartel, the Court held the activity illegal. It rejected both *Noerr-Pennington* and First Amendment defenses.

V. The Commerce and Supremacy Clauses and the Reach of Competition Policy

The Commerce Clause of the Constitution of the United States provides that Congress shall regulate interstate commerce. State regulatory statutes may run afoul of the Commerce Clause if they discriminate against interstate commerce, regulate wholly out-of-state commerce, or impose an undue burden on interstate commerce. A Connecticut statute required out-of-state shippers of beer to affirm that their posted prices for beer sold to Connecticut wholesalers were no higher than the prices at which the shippers sold the same products in bordering states at the time of the posting. The Supreme Court held that the statute impermissibly burdened and discriminated against interstate commerce and was unconstitutional. Healy v. Beer Institute, Inc., 491 U.S. 324 (1989).

In West Lynn Creamery v. Healy, 512 U.S. 186 (1994), the Supreme Court held unconstitutional a Massachusetts pricing order that taxed all milk sold in or into the state, and directed the distribution of all of these tax moneys to the Massachusetts dairy farmers, who were struggling to compete with lower-cost out-of-state dairy farmers. The Supreme Court characterized the order as "economic protectionism" which the dormant commerce clause prohibits. Note, however, that U.S. law, unlike European Union law, does not prohibit state subsidies, and the Court was able to reach its conclusion only in view of the fact that a tax was involved, even though the tax itself was non-discriminatory.

The Supremacy Clause provides that federal law shall be supreme; it prevails over, or preempts, any inconsistent state law to the extent that interstate commerce is implicated. Federal law can preempt state law by express language or by language from which Congress's intent to preempt is made clear. Also, federal law can preempt state law by occupying an entire field so that there is no room for state law; and federal law is preemptive where the state law will necessarily undermine the scheme of the federal law. Courts are reluctant to find preemption by implication, however. In CTS Corp. v. Dynamics Corp. of America, 481 U.S. 69 (1987), the Supreme Court held that a state takeover statute that gave extra benefits to a local takeover target was not preempted by the Williams Act (and also that it did not impose an undue burden on interstate commerce in securities); and in California v. ARC America, 490 U.S. 93 (1989), the Supreme Court held that a state antitrust law that allowed indirect purchasers to recover their antitrust damages was not preempted by the Clayton Act, even though the Clayton Act (under the *Illinois Brick* doctrine) disallows damage recovery by indirect purchasers, largely because proof complications would unduly burden the system.

In connection with mergers that threaten to cause both local and interstate effects, both state and federal law may apply to the same transaction. The laws of several foreign nations may apply as well if the merger has a transnational dimension. In the 1980s, Mobil Oil, based in Texas, pursued a hostile takeover of Marathon Oil, based in Ohio. The case was settled when Mobil worked out a consent decree with the federal government agreeing to spin off its Yates oil field. With the spin-off, the federal government regarded the takeover as procompetitive. But Marathon sued under the Ohio antitrust law and the Ohio state court judge had a negative view of the competitive effects of the takeover. Could the Ohio court enjoin the merger? Would the federal merger laws preempt the Ohio law, in its application? Would the Ohio injunction constitute an undue burden on interstate commerce? One of the few opinions analyzing this issue is the concurring and dissenting opinion of Judge Mosk in State of California v. Texaco, Inc., 762 P.2d 385, 399, 425–30 (Cal. Sup. Ct. 1988), regarding the possible application of California antitrust law to a leading interstate oil company's acquisition of the California assets of another interstate oil company. Judge Mosk observed that the state had an interest in "a free and competitive market in the supply and transportation of crude oil." He concluded that the merger was not beyond the state's power to regulate, and that a state prohibition would not have been an undue burden on interstate commerce under the Commerce Clause.

Public policy issues of this sort, raised to a global level, are magnified in a more nearly integrated world of multitudinous antitrust enforcers.

VI. End Note

This essay sets out procedural, legislative and jurisdictional scope and limits of U.S. antitrust law and examines the scope for and balances between various centers of sovereign authority. The main body of the Casebook addresses the substantive scope of antitrust, with occasional reference to the procedural and jurisdictional framework of the law.

There has been a perceptible interplay between substance, procedure, limits of competence, and enforcement patterns. When substantive scope is thought to have expanded too far (as was perceived in the early 1980s), new procedural rules and doctrine—such as standing rules—tend to develop to rein it in. When the prime U.S. enforcer (the federal government) under-enforces the law, other enforcers—such as the states—step in. When a nation treads too far on to the territory of another nation, the response of the offended sovereign, and counter-reactions of the first, set in motion the emergence of a new equilibrium.

Reflect on whether U.S. law has struck an appropriate balance between national concerns and foreign concerns, between federal concerns and state and local concerns, and between competition policy and other federal policies.

APPENDIX B

U.S. STATUTES AND EUROPEAN UNION TREATIES

■ ■ ■

Table of Contents

I. U.S. Statutes

A. THE SHERMAN ACT 1890, as amended 15 U.S.C. §§ 1–7

Section 1. Every contract, combination in the form of trust or otherwise, or conspiracy, in restraint of trade or commerce among the several States, or with foreign nations, is declared to be illegal. Every person who shall make any contract or engage in any combination or conspiracy hereby declared to be illegal shall be deemed guilty of a felony, and, on conviction thereof, shall be punished by fine not exceeding $100,000,000 if a corporation, or, if any other person, $1,000,000, or by imprisonment not exceeding 10 years, or by both said punishments, in the discretion of the court.

Section 2. Every person who shall monopolize, or attempt to monopolize, or combine or conspire with any other person or persons, to monopolize any part of the trade or commerce among the several States, or with foreign nations, shall be deemed guilty of a felony, and, on conviction thereof, shall be punished by fine not exceeding $100,000,000 if a corporation, or, if any other person, $1,000,000, or by imprisonment not exceeding 10 years, or by both said punishments, in the discretion of the court.*

Section 3. (a) Every contract, combination in form of trust or otherwise, or conspiracy, in restraint of trade or commerce in any Territory of the United States or of the District of Columbia, or in restraint of trade or commerce between any such Territory and another, or between any such Territory or Territories and any State or States or the District of Columbia, or with foreign nations, or between the District of Columbia and any State or States or foreign nations, is declared illegal. Every person who shall make any such contract or engage in any such combination or conspiracy, shall be deemed guilty of a felony, and, on conviction thereof, shall be punished by fine not exceeding $100,000,000 if a corporation, or, if any other person, $1,000,000, or by imprisonment not exceeding 10 years, or by both said punishments, in the discretion of the court. (b) Every person who shall monopolize, or attempt to monopolize, or combine or conspire with any other person or persons, to monopolize any part of the trade or commerce in any Territory of the United States or of the District of Columbia, or between any such Territory and another, or between any such Territory or Territories and any State or States or the District of Columbia, or with foreign nations, or between the District of Columbia, and any State or States or foreign nations, shall be deemed guilty of a felony, and, on conviction thereof, shall be punished by fine not exceeding $100,000,000 if a corporation, or, if any other person, $1,000,000, or by imprisonment not exceeding 10 years, or by both said punishments, in the discretion of the court.

Section 4. The several district courts of the United States are invested with jurisdiction to prevent and restrain violations of sections 1 to 7 of this title; and it shall be the duty of the several United States attorneys, in their respective districts, under the direction of the Attorney General, to institute proceedings in equity to prevent and restrain such violations. Such proceedings may be by way of petition setting forth the case and praying that such violation shall be enjoined or otherwise prohibited. When the parties complained of shall have been duly notified of such petition the court shall proceed, as soon as may be, to the hearing and determination of the case; and pending such petition and before final decree, the court may at any time make such temporary restraining order or prohibition as shall be deemed just in the premises.

* * *

Section 6. Any property owned under any contract or by any combination, or pursuant to any conspiracy (and being the subject thereof) mentioned in section [one of this Act], and being in the course of transportation from one State to another, or to a foreign country, shall be forfeited to the United States, and may be seized and condemned by like proceedings as those provided by law for the forfeiture, seizure, and

* The Sentencing Reform Act of 1984, 18 U.S.C. § 3571, specifies an alternative fine of not more than the greater of twice the gain or loss from the violation.

condemnation of property imported into the United States contrary to law.

Section 7. [added by the Foreign Trade Antitrust Improvements Act of 1982, 15 U.S.C. § 6A]. Sections 1 to 7 of this title [the Sherman Act] shall not apply to conduct involving trade or commerce (other than import trade or import commerce) with foreign nations unless

(1) such conduct has a direct, substantial, and reasonably foreseeable effect

(A) on trade or commerce which is not trade or commerce with foreign nations, or on import trade or import commerce with foreign nations; or

(B) on export trade or export commerce with foreign nations, of a person engaged in such trade or commerce in the United States; and

(2) such effect gives rise to a claim under the provisions of [this Act], other than this section.

If sections 1 to 7 of this title apply to such conduct only because of the operation of paragraph (1)(B), then sections 1 to 7 of this title shall apply to such conduct only for injury to export business in the United States.

B. THE CLAYTON ACT 1914, as amended 15 U.S.C. §§ 12–27

Section 1. (a) "Antitrust laws," as used herein, includes the Act entitled "An Act to protect trade and commerce against unlawful restraints and monopolies," approved July second, eighteen hundred and ninety; sections [of Wilson Tariff Act amendments, prohibiting combinations in import trade]; and also this Act.

"Commerce," as used herein, means trade or commerce among the several States and with foreign nations, or between the District of Columbia or any Territory of the United States and any State, Territory, or foreign nation, or between any insular possessions or other places under the jurisdiction of the United States, or between any such possession or place and any State or Territory of the United States or the District of Columbia or any foreign nation, or within the District of Columbia or any Territory or any insular possession or other place under the jurisdiction of the United States: *Provided,* That nothing in this Act contained shall apply to the Philippine Islands.

The word "person" or "persons" wherever used in this Act shall be deemed to include corporations and associations existing under or authorized by the laws of either the United States, the laws of any of the Territories, the laws of any State, or the laws of any foreign country.

(b) This Act may be cited as the "Clayton Act".

Section 2. [See Robinson–Patman Act, infra.]

Section 3. It shall be unlawful for any person engaged in commerce, in the course of such commerce, to lease or make a sale or contract for sale of goods, wares, merchandise, machinery, supplies, or other commodities, whether patented or unpatented, for use, consumption, or resale within the United States or any Territory thereof or the District of Columbia or any insular possession or other place under the jurisdiction of the United States, or fix a price charged therefor, or discount from, or rebate upon, such price, on the condition, agreement, or understanding that the lessee or purchaser thereof shall not use or deal in the goods, wares, merchandise, machinery, supplies, or other commodities of a competitor or competitors of the lessor or seller, where the effect of such lease, sale, or contract for sale or such condition, agreement, or understanding may be to substantially lessen competition or tend to create a monopoly in any line of commerce.

Section 4. (a) Except as provided in subsection (b) of this section, any person who shall be injured in his business or property by reason of anything forbidden in the antitrust laws may sue therefor in any district court of the United States in the district in which the defendant resides or is found or has an agent, without respect to the amount in controversy, and shall recover threefold the damages by him sustained, and the cost of suit, including a reasonable attorney's fee....

> (b)(1) Except as provided in paragraph (2), any person who is a foreign state may not recover under subsection (a) of this section an amount in excess of the actual damages sustained by it and the cost of suit, including a reasonable attorney's fee.
>
> (2) Paragraph (1) shall not apply to a foreign state if—
>
> (A) such foreign state would be denied, under section 1605(a)(2) of Title 28, immunity in a case in which the action is based upon a commercial activity, or an act, that is the subject matter of its claim under this section;
>
> (B) such foreign state waives all defenses based upon or arising out of its status as a foreign state, to any claims brought against it in the same action;
>
> (C) such foreign state engages primarily in commercial activities; and
>
> (D) such foreign state does not function, with respect to the commercial activity, or the act, that is the subject matter of its claim under this section as a procurement entity for itself or for another foreign state.

(c) For purposes of this section—

(1) the term "commercial activity" shall have the meaning given it in section 1603(d) of Title 28, and

(2) the term "foreign state" shall have the meaning given it in section 1603(a) of Title 28.

Section 4A. Whenever the United States is hereafter injured in its business or property by reason of anything forbidden in the antitrust laws it may sue therefor in the United States district court for the district in which the defendant resides or is found or has an agent, without respect to the amount in controversy, and shall recover actual damages by it sustained and the cost of suit....

Section 4B. Any action to enforce any cause of action under section [4, 4A or 4C of this Act] shall be forever barred unless commenced within four years after the cause of action accrued. No cause of action barred under existing law on the effective date of this Act shall be revived by this Act.

Section 4C. (a)(1) Any attorney general of a State may bring a civil action in the name of such State, as parens patriae on behalf of natural persons residing in such State, in any district court of the United States having jurisdiction of the defendant, to secure monetary relief as provided in this section for injury sustained by such natural persons to their property by reason of any violation of the Sherman Act. The court shall exclude from the amount of monetary relief awarded in such action any amount of monetary relief (A) which duplicates amounts which have been awarded for the same injury, or (B) which is properly allocable to (i) natural persons who have excluded their claims pursuant to subsection (b)(2) of this section, and (ii) any business entity.

(2) The court shall award the State as monetary relief threefold the total damage sustained as described in paragraph (1) of this subsection, and the cost of suit, including a reasonable attorney's fee....

* * *

Section 6. The labor of a human being is not a commodity or article of commerce. Nothing contained in the antitrust laws shall be construed to forbid the existence and operation of labor, agricultural, or horticultural organizations, instituted for the purposes of mutual help, and not having capital stock or conducted for profit, or to forbid or restrain individual members of such organizations from lawfully carrying out the legitimate objects thereof; nor shall such organizations, or the members thereof, be held or construed to be illegal combinations or conspiracies in restraint of trade, under the antitrust laws.

Section 7. No person engaged in commerce or in any activity affecting commerce shall acquire, directly or indirectly, the whole or any part of the stock or other share capital and no person subject to the jurisdiction of the Federal Trade Commission shall acquire the whole or any part of the assets of another person engaged also in commerce or in any activity affecting commerce, where in any line of commerce or in any activity affecting commerce in any section of the country, the effect of such acquisition may be substantially to lessen competition, or to tend to create a monopoly.

No person shall acquire, directly or indirectly, the whole or any part of the stock or other share capital and no person subject to the jurisdiction of the Federal Trade Commission shall acquire the whole or any part of the assets of one or more persons engaged in commerce or in any activity affecting commerce, where in any line of commerce or in any activity affecting commerce in any section of the country, the effect of such acquisition, of such stocks or assets, or of the use of such stock by the voting or granting of proxies or otherwise, may be substantially to lessen competition, or to tend to create a monopoly.

This section shall not apply to persons purchasing such stock solely for investment and not using the same by voting or otherwise to bring about, or in attempting to bring about, the substantial lessening of competition. Nor shall anything contained in this section prevent a corporation engaged in commerce or in any activity affecting commerce from causing the formation of subsidiary corporations for the actual carrying on of their immediate lawful business, or the natural and legitimate branches or extensions thereof, or from owning and holding all or a part of the stock of such subsidiary corporations, when the effect of such formation is not to substantially lessen competition.

Nor shall anything herein contained be construed to prohibit any common carrier subject to the laws to regulate commerce from aiding in the construction of branches or short lines so located as to become feeders to the main line of the company so aiding in such construction or from acquiring or owning all or any part of the stock of such branch lines, nor to prevent any such common carrier from acquiring and owning all or any part of the stock of a branch or short line constructed by an independent company where there is no substantial competition between the company owning the branch line so constructed and the company owning the main line acquiring the property or an interest therein, nor to prevent such common carrier from extending any of its lines through the medium of the acquisition of stock or otherwise of any other common carrier where there is no substantial competition between the company extending its lines and the company whose stock, property, or an interest therein is so acquired.

Nothing contained in this section shall be held to affect or impair any right heretofore legally acquired: *Provided,* That nothing in this section shall be held or construed to authorize or make lawful anything heretofore prohibited or made illegal by the antitrust laws, nor to exempt any person from the penal provisions thereof or the civil remedies therein provided.

Nothing contained in this section shall apply to transactions duly consummated pursuant to authority given by the Civil Aeronautics Board, Federal Communications Commission, Federal Power Commission, Interstate Commerce Commission, the Securities and Exchange Commission in the exercise of its jurisdiction under section 79j of this title, the United States Maritime Commission, or the Secretary of Agriculture under any statutory provision vesting such power in such Commission, Secretary, or Board.

* * *

Section 7A [The Hart–Scott–Rodino Act] Premerger notification and waiting period

(a) Filing

Except as exempted pursuant to subsection (c), no person shall acquire, directly or indirectly, any voting securities or assets of any other person, unless both persons (or in the case of a tender offer, the acquiring person) file notification pursuant to rules under subsection (d)(1) and the waiting period described in subsection (b)(1) has expired, if—

(1) the acquiring person, or the person whose voting securities or assets are being acquired, is engaged in commerce or in any activity affecting commerce; and

(2) as a result of such acquisition, the acquiring person would hold an aggregate total amount of the voting securities and assets of the acquired person—

(A) in excess of $200,000,000 (as adjusted and published for each fiscal year beginning after September 30, 2004, in the same manner as provided in section 8(a)(5) to reflect the percentage change in the gross national product for such fiscal year compared to the gross national product for the year ending September 30, 2003); or

(B)(i) in excess of $50,000,000 (as so adjusted and published) but not in excess of $200,000,000 (as so adjusted and published); and

(ii)(I) any voting securities or assets of a person engaged in manufacturing which has annual net sales or total assets of $10,000,000 (as so adjusted and published) or more are being acquired by any person which has total assets or annual net sales of $100,000,000 (as so adjusted and published) or more;

(II) any voting securities or assets of a person not engaged in manufacturing which has total assets of $10,000,000 (as so adjusted and published) or more are being acquired by any person which has total assets or annual net sales of $100,000,000 (as so adjusted and published) or more; or

(III) any voting securities or assets of a person with annual net sales or total assets of $100,000,000 (as so adjusted and published) or more are being acquired by any person with total assets or annual net sales of $10,000,000 (as so adjusted and published) or more.

In the case of a tender offer, the person whose voting securities are sought to be acquired by a person required to file notification under this subsection shall file notification pursuant to rules under subsection (d).

(b) Waiting period; publication; voting securities

(1) The waiting period required under subsection (a) of this section shall—

(A) begin on the date of the receipt by the Federal Trade Commission and the Assistant Attorney General in charge of the Antitrust Division of the Department of Justice (hereinafter referred to in this section as the "Assistant Attorney General") of—

(i) the completed notification required under subsection (a) of this section,

or

(ii) if such notification is not completed, the notification to the extent completed and a statement of the reasons for such noncompliance, from both persons, or, in the case of a tender offer, the acquiring person; and

(B) end on the thirtieth day after the date of such receipt (or in the case of a cash tender offer, the fifteenth day), or on such later date as may be set under subsection (e)(2) or (g)(2) of this section.

(2) The Federal Trade Commission and the Assistant Attorney General may, in individual cases, terminate the waiting period specified in paragraph (1) and allow any person to proceed with any acquisition subject to this section, and promptly shall cause to be published in the Federal Register a notice that neither intends to take any action within such period with respect to such acquisition.

(3) As used in this section—

(A) The term "voting securities" means any securities which at present or upon conversion entitle the owner or holder thereof to vote for the election of directors of the issuer or, with respect to unincorporated issuers, persons exercising similar functions.

(B) The amount or percentage of voting securities or assets of a person which are acquired or held by another person shall be determined by aggregating the amount or percentage of such voting securities or assets held or acquired by such other person and each affiliate thereof.

(c) Exempt transactions [omitted]

(d) Commission rules [omitted]

(e) Additional information; waiting period extensions

(1)(A) The Federal Trade Commission or the Assistant Attorney General may, prior to the expiration of the 30–day waiting period (or in the case of a cash tender offer, the 15–day waiting period) specified in subsection (b)(1) of this section, require the submission of additional information or documentary material relevant to the proposed acquisition, from a person required to file notification with respect to such acquisition under subsection (a) of this section prior to the expiration of the waiting period specified in subsection (b)(1) of this section, or from any officer, director, partner, agent, or employee of such person.

(B)(i) The Assistant Attorney General and the Federal Trade Commission shall each designate a senior official who does not have direct responsibility for the review of any enforcement recommendation under this section concerning the transaction at issue, to hear any petition filed by such person to determine–

(I) whether the request for additional information or documentary material is unreasonably cumulative, unduly burdensome, or duplicative; or

(II) whether the request for additional information or documentary material has been substantially complied with by the petitioning person.

(ii) Internal review procedures for petitions filed pursuant to clause (i) shall include reasonable deadlines for expedited review of such petitions, after reasonable negotiations with investigative staff, in order to avoid undue delay of the merger review process.

(iii) Not later than 90 days after the date of the enactment of this Act, the Assistant Attorney General and the Federal Trade Commission shall conduct an internal review and implement reforms of the merger review process in order to eliminate unnecessary burden, remove costly duplication, and eliminate undue delay, in order to achieve a more effective and more efficient merger review process.

(iv) Not later than 120 days after the date of enactment of this Act, the Assistant Attorney General and the Federal Trade Commission shall issue or amend their respective industry guidance, regulations, operating manuals and relevant policy documents, to the extent appropriate, to implement each reform in this subparagraph.

(v) Not later than 180 days after the date the of enactment of this Act, the Assistant Attorney General and the Federal Trade Commission shall each report to Congress—

(I) which reforms each agency has adopted under this subparagraph;

(II) which steps each has taken to implement such internal reforms; and

(III) the effects of such reforms.

(2) The Federal Trade Commission or the Assistant Attorney General, in its or his discretion, may extend the 30–day waiting period (or in the case of a cash tender offer, the 15–day waiting period) specified in subsection (b)(1) of this section for an additional period of not more than 30 days (or in the case of a cash tender offer, 10 days) after the date on which the Federal Trade Commission or the Assistant Attorney General, as the case may be, receives from any person to whom a request is made under paragraph (1), or in the case of tender offers, the acquiring person, (A) all the information and documentary material required to be submitted pursuant to such a request, or (B) if such request is not fully complied with, the information and documentary material submitted and a statement of the reasons for such noncompliance. Such additional period may be further extended only by the United States district court, upon an application by the Federal

Trade Commission or the Assistant Attorney General pursuant to subsection (g)(2) of this section.

(f) Preliminary injunctions; hearings

If a proceeding is instituted or an action is filed by the Federal Trade Commission, alleging that a proposed acquisition violates section 18 of this title, or section 45 of this title, or an action is filed by the United States, alleging that a proposed acquisition violates such section 18 of this title, or section 1 or 2 of this title, and the Federal Trade Commission or the Assistant Attorney General (1) files a motion for a preliminary injunction against consummation of such acquisition pendente lite, and (2) certifies the United States district court for the judicial district within which the respondent resides or carries on business, or in which the action is brought, that it or he believes that the public interest requires relief pendente lite pursuant to this subsection, then upon the filing of such motion and certification, the chief judge of such district court shall immediately notify the chief judge of the United States court of appeals for the circuit in which such district court is located, who shall designate a United States district judge to whom such action shall be assigned for all purposes.

(g) Civil penalty; compliance; power of court

(1) Any person, or any officer, director, or partner thereof, who fails to comply with any provision of this section shall be liable to the United States for a civil penalty of not more than $10,000 for each day during which such person is in violation of this section. Such penalty may be recovered in a civil action brought by the United States.

[NOTE: $10,000 has been changed to $11,000 pursuant to the Debt Collections Improvement Act of 1996.]

(2) If any person, or any officer, director, partner, agent, or employee thereof, fails substantially to comply with the notification requirement under subsection (a) of this section or any request for the submission of additional information or documentary material under subsection (e)(1) of this section within the waiting period specified in subsection (b)(1) of this section and as may be extended under subsection (e)(2) of this section, the United States district court—

(A) may order compliance;

(B) shall extend the waiting period specified in subsection (b)(1) of this section and as may have been extended under subsection (e)(2) of this section until there has been substantial compliance, except that, in the case of a tender offer, the court may not extend such waiting period on the basis of a failure, by the person whose stock is sought to be acquired, to comply substantially with such notification requirement or any such request; and

(C) may grant such other equitable relief as the court in its discretion determines necessary or appropriate, upon application of the Federal Trade Commission or the Assistant Attorney General.

[Disclosure, exemption, construction, and report to Congress omitted]
* * *

Section 8. [Interlocking directorates and officers]

(a)(1) No person shall, at the same time, serve as a director or officer in any two corporations (other than banks, banking associations, and trust companies) that are—

(A) engaged in whole or in part in commerce; and

(B) by virtue of their business and location of operation, competitors, so that the elimination of competition by agreement between them would constitute a violation of any of the antitrust laws;

if each of the corporations has capital, surplus, and undivided profits aggregating more than $10,000,000 as adjusted pursuant to paragraph (5) of this subsection.

(2) Notwithstanding the provisions of paragraph (1), simultaneous service as a director or officer in any two corporations shall not be prohibited by this section if—

(A) the competitive sales of either corporation are less than $1,000,000 as adjusted pursuant to paragraph (5) of this subsection;

(B) the competitive sales of either corporation are less than 2 per centum of that corporation's total sales; or

(C) the competitive sales of each corporation are less than 4 per centum of that corporation's total sales.

For purposes of this paragraph, "competitive sales" means the gross revenues for all products and services sold by one corporation in competition with the other, determined on the basis of annual gross revenues for such products and services in that corporation's last completed fiscal year. For the purposes of this paragraph, "total sales" means the gross revenues for all products and services sold by one corporation over that corporation's last completed fiscal year.

(3) The eligibility of a director or officer under the provisions of paragraph (1) shall be determined by the capital, surplus and undivided profits, exclusive of dividends declared but not paid to stockholders, of each corporation at the end of that corporation's last completed fiscal year.

(4) For purposes of this section, the term "officer" means an officer elected or chosen by the Board of Directors.

(5) For each fiscal year commencing after September 30, 1990, the $10,000,000 and $1,000,000 thresholds in this subsection shall be increased (or decreased) as of October 1 each year by an amount equal to the percentage increase (or decrease) in the gross national product,

as determined by the Department of Commerce or its successor, for the year then ended over the level so established for the year ending September 30, 1989. As soon as practicable, but not later than January 31 of each year, the Federal Trade Commission shall publish the adjusted amounts required by this paragraph.*

(b) When any person elected or chosen as a director or officer of any corporation subject to the provisions hereof is eligible at the time of his election or selection to act for such corporation in such capacity, his eligibility to act in such capacity shall not be affected by any of the provisions hereof by reason of any change in the capital, surplus and undivided profits, or affairs of such corporation from whatever cause, until the expiration of one year from the date on which the event causing ineligibility occurred.

* * *

Section 12. Any suit, action, or proceeding under the antitrust laws against a corporation may be brought not only in the judicial district whereof it is an inhabitant, but also in any district wherein it may be found or transacts business; and all process in such cases may be served in the district of which it is an inhabitant, or wherever it may be found.

* * *

Section 14. Whenever a corporation shall violate any of the penal provisions of the antitrust laws, such violation shall be deemed to be also that of the individual directors, officers, or agents of such corporation who shall have authorized, ordered, or done any of the acts constituting in whole or in part such violation, and such violation shall be deemed a misdemeanor, and upon conviction therefor of any such director, officer, or agent he shall be punished by a fine of not exceeding $5,000 or by imprisonment for not exceeding one year, or by both, in the discretion of the court.

Section 15. The several district courts of the United States are invested with jurisdiction to prevent and restrain violations of this Act, and it shall be the duty of the several United States attorneys, in their respective districts, under the direction of the Attorney General, to institute proceedings in equity to prevent and restrain such violations....

Section 16. Any person, firm, corporation, or association shall be entitled to sue for and have injunctive relief, in any court of the United States having jurisdiction over the parties, against threatened loss or damage by a violation of the antitrust laws, including sections [two, three, seven and eight of this Act], when and under the same conditions and principles as injunctive relief against threatened conduct that will cause loss or damage is granted by courts of equity, under the rules governing such proceedings, and upon the execution of proper bond against damages

* Editors' note: On Jan. 27, 2012, the thresholds were adjusted to $27,784,000 and $2,778,400 respectively.

for an injunction improvidently granted and a showing that the danger of irreparable loss or damage is immediate, a preliminary injunction may issue: *Provided,* That nothing herein contained shall be construed to entitle any person, firm, corporation, or association, except the United States, to bring suit in equity for injunctive relief against any common carrier subject to the provisions of [the Act to regulate commerce, approved February fourth, eighteen hundred and eighty-seven], in respect of any matter subject to the regulation, supervision, or other jurisdiction of the Interstate Commerce Commission. In any action under this section in which the plaintiff substantially prevails, the court shall award the cost of suit, including a reasonable attorney's fee, to such plaintiff.

C. Antitrust Criminal Penalty Enhancement and Reform Act of 2004 (ACPERA), as amended Pub. L. No. 108–237 (sunsets in 2020)

Section 213. (a) IN GENERAL.—Subject to subsection (d), in any civil action alleging a violation of section 1 or 3 of the Sherman Act, or alleging a violation of any similar State law, based on conduct covered by a currently effective antitrust leniency agreement, the amount of damages recovered by or on behalf of a claimant from an antitrust leniency applicant who satisfies the requirements of subsection (b), together with the amounts so recovered from cooperating individuals who satisfy such requirements, shall not exceed that portion of the actual damages sustained by such claimant which is attributable to the commerce done by the applicant in the goods or services affected by the violation.

(b) REQUIREMENTS.—Subject to subsection (c), an antitrust leniency applicant or cooperating individual satisfies the requirements of this subsection with respect to a civil action described in subsection (a) if the court in which the civil action is brought determines, after considering any appropriate pleadings from the claimant, that the applicant or cooperating individual, as the case may be, has provided satisfactory cooperation to the claimant with respect to the civil action, which cooperation shall include—

(1) providing a full account to the claimant of all facts known to the applicant or cooperating individual, as the case may be, that are potentially relevant to the civil action;

(2) furnishing all documents or other items potentially relevant to the civil action that are in the possession, custody, or control of the applicant or cooperating individual, as the case may be, wherever they are located; and

(3)(A) in the case of a cooperating individual—

(i) making himself or herself available for such interviews, depositions, or testimony in connection with the civil action as the claimant may reasonably require; and

(ii) responding completely and truthfully, without making any attempt either falsely to protect or falsely to implicate any person or entity, and without intentionally withholding any potentially relevant information, to all questions asked by the claimant in interviews, depositions, trials, or any other court proceedings in connection with the civil action; or

(B) in the case of an antitrust leniency applicant, using its best efforts to secure and facilitate from cooperating individuals covered by the agreement the cooperation described in clauses (i) and (ii) and subparagraph (A).

(c) TIMELINESS.—If the initial contact by the antitrust leniency applicant with the Antitrust Division regarding conduct covered by the antitrust leniency agreement occurs after a State, or subdivision of a State, has issued compulsory process in connection with an investigation of allegations of a violation of section 1 or 3 of the Sherman Act or any similar State law based on conduct covered by the antitrust leniency agreement or after a civil action described in subsection (a) has been filed, then the court shall consider, in making the determination concerning satisfactory cooperation described in subsection (b), the timeliness of the applicant's initial cooperation with the claimant.

(d) CONTINUATION.—Nothing in this section shall be construed to modify, impair, or supersede the provisions of sections 4, 4A, and 4C of the Clayton Act relating to the recovery of costs of suit, including a reasonable attorney's fee, and interest on damages, to the extent that such recovery is authorized by such sections.

D. THE FEDERAL TRADE COMMISSION ACT 1914, as amended 15 U.S.C. §§ 41–58

* * *

Section 5. (a)(1) Unfair methods of competition in or affecting commerce, and unfair or deceptive acts or practices in or affecting commerce, are declared unlawful.

(2) The Commission is empowered and directed to prevent persons, partnerships, or corporations, except banks, savings and loan institutions described in section [18(f)(3) of this Act], common carriers subject to the Acts to regulate commerce, air carriers and foreign air carriers subject to the Federal Aviation Act of 1958, and persons, partnerships, or corporations insofar as they are subject to the Packers and Stockyards Act, 1921, as amended, except as provided in section 406(b) of said Act, from using unfair methods of competition in or affecting commerce and unfair or deceptive acts or practices in or affecting commerce.

(3) This subsection shall not apply to unfair methods of competition involving commerce with foreign nations (other than import commerce) unless—

(A) such methods of competition have a direct, substantial, and reasonably foreseeable effect—

(i) on commerce which is not commerce with foreign nations, or on import commerce with foreign nations; or

(ii) on export commerce with foreign nations, of a person engaged in such commerce in the United States; and

(B) such effect gives rise to a claim under the provisions of this subsection, other than this paragraph.

If this subsection applies to such methods of competition only because of the operation of subparagraph (A)(ii), this subsection shall apply to such conduct only for injury to export business in the United States.

* * *

Section 6. The Commission shall also have power—

(a) To gather and compile information concerning, and to investigate from time to time the organization, business, conduct, practices, and management of any person, partnership, or corporation engaged in or whose business affects commerce, excepting banks, savings and loan institutions described in section [18(f)(3) of this Act], and common carriers subject to the Act to regulate commerce, and its relation to other persons, partnerships, and corporations.

(b) To require, by general or special orders, persons, partnerships, and corporations, engaged in or whose business affects commerce, excepting banks, savings and loan institutions described in section [18(f)(3) of this Act], and common carriers subject to the Act to regulate commerce, or any class of them, or any of them, respectively, to file with the Commission in such form as the Commission may prescribe annual or special, or both annual and special, reports or answers in writing to specific questions, furnishing to the Commission such information as it may require as to the organization, business, conduct, practices, management, and relation to other corporations, partnerships, and individuals of the respective persons, partnerships, and corporations filing such reports or answers in writing. Such reports and answers shall be made under oath, or otherwise, as the Commission may prescribe, and shall be filed with the Commission within such reasonable period as the Commission may prescribe, unless additional time be granted in any case by the Commission.

(c) Whenever a final decree has been entered against any defendant corporation in any suit brought by the United States to prevent and restrain any violation of the antitrust Acts, to make investigation, upon its own initiative, of the manner in which the decree has been or is being carried out, and upon the application of the Attorney General it shall be its duty to make such investigation. It shall transmit to the Attorney General a report embodying its findings and recommendations as a result of any such investigation, and the report shall be made public in the discretion of the Commission.

(d) Upon the direction of the President or either House of Congress to investigate and report the facts relating to any alleged violations of the antitrust Acts by any corporation.

(e) Upon the application of the Attorney General to investigate and make recommendations for the readjustment of the business of any corporation alleged to be violating the antitrust Acts in order that the corporation may thereafter maintain its organization, management, and conduct of business in accordance with law.

(f) To make public from time to time such portions of the information obtained by it hereunder as are in the public interest; and to make annual and special reports to the Congress and to submit therewith recommendations for additional legislation; and to provide for the publication of its reports and decisions in such form and manner as may be best adapted for public information and use: *Provided,* That the Commission shall not have any authority to make public any trade secret or any commercial or financial information which is obtained from any person and which is privileged or confidential, except that the Commission may disclose such information to officers and employees of appropriate Federal law enforcement agencies or to any officer or employee of any State law enforcement agency upon the prior certification of an officer of any such Federal or State law enforcement agency that such information will be maintained in confidence and will be used only for official law enforcement purposes.

(g) From time to time to classify corporations and (except as provided in section [18(a)(2) of this Act]) to make rules and regulations for the purpose of carrying out the provisions of [this Act].

* * *

E. THE ROBINSON–PATMAN ACT 1936, as amended 15 U.S.C. § 13

Section 2. (a) It shall be unlawful for any person engaged in commerce, in the course of such commerce, either directly or indirectly, to discriminate in price between different purchasers of commodities of like grade and quality, where either or any of the purchases involved in such discrimination are in commerce, where such commodities are sold for use, consumption, or resale within the United States or any Territory thereof or the District of Columbia or any insular possession or other place under the jurisdiction of the United States, and where the effect of such discrimination may be substantially to lessen competition or tend to create a monopoly in any line of commerce, or to injure, destroy, or prevent competition with any person who either grants or knowingly receives the benefit of such discrimination, or with customers of either of them: *Provided,* That nothing herein contained shall prevent differentials which make only due allowance for differences in the cost of manufacture, sale, or delivery resulting from the differing methods or quantities in which such commodities are to such purchasers sold or delivered: *Provided, however,* That the Federal Trade Commission may, after due investigation and hearing to all interested parties, fix and establish quantity limits, and revise the same as it finds necessary, as to particular commodities or classes of commodities, where it finds that available purchasers in greater quantities are so few as to render differentials on account thereof unjustly discriminatory or promotive of monopoly in any line of commerce; and the foregoing shall then not be construed to permit differentials based on differences in quantities greater than those so fixed and established: *And provided further,* That nothing herein contained shall prevent persons engaged in selling goods, wares, or merchandise in commerce from selecting their own customers in bona fide transactions and not in restraint of trade: *And provided further,* That nothing herein contained shall prevent price changes from time to time where in response to changing conditions affecting the market for or the marketability of the goods concerned, such as but not limited to actual or imminent deterioration of perishable goods, obsolescence of seasonal goods, distress sales under court process, or sales in good faith in discontinuance of business in the goods concerned.

(b) Upon proof being made, at any hearing on a complaint under this section, that there has been discrimination in price or services or facilities furnished, the burden of rebutting the prima-facie case thus made by showing justification shall be upon the person charged with a violation of this section, and unless justification shall be affirmatively shown, the Commission is authorized to issue an order terminating the discrimination: *Provided, however,* That nothing herein contained shall prevent a seller rebutting the prima-facie case thus made by showing that his lower price or the furnishing of services or facilities to any purchaser or purchasers was made in good faith to meet an equally low price of a competitor, or the services or facilities furnished by a competitor.

(c) It shall be unlawful for any person engaged in commerce, in the course of such commerce, to pay or grant, or to receive or accept, anything of value as a commission, brokerage, or other compensation, or any allowance or discount in lieu thereof, except for services rendered in connection with the sale or purchase of goods, wares, or merchandise, either to the other party to such transaction or to an agent, representative, or other intermediary therein where such intermediary is acting in fact for or in behalf, or is subject to the direct or indirect control, of any party to such transaction other than the person by whom such compensation is so granted or paid.

(d) It shall be unlawful for any person engaged in commerce to pay or contract for the payment of anything of value to or for the benefit of a customer of such person in the course of such commerce as compensation or in consideration for any services or facilities furnished by or through such customer in connection with the processing, handling, sale, or offering for sale of any products or commodities manufactured, sold, or offered for sale by such person, unless such payment or consideration is available on proportionally equal terms to all other customers competing in the distribution of such products or commodities.

(e) It shall be unlawful for any person to discriminate in favor of one purchaser against another purchaser or purchasers of a commodity bought for resale, with or without processing, by contracting to furnish or furnishing, or by contributing to the furnishing of, any services or facilities connected with the processing, handling, sale, or offering for sale of such commodity so purchased upon terms not accorded to all purchasers on proportionally equal terms.

(f) It shall be unlawful for any person engaged in commerce, in the course of such commerce, knowingly to induce or receive a discrimination in price which is prohibited by this section.

Section 3. It shall be unlawful for any person engaged in commerce, in the course of such commerce, to be a party to, or assist in, any transaction of sale, or contract to sell, which discriminates to his knowledge against competitors of the purchaser, in that, any discount, rebate, allowance, or advertising service charge is granted to the purchaser over and above any discount, rebate, allowance, or advertising service charge available at the time of such transaction to said competitors in respect of a sale of goods of like grade, quality, and quantity; to sell, or contract to sell, goods in any part of the United States at prices lower than those exacted by said person elsewhere in the United States for the purpose of destroying competition, or eliminating a competitor in such part of the United States; or, to sell, or contract to sell, goods at unreasonably low prices for the purpose of destroying competition or eliminating a competitor.

Any person violating any of the provisions of this section shall, upon conviction thereof, be fined not more than $5,000 or imprisoned not more than one year, or both.

Section 4. Nothing in [this Act], shall apply to purchases of their supplies for their own use by schools, colleges, universities, public libraries, churches, hospitals, and charitable institutions not operated for profit.

F. THE EXPORT TRADING COMPANY ACT OF 1982 Pub. L. No. 97–290, 96 Stat. 1233

Section 102. (a) The Congress finds that—

(1) United States exports are responsible for creating and maintaining one out of every nine manufacturing jobs in the United States and for generating one out of every seven dollars of total United States goods produced;

(2) the rapidly growing service-related industries are vital to the well-being of the United States economy inasmuch as they create jobs for seven out of every ten Americans, provide 65 per centum of the Nation's gross national product, and offer the greatest potential for significantly increased industrial trade involving finished products;

(3) trade deficits contribute to the decline of the dollar on international currency markets and have an inflationary impact on the United States economy;

(4) tens thousands of small- and medium-sized United States businesses produce exportable goods or services but do not engage in exporting;

(5) although the United States is the world's leading agricultural exporting nation, many farm products are not marketed as widely and effectively abroad as they could be through export trading companies;

(6) export trade services in the United States are fragmented into a multitude of separate functions, and companies attempting to offer export trade services lack financial leverage to reach a significant number of potential United States exporters;

(7) the United States needs well-developed export trade intermediaries which can achieve economies of scale and acquire expertise enabling them to export goods and services profitably, at low per unit cost to producers;

(8) the development of export trading companies in the United States has been hampered by business attitudes and by Government regulations;

(9) those activities of State and local governmental authorities which initiate, facilitate, or expand exports of goods and services can be an important source for expansion of total United States exports, as well as for experimentation in the development of innovative export programs keyed to local, State, and regional economic needs;

(10) if United States trading companies are to be successful in promoting United States exports and in competing with foreign trading companies, they should be able to draw on the resources, expertise, and knowledge of the United States banking system, both in the United States and abroad; and

(11) the Department of Commerce is responsible for the development and promotion of United States exports, and especially for facilitating the export of finished products by United States manufacturers.

(b) It is the purpose of this chapter to increase United States exports of products and services by encouraging more efficient provision of export trade services to United States producers and suppliers, in particular by establishing an office within the Department of Commerce to promote the formation of export trade associations and export trading companies, by permitting bank holding companies, bankers' banks, and Edge Act corporations and agreement corporations that are subsidiaries of bank holding companies to invest in export trading companies, by reducing restrictions on trade financing provided by financial institutions, and by modifying the application of the antitrust laws to certain export trade.

Section 103. (a) For purposes of this subchapter—

(1) the term "export trade" means trade or commerce in goods or services produced in the United States which are exported, or in the course of being exported, from the United States to any other country;

(2) the term "services" includes, but is not limited to, accounting, amusement, architectural, automatic data processing, business, communications, construction franchising and licensing, consulting, engi-

neering, financial, insurance, legal, management, repair, tourism, training, and transportation services;

(3) the term "export trade services" includes, but is not limited to, consulting, international market research, advertising, marketing, insurance, product research and design, legal assistance, transportation, including trade documentation and freight forwarding, communication and processing of foreign orders to and for exporters and foreign purchasers, warehousing, foreign exchange, financing, and taking title to goods, when provided in order to facilitate the export of goods or services produced in the United States;

(4) the term "export trading company" means a person, partnership, association, or similar organization, whether operated for profit or as a nonprofit organization, which does business under the laws of the United States or any State and which is organized and operated principally for purposes of—

(A) exporting goods or services produced in the United States; or

(B) facilitating the exportation of goods or services produced in the United States by unaffiliated persons by providing one or more export trade services;

(5) the term "State" means any of the several States of the United States, the District of Columbia, the Commonwealth of Puerto Rico, the Virgin Islands, American Samoa, Guam, the Commonwealth of the Northern Mariana Islands, and the Trust Territory of the Pacific Islands;

(6) the term "United States" means the several States of the United States, the District of Columbia, the Commonwealth of Puerto Rico, the Virgin Islands, American Samoa, Guam, the Commonwealth of the Northern Mariana Islands, and the Trust Territory of the Pacific Islands; and

(7) the term "antitrust laws" means the antitrust laws as defined in section [(a) of the first section of the Clayton Act, section 5 of the Federal Trade Commission Act to the extent that section 5] applies to unfair methods of competition, and any State antitrust or unfair competition law.

(b) The Secretary of Commerce may by regulation further define any term defined in subsection (a) of this section, in order to carry out this subchapter.

Section 104. The Secretary of Commerce shall establish within the Department of Commerce an office to promote and encourage to the greatest extent feasible the formation of export trade associations and export trading companies. Such office shall provide information and advice to interested persons and shall provide a referral service to facilitate contact between producers of exportable goods and services and firms offering export trade services.

* * *

Section 301. To promote and encourage export trade, the Secretary may issue certificates of review and advise and assist any person with respect to applying for certificates of review.

Section 302. (a) To apply for a certificate of review, a person shall submit to the Secretary a written application which—

(1) specifies conduct limited to export trade, and

(2) is in a form and contains any information, including information pertaining to the overall market in which the applicant operates, required by rule or regulation promulgated under section [310 of this Act].

* * *

Section 303. (a) A certificate of review shall be issued to any applicant that establishes that its specified export trade, export trade activities, and methods of operation will

(1) result in neither a substantial lessening of competition or restraint of trade within the United States nor a substantial restraint of the export trade of any competitor of the applicant;

(2) not unreasonably enhance, stabilize, or depress prices within the United States of the goods, wares, merchandise, or services of the class exported by the applicant;

(3) not constitute unfair methods of competition against competitors engaged in the export of goods, wares, merchandise, or services of the class exported by the applicant; and

(4) not include any act that may reasonably be expected to result in the sale for consumption or resale within the United States of the goods, wares, merchandise, or services exported by the applicant.

(b) Within ninety days after the Secretary receives an application for a certificate of review, the Secretary shall determine whether the applicant's export trade, export trade activities, and methods of operation meet the standards of subsection (a) of this section. If the Secretary, with the concurrence of the Attorney General, determines that such standards are met, the Secretary shall issue to the applicant a certificate of review. The certificate of review shall specify—

(1) the export trade, export trade activities, and methods of operation to which the certificate applies,

(2) the person to whom the certificate of review is issued, and

(3) any terms and conditions the Secretary or the Attorney General deems necessary to assure compliance with the standards of subsection (a) of this section.

* * *

Section 306. (a) Except as provided in subsection (b) of this section, no criminal or civil action may be brought under the antitrust laws against a person to whom a certificate of review is issued which is based on conduct which is specified in, and complies with the terms of, a certificate issued under section 4013 of this title which certificate was in effect when the conduct occurred.

(b)(1) Any person who has been injured as a result of conduct engaged in under a certificate of review may bring a civil action for injunctive relief, actual damages, the loss of interest on actual damages, and the cost of suit (including a reasonable attorney's fee) for the failure to comply with the standards of section [303(a) of this Act]. Any action commenced under this subchapter shall proceed as if it were an action commenced under section 4 or section 16 of the Clayton Act, except that the standards of section [303(a) of this Act] and the remedies provided in this paragraph shall be the exclusive standards and remedies applicable to such action.

(2) Any action brought under paragraph (1) shall be filed within two years of the date the plaintiff has notice of the failure to comply with the standards of section 4013(a) of this title but in any event within four years after the cause of action accrues.

(3) In any action brought under paragraph (1), there shall be a presumption that conduct which is specified in and complies with a certificate of review does comply with the standards of section [303(a) of this Act].

(4) In any action brought under paragraph (1), if the court finds that the conduct does comply with the standards of section [303(a) of this Act], the court shall award to the person against whom the claim is brought the cost of suit attributable to defending against the claim (including a reasonable attorney's fee).

(5) The Attorney General may file suit pursuant to section 15 of the Clayton Act (15 U.S.C. § 25) to enjoin conduct threatening clear and irreparable harm to the national interest.

* * *

Section 310. The Secretary, with the concurrence of the Attorney General, shall promulgate such rules and regulations as are necessary to carry out the purposes of this chapter.

G. THE NATIONAL COOPERATIVE RESEARCH AND PRODUCTION ACT OF 1993 15 U.S.C. §§ 4301–4305

Section 2. (a) For purposes of this Act:

(1) The term "antitrust laws" has the meaning given it in subsection (a) of the first section of the Clayton Act, except that such term includes section 5 of the Federal Trade Commission Act to the extent that such section 5 applies to unfair methods of competition.

(2) The term "Attorney General" means the Attorney General of the United States.

(3) The term "Commission" means the Federal Trade Commission.

(4) The term "person" has the meaning given it in subsection (a) of the first section of the Clayton Act.

(5) The term "State" has the meaning given it in section 4G(2) of the Clayton Act.

(6) The term "joint venture" means any group of activities, including attempting to make, making, or performing a contract, by two or more persons for the purpose of—

(A) theoretical analysis, experimentation, or systematic study of phenomena or observable facts,

(B) the development or testing of basic engineering techniques,

(C) the extension of investigative findings or theory of a scientific or technical nature into practical application for experimental and demonstration purposes, including the experimental production and testing of models, prototypes, equipment, materials, and processes,

(D) the production of a product, process, or service,

(E) the testing in connection with the production of a product, process, or service by such venture,

(F) the collection, exchange, and analysis of research or production information, or

(G) any combination of the purposes specified in subparagraphs (A), (B), (C), (D), (E), and (F),

and may include the establishment and operation of facilities for the conducting of such venture, the conducting of such venture on a protected and proprietary basis, and the prosecuting of applications for patents and the granting of licenses for the results of such venture, but does not include any activity specified in subsection (b).

(7) The term "standards development activity" means any action taken by a standards development organization for the purpose of developing, promulgating, revising, amending, reissuing, interpreting, or otherwise maintaining a voluntary consensus standard, or using such standard in conformity assessment activities, including actions relating to the intellectual property policies of the standards development organization.

(8) The term "standards development organization" means a domestic or international organization that plans, develops, establishes, or coordinates voluntary consensus standards using procedures that incorporate the attributes of openness, balance of interests, due process, an appeals process, and consensus in a manner consistent with the Office of Management and Budget Circular Number A–119, as revised February 10, 1998. The term "standards development

organization'' shall not, for purposes of this chapter, include the parties participating in the standards development organization.

(9) The term ''technical standard'' has the meaning given such term in section 12(d)(4) of the National Technology Transfer and Advancement Act of 1995.

(10) The term ''voluntary consensus standard'' has the meaning given such term in Office of Management and Budget Circular Number A–119, as revised February 10, 1998.

(b) The term ''joint venture'' excludes the following activities involving two or more persons:

(1) exchanging information among competitors relating to costs, sales, profitability, prices, marketing, or distribution of any product, process, or service if such information is not reasonably required to carry out the purpose of such venture,

(2) entering into any agreement or engaging in any other conduct restricting, requiring, or otherwise involving the marketing, distribution, or provision by any person who is a party to such venture of any product, process, or service, other than—

(A) the distribution among the parties to such venture, in accordance with such venture, of a product, process, or service produced by such venture,

(B) the marketing of proprietary information, such as patents and trade secrets, developed through such venture formed under a written agreement entered into before the date of the enactment of the National Cooperative Production Amendments of 1993, or

(C) the licensing, conveying, or transferring of intellectual property, such as patents and trade secrets, developed through such venture formed under a written agreement entered into on or after the date of the enactment of the National Cooperative Production Amendments of 1993,

(3) entering into any agreement or engaging in any other conduct—

(A) to restrict or require the sale, licensing, or sharing of inventions, developments, products, processes or services not developed through, or produced by such venture, or

(B) to restrict or require participation by any person who is a party to such venture in other research and development activities, that is not reasonably required to prevent misappropriation of proprietary information contributed by any person who is a party to such venture or of the results of such venture.

(4) entering into any agreement or engaging in any other conduct allocating a market with a competitor,

(5) exchanging information among competitors relating to production (other than production by such venture) of a product, process, or

service if such information is not reasonably required to carry out the purpose of such venture,

(6) entering into any agreement or engaging in any other conduct restricting, requiring, or otherwise involving the production (other than the production by such venture) of a product, process, or service,

(7) using existing facilities for the production of a product, process, or service by such venture unless such use involves the production of a new product or technology, and

(8) except as provided in paragraphs (2), (3), and (6), entering into any agreement or engaging in any other conduct to restrict or require participation by any person who is a party to such venture, in any unilateral or joint activity that is not reasonably required to carry out the purpose of such venture.

(c) The term "standards development activity" excludes the following activities:

(1) Exchanging information among competitors relating to cost, sales, profitability, prices, marketing, or distribution of any product, process, or service that is not reasonably required for the purpose of developing or promulgating a voluntary consensus standard, or using such standard in conformity assessment activities.

(2) Entering into any agreement or engaging in any other conduct that would allocate a market with a competitor.

(3) Entering into any agreement or conspiracy that would set or restrain prices of any good or service.

Section 3. In any action under the antitrust laws, or under any State law similar to the antitrust laws, the conduct of (1) any person in making or performing a contract to carry out a joint venture, or (2) a standards development organization while engaged in a standards development activity, shall not be deemed illegal per se; such conduct shall be judged on the basis of its reasonableness, taking into account all relevant factors affecting competition, including, but not limited to, effects on competition in properly defined, relevant research, development, product, process, and service markets. For the purpose of determining a properly defined, relevant market, worldwide capacity shall be considered to the extent that it may be appropriate in the circumstances.

Section 4. [(a) Amount recoverable] Notwithstanding section 15 of this title and in lieu of the relief specified in such section, any person who is entitled to recovery on a claim under such section shall recover the actual damages sustained by such person, interest calculated at the rate specified in section 1961 of Title 28 on such actual damages as specified in subsection (d) of this section, and the cost of suit attributable to such claim, including a reasonable attorney's fee pursuant to section 4304 of this title if such claim—

(1) results from conduct that is within the scope of a notification that has been filed under section 4305(a) of this title for a joint venture, or for a standards development activity engaged in by a standards development organization against which such claim is made, and

(2) is filed after such notification becomes effective pursuant to section 4305(c) of this title.

[(b) Recovery by States] Notwithstanding section 15c of this title, and in lieu of the relief specified in such section, any State that is entitled to monetary relief on a claim under such section shall recover the total damage sustained as described in subsection (a)(1) of such section, interest calculated at the rate specified in section 1961 of Title 28 on such total damage as specified in subsection (d) of this section, and the cost of suit attributable to such claim, including a reasonable attorney's fee pursuant to section 15c of this title if such claim—

(1) results from conduct that is within the scope of a notification that has been filed under section 4305(a) of this title for a joint venture, or for a standards development activity engaged in by a standards development organization against which such claim is made, and

(2) is filed after such notification becomes effective pursuant to section 4305(c) of this title.

[(c) Conduct similar under State law] Notwithstanding any provision of any State law providing damages for conduct similar to that forbidden by the antitrust laws, any person who is entitled to recovery on a claim under such provision shall not recover in excess of the actual damages sustained by such person, interest calculated at the rate specified in section 1961 of Title 28 on such actual damages as specified in subsection (d) of this section, and the cost of suit attributable to such claim, including a reasonable attorney's fee pursuant to section 4304 of this title if such claim—

(1) results from conduct that is within the scope of a notification that has been filed under section 4305(a) of this title for a joint venture, or for a standards development activity engaged in by a standards development organization against which such claim is made, and

(2) is filed after notification has become effective pursuant to section 4305(c) of this title.

(d) Interest. Interest shall be awarded on the damages involved for the period beginning on the earliest date for which injury can be established and ending on the date of judgment, unless the court finds that the award of all or part of such interest is unjust in the circumstances.

(e) Subsections (a), (b), and (c) of this section shall not be construed to modify the liability under the antitrust laws of any person (other than a standards development organization) who—

(1) directly (or through an employee or agent) participates in a standards development activity with respect to which a violation of any of the antitrust laws is found,

(2) is not a fulltime employee of the standards development organization that engaged in such activity, and

(3) is, or is an employee or agent of a person who is, engaged in a line of commerce that is likely to benefit directly from the operation of the standards development activity with respect to which such violation is found.

[(f) Applicability] This section shall be applicable only if the challenged conduct of a person defending against a claim is not in violation of any decree or order, entered or issued after October 11, 1984, in any case or proceeding under the antitrust laws or any State law similar to the antitrust laws challenging such conduct as part of a joint venture, or of a standards development activity engaged in by a standards development organization.

Section 5. (a) Notwithstanding sections 4 and 16 of the Clayton Act, in any claim under the antitrust laws, or any State law similar to the antitrust laws, based on the conducting of a joint venture, or of a standards development activity engaged in by a standards development organization, the court shall, at the conclusion of the action—

(1) award to a substantially prevailing claimant the cost of suit attributable to such claim, including a reasonable attorney's fee, or

(2) award to a substantially prevailing party defending against any such claim the cost of suit attributable to such claim, including a reasonable attorney's fee, if the claim, or the claimant's conduct during the litigation of the claim, was frivolous, unreasonable, without foundation, or in bad faith.

(b) The award made under subsection (a) of this section may be offset in whole or in part by an award in favor of any other party for any part of the cost of suit, including a reasonable attorney's fee, attributable to conduct during the litigation by any prevailing party that the court finds to be frivolous, unreasonable, without foundation, or in bad faith.

(c) Subsections (a) and (b) of this section shall not apply with respect to any person who—

(1) directly participates in a standards development activity with respect to which a violation of any of the antitrust laws is found,

(2) is not a fulltime employee of a standards development organization that engaged in such activity, and

(3) is, or is an employee or agent of a person who is, engaged in a line of commerce that is likely to benefit directly from the operation of the standards development activity with respect to which such violation is found.

Section 6. (a)(1) Written notifications; filing. Any party to a joint venture, acting on such venture's behalf, may, not later than 90 days after entering into a written agreement to form such venture or not later than 90 days after October 11, 1984, whichever is later, file simultaneously with the Attorney General and the Commission a written notification disclosing—

(A) the identities of the parties to such venture,

(B) the nature and objectives of such venture, and

(C) if a purpose of such venture is the production of a product, process, or service, as referred to in section 4301(a)(6)(D) of this title, the identity and nationality of any person who is a party to such venture, or who controls any party to such venture whether separately or with one or more other persons acting as a group for the purpose of controlling such party.

Any party to such venture, acting on such venture's behalf, may file additional disclosure notifications pursuant to this section as are appropriate to extend the protections of section 4303 of this title. In order to maintain the protections of section 4303 of this title, such venture shall, not later than 90 days after a change in its membership, file simultaneously with the Attorney General and the Commission a written notification disclosing such change.

(2) A standards development organization may, not later than 90 days after commencing a standards development activity engaged in for the purpose of developing or promulgating a voluntary consensus standards or not later than 90 days after June 22, 2004, whichever is later, file simultaneously with the Attorney General and the Commission, a written notification disclosing—

(A) the name and principal place of business of the standards development organization, and

(B) documents showing the nature and scope of such activity.

Any standards development organization may file additional disclosure notifications pursuant to this section as are appropriate to extend the protections of section 4303 of this title to standards development activities that are not covered by the initial filing or that have changed significantly since the initial filing.

(b) Publication; Federal Register; notice

Except as provided in subsection (e) of this section, not later than 30 days after receiving a notification filed under subsection (a) of this section, the Attorney General or the Commission shall publish in the Federal Register a notice with respect to such venture that identifies the parties to such venture and that describes in general terms the area of planned activity of such venture, or a notice with respect to such standards development activity that identifies the standards development organization engaged in such activity and that describes such activity in general terms. Prior to its publication, the contents of such notice shall be made available to the parties to such venture or available to such organization, as the case may be.

(c) Effect of notice. If with respect to a notification filed under subsection (a) of this section, notice is published in the Federal Register, then such notification shall operate to convey the protections of section 4303 of this title as of the earlier of—

(1) the date of publication of notice under subsection (b) of this section,

or

(2) if such notice is not so published within the time required by subsection

(b) of this section, after the expiration of the 30–day period beginning on the date the Attorney General or the Commission receives the applicable information described in subsection (a) of this section.

(d) Exemption; disclosure; information. Except with respect to the information published pursuant to subsection (b) of this section—

(1) all information and documentary material submitted as part of a notification filed pursuant to this section, and

(2) all other information obtained by the Attorney General or the Commission in the course of any investigation, administrative proceeding, or case, with respect to a potential violation of the antitrust laws by the joint venture, or the standards development activity, with respect to which such notification was filed, shall be exempt from disclosure under section 552 of Title 5, and shall not be made publicly available by any agency of the United States to which such section applies except in a judicial or administrative proceeding in which such information and material is subject to any protective order.

(e) Withdrawal of notification. Any person or standards development organization that files a notification pursuant to this section may withdraw such notification before notice of the joint venture involved is published under subsection (b) of this section. Any notification so withdrawn shall not be subject to subsection (b) of this section and shall not confer the protections of section 4303 of this title on any person or any standards development organization with respect to whom such notification was filed.

(f) Judicial review; inapplicable with respect to notifications

Any action taken or not taken by the Attorney General or the Commission with respect to notifications filed pursuant to this section shall not be subject to judicial review.

(g) Admissibility into evidence; disclosure of conduct; publication of notice; supporting or answering claims under antitrust laws

(1) Except as provided in paragraph (2), for the sole purpose of establishing that a person or standards development organization is

entitled to the protections of section 4303 of this title, the fact of disclosure of conduct under subsection (a) of this section and the fact of publication of a notice under subsection (b) of this section shall be admissible into evidence in any judicial or administrative proceeding.

(2) No action by the Attorney General or the Commission taken pursuant to this section shall be admissible into evidence in any such proceeding for the purpose of supporting or answering any claim under the antitrust laws or under any State law similar to the antitrust laws.

Section 7. Notwithstanding sections 4 and 6, the protections of section 4 shall not apply with respect to a joint venture's production of a product, process, or service, as referred to in section 2(a)(6)(D), unless—

(1) the principle facilities for such production are located in the United States or its territories, and

(2) each person who controls any party to such venture (including such party itself) is a United States person, or a foreign person from a country whose law accords antitrust treatment no less favorable to United States persons than to such country's domestic persons with respect to participation in joint ventures for production.

* * *

II. European Union Treaties

A. Treaty on European Union 1992 (as amended)

Article 3(3) The Union shall establish an internal market. It shall work for the sustainable development of Europe based on balanced economic growth and price stability, a highly competitive social market economy, aiming at full employment and social progress, and a high level of protection and improvement of the quality of the environment. It shall promote scientific and technological advance. It shall combat social exclusion and discrimination, and shall promote social justice and protection, equality between women and men, solidarity between generations and protection of the rights of the child. It shall promote economic, social and territorial cohesion, and solidarity among Member States. It shall respect its rich cultural and linguistic diversity, and shall ensure that Europe's cultural heritage is safeguarded and enhanced. * * *

Article 4(3). Pursuant to the principle of sincere co-operation, the Union and the Member States shall, in full mutual respect, assist each other in carrying out tasks which flow from the Treaties. The Member States shall take any appropriate measure, general or particular, to ensure fulfillment of the obligations arising out of the Treaties or resulting from the acts of the institutions of the Union. The Member States shall facilitate the achievement of the Union's tasks and refrain from any measure which could jeopardize the attainment of the Union's objectives.

B. Treaty on the Functioning of the European Union 1957 (as renamed and amended)

Article 18. Within the scope of application of the Treaties, and without prejudice to any special provisions contained therein, any discrimination on grounds of nationality shall be prohibited. The European Parliament and the Council, acting in accordance with the ordinary legislative procedure, may adopt rules designed to prohibit such discrimination.

* * *

Article 101(1). The following shall be prohibited as incompatible with the internal market: all agreements between undertakings, decisions by associations of undertakings and concerted practices which may affect trade between Member States and which have as their object or effect the prevention, restriction or distortion of competition within the internal market, and in particular those which:

(a) directly or indirectly fix purchase or selling prices or any other trading conditions;

(b) limit or control production, markets, technical development, or investment;

(c) share markets or sources of supply;

(d) apply dissimilar conditions to equivalent transactions with other trading parties, thereby placing them at a competitive disadvantage;

(e) make the conclusion of contracts subject to acceptance by the other parties of supplementary obligations which, by their nature or according to commercial usage, have no connection with the subject of such contracts.

(2) Any agreements or decisions prohibited pursuant to this Article shall be automatically void.

(3) The provisions of paragraph 1 may, however, be declared inapplicable in the case of:

–any agreement or category of agreements between undertakings,

–any decision or category of decisions by associations of undertakings,

–any concerted practice or category of concerted practices,

which contributes to improving the production or distribution of goods or to promoting technical or economic progress, while allowing consumers a fair share of the resulting benefit, and which does not:

(a) impose on the undertakings concerned restrictions which are not indispensable to the attainment of these objectives;

(b) afford such undertakings the possibility of eliminating competition in respect of a substantial part of the products in question.

Article 102. Any abuse by one or more undertakings of a dominant position within the internal market or in a substantial part of it shall be prohibited as incompatible with the internal market in so far as it may affect trade between Member States. Such abuse may, in particular, consist in:

(a) directly or indirectly imposing unfair purchase or selling prices or other unfair trading conditions;

(b) limiting production, markets or technical development to the prejudice of consumers;

(c) applying dissimilar conditions to equivalent transactions with other trading parties, thereby placing them at a competitive disadvantage;

(d) making the conclusion of contracts subject to acceptance by the other parties of supplementary obligations which, by their nature or according to commercial usage, have no connection with the subject of such contracts.

* * *

Article 106(1). In the case of public undertakings and undertakings to which Member States grant special or exclusive rights, Member States shall neither enact nor maintain in force any measure contrary to the rules contained in the Treaties, in particular to those rules provided for in Article 18 and Articles 101 to 109.

(2) Undertakings entrusted with the operation of services of general economic interest or having the character of a revenue-producing monopoly shall be subject to the rules contained in the Treaties, in particular to the rules on competition, in so far as the application of such rules does not obstruct the performance, in law or in fact, of the particular tasks assigned to them. The development of trade must not be affected to such an extent as would be contrary to the interests of the Union.

(3) The Commission shall ensure the application of the provisions of this Article and shall, where necessary, address appropriate directives or decisions to Member States.

Article 107(1). Save as otherwise provided in the Treaties, any aid granted by a Member State or through State resources in any form whatsoever which distorts or threatens to distort competition by favouring certain undertakings or the production of certain goods shall, in so far as it affects trade between Member States, be incompatible with the internal market.

(2) The following shall be compatible with the internal market:

(a) aid having a social character, granted to individual consumers, provided that such aid is granted without discrimination related to the origin of the products concerned;

(b) aid to make good the damage caused by natural disasters or exceptional occurrences;

(c) aid granted to the economy of certain areas of the Federal Republic of Germany affected by the division of Germany, in so far as such aid is required in order to compensate for the economic disadvantages caused by that division. Five years after the entry into force of the Treaty of Lisbon, the Council, acting on a proposal from the Commission, may adopt a decision repealing this point.

(3) The following may be considered to be compatible with the internal market:

(a) aid to promote the economic development of areas where the standard of living is abnormally low or where there is serious underemployment, and of the regions referred to in Article 349, in view of their structural, economic and social situation;

(b) aid to promote the execution of an important project of common European interest or to remedy a serious disturbance in the economy of a Member State;

(c) aid to facilitate the development of certain economic activities or of certain economic areas, where such aid does not adversely affect trading conditions to an extent contrary to the common interest;

(d) aid to promote culture and heritage conservation where such aid does not affect trading conditions and competition in the Union to an extent that is contrary to the common interest;

(e) such other categories of aid as may be specified by decision of the Council on a proposal from the Commission.

* * *

Article 108(1). The Commission shall, in cooperation with Member States, keep under constant review all systems of aid existing in those States. It shall propose to the latter any appropriate measures required by the progressive development or by the functioning of the internal market.

(2) If, after giving notice to the parties concerned to submit their comments, the Commission finds that aid granted by a State or through State resources is not compatible with the internal market having regard to Article 107, or that such aid is being misused, it shall decide that the State concerned shall abolish or alter such aid within a period of time to be determined by the Commission.

If the State concerned does not comply with this decision within the prescribed time, the Commission or any other interested State may, in derogation from the provisions of Articles 258 and 259, refer the matter to the Court of Justice of the European Union direct.

On application by a Member State, the Council may, acting unanimously, decide that aid which that State is granting or intends to grant shall be considered to be compatible with the internal market, in derogation from the provisions of Article 107 or from the regulations provided for in Article 109, if such a decision is justified by exceptional circumstances. If, as regards the aid in question, the Commission has already initiated the procedure provided for in the first subparagraph of this paragraph, the fact that the State concerned has made its application to the Council shall have the effect of suspending that procedure until the Council has made its attitude known.

If, however, the Council has not made its attitude known within three months of the said application being made, the Commission shall give its decision on the case.

(3) The Commission shall be informed, in sufficient time to enable it to submit its comments, of any plans to grant or alter aid. If it considers that any such plan is not compatible with the internal market having regard to Article 107, it shall without delay initiate the procedure provided for in paragraph 2. The Member State concerned shall not put its proposed measures into effect until this procedure has resulted in a final decision.

(4) The Commission may adopt regulations relating to the categories of State aid that the Council has, pursuant to Article 109, determined may be exempted from the procedure provided for by paragraph 3 of this Article.

* * *

APPENDIX C

2010 HORIZONTAL MERGER GUIDELINES

■ ■ ■

U.S. Justice Department and Federal Trade Commission
August 19, 2010

* * *

Table of Contents

1. Overview

These Guidelines outline the principal analytical techniques, practices, and the enforcement policy of the Department of Justice and the Federal Trade Commission (the "Agencies") with respect to mergers and acquisitions involving actual or potential competitors ("horizontal mergers") under the federal antitrust laws.[1] The relevant statutory provisions include Section 7 of the Clayton Act, 15 U.S.C. § 18, Sections 1 and 2 of the Sherman Act, 15 U.S.C. §§ 1, 2, and Section 5 of the Federal Trade Commission Act, 15 U.S.C. § 45. Most particularly, Section 7 of the Clayton Act prohibits mergers if "in any line of commerce or in any activity affecting commerce in any section of the country, the effect of such acquisition may be substantially to lessen competition, or to tend to create a monopoly."

The Agencies seek to identify and challenge competitively harmful mergers while avoiding unnecessary interference with mergers that are either competitively beneficial or neutral. Most merger analysis is necessarily predictive, requiring an assessment of what will likely happen if a merger proceeds as compared to what will likely happen if it does not. Given this inherent need for prediction, these Guidelines reflect the congressional intent that merger enforcement should interdict competitive problems in their incipiency and that certainty about anticompetitive effect is seldom possible and not required for a merger to be illegal.

These Guidelines describe the principal analytical techniques and the main types of evidence on which the Agencies usually rely to predict whether a horizontal merger may substantially lessen competition. They are not intended to describe how the Agencies analyze cases other than horizontal mergers. These Guidelines are intended to assist the business community and antitrust practitioners by increasing the transparency of the analytical process underlying the Agencies' enforcement decisions. They may also assist the courts in developing an appropriate framework for interpreting and applying the antitrust laws in the horizontal merger context.

---

1. These Guidelines replace the Horizontal Merger Guidelines issued in 1992, revised in 1997. They reflect the ongoing accumulation of experience at the Agencies. The Commentary on the Horizontal Merger Guidelines issued by the Agencies in 2006 remains a valuable supplement to these Guidelines. These Guidelines may be revised from time to time as necessary to reflect significant changes in enforcement policy, to clarify existing policy, or to reflect new learning. These Guidelines do not cover vertical or other types of non-horizontal acquisitions.

These Guidelines should be read with the awareness that merger analysis does not consist of uniform application of a single methodology. Rather, it is a fact-specific process through which the Agencies, guided by their extensive experience, apply a range of analytical tools to the reasonably available and reliable evidence to evaluate competitive concerns in a limited period of time. Where these Guidelines provide examples, they are illustrative and do not exhaust the applications of the relevant principle.[2]

The unifying theme of these Guidelines is that mergers should not be permitted to create, enhance, or entrench market power or to facilitate its exercise. For simplicity of exposition, these Guidelines generally refer to all of these effects as enhancing market power. A merger enhances market power if it is likely to encourage one or more firms to raise price, reduce output, diminish innovation, or otherwise harm customers as a result of diminished competitive constraints or incentives. In evaluating how a merger will likely change a firm's behavior, the Agencies focus primarily on how the merger affects conduct that would be most profitable for the firm.

A merger can enhance market power simply by eliminating competition between the merging parties. This effect can arise even if the merger causes no changes in the way other firms behave. Adverse competitive effects arising in this manner are referred to as "unilateral effects." A merger also can enhance market power by increasing the risk of coordinated, accommodating, or interdependent behavior among rivals. Adverse competitive effects arising in this manner are referred to as "coordinated effects." In any given case, either or both types of effects may be present, and the distinction between them may be blurred.

These Guidelines principally describe how the Agencies analyze mergers between rival suppliers that may enhance their market power as sellers. Enhancement of market power by sellers often elevates the prices charged to customers. For simplicity of exposition, these Guidelines generally discuss the analysis in terms of such price effects. Enhanced market power can also be manifested in non-price terms and conditions that adversely affect customers, including reduced product quality, reduced product variety, reduced service, or diminished innovation. Such non-price effects may coexist with price effects, or can arise in their absence. When the Agencies investigate whether a merger may lead to a substantial lessening of non-price competition, they employ an approach analogous to that used to evaluate price competition. Enhanced market power may also make it more likely that the merged entity can profitably and effectively engage in exclusionary conduct. Regardless of how enhanced market power likely would be manifested, the Agencies normally evaluate mergers based on their impact on customers. The Agencies examine effects on either or both of the direct customers and the final consumers. The Agencies presume,

2. These Guidelines are not intended to describe how the Agencies will conduct the litigation of cases they decide to bring. Although relevant in that context, these Guidelines neither dictate nor exhaust the range of evidence the Agencies may introduce in litigation.

absent convincing evidence to the contrary, that adverse effects on direct customers also cause adverse effects on final consumers.

Enhancement of market power by buyers, sometimes called "monopsony power," has adverse effects comparable to enhancement of market power by sellers. The Agencies employ an analogous framework to analyze mergers between rival purchasers that may enhance their market power as buyers. See Section 12.

2. Evidence of Adverse Competitive Effects

The Agencies consider any reasonably available and reliable evidence to address the central question of whether a merger may substantially lessen competition. This section discusses several categories and sources of evidence that the Agencies, in their experience, have found most informative in predicting the likely competitive effects of mergers. The list provided here is not exhaustive. In any given case, reliable evidence may be available in only some categories or from some sources. For each category of evidence, the Agencies consider evidence indicating that the merger may enhance competition as well as evidence indicating that it may lessen competition.

2.1 Types of Evidence

2.1.1 Actual Effects Observed in Consummated Mergers

When evaluating a consummated merger, the ultimate issue is not only whether adverse competitive effects have already resulted from the merger, but also whether such effects are likely to arise in the future. Evidence of observed post-merger price increases or other changes adverse to customers is given substantial weight. The Agencies evaluate whether such changes are anticompetitive effects resulting from the merger, in which case they can be dispositive. However, a consummated merger may be anticompetitive even if such effects have not yet been observed, perhaps because the merged firm may be aware of the possibility of post-merger antitrust review and moderating its conduct. Consequently, the Agencies also consider the same types of evidence they consider when evaluating unconsummated mergers.

2.1.2 Direct Comparisons Based on Experience

The Agencies look for historical events, or "natural experiments," that are informative regarding the competitive effects of the merger. For example, the Agencies may examine the impact of recent mergers, entry, expansion, or exit in the relevant market. Effects of analogous events in similar markets may also be informative.

The Agencies also look for reliable evidence based on variations among similar markets. For example, if the merging firms compete in some locales but not others, comparisons of prices charged in regions where they do and do not compete may be informative regarding post-merger prices. In some cases, however, prices are set on such a broad geographic basis that such comparisons are not informative. The Agencies also may examine how prices in similar markets vary with the number of significant competitors in those markets.

2.1.3 Market Shares and Concentration in a Relevant Market

The Agencies give weight to the merging parties' market shares in a relevant market, the level of concentration, and the change in concentration caused by the merger. See Sections 4 and 5. Mergers that cause a significant increase in concentration and result in highly concentrated markets are presumed to be likely to enhance market power, but this presumption can be rebutted by persuasive evidence showing that the merger is unlikely to enhance market power.

2.1.4 Substantial Head-to-Head Competition

The Agencies consider whether the merging firms have been, or likely will become absent the merger, substantial head-to-head competitors. Such evidence can be especially relevant for evaluating adverse unilateral effects, which result directly from the loss of that competition. See Section 6. This evidence can also inform market definition. See Section 4.

2.1.5 Disruptive Role of a Merging Party

The Agencies consider whether a merger may lessen competition by eliminating a "maverick" firm, i.e., a firm that plays a disruptive role in the market to the benefit of customers. For example, if one of the merging firms has a strong incumbency position and the other merging firm threatens to disrupt market conditions with a new technology or business model, their merger can involve the loss of actual or potential competition. Likewise, one of the merging firms may have the incentive to take the lead in price cutting or other competitive conduct or to resist increases in industry prices. A firm that may discipline prices based on its ability and incentive to expand production rapidly using available capacity also can be a maverick, as can a firm that has often resisted otherwise prevailing industry norms to cooperate on price setting or other terms of competition.

2.2 Sources of Evidence

The Agencies consider many sources of evidence in their merger analysis. The most common sources of reasonably available and reliable evidence are the merging parties, customers, other industry participants, and industry observers.

2.2.1 Merging Parties

The Agencies typically obtain substantial information from the merging parties. This information can take the form of documents, testimony, or data, and can consist of descriptions of competitively relevant conditions or reflect actual business conduct and decisions. Documents created in the normal course are more probative than documents created as advocacy materials in merger review. Documents describing industry conditions can be informative regarding the operation of the market and how a firm identifies and assesses its rivals, particularly when business decisions are made in reliance on the accuracy of those descriptions. The business decisions taken by the merging firms also can be informative about industry conditions. For example, if a firm sets price well above incremental cost, that normally indicates either that the firm believes its customers are not highly sensitive to price (not in itself of antitrust concern, see Section 4.1.3[3]) or that the firm and its rivals are engaged in coordinated interaction (see Section 7). Incremental cost depends on the relevant increment in output as well as on the time period involved, and in the case of large increments and sustained changes in output it may include some costs that would be fixed for smaller increments of output or shorter time periods.

Explicit or implicit evidence that the merging parties intend to raise prices, reduce output or capacity, reduce product quality or variety, withdraw products or delay their introduction, or curtail research and development efforts after the merger, or explicit or implicit evidence that the ability to engage in such conduct motivated the merger, can be highly informative in evaluating the likely effects of a merger. Likewise, the Agencies look for reliable evidence that the merger is likely to result in efficiencies. The Agencies give careful consideration to the views of individuals whose responsibilities, expertise, and experience relating to the issues in question provide particular indicia of reliability. The financial terms of the transaction may also be informative regarding competitive effects. For example, a purchase price in excess of the acquired firm's stand-alone market value may indicate that the acquiring firm is paying a premium because it expects to be able to reduce competition or to achieve efficiencies.

2.2.2 Customers

Customers can provide a variety of information to the Agencies, ranging from information about their own purchasing behavior and choices to their views about the effects of the merger itself.

Information from customers about how they would likely respond to a price increase, and the relative attractiveness of different products or suppliers, may be highly relevant, especially when corroborated by other evidence such as historical purchasing patterns and practices. Customers also can provide valuable information about the impact of historical events such as entry by a new supplier.

The conclusions of well-informed and sophisticated customers on the likely impact of the merger itself can also help the Agencies investigate competitive effects, because customers typically feel the consequences of

3. High margins commonly arise for products that are significantly differentiated. Products involving substantial fixed costs typically will be developed only if suppliers expect there to be enough differentiation to support margins sufficient to cover those fixed costs. High margins can be consistent with incumbent firms earning competitive returns.

both competitively beneficial and competitively harmful mergers. In evaluating such evidence, the Agencies are mindful that customers may oppose, or favor, a merger for reasons unrelated to the antitrust issues raised by that merger.

When some customers express concerns about the competitive effects of a merger while others view the merger as beneficial or neutral, the Agencies take account of this divergence in using the information provided by customers and consider the likely reasons for such divergence of views. For example, if for regulatory reasons some customers cannot buy imported products, while others can, a merger between domestic suppliers may harm the former customers even if it leaves the more flexible customers unharmed. See Section 3.

When direct customers of the merging firms compete against one another in a downstream market, their interests may not be aligned with the interests of final consumers, especially if the direct customers expect to pass on any anticompetitive price increase. A customer that is protected from adverse competitive effects by a long-term contract, or otherwise relatively immune from the merger's harmful effects, may even welcome an anticompetitive merger that provides that customer with a competitive advantage over its downstream rivals.

> *Example 1:* As a result of the merger, Customer C will experience a price increase for an input used in producing its final product, raising its costs. Customer C's rivals use this input more intensively than Customer C, and the same price increase applied to them will raise their costs more than it raises Customer C's costs. On balance, Customer C may benefit from the merger even though the merger involves a substantial lessening of competition.

2.2.3 Other Industry Participants and Observers

Suppliers, indirect customers, distributors, other industry participants, and industry analysts can also provide information helpful to a merger inquiry. The interests of firms selling products complementary to those offered by the merging firms often are well aligned with those of customers, making their informed views valuable.

Information from firms that are rivals to the merging parties can help illuminate how the market operates. The interests of rival firms often diverge from the interests of customers, since customers normally lose, but rival firms gain, if the merged entity raises its prices. For that reason, the Agencies do not routinely rely on the overall views of rival firms regarding the competitive effects of the merger. However, rival firms may provide relevant facts, and even their overall views may be instructive, especially in cases where the Agencies are concerned that the merged entity may engage in exclusionary conduct.

> *Example 2:* Merging Firms A and B operate in a market in which network effects are significant, implying that any firm's product is significantly more valuable if it commands a large market share or if

it is interconnected with others that in aggregate command such a share. Prior to the merger, they and their rivals voluntarily interconnect with one another. The merger would create an entity with a large enough share that a strategy of ending voluntary interconnection would have a dangerous probability of creating monopoly power in this market. The interests of rivals and of consumers would be broadly aligned in preventing such a merger.

3. Targeted Customers and Price Discrimination

When examining possible adverse competitive effects from a merger, the Agencies consider whether those effects vary significantly for different customers purchasing the same or similar products. Such differential impacts are possible when sellers can discriminate, e.g., by profitably raising price to certain targeted customers but not to others. The possibility of price discrimination influences market definition (see Section 4), the measurement of market shares (see Section 5), and the evaluation of competitive effects (see Sections 6 and 7).

When price discrimination is feasible, adverse competitive effects on targeted customers can arise, even if such effects will not arise for other customers. A price increase for targeted customers may be profitable even if a price increase for all customers would not be profitable because too many other customers would substitute away. When discrimination is reasonably likely, the Agencies may evaluate competitive effects separately by type of customer. The Agencies may have access to information unavailable to customers that is relevant to evaluating whether discrimination is reasonably likely.

For price discrimination to be feasible, two conditions typically must be met: differential pricing and limited arbitrage.

First, the suppliers engaging in price discrimination must be able to price differently to targeted customers than to other customers. This may involve identification of individual customers to which different prices are offered or offering different prices to different types of customers based on observable characteristics.

Example 3: Suppliers can distinguish large buyers from small buyers. Large buyers are more likely than small buyers to self-supply in response to a significant price increase. The merger may lead to price discrimination against small buyers, harming them, even if large buyers are not harmed. Such discrimination can occur even if there is no discrete gap in size between the classes of large and small buyers.

In other cases, suppliers may be unable to distinguish among different types of customers but can offer multiple products that sort customers based on their purchase decisions.

Second, the targeted customers must not be able to defeat the price increase of concern by arbitrage, e.g., by purchasing indirectly from or through other customers. Arbitrage may be difficult if it would void warranties or make service more difficult or costly for customers. Arbitrage is inherently impossible for many services. Arbitrage between customers at different geographic locations may be impractical due to transportation costs. Arbitrage on a modest scale may be possible but sufficiently costly or limited that it would not deter or defeat a discriminatory pricing strategy.

4. Market Definition

When the Agencies identify a potential competitive concern with a horizontal merger, market definition plays two roles. First, market definition helps specify the line of commerce and section of the country in which the competitive concern arises. In any merger enforcement action, the Agencies will normally identify one or more relevant markets in which the merger may substantially lessen competition. Second, market definition allows the Agencies to identify market participants and measure market shares and market concentration. See Section 5. The measurement of market shares and market concentration is not an end in itself, but is useful to the extent it illuminates the merger's likely competitive effects.

The Agencies' analysis need not start with market definition. Some of the analytical tools used by the Agencies to assess competitive effects do not rely on market definition, although evaluation of competitive alternatives available to customers is always necessary at some point in the analysis.

Evidence of competitive effects can inform market definition, just as market definition can be informative regarding competitive effects. For example, evidence that a reduction in the number of significant rivals offering a group of products causes prices for those products to rise significantly can itself establish that those products form a relevant market. Such evidence also may more directly predict the competitive effects of a merger, reducing the role of inferences from market definition and market shares.

Where analysis suggests alternative and reasonably plausible candidate markets, and where the resulting market shares lead to very different inferences regarding competitive effects, it is particularly valuable to examine more direct forms of evidence concerning those effects.

Market definition focuses solely on demand substitution factors, i.e., on customers' ability and willingness to substitute away from one product to another in response to a price increase or a corresponding non-price change such as a reduction in product quality or service. The responsive actions of suppliers are also important in competitive analysis. They are considered in these Guidelines in the sections addressing the identification of market participants, the measurement of market shares, the analysis of competitive effects, and entry.

Customers often confront a range of possible substitutes for the products of the merging firms. Some substitutes may be closer, and others more distant, either geographically or in terms of product attributes and perceptions. Additionally, customers may assess the proximity of different products differently. When products or suppliers in different geographic areas are substitutes for one another to varying degrees, defining a market to include some substitutes and exclude others is inevitably a simplification that cannot capture the full variation in the extent to which different products compete against each other. The principles of market definition outlined below seek to make this inevitable simplification as useful and informative as is practically possible. Relevant markets need not have precise metes and bounds.

Defining a market broadly to include relatively distant product or geographic substitutes can lead to misleading market shares. This is because the competitive significance of distant substitutes is unlikely to be commensurate with their shares in a broad market. Although excluding more distant substitutes from the market inevitably understates their competitive significance to some degree, doing so often provides a more accurate indicator of the competitive effects of the merger than would the alternative of including them and overstating their competitive significance as proportional to their shares in an expanded market.

> *Example 4:* Firms A and B, sellers of two leading brands of motorcycles, propose to merge. If Brand A motorcycle prices were to rise, some buyers would substitute to Brand B, and some others would substitute to cars. However, motorcycle buyers see Brand B motorcycles as much more similar to Brand A motorcycles than are cars. Far more cars are sold than motorcycles. Evaluating shares in a market that includes cars would greatly underestimate the competitive significance of Brand B motorcycles in constraining Brand A's prices and greatly overestimate the significance of cars.

Market shares of different products in narrowly defined markets are more likely to capture the relative competitive significance of these products, and often more accurately reflect competition between close substitutes. As a result, properly defined antitrust markets often exclude some substitutes to which some customers might turn in the face of a price increase even if such substitutes provide alternatives for those customers. However, a group of products is too narrow to constitute a relevant market if competition from products outside that group is so ample that even the complete elimination of competition within the group would not significantly harm either direct customers or downstream consumers. The hypothetical monopolist test (see Section 4.1.1) is designed to ensure that candidate markets are not overly narrow in this respect.

The Agencies implement these principles of market definition flexibly when evaluating different possible candidate markets. Relevant antitrust markets defined according to the hypothetical monopolist test are not always intuitive and may not align with how industry members use the term "market."

Section 4.1 describes the principles that apply to product market definition, and gives guidance on how the Agencies most often apply those principles. Section 4.2 describes how the same principles apply to geographic market definition. Although discussed separately for simplicity of exposition, the principles described in Sections 4.1 and 4.2 are combined to define a relevant market, which has both a product and a geographic dimension. In particular, the hypothetical monopolist test is applied to a group of products together with a geographic region to determine a relevant market.

4.1 Product Market Definition

When a product sold by one merging firm (Product A) competes against one or more products sold by the other merging firm, the Agencies define a relevant product market around Product A to evaluate the importance of that competition. Such a relevant product market consists of a group of substitute products including Product A. Multiple relevant product markets may thus be identified.

4.1.1 The Hypothetical Monopolist Test

The Agencies employ the hypothetical monopolist test to evaluate whether groups of products in candidate markets are sufficiently broad to constitute relevant antitrust markets. The Agencies use the hypothetical monopolist test to identify a set of products that are reasonably interchangeable with a product sold by one of the merging firms.

The hypothetical monopolist test requires that a product market contain enough substitute products so that it could be subject to post-merger exercise of market power significantly exceeding that existing absent the merger. Specifically, the test requires that a hypothetical profit-maximizing firm, not subject to price regulation, that was the only present and future seller of those products ("hypothetical monopolist") likely would impose at least a small but significant and non-transitory increase in price ("SSNIP") on at least one product in the market, including at least one product sold by one of the merging firms.[4] For the purpose of analyzing this issue, the terms of sale of products outside the candidate market are held constant. The SSNIP is employed solely as a methodological tool for performing the hypothetical monopolist test; it is not a tolerance level for price increases resulting from a merger.

Groups of products may satisfy the hypothetical monopolist test without including the full range of substitutes from which customers choose. The hypothetical monopolist test may identify a group of products as a relevant market even if customers would substitute significantly to products outside that group in response to a price increase.

---

4. If the pricing incentives of the firms supplying the products in the candidate market differ substantially from those of the hypothetical monopolist, for reasons other than the latter's control over a larger group of substitutes, the Agencies may instead employ the concept of a hypothetical profit-maximizing cartel comprised of the firms (with all their products) that sell the products in the candidate market. This approach is most likely to be appropriate if the merging firms sell products outside the candidate market that significantly affect their pricing incentives for products in the candidate market. This could occur, for example, if the candidate market is one for durable equipment and the firms selling that equipment derive substantial net revenues from selling spare parts and service for that equipment.

Example 5: Products A and B are being tested as a candidate market. Each sells for $100, has an incremental cost of $60, and sells 1200 units. For every dollar increase in the price of Product A, for any given price of Product B, Product A loses twenty units of sales to products outside the candidate market and ten units of sales to Product B, and likewise for Product B. Under these conditions, economic analysis shows that a hypothetical profit-maximizing monopolist controlling Products A and B would raise both of their prices by ten percent, to $110. Therefore, Products A and B satisfy the hypothetical monopolist test using a five percent SSNIP, and indeed for any SSNIP size up to ten percent. This is true even though two-thirds of the sales lost by one product when it raises its price are diverted to products outside the relevant market.

When applying the hypothetical monopolist test to define a market around a product offered by one of the merging firms, if the market includes a second product, the Agencies will normally also include a third product if that third product is a closer substitute for the first product than is the second product. The third product is a closer substitute if, in response to a SSNIP on the first product, greater revenues are diverted to the third product than to the second product.

Example 6: In Example 5, suppose that half of the unit sales lost by Product A when it raises its price are diverted to Product C, which also has a price of $100, while one-third are diverted to Product B. Product C is a closer substitute for Product A than is Product B. Thus Product C will normally be included in the relevant market, even though Products A and B together satisfy the hypothetical monopolist test.

The hypothetical monopolist test ensures that markets are not defined too narrowly, but it does not lead to a single relevant market. The Agencies may evaluate a merger in any relevant market satisfying the test, guided by the overarching principle that the purpose of defining the market and measuring market shares is to illuminate the evaluation of competitive effects. Because the relative competitive significance of more distant substitutes is apt to be overstated by their share of sales, when the Agencies rely on market shares and concentration, they usually do so in the smallest relevant market satisfying the hypothetical monopolist test.

Example 7: In Example 4, including cars in the market will lead to misleadingly small market shares for motorcycle producers. Unless motorcycles fail the hypothetical monopolist test, the Agencies would not include cars in the market in analyzing this motorcycle merger.

4.1.2 Benchmark Prices and SSNIP Size

The Agencies apply the SSNIP starting from prices that would likely prevail absent the merger. If prices are not likely to change absent the merger, these benchmark prices can reasonably be taken to be the prices prevailing prior to the merger.[5] If prices are likely to change absent the merger, e.g., because of innovation or entry, the Agencies may use anticipated future prices as the benchmark for the test. If prices might fall absent the merger due to the breakdown of pre-merger coordination, the Agencies may use those lower prices as the benchmark for the test. In some cases, the techniques employed by the Agencies to implement the hypothetical monopolist test focus on the difference in incentives between pre-merger firms and the hypothetical monopolist and do not require specifying the benchmark prices.

The SSNIP is intended to represent a "small but significant" increase in the prices charged by firms in the candidate market for the value they contribute to the products or services used by customers. This properly directs attention to the effects of price changes commensurate with those that might result from a significant lessening of competition caused by the merger. This methodology is used because normally it is possible to quantify "small but significant" adverse price effects on customers and analyze their likely reactions, not because price effects are more important than non-price effects.

The Agencies most often use a SSNIP of five percent of the price paid by customers for the products or services to which the merging firms contribute value. However, what constitutes a "small but significant" increase in price, commensurate with a significant loss of competition caused by the merger, depends upon the nature of the industry and the merging firms' positions in it, and the Agencies may accordingly use a price increase that is larger or smaller than five percent. Where explicit or implicit prices for the firms' specific contribution to value can be identified with reasonable clarity, the Agencies may base the SSNIP on those prices.

> *Example 8:* In a merger between two oil pipelines, the SSNIP would be based on the price charged for transporting the oil, not on the price of the oil itself. If pipelines buy the oil at one end and sell it at the other, the price charged for transporting the oil is implicit, equal to the difference between the price paid for oil at the input end and the price charged for oil at the output end. The relevant product sold by the pipelines is better described as "pipeline transportation of oil from point A to point B" than as "oil at point B."

> *Example 9:* In a merger between two firms that install computers purchased from third parties, the SSNIP would be based on their fees, not on the price of installed computers. If these firms purchase the computers and charge their customers one package price, the implicit installation fee is equal to the package charge to customers less the price of the computers.

> *Example 10:* In Example 9, suppose that the prices paid by the merging firms to purchase computers are opaque, but account for at

5. Market definition for the evaluation of non-merger antitrust concerns such as monopolization or facilitating practices will differ in this respect if the effects resulting from the conduct of concern are already occurring at the time of evaluation.

least ninety-five percent of the prices they charge for installed computers, with profits or implicit fees making up five percent of those prices at most. A five percent SSNIP on the total price paid by customers would at least double those fees or profits. Even if that would be unprofitable for a hypothetical monopolist, a significant increase in fees might well be profitable. If the SSNIP is based on the total price paid by customers, a lower percentage will be used.

4.1.3 Implementing the Hypothetical Monopolist Test

The hypothetical monopolist's incentive to raise prices depends both on the extent to which customers would likely substitute away from the products in the candidate market in response to such a price increase and on the profit margins earned on those products. The profit margin on incremental units is the difference between price and incremental cost on those units. The Agencies often estimate incremental costs, for example using merging parties' documents or data the merging parties use to make business decisions. Incremental cost is measured over the change in output that would be caused by the price increase under consideration.

In considering customers' likely responses to higher prices, the Agencies take into account any reasonably available and reliable evidence, including, but not limited to:

- ☐ how customers have shifted purchases in the past in response to relative changes in price or other terms and conditions;
- ☐ information from buyers, including surveys, concerning how they would respond to price changes;
- ☐ the conduct of industry participants, notably:
  - o sellers' business decisions or business documents indicating sellers' informed beliefs concerning how customers would substitute among products in response to relative changes in price;
  - o industry participants' behavior in tracking and responding to price changes by some or all rivals;
- ☐ objective information about product characteristics and the costs and delays of switching products, especially switching from products in the candidate market to products outside the candidate market;
- ☐ the percentage of sales lost by one product in the candidate market, when its price alone rises, that is recaptured by other products in the candidate market, with a higher recapture percentage making a price increase more profitable for the hypothetical monopolist;
- ☐ evidence from other industry participants, such as sellers of complementary products;
- ☐ legal or regulatory requirements; and
- ☐ the influence of downstream competition faced by customers in their output markets.

When the necessary data are available, the Agencies also may consider a "critical loss analysis" to assess the extent to which it corroborates inferences drawn from the evidence noted above. Critical loss analysis asks whether imposing at least a SSNIP on one or more products in a candidate market would raise or lower the hypothetical monopolist's profits. While this "breakeven" analysis differs from the profit-maximizing analysis called for by the hypothetical monopolist test in Section 4.1.1, merging parties sometimes present this type of analysis to the Agencies. A price increase raises profits on sales made at the higher price, but this will be offset to the extent customers substitute away from products in the candidate market. Critical loss analysis compares the magnitude of these two offsetting effects resulting from the price increase. The "critical loss" is defined as the number of lost unit sales that would leave profits unchanged. The "predicted loss" is defined as the number of unit sales that the hypothetical monopolist is predicted to lose due to the price increase. The price increase raises the hypothetical monopolist's profits if the predicted loss is less than the critical loss.

The Agencies consider all of the evidence of customer substitution noted above in assessing the predicted loss. The Agencies require that estimates of the predicted loss be consistent with that evidence, including the pre-merger margins of products in the candidate market used to calculate the critical loss. Unless the firms are engaging in coordinated interaction (see Section 7), high pre-merger margins normally indicate that each firm's product individually faces demand that is not highly sensitive to price.[6] Higher pre-merger margins thus indicate a smaller predicted loss as well as a smaller critical loss. The higher the pre-merger margin, the smaller the recapture percentage necessary for the candidate market to satisfy the hypothetical monopolist test.

Even when the evidence necessary to perform the hypothetical monopolist test quantitatively is not available, the conceptual framework of the test provides a useful methodological tool for gathering and analyzing evidence pertinent to customer substitution and to market definition. The Agencies follow the hypothetical monopolist test to the extent possible given the available evidence, bearing in mind that the ultimate goal of market definition is to help determine whether the merger may substantially lessen competition.

4.1.4 Product Market Definition with Targeted Customers

If a hypothetical monopolist could profitably target a subset of customers for price increases, the Agencies may identify relevant markets defined around those targeted customers, to whom a hypothetical monopolist would profitably and separately impose at least a SSNIP. Markets to serve targeted customers are also known as price discrimination markets. In practice, the Agencies identify price discrimination markets only where

---

6. While margins are important for implementing the hypothetical monopolist test, high margins are not in themselves of antitrust concern.

they believe there is a realistic prospect of an adverse competitive effect on a group of targeted customers.

> *Example 11:* Glass containers have many uses. In response to a price increase for glass containers, some users would substitute substantially to plastic or metal containers, but baby food manufacturers would not. If a hypothetical monopolist could price separately and limit arbitrage, baby food manufacturers would be vulnerable to a targeted increase in the price of glass containers. The Agencies could define a distinct market for glass containers used to package baby food.

The Agencies also often consider markets for targeted customers when prices are individually negotiated and suppliers have information about customers that would allow a hypothetical monopolist to identify customers that are likely to pay a higher price for the relevant product. If prices are negotiated individually with customers, the hypothetical monopolist test may suggest relevant markets that are as narrow as individual customers (see also Section 6.2 on bargaining and auctions). Nonetheless, the Agencies often define markets for groups of targeted customers, i.e., by type of customer, rather than by individual customer. By so doing, the Agencies are able to rely on aggregated market shares that can be more helpful in predicting the competitive effects of the merger.

4.2 Geographic Market Definition

The arena of competition affected by the merger may be geographically bounded if geography limits some customers' willingness or ability to substitute to some products, or some suppliers' willingness or ability to serve some customers. Both supplier and customer locations can affect this. The Agencies apply the principles of market definition described here and in Section 4.1 to define a relevant market with a geographic dimension as well as a product dimension.

The scope of geographic markets often depends on transportation costs. Other factors such as language, regulation, tariff and non-tariff trade barriers, custom and familiarity, reputation, and service availability may impede long-distance or international transactions. The competitive significance of foreign firms may be assessed at various exchange rates, especially if exchange rates have fluctuated in the recent past.

In the absence of price discrimination based on customer location, the Agencies normally define geographic markets based on the locations of suppliers, as explained in subsection 4.2.1. In other cases, notably if price discrimination based on customer location is feasible as is often the case when delivered pricing is commonly used in the industry, the Agencies may define geographic markets based on the locations of customers, as explained in subsection 4.2.2.

4.2.1 Geographic Markets Based on the Locations of Suppliers

Geographic markets based on the locations of suppliers encompass the region from which sales are made. Geographic markets of this type often apply when customers receive goods or services at suppliers' locations. Competitors in the market are firms with relevant production, sales, or service facilities in that region. Some customers who buy from these firms may be located outside the boundaries of the geographic market.

The hypothetical monopolist test requires that a hypothetical profit-maximizing firm that was the only present or future producer of the relevant product(s) located in the region would impose at least a SSNIP from at least one location, including at least one location of one of the merging firms. In this exercise the terms of sale for all products produced elsewhere are held constant. A single firm may operate in a number of different geographic markets, even for a single product.

> *Example 12:* The merging parties both have manufacturing plants in City X. The relevant product is expensive to transport and suppliers price their products for pickup at their locations. Rival plants are some distance away in City Y. A hypothetical monopolist controlling all plants in City X could profitably impose a SSNIP at these plants. Competition from more distant plants would not defeat the price increase because supplies coming from more distant plants require expensive transportation. The relevant geographic market is defined around the plants in City X.

When the geographic market is defined based on supplier locations, sales made by suppliers located in the geographic market are counted, regardless of the location of the customer making the purchase.

In considering likely reactions of customers to price increases for the relevant product(s) imposed in a candidate geographic market, the Agencies consider any reasonably available and reliable evidence, including:

- ☐ how customers have shifted purchases in the past between different geographic locations in response to relative changes in price or other terms and conditions;
- ☐ the cost and difficulty of transporting the product (or the cost and difficulty of a customer traveling to a seller's location), in relation to its price;
- ☐ whether suppliers need a presence near customers to provide service or support;
- ☐ evidence on whether sellers base business decisions on the prospect of customers switching between geographic locations in response to relative changes in price or other competitive variables;
- ☐ the costs and delays of switching from suppliers in the candidate geographic market to suppliers outside the candidate geographic market; and
- ☐ the influence of downstream competition faced by customers in their output markets.

4.2.2 Geographic Markets Based on the Locations of Customers

When the hypothetical monopolist could discriminate based on customer location, the Agencies may define geographic markets based on the locations of targeted customers.[7] Geographic markets of this type often apply when suppliers deliver their products or services to customers' locations. Geographic markets of this type encompass the region into which sales are made. Competitors in the market are firms that sell to customers in the specified region. Some suppliers that sell into the relevant market may be located outside the boundaries of the geographic market.

The hypothetical monopolist test requires that a hypothetical profit-maximizing firm that was the only present or future seller of the relevant product(s) to customers in the region would impose at least a SSNIP on some customers in that region. A region forms a relevant geographic market if this price increase would not be defeated by substitution away from the relevant product or by arbitrage, e.g., customers in the region travelling outside it to purchase the relevant product. In this exercise, the terms of sale for products sold to all customers outside the region are held constant.

Example 13: Customers require local sales and support. Suppliers have sales and service operations in many geographic areas and can discriminate based on customer location. The geographic market can be defined around the locations of customers.

Example 14: Each merging firm has a single manufacturing plant and delivers the relevant product to customers in City X and in City Y. The relevant product is expensive to transport. The merging firms' plants are by far the closest to City X, but no closer to City Y than are numerous rival plants. This fact pattern suggests that customers in City X may be harmed by the merger even if customers in City Y are not. For that reason, the Agencies consider a relevant geographic market defined around customers in City X. Such a market could be defined even if the region around the merging firms' plants would not be a relevant geographic market defined based on the location of sellers because a hypothetical monopolist controlling all plants in that region would find a SSNIP imposed on all of its customers unprofitable due to the loss of sales to customers in City Y.

When the geographic market is defined based on customer locations, sales made to those customers are counted, regardless of the location of the supplier making those sales.

Example 15: Customers in the United States must use products approved by U.S. regulators. Foreign customers use products not approved by U.S. regulators. The relevant product market consists of products approved by U.S. regulators. The geographic market is defined around U.S. customers. Any sales made to U.S. customers by foreign suppliers are included in the market, and those foreign

7. For customers operating in multiple locations, only those customer locations within the targeted zone are included in the market.

suppliers are participants in the U.S. market even though located outside it.

5. Market Participants, Market Shares, and Market Concentration

The Agencies normally consider measures of market shares and market concentration as part of their evaluation of competitive effects. The Agencies evaluate market shares and concentration in conjunction with other reasonably available and reliable evidence for the ultimate purpose of determining whether a merger may substantially lessen competition.

Market shares can directly influence firms' competitive incentives. For example, if a price reduction to gain new customers would also apply to a firm's existing customers, a firm with a large market share may be more reluctant to implement a price reduction than one with a small share. Likewise, a firm with a large market share may not feel pressure to reduce price even if a smaller rival does. Market shares also can reflect firms' capabilities. For example, a firm with a large market share may be able to expand output rapidly by a larger absolute amount than can a small firm. Similarly, a large market share tends to indicate low costs, an attractive product, or both.

5.1 Market Participants

All firms that currently earn revenues in the relevant market are considered market participants. Vertically integrated firms are also included to the extent that their inclusion accurately reflects their competitive significance. Firms not currently earning revenues in the relevant market, but that have committed to entering the market in the near future, are also considered market participants.

Firms that are not current producers in a relevant market, but that would very likely provide rapid supply responses with direct competitive impact in the event of a SSNIP, without incurring significant sunk costs, are also considered market participants. These firms are termed "rapid entrants." Sunk costs are entry or exit costs that cannot be recovered outside the relevant market. Entry that would take place more slowly in response to adverse competitive effects, or that requires firms to incur significant sunk costs, is considered in Section 9.

Firms that produce the relevant product but do not sell it in the relevant geographic market may be rapid entrants. Other things equal, such firms are most likely to be rapid entrants if they are close to the geographic market.

> *Example 16:* Farm A grows tomatoes halfway between Cities X and Y. Currently, it ships its tomatoes to City X because prices there are two percent higher. Previously it has varied the destination of its shipments in response to small price variations. Farm A would likely be a rapid entrant participant in a market for tomatoes in City Y.

Example 17: Firm B has bid multiple times to supply milk to School District S, and actually supplies milk to schools in some adjacent areas. It has never won a bid in School District S, but is well qualified to serve that district and has often nearly won. Firm B would be counted as a rapid entrant in a market for school milk in School District S.

More generally, if the relevant market is defined around targeted customers, firms that produce relevant products but do not sell them to those customers may be rapid entrants if they can easily and rapidly begin selling to the targeted customers.

Firms that clearly possess the necessary assets to supply into the relevant market rapidly may also be rapid entrants. In markets for relatively homogeneous goods where a supplier's ability to compete depends predominantly on its costs and its capacity, and not on other factors such as experience or reputation in the relevant market, a supplier with efficient idle capacity, or readily available "swing" capacity currently used in adjacent markets that can easily and profitably be shifted to serve the relevant market, may be a rapid entrant.[8] However, idle capacity may be inefficient, and capacity used in adjacent markets may not be available, so a firm's possession of idle or swing capacity alone does not make that firm a rapid entrant.

5.2 Market Shares

The Agencies normally calculate market shares for all firms that currently produce products in the relevant market, subject to the availability of data. The Agencies also calculate market shares for other market participants if this can be done to reliably reflect their competitive significance.

Market concentration and market share data are normally based on historical evidence. However, recent or ongoing changes in market conditions may indicate that the current market share of a particular firm either understates or overstates the firm's future competitive significance. The Agencies consider reasonably predictable effects of recent or ongoing changes in market conditions when calculating and interpreting market share data. For example, if a new technology that is important to long-term competitive viability is available to other firms in the market, but is not available to a particular firm, the Agencies may conclude that that firm's historical market share overstates its future competitive significance. The Agencies may project historical market shares into the foreseeable future when this can be done reliably.

The Agencies measure market shares based on the best available indicator of firms' future competitive significance in the relevant market. This may depend upon the type of competitive effect being considered, and on the availability of data. Typically, annual data are used, but where individual

8. If this type of supply side substitution is nearly universal among the firms selling one or more of a group of products, the Agencies may use an aggregate description of markets for those products as a matter of convenience.

transactions are large and infrequent so annual data may be unrepresentative, the Agencies may measure market shares over a longer period of time.

In most contexts, the Agencies measure each firm's market share based on its actual or projected revenues in the relevant market. Revenues in the relevant market tend to be the best measure of attractiveness to customers, since they reflect the real-world ability of firms to surmount all of the obstacles necessary to offer products on terms and conditions that are attractive to customers. In cases where one unit of a low-priced product can substitute for one unit of a higher-priced product, unit sales may measure competitive significance better than revenues. For example, a new, much less expensive product may have great competitive significance if it substantially erodes the revenues earned by older, higher-priced products, even if it earns relatively few revenues. In cases where customers sign long-term contracts, face switching costs, or tend to re-evaluate their suppliers only occasionally, revenues earned from recently acquired customers may better reflect the competitive significance of suppliers than do total revenues.

In markets for homogeneous products, a firm's competitive significance may derive principally from its ability and incentive to rapidly expand production in the relevant market in response to a price increase or output reduction by others in that market. As a result, a firm's competitive significance may depend upon its level of readily available capacity to serve the relevant market if that capacity is efficient enough to make such expansion profitable. In such markets, capacities or reserves may better reflect the future competitive significance of suppliers than revenues, and the Agencies may calculate market shares using those measures. Market participants that are not current producers may then be assigned positive market shares, but only if a measure of their competitive significance properly comparable to that of current producers is available. When market shares are measured based on firms' readily available capacities, the Agencies do not include capacity that is committed or so profitably employed outside the relevant market, or so high-cost, that it would not likely be used to respond to a SSNIP in the relevant market.

> *Example 18:* The geographic market is defined around customers in the United States. Firm X produces the relevant product outside the United States, and most of its sales are made to customers outside the United States. In most contexts, Firm X's market share will be based on its sales to U.S. customers, not its total sales or total capacity. However, if the relevant product is homogeneous, and if Firm X would significantly expand sales to U.S. customers rapidly and without incurring significant sunk costs in response to a SSNIP, the Agencies may base Firm X's market share on its readily available capacity to serve U.S. customers.

When the Agencies define markets serving targeted customers, these same principles are used to measure market shares, as they apply to those customers. In most contexts, each firm's market share is based on its actual or projected revenues from the targeted customers. However, the Agencies may instead measure market shares based on revenues from a broader group of customers if doing so would more accurately reflect the competitive significance of different suppliers in the relevant market. Revenues earned from a broader group of customers may also be used when better data are thereby available.

5.3 Market Concentration

Market concentration is often one useful indicator of likely competitive effects of a merger. In evaluating market concentration, the Agencies consider both the post-merger level of market concentration and the change in concentration resulting from a merger. Market shares may not fully reflect the competitive significance of firms in the market or the impact of a merger. They are used in conjunction with other evidence of competitive effects. See Sections 6 and 7.

In analyzing mergers between an incumbent and a recent or potential entrant, to the extent the Agencies use the change in concentration to evaluate competitive effects, they will do so using projected market shares. A merger between an incumbent and a potential entrant can raise significant competitive concerns. The lessening of competition resulting from such a merger is more likely to be substantial, the larger is the market share of the incumbent, the greater is the competitive significance of the potential entrant, and the greater is the competitive threat posed by this potential entrant relative to others.

The Agencies give more weight to market concentration when market shares have been stable over time, especially in the face of historical changes in relative prices or costs. If a firm has retained its market share even after its price has increased relative to those of its rivals, that firm already faces limited competitive constraints, making it less likely that its remaining rivals will replace the competition lost if one of that firm's important rivals is eliminated due to a merger. By contrast, even a highly concentrated market can be very competitive if market shares fluctuate substantially over short periods of time in response to changes in competitive offerings. However, if competition by one of the merging firms has significantly contributed to these fluctuations, perhaps because it has acted as a maverick, the Agencies will consider whether the merger will enhance market power by combining that firm with one of its significant rivals.

The Agencies may measure market concentration using the number of significant competitors in the market. This measure is most useful when there is a gap in market share between significant competitors and smaller rivals or when it is difficult to measure revenues in the relevant market. The Agencies also may consider the combined market share of the merging firms as an indicator of the extent to which others in the market may not be able readily to replace competition between the merging firms that is lost through the merger.

The Agencies often calculate the Herfindahl–Hirschman Index ("HHI") of market concentration. The HHI is calculated by summing the squares of the individual firms' market shares,[9] and thus gives proportionately greater weight to the larger market shares. When using the HHI, the Agencies consider both the post-merger level of the HHI and the increase in the HHI resulting from the merger. The increase in the HHI is equal to twice the product of the market shares of the merging firms.[10]

Based on their experience, the Agencies generally classify markets into three types:

- ☐ Unconcentrated Markets: HHI below 1500
- ☐ Moderately Concentrated Markets: HHI between 1500 and 2500
- ☐ Highly Concentrated Markets: HHI above 2500

The Agencies employ the following general standards for the relevant markets they have defined:

- ☐ *Small Change in Concentration:* Mergers involving an increase in the HHI of less than 100 points are unlikely to have adverse competitive effects and ordinarily require no further analysis.
- ☐ *Unconcentrated Markets:* Mergers resulting in unconcentrated markets are unlikely to have adverse competitive effects and ordinarily require no further analysis.
- ☐ *Moderately Concentrated Markets:* Mergers resulting in moderately concentrated markets that involve an increase in the HHI of more than 100 points potentially raise significant competitive concerns and often warrant scrutiny.
- ☐ *Highly Concentrated Markets:* Mergers resulting in highly concentrated markets that involve an increase in the HHI of between 100 points and 200 points potentially raise significant competitive concerns and often warrant scrutiny. Mergers resulting in highly concentrated markets that involve an increase in the HHI of more than 200 points will be presumed to be likely to enhance market power. The presumption may be rebutted by persuasive evidence showing that the merger is unlikely to enhance market power.

The purpose of these thresholds is not to provide a rigid screen to separate competitively benign mergers from anticompetitive ones, although high levels of concentration do raise concerns. Rather, they provide one way to identify some mergers unlikely to raise competitive concerns and some others for which it is particularly important to examine whether other competitive factors confirm, reinforce, or counteract the potentially harm-

9. For example, a market consisting of four firms with market shares of thirty percent, thirty percent, twenty percent, and twenty percent has an HHI of 2600 (302 + 302 + 202 + 202 = 2600). The HHI ranges from 10,000 (in the case of a pure monopoly) to a number approaching zero (in the case of an atomistic market). Although it is desirable to include all firms in the calculation, lack of information about firms with small shares is not critical because such firms do not affect the HHI significantly.

10. For example, the merger of firms with shares of five percent and ten percent of the market would increase the HHI by 100 ($5 \times 10 \times 2 = 100$).

ful effects of increased concentration. The higher the post-merger HHI and the increase in the HHI, the greater are the Agencies' potential competitive concerns and the greater is the likelihood that the Agencies will request additional information to conduct their analysis.

6. Unilateral Effects

The elimination of competition between two firms that results from their merger may alone constitute a substantial lessening of competition. Such unilateral effects are most apparent in a merger to monopoly in a relevant market, but are by no means limited to that case. Whether cognizable efficiencies resulting from the merger are likely to reduce or reverse adverse unilateral effects is addressed in Section 10.

Several common types of unilateral effects are discussed in this section. Section 6.1 discusses unilateral price effects in markets with differentiated products. Section 6.2 discusses unilateral effects in markets where sellers negotiate with buyers or prices are determined through auctions. Section 6.3 discusses unilateral effects relating to reductions in output or capacity in markets for relatively homogeneous products. Section 6.4 discusses unilateral effects arising from diminished innovation or reduced product variety. These effects do not exhaust the types of possible unilateral effects; for example, exclusionary unilateral effects also can arise.

A merger may result in different unilateral effects along different dimensions of competition. For example, a merger may increase prices in the short term but not raise longer-term concerns about innovation, either because rivals will provide sufficient innovation competition or because the merger will generate cognizable research and development efficiencies. See Section 10.

6.1 Pricing of Differentiated Products

In differentiated product industries, some products can be very close substitutes and compete strongly with each other, while other products are more distant substitutes and compete less strongly. For example, one high-end product may compete much more directly with another high-end product than with any low-end product.

A merger between firms selling differentiated products may diminish competition by enabling the merged firm to profit by unilaterally raising the price of one or both products above the pre-merger level. Some of the sales lost due to the price rise will merely be diverted to the product of the merger partner and, depending on relative margins, capturing such sales loss through merger may make the price increase profitable even though it would not have been profitable prior to the merger.

The extent of direct competition between the products sold by the merging parties is central to the evaluation of unilateral price effects. Unilateral price effects are greater, the more the buyers of products sold by one merging firm consider products sold by the other merging firm to be their next choice. The Agencies consider any reasonably available and reliable information to evaluate the extent of direct competition between the products sold by the merging firms. This includes documentary and testimonial evidence, win/loss reports and evidence from discount approval processes, customer switching patterns, and customer surveys. The types of evidence relied on often overlap substantially with the types of evidence of customer substitution relevant to the hypothetical monopolist test. See Section 4.1.1.

Substantial unilateral price elevation post-merger for a product formerly sold by one of the merging firms normally requires that a significant fraction of the customers purchasing that product view products formerly sold by the other merging firm as their next-best choice. However, unless pre-merger margins between price and incremental cost are low, that significant fraction need not approach a majority. For this purpose, incremental cost is measured over the change in output that would be caused by the price change considered. A merger may produce significant unilateral effects for a given product even though many more sales are diverted to products sold by non-merging firms than to products previously sold by the merger partner.

> *Example 19:* In Example 5, the merged entity controlling Products A and B would raise prices ten percent, given the product offerings and prices of other firms. In that example, one-third of the sales lost by Product A when its price alone is raised are diverted to Product B. Further analysis is required to account for repositioning, entry, and efficiencies.

In some cases, the Agencies may seek to quantify the extent of direct competition between a product sold by one merging firm and a second product sold by the other merging firm by estimating the diversion ratio from the first product to the second product. The diversion ratio is the fraction of unit sales lost by the first product due to an increase in its price that would be diverted to the second product. Diversion ratios between products sold by one merging firm and products sold by the other merging firm can be very informative for assessing unilateral price effects, with higher diversion ratios indicating a greater likelihood of such effects. Diversion ratios between products sold by merging firms and those sold by non-merging firms have at most secondary predictive value.

Adverse unilateral price effects can arise when the merger gives the merged entity an incentive to raise the price of a product previously sold by one merging firm and thereby divert sales to products previously sold by the other merging firm, boosting the profits on the latter products. Taking as given other prices and product offerings, that boost to profits is equal to the value to the merged firm of the sales diverted to those products. The value of sales diverted to a product is equal to the number of units diverted to that product multiplied by the margin between price and incremental cost on that product. In some cases, where sufficient information is available, the Agencies assess the value of diverted sales, which can serve as an indicator of the upward pricing pressure on the first product resulting from the merger. Diagnosing unilateral price effects based on the value of diverted sales need not rely on market definition or the calculation of market shares and concentration. The Agencies rely much more on the value of diverted sales than on the level of the HHI for diagnosing unilateral price effects in markets with differentiated products. If the value of diverted sales is proportionately small, significant unilateral price effects are unlikely.[11]

Where sufficient data are available, the Agencies may construct economic models designed to quantify the unilateral price effects resulting from the merger. These models often include independent price responses by non-merging firms. They also can incorporate merger-specific efficiencies. These merger simulation methods need not rely on market definition. The Agencies do not treat merger simulation evidence as conclusive in itself, and they place more weight on whether their merger simulations consistently predict substantial price increases than on the precise prediction of any single simulation.

A merger is unlikely to generate substantial unilateral price increases if non-merging parties offer very close substitutes for the products offered by the merging firms. In some cases, non-merging firms may be able to reposition their products to offer close substitutes for the products offered by the merging firms. Repositioning is a supply-side response that is evaluated much like entry, with consideration given to timeliness, likelihood, and sufficiency. See Section 9. The Agencies consider whether repositioning would be sufficient to deter or counteract what otherwise would be significant anticompetitive unilateral effects from a differentiated products merger.

6.2 Bargaining and Auctions

In many industries, especially those involving intermediate goods and services, buyers and sellers negotiate to determine prices and other terms of trade. In that process, buyers commonly negotiate with more than one seller, and may play sellers off against one another. Some highly structured forms of such competition are known as auctions. Negotiations often combine aspects of an auction with aspects of one-on-one negotiation, although pure auctions are sometimes used in government procurement and elsewhere.

A merger between two competing sellers prevents buyers from playing those sellers off against each other in negotiations. This alone can significantly enhance the ability and incentive of the merged entity to obtain a result more favorable to it, and less favorable to the buyer, than the merging firms would have offered separately absent the merger. The Agencies analyze unilateral effects of this type using similar approaches to those described in Section 6.1.

---

11. For this purpose, the value of diverted sales is measured in proportion to the lost revenues attributable to the reduction in unit sales resulting from the price increase. Those lost revenues equal the reduction in the number of units sold of that product multiplied by that product's price.

Anticompetitive unilateral effects in these settings are likely in proportion to the frequency or probability with which, prior to the merger, one of the merging sellers had been the runner-up when the other won the business. These effects also are likely to be greater, the greater advantage the runner-up merging firm has over other suppliers in meeting customers' needs. These effects also tend to be greater, the more profitable were the pre-merger winning bids. All of these factors are likely to be small if there are many equally placed bidders.

The mechanisms of these anticompetitive unilateral effects, and the indicia of their likelihood, differ somewhat according to the bargaining practices used, the auction format, and the sellers' information about one another's costs and about buyers' preferences. For example, when the merging sellers are likely to know which buyers they are best and second best placed to serve, any anticompetitive unilateral effects are apt to be targeted at those buyers; when sellers are less well informed, such effects are more apt to be spread over a broader class of buyers.

6.3 Capacity and Output for Homogeneous Products

In markets involving relatively undifferentiated products, the Agencies may evaluate whether the merged firm will find it profitable unilaterally to suppress output and elevate the market price. A firm may leave capacity idle, refrain from building or obtaining capacity that would have been obtained absent the merger, or eliminate pre-existing production capabilities. A firm may also divert the use of capacity away from one relevant market and into another so as to raise the price in the former market. The competitive analyses of these alternative modes of output suppression may differ.

A unilateral output suppression strategy is more likely to be profitable when (1) the merged firm's market share is relatively high; (2) the share of the merged firm's output already committed for sale at prices unaffected by the output suppression is relatively low; (3) the margin on the suppressed output is relatively low; (4) the supply responses of rivals are relatively small; and (5) the market elasticity of demand is relatively low.

A merger may provide the merged firm a larger base of sales on which to benefit from the resulting price rise, or it may eliminate a competitor that otherwise could have expanded its output in response to the price rise.

> *Example 20:* Firms A and B both produce an industrial commodity and propose to merge. The demand for this commodity is insensitive to price. Firm A is the market leader. Firm B produces substantial output, but its operating margins are low because it operates high-cost plants. The other suppliers are operating very near capacity. The merged firm has an incentive to reduce output at the high-cost plants, perhaps shutting down some of that capacity, thus driving up the price it receives on the remainder of its output. The merger harms customers, notwithstanding that the merged firm shifts some output from high-cost plants to low-cost plants.

In some cases, a merger between a firm with a substantial share of the sales in the market and a firm with significant excess capacity to serve that market can make an output suppression strategy profitable.[12] This can occur even if the firm with the excess capacity has a relatively small share of sales, if that firm's ability to expand, and thus keep price from rising, has been making an output suppression strategy unprofitable for the firm with the larger market share.

6.4 Innovation and Product Variety

Competition often spurs firms to innovate. The Agencies may consider whether a merger is likely to diminish innovation competition by encouraging the merged firm to curtail its innovative efforts below the level that would prevail in the absence of the merger. That curtailment of innovation could take the form of reduced incentive to continue with an existing product-development effort or reduced incentive to initiate development of new products.

The first of these effects is most likely to occur if at least one of the merging firms is engaging in efforts to introduce new products that would capture substantial revenues from the other merging firm. The second, longer-run effect is most likely to occur if at least one of the merging firms has capabilities that are likely to lead it to develop new products in the future that would capture substantial revenues from the other merging firm. The Agencies therefore also consider whether a merger will diminish innovation competition by combining two of a very small number of firms with the strongest capabilities to successfully innovate in a specific direction.

The Agencies evaluate the extent to which successful innovation by one merging firm is likely to take sales from the other, and the extent to which post-merger incentives for future innovation will be lower than those that would prevail in the absence of the merger. The Agencies also consider whether the merger is likely to enable innovation that would not otherwise take place, by bringing together complementary capabilities that cannot be otherwise combined or for some other merger-specific reason. See Section 10.

The Agencies also consider whether a merger is likely to give the merged firm an incentive to cease offering one of the relevant products sold by the merging parties. Reductions in variety following a merger may or may not be anticompetitive. Mergers can lead to the efficient consolidation of products when variety offers little in value to customers. In other cases, a merger may increase variety by encouraging the merged firm to reposition its products to be more differentiated from one another.

If the merged firm would withdraw a product that a significant number of customers strongly prefer to those products that would remain available, this can constitute a harm to customers over and above any effects on the

12. Such a merger also can cause adverse coordinated effects, especially if the acquired firm with excess capacity was disrupting effective coordination.

price or quality of any given product. If there is evidence of such an effect, the Agencies may inquire whether the reduction in variety is largely due to a loss of competitive incentives attributable to the merger. An anticompetitive incentive to eliminate a product as a result of the merger is greater and more likely, the larger is the share of profits from that product coming at the expense of profits from products sold by the merger partner. Where a merger substantially reduces competition by bringing two close substitute products under common ownership, and one of those products is eliminated, the merger will often also lead to a price increase on the remaining product, but that is not a necessary condition for anticompetitive effect.

> *Example 21:* Firm A sells a high-end product at a premium price. Firm B sells a mid-range product at a lower price, serving customers who are more price sensitive. Several other firms have low-end products. Firms A and B together have a large share of the relevant market. Firm A proposes to acquire Firm B and discontinue Firm B's product. Firm A expects to retain most of Firm B's customers. Firm A may not find it profitable to raise the price of its high-end product after the merger, because doing so would reduce its ability to retain Firm B's more price-sensitive customers. The Agencies may conclude that the withdrawal of Firm B's product results from a loss of competition and materially harms customers.

7. Coordinated Effects

A merger may diminish competition by enabling or encouraging post-merger coordinated interaction among firms in the relevant market that harms customers. Coordinated interaction involves conduct by multiple firms that is profitable for each of them only as a result of the accommodating reactions of the others. These reactions can blunt a firm's incentive to offer customers better deals by undercutting the extent to which such a move would win business away from rivals. They also can enhance a firm's incentive to raise prices, by assuaging the fear that such a move would lose customers to rivals.

Coordinated interaction includes a range of conduct. Coordinated interaction can involve the explicit negotiation of a common understanding of how firms will compete or refrain from competing. Such conduct typically would itself violate the antitrust laws. Coordinated interaction also can involve a similar common understanding that is not explicitly negotiated but would be enforced by the detection and punishment of deviations that would undermine the coordinated interaction. Coordinated interaction alternatively can involve parallel accommodating conduct not pursuant to a prior understanding. Parallel accommodating conduct includes situations in which each rival's response to competitive moves made by others is individually rational, and not motivated by retaliation or deterrence nor intended to sustain an agreed-upon market outcome, but nevertheless emboldens price increases and weakens competitive incentives to reduce prices or offer customers better terms. Coordinated interaction includes conduct not otherwise condemned by the antitrust laws.

The ability of rival firms to engage in coordinated conduct depends on the strength and predictability of rivals' responses to a price change or other competitive initiative. Under some circumstances, a merger can result in market concentration sufficient to strengthen such responses or enable multiple firms in the market to predict them more confidently, thereby affecting the competitive incentives of multiple firms in the market, not just the merged firm.

7.1 Impact of Merger on Coordinated Interaction

The Agencies examine whether a merger is likely to change the manner in which market participants interact, inducing substantially more coordinated interaction. The Agencies seek to identify how a merger might significantly weaken competitive incentives through an increase in the strength, extent, or likelihood of coordinated conduct. There are, however, numerous forms of coordination, and the risk that a merger will induce adverse coordinated effects may not be susceptible to quantification or detailed proof. Therefore, the Agencies evaluate the risk of coordinated effects using measures of market concentration (see Section 5) in conjunction with an assessment of whether a market is vulnerable to coordinated conduct. See Section 7.2. The analysis in Section 7.2 applies to moderately and highly concentrated markets, as unconcentrated markets are unlikely to be vulnerable to coordinated conduct.

Pursuant to the Clayton Act's incipiency standard, the Agencies may challenge mergers that in their judgment pose a real danger of harm through coordinated effects, even without specific evidence showing precisely how the coordination likely would take place. The Agencies are likely to challenge a merger if the following three conditions are all met: (1) the merger would significantly increase concentration and lead to a moderately or highly concentrated market; (2) that market shows signs of vulnerability to coordinated conduct (see Section 7.2); and (3) the Agencies have a credible basis on which to conclude that the merger may enhance that vulnerability. An acquisition eliminating a maverick firm (see Section 2.1.5) in a market vulnerable to coordinated conduct is likely to cause adverse coordinated effects.

7.2 Evidence a Market is Vulnerable to Coordinated Conduct

The Agencies presume that market conditions are conducive to coordinated interaction if firms representing a substantial share in the relevant market appear to have previously engaged in express collusion affecting the relevant market, unless competitive conditions in the market have since changed significantly. Previous express collusion in another geographic market will have the same weight if the salient characteristics of that other market at the time of the collusion are comparable to those in the relevant market. Failed previous attempts at collusion in the relevant market suggest that successful collusion was difficult pre-merger but not so difficult as to deter attempts, and a merger may tend to make success more likely. Previous collusion or attempted collusion in another product market may also be given substantial weight if the salient characteristics of that other market at the time of the collusion are closely comparable to those in the relevant market.

A market typically is more vulnerable to coordinated conduct if each competitively important firm's significant competitive initiatives can be promptly and confidently observed by that firm's rivals. This is more likely to be the case if the terms offered to customers are relatively transparent. Price transparency can be greater for relatively homogeneous products. Even if terms of dealing are not transparent, transparency regarding the identities of the firms serving particular customers can give rise to coordination, e.g., through customer or territorial allocation. Regular monitoring by suppliers of one another's prices or customers can indicate that the terms offered to customers are relatively transparent.

A market typically is more vulnerable to coordinated conduct if a firm's prospective competitive reward from attracting customers away from its rivals will be significantly diminished by likely responses of those rivals. This is more likely to be the case, the stronger and faster are the responses the firm anticipates from its rivals. The firm is more likely to anticipate strong responses if there are few significant competitors, if products in the relevant market are relatively homogeneous, if customers find it relatively easy to switch between suppliers, or if suppliers use meeting-competition clauses.

A firm is more likely to be deterred from making competitive initiatives by whatever responses occur if sales are small and frequent rather than via occasional large and long-term contracts or if relatively few customers will switch to it before rivals are able to respond. A firm is less likely to be deterred by whatever responses occur if the firm has little stake in the status quo. For example, a firm with a small market share that can quickly and dramatically expand, constrained neither by limits on production nor by customer reluctance to switch providers or to entrust business to a historically small provider, is unlikely to be deterred. Firms are also less likely to be deterred by whatever responses occur if competition in the relevant market is marked by leapfrogging technological innovation, so that responses by competitors leave the gains from successful innovation largely intact.

A market is more apt to be vulnerable to coordinated conduct if the firm initiating a price increase will lose relatively few customers after rivals respond to the increase. Similarly, a market is more apt to be vulnerable to coordinated conduct if a firm that first offers a lower price or improved product to customers will retain relatively few customers thus attracted away from its rivals after those rivals respond.

The Agencies regard coordinated interaction as more likely, the more the participants stand to gain from successful coordination. Coordination generally is more profitable, the lower is the market elasticity of demand.

Coordinated conduct can harm customers even if not all firms in the relevant market engage in the coordination, but significant harm normally is likely only if a substantial part of the market is subject to such conduct. The prospect of harm depends on the collective market power, in the relevant market, of firms whose incentives to compete are substantially weakened by coordinated conduct. This collective market power is greater, the lower is the market elasticity of demand. This collective market power is diminished by the presence of other market participants with small market shares and little stake in the outcome resulting from the coordinated conduct, if these firms can rapidly expand their sales in the relevant market.

Buyer characteristics and the nature of the procurement process can affect coordination. For example, sellers may have the incentive to bid aggressively for a large contract even if they expect strong responses by rivals. This is especially the case for sellers with small market shares, if they can realistically win such large contracts. In some cases, a large buyer may be able to strategically undermine coordinated conduct, at least as it pertains to that buyer's needs, by choosing to put up for bid a few large contracts rather than many smaller ones, and by making its procurement decisions opaque to suppliers.

8. Powerful Buyers

Powerful buyers are often able to negotiate favorable terms with their suppliers. Such terms may reflect the lower costs of serving these buyers, but they also can reflect price discrimination in their favor.

The Agencies consider the possibility that powerful buyers may constrain the ability of the merging parties to raise prices. This can occur, for example, if powerful buyers have the ability and incentive to vertically integrate upstream or sponsor entry, or if the conduct or presence of large buyers undermines coordinated effects. However, the Agencies do not presume that the presence of powerful buyers alone forestalls adverse competitive effects flowing from the merger. Even buyers that can negotiate favorable terms may be harmed by an increase in market power. The Agencies examine the choices available to powerful buyers and how those choices likely would change due to the merger. Normally, a merger that eliminates a supplier whose presence contributed significantly to a buyer's negotiating leverage will harm that buyer.

> *Example 22:* Customer C has been able to negotiate lower pre-merger prices than other customers by threatening to shift its large volume of purchases from one merging firm to the other. No other suppliers are as well placed to meet Customer C's needs for volume and reliability. The merger is likely to harm Customer C. In this situation, the Agencies could identify a price discrimination market consisting of Customer C and similarly placed customers. The merger threatens to end previous price discrimination in their favor.

Furthermore, even if some powerful buyers could protect themselves, the Agencies also consider whether market power can be exercised against other buyers.

Example 23: In Example 22, if Customer C instead obtained the lower pre-merger prices based on a credible threat to supply its own needs, or to sponsor new entry, Customer C might not be harmed. However, even in this case, other customers may still be harmed.

9. Entry

The analysis of competitive effects in Sections 6 and 7 focuses on current participants in the relevant market. That analysis may also include some forms of entry. Firms that would rapidly and easily enter the market in response to a SSNIP are market participants and may be assigned market shares. See Sections 5.1 and 5.2. Firms that have, prior to the merger, committed to entering the market also will normally be treated as market participants. See Section 5.1. This section concerns entry or adjustments to pre-existing entry plans that are induced by the merger.

As part of their full assessment of competitive effects, the Agencies consider entry into the relevant market. The prospect of entry into the relevant market will alleviate concerns about adverse competitive effects only if such entry will deter or counteract any competitive effects of concern so the merger will not substantially harm customers.

The Agencies consider the actual history of entry into the relevant market and give substantial weight to this evidence. Lack of successful and effective entry in the face of non-transitory increases in the margins earned on products in the relevant market tends to suggest that successful entry is slow or difficult. Market values of incumbent firms greatly exceeding the replacement costs of their tangible assets may indicate that these firms have valuable intangible assets, which may be difficult or time consuming for an entrant to replicate.

A merger is not likely to enhance market power if entry into the market is so easy that the merged firm and its remaining rivals in the market, either unilaterally or collectively, could not profitably raise price or otherwise reduce competition compared to the level that would prevail in the absence of the merger. Entry is that easy if entry would be timely, likely, and sufficient in its magnitude, character, and scope to deter or counteract the competitive effects of concern.

The Agencies examine the timeliness, likelihood, and sufficiency of the entry efforts an entrant might practically employ. An entry effort is defined by the actions the firm must undertake to produce and sell in the market. Various elements of the entry effort will be considered. These elements can include: planning, design, and management; permitting, licensing, or other approvals; construction, debugging, and operation of production facilities; and promotion (including necessary introductory discounts), marketing, distribution, and satisfaction of customer testing and qualification requirements. Recent examples of entry, whether successful or unsuccessful, generally provide the starting point for identifying the elements of practical entry efforts. They also can be informative regarding the scale necessary for an entrant to be successful, the presence or absence of entry barriers, the factors that influence the timing of entry, the costs and risk associated with entry, and the sales opportunities realistically available to entrants.

If the assets necessary for an effective and profitable entry effort are widely available, the Agencies will not necessarily attempt to identify which firms might enter. Where an identifiable set of firms appears to have necessary assets that others lack, or to have particularly strong incentives to enter, the Agencies focus their entry analysis on those firms. Firms operating in adjacent or complementary markets, or large customers themselves, may be best placed to enter. However, the Agencies will not presume that a powerful firm in an adjacent market or a large customer will enter the relevant market unless there is reliable evidence supporting that conclusion.

In assessing whether entry will be timely, likely, and sufficient, the Agencies recognize that precise and detailed information may be difficult or impossible to obtain. The Agencies consider reasonably available and reliable evidence bearing on whether entry will satisfy the conditions of timeliness, likelihood, and sufficiency.

9.1 Timeliness

In order to deter the competitive effects of concern, entry must be rapid enough to make unprofitable overall the actions causing those effects and thus leading to entry, even though those actions would be profitable until entry takes effect.

Even if the prospect of entry does not deter the competitive effects of concern, post-merger entry may counteract them. This requires that the impact of entrants in the relevant market be rapid enough that customers are not significantly harmed by the merger, despite any anticompetitive harm that occurs prior to the entry.

The Agencies will not presume that an entrant can have a significant impact on prices before that entrant is ready to provide the relevant product to customers unless there is reliable evidence that anticipated future entry would have such an effect on prices.

9.2 Likelihood

Entry is likely if it would be profitable, accounting for the assets, capabilities, and capital needed and the risks involved, including the need for the entrant to incur costs that would not be recovered if the entrant later exits. Profitability depends upon (a) the output level the entrant is likely to obtain, accounting for the obstacles facing new entrants; (b) the price the entrant would likely obtain in the post-merger market, accounting for the impact of that entry itself on prices; and (c) the cost per unit the entrant would likely incur, which may depend upon the scale at which the entrant would operate.

9.3 Sufficiency

Even where timely and likely, entry may not be sufficient to deter or counteract the competitive effects of concern. For example, in a differentiated product industry, entry may be insufficient because the products offered by entrants are not close enough substitutes to the products offered by the merged firm to render a price increase by the merged firm unprofitable. Entry may also be insufficient due to constraints that limit entrants' competitive effectiveness, such as limitations on the capabilities of the firms best placed to enter or reputational barriers to rapid expansion by new entrants. Entry by a single firm that will replicate at least the scale and strength of one of the merging firms is sufficient. Entry by one or more firms operating at a smaller scale may be sufficient if such firms are not at a significant competitive disadvantage.

10. Efficiencies

Competition usually spurs firms to achieve efficiencies internally. Nevertheless, a primary benefit of mergers to the economy is their potential to generate significant efficiencies and thus enhance the merged firm's ability and incentive to compete, which may result in lower prices, improved quality, enhanced service, or new products. For example, merger-generated efficiencies may enhance competition by permitting two ineffective competitors to form a more effective competitor, e.g., by combining complementary assets. In a unilateral effects context, incremental cost reductions may reduce or reverse any increases in the merged firm's incentive to elevate price. Efficiencies also may lead to new or improved products, even if they do not immediately and directly affect price. In a coordinated effects context, incremental cost reductions may make coordination less likely or effective by enhancing the incentive of a maverick to lower price or by creating a new maverick firm. Even when efficiencies generated through a merger enhance a firm's ability to compete, however, a merger may have other effects that may lessen competition and make the merger anticompetitive.

The Agencies credit only those efficiencies likely to be accomplished with the proposed merger and unlikely to be accomplished in the absence of either the proposed merger or another means having comparable anticompetitive effects. These are termed merger-specific efficiencies.[13] Only alternatives that are practical in the business situation faced by the merging firms are considered in making this determination. The Agencies do not insist upon a less restrictive alternative that is merely theoretical.

---

13. The Agencies will not deem efficiencies to be merger-specific if they could be attained by practical alternatives that mitigate competitive concerns, such as divestiture or licensing. If a merger affects not whether but only when an efficiency would be achieved, only the timing advantage is a merger-specific efficiency.

Efficiencies are difficult to verify and quantify, in part because much of the information relating to efficiencies is uniquely in the possession of the merging firms. Moreover, efficiencies projected reasonably and in good faith by the merging firms may not be realized. Therefore, it is incumbent upon the merging firms to substantiate efficiency claims so that the Agencies can verify by reasonable means the likelihood and magnitude of each asserted efficiency, how and when each would be achieved (and any costs of doing so), how each would enhance the merged firm's ability and incentive to compete, and why each would be merger-specific.

Efficiency claims will not be considered if they are vague, speculative, or otherwise cannot be verified by reasonable means. Projections of efficiencies may be viewed with skepticism, particularly when generated outside of the usual business planning process. By contrast, efficiency claims substantiated by analogous past experience are those most likely to be credited.

Cognizable efficiencies are merger-specific efficiencies that have been verified and do not arise from anticompetitive reductions in output or service. Cognizable efficiencies are assessed net of costs produced by the merger or incurred in achieving those efficiencies.

The Agencies will not challenge a merger if cognizable efficiencies are of a character and magnitude such that the merger is not likely to be anticompetitive in any relevant market.[14] To make the requisite determination, the Agencies consider whether cognizable efficiencies likely would be sufficient to reverse the merger's potential to harm customers in the relevant market, e.g., by preventing price increases in that market.[15] In conducting this analysis, the Agencies will not simply compare the magnitude of the cognizable efficiencies with the magnitude of the likely harm to competition absent the efficiencies. The greater the potential adverse competitive effect of a merger, the greater must be the cognizable efficiencies, and the more they must be passed through to customers, for the Agencies to conclude that the merger will not have an anticompetitive effect in the relevant market. When the potential adverse competitive effect of a merger is likely to be particularly substantial, extraordinarily great cognizable efficiencies would be necessary to prevent the merger from being anticompetitive. In adhering to this approach, the Agencies are

---

14. The Agencies normally assess competition in each relevant market affected by a merger independently and normally will challenge the merger if it is likely to be anticompetitive in any relevant market. In some cases, however, the Agencies in their prosecutorial discretion will consider efficiencies not strictly in the relevant market, but so inextricably linked with it that a partial divestiture or other remedy could not feasibly eliminate the anticompetitive effect in the relevant market without sacrificing the efficiencies in the other market(s). Inextricably linked efficiencies are most likely to make a difference when they are great and the likely anticompetitive effect in the relevant market(s) is small so the merger is likely to benefit customers overall.

15. The Agencies normally give the most weight to the results of this analysis over the short term. The Agencies also may consider the effects of cognizable efficiencies with no short-term, direct effect on prices in the relevant market. Delayed benefits from efficiencies (due to delay in the achievement of, or the realization of customer benefits from, the efficiencies) will be given less weight because they are less proximate and more difficult to predict. Efficiencies relating to costs that are fixed in the short term are unlikely to benefit customers in the short term, but can benefit customers in the longer run, e.g., if they make new product introduction less expensive.

mindful that the antitrust laws give competition, not internal operational efficiency, primacy in protecting customers.

In the Agencies' experience, efficiencies are most likely to make a difference in merger analysis when the likely adverse competitive effects, absent the efficiencies, are not great. Efficiencies almost never justify a merger to monopoly or near-monopoly. Just as adverse competitive effects can arise along multiple dimensions of conduct, such as pricing and new product development, so too can efficiencies operate along multiple dimensions. Similarly, purported efficiency claims based on lower prices can be undermined if they rest on reductions in product quality or variety that customers value.

The Agencies have found that certain types of efficiencies are more likely to be cognizable and substantial than others. For example, efficiencies resulting from shifting production among facilities formerly owned separately, which enable the merging firms to reduce the incremental cost of production, are more likely to be susceptible to verification and are less likely to result from anticompetitive reductions in output. Other efficiencies, such as those relating to research and development, are potentially substantial but are generally less susceptible to verification and may be the result of anticompetitive output reductions. Yet others, such as those relating to procurement, management, or capital cost, are less likely to be merger-specific or substantial, or may not be cognizable for other reasons.

When evaluating the effects of a merger on innovation, the Agencies consider the ability of the merged firm to conduct research or development more effectively. Such efficiencies may spur innovation but not affect short-term pricing. The Agencies also consider the ability of the merged firm to appropriate a greater fraction of the benefits resulting from its innovations. Licensing and intellectual property conditions may be important to this enquiry, as they affect the ability of a firm to appropriate the benefits of its innovation. Research and development cost savings may be substantial and yet not be cognizable efficiencies because they are difficult to verify or result from anticompetitive reductions in innovative activities.

11. Failure and Exiting Assets

Notwithstanding the analysis above, a merger is not likely to enhance market power if imminent failure, as defined below, of one of the merging firms would cause the assets of that firm to exit the relevant market. This is an extreme instance of the more general circumstance in which the competitive significance of one of the merging firms is declining: the projected market share and significance of the exiting firm is zero. If the relevant assets would otherwise exit the market, customers are not worse off after the merger than they would have been had the merger been enjoined.

The Agencies do not normally credit claims that the assets of the failing firm would exit the relevant market unless all of the following circumstances are met: (1) the allegedly failing firm would be unable to meet its financial obligations in the near future; (2) it would not be able to reorganize successfully under Chapter 11 of the Bankruptcy Act; and (3) it has made unsuccessful good-faith efforts to elicit reasonable alternative offers that would keep its tangible and intangible assets in the relevant market and pose a less severe danger to competition than does the proposed merger.[16]

Similarly, a merger is unlikely to cause competitive harm if the risks to competition arise from the acquisition of a failing division. The Agencies do not normally credit claims that the assets of a division would exit the relevant market in the near future unless both of the following conditions are met: (1) applying cost allocation rules that reflect true economic costs, the division has a persistently negative cash flow on an operating basis, and such negative cash flow is not economically justified for the firm by benefits such as added sales in complementary markets or enhanced customer goodwill;[17] and (2) the owner of the failing division has made unsuccessful good-faith efforts to elicit reasonable alternative offers that would keep its tangible and intangible assets in the relevant market and pose a less severe danger to competition than does the proposed acquisition.

12. Mergers of Competing Buyers

Mergers of competing buyers can enhance market power on the buying side of the market, just as mergers of competing sellers can enhance market power on the selling side of the market. Buyer market power is sometimes called "monopsony power."

To evaluate whether a merger is likely to enhance market power on the buying side of the market, the Agencies employ essentially the framework described above for evaluating whether a merger is likely to enhance market power on the selling side of the market. In defining relevant markets, the Agencies focus on the alternatives available to sellers in the face of a decrease in the price paid by a hypothetical monopsonist.

Market power on the buying side of the market is not a significant concern if suppliers have numerous attractive outlets for their goods or services. However, when that is not the case, the Agencies may conclude that the merger of competing buyers is likely to lessen competition in a manner harmful to sellers.

The Agencies distinguish between effects on sellers arising from a lessening of competition and effects arising in other ways. A merger that does not enhance market power on the buying side of the market can nevertheless lead to a reduction in prices paid by the merged firm, for example, by

16. Any offer to purchase the assets of the failing firm for a price above the liquidation value of those assets will be regarded as a reasonable alternative offer. Liquidation value is the highest value the assets could command for use outside the relevant market.

17. Because the parent firm can allocate costs, revenues, and intra-company transactions among itself and its subsidiaries and divisions, the Agencies require evidence on these two points that is not solely based on management plans that could have been prepared for the purpose of demonstrating negative cash flow or the prospect of exit from the relevant market.

reducing transactions costs or allowing the merged firm to take advantage of volume-based discounts. Reduction in prices paid by the merging firms not arising from the enhancement of market power can be significant in the evaluation of efficiencies from a merger, as discussed in Section 10.

The Agencies do not view a short-run reduction in the quantity purchased as the only, or best, indicator of whether a merger enhances buyer market power. Nor do the Agencies evaluate the competitive effects of mergers between competing buyers strictly, or even primarily, on the basis of effects in the downstream markets in which the merging firms sell.

> *Example 24:* Merging Firms A and B are the only two buyers in the relevant geographic market for an agricultural product. Their merger will enhance buyer power and depress the price paid to farmers for this product, causing a transfer of wealth from farmers to the merged firm and inefficiently reducing supply. These effects can arise even if the merger will not lead to any increase in the price charged by the merged firm for its output.

13. Partial Acquisitions

In most horizontal mergers, two competitors come under common ownership and control, completely and permanently eliminating competition between them. This elimination of competition is a basic element of merger analysis. However, the statutory provisions referenced in Section 1 also apply to one firm's partial acquisition of a competitor. The Agencies therefore also review acquisitions of minority positions involving competing firms, even if such minority positions do not necessarily or completely eliminate competition between the parties to the transaction.

When the Agencies determine that a partial acquisition results in effective control of the target firm, or involves substantially all of the relevant assets of the target firm, they analyze the transaction much as they do a merger. Partial acquisitions that do not result in effective control may nevertheless present significant competitive concerns and may require a somewhat distinct analysis from that applied to full mergers or to acquisitions involving effective control. The details of the post-acquisition relationship between the parties, and how those details are likely to affect competition, can be important. While the Agencies will consider any way in which a partial acquisition may affect competition, they generally focus on three principal effects.

First, a partial acquisition can lessen competition by giving the acquiring firm the ability to influence the competitive conduct of the target firm. A voting interest in the target firm or specific governance rights, such as the right to appoint members to the board of directors, can permit such influence. Such influence can lessen competition because the acquiring firm can use its influence to induce the target firm to compete less aggressively or to coordinate its conduct with that of the acquiring firm.

Second, a partial acquisition can lessen competition by reducing the incentive of the acquiring firm to compete. Acquiring a minority position in a rival might significantly blunt the incentive of the acquiring firm to compete aggressively because it shares in the losses thereby inflicted on that rival. This reduction in the incentive of the acquiring firm to compete arises even if cannot influence the conduct of the target firm. As compared with the unilateral competitive effect of a full merger, this effect is likely attenuated by the fact that the ownership is only partial.

Third, a partial acquisition can lessen competition by giving the acquiring firm access to non-public, competitively sensitive information from the target firm. Even absent any ability to influence the conduct of the target firm, access to competitively sensitive information can lead to adverse unilateral or coordinated effects. For example, it can enhance the ability of the two firms to coordinate their behavior, and make other accommodating responses faster and more targeted. The risk of coordinated effects is greater if the transaction also facilitates the flow of competitively sensitive information from the acquiring firm to the target firm.

Partial acquisitions, like mergers, vary greatly in their potential for anticompetitive effects. Accordingly, the specific facts of each case must be examined to assess the likelihood of harm to competition. While partial acquisitions usually do not enable many of the types of efficiencies associated with mergers, the Agencies consider whether a partial acquisition is likely to create cognizable efficiencies.

APPENDIX D

1984 NON-HORIZONTAL MERGER GUIDELINES

■ ■ ■

U.S. Department of Justice
June 14, 1984

* * *

Table of Contents

---

4. Horizontal Effect From Non-horizontal Mergers

4.0 By definition, non-horizontal mergers involve firms that do not operate in the same market. It necessarily follows that such mergers produce no immediate change in the level of concentration in any relevant market as defined in Section 2 of these Guidelines. Although non-horizontal mergers are less likely than horizontal mergers to create competitive problems, they are not invariably innocuous. This section describes the principal theories under which the Department is likely to challenge non-horizontal mergers.

4.1 Elimination of Specific Potential Entrants

4.11 The Theory of Potential Competition

In some circumstances, the non-horizontal merger[1] of a firm already in a market (the "acquired firm") with a potential entrant to that market (the "acquiring firm")[2] may adversely affect competition in the market. If the merger effectively removes the acquiring firm from the edge of the market, it could have either of the following effects:

4.111 Harm to "Perceived Potential Competition"

By eliminating a significant present competitive threat that constrains the behavior of the firms already in the market, the merger could result in an immediate deterioration in market performance. The economic theory of limit pricing suggests that monopolists and groups of colluding firms may find it profitable to restrain their pricing in order to deter new entry that is likely to push prices even lower by adding capacity to the market. If the acquiring firm had unique advantages in entering the market, the firms in the market might be able to set a new and higher price after the threat of entry by the acquiring firm was eliminated by the merger.

4.112 Harm to "Actual Potential Competition"

By eliminating the possibility of entry by the acquiring firm in a more procompetitive manner, the merger could result in a lost opportunity for improvement in market performance resulting from the addition of a significant competitor. The more procompetitive alternatives include both new entry and entry through a "toehold" acquisition of a present small competitor.

4.12 Relation Between Perceived and Actual Competition

If it were always profit-maximizing for incumbent firms to set price in such a way that all entry was deterred and if information and coordination were sufficient to implement this strategy, harm to perceived potential competition would be the only competitive problem to address. In practice, however, actual potential competition has independent importance. Firms already in the market may not find it optimal to set price low enough to

1. Under traditional usage, such a merger could be characterized as either "vertical" or "conglomerate," but the label adds nothing to the analysis.

2. The terms "acquired" and "acquiring" refer to the relationship of the firms to the market of interest, not to the way the particular transaction is formally structured.

deter all entry; moreover, those firms may misjudge the entry advantages of a particular firm and, therefore, the price necessary to deter its entry.[3]

4.13 Enforcement Standards

Because of the close relationship between perceived potential competition and actual potential competition, the Department will evaluate mergers that raise either type of potential competition concern under a single structural analysis analogous to that applied to horizontal mergers. The Department first will consider a set of objective factors designed to identify cases in which harmful effects are plausible. In such cases, the Department then will conduct a more focused inquiry to determine whether the likelihood and magnitude of the possible harm justify a challenge to the merger. In this context, the Department will consider any specific evidence presented by the merging parties to show that the inferences of competitive harm drawn from the objective factors are unreliable.

The factors that the Department will consider are as follows:

4.131 Market Concentration

Barriers to entry are unlikely to affect market performance if the structure of the market is otherwise not conducive to monopolization or collusion. Adverse competitive effects are likely only if overall concentration, or the largest firm's market share, is high. The Department is unlikely to challenge a potential competition merger unless overall concentration of the acquired firm's market is above 1800 HHI (a somewhat lower concentration will suffice if one or more of the factors discussed in Section 3.4 indicate that effective collusion in the market is particularly likely). Other things being equal, the Department is increasingly likely to challenge a merger as this threshold is exceeded.

4.132 Conditions of Entry Generally

If entry to the market is generally easy, the fact that entry is marginally easier for one or more firms is unlikely to affect the behavior of the firms in the market. The Department is unlikely to challenge a potential competition merger when new entry into the acquired firm's market can be accomplished by firms without any specific entry advantages under the conditions stated in Section 3.3. Other things being equal, the Department is increasingly likely to challenge a merger as the difficulty of entry increases above that threshold.

4.133 The Acquiring Firm's Entry Advantage

If more than a few firms have the same or a comparable advantage in entering the acquired firm's market, the elimination of one firm is unlikely to have any adverse competitive effect. The other similarly situated firm(s) would continue to exert a present restraining influence,

3. When collusion is only tacit, the problem of arriving at and enforcing the correct limit price is likely to be particularly difficult.

or, if entry would be profitable, would recognize the opportunity and enter. The Department is unlikely to challenge a potential competition merger if the entry advantage ascribed to the acquiring firm (or another advantage of comparable importance) is also possessed by three or more other firms. Other things being equal, the Department is increasingly likely to challenge a merger as the number of other similarly situated firms decreases below three and as the extent of the entry advantage over non-advantaged firms increases.

If the evidence of likely actual entry by the acquiring firm is particularly strong,[4] however, the Department may challenge a potential competition merger, notwithstanding the presence of three or more firms that are objectively similarly situated. In such cases, the Department will determine the likely scale of entry, using either the firm's own documents or the minimum efficient scale in the industry. The Department will then evaluate the merger much as it would a horizontal merger between a firm the size of the likely scale of entry and the acquired firm.

4.134 The Market Share of the Acquired Firm

Entry through the acquisition of a relatively small firm in the market may have a competitive effect comparable to new entry. Small firms frequently play peripheral roles in collusive interactions, and the particular advantages of the acquiring firm may convert a fringe firm into a significant factor in the market.[5] The Department is unlikely to challenge a potential competition merger when the acquired firm has a market share of five percent or less. Other things being equal, the Department is increasingly likely to challenge a merger as the market share of the acquired firm increases above that threshold. The Department is likely to challenge any merger satisfying the other conditions in which the acquired firm has a market share of 20 percent or more.

4.135 Efficiencies

As in the case of horizontal mergers, the Department will consider expected efficiencies in determining whether to challenge a potential competition merger. See Section 3.5 (Efficiencies).

4.2 Competitive Problems from Vertical Mergers

4.21 Barriers to Entry from Vertical Mergers

In certain circumstances, the vertical integration resulting from vertical mergers could create competitively objectionable barriers to entry. Stated generally, three conditions are necessary (but not sufficient) for this problem to exist. First, the degree of vertical integration between the

4. For example, the firm already may have moved beyond the stage of consideration and have made significant investments demonstrating an actual decision to enter.

5. Although a similar effect is possible with the acquisition of larger firms, there is an increased danger that the acquiring firm will choose to acquiesce in monopolization or collusion because of the enhanced profits that would result from its own disappearance from the edge of the market.

two markets must be so extensive that entrants to one market (the "primary market") also would have to enter the other market (the "secondary market")[6] simultaneously. Second, the requirement of entry at the secondary level must make entry at the primary level significantly more difficult and less likely to occur. Finally, the structure and other characteristics of the primary market must be otherwise so conducive to non-competitive performance that the increased difficulty of entry is likely to affect its performance. The following standards state the criteria by which the Department will determine whether these conditions are satisfied.

4.211 Need for Two–Level Entry

If there is sufficient unintegrated capacity[7] in the secondary market, new entrants to the primary market would not have to enter both markets simultaneously. The Department is unlikely to challenge a merger on this ground where post-merger sales (purchases) by unintegrated firms in the secondary market would be sufficient to service two minimum-efficient-scale plants in the primary market. When the other conditions are satisfied, the Department is increasingly likely to challenge a merger as the unintegrated capacity declines below this level.

4.212 Increased Difficulty of Simultaneous Entry to Both Markets

The relevant question is whether the need for simultaneous entry to the secondary market gives rise to a substantial incremental difficulty as compared to entry into the primary market alone. If entry at the secondary level is easy in absolute terms, the requirement of simultaneous entry to that market is unlikely adversely to affect entry to the primary market. Whatever the difficulties of entry into the primary market may be, the Department is unlikely to challenge a merger on this ground if new entry into the secondary market can be accomplished under the conditions stated in Section 3.3.[8] When entry is not possible under those conditions, the Department is increasingly concerned about vertical mergers as the difficulty of entering the secondary market increases. The Department, however, will invoke this theory only where the need for secondary market

6. This competitive problem could result from either upstream or downstream integration, and could affect competition in either the upstream market or the downstream market. In the text, the term "primary market" refers to the market in which the competitive concerns are being considered, and the term "secondary market" refers to the adjacent market.

7. Ownership integration does not necessarily mandate two-level entry by new entrants to the primary market. Such entry is most likely to be necessary where the primary and secondary markets are completely integrated by ownership and each firm in the primary market uses all of the capacity of its associated firm in the secondary market. In many cases of ownership integration, however, the functional fit between vertically integrated firms is not perfect, and an outside market exists for the sales (purchases) of the firms in the secondary market. If that market is sufficiently large and diverse, new entrants to the primary market may be able to participate without simultaneous entry to the secondary market. In considering the adequacy of this alternative, the Department will consider the likelihood of predatory price or supply "squeezes" by the integrated firms against their unintegrated rivals.

8. Entry into the secondary market may be greatly facilitated in that an assured supplier (customer) is provided by the primary market entry.

entry significantly increases the costs (which may take the form of risks) of primary market entry.

More capital is necessary to enter two markets than to enter one. Standing alone, however, this additional capital requirement does not constitute a barrier to entry to the primary market. If the necessary funds were available at a cost commensurate with the level of risk in the secondary market, there would be no adverse effect. In some cases, however, lenders may doubt that would-be entrants to the primary market have the necessary skills and knowledge to succeed in the secondary market and, therefore, in the primary market. In order to compensate for this risk of failure, lenders might charge a higher rate for the necessary capital. This problem becomes increasingly significant as a higher percentage of the capital assets in the secondary market are long-lived and specialized to that market and, therefore, the Department will consider both the degree of similarity in the essential skills in the primary and secondary markets and the economic life and degree of specialization of the capital assets in the secondary market.

Economies of scale in the secondary market may constitute an additional barrier to entry to the primary market in some situations requiring two-level entry. The problem could arise if the capacities of minimum-efficient-scale plants in the primary and secondary markets differ significantly. For example, if the capacity of a minimum-efficient-scale plant in the secondary market were significantly greater than the needs of a minimum-efficient-scale plant in the primary market, entrants would have to choose between inefficient operation at the secondary level (because of operating an efficient plant at an inefficient output or because of operating an inefficiently small plant) or a larger than necessary scale at the primary level. Either of these effects could cause a significant increase in the operating costs of the entering firm.[9]

4.213 Structure and Performance of the Primary Market

Barriers to entry are unlikely to affect performance if the structure of the primary market is otherwise not conducive to monopolization or collusion.[10] The Department is unlikely to challenge a merger on this ground unless overall concentration of the primary market is above 1800 HHI (a somewhat lower concentration will suffice if one or more of the factors discussed in Section 3.4 indicate that effective collusion is particularly likely). Above that threshold, the Department is increasingly likely to challenge a merger that meets the other criteria set forth above as the concentration increases.

---

9. It is important to note, however, that this problem would not exist if a significant outside market exists at the secondary level. In that case, entrants could enter with the appropriately scaled plants at both levels, and sell or buy in the market as necessary.

10. For example, a market with 100 firms of equal size would perform competitively despite a significant increase in entry barriers.

4.22 Facilitating Collusion Through Vertical Mergers

4.221 Vertical Integration to the Retail Level

A high level of vertical integration by upstream firms into the associated retail market may facilitate collusion in the upstream market by making it easier to monitor price. Retail prices are generally more visible than prices in upstream markets, and vertical mergers may increase the level of vertical integration to the point at which the monitoring effect becomes significant. Adverse competitive consequences are unlikely unless the upstream market is generally conducive to collusion and a large percentage of the products produced there are sold through vertically integrated retail outlets.

The Department is unlikely to challenge a merger on this ground unless 1) overall concentration of the upstream market is above 1800 HHI (a somewhat lower concentration will suffice if one or more of the factors discussed in Section 3.4 indicate that effective collusion is particularly likely), and 2) a large percentage of the upstream product would be sold through vertically-integrated retail outlets after the merger. Where the stated thresholds are met or exceeded, the Department's decision whether to challenge a merger on this ground will depend upon an individual evaluation of its likely competitive effect.

4.222 Elimination of a Disruptive Buyer

The elimination by vertical merger of a particularly disruptive buyer in a downstream market may facilitate collusion in the upstream market. If upstream firms view sales to a particular buyer as sufficiently important, they may deviate from the terms of a collusive agreement in an effort to secure that business, thereby disrupting the operation of the agreement. The merger of such a buyer with an upstream firm may eliminate that rivalry, making it easier for the upstream firms to collude effectively. Adverse competitive consequences are unlikely unless the upstream market is generally conducive to collusion and the disruptive firm is significantly more attractive to sellers than the other firms in its market.

The Department is unlikely to challenge a merger on this ground unless 1) overall concentration of the upstream market is 1800 HHI or above (a somewhat lower concentration will suffice if one or more of the factors discussed in Section 3.4 indicate that effective collusion is particularly likely), and 2) the allegedly disruptive firm differs substantially in volume of purchases or other relevant characteristics from the other firms in its market. Where the stated thresholds are met or exceeded, the Department's decision whether to challenge a merger on this ground will depend upon an individual evaluation of its likely competitive effect.

4.23 Evasion of Rate Regulation

Non-horizontal mergers may be used by monopoly public utilities subject to rate regulation as a tool for circumventing that regulation. The clearest example is the acquisition by a regulated utility of a supplier of its fixed or variable inputs. After the merger, the utility would be selling to itself and might be able arbitrarily to inflate the prices of internal transactions. Regulators may have great difficulty in policing these practices, particularly if there is no independent market for the product (or service) purchased from the affiliate.[11] As a result, inflated prices could be passed along to consumers as "legitimate" costs. In extreme cases, the regulated firm may effectively preempt the adjacent market, perhaps for the purpose of suppressing observable market transactions, and may distort resource allocation in that adjacent market as well as in the regulated market. In such cases, however, the Department recognizes that genuine economies of integration may be involved. The Department will consider challenging mergers that create substantial opportunities for such abuses.[12]

*

4.24 Efficiencies

As in the case of horizontal mergers, the Department will consider expected efficiencies in determining whether to challenge a vertical merger. See Section 3.5 (Efficiencies). An extensive pattern of vertical integration may constitute evidence that substantial economies are afforded by vertical integration. Therefore, the Department will give relatively more weight to expected efficiencies in determining whether to challenge a vertical merger than in determining whether to challenge a horizontal merger.

---

11. A less severe, but nevertheless serious, problem can arise when a regulated utility acquires a firm that is not vertically related. The use of common facilities and managers may create an insoluble cost allocation problem and provide the opportunity to charge utility customers for non-utility costs, consequently distorting resource allocation in the adjacent as well as the regulated market.

12. Where a regulatory agency has the responsibility for approving such mergers, the Department may express its concerns to that agency in its role as competition advocate.

APPENDIX E

STATEMENT OF ANTITRUST ENFORCEMENT POLICY REGARDING ACCOUNTABLE CARE ORGANIZATIONS

■ ■ ■

U.S. Justice Department and Federal Trade Commission
2011

I. Introduction

The Patient Protection and Affordable Care Act and the Health Care and Education Reconciliation Act of 2010 (collectively, the "Affordable Care Act") seek to improve the quality and reduce the costs of health care services in the United States by, among other things, encouraging physicians, hospitals, and other health care providers to become accountable for a patient population through integrated health care delivery systems.[1] One delivery system reform is the Affordable Care Act's Medicare Shared Savings Program (the "Shared Savings Program"), which promotes the formation and operation of Accountable Care Organizations ("ACOs"[2]) to serve Medicare fee-for-service beneficiaries.[3] Under this provision, "groups of providers of services and suppliers meeting criteria specified by the [Department of Health and Human Services] Secretary may work together to manage and coordinate care for Medicare fee-for-service beneficiaries through an [ACO]."[4] An ACO may share in some portion of any savings it creates if the ACO meets certain quality performance standards established by the Secretary of Health and Human Services through the Centers for Medicare and Medicaid Services ("CMS"). The Affordable Care Act requires an ACO that wishes to participate in the Shared Savings Program to enter into an agreement with CMS for not less than three years.[5]

---

1. Health Care and Education Reconciliation Act of 2010, Pub. L. No. 111–52, 124 Stat. 1029 (2010); Patient Protection and Affordable Care Act, Pub. L. No. 111–48, 124 Stat. 119 (2010).

2. As used in this document, "ACO" refers to Accountable Care Organizations under the Medicare Shared Savings Program, which also may operate in commercial markets. Patient Protection and Affordable Care Act § 3022, 124 Stat. at 395–99.

3. *Id.*

4. *Id.* at 395.

Recent commentary suggests that some health care providers are likely to create and participate in ACOs that serve both Medicare beneficiaries and commercially insured patients.[6] The Federal Trade Commission and the Antitrust Division of the Department of Justice (the "Agencies") recognize that ACOs may generate opportunities for health care providers to innovate in both the Medicare and commercial markets and achieve for many other consumers the benefits Congress intended for Medicare beneficiaries through the Shared Savings Program. Therefore, to maximize and foster opportunities for ACO innovation and better health for patients, the Agencies wish to clarify their antitrust enforcement policy regarding collaborations among independent providers that seek to become ACOs in the Shared Savings Program. The Agencies recognize that not all such ACOs are likely to benefit consumers, and under certain conditions ACOs could reduce competition and harm consumers through higher prices or lower quality of care. Thus, the antitrust analysis of ACO applicants to the Shared Savings Program seeks to protect both Medicare beneficiaries and commercially insured patients from potential anticompetitive harm while allowing ACOs the opportunity to achieve significant efficiencies.

To achieve these goals, the Agencies have developed this *Statement of Antitrust Enforcement Policy Regarding Accountable Care Organizations Participating in the Medicare Shared Savings Program* (the "Policy Statement"). The Policy Statement is intended to ensure that health care providers have the antitrust clarity and guidance needed to form procompetitive ACOs that participate in both the Medicare and commercial markets. The Policy Statement describes (1) the ACOs to which the Policy Statement will apply;[7] (2) when the Agencies will apply rule of reason treatment to those ACOs; (3) an antitrust safety zone; and (4) additional antitrust guidance for ACOs that are outside the safety zone, including a voluntary expedited antitrust review process for newly formed ACOs.[8]

II. Applicability of the Policy Statement

The Policy Statement applies to collaborations among otherwise independent providers and provider groups[9] that are eligible and intend, or

5. *Id.* at 396.

6. Fed. Trade Comm'n & Dep't of Health and Human Serv., Workshop Regarding Accountable Care Organizations, and Implications Regarding Antitrust, Physician Self-Referral, Anti-Kickback, and Civil Monetary Penalty (CMP) Laws (Oct. 5, 2010).

7. The analytical principles underlying the Policy Statement also would apply to various ACO initiatives undertaken by the Innovation Center within CMS as long as those ACOs are substantially clinically or financially integrated.

8. The Policy Statement provides guidance to assist ACOs in determining whether they are likely to present competitive concerns. It does not reflect the full analysis that the Agencies may use in evaluating ACOs or any other transaction or course of conduct. "Newly formed ACOs" are defined *infra* at note 23.

9. A "collaboration" comprises an agreement or set of agreements, other than merger agreements, among otherwise independent entities jointly to engage in economic activity, and the resulting economic activity.

have been approved, to participate in the Shared Savings Program. For ease of reference, the Policy Statement refers to such collaborations as ACOs, although they may not yet have been approved to participate as ACOs in the Shared Savings Program. The Policy Statement refers to the otherwise independent providers and provider groups that constitute the ACO as ACO participants.[10] The Policy Statement does not apply to mergers. Merger transactions, including transactions that meet the criteria set forth in Section 1.3 of the *Antitrust Guidelines for Collaborations Among Competitors*,[11] will be evaluated under the Agencies' *Horizontal Merger Guidelines*.[12] The Policy Statement also does not apply to single, fully integrated entities.

III. The Agencies Will Apply Rule of Reason Analysis to ACOs That Meet Certain Conditions

The antitrust laws treat naked price-fixing and market-allocation agreements among competitors as per se illegal. Joint price agreements among competing health care providers are evaluated under the rule of reason, however, if the providers are financially or clinically integrated and the agreement is reasonably necessary to accomplish the procompetitive benefits of the integration.

A rule of reason analysis evaluates whether the collaboration is likely to have anticompetitive effects and, if so, whether the collaboration's potential procompetitive efficiencies are likely to outweigh those effects. The greater the likely anticompetitive effects, the greater the likely efficiencies must be for the collaboration to pass muster under the antitrust laws. The Agencies have articulated the standards for both financial and clinical integration in various policy statements, speeches, business reviews, and advisory opinions. For example, the Agencies' *Statements of Antitrust Enforcement Policy in Health Care* (the "Health Care Statements") explain that where participants in physician or multiprovider joint ventures have agreed to share substantial financial risk as defined in the Health Care Statements, their risk-sharing arrangement generally establishes both an overall efficiency goal for the venture and the incentives for the participants to meet that goal.[13] Accordingly, the setting of price is integral to the venture's use of such an arrangement and therefore warrants evaluation under the rule of reason.[14] The Health

U.S. DEP'T OF JUSTICE & FED. TRADE COMM'N, ANTITRUST GUIDELINES FOR COLLABORATIONS AMONG COMPETITORS § 1.1 (2000) [hereinafter COLLABORATION GUIDELINES], *available at* http://www.ftc.gov/os/2000/04/ftcdojguidelines.pdf.

10. An ACO participant can be an independent physician solo practice, a fully integrated physician group practice, an inpatient facility, or an outpatient facility. The Policy Statement's definition of ACO participant may differ from CMS's use of the term.

11. COLLABORATION GUIDELINES, *supra* note 9, § 1.3.

12. U.S. DEP'T OF JUSTICE & FED. TRADE COMM'N, HORIZONTAL MERGER GUIDELINES (rev. ed. 2010), *available at* http://www.justice.gov/atr/public/guidelines/hmg-2010.pdf.

13. U.S. DEP'T OF JUSTICE & FED. TRADE COMM'N, STATEMENTS OF ANTITRUST ENFORCEMENT POLICY IN HEALTH CARE, Statements 8 and 9 (1996) [hereinafter HEALTH CARE STATEMENTS], *available at* http://www.ftc.gov/reports/hlth3s.pdf.

14. *Id.*

Care Statements provide examples of financial risk-sharing arrangements that can satisfy this standard, but also recognize that other acceptable financial risk-sharing arrangements might develop.[15]

The Health Care Statements further explain that provider joint ventures also may involve clinical integration sufficient to ensure that the venture is likely to produce significant efficiencies.[16] Clinical integration can be evidenced by the joint venture implementing an active and ongoing program to evaluate and modify practice patterns by the venture's providers and to create a high degree of interdependence and cooperation among the providers to control costs and ensure quality.[17] Federal Trade Commission staff advisory opinions discuss evidence that appears sufficient to demonstrate clinical integration in specific factual circumstances.[18]

The Affordable Care Act provides that CMS may approve ACOs that meet certain eligibility criteria, including (1) a formal legal structure that allows the ACO to receive and distribute payments for shared savings; (2) a leadership and management structure that includes clinical and administrative processes; (3) processes to promote evidence-based medicine and patient engagement; (4) reporting on quality and cost measures; and (5) coordinated care for beneficiaries.[19] CMS has further defined these eligibility criteria through regulations.[20]

By contrast, the Agencies have not previously listed specific criteria required to establish clinical integration, but instead have responded to detailed proposals from health care providers who have decided on specific ways to integrate their health care delivery systems to improve quality and lower costs.[21] The Agencies have chosen to avoid prescribing how clinical integration should take place. Nonetheless, the Agencies recognize that health care providers seeking to create ACOs in the context of the Shared Savings Program could benefit from additional antitrust guidance in evaluating whether an ACO that satisfies the CMS eligibility criteria could be subject to an antitrust investigation and potential challenge as engaging in per se illegal conduct.

The Agencies have determined that CMS's eligibility criteria are broadly consistent with the indicia of clinical integration that the Agencies

---

15. *Id.*

16. *Id.*

17. *See, e.g.*, Christine A. Varney, Assistant Attorney Gen., Antitrust Div., U.S. Dep't of Justice, Antitrust and Healthcare at 12 (May 24, 2010), *available at* http://www.justice.gov/atr/public/speeches/258898.pdf.

18. *See* FED. TRADE COMM'N, ADVISORY OPINIONS (1982–2010), *available at* http://www.ftc.gov/bc/healthcare/industryguide/advisory.htm#2010.

19. Patient Protection and Affordable Care Act, Pub. L. No. 111–48, § 3022, 124 Stat. 119, 395–99 (2010).

20. Medicare Program; Medicare Shared Savings Program: Accountable Care Organizations, 42 C.F.R. pt. 425 (2011) [hereinafter CMS ACO Rule].

21. *See generally* FTC Staff Advisory Opinions (2002–Present), *available at* www.ftc.gov/bc/healthcare/industryguide/opinionguidance.htm; *see also* U.S. DEP'T OF JUSTICE & FED. TRADE COMM'N, IMPROVING HEALTH CARE: ANOTHER DOSE OF COMPETITION ch. 2 at 34–41 (July 2004), *available at* http://www.ftc.gov/reports/healthcare/040723healthcarerpt.pdf.

previously set forth in the Health Care Statements and identified in the context of specific proposals for clinical integration from health care providers.[22] The Agencies also have determined that organizations meeting the eligibility requirements for the Shared Savings Program are reasonably likely to be bona fide arrangements intended to improve the quality, and reduce the costs, of providing medical and other health care services through their participants' joint efforts.

To assess whether an ACO has improved quality and reduced costs to Medicare, CMS will collect and evaluate cost, utilization, and quality metrics relating to each ACO's performance in the Shared Savings Program. The results of this monitoring will help the Agencies determine whether the CMS eligibility criteria have required a sufficient level of clinical integration to produce cost savings and quality improvements, and may help inform the Agencies' future analysis of ACOs and other provider organizations.

In light of CMS's eligibility criteria, and its monitoring of each ACO's results, the Agencies will treat joint negotiations with private payers as reasonably necessary to an ACO's primary purpose of improving health care delivery, and will afford rule of reason treatment to an ACO that meets CMS's eligibility requirements for, and participates in, the Shared Savings Program and uses the same governance and leadership structures and clinical and administrative processes it uses in the Shared Savings Program to serve patients in commercial markets. The Agencies further note that CMS's regulations allow an ACO to propose alternative ways to establish clinical management and oversight of the ACO, and the Agencies are willing to consider other proposals for clinical integration as well.

IV. The Agencies' Antitrust Analysis of ACOs That Meet CMS Eligibility Criteria

The following Sections provide additional antitrust guidance for ACOs that are eligible and intend, or have been approved, to participate in the Shared Savings Program, including those ACOs that also plan to operate in the commercial market. Section A sets forth a safety zone for certain ACOs that are highly unlikely to raise significant competitive concerns and, therefore, will not be challenged by the Agencies under the antitrust laws, absent extraordinary circumstances.

The Agencies emphasize that ACOs outside the safety zone may be procompetitive and legal. An ACO that does not impede the functioning of a competitive market will not raise competitive concerns. The creation of a safety zone reflects the view that ACOs that fall within the safety zone are highly unlikely to raise significant competitive concerns; it does not imply that ACOs outside the safety zone necessarily present competitive concerns.

22. *Id. See also, e.g.*, TriState Health Partners, Inc. Advisory Opinion from FTC Staff (Apr. 13, 2009) (evaluating TriState Health Partners' proposal and stating that, if implemented as proposed, FTC staff would not recommend that the Commission challenge the proposed program), *available at* www.ftc.gov/os/closings/staff/090413tristateaoletter.pdf.

Section B offers options for ACOs that seek additional antitrust guidance. It describes certain conduct all ACOs generally should avoid, other conduct that ACOs with high Primary Service Area ("PSA") shares or other possible indicia of market power may wish to avoid, and the process by which a newly formed ACO[23] may obtain a voluntary expedited antitrust review.

A. The Antitrust Safety Zone for ACOs in the Shared Savings Program

This Section sets forth an antitrust safety zone for ACOs that meet the CMS eligibility criteria for and intend, or have been approved, to participate in the Shared Savings Program and are highly unlikely to raise significant competitive concerns. The Agencies will not challenge ACOs that fall within the safety zone, absent extraordinary circumstances.[24]

To determine whether it falls within the safety zone, an ACO should evaluate the ACO's share of services in each ACO participant's PSA. Although a PSA does not necessarily constitute a relevant antitrust geographic market, it nonetheless serves as a useful screen for evaluating potential competitive effects.

The Policy Statement focuses on PSA shares for three major categories of services: physician specialties, major diagnostic categories ("MDCs") for inpatient facilities, and outpatient categories, as defined by CMS, for outpatient facilities.[25]

Although these services are useful in evaluating potential anticompetitive effects, they do not necessarily constitute relevant antitrust product markets. The Appendix to the Policy Statement describes how to calculate an ACO's shares of these services in the relevant PSAs, identifies data sources available for these calculations, and provides illustrative examples.[26]

For an ACO to fall within the safety zone, independent ACO participants that provide the same service (a "common service") must have a combined share of 30 percent or less of each common service in each participant's PSA, wherever two or more ACO participants provide that service to patients from that PSA.[27] As noted above, a service is defined as

---

23. "Newly formed ACOs" are those ACOs that, as of March 23, 2010, the date on which the Patient Protection and Affordable Care Act was enacted, had not yet signed or jointly negotiated any contracts with private payers, and have not yet participated in the Shared Savings Program. Patient Protection and Affordable Care Act, Pub. L. No. 111–48, 124 Stat. 119 (2010). An ACO is not newly formed if it comprises only the same, or a subset of the same, providers that signed or jointly negotiated contracts with private payers on or before March 23, 2010.

24. Extraordinary circumstances could include, for example, ACO participants engaging in collusion or improper exchanges of price information or other competitively sensitive information with respect to their sale of competing services outside the ACO. *See infra* IV(B)(1)(a).

25. The Policy Statement does not apply to other types of providers (e.g., clinical laboratories or nursing homes). Nonetheless, the Agencies recognize that those providers may participate in ACOs.

26. The ACO may send questions regarding PSA share calculations to aco_psa_questions@ftc.gov.

27. Thus, if two otherwise independent physician group practices form an ACO and each includes cardiologists and oncologists, each physician group practice would be an independent

a primary specialty for physicians, an MDC for inpatient facilities, or an outpatient category for outpatient facilities. The PSA for each participant is defined as "the lowest number of postal zip codes from which the [ACO participant] draws at least 75 percent of its [patients],"[28] separately for all physician, inpatient, or outpatient services. Thus, for purposes of determining whether the ACO is eligible for the safety zone, each independent physician solo practice, each fully integrated physician group practice, each inpatient facility (even if part of a hospital system), and each outpatient facility will have its own PSA. In addition, each inpatient facility hospital will have separate PSAs for its (1) inpatient services, (2) outpatient services, and (3) physician services provided by its physician employees, if any.[29]

As described below, the availability of the PSA safety zone differs in some cases depending on whether an ACO participant is exclusive or non-exclusive to the ACO. To participate in an ACO on a non-exclusive basis, a participant must be allowed to contract with private payers through entities other than the ACO, including contracting individually or through other ACOs or analogous collaborations. The ACO must be non-exclusive in fact and not just in name. Exclusivity may be present explicitly or implicitly, formally or informally, through a written or de facto agreement as shown by conduct.[30]

Hospitals and Ambulatory Surgical Centers. Any hospital or ambulatory surgery center ("ASC") participating in an ACO must be non-exclusive to the ACO to fall within the safety zone, regardless of its PSA share.

Physicians. The safety zone for physicians (regardless of whether the physicians are hospital employees) does not differ based on whether the physicians are exclusive or non-exclusive to the ACO, unless they fall within the rural exception or dominant participant limitation described below.

1. Rural Exception

An ACO that exceeds the 30 percent PSA share may still fall within the safety zone if it qualifies for this rural exception. The rural exception allows such an ACO to include one physician or physician group practice[31]

participant in the ACO, and cardiology and oncology would be common services. If, on the other hand, one physician group practice consists only of cardiologists and the other only of oncologists, then there would be no common services and the ACO would fall within the safety zone regardless of its share, subject to the dominant participant limitation described below.

28. Medicare Program: Physicians' Referrals to Health Care Entities With Which They Have Financial Relationships (Phase II), 69 Fed. Reg. 16,094 (Mar. 26, 2004).

29. *See* Appendix to the Policy Statement.

30. The Health Care Statements further explain the indicia of non-exclusivity that the Agencies consider relevant to this evaluation. HEALTH CARE STATEMENTS, *supra* note 13, at 66–67.

31. To qualify for the rural exception, the physician group practice must be treating patients as a fully integrated practice group as of the date of the Policy Statement. The practice group can add or eliminate physicians and still remain in the safety zone, as long as the number of full-time equivalent physicians in the practice group does not increase during the ACO's Shared Savings Program agreement period. For the purposes of the Policy Statement, Federally Qualified Health per specialty from each rural area[32] *on a non-exclusive basis* and still fall within the safety zone, provided the physician's or physician group practice's primary office is in a zip code that is classified as "isolated rural" or "other small rural."[33] Thus, an ACO may qualify for the safety zone as long as it includes only one physician or physician group practice per specialty for each county that contains at least one "isolated rural" or "other small rural" zip code, even if the inclusion of these physicians causes the ACO's share of any common service to exceed 30 percent in any ACO participant's PSA.

Likewise, an ACO may include Rural Hospitals[34] *on a non-exclusive basis* and qualify for the safety zone, even if the inclusion of a Rural Hospital causes the ACO's share of any common service to exceed 30 percent in any ACO participant's PSA.

2. Dominant Participant Limitation

The dominant participant limitation applies to any ACO that includes a participant with a greater than 50 percent share in its PSA of any service that no other ACO participant provides to patients in that PSA. Under these conditions, the ACO participant must be *non-exclusive* to the ACO for the ACO to fall within the safety zone.[35] In addition, to fall within the safety zone, an ACO with a dominant participant cannot

Centers and Rural Health Clinics, as defined by the Social Security Act, are considered physician group practices. 42 U.S.C. § 1396d (2006); 42 U.S.C. § 1395x(aa) (2006). A physician or physician group practice that qualifies for the rural exception may obtain "call coverage" from other physicians in the same rural area without losing its safety zone status as long as those physicians do not participate in the ACO.

32. For the purposes of the Policy Statement, a "rural area" means any county containing at least one zip code that has been classified as "isolated rural," or "other small rural," according to the WWAMI Rural Health Research Center of the University of Washington's seven category classification. http://depts.washington.edu/uwruca/ruca-maps.php. These are zip codes that have a Rural Urban Commuting Area ("RUCA") code of 10.0, 10.2–10.6, 8.0, 8.2–8.4, or 9.0–9.2 as developed by the WWAMI Rural Health Research Center of the University of Washington and the U.S. Department of Agriculture's Economic Research Service. http://www.ers.usda.gov/briefing/Rurality/RuralUrbanCommutingAreas/. The RUCA code for any particular zip code can be found at http://depts.washington.edu/uwruca/ruca-download.php.

33. A physician's or physician group practice's primary office is the office in which the majority of the physician's or physician group practice's patient visits take place. If no office serves a majority of a physician's patients, the majority of patient visits must take place in offices located in "isolated rural" or "other small rural" zip codes to qualify for the rural exception.

34. For the purposes of the Policy Statement, a Rural Hospital is defined as a Sole Community Hospital, a Critical Access Hospital, or any other acute care hospital located in a rural area that has no more than 50 acute care inpatient beds and is located at least 35 miles from any other inpatient acute care hospital. A Sole Community Hospital is a hospital that is paid under the Medicare hospital inpatient prospective payment system and meets the criteria for Sole Community Hospital status as specified at 42 C.F.R. § 412.92. *See also* DEP'T OF HEALTH AND HUMAN SERVS., CTRS. FOR MEDICARE & MEDICAID SERVS., SOLE COMMUNITY HOSPITAL, RURAL HEALTH FACT SHEET SERIES (Oct. 2010), *available at* https://www.cms.gov/MLNProducts/downloads/SoleCommHospfctsht508–09.pdf; Social Security Act, 42 U.S.C. § 1395ww(d)(5)(D)(iii) (2006). A Critical Access Hospital is a hospital that has been certified as a Medicare Critical Access Hospital, as described in 42 C.F.R. § 485 Subpart F. *See also* 42 U.S.C. § 1395i–4(c)(2).

35. For example, a physician group participating in the ACO may comprise a specialty not found in any other ACO participant. In this case, the ACO may be eligible for the safety zone even if the physician group's share exceeds 50 percent, but only if the physician group participates in the ACO on a non-exclusive basis and the ACO does not restrict a private payer's ability to contract or deal with other ACOs or provider groups.

require a private payer to contract exclusively with the ACO or otherwise restrict a private payer's ability to contract or deal with other ACOs or provider networks.

* * *

The safety zone will remain in effect for the duration of an ACO's agreement with CMS, provided the ACO continues to meet the safety zone's requirements. An ACO will not lose its safety zone status solely because it attracts more patients.

B. ACOs Outside the Safety Zone

ACOs that fall outside the safety zone may be procompetitive and lawful. An ACO that does not impede the functioning of a competitive market will not raise competitive concerns.[36]

Nonetheless, there may be circumstances in which an ACO would raise competitive concerns. This section describes some types of conduct by an ACO that, under certain circumstances, may raise competitive concerns and outlines how an ACO may obtain further antitrust guidance from the Agencies.

1. Conduct to Avoid

a. Improper Sharing of Competitively Sensitive Information

Regardless of an ACO's PSA shares or other indicia of market power, significant competitive concerns can arise when an ACO's operations lead to price-fixing or other collusion among ACO participants in their sale of competing services outside the ACO. For example, improper exchanges of prices or other competitively sensitive information among competing participants could facilitate collusion and reduce competition in the provision of services outside the ACO, leading to increased prices or reduced quality or availability of health care services.[37] ACOs should refrain from, and implement appropriate firewalls or other safeguards against, conduct that may facilitate collusion among ACO participants in the sale of competing services outside the ACO.[38]

---

36. The Agencies emphasize that PSA shares are useful as a screening device and that alternative data and information also may be useful in evaluating the likely competitive significance of a particular ACO. The Agencies recognize that an ACO may have reliable evidence other than PSA shares from which the ACO may reasonably conclude that the ACO is unlikely to raise competitive concerns.

37. Health Care Statements 4, 5, and 6 relate to the sharing of data and information among competing providers. The Health Care Statements set forth safety zones for providers' collective provision of fee- and non-fee-related information to health care purchasers and participation in exchanges of price and cost information. The Health Care Statements also provide further guidance on the distinctions between legitimate information sharing and information sharing that may facilitate collusion or otherwise raise competitive concerns. HEALTH CARE STATEMENTS, *supra* note 13, at 40–52.

38. ACOs within the safety zone should also refrain from this conduct. *See supra* note 24.

b. Conduct by ACOs with High PSA Shares or Other Possible Indicia of Market Power That May Raise Competitive Concerns

For ACOs with high PSA shares or other possible indicia of market power, the Agencies identify four types of conduct that may raise competitive concerns.[39] The Agencies recognize that some of the conduct described in (1) through (4) below may be competitively neutral or even procompetitive, depending on the circumstances, including whether the ACO has market power. For example, an ACO that requires its participants to contract exclusively through the ACO to increase the ACO's efficiency is generally less likely to raise competitive concerns the greater the number of competing ACOs or independent providers available to contract with private payers or to participate in competing ACOs or other analogous collaborations.

An ACO with high PSA shares or other possible indicia of market power may wish to avoid the conduct set forth in (1) through (4) below. Depending on the circumstances, the conduct identified below may prevent private payers from obtaining lower prices and better quality service for their enrollees:

1. Preventing or discouraging private payers from directing or incentivizing patients to choose certain providers, including providers that do not participate in the ACO, through "anti-steering," "anti-tiering," "guaranteed inclusion," "most-favored-nation," or similar contractual clauses or provisions
2. Tying sales (either explicitly or implicitly through pricing policies) of the ACO's services to the private payer's purchase of other services from providers outside the ACO (and vice versa), including providers affiliated with an ACO participant (e.g., an ACO should not require a purchaser to contract with *all* of the hospitals under common ownership with a hospital that participates in the ACO)
3. Contracting on an exclusive basis with ACO physicians, hospitals, ASCs, or other providers, thereby preventing or discouraging those providers from contracting with private payers outside the ACO, either individually or through other ACOs or analogous collaborations[40]
4. Restricting a private payer's ability to make available to its health plan enrollees cost, quality, efficiency, and performance information to aid enrollees in evaluating and selecting providers in the health plan, if that information is similar to the cost, quality, efficiency, and performance measures used in the Shared Savings Program

---

39. ACOs with high PSA shares or other possible indicia of market power also should consider the likely competitive effects of other types of conduct in which they engage.

40. Note that, although CMS requires the physician practice through which physicians bill for primary care services and to which Medicare beneficiaries are assigned to contract exclusively with one ACO for the purposes of beneficiary assignment, CMS does *not* require either those individual physicians or physician practices to contract exclusively through the same ACO for the purposes of providing services to private health plans' enrollees. CMS ACO Rule, *supra* note 20.

2. Availability of Expedited Voluntary Antitrust Review

Any newly formed ACO[41] that desires further antitrust guidance regarding its formation and planned operation can seek expedited 90 day review from the Agencies.[42] During expedited review, the reviewing Agency will examine whether the ACO will likely harm competition by increasing the ACO's ability or incentive profitably to raise prices above competitive levels or reduce output, quality, service, or innovation below what likely would prevail in the absence of the ACO.[43] To the extent possible in the 90 day review period, the Agency will consider factors in the rule of reason analysis as explained in the *Antitrust Guidelines for Collaborations Among Competitors* and the Health Care Statements.[44]

The ACO should submit its request for expedited review, along with a completed cover sheet (available on the Agencies' websites), to both Agencies before its entrance into the Shared Savings Program, and the Agencies will then promptly determine, and notify the applicant, which Agency will be the reviewing Agency.[45] As soon as the Agencies notify the applicant which Agency will be the reviewing Agency, the applicant should provide all of the documents and information listed below to the reviewing Agency. The Agencies shall establish a Federal Trade Commission/Department of Justice ACO Working Group to collaborate and discuss issues arising out of the ACO reviews. This process will allow ACOs to rely on the expertise of both Agencies and ensure efficient, cooperative, and expeditious reviews.[46]

To start the 90 day review, the reviewing Agency must receive all of the following documents and information:[47]

1. The application and all supporting documents that the ACO plans to submit, or has submitted, to CMS, including a sample of each type of participation agreement and each type of document that reflects a financial arrangement between or among the ACO and

---

41. *See supra* note 23.

42. When the Federal Trade Commission is the reviewing Agency, Commission staff will perform the ACO review pursuant to the Commission's authorization of its staff in 16 C.F.R. § 1.1(b). When the Antitrust Division is the reviewing Agency, the Assistant Attorney General in charge of the Antitrust Division or the Assistant Attorney General's delegate will sign the review letter. 28 C.F.R § 50.6.

43. *See* COLLABORATION GUIDELINES, *supra* note 9, § 1.2.

44. *See id.* § 3.3; HEALTH CARE STATEMENTS, *supra* note 13, Statements 8 and 9.

45. A request for an expedited review must be submitted in writing to either (1) the Office of the Assistant Attorney General, Antitrust Division, Department of Justice, Main Justice Building, Room 3109, 950 Pennsylvania Avenue, NW, Washington, DC 20530 (for non-U.S. Postal Service deliveries, use ZIP code 20004), and to the Federal Trade Commission, Bureau of Competition, Premerger Notification Office, Room 303, 600 Pennsylvania Avenue, NW, Washington, DC 20580 or (2) acorequest@usdoj.gov and acorequest@ftc.gov.

46. For example, it has been standard practice for the Agencies to share with each other their proposed health care business review and staff advisory opinion letters before issuing them in final form to ensure application of consistent standards of antitrust review.

47. The ACO must represent in writing that it has undertaken a good-faith search for the documents and information specified in the Policy Statement and, where applicable, provided all responsive material.

Moreover, the Agencies may request additional documents and information where necessary to evaluate the ACO. A request for additional documents and information, however, will not extend the 90 day review period.

its participants, as well as the ACO's bylaws and operating policies

2. Documents discussing

   a. the ACO's business strategies or plans to compete in the Medicare and commercial markets, including those relating to the ACO's likely impact on the prices, cost, or quality of any service provided by the ACO to Medicare beneficiaries, commercial health plans, or other payers; and

   b. the level and nature of competition among participants in the ACO, and the competitive significance of the ACO and ACO participants in the markets in which they provide services

3. Information sufficient to show the following:

   a. The common services that two or more ACO participants provide to patients from the same PSA, as described in the Appendix, and the identity of the ACO participants or providers providing those services

   b. The PSA of each ACO participant, and either PSA share calculations the ACO may have performed or other data that show the current competitive significance of the ACO or ACO participants, including any data that describe the geographic service area of each participant and the size of each participant relative to other providers serving patients from that area

   c. Restrictions that prevent ACO participants from obtaining information regarding prices that other ACO participants charge private payers that do not contract through the ACO

   d. The identity, including points of contact, of the five largest commercial health plans or other private payers, actual or projected, for the ACO's services

   e. The identity of any other existing or proposed ACO known to operate, or known to plan to operate, in any market in which the ACO will provide services

Moreover, the ACO may submit any other documents and information that it believes may be helpful to the Agency in assessing the ACO's likely impact on competition. The documents and information may include anything that may establish a clearer picture of competitive realities in the market, including

1. evidence that the ACO is not likely to have market power in the relevant market;

2. any substantial procompetitive justification for why the ACO needs its proposed composition to provide high-quality, cost-effective care to Medicare beneficiaries and patients in the commercial market; and

3. if relevant, an explanation as to why the ACO engaging in any of the four types of conduct listed in Section IV.B of the Policy Statement would not be anticompetitive or might even be procompetitive.

Within 90 days of receiving all of the above documents and information,[48] the reviewing Agency will advise the ACO that the ACO's formation and operation, as described in the documents and information provided to the Agency,

1. does not likely raise competitive concerns or, if appropriate, does not likely raise competitive concerns conditioned on the ACO's written agreement to take specific steps to remedy concerns raised by the Agency;
2. potentially raises competitive concerns; or
3. likely raises competitive concerns.

As is current practice, both the request letter and the reviewing Agency's response will be made public consistent with applicable confidentiality provisions.[49] Also, consistent with current practice, if it appears that an ACO's formation or conduct may be anticompetitive, the Agency may investigate the ACO and, if appropriate, take enforcement action at any time before or during the ACO's participation in the Shared Savings Program.

---

48. Upon the applicant's request, the reviewing Agency may extend the review beyond 90 days, subject to the availability of resources or other discretionary considerations.

49. The provisions regarding public access to review information, non-disclosure of competitively sensitive or business confidential information, and retention of review information set forth in 28 C.F.R. § 50.6 (2010) (U.S. Department of Justice business review letters) and 16 C.F.R. §§ 1.1–1.4 (2010) (FTC advisory opinions) will generally apply to the expedited review process. Requesters should follow applicable Agency procedures governing the designation of competitively sensitive business information and other information the requesters wish not to be made public in connection with a review request. *See* 28 C.F.R. § 50.56 (U.S. Department of Justice procedures); 16 C.F.R. §§ 4.2, 4.9, and 4.10 (FTC procedures).

Appendix

This Appendix explains how to calculate the PSA shares of common services discussed in the Policy Statement.[50] There are three steps:

1. Identify each service provided by at least two independent ACO participants (i.e., each common service). A service is defined as follows:
    a. For physicians, a service is the physician's primary specialty, as designated on the physician's Medicare Enrollment Application. Each specialty is identified by its Medicare Specialty Code ("MSC"), as defined by CMS.[51]
    b. For inpatient facilities (e.g., hospitals), a service is an MDC.[52]
    c. For outpatient facilities (e.g., ASCs or hospitals), a service is an outpatient category, as defined by CMS.[53]
2. Identify the PSA(s) for each participant (e.g., physician group, inpatient facility, or outpatient facility) in the ACO that provides any common service. For each participant, the PSA is defined as the lowest number of postal zip codes from which the participant draws at least 75 percent of its patients.[54] Each independent physician solo practice, each fully integrated physician group practice, each inpatient facility (even if part of a hospital system), and each outpatient facility will have its own PSA. In addition, each inpatient facility will have a separate PSA for inpatient services, outpatient services, and physician services provided by its physician employees.
3. Separately for each common service, calculate the ACO's PSA share in the PSA of each participant that provides that service if at least two participants provide that service to patients from that PSA. If an entity owned by an ACO participant provides services in a PSA, those services should be included in the share calculation regardless of whether the affiliated organization participates in the ACO.
    a. For physician services, the ACO should calculate its shares of Medicare fee-for-service allowed charges (i.e., the amount that a provider is entitled to receive for the service provided) during the most recent calendar year for which data are

50. Any ACO participant that wants to determine whether it meets the dominant participant limitation of the safety zone should calculate its PSA share in a similar manner.

51. CMS will make publicly available the most current list of applicable specialties. Specialty Codes 01 (general practice), 08 (family practice), 11 (internal medicine), and 38 (geriatric medicine) are considered "Primary Care" specialties, and are treated as a single service for the purposes of the Policy Statement.

52. CMS will make publicly available the most current list of MDCs.

53. CMS will make publicly available a list of applicable outpatient categories as well as data necessary to assign procedure codes to the appropriate category.

54. This PSA calculation is based on the Stark II regulations. Medicare Program: Physicians' Referrals to Health Care Entities With Which They Have Financial Relationships (Phase II), 69 Fed. Reg. 16,094 (Mar. 26, 2004).

available. CMS will make public the data necessary to identify the full range of services and the aggregate fee-for-service allowed charges for each service, by zip code.

b. For inpatient services, the ACO should calculate its shares of inpatient discharges, using state-level all-payer hospital discharge data where available, for the most recent calendar year for which data are available. For ACOs located in a state where all-payer hospital discharge data are not available, the ACO should calculate its shares of Medicare fee-for-service payments during the most recent federal fiscal year for which data are available. CMS will make public the data necessary to identify the full range of services and the aggregate fee-for-service payments for each service, by zip code.

c. For outpatient services, the ACO should calculate its shares of Medicare fee-for-service payments for hospitals and fee-for-services allowed charges for ASCs during the most recent calendar year for which data are available, or the ACO can use state-level all-payer claims data, if available. CMS will make public the data necessary to identify the full range of services and the aggregate fee-for-service payments and allowed charges for each service, by zip code.

For those services that are rarely used by Medicare beneficiaries (e.g., pediatrics, obstetrics, gynecology, and neonatal care) and for which all-payer data are not available, the ACO may use other available data to determine the relevant shares. For example, for those services, data on the number of active physicians within the specialty and located within the PSA may be a reasonable alternative for the purposes of calculating shares of physician services.

Example of How to Calculate an ACO's PSA Shares

The following example illustrates how to calculate the ACO's relevant PSA shares. Assume that two independent physician practices, two independent hospitals, and an ASC propose to form an ACO. For purposes of this example, further assume that the hospitals do not directly employ physicians. If they do, then services provided by the hospitals' employed physicians would need to be taken into account in determining the PSA and calculating the ACO's shares for each common physician service where at least two participants provide that service to patients from the same PSA.

For the physician groups:

1. Identify the physician groups' common MSCs. In this example, Physician Group A ("PG A") has physicians with general surgery (MSC 02) and orthopedic surgery specialties (MSC 20). Physician Group B ("PG B") has physicians with orthopedic surgery (MSC 20) and cardiology (MSC 06) specialties. The only common service is orthopedic surgery, not general surgery or cardiology, because

PG A does not have cardiologists and PG B does not have general surgeons.

2. Identify the zip codes that make up the PSA for each physician group. In this example, there will be two PSAs: one for PG A ("PSA A") and one for PG B ("PSA B").
3. Determine the ACO's share in each of the PSAs. In this example, both PG A's and PG B's orthopedic surgeons serve patients located in both PSAs. Thus, shares need to be calculated in PSA A and PSA B. The ACO's share of orthopedic surgery in PSA A would be the total Medicare allowed charges for claims billed by the ACO's orthopedic surgeons (which are PG A's and PG B's total allowed charges for claims billed by orthopedic surgeons for Medicare beneficiaries in PSA A's zip codes) divided by the total allowed charges for orthopedic surgery for all Medicare beneficiaries in PSA A. Likewise, the ACO's share of orthopedic surgery services in PSA B would be the total Medicare allowed charges for claims billed by the ACO's orthopedic surgeons (which are PG A's and PG B's total allowed charges for claims billed by orthopedic surgeons for Medicare beneficiaries in PSA B's zip codes) divided by the total allowed charges for orthopedic surgery for all Medicare beneficiaries in PSA B.

For the inpatient services:

1. Identify the hospitals' common MDCs. In this example, Hospital 1 and Hospital 2 each provide services in 10 MDCs, but only two are common services: cardiac care (i.e., services related to diseases and disorders of the circulatory system—MDC 05) and orthopedic care (i.e., services related to diseases and disorders of the musculoskeletal system and connective tissue—MDC 08).
2. Identify the zip codes that make up the PSA for inpatient services for each hospital. In this example, there will be two PSAs: Hospital 1's PSA and Hospital 2's PSA.
3. Determine the ACO's share in each of the PSAs. In this example, Hospital 1 and Hospital 2 both serve cardiac patients located in each hospital's PSA and both serve orthopedic patients in each hospital's PSA. Thus, shares need to be calculated in both PSAs, resulting in four shares. This hypothetical ACO is located in a state for which all-payer hospital discharge data are available, so the ACO's share of cardiac care in Hospital 1's PSA would be the ACO's total number of inpatient discharges for MDC 05 (which are Hospital 1's and Hospital 2's total inpatient discharges for cardiac care in Hospital 1's PSA) divided by the total number of inpatient discharges for MDC 05 for all residents of this PSA. Use the analogous process to calculate the ACO's share of cardiac care in Hospital 2's PSA, the ACO's share of orthopedic care in Hospital 1's PSA, and the ACO's share of orthopedic care in Hospital 2's PSA.

For the outpatient services:

1. Identify the hospitals' and ASC's common outpatient categories. In this example, Hospital 1 does not provide outpatient services, while Hospital 2 and the ASC each provide services in 10 outpatient categories, but only two are common services: cardiovascular tests/procedures (outpatient category 2) and musculoskeletal procedures (outpatient category 5).
2. Identify the zip codes that make up the PSA for outpatient services for Hospital 2 and the ASC. In this example, there will be two PSAs: Hospital 2's PSA for outpatient services and the ASC's PSA.
3. Determine the ACO's share in each of the PSAs. In this example, Hospital 2 and the ASC both provide cardiovascular tests/procedures to patients located in each facility's PSA, and both provide musculoskeletal procedures to patients located in each facility's PSA. Thus, shares need to be calculated in both PSAs, resulting in four shares. The ACO's share of cardiovascular tests/procedures in Hospital 2's PSA would be the ACO's total Medicare fee-for-service payments/charges for outpatient category 2 (which are Hospital 2's total payments and the ASC's total allowed charges for outpatient cardiovascular tests/procedures for Medicare beneficiaries in Hospital 2's PSA) divided by the total payments/charges for outpatient category 2 for all Medicare beneficiaries in this PSA. Use the analogous process to calculate the ACO's share of cardiovascular tests/procedures in the ASC's PSA, the ACO's share of musculoskeletal procedures in Hospital 2's PSA, and the ACO's share of musculoskeletal procedures in the ASC's PSA.

Application to the Safety Zone: In this example, the ACO would calculate ten PSA shares. If *all* of the shares are 30 percent or below, and the hospitals and the ASC are non-exclusive to the ACO, then the ACO would fall within the safety zone. In other words, the 30 percent threshold must be met in *each* relevant PSA for each common service. If that condition is not met, then the ACO does not fall within the safety zone, unless it qualifies for the rural exception.

For the Antitrust Division of the Department of Justice.

Sharis A. Pozen
Acting Assistant Attorney General

For the Federal Trade Commission.

Donald S. Clark
Secretary

APPENDIX F

ANTITRUST ENFORCEMENT GUIDELINES FOR INTERNATIONAL OPERATIONS

■ ■ ■

U.S. Department of Justice and Federal Trade Commission
April 1995

* * *

Table of Contents

1. Introduction

For more than a century, the U.S. antitrust laws have stood as the ultimate protector of the competitive process that underlies our free market economy. Through this process, which enhances consumer choice and promotes competitive prices, society as a whole benefits from the best possible allocation of resources.

Although the federal antitrust laws have always applied to foreign commerce, that application is particularly important today. Throughout the world, the importance of antitrust law as a means to ensure open and free markets, protect consumers, and prevent conduct that impedes competition is becoming more apparent. The Department of Justice ("the Department") and the Federal Trade Commission ("the Commission" or "FTC")(when referred to collectively, "the Agencies"), as the federal agencies charged with the responsibility of enforcing the antitrust laws, thus have made it a high priority to enforce the antitrust laws with respect to international operations and to cooperate wherever appropriate with foreign authorities regarding such enforcement. In furtherance of this priority, the Agencies have revised and updated the Department's 1988 Antitrust Enforcement Guidelines for International Operations, which are hereby withdrawn.[1]

The 1995 Antitrust Enforcement Guidelines for International Operations (hereinafter "Guidelines") are intended to provide antitrust guidance to businesses engaged in international operations on questions that relate specifically to the Agencies' international enforcement policy.[2] They

1. The U.S. Department of Justice and Federal Trade Commission Antitrust Guidelines for the Licensing of Intellectual Property (1995), the U.S. Department of Justice and Federal Trade Commission Horizontal Merger Guidelines (1992), and the Statements of Antitrust Enforcement Policy and Analytical Principles Relating to Health Care and Antitrust, Jointly Issued by the U.S. Department of Justice and Federal Trade Commission (1994), are not qualified, modified, or otherwise amended by the issuance of these Guidelines.

2. Readers should separately evaluate the risk of private litigation by competitors, consumers and suppliers, as well as the risk of enforcement by state prosecutors under state and federal antitrust laws.

do not, therefore, provide a complete statement of the Agencies' general enforcement policies. The topics covered include the Agencies' subject matter jurisdiction over conduct and entities outside the United States and the considerations, issues, policies, and processes that govern their decision to exercise that jurisdiction; comity; mutual assistance in international antitrust enforcement; and the effects of foreign governmental involvement on the antitrust liability of private entities. In addition, the Guidelines discuss the relationship between antitrust and international trade initiatives. Finally, to illustrate how these principles may operate in certain contexts, the Guidelines include a number of examples.

As is the case with all sidelines, users should rely on qualified counsel to assist them in evaluating the antitrust risk associated with any contemplated transaction or activity. No set of guidelines can possibly indicate how the Agencies will assess the particular facts of every case. Persons seeking more specific advance statements of enforcement intentions with respect to the matters treated in these Guidelines should use the Department's Business Review procedure,[3] the Commission's Advisory Opinion procedure[4] or one of the more specific procedures described below for particular types of transactions.

2. Antitrust Laws Enforced by the Agencies

Foreign commerce cases can involve almost any provision of the antitrust laws. The Agencies do not discriminate in the enforcement of the antitrust laws on the basis of the nationality of the parties. Nor do the Agencies employ their statutory authority to further non-antitrust goals. Once jurisdictional requirements, comity, and doctrines of foreign governmental involvement have been considered and satisfied, the same substantive rules apply to all cases.

The following is a brief summary of the laws enforced by the Agencies that are likely to have the greatest significance for international transactions.

2.1 Sherman Act

Section 1 of the Sherman Act, 15 U.S.C.A. § 1, sets forth the basic antitrust prohibition against contracts, combinations, and conspiracies "in restraint of trade or commerce among the several States or with foreign nations." Section 2 of the Act, 15 U.S.C.A. § 2, prohibits "monopolization, attempts to monopolize, and conspiracies to monopolize any part of trade or commerce among the several States or with foreign nations." Section 6a of the Sherman Act, 15 U.S.C.A. § 6a, defines the jurisdictional reach of the Act with respect to non-import foreign commerce.

Violations of the Sherman Act may be prosecuted as civil or criminal offenses. Conduct that the Department prosecutes criminally is limited to traditional *per se* offenses of the law, which typically involve price-fixing,

---

3. 28 C.F.R. § 50.6 (1994).

4. 16 C.F.R. §§ 1.1–1.14 (1994).

customer allocation, bid-rigging or other cartel activities that would also be violations of the law in many countries. Criminal violations of the Act are punishable by fines and imprisonment. The Sherman Act provides that corporate defendants may be fined up to $10 million, other defendants may be fined up to $350,000, and individuals may be sentenced to up to 3 years imprisonment.[5] The Department has sole responsibility for the enforcement of the Sherman Act. In a civil proceeding, the Department may obtain injunctive relief against prohibited practices. It may also obtain treble damages if the U.S. government is the purchase of affected goods or services.[6] Private plaintiffs may also obtain injunctive and treble damage relief for violations of the Sherman Act.[7] Before the Commission, conduct that violates the Sherman Act may be challenged pursuant to the Commission's power under Section 5 of the Federal Trade Commission Act, described below.

2.2 Clayton Act

The Clayton Act, 15 U.S.C.A. §§ 12 *et seq.*, expands on the general prohibitions of the Sherman Act and addresses anticompetitive problems in their incipiency.[8] Section 7 of the Clayton Act, 15 U.S.C.A. § 18, prohibits any merger or acquisition of stock or assets "where in any line of commerce, or in any activity affecting commerce in any section of the country, the effect of such acquisition may be substantially to lessen competition, or to tend to create a monopoly."[9] Section 15 of the Clayton Act empowers the Attorney General, and Section 13(b) of the FTC Act empowers the Commission, to seek a court order enjoining consummation of a merger that would violate Section 7. In addition, the Commission may seek a cease and desist order in an administrative proceeding against a merger under Section 11 of the Clayton Act, Section 5 of the FTC Act, or both. Private parties may also seek injunctive relief under 15 U.S.C.A. § 26.

Section 3 of the Clayton Act prohibits any person engaged in commerce from conditioning the lease or sale of goods or commodities upon the purchaser's agreement not to use the products of a competitor, if the effect may be "to substantially lessen competition or to tend to create a monopoly in any line of commerce."[10] In evaluating transactions, the

5. Defendants may be fined up to twice the gross pecuniary gain or loss caused by their offense in lieu of the Sherman Act fines, pursuant to 18 U.S.C.A. § 3571(d) (1988 & Supp. 1993). In addition, the U.S. Sentencing Commission Guidelines provide further information about possible criminal sanctions for individual antitrust defendants in § 2R1.1 and for organizational defendants in Chapter 8.

6. See 15 U.S.C.A. § 4 (1988) (injunctive relief); 15 U.S.C.A. § 15(a) (1988 & Supp. 1993) (damages).

7. See 15 U.S.C.A. §§ 16, 26 (1988).

8. Under the Clayton Act, "commerce" includes "trade or commerce among the several States and with foreign nations." "Persons" include corporations or associations existing under or authorized either by the laws of the United States or any of its states or territories, or by the laws of any foreign country. 15 U.S.C.A. § 12 (1988 & Supp. 1993).

9. 15 U.S.C.A. § 18 (1988). The asset acquisition clause applies to "person[s] subject to the jurisdiction of the Federal Trade Commission" under the Clayton Act.

10. 15 U.S.C.A. § 14 (1988).

trend of recent authority is to use the same analysis employed in the evaluation of tying under Section 1 of the Sherman Act to assess a defendant's liability under Section 3 of the Clayton Act.[11] Section 2 of the Clayton Act, known as the Robinson–Patman Act,[12] prohibits price discrimination in certain circumstances. In practice, the Commission has exercised primary enforcement responsibility for this provision.

2.3 Federal Trade Commission Act

Section 5 of the Federal Trade Commission Act ("FTC Act") declares unlawful "unfair methods of competition in or affecting commerce, and unfair or deceptive acts or practices in or affecting commerce."[13] Pursuant to its authority over unfair methods of competition, the Commission may take administrative action against conduct that violates the Sherman Act and the Clayton Act, as well as anticompetitive practices that do not fall within the scope of the Sherman or Clayton Acts. The Commission may also seek injunctive relief in federal court against any such conduct under Section 13(b) of the FTC Act. Although enforcement at the Commission relating to international deceptive practices has become increasingly important over time, these Guidelines are limited to the Commission's antitrust authority under the unfair methods of competition language of Section 5.

2.4 Hart–Scott–Rodino Antitrust Improvements Act of 1976

Title II of the Hart–Scott–Rodino Antitrust Improvements Act of 1976 ("HSR Act"), 15 U.S.C.A. § 18a, provides the Department and the Commission with several procedural devices to facilitate enforcement of the antitrust laws with respect to anticompetitive mergers and acquisitions.[14] The HSR Act requires persons engaged in commerce or in any activity affecting commerce to notify the Agencies of proposed mergers or acquisitions that would exceed statutory size-of-party and size-of-transaction

11. See, e.g., Mozart Co. v. Mercedes–Benz of N. Am, Inc., 833 F.2d 1342, 1352 (9th Cir.1987), cert. denied, 488 U.S. 870 (1988).

12. 15 U.S.C.A. §§ 13–13b, 21a (1988). The Robinson–Patman Act applies only to purchases involving commodities "for use, consumption, or resale within the United States." Id. at § 13. It has been construed not to apply to sales for export. See, e.g., General Chem., Inc. v. Exxon Chem. Co. 625 F.2d 1231, 1234 (5th Cir.1980). Intervening domestic sales, however, would be subject to the Act. See Raul Int'l Corp. v. Sealed Power Corp., 586 F.Supp. 349, 351–55 (D.N.J.1984).

13. 15 U.S.C.A. § 45 (1988 & Supp. 1993).

14. The scope of the Agencies' jurisdiction under Clayton § 7 exceeds the scope of those transactions subject to the premerger notification requirements of the HSR Act. Whether or not the HSR Act premerger notification thresholds are satisfied, either Agency may request the parties to a merger affecting U.S. Commerce to provide information voluntarily concerning the transaction. In addition, the Department may issue Civil Investigative Demands ("CIDs") pursuant to the Antitrust Civil Process Act, 15 U.S.C.A. §§ 1311–1314 (1988), and the Commission may issued administrative CIDs pursuant to the Act of Aug. 26, 1994, Pub. L. No. 103–312, § 7; 108 Stat. 1691 (1994). The Commission may also issue administrative subpoenas and orders to file special reports under Sections 9 and 6(b) of the FTC Act, respectively. 15 U.S.C.A. §§ 49, 46(b) (1988). Authority in particular cases is allocated to either the Department or the Commissions pursuant to a voluntary clearance protocol. See Antitrust & Trade Reg. Daily (BNA), Dec. 6, 1993, and U.S. Department of Justice and Federal Trade Commission, Hart–Scott–Rodino Premerger Program Improvements (March 23, 1995).

thresholds,[15] to provide certain information relating to reportable transactions, and to wait for a prescribed period—15 days for cash tender offers and 30 days for most other transactions—before consummating the transaction.[16] The Agency may, before the end of the waiting period, request additional information concerning a transaction (make a "Second Request") and thereby extend the waiting period beyond the initial one prescribed, to a specified number of days after the receipt of the material required by the Second Request—10 days for cash tender offers and 20 days for most other transactions[17]

The HSR Act and the FTC rules implementing the HSR Act[18] exempt from the premerger notification requirements certain international transactions (typically those having little nexus to U.S. commerce) that otherwise meet the statutory thresholds.[19] Failure to comply with the HSR Act is punishable by court-imposed civil penalties of up to $10,000 for each day a violation continues. The court may also order injunctive relief to remedy a failure substantially to comply with the HSR Act. Businesses may seek an interpretation of their obligations under the HSR Act from the Commission.[20]

2.5 National Cooperative Research and Production Act

The National Cooperative Research and Production Act ("NCRPA"), 15 U.S.C.A. §§ 4301–06, clarifies the substantive application of the U.S. antitrust laws to joint research and development ("R & D") activities and joint production activities. Originally drafted to encourage research and development by providing a special antitrust regime for research and development joint ventures, the NCRPA requires U.S. courts to judge the competitive effects of a challenged joint R&D or joint production venture,

---

15. Unless exempted pursuant to the HSR Act, the parties must provide premerger notification to the Agencies if (1) the acquiring person, or the person whose voting securities or assets are being acquired, is engaged in commerce or any activity affecting commerce; and (2)(a) any voting securities or asset of a person engaged in manufacturing which has annual net sales total assets of $10 million or more are being acquired by any person which has total assets or annual net sales of $100 million or more, or (b) any voting securities or assets of a person not engaged in manufacturing which has total assets of $10 million or more are being acquired by any person which has total assets or annual sales of $100 million or more; or (c) any voting securities or assets of a person with annual net sales or total assets of $100 million or more are being acquired by any person with total assets or annual net sales of $10 million on more; and (3) as a result of such acquisition, the acquiring person would hole (a) 15 percent or more of the voting securities or assets of the acquired person, or (b) an aggregate total amount of the voting securities and assets of the acquired person of $15 million. 15 U.S.C.A. § 18a(a) (1988). The size of the transaction test set forth in (3) must be read in conjunction with 16 C.F.R. § 802.20 (1994). This Section exempts asset acquisitions valued at $15 million or less. It also exempts voting securities acquisitions of $15 million or less unless, if as a result of the acquisition, the acquiring person would hold 50 percent or more of the voting securities of an issuer that has annual net sales or total assets of $25 million or more. The HSR rules are necessarily technical, contain other exemptions, and should be consulted, rather than relying on this summary.

16. 15 U.S.C.A. § 18a(b) (1988 & Supp. 1993); 16 C.F.R. § 803.1 (1994); see also 11 U.S.C.A. § 363(b)(2).

17. 15 U.S.C.A. § 18a(e) (1988).

18. 16 C.F.R. §§ 801–803 (1994).

19. 16 C.F.R. §§ 801.1(e),(k), 802.50–52 (1994). See infra at Section 4.22.

20. See 16 C.F.R. § 803.30 (1994).

or a combination of the two, in properly defined relevant markets and under a rule-of-reason standard. The statute specifies that the conduct "shall be judged on the basis of its reasonableness, taking into account all relevant factors affecting competition, including, but not limited to, effects on competition in properly defined, relevant research, development, product, process, and service markets."[21] This approach is consistent with the Agencies' general analysis of joint ventures.[22]

The NCRPA also establishes a voluntary procedure pursuant to which the Attorney General and the FTC may be notified of a joint R & D or production venture. The statute limits the monetary relief that may be obtained in private civil suits against the participants in a notified venture to actual rather than treble damages, if the challenged conduct is within the scope of the notification. With respect to joint production ventures, the National Cooperative Production Amendments of 1999[23] provide that the benefits of the limitation on recoverable damages for claims resulting from conduct within the scope of a notification are not available unless (1) the principal facilities for the production are located within the United States or its territories, and (2) "each person who controls any party to such venture (including such party itself) is a United States person, or a foreign person from a country whose law accords antitrust treatment no less favorable to United States persons than to such country's domestic persons with respect to participation in joint ventures for production."[24]

2.6 Webb–Pomerene Act

The Webb–Pomerene Act, 15 U.S.C.A. § 6145, provides a limited antitrust exemption for the formation and operation of associations of otherwise competing businesses to engage in collective export sales. The exemption applies only to the export of "goods, wares, or merchandise."[25] It does not apply to conduct that has an anticompetitive effect in the United States or that injures domestic competitors of the members of an export association. Nor does it provide any immunity from prosecution under foreign antitrust laws.[26] Associations seeking an exemption under the Webb–Pomerene Act must file their articles of agreement and annual reports with the Commission, but preformation approval from the Commission is not required.

---

21. 15 U.S.C.A. § 4302 (1988 & Supp. 1993).

22. See, e.g., U.S. Department of Justice and Federal Trade Commission Antitrust Guidelines for the Licensing of Intellectual Property, § 4 (1995); Statements of Antitrust Enforcement Policy and Analytical Principles Relating to Health Care and Antitrust, Jointly Issued by the U.S. Department of Justice and the Federal Trade Commission (1994), Statement 2 (outlining a four-step approach for joint venture analysis). See generally National Collegiate Athletic Ass'n v. Board of Regents of Univ. of Okla, 468 U.S. 85 (1984); Federal Trade Comm'n v. Indiana Fed'n of Dentists, 476 U.S. 447 (1986). See also Massachusetts Board of Registration in Optometry, 110 F.T.C. 549 (1988).

23. Pub. L. No. 103–42, 107 Stat. 117, 119 (1993).

24. 15 U.S.C.A. § 4306(2) (Supp. 1993).

25. 15 U.S.C.A. § 61 (1988).

26. See, e.g., Cases 89/85, etc., Ahlstrom Osakeyhtio v. Commission ("Wood Pulp"), 1988 E.C.R. 5193, [1987–1988 Transfer Binder] Common Mkt. Rep. (CCH) ¶ 14,491 (1988).

2.7 *Export Trading Company Act of 1982*

The Export Trading Company Act of 1982 (the "ETC Act"), Pub. L. No. 97–290, 96 Stat. 1234, is designed to increase U.S. exports of goods and services. It addresses that goal in several ways. First, in Title II, it encourages more efficient provision of export trade services to U.S. producers and suppliers by reducing restrictions on trade financing provided by financial institutions.[27] Second, in Title III, it reduces uncertainty concerning the application of the U.S. antitrust laws to export trade through the creation of a procedure by which persons engaged in U.S. export trade may obtain an export trade certificate of review ("ETCR").[28] Third, in Title IV, it clarifies the jurisdictional rules applicable to non-import cases brought under the Sherman Act and the FTC Act.[29] The Title III certificates are discussed briefly here; the jurisdictional rules are treated below in Section 3.1.

Export trade certificates of review are issued by the Secretary of Commerce with the concurrence of the Attorney General. Persons named in the ETCR obtain limited immunity from suit under both state and federal antitrust laws for activities that are specified in the certificate and that comply with the terms of the certificate. To obtain an ETCR, an applicant must show that proposed export conduct will:

(1) result in neither a substantial lessening of competition or restraint of trade within the United States nor a substantial restraint of the export trade of any competitor of the applicant;

(2) not unreasonably enhance, stabilize, or depress prices in the United States of the class of goods or services covered by the application;

(3) not constitute unfair methods of competition against competitors engaged in the export of the class of goods or services exported by the applicant; and

(4) not include any act that may reasonably be expected to result in the sale for consumption or resale in the United States of such goods or services.[30]

Congress intended that these standards "encompass the full range of the antitrust laws," as defined in the ETC Act.[31]

Although an ETCR provides significant protection under the antitrust laws, it has certain limitations. First, conduct that falls outside the scope of a certificate remains fully subject to private and governmental enforcement actions. Second, an ETCR that is obtained by fraud is void from the outset and thus offers no protection under the antitrust laws. Third, any

27. See 12 U.S.C.A. §§ 372, 635 a–4, 1841, 1843 (1988 & Supp. 1993) (because Title II does not implicate the antitrust laws, it is not discussed further in these Guidelines.)

28. 15 U.S.C.A. §§ 4011–21 (1988 & Supp. 1993).

29. 15 U.S.C.A. § 6a (1988); 15 U.S.C.A. § 45(a)(3) (1988).

30. 15 U.S.C.A. § 4013(a) (1988).

31. H.R. Rep. No. 924, 97th Cong., 2d Sess. 26 (1982). See 15 U.S.C.A. § 4021(6).

person that has been injured by certified conduct may recover actual (though not treble) damages if that conduct is found to violate any of the statutory criteria described above. In any such action, certified conduct enjoys a presumption of legality, and the prevailing party is entitled to recover costs and attorneys' fees.[32] Fourth, an ETCR does not constitute, explicitly or implicitly, an endorsement or opinion by the Secretary of Commerce or by the Attorney General concerning the legality of such business plans under the laws of any foreign country.

The Secretary of Commerce may revoke or modify an ETCR if the Secretary or the Attorney General determines that the applicant's export activities have ceased to comply with the statutory criteria for obtaining a certificate. The Attorney General may also bring suit under Section 15 of the Clayton Act to enjoin conduct that threatens "a clear and irreparable harm to the national interest,"[33] even if the conduct has been pre-approved as part of an ETCR.

The Commerce Department, in consultation with the Department, has issued guidelines setting forth the standards used in reviewing ETCR applications.[34] The ETC Guidelines contain several examples illustrating application of the certification standards to specific export trade conduct, including the use of vertical and horizontal restraints and technology licensing arrangements. In addition, the Commerce Department's Export Trading Company Guidebook[35] provides information on the functions and advantages of establishing or using an export trading company, including factors to consider in applying for an ETCR. The Commerce Department's Office of Export Trading Company Affairs provides advice and information on the formation of export trading companies and facilitates contacts between producers of exportable goods and services and firms offering export trade services.

2.8 Other Pertinent Legislation

2.81 Wilson Tariff Act

The Wilson Tariff Act, 15 U.S.C.A. §§ 8–11, prohibits "every combination, conspiracy, trust, agreement, or contract" made by or between two or more persons or corporations, either of whom is engaged in importing any article from a foreign country into the United States, where the agreement is intended to restrain trade or increase the market price in any part of the United States of the imported articles, or of "any manufacture into which such imported article enters or is intended to enter." Violation of the Act is a misdemeanor, punishable by a maximum

32. See 15 U.S.C.A. § 4016(b)(1) (1988) (injured party) and § 4016(b)(4) (1988) (party against whom claim is brought).

33. 15 U.S.C.A. § 4016(b)(5) (1988); see 15 U.S.C.A. § 15 (1988).

34. See Department of Commerce, International Trade Administration, Guidelines for the Issuance of Export Trade Certificates of Review (2d ed.), 50 Fed. Reg. 1786 (1985) (hereinafter "ETC Guidelines").

35. U.S. Department of Commerce, International Trade Administration, The Export Trading Company Guidebook (1984).

fine of $5,000 or one year in prison. The Act also provides for seizure of the imported articles.[36]

2.82 Antidumping Act of 1916

The Revenue Act of 1916, better known as the Antidumping Act, 15 U.S.C.A. §§ 71–74, is not an antitrust statute, but its subject matter is closely related to the antitrust rules regarding predation. It is a trade statute that creates a private claim against importers who sell goods into the United States at prices substantially below the prices charged for the same goods in their home market. In order to state a claim, a plaintiff must show both that such lower prices were commonly and systematically charged, and that the importer had the specific intent to injure or destroy an industry in the United States, or to prevent the establishment of an industry. Dumping cases are more commonly brought using the administrative procedures of the Tariff Act of 1930, discussed below.

2.83 Tariff Act of 1930

A comprehensive discussion of the trade remedies available under the Tariff Act is beyond the scope of these Guidelines. However, because antitrust questions sometimes arise in the context of trade actions, it is appropriate to describe these laws briefly.

2.831 Countervailing Duties

Pursuant to Title VII.A of the Tariff Act,[37] U.S. manufacturers, producers, wholesalers, unions, and trade associations may petition for the imposition of offsetting duties on subsidized foreign imports.[38] The Department of Commerce's International Trade Administration ("ITA") must make a determination that the foreign government in question is subsidizing the imports, and in almost all cases the International Trade Commission ("ITC") must determine that a domestic industry is materially injured or threatened with material injury by reason of these imports.

2.832 Antidumping Duties

Pursuant to Title VII.B of the Tariff Act,[39] parties designated in the statute (the same parties as in the countervailing duties provision) may petition for antidumping duties, which must be imposed on foreign merchandise that is being, or is likely to be, sold in the United States at "less than fair value" ("LTFV"), if the U.S. industry is materially injured or threatened with material injury by imports of the foreign merchandise.

36. 15 U.S.C.A. § 11 (1988).

37. See 19 U.S.C.A. §§ 1671 *et seq.* (1988 & Supp. 1993), amended by Uruguay Round Agreements Act, Pub. L. No. 103–465, 108 Stat. 4809 (1994).

38. Some alternative procedures exist under Tariff Act § 701(c) for countries that have not subscribed to the World Trade Organization ("WTO") Agreement on Subsidies and Countervailing Measures or measures equivalent to it. 19 U.S.C.A. § 1671(c) (1988 & Supp. 1993), amended by the Uruguay Round Agreements Act, Pub. L. No. 103–465, 108 Stat. 4809 (1994).

39. See 19 U.S.C.A. §§ 1673 *et seq.* (1988).

The ITA makes the LTFV determination, and the ITC is responsible for the injury decision.

2.833 Section 337

Section 337 of the Tariff Act, 19 U.S.C.A. § 1337, prohibits "unfair methods of competition and unfair acts in the importation of articles into the United States," if the effect is to destroy or substantially injure a U.S. industry, or where the acts relate to importation of articles infringing U.S. patents, copyrights, trademarks, or registered mask works.[40] Complaints are filed with the ITC. The principal remedies under Section 337 are an exclusion order directing that any offending goods be excluded from entry into the United States, and a cease and desist order directed toward any offending U.S. firms and individuals.[41] The ITC is required to give the Agencies an opportunity to comment before making a final determination.[42] In addition, the Department participates in the interagency group that prepares recommendations for the President to approve, disapprove, or allow to take effect the import relief proposed by the ITC.

2.84 Trade Act of 1974

2.841 Section 201

Section 201 of the Trade Act of 1974, 19 U.S.C.A. §§ 2251 *et seq.*, provides that American businesses claiming serious injury due to significant increases in imports may petition the ITC for relief or modification under the so-called "escape clause." If the ITC makes a determination that "an article is being imported into the United States in such increased quantities as to be a substantial cause of serious injury, or the threat thereof, to the domestic industry producing an article like or directly competitive with the imported article," and formulates its recommendation for appropriate relief, the Department participates in the interagency committee that conducts the investigations and advises the President whether to adopt, modify, or reject the import relief recommended by the ITC.

2.842 Section 301

Section 301 of the Trade Act of 1974, 19 U.S.C.A. § 2411, provides that the U.S. Trade Representative ("USTR"), subject to the specific direction, if any, of the President, may take action, including restricting imports, to enforce rights of the United States under any trade agreement, to address acts inconsistent with the international legal rights of the United States, or to respond to unjustifiable, unreasonable or discriminatory practices of foreign governments that burden or restrict U.S. commerce. Interested parties may initiate such actions through petitions to

---

40. 19 U.S.C.A. § 1337 (1988), amended by the Uruguay Round Agreements Act, Pub. L. No. 103–465, 108 Stat. 4809 (1994).

41. 19 U.S.C.A. §§ 1337(d), (f) (1988).

42. 19 U.S.C.A. § 1337(b)(2) (1988).

the USTR, or the USTR may itself initiate proceedings.[43] Of particular interest to antitrust enforcement is Section 301(d)(3)(B)(i)(IV), which includes among the "unreasonable" practices of foreign governments that might justify a proceeding the "toleration by a foreign government of systematic anticompetitive activities by enterprises or among enterprises in the foreign country that have the effect of restricting ... access of United States goods or services to a foreign market."[44] The Department participates in the interagency committee that makes recommendations to the President on what actions, if any, should be taken.

2.9 *Relevant International Agreements*

To further the twin goals of promoting enforcement cooperation between the United States and foreign governments and of reducing any tensions that may arise in particular proceedings, the Agencies have developed close relationships with antitrust and competition policy officials of many different countries. In some instances, understandings have been reached with respect to notifications, consultations, and cooperation in antitrust matters.[45] In other instances, more general rules endorsed by multilateral organizations such as the Organization for Economic Cooperation and Development ("OECD") provide the basis for the Agencies' cooperative policies. Finally, even in the absence of specific or general international understandings or recommendations, the Agencies often seek cooperation with foreign authorities.

2.91 Bilateral Cooperation Agreements

Formal written bilateral arrangements exist between the United States and the Federal Republic of Germany, Australia, and Canada.[46]

---

43. 19 U.S.C.A. § 2412(a), (b) (1988), amended by the Uruguay Round Agreements Act, Pub. L. No. 103–465, 108 Stat. 4809 (1994); see also Identification of Trade Expansion Priorities, Exec. Order No. 12,901, 59 Fed. Reg. 10,727 (1994).

44. 19 U.S.C.A. § 2411(d)(3)(B)(i)(IV) (1988), amended by the Uruguay Round Agreements Act, Pub. L. No. 103–465, 108 Stat. 4809 (1994), § 314(c).

45. Chapter 15 of the North American Free Trade Agreement ("NAFTA") addresses competition policy matters and commits the Parties to cooperate on antitrust matters. North American Free Trade Agreement Between the Government of the United States of America, the Government of Canada and the Government of the United Mexican States, 32 I.L.M. 605, 663 (1993), reprinted in H.R. Doc. No. 159, 103d Cong., 1st Sess. 712, 1170–1174 (1993).

46. See Agreement Relating to Mutual Cooperation Regarding Restrictive Business Practices, June 23, 1976, U.S.–Federal Republic of Germany, 27 U.S.T. 1956, T.I.S. No. 8291, reprinted in 4 Trade Reg. Rep. (CCH) ¶ 13,501; Agreement Between the Government of the Untied States of America and the Government of Australia Relating to Cooperation on Antitrust Matters, June 29, 1982, U.S.–Australia, T.I.A.S. No. 10365, reprinted in 4 Trade Reg. Rep. (CCH) ¶ 13,502; and Memorandum of Understanding as to Notification, Consultation, and Cooperation with Respect to the Application of National Antitrust Laws, March 9, 1984, U.S.–Canada, reprinted in 4 Trade Reg. Rep. (CCH) ¶ 13,503. The Agencies also signed a similar agreement with the Commission of the European Communities in 1991. See Agreement Between the Government of the United States of America and the Commission of the European Communities Regarding the Application of Their Competition Laws, Sept. 23, 1991, 30 I.L.M. 1491 (Nov. 1991), reprinted in 4 Trade Reg. Rep. (CCH) ¶ 13,504. However, on August 9, 1994, the European Court of Justice ruled that the conclusion of the Agreement did not comply with institutional requirements of the law of the European Union ("EU"). Under the Court's decision, action by the EU Council of Ministers is necessary for this type of agreement. See French Republic v. Commission of European Communities (No. C–327/91) (Aug. 9, 1994).

International antitrust cooperation can also occur through mutual legal assistance treaties ("MLATs"), which are treaties of general application pursuant to which the United States and a foreign country agree to assist one another in criminal law enforcement matters. MLATs currently are in force with over one dozen countries, and many more are in the process of ratification or negotiation. However, only the MLAT with Canada has been used to date to obtain assistance in antitrust investigations.[47] The Agencies also hold regular consultations with the antitrust officials of Canada, the European Commission, and Japan, and have close, informal ties with the antitrust authorities of many other countries. Since 1990, the Agencies have cooperated closely with countries in the process of establishing competition agencies, assisted by funding provided by the Agency for International Development.

On November 2, 1994, President Clinton signed into law the International Antitrust Enforcement Assistance Act of 1994,[48] which authorizes the Agencies to enter into antitrust mutual assistance agreements in accordance with the legislation.

2.92 International Guidelines and Recommendation

The Agencies have agreed with respect to member countries of the OECD to consider the legitimate interests of other nations in accordance with relevant OECD recommendations.[49] Under the terms of a 1986 recommendation, the United States agency with responsibility for a particular case notifies a member country whenever an antitrust enforcement action may affect important interests of that country or its nationals.[50] Examples of potentially notifiable actions include requests for documents located outside the United States, attempts to obtain information from potential witnesses located outside the United States, and cases or investigations with significant foreign conduct or involvement of foreign persons.

3. Threshold International Enforcement Issues

3.1 Jurisdiction

Just as the acts of U.S. citizens in a foreign nation ordinarily are subject to the law of the country in which they occur, the acts of foreign citizen in the United States ordinarily are subject to U.S. law. The reach of the U.S. antitrust laws is not limited, however, to conduct and transac-

47. Treaty with Canada on Mutual Legal Assistance in Criminal Matters, S. Treaty Doc. No. 28, 100th Cong., 2d Sess. (1988).

48. Pub. L. No. 103–438, 108 Stat. 4597 (1994).

49. See Revised Recommendation of the OECD Council Concerning Cooperation Between Member Countries on Restrictive Business Practices Affecting International Trade, OECD Doc. No. C(86)44 (Final) (May 21, 1986). The Recommendation also calls for countries to consult with each other in appropriate situations, with the aim of promoting enforcement cooperation and minimizing differences that may arise.

50. The OECD has 25 member countries and the European Commission takes part in its work. The OECD's membership includes many of the most advanced market economies in the world. The OECD also has several observer nations, which have made rapid progress toward open market economies. The Agencies follow recommended OECD practices with respect to all member countries.

tions that occur within the boundaries of the United States. Anticompetitive conduct that affects U.S. domestic or foreign commerce may violate the U.S. antitrust laws regardless of where such conduct occurs or the nationality of the parties involved.

Under the Sherman Act and the FTC Act, there are two principal tests for subject matter jurisdiction in foreign commerce cases. With respect to foreign import commerce, the Supreme Court has recently stated in *Hartford Fire Insurance Co. v. California* that "the Sherman Act applies to foreign conduct that was meant to produce and did in fact produce some substantial effect in the United States".[51] There has been no such authoritative ruling on the scope of the FTC Act, but both Acts apply to commerce "with foreign nations" and the Commission has held that terms used by both Acts should be construed together.[52] Second, with respect to foreign commerce other than imports, the Foreign Trade Antitrust Improvements Act of 1982 ("FTAIA") applies to foreign conduct that has a direct, substantial, and reasonably foreseeable effect on U.S. commerce.[53]

3.11 Jurisdiction Over Conduct Involving Import Commerce

Imports into the United States by definition affect the U.S. domestic market directly, and will, therefore, almost invariably satisfy the intent part of the *Hartford Fire* test. Whether they in fact produce the requisite substantial effects will depend on the facts of each case.

ILLUSTRATIVE EXAMPLE A[54]

Situation: A, B, C, and D are foreign companies that produce a product in various foreign countries. None has any U.S. production, nor any U.S. subsidiaries. They organize a cartel for the purpose of raising the price for the product in question. Collectively, the cartel members make substantial sales into the United States, both in absolute terms and relative to total U.S. consumption.

Discussion: These facts present the straightforward case of cartel participants selling products directly into the United States. In this

---

51. 509 U.S. 764, 796 (1993). In a world in which economic transactions observe no boundaries, international recognition of the "effects doctrine" of jurisdiction has become more widespread. In the context of import trade, the "implementation" test adopted in the European Court of Justice usually produces the same outcome as the "effects" test employed in the Untied States. See Cases 89/85, etc., Ahlstrom v. Commission, supra at note 26. The merger laws of the European Union, Canada, Germany, France, Australia, and the Czech and Slovak Republics, among others, take a similar approach.

52. In re Massachusetts Bd. of Registration in Optometry, 110 F.T.C. 598, 609 (1988).

53. 15 U.S.C.A. § 6a (1988) (Sherman Act) and § 45(a)(3) (1988) (FTC Act).

54. The examples incorporated into the text are intended solely to illustrate how the Agencies would apply the principles articulated in the Guidelines in differing fact situations. In each case, of course, the ultimate outcome of the analysis, i.e., whether or not a violation of the antitrust laws has occurred, would depend on the specific facts and circumstances in the case. These examples, therefore, do not address many of the factual and economic questions the Agencies would ask in analyzing particular conduct or transactions under the antitrust laws. Therefore, certain hypothetical situations presented here may, when fully analyzed, not violate nay provision of the antitrust laws.

situation, the transaction is unambiguously an import into the U.S. market and the sale is not complete until the goods teach the United States. Thus, U.S. subject matter jurisdiction is clear under the general principles of antitrust law expressed most recently in *Hartford Fire*. The facts presented here demonstrate actual and intended participation in U.S. commerce.[55] The separate question of personal jurisdiction under the facts presented here would be analyzed using the principles discussed infra in Section 4.1.

3.12 Jurisdiction Over Conduct Involving Other Foreign Commerce

With respect to foreign commerce other than imports, the jurisdictional limits of the Sherman Act and the FTC Act are delineated in the FTAIA. The FTAIA amended the Sherman Act to declare that it:

> shall not apply to conduct involving trade or commerce (other than import trade or commerce) with foreign nations unless
>
> (1) such conduct has a direct, substantial, and reasonably foreseeable effect:
>
> (A) on trade or commerce which is not trade or commerce with foreign nations, or on import trade or import commerce with foreign nations; or (B) on export trade or export commerce with foreign nations, of a person engaged in such trade or commerce in the United States;[56]
>
> (2) such effect gives rise to a claim under the provisions of [the Sherman Act], other than this section.

The FTAIA uses slightly different statutory language for the FTC Act,[57] but produces the same jurisdictional outcomes.

3.121 Jurisdiction in Cases Under Subsection 1 (A) of the FTAIA

To the extent that conduct in foreign countries does not "involve" import commerce but does have an "effect" on either import transactions or commerce within the United States, the Agencies apply the "direct, substantial, and reasonably foreseeable" standard of the FTAIA. That standard is applied, for example, in cases in which a cartel of foreign enterprises, or a foreign monopolist, reaches the U.S. market through any mechanism that goes beyond direct sales, such as the use of an unrelated intermediary, as well as in cases in which foreign vertical restrictions or intellectual licensing arrangements have an anticompetitive effect on U.S. commerce.

ILLUSTRATIVE EXAMPLE B

Situation: As in Illustrative Example A, the foreign cartel produces a product in several foreign countries. None of its members has any U.S.

55. See infra at Section 3.12.

56. If the Sherman Act applies to such conduct only because of the operation of paragraph (1)(B), then that Act shall apply to such conduct only for injury to export business in the United States. 15 U.S.C.A. § 6a (1988).

57. See 15 U.S.C. § 45(a)(3) (1988).

production, nor do any of them have U.S. subsidiaries. They organize a cartel for the purpose of raising the price for the product in question. Rather than selling directly into the United States, however, the cartel sells to an intermediary outside the United States, which they know will resell the product in the United States. The intermediary is not part of the cartel.

Discussion: The jurisdictional analysis would change slightly from the one presented in example A, because not only is the conduct being challenged entered into by cartel lists in a foreign but it is also initially implemented through a sale made in a foreign country. Despite the different test, however, the outcome on these facts would in all likelihood remain the same. The fact that the illegal conduct occurs prior to the import would trigger the application of the FTAIA. Agencies would have to determine whether the challenged conduct had "direct, substantial and reasonably foreseeable effects" on U.S. domestic or import commerce. Furthermore, since "the essence of any violation of Section 1 [of the Sherman Act] is the illegal agreement itself—rather than the overt acts performed in furtherance of it,"[58] the Agencies would focus on the potential harm that would ensue if the conspiracy were successful, not on whether the actual conduct in furtherance of the conspiracy had in fact the prohibited effect upon interstate or foreign commerce.

ILLUSTRATIVE EXAMPLE C

Situation: Variant (1): Widgets are manufactured in both the United States and various other countries around the world. The non-U.S. manufacturers Meet privately outside the United States and agree among themselves to raise prices to specified levels. Their agreement clearly indicates that sales in or into the United States are not within the scope of the agreement, and thus that each participant is free independently to set its prices for the U.S. market. Over time, the cartel members begin to sell excess production into the United States. These sales have the effect of stabilizing the cartel for the foreign markets. In the U.S. market, these "excess" sales are priced at levels below those that would have prevailed in the U.S. market but for the cartel, but there is no evidence that prices are predatory. As a result of these events, several U.S. widget manufacturers curtail their production, overall domestic output falls, and remaining manufacturers fail to invest in new or improved capacity.

Variant (2): Assume now that the cartel agreement specifically provides that cartel members will set agreed prices for the U.S. market at levels designed to soak up excess quantities that arise as a result of price increases in foreign markets. The U.S. price level is set at periodic meetings where each participant indicates how much it must off-load in this way. Thus, the cartel members sell goods in the U.S. market at fixed prices that undercut prevailing U.S. price levels, with consequences similar to those in Variant 1.

---

58. Summit Health, Ltd. v. Pinhas, 500 U.S. 322, 330–31 (1991).

Discussion: Variant (1): The jurisdictional issue is whether the predictable economic consequences of the original cartel agreement and the independent sales into the United States are sufficient to support jurisdiction. The mere fact that the existence of U.S. sales or the level of U.S. prices may ultimately be affected by the cartel agreement is not enough for either *Hartford Fire* jurisdiction or the FTAIA.[59] Furthermore, in the absence of an agreement with respect to the U.S. market, sales into the U.S. market at non-predatory levels do not raise antitrust concerns.[60]

Variant (2): The critical element of a foreign price-fixing agreement with direct, intended effects in the United States is now present. The fact that the cartel believes its U.S. prices are "reasonable," or that it may be exerting downward pressure on U.S. price levels, does not exonerate it.[61] Variant 2 presents a case where the Agencies would need clear evidence of the prohibited agreement before they would consider moving forward. They would be particularly cautious if the apparent effects in the U.S. market appeared to be beneficial to consumers.

3.122 Jurisdiction in Cases Under Subsection 1(B) of the FTAIA

Two categories of "export cases" fall within the FTAIA's jurisdictional test. First, the Agencies may, in appropriate cases, take enforcement action against anticompetitive conduct, wherever occurring, that restrains U.S. exports, if (1) the conduct has a direct, substantial, and reasonably foreseeable effect on exports of goods or services from the United States, and (2) the U.S. courts can obtain jurisdiction over persons or corporations engaged in such conduct.[62] As Section 3.2 below explains more fully, if the conduct is unlawful under the importing country's antitrust laws as well, the Agencies are also prepared to work with that country's authorities if they are better situated to remedy the conduct, and if they are prepared to take action that will address the U.S. concerns, pursuant to their antitrust laws.

Second, the Agencies may in appropriate cases take enforcement action against conduct by U.S. exporters that has a direct, substantial, and reasonably foreseeable effect on trade or commerce within the United States, or on import trade or commerce. This can arise in two principal ways. First, if U.S. supply and demand were not particularly elastic, an

59. If the Agencies lack jurisdiction under the FTAIA to challenge the cartel, the facts of this example would nonetheless lend themselves well to cooperative enforcement action among antitrust agencies. Virtually every country with an antitrust law prohibits horizontal cartels and the Agencies would willingly cooperate with foreign authorities taking direct action against the cartel in the countries where the agreement has raised the price of widgets to the extent such corporation is allowed under U.S. law and any agreement executed pursuant to U.S. law with foreign agencies or governments.

60. Cf. Matsushita Elec. Indus. Co. v. Zenith Radio Corp., 475 U.S. 574 (1986).

61. Cf. Arizona v. Maricopa County Medical Soc'y, 457 U.S. 332 (1982); United States v. Socony–Vacuum Oil Co., 310 U.S. 150 (1940); United States v. Trenton Potteries Co., 273 U.S. 392 (1927).

62. See U.S. Department of Justice Press Release dated April 3, 1992 (announcing enforcement policy that would permit the Department to challenge foreign business conduct that harms U.S. exports when the conduct would have violated U.S. antitrust laws if it occurred in the United States).

agreement among U.S. firms accounting for a substantial share of the relevant market, regarding the level of their exports, could reduce supply and raise prices in the United States.[63] Second, conduct ostensibly export-related could affect the price of products sold or resold in the United States. This kind of effect could occur if, for example, U.S. firms fixed the price of an input used to manufacture a product overseas for ultimate resale in the United States.

ILLUSTRATIVE EXAMPLE D

Situation: Companies E and F are the only producers of product Q in country Epsilon, one of the biggest markets for sales of Q in the world. E and F together account for 99 percent of the sales of product Q in Epsilon.[64] In order to prevent a competing U.S. producer from entering the market in Epsilon, E and F agree that neither one of them will purchase or distribute the U.S. product, that they will take "all feasible" measures to keep the U.S. company out of their market. Without specifically discussing what other measures they will take to carry out this plan, E and F meet with their distributors and, through a variety of threats and inducements, obtain agreement of all of the distributors not to carry the U.S. product. There are no commercially feasible substitute distribution channels available to the U.S. producer. Because of the actions of E and F, the U.S. producer cannot find any distributors to carry its product and is unable to make any sales in Epsilon.

Discussion: The agreement between E and F not to purchase or distribute the U.S. product would clearly have a direct and reasonably foreseeable effect on U.S. export commerce, since it is aimed at a U.S. exporter. The substantiality of the effects on U.S. exports would depend on the significance of E and F as purchasers and distributors of Q, although on these facts the virtually total foreclosure from Epsilon would almost certainly qualify as a substantial effect for jurisdictional purposes. However, if the Agencies believe that they may encounter difficulties in establish personal jurisdiction or in obtaining effective relief, the case may be one in which the Agencies would seek to resolve their concerns by working with other authorities who are examining the transaction.

ILLUSTRATIVE EXAMPLE E

Situation: Companies P, Q, R, and S, organized under the laws of country Alpha, all manufacture and distribute construction equipment. Much of that equipment is protected by patents in the various countries where it is sold, including Alpha. The companies all belong to a private

63. One would need to know more than indirect price effects resulting from legitimate export efforts to support an antitrust challenge. See ETC Guidelines, supra at note 34, 50 Fed. Reg. at 1791.

64. That E and F together have an overwhelmingly dominant share in Epsilon may or may not, depending on the market conditions for Q, satisfy the requirement of "substantial effect on U.S. exports" as required by the FTAIA. Foreclosure of exports to a single country, such as Epsilon, may satisfy the statutory threshold if that country's market accounts for a significant part of the export opportunities for U.S. firms.

trade association, which develops industry standards that are often (although not always) adopted by Alpha's regulatory authorities. Feeling threatened by competition from the United States, the companies agree at a trade association meeting (1) to refuse to adopt any U.S. company technology as an industry standard, and (2) to boycott the distribution of U.S. construction equipment. The U.S. companies have taken all necessary steps to protect their intellectual property under the law of Alpha.

Discussion: In this example, the collective activity impedes U.S. companies in two ways: their technology is boycotted (even if U.S. companies are willing to license their intellectual property) and they are foreclosed from access to distribution channels. The jurisdictional question is whether these actions create a direct, substantial, and reasonably foreseeable effect on the exports of U.S. companies. The mere fact that only the market of Alpha appears to be foreclosed is not enough to defeat such an effect. Only if exclusion from Alpha as a quantitative measure whom so *de minimis* in terms of actual volume of trade that there would not be a substantial effect on U.S. export commerce would jurisdiction be lacking. Given that this example involves construction equipment, a generally highly priced capital good, the exclusion from Alpha would probably satisfy the substantiality requirement for FTAIA jurisdiction. This arrangement appear to have been created with particular reference to competition from the United States, which indicates that the effects U.S. exports are both direct and foreseeable.

3.13 Jurisdiction When U.S. Government Finances or Purchases

The Agencies may, in appropriate cases, take enforcement action when the U.S. Government is a purchaser, or substantially funds the purchase, of goods or services for consumption or use abroad. Cases in which the effect of anticompetitive conduct with respect to the sale of these goods or services falls primarily on U.S. taxpayers may qualify for redress under the federal antitrust laws.[65] As a general matter, the Agencies consider there to be a sufficient effect on U.S. commerce to support the assertion of jurisdiction if, as a result of its payment or financing, the U.S. Government bears more than half the cost of the transaction. For purposes of this determination, the Agencies apply the standards used in certifying export conduct under the ETC Act of 1982, 15 U.S.C.A. §§ 4011–21 (1982).[66]

---

65. Cf. United States v. Concentrated Phosphate Export Ass'n, 393 U.S. 199, 208 (1968) ("[A]though the fertilizer shipments were consigned to Korea and although in most cases Korea formally let the contracts, American participation was the overwhelmingly dominant feature. The burden of noncompetitive pricing fell, not on any foreign purchaser, but on the American taxpayer. The United States was, in essence, furnishing fertilizer to Korea.... The foreign elements in the transaction were, by comparison, insignificant."); United States v. Standard Tallow Corp., 1988–1 Trade Cas. (CCH) ¶ 67,913 (S.D.N.Y.1988) (consent decree) (barring suppliers from fixing prices or rigging bids for the sale of tallow financed in whole or in part through grants or loans by the U.S. Government); United States v. Anthracite Export Ass'n, 1970 Trade Cas. (CCH) ¶ 73,348 (M.D.Pa.1970) (consent decree) (barring price-fixing, bid-rigging, and market allocation in Army foreign aid program).

66. See ETC Guideline, supra at note 34, 50 Fed. Reg. at 1799–1800. The requisite U.S. Government involvement could include the actual purchase of goods by the U.S. Government for

ILLUSTRATIVE EXAMPLE F

Situation: A combination of U.S. firm and local firms in country Beta create a U.S.-based joint venture for the purpose of building a major pollution control facility for Beta's Environmental Control Agency ("BECA"). The venture has received preferential funding from the U.S. Government, which has the effect of making the present value of expected future repayment of the principal and interest on the loan less than half its face value. Once the venture has begun work, it appears that its members secretly have agreed to inflate the price quoted to BECA, in order to secure more funding.

Discussion: The fact that the U.S. Government bears more than half the financial risk of the transaction is sufficient for jurisdiction. With jurisdiction established, the Agencies would proceed to investigate whether the apparent bid-rigging actually occurred.[67]

ILLUSTRATIVE EXAMPLE G

Situation: The United States has many military bases and other facilities located in other countries. These facilities procure substantial goods and services from suppliers in the host country. In country X, it comes to the attention of the local U.S. military base commander that bids to supply certain construction services have been rigged.

Discussion: Sales made by a foreign party to the U.S. Government, including to a U.S. facility located in a foreign country, are within U.S. antitrust jurisdiction when they fall within the rule of Section 3.13. Bid-rigging of sales to the U.S. Government represents the kind of conduct that can lead to an antitrust action. Indeed, in the United States this type of behavior is normally prosecuted by the Department as a criminal offense. In practice, the Department has whenever possible worked closely with the host country antitrust authorities to explore remedies under local law. This has been successful in a number of instances.[68]

3.14 Jurisdiction Under Section 7 of the Clayton Act

Section 7 of the Clayton Act applies to mergers and acquisitions between firms that are engaged in commerce or in any activity affecting commerce. The Agencies would apply the same principles regarding their foreign commerce jurisdiction to Clayton Section 7 cases as they would apply in Sherman Act cases.

---

shipment abroad, a U.S. Government grant to a foreign government that is specifically earmarked for the transaction, or a U.S. Government loan specifically earmarked for the transaction that is made on such generous terms that it amounts to a grant. U.S. Government interests would not be considered to be sufficiently implicated with respect to a transaction that is funded by an international agency, or a transaction in which the foreign government received non-earmarked funds from the United States as part of a general government-to-government aid program.

67. Such conduct might also violate the False Claims Act, 31 U.S.C.A. §§ 3729–3733 (1988 & Supp. 1993).

68. If, however, local law does not provide adequate remedies, or the local authorities are not prepared to take action, the Department will weigh the comity factors, discussed infra at Section 3.2, and take such action as is appropriate.

ILLUSTRATIVE EXAMPLE H

Situation: Two foreign firms, one in Europe and the other in Canada, account together for a substantial percentage of U.S. sales of a particular product through direct imports. Both firms have sales offices and are subject to personal jurisdiction in the United States, although neither has productive assets in the United States. They enter into an agreement to merge.

Discussion: The express language of Section 7 of the Clayton Act reaches the stock and asset acquisitions of persons engaged in trade and commerce "with foreign nations."[69] Thus, in assessing jurisdiction for this merger outside the United States the Agencies could establish U.S. subject matter jurisdiction based on its effect on U.S. imports.

If the facts stated above were modified to show that the proposed merger would have effects on U.S. export commerce, as opposed to import trade, then in assessing jurisdiction under the Clayton Act the Agencies would analyze the question of effects on commerce in a manner consistent the FTAIA: that is, they would look to see whether the effects on U.S. domestic or import commerce are direct, substantial, and reasonably foreseeable.[70] It is appropriate to do so because the FTAIA sheds light on the type of effects Congress considered necessary for foreign commerce cases, even though the FTAIA did not amend the Clayton Act.

In both these situations, the Agencies would conclude that Section 7 jurisdiction technically exists. However, if effective relief is difficult to obtain, the case may be one in which the Agency would seek to coordinate their efforts with other authorities who are examining the transaction.[71]

3.2 Comity

In enforcing the antitrust laws, the Agencies consider international comity. Comity itself reflects the broad concept of respect among co-equal sovereign nations and plays a role in determining "the recognition which one nation allows within its territory to the legislative, executive or judicial acts of another nation.[72] Thus, in determining whether to assert jurisdiction to investigate or bring an action, or to seek particular remedies in a given case," each Agency takes into account whether significant interests of any foreign sovereign would be affected.[73]

In performing a comity analysis, the Agencies take into account all relevant factors. Among others, these may include (1) the relative significance to the alleged violation of conduct within the United States, as

69. Clayton Act § 1, 15 U.S.C.A. § 12 (1988).

70. See supra at Section 3.121.

71. Through concepts such as "positive comity," one country's authorities may ask another country to take measures that address possible harm to competition in the requesting country's market.

72. Hilton v. Guyot, 159 U.S. 113, 164 (1895).

73. The Agencies have agreed to consider the legitimate interests of other nations in accordance with the recommendations of the OECD and various bilateral agreements, see supra at Section 2.9.

compared to conduct abroad; (2) the nationality of the persons involved in or affected by the conduct; (3) the presence or absence of a purpose to affect U.S. consumers, markets or exporters; (4) the relative significance and foreseeability of the effects of the conduct on the United States as compared to the effects abroad; (5) the existence of reasonable expectations that would be furthered or defeated by the action; (6) the degree of conflict with foreign law or articulated foreign economic policies; (7) the extent to which the enforcement activities of another country with respect to the same persons, including remedies resulting from those activities, may be affected; and (8) the effectiveness of foreign enforcement as compared to U.S. enforcement action.[74]

The relative weight that each factor should be given depends on the facts and circumstances of each case. With respect to the factor concerning conflict with foreign law, the Supreme Court made clear in *Hartford Fire*[75] that no conflict exists for purposes of an international comity analysis in the courts if the person subject to regulation by two states can comply with the laws of both. Bearing this in mind, the Agencies first ask what laws or policies of the arguably interested foreign jurisdictions are implicated by the conduct in question. There may be no actual conflict between the antitrust enforcement interests of the United States and the laws or policies of a foreign sovereign. This is increasingly true as more countries adopt antitrust or competition laws that are compatible with those of the United States. In these cases, the anticompetitive conduct in question may also be prohibited under the pertinent foreign laws, and thus the possible conflict would relate to enforcement practices or remedy. If the laws or policies of a foreign nation are neutral, it is again possible for the parties in question to comply with the U.S. prohibition without violating foreign law.

The Agencies also take full account of comity factors beyond whether there is a conflict with foreign law. In deciding whether or not to challenge an alleged antitrust violation, the Agencies would, as part of a comity analysis, consider whether one country encourages a certain course of conduct, leaves parties free to choose among different strategies, or prohibits some of those strategies. In addition, the Agencies take into account the effect of their enforcement activities on related enforcement activities of a foreign antitrust authority. For example, the Agencies would consider whether their activities would interfere with or reinforce the objectives of the foreign proceeding, including any remedies contemplated or obtained by the foreign antitrust authority.

The Agencies also will consider whether the objectives sought to be obtained by the assertion of U.S. law would be achieved in a particular instance by foreign enforcement. In lieu of bringing an enforcement action, the Agencies may consult with interested foreign sovereigns

74. The first six of these factors are based on previous Department Guidelines. The seventh and eighth factors are derived from considerations in the U.S.—EC Antitrust Cooperation Agreement. See supra at note 46.

75. 509 U.S. 764, 798.

through appropriate diplomatic channels to attempt to eliminate anticompetitive effects in the United States.

In cases when the United States decides to prosecute an antitrust action, such a decision represents a determination by the Executive Branch that the importance of antitrust enforcement outweighs any relevant foreign policy concerns.[76] The Department does not believe that it is the role of the courts to "second-guess the executive branch's judgment as to the proper role of comity concerns under these circumstances."[77] To date, no Commission cases have presented the issue of the degree of deference that courts should give to the Commission's comity decisions.[78] It is important also to note that in disputes between private parties, many courts are willing to undertake a comity analysis.[79]

ILLUSTRATIVE EXAMPLE I

Situation: A group of buyers in one foreign country decide that they will agree on the price that they will offer to U.S. suppliers of a particular product. The agreement results in substantial loss of sales and capacity reductions in the United States.

Discussion: From a jurisdictional point of view, the FTAIA standard appears to be satisfied because the effects on U.S. exporters presented here are direct and the percentage of supply accounted for by the buyers' cartel is substantial given the fact that the U.S. suppliers are major. The Agencies, however, would also take into consideration the comity aspects presented before deciding whether or not to proceed.

Consistent with their consideration of comity and its obligations under various international agreements, the Agencies would ordinarily notify the antitrust authority in the cartel's home country. If that authority were in a better position to address the competitive problem, and were prepared to take effective action to address the adverse effects on U.S. commerce, the Agencies would consider working cooperatively with the foreign authority or staying their own remedy pending enforcement efforts by the foreign country. In deciding whether to proceed, the Agencies would weigh the factors relating to comity set forth above. Factors weighing in favor of bringing such an action include the substantial and purposeful harm caused by the cartel to the United States.

ILLUSTRATIVE EXAMPLE J

Situation: A and B manufacture a consumer product for which there are no readily available substitutes in ten different countries around the

---

76. Foreign policy concerns may also lead the United States not to prosecute a case. See, e.g., U.S. Department of Justice Press Release dated Nov. 19, 1984 (announcing the termination, based on foreign policy concerns, of a grand jury investigation into passenger air travel between the United States and the United Kingdom).

77. United States v. Baker Hughes, Inc., 731 F.Supp. 3, 6 n.5 (D.D.C.1990), aff'd, 908 F.2d 981 (D.C.Cir.1990).

78. Like the Department, the Commission considers comity issues and consults with foreign antitrust authorities, but the Commission in not part of the Executive Branch.

79. See, e.g., Timberlane Lumber Co. v. Bank of America, 549 F.2d 597 (9th Cir.1976).

world, including the United States, Canada, Mexico, Spain, Australia, and others. When they decide to merge, it becomes necessary for them to file premerger notifications in many of these countries, and to subject themselves to the merger law of all ten.[80]

Discussion: Under the 1986 OECD Recommendation, OECD countries notify one another when a proceeding such as a merger review is underway that might affect the interests of other countries. Within the strict limits of national confidentiality laws, agencies attempt to cooperate with one another in processing these reviews. This might extend to exchanges of publicly available information, agreements to let the other agencies know when a decision to institute a proceeding is taken, and to consult for purposes of international comity with respect to proposed remedial measures and investigatory methods. The parties can facilitate faster resolution of these cases if they are willing voluntarily to waive confidentiality protections and to cooperate with a joint investigation. At present, confidentiality provisions in U.S. and foreign laws do not usually permit effective coordination of a single international investigation in the absence of such waivers.

3.3 Effects of Foreign Government Involvement

Foreign governments may be involved in a variety of ways in conduct that may have antitrust consequences. To address the implications of such foreign governmental involvement, Congress and the courts have developed four special doctrines: the doctrine of foreign sovereign immunity; the doctrine of foreign sovereign compulsion; the act of state doctrine; and the application of the *Noerr–Pennington* doctrine to immunize the lobbying of foreign governments. Although these doctrines are interrelated, for purposes of discussion the Guidelines discuss each one individually.

3.31 Foreign Sovereign Immunity

The scope of immunity of a foreign government or its agencies and instrumentalities (hereinafter foreign government)[81] from the jurisdiction of the U.S. courts for all causes of action, including antitrust, is governed by the Foreign Sovereign Immunities Act of 1976 ("FSIA").[82] Subject to the treaties in place at the time of FSIA's enactment, a foreign government is immune from suit except where designated in the FSIA.[83]

80. Not every country has compulsory premerger notification, and the events triggering duties to notify vary from country to country.

81. Section 1603(b) of the Foreign Sovereign Immunities Act of 1976 defines an "agency or instrumentality of a foreign state" to be any entity "(1) which is a separate legal person, corporate or otherwise; and (2) which is an organ of a foreign state or political subdivision thereof, or a majority of whose shares or other ownership interest is owned by a foreign state or political subdivision thereof; and (3) which is neither a citizen of a State of the United States as defined in Section 1332(c) and (d) of [Title 28, U.S. Code], nor created under the laws of any third country." 28 U.S.C.A. § 1603(b) (1988). It is not uncommon in antitrust cases to see state-owned enterprises meeting this definition.

82. 28 U.S.C.A. §§ 1602, *et seq.* (1988).

83. 28 U.S.C.A. § 1604 (1988) & Supp. (1993).

Under the FSIA, a U.S. court has jurisdiction if the foreign government has:

(a) waived its immunity explicitly or by implication,

(b) engaged in commercial activity as described in the statute,

(c) expropriated property in violation of international law,

(d) acquired rights to U.S. property,

(e) committed certain torts within the United States, or agreed to arbitration of a dispute.[84]

The commercial activities exception is a frequently invoked exception to sovereign immunity under the FSIA. Under the FSIA, a foreign government is not immune in any case: in which the action is based upon a commercial activity carried on in the United States by the foreign state; or upon an act performed in the United States in connection with a commercial activity of the foreign state elsewhere: or upon an act outside the territory of the United States in connection with a commercial activity of the foreign state elsewhere and that act causes a direct effect in the United States.[85]

"Commercial activity of the foreign state" is not defined in the FSIA, but is to be determined by the "nature of the course of conduct or particular transaction or act, rather than by reference to its purpose."[86] In attempting to differentiate commercial from sovereign activity, courts have considered whether the conduct being challenged is customarily performed for profit[87] and whether the conduct is of a type that only a sovereign government can perform.[88] As a practical matter, most activities of foreign government-owned corporations operating in the commercial marketplace will be subject to U.S. antitrust laws to the same extent as the activities of foreign privately-owned firms.

The commercial activity also must have a substantial nexus with the United States before a foreign government is subject to suit. The FSIA sets out three different standards for meeting this requirement. First, the challenged conduct by the foreign government may occur in the United States.[89] Alternatively, the challenged commercial activity may entail an act performed in the United States in connection with a commercial

84. 28 U.S.C.A. § 1605(a)(1–6) (1988).

85. 28 U.S.C.A. § 1605(a)(2) (1988).

86. 28 U.S.C.A. § 1603(d) (1988).

87. See, e.g., Republic of Argentina v. Weltover, Inc., 504 U.S. 607 (1992); Schoenberg v. Exportadora de Sal, S.A. de C.V., 930 F.2d 777 (9th Cir.1991); Rush–Presbyterian–St. Luke's Medical Ctr. v. Hellenic Republic, 877 F.2d 574, 578 n.4 (7th Cir.), cert. denied, 493 U.S. 937 (1989).

88. See, e.g., Saudi Arabia v. Nelson, 507 U.S. 349 (1993); de Sanchez v. Banco Central de Nicaragua, 770 F.2d 1385 (5th Cir.1985); Letelier v. Republic of Chile, 748 F.2d 790, 797–98 (2d Cir.1984), cert. denied, 471 U.S. 1125 (1985); International Association of Machinists & Aerospace Workers v. Organization of Petroleum Exporting Countries, 477 F.Supp. 553 (C.D.Cal.1979); cert. denied, aff'd on other grounds, 649 F.2d 1354 (9th Cir.1981), cert. denied 454 U.S. 1163 (1982).

89. 28 U.S.C.A. § 1603(e) (1988).

activity of the foreign government elsewhere.[90] Or, finally, the challenged commercial activity of a foreign government outside of the United States may produce a direct effect within the United States, i.e., an effect which follows "as an immediate consequence of the defendant's ... activity."[91]

3.32 Foreign Sovereign Compulsion

Although U.S. antitrust jurisdiction extends to conduct and parties in foreign countries whose actions have the required effects on U.S, commerce, as discussed above, those parties may find themselves subject to conflicting requirements from the other country (or countries) where they are located.[92] Under Hartford Fire, if it is possible for the party to comply both with the foreign law and the U.S. antitrust laws, the existence of the foreign law does not provide any legal excuse for actions that do not comply with U.S. law. However, a direct conflict may arise when the facts demonstrate that the foreign sovereign has compelled the very conduct that the U.S. antitrust law prohibits.

In these circumstances, at least one court has recognized a defense under the U.S. antitrust laws, and the Agencies will also recognize it.[93] There are two rationales underlying the defense of foreign sovereign compulsion. First, Congress enacted the U.S. antitrust laws against the background of well recognized principles of international law and comity among nations, pursuant to which U.S. authorities give due deference to the official acts of foreign governments. A defense for actions taken under the circumstances spelled out below serves to accommodate two equal sovereigns. Second, important considerations of fairness to the defendant

---

90. See H.R. Rep. No. 1487, 94th Cong., 2d Sess. 18–19 (1976), reprinted in 1976 U.S.C.C.A.N. 6604, 6617–18 (providing as an example the wrongful termination in the United States of an employee of a foreign state employed in connection with commercial activity in a third country.) But see Filus v. LOT Polish Airlines, 907 F.2d 1328, 1333 (2d Cir.1990) (holding as too attenuated the failure to warn of a defective product sold outside of the United States in connection with an accident outside the United States).

91. Republic of Argentina, 504 U.S. at 618. This test is similar to proximate cause formulations adopted by other courts. See Martin v. Republic of South Africa, 836 F.2d 91, 95 (2d Cir.1987) (a direct effect is one with no intervening element which flows in a straight line without deviation or interruption), quoting Upton v. Empire of Iran, 459 F.Supp. 264, 266 (D.D.C. 1978), aff'd mem., 607 F.2d 494 (D.C.Cir.1979).

92. Conduct by private entities not required by law is entirely outside of the protections afforded by this defense. See Continental Ore Co. v. Union Carbide & Carbon Corp., 370 U.S. 690, 706 (1962); United States v. Watchmakers of Switzerland Info. Ctr., Inc., 1963 Trade Cas. (CCH) ¶ 70,600 at 77,456–57 (S.D.N.Y.1962) ("[T]he fact that the Swiss Government may, as a practical matter, approve the effects of this private activity cannot convert what is essentially a vulnerable private conspiracy into an unassailable system resulting from a foreign government mandate.") See supra at Section 3.2.

93. Interamerican Refining Corp. v. Texaco Maracaibo, Inc., 307 F.Supp. 1291 (D.Del.1970) (defendant, having been ordered by the government of Venezuela not to sell oil to a particular refiner out of favor with the current political regime, held not subject to antitrust liability under the Sherman Act for an illegal group boycott). The defense of foreign sovereign compulsion is distinguished from the federalism-based state action doctrine. The state action doctrine applies not just to the actions of states and their subdivisions, but also to private anticompetitive conduct that is both undertaken pursuant to clearly articulated state policies, and is actively supervised by the state. See Federal Trade Comm'n v. Ticor Title Insurance Co., 504 U.S. 621 (1992); California Retail Liquor Dealers Ass'n v. Midcal Aluminum, Inc., 445 U.S. 97, 105 (1980); Parker v. Brown, 317 U.S. 341 (1943).

require some mechanism that provides a predictable rule of decision for those seeking to conform their behavior to all pertinent laws.

Because of the limited scope of the defense, the Agencies will refrain from enforcement actions on the ground of foreign sovereign compulsion only when certain criteria are satisfied. First, the foreign government must have compelled the anticompetitive conduct under circumstances in which a refusal to comply with the foreign government's command would give rise to the imposition of penal or other severe sanctions. As a general matter, the Agencies regard the foreign government's formal representation that refusal to comply with its command would have such a result as being sufficient to establish that the conduct in question has been compelled, as long as that representation contains sufficient detail to enable the Agencies to see precisely how the compulsion would be accomplished under local law.[94] Foreign government measures short of compulsion do not suffice for this defense, although they can be relevant in a comity analysis.

Second, although there can be no strict territorial test for this defense, the defense normally applies only when the foreign government compels conduct which can be accomplished entirely within its own territory. If the compelled conduct occurs in the United States, the Agencies will not recognize the defense.[95] For example, no defense arises when a foreign government requires the U.S. subsidiaries of several firms to organize a cartel in the United States to fix the price at which products would be sold in the United States, or when it requires its firms to fix mandatory resale prices for their U.S. distributors to use in the United States.

Third, with reference to the discussion of foreign sovereign immunity in Section 3.31 above, the order must come from the foreign government acting in its governmental capacity. The defense does not arise from conduct that would fall within the FSIA commercial activity exception.

ILLUSTRATIVE EXAMPLE K

Situation: Greatly increased quantities of commodity X have flooded into the world market over the last two or three years, including substantial amounts indirectly coming into the United States. Because they are unsure whether they would prevail in an antidumping and countervailing duty case, U.S. industry participants have refrained from filing trade law petitions. The officials of three foreign countries meet with their respective domestic firms and urge them to "rationalize" production by cooperatively cutting back. Going one step further, one of the interested governments orders cutbacks from its firms, subject to substantial penalties for non-compliance. Producers from the other two countries agree among

94. For example, the Agencies may not regard as dispositive a statement that is ambiguous or that on its face appears to be internally inconsistent. The Agencies may inquire into the circumstances underlying the statement and they may also request further information if the source of the power to compel is unclear.

95. See Linseman v. World Hockey Ass'n, 439 F.Supp. 1315, 1325 (D.Conn.1977).

themselves to institute comparable cutbacks, but their governments do not require them to do so.

Discussion: Assume for the purpose of this example that the overseas production cutbacks have the necessary effects on U.S. commerce to support jurisdiction. As for the participants from the two countries that did not impose any penalty for a failure to reduce production, the Agencies would not find that sovereign compulsion precluded prosecution of this agreement.[96] As for participants from the country that did compel production cut-backs through the imposition of severe penalties, the Agencies would acknowledge a defense of sovereign compulsion.

3.33 Acts of State

The act of state doctrine is a judge-made rule of federal common law.[97] It is a doctrine of judicial abstention based on considerations of international comity and separation of powers, and applies only if the specific conduct complained of is a public act of the foreign sovereign within its territorial jurisdiction on matters pertaining to its governmental sovereignty. The act of state doctrine arises when the validity of the acts of a foreign government is an unavoidable issue in a case.[98]

Courts have refused to adjudicate claims or issues that would require the court to judge the legality (as a matter of U.S. law or international law) of the sovereign act of a foreign state.[99] Although in some cases the sovereign act in question may compel private behavior, such compulsion is not required by the doctrine.[100] While the act of state doctrine does not compel dismissal as a matter of course, judicial abstention is appropriate in a case where the court must "declare invalid, and thus ineffective as a rule of decision in the U.S. courts, ... the official act of a foreign sovereign."[101]

When a restraint on competition arises directly from the act of a foreign sovereign, such as the grant of a license, award of a contract, expropriation of property, or the like, the Agencies may refrain from bringing an enforcement action based on the act of state doctrine. For example, the Agencies will not challenge foreign acts of state if the facts and circumstances indicate that: (1) the specific conduct complained of is a public act of the sovereign, (2) the act was taken within the territorial jurisdiction of the sovereign, and (3) the matter is governmental, rather than commercial.

---

96. As in all such cases, the Agencies would consider comity factors as part of their analysis. See supra at Section 3.2.

97. Banco Nacional de Cuba v. Sabbatino, 376 U.S. 398, 421–22 n.21 (1964) (noting that other countries do not adhere in any formulaic way to an act of state doctrine).

98. See W.S. Kirkpatrick & Co. v. Environmental Tectonics Corp., 493 U.S. 400 (1900).

99. International Ass'n of Machinists and Aerospace Workers v. Organization of Petroleum Exporting Countries, 649 F.2d 1354, 1358 (9th Cir.1981), cert. denied, 454 U.S. 1163 (1982).

100. See Timberlane, supra at note 79, 549 F.2d at 606–08.

101. Kirkpatrick, 493 U.S. at 405, quoting Ricaud v. American Metal Co., 246 U.S. 304, 310 (1918).

3.34 Petitioning of Sovereigns

Under the *Noerr–Pennington* doctrine, a genuine effort to obtain or influence action by governmental entities in the United States is immune from application of the Sherman Act, even if the intent or effect of that effort is to restrain or monopolize trade.[102] Whatever the basis asserted for *Noerr–Pennington* immunity (either as an application of the First Amendment or as a limit on the statutory reach of the Sherman Act, or both), the Agencies will apply it in the same manner to the petitioning of foreign governments and the U.S. Government.

ILLUSTRATIVE EXAMPLE L

Situation: In the course of preparing an antidumping case, which requires the U.S. industry to demonstrate that it has been injured through the effects of the dumped imports, producers representing 75 percent of U.S. output exchange the information required for the adjudication. All the information is exchanged indirectly through third parties and in an aggregated form that makes the identity of any particular producer's information impossible to discern.

Discussion: Information exchanged by competitors within the context of an antidumping proceeding implicates the *Noerr–Pennington* petitioning immunity. To the extent that these exchanges are reasonably necessary in order for them to prepare their joint petition, which is permitted under the trade laws, *Noerr* is available to protect against antitrust liability that would otherwise arise. On these facts the parties are likely to be immunized by *Noerr* if they have taken the necessary measures to ensure that the provision of sensitive information called for by the Commerce Department and the ITC cannot be used for anticompetitive purposes. In such a situation, the information exchange is incidental to genuine petitioning and is not subject to the antitrust laws.

Conversely, were the parties directly to exchange extensive information relating to their costs, the prices each has charged for the product, pricing trends, and profitability, including information about specific transactions that went beyond the scope of those facts required for the adjudication, such conduct would go beyond the contemplated protection of *Noerr* immunity.

3.4 Antitrust Enforcement and International Trade Regulation

There has always been a close relationship between the international application of the antitrust laws and the policies and rules governing the

102. See Eastern R.R. Presidents Conference v. Noerr Motor Freight, Inc., 365 U.S. 127 (1961); United Mine Workers of Am. v. Pennington, 381 U.S. 657 (1965); California Motor Transport Co. v. Trucking Unlimited, 404 U.S. 508 (1972) (extending protection to petitioning before "all departments of Government," including the courts); Professional Real Estate Investors, Inc. v. Columbia Pictures Indus., 508 U.S. 49 (1993). However, this immunity has never applied to "sham" activities, in which petitioning "ostensibly directed toward influencing governmental action, is a mere sham to cover ... an attempt to interfere directly with the business relationships of a competitor." Professional Real Estate Investors, 508 U.S. at 56, quoting Noerr, 365 U.S. at 144. See also USS–Posco Indus. v. Contra Costa Cty. Bldg. & Constr. Trades Council, AFL–CIO, 31 F.3d 800 (9th Cir.1994).

international trade of the United States. Restrictions such as tariffs or quotas on the free flow of goods affect market definition, consumer choice, and supply options for U.S. producers. In certain instances, the U.S. trade laws set forth specific procedures for settling disputes under those laws, which can involve price and quantity agreements by the foreign firms involved. When those are followed, an implied antitrust immunity results.[103] However, agreements among competitors that do not comply with the law, or so beyond the measures authorized by the law, do not enjoy antitrust immunity. In the absence of legal authority, the fact, without more, that U.S. or foreign government officials were involved in or encouraged measures that would otherwise violate the antitrust laws does not immunize such arrangements.[104]

If a particular voluntary export restraint does not qualify for express or implied immunity form the antitrust laws, then the legality of the arrangement would depend upon the existence of the ordinary elements of an antitrust offense, such as whether or not a prohibited agreement exists or whether defenses such as foreign sovereign compulsion can be invoked.

ILLUSTRATIVE EXAMPLE M

Situation: Six U.S. producers of product Q have initiated an antidumping action alleging that imports of Q from country Sigma at less than fair value are causing material injury to the U.S. Q industry. The ITC has made a preliminary decision that there is a reasonable indication that the U.S. industry is suffering material injury from Q imported from Sigma. The Department of Commerce has preliminarily concluded that the foreign market value of Q imported into the United States by Sigma's Q producers exceeds the price at which they are selling Q in this country by margins of 10 to 40 percent. Sigma's Q producers jointly initiate discussions with the Department of Commerce that lead to suspension of the investigation in accordance with Section 734 of the Tariff Act of 1930, 19 U.S.C.A. § 1673c. The suspension agreement provides that each of Sigma's Q producers will sell product Q in the United States at no less than its individual foreign market value, as determined periodically by the Department of Commerce in accordance with the Tariff Act. Before determining to suspend the investigation, the Department of Commerce provides copies of the proposed agreement to the U.S. Q producers, who

103. See, e.g., Letter from Charles F. Rule, Acting Assistant Attorney General, Antitrust Division, Department of Justice, to Mr. Makoto Kuroda, Vice–Minister for International Affairs, Japanese Ministry of International Trade and Industry, July 30, 1986 (concluding that a suspension agreement did not violate U.S. antitrust laws on the basis of factual representations that the agreement applied only to products under investigation, that it did not require pricing above levels needed to eliminate sales below foreign market value, and that assigning weighted-average foreign market values to exporters who were not respondents in the investigation was necessary to achieve the purpose of the antidumping law).

104. Cf. United States v. Socony–Vacuum Oil Co., 310 U.S. 150, 226 (1940) ("Though employees of the government may have known of those programs and winked at them or tacitly approved them, no immunity would have thereby been obtained. For Congress had specified the precise manner and method of securing immunity [in the National Industrial Recovery Act]. None other would suffice...."); see also Otter Tail Power Co. v. United States, 410 U.S. 366, 378–79 (1973).

jointly advise the that they do not object to the suspension of the investigation on the terms proposed. The Department also determines that suspension of the investigation would be in the public interest. As a result of the suspension agreement, prices in the United States of Q imported from Sigma rise by an average of 25 percent from the prices that prevailed before the antidumping action was initiated.

Discussion: While an unsupervised agreement among foreign firms to raise their U.S. sales prices ordinarily would violate the Sherman Act, the suspension agreement outlined above qualifies for an implied immunity from the antitrust laws. As demonstrated here, the parties have engaged only in conduct contemplated by the Tariff Act and none of the participants have engaged in conduct beyond what is necessary to implement that statutory scheme.

ILLUSTRATIVE EXAMPLE N

Situation: The Export Association is a Webb–Pomerene association that has filed the appropriate certificates and reports with the Commission. The Association exports a commodity to markets around the world, and fixes the price at which all of its members sell the commodity in the foreign markets. Nearly 80 percent of all U.S. producers of the commodity belong to the Association, and on a world-wide level, the Association's member account for approximately 40 percent of annual sales.

Discussion: The Webb–Pomerene Act addresses only the question of antitrust liability under U.S. law. Although the U.S. antitrust laws confer an immunity on such associations, the Act does not purport to confer immunity under the law of any foreign country, nor does the Act compel the members of a Webb–Pomerene association to act in any particular way. Thus, a foreign government retains the ability to initiate proceedings if such an association allegedly violates that country's competition law.

4. Personal Jurisdiction and Procedural Rules

4.1 Personal Jurisdiction and Venue

The Agencies will bring suit only if they conclude that personal jurisdiction exists under the due process clause of the U.S. Constitution.[105] The Constitution requires that the defendant have affiliating or minimum contacts with the United States, such that the proceeding comports with "fair play and substantial justice."[106]

Section 12 of the Clayton Act, 15 U.S.C.A. § 22, provides that any suit under the antitrust laws against a corporation may be brought in the judicial district where it is an inhabitant, where it may be found, or where it transacts business. The concept of transacting business is interpreted

105. See also International Shoe Co. v. Washington, 326 U.S. 310 (1945); Asahi Metal Industry Co., Ltd. v. Superior Court, 480 U.S. 102 (1987).

106. Go–Video, Inc. v. Akai Elec. Co., Ltd., 885 F.2d 1406, 1414 (9th Cir.1989); Wells Fargo & Co. v. Wells Fargo Express Co., 556 F.2d 406, 418 (9th Cir.1977). To establish jurisdiction, parties must also be served in accordance with the Federal Rules of Civil Procedure or other relevant authority. Fed. R. Civ. P. 4(k); 15 U.S.C.A. §§ 22, 44.

pragmatically by the Agencies. Thus, a company may transact business in a particular district directly through an agent, or through a related corporation that is actually the "alter ego" of the foreign party.[107]

4.2 Investigatory Practice Relating to Foreign Nations

In conducting investigations that require documents that are located outside the United States, or contacts with persons located outside the United States, the Agencies first consider requests for voluntary cooperation when practical and consistent with enforcement objectives. When compulsory measures are needed, they seek whenever possible to work with the foreign government involved. U.S. law also provides authority in some circumstances for the use of compulsory measures directed to parties over whom the courts have personal jurisdiction, which the Agencies may use when other efforts to obtain information have been exhausted or would be unavailing.[108]

Conflicts can arise, however, where foreign statutes purport to prevent persons from disclosing documents or information for use in U.S. proceedings. However, the mere existence of such statutes does not excuse noncompliance with a request for information from one of the Agencies.[109] To enable the Agencies to obtain evidence located abroad more Effectively, as noted in Section 2.91 above, Congress recently his enacted legislation authorizing the Agencies to negotiate bilateral agreements with foreign governments or antitrust enforcement agencies to facilitate the exchange of documents and evidence in civil and criminal investigations.[110]

*4.22 Hart-Scott-Rodino: Special Foreign Commerce Rules**

As noted above in Section 2.4, qualifying mergers and acquisitions, defined both in terms of size of party and size of transaction, must be reported to the Agencies, along with certain information about the parties and the transaction, prior to their consummation, pursuant to the HSR Amendments to the Clayton Act, 15 U.S.C.A. § 18a.

In some instances, the HSR implementing regulations exempt otherwise reportable foreign transactions.[111] First, some acquisitions by U.S.

107. See, e.g., Letter from Donald S. Clark, Secretary of the Federal Trade Commission, to Caswell O. Hobbs, Esq., Morgan, Lewis & Bockius, Jan. 17, 1990 (Re: Petition to Quash Subpoena Nippon Sheet Glass, *et al.*, File No. 891–0088, at page 3) ("The Commission . . . may exercise jurisdiction over and serve process on, a foreign entity that has a related company in the United States acting as its agent or alter ego."); see also Fed. R. Civ. P. 4; Volkswagenwerk AG v. Schlunk, 486 U.S. 694, 707–708 (1988); United States v. Scophony Corp., 333 U.S. 795, 810–818 (1948).

108. For example, 28 U.S.C.A. § 1783(a) (1988) authorizes a U.S. court to order the issuance of a subpoena "requiring the appearance as a witness before it, or before a person or body designated by it, of a national or resident of the United States who is in a foreign country, or requiring the production of a specified document or other thing by him," under circumstances spelled out in the statute.

109. See Société Internationale pour Participations Industrielles et Commerciales, S.A. v. Rogers, 357 U.S. 197 (1958).

110. International Antitrust Enforcement Assistance Act of 1944, Pub. L. No. 103–438, 108 Stat. 4597 (1994).

* *Editors' note: Consult current rules. The rules have been amended.*

persons are exempt. Acquisitions of foreign assets by a U.S. person are exempt when (i) no sales in or into the United States are attributable to those assets, or (ii) some sales in or into the United States are attributable to those assets, but the acquiring person would not hold assets of the acquired person to which $25 million or more of such sales in the acquired person's most recent fiscal year were attributable.[112] Acquisitions by a U.S. person of voting securities of a foreign issuer are exempt unless the issuer holds assets in the United States having an aggregate book value of $15 million or more, or made aggregate sales in or into the United States of $25 million or more in its most recent fiscal year.[113]

Second, some acquisitions by foreign persons are exempt. An exemption exists for acquisitions by foreign persons if (i) the acquisition is of voting securities of a foreign issuer and would not confer control of a U.S. issuer having annual net sales or total assets of $25 million or more, or of any issuer with assets located in the United States having a book value of $15 million or more; or (ii) the acquired person is also a foreign person and the aggregate annual net sales of the merging firms or into the United States is less than $110 million and their aggregate total assets in the United States is less than $110 million.[114] In addition, an acquisition by a foreign person of assets located outside the United States is exempt. Acquisition by foreign persons of U.S. issuers or assets are not exempt.

Finally, acquisitions are exempt if the ultimate parent entity of either the acquiring or the acquired person is controlled by a foreign state, and the acquisition is of assets located within that foreign state, or of voting securities of an issuer organized under its laws.[115] The HSR rules are necessarily technical, and should be consulted rather than relying on the summary description herein.

---

111. See 16 C.F.R. §§ 802.50–52 (1994).

112. See 16 C.F.R. § 802.50(a) (1994).

113. See 16 C.F.R. § 802.50(b) (1994).

114. See 16 C.F.R. § 802.51 (1994).

115. See 16 C.F.R. § 802.52 (1994).

APPENDIX G

ANTITRUST GUIDELINES FOR THE LICENSING OF INTELLECTUAL PROPERTY

■ ■ ■

U.S. DEPARTMENT OF JUSTICE AND THE FEDERAL TRADE COMMISSION
APRIL 1995

* * *

Table of Contents

1. Intellectual Property Protection and the Antitrust Laws

1.0 These Guidelines state the antitrust enforcement policy of the U.S. Department of Justice and the Federal Trade Commission (individually, "the Agency," and collectively, "the Agencies") with respect to the licensing of intellectual property protected by patent, copyright, and trade secret law, and of know-how.[1] By stating their general policy, the Agencies hope to assist those who need to predict whether the Agencies will challenge a practice as anticompetitive. However, these Guidelines cannot remove judgment and discretion in antitrust law enforcement. Moreover, the standards set forth in these Guidelines must be applied in unforeseeable circumstances. Each case will be evaluated in light of its own facts, and these Guidelines will be applied reasonably and flexibly.[2]

In the United States, patents confer rights to exclude others from making, using, or selling in the United States the invention claimed by the patent for a period of seventeen years from the date of issue.[3] To gain patent protection, an invention (which may be a product, process, machine, or composition of matter) must be novel, nonobvious, and useful. Copyright protection applies to original works of authorship embodied in a tangible medium of expression.[4] A copyright protects only the expression, not the underlying ideas.[5] Unlike a patent, which protects an invention not only from copying but also from independent creation, a copyright does not preclude others from independently creating similar expression. Trade secret protection applies to information whose economic value depends on its not being generally known.[6] Trade secret protection is conditioned upon efforts to maintain secrecy and has no fixed term. As with copyright protection, trade secret protection does not preclude independent creation by others.

---

1. These Guidelines do not cover the antitrust treatment of trademarks. Although the same general antitrust principles that apply to other forms of intellectual property apply to trademarks as well, these Guidelines deal with technology transfer and innovation-related issues that typically arise with respect to patents, copyrights, trade secrets, and know-how agreements, rather than with product-differentiation issues that typically arise with respect to trademarks.

2. As is the case with all guidelines, users should rely on qualified counsel to assist them in evaluating the antitrust risk associated with any contemplated transaction or activity. No set of guidelines can possibly indicate how the Agencies will assess the particular facts of every case. Parties who wish to know the Agencies' specific enforcement intentions with respect to any particular transaction should consider seeking a Department of Justice business review letter pursuant to 28 C.F.R. § 50.6 or a Federal Trade Commission Advisory Opinion pursuant to 16 C.F.R. §§ 1.1–1.4.

3. See 35 U.S.C.A. § 154 (1988). Section 532(a) of the Uruguay Round Agreements Act, Pub. L. No. 103–465, 108 Stat. 4809, 4983 (1994) would change the length of patent protection to a term beginning on the date at which the patent issues and ending twenty years from the date on which the application for the patent was filed.

4. See 17 U.S.C.A. § 102 (1988 & Supp. V 1993). Copyright protection lasts for the author's life plus 50 years, or 75 years from first publication (or 100 years from creation, whichever expires first) for works made for hire. See 17 U.S.C.A. § 302 (1988). The principles stated in these Guidelines also apply to protection of mask works fixed in a semiconductor chip product (see 17 U.S.C.A. § 901 *et seq.* (1988)), which is analogous to copyright protection for works of authorship.

5. See 17 U.S.C.A. § 102(b) (1988).

6. Trade secret protection derives from state law. See generally Kewanee Oil Co. v. Bicron Corp., 416 U.S. 470 (1974).

The intellectual property laws and the antitrust laws share the common purpose of promoting innovation and enhancing consumer welfare.[7] The intellectual property laws provide incentives for innovation and its dissemination and commercialization by establishing enforceable property rights for the creators of new and useful products, more efficient processes, and original works of expression. In the absence of intellectual property rights, imitators could more rapidly exploit the efforts of innovators and investors without compensation. Rapid imitation would reduce the commercial value of innovation and erode incentives to invest, ultimately to the detriment of consumers. The antitrust laws promote innovation and consumer welfare by prohibiting certain actions that may harm competition with respect to either existing or new ways of serving consumers.

2. General Principles

2.0 These Guidelines embody three general principles: (a) for the purpose of antitrust analysis, the Agencies regard intellectual property as being essentially comparable to any other form of property; (b) the Agencies do not presume that intellectual property creates market power in the antitrust context; and (c) the Agencies recognize that intellectual property licensing allows firms to combine complementary factors of production and is generally procompetitive.

2.1 Standard Antitrust Analysis Applies to Intellectual Property

The Agencies apply the same general antitrust principles to conduct involving intellectual property that they apply to conduct involving any other form of tangible or intangible property. That is not to say that intellectual property is in all respects the same as any other form of property. Intellectual property has important characteristics, such as ease of misappropriation, that distinguish it from many other forms of property. These characteristics can be taken into account by standard antitrust analysis, however, and do not require the application of fundamentally different principles.[8]

Although there are clear and important differences in the purpose, extent, and duration of protection provided under the intellectual property regimes of patent, copyright, and trade secret, the governing antitrust principles are the same. Antitrust analysis takes differences among these forms of intellectual property into account in evaluating the specific market circumstances in which transactions occur, just as it does with other particular market circumstances.

Intellectual property law bestows on the owners of intellectual property certain rights to exclude others. These rights help the owners to profit

---

7. "[T]he aims and objectives of patent and antitrust laws may seem, at first glance, wholly at odds. However, the two bodies of law are actually complementary, as both are aimed at encouraging innovation, industry and competition." Atari Games Corp. v. Nintendo of America, Inc., 897 F.2d 1572, 1576 (Fed.Cir.1990).

8. As with other forms of property, the power to exclude others from the use of intellectual property may vary substantially, depending on the nature of the property and its status under federal or state law. The greater or lesser legal power of an owner to exclude others is also taken into account by standard antitrust analysis.

from the use of their property. An intellectual property owner's rights to exclude are similar to the rights enjoyed by owners of other forms of private property. As with other forms of private property, certain types of conduct with respect to intellectual property may have anticompetitive effects against which the antitrust laws can and do protect. Intellectual property is thus neither particularly free from scrutiny under the antitrust laws, nor particularly suspect under them.

The Agencies recognize that the licensing of intellectual property is often international. The principles of antitrust analysis described in these Guidelines apply equally to domestic and international licensing arrangements. However, as described in the 1995 Department of Justice and Federal Trade Commission Antitrust Enforcement Guidelines for International Operations, considerations particular to international operations, such as jurisdiction and comity, may affect enforcement decisions when the arrangement is in an international context.

2.2 *Intellectual Property and Market Power*

Market power is the ability profitably to maintain prices above, or output below, competitive levels for a significant period of time.[9] The Agencies will not presume that a patent, copyright, or trade secret necessarily confers market power upon its owner. Although the intellectual property right confers the power to exclude with respect to the *specific* product, process, or work in question, there will often be sufficient actual or potential close substitutes for such product, process, or work to prevent the exercise of market power.[10] If a patent or other form of intellectual property does confer market power, that market power does not by itself offend the antitrust laws. As with any other tangible or intangible asset that enables its owner to obtain significant supracompetitive profits, market power (or even a monopoly) that is solely "a consequence of a superior product, business acumen, or historic accident" does not violate the antitrust laws.[11] Nor does such market power impose on the intellec-

9. Market power can be exercised in other economic dimensions, such as quality, service, and the development of new or improved goods and processes. It is assumed in this definition that all competitive dimensions are held constant except the ones in which market power is being exercised; that a seller is able to charge higher prices for a higher-quality product does not alone indicate market power. The definition in the text is stated in terms of a seller with market power. A buyer could also exercise market power (e.g., by maintaining the price below the competitive level, thereby depressing output).

10. The Agencies note that the law is unclear on this issue. Compare Jefferson Parish Hospital District No. 2 v. Hyde, 466 U.S. 2, 16 (1984) (expressing the view in dictum that if a product is protected by a patent, "it is fair to presume that the inability to buy the product elsewhere gives the seller market power") with id. at 37 n.7 (O'Connor, J., concurring) ("[A] patent holder has no market power in any relevant sense if there are close substitutes for the patented product."). Compare also Abbott Laboratories v. Brennan, 952 F.2d 1346, 1354–55 (Fed. Cir.1991) (no presumption of market power from intellectual property right), cert. denied, 505 U.S. 1205 (1992) with Digidyne Corp. v. Data General Corp., 734 F.2d 1336, 1341–42 (9th Cir.1984) (requisite economic power is presumed from copyright), cert. denied, 473 U.S. 908 (1985).

11. United States v. Grinnell Corp., 384 U.S. 563, 571 (1966); see also United States v. Aluminum Co. of America, 148 F.2d 416, 430 (2d Cir.1945) (Sherman Act is not violated by the attainment of market power solely through "superior skill, foresight and industry").

tual property owner an obligation to license the use of that property to others. As in other antitrust contexts, however, market power could be illegally acquired or maintained, or, even if lawfully acquired and maintained, would be relevant to the ability of an intellectual property owner to harm competition through unreasonable conduct in connection with such property.

2.3 Procompetitive Benefits of Licensing

Intellectual property typically is one component among many in a production process and derives value from its combination with complementary factors. Complementary factors of production include manufacturing and distribution facilities, workforces, and other items of intellectual property. The owner of intellectual property has to arrange for its combination with other necessary factors to realize its commercial value. Often, the owner finds it most efficient to contract with others for these factors, to sell rights to the intellectual property, or to enter into a joint venture arrangement for its development, rather than supplying these complementary factors itself.

Licensing, cross-licensing, or otherwise transferring intellectual property (hereinafter "licensing") can facilitate integration of the licensed property with complementary factors of production. This integration can lead to more efficient exploitation of the intellectual property, benefiting consumers through the reduction of costs and the introduction of new products. Such arrangements increase the value of intellectual property to consumers and to the developers of the technology. By potentially increasing the expected returns from intellectual property, licensing also can increase the incentive for its creation and thus promote greater investment in research and development.

Sometimes the use of one item of intellectual property requires access to another. An item of intellectual property "blocks" another when the second cannot be practiced without using the first. For example, an improvement on a patented machine can be blocked by the patent on the machine. Licensing may promote the coordinated development of technologies that are in a blocking relationship.

Field-of-use, territorial, and other limitations on intellectual property licenses may serve procompetitive ends by allowing the licensor to exploit its property as efficiently and effectively as possible. These various forms of exclusivity can be used to give a licensee an incentive to invest in the commercialization and distribution of products embodying the licensed intellectual property and to develop additional applications for the licensed property. The restrictions may do so, for example, by protecting the licensee against free-riding on the licensee's investments by other licensees or by the licensor. They may also increase the licensor's incentive to license, for example, by protecting the licensor from competition in the licensor's own technology in a market niche that it prefers to keep to itself. These benefits of licensing restrictions apply to patent, copyright, and trade secret licenses, and to know-how agreements.

Example 1[12]

Situation: ComputerCo develops a new, copyrighted software program for inventory management. The program has wide application in the health field. ComputerCo licenses the program in an arrangement that imposes both field of use and territorial limitations. Some of ComputerCo's licenses permit use only in hospitals; others permit use only in group medical practices. ComputerCo charges different royalties for the different uses. All of ComputerCo's licenses permit use only in specified portions of the United States and in specified foreign countries.[13] The licenses contain no provisions that would prevent or discourage licensees from developing, using, or selling any other program, or from competing in any other good or service other than in the use of the licensed program. None of the licensees are actual or likely potential competitors of ComputerCo in the sale of inventory management programs.

Discussion: The key competitive issue raised by the licensing arrangement is whether it harms competition among entities that would have been actual or likely potential competitors in the absence of the arrangement. Such harm could occur if, for example, the licenses anticompetitively foreclose access to competing technologies (in this case, most likely competing computer programs), prevent licensees from developing their own competing technologies (again, in this case, most likely computer programs), or facilitate market allocation or price-fixing for any product or service supplied by the licensees. (See section 3.1.) If the license agreements contained such provisions, the Agency evaluating the arrangement would analyze its likely competitive effects as described in parts 3–5 of these Guidelines. In this hypothetical, there are no such provisions and thus the arrangement is merely a subdivision of the licensor's intellectual property among different fields of use and territories. The licensing arrangement does not appear likely to harm competition among entities that would have been actual or likely potential competitors if ComputerCo had chosen not to license the software program. The Agency therefore would be unlikely to object to this arrangement. Based on these facts, the result of the antitrust analysis would be the same whether the technology was protected by patent, copyright, or trade secret. The Agency's conclusion as to likely competitive effects could differ if, for example, the license barred licensees from using any other inventory management program.

3. Antitrust Concerns and Modes of Analysis

3.1 Nature of the Concerns

While intellectual property licensing arrangements are typically welfare-enhancing and procompetitive, antitrust concerns may nonetheless arise. For example, a licensing arrangement could include restraints that adversely affect competition in goods markets by dividing the markets

12. The examples in these Guidelines are hypothetical and do not represent judgments about, or analysis of, any actual market circumstances of the named industries.

13. These Guidelines do not address the possible application of the antitrust laws of other countries to restraints such as territorial restrictions in international licensing arrangements.

among firms that would have competed using different technologies. See, e.g., Example 7. An arrangement that effectively merges the research and development activities of two of only a few entities that could plausibly engage in research and development in the relevant field might harm competition for development of new goods and services. See section 3.2.3. An acquisition of intellectual property may lessen competition in a relevant antitrust market. See section 5.7. The Agencies will focus on the actual effects of an arrangement, not on its formal terms.

The Agencies will not require the owner of intellectual property to create competition in its own technology. However, antitrust concerns may arise when a licensing arrangement harms competition among entities that would have been actual or likely potential competitors[14] in a relevant market in the absence of the license (entities in a "horizontal relationship"). A restraint in a licensing arrangement may harm such competition, for example, if it facilitates market division or price-fixing. In addition, license restrictions with respect to one market may harm such competition in another market by anticompetitively foreclosing access to, or significantly raising the price of, an important input,[15] or by facilitating coordination to increase price or reduce output. When it appears that such competition may be adversely affected, the Agencies will follow the analysis set forth below. See generally sections 3.4 and 4.2.

3.2 Markets Affected by Licensing Arrangements

Licensing arrangements raise concerns under the antitrust laws if they are likely to affect adversely the prices, quantities, qualities, or varieties of goods and services[16] either currently or potentially available. The competitive effects of licensing arrangements often can be adequately assessed within the relevant markets for the goods affected by the arrangements. In such instances, the Agencies will delineate and analyze only goods markets. In other cases, however, the analysis may require the delineation of markets for technology or markets for research and development (innovation markets).

3.2.1 Goods Markets

A number of different goods markets may be relevant to evaluating the effects of a licensing arrangement. A restraint in a licensing arrangement may have competitive effects in markets for final or intermediate goods made using the intellectual property, or it may have effects upstream, in markets for goods that are used as inputs, along with the intellectual property, to the production of other goods. In general, for goods markets affected by a licensing arrangement, the Agencies will approach the delineation of relevant market and the measurement of

14. A firm will be treated as a likely potential competitor if there is evidence that entry by that firm is reasonably probable in the absence of the licensing arrangement.

15. As used herein, "input" includes outlets for distribution and sales, as well as factors of production. See, e.g., sections 4.1.1 and 5.3–5.5 for further discussion of conditions under which foreclosing access to, or raising the price of, an input may harm competition in a relevant market.

16. Hereinafter, the term "goods" also includes services.

market share in the intellectual property area as in section I of the U.S. Department of Justice and Federal Trade Commission Horizontal Merger Guidelines.[17]

3.2.2 Technology Markets

Technology markets consist of the intellectual property that is licensed (the "licensed technology") and its close substitutes–that is, the technologies or goods that are close enough substitutes significantly to constrain the exercise of market power with respect to the intellectual property that is licensed.[18] When rights to intellectual Property are marketed separately from the products in which they are used,[19] the Agencies may rely on technology markets to analyze the competitive effects of a licensing arrangement.

Example 2

Situation: Firms Alpha and Beta independently develop different patented process technologies to manufacture the same off-patent drug for the treatment of a particular disease. Before the firms use their technologies internally or license them to third parties, they announce plans jointly to manufacture the drug, and to assign their manufacturing processes to the new manufacturing venture. Many firms are capable of using and have the incentive to use the licensed technologies to manufacture and distribute the drug; thus, the market for drug manufacturing and distribution is competitive. One of the Agencies is evaluating the likely competitive effects of the planned venture.

Discussion: The Agency would analyze the competitive effects of the proposed joint venture by first defining the relevant markets in which competition may be affected and then evaluating the likely competitive effects of the joint venture in the identified markets. (See Example 4 for a discussion of the Agencies' approach to joint venture analysis.) In this example, the structural effect of the joint venture in the relevant goods market for the manufacture and distribution of the drug is unlikely to be significant, because many firms in addition to the joint venture compete in that market. The joint venture might, however, increase the prices of the drug produced using Alpha's or Beta's technology by reducing competition in the relevant market for technology to manufacture the drug.

---

17. U.S. Department of Justice and Federal Trade Commission, Horizontal Merger Guidelines (April 2, 1992) (hereinafter "1992 Horizontal Merger Guidelines"). As stated in section 1.41 of the 1992 Horizontal Merger Guidelines, market shares for goods markets "can be expressed either in dollar terms through measurement of sales, shipments, or production, or in physical terms through measurement of sales, shipments, production, capacity or reserves."

18. For example, the owner of a process for producing a particular good may be constrained in its conduct with respect to that process not only by other processes for making that good, but also by other goods that compete with the downstream good and by the processes used to produce those other goods.

19. Intellectual property is often licensed, sold, or transferred as an integral part of a marketed good. An example is a patented product marketed with an implied license permitting its use. In such circumstances, there is no need for a separate analysis of technology markets to capture relevant competitive effects.

The Agency would delineate a technology market in which to evaluate likely competitive effects of the proposed joint venture. The Agency would identify other technologies that can be used to make the drug with levels of effectiveness and cost per dose comparable to that of the technologies owned by Alpha and Beta. In addition, the Agency would consider the extent to which competition from other drugs that are substitutes for the drug produced using Alpha's or Beta's technology would limit the ability of a hypothetical monopolist that owned both Alpha's and Beta's technology to raise its price.

To identify a technology's close substitutes and thus to delineate the relevant technology market, the Agencies will, if the data permit, identify the smallest group of technologies and goods over which a hypothetical monopolist of those technologies and goods likely would exercise market power–for example, by imposing a small but significant and nontransitory price increase.[20] The Agencies recognize that technology often is licensed in ways that are not readily quantifiable in monetary terms.[21] In such circumstances, the Agencies will delineate the relevant market by identifying other technologies and goods which buyers would substitute at a cost comparable to that of using the licensed technology.

In assessing the competitive significance of current and likely potential participants in a technology market, the Agencies will take into account all relevant evidence. When market share data are available and accurately reflect the competitive significance of market participants, the Agencies will include market share data in this assessment. The Agencies also will seek evidence of buyers' and market participants' assessments of the competitive significance of technology market participants. Such evidence is particularly important when market share data are unavailable, or do not accurately represent the competitive significance of market participants. When market share data or other indicia of market power are not available, and it appears that competing technologies are comparably efficient,[22] the Agencies will assign each technology the same market share. For new technologies, the Agencies generally will use the best available information to estimate market acceptance over a two-year period, beginning with commercial introduction.

3.2.3 Research and Development: Innovation Markets

If a licensing arrangement may adversely affect competition to develop new or improved goods or processes, the Agencies will analyze such an

---

20. This is conceptually analogous to the analytical approach to goods markets under the 1992 Horizontal Merger Guidelines. Cf. § 1.11. Of course, market power also can be exercised in other dimensions, such as quality, and these dimensions also may be relevant to the definition and analysis of technology markets.

21. For example, technology may be licensed royalty-free in exchange for the right to use other technology, or it may be licensed as part of a package license.

22. The Agencies will regard two technologies as "comparably efficient" if they can be used to produce close substitutes at comparable costs.

impact either as a separate competitive effect in relevant goods or technology markets, or as a competitive effect in a separate innovation market. A licensing arrangement may have competitive effects on innovation that cannot be adequately addressed through the analysis of goods or technology markets. For example, the arrangement may affect the development of goods that do not yet exist.[23] Alternatively, the arrangement may affect the development of new or improved goods or processes in geographic markets where there is no actual or likely potential competition in the relevant goods.[24]

An innovation market consists of the research and development directed to particular new or improved goods or processes, and the close substitutes for that research and development. The close substitutes are research and development efforts, technologies, and goods[25] that significantly constrain the exercise of market power with respect to the relevant research and development, for example by limiting the ability and incentive of a hypothetical monopolist to retard the pace of research and development. The Agencies will delineate an innovation market only when the capabilities to engage in the relevant research and development can be associated with specialized assets or characteristics of specific firms.

In assessing the competitive significance of current and likely potential participants in an innovation market, the Agencies will take into account all relevant evidence. When market share data are available and accurately reflect the competitive significance of market participants, the Agencies will include market share data in this assessment. The Agencies also will seek evidence of buyers' and market participants' assessments of the competitive significance of innovation market participants. Such evidence is particularly important when market share data are unavailable or do not accurately represent the competitive significance of market participants. The Agencies may base the market shares of participants in an innovation market on their shares of identifiable assets or characteristics upon which innovation depends, on shares of research and development expenditures, or on shares of a related product. When entities have comparable capabilities and incentives to pursue research and development that is a close substitute for the research and development activities of the parties to a licensing arrangement, the Agencies may assign equal market shares to such entities.

23. E.g., Sensormatic, FTC Inv. No. 941–0126, 60 Fed. Reg. 5428 (accepted for comment Dec. 28, 1994); Wright Medical Technology, Inc., FTC Inv. No. 951–0015, 60 Fed. Reg. 460 (accepted for comment Dec. 8, 1994); American Home Products, FTC Inv. No. 941–0116, 59 Fed. Reg. 60,807 (accepted for comment Nov. 28, 1994); Roche Holding Ltd., 113 F.T.C. 1086 (1990); United States v. Automobile Mfrs. Ass'n, 307 F.Supp. 617 (C.D.Cal.1969), appeal dismissed sub nom. City of New York v. United States, 397 U.S. 248 (1970), modified sub nom. United States v. Motor Vehicles Mfrs. Ass'n, 1982–83 Trade Cas. (CCH) ¶ 65,088 (C.D.Cal.1982).

24. See Complaint, United States v. General Motors Corp., Civ. No. 93–530 (D. Del., filed Nov. 16, 1993).

25. For example, the licensor of research and development may be constrained in its conduct not only by competing research and development efforts but also by other existing goods that would compete with the goods under development.

Example 3

Situation: Two companies that specialize in advanced metallurgy agree to cross-license future patents relating to the development of a new component for aircraft jet turbines. Innovation in the development of the component requires the capability to work with very high tensile strength materials for jet turbines. Aspects of the licensing arrangement raise the possibility that competition in research and development of this and related components will be lessened. One of the Agencies is considering whether to define an innovation market in which to evaluate the competitive effects of the arrangement.

Discussion: If the firms that have the capability and incentive to work with very high tensile strength materials for jet turbines can be reasonably identified, the Agency will consider defining a relevant innovation market for development of the new component. If the number of firms with the required capability and incentive to engage in research and development of very high tensile strength materials for aircraft jet turbines is small, the Agency may employ the concept of an innovation market to analyze the likely competitive effects of the arrangement in that market, or as an aid in analyzing competitive effects in technology or goods markets. The Agency would perform its analysis as described in parts 3–5.

If the number of firms with the required capability and incentive is large (either because them are a large number of such firms in the jet turbine industry, or because there are many firms in other industries with the required capability and incentive), then the Agency will conclude that the innovation market is competitive. Under these circumstances, it is unlikely that any single firm or plausible aggregation of firms could acquire a large enough share of the assets necessary for innovation to have an adverse impact on competition.

If the Agency cannot reasonably identify the firms with the required capability and incentive, it will not attempt to define an innovation market.

Example 4

Situation: Three of the largest producers of a plastic used in disposable bottles plan to engage in joint research and development to produce a new type of plastic that is rapidly biodegradable. The joint venture will grant to its partners (but to no one else) licenses to all patent rights and use of know-how. One of the Agencies is evaluating the likely competitive effects of the proposed joint venture.

Discussion: The Agency would analyze the proposed research and development joint venture using an analysis similar to that applied to other joint ventures.[26] The Agency would begin by defining the relevant

---

26. See, e.g. U.S. Department of Justice and Federal Trade Commission, Statements of Enforcement Policy and Analytical Principles Relating to Health Care and Antitrust 20–23, 37–

markets in which to analyze the joint venture's likely competitive effects. In this case, a relevant market is an innovation market–research and development for biodegradable (and other environmentally friendly) containers. The Agency would seek to identify any other entities that would be actual or likely potential competitors with the joint venture in that relevant market. This would include those firms that have the capability and incentive to undertake research and development closely substitutable for the research and development proposed to be undertaken by the joint venture, taking into account such firms' existing technologies and technologies under development, R & D facilities, and other relevant assets and business circumstances. Firms possessing such capabilities and incentives would be included in the research and development market even if they are not competitors in relevant markets for related goods, such as the plastics currently produced by the joint venturers, although competitors in existing goods markets may often also compete in related innovation markets.

Having defined a relevant innovation market, the Agency would assess whether the joint venture is likely to have anticompetitive effects in that market. A starting point in this analysis is the degree of concentration in the relevant market and the market shares of the parties to the joint venture. If, in addition to the parties to the joint venture (taken collectively), there are at least four other independently controlled entities that possess comparable capabilities and incentives to undertake research and development of biodegradable plastics, or other products that would be close substitutes for such new plastics, the joint venture ordinarily would be unlikely to adversely affect Competition in the relevant innovation market (cf. section 4.3). If there are fewer than four other independently controlled entities with similar capabilities and incentives, the Agency would consider whether the joint venture would give the parties to the joint venture an incentive and ability collectively to reduce investment in, or otherwise to retard the pace or scope of, research and development efforts. If the joint venture creates a significant risk of anticompetitive effects in the innovation market, the Agency would proceed to consider efficiency justifications for the venture, such as the potential for combining complementary R & D assets in such a way as to make successful innovation more likely, or to bring it about sooner, or to achieve cost reductions in research and development.

The Agency would also assess the likelihood that the joint venture would adversely affect competition in other relevant markets, including markets for products produced by the parties to the joint venture. The risk of such adverse competitive effects would be increased to the extent that, for example, the joint venture facilitates the exchange among the parties of competitively sensitive information relating to goods markets in which the parties currently compete or facilitates the coordination of competitive activities in such markets. The Agency would examine wheth-

---

40, 72–74 (September 27, 1994). This type of transaction may qualify for treatment under the National Cooperative Research and Production Act of 1993, 15 U.S.C.A. §§ 4301–05.

er the joint venture imposes collateral restraints that might significantly restrict competition among the joint venturers in goods markets, and would examine whether such collateral restraints were reasonably necessary to achieve any efficiencies that are likely to be attained by the venture.

3.3 Horizontal and Vertical Relationships

As with other property transfers, antitrust analysis of intellectual property licensing arrangements examines whether the relationship among the parties to the arrangement is primarily horizontal or vertical in nature, or whether it has substantial aspects of both. A licensing arrangement has a vertical component when it affects activities that are in a complementary relationship, as is typically the case in a licensing arrangement. For example, the licensor's primary line of business may be in research and development, and the licensees, as manufacturers, may be buying the rights to use technology developed by the licensor. Alternatively, the licensor may be a component manufacturer owning intellectual property rights in a product that the licensee manufactures by combining the component with other inputs, or the licensor may manufacture the product, and the licensees may operate primarily in distribution and marketing.

In addition to this vertical component, the licensor and its licensees may also have a horizontal relationship. For analytical purposes, the Agencies ordinarily will treat a relationship between a licensor and its licensees, or between licensees, as horizontal when they would have been actual or likely potential competitors in a relevant market in the absence of the license.

The existence of a horizontal relationship between a licensor and its licensees does not, in itself, indicate that the arrangement is anticompetitive. Identification of such relationships is merely an aid in determining whether there may be anticompetitive effects arising from a licensing arrangement. Such a relationship need not give rise to an anticompetitive effect, nor does a purely vertical relationship assure that there are no anticompetitive effects.

The following examples illustrate different competitive relationships among a licensor and its licensees.

Example 5

Situation: AgCo, a manufacturer of farm equipment, develops a new, patented emission control technology for its tractor engines and licenses it to FarmCo, another farm equipment manufacturer. AgCo's emission control technology is far superior to the technology currently owned and used by FarmCo, so much so that FarmCo's technology does not significantly constrain the prices that AgCo could charge for its technology. AgCo's emission control patent has a broad scope. It is likely that any improved emissions control technology that FarmCo could develop in the foreseeable future would infringe AgCo's patent.

Discussion: Because FarmCo's emission control technology does not significantly constrain AgCo's competitive conduct with respect to its emission control technology, AgCo's and FarmCo's emission control technologies are not close substitutes for each other. FarmCo is a consumer of AgCo's technology and is not an actual competitor of AgCo in the relevant market for superior emission control technology of the kind licensed by AgCo. Furthermore, FarmCo is not a likely potential competitor of AgCo in the relevant market because, even if FarmCo could develop an improved emission control technology, it is likely that it would infringe AgCo's patent. This means that the relationship between AgCo and FarmCo with regard to the supply and use of emissions control technology is vertical. Assuming that AgCo and FarmCo are actual or likely potential competitors in sales of farm equipment products, their relationship is horizontal in the relevant markets for farm equipment.

Example 6

Situation: FarmCo develops a new valve technology for its engines and enters into a cross-licensing arrangement with AgCo, whereby AgCo licenses its emission control technology to FarmCo and FarmCo licenses its valve technology to AgCo. AgCo already owns an alterative valve technology that can be used to achieve engine performance similar to that using FarmCo's valve technology and at a comparable cost to consumers. Before adopting FarmCo's technology, AgCo was using its own valve technology in its production of engines and was licensing (and continues to license) that technology for use by others. As in Example 5, FarmCo does not own or control an emission control technology that is a close substitute for the technology licensed from AgCo. Furthermore, as in Example 5, FarmCo is not likely to develop an improved emission control technology that would be a close substitute for AgCo's technology, because of AgCo's blocking patent.

Discussion: FarmCo is a consumer and not a competitor of AgCo's emission control technology. As in Example 5, their relationship is vertical with regard to this technology. The relationship between AgCo and FarmCo in the relevant market that includes engine valve technology is vertical in part and horizontal in part. It is vertical in part because AgCo and FarmCo stand in a complementary relationship, in which AgCo is a consumer of a technology supplied by FarmCo. However, the relationship between AgCo and FarmCo in the relevant market that includes engine valve technology is also horizontal in part, because FarmCo and AgCo are actual competitors in the licensing of valve technology that can be used to achieve similar engine performance at a comparable cost. Whether the firms license their valve technologies to others is not important for the conclusion that the firms have a horizontal relationship in this relevant market. Even if AgCo's use of its valve technology were solely captive to its own production, the fact that the two valve technologies are substitutable at comparable cost means that the two firms have a horizontal relationship.

As in Example 5, the relationship between AgCo and FarmCo is horizontal in the relevant markets for farm equipment.

3.4 Framework for Evaluating Licensing Restraints

In the vast majority of cases, restraints in intellectual property licensing arrangements are evaluated under the rule of reason. The Agencies' general approach in analyzing a licensing restraint under the rule of reason is to inquire whether the restraint is likely to have anticompetitive effects and, if so, whether the restraint is reasonably necessary to achieve procompetitive benefits that outweigh those anticompetitive effects. See Federal Trade Commission v. Indiana Federation of Dentists, 476 U.S. 447 (1986); NCAA v. Board of Regents of the University of Oklahoma, 468 U.S. 85 (1984); Broadcast Music, Inc. v. Columbia Broadcasting System, Inc., 441 U.S. 1 (1979); 7 Phillip E. Areeda, Antitrust Law § 1502 (1986). See also part 4.

In some cases, however, the courts conclude that a restraint's "nature and necessary effect are so plainly anticompetitive" that it should be treated as unlawful per se, without an elaborate inquiry into the restraint's likely competitive effect. Federal Trade Commission v. Superior Court Trial Lawyers Association, 493 U.S. 411, 433 (1990); National Society of Professional Engineers v. United States, 435 U.S. 679, 692 (1978). Among the restraints that have been held per se unlawful are naked price-fixing, output restraints, and market division among horizontal competitors, as well as certain group boycotts and resale price maintenance.

To determine whether a particular restraint in a licensing arrangement is given per se or rule of reason treatment, the Agencies will assess whether the restraint in question can be expected to contribute to an efficiency-enhancing integration of economic activity. See *Broadcast Music,* 441 U.S. at 16–24. In general, licensing arrangements promote such integration because they facilitate the combination of the licensor's intellectual property with complementary factors of production owned by the licensee. A restraint in a licensing arrangement may further such integration by, for example, aligning the incentives of the licensor and the licensees to promote the development and marketing of the licensed technology, or by substantially reducing transactions costs. If there is no efficiency-enhancing integration of economic activity and if the type of restraint is one that has been accorded per se treatment, the Agencies will challenge the restraint under the per se rule. Otherwise, the Agencies will apply a rule of reason analysis.

Application of the rule of reason generally requires a comprehensive inquiry into market conditions. (See sections 4.1–4.3.) However, that inquiry may be truncated in certain circumstances. If the Agencies conclude that a restraint has no likely anticompetitive effects, they will treat it as reasonable, without an elaborate analysis of market power or the justifications for the restraint. Similarly, if a restraint facially appears to be of a kind that would always or almost always tend to reduce output or increase prices,[27] and the restraint is not reasonably related to efficiencies, the Agencies will likely challenge the restraint without an elaborate analysis of particular industry circumstances.[28] See Indiana Federation of Dentists, 476 U.S. at 459–60; *NCAA*, 468 U.S. at 109.

Example 7

Situation: Gamma, which manufactures Product X using its patented process, offers a license for its process technology to every other manufacturer of Product X, each of which competes world-wide with Gamma in the manufacture and sale of X. The process technology does not represent an economic improvement over the available existing technologies. Indeed, although most manufacturers accept licenses from Gamma, none of the licensees actually uses the licensed technology. The licenses provide that each manufacturer has an exclusive right to sell Product X manufactured using the licensed technology in a designated geographic area and that no manufacturer may sell Product X, however manufactured, outside the designated territory.

Discussion: The manufacturers of Product X are in a horizontal relationship in the goods market for Product X. Any manufacturers of Product X that control technologies that are substitutable at comparable cost for Gamma's process are also horizontal competitors of Gamma in the relevant technology market. The licensees of Gamma's process technology are technically in a vertical relationship, although that is not significant in this example because they do not actually use Gamma's technology.

The licensing arrangement restricts competition in the relevant goods market among manufacturers of Product X by requiring each manufacturer to limit its sales to an exclusive territory. Thus, competition among entities that would be actual competitors in the absence of the licensing arrangement is restricted. Based on the facts set forth above, the licensing arrangement does not involve a useful transfer of technology, and thus it is unlikely that the restraint on sales outside the designated territories contributes to an efficiency-enhancing integration of economic activity. Consequently, the evaluating Agency would be likely to challenge the arrangement under the per se rule as a horizontal territorial market allocation scheme and to view the intellectual property aspects of the arrangement as a sham intended to cloak its true nature.

---

27. Details about the Federal Trade Commission's approach are set forth in Massachusetts Board of Registration in Optometry, 110 F.T.C. 549, 604 (1988). In applying its truncated rule of reason inquiry, the FTC uses the analytical category of "inherently suspect" restraints to denote facially anticompetitive restraints that would always or almost always tend to decrease output or increase prices, but that may be relatively unfamiliar or may not fit neatly into traditional per se categories.

28. Under the FTC's *Mass. Board* approach, asserted efficiency justifications for inherently suspect restraints are examined to determine whether they are plausible and, if so, whether they are valid in the context of the market at issue. *Mass. Board,* 110 F.T.C. at 604.

If the licensing arrangement could be expected to contribute to an efficiency-enhancing integration of economic activity, as might be the case if the licensed technology were an advance over existing processes and used by the licensees, the Agency would analyze the arrangement under the rule of reason applying the analytical framework described in this section.

In this example, the competitive implications do not generally depend on whether the licensed technology is protected by patent, is a trade secret or other know-how, or is a computer program protected by copyright; nor do the competitive implications generally depend on whether the allocation of markets is territorial, as in this example, or functional, based on fields of use.

4. General Principles Concerning the Agencies' Evaluation of Licensing Arrangements Under the Rule of Reason

4.1 Analysis of Anticompetitive Effects

The existence of anticompetitive effects resulting from a restraint in a licensing arrangement will be evaluated on the basis of the analysis described in this section.

4.1.1 Market Structure, Coordination, and Foreclosure

When a licensing arrangement affects parties in a horizontal relationship, a restraint in that arrangement may increase the risk of coordinated pricing, output restrictions, or the acquisition or maintenance of market power. Harm to competition also may occur if the arrangement poses a significant risk of retarding or restricting the development of new or improved goods or processes. The potential for competitive harm depends in part on the degree of concentration in, the difficulty of entry into, and the responsiveness of supply and demand to changes in price in the relevant markets. Cf. 1992 Horizontal Merger Guidelines ¶ 1.5.3.

When the licensor and licensees are in a vertical relationship, the Agencies will analyze whether the licensing arrangement may harm competition among entities in a horizontal relationship at either the level of the licensor or the licensees, or possibly in another relevant market. Harm to competition from a restraint may occur if it anticompetitively forecloses access to, or increases competitors' costs of obtaining, important inputs, or facilitates coordination to raise price or restrict output. The risk of anticompetitively foreclosing access or increasing competitors' costs is related to the proportion of the markets affected by the licensing restraint; other characteristics of the relevant markets, such as concentration, difficulty of entry, and the responsiveness of supply and demand to changes in price in the relevant markets; and the duration of the restraint. A licensing arrangement does not foreclose competition merely because some or all of the potential licensees in an industry choose to use the licensed technology to the exclusion of other technologies. Exclusive use may be an efficient consequence of the licensed technology having the lowest cost or highest value.

Harm to competition from a restraint in a vertical licensing arrangement also may occur if a licensing restraint facilitates coordination among entities in a horizontal relationship to raise prices or reduce output in a relevant market. For example, if owners of competing technologies impose similar restraints on their licensees, the licensors may find it easier to coordinate their pricing. Similarly, licensees that are competitors may find it easier to coordinate their pricing if they are subject to common restraints in licenses with a common licensor or competing licensors. The risk of anticompetitive coordination is increased when the relevant markets are concentrated and difficult to enter. The use of similar restraints may be common and procompetitive in an industry, however, because they contribute to efficient exploitation of the licensed property.

4.1.2 Licensing Arrangements Involving Exclusivity

A licensing arrangement may involve exclusivity in two distinct respects. First, the licensor may grant one or more *exclusive licenses,* which restrict the right of the licensor to license others and possibly also to use the technology itself. Generally, an exclusive license may raise antitrust concerns only if the licensees themselves, or the licensor and its licensees, are in a horizontal relationship. Examples of arrangements involving exclusive licensing that may give rise to antitrust concerns include cross-licensing by parties collectively possessing market power (see section 5.5), grantbacks (see section 5.6), and acquisitions of intellectual property rights (see section 5.7).

A non-exclusive license of intellectual property that does not contain any restraints on the competitive conduct of the licensor or the licensee generally does not present antitrust concerns even if the parties to the license are in a horizontal relationship, because the non-exclusive license normally does not diminish competition that would occur in its absence.

A second form of exclusivity, *exclusive dealing,* arises when a license prevents or restrains the licensee from licensing, selling, distributing, or using competing technologies. See section 5.4. Exclusivity may be achieved by an explicit exclusive dealing term in the license or by other provisions such as compensation terms or other economic incentives. Such restraints may anticompetitively foreclose access to, or increase competitors' costs of obtaining, important inputs, or facilitate coordination to raise price or reduce output, but they also may have procompetitive effects. For example, a licensing arrangement that prevents the licensee from dealing in other technologies may encourage the licensee to develop and market the licensed technology or specialized applications of that technology. See, e.g., Example 8. The Agencies will take into account such procompetitive effects in evaluating the reasonableness of the arrangement. See section 4.2.

The antitrust principles that apply to a licensor's grant of various forms of exclusivity to and among its licensees are similar to those that apply to comparable vertical restraints outside the licensing context, such as exclusive territories and exclusive dealing. However, the fact that intellectual property may in some cases be misappropriated more easily than other forms of property may justify the use of some restrictions that might be anticompetitive in other contexts.

As noted earlier, the Agencies will focus on the actual practice and its effects, not on the formal terms of the arrangement. A license denominated as non-exclusive (either in the sense of exclusive licensing or in the sense of exclusive dealing) may nonetheless give rise to the same concerns posed by formal exclusivity. A non-exclusive license may have the effect of exclusive licensing if it is structured so that the licensor is unlikely to license others or to practice the technology itself. A license that does not explicitly require exclusive dealing may have the effect of exclusive dealing if it is structured to increase significantly a licensee's cost when it uses competing technologies. However, a licensing arrangement will not automatically raise these concerns merely because a party chooses to deal with a single licensee or licensor, or confines his activity to a single field of use or location, or because only a single licensee has chosen to take a license.

Example 8

Situation: NewCo, the inventor and manufacturer of a new flat panel display technology, lacking the capability to bring a flat panel display product to market, grants BigCo an exclusive license to sell a product embodying NewCo's technology. BigCo does not currently sell, and is not developing (or likely to develop), a product that would compete with the product embodying the new technology and does not control rights to another display technology. Several firms offer competing displays, BigCo accounts for only a small proportion of the outlets for distribution of display products, and entry into the manufacture and distribution of display products is relatively easy. Demand for the new technology is uncertain and successful market penetration will require considerable promotional effort. The license contains an exclusive dealing restriction preventing BigCo from selling products that compete with the product embodying the licensed technology.

Discussion: This example illustrates both types of exclusivity in a licensing arrangement. The license is exclusive in that it restricts the right of the licensor to grant other licenses. In addition, the license has an exclusive dealing component in that it restricts the licensee from selling competing products.

The inventor of the display technology and its licensee are in a vertical relationship and are not actual or likely potential competitors in the manufacture or sale of display products or in the sale or development of technology. Hence, the grant of an exclusive license does not affect competition between the licensor and the licensee. The exclusive license may promote competition in the manufacturing and sale of display products by encouraging BigCo to develop and promote the new product in the face of uncertain demand by rewarding BigCo for its efforts if they lead to large sales. Although the license bars the licensee from selling competing products, this exclusive dealing aspect is unlikely in this example to harm competition by anticompetitively foreclosing access, raising competitors' costs of inputs, or facilitating anticompetitive pricing because the relevant product market is unconcentrated, the exclusive dealing restraint affects only a small proportion of the outlets for distribution of display products, and entry is easy. On these facts, the evaluating Agency would be unlikely to challenge the arrangement.

4.2 Efficiencies and Justifications

If the Agencies conclude, upon an evaluation of the market factors described in section 4.1, that a restraint in a licensing arrangement is unlikely to have an anticompetitive effect, they will not challenge the restraint. If the Agencies conclude that the restraint has, or is likely to have, an anticompetitive effect, they will consider whether the restraint is reasonably necessary to achieve procompetitive efficiencies. If the restraint is reasonably necessary, the Agencies will balance the procompetitive efficiencies and the anticompetitive effects to determine the probable net effect on competition in each relevant market.

The Agencies' comparison of anticompetitive harms and procompetitive efficiencies is necessarily a qualitative one. The risk of anticompetitive effects in a particular case may be insignificant compared to the expected efficiencies, or vice versa. As the expected anticompetitive effects in a particular licensing arrangement increase, the Agencies will require evidence establishing a greater level of expected efficiencies.

The existence of practical and significantly less restrictive alternatives is relevant to a determination of whether a restraint is reasonably necessary. If it is clear that the parties could have achieved similar efficiencies by means that are significantly less restrictive, then the Agencies will not give weight to the parties' efficiency claim. In making this assessment, however, the Agencies will not engage in a search for a theoretically least restrictive alternative that is not realistic in the practical prospective business situation faced by the parties.

When a restraint has, or is likely to have, an anticompetitive effect, the duration of that restraint can be an important factor in determining whether it is reasonably necessary to achieve the putative procompetitive efficiency. The effective duration of a restraint may depend on a number of factors, including the option of the affected party to terminate the arrangement unilaterally and the presence of contract terms (e.g., unpaid balances on minimum purchase commitments) that encourage the licensee to renew a license arrangement. Consistent with their approach to less restrictive alternative analysis generally, the Agencies will not attempt to draw fine distinctions regarding duration; rather, their focus will be on situations in which the duration clearly exceeds the period needed to achieve the procompetitive efficiency.

The evaluation of procompetitive efficiencies, of the reasonable necessity of a restraint to achieve them, and of the duration of the restraint, may depend on the market context. A restraint that may be justified by the needs of a new entrant, for example, may not have a procompetitive efficiency justification in different market circumstances. Cf. United States v. Jerrold Electronics Corp., 187 F.Supp. 545 (E.D.Pa.1960), aff'd per curiam, 365 U.S. 567 (1961).

4.3 Antitrust "Safety Zone"

Because licensing arrangements often promote innovation and enhance competition, the Agencies believe that an antitrust "safety zone" is useful in order to provide some degree of certainty and thus to encourage such activity.[29] Absent extraordinary circumstances, the Agencies will not challenge a restraint in an intellectual property licensing arrangement if (1) the restraint is not facially anticompetitive[30] and (2) the licensor and its licensees collectively account for no more than twenty percent of each relevant market significantly affected by the restraint. This "safety zone" does not apply to those transfers of intellectual property rights to which a merger analysis is applied. See section 5.7.

Whether a restraint falls within the safety zone will be determined by reference only to goods markets unless the analysis of goods markets alone would inadequately address the effects of the licensing arrangement on competition among technologies or in research and development.

If an examination of the effects on competition among technologies or in research development is required, and if market share data are unavailable or do not accurately represent competitive significance, the following safety zone criteria will apply. Absent extraordinary circumstances, the Agencies will not challenge a restraint in an intellectual property licensing arrangement that may affect competition in a technology market if (1) the restraint is not facially anticompetitive and (2) there are four or more independently controlled technologies in addition to the technologies controlled by the parties to the licensing arrangement that may be substitutable for the licensed technology at a comparable cost to the user. Absent extraordinary circumstances, the Agencies will not challenge a restraint in an intellectual property licensing arrangement that may affect competition in an innovation market if (1) the restraint is not facially anticompetitive and (2) four or more independently controlled entities in addition to the parties to the licensing arrangement possess the required specialized assets or characteristics and the incentive to engage in research and development that is a close substitute of the research and development activities of the parties to the licensing agreement.[31]

---

29. The antitrust "safety zone" does not apply to restraints that are not in a licensing arrangement, or to restraints that are in a licensing arrangement but are unrelated to the use of the licensed intellectual property.

30. "Facially anticompetitive" refers to restraints that normally warrant per se treatment, as well as other restraints of a kind that would always or almost always tend to reduce output or increase prices. See section 3.4.

31. This is consistent with congressional intent in enacting the National Cooperative Research Act. See H.R. Conf. Rpt. No. 1044, 98th Cong., 2d Sess., 10, reprinted in 1984 U.S.C.C.A.N. 3105, 3134–35.

The Agencies emphasize that licensing arrangements are not anticompetitive merely because they do not fall within the scope of the safety zone. Indeed, it is likely that the great majority of licenses falling outside the safety zone are lawful and procompetitive. The safety zone is designed to provide owners of intellectual property with a degree of certainty in those situations in which anticompetitive effects are so unlikely that the arrangements may be presumed not to be anticompetitive without an inquiry into particular industry circumstances. It is not intended to suggest that parties should conform to the safety zone or to discourage parties falling outside the safety zone from adopting restrictions in their license arrangements that are reasonably necessary to achieve an efficiency-enhancing integration of economic activity. The Agencies will analyze arrangements falling outside the safety zone based on the considerations outlined in parts 3–5.

The status of a licensing arrangement with respect to the safety zone may change over time. A determination by the Agencies that a restraint in a licensing arrangement qualifies for inclusion in the safety zone is based on the factual circumstances prevailing at the time of the conduct at issue.[32]

5. Application of General Principles

5.0 This section illustrates the application of the general principles discussed above to particular licensing restraints and to arrangements that involve the cross-licensing, pooling, or acquisition of intellectual property. The restraints and arrangements identified are typical of those that are likely to receive antitrust scrutiny; however, they are not intended as an exhaustive list of practices that could raise competitive concerns.

5.1 Horizontal Restraints

The existence of a restraint in a licensing arrangement that affects parties in a horizontal relationship (a "horizontal restraint") does not necessarily cause the arrangement to be anticompetitive. As in the case of joint ventures among horizontal competitors, licensing arrangements among such competitors may promote rather than hinder competition if they result in integrative efficiencies. Such efficiencies may arise, for example, from the realization of economies of scale and the integration of complementary research and development, production, and marketing capabilities.

Following the general principles outlined in section 3.4, horizontal restraints often will be evaluated under the rule of reason. In some circumstances, however, that analysis may be truncated; additionally, some restraints may merit per se treatment, including price fixing, allocation of markets or customers, agreements to reduce output, and certain group boycotts.

---

32. The conduct at issue may be the transaction giving rise to the restraint or the subsequent implementation of the restraint.

Example 9

Situation: Two of the leading manufacturers of a consumer electronic product hold patents that cover alternative circuit designs for the product. The manufacturers assign their patents to a separate corporation wholly owned by the two firms. That corporation licenses the right to use the circuit designs to other consumer product manufacturers and establishes the license royalties. None of the patents is blocking; that is, each of the patents can be used without infringing a patent owned by the other firm. The different circuit designs are substitutable in that each permits the manufacture at comparable cost to consumers of products that consumers consider to be interchangeable. One of the Agencies is analyzing the licensing arrangement.

Discussion: In this example, the manufacturers are horizontal competitors in the goods market for the consumer product and in the related technology markets. The competitive issue with regard to a joint assignment of patent rights is whether the assignment has an adverse impact on competition in technology and goods markets that is not outweighed by procompetitive efficiencies, such as benefits in the use or dissemination of the technology. Each of the patent owners has a right to exclude others from using its patent. That right does not extend, however, to the agreement to assign rights jointly. To the extent that the patent rights cover technologies that are close substitutes, the joint determination of royalties likely would result in higher royalties and higher goods prices than would result if the owners licensed or used their technologies independently. In the absence of evidence establishing efficiency-enhancing integration from the joint assignment of patent rights, the Agency may conclude that the joint marketing of competing patent rights constitutes horizontal price fixing and could be challenged as a per se unlawful horizontal restraint of trade. If the joint marketing arrangement results in an efficiency-enhancing integration, the Agency would evaluate the arrangement under the rule of reason. However, the Agency may conclude that the anticompetitive effects are sufficiently apparent, and the claimed integrative efficiencies are sufficiently weak or not reasonably related to the restraints, to warrant challenge of the arrangement without an elaborate analysis of particular industry circumstances (see section 3.4).

5.2 Resale Price Maintenance

Resale price maintenance is illegal when "commodities have passed into the channels of trade and are owned by dealers." Dr. Miles Medical Co. v. John D. Park & Sons Co., 220 U.S. 373, 408 (1911).* It has been held per se illegal for a licensor of an intellectual property right in a product to fix a licensee's *resale* price of that product. United States v. Univis Lens Co., 316 U.S. 241 (1942); Ethyl Gasoline Corp. v. United States, 309 U.S. 436 (1940).[33] Consistent with the principles set forth in

* Editors' note: *Dr. Miles* has been overruled.

33. But cf. United States v. General Electric Co., 272 U.S. 476 (1926) (holding that an owner of a product patent may condition a license to manufacture the product on the fixing of the *first* section 3.4, the Agencies will enforce the per se rule against resale price maintenance in the intellectual property context.

5.3 Tying Arrangements

A "tying" or "tie-in" or "tied sale" arrangement has been defined as "an agreement by a party to sell one product ... on the condition that the buyer also purchases a different (or tied) product, or at least agrees that he will not purchase that [tied] product from any other supplier." Eastman Kodak Co. v. Image Technical Services, Inc., 504 U.S. 451, 461 (1992). Conditioning the ability of a licensee to license one or more items of intellectual property on the licensee's purchase of another item of intellectual property or a good or a service has been held in some cases to constitute illegal tying.[34] Although tying arrangements may result in anticompetitive effects, such arrangements can also result in significant efficiencies and procompetitive benefits. In the exercise of their prosecutorial discretion, the Agencies will consider both the anticompetitive effects and the efficiencies attributable to a tie-in. The Agencies would be likely to challenge a tying arrangement if: (1) the seller has market power in the tying product,[35] (2) the arrangement has an adverse effect on competition in the relevant market for the tied product, and (3) efficiency justifications for the arrangement do not outweigh the anticompetitive effects.[36] The Agencies will not presume that a patent, copyright, or trade secret necessarily confers market power upon its owner.

Package licensing—the licensing of multiple items of intellectual property in a single license or in a group of related licenses—may be a form of tying arrangement if the licensing of one product is conditioned upon the acceptance of a license of another, separate product. Package licensing can be efficiency-enhancing under some circumstances. When multiple licenses are needed to use any single item of intellectual property, for example, a package license may promote such efficiencies. If a package license constitutes a tying arrangement, the Agencies will evaluate its competitive effects under the same principles they apply to other tying arrangements.

---

sale price of the patented product). Subsequent lower court decisions have distinguished the *GE* decision in various contexts. See, e.g., Royal Indus. v. St. Regis Paper Co., 420 F.2d 449, 452 (9th Cir.1969) (observing that *GE* involved a restriction by a patentee who also manufactured the patented product and leaving open the question whether a nonmanufacturing patentee may fix the price of the patented product); Newburgh Moire Co. v. Superior Moire Co., 237 F.2d 283, 293–94 (3d Cir.1956) (grant of multiple licenses each containing price restrictions does not come within the *GE* doctrine); Cummer–Graham Co. v. Straight Side Basket Corp., 142 F.2d 646, 647 (5th Cir.) (owner of an intellectual property right in a process to manufacture an unpatented product may not fix the sale price of that product), cert. denied, 323 U.S. 726 (1944); Barber–Colman Co. v. National Tool Co., 136 F.2d 339, 343–44 (6th Cir.1943) (same).

34. See, e.g., United States v. Paramount Pictures, Inc., 334 U.S. 131, 156–58 (1948) (copyrights); International Salt Co. v. United States, 332 U.S. 392 (1947) (patent and related product).

35. Cf. 35 U.S.C.A. § 271(d) (1988 & Supp. V 1993) (requirement of market power in patent misuse cases involving tying).

36. As is true throughout these Guidelines, the factors listed are those that guide the Agencies' internal analysis in exercising their prosecutorial discretion. They are not intended to circumscribe how the Agencies will conduct the litigation of cases that they decide to bring.

5.4 Exclusive Dealing

In the intellectual property context, exclusive dealing occurs when a license prevents the licensee from licensing, selling, distributing, or using competing technologies. Exclusive dealing arrangements are evaluated under the rule of reason. See Tampa Electric Co. v. Nashville Coal Co., 365 U.S. 320 (1961)(evaluating legality of exclusive dealing under section 1 of the Sherman Act and section 3 of the Clayton Act); Beltone Electronics Corp., 100 F.T.C. 68 (1982)(evaluating legality of exclusive dealing under section 5 of the Federal Trade Commission Act). In determining whether an exclusive dealing arrangement is likely to reduce competition in a relevant market, the Agencies will take into account the extent to which the arrangement (1) promotes the exploitation and development of the licensor's technology and (2) anticompetitively forecloses the exploitation and development of, or otherwise constrains competition among, competing technologies.

The likelihood that exclusive dealing may have anticompetitive effects is related, inter alia, to the degree of foreclosure in the relevant market, the duration of the exclusive dealing arrangement, and other characteristics of the input and output markets, such as concentration, difficulty of entry, and the responsiveness of supply and demand to changes in price in the relevant markets. (See sections 4.1.1 and 4.1.2.) If the Agencies determine that a particular exclusive dealing arrangement may have an anticompetitive effect, they will evaluate the extent to which the restraint encourages licensees to develop and market the licensed technology (or specialized applications of that technology), increases licensors' incentives to develop or refine the licensed technology, or otherwise increases competition and enhances output in a relevant market. (See section 4.2 and Example 8.)

5.5 Cross-licensing and Pooling Arrangements

Cross-licensing and pooling arrangements are agreements of two or more owners of different items of intellectual property to license one another or third parties. These arrangements may provide procompetitive benefits by integrating complementary technologies, reducing transaction costs, clearing blocking positions, and avoiding costly infringement litigation. By promoting the dissemination of technology, cross-licensing and pooling arrangements are often procompetitive.

Cross-licensing and pooling arrangements can have anticompetitive effects in certain circumstances. For example, collective price or output restraints in pooling arrangements, such as the joint marketing of pooled intellectual property rights with collective price setting or coordinated output restrictions, may be deemed unlawful if they do not contribute to an efficiency-enhancing integration of economic activity among the participants. Compare *NCAA* 468 U.S. at 114 (output restriction on college football broadcasting held unlawful because it was not reasonably related to any purported justification) with *Broadcast Music,* 441 U.S. at 23 (blanket license for music copyrights found not per se illegal because the cooperative price was necessary to the creation of a new product). When cross-licensing or pooling arrangements are mechanisms to accomplish naked price fixing or market division, they are subject to challenge under the per se rule. See United States v. New Wrinkle, Inc., 342 U.S. 371 (1952) (price fixing).

Settlements involving the cross-licensing of intellectual property rights can be an efficient means to avoid litigation and, in general, courts favor such settlements. When such cross-licensing involves horizontal competitors, however, the Agencies will consider whether the effect of the settlement is to diminish competition among entities that would have been actual or likely potential competitors in a relevant market in the absence of the cross-license. In the absence of offsetting efficiencies, such settlements may be challenged as unlawful restraints of trade. Cf. United States v. Singer Manufacturing Co., 374 U.S. 174 (1963) (cross-license agreement was part of broader combination to exclude competitors).

Pooling arrangements generally need not be open to all who would like to join. However, exclusion from cross-licensing and pooling arrangements among parties that collectively possess market power may, under some circumstances, harm competition. Cf. Northwest Wholesale Stationers, Inc. v. Pacific Stationery & Printing Co., 472 U.S. 284 (1985) (exclusion of a competitor from a purchasing cooperative not per se unlawful absent a showing of market power). In general, exclusion from a pooling or crosslicensing arrangement among competing technologies is unlikely to have anticompetitive effects unless (1) excluded firms cannot effectively compete in the relevant market for the good incorporating the licensed technologies and (2) the pool participants collectively possess market power in the relevant market. If these circumstances exist, the Agencies will evaluate whether the arrangement's limitations on participation are reasonably related to the efficient development and exploitation of the pooled technologies and will assess the net effect of those limitations in the relevant market. See section 4.2.

Another possible anticompetitive effect of pooling arrangements may occur if the arrangement deters or discourages participants from engaging in research and development, thus retarding innovation. For example, a pooling arrangement that requires members to grant licenses to each other for current and future technology at minimal cost may reduce the incentives of its members to engage in research and development because members of the pool have to share their successful research and development and each of the members can free ride on the accomplishments of other pool members. See generally United States v. Mfrs. Aircraft Ass'n, Inc., 1976–1 Trade Cas. (CCH) ¶ 60,810 (S.D.N.Y.1975); United States v. Automobile Mfrs. Ass'n, 307 F.Supp. 617 (C.D.Cal.1969), appeal dismissed sub nom. City of New York v. United States, 397 U.S. 248 (1970), modified sub nom. United States v. Motor Vehicle Mfrs. Ass'n, 1982–83 Trade Cas. (CCH) ¶ 65,088 (C.D.Cal.1982). However, such an arrangement can have procompetitive benefits, for example, by exploiting economies of scale and integrating complementary capabilities of the pool members, (including the clearing of blocking positions), and is likely to cause competitive problems only when the arrangement includes a large fraction of the potential research and development in an innovation market. See section 3.2.3 and Example 4.

Example 10

Situation: As in Example 9, two of the leading manufacturers of a consumer electronic product hold patents that cover alternative circuit designs for the product. The manufacturers assign several of their patents to a separate corporation wholly owned by the two firms. That corporation licenses the right to use the circuit designs to other consumer product manufacturers and establishes the license royalties. In this example, however, the manufacturers assign to the separate corporation only patents that are blocking. None of the patents assigned to the corporation can be used without infringing a patent owned by the other firm.

Discussion: Unlike the previous example, the joint assignment of patent rights to the wholly owned corporation in this example does not adversely affect competition in the licensed technology among entities that would have been actual or likely potential competitors in the absence of the licensing arrangement. Moreover, the licensing arrangement is likely to have procompetitive benefits in the use of the technology. Because the manufacturers' patents are blocking, the manufacturers are not in a horizontal relationship with respect to those patents. None of the patents can be used without the right to a patent owned by the other firm, so the patents are not substitutable. As in Example 9, the firms are horizontal competitors in the relevant goods market. In the absence of collateral restraints that would likely raise price or reduce output in the relevant goods market or in any other relevant antitrust market and that are not reasonably related to an efficiency-enhancing integration of economic activity, the evaluating Agency would be unlikely to challenge this arrangement.

5.6 Grantbacks

A grantback is an arrangement under which a licensee agrees to extend to the licensor of intellectual property the right to use the licensee's improvements to the licensed technology. Grantbacks can have procompetitive effects, especially if they are nonexclusive. Such arrangements provide a means for the licensee and the licensor to share risks and reward the licensor for making possible further innovation based on or informed by the licensed technology, and both promote innovation in the first place and promote the subsequent licensing of the results of the innovation. Grantbacks may adversely affect competition, however, if they substantially reduce the licensee's incentives to engage in research and development and thereby limit rivalry in innovation markets.

A non-exclusive grantback allows the licensee to practice its technology and license it to others. Such a grantback provision may be necessary to ensure that the licensor is not prevented from effectively competing because it is denied access to improvements developed with the aid of its own technology. Compared with an exclusive grantback, a non-exclusive grantback, which leaves the licensee free to license improvements technology to others, is less likely to have anticompetitive effects.

The Agencies will evaluate a grantback provision under the rule of reason, see generally Transparent–Wrap Machine Corp. v. Stokes & Smith Co., 329 U.S. 637, 645–48 (1947) (grantback provision in technology license is not per se unlawful), considering its likely effects in light of the overall structure of the licensing arrangement and conditions in the relevant markets. An important factor in the Agencies' analysis of a grantback will be whether the licensor has market power in a relevant technology or innovation market. If the Agencies determine that a particular grantback provision is likely to reduce significantly licensees' incentives to invest in improving the licensed technology, the Agencies will consider the extent to which the grantback provision has offsetting procompetitive effects, such as (1) promoting dissemination of licensees' improvements to the licensed technology, (2) increasing the licensors' incentives to disseminate the licensed technology, or (3) otherwise increasing competition and output in a relevant technology or innovation market. See section 4.2. In addition, the Agencies will consider the extent to which grantback provisions in the relevant markets generally increase licensors' incentives to innovate in the first place.

5.7 Acquisition of Intellectual Property Rights

Certain transfers of intellectual property rights are most appropriately analyzed by applying the principles and standards used to analyze mergers, particularly those in the 1992 Horizontal Merger Guidelines. The Agencies will apply a merger analysis to an outright sale by an intellectual property owner of all of its rights to that intellectual property and to a transaction in which a person obtains through grant, sale, or other transfer an exclusive license for intellectual property (i.e., a license that precludes all other persons, including the licensor, from using the licensed intellectual property).[37] Such transactions may be assessed under section 7 of the Clayton Act, sections 1 and 2 of the Sherman Act, and section 5 of the Federal Trade Commission Act.

Example 11

Situation: Omega develops a new, patented pharmaceutical for the treatment of a particular disease. The only drug on the market approved for the treatment of this disease is sold by Delta. Omega's patented drug has almost completed regulatory approval by the Food and Drug Administration. Omega has invested considerable sums in product development and market testing, and initial results show that Omega's drug would be a significant competitor to Delta's. However, rather than enter the market as a direct competitor of Delta, Omega licenses to Delta the right to

37. The safety zone of section 4.3 does not apply to transfers of intellectual property such as those described in this section.

manufacture and sell Omega's patented drug. The license agreement with Delta is nominally nonexclusive. However, Omega has rejected all requests by other firms to obtain a license to manufacture and sell Omega's patented drug, despite offers by those firms of terms that are reasonable in relation to those in Delta's license.

Discussion: Although Omega's license to Delta is nominally nonexclusive, the circumstances indicate that it is exclusive in fact because Omega has rejected all reasonable offers by other firms for licenses to manufacture and sell Omega's patented drug. The facts of this example indicate that Omega would be a likely potential competitor of Delta in the absence of the licensing arrangement, and thus they are in a horizontal relationship in the relevant goods market that includes drugs for the treatment of this particular disease. The evaluating Agency would apply a merger analysis to this transaction, since it involves an acquisition of a likely potential competitor.

6. Enforcement of Invalid Intellectual Property Rights

The Agencies may challenge the enforcement of invalid intellectual property rights as antitrust violations. Enforcement or attempted enforcement of a patent obtained by fraud on the Patent and Trademark Office or the Copyright Office may violate section 2 of the Sherman Act, if all the elements otherwise necessary to establish a section 2 charge are proved, or section 5 of the Federal Trade Commission Act. Walker Process Equipment, Inc. v. Food Machinery & Chemical Corp., 382 U.S. 172 (1965) (patents); American Cyanamid Co., 72 F.T.C. 623, 684–85 (1967), aff'd sub. nom. Charles Pfizer & Co., 401 F.2d 574 (6th Cir.1968), cert. denied, 394 U.S. 920 (1969) (patents); Michael Anthony Jewelers, Inc. v. Peacock Jewelry, Inc., 795 F.Supp. 639, 647 (S.D.N.Y.1992) (copyrights). Inequitable conduct before the Patent and Trademark Office will not be the basis of a section 2 claim unless the conduct also involves knowing and willful fraud and the other elements of a section 2 claim are present. Argus Chemical Corp. v. Fibre Glass–Evercoat, Co., Inc., 812 F.2d 1381, 1384–85 (Fed.Cir.1987). Actual or attempted enforcement of patents obtained by inequitable conduct that falls short of fraud under some circumstances may violate section 5 of the Federal Trade Commission Act, *American Cyanamid Co.*, supra. Objectively baseless litigation to enforce invalid intellectual property rights may also constitute an element of a violation of the Sherman Act. See Professional Real Estate Investors, Inc. v. Columbia Pictures Industries, Inc., 508 U.S. 49, 60 (1993) (copyrights); Handgards, Inc. v. Ethicon, Inc., 743 F.2d 1282, 1289 (9th Cir.1984), cert. denied, 469 U.S. 1190 (1985) (patents); Handgards, Inc. v. Ethicon, Inc., 601 F.2d 986, 992–96 (9th Cir.1979), cert. denied, 444 U.S. 1025 (1980) (patents); CVD, Inc. v. Raytheon Co., 769 F.2d 842 (1st Cir.1985) (trade secrets), cert. denied, 475 U.S. 1016 (1986).

APPENDIX H

CASE STUDY—LOYALTY DISCOUNTS & REBATES

International Competition Network, Unilateral Conduct Working Group 2010*

■ ■ ■

For use with Chapter 3: Monopoly and Dominance

Background

1. Cerveja is the largest brewer in ICNland with a national market share of 73% of all branded beer sales. It sells one brand of beer and has held a greater than 70% market share for the last 20 years. Cerveja is headquartered in ICNland and has annual global turnover of approximately $1 billion.

2. ICNland is a middle income country, with a hot climate, a few very large cities and large mainly rural regions with smaller towns and cities as centres for the largely agricultural and mining economic bases of the regions. It has three states: Urbania, Mineralia and Agrilandia.

Beer Sales Market(s) & Distribution

3. In ICNland there is a downstream retail beer sales market, consisting of two main types of sellers. (1) Seventy percent of ICNlandian beer is sold in unrefrigerated bottles or cans by large supermarkets. (2) Thirty percent is sold in chilled bottles in small retail outlets, most of which double up as bars. A very small proportion (<1%) is sold in high end pubs and restaurants, including some served from kegs 'on tap'.

4. For decades, Cerveja has been the most popular brand of beer in ICNland, with widespread consumer appeal. As a result, sellers in both distribution channels have generally maintained around 70% to 80% of their stocks as Cerveja brand beer. This reflects local taste, as reflected in historic demand for Cerveja beer. Smaller

* Printed with thanks to the International Competition Network.

outlets have generally stocked a higher share of Cerveja than the supermarkets.

5. Cerveja and other beer manufacturers sell their products directly to the two categories of downstream outlets. Existing ICNland health regulations prevent the commercial importation of beer brewed abroad, meaning that all beer sold in ICNland is brewed within the country.

6. Based on industry data, the national market share of Cerveja and its competitors in the downstream distribution of beer to all retailers is the following:

Table 1

Company	2007	2008	2009
Cerveja	80%	76%	73%
Hollandia	......	18%	23%
Pappabeer	13%	.....	......
Others	7%	6%	4%

7. Hollandia's share growth has mostly occurred in sales to supermarkets as opposed to sales in smaller outlets.

The competitors to Cerveja are the following:

8. **Hollandia** is a leading international brewer and distributor of beer, with operations in 20 countries, including in ICNland. It entered ICNland in 2008 through its acquisition of **Pappabeer**, which traditionally was the second largest brewer and distributor of beer in ICNland. Hollandia's annual global turnover is around $10 billion, ten times the size of Cerveja's global turnover. Hollandia rebranded Pappabeer's one and only brand as "Hollandia Brew" in 2008, and grew its market share by more than one third—from 13% to 18%—within a year. Since its acquisition of Pappabeer Hollandia as invested $50 million in modernizing Pappabeer's existing brewing facilities, in addition to building two new modern brewing facilities within ICNland. (Cerveja has not made a major investment in its beer production facilities since 1990, other than incremental expansions to existing facilities and routine maintenance.) In 2008 Hollandia also announced that it will be looking for "new up and coming" local beer brands to "grow its portfolio" in ICNland.

9. The "**Others**" are comprised of around 30 small local breweries located throughout ICNland. No small brewer has an annual turnover of more than $50 million. The number of small local breweries has been contracting over the past 20 years, and few new brands have been introduced during the last 5 years. The local brewers products have a shorter shelf life and do not have the same type of distribution networks meaning they cannot provide the same guarantee as to frequent deliveries and deliver-

ies on short notice. The smaller brewers generally have had a larger impact in the small retail outlets, compared to supermarkets. Specifically, no new small brewer has been able to penetrate the supermarket sector in the past 5 years, nor have existing small brands carried by large supermarkets been able to raise their small market shares during that time.

10. Retail beer sales markets are local in ICNland. Consumer prices vary in different retail markets, depending upon income levels, number of competitors (some localities have many small outlets and supermarkets, others very few), local taste, and other factors. Within a local market, prices per unit of beer sold are the lowest in supermarkets, with small outlet prices somewhat higher; differences between supermarket and small outlet prices vary according to the local market. Large supermarkets are in middle and upper income areas, in the bigger cities, along with many smaller outlets, that also stay open much later.

11. Since its entry into ICNland in 2008, Hollandia has focussed mostly on growing its sales of Hollandia Brew through large supermarkets. It has done this through national marketing campaigns and promotions. Its sales of Hollandia Brew in the other sectors have been more limited so far.

12. Traditionally, distribution through small retailers and bars has been critical to the introduction and market growth of new small beer brands. New small brands initially do not have the capital to support the national media advertising campaigns, large-scale distribution networks, or favourable shelf space placements to induce large supermarkets to carry them. Moreover, the small retailer channel is viewed as important to build consumer recognition and loyalty. No new brand has entered the large supermarket channel in over 5 years, nor have existing small brands carried by large supermarkets been able to raise their small market shares during that time. Indeed, very few new brands have entered the market in recent years.

13. Cerveja, which is carried by all large supermarkets, negotiates individual contracts with different supermarket chains.

14. A cost breakdown for Cerveja, as given by Cerveja in a presentation to investors in 2008, is as follows, as % of revenue net of all rebates and discounts:

    - ☐ Brewing and bottling: 50%
    - ☐ Advertising and marketing: 15%
    - ☐ Distribution (done by Cerveja through network of depots and contracted freight and delivery companies): 15%

Loyalty Program

15. Cerveja established in 2009 a loyalty program called "So Hoppy Together." This "two facet" program applies only to small

retailers. Small retailers are eligible for rebates under both facets if they meet the specified qualifications. A retailer must have qualified for a cash rebate under the first facet for 4 consecutive quarters to be eligible for a rebate under the second facet rebate for that year.

16. First facet. Cerveja will grant each small retailer a cash rebate on a quarterly basis, as a percentage of all the retailer's Cerveja sales over the quarter, if the retailer hits targets as follows: (1) 2% if the outlet has the same dollar sales volume as in the same quarter the previous year; (2) an extra 1% if it achieves at least a 5% growth in sales volume over the same quarter the previous year; (3) an extra 1% if it achieves at least a 10% growth in sales volume over the same quarter the previous year. Thus, under the first facet, a small retailer can achieve a cash rebate of up to 4%.

17. Second facet. Cerveja will, at the end of every one year period under the program, grant each small retailer a 3% cash rebate for each case of Cerveja beer sold.

18. Cerveja has stated publicly that the "So Hoppy Together" program is open to all small retailers in ICNland.

19. Cerveja typically recommended a maximum retail price for smaller outlets which was around $2.50 per case above the wholesale delivered price. If outlets were found to be pricing above the recommended price Cerveja might not provide signage, marketing and promotional materials. The outlets would also likely not be included in specials, where a discount might be run around an event such as a soccer final or public holiday, and outlets would be expected to pass on the discounts and not increase their margins.

20. On introducing the Hoppy program the wholesale price was increased, such that the recommended retail price was now just $1 higher than the wholesale price. With rebates of around 5% to 6% the same margin as before would be earned by the outlets.

21. Cerveja has indicated to the outlets that it wants to reward performance, where outlets doing better in terms of growth get the benefit in their margin, and outlets performing on par with before should be no worse off.

The Complaints

22. Since Cerveja's introduction of the So Hoppy Together program, the ICNland Competition Authority has received the following complaints:

    - ☐ Individual complaints from over 70 small retailers in ICNland that Cerveja has dropped them from the So Hoppy Together program. Many of these complaints share a common theme:

that Cerveja isn't providing adequate marketing and financial support to allow them to qualify for rebates.

☐ A group complaint from 17 small local breweries that the So Hoppy Together program is an abuse of dominance having the effect of eliminating small local breweries that meet customer needs and preferences.

Loyalty Discounts & Rebates Case Study: Document Annex

1. Complaint from Small Retailers, attaching 3 emails
2. Complaint from Small Breweries
3. Cerveja memorandum
4. Small Retailers Association memorandum
5. Hollandia memorandum
6. Cerveja E-mail
7. Independent market analyst report
8. Excel Spreadsheet with data on costs, prices, market shares, over time

Evidence from the investigation

Market shares, % by brewer

National	2005	2006	2007	2008	2009
Cerveja	76	76	80	76	73
Hollandia	..	..	..	18	23
Pappabeer	14	15	13	..	..
Others	10	9	7	6	4

Supermarkets	2005	2006	2007	2008	2009
Cerveja	82	81	82	74	68
Hollandia	..	..	..	22	29
Pappabeer	13	14	13	..	..
Others	5	5	5	4	3

Small outlets	2005	2006	2007	2008	2009
Cerveja	68	70	78	79	81
Hollandia	..	..	..	13	13
Pappabeer	17	18	14	..	..
Others	15	12	8	8	6

Small outlets share of beer sales by state,%

	2005	2006	2007	2008	2009
Urbania state	22	18	16	16	15
Mineralia state	45	44	43	41	40
Agrilandia state	53	54	52	49	50
National	40	38	36	32	30

Overall sales growing more in Urbania, reflecting patterns of economic growth and migration

$ per unit (case of 24), NB inflation is zero

Average delivered prices to supermarket channel (after discounts etc.)

	2005	2006	2007	2008	2009
Cerveja	25	26	26	21	20
Hollandia				22	22
Average for Small Brewers	26	27	27	24	24

Average delivered prices to small outlets (after rebates)

	2005	2006	2007	2008	2009
Cerveja	27	27	28	27	25
Hollandia				27	25
Average for Small Brewers	26	26	27	27	26

Distribution costs, $ per case, for Cerveja

Approx dist costs to supermarkets	2
Approx dist costs to small outlets	6

Average unit costs, $ per case

Cerveja, all sales

	2005	2006	2007	2008	2009
Variable costs	10	10	10	10	10
Fixed costs	2	2	2	2	2
Total brewing & bottling	*13*	*13*	*13*	*12*	*12*
National campaigns	1.5	1.5	1.5	2	3
Local promotional materials	1.5	1.5	1.5	1.5	1.5
Advertising & marketing	3	3	3	3.5	4.5
Distribution	*3.5*	*3.5*	*3.5*	*3.5*	*3.5*
Total costs	19.5	19.5	19.5	19	20
Margin before tax and depreciation	6.5	7	7	4	2
Avg delivered price	*26*	*26.5*	*26.5*	*23*	*22*

Costs and margins for supermarkets

ATC	18	18	18	17.5	18.5
Price	25	26	26	21	20
Margin	7	8	8	3.5	1.5

Costs and margins for small outlets

ATC	22	22	22	21.5	22.5
Price	27	27	28	27	25
Margin	5	5	6	5.5	2.5

Hollandia, supermarkets

	2008	2009
Variable costs	9	9
Fixed costs	2	2
Total brewing & bottling	*11*	*11*

National campaigns	4	4
Local promotional materials	1	1
Advertising & marketing	*5*	*5*
Distribution	*2.5*	*2.5*
Total costs	*18.5*	*18.5*
Margin before tax and depreciation	3.5	2.5
Avg delivered price	*22*	*21*

Small Brewers, All sales

	2005	2006	2007	2008	2009
Variable costs	11	11	12	12	13
Fixed costs	3	3	3	3	4
Total brewing & bottling	*14*	*14*	*15*	*15*	*17*
National campaigns	0.5	0.5	0.5	0.5	0.5
Local promotional materials	1.5	1.5	1.5	2	2
Advertising & marketing	*2*	*2*	*2*	*2.5*	*2.5*
Distribution	*5*	*6*	*6*	*7*	*7*
Total Costs	*21*	*22*	*23*	*24.5*	*26.5*
Margin before tax and depreciation	5	4	4	2.5	-0.5
Avg delivered price	*26*	*26*	*27*	*27*	*26*

Hollandia Unit costs for small retail outlets

Given the small scale, distribution costs are around 9 per unit for Hollandia

Notes:

The prices given above are net of rebates; Cerveja's actual delivered wholesale prices in 2009 (i.e. before rebates) to small outlets are around 1.50 higher than this. Cerveja recommends (maximum) retail prices. If outlets mark-up above this then Cerveja is likely to withdraw signage, marketing and promotional materials. The recommended maximum retail prices were around 2.5 above the wholesale prices before the Hoppy programme; in 2009 they were 1 above the wholesale price.

Summary of Complaint to ICNland Competition Agency from Small Retailers

The Cerveja brand is viewed as a "must carry" product by all retail categories, due to its strong public recognition supported by heavy advertising to consumers. Indeed, the brand identity of Cerveja is seen as aligned with that of the country.

While we applaud Cerveja for its position and role in supporting responsible drinking, we are concerned that its recent 'So Hoppy Together' is unfair in restricting the freedom of our members, a crucial part of Cerveja's own route to market, to choose how to run their businesses. As you know, people buy their beers through the corner stores and bars on every block, that are part of our communities, where people can meet and catch up on the latest gossip.

As we all know, Cerveja is particularly strong in the mass of the population, who can get it wherever they are in the country. The rivalry posed by Hollandia is, in our view, mainly aimed at middle class drinkers in the big cities who like the international association of the Hollandia beers and either drink in up-market pubs or buy in large supermarkets.

Hollandia does not seem interested in our members who are more oriented to their local areas and need the freedom to offer, in addition to Cerveja, local beers. The importance of these beers differs a lot from area to area, reflecting local drinking habits. These beers may not be perceived as being of the same quality, do not have the same attractive labelling as Cerveja and tend to have a shorter shelf life, but they have generally also been cheaper!

The effect of the Hoppy programme is that our members must at minimum maintain their sales of Cerveja (this will get them a 5% rebate—adding the 2% from the first facet to the 3% from the second facet), and aim hard to grow by at least 5% per year. With the relatively slow growth in the economy, and the mature nature of beer as a product this means that our members cannot allow other brands to be attractive. Losing the Hoppy rebate would mean they would go out of business given the cut-throat margins! Where demand is declining because of depressed local conditions and/or the increased penetration of supermarkets, this means that the small outlets are even more at risk. We believe that Cerveja does not provide enough support and promotions for our members to meet these challenges.

We have attached two emails which illustrate that if retailers do not meet the targets they are cut out of the rebate programme. These outlets are currently struggling to stay alive. A third email shows what everybody in the industry knows—that Cerveja is scared about Hollandia and whether it gets the marketing space it needs to grow in our markets.

E-MAIL 1

From: Hernandez, Armand [A.Hernandez@cerveja.com]
To: Bessille, Tony [T.Bassille@gserve.net]
Date: 20 February 2010
Subject: So Hoppy Together Program

I regret to inform you that because of your decreasing sales of Cerveja during the calendar year 2009, you are no longer eligible for participation in the So Hoppy Together program. If your quarterly sales in 2010 meet or beat the sales for the same period in the previous year then you will of course get the relevant rebate and, if you qualify for each quarter over the year, then you would be again eligible for the annual reward at the end of 2010.

We wish to assure you of our confidence and support, and have no doubt that with your marketing skills you will perform well once again!

Best Regards,

Armand Hernandez
Regional Sales Manager 2
Cerveja S.r.l.

"Grab a Cerveja and have fun today"

E-MAIL 2

From: Pascal, Louise [L.Pascal@cerveja.com]
To: Smith, Jesus [J.Smith@shoptoday.co.icn]
Date: 24 May 2010
Subject: So Hoppy Together Program

Dear Mr Smith:

I regret to inform you that due to the 3% drop in total Cerveja sales during the fourth quarter of 2009, Cerveja has decided to no longer offer the So Hoppy Together program to your store, Shop Today. We hope you get back on track quickly and, of course, will give you the due recognition on a quarterly basis, as set out in the reward schedule. Keeping this up over the year will also mean you qualify once more for the annual performance recognition.

I look forward to welcoming you back,

Louise Pascal
Regional Sales Manager 7
Cerveja S.r.l.

"Grab a Cerveja and have fun today"

E–MAIL 3

From: Irunde, Sammy [S.Irunde@cerveja.com]
To: Irunde, Pablo [P.Irunde@coldmail.com]
Date: 2 June 2010
Subject: WAKE UP!!!!!!!

Pablo, what's the deal man???? I was in your store the other day and Hollandia is positioned right up front, with that huge, obnoxious big Hollandia advertisement when you just enter the store with those horrible green and white colors! Yuck! Brother, I already told you what I overheard Louise and Armand from sales talking about the other day—that Cerveja isn't going to tolerate small stores being too friendly with Hollandia!!! I know you're depending on that big rebate from Cerveja, so **please** wake up and smell the coffee before its dumped over your head!

Anyway, look forward to seeing you, Adriana and the kids on Saturday. We'll be having lamb and beans, your favorite. See you around 3!

Take Care,

Sammy

Samuel IRUNDE

Assistant to the Region 2 Stock Manager

Cerveja S.r.l.

"Grab a Cerveja and have fun today"

Summary of Complaint to ICNland Competition Agency from Small Breweries

We represent a large number of small breweries that are a dying breed due to the blatant bullying by Cerveja of the smaller outlets and the callous disregard for local sensibilities by the national supermarket chains.

As we would think is common sense, consumers should have the option to buy their local beers, reflecting local tastes. The breweries established by our members over decades make quality products that meet all the necessary regulatory standards. However, the unreasonable demands of the supermarkets regarding delivery schedules and shelf life are used as an excuse not to stock our members' products. And, of course, being locally based, our members cannot do the national promotions with big branding and gimmicks that the supermarkets seem to like. The scale and reach to sustain the distribution, marketing and advertising campaigns simply mean our members are not given the chance by the supermarkets.

This has not been so important until now as we could sell to the man and woman in the street through the outlets closest to them in the most convenient way. But, Cerveja's new loyalty program, misleadingly called 'So Hoppy Together', will kill us—lots of our weaker brewery members will be driven out of business with a huge loss to the fabric of local life.

We recognize the strong pull of the Cerveja brand and applaud their success and support for our national symbols such as the soccer team. We are merely pointing out that consumers deserve a real choice.

It is already easier for outlets to just push Cerveja as we cannot match its delivery network and its promotional materials. Our members distribute through smaller, local trucking companies and support the local economies, and people know our brands as they have been passed on from one generation to the next.

As we understand it, the Hoppy programme does not on the face of it look as if it would necessarily squeeze our members out, as the outlets only have to meet the existing Cerveja volumes for a rebate. But, it seems as if the outlets have pushed Cerveja hard in response to it because they are either scared of missing the target, or because there are some other incentives at work.

We don't know the details, but we trust the ICNLandia competition authority will protect local choice and local businesses.

September 1, 2008

MEMORANDUM FOR RICARDO SALAZAR, PRESIDENT OF CERVEJA

FROM: Jose Perez, Vice President for Marketing, Cerveja

SUBJECT: The Hollandia Threat

Our marketing team reports disturbing news about Hollandia's threat in the ICNland beer market. Ever since Hollandia acquired Pappabeer and rebranded it as Hollandia Brew, Hollandia's market share in the large supermarket niche has risen sharply. Some supermarkets even are giving Hollandia Brew superior shelf placement! Although longstanding customer loyalty provides us some defense, I fear that long-term Hollandia will be able to use its deep pockets to match us in mass media markets and for supermarket placement.

To put it bluntly, we do not have Hollandia's financial resources. We can maintain, and ramp up, our adspend based on our large volumes, but Hollandia can match this if they choose to. What we can do, however, is fortify our traditionally strong customer loyalty through the small retailer channel. As you know, the small retail sector is essential for the ubiquity of Cerveja. Hollandia also needs to have national reach if it is going to seriously challenge the number one position of Cerveja. Hollandia now seems to recognize the importance of the sector, as our sales teams report seeing Hollandia Brew more frequently in small retailers, and there are rumors that Hollandia may also be looking to expand by acquiring or developing new indigenous ICNland brands. The small retail sector is also the birthplace of new brands and customer loyalty. If we can kill brand development in the small retailer channel, it may make it harder for Hollandia to acquire an "attractive" brand and/or to take Hollandia Brew itself to the mass market. Hollandia may then decide just to remain a high end niche player with Hollandia Brew, and not take us on seriously. That would be a relief.

With these facts in mind, I have developed a draft program called "So Hoppy Together," aimed solely at our small retail channel. This program will involve targeted discounts to small retailers that show loyalty to Cerveja (details to follow next week). It may kill any attempts by Hollandia to increase customer acceptance of Hollandia Brew and develop small brands in the small retailer channel, and thus help us as we combat Hollandia. Importantly, the maximum payment for reaching the target is on all units sold taking advantage of the fact that studies have shown that customers are very unlikely to switch in significant numbers in the short to medium term to other similarly priced beers. Outlets have no choice but to promote our leading beer. Indeed, with our jacked up marketing we think customer loyalty is at least around 75–80%, even if rivals match our adspend.

If you and the Cerveja board approve the program, marketing would be able to introduce it as early as the beginning of 2009. Let me know what you think.

March 1, 2010

From: Paolo Gomez, President, Small Retailers Association (SRA) of ICNland

To: Member Small Retail Owners

Re: So Hoppy Together: Threat or Opportunity

I have heard conflicting reports about the Hoppy program. Some SRA members—those that qualify for large Hoppy rebates—report that their overall sales and net profit margins have risen and that consumers are pleased. Others—mainly those that have not qualified for rebates—report that they do not want to disappoint local customers who want alternatives to Cerveja but at the same time feel they may suffer long term if they do not give in to Cerveja's "Hoppy" demands. In the latter category, many small retailers report that "Hoppy" is more a threat than a benefit—one that precludes the opportunity to try out new brands and perhaps get noticed by Hollandia.

As you know, so far Hollandia seems to have focused its marketing efforts on large supermarkets. As a result, the penetration of Hollandia Brew among small retailers has been relatively modest to date. However, we've heard increasingly that Hollandia is turning its focus more to small retailers. In addition to trying to promote Hollandia Brew, we heard that Hollandia sales reps have been asking small retailers to help them identify "hot" new brands. Hollandia has very deep pockets and may offer great long term potential, but great risk as well—who knows how long they will stay in the INCland market? And, of course, becoming close to Hollandia may have a blow-back effect on a retailer's existing relationship with Cerveja.

I leave it up to you, member owners, to follow the policy that works best for you, either aggressively working to promote Cerveja fully; partially going along with Hoppy inducements; or dropping Hoppy altogether. From my perspective, however, it seems to me it would be highly risky not to do your best to keep on the best of terms with Cerveja.

May 5, 2010

MEMORANDUM FOR THE PRESIDENT OF HOLLANDIA, INC.

FROM: Hans Huizinga, Hollandia Regional Vice President for ICNland

SUBJECT: Update on the ICNland Market

As you know, Hollandia has rapidly increased its market share in ICNland since the 2008 Pappabeer acquisition.

While this is good news, longer term prospects are uncertain. Our sales are mostly through large supermarkets, and we have had to grant major promotional concessions to grow the Hollandia Brew brand in these outlets. We simply cannot afford to continue to "buy" market share through large advertising campaigns. Furthermore, our recent market research indicates that we need to both increase customer acceptance of Hollandia Brew (despite our marketing efforts, our surveys show that it's still way behind Cerveja in terms of customer preference) and diversify into new brands. Our marketing surveys also indicate that only brands that have gained a critical acceptance level through small local retail sales are likely to do well in the long-term.

To further grow in ICNland and challenge Cerveja for supremacy, we simply can't just keep throwing money at supermarket promotions. We need to redouble our efforts to promote the Hollandia Brew label within the small retailer channel, and also should expand our portfolio by developing or acquiring one or two new "hot" brands. Regrettably, Cerveja must recognize this and it has been granting small local retailers incentives to protect its turf. Clearly, further growth in ICNland will require more investment on our part, to which Cerveja may retaliate further in kind. Moreover, there may be other, more immediately profitable opportunities in other countries. I leave this question up to you and the board, of course.

Long term, we will have to decide whether (1) to withdraw entirely from the Cerveja market, (2) to maintain Hollandia Brew as a niche number two brand with limited growth potential, of (3) aggressively promote Hollandia Brew at small retailers and also seek to proliferate brands and try to dominate the ICNland market. Over the next few months, I will be meeting with major supermarket chains, the small local retailers' association, and marketing survey firms as I contemplate next steps. I will report back to you by the end of the year on developments and further steps, if any, we should consider taking.

E–MAIL

From: da Silva, Joao [J.dasilva@cerveja.com]

To: Perez, Jose [J.Perez@cerveja.com]

Date: 2 July 2010

Subject: So Hoppy Together Program

Jose:

You are a marketing genius, my friend! 2009 was indeed a tough year but based on the most recent data for this year (2010) collected by my analysts, Cerveja sales at SHTP stores are up, on average, 15% this year compared to last! Take that, Hollandia! And we've been able to prevent prices falling further in the small outlet channel. These increased volumes more than make up for the rebates we're giving out here—our overall profitability is actually up over the same period for this business! Also, the increased volumes we're producing, combined with the new production software package we installed last year, means overall costs are down 2%, on average, at our breweries. A true win, win, win situation—for everyone except our competitors!!!!!

You have my vote for employee of the year! I think you get a nice plaque in your office if you win! ;-)

Joao da Silva
Director of Accounting
Cerveja S.r.l.

"Grab a Cerveja and have fun today"

Summary of Independent Marketing/Industry Study, 2009

This is a fascinating time for analysts of the beer industry with serious rivalry from an established player threatening to shake up the market in a more significant way than we have seen for decades.

Hollandia have put up breweries using latest production technologies which means, despite substantial capital costs, they should be very cost competitive. On the other side, massive advertising is necessary to position its main brands for growth, and the returns to these advertising costs require being able to ramp up volumes.

Preference trends for beer in ICNLandia

The overall market is growing, as would be expected with economic growth averaging around 4%. But the growth in beer consumption is much slower as the extra disposable income tends to go on things such as mobile phones and electronic devices. Drinking choices, especially in the middle income market segment where the economic growth is concentrated, are also looking to products such as wine reflecting habits shifting to drinking with meals and less at bars. However, beer is still overwhelmingly the alcoholic beverage of choice.

Our assessment is that the many local beers are in long-term decline for several reasons. Their main market is older people, mainly men, who have grown up with the beer. Younger drinkers have wider frame of reference—in national and international terms and want to engage in a drinking experience which they feel links them into wider communities. While Cerveja's national identity undoubtedly keeps it right up there, coupled with their new moves to bring in fashion brand derivatives such as their new 'ice' beer, Hollandia's international reach places them in a good position.

Smaller beers need to make themselves appealing as a 'craft' product, but have failed to do so, with unimaginative branding tending to emphasise their 'localness', something which people relate to less and less when it comes to beer. We also doubt whether the smaller breweries have the finance base to lay-out the adspend necessary to make such a re-positioning strategy work.

Evolution of different routes to market

Along with long-term shifts in preferences we see similar changes in the routes to market for beer producers. The inexorable roll-out of large supermarkets, most who are part of national chains, is the product of improved logistics and stock control technologies coupled with greater car ownership. While the trend is in one direction, it is important not to get carried away, however. Although it may seem from the wealthier large cities that this is the big story, and it accounts for a lot of consumption spend, in the poorer states, relying on mining or agriculture levels, of car ownership are much lower and these shifts are much slower.

The smaller outlets in the states of Mineralia and Agrilandia, as well as in rural areas of Urbania, are crucial to get product to the population conveniently, when they want it. The importance of habit means that not having a brand available on a close to universal basis means its growth will be limited.

Likely Hollandia strategy?

All this suggests very interesting choices face Hollandia, especially in light of Cerveja's apparent response.

On the one hand, Cerveja is not likely to be a particularly efficient overall operator given that it has been in such a comfortable position for so long. Its strengths, however, include its very effective distribution network through its own and contracted drivers meaning that it is able to meet orders at very short notice and guarantee its beer is on hand to customers anywhere in the country. It also has the cash pile to respond to any threat, whether with advertising and promotion blitzes which it can carry on its massive national sales base, or in hiring the best external marketing experts to look at launching new brands where necessary.

On the other hand, Hollandia has world class logistics capabilities especially in meeting the needs of the large supermarket chains. It just needs to get the scale to bring its unit costs down. It has the brands and the appeal.

We see the big choice facing Hollandia is whether to locate its beers in a somewhat premium 'international' niche, with strong marketing aimed at middle income urban drinkers, as against the importance for growth of having its beer available in all outlets. We must remember that middle class urban drinkers also frequent street corner outlets and beachfront stands.

It has come in at very price competitive levels, really shaking up the market, but it has, wisely in our opinion, not followed Cerveja down in its pricing.

We will be watching closely as events unfold, and also looking to see the effect of the latest tactic, Cerveja's loyalty programme 'So Hoppy Together'.

INDEX

References are to Pages

References are to Pages

†